International Economics

Sixteenth Edition

REGENT'S
UNIVERSITY LONDON

Thomas A. Pugel
New York University

Mc
Graw
Hill
Education

INTERNATIONAL ECONOMICS: SIXTEENTH EDITION

Published by McGraw-Hill Education, 2 Penn Plaza, New York, NY 10121. Copyright © 2016 by McGraw-Hill Education. All rights reserved. Printed in the United States of America. Previous editions © 2012, 2009, and 2007. No part of this publication may be reproduced or distributed in any form or by any means, or stored in a database or retrieval system, without the prior written consent of McGraw-Hill Education, including, but not limited to, in any network or other electronic storage or transmission, or broadcast for distance learning.

Some ancillaries, including electronic and print components, may not be available to customers outside the United States.

This book is printed on acid-free paper.

1 2 3 4 5 6 7 8 9 0 DOC/DOC 1 0 9 8 7 6 5

ISBN 978-0-07-802177-0
MHID 0-07-802177-4

Senior Vice President, Products & Markets: *Kurt L. Strand*
Vice President, General Manager, Products & Markets: *Marty Lange*
Vice President, Content Design & Delivery: *Kimberly Meriwether David*
Managing Director: *James Heine*
Lead Product Developer: *Michele Janicek*
Senior Product Developer: *Christina Kouvelis*
Director of Marketing: *Lynn Breithaupt*
Director, Content Design & Delivery: *Linda Avenarius*
Senior Content Project Manager: *Lisa Bruflodt*
Buyer: *Laura M. Fuller*
Cover Image: *Design Pics/Ryan Briscall*
Compositor: *Laserwords Private Limited*
Printer: *R. R. Donnelley*

All credits appearing on page or at the end of the book are considered to be an extension of the copyright page.

Library of Congress Cataloging-in-Publication Data

Pugel, Thomas A.
  International economics/Thomas A. Pugel.—Sixteenth edition.
    pages cm
  ISBN 978-0-07-802177-0 (alk. paper)
  1. Commercial policy. 2. Foreign exchange. I. Title.
HF1411.L536 2016
337—dc23

                                                    2014040055

The Internet addresses listed in the text were accurate at the time of publication. The inclusion of a website does not indicate an endorsement by the authors or McGraw-Hill Education, and McGraw-Hill Education does not guarantee the accuracy of the information presented at these sites.

www.mhhe.com

International Economics

Sixteenth Edition

The McGraw-Hill Series in Economics

In memory of my parents, Adele and Edmund, and my parents-in-law, Vivian and Freeman, with my deepest appreciation and gratitude for all that they did to benefit the generations that follow.

About the Author

Thomas A. Pugel

Thomas A. Pugel is Professor of Economics and Global Business at the Stern School of Business, New York University, and a Fellow of the Teaching Excellence Program at the Stern School. His research and publications focus on international industrial competition and government policies toward international trade and industry. Professor Pugel has been Visiting Professor at Aoyama Gakuin University in Japan and a member of the U.S. faculty at the National Center for Industrial Science and Technology Management Development in China. He received the university-wide Distinguished Teaching Award at New York University in 1991, and twice he was voted Professor of the Year by the graduate students at the Stern School of Business. He studied economics as an undergraduate at Michigan State University and earned a PhD in economics from Harvard University.

Preface

International economics combines the excitement of world events and the incisiveness of economic analysis. We are now deeply into the second great wave of globalization, in which product, capital, and labor markets are becoming more integrated across countries. This second wave, which began in about 1950 and picked up steam in the 1980s, has now lasted longer than the first, which began in about 1870 and ended with World War I (or perhaps with the onset of the Great Depression in 1930).

As indicators of the current process of globalization, we see that international trade, foreign direct investment, cross-border lending, and international portfolio investments have been growing faster than world production. Information, data, and rumors now spread around the world instantly through the Internet and other global electronic media.

As the world becomes more integrated, countries become more interdependent. Increasingly, events and policy changes in one country affect many other countries. Also increasingly, companies make decisions about production and product development based on global markets.

My goal in writing and revising this book is to provide the best blend of events and analysis, so that the reader builds the abilities to understand global economic developments and to evaluate proposals for changes in economic policies. The book is informed by current events and by the latest in applied international research. My job is to synthesize all of this to facilitate learning. The book

Combines rigorous economic analysis with attention to the issues of economic policy that are alive and important today.

Is written to be concise and readable.

Uses economic terminology when it enhances the analysis but avoids jargon for jargon's sake.

I follow these principles when I teach international economics to undergraduates and master's degree students. I believe that the book benefits as I bring into it what I learn from the classroom.

THE SCHEME OF THE BOOK

The examples presented in Chapter 1 show that international economics is exciting and sometimes controversial because there are both differences between countries and interconnections among countries. Still, international economics is like other economics in that we will be examining the fundamental challenge of scarcity of resources—how we can best use our scarce resources to create the most value and the most benefits. We will be able to draw on many standard tools and concepts of economics, such as supply and demand analysis, and extend their use to the international arena.

We begin our in-depth exploration of international economics with international trade theory and policy. In Chapters 2–7 we look at why countries trade goods and services. In Chapters 8–15 we examine what government policies toward trade would bring benefits and to whom. This first half of the book might be called international microeconomics.

Our basic theory of trade, presented in Chapter 2, says that trade usually results from the interaction of competitive demand and supply. It shows how the gains that trade brings to some people and the losses it brings to others can sum to overall global and national gains from trade. Chapter 3 launches an exploration of what lies behind the demand and supply curves and discovers the concept of comparative advantage. Chapter 4 shows that countries have different comparative advantages for the fundamental reason that people, and therefore countries, differ from each other in the productive resources they own. Chapter 5 looks at the strong impacts of trade on people who own those productive resources—the human labor and skills, the capital, the land, and other resources. Some ways of making a living are definitely helped by trade, while others are hurt. Chapter 6 examines how actual trade may reflect forces calling for theories that go beyond our basic ideas of demand and supply and of comparative advantage. Chapter 7 explores some key links between trade and economic growth.

Chapters 8–15 use the theories of the previous chapters to analyze a broad range of government policy issues. Chapters 8–10 set out on a journey to map the border between good trade barriers and bad ones. This journey turns out to be intellectually challenging, calling for careful reasoning. Chapter 11 explores how firms and governments sometimes push for more trade rather than less, promoting exports more than a competitive marketplace would. Chapter 12 switches to the economics of trade blocs like the European Union and the North American Free Trade Area. Chapter 13 faces the intense debate over how environmental concerns should affect trade policy. Chapter 14 looks at how trade creates challenges and opportunities for developing countries. Chapter 15 examines the economics of emigration and immigration and the roles of global companies in the transfer of resources, including technology, between countries.

The focus of the second half of the book shifts to international finance and macroeconomics. In Chapters 16–21 we enter the world of different moneys, the exchange rates between these moneys, and international investors and speculators. Chapters 22–25 survey the effects of a national government's choice of exchange-rate policy on the country's macroeconomic performance, especially unemployment and inflation.

Chapter 16 presents the balance of payments, a way to keep track of all the economic transactions between a country and the rest of the world. In Chapter 17 we explore the basics of exchange rates between currencies and the functioning and enormous size of the foreign exchange market. Chapter 18 provides a tour of the returns to and risks of foreign financial investments. Exchange rates are prices, and in Chapter 19 we look behind basic supply and demand in the foreign exchange market, in search of fundamental economic determinants of exchange-rate values. Chapter 20 examines government policies toward the foreign-exchange market, first using description and analysis, and then presenting the history of exchange-rate regimes, starting with the gold standard and finishing with the current mash-up of different national policies. Well-behaved international lending and borrowing can create global gains, but Chapter 21 also examines financial crises that can arise from some kinds of foreign borrowing and that can spread across countries, a clear downside of globalization.

Chapter 22 begins our explication of international macroeconomics by developing a framework for analyzing a national economy that is linked to the rest of the world through international trade and international financial investing. We use this framework in the next two chapters to explore the macroeconomic performance of a country that maintains a fixed exchange-rate value for its currency (Chapter 23) and of a country that allows a floating, market-driven exchange-rate value for its currency (Chapter 24). Chapter 25 uses what we have learned throughout the second half of the book to examine the benefits and costs of alternatives for a country's exchange-rate policy. While rather extreme versions of fixed exchange rates serve some countries well, the general trend is toward more flexible exchange rates.

In a few places the book's scheme (international trade first, international finance second) creates some momentary inconvenience, as when we look at the exchange-rate link between cutting imports and reducing exports in Chapter 5 before we have discussed exchange rates in depth. Mostly the organization serves us well. The understanding we gain about earlier topics provides us with building blocks that allow us to explore broader issues later in the book.

CURRENT EVENTS AND NEW EXAMPLES

It is a challenge and a pleasure for me to incorporate the events and policy changes that continue to transform the global economy, and to find the new examples that show the effects of globalization (both its upside and its downside). Here are some of the current and recent events and issues that are included in this edition to provide new examples that show the practical use of our international economic analysis:

- The euro crisis that began in Greece in 2010 spread to several other countries in the euro area and during 2011–2012 seemed to threaten the continued existence of the euro itself. Still, in the face of continued weak economic performance in the euro area, Latvia adopted the euro at the beginning of 2014, bringing the number of countries in the euro area to 18.
- Beginning in 2007 the United States rapidly expanded its production of natural gas using horizontal drilling and hydraulic fracturing. A large number of U.S. firms sought approval to export natural gas, but a U.S. law prohibits export unless it is in the national interest. The U.S. government has been slow to act; as of mid-2014, only one U.S. facility had received full approval to export.
- Immigration continues to be a hot issue. In 2014 Swiss voters approved limitations on immigration into the country. Prime Minister Cameron pledged to greatly reduce immigration into Britain by 2015. In 2013 the U.S. government again failed to pass a revision of its immigration laws.
- Chinese government holdings of foreign exchange reserve assets reached $4 trillion in mid-2014, the result of continued official intervention to prevent the exchange-rate value of China's currency from rising too quickly.
- Pressure from the growth of the countries' exports led to rapidly rising wages for workers in China and in India.
- After nearly two decades of negotiations, Russia joined the World Trade Organization (WTO) in 2012.

- In 2013 the members of the WTO reached a new multilateral agreement on trade facilitation, but in 2014 its implementation was held up by a single country, India.
- In response to rapidly growing imports, American steel producers sent a large number of new complaints to the U.S. government, alleging dumping by foreign producers and seeking hefty new antidumping duties.
- The WTO ruled that European governments had violated WTO rules by offering massive subsidies to Airbus and that the U.S. government had violated WTO rules by offering massive subsidies to Boeing. But, then, the situation seemed to reach a stalemate.
- After approval from the U.S. Congress, the United States implemented free-trade agreements with Colombia, South Korea, and Panama.
- In 2012, Venezuela became a member of MERCOSUR, the South American regional trade area.
- Croatia joined the European Union in 2013 as its 28th member country.
- The first phase of the Kyoto Protocol was completed in 2012. For a number of reasons, the effects were minor, and global warming continues as a major global environmental challenge.
- Led by increases in international financial investments and computer-driven trading, the size of the foreign exchange market continued to grow, with trading of one currency for another reaching $5 trillion *per day* in 2013. Foreign exchange trading has more than tripled since 2004.
- The market-driven exchange-rate value of the Japanese yen increased during the week after a tsunami caused the nuclear disaster at Fukushima in 2011, prompting a large official intervention in the foreign exchange market.
- Starting in 2008, the International Monetary Fund (IMF) rapidly expanded its lending to countries in crisis, with loans outstanding reaching $125 billion in mid-2014. Most of these IMF loans are to advanced countries—Iceland, Greece, Ireland, and Portugal—a sharp contrast to the lending to developing countries that had been predominant since 1980.
- The United States pursued a third round of quantitative easing during 2012–2014 as a continuation of unconventional monetary policy for an economy stuck in a liquidity trap. In this third round, the Fed bought about $1.5 trillion of Treasury securities and mortgage-backed securities, but this round seemed to have less effect on the exchange-rate value of the U.S. dollar than did previous rounds.

IMPROVING THE BOOK: TOPICS

In this edition I introduce and extend a number of improvements to the pedagogical structure and topical coverage of the book.
- The euro crisis that began in 2010 and intensified in 2011 and 2012 has had profound effects on the member countries of the euro area—the countries that have replaced their national currencies with the euro in a monetary union.

This edition interweaves the causes and impacts of the euro crisis across its chapters. The overview of the euro crisis in Chapter 1 shows that it began in different ways, as a fiscal crisis in Greece and as a burst housing-price bubble in Ireland that led to a banking crisis. Portugal then had a debt-driven crisis, and contagion spread the crisis pressures to Spain and Italy. The European Central Bank needed to play a key role, and a new program announced in July 2012 and adopted in September was the turning point in addressing the worst of the crisis. I then present discussions of important aspects of the crisis in a series of new shaded *Euro Crisis* boxes, which join the other six series of boxes: *Global Crisis, Focus on China, Global Governance, Focus on Labor, Case Studies,* and *Extensions.* For the *Euro Crisis* series, the new box in Chapter 16 shows how attention to current account balances and net international investment positions of the countries at the center of the crisis would have given signals of rising risk. Chapter 18 has a combination of a *Global Crisis* and *Euro Crisis* box, which shows how a key parity relationship among interest rates and exchange rates weakened under crisis conditions. The new box in Chapter 21 explains how the euro crisis was actually three interrelated crises that reinforced each other—sovereign debt or fiscal crisis, banking crisis, and macroeconomic crisis. While the sovereign debt and banking crises have calmed, the macroeconomic performance of the euro area remained very weak and Greece was in depression. The concluding section of Chapter 25 examines the benefits and costs of European monetary union, with special attention to fiscal policy. The euro area lacks area-wide taxation and government spending, National fiscal policies have a double edge, as both the principal remaining tool for national governments to address their macroeconomic performance problems and a potential source of instability that can threaten the entire union.

- The global financial and economic crisis that began in 2007 is the most important global trauma of the past 70 years, and it was a major contributor to the onset of the euro crisis. A new section of the text of Chapter 21 describes the global crisis, including the start of the crisis as the result of losses on sub-prime mortgages in the United States and on assets backed by these mortgages, and the terrible worsening of the crisis in 2008 with the failure of Lehman Brothers. This discussion of the global crisis also shows how the analysis of the series of financial crises that hit developing countries during 1982–2002 helps us to understand the causes and spread of the global crisis. The *Global Crisis* series of boxes examines other aspects of the crisis, including the collapse of international trade (Chapter 2), the avoidance of new protectionism (Chapter 9), the use of quantitative easing as nontraditional monetary policy once short-term interest rates are essentially zero (Chapter 24), and the increased use of currency swaps among central banks (Chapter 24).

- China continues its rise as a force in the global economy. The presentation of China's global role, including the series of boxes *Focus on China,* continues to be a strength of the text. Chapters 1 and 20 discuss the development of China's controversial policies toward the exchange-rate value of its currency. In the box in Chapter 9, the presentation of China's rising involvement in the dispute settlement process at the World Trade Organization, both as a respondent (alleged violator) and as a complainant, has been updated and rewritten. Among other recent cases, the WTO ruled in 2014 that China's restrictions on exports of rare earths were a violation of its WTO commitments.

- A major strength of the book remains in-depth analysis of a range of trade and trade-policy issues. The discussion of monopolistic competition and intra-industry trade in Chapter 6 has been expanded to incorporate the conclusions from research based on differences across firms in their cost levels. Opening to international trade favors the survival and expansion of lower-cost firms. This discussion also includes an estimate of the global gains from greater product variety. The section on trade embargoes in Chapter 12 has been revised, with a current case, Iran, being used as the example of the effects of international sanctions on the target country. Estimates of national factor endowments presented in Chapter 5 are completely updated and include better data on physical capital stocks and more countries in total. Data on national intra-industry trade shares in Chapter 6 include new estimates for 2012.

- Chapter 13 on trade and the environment continues as a unique and powerful treatment of issues of interest to many students. The discussion of global warming has been revised to incorporate data and projections from recent studies. The discussion of the Kyoto Protocol has been updated to include the outcomes from the first phase that ended in 2012 and the continued increase in global greenhouse gas emissions.

- The box on the fiscal effects of immigration in Chapter 15 has been substantially rewritten to incorporate the results of a recent Organization for Economic Cooperation and Development study of the effects of immigrants on government revenues and expenditures.

- In Chapter 18 a new section of text explains the definitions and uses of real exchange rates and effective exchange rates. The four ways to measure the exchange-rate value of a currency had previously been a box in the chapter, but the increasing importance of these concepts motivated the shift to a text section.

- Chapter 21 has been substantially revised. It incorporates the global financial and economic crisis into the text of the chapter and has a new box on the euro crisis. Some other aspects of the chapter have been streamlined. The short subsections on the Brazilian mini-crisis of 1999 and the Turkish crisis of 2001 have been removed, as has one of the two boxes on the International Monetary Fund.

- I used the latest available sources to update the wide range of data and information presented in the figures and text of the book. Among other updates, the book offers the latest information on international trade in specific products for the United States, China, and Japan; national average tariff rates; dumping and subsidy cases; levels and growth rates of national incomes per capita; trends in the relative prices of primary products; patterns of foreign direct investments broadly and by major home country; rates of immigration into the United States, Canada, and the European Union; the U.S. balance of payments and the U.S. international investment position; the sizes of foreign exchange trading and foreign exchange futures, swaps, and options; levels and trends for nominal exchange rates; effective exchange-rate values for the U.S. dollar; evidence about relative purchasing power parity; the exchange-rate policies chosen by national governments; the flows of international financing to and the outstanding foreign debt of developing countries; and gold prices.

NEW QUESTIONS AND PROBLEMS

In this edition I provide additional opportunities for students to engage with the book's contents by adding new questions that students can use to build their facility in using the concepts and analysis of international economics.

- Forty-eight new questions and problems have been added, two new questions and problems to each of the chapters that have end-of-chapter materials. These new questions and problems are targeted to cover chapter topics that were previously underrepresented.
- A discussion question has been added at the end of each Case Study box, a total of 24 new questions that focus on the issues raised in the case studies.

FORMAT AND STYLE

I have been careful to retain the goals of clarity and honesty that have made *International Economics* an extraordinary success in classrooms and courses around the world. There are plenty of quick road signs at the start of and within chapters. The summaries at the ends of the chapters offer an integration of what has been discussed. Students get the signs, "Here's where we are going; here's where we have just been." I use bullet-point and numbered lists to add to the visual appeal of the text and to emphasize sets of determinants or effects. I strive to keep paragraphs to reasonable lengths, and I have found ways to break up some long paragraphs to make the text easier to read.

I am candid about ranking some tools or facts ahead of others. The undeniable power of some of the economist's tools is applied repeatedly to events and issues without apology. Theories and concepts that fail to improve on common sense are not oversold.

The format of the book is fine-tuned for better learning. Students need to master the language of international economics. Most exam-worthy **terms** appear in boldface in the text, with their definitions usually contiguous. The material at the end of each chapter includes a listing of these *Key Terms*, and an online *Glossary* has definitions of each term. Words and phrases that deserve *special emphasis* are in italics.

Each chapter (except for the short introductory chapter) has at least 12 questions and problems. The answers to all odd-numbered questions and problems are included in the material at the end of the book. As a reminder, these odd-numbered questions are marked with a ✦.

Box

Shaded boxes appear in different font with a different right-edge format and two columns per page, in contrast to the style of the main text. The boxes are labeled by type and provide discussions of the euro crisis that began in 2010, the global financial and economic crisis that began in 2007, the roles of the WTO and the IMF in global governance, China's international trade and investment, labor issues, case studies, and extensions of the concepts presented in the text.

SUPPLEMENTS

The following ancillaries are available for quick download and convenient access via the Instructor Resource material available through McGraw-Hill Connect®.

- **PowerPoint Presentations:** Revised by Farhad Saboori of Albright College, the PowerPoint slides now include a brief, detailed review of the important ideas covered in each chapter, accompanied by relevant tables and figures featured within the text. You can edit, print, or rearrange the slides to fit the needs of your course.
- **Test Bank:** Updated by Robert Allen of Columbia Southern University, the test bank offers well over 1,500 questions categorized by level of difficulty, AACSB learning categories, Bloom's taxonomy, and topic.
- **Computerized Test Bank:** McGraw-Hill's EZ Test is a flexible and easy-to-use electronic testing program that allows you to create tests from book-specific items. It accommodates a wide range of question types, and you can add your own questions. Multiple versions of the test can be created, and any test can be exported for use with course management systems. EZ Test Online gives you a place to administer your EZ Test–created exams and quizzes online. Additionally, you can access the test bank through McGraw-Hill Connect.
- **Instructor's Manual:** Written by the author, the instructor's manual contains chapter overviews, teaching tips, and suggested answers to the discussion questions featured among the case studies as well as the end-of-chapter questions and problems. To increase flexibility, the Tips section in each chapter often provides the author's thoughts and suggestions for customizing the coverage of certain sections and chapters.

DIGITAL SOLUTIONS

McGraw-Hill Connect® Economics

Less Managing. More Teaching. Greater Learning. McGraw-Hill's *Connect® Economics* is an online assessment solution that connects students with the tools and resources they'll need to achieve success.

McGraw-Hill's *Connect Economics* Features

Connect Economics allows faculty to create and deliver exams easily with selectable test bank items. Instructors can also build their own questions into the system for homework or practice. Other features include:

Instructor Library The *Connect Economics* Instructor Library is your repository for additional resources to improve student engagement in and out of class. You can select and use any asset that enhances your lecture. The *Connect Economics* Instructor Library includes all of the instructor supplements for this text.

Student Resources Any supplemental resources that align with the text for student use will be available through *Connect*.

Student Progress Tracking *Connect Economics* keeps instructors informed about how each student, section, and class is performing, allowing for more productive use of lecture and office hours. The progress-tracking function enables you to

- View scored work immediately and track individual or group performance with assignment and grade reports.
- Access an instant view of student or class performance relative to learning objectives.
- Collect data and generate reports required by many accreditation organizations, such as AACSB.

Diagnostic and Adaptive Learning of Concepts: LearnSmart and SmartBook offer the first and only adaptive reading experience designed to change the way students read and learn.

LEARNSMART° Students want to make the best use of their study time. The LearnSmart adaptive self-study technology within *Connect Economics* provides students with a seamless combination of practice, assessment, and remediation for every concept in the textbook. LearnSmart's intelligent software adapts to every student's response and automatically delivers concepts that advance students' understanding while reducing time devoted to the concepts already mastered. The result for every student is the fastest path to mastery of the chapter concepts. LearnSmart

- Applies an intelligent concept engine to identify the relationships between concepts and to serve new concepts to each student only when he or she is ready.
- Adapts automatically to each student, so students spend less time on the topics they understand and practice more those they have yet to master.
- Provides continual reinforcement and remediation but gives only as much guidance as students need.
- Integrates diagnostics as part of the learning experience.
- Enables you to assess which concepts students have efficiently learned on their own, thus freeing class time for more applications and discussion.

 Smartbook is an extension of LearnSmart—an adaptive eBook that helps students focus their study time more effectively. As students read, Smartbook assesses comprehension and dynamically highlights where they need to study more.

For more information about *Connect*, go to **connect.mheducation.com**, or contact your local McGraw-Hill sales representative.

McGraw-Hill's Customer Experience Group

We understand that getting the most from your new technology can be challenging. That's why our services don't stop after you purchase our products. You can e-mail our Product Specialists 24 hours a day to get product-training online. Or you can search our knowledge bank of Frequently Asked Questions on our support website. For Customer Support, call 800-331-5094, or visit www.mhhe.com/support.

Create

 McGraw-Hill Create™ is a self-service website that allows you to create customized course materials using McGraw-Hill's comprehensive, cross-disciplinary content and digital products. You can even access third-party content such as readings, articles, cases, videos, and more. Arrange the content you've selected to match the scope and sequence of your course. Personalize your book with a cover design and choose the best format for your students—eBook, color print, or black-and-white print. And, when you are done, you'll receive a PDF review copy in just minutes!

CourseSmart

 Go paperless with eTextbooks from CourseSmart and move light-years beyond traditional print textbooks. Read online or offline anytime, anywhere. Access your eTextbook on multiple devices with or without an Internet connection. CourseSmart eBooks include convenient, built-in tools that let you search topics quickly, add notes and highlights, copy/paste passages, and print any page.

Acknowledgments

I offer my deepest thanks to the many people whose advice helped me to improve *International Economics* in its sixteenth edition. My first thanks are to Peter H. Lindert, my co author on several previous editions. I learned much from him about the art of writing for the community of students who want to deepen their knowledge and understanding of the global economy.

I love teaching international economics, and I am grateful to my students for the many suggestions and insights that I have received from them. I thank my friends and colleagues from other colleges and universities who took the time to e-mail me with corrections and ideas for changes. I especially thank my faculty colleagues at the NYU Stern School for information and suggestions. I am indebted to Natalia Tamirisa of the International Monetary Fund for providing the data used in Figure 13.6, Carbon Tax to Stabilize Atmospheric Carbon Dioxide; to Richard M. Levich of the NYU Stern School of Business for providing data used in the box "Covered Interest Parity Breaks Down" in Chapter 18; and to Ravi Balakrishnan and Volodymyr Tulin of the International Monetary Fund for the data used in Figure 18.3, Uncovered Interest Differentials: The United States against Germany and Japan, 1991–2005. I also thank my brother, Michael Pugel, who shared with me his knowledge of technology issues from his perspective as a patent attorney and electrical engineer.

I express my gratitude to the reviewers whose detailed and thoughtful comments and critiques provided guidance as I wrote the sixteenth edition:

Adhip Chaudhuri, Georgetown University; Baizhu Chen, University of Southern California; Tran Dung, Wright State University; Wei Ge, Bucknell University; Pedro Gete, Georgetown University; Kirk Gifford, Brigham Young University; Nam Pham, George Washington University; Courtney Powell-Thomas, Virginia Tech University; Farhad Saboori, Albright College; George Sarraf, University of California–Irvine; Paul Wachtel, New York University; Lou Zaera, Fashion Institute of Technology.

I remain grateful to the reviewers whose suggestions for improvements to the previous editions continued to redound to my benefit as I prepared the sixteenth:

Vera Adamchik, University of Houston–Victoria; Gregory W. Arbum, The University of Findlay; Manoj Atolia, Florida State University; Mina Baliamoune, University of North Florida; Michael P. Barry, Mount St. Mary's University; Trisha Bezmen, Old Dominion University; Frank Biggs, Principia College; Philip J. Bryson, Brigham Young University; Philip E. Burian, Colorado Technical University at Sioux Falls; James Butkiewicz, University of Delaware; Debasish Chakraborty, Central Michigan University; Roberto Chang, Rutgers University; Shah Dabirian, California State University Long Beach; Jamshid Damooei, California Lutheran University; Manjira Datta, Arizona State University; Dennis Debrecht, Carroll College; Carol Decker, Tennessee Wesleyan College; John R. Dominguez, University of Wisconsin–Whitewater; Eric Drabkin, Hawaii Pacific University; Robert Driskill, Vanderbilt University; Patrick M. Emerson, Oregon State University; Carole Endres, Wright State University; Nicolas Ernesto Magud, University of Oregon; Hisham Foad, San Diego State University; Yoshi Fukasawa, Midwestern State University; John Gilbert, Utah State University; Chris Gingrich, Eastern Mennonite University;

Amy Glass, Texas A&M University; Omer Gokcekus, Seton Hall University; William Hallagan, Washington State University; Tom Head, George Fox University; Barbara Heroy John, University of Dayton; Farid Islam, Woodbury School of Business; Brian Jacobsen, Wisconsin Lutheran College; Geoffrey Jehle, Vassar College and Columbia University; Jack Julian, Indiana University of Pennsylvania; Ghassan Karam, Pace University; Vani V. Kotcherlakota, University of Nebraska at Kearney; Quan Le, Seattle University; Kristina Lybecker, The Colorado College; John Marangos, Colorado State University; John Mukum Mbaku, Weber State University; John McLaren, University of Virginia; Michael A. McPherson, University of North Texas; Matthew McPherson, Gonzaga University; Norman C. Miller, Miami University; Karla Morgan, Whitworth College; Stefan Norrbin, Florida State University; Joseph Nowakowski, Muskingum College; Rose Marie Payan, California Polytechnic University; Harvey Poniachek, Rutgers University; Dan Powroznik, Chesapeake College; Ed Price, Oklahoma State University; Kamal Saggi, Southern Methodist University; Jawad Salimi, West Virginia University–Morgantown; Andreas Savvides, Oklahoma State University; Philip Sprunger, Lycoming College; John Stiver, University of Connecticut; William J. Streeter, Olin Business School–Washington University in St. Louis; Kay E. Strong, Bowling Green State University–Firelands; Kishor Thanawala, Villanova University; Victoria Umanskaya, University of California-Riverside; Doug Walker, Georgia College and State University; Dr. Evelyn Wamboye, University of Wisconsin–Stout; Dave Wharton, Washington College; Elizabeth M. Wheaton, Southern Methodist University; Jiawen Yang, George Washington University; Bassam Yousif, Indiana State University Hamid Zangeneh, Widener University;

I offer my thanks and admiration to the great group at McGraw-Hill/Irwin who worked with me closely in preparing this edition, including Michele Janicek, lead product developer; Christina Kouvelis, senior product developer; Lisa Bruflodt, senior project manager; and Sourav Majumdar, project manager at SPi Global.

My final acknowledgment is in remembrance of the late Charles P. Kindleberger, who was one of my teachers during my graduate studies. He started this book over 60 years ago, and I strive to meet the standards of excellence and relevance that he set for the book.

Thomas A. Pugel

Brief Contents

Contents

Chapter 15

Multinationals and Migration: International Factor Movements   334

Chapter 16

Payments among Nations   370

Chapter 17

The Foreign Exchange Market   389

Chapter **One**

International Economics Is Different

Nations are not like regions or families. They are sovereign, meaning that no central court can enforce its will on them with a global police force. Being sovereign, nations can put all sorts of barriers between their residents and the outside world. A region or family must deal with the political reality that others within the same nation can out-vote it and can therefore coerce it or tax it. A family or region has to compromise with others who have political voice. A nation feels less pressure to compromise and often ignores the interests of foreigners. A nation uses policy tools that are seldom available to a region and never available to a family. A nation can have its own currency, its own barriers to trading with foreigners, its own government taxing and spending, and its own laws of citizenship and residence.

As long as countries exist, international economics will be a body of analysis distinct from the rest of economics. The special nature of international economics makes it fascinating and sometimes difficult. Let's look at four controversial developments that frame the scope of this book.

FOUR CONTROVERSIES

U.S. Exports of Natural Gas

Natural gas has wide-ranging uses as a source of energy, from heating homes and commercial buildings, to generating electricity, to the production of such products as steel, paper, cement, and glass, to providing the feedstock for the production of chemicals, fertilizers, and plastics. For the U.S. market for natural gas during the decade to 2006, several trends were clear. U.S. production of natural gas had been about flat since the mid-1990s. As U.S. consumption increased, imports rose from 13 percent of consumption in the mid-1990s to over 19 percent in 2006, with nearly all of the imports from Canada through pipelines. The cost of production from new wells in the United States (and in Canada) was rising, as the lowest-cost sources (using standard production technologies) were exhausted. The typical producer price of natural gas in the United States rose from $2 per million British thermal units (MMBtu) to $6 in the mid-2000s. The expectation was the United States would soon need to ramp up high-cost imports of liquefied natural gas (LNG) to meet continued growth in consumption.

Then a revolution in extraction technology hit and everything changed. U.S. producers used the combination of hydraulic fracturing and horizontal drilling (a process called "fracking") to extract natural gas from shale deep underground. U.S. production of natural gas increased by 31 percent during 2006–2013, and imports fell to 11 percent of U.S. consumption. The typical producer price of natural gas hovered at about $4 during 2009–2013, and the price briefly fell below $2 in early 2012.

As U.S. production continues to increase, U.S. firms should be looking for new customers. But, if the new customers are foreign, then expanding exports can be controversial, and the United States is a sovereign nation. A 1938 law prohibits exports unless the exporting firm can convince the government that the exports are in the "public interest." The definition of public interest in the law is not precise but broadly includes adequate supply for domestic users and consumers, environmental impact, geopolitics, and energy security. (There is an exception for exports to 20 countries with which the United States has free trade agreements. However, with the exception of South Korea, the most promising potential foreign buyers of U.S. natural gas, including Japan, India, China, and some European countries, do not have free trade agreements with the United States.)

Should the United States export more natural gas (than the very small amount it has been exporting by pipeline to Canada and Mexico)? That is, are larger amounts of natural gas exports in the U.S. public or national interest? Dow Chemical led a group of major U.S. users of natural gas that urged caution and limits on U.S. exports. In a *Wall Street Journal* article,[1] Andrew N. Liveris, chairman and CEO of Dow Chemical, argued that plentiful low-cost U.S. production of natural gas should be used within the United States to produce general benefits rather than short-term profits to U.S. exporters that lead to long-run costs to the rest of the economy. He concluded that the United States must "consider what is in the nation's best interest . . . before it exports all of its gas away."

How would exports work? The new large buyers would be in Asia and Europe, so U.S. firms could not send gas to them by low-cost pipelines. Instead, the gas would need to be liquefied and sent in special ships, an expensive process that costs about $4 to $5 per MMBtu. Could U.S. firms still make a profit? U.S. natural gas prices are about $4, so the combined cost of natural gas and getting it to, say Japan, is about $9. After the tsunami that caused the disaster at Fukushima in 2011, Japan shut down all of its nuclear generation of electricity and greatly increased its demand for natural gas, nearly all of which is met through LNG imports. Prices rose to $14 to $19. At these initial prices and cost, a U.S. firm that could export to Japan would earn a large profit from the arbitrage ($5 to $10 per MMBtu). The more typical price for Japan LNG imports has been about $10, so there would still be an arbitrage profit, but it would not be as large.

What would happen if the U.S. government permitted substantial amounts of ongoing U.S. exports? Are the effects as dangerous as Dow Chemical suggests? Let's preview some of the results from the economic analysis of international trade in Chapters 2 and 8. First, the United States will *not* "export all of its gas away." Instead,

---

[1]Andrew N. Liveris, "Wanted: A Balanced Approach to Shale Gas Exports," *The Wall Street Journal* (February 25, 2013).

the international natural gas market would reach an equilibrium. The extra foreign demand would increase the U.S. price somewhat. U.S. production of natural gas would increase somewhat, and U.S. consumption would decrease somewhat. (In an importing country like Japan, comparable effects would occur. For Japan, which has almost no domestic production, the price in Japan would fall and consumption would increase.) Second, there will be winners and losers, as Dow indicates. In the United States, natural gas producers and export distributors would benefit and U.S. consumers and users would be harmed.

Third, what is the overall effect on the U.S. national interest? Economic analysis provides a clear answer. If we ignore environmental effects, as Dow does, the United States gains from the increased exports of natural gas. U.S. producers gain more than U.S. consumers lose. Interestingly, Dow Chemical will still get much of what it wants even in this freer trade situation. The large LNG transport costs will keep the U.S. price low, about $5 less than in importing countries like Japan. Chemical firms and other industrial users in the United States will still have an advantage internationally based on their access to relatively low-priced U.S. natural gas.

What about environmental effects? First, noxious chemicals are used in the fracking process, and these can leak into groundwater supplies if the fracking is not done carefully. Second, burning natural gas releases carbon dioxide, a greenhouse gas that is contributing to global warming, and there is a risk of leaks of methane, another greenhouse gas, during the extraction process. A more subtle analysis of the effects on greenhouse gas emissions would also examine the alternative to increased natural gas use. For example, if natural gas replaces coal, then the net effect is to lower greenhouse gas emissions. Adverse environmental effects are actual or potential negative spillovers (a "negative externality"), and the full cost of producing and using natural gas increases. Chapter 13 provides economic analysis of the interplay between environmental issues and international trade. With external environmental costs, the country will export too much. Most observers think that the risks of chemical leaks are not large in the United States because government regulations and the threat of damage lawsuits impel producers generally to be careful. If the net effects on greenhouse gases are also not that large, then the over-exporting effect is not large.

What has actually happened? As of mid-2014, the U.S. government had only provided full approval to one LNG export facility, and it was expected to begin exporting at about the end of 2015. Six other facilities had conditional approval that their exports would be in the public interest, but they had not yet received separate approval for compliance with environmental and safety norms. Another 26 applications were under review.

National government officials have the power to enact policies that can limit international transactions like exporting. If the whole world were one country, the issue of shifts in selling would be left to the marketplace. Within a country, it is usually impermissible for one region to restrict commerce with another region. But the world is split into different countries, each with national policies. Overall, the U.S. economy is likely to benefit from increased exports of national gas. This is the essence of both comparative advantage as a basis for international trade and the gains from trading, topics examined in Chapters 2–7. The slow process of facility approval is a reflection of the controversy about allowing U.S. exports of natural gas. Powerful users like Dow

Chemical can pursue their own benefits by seeking to limit exports through political action. Environmental groups can focus on their own interests. Economic analysis provides a sound way to add everything up to get to the national interest, but that does not make the controversy go away.

Immigration

About 230 million people, 3 percent of the world's population, live outside the country of their birth. For most industrialized countries (an exception is Japan), the percentage of the country's population that is foreign-born is rather high—14 percent for the United States and for Germany, 20 percent for Canada, 12 percent for Britain and for France, 15 percent for Sweden, and 27 percent for Switzerland and for Australia—and rising. Many of the foreign-born are illegal immigrants—over one-fourth of the total for the United States. The rising immigration has set off something of a backlash.

In 2007 the U.S. Congress considered and rejected a bill to enact comprehensive reform of U.S. policies toward immigration. The bill, backed by President Bush and many congressional leaders, would have shifted U.S. policy toward favoring new immigrants with more education and skills, created a new temporary guest worker program, increased requirements for employers to verify the legal status of their employees, built new fences along the U.S. border with Mexico and added new border guards, and created a complex process for illegal immigrants to gain legal status. After different groups in the United States raised their objections, including conservatives who focused on the latter provision and labeled it an unacceptable amnesty, support for the bill unraveled. A renewed effort to pass a comprehensive reform of U.S. immigration laws failed to gain traction in Congress in 2013.

In the absence of federal changes, individual states have enacted hundreds of state laws about immigrants in recent years, many of them tightening up against illegal immigrants. For instance, Arizona has passed a series of laws, beginning in 2004, that stop government assistance to illegal immigrants (unless federal law explicitly requires it), that can revoke a firm's right to do business if it employs illegal immigrants, that make it a crime for an illegal immigrant to solicit work or hold a job, and that require police to check the immigration status of any person whom they suspect is an illegal immigrant. The latter requirement is likely to encourage racial profiling. The sheriff of Phoenix has been particularly outspoken and aggressive in arresting illegal immigrants.

Anti-immigrant rhetoric and actions have been rising in other countries. Voters in France, the Netherlands, Austria, Denmark, and Norway have shifted toward candidates who promise to reduce and restrict immigration. In 2014, Swiss voters, driven by concerns that rising immigration was hurting employment of Swiss nationals, pushing up housing prices, and overburdening transportation systems, passed the Stop Mass Immigration referendum to impose numerical limits for foreign workers by 2017. In Britain, Prime Minister David Cameron pledged to achieve a large reduction in net migration into the country by 2015. Because Britain cannot do much to limit immigration from fellow European Union countries, the government has tightened immigration from other countries, including reductions in visas for college students. In the Australian election of 2010, the leader of one of the two major parties was an immigrant and the leader of the other was foreign-born to Australian parents. However, both were compelled by public opinion to promise to substantially reduce immigration by tightening policies.

Opponents of immigration stress a range of problems that they believe arise from immigration, including general losses to the economy; the fiscal burden that may arise from immigrants' use of government services (such as health care and schooling); slow integration of immigrants into the new national culture, values, and language; increased crime; and links of some immigrants to terrorism. What should one make of the claims of the opponents? Most immigrants move to obtain jobs at pay that is better than they can receive in their home countries, so it seems important to examine the economic effects.

How much harm do immigrants do to the economies of the countries they move to? International economic analysis helps us to think through the issue objectively, without being diverted by emotional traps. The answer is perhaps surprising, given the heat from immigration's opponents.

As we will see in more depth in Chapter 15, such job-seeking immigration brings net economic benefits not only to the immigrants, but also to the receiving country overall. The basic analysis shows that there are winners and losers within the receiving country. The winners include the firms that employ the immigrants and the consumers who buy the products that the immigrants help to produce. The group that loses is the workers who compete with the immigrants for jobs. For instance, for the industrialized countries, the real wages of low-skilled workers have been depressed by the influx of low-skilled workers from developing countries. Putting all of this together, we find that the net effect for the receiving country is positive—the winners win more than the losers lose.

It is important to recognize economic net benefits, but there will be fights over immigration as long as there are national borders. National governments have the ability to impose limits on immigration, and many do. If legal immigration is severely restricted by national policies, some immigrants move illegally. Migration, both legal and illegal, brings major gains in global economic well-being. But it remains socially and politically controversial.

China's Exchange Rate

An exchange rate is the value of a country's currency in terms of some other country's currency. Exchange rates are often sources of controversy, with conflict over the exchange-rate value of China's currency (the yuan, also called the renminbi) as the most intense in recent years.

In 1994 the Chinese government switched from a system of having several different exchange rates, each applying to different kinds of international transactions, to an unofficial but unmistakable fixed rate to the U.S. dollar. In fact, the exchange rate was locked at about 8.28 yuan per U.S. dollar from 1997 to 2005. During the Asian crisis of 1997–1998, the U.S. government praised the Chinese government's fixed exchange rate as a source of stability in an otherwise unstable region.

However, by 2003 the U.S. government had begun to complain that China's fixed-rate policy was actually unacceptable currency manipulation. In 2004 the U.S. trade deficit (the amount by which imports exceed exports) with China was $161 billion, a substantial part of the total U.S. trade deficit of $609 billion with the entire world. These deficits were headed even higher in 2005, and the pressure from the U.S. government intensified. Bills introduced in the U.S. Congress threatened reprisals, including large new tariffs on imports from China, unless the Chinese government implemented a large increase in the exchange-rate value of the yuan. The European Union also had a large trade deficit with China, and it was also pressuring China to revalue the yuan.

Can keeping the exchange rate steady be manipulation? What this must mean is that the exchange-rate value should have changed but did not. What was the evidence? The bottom-line evidence was that, especially after 2001, the Chinese government continually had to go into the foreign exchange market to buy dollars and to sell yuan, to keep the market rate equal to the fixed-rate target. If it had not done so, the strong private demand for yuan would have led to a rise in the price (the exchange-rate value) of the yuan. (Equivalently, the large private supply of dollars that were being sold to get yuan would have led to a decline in the value of the dollar against the yuan.)

There was evidence that the exchange-rate value of the Chinese currency was too low, but by how much? Various estimates of the degree of undervaluation were offered by economists, and most were in the range of 15 to 40 percent. Even for the experts, there are challenges in making this estimate.

First, while China had substantial trade surpluses with the United States and the European Union, it had trade deficits with many other countries, including South Korea, Thailand, the Philippines, Australia, Russia, Japan, and Brazil. Overall China had a trade surplus. It was not that large in 2004, though it was increasing.

Second, China has a remarkably high national saving rate. For a typical developing country, its low saving rate usually leads to a trade deficit, but China is not typical. So there is some economic sense for China to have a trade surplus.

Third, as the official pressure built on the Chinese government to change the exchange rate, private speculators began to move "hot money" into the country in the hopes of profiting when the value of the yuan increased. A substantial part of the government's purchase of dollars was buying this hot money, and the hot money flow will reverse once the speculators think that the play is done.

For a few years, the Chinese government resisted the foreign pressure to change its exchange-rate policy. The fixed exchange rate to the U.S. dollar had served the Chinese economy well. The Chinese government did not want to appear to be giving in to the foreign pressure, and it stated repeatedly that it alone would make any decisions about its exchange-rate policy as it saw fit for the good of China's economy.

Then, on July 21, 2005, the Chinese government announced and implemented changes in its policy toward the exchange-rate value of the yuan. It increased the value from 8.28 yuan per U.S. dollar to 8.11 yuan per dollar, a revaluation of 2.1 percent. (Yes, that does look odd, but the lower number means a higher value for the yuan. Welcome to the sometimes confusing world of foreign exchange. As stated, the numbers show a decrease in the value of a dollar, which is the same as an increase in the value of the yuan.) Thereafter, the Chinese government followed a policy best described as a "crawling peg," in which the government allows small daily changes that result in a slow, tightly controlled change over time in the exchange-rate value. By July 2008 the yuan had increased by a total of about 21 percent, to a value of about 6.83 yuan per dollar. But the Chinese government was worried about the worsening global financial and economic crisis. The government decided to return to a steady fixed rate to the U.S. dollar, and the yuan was kept at about 6.83 per dollar for nearly two years.

China continued to run a trade surplus and foreign investment continued to flow into China. China continued to intervene in the foreign exchange market, buying dollars and selling yuan, to prevent the yuan from appreciating. China continued to add the dollars to its holdings of official international reserve assets. These government holdings of foreign-currency-denominated financial investments and similar assets had been $166 billion at the beginning of 2001, grew to $711 billion in mid-2005, and reached $2.45 trillion by mid-2010.

As the world recovered from the worst of the global crisis, the United States and other countries resumed pressure on China to increase the exchange-rate value of the yuan. Although again there was a wide range of estimates, a number of credible analysts concluded that the yuan was still undervalued by perhaps 15 to 30 percent. On June 18, 2010, the Chinese government resumed allowing a slow increase in the exchange-rate value of the yuan, and by August 2014 it rose in value by another 11 percent.

While foreign pressure may have had some effect, the most important reason that China's government resumed yuan appreciation was that conditions in China's national economy had changed. As the government intervened in the foreign exchange market to buy dollars, it was also selling yuan. The yuan money supply in China grew too rapidly, encouraging local borrowing and spending that created upward pressure on the inflation rate in China. Given these conditions, the increase in the exchange-rate value of the yuan can assist the Chinese government to manage its domestic economy better, through at least three channels. First, it lowers import prices in China, thereby reducing inflation pressures in China. Second, it slows the growth of China's exports, removing some of the demand pressure on the prices of resources and products. Third, it reduces the amount of intervention needed, reducing the pressure for growth of China's domestic money supply.

The international controversy over China's exchange rate was very much alive in mid-2014, as exchange market intervention continued and China's official international reserves rose to a staggering $4 trillion in June 2014. As the conflict over China's exchange-rate policy shows clearly, policy decisions by one country have effects that spill over onto other countries. The exchange rate is a key price that affects international trade flows of goods and services and international financial flows.

In the second half of this book, we will examine in depth many of the issues raised in the description of this controversial situation. For example, in Chapter 16 we will examine trade surpluses and trade deficits in the context of a country's balance of payments. In Chapter 18 we will explore foreign financial investments and the role of currency speculation. In Chapters 22–24 we will examine how exchange rates and official intervention in the foreign exchange market affect not only a country's trade balance but also its national production, unemployment, and inflation rate. And in Chapters 20 and 25 we will look at why a country would or would not choose to have a fixed exchange rate.

Euro Crisis

The European Union (EU), founded in 1957–1958, is the most successful regional trade agreement. It has expanded from 6 countries to 28 and has largely eliminated barriers to trade in goods and services and movement of people and financial capital among its member countries. As a major step toward economic and monetary union, 11 EU countries established the euro as their common currency in 1999, with the European Central Bank (ECB) in charge of monetary policy for the new euro area.

In its first decade the euro worked well. With national currencies replaced by the euro, the transactions costs of doing business across euro-area countries fell, risks of unexpected exchange-rate changes within the area were eliminated, international trade among the euro-area countries increased, and financial markets became more integrated. By 2009 the number of EU countries in the euro area had increased to 16 (and two more would join by 2014). The annual growth of real GDP for the euro area was a little more than 3 percent during 2006–2007, unemployment fell below 8 percent, and the annual inflation rate was a little above 2 percent.

The global financial and economic crisis began in 2007. The United States had had a credit boom that increased debt generally, with a surge specifically in sub-prime mortgages, those made to high-risk borrowers, that were then packaged into debt securities and sold to investors. The credit boom had funded a housing bubble, with U.S. housing prices rising rapidly and peaking in April 2006. When sub-prime mortgages increasingly went into default, investors, including many financial institutions, that had purchased the mortgage-backed securities suffered losses. Short-term debt markets froze as financial institutions and other investors became wary of lending to other financial institutions.

The global crisis intensified with the failure of Lehman Brothers in September 2008. Europe was involved in four major ways. First, some European countries had their own credit booms, with housing bubbles in Ireland, Spain, and several other countries. Second, many European banks bought mortgage-backed securities and suffered losses on their holdings. Third, the freezing of short-term funding markets hurt many European banks. Fourth, the recession that began in the United States spread to other countries. As U.S. production and income declined, the United States imported fewer foreign goods and services. That is, other countries exported less, and aggregate demand for their products fell.

Along with the rest of the world, the euro area went into a deep recession, with real GDP falling by over 4 percent during 2009. Government policy responses, including aggressive actions by the U.S. Federal Reserve, had largely stabilized financial markets by late 2009. The recession in the euro area ended in mid-2009, and it looked like the euro area was on a steady path to recovery.

Two festering problems were about to explode, causing several national crises that eventually threatened the euro's existence. First, the recession drove increased fiscal deficits in most euro-area countries. Greece's fiscal deficit was almost 16 percent of its GDP in 2009, and its outstanding government debt rose to 130 percent of its GDP. Second, burst housing bubbles in some countries led to rising defaults on mortgages, threatening the solvency of the banks that had made the loans. The Irish government addressed the weakness of its banking system by decreeing in 2008 that the government guaranteed all deposits and debts of large Irish banks. As bank losses mounted, the government provided massive assistance. Ireland's fiscal deficit jumped to 30 percent of its GDP in 2010, and outstanding government debt rose from 25 percent of GDP in 2007 to over 100 percent by 2011.

With the success of the euro in integrating financial markets across the euro area, and with generally strong economic performance, the interest rates on the government debts of different countries were very close to each other up to 2008. Essentially, the markets viewed the credit risk of the Greek government and other euro area governments to be nearly the same as the risk of the German government. In 2009, with the realization that the Greek deficit was much larger than the Greek government had previously indicated, the interest rates on Greek government debt began to rise well above those for Germany's government debt, with the interest rate on 10-year Greek government bonds close to 5 percentage points higher by April 2010. The Greek government concluded that it could not take on such expensive financing, and the euro crisis began. In May 2010 the Greek government received a bailout package of €110 billion (equal to U.S. $138 billion at the exchange rate at that time of about $1.256 per euro), funded by the other euro-area countries through the newly formed European Financial Stability Facility (EFSF), the EU, and the International Monetary Fund. To access periodic loans to cover its fiscal deficits, the Greek government had to reduce its fiscal deficit over time by reducing government expenditures and raising taxes, and to enact structural reforms to loosen regulations on labor markets and product markets.

Driven by concerns about the rising costs of the bank bailouts, the interest rates on Irish government debt spiked beginning in March 2010. In November the euro crisis spread, with the Irish government receiving a bailout package that totaled €85 billion. In Portugal a credit boom led to a mix of excessive government debt and excessive private debt. The interest rates on Portuguese government debt rose rapidly, and the Portuguese government received a bailout package of €78 billion in May 2011.

Investors increasingly wondered about other euro countries, and the euro crisis expanded and intensified in mid-2011. Spain had its own housing bubble that had burst in late 2007, and a number of Spanish banks were shaky. The Spanish fiscal deficit was close to 10 percent in 2009 and 2010, and it was expected to continue at that high level. Yet, Spain began with a relatively low government debt, so that by 2010 its outstanding government debt was only about 60 percent of its GDP. Still, beginning in April 2011 nervous investors drove up interest rates on Spanish government debt. Italy had a large outstanding government debt, which had been above 100 percent of GDP since the euro began, but it had a relatively manageable fiscal deficit, below 5 percent in 2010 and falling. Nonetheless, interest rates on Italian government debt spiked beginning in June 2011. And, by July 2011, jitters in the debt markets increased generally as euro-area leaders began to discuss that Greece would have to default on it government debt, and as fears intensified that Greece would be forced to try to find a way to exit from the euro.

Spain and Italy were too large—the EFSF and the International Monetary Fund did not have enough resources to provide Spain and Italy with bailout packages comparable to those provided to Greece, Ireland, and Portugal. The European Central Bank (ECB) had the resource capability to respond, but its role had been limited, and even somewhat perverse, to this point in the euro crisis.

By statute the ECB's primary objective is price stability (a low inflation rate, defined as less than but close to 2 percent), and the ECB is prohibited from direct lending to national governments or direct purchase of national government debt. Although not prohibited, the ECB was reluctant to purchase existing national government debt in secondary markets as this was viewed as too close to direct purchase. Through its new Securities Market Program, the ECB purchased modest amounts of existing Greek, Irish, and Portuguese government bonds during May 2010–March 2011, and modest amounts of Spanish and Italian government bonds during August 2011–February 2012, with total purchases of about €212 billion. Yet, in 2011, the ECB also became worried that the area's inflation rate was rising above its target. In two steps (April and July) it raised its interest rate target (in the middle of the crisis) by half a percentage point, even as a new euro-area recession began in the middle of the year. The ECB reversed the interest rate increase in December.

By November 2011 the interest rates on 10-year Spanish and Italian government bonds were 4–5 percentage points higher than the rates on comparable German bonds. In December the ECB finally swung into serious action, announcing a series of two large offerings (December 2011 and February 2012) of long-term loans to banks in the euro area. The banks, net new borrowing was about €520 billion in total. Banks used some of these funds to buy government bonds, and Spanish and Italian interest rates declined.

The respite was short-lived. In March 2012 the Greek government received a second bailout program that added €130 billion to the first one, and the Greek government defaulted on its privately held bonds, decreasing its outstanding debt by €100 billion. Investors again became worried about risks in individual euro-area countries and risks to the continued existence of the euro. Interest rates on Spanish and Italian government bonds jumped again.

On July 26, 2012, ECB President Mario Draghi delivered a speech that more fully addressed the crisis and began to wind it down. He stated that "the ECB is ready to do whatever it takes to preserve the euro. And believe me, it will be enough." In September the ECB approved the new Outright Monetary Transactions program. To prevent distortions in financial markets, the ECB is willing to purchase potentially large amounts of national government bonds if the government also has a program with the European Stability Mechanism (ESM—the EU is fond of acronyms), which replaced the EFSF. The ECB insisted on a program with the ESM because the ESM imposes conditions for national adjustment (the ECB cannot do so).

In July the interest rates on Italian, Spanish, Greek, Portuguese, and Irish bonds went into rapid decline, and by 2014 all 10-year bond rates except those of Greece were back to within 2 percentage points of the rates on German government bonds. The worst of the euro crisis was over, although in late 2012 Spain received a loan from the ESM to recapitalize its banks and in March 2013 Cyprus received a bailout program.

Each country must choose a policy for the exchange rate (international value) of its currency, and the countries of the euro area have chosen monetary union, an extreme and controversial form of "fixed exchange rates" within the area. Monetary union is a step well beyond a regional trade bloc, and we discuss the euro and its crisis throughout the second half of the book. In Chapter 16 we examine current account balances and net international financial asset positions as indicators of potential problems in the countries at the center of the euro crisis. In Chapter 21 we describe and analyze financial crises that have occurred during the past 40 years, and we explicate the euro crisis as a set of three mutually reinforcing crises—sovereign (government) debt crisis, banking crisis, and macroeconomic performance crisis. In Chapter 25 we specifically analyze the benefits and costs of European Monetary Union. Two controversies emerge. First, what is the cost to a member country of giving up both national monetary policy and the ability to change its exchange rate with other member countries? Second, is it possible to manage the tension between national fiscal policy as an important tool for the government to improve the country's macroeconomic performance and national fiscal policy as a source of instability (and even crisis) for the monetary union?

ECONOMICS AND THE NATION-STATE

It should be clear from the four controversies described above that international economics is a special field of study because nations are sovereign. Each nation has its own government policies. For each nation, these policies are almost always designed to serve some group(s) inside that nation. Countries almost never care as much about the interests of foreigners as they do about national interests. Think of the debate about U.S. exports of natural gas. How loudly have Americans spoken out about the harm to Japan because of the high cost of its natural gas imports?

The fact that nations have their sovereignty, their separate self-interests, and their separate policies means that *nobody is in charge of the whole world economy.* The global economy has no global government, benevolent or otherwise. It is true that there are international organizations that try to manage aspects of the global economy, particularly the World Trade Organization, the International Monetary Fund, the United Nations, and the World Bank. But each country has the option to ignore or defy these global institutions if it really wants to.

Among the most important policies that each country can manipulate separately are policies toward the international movement of productive resources (people and financial capital), policies toward government taxation and spending, and policies toward money and exchange rates.

Factor Mobility

In differentiating international from domestic economics, classical economists stressed the behavior of the factors of production. Labor, land, and capital were seen as mobile within a country, in the sense that these resources could be put to different productive uses within the country. For example, a country's land could be used to grow wheat or to raise dairy cattle or as the site for a factory. But, the classical economists believed, these resources were not mobile across national borders. Outside of war land does not move from one country to another. They also downplayed the ability of workers or capital to move from one country to another.

If true, this difference between intranational factor mobility and international factor immobility would have implications for many features of the global economy. For instance, the wages of French workers of a given training and skill would be more or less the same, regardless of which industry the workers happened to be part of. But this French wage level could be very different from the wage for comparable workers in Germany, Italy, Canada, or Australia. The same equality of return within a country, but differences internationally, was believed to be true for land and capital.

This distinction of the classical economists is partly valid today. Land is the least mobile factor internationally. Workers and capital do move internationally, in response to opportunities for economic gain. Still, there appear to be differences of degree in mobility interregionally and internationally. People usually migrate within their own country more readily than they emigrate abroad. This is true partly because identity of language, customs, and tradition is more likely to exist within a country than between countries. In addition, national governments impose greater limitations on international migration than they do on relocation within the country. Capital is also more mobile within than between countries. Even financial capital, which in many ways is free to move internationally, is subject to a "home bias" in which people prefer to invest within their own country. In our analysis of international trade in the first half of this book, we will generally presume that some key resource inputs (to production of the traded products) cannot easily move directly between countries. We then examine international resource mobility, including immigration, in Chapter 15 and examine aspects of international financial investments in Chapters 16–21.

Different Fiscal Policies

For each sovereign country, its separate government has its own public spending, power to tax, and power to regulate. Governments use these policies to limit international transactions when they use taxes or regulations that reduce imports, exports, immigration, and financial flows. Other aspects of fiscal policy, including subsidies to exports, encourage more international transactions. Differences across countries in tax and regulatory policies can also cause larger flows of funds and products. Banks set up shop in the Bahamas, where their capital gains are less taxed and their books less scrutinized. Shipping firms register in Liberia or Panama, where registration costs little and where they are free from other countries' requirements to use higher-cost national maritime workers. We examine the microeconomic effects of policies toward international trade in Chapters 8–14 and the macroeconomic effects of different fiscal policies in Chapters 22–24.

Different Moneys

To many economists, and especially to noneconomists, the principal difference between domestic and international trade and investment is that international transactions often involve the use of different moneys. That is very different from transactions within a country. You cannot issue your own money, nor can your family, nor can the state of Ohio.

The existence of separate moneys means that the value of one money relative to another can change. We could imagine otherwise. If a U.S. dollar were worth exactly 10 Swedish kronor for 10 centuries, people would certainly come to think of a krona and a dime as the same money. But this does not happen. Since the 1970s the price ratios between the major currencies have been fluctuating by the minute. We must treat the dollar and the krona, for example, as different moneys. And the exchange-rate values can be contentious, as we saw for China's yuan.

Most countries have their own national money, though some countries share the same money, as we saw for the euro area. The supply of each kind of money is controlled by the monetary authority or central bank in charge of that money. Monetary policy affects not only the country using that money but also other countries, even if they use different moneys. Chapters 17–25 explore the special relationships between national moneys.

Chapter **Two**

The Basic Theory Using Demand and Supply

For centuries people have been fighting over whether governments should allow trade between countries. There have been, and probably always will be, two sides to the argument. Some argue that just letting everybody trade freely is best for both the country and the world. Others argue that trade with other countries makes it harder for some people to make a good living. Both sides are at least partly right.

International trade matters a lot. Its effects on the economic life of people in a country are enormous. Imagine a world in which your country did not trade at all with other countries. It isn't hard to do. Imagine what kind of job you would be likely to get, and think of what products you could buy (or not buy) in such a world. For the United States, for example, start by imagining that it lived without its $300 billion a year in imported oil. Americans would have to cut back on energy use because the remaining domestic oil (and natural gas and other energy sources) would be more expensive. Americans who produce oil and other energy sources might be pleased with such a scenario. Those who work in the auto industry and those who need to heat their homes would not. Similar impacts would be felt by producers and consumers in other parts of the economy suddenly stripped of imports like LCD televisions and clothing. On the export side, suppose that Boeing could sell airplanes and American farmers could sell their crops only within the United States, and that U.S. universities could admit only domestic students. In each case there are people who gain and people who lose from cutting off international trade. Every one of these differences between less trade and more trade has strong effects on what career you choose. Little wonder, then, that people are always debating the issue of having less or more trade.

Each side of the trade debate needs a convincing story of just how trade matters and to whom. Yet that story, so useful in the arena of policy debate, requires an even more basic understanding of why people trade as they do when allowed to trade, exporting some products and importing others. If we do not know how people decide what goods and services to trade, it is hard to say what the effects of trade are or whether trade should be restricted by governments.

FOUR QUESTIONS ABOUT TRADE

This chapter and subsequent Chapters 3–7 tackle the issue of how trade works by comparing two worlds. In one world no trade is allowed. In the other, governments just stand aside and let individual businesses and households trade freely across national borders. We seek answers to four key questions:

1. Why do countries trade? More precisely, what determines which products a country exports and which products it imports?
2. How does trade affect production and consumption in each country?
3. How does trade affect the economic well-being of each country? In what sense can we say that a country gains or loses from trade?
4. How does trade affect the distribution of economic well-being or income among various groups within the country? Can we identify specific groups that gain from trade and other groups that lose because of trade?

Our basic theory of trade says that trade usually results from the interaction of competitive demand and supply. This chapter goes straight to the basic picture of demand and supply. It suggests answers to the four questions about trade, including how to measure the gains that trade brings to some people and the losses it brings to others.

We are embarking on an extended exploration of international trade. The first box in this chapter, "Trade Is Important," provides information that sets the stage for our journey. The chapter's second box, "The Trade Mini-Collapse of 2009," shows how trade declined much more than general economic activity during the global financial and economic crisis.

DEMAND AND SUPPLY

Let's review the economics of demand and supply before we apply these tools to examine international trade. The product that we use as an example is motorbikes. We assume that the market for motorbikes is competitive. Although the analysis appears to be only about a single product (here, motorbikes), it actually is broader than this. Demanders make decisions about buying this product instead of other products. Suppliers use resources to produce this product, and the resources used in producing motorbikes are not available to produce other products. What we are studying is actually one product relative to all other goods and services in the economy.

Demand

What determines how much of a product is demanded? A consumer's problem is to get as much happiness or well-being (in economists' jargon, utility) as possible by spending the limited income that the consumer has available. A basic determinant of how much a consumer buys of a product is the person's taste, preferences, or opinions of the product. Given the person's tastes, the price of the product (relative to the prices of other products) also has a major influence on how much of the product is purchased. At a higher price for this product, the consumer usually economizes and reduces the quantity purchased. Another major influence is the consumer's income. If the consumer's income increases, the consumer buys more of many products, probably including more of this

FIGURE 2.1

Demand and
Supply for
Motorbikes

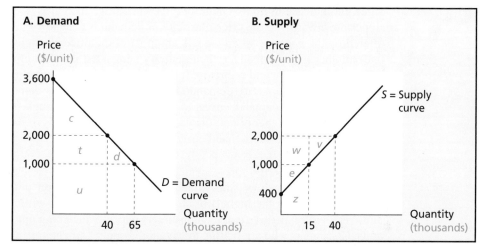

The market demand curve for motorbikes slopes downward. A lower price results in a larger
quantity demanded. The market supply curve for motorbikes slopes upward. A higher price
results in a larger quantity supplied.

product. (The consumer buys more if this product is a *normal good.* This is not the only
possibility—quantity purchased is unchanged if demand is independent of income, and
quantity goes down if the product is an *inferior good.* In this text we almost always
examine only normal goods, as we consider these to be the usual case.)

How much the consumer demands of the product thus depends on a number of
influences: tastes, the price of this product, the prices of other products, and income.
We would like to be able to picture demand. We do this by focusing on one major
determinant, the product's price. After we add up all consumers of the product, we
use a market demand curve like the demand curve for motorbikes shown as *D* in
Figure 2.1A.[1] We have a strong presumption that the demand curve slopes downward.
An increase in the product's price (say, from $1,000 per motorbike to $2,000) results
in a decrease in quantity demanded (from 65,000 to 40,000 motorbikes purchased per
year). This is a movement along the demand curve because of a change in the product's
price. The increase in price results in a lower quantity demanded as people (somewhat
reluctantly) switch to substitute products (e.g., bicycles) or make do with less of the
more expensive product (forgo buying a second motorbike of a different color).

How responsive is quantity demanded to a change in price? One way to measure
responsiveness is by the slope of the demand curve (actually, by the inverse of the slope
because price is on the vertical axis). A steep slope indicates low responsiveness of quantity
to a change in price (quantity does not change that much). A flatter slope indicates more
responsiveness. The slope is a measure of responsiveness, but it can also be misleading.
By altering the units used on the axes, the demand curve can be made to look flat or steep.

A measure of responsiveness that is "unit-free" is elasticity, the *percent* change
in one variable resulting from a 1 *percent* change in another variable. The price
elasticity of demand is the percent change in quantity demanded resulting from a

---

[1]The equation for this demand curve is $Q_D = 90{,}000 - 25P$ (or $P = 3{,}600 - 0.04Q_D$).

1 percent increase in price. Quantity falls when price increases (if the demand curve slopes downward), so the price elasticity of demand is a negative number (though we often drop the *negative* when we talk about it). If the price elasticity is a large (negative) number (greater than 1), then quantity demanded is substantially responsive to a price change—demand is *elastic*. If the price elasticity is a small (negative) number (less than 1), then quantity demanded is not that responsive—demand is *inelastic*.

In drawing the demand curve, we assume that other things that can influence demand—income, other prices, and tastes—are constant. If any of the other influences changes, then the entire demand curve shifts.

Consumer Surplus

The demand curve shows the value that consumers place on units of the product because it indicates the highest price that some consumer is willing to pay for each unit. Yet, in a competitive market, consumers pay only the going market price for these units. Consumers who are willing to pay more benefit from buying at the market price. Their well-being is increased, and we can measure how much it increases.

To see this, consider first the value that consumers place on the total quantity of the product that they actually purchase. We can measure the value unit by unit. For the first motorbike demanded, the demand curve in Figure 2.1A tells us that somebody would be willing to pay a very high price (about $3,600)—the price just below where the demand curve hits the price axis. The demand curve tells us that somebody is willing to pay a slightly lower price for the second motorbike, and so on down the demand curve for each additional unit.

By adding up all of the demand curve heights for each unit that is demanded, we see that the whole area under the demand curve (up to the total consumption quantity) measures the total value to consumers from buying this quantity of motorbikes. For instance, for 40,000 motorbikes the total value to consumers is $112 million, equal to area $c + t + u$. This amount can be calculated as the sum of two areas that are easier to work with: the area of the rectangle $t + u$ formed by price and quantity, equal to $2,000 \times 40,000$, plus the area of triangle c above this rectangle, equal to $(1/2) \times (\$3,600 - \$2,000) \times 40,000$. (Recall that the area of a triangle like c is equal to one-half of the product of its height and base.) This total value can be measured as a money amount, but it ultimately represents the *willingness* of consumers, if necessary, to forgo consuming other goods and services to buy this product.

The marketplace does not give away motorbikes for free, of course. The buyers must pay the market price (a money amount, but ultimately the value of other goods and services that the buyers must give up to buy this product). For instance, at a price of $2,000 per motorbike, consumers buy 40,000 motorbikes and pay $80 million in total (price times quantity, equal to area $t + u$).

Because many consumers value the product more highly than $2,000 per motorbike, paying the going market price still leaves consumers with a *net gain* in economic well-being. The net gain is the difference between the value that consumers place on the product and the payment that they must make to buy the product. This net gain is called **consumer surplus**, the increase in the economic well-being of consumers who are able to buy the product at a market price lower than the highest price that they are willing and able to pay for the product. For a market price of $2,000 in

Case Study   Trade Is Important

To understand stories about how trade works, it is useful to know some of the key facts about trade. A good start is a broad overview of the products traded and trade's growing importance.

How large is international trade? What products are traded? The table below shows exports by major product categories, for the world overall and for two broad economic groups of countries, the industrialized (or developed or advanced) countries and the developing countries.

In 2012, world trade was nearly $23 trillion, with the industrialized countries contributing a little over half of world exports. Most goods are traded across national borders, as are many services, including transportation, computer and information services, as well as insurance, consulting, and educational services. For the world, about half of trade is in manufactured products, with the rest of trade split between primary products and services. By comparing the details across the columns, we can see that the broad pattern of exporting by the industrialized countries has some differences from the pattern for developing countries. Industrialized countries export

relatively less of primary products, especially fuels. In manufactured products, industrialized countries export relatively more of chemicals, while developing countries export relatively more of textiles and clothing. Industrialized countries are relatively strong in exporting services. We will use this kind of observation—looking at trade across product categories—as we examine why countries trade with each other.

How important is international trade in the economies of various countries? The second table in this box examines one measure of the importance of trade to a country, the ratio of the sum of a country's total trade (exports plus imports) to the country's gross domestic product (GDP, a standard way of measuring the size of a country's economy). These measures are not completely comparable (exports and imports measure full sales values, while GDP measures value added). Still, they provide a reasonable way of comparing the importance of trade across time and across countries.

Here are a few observations about what we see in this table. First, for each of the countries

Exports, 2012 (billions of U.S. dollars)

	World	Industrialized Countries	Developing Countries
Total	22,777	12,283	10,494
Primary products	6,293	2,454	3,839
Agricultural	1,666	942	724
Fuels	3,451	927	2,524
Ores	1,176	585	590
Manufactured products	11,486	6,426	5,060
Chemicals	1,945	1,349	596
Machinery and transport equipment	5,829	3,247	2,582
Textiles and clothing	733	213	520
Other	2,979	1,617	1,362
Services	4,426	2,951	1,475

Note: Sum of primary products, manufactured products, and services does not equal total because of a small amount of unclassified goods.

Source: UNCTAD, UNCTADStat.

—Continued on next page

Exports Plus Imports as a Percentage of GDP

	1970	2012
United States	11.1	30.4
Canada	42.0	62.1
Japan	20.3	31.3
France	31.1	57.1
United Kingdom	43.6	65.3
Australia	25.9	41.5
Denmark	57.3	104.5
China	5.3	51.3
India	8.0	55.4
Korea	37.7	109.9
Brazil	14.9	26.5

Source: International Monetary Fund, *International Financial Statistics.*

shown in the table (and for most other countries), international trade has become more important. Trade's increasing importance is one part of the process of globalization—in which

rising international transactions increasingly link together what had been relatively separate national economies. Second, trade tends to be more important for countries with smaller economies (such as Canada and Denmark) and somewhat less important for very large economies (such as the United States and Japan). Third, both China and India have gone from being mostly closed to trade to much more open and involved. The experiences of China and India in the past several decades are rather close to the approach we will take in Chapters 2–7—imagining a national economy with no trade and then drawing out what will happen when the country opens up to free trade.

DISCUSSION QUESTION

Given the trends shown here, do you think that international trade should have become more controversial or less controversial than it was several decades ago?

Figure 2.1A, the consumer surplus is the difference between the total value to consumers (area $c + t + u$) and the total payments to buy the product (area $t + u$). Consumer surplus thus is equal to area c, the area below the demand curve and above the price line. This contribution to the economic well-being of consumers through the use of this market is $32 million, equal to $(1/2) \times (\$3,600 - \$2,000) \times 40,000$.

A major use of consumer surplus is to measure the impact on consumers of a change in market price. For instance, what is the effect in our example if the market price of motorbikes is $1,000 instead of $2,000? Consumers are better off—they pay a lower price and decide to buy more. How much better off? Consumer surplus increases from a smaller triangle (extending down to the $2,000 price line) to a larger triangle (extending down to the $1,000 price line). The *increase* in consumer surplus is area $t + d$. This increase can be calculated as the area of rectangle t, equal to $(\$2,000 - \$1,000) \times 40,000$, plus the area of triangle d, equal to $(1/2) \times (\$2,000 - \$1,000) \times (65,000 - 40,000)$. The increase in consumer surplus is $52.5 million. The lower market price results in both an increase in economic well-being for consumers who would have bought anyway at the higher price (area t) and an increase in economic well-being for those consumers who are drawn into purchasing by the lower price (area d).

Supply

What determines how much of a product is supplied by a business firm (or other producer) into a market? A firm supplies the product because it is trying to earn a profit on its production and sales activities. One influence on how much a firm supplies is the price that the firm receives for its sales. The other major influence is the cost of producing and selling the product.

For a competitive firm, if the price at which the firm can sell another unit of its product exceeds the extra (or marginal) cost of producing it, then the firm should supply that unit because it makes a profit on it. The firm then will supply units up to the point at which the price received just about equals the extra cost of another unit. The cost of producing another unit depends on two things: the resources or inputs (such as labor, capital, land, and materials) needed to produce the extra unit and the prices that have to be paid for these inputs.

We would like to be able to picture supply, and we do so by focusing on how the price of the product affects quantity supplied. After we add up all producers of the product, we use a market supply curve like the supply curve *S* for motorbikes in Figure 2.1B.[2] We usually presume that the supply curve slopes upward. An increase in the product's price (say, from $1,000 per motorbike to $2,000) results in an increase in quantity supplied (from 15,000 to 40,000 motorbikes produced and sold per year). This is a movement along the supply curve. In a competitive industry, an additional motorbike is supplied if the price received covers the extra cost of producing and selling this additional unit. If additional units can be produced only at a rising extra or marginal cost, then a higher price is necessary to draw out additional quantity supplied. The supply curve turns out to be the same as the curve showing the marginal cost of producing each unit.

How responsive is quantity supplied to a change in the market price? One way to measure responsiveness is by the slope of the supply curve. Quantity supplied is more responsive if the slope is flatter. A "unit-free" measure is the **price elasticity of supply**—the percent increase in quantity supplied resulting from a 1 percent increase in market price. Quantity supplied is not that responsive to price—supply is inelastic—if the price elasticity is less than 1. Quantity supplied is substantially responsive—supply is elastic—if the price elasticity is greater than 1.

In drawing the supply curve, we assume that other things influencing supply are constant. These other things include the conditions of availability of inputs and the technology that determines what inputs are needed to produce extra units of the product. If any of these other influences changes, then the entire supply curve shifts.

Producer Surplus

The supply curve shows the lowest possible price at which some producer would be willing to supply each unit. Producers actually receive the going market price for these units. Producers who would have been willing to supply at a lower price benefit from selling at the market price. Indeed, we can measure how much their well-being increases.

To see this, consider first the total (variable) costs of producing and selling the total quantity that is actually supplied. We can measure this cost unit by unit. For the first motorbike supplied into the market, the supply curve in Figure 2.1B tells us that some producer would be willing to supply this for about $400, the price just above where the supply curve hits the axis. This amount just covers the extra cost of producing and

---

[2]The equation for this supply curve is $Q_S = -10,000 + 25P$ (or $P = 400 + 0.04Q_S$).

Global Crisis   The Trade Mini-Collapse of 2009

The global crisis that began in 2007 and deepened in late 2008 spread well beyond financial markets. The crisis caused the first large-scale downturn in world trade in more than half a century, ending decades in which, nearly year after year, international trade grew faster than world production. First, let's look at the growth of trade over decades, then we'll examine the unexpected mini-collapse.

The diagram shows world exports of goods and services and world production of goods and services. Each is adjusted for price inflation, so we are seeing what happened to the quantity or volume. Each is measured as an index number, with its value set to be equal to 100 in 1960. Using the index values, we can see how each has changed during the past half century.

Looking at the entire time period, the explosive growth of world exports is clear. Since 1960, world production has increased by a factor of

6 (from the initial 100 in 1960 to about 600 in 2013). *Since 1960, world trade has increased by a factor of over 20.* This is another way to see what we highlighted in the previous box—the increasing importance of trade.

The diagram also shows the surprising recent decline of world trade. Starting in late 2008, world trade declined by about 11 percent. The trade decline was much larger than the 2 percent decline in world production. Why was the trade decline so large? Two specific features matter. First, a relatively large part of trade is in durable goods like machinery and automobiles. In the crisis-driven global recession, purchases of durable goods were postponed or canceled, and trade in these products collapsed. The trade decline was amplified because production of these products often involves a global supply chain in which materials and components are traded across borders before final assembly. A decrease of, say, $100 in the sale

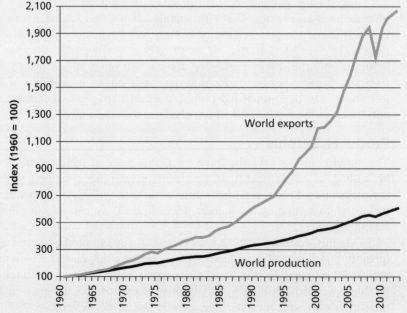

Volume of World Trade and World Production, 1960–2013

Source: World Bank, *World Development Indicators.*

of a final good can result in a decrease of well more than $100 in the cumulated value of trade in materials, components, and the final good itself. Second, but of much less importance, most trade requires financing, and there was some crisis-driven decline in working-capital financing for export production and in trade financing for export–import transactions. For both of these reasons, the crisis-recession decline in world production and final sales led to a magnified decline in world trade.

The collapse in world trade in 2009 resurrected memories of the Great Depression of the 1930s, when trade declined by 25 percent during the four years from 1929 to 1933. Fortunately for the world, and for us, the recent decline in trade was a mini-collapse, and robust trade growth returned beginning in mid-2009. Then, the euro crisis that began in 2010 caused some slowdown in the growth rate of world exports in 2012 and 2013, but not an actual decline in trade volume.

selling this first unit. The supply curve tells us that some producer is willing to supply the second motorbike for a slightly higher price because the extra cost of the second unit is a little higher, and so on.

By adding up all of the supply curve heights for each unit supplied, we find that the whole area under the supply curve (up to the total quantity supplied) is the total cost of producing and selling this quantity of motorbikes. For instance, the total cost of producing 15,000 motorbikes is equal to area z in Figure 2.1B. This total cost can be measured as a money amount, but for the whole economy it ultimately represents an **opportunity cost**—the value of other goods and services that are not produced because resources are instead used to produce this product (motorbikes).

The total revenue received by producers is the product of the market price and the quantity sold. For instance, at a price of $1,000 per motorbike, producers sell 15,000 motorbikes, so they receive $15 million in total revenue (equal to area $e + z$).

Because producers would have been willing to supply some motorbikes at a price below $1,000, receiving the going market price for all units results in a *net gain* in their economic well-being. The net gain is the difference between the revenues received and the costs incurred. This net gain is called **producer surplus,** the increase in the economic well-being of producers who are able to sell the product at a market price higher than the lowest price that would have drawn out their supply. For a market price of $1,000 in Figure 2.1B, the producer surplus is the difference between total revenues (area $e + z$) and total costs (area z). Producer surplus is thus equal to area e, the area above the supply curve and below the price line. Producer surplus in this case is $4.5 million, equal to $(1/2) \times (\$1,000 - \$400) \times 15,000$.

A major use of producer surplus is to measure the impact on producers of a change in market price. For instance, what is the effect if the market price is $2,000 instead of $1,000? Producers are better off—they receive a higher price and decide to produce and sell more. Producer surplus increases from a smaller triangle (extending up to the $1,000 price line) to a larger triangle (extending up to the $2,000 price line). The *increase* in producer surplus is equal to area $w + v$,

FIGURE 2.2

The Market for Motorbikes: Demand and Supply

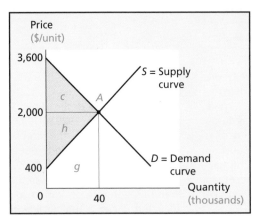

The market for motorbikes can be pictured using demand and supply curves. In this example, which may be a national market with no international trade, the market reaches equilibrium at a price of $2,000 per motorbike, with 40,000 motorbikes produced and purchased during the time period (e.g., a year). Under these conditions, consumers get consumer surplus equal to area c and producers get producer surplus equal to area h.

or ($2,000 − $1,000) × 15,000 plus (1/2) × ($2,000 − $1,000) × (40,000 − 15,000), which equals $27.5 million. The higher market price results in both an increase in economic well-being for producers who would have supplied anyway at the lower price (area *w*) and an increase in well-being for producers of the additional units supplied (area *v*).

A National Market with No Trade

If *D* in Figure 2.1A represents the *national* demand for the product and *S* in Figure 2.1B represents the *national* supply, we can combine these into the single picture for the national market for this product, as shown in Figure 2.2. If there is no international trade, then equilibrium occurs at the price at which the market clears domestically, with national quantity demanded equal to national quantity supplied. In Figure 2.2 this no-trade equilibrium occurs at point *A*, with a price of $2,000 per motorbike and total quantity supplied and demanded of 40,000 motorbikes. Both consumers and producers benefit from having this market, as consumer surplus is area *c* and producer surplus is area *h* (the same as area *e* + *w* + *v* in Figure 2.1B). In this example, both gain the same amount of surplus, $32 million each. In general, these two areas do not have to be equal, though both will be positive amounts. For instance, consumer surplus will be larger than producer surplus if the demand curve is steeper (more inelastic) or the supply curve is flatter (more elastic) than those shown in Figure 2.2.

TWO NATIONAL MARKETS AND THE OPENING OF TRADE

To discuss international trade in motorbikes, we need at least two countries. We will call the country whose national market is shown in Figure 2.2 the United States. This U.S. national market is also shown in the left-hand graph of Figure 2.3; we add the

FIGURE 2.3   The Effects of Trade on Production, Consumption, and Price, Shown with Demand and Supply Curves

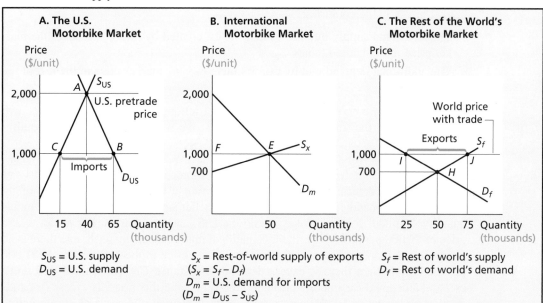

In the international market for motorbikes, the desire to trade is the (horizontal) difference between national demand and supply. The difference between U.S. demand and supply, on the left, is graphed in the center diagram as the U.S. demand for imports (the D_m curve). The difference between foreign supply and demand, on the right, is graphed in the center diagram as the foreign supply of exports (the S_x curve). The interactions of demand and supply in both countries determine the world price of motorbikes and the quantities produced, traded, and consumed.

Effects of Trade	Price	Quantity Supplied	Quantity Demanded
United States	Down	Down	Up
Rest of the world	Up	Up	Down

subscript US to make this clear. We will call the other country the "rest of the world." The "national" market for the rest of the world is shown in the right-hand graph of Figure 2.3. Demand for motorbikes within the rest of the world is D_f, and supply is S_f. With no trade, the market equilibrium in the rest of the world occurs at point H, with a price of $700 per motorbike. To focus on the basic aspects of the situation, we will assume that prices in the two countries are stated in the same monetary units.

Starting from this initial situation of no trade in motorbikes between the two countries, can an observant person profit by initiating some trade? Using the principle of "buy low, sell high," the person could profit by buying motorbikes for $700 per motorbike in the rest of the world and selling them for $2,000 per motorbike in the United States, earning profit (before any other expenses) of $1,300 per motorbike. This is called **arbitrage**—buying something in one market and reselling the same thing in another market to profit from a price difference.

Free-Trade Equilibrium

As international trade in motorbikes develops between these two countries, it affects market prices in the countries:

- The additional supply into the United States, created by imports, reduces the market price in the United States.
- The additional demand met by exports increases the market price in the rest of the world.

In fact, if there are no transport costs or other frictions, free trade results in the two countries having the same price for motorbikes. We will call this free-trade equilibrium price the international price or world price.

What will this free-trade equilibrium price be? We can picture the price by constructing the market for international trade in motorbikes. The U.S. demand for imports can be determined for each possible price at which the United States might import. This demand for imports is the excess demand (quantity demanded minus quantity supplied) for motorbikes within the U.S. national market. For instance, at a price of $2,000 per motorbike, the U.S. national market clears by itself, and there is no excess demand and no demand for imports. If the price in the U.S. market is $1,000 per motorbike, then there is excess demand of distance *CB*, equal to 50,000 units, creating a demand for imports of 50,000 motorbikes at this price. If excess demands at other prices below $2,000 per motorbike are measured, the curve D_m, representing U.S. demand for imports, can be drawn, as shown in the middle graph of Figure 2.3.

The export supply from the rest of the world can be determined in a similar way. The supply of exports is the excess supply (quantity supplied minus quantity demanded) of motorbikes in the rest-of-the-world market. For instance, at a price of $700 per unit, this market clears by itself, and there is no excess supply and no export supply. If the price in this market is $1,000 per motorbike, then excess supply is distance *IJ* equal to 50,000 units, creating a supply of exports of 50,000 motorbikes at this price. If excess supplies for other prices above $700 per motorbike are measured, the curve S_x, representing export supply from the rest of the world, can be drawn, as shown in the middle graph of Figure 2.3.

Free-trade equilibrium occurs at the price that clears the international market. In Figure 2.3 this is at point *E*, where quantity demanded of imports equals quantity supplied of exports. The volume of trade (*FE*) is 50,000 motorbikes and the free-trade equilibrium price is $1,000 per motorbike.

This equilibrium can also be viewed as equating total world demand and supply. The international price is the price in each national market with free trade. At the price of $1,000 per motorbike, total world quantity demanded is 90,000 units (65,000 in the United States and 25,000 in the rest of the world), and total world quantity supplied is also 90,000 units (15,000 plus 75,000). The excess demand within the U.S. market (*CB*) of 50,000 motorbikes is met by the excess supply from the rest-of-the-world market (*IJ*).

What would happen if the world price for some reason was (temporarily) different from $1,000 per motorbike? At a slightly higher price (say, $1,100 per motorbike):

- The U.S. excess (or import) demand would be less than 50,000 motorbikes.
- The rest of the world's excess (or export) supply would be above 50,000 units.

Because export quantity supplied exceeds import quantity demanded, the imbalance creates pressure for the price to fall back to the equilibrium value of $1,000 per motorbike. Conversely, a price below $1,000 would not last because U.S. import quantity demanded would be greater than the foreign export quantity supplied.

Effects in the Importing Country

Opening trade in motorbikes has effects on economic well-being (in economists' jargon, *welfare*) in both the United States and the rest of the world. We will first examine changes in the importing country, the United States. Figure 2.4 reproduces Figure 2.3 and adds labels for the areas relevant to consumer and producer surplus.

Effects on Consumers and Producers

For the United States (the importing country), the shift from no trade to free trade lowers the market price. U.S. consumers of the product benefit from this change and increase their quantity consumed. The concept of consumer surplus allows us

FIGURE 2.4   The Effects of Trade on Well-Being of Producers, Consumers, and the Nation as a Whole

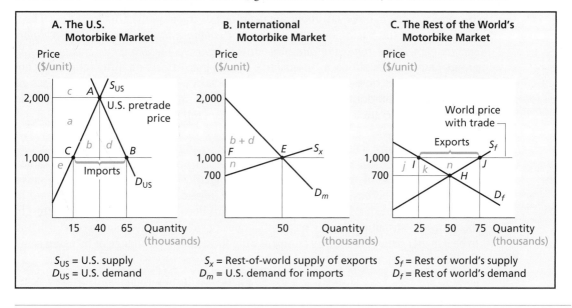

Welfare Effects of Free Trade

	United States			Rest of the World	
Group	Surplus with Free Trade	Surplus with No Trade	Net Effect of Trade	Group	Net Effect of Trade
Consumers	$a + b + c + d$	c	$a + b + d$	Consumers	$-(j + k)$ [a loss]
Producers	e	$a + e$	$-a$ [a loss]	Producers	$j + k + n$
U.S. as a whole (consumers plus producers)	$a + b + c + d + e$	$c + a + e$	$b + d$	Rest of the world as a whole	n

to quantify what the lower price is worth to consumers. With free trade, consumer surplus is the area below the demand curve and above the international price line of $1,000 per motorbike, equal to area $a + b + c + d$ (the same as area $t + c + d$ in Figure 2.1A). Thus, in comparison with the no-trade consumer surplus of area c, the opening of trade brings consumers of this product a gain of area $a + b + d$ (equal to $52.5 million, area $t + d$ in Figure 2.1A). This gain is spread over many people who consume this product (including some who are also producers of the product).

U.S. producers of this product (in their role as producers) are hurt by the shift from no trade to free trade. They receive a lower price for their product and shrink production. Producer surplus decreases from area $e + a$ with no trade (the same as area $e + w + v$ in Figure 2.1B) to only area e. The loss in producer surplus is area a (equal to $27.5 million). Area a is a loss of producer surplus both on the 15,000 motorbikes still produced in the United States and on the 25,000 that are no longer produced in the United States as imports capture this part of the market.[3]

Net National Gains

If U.S. consumers gain area $a + b + d$ from the opening of trade and U.S. producers lose area a, what can we say about the net effect of trade on the United States? There is no escaping the basic point that *we cannot compare the welfare effects on different groups without imposing our subjective weights to the economic stakes of each group*. Our analysis allows us to quantify the separate effects on different groups, but it does not tell us how important each group is to us. In our example, how much of the consumer gain does the producer loss of $27.5 million offset in our minds? No theorem or observation of economic behavior can tell us. The result depends on our value judgments.

Economists have tended to resolve the matter by imposing the value judgment that we call the one-dollar, one-vote metric—each dollar of gain or loss is valued equally, regardless of who experiences it. The metric implies a willingness to judge trade issues on the basis of their effects on aggregate well-being, without regard to their effects on the distribution of well-being. This does not signify a lack of interest in the issue of distribution. It only means that one considers the distribution of well-being to be a matter better handled by compensating those hurt by a change or by using some

---

[3]Figure 2.4 does not enable us to identify the "producers" experiencing these losses of producer surplus. If one views the supply curve as the marginal cost curve for competitive entrepreneurs who face fixed prices for inputs, then the change in producer surplus is the change in these entrepreneurs' profits. Taking this approach implicitly assumes that workers and suppliers of capital are completely unaffected by the fortunes of the industry because they can just take their labor and capital elsewhere and earn exactly the same returns. Yet this narrow focus is not justified, either by the real world or by the larger model that underlies the demand and supply curves.

Though the present diagrams cannot show the entire model of international trade at once, they are based on a general equilibrium model that shows how trade affects the rates of pay of productive inputs as well as product prices and quantities. As we shall see in Chapter 5, anything that changes the relative price of a product also changes the distribution of income within the nation. The issue of how trade affects the distribution of income will be taken up later. Now the key point is simply that as the price of motorbikes drops and the economy moves from point *A* to point *C*, the producer surplus being lost probably is a loss to workers and other input suppliers to the industry, not just a loss to the industry's entrepreneurs. To know how the change in producer surplus is divided among these groups, one would have to consult the full model, which will be complete by the end of Chapter 5.

other direct means of redistributing well-being toward those groups (for example, the poor) whose dollars of well-being seem to matter more to us.

You need not accept this value judgment. You may feel that the stake of, say, motorbike producers matters much more to you, dollar for dollar, than the stake of motorbike consumers. You might feel this way, for example, if you knew that the producers are poor, unskilled laborers, whereas the consumers are rich. And you might also feel that there is no politically feasible way to compensate the poor workers for their income losses from the opening of trade. If so, you may wish to say that each dollar lost by producers means five or six times as much to you as each dollar gained by consumers. Taking this stand leads you to conclude that opening trade violates your conception of the national interest. Even in this case, however, you could still find the demand−supply analysis useful. It is a way of quantifying the separate stakes of groups whose interests you weight unequally.

If the one-dollar, one-vote metric is accepted, then the net national gains from trade equal the difference between what one group gains and what the other group loses. If motorbike consumers gain area $a + b + d$ and motorbike producers lose area a, the net national gain from trade is area $b + d$, or a triangular area worth \$25 million per year $[= (1/2) \times (65{,}000 - 15{,}000 \text{ motorbikes}) \times (\$2{,}000 - \$1{,}000) \text{ per motorbike}]$. It turns out that very little information is needed to measure the net national gain. All that is needed is an estimate of the amount of trade and an estimate of the change in price brought about by trade.

Effects in the Exporting Country

For the rest of the world (the exporting country), the analysis follows a similar path. Here the shift from no trade to free trade increases the market price. The increase in price benefits motorbike producers in the rest of the world, whose producer surplus increases by area $j + k + n$ in Figure 2.4. The increase in price hurts motorbike consumers, whose consumer surplus decreases by area $j + k$. In the exporting country, producers of the product gain and consumers lose. Using the one-dollar, one-vote metric, we can say that the rest of the world gains from trade, and that its net gain from trade equals area n.

Which Country Gains More?

This analysis shows that each country gains from international trade, so it is clear that the whole world gains from trade. Trade is a positive-sum activity. At the same time, the gains to the countries generally are not equal—area $b + d$ is generally not equal to area n. These two triangles can be compared rather easily. They both have the same base (equal to 50,000 units, the volume of trade). The height of each triangle is the change in price in the shift from no trade to free trade for each country. Thus, the country that experiences the larger price change has a larger value of the net gains from trade.

The gains from opening trade are divided in direct proportion to the price changes that trade brings to the two sides. If a nation's price changes x percent (as a percentage of the free-trade price) and the price in the rest of the world changes y percent, then

$$\frac{\text{Nation's gain}}{\text{Rest of world's gain}} = \frac{x}{y}$$

The side with the less elastic (steeper) trade curve (import demand curve or export supply curve) gains more.

In Figure 2.4, the United States gains more. Its gains from trade in this product are $25 million. Its price changes from $2,000 to $1,000, equal to 100 percent of the free-trade price $1,000. The gains from trade for the rest of the world are $7.5 million. Its price changes from $700 to $1,000, equal to 30 percent of the free-trade price.

Summary: Early Answers to the Four Trade Questions	Extending the familiar demand—supply framework to international trade has given us useful preliminary answers to the four basic questions about international trade. The contrast between no trade and free trade offers these conclusions: 1. Why do countries trade? Demand and supply conditions differ between countries, so prices differ between countries if there is no international trade. Trade begins as someone conducts arbitrage to earn profits from the price difference between previously separated markets. A product will be exported from countries where its price was lower without trade to countries where its price was higher. 2. How does trade affect production and consumption in each country? The move from no trade to a free-trade equilibrium changes the product price from its no-trade value to the free-trade equilibrium international price or world price. The price change in each country results in changes in quantities consumed and produced. In the country importing the product, trade raises the quantity consumed and lowers the quantity produced of that product. In the exporting country, trade raises the quantity produced and lowers the quantity consumed of the product. 3. Which country gains from trade? If we use the one-dollar, one-vote metric, then both do. Each country's net national gains from trade are proportional to the change in its price that occurs in the shift from no trade to free trade. The country whose prices are disrupted more by trade gains more. 4. Within each country, who are the gainers and losers from opening trade? The gainers are the consumers of imported products and the producers of exportable products. Those who lose are the producers of import-competing products and the consumers of exportable products.

Key Terms			
	Elasticity	Opportunity cost	Supply of exports
	Price elasticity of	Producer surplus	One-dollar, one-vote
	demand	Arbitrage	metric
	Consumer surplus	International price	Net national gains from
	Price elasticity of	World price	trade
	supply	Demand for imports	

Suggested Reading

Suranovic (2000) discusses seven types of fairness and applies them to international trade. He calls our one-dollar, one-vote metric "maximum benefit fairness." Bems et al. (2013) survey the causes of the 2009 trade collapse.

Questions and Problems

◆ 1. What is consumer surplus? Using real-world data, what information would you need to measure consumer surplus for a product?

2. What is producer surplus? Using real-world data, what information would you need to measure producer surplus for a product?

◆ 3. How can a country's supply and demand curves for a product be used to determine the country's supply-of-exports curve? What does the supply-of-exports curve mean?

4. How can a country's supply and demand curves for a product be used to determine the country's demand-for-imports curve? What does the demand-for-imports curve mean?

◆ 5. A tropical country can produce winter coats, but there is no domestic demand for these coats. Explain how this country can gain from free trade in winter coats.

6. The United States exports a substantial amount of scrap iron and steel to Turkey, China, Canada, and other countries. Why do some U.S. users of scrap iron and steel support a prohibition on these exports?

◆ 7. Explain what is wrong with the following statement: "Trade is self-eliminating. Opening up trade opportunities drives prices and costs into equality between countries. But once prices and costs are equalized, there is no longer any reason to trade the product from one country to another, and trade stops."

8. In 2012, the United States imported about 3.1 billion barrels of oil. Perhaps it would be better for the United States if it could end the billions of dollars of payments to foreigners by not importing this oil. After all, the United States can produce its own oil (or other energy products that substitute for oil). If the United States stopped all oil imports suddenly, it would be very disruptive. But perhaps the United States could gain if it gradually restricted and then ended oil imports in an orderly transition. If we allow time for adjustments by U.S. consumers and producers of oil, and we perhaps are optimistic about how much adjustment is possible, then the following two equations show domestic demand and supply conditions in the United States:

$$\text{Demand: } P = 364 - 48 \cdot Q_D$$
$$\text{Supply: } P = 4 + 40 \cdot Q_S$$

where quantity Q is in billions of barrels per year and price P is in dollars per barrel.

a. With free trade and an international price of $100 per barrel, how much oil does the United States produce domestically? How much does it consume? Show the demand and supply curves on a graph and label these points. Indicate on the graph the quantity of U.S. imports of oil.

b. If the United States stopped all imports of oil (in a way that allowed enough time for orderly adjustments as shown by the equations), how much oil would be produced in the United States? How much would be consumed? What would be the price of oil in the United States with no oil imports? Show all of this on your graph.

c. If the United States stopped all oil imports, which group(s) in the United States would gain? Which group(s) would lose? As appropriate, refer to your graph in your answer.

◆ 9. Consider Figure 2.3, which shows free trade in motorbikes. Assume that consumers in the United States shift their tastes in favor of motorbikes. What is the effect on the U.S. domestic demand and/or supply curve(s)? What is the effect on the U.S. demand-for-imports curve? What is the effect on the equilibrium international price?

10. Consider again Figure 2.3, which shows free trade in motorbikes. Assume that U.S. productivity in producing motorcycles increases. What is the effect on the U.S. domestic demand and/or supply curve(s)? What is the effect on the U.S. demand-for-imports curve? What is the effect on the equilibrium international price?

◆ 11. Consider a two-country world. Each country has an upward-sloping national supply curve for raisins and a downward-sloping national demand curve for raisins. With no trade in raisins, the no-trade equilibrium price for raisins in one country would be $2.00 per kilogram and the no-trade equilibrium price for raisins in the other country would be $3.20 per kilogram. If the countries allow free trade in raisins, explain why $3.50 per kilogram cannot be the free-trade equilibrium world price for raisins. In your answer, draw and refer to graphs of supply and demand curves for the two national markets.

12. Consider a world in which everyone agrees that changes in consumers' well-being are more important than changes in producers' well-being in analyzing the effects of free trade in furniture. (This belief is a deviation from the one-dollar, one-vote metric.) Does the importing country still gain from free trade in furniture? Does the exporting country still gain from free trade in furniture?

◆ 13. The equation for the demand curve for writing paper in Belgium is

$$Q_D = 350 - (P/2) \text{ [or } P = 700 - 2Q_D]$$

The equation for the supply curve for writing paper in Belgium is

$$Q_S = -200 + 5P \text{ [or } P = 40 + (Q_S/5)]$$

a. What are the equilibrium price and quantity if there is no international trade?

b. What are the equilibrium quantities for Belgium if the nation can trade freely with the rest of the world at a price of 120?

c. What is the effect of the shift from no trade to free trade on Belgian consumer surplus? On Belgian producer surplus? What is the net national gain or loss for Belgium?

14. Country I has the usual demand and supply curves for Murky Way candy bars. Country II has a typical demand curve, too, but it cannot produce Murky Way candy bars.

a. Use supply and demand curves for the domestic markets and for the international market. Show in a set of graphs the free-trade equilibrium for Murky Way candy bars. Indicate the equilibrium world price. How does this world price compare to the no-trade price in Country I? Indicate how many Murky Ways are traded during each time period with free international trade.

b. Show graphically and explain the effects of the shift from no trade to free trade on surpluses in each country. Indicate the net national gain or loss from free trade for each country.

Chapter **Three**

Why Everybody Trades: Comparative Advantage

Chapter 2 examined international trade focusing on a single product. That analysis helped answer some major questions about international trade but only indirectly addressed some others. For an industry with expanding production, where do the additional resources come from? For a shrinking industry, what happens to the resources no longer needed? If consumers increase or decrease the quantity demanded of one product, what effect does this have on demand for other products?

Full analysis of international trade requires consideration of the entire economy. Yet the entire economy is very complex—it consists of thousands of products and the various resources needed to produce them. Fortunately, we can gain major insights by considering an economy composed of just two products. For international trade, one product can be exported and the other imported. This two-product economy captures an essential feature of international trade: A country tends to be a net exporter of some products and a net importer of others.

This chapter begins our examination of the general equilibrium of a two-product economy. We focus on the first of our four basic trade questions: Why do countries trade? In fact, why does everybody—every country as well as every person—find it worthwhile to produce and export (sell) some things and to import (buy) other things? We proceed in three steps:

1. We start with Adam Smith's original explanation, which he developed as he battled mercantilist thinking.
2. We then see that David Ricardo's principle of comparative advantage allows us to explain trade better than most people's intuition and better than Adam Smith's original explanation.
3. We begin our development of tools for analyzing a two-product economy. The production-possibility curve summarizes national production capabilities. We can use it to show how trading based on comparative advantage can enhance the well-being of a country.

As you read this chapter, pay attention to the basic message: the power of comparative advantage. If you think that the framework is much too simple, don't despair. Subsequent chapters will build on the key insights of this chapter by adding more realistic features to the economy.

ADAM SMITH'S THEORY OF ABSOLUTE ADVANTAGE

In the late 18th and early 19th centuries, first Adam Smith and then David Ricardo explored the basis for international trade as part of their efforts to make a case for free trade. Their writings were responses to the doctrine of mercantilism prevailing at the time. (See the box "Mercantilism.") Their classic theories swayed policymakers for a whole century, even though today we view them as only special cases of a more basic, and more powerful, theory of trade.

In his *Wealth of Nations,* Adam Smith promoted free trade by comparing nations to households. Every household finds it worthwhile to produce only some of the products it consumes, and to buy other products using the proceeds from what the household can sell to others. The same should apply to nations:

> It is the maxim of every prudent master of a family, never to attempt to make at home what it will cost . . . more to make than to buy. The tailor does not attempt to make his own shoes, but buys them from the shoemaker . . .
>   What is prudence in the conduct of every private family, can scarce be folly in that of a great kingdom. If a foreign country can supply us with a commodity cheaper than we ourselves can make it, better buy it of them with some part of the product of our own industry, employed in a way in which we have some advantage.

An example can show Smith's reasoning. The two "countries" in the example are the United States and the rest of the world. The two products are wheat and cloth (perhaps broadly representing agricultural products and manufactured products). Each product is produced using one resource called labor. (Smith focused on labor because he thought that all "value" was determined by and measured in hours of labor. In this respect he was imitated by David Ricardo and Karl Marx, who also believed that labor was the basis for all value. We don't have to take this literally—we can consider "labor" to be a bundle of resources used to produce products.)

Suppose that the United States is better than the rest of the world at producing wheat, and the rest of the world is better than the United States at producing cloth. It is probably not a surprise that international trade can create benefits because the United States can focus on producing what it does best (wheat) and export it, and the rest of the world can focus on producing what it does best (cloth) and export it. Let's look at this more closely.

What do we mean by "better at producing"? We can indicate each country's ability to produce each product in one of two equivalent ways. First, we can measure labor productivity—the number of units of output that a worker can produce in one hour. Second, we can look at the number of hours that it takes a worker to produce one unit of output—this is just the reciprocal of labor productivity. Here are some numbers for our example:

Case Study   Mercantilism: Older Than Smith—and Alive Today

Mercantilism was the philosophy that guided European thinking about international trade in the several centuries before Adam Smith published his *Wealth of Nations* in 1776. Mercantilists viewed international trade as a source of major benefits to a nation. Merchants engaged in trade, especially those selling exports, were good—hence the name *mercantilism*. But mercantilists also maintained that government regulation of trade was necessary to provide the largest national benefits. Trade merchants would serve their own interests and not the national interest, in the absence of government guidance.

A central belief of mercantilism was that national well-being or wealth was based on national holdings of gold and silver (specie or bullion). Given this view of national wealth, exports were viewed as good and imports (except for raw materials not produced at home) were seen as bad. If a country sells (exports) more to foreign buyers than the foreigners sell to the country (the country's imports), then the foreigners have to pay for the excess of their purchases by shipping gold and silver to the country. The gain in gold and silver increases the country's well-being, according to the mercantilist belief. Imports are undesirable because they reduce the country's ability to accumulate these precious metals. Imports were also feared because they might not be available to the country in time of war. In addition, gold and silver accruing to the national rulers could be especially valuable in helping to maintain a large military for the country. Based on mercantilist thinking, governments (1) imposed an array of taxes and prohibitions designed to limit imports and (2) subsidized and encouraged exports.

Because of its peculiar emphasis on gold and silver, mercantilism viewed trade as a zero-sum activity—one country's gains come at the expense of some other countries, since a surplus in international trade for one country must be a deficit for some other(s). The focus on promoting exports and limiting imports also provided major benefits for domestic producer interests (in both exporting and import-competing industries).

Adam Smith and economists after him pointed out that the mercantilists' push for more exports and fewer imports turns social priorities upside down. Here are the key points that refute mercantilist thinking:

- National well-being is based on the ability to consume products (and other "goods" such as leisure and a clean environment) now and in the future. Imports are part of the expanding national consumption that a nation seeks, not an evil to be suppressed.

- The importance of national production and exports is only indirect: They provide the income to buy products to consume. Exports are not desirable on their own; rather, exports are useful because they pay for imports.

- Trade freely transacted between countries generally leads to gains for all countries—trade is a positive-sum activity.

In addition, even the goal of acquiring gold and silver can be self-defeating if this acquisition expands the domestic money supply and leads to domestic inflation of product prices—an argument first expounded by David Hume even before Smith did his writing.

Although the propositions of the mercantilists have been refuted, and countries no longer focus on piling up gold and silver, mercantilist thinking is very much alive today. It now has a sharp focus on employment. Neo-mercantilists believe that exports are good because they create jobs in the country. Imports are bad because they take jobs from the country and give them to foreigners. Neo-mercantilists continue to depict trade as a zero-sum activity. There is no recognition that trade can bring gains to all countries (including mutual gains in employment as prosperity rises throughout the world). Mercantilist thinking, though misguided, still pervades discussions of international trade in countries all over the world.

DISCUSSION QUESTION
Proponents of national competitiveness focus on whether our country is winning the battle for global market share in an industry. Is this a kind of mercantilist thinking? Why or why not?

	In the United States		In the Rest of the World
Productivity:			
Units of cloth per labor hour	0.25	<	1.0
Units of wheat per labor hour	0.5	>	0.4
Labor hours to make:			
1 unit of cloth	4.0	>	1.0
1 unit of wheat	2.0	<	2.5

In this numerical example, the United States has an **absolute advantage** in producing wheat because the U.S. labor productivity in wheat is higher than the rest of the world's labor productivity in wheat. Similarly, the rest of the world has an absolute advantage in producing cloth.

If there is no trade, then each country will have to produce both products to satisfy its demand for the products. If the countries then open to free trade, each can shift its labor resources toward producing the good in which it has the absolute advantage. Total world production increases. In the United States, shifting one hour of labor results in a decrease of 0.25 unit of cloth and an increase of 0.5 unit of wheat. In the rest of the world, shifting one hour of labor results in a decrease of 0.4 unit of wheat and an increase of 1 unit of cloth. For each product, production using labor that has high productivity replaces production using labor that has low productivity.

International trade makes these shifts in production possible even if consumers in each country want to buy something different from what is produced in the country. For instance, in the United States the apparent shortage of (or apparent excess demand for) cloth (as cloth production decreases) is met by imports of cloth from the rest of the world. The United States pays for these imports of cloth by exporting some of the extra wheat produced.

Thus, Adam Smith showed the benefits of free trade by showing that global production efficiency is enhanced because trade allows each country to exploit its absolute advantage in producing some product(s). At least one country is better off with trade, and this country's gain is not at the expense of the other country. In many cases both countries will gain from trade by splitting the benefits of the enhanced global production.

Smith's reasoning was fundamentally correct, and it helped to persuade some governments to dismantle inefficient barriers to international trade over the 100 years after he wrote *Wealth of Nations*. Yet his argument failed to put to rest a fear that others had already expressed even before he wrote. What if our country has no absolute advantage? What if the foreigners are better at producing everything than we are? Will they want to trade? If they do, should we want to?

That fear existed in the minds of many of Smith's English contemporaries, who worried that the Dutch were more productive than they at making anything. The fear reappears often. In the wake of World War II, many nations thought they could not possibly compete with the highly productive Americans at anything and wondered how they could gain from free trade. Today some Americans have the same fear in reverse: Aren't foreigners getting better at making everything that enters international trade, and won't the United States be hurt by free trade? We turn next to the theory that first answered these fears and established a fundamental principle of international trade.

RICARDO'S THEORY OF COMPARATIVE ADVANTAGE

David Ricardo's main contribution to our understanding of international trade was to show that there is a basis for beneficial trade whether or not countries have any absolute advantage. His contribution is based on a careful examination of opportunity cost. The **opportunity cost** of producing more of a product in a country is the amount of production of the other product that is given up. The opportunity cost exists because production resources must be shifted from the other product to this product. (We already used this idea in the discussion of absolute advantage, when we shifted labor from producing one product to producing the other product.)

Ricardo's writings in the early 19th century demonstrated the **principle of comparative advantage:** A country will export the goods and services that it can produce at a low opportunity cost and import the goods and services that it would otherwise produce at a high opportunity cost.

The key word here is *comparative,* meaning "relative" and "not necessarily absolute." Even if one country is absolutely more productive at producing everything and the other country is absolutely less productive, they both can gain by trading with each other as long as their relative (dis)advantages in making different goods are different. Each country can benefit from trade by exporting products in which it has the greatest relative advantage (or least relative disadvantage) and importing products in which it has the least relative advantage (or the greatest relative disadvantage). Ricardo's approach is actually a double comparison—between countries and between products.

Ricardo drove home the point with a simple numerical example of gains from trading two products (cloth and wine) between two countries (England and Portugal). Here is a similar illustration, using wheat and cloth in the United States and the rest of the world:

	In the United States		In the Rest of the World
Productivity:			
Units of cloth per labor hour	0.25	<	1.0
Units of wheat per labor hour	0.5	<	0.67
Labor hours to make:			
1 unit of cloth	4.0	>	1.0
1 unit of wheat	2.0	>	1.5

Here, one country has inferior productivity in both goods. The United States has absolute disadvantages in both goods—lower productivity or larger numbers of hours to produce one unit of each good. What products (if any) will the United States export or import? Can trade bring net national gains to both countries?

As in the absolute-advantage case, we can begin by imagining the two countries separately with no trade between them. Each country will have to produce both products to meet local demands for the two products. What will the product prices be in each country? With no trade, the prices of the two products within each country will be determined by conditions within each country. To keep our focus on real values and activities, we are going to try to ignore money for as long as we can. Rather than looking at money prices (dollars per cloth unit or dollars per wheat unit), we will use the **relative price**—the ratio of one product price to another product price. It's as if we are in a world without money, a world of barter between real products like wheat and cloth.[1]

Ricardo, like Smith, believed that, in competitive markets, product prices reflect the costs of the labor needed to produce the products. With no trade, four hours of labor in the United States could produce either 2 wheat units or 1 cloth unit. The price of 1 cloth unit is then 2 wheat units in the United States. (Two wheat units is also the opportunity cost of producing cloth in the United States—product prices reflect costs.) In the rest of the world, one hour of labor could produce 1 cloth unit or 2/3 wheat unit. The price (and the opportunity cost) of a cloth unit is 0.67 wheat unit in the rest of the world. Thus, within the two isolated economies, national prices would follow the relative labor costs of cloth and wheat:

	In the United States	In the Rest of the World
With no international trade:		
Price of cloth	2.0 *W/C*	0.67 *W/C*
Price of wheat	0.5 *C/W*	1.5 *C/W*

We will use the notation *W* to refer to wheat units and *C* to refer to cloth units. The relative price of cloth is measured as wheat units per unit of cloth (*W/C*), and the relative price of wheat as *C/W*. Note that there is really only one ratio in each country because the price of wheat is just the reciprocal of the price of cloth.

Now let trade be possible between the United States and the rest of the world. Somebody will notice the difference between the national prices for each good and will try to profit from that difference. The principle is simple and universal: As long as prices differ in two places (by more than any cost of transporting between the places), there is a way to profit through **arbitrage**—buying at the low price in one place and selling at the high price in the other place.

Perhaps the first alert person will think of sending cloth to the United States in exchange for U.S. wheat. Consider the arbitrage profit that the person could make. She acquires cloth in the rest of the world, giving up 0.67 *W* for each cloth unit. She

---

[1]We keep money hiding in the wings throughout most of Chapters 2–15, allowing it to take center stage only in the more macroeconomic Chapters 16–25. Money appears briefly in the box later in this chapter titled "What If Trade Doesn't Balance?" and again in Chapter 5, both times to help us think about how exchange rates relate to real prices like the "wheat units per unit of cloth" prices used here. Chapters 8–15 switch to what look like ordinary money prices, such as dollars per bicycle in Chapter 8. Even there, however, the prices do not have much to do with money. As in Chapter 2, the dollars are really units of all products other than the one being pictured (e.g., motorbikes).

then ships this cloth to the United States and sells it there for 2.0 *W* per cloth unit. To keep things simple, we will usually assume that the cost of transporting products between the countries is zero.[2] Therefore, by buying low (at 0.67) and selling high (at 2.0), she can make an arbitrage profit of 1.33 *W* for each cloth unit that she exports from the rest of the world (and imports into the United States). Somebody else could profit by acquiring wheat in the United States at the low price of 0.5 *C* per wheat unit, shipping the wheat to the rest of the world, and selling it for the higher price of 1.5 *C* per wheat unit.

The opening of profitable international trade will start pushing the two separate national price ratios toward a new worldwide equilibrium. As people remove cloth from the rest of the world by exporting it, cloth becomes more expensive relative to wheat in the rest of the world. Meanwhile, cloth becomes cheaper in the United States, thanks to the additional supply of cloth imported from the rest of the world. So, cloth tends to get more expensive where it was cheap at first, and cheaper where it was more expensive. (A similar process occurs for wheat.)

The tendencies continue until the two national relative prices become one world equilibrium relative price. Normal trade on an ongoing basis will be conducted at this equilibrium relative price.

What will the equilibrium international price be? We cannot say for sure without knowing how strongly the two countries demand each of the two products. We do know something—the equilibrium international price ratio must fall within the range of the two price ratios that prevailed in each country before trade began:

$$2.0 \ W/C \geq \text{International price of cloth} \geq 0.67 \ W/C$$

or, equivalently,

$$0.5 \ C/W \leq \text{International price of wheat} \leq 1.5 \ C/W$$

Why? Consider what would happen if this were *not* true. For instance, consider an international price of only 0.4 *W/C*. At this low price of cloth, the rest of the world would want to import cloth and export wheat because the price of cloth on the international market is now below the cost of producing cloth at home (0.67 *W/C*). No deal could be made, though. At this low cloth price the United States would also want to import cloth and export wheat. No equilibrium is possible, and the cloth price would be pushed up as a result of the excess demand for cloth. (Similar reasoning applies to show the lack of an equilibrium if the cloth price is above 2 *W/C*.) The only way for the two sides to agree on trading is to have the cloth price somewhere in the range 0.67 to 2.0 *W/C*.

---

[2]The assumption of zero transport costs is relatively harmless. If transport costs are positive but not too large, they reduce the gains from trading but do not reverse any of our major conclusions. In addition, in a world with many products, high transport costs for some products could prevent any trade in those products. For instance, many services are nontraded products because the cost of getting the seller and buyer together is too high. (No Canadian or American would travel to China just to get a cheap haircut.) Yet other services can be and are traded at low cost, especially if the service is "transported" electronically. For instance, the author of this book recently completed consulting research for the European Union in which all communication, including the delivery of completed work, was conducted by e-mail and telephone.

Suppose that the strengths of demand for the products, which we will examine more closely in the next chapter, lead to an equilibrium international cloth price that has the convenient value of 1 *W/C*. Then both countries gain from international trade. The United States gains:

- It produces a unit of wheat by giving up only 0.5 unit of cloth.
- It can export this wheat unit and receive 1 unit of cloth.

The rest of the world gains:

- It produces a unit of cloth by giving up only 0.67 unit of wheat.
- It can export this cloth unit and receive 1 unit of wheat.

How do absolute advantage and comparative advantage relate to each other? There are two parts to the answer. First, Smith's example of each country having an absolute advantage in one product is also a case of comparative advantage. Our detailed analysis of comparative advantage could be applied to the numerical example of absolute advantage in the previous section.

Second, comparative advantage is more general and powerful. What matters is that the two countries have different price ratios if there is no trade. A country will have a comparative advantage even if it has no absolute advantage. The basis for trade and the gains from trade arise from differences between the countries in opportunity costs of the goods. In our numerical example of comparative advantage, the opportunity cost of a unit of wheat within the United States (0.5 *C/W*) is lower than this opportunity cost in the rest of the world (1.5 *C/W*). The United States will export wheat, even though it has an absolute disadvantage in producing both wheat and cloth.

So is comparative advantage everything? Not exactly. While absolute advantage does not determine the trade pattern in cases like this, it is a key to differences in living standards. Having an absolute disadvantage in all products means that the country is less productive than other countries are. Low-productivity countries have low real wages and are poor countries. High-productivity countries have high real wages and are rich countries. See the box titled "Absolute Advantage Does Matter."

RICARDO'S CONSTANT COSTS AND THE PRODUCTION-POSSIBILITY CURVE

Ricardo's numerical illustration succeeded in proving the principle of comparative advantage. We can also show Ricardo's comparative advantage using diagrams indicating what each country can produce and consume.

Figure 3.1 pictures production, consumption, and trade for the United States and the rest of the world. Let's examine national production first. Each country can use its resources (labor) to produce various amounts of the two products, wheat and cloth. To show what a nation is capable of producing requires a curve (or line) that shows all of these possibilities. For example, consider that the United States has 100 billion hours of labor available during the year and that labor productivities are as shown in the Ricardian numerical example (0.5 wheat unit per hour and 0.25 cloth unit per hour). Then, the United States can make 50 billion wheat units per year if it produces only

FIGURE 3.1
The Gains from Trade, Shown for Ricardo's Constant-Cost Case

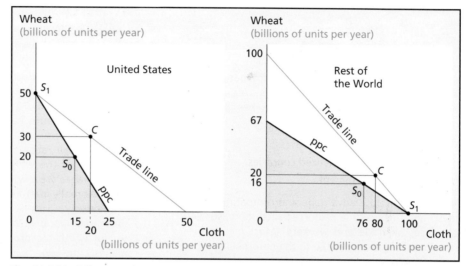

The thick black lines are the production-possibility curves (ppc's), showing what each nation can produce. With no trade, each country's consumption is limited by its ability to produce so that consumption occurs at a point like S_0 in each country. With free trade, each country specializes in producing only one good, at S_1. Each country can reach its desirable levels of consumption (consuming at a point like C) by trading along the colored trade line.

Result: Both countries gain from trade. For each country, specializing and trading make it possible to consume more of both goods at C, relative to a no-trade point like S_0 on the ppc.

wheat—or it can make 25 billion cloth units per year if instead it makes only cloth. The United States can also produce a mix of wheat and cloth, say, 20 billion wheat units and 15 billion cloth units. If we graph all of these points, we have the country's **production-possibility curve (ppc),** which shows all combinations of amounts of different products that an economy can produce with full employment of its resources and maximum feasible productivity of these resources.

The thick black lines in Figure 3.1 are the ppc's for the United States and the rest of the world (assuming that the rest of the world also has 100 billion hours of labor available annually). Note that each is a straight line with a constant (negative) slope. This slope indicates the cost of extra cloth, the number of wheat units each country would have to give up to make each extra cloth unit. In this case, the cost is always 50/25 = 2 *W/C* for the United States, the same opportunity cost of cloth as in the numerical example. With no trade and competitive markets, this cost is also the relative price of cloth in the United States. For the rest of the world the cost of extra cloth is 67/100 = 2/3 *W/C*. This is also the relative price of cloth in the rest of the world with competitive markets and no trade. The ppc's in Figure 3.1 are drawn as straight lines to reflect Ricardo's belief that each labor-productivity value is constant. Constant productivities imply that the trade-off in production—the marginal or opportunity cost of each good—is constant in each country.

We can use Figure 3.1 to restate Ricardo's conclusions about the basis for trade and the gains from trade. If neither country traded, each could consume and enjoy

Focus on Labor   Absolute Advantage Does Matter

If free trade is so good, why do so many people fear it? Activists and protesters have recently been complaining loudly that trade has bad effects on

- Workers in developing countries.
- Workers in the industrialized countries.
- The natural environment.

Analysis of absolute advantage and comparative advantage focuses on a resource called labor, so let's focus on trade and workers. (Most of our examination of issues related to the natural environment is concentrated in Chapter 13.)

Can the classical analysis pioneered by Smith and Ricardo really tell us anything about current controversies? The most interesting case is the one presented in the text, in which one country (now call it the North) has an absolute advantage in the production of all products, and the other country (now call it the South) has an absolute disadvantage. Three prominent questions can be examined within this framework:

1. If labor in the North is so productive, will workers in the South be overwhelmed so that free trade makes the South poorer?
2. If wages in the South are so low, will workers in the North be overwhelmed so that free trade makes the North poorer?
3. Does trade lead to harm to and exploitation of workers in the South, as indicated by the low wages (and/or poor working conditions)?

The text has already answered the first question. The South will have a *comparative advantage* in some set of products, and production of these products will thrive in that country. The opening of trade will lead to reductions of jobs producing the products that are imported from the North, but these workers can shift to the expanding export-oriented industries. While there may be some transition costs borne by the workers who must shift from one industry to another, the South still gets the gains from trade—generally, it becomes richer, not poorer.

How is it that some products produced by (absolutely) low-productivity workers in the South can compete successfully? The answer must be that workers in the South have low wages. The cost of producing a unit of a product is the ratio between the wage rate paid to a worker and the productivity of the worker. Production cost can be low if wages are low, or if productivity is high, and what really matters is the relationship between the two.

For the South's comparative-advantage products (the ones for which the productivity disadvantage is smallest), the lower wages lead to low production costs and the ability to export successfully. For the comparative-disadvantage products, the large productivity disadvantage is not offset by the lower wages, and these products are imported from the North.

But if wages in the South are low, how can products produced by high-wage workers in the North compete? The answer to this second question is the other side of the answer to the first. The North has *comparative advantage* in a set of products because in these products its (absolute) productivity advantage is the largest. Even with high wages, the cost of producing these products is low because the workers are highly productive. The North can successfully export these products because high productivity leads to low production costs. By using its comparative advantage (maximizing its absolute productivity advantage), the North gets the gains from trade—generally it also becomes richer, not poorer.

But is this fair? Why should the workers in the North have high wages and the workers in the South have low wages? Does this show that the workers in the South are being exploited by trade? A big part of the answer to these questions is that *absolute advantage does matter*. But it matters not for determining the trade pattern but rather *for determining national wage levels and national living standards*. Workers can receive high wages and enjoy high living standards if they are highly productive. Workers with low productivity are paid low wages. (See the accompanying figure for recent evidence for a number of countries that shows how true this is.) The low wages in the South are the result of the low labor productivity, and wages in the South are going to be low with or without trade. Trade does not exploit these workers. In fact, because of the gains from trade, workers in the South can earn somewhat higher wages and have somewhat better living standards. Still, as long as productivity remains low in the South, workers in the South will remain relatively poor, even with free trade.

Is there anything we can do if we still think that it is unfair that workers in the South earn such low wages? Trade by itself is not the solution (though it also is not the culprit). Some kind of government mandate to pay higher wages in

the South is also not the solution. Forcing higher wages would raise production costs, and this would just shrink some of the export-oriented industries that have productivity levels not much below the productivity levels in the North.

The true solution must be to find ways to increase the productivity of workers in the South. While Ricardo's approach does not indicate what determines labor productivity, we know some changes that would be desirable: increasing worker quality by enhancing education and health, upgrading production technologies and management practices, and reforming or liberalizing restrictive and distortionary government policies. In short, absolute advantage matters—to raise wages and living standards, we need to raise productivity.

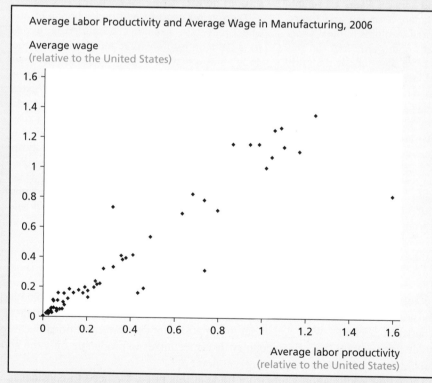

Average Labor Productivity and Average Wage in Manufacturing, 2006

For the manufacturing sector of each of 63 countries, the average labor productivity and average wage are measured relative to the United States, for 2006. The figure shows that there is a strong tendency for the average wage to be higher in countries with higher average labor productivity. (For the curious, the outlier on labor productivity is Ireland.)

Sources: For 28 industrialized and other European countries, value added per hour and labor compensation per hour from EU KLEMS, Growth and Productivity Accounts, November 2009 Release. For 35 other developing countries, value added per employee and wage per employee from UNIDO, *International Yearbook of Industrial Statistics, 2010*. Based on Golub (1999).

Extension   What If Trade Doesn't Balance?

You may be struck by a contradiction between the spirit of the trade theory and recent headlines about international trade.

The theory assumes that trade balances. In diagrams like Figure 3.1, the theory assumes equality between the market value of a country's exports and the market value of its imports (both values calculated using the international price ratio). The balance seems guaranteed by the absence of money from the diagram, as noted in this chapter's footnote 1. As long as countries are just bartering wheat for cloth, they must think U.S. wheat exports have exactly the same market value as U.S. cloth imports. Trade must balance.

Yet the news media have been announcing huge U.S. trade deficits every year since 1975. Imports of goods and services keep exceeding exports. (Conversely, Japan, Germany, and France have been running trade surpluses in most years since that time.) What's going on? How can the basic theory of trade be so silent about the most newsworthy aspect of international trade flows? Isn't the theory wrong in its statements about the reasons for trade or the gains from trade? Maybe Ricardo was too optimistic about every country's having enough comparative advantage to balance its overall trade.

These are valid questions, and they deserve a better answer than simply "Well, the model assumes balanced trade." In later chapters, we will add details about how trade deficits and surpluses relate to exchange rates, money, and finance. But the real answer is more fundamental: The model is not really wrong in assuming balanced trade, even for a country that currently has a huge trade deficit or trade surplus!

Take the case of the U.S. trade deficit. It looks as though exports are always less than imports. Well, yes and no. Yes, the trade balance (more precisely the "current-account" balance in Chapter 16) has stayed negative for many years. But a country with a current-account deficit pays for it by either piling up debts or giving up assets to foreigners. Such a country is *exporting* paper IOUs, such as bonds, that are a present claim on future goods and services. The value of these net exports of paper IOUs matches the value of the ordinary current-account deficit.

There is no need to add paper bonds to our wheat-and-cloth examples because the bonds are a claim on future wheat and cloth. Today the United States may be importing more cloth than it is exporting wheat, but this deficit is matched by the expected value of its net exports of extra wheat someday when it pays off the debt. Trade is expected to balance over the very long run. That expectation could prove wrong in the future: Maybe the United States will default on some of its foreign debts, or maybe price inflation (deflation) will make it give up less (more) wheat than expected. Still, today's transactions are based on the expectation that trade will balance in the long run.

only combinations of wheat and cloth that are on (or below) its ppc, combinations like those shown as S_0 in Figure 3.1. When trade is opened, each nation can trade at a price between 2/3 and 2 *W/C*. Again, let us suppose that demand conditions make the free-trade price equal 1 *W/C*. Each country then specializes in producing only the good in which it has a comparative advantage, at point S_1.

To show how each nation gains from trade at this price, we need to consider how trade should be drawn on the diagram. When a nation sells its exports to get imports, it ends up consuming a different set of goods. How different? In a diagram such as Figure 3.1, the line connecting where a nation produces and where it consumes is a line along which wheat trades for cloth at the world price ratio, 1 *W/C*. Two trade (or world price) lines are shown in Figure 3.1.

If the United States specializes in making only wheat, at S_1, it can export wheat for cloth imports at the world price ratio, moving along the trade line. Giving up wheat and gaining cloth imports means moving southeast along the trade line. If the world price is 1 *W/C*, the United States could consume anywhere along this thin colored line. Clearly, this is a better set of consumption options than if the United States did not trade. For each point like S_0, where the nation consumes what it produces, there are better consumption points like *C*, where it can end up consuming more of everything by specializing and trading. The United States gains from trade. It is equally clear that the rest of the world also gains from specializing in cloth production (at S_1) and trading some of that cloth for wheat, moving northwest along its trade line to consume at some point like *C*. Thus, Figure 3.1 is a different way to view the workings of comparative advantage with Ricardian constant costs.

This analysis is clear and powerful, but it also shows a serious shortcoming. The constancy of marginal costs in Figure 3.1 leads us to conclude that each country would maximize its gain by specializing its production completely in its comparative-advantage good.[3]

The real world fails to show total specialization. In Ricardo's day, it may have been reasonable for him to assume that England grew no wine grapes and relied on foreign grapes and wines. However, even with cloth imports from England, the other country in his example, Portugal, made most of its own cloth. Complete specialization is no more common today. The United States and Canada continue to produce some of their domestic consumption of products that they partially import—textiles, cars, and furniture, for example. We take up the more realistic case of increasing marginal cost and incomplete specialization in the next chapter.

Summary

International trade occurs because product prices would differ if there were no trade. This chapter begins our analysis of theories emphasizing production-side differences between countries as the reason for product prices to differ without trade. In Adam Smith's theory of absolute advantage, each country exports the product in which the country has the higher labor productivity. David Ricardo's principle of comparative advantage shows that beneficial trade can occur even if one country is worse (less productive) at producing all products.

The principle of comparative advantage is based on the importance of opportunity cost—the amount of other products that must be forgone to produce more of a particular product. The principle states that a country will export products that it can produce at low opportunity cost in return for imports of products that it would otherwise produce at high opportunity cost.

[3]With constant costs, one of the two trading countries can fail to specialize completely only in the special case in which the international price ratio settles at the same price ratio prevailing in that country with no trade. In this case the country whose price ratio does not change is a "large" country and the other country is a "small" country. The large country continues to produce both goods with free trade because the small country cannot export enough to satisfy all demand for this product in the large country. Figure 3.1 assumes that the countries are of sufficiently similar "size" that both completely specialize in production.

We can picture a country's production capabilities using a **production-possibility curve (ppc)**. Ricardo's approach assumes constant marginal costs, so a country's ppc is a straight line. We can use graphs with countries' production-possibility curves to illustrate why countries trade according to comparative advantage and to show that both countries can gain by trading. Contrary to mercantilist thinking, trade is *not* a zero-sum game in which one country gains only when the other country loses.

Key Terms	Labor productivity	Principle of comparative	Production-possibility
	Mercantilism	advantage	curve (ppc)
	Absolute advantage	Relative price	
	Opportunity cost	Arbitrage	

Suggested Reading

Irwin (1996) provides a good survey of thoughts about the advantages and disadvantages of free trade, starting with the ancient Greeks and continuing through mercantilists, Smith, Ricardo, and recent economic analysis. Bhagwati (2004) and Wolf (2004) analyze and respond to the complaints and charges made by the critics of freer trade (and of economic globalization more generally).

Questions and Problems

◆ 1. "According to Ricardo's analysis, a country exports any good whose production requires fewer labor hours per unit than the labor hours per unit needed to produce the good in the foreign country. That is, the country exports any good in which its labor productivity is higher than the labor productivity for this good in the foreign country." Do you agree or disagree? Why?

2. "For my country, imports are the good thing about international trade, whereas exports are more like the necessary evil." Do you agree or disagree? Why?

◆ 3. "Mercantilism recommends that a country should limit its exports, so that more of the otherwise-exportable products are instead available for local consumption." Do you agree or disagree with this characterization of mercantilism's message? Explain.

4. Consider the two economies shown in Figure 3.1. When there is free trade, are we sure that each country should specialize completely in producing only one of the products? For instance, perhaps each country should shift along its production-possibility curve only about halfway from the no-trade production point S_0 to the intercept point S_1. If the countries still traded with each other at the relative price of 1 W/C, would producing at the halfway point be better or worse for each country (compared to completely specializing at point S_1)?

◆ 5. Consider the numerical example that we used to demonstrate the thinking of Adam Smith (page 34). Assume that there is now no international trade. You are the first person to notice the differences between the countries and the possibility of international trade. How would you engage in arbitrage? How much can you profit from your first small amount of arbitrage?

6. Again, consider the numerical example that we used to demonstrate the thinking of Adam Smith (page 34). When these countries open to free trade, is it *possible* that the free-trade equilibrium world relative price of cloth is 1.5 W/C?

◆ 7. You are given the information shown in the table about production relationships in Pugelovia and the rest of the world.

	Inputs per Unit of Rice Output	Inputs per Unit of Cloth Output
Pugelovia	75	100
Rest of the world	50	50

You make several Ricardian assumptions: These are the only two commodities, there are constant ratios of input to output whatever the level of output of rice and cloth, and competition prevails in all markets.

a. Does Pugelovia have an absolute advantage in producing rice? Cloth?
b. Does Pugelovia have a comparative advantage in producing rice? Cloth?
c. If no international trade were allowed, what price ratio would prevail between rice and cloth within Pugelovia?
d. If free international trade is opened up, what are the limits for the equilibrium international price ratio? What product will Pugelovia export? Import?

8. Consider another Ricardian example, using standard Ricardian assumptions:

	Labor Hours per Bottle of Wine	Labor Hours per Kilogram of Cheese
Vintland	15	10
Moonited Republic	10	4

Vintland has 30 million hours of labor in total per year. Moonited Republic has 20 million hours of labor per year.

a. Which country has an absolute advantage in wine? In cheese?
b. Which country has a comparative advantage in wine? In cheese?
c. Graph each country's production-possibility curve. Show the no-trade production point for each country, assuming that with no trade Vintland consumes 1.5 million kilos of cheese and Moonited Republic consumes 3 million kilos of cheese.
d. When trade is opened, which country exports which good? If the equilibrium international price ratio is ½ bottle of wine per kilo of cheese, what happens to production in each country?
e. In this free-trade equilibrium, 2 million kilos of cheese and 1 million bottles of wine are traded. What is the consumption point in each country with free trade? Show this graphically.
f. Does each country gain from trade? Explain, referring to your graphs as is appropriate.

◆ 9. The real wage is the purchasing power of one hour of labor. That is, for each product it is the number of units of the product that a worker can buy with his earnings from one hour of work. In a Ricardian model, for any product actually produced by the worker, the worker is simply paid according to her productivity (units of output per hour). This is then her real wage in terms of this product. In your answer to this question, use the numerical example from the section on Ricardo's theory of comparative advantage.

   a. With no trade, what is the real wage of labor with respect to each good in the United States? In the rest of the world? Which country's labor has the higher "average" real wage?

   b. With free trade and an equilibrium price ratio of 1 *W/C*, each country completely specializes. What is the real wage with respect to wheat in the United States? By using international trade to obtain cloth, what is the new value of the real wage with respect to cloth in the United States? What does this tell us about gains from trade for the United States? What is the real wage with respect to cloth in the rest of the world? By using international trade to obtain wheat, what is the new value of the real wage with respect to wheat in the rest of the world? What does this tell us about the gains from trade for the rest of the world?

   c. With free trade, which country's labor has the higher "average" real wage? In what sense does absolute advantage matter?

10. In your answer to this question, use the numerical example from the section on Ricardo's theory of comparative advantage. What is the effect on the pattern of trade predicted by the Ricardian analysis if the number of labor hours required to make a unit of wheat in the United States is reduced by half (that is, if its productivity doubles)? Now return to the initial numbers. What is the effect on the pattern of trade if instead the number of hours required to make a unit of cloth in the United States is reduced by half (productivity doubles)?

◆ 11. Consider the international trade shown in Figure 3.1. Suppose that the equilibrium international cloth price is 1.2 *W/C*, instead of 1 *W/C*. At the equilibrium international price of 1.2 *W/C*, does the United States probably gain more or less from free trade (than it would if, instead, the equilibrium international price is 1 *W/C*)? Does the rest of the world probably gain more or less? Explain, and refer to the figure's graphs in your explanation.

12. You know the following information about labor productivity (units of output per hour of labor) in a country:

   A worker can produce 8 units of product V in one hour.

   A worker can produce 4 units of product Z in one hour.

   a. With no international trade, what is the opportunity cost of product Z for this country?

   b. The country now opens to free trade, and the equilibrium world price of product Z is 1.5 *V/Z*. In comparison with no trade, which product will the country shift toward producing more of?

   c. For free trade with an equilibrium world price of product Z equal to 1.5 *V/Z*, is it possible that the labor productivities in the other country (the one that this country trades with) are 6 units of product V per labor hour and 6 units of product Z per labor hour? Why or why not?

Chapter **Four**

Trade: Factor Availability and Factor Proportions Are Key

Chapter 3 presented the powerful concept of comparative advantage in a simple setting like the one that Ricardo first used. As we noted at the end of the chapter, a drawback to Ricardo's approach is the assumption of constant marginal opportunity costs. Many industries incur rising, rather than constant, marginal opportunity costs. For instance, efforts to expand U.S. wheat production would fairly quickly run into rising costs caused by limits on (1) how much more land could be drawn into wheat production and how suitable this additional land would be for wheat production, (2) the availability of additional workers willing and suitable to work on the farms, and/or (3) the availability of seeds, fertilizers, and other material inputs.

This chapter presents the analysis of trade with increasing marginal costs of production, an approach that is usually considered to be the standard modern theory of trade. The first part of the chapter presents the development of tools to analyze the general equilibrium of our two-product economy. First, we show that with rising marginal costs the production-possibility curve will have a bowed-out shape. Second, we introduce community indifference curves to illustrate consumers' decisions about how much to buy of each of the two products. Third, we use these tools to show a country's economic situation with no trade and with free trade.

In the second half of the chapter we use this framework to explore the answers to three of our four key questions about trade: the basis for trade, the gains from trade, and the effects on production and consumption. The analysis shows that there are three possible bases for trade. One possibility is that there are differences in the demands for the products in the different countries. A second possibility is that differences in technologies or resource productivities can create comparative advantage, just as they did in Ricardo's approach.

The chapter culminates in the presentation of the third possible basis for international trade. The Heckscher–Ohlin theory of trade emphasizes international differences in the abundance of the *factors of production* (land, labor, skills, capital, and natural resources). Differences in factor availability are a source of comparative advantage because there are also differences in the use of each factor in the production of different products.

PRODUCTION WITH INCREASING MARGINAL COSTS

In the standard modern theory of international trade, economists replace the constant-cost assumption used in the Ricardian approach with a more realistic assumption about marginal costs. They assume increasing marginal costs: As one industry expands at the expense of others, increasing amounts of the other products must be given up to get each extra unit of the expanding industry's product.

A country's production-possibility curve (ppc) shows the combinations of amounts of different products that a country can produce, given the country's available factor resources and maximum feasible productivities. What does the ppc look like with increasing marginal costs? It is "bowed out," as shown in the top half of Figure 4.1. To see why a bowed-out ppc shows increasing marginal costs, consider what happens to the marginal cost of producing an extra unit of cloth as we shift more and more resources from wheat production to cloth production. When the economy is producing only 20 billion units of cloth, the slope of the production-possibility curve at point S_1 tells us that one extra cloth unit could be made each year by giving up one unit of wheat. When 40 billion cloth units are being made each year, getting the resources to make another cloth unit a year means giving up two units of wheat, as shown by the steeper slope at point S_0. To push cloth production up to 60 billion cloth units per year requires giving up wheat in amounts that rise to three wheat units for the last unit of cloth.

The increasing costs of extra cloth are also increasing costs of producing extra wheat. When one starts from a cloth-only economy at point S_2 and shifts increasing amounts of resources into growing wheat, the cost of an extra wheat unit rises (from 1/3 cloth unit at S_2 to 1/2 cloth unit at S_0, 1 cloth unit at S_1, and so forth).

The increasing marginal costs reappear in a familiar form in the lower half of Figure 4.1. Here the vertical axis shows the marginal costs of extra cloth, which are the slopes in the upper half of the figure. The resulting curve is a *supply curve* for cloth. The set of competitive U.S. cloth producers would use the marginal costs of producing extra cloth to decide how much cloth to supply at each possible market price of cloth. So, we have two ways to picture increasing marginal costs, the two-product bowed-out ppc and the upward-sloping supply curve that focuses on one of these products.

What's Behind the Bowed-Out Production-Possibility Curve?

What information do we need to derive the production-possibility curve of each country? Why are increasing-cost curves (bowed-out in shape) more realistic than constant-cost (straight-line) production-possibility curves?

A country's production-possibility curve is derived from information on both total factor (resource) supplies and the production functions that indicate how factor inputs can be used to produce outputs in various industries. In Appendix B we show how the

FIGURE 4.1

Production
Possibilities
under Increasing
Costs

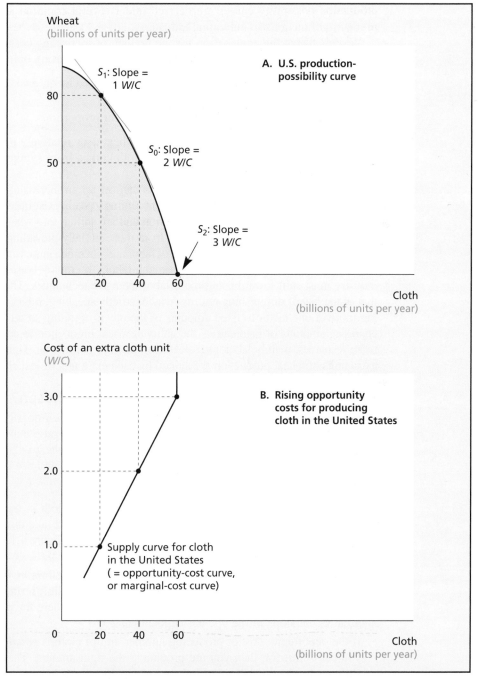

**A. U.S. production-
possibility curve**

S_1: Slope =
1 W/C

S_0: Slope =
2 W/C

S_2: Slope =
3 W/C

Wheat
(billions of units per year)

Cloth
(billions of units per year)

**B. Rising opportunity
costs for producing
cloth in the United States**

Cost of an extra cloth unit
(W/C)

Supply curve for cloth
in the United States
(= opportunity-cost curve,
or marginal-cost curve)

Cloth
(billions of units per year)

Increasing opportunity costs can be shown in either of two equivalent ways: as changing slopes along a bowed-out production-possibility curve or as an upward-sloping supply (or marginal-cost) curve. Note: For the analysis of the production-possibility curve, we ignore the fact that the slopes of the tangent lines are negative.

production-possibility curves are derived under several common assumptions about production functions in individual industries.

We can sketch the explanation for the realism of increasing costs (and the bowed-out shape) even without a rigorous demonstration. The starting points are that

- There are several kinds of factor inputs (land, skilled labor, unskilled labor, capital, and so forth).
- Different products use factor inputs in different proportions.

To stay with our wheat-and-cloth example, wheat uses relatively more land and less labor than cloth, whether the yarn for the cloth comes from synthetic fibers or from natural fibers such as cotton or silk.

This basic variation in input proportions can set up an increasing-cost (bowed-out) production-possibility curve even if constant returns to scale exist in each industry. When resources are released from cloth production and are shifted into wheat production, they will be released in proportions different from those initially prevailing in wheat production. The cloth industry will release a lot of labor and not much land. But wheat production generally requires a lot of land and not much labor. To employ these factors, the wheat industry must shift toward using more labor-intensive techniques. The effect is close to that of the law of diminishing returns (which, strictly speaking, refers to the case of adding more of one factor to fixed amounts of the others): Adding so much labor to slowly changing amounts of land causes the gains in wheat production to decline as more and more resources, mainly labor, are released from cloth production. Thus, fewer and fewer extra units of wheat production are gained by each extra unit of lost cloth production.

What Production Combination Is Actually Chosen?

Out of all the possible production points along the production-possibility curve, which one point does the nation select? That depends on the price ratio that competitive firms face. Suppose that the market price of cloth in terms of wheat is 2 *W/C*. If you are a competitive firm vying with other firms around you, you will see one of these three conditions at any production point:

- If the opportunity cost of producing another unit of cloth is *less* than the 2 *W/C* that you can sell it for, then try to make more cloth (and take resources away from wheat). Firms would react this way at a point like S_1 in Figure 4.1, where the opportunity cost is less (the slope of the ppc is flatter) than 2 *W/C*.
- If the opportunity cost of producing another unit of cloth is *more* than the 2 *W/C* that you can sell it for, then try to make less cloth (and shift resources into growing wheat). Firms would react this way at a point like S_2, where the opportunity cost is greater (the slope of the ppc is steeper) than 2 *W/C*.
- If the opportunity cost of producing another unit of cloth is *equal* to the 2 *W/C* that you can sell it for, then you are producing the right amount. There is no reason to shift any production between cloth and wheat. Firms would react this way at point S_0.

By choosing to produce at S_0 (40 billion cloth and 50 billion wheat) when the price is 2 *W/C*, firms end up maximizing the value of national production. The price is represented by a price line whose slope is 2 *W/C*. The price line with this slope is tangent to the ppc at S_0.[1] The tangent point is important. For the price shown by the slope of the price line, you cannot increase the value of national production, measured in either cloth units or wheat units, by moving to any other point on the production-possibility curve.[2]

What will happen if the relative price of cloth declines to 1 *W/C*? With a lower price of cloth, we expect that cloth production will decrease. The resources released as cloth production decreases are shifted into wheat production, and wheat output increases. After a period of transition, during which resources are shifted from the cloth industry to the wheat industry, the production point chosen by the country will shift to point S_1. The tangent line at S_1 has a slope of 1 *W/C* and represents a new price line. The production combination chosen has less cloth (20) and more wheat (80).

COMMUNITY INDIFFERENCE CURVES

The production-possibility curve pictures the production side of a country's economy. To complete the picture of the economy, we need a way to depict the determinants of demand for two products simultaneously.

For an individual, economists typically begin with the notion that each individual derives well-being (or happiness or utility) from consuming various goods and services. Figure 4.2 shows the usual way of relating an individual's well-being to amounts of two goods, again wheat and cloth, that the individual consumes. Instead of drawing the level of well-being in a third dimension rising out of the printed page, economists draw contours called indifference curves. An **indifference curve** shows the various combinations of consumption quantities (here wheat and cloth) that lead to the same level of well-being or happiness. For example, the indifference curve I_0 shows that the individual is *indifferent* between points A, B, and C, each of which gives the same level of well-being. That is, the individual would be equally happy consuming 80 units of wheat and 20 units of cloth, *or* 40 of both, *or* 20 of wheat and 80 of cloth.

Any consumption point below and to the left of I_0 is worse than A or B or C in the eyes of this individual. Points above and to the right of I_0 are better. For example, point D, on the better indifference curve I_1, yields a higher level of happiness than A or B or C. Point E, on I_2, is even more preferred.

Each indifference curve is typically presumed to have a bowed shape, as shown in the figure. The individual has an infinite number (a complete map) of indifference curves, representing infinitesimally small differences in well-being and showing the person's preferences regarding various combinations of the products. Our diagrams typically show only a small number of indifference curves from this complete map.

---

[1] To make our descriptions less cluttered, we will consistently use positive values for the slopes of price lines (and similar lines like tangents to a ppc), even though the slopes are actually negative.

[2] This can be seen by extending the 2 *W/C* price line from point S_0 to touch either axis in Figure 4.1. The point where the extended line hits the horizontal axis is the value of the whole national production of wheat plus cloth, expressed as the amount of cloth that it could be traded for. Similarly, the point where the extended line hits the vertical axis is the value of the same national production, expressed in units of wheat. You can see that this value is greater when the nation produces at S_0 than when it produces at any other point on the ppc, as long as the price (and the slope of a price line through this other point) is 2 *W/C*.

FIGURE 4.2

Indifference
Curves Relating
an Individual's
Level of
Well-Being to
Consumption of
Two Goods

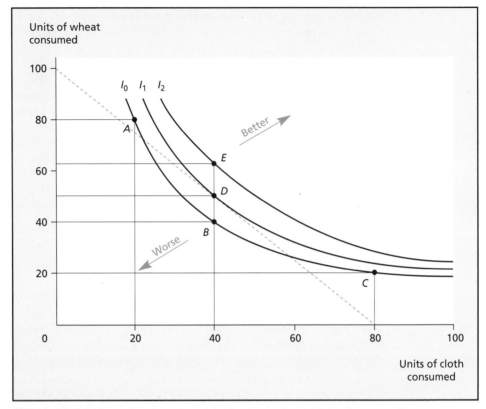

Different combinations of consumption quantities that each would give the person the same
level of well-being are points on a single indifference curve. (Example: points A, B, and C on
I_0.) A consumption point that would give the person a higher level of well-being is on a higher
indifference curve. (Example: point E on I_2 is better than any point on I_1.) If the budget constraint
is the dashed colored line, then the person would achieve his highest feasible well-being by
purchasing and consuming the consumption quantities shown by point D because indifference
curve I_1 is the highest one that he can reach.

The actual consumption point chosen by the individual depends on the budget constraint facing the person—the income that the individual has available to
spend on these products and the prices of the products. The budget constraint is
$Y = P_W \cdot Q_W + P_C \cdot Q_C$, assuming that the individual spends all his income, Y, on the
two products wheat (W) and cloth (C). For given income and prices, the equation is
a straight line showing combinations of cloth and wheat that the individual is able
to purchase with this income: $Q_W = (Y/P_W) - (P_C/P_W) \cdot Q_C$. The slope of this budget
constraint is the (negative of the) price ratio P_C/P_W, the relative price of cloth, so
we usually refer to this budget constraint as a price line.
    Given the budget constraint or price line, the individual chooses consumption to
be as well off as possible—to reach the highest feasible indifference curve. This is
the indifference curve that is just tangent to the price line. In Figure 4.2, the dashed
colored line shows the budget constraint for an individual who could purchase
100 wheat units if he spent all of his income on wheat ($Y/P_W = 100$) and who faces the

relative price of cloth equal to 1.25 in the markets ($P_C/P_W = 1.25$). Given this budget constraint, the individual should choose to consume 50 wheat units and 40 cloth units (at point *D*). The consumer reaches the level of well-being shown by I_1.

When exploring trade issues, we want to portray how the entire nation, not just one individual, decides on consumption quantities and what this decision implies for the economic well-being of the nation as a whole. Can we portray a large group of people (like a country) as having a set of indifference curves? There are problems with this portrayal, and we will discuss these in the next paragraph. Yet, a single set of indifference curves for a group of people is remarkably useful as a tool for our analysis. We will utilize community indifference curves, which purport to show how the economic well-being of a whole group depends on the whole group's consumption of products. In what follows, we look at sets of indifference curves like those in Figure 4.2 as if they were community indifference curves for thousands or millions of people. We will use community indifference curves, along with the price line representing the national budget (or income) constraint, as the basis for the choice of national quantities demanded and consumed of wheat and cloth.

Nonetheless, we must keep in mind that economic theory raises difficult questions about community indifference curves. First, the shapes of individual indifference curves differ from person to person. There is no completely clear way to "add up" individuals' indifference curves to obtain community indifference curves. Second, the concept of national well-being or welfare is not well defined. How can we say whether the community is better off with an average of 40 wheat units less and 40 cloth units more? As a result of this change, usually some members of the community gain, while others lose. Who can say that the increase in happiness of the one is greater than the decrease in happiness of the other? Levels of happiness or well-being cannot be compared from one person to another.

These are real difficulties. We will use community indifference curves because they are convenient and neat. They are reasonable for depicting the basis for national demand patterns for two products simultaneously. Under certain assumptions they provide information on national well-being, but some caution is needed in using them in this way. Higher national well-being, as shown by a higher community indifference curve, does not mean that each person is actually better off.

PRODUCTION AND CONSUMPTION TOGETHER

Figure 4.3 summarizes information on the U.S. economy. The production capabilities of the United States are shown by the bowed-out (increasing-cost) production-possibility curve, and U.S. consumption preferences are shown by a map of community indifference curves, of which three are shown.

Without Trade

With no trade the United States must be self-sufficient and must find the combination of domestically produced wheat and cloth that will maximize community well-being. In this case, I_1 is the best (highest) indifference curve that the United States can achieve. To reach I_1, the United States must produce at S_0 on its production-possibility curve. At this tangent point, the United States produces and consumes 40 billion units

FIGURE 4.3

Indifference
Curves and
Production
Possibilities
without Trade

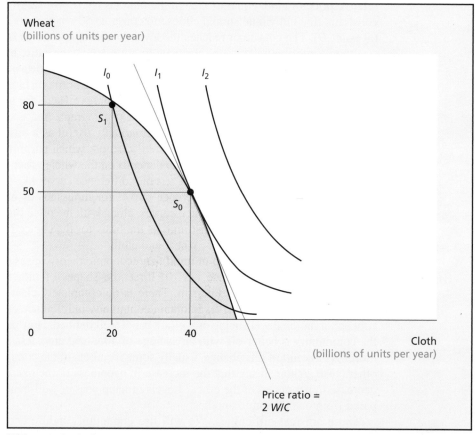

Without trade, the best an economy can do is to move to the production point that touches the highest community indifference curve. This best no-trade point is S_0, where the nation both produces and consumes, reaching indifference curve I_1.

of cloth and 50 billion units of wheat. The relative price of cloth in the United States with no trade is 2 *W/C*.

Point S_0 is the no-trade equilibrium for the United States. If, instead, the United States found itself at any other point on the U.S. production-possibility curve, consumers or producers would want to shift toward S_0. To see this, consider the example in which the economy begins at S_1, with a price ratio set by the slope of the ppc (a relative price of 1 *W/C*). Consumers would find that this makes cloth look so cheap that they would rather buy more cloth than 20 billion units and less wheat than 80 billion units. Producers will follow this change in demand and shift resources into cloth production and out of wheat. The tendency to alter production will persist until the economy produces and consumes at S_0, the no-trade (or autarky) equilibrium.

With Trade

To show the effects of opening the world to international trade, we examine the economies of both countries. The left side of Figure 4.4A shows the U.S. economy (the same as in Figure 4.3). The right side shows the economy of the rest of the world.

FIGURE 4.4
Two Views of
Free Trade and
Its Effects

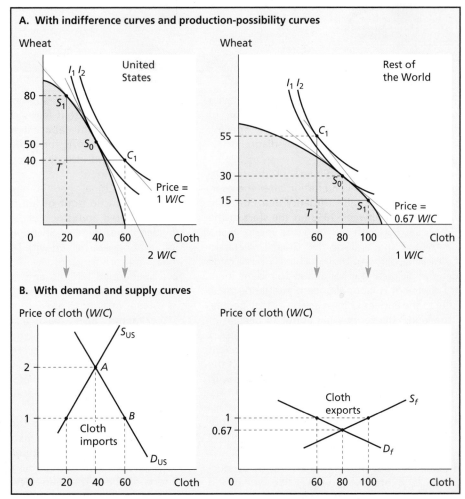

There are two convenient ways to portray a free-trade equilibrium. The upper panel shows trade between two countries for two products, with each country producing at its point S_1 and consuming at its point C_1. The lower panel shows the same thing using supply and demand curves that focus on one product (cloth).

The no-trade equilibrium in each country is at point S_0. With no trade the U.S. relative price of cloth would be 2 *W/C*, while the relative price in the rest of the world would be 0.67 *W/C*.

As in previous examples, the difference in price ratios with no trade provides the immediate basis for trade. With free trade the United States imports cloth from the rest of the world and exports wheat to the rest of the world. This trade tends to decrease the relative price of cloth in the United States and increase the relative price of cloth in the rest of the world. With free trade (and assuming no transport costs), trade results in an equilibrium international price ratio in the range of 0.67 *W/C* to 2 *W/C*. The price ratio for this free-trade equilibrium is the price that results in the quantity of wheat exported by the United States being equal to the quantity of wheat imported by the rest of the

Focus on China   The Opening of Trade and China's Shift Out of Agriculture

The real world does in fact reveal the behavior portrayed in the diagrams and discussion of this chapter. Countries do react to the opening of trade in the ways predicted by diagrams like those in Figure 4.4.

A good example is China's progression to becoming a major trading nation after the near-total isolation and self-sufficiency that Chairman Mao imposed between 1958 (at the start of the Great Leap Forward) and 1976 (the year of Mao's death and the end of the Great Proletarian Cultural Revolution). Though China covers a huge geographic area, it is not a land-abundant country. Rather, it is labor-abundant and land-scarce. True to the ancient Chinese saying "Many people, little land," the country has about 19 percent of the world's population but only about 10 percent of its farmable land. For such a labor-abundant country, this chapter's theories would predict the following responses to the chance to trade with the rest of the world:

- China should export labor-intensive products like clothing and import land-intensive products like wheat.
- China should shift resources out of producing land-intensive products like wheat and into producing labor-intensive products like clothing.
- China's production specialization should be incomplete. The country should go on producing some land-intensive products, though these should be a lower share of production than before.
- China should be a more prosperous country with trade than without trade. The theory even allows for the possibility that China could consume more of all goods, including both wheat and clothing.

All these predictions have been coming true in China since 1976. The trade pattern is what we would expect: China has become a strong exporter of all sorts of manufactured products, including clothing, that take advantage of the country's abundant labor supply. China has also turned to imports for a portion of its consumption of land-intensive products, including wheat.

All over China, people have noticed the shift of production out of agriculture and into export-oriented industry. For example, in the crowded countryside of Shandong province, villages that once struggled with poor soil to grow wheat and corn for cities like Tianjin and Beijing have abandoned farming and now make furniture and pharmaceuticals. Even the relatively fertile villages of Jiangsu province, near the mouth of the Yangtse River, make textiles, steel, and other industrial goods. Similarly, in the south, Guangdong province used to send its rice north to Beijing. Now Guangdong, a leader in China's rapid industrialization, consumes more rice than it produces, supplementing local crops with rice imports from Thailand.

Both public opinion and the available statistics agree that the great majority of China's population have gained purchasing power. Some Chinese do fear becoming dependent on imports of food. The fears seem to be greater in the government than in the population at large. The government in the 1990s decided to channel a larger share of taxpayers' money into promoting agricultural production, to retard the shift away from being self-sufficient in food. Yet many are less worried. Wu Xiedong, leader of one of those Jiangsu villages that switched from growing grain to making textiles and steel, is optimistic about the shift. As he put it in 1995, "As long as the present policy that allows farmers to go into industry doesn't change, we will continue to grow very fast." As for relying on imported food, Wu says, "America has lots of grain, right? If America buys my steel, I'll buy America's grain. Then we can all get rich."*

China's experience mirrors what happened earlier to Japan, Korea, Taiwan, and Hong Kong. All of these labor-abundant and land-scarce areas reacted to the opening of trade by shifting into labor-intensive industry and out of land-intensive agriculture, and all of them prospered.

*Note the "if" part of this statement. If U.S. policy blocked imports of industrial products from China, the Chinese would also reduce imports from the United States. The gains from trade then would be reduced.

Source: Source of the two quotes from Wu Xiedong: *Wall Street Journal*, March 10, 1995.

world, and the quantity of cloth exported by the rest of the world being equal to the quantity of cloth imported by the United States.

For the conditions in each country shown by their production-possibility curves and community indifference curves, the free-trade equilibrium occurs at a price ratio of 1 W/C. In the shift from no trade to free trade, producers in the United States respond to the lower relative price of cloth (and thus higher relative price of wheat) by reducing production of cloth and increasing production of wheat, shifting production from point S_0 to S_1. With production at S_1, the United States can trade wheat for cloth with the rest of the world at the price of 1 W/C. Consumption can be at any point along the price line that is tangent to the ppc at point S_1 (a line indicating a price ratio of 1 W/C). Along this price line, the United States will consume at point C_1, the tangent point with the highest achievable community indifference curve I_2.

In the rest of the world, the shift from no trade to free trade increases the relative price of cloth. Producers respond by increasing production of cloth and decreasing production of wheat from point S_0 to S_1. The rest of the world can trade away from its production point at the international equilibrium price ratio. Consumption can be at any point along the price line tangent to the ppc at S_1. Given this price line, the rest of the world will consume at point C_1.

At the international price ratio of 1 W/C, the United States is willing to export 40 billion units of wheat, the difference between the 80 produced domestically at point S_1 and the 40 consumed domestically at point C_1. The rest of the world wants to import 40 billion units of wheat, equal to the difference between the 55 consumed domestically and the 15 produced domestically. At this price ratio, the United States wants to import 40 billion cloth units (60 consumed minus 20 produced domestically). The rest of the world is willing to export 40 billion cloth units (100 produced minus 60 consumed domestically). Thus, the international trade markets for both products are in equilibrium, confirming that the price ratio of 1 W/C is the international equilibrium price ratio.

The export–import quantities in each country can be summarized by the *trade triangles* that show these quantities. The trade triangle for the United States is shown by the right triangle S_1TC_1, and that for the rest of the world is C_1TS_1. International equilibrium is achieved when these two trade triangles are the same size so that both sides agree on the amounts traded.

We will generally assume that there is only one free-trade equilibrium international price ratio for a given set of supply and demand conditions in each country. To see why a price ratio other than 1 W/C generally will not be an international equilibrium, consider a price line flatter (making cloth even cheaper) than the price of 1 W/C. The United States would respond to such a price by producing above and to the left of point S_1 and trading large volumes of wheat for cloth to consume out beyond C_1. The catch, however, is that the rest of the world would not want to trade so much at a price ratio that makes its cloth cheaper than 1 W/C. This can be seen by finding the tangency of the new flat price line to the rest of the world's production-possibility and indifference curves on the right side of Figure 4.4A. The result of a price ratio making cloth cheaper than 1 W/C is closer to S_0, the no-trade point. With the rest of the world willing to export only a small amount of cloth at such a price, the excess demand for imported cloth by the United States would increase the relative price of cloth. The price would return to the equilibrium unitary price shown in Figure 4.4.

Demand and Supply Curves Again

The community indifference curves also can be combined with the production-possibility curves to plot out demand curves for cloth or wheat. A demand curve for cloth shows how the quantity of cloth demanded responds to its price. To derive the U.S. demand curve for cloth, start in Figure 4.4A with a price ratio and find how much cloth the United States would be willing and able to consume at that price. At 2 W/C, the United States is willing and able to consume 40 billion cloth units a year (at S_0). At 1 W/C, the United States would consume 60 billion cloth units (at C_1). These demand points could be replotted in Figure 4.4B, with the prices on the vertical axis. Point S_0 above becomes point A below, point C_1 above becomes point B below, and so forth. The same could be done for the rest of the world. (The demand-curve derivation is like that found in ordinary price-theory textbooks, except that the nation's income constraint slides along a production-possibility surface instead of rotating on a fixed-income point.) In this way the handy demand–supply framework can be derived from community indifference curves and production-possibility curves. The international equilibrium focusing on a single product (the approach discussed in Chapter 2 and shown in Figure 4.4B) is therefore consistent with the general equilibrium approach using two products.[3]

THE GAINS FROM TRADE

There are two ways to use a figure like Figure 4.4A to show that each nation gains from international trade. First, trade allows each country to consume at a point (C_1) that lies beyond its own ability to produce (its production-possibility curve). This is a gain from trade as long as we view more consumption as desirable. It is the same

---

[3]The theoretical literature on international trade often uses the indifference curves and production-possibility curve to derive an *offer curve*. An offer curve is a way of showing how a nation's offer of exports for imports from the rest of the world depends on the international price ratio. A nation's offer curve shows the same information as its export supply or import demand curve. Appendix C discusses how an offer curve can be derived and used.

demonstration of the gains from trade that we used for the Ricardian approach in Chapter 3. Second, trade allows each country to achieve a higher community indifference curve (I_2 rather than I_1 with no trade). However, the use of community indifference curves to show national gains from trade may hide the fact that opening trade actually hurts some groups while bringing gains to others. We take up this issue of the distribution of gains and losses in the next chapter.

How much each country gains from trade depends on the international price ratio in the ongoing international trade equilibrium. As individuals we benefit from receiving high prices for the things that we sell (such as our labor services) and paying low prices for the things that we buy. A similar principle applies to countries.

A country gains more from trade if it receives a higher price for its exports relative to the price that it pays for its imports. For each country, the gains from trade depend on the country's international **terms of trade,** which are the price the country receives from foreign buyers for its export product(s), relative to the price that the country pays foreign sellers for its import product(s).

In our example, the rest of the world exports cloth and imports wheat, so the terms of trade for the rest of the world are the relative price of cloth. In Figure 4.4A we can show that the rest of the world would gain more from trade if its terms of trade were better—if the equilibrium international relative price of cloth were higher. Then the international price line would be steeper than the line through S_1 and C_1, and the rest of the world could reach a community indifference curve higher than I_2.

For the United States, its terms of trade are the relative price of wheat, its export good. The United States would gain more from trade if the equilibrium relative price of wheat were higher, resulting in a flatter international price line than the line through S_1 and C_1. Then the United States could reach a community indifference curve higher than I_2.

TRADE AFFECTS PRODUCTION AND CONSUMPTION

Figure 4.4A shows that there are substantial effects on production quantities when trade is opened. The opening has two types of implications for production. First, *within each country* output expands for the product that the country exports—more wheat produced in the United States and more cloth produced in the rest of the world. In each country, the growing industry expands by acquiring factor resources from the other industry in the economy. The import-competing industry reduces its domestic production—cloth in the United States and wheat in the rest of the world. Although production shifts in each country, the countries do not (necessarily) specialize completely in producing their export product if the production-possibility curve is bowed out because of increasing costs.

Second, the shift from no trade to free trade results in more efficient *world* production as each country expands output of the product in which it is initially the lower-cost producer. In the particular case shown in Figure 4.4A, the efficiency gains show up as an increase in world production of wheat (from $50 + 30 = 80$ with no trade to $80 + 15 = 95$ with trade), while world cloth production is unchanged at 120.

In each country, opening to trade also alters the quantities consumed of each product, as the consumption point shifts from S_0 with no trade to C_1 with free trade.

Consumer theory indicates that the quantity consumed of the importable product in each country will increase. The relative price of the importable product declines in each country, so consumers in the country buy more of it (a positive substitution effect). Meanwhile, real income rises in each country (as a result of the gains from trade), so consumers buy even more (a positive income effect). The quantity consumed of the exportable product in each country could increase, stay the same, or decrease because of opposing pressures from a negative substitution effect (resulting from the higher relative price of the exportable good) and a positive income effect (as real income rises). In the particular case shown in Figure 4.4A, the quantities consumed of the exportable product actually decrease (50 to 40 for wheat in the United States and 80 to 60 for cloth in the rest of world), but other outcomes for these two consumption quantities are possible.

WHAT DETERMINES THE TRADE PATTERN?

Our general view of national economies engaged in international trade is shown in Figure 4.4A. The immediate basis for the pattern of international trade that we see here is that relative product prices would differ between the two countries if there were no trade. But why would product prices differ with no trade? They can differ because

- Production conditions differ—the relative shapes of the production-possibility curves differ between the countries.
- Demand conditions differ—the relative shapes and positions of the community indifference curves differ between the countries.
- Some combination of these two differences.

In our example the basis for the United States to import cloth could be that the United States has a high demand for cloth, perhaps due to a harsh climate or fashion consciousness. Although this kind of explanation may apply to a few products, most analyses focus on production-side differences as the basis for no-trade price differences, assuming that demand patterns are similar for the countries.

Production-side differences can be a basis for the international trade pattern when the relative shapes of the production-possibility curves differ. For instance, in Figure 4.4A, the ppc for the United States is skewed toward production of wheat, and the ppc for the rest of the world is skewed toward production of cloth. Why do we see these production-side differences? There are two basic reasons.

First, the production technologies or resource productivities may differ between countries. For instance, the United States may have superior technology to produce wheat and somehow keep its secret from the rest of the world. The better technology results in relatively high resource productivity in U.S. wheat production. This will skew the U.S. production-possibility curve toward producing larger amounts of wheat, resulting in a comparative advantage for the United States to produce and export wheat. This type of comparative advantage was the basis for trade in the Ricardian approach.

Although technology or productivity differences can be a production-side basis for comparative advantage, for the remainder of this chapter and in the next chapter, we assume that they are not. Instead, we assume that both countries have access to the same technologies for production and are capable of achieving similar levels of resource productivity. This assumption is plausible if technology spreads internationally because it is difficult for a country to keep its technology secret. (Issues related to technology will be taken up in later chapters.)

The second reason that the relative shapes of the production-possibility curves can differ is more subtle but has become the basis for the standard modern theory of comparative advantage. It is the Heckscher–Ohlin theory based on (1) differences across countries in the availability of factor resources and (2) differences across products in the use of these factors in producing the products.

THE HECKSCHER–OHLIN (H–O) THEORY

The leading theory of what determines nations' trade patterns emerged in Sweden. Eli Heckscher, the noted Swedish economic historian, developed the core idea in a brief article in 1919. A clear overall explanation was developed and publicized in the 1930s by Heckscher's student Bertil Ohlin. Ohlin, like Keynes, managed to combine a distinguished academic career—professor at Stockholm and later a Nobel laureate—with political office (Riksdag member, party leader, and government official during World War II). Ohlin's persuasive narrative of the theory and the evidence that seemed to support it were later reinforced by another Nobel laureate, Paul Samuelson, who derived mathematical conditions under which the Heckscher–Ohlin (H–O) prediction was strictly correct.[4]

The Heckscher–Ohlin theory of trade patterns says, in Ohlin's own words,

> Commodities requiring for their production much of [abundant factors of production] and little of [scarce factors] are exported in exchange for goods that call for factors in the opposite proportions. Thus indirectly, factors in abundant supply are exported and factors in scanty supply are imported. (Ohlin, 1933, p. 92)

Or, more succinctly, the Heckscher–Ohlin theory predicts that a country exports the product (or products) that uses its relatively abundant factor(s) intensively and imports the product (or products) that uses its relatively scarce factor(s) intensively.

To judge this plausible and testable argument more easily, we need definitions of factor abundance and factor-use intensity. Consider labor:

- A country is relatively labor-abundant if it has a higher ratio of labor to other factors than does the rest of the world.
- A product is relatively labor-intensive if labor costs are a greater share of its value than they are of the value of other products.

The H–O explanation of trade patterns begins with a specific hunch as to why product prices might differ between countries before they open trade. Heckscher and Ohlin predicted that the key to comparative costs lies in factor proportions used in

---

[4]Ohlin backed the H–O theory with real-world observation and appeals to intuition. Samuelson took the mathematical road, adding assumptions that allowed a strict proof of the theory's main prediction. Samuelson assumed that (1) there are two countries, two goods, and two factors (the parsimonious "$2 \times 2 \times 2$" simplification); (2) factor supplies are fixed for each country, fully employed, and mobile between sectors within each country, but immobile between countries; (3) the consumption patterns of the two countries are identical; and (4) both countries share the same constant-returns-to-scale production technologies. The H–O predictions follow logically in Samuelson's narrow case and seem broadly accurate in the real world. Our analysis in the text is based on Samuelson's depiction of the theory.

production. If cloth costs 2 *W/C* in the United States and less than 1 *W/C* elsewhere, it must be primarily because the United States has relatively less of the factors that cloth uses intensively, and relatively more of the factors that wheat uses intensively, than does the rest of the world.

Let *land* be the factor that wheat uses more intensively and *labor* be the factor that cloth uses more intensively. Let all costs be decomposable into land and labor costs (e.g., it takes certain amounts of land and labor to make fertilizer for growing wheat and certain other amounts of land and labor to make cotton inputs for cloth making). The H–O theory predicts that the United States exports wheat and imports cloth because wheat is land-intensive and cloth is labor-intensive and

$$\frac{\text{(U.S. land supply)}}{\text{(U.S. labor supply)}} > \frac{\text{(Rest of world's land supply)}}{\text{(Rest of world's labor supply)}}$$

Under these conditions[5] with no international trade, land should rent more cheaply in the United States than elsewhere because land is relatively abundant in the United States and relatively scarce in the rest of the world. The cheapness of land cuts costs more in wheat farming than in cloth making, so the United States is the lower-cost producer of wheat. Conversely, the scarcity of labor should make the wage rate higher in the United States than elsewhere, so cloth is relatively expensive to produce in the United States. This, according to H–O, is why product prices differ in the direction they do before trade begins. And, the theory predicts, it is the combination of the difference in relative factor endowments and the pattern of factor intensities that makes the United States export wheat instead of cloth (and import cloth instead of wheat) when trade opens up.

Summary

The standard modern theory of trade is based on increasing marginal costs of producing more of a product, so that the production-possibility curve is bowed out. We can combine bowed-out production-possibility curves with community indifference curves to show how countries are affected by opening to trade.

Trade is positive-sum activity. The whole world gains from trade, and each country is at least as well off with free trade as with no trade. The gains from trade for each country can be demonstrated in two ways. First, trade allows the country to consume beyond its own ability to produce—it allows consumption outside of its production-possibility curve. Second, trade allows the country to reach a higher community indifference curve, indicating that the country reaches a higher level of national economic well-being.

The analysis provides key insights into the basis for the pattern of international trade (what is exported and what is imported) by each country. While trade can be

---

[5]Take care not to misread the relative factor endowment inequality. It does not say the United States has absolutely more land than the rest of the world. Nor does it say that the United States has less labor. In fact, the United States really has less of both. Nor does it say the United States has more land than it has labor—a meaningless statement in any case. (How many acres or hectares are "more than" how many hours of labor?)

Rather it is an inequality between relative endowments. Here are two correct ways of stating it: (1) There is more land per laborer in the United States than in the rest of the world and (2) the U.S. share of the world's land is greater than its share of the world's labor.

driven by differences in demand, most of our attention is on production-side differences. Production-side differences cause the countries' production-possibility curves to skew in different ways, reflecting different comparative advantages. One source of production-side differences is differences in technologies or factor productivities.

The Heckscher–Ohlin (H–O) theory focuses on another important source of production-side differences. International differences in the shapes of bowed-out ppc's can occur because (1) different products use the factors of production in different proportions and (2) countries differ in their relative factor endowments. The H–O theory of trade patterns predicts that a country exports products that are produced with more intensive use of the country's relatively abundant factors in exchange for imports of products that use the country's relatively scarce factors more intensively.

Key Terms	Increasing marginal costs	Indifference curve	Heckscher–Ohlin theory
	Production-possibility curve (ppc)	Community indifference curves	Labor-abundant
		Terms of trade	Labor-intensive

Suggested Reading

For advanced technical surveys of the economic analysis of free trade, see Chapters 1–3, 7, and 8 of Jones and Kenen, Vol. I (1984). Ruffin (1988) improved the Ricardian model of comparative advantage so that it generates the predictions of the Heckscher–Ohlin model. He does so by interpreting productivity differences in the one-factor Ricardian approach as differences in relative factor endowments. Chor (2010) examines comparative advantage based on differences across countries in institutions (such as security of contact enforcement and labor market regulations) that are more important to some industries than to others.

Bernhofen and Brown (2005) find that the gains to Japan from its opening to trade in the 19th century were equal to about 8 percent of its GDP at that time.

Questions and Problems

◆ 1. "According to the Heckscher–Ohlin theory, two countries that have the same production technologies for the various products that they produce are unlikely to trade much with each other." Do you agree or disagree? Why?

2. "For a world in which international trade would be based only on the differences featured in the Heckscher–Ohlin theory, the shift from no trade to free trade is like a zero-sum game." Do you agree or disagree? Why?

◆ 3. The country of Pugelovia has an endowment (total supply) of 20 units of labor and 3 units of land, whereas the rest of the world has 80 units of labor and 7 units of land. Is Pugelovia labor-abundant? Is Pugelovia land-abundant? If wheat is land-intensive and cloth is labor-intensive, what is the Heckscher–Ohlin prediction for the pattern of trade between Pugelovia and the rest of the world?

4. Explain how a supply curve can be obtained or derived from an increasing-cost production-possibility curve. Use Figure 4.3 to derive the supply curve for cloth. For a bit more challenge, use Figure 4.3 to derive the supply curve for wheat.

◆ 5. In your answer to this question, use a diagram like Figure 4.3, making it large enough so that you can see the curves and quantities clearly. The no-trade point is as shown in Figure 4.3, a price ratio of 2 *W/C* and 40 units of cloth demanded. Sketch the derivation of the portion of the country's cloth demand curve for cloth prices of 2 and below. (To do this, examine a price of about 1.5, then 1.0, and then 0.5. In your analysis you will need to show additional community indifference curves—ones that exist but are not shown explicitly in Figure 4.3.)

6. Return to your answer for question 5. For prices below 2, which good does the country export? Which good does it import? How does the quantity (demanded or needed) of imports change as the price changes? What is happening to the country's terms of trade as the price declines? What is happening to the country's well-being or welfare as the price declines?

◆ 7. The country of Puglia produces and consumes two products, pasta (*P*) and togas (*T*), with increasing marginal opportunity costs of producing more of either product. With no international trade the relative price of pasta is 4 *T/P*.

   a. Show Puglia's economy, using a graph with a production-possibility curve and community indifference curves.

   b. Puglia now opens to international trade. With free trade the world relative price of pasta is 3 *T/P*. Which product will Puglia export? Which product will it import? On the same graph that you used for part *a*, show the free-trade equilibrium for Puglia.

   c. Use your graph to explain whether or not Puglia gains from free trade.

8. Consider the rest of the world with free trade (production at S_1 and consumption at C_1), as shown in the graph on the right in Figure 4.4A. The international relative price of cloth now changes to 1.3 *W/C*.

   a. Using a graph, show the effects of this change in the international relative price on production and consumption in the rest of the world.

   b. Is this change in the international relative price an improvement or deterioration in the terms of trade of the rest of the world? According to your graph, does the rest of the world gain or lose well-being? Explain.

◆ 9. Consider Figure 4.4A. According to the logic of the Heckscher–Ohlin theory, why is the shape of the U.S. production-possibility curve different from the shape of the production-possibility curve for the rest of the world?

10. In your answer to this question, use a diagram like Figure 4.3 and start from a no-trade point like S_0 with a no-trade price ratio of 2 *W/C*. Now trade is opened and the country can trade whatever it wants at an international price ratio of 1 *W/C*. (In your answers, you will need to picture additional community indifference curves that exist but are not shown explicitly in Figure 4.3.)

   a. Show that the country can gain from trade even if the country does not change its production point. (Production stays at point S_0.) (*Hint:* The price line with slope of 1 will go through point S_0 but will not be tangent to the production-possibility curve.)

   b. Show that the country can gain even more from trade if it also adjusts the production point to its optimal position (given the price ratio of 1).

c. What happens to the volume of trade as the country's position shifts from that shown in part *a* to that shown in part *b*?

✦ 11. Extending what you know about production-possibility curves, try to draw the ppc for a nation consisting of four individuals who work separately. The four individuals have these different abilities:

Person A   can make 1 unit of cloth or 2 units of wheat or any combination in between (e.g., can make 0.5 cloth and 1 wheat by spending half time on each).

Person B   can make 2 cloth or 1 wheat or any combination in between.

Person C   can make 1 cloth or 1 wheat or any combination in between.

Person D   can make 2 cloth or 3 wheat or any combination in between.

What is the best they can all produce? That is, draw the ppc for the four of them. Try it in these stages:

a. What is the most wheat they could grow if they spent all of their time growing wheat only? Plot that point on a cloth–wheat graph.

b. What is the most cloth they could make? Plot that point.

c. Now here's the tricky part. Find the best combinations they could produce when producing some of both, where *best* means they could make that combination but could not make more of one good without giving up some of the other.

12. The world consists of two countries. One country (call it Hiland) has a strong legal system for contract enforcement, and the other country (call it Loland) has a legal system in which enforcement of contracts is uncertain, slow, and costly. In other basic ways the two countries are quite similar.

For some final-goods industries, key material inputs into production are obtained on spot markets, using short-lived purchasing agreements. For other final-goods industries, key material inputs into production are best obtained through complicated, longer-term contracts to assure steady availability of the inputs.

What do you predict about the pattern of trade in final goods between these two countries? Why?

Chapter Five

Who Gains and Who Loses from Trade?

If countries gain from opening trade, why do free-trade policies have so many opponents year in and year out? The answer does not lie mainly in public ignorance about the effects of trade. Trade *does* typically hurt some groups within any country. Many opponents of freer trade probably perceive this point correctly. A full analysis of trade requires that we identify the winners and losers from freer trade. The chapter on the analysis of supply and demand provided one look at these groups by focusing on producers and consumers of a product. But this distinction is not completely valid. People who are consumers also own and provide factor resources that are used in production. Is there another useful way to examine the winners and losers?

A virtue of the Heckscher–Ohlin (H–O) theory of trade patterns is that it offers realistic predictions of how trade affects the incomes of groups representing different factors of production (e.g., landlords, workers). In each country international trade divides society into gainers from trade and losers from trade because changes in relative product prices are likely to raise the rewards to some factors and lower the rewards to others. A key purpose of this chapter is to show the implications of the Heckscher–Ohlin theory for the incomes received by the different factors of production.

The Heckscher–Ohlin theory claims to provide powerful insights into the basis for trade and the effects of trade, including the gains and losses for different production factors. How well does it actually fit the world's trade? A second key purpose of the chapter is to examine the empirical evidence on Heckscher–Ohlin. Does Heckscher–Ohlin explain actual trade patterns? Does it identify the factors that gain and lose from trade?

WHO GAINS AND WHO LOSES WITHIN A COUNTRY

According to the Heckscher–Ohlin approach, trade arises from differences in the availability of factor inputs in different countries and differences in the proportions in which these factors are used in producing different products. Opening to trade alters domestic production (for instance, from S_0 to S_1 in Figure 4.4A in the previous chapter). There is expansion in the export-oriented sector (the one using the country's abundant factor intensively in production). There is contraction in the import-competing sector (the one using the country's scarce factor intensively). The changes in production have one set of effects on incomes in the short run but another in the long run.

Short-Run Effects of Opening Trade

In the **short run,** laborers, plots of land, and other inputs are tied to their current lines of production. The demand for these factors, and therefore the incomes or returns they earn, depend on the sector in which they are employed. Some people will enjoy higher demand for the factors they have to offer because their factors are employed in the sector that is attempting to expand its production. With the opening to free trade, the expanding industries in our example are wheat in the United States and cloth in the rest of the world. In the United States landlords in wheat-growing areas can charge higher rents because their land is in strong demand. U.S. farmworkers in wheat-growing areas are likely to get (temporarily) higher wages. Foreign clothworkers can also demand and get higher wage rates. Foreign landlords in the areas raising cotton and wool for cloth-making can also get higher rents.

Meanwhile, the sellers of factors to the declining industries—U.S. clothworkers, U.S. landlords in areas supplying the cloth-making industry, foreign wheat-area landlords and farmhands—lose income through reduced demand and therefore reduced prices for their services.

For the short run, then, gains and losses divide by output sector: All groups tied to rising sectors gain, and all groups tied to declining sectors lose. One would expect employers, landlords, and workers in the declining sectors to unite in protest.

The Long-Run Factor-Price Response

In the **long run,** factors can move between sectors in response to differences in returns. Sellers of the same factor will eventually respond to the income gaps that opened up in the short run. Some U.S. clothworkers will find better-paying jobs in the wheat sector. As the supply of labor into the wheat sector increases, wages in the wheat sector decline. As the remaining supply of labor to the cloth sector shrinks, wages in the cloth sector increase. Some U.S. cotton- and wool-raising land will also get better rents by converting to wheat-related production, bringing rents in different areas back in line. Similarly, foreign farmhands and landlords will find the pay better in the cloth-related sector. As the supplies of the factors to the two sectors change in the long run, wages and rents in the cloth sector decrease, and wages and rents in the wheat sector increase. The full process of the effects of opening trade on factor prices in the long run is summarized in Figure 5.1.

When the factors respond by moving to the better-paying sectors, will all wages and rents be bid back to their pretrade levels? No, they will not. In the long run, wage rates end up lower for all U.S. workers and higher for all foreign workers (each relative to its level with no trade). All land rents end up higher in the United States and lower in the rest of the world (each relative to its level with no trade).

What drives this crucial result is the imbalance in the changes in factor supply and demand. Wheat growing is more land-intensive and less labor-intensive than cloth making. Therefore, the amounts of each factor being hired in the expanding sector will not match the amounts being released in the other sector. The imbalances create pressures for factor prices to adjust.

In the United States, for example, expanding wheat production creates demand for a lot of land and very few workers, whereas cutting cloth production releases a lot of

FIGURE 5.1

How Free Trade
Affects Income
Distribution
in the Long
Run: The
Whole Chain of
Influence

	In the United States	In the Rest of the World
Initial product prices:	Wheat cheap, cloth expensive	Wheat expensive, cloth cheap
	Trade opens: —— wheat ⟶ ⟵ cloth ——	
Product prices respond to trade	P_{wheat} up, P_{cloth} down	P_{wheat} down, P_{cloth} up
Production responds to product prices*	Produce more wheat Produce less cloth	Produce less wheat Produce more cloth
Crucial step— National factor markets change	For each unit of cloth sacrificed, many workers and a small amount of land laid off; extra wheat demands few workers and much land	For each unit of wheat sacrificed, much land and few workers laid off; extra cloth demands many workers and little land
National factor prices respond	Wage rates fall and rents rise (in both sectors)	Wage rates rise and rents fall (in both sectors)
Long-run results:	Product prices equalized between countries. Net gains for both countries but different effects on different groups. Winners: U.S. landowners, foreign workers. Losers: U.S. workers, foreign landowners	

*At this point, the short-run effects come into play, but the economy continues to move toward the longer-run effects shown in the rest of this figure.

workers and not so much land.[1] Something has to give. The only way the employment of labor and land can adjust to the available national supplies is for factor prices to change. The production shift toward land-intensive, labor-sparing wheat raises rents and cuts wages *throughout* the United States in the long run. The rise in rents and the fall in wages both continue until producers come up with more land-saving and labor-using ways of making wheat and cloth. Once they do, rents and wages stabilize—but U.S. rents still end up higher and wages lower than before trade opened up. The same kind of reasoning makes the opposite results hold for the rest of the world.

Trade, then, makes some people absolutely better off and others absolutely worse off in each of the trading countries. The gainers and losers in the short run are somewhat different from those in the long run because more adjustment can occur in the long run. Figure 5.2 summarizes the discussion of winners and losers in the short and long runs.

[1]This passage uses convenient shorthand that is quantitatively vague: "a lot of" land, "very few" workers, and so on. These should give the right impressions with a minimum of verbiage. For more precision about the implied inequalities, see the numerical example in the box "A Factor-Ratio Paradox."

FIGURE 5.2
Winners and
Losers: Short
Run Versus
Long Run

Effects of Free Trade in the Short Run

(After product prices change and production attempts to respond, but before factors move between sectors)

	In the United States		In the Rest of the World	
	Landowners	Laborers	Landowners	Laborers
In wheat	Gain	Gain	Lose	Lose
In cloth	Lose	Lose	Gain	Gain

Effects of Free Trade in the Long Run

(After factors move between sectors in response to changes in factor demands, as shown in Figure 5.1)

	In the United States		In the Rest of the World	
	Landowners	Laborers	Landowners	Laborers
In wheat	Gain	Lose	Lose	Gain
In cloth	Gain	Lose	Lose	Gain

Reminder: The gains and losses to the different groups do not cancel out leaving zero net gain. In the long run, both countries get net gains. In the short run, net national gains or losses depend partly on the severity of any temporary unemployment of displaced factors.

THREE IMPLICATIONS OF THE H–O THEORY

The Heckscher–Ohlin model has three major implications for factor incomes. These implications follow from the sort of analysis done in the previous section.

The Stolper–Samuelson Theorem

The conclusion that opening to trade splits a country into specific gainers and losers in the long run is an application of a general relationship called the **Stolper–Samuelson theorem**.[2] This theorem states that, given certain conditions and assumptions, including full adjustment to a new long-run equilibrium, an event that changes relative product prices in a country unambiguously has two effects:

- It raises the real return to the factor used intensively in the rising-price industry.
- It lowers the real return to the factor used intensively in the falling-price industry.

[2]Four important conditions and assumptions are needed for the Stolper–Samuelson theorem: (1) The country produces positive amounts of two goods (e.g., wheat and cloth) with two factors of production (e.g., land and labor) used in producing each good. One good (wheat) is relatively land-intensive; the other (cloth) is relatively labor-intensive. (2) Factors are mobile between sectors and fully employed overall in the economy. In addition, it is often assumed that total factor supplies (factor endowment sizes) are fixed, though this can be relaxed somewhat. (3) Competition prevails in all markets. (4) Production technology involves constant returns to scale (e.g., if all factors used in producing a product double, then output of the product doubles).

Extension   A Factor-Ratio Paradox

The effects of trade on factor use have their paradoxical side. By assumption, the same fixed amounts of factor supplies get reemployed in the long run. But everything else about factor use changes. To deepen understanding of several subtleties that help explain how trade makes gainers and losers, this box poses a paradox:

> In one country, trade makes the land/labor ratio fall in both industries—but this ratio stays the same for the country as a whole. In the rest of the world, the same kind of paradox holds in the other direction: Trade makes the land/labor ratio rise in both industries—but this ratio again stays the same overall.

How, in the United States, could something that falls in both industries stay the same for the

two industries together? How, in the rest of the world, could it rise in both yet stay the same for the two together?

The explanation hinges on a tug-of-war that is only hinted at in the main text of this chapter. Here is what the tug-of-war looks like for the United States in our ongoing example. Trade shifts both land and labor toward the land-intensive wheat sector, yet rising rents and falling wages induce both sectors to come up with more labor-intensive ways of producing. The two effects just offset each other and remain consistent with the same fixed total factor supplies.

Let's look at a set of numbers illustrating how our wheat–cloth trade might plausibly change factor-use ratios in the United States and the rest of the world:

| | United States Before (with No Trade) | | | | Rest of the World Before (with No Trade) | | | |
Sector	Output	Land Use	Labor Use	Land/Labor Ratio	Output	Land Use	Labor Use	Land/Labor Ratio
Wheat	50	35	35	1.000	30	16	32	0.500
Cloth	40	18	65	0.277	80	18	160	0.113
Whole economy		53	100	0.530		34	192	0.177

| | After (with Free Trade) | | | | After (with Free Trade) | | | |
Sector	Output	Land Use	Labor Use	Land/Labor Ratio	Output	Land Use	Labor Use	Land/Labor Ratio
Wheat	80	48	64	0.750 (down)	15	9	12	0.750 (up)
Cloth	20	5	36	0.139 (down)	100	25	180	0.139 (up)
Whole economy		53	100	0.530 (same)		34	192	0.177 (same)

Here we have both the factor-ratio paradox and its explanation. In the United States the change in factor prices has induced both wheat producers and cloth producers to come up with production methods having lower land/labor ratios (more labor-intensive techniques). Yet the same fixed factor supplies are employed.

One can see that the key is the shift of U.S. output toward land-intensive wheat. If it had been

the only change, the national land/labor ratio would have risen. This is what induced the rise in rents and the fall in wages. The increase in the cost of land and the decrease in the cost of labor in turn induce firms to shift to more labor-intensive (less land-intensive) production techniques in both industries. (The same points apply in mirror image for the rest of the world.)

A shift from no trade to free trade is an event that changes product prices. For instance, in our example, the opening of trade increases the relative price of wheat in the United States. The Stolper–Samuelson theorem then predicts a rise in the real income of the owners of land (the factor used intensively in producing wheat) and a decline in the real income of the providers of labor (the factor used intensively in producing cloth). In the rest of the world, the real income of labor increases and the real income of landowners decreases.

Stolper and Samuelson showed that this result does not depend at all on how much of each product is consumed by the households of landowners and laborers. The result clashed with an intuition many economists had shared. It seemed, for instance, that if U.S. laborers spent a very large share of their incomes on cloth, they could gain from free trade by having cheaper cloth. Not so, according to the theorem. Opening trade must enable one of the two factors to buy more of either good. It will make the other factor poorer in its ability to buy either good.

Let's use an example to see why. Under competition, the price of each product must equal its marginal cost. In our wheat–cloth economy, price must equal the marginal land and labor costs in each sector:

$$P_{wheat} = \text{Marginal cost of wheat} = ar + bw$$

and

$$P_{cloth} = \text{Marginal cost of cloth} = cr + dw$$

where the product prices are measured in the same units (e.g., units of a commodity, or dollars), r is the rental rate earned on land, and w is the wage rate paid to labor. The coefficients a, b, c, and d are physical input/output ratios. These indicate how much land (a and c) or labor (b and d) is required to produce one unit of each good. The easiest case to consider is one where these input/output coefficients are constant.

Suppose that the price of wheat rises 10 percent and the price of cloth stays the same. The higher price of wheat (and the resulting expansion of wheat production) will bid up the return to at least one factor. In fact, it is likely to raise the rental rate for land because growing wheat uses land intensively. So r rises. Now look at the equation for the cloth sector. If r rises and the price of cloth stays the same, then the wage rate w must fall absolutely. The contraction of cloth production drives down the wage rate. Next take the fall of w back to the equation for the wheat sector. If w is falling and P_{wheat} is rising 10 percent, then r must be rising *more* than 10 percent to keep the equation valid. So if wheat is the land-intensive sector,

$$P_{wheat} \uparrow \text{ by 10\% and } P_{cloth} \text{ steady means } r \uparrow \text{ more than 10\% and } w \downarrow.$$

Thus a shift in relative product prices brings an even more magnified response in factor prices. The factor used intensively in production in the rising-price sector has its market reward (e.g., r in our example) rise even faster than the product price rises. Therefore, its real return (its purchasing power with respect to either product) rises. A factor used intensively in the other sector has its real purchasing power cut. In our example, the lower wage rate means workers lose purchasing power with respect to both the higher-priced wheat and the stable-priced cloth. The real wage rate decreases.

The same principle emerges no matter how we change the example (e.g., even if we let the price of wheat stay the same and increase the price of cloth instead, so that the real wage rate rises and the real rental rate declines, or even if we let producers change the input/output coefficients a, b, c, and d in response to changes in r and w).[3] The principle really just follows from the fact that price must equal marginal cost under competition, both before and after trade (or some other event) has changed the price ratio between wheat and cloth.

The Specialized-Factor Pattern

The Stolper–Samuelson theorem uses only two factors and two products. Its results are part of a broader pattern, one that tends to hold for any number of factors and products.

- The more a factor is specialized, or concentrated, in the production of a product whose relative price is rising, the more this factor stands to gain from the change in the product price.
- The more a factor is concentrated into the production of a product whose relative price is falling, the more it stands to lose from the change in product price.

This pattern should seem plausible. You may wonder whether it is meant as a pattern for the short run, when factors are immobile, or for the long run. The answer is both. Consider the issue of opening to free trade. The longer a factor continues to be associated with producing exportables, the greater its stake in freer trade. The longer it is associated with production threatened by imports, the more it gains from limits on trade. In the extreme case, a factor that can be used only in one sector has a lifelong or permanent stake in the price of that sector's product. A good example of such an immobile factor is farmland that is suited to growing only one type of crop, so it has almost no alternative use. There is little difference between the short run and the long run when it comes to this land. If the land is of a type that will always be good only for growing an import-competing crop, there is nothing subtle about the landowner's stake in policies that keep out imports of that crop.

The Factor-Price Equalization Theorem

The same Heckscher–Ohlin trade model that leads to the Stolper–Samuelson result also leads to an even more-surprising prediction about the effects of trade on factor prices in different countries. Beginning with a proof by Paul Samuelson in the late 1940s, the **factor-price equalization theorem** was established about the effect

---

[3]For a numerical example, let both prices start at 100, let r and w both start at 1, and let $a = 40$, $b = 60$, $c = 25$, and $d = 75$. Let the price of wheat rise by 10 percent to 110. Your task is to deduce what values of r and w could satisfy the new wheat equation $110 = 40\,r + 60\,w$, while still satisfying the cloth equation $100 = 25\,r + 75\,w$. You should get that r rises to 1.5 and w falls to 5/6.

The text says that the result still holds even if a, b, c, and d change. To be more precise, the result still holds if a or c falls when r rises, or if b or d falls when w rises. These are the economically plausible directions of response, so the result holds in all plausible cases.

of trade on international differences in factor prices.[4] This theorem states that, given certain conditions and assumptions, free trade equalizes not only product prices but also the prices of individual factors between the two countries. To see what this means, consider our standard example of free trade in cloth and wheat. The theorem predicts that, even if factors cannot migrate between countries directly, with free trade

- Laborers (of the same skill level) earn the same wage rate in both countries.
- Units of land (of comparable quality) earn the same rental return in both countries.

This is a remarkable conclusion. It follows from the effects of opening trade on factor prices in each country. With no trade, workers in the United States, the labor-scarce country, earn a high wage rate, and workers in the rest of the world (labor-abundant) earn a low wage rate. The opening of trade results in a lowering of the wage rate in the United States and a rise of the wage rate in the rest of the world (recall Figure 5.1). If product prices are the same in the two countries with free trade, if production technologies are the same, and if both countries produce both products (among other necessary conditions), then the wage rate is also the same for the two countries with free trade. (You might try to develop similar reasoning for land rents.)

The factor-price equalization theorem implies that laborers will end up earning the same wage rate in all countries, even if labor migration between countries is not allowed. Trade makes this possible, within the assumptions of the model, because the factors that cannot migrate between countries end up being implicitly shipped between countries in commodity form. Trade makes the United States export wheat and import cloth. Since wheat is land-intensive and cloth is labor-intensive, trade is in effect sending a land-rich commodity to the rest of the world in exchange for labor-rich cloth. It is as though each factor were migrating toward the country in which it was scarcer before trade.

DOES HECKSCHER–OHLIN EXPLAIN ACTUAL TRADE PATTERNS?

The Heckscher–Ohlin approach to trade provides important insights, in theory, about the gains from trade, the effects of trade on production and consumption, and the effects of trade on the incomes of production factors. These insights are based on the hunch by Heckscher and Ohlin about the basis for trade—why countries export some products and import others. To know if the Heckscher–Ohlin theory actually is useful, we must consider whether this hunch is right. Does it help to explain real-world trade patterns?

The first formal efforts to test the H–O theory used the simple model of two factors of production and U.S. trade data. These tests failed to confirm the H–O theory.

---

[4]The important conditions and assumptions needed for the factor-price equalization theorem include all four of those for the Stolper–Samuelson theorem (see footnote 2) and the following additional ones: (5) Both countries produce positive amounts of both goods with free trade. (Both are incompletely specialized in production.) (6) Trade is free of government restrictions or barriers to trade (like tariffs). (7) There are no transport costs. (8) The technologies available (or the production functions) are the same for both countries. (9) There are no factor-intensity reversals. (If wheat is the relatively land-intensive good in one country, then it is also the relatively land-intensive good in the other country.)

(See the box "The Leontief Paradox.") More recent tests recognize that more than two types of production factors are relevant to the H–O explanation of trade patterns.

Economists have tested the H–O theory in several ways. Complete tests require information on the factor endowments of different countries, international trade for various products, and the factor proportions used in producing these products. The upshot of these tests can be seen through a look at factor endowments and trade patterns.

Factor Endowments

Figure 5.3 shows the shares of several countries in the "world" endowments of certain factors of production. To recognize the patterns of relative abundance and scarcity here, a country's share of the world endowment of one factor should be compared to that country's shares of the world endowments of other factors. Physical (or nonhuman) capital is relatively abundant in the industrialized countries, including the United States and the five other countries shown specifically in the figure.

Highly skilled labor, represented here by those who have some college or a similar post-secondary education (whether or not they graduated), is also relatively abundant in the industrialized countries. This category includes scientists and engineers, a key input into the research and development (R&D) that influences international competition in high-technology goods.

Unskilled labor, represented here by those who have no formal education plus those who have not completed primary school, is relatively scarce in the developed countries. The developing countries show the opposite pattern of abundance and scarcity for physical capital, highly skilled labor, and unskilled labor. For medium-skilled labor, the international contrasts are not nearly so sharp. Countries have them in shares that tend to be in the middle of the abundance–scarcity spectrum, with China being an interesting exception.

FIGURE 5.3   Shares of the World's Factor Endowments, 2010–2011

	Physical Capital	Highly Skilled Labor[a]	Medium- Skilled Labor[b]	Unskilled Labor[c]	Crop Land	Pasture Land	Forestland
United States	16.8%	19.0%	3.9%	0.2%	11.1%	8.1%	7.9%
Canada	1.4	1.5	0.6	0.1	3.3	0.5	8.1
Japan	7.5	6.1	2.2	0.4	0.3	0.0	0.7
Germany	4.2	1.9	1.8	0.4	0.8	0.2	0.3
France	3.6	1.5	1.2	0.5	1.3	0.3	0.4
United Kingdom	2.6	1.7	1.2	0.4	0.4	0.4	0.1
Other industrialized countries	16.8	9.5	5.9	1.6	6.6	13.1	7.0
China	18.3	12.9	27.8	15.7	8.6	12.8	5.5
Other developing countries	28.9	45.9	55.4	80.8	67.5	64.7	70.1

Notes: All values are approximations. The "world" refers to 138 countries (29 industrialized countries and 109 developing countries) for which reasonable data are available. Physical capital and the land categories are for 2011, and the labor categories are for 2010.

[a]Adults who have some college (post-secondary education).

[b]Adults who have completed primary (first-level) education but have no college (post-secondary education).

[c]Adults who have not completed primary (first-level) education.

Sources: Physical capital (capital stock at current PPPs) from Feenstra, Inklaar, and Timmer (2013). Data on labor from Barro and Lee (2013), except four countries from Cohen and Soto (2007). Data on land from World Bank, *World Development Indicators*.

Case Study   The Leontief Paradox

What we now know about the mixtures of productive factors that make up the exports and imports of leading nations has been learned largely because Wassily Leontief was puzzled in the 1950s. Leontief, a Nobel Prize winner in economics, set off a generation of fruitful debate by following the soundest of scientific instincts: testing whether the predictions of a theory really fit the facts.

Leontief decided to test the Heckscher–Ohlin theory that countries will export products whose production requires more of the country's abundant factors and import products whose production relies more on the country's scarce factors. He assumed that the U.S. economy at that time was capital-abundant (and labor-scarce) relative to the rest of the world.

LEONTIEF'S *K/L* TEST

Leontief computed the ratios of capital stocks to numbers of workers in the U.S. export and import-competing industries in 1947. This computation required figuring out not only how much capital and labor were used directly in each of these several dozen industries but also how much capital and labor were used in producing the materials purchased from other industries. As the main pioneer in input–output analysis, he had the advantage of knowing just how to multiply the input–output matrix of the U.S. economy by vectors of capital and labor inputs, export values, and import values to derive the desired estimates of capital/labor ratios in exports and import-competing production. So the test of the H–O theory was set. If the United States was relatively capital-abundant, then the U.S. export bundle should embody a higher capital/labor ratio (K_x/L_x) than the capital/labor ratio embodied in the U.S. production that competed with imports (K_m/L_m).

Leontief's results posed a paradox that puzzled him and others: In 1947, the United States was exporting relatively labor-intensive goods to the rest of the world in exchange for relatively capital-intensive imports! The key ratio $(K_x/L_x)/(K_m/L_m)$ was only 0.77 when H–O said it should be well above unity. Other studies confirmed the bothersome Leontief paradox for the United States between World War II and 1970.

BROADER AND BETTER TESTS

The most fruitful response to the paradox was to introduce other factors of production besides just capital and labor. Perhaps, reasoned many economists (including Leontief himself), we should make use of the fact that there are different kinds of labor, different kinds of natural resources, different kinds of capital, and so forth. Broader calculations of factor content have paid off in extra insights into the basis for U.S. trade. True, the United States was somewhat capital-abundant, yet it failed to export capital-intensive products. But the post-Leontief studies showed that the United States was also abundant in farmland and highly skilled labor. And the United States was indeed a net exporter of products that use these factors intensively, as H–O predicts.

DISCUSSION QUESTION

When Leontief published his results, should economists have abandoned Heckscher–Ohlin as a theory of international trade?

Figure 5.3 confirms what we know about the distribution of the world's crop land, pasture land, and forestland. These types of land are relatively concentrated in North America and certain other developed and developing countries (e.g., Australia, Argentina, Brazil). Europe and Japan are poorly endowed.

Although not shown in Figure 5.3, we do have some information on endowments of natural resources in the form of fuels in the ground. Almost two-thirds of the proved reserves of crude oil and of natural gas are in the countries of the Middle East. Proved reserves of coal are more dispersed, with the United States, Russia, and Australia having a relative abundance. Unfortunately, we have limited data on other natural resources (minerals and metal ores in the ground). Still, we can surmise some patterns. Canada is relatively abundantly endowed, though the United States generally is not. Certain countries, including Australia, Bolivia, Chile, Jamaica, and Zambia, are endowed with abundance of various metal ores.

International Trade

If Heckscher and Ohlin have given us the right prediction, the unequal distribution of factors should be mirrored in the patterns of trade, with each country exporting those goods and services that use its abundant factors relatively intensively.

International trade patterns are broadly consistent with the H–O prediction that nations tend to export the products using their abundant factors intensively. Consider first the United States. U.S. exports and imports for selected goods are shown in Figure 5.4.

FIGURE 5.4
U.S. International Trade in Selected Products, 2012

Source: United Nations, Statistics Division, *UN Comtrade Database.*

A. Products Whose Trade Is Consistent with H–O Theory

	U.S. Exports ($ billions)	U.S. Imports ($ billions)	Net Exports as a Percentage of Total Trade*
Wheat (041)	8.17	0.85	+81
Corn (044)	9.71	1.02	+81
Coffee (071)	1.28	7.26	−70
Soybeans (2222)	24.74	0.35	+97
Coal (321)	14.88	0.93	+88
Crude petroleum (333)	2.40	321.86	−99
Primary plastic materials (57)	34.49	13.80	+43
Insecticides and herbicides (591)	3.31	0.89	+58
Aircraft (792)	104.20	24.31	+62
Clothing and accessories (84)	5.58	87.96	−88
Shoes and other footwear (85)	1.33	24.86	−90
Toys (8942)	0.96	11.55	−85

B. Products Whose Trade Appears to Be Inconsistent with H–O Theory

	U.S. Exports ($ billions)	U.S. Imports ($ billions)	Net Exports as a Percentage of Total Trade*
Pharmaceuticals (54)	44.59	68.66	−21
Perfumes and cosmetics (553)	8.21	7.05	+8
Iron and steel (67)	20.82	44.96	−37
Automobiles (7812)	53.90	149.14	−47
Medical instruments (872)	21.46	16.20	+14

Note: Commodity numbers from the Standard International Trade Classification, revision 3, are shown in parentheses.
*Net exports as a percentage of total trade equals exports of this product minus imports of this product, divided by exports plus imports of this product. This percentage is an indicator of "revealed comparative advantage" in the product.

The United States is relatively abundant in crop land, and it tends to be a net exporter (exports exceed imports) of temperate-zone agricultural products, such as wheat, corn, and soybeans. The United States is an importer of tropical-zone agricultural products like coffee. The United States has abundant endowments of some natural resources, such as coal, and tends to be a net exporter of these resource products. It is a net importer (imports exceed exports) of many other natural resource products, such as petroleum, which are found more abundantly in some other countries.

The United States is relatively abundant in skilled labor, including scientists and engineers employed in R&D, and tends to be a net exporter of products that are skilled-labor-intensive or technology-intensive, including primary plastic materials, insecticides and herbicides, and aircraft. Less-skilled labor is relatively scarce in the United States, so the country is a net importer of less-skilled-labor-intensive products like clothing, shoes, and toys. (The United States is also a major net exporter of business services—for instance, marketing, management, accounting, and consulting—reflecting the abundance of skilled labor that is important in producing these services.)

The pattern of U.S. trade in some other goods appears to be inconsistent with H–O. Five of these are shown in Figure 5.4. The United States is a net importer of steel and automobiles. The United States both exports and imports large amounts of pharmaceuticals, perfumes and cosmetics, and medical instruments. Factor proportions do not seem to be able to explain U.S. trade patterns for these products. In the next chapter, we will examine other theories that may explain them.

The trade pattern of Japan is also broadly consistent with H–O. Land and natural resources are scarce in Japan, which is crucially dependent on imports of agricultural, fishing, forestry, and mineral products. Without trade, Japan would be a far poorer country. Japan has relatively abundant skilled labor (including scientists and engineers) and tends to export skilled-labor-intensive manufactured products. Although Japan 60 years ago was a net exporter of less-skilled-labor-intensive products, the country now is a net importer of these products, a pattern consistent with its current relative scarcity in less-skilled labor.

Canada is relatively abundant in natural resources and tends to export primary products. Even its exports of manufactures tend to be intensive in natural resources used as important inputs into the manufacturing process. Examples include fertilizers, nonferrous metals, wood products, and paper.

The trade patterns of developing countries largely follow the H–O theory. For a closer look at the trade of one developing country, see the box "China's Exports and Imports."

In general, trade patterns fit the H–O theory reasonably well but certainly not perfectly.[5]

[5]A comprehensive test by Bowen, Leamer, and Sveikauskas (1987) measured the ability of factor endowments and U.S. input–output patterns to predict the net factor flows through trade in 1967. Out of 324 cases, defined by 12 factors and 27 countries, H–O correctly predicted the sign of net exports in 61 percent of the cases. This share was better than a coin flip, but only modestly so. The results of testing by Trefler (1995) indicate that all three of the bases for trade noted in Chapter 4 may be important for explaining actual trade—namely, factor endowment differences, technology differences, and a demand bias toward consuming domestically produced products. The magnitudes of the technology differences that Trefler finds are similar to the differences in labor productivity shown on the horizontal axis of the figure in Chapter 3's box on absolute advantage (p. 40). Research by Davis and Weinstein (2001), Schott (2003), and Trefler and Zhu (2010) includes further refinements and shows that factor endowment differences are an important part of predicting trade patterns.

WHAT ARE THE EXPORT-ORIENTED
AND IMPORT-COMPETING FACTORS?

The link of factor endowments to international trade patterns emphasized in the H–O theory also suggests, through the logic of the Stolper–Samuelson theorem, the effects of trade on factor groups' incomes and purchasing power. National policymakers need to know which factor groups are likely to gain and lose from liberalizing trade. The policymakers can then anticipate different groups' views on trade or plan ahead for ways to compensate groups that are harmed, if society wishes to do so.

The U.S. Pattern

Figure 5.5 shows the factor content of U.S. exports and of U.S. imports competing with domestic production. Overall, labor incomes account for a greater share of the value of U.S. exports than of the value of U.S. imports. This reflects two facts. First, the number of jobs associated with U.S. exports is about the same as the number associated with an equal value of imports. (See the box "U.S. Jobs and Foreign Trade.") Second, the average skill and pay levels are higher on the export side. In fact, it seems wise to divide labor into at least two types—skilled and unskilled—as in Figure 5.5. Skilled labor in the United States is an export-oriented factor, while unskilled labor is an import-competing factor. Farmland is another export-oriented factor. Physical capital (as suggested by the Leontief paradox) and mineral rights generally are import-competing factors.

FIGURE 5.5
A Schematic View of the Factor Content of U.S. Exports and Competing Imports

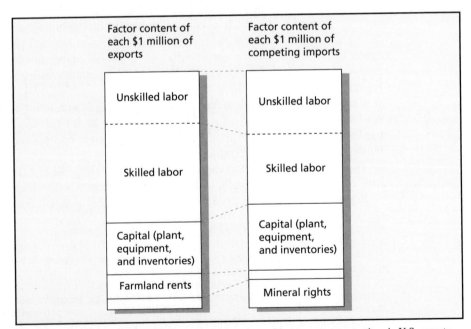

Note: Vertical distances are meant to give rough impressions of factor-content proportions in U.S. exports and the set of outputs that would replace the U.S. imports that compete with domestic products.

The Canadian Pattern

Canada, by contrast, implicitly exports and imports the factor mixtures sketched in Figure 5.6. One clear similarity to the U.S. pattern is that both countries are net exporters of the services of farmland through their positions as major grain exporters. Another similarity is that Canada is a net importer of unskilled labor. In contrast to the United States, Canada is a net importer of labor overall and a slight net exporter of nonhuman capital. Finally, Canada is a heavy net exporter of mineral-rights services through its exports of both the minerals extracted from the ground and manufactured products made with these minerals.

Patterns in Other Countries

The patterns of factor content have also been roughly measured for other countries. Two such results deserve quick mention here.

The factor content of *oil-exporting countries* is not surprising. They explicitly export mineral rights in large amounts, of course. The less populous oil exporters, particularly the oil nations of the Arabian peninsula, also export capital services through the foreign investment of much of their financial wealth. The same countries implicitly import just about every other factor: all human factors and farmland.

The *oil-importing developing countries* implicitly import capital and human skills as well as oil. They export unskilled labor, the services of agricultural land, and minerals other than oil. This pattern has important implications for the distributional effects of trade. For many developing countries, lower-income groups selling unskilled labor or working small farm plots have the greatest positive stake

FIGURE 5.6
The Factor Content of Canada's Exports and Competing Imports

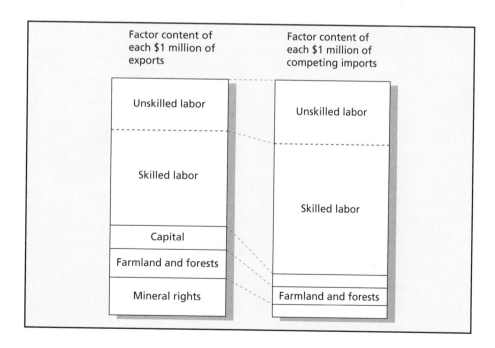

Focus on China   China's Exports and Imports

One of the most striking features of the global economy is the rise of China as a trading force after it opened to international trade beginning in the 1970s. China accounted for less than 1 percent of international trade in 1980. Its exports and imports have grown rapidly, so that by 2012 China's trade averaged over 9 percent of world trade.

Many media stories and commentators make it sound as though China is a ruthless mercantilist trader, focused on exporting its way to economic success. But the actual evidence is quite different. China is much closer to fitting our presumption that changes in export values roughly match changes in import values, so that trade is close to being balanced over time. The figure on the next page shows the paths of the value of exports and value of imports for China during 1976–2012. The rapid growth is evident. It is also clear that the value of exports almost exactly equaled the value of imports up to about 1996. While exports and imports continued to grow rapidly, exports exceeded imports by a moderate amount each year from 1996 to 2004. Then the gap increased to about $350 billion in 2008, before declining to about $230 billion in 2012. Still, with generally rapid growth in both exports and imports, China's trade expansion is closer to the textbook model of balanced overall trade than it is to an export-only mercantilism.

What does China trade? Do the patterns across export and import products match with what the Heckscher–Ohlin theory predicts? As shown in Figure 5.3, China is relatively abundant in medium-skilled labor, and it is relatively scarce in forestland, crop land, and highly skilled labor. Although it is not shown in this figure, we also know that China is relatively scarce in most natural resources in the ground.

The table below lists some representative products in China's international trade in 2012.

As is true for other countries, much but not all of China's international trade is consistent with the Heckscher–Ohlin theory. First, the theory predicts that China will be a net importer of land-intensive agricultural products like soybeans. Second, the theory predicts that China will be a net importer of natural resources like metal ores and crude petroleum. Third, the theory predicts that China will be a net importer of skilled-labor-intensive manufactured products like metalworking machinery,

	China's Exports ($ billions)	China's Imports ($ billions)
Soybeans (2222)	0.3	35.0
Metal ores (28)	0.5	158.7
Crude petroleum (333)	2.2	220.8
Metalworking machinery (73)	6.9	18.2
Computers (752)	169.4	35.1
Audio equipment (763)	20.0	10.1
Electronic microcircuits (7764)	54.3	192.7
Aircrafts (792)	1.6	17.6
Clothing and accessories (84)	159.6	4.5
Shoes and other footwear (85)	46.8	1.8
Toys (8942)	11.5	0.3
Vegetables (054 and 056)	10.6	2.7
Textiles and leather machinery (724)	4.7	4.6

Note: Commodity numbers from the Standard International Trade Classification, revision 3, are shown in parentheses.

Source: United Nations, Statistics Division, *UN Comtrade Database*.

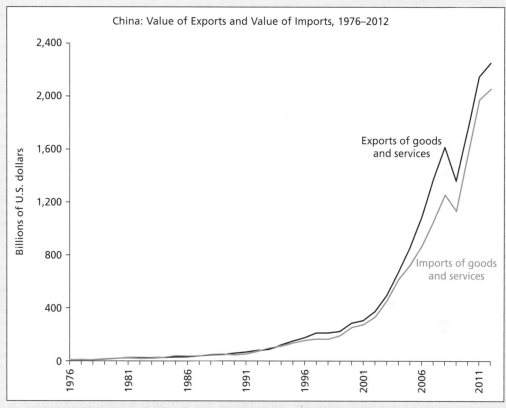

China: Value of Exports and Value of Imports, 1976–2012

Exports of goods and services

Imports of goods and services

Source: World Bank, *World Development Indicators.*

electronic microcircuits, and aircrafts. Fourth, the theory predicts that China will be a net exporter of lower-skilled-labor-intensive products like cloth-ing, footwear, and toys.

But then we are left with a fifth group that appears superficially puzzling. Why is China a net exporter of such products as computers and audio equipment? Here we must be careful to note that the part of the production process that occurs in China is mainly the assembly of these products, and the assembly processes use lower-skilled labor intensively. Essentially, China is a net importer of the materials and components that go into these products (as well as importing the product designs and the machinery used in pro-duction). China's production focuses on using its

abundant less-skilled and medium-skilled work-ers to assemble the final products, which are then exported.

While much of China's international trade does match with the Heckscher–Ohlin theory, there are some products that do not, including vegetables and textile machinery, as shown at the bottom of the listing.

Overall, China fits our textbook stories re-markably well. First, its trade has been roughly balanced—the value of exports has roughly equaled the value of imports, even though both are growing rapidly. Second, much of its pat-tern of net exports and net imports of different products is just what Heckscher and Ohlin would predict.

in foreign trade because their products are the exportable ones. Restrictions on international trade can widen the income gaps between rich and poor in developing countries. We examine trade issues for developing countries in depth in Chapter 14.

DO FACTOR PRICES EQUALIZE INTERNATIONALLY?

Perhaps the most remarkable conclusion of the Heckscher–Ohlin theory is that trade can equalize the price of each factor of production across countries. The factor-price equalization theorem is more than just remarkable. It is also clearly wrong in the strong form in which it is stated. Even the most casual glance at the real world shows that factor prices are not fully equalized across countries. For example, the same labor skill does not earn the same real pay in all countries. Machine operators do not earn the same pay in Mexico or India as in the United States or Canada. Neither do hair stylists. Given the large number of assumptions—some of them not realistic—that are necessary to prove the strong form of the factor-price equalization theorem, it is not surprising that the real world is not fully consistent with the theorem. For instance, in the real world governments do impose barriers to free trade, and technologies (or production functions) are not exactly the same in all countries.

Does a weaker form of the theorem work? That is, does trade tend to make prices for a factor more similar across countries than they would be with no trade? In our ongoing example, with no trade the return to land (the abundant factor) in the United States would be low, and the return to land (the scarce factor) in the rest of the world would be high. Opening to trade increases the return to land in the United States and reduces the return to land in the rest of the world—an example of a *tendency* toward international factor-price equalization.

That is exactly what happened before World War I: As Europe expanded its trade with land-rich America and Australia, the high land rents in Europe tended to stagnate while the low land rents of America and Australia shot up, reducing the global inequality of land rent. More recently, we see this tendency toward equalization in the rise of wages in China and India. As China has integrated into world trade and expanded its exports of less-skilled, labor-intensive manufactured goods, increases in demand for less-skilled workers has led to real wages for a typical factory worker rising at about 10 percent per year since the early 2000s, narrowing the wage gap between China and the industrialized countries. In India, the growth of export-oriented production of business services (sometimes referred to as offshore outsourcing) has also affected wages in the past decade or so. Worker compensation in business services in India had been about one-fifth the compensation for comparably skilled workers in the United States. By 2013 compensation in India had risen to about three-fifths. Although we still do not see full factor-price equalization in the real world, there appear to be tendencies toward equalization.

Focus on Labor   U.S. Jobs and Foreign Trade

The U.S. Congress has sometimes come close to passing comprehensive bills to slash U.S. imports through tariffs or other barriers. These attempts have been defended as necessary to protect U.S. jobs. Does more trade mean fewer U.S. jobs? Does less trade mean more U.S. jobs? Economists have developed a relatively clear and surprising answer.

Consider general restrictions that reduce U.S. imports across the board. Such restrictions are likely to result in no increase in U.S. jobs at given wage rates! This is because (1) reducing U.S. imports also tends to reduce U.S. exports and (2) the average job content of U.S. exports is about equal to that of U.S. imports.

There are four reasons to think that reducing imports reduces exports. First, exports use importable inputs. If these imports are not so readily available, U.S. exports become less competitive. Second, foreigners who lose sales to us cannot buy so much from us. As foreigners lose income from exports to us, they buy less of many things, including less of our exports. Third, foreign governments may retaliate by increasing their own protection against imports. U.S. exports decline as they face additional foreign barriers.

Fourth, cutting our imports may create pressures for changes in exchange rates. We will discuss exchange rates further in Chapters 17–25. Here we depart briefly from barter trade to recognize that most trade is paid for with national currencies. Reducing demand for imports also reduces demand for foreign currencies used to pay for the imports. If the foreign currencies then lose value—thus increasing the exchange-rate value of the U.S. dollar—the higher dollar value tends to make U.S. goods more expensive to foreign buyers. In response they buy less of our exports.

The combination of these four effects results in roughly a dollar-for-dollar cut in exports if imports are cut. If both exports and imports are cut, the effect on U.S. jobs then depends on whether more jobs are created in the expanding import-competing industries than are lost in the declining-export industries. Estimates from different studies vary somewhat. Overall, the studies indicate that the net change in total jobs would probably be small if U.S. imports and U.S. exports decreased by the same amount. (In addition, the average wage rate tends to be higher in export industries.)

If a sweeping cut in imports would probably not increase jobs much, why would labor groups favor such import cuts? The largest lobbyist for protection against imports is the American Federation of Labor–Congress of Industrial Organizations (AFL–CIO). The goods-sector membership of this organization is concentrated in industries that are more affected by import competition than is the economy (or labor) as a whole. It is practical for the AFL–CIO to lobby for protectionist bills that would defend the jobs of AFL–CIO members and their wages even if these bills would cost many jobs and wages outside of this labor group. To understand who is pushing for protection, it is important to know whose incomes are most tied to competition from imports.

This discussion refers to a general restriction against U.S. imports. Selective barriers against specific imports would alter the net effect on U.S. jobs. For instance, studies of existing U.S. barriers, which are selective, show that they are most restrictive on goods having a higher-than-average jobs content, especially in less-skilled jobs categories. Thus, existing U.S. import barriers may bring some increase in U.S. jobs, even though raising new barriers against all imports probably would not increase U.S. jobs.

We conclude by noting that the validity of focusing on jobs gained and lost through trade is itself debatable. Jobs gained or lost through changes in international trade are themselves a small part of overall changes in jobs in the economy. Many different sources of pressure for change, including shifts in demand and changes in technologies, result in changes in the number and types of jobs in the country. A well-functioning economy is dynamic—employment shifts between sectors to reallocate workers (and other resources) to their highest-value uses. While there are disruptions in the short run, the reallocations are crucial to economic growth.

Summary:
Fuller
Answers
to the
Four
Trade
Questions

This chapter examines the effects of trade on income distribution. Combining these insights with the basic view of trade offered in Chapters 2, 3, and 4, we can summarize by answering the four basic questions about trade introduced at the start of Chapter 2.

1. Why do countries trade? Supply and demand conditions differ between countries because production conditions and consumer tastes differ. The main theories emphasize differences in production conditions rather than in tastes. Ricardo argued that trade is profitable because countries have different comparative advantages in producing different goods. His examples stressed differences in resource productivities. The Heckscher–Ohlin theory agrees that comparative advantages in production are the basis for trade, but H–O explains comparative advantage in terms of underlying differences in factor endowments. Each country tends to export those goods that intensively use its relatively abundant factors of production. The evidence is that the Heckscher–Ohlin theory explains a good part of the world's actual trade patterns reasonably well, but that some important aspects of trade patterns do not square easily with H–O.

2. How does trade affect production and consumption in each country? In the country importing a good, it will raise consumption and lower production of that good. In the exporting country, it will raise production of that good, but in the general case we cannot say for sure what happens to the quantity consumed of that good. With the exception of the latter conclusion, these answers are unchanged since Chapter 2.

3. Which country gains from trade? Both countries gain. Trade makes every nation better off in the net national sense defined in Chapter 2. Each country's net national gains are proportional to the change in its price from its no-trade value, so the country whose prices are disrupted more by trade gains more. (Later chapters will show how an already-trading nation can be made worse off by trading more, but some trade is better than no trade at all.)

4. Within each country, who are the gainers and losers from opening trade? This chapter has concentrated on this fourth question. Its answers go well beyond those summarized at the end of Chapter 2.

In the **short run,** with factors unable to move much between sectors, the gainers and losers are defined by the product sector, not by what factors of production the people are selling. The gainers are those who consume imported goods and produce exportable goods. Those who lose are the producers of import-competing goods and consumers of exportable goods. So far, the answer remains close to the answer given at the end of Chapter 2.

In the **long run,** when factors can move between sectors and the economy achieves full employment, the division between gainers and losers looks different. Application of the general **Stolper–Samuelson theorem** to the case of opening trade shows that

- If you make your living selling a factor that is relatively abundant in your country, you gain from trade (by receiving a higher real income), regardless of what sector you work in or what goods you consume. Examples are scientists and grain-area landowners in the United States and less-skilled laborers in China.

- If you make your living selling a factor that is relatively scarce in your country, you lose from trade (by receiving a lower real income), regardless of what sector you work in or what goods you consume. Examples are less-skilled laborers in the United States and scientists and grain-area landowners in China.

A corollary of these long-run effects on different groups' fortunes is that trade can reduce international differences in how well a given factor of production is paid. A factor of production (for instance, less-skilled labor) tends to lose its high reward in countries where it was scarce before trade and to gain in countries where it was abundant before trade. Under certain conditions the **factor-price equalization theorem** holds: Free trade in products will equalize a factor's rate of pay in all countries, even if the factor itself is not free to move between countries. Those conditions for perfect equalization are not often met in the real world, but there is real-world evidence that opening trade tends to make factor prices less unequal between countries.

Key Terms

Short run	Stolper–Samuelson	Factor-price
Long run	theorem	equalization theorem

Suggested Reading

For excellent surveys of empirical tests of trade theories, see Deardorff (1984), Leamer and Levinsohn (1995), and Davis and Weinstein (2003). Tough tests of the Heckscher–Ohlin theory appear in Bowen, Leamer, and Sveikauskas (1987); Trefler (1993, 1995); Davis and Weinstein (2001); Schott (2003); and Trefler and Zhu (2010).

Hanson (2012) discusses the role of comparative advantage in the trade of developing countries. Explorations of the effects of trade (and other aspects of globalization) on the earnings of different groups in developing countries include Goldberg and Pavcnik (2007); Gonzaga, Menezes Filho, and Terra (2006); and Robertson (2007). O'Rourke et al. (1996) and O'Rourke and Williamson (1994) explore factor price convergence in the late 19th century.

Questions and Problems

◆ 1. As a result of the North American Free Trade Agreement (NAFTA), the United States and Canada shifted toward free trade with Mexico. According to the Stolper–Samuelson theorem, how is this shift affecting the real wage of unskilled labor in Mexico? In the United States or Canada? How is it affecting the real wage of skilled labor in Mexico? In the United States or Canada?

2. "The factor-price equalization theorem indicates that with free trade the real wage earned by labor becomes equal to the real rental rate earned by landowners." Is this correct or not? Why?

◆ 3. "Opening up free trade does hurt people in import-competing industries in the short run. But in the long run, when people and resources can move between industries, everybody ends up gaining from free trade." Do you agree or disagree? Explain.

4. One of your relatives suggests to you that our country should stop trading with other countries because imports take away jobs and lower our national well-being. How would you try to convince him that this is probably not the right way to look at international trade and its effects on the country?

◆ 5. The empirical results that Leontief found in his tests are viewed as a paradox. Why?

6. Consider our standard model of the economy, with two goods (wheat and cloth) and two factors (land and labor). A decrease now occurs in the relative price of wheat.

What are the short-run and long-run effects on the earnings of each of the following: Labor employed in the wheat industry? Labor in the cloth industry? Land used in the wheat industry? Land in the cloth industry?

◆ 7. In shipbuilding there are two types of ships. Producing basic bulk-carrying ships is labor intensive. Production of complex ships, including the largest container ships and very deepwater oil-drilling ships, depends more on technical skills and design capabilities. Both China and South Korea have large shipbuilding industries. China's factor endowments are shown in Figure 5.3, and comparable data for South Korea, reading across the columns, are 2.3%, 2.6%, 0.7%, 0.1%, 0.1%, 0.0%, 0.0%, and 0.2%. If China exports mostly basic bulk-carrying ships and South Korea exports mostly complex ships, is this pattern consistent with the Heckscher–Ohlin theory?

8. Indian exports of computer software development services have grown rapidly since the early 2000s. In the early 2000s the cost to employ programmers in India was about half the cost of programmers with comparable skills in the United States. In 2013 the cost in India was about two-thirds the cost in the United States. What trade theory or theories help us to understand the change?

◆ 9. In the long run in a perfectly competitive industry, price equals marginal cost and firms earn no economic profits. The following two equations describe this long-run situation for prices and costs, where the numbers indicate the amounts of each input (labor and land) needed to produce a unit of each product (wheat and cloth):

$$P_{wheat} = 60w + 40r$$

$$P_{cloth} = 75w + 25r$$

  a. If the price of wheat is initially 100 and the price of cloth is initially 100, what are the values for the wage rate, w, and the rental rate, r? What is the labor cost per unit of wheat output? Per unit of cloth? What is the rental cost per unit of wheat? Per unit of cloth?

  b. The price of cloth now increases to 120. What are the new values for w and r (after adjustment to the new long-run situation)?

  c. What is the change in the real wage (purchasing power of labor income) with respect to each good? Is the real wage higher or lower "on average"? What is the change in the real rental rate (purchasing power of land income) with respect to each good? Is the real rental rate higher or lower "on average"?

  d. Relate your conclusions in part *c* to the Stolper–Samuelson theorem.

10. You are given the following input cost shares in the corn and vehicle industries for the country of Pugelovia:

	For Each Dollar of		
	Corn Output	Vehicle Output	Overall National Income
Total labor input	$0.60	$0.59	$0.60
Total land input	0.15	0.06	0.10
Total capital input	0.25	0.35	0.30
	$1.00	$1.00	$1.00

Suppose that a change in demand conditions in the rest of the world raises the price of corn relative to vehicles, so producers in Pugelovia try to expand production of corn in order to export more corn.

a. If all factors are *immobile* between the corn and vehicle sectors, who gains from this change? Who loses?

b. If all factors are freely *mobile* between the corn and vehicle sectors, who gains from this change? Who loses?

✦ 11. From the following information calculate the total input shares of labor and capital in each dollar of cloth output:

	For Each Dollar of		
	Cloth Output	Synthetic Fiber Output	Cotton Fiber Output
Direct labor input	$0.50	$0.30	$0.60
Direct capital input	0.20	0.70	0.40
Synthetic fiber input	0.10	0.00	0.00
Cotton fiber input	0.20	0.00	0.00
All inputs	$1.00	$1.00	$1.00

Cloth is the only product that this country exports. The total input share of labor in producing $1.00 of import substitutes in this country is $0.55, and the total input share of capital is $0.45. Is this trade pattern consistent with the fact that this country is relatively labor-abundant and capital-scarce?

12. Consider the following data on some of Japan's exports and imports in 2012, measured in billions of U.S. dollars:

Product	Japanese Exports	Japanese Imports
Food (0)	3.7	64.2
Metal ores (28)	6.5	39.7
Crude petroleum (333)	0.0	153.1
Pharmaceuticals (54)	4.0	24.3
Soaps and cleaners (554)	1.2	0.8
Iron and steel (67)	43.8	10.1
Automobiles (7812)	97.3	10.9
Aircraft (792)	3.9	7.3
Clothing and accessories (84)	0.6	33.9
Shoes and other footwear (85)	0.1	5.9
Medical instruments (872)	2.8	6.0

Note: Commodity numbers from the Standard International Trade Classification are shown in parentheses.

For which of these products do Japan's exports and imports appear to be consistent with the predictions of the Heckscher–Ohlin theory? Which appear to be inconsistent?

Chapter **Six**

Scale Economies, Imperfect Competition, and Trade

According to our standard theories of comparative advantage, countries should trade to exploit the relative cost differences that arise from differences in factor endowments and differences in technology and productivity. As we discussed in the previous chapter, much international trade conforms to this predicted pattern. Industrialized countries trade with developing countries. Countries with substantial reserves of oil trade with countries that lack crude in the ground.

However, another part of international trade does not conform. According to comparative advantage, countries that are similar should trade little with each other. Industrialized countries are similar to each other in many aspects of their relative factor endowments (physical capital, skilled labor, unskilled labor) and also in their technologies and technological capabilities. Yet, they trade extensively with each other. About two-thirds of the exports of industrialized countries are shipped to other industrialized countries, and about one-third of total world trade is industrialized countries trading with each other.

According to our standard theories of comparative advantage, each country should export some products (if the country has a relative cost advantage) and import other products (if the country has a relative cost disadvantage). Much trade is in this form. For instance, a country that exports large amounts of oil usually does not also import much oil, but rather it imports other products like machinery. But, again, another part of international trade does not conform. For instance, much of the trade of an industrialized country is two-way trade in which the country both exports and imports the same or very similar products.

To understand why industrialized countries trade so much with each other, and why they have so much two-way trade in very similar products, we need to extend our models of trade beyond standard comparative advantage, with its assumption of perfect competition. In this chapter we will incorporate additional important features of rivalry in actual global markets, features that represent aspects of imperfect competition.

We begin by reviewing what we need to know about scale economies, in which large size leads to lower per-unit costs of production. Scale economies play an important role in departures from perfect competition. Then we look carefully at intra-industry trade—two-way trade in which a country both exports and imports the same or very similar products.

With these concepts in hand, we turn to the main task of the chapter, the development of three theories that add to our understanding of trade. Each theory is based on a type of market structure that differs from perfect competition, specifically:

- Product differentiation and monopolistic competition.
- Dominance of large firms in global oligopoly.
- Clustering of firms to exploit cost advantages of locating close to each other.

Each of these theories applies to industries with specific characteristics. As you will see, each adds to our ability to answer the four major questions about trade.

SCALE ECONOMIES

For types of imperfect competition that are the focus of this chapter, scale economies play an important role. But what are scale economies? Where do they come from? We are entering new territory because our standard theory of international trade has assumed constant returns to scale.

Consider how cost changes as a firm alters the amount that it wants to produce, assuming that the firm can make full or long-run adjustments of all factor inputs and that factor prices are constant. Total cost increases if the firm wants to produce more, so the proportionate changes in total cost and output quantity are the key issues. With **constant returns to scale,** input use and total cost rise in the same proportion as output increases. For an industry such as production of basic clothing items, production is probably very close to constant returns to scale.

What is the implication for *average cost*, which is total cost divided by the number of units produced? For constant returns to scale, total cost and output go up by the same proportion, so average cost (the ratio between them) is constant (or steady). Here is a simple example of constant returns to scale. If a firm wants to double output, it must double all the inputs that it uses. If input prices are constant, then total cost also doubles. If both total cost and output double, then average cost is unchanged.

Of course, constant returns to scale are not the only possibility. In fact, we believe that for many industries there is a range of output for which scale economies exist. With **scale economies,** output quantity goes up by a larger proportion than does total cost, as output increases. If output quantity expands faster than total cost increases, then the average cost of producing a unit of output decreases as output increases. (Remember, we are assuming all useful long-run adjustments are made to vary the production inputs as the output quantity changes, and we are assuming that input prices are constant.)

Figure 6.1 shows how scale economies affect average costs. The basic data for total cost that would be incurred to produce each of several different levels of output are shown toward the bottom of the figure, and the average cost for each of these output levels can be computed as total cost divided by output quantity. According to Figure 6.1, if the output level for this time period is only 25,000 units, the average cost for producing these units would be $26 per unit. If, instead, the output level is 50,000 units, the average cost would be $23 per unit, and for 75,000 units the average cost would be $21 per unit. For the output level of 100,000 units, the average cost would be $20 per unit. For output levels up to 100,000 units, scale economies can

FIGURE 6.1
Scale
Economies

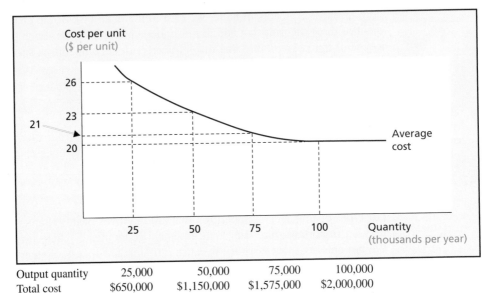

Output quantity	25,000	50,000	75,000	100,000
Total cost	$650,000	$1,150,000	$1,575,000	$2,000,000

Scale economies exist for the range of production up to 100,000 units, so average cost is declining as output increases in this range.

be achieved, so average cost declines as output increases. (For output levels above 100,000, constant returns to scale apply, and the average cost curve is a flat line.)

Internal Scale Economies

Where do scale economies come from? There are actually two types of scale econo-mies. First, scale economies can be internal to the individual firm. The actions and decisions of the individual firm itself result in **internal scale economies.** A larger firm may have a lower average cost for a number of different reasons. Here are a few examples. (1) There are often up-front costs before any production occurs. For instance, the cost of designing and developing a new large civilian aircraft is often close to $10 billion. As more planes of this model can be produced, the average cost of each airplane will be lower because the up-front fixed development cost is spread over the larger number of planes. (2) There are sometimes advantages to using large, special-ized capital equipment that operates at high volume. Bottling or canning beer achieves lowest cost per unit using high-speed automated filling and sealing machines, but use of such a machine is economical only if it can be run to produce more than a thousand bottles or cans per minute. (3) Tanks, vats, and pipes are a source of scale economies in producing chemicals. The cost of this type of input is based largely on its surface area, but its contribution to output is based on the volume that it contains. As size increases, volume increases proportionately more than surface area.

Scale economies that are *internal* to the firm can drive an industry away from textbook-perfect competition because they drive individual firms to be larger than the (very) small firms that populate perfectly competitive industries. But how far away? This depends on the size or extent of the scale economies. How large does a firm have to be to achieve all or most of the available scale economies? For instance, in Figure 6.1 low average cost is achieved at an output size of 100,000 units. And how large is the unit-cost penalty for smaller output levels? In Figure 6.1 the average cost penalty for a scale of 50,000 units, compared with lowest average cost at 100,000 units, is about 15 percent ($= (23 - 20)/20$). The answers to these questions are important for the type of structure that arises on the seller side of the market.

If scale economies are modest or moderate, then there is room in the industry for a large number of firms. If, in addition, products are differentiated, then we have a mild form of imperfect competition called monopolistic competition, a type of market structure in which a large number of firms compete vigorously with each other in producing and selling varieties of the basic product. Because each firm's product is somewhat different, each firm has some control over the price that it charges for its product. This contrasts with the perfectly competitive market structure used in standard trade theory. With perfect competition, each of the industry's many small firms produces an identical commodity-like product, takes the market price as given, and believes that it has no direct control or influence on this market price.

If scale economies are substantial over a large range of output, then it is likely that a few firms will grow to be large in order to reap the scale economies. If a few large firms dominate the global industry, perhaps because of substantial scale economies, then we have an oligopoly. The large firms in an oligopoly know that they can control or influence prices. A key issue in an oligopoly is how actively these large firms compete with each other. If they do not compete too aggressively, then it is possible for the firms to earn economic (or pure) profit, profit greater than the normal return to invested capital.

In a later section of this chapter, we present in-depth analysis of how we can use monopolistic competition to better understand the drivers and implications of international trade. We then take a look at the role of oligopoly in international trade.

External Scale Economies

The second type of scale economies is external to any individual firm. External scale economies are based on the size of an entire industry within a specific geographic area. The average cost of the typical firm producing the product in this area declines as the output of the *industry* (all the local firms producing this product) within the area is larger. External economies explain the *clustering* of the production of some products in specific geographic areas. What are the sources of external scale economies? There are several possibilities.

External economies can arise if concentration of an industry's firms in a geographic area attracts greater local supplies of specialized services for the industry or larger pools of specialized kinds of labor required by the industry. One reason that filmmaking firms cluster in Hollywood (and in Mumbai, formerly Bombay, India, known as Bollywood) is that a deep pool of workers skilled in the various aspects of filmmaking and a range of companies providing special services to facilitate filmmaking are available in these locations. (You can also see the self-reinforcing aspect of external scale economies—if you want to break into films and filmmaking, or to offer services to film companies, you know where you need to go.) External economies can also result as new knowledge about product and production technology (or other useful business information) diffuses quickly among firms in the area, through direct contacts among the firms or as skilled workers transfer from firm to firm. Knowledge diffusion is rapid and personnel are continually shifting among the high-technology computer, software, semiconductor, and related firms in Silicon Valley. Other examples of clustering driven by external scale economies include banking and finance in London and in New York City; stylish clothing, shoes, and accessories in Italy; and watches in Switzerland.

The final section of this chapter examines how external scale economies add to our ability to analyze international trade.

INTRA-INDUSTRY TRADE

According to our basic theories of comparative advantage, if a country trades in a product, it should either mostly export the product (based on its relatively low production costs) or mostly import the product (as a result of its relatively high production costs). We would see only **inter-industry trade,** in which a country exports some products in trade for imports of other, quite different products.

While much trade is inter-industry, especially in agricultural products and other primary products, there is also substantial **intra-industry trade (IIT)**—two-way trade in which a country both exports and imports the same or very similar products (product varieties that are such close substitutes that they are classified within the same industry). Figure 6.2 provides some examples of product categories in which the United States engages in intra-industry trade. For example, for each of perfumes and cosmetics, the amount that the United States exports is close to the amount that it imports.

We can quantify the relative importance of IIT in a country's trade in a product by splitting the total trade (the sum of exports plus imports) into two components. The first component is **net trade,** the difference between exports and imports of that product. Net trade is not intra-industry trade. Rather, net trade shows the product's importance in the country's inter-industry trade, in which some products are (net) exported and other products are (net) imported. In measurement we often use the convention that net trade is a positive value if the country is a net exporter of the product, and it is a negative value if the country is a net importer of the product. (The "positive" and "negative" are not value judgments, just ways of measuring.)

Intra-industry trade is then the other component of the country's total trade in the product, the amount of trade in which the country is both exporting and importing in the same product category. There are two equivalent ways to measure the amount of a country's intra-industry trade in a product. First, it is equal to twice the value of the smaller of exports or imports (capturing the amount of exporting of the product that is matched by the same amount of importing of the product). Second, IIT is the part of total trade in the product (exports plus imports) that is not net trade. Using this latter approach,

$$IIT = (X + M) - |X - M|$$

where X is the value of exports of the product and M is the value of imports of the product. Furthermore, we often want to compare the importance of IIT across different products or different countries. Because the total amount of trade in a product differs naturally for different products or different countries, we can measure the *relative* importance of intra-industry trade as a share of total trade in the product:

$$\text{IIT share} = \frac{\text{IIT}}{\text{Total trade}} = \frac{(X + M) - |X - M|}{(X + M)} = 1 - \frac{|X - M|}{(X + M)}$$

FIGURE 6.2   Intra-Industry Trade for the United States, Selected Products, 2012

	U.S. Exports (X) ($ millions)	U.S. Imports (M) ($ millions)	Total Trade (X + M) ($ millions)	Net Trade (X − M) ($ millions)	Intra-Industry Trade ($ millions)	IIT Share (percentage)
Perfumes (55310)	1,723	1,962	3,684	(−)239	3,445	93.5
Cosmetics (55320)	3,710	3,058	6,768	(+)651	6,117	90.4
Household clothes washing machines (77511)	205	308	512	(−)103	410	79.9
Electronic microcircuits (77640)	33,483	27,490	60,973	(+)5,993	54,979	90.2
Automobiles (78120)	53,901	149,142	203,042	(−)95,241	107,802	53.1
Photographic cameras (88111)	323	134	456	(+)189	267	58.6
Books and brochures (89219)	2,414	1,712	4,126	(+)701	3,425	83.0

For each product, intra-industry trade is the difference between total trade and (the absolute value of) net trade. The IIT share is intra-industry trade as a percentage of total trade.

The numbers in parentheses are the 5-digit code, Standard International Trade Classification, Revision 3.

Source: Data on exports and imports from United Nations, Commodity Division, *UN Comtrade Database.*

The values of these various measures are shown in Figure 6.2. For these seven products, over half of U.S. total trade in the product is IIT.

How Important Is Intra-Industry Trade?

How large is intra-industry trade in general? It is more important for trade in manufactured products than it is for trade in agricultural products and other primary products, so let's focus on nonfood manufactured products. Figure 6.3 shows the average share of IIT in the nonfood manufactures trade of six industrialized countries. The estimates are based on dividing the sector into over 1,300 different products. To develop the estimates, the IIT share is calculated for *each* of these products, and then the *weighted average* is calculated across all these products (using the country's total trade in the product as weights, so that products with more total trade receive more weight in the overall average).[1] The fine level of product detail is necessary so that we have meaningful, narrowly defined industries. We try to avoid biasing the measurement of IIT

---

[1] We can show the formula for this weighted average of IIT shares. To be clear, let us add the subscript i to the value for each product's exports and imports, to emphasize that we are averaging over a number of different product categories.

$$\text{Weighted average of IIT shares} = \sum_i \left[\left[\frac{(X_i + M_i)}{\sum_i (X_i + M_i)} \right] \cdot (\text{IIT share})_i \right]$$

In this formula, the first (ratio) term is the proportionate weight for each product category, and the second term is the calculated IIT share for that product category.

FIGURE 6.3

Average
Percentage
Shares of Intra-
Industry Trade
in the Country's
Total Trade
in Nonfood
Manufactured
Products

Country	1989	2005	2012
United States	55.3	58.3	63.6
Canada	54.3	63.2	55.4
Japan	27.8	41.2	38.0
Germany	62.6	67.5	67.2
France	71.3	73.9	71.5
United Kingdom	69.0	71.7	71.6

For trade in nonfood manufactured goods (SITC 5 through 8), intra-industry trade is more than half of overall trade for most industrialized countries. The estimates are based on over 1,300 different individual product categories (the 5-digit level of the SITC, Revision 2).

Source: Authors' calculations, based on data for 1989 and 2005 from Organization for Economic Cooperation and Development, *SourceOECD ITCS International Trade by Commodity Database,* and data for 2012 from United Nations, Commodity Division, *UN Comtrade Database.*

upward, which could happen if we instead used broad product categories in which we would be (mistakenly) finding IIT when a country exports "apples" and imports "oranges" (if the too-broad product category was "fruit").[2]

As we can see in Figure 6.3, the importance of IIT rose from 1989 to 2005 for these six countries. The increase was especially large for Japan. In this aspect of its trade, Japan is still different from most other industrialized countries, but it is less different than it used to be. After 2005, the importance of IIT has roughly plateaued, except for the continued increase in U.S. IIT. For five of these six countries, IIT is more than half of total trade in nonfood manufactured products.

We know from other studies that IIT is more prevalent where trade barriers and transport costs are low, as within preferential-trade areas like the European Union. In Figure 6.3, the average IIT shares are particularly high for the three European countries. Furthermore, IIT is more characteristic of the (high-income) industrialized countries, and average IIT shares tend to be lower for the (low-income) developing countries. For instance, for China's trade in 1992, the average IIT share for its trade in nonfood manufactures was 20.9 percent. Even this difference has narrowed for developing countries like China that have been integrating into the global economy. By 2004, the average share of IIT in China's trade in nonfood manufactured products had risen to 41.1 percent, and it was 39.2 percent in 2012.

What Explains Intra-Industry Trade?

Why do we see so much intra-industry trade? There are several reasons. Some measured IIT probably reflects trade driven by comparative advantage. For instance, a product category may still be too broad, so that it includes different products that are produced using different production methods. Within a category, for instance, the United States may export specific products that are produced using skilled labor intensively

[2]In the analysis of intra-industry trade, a well-defined product category consists of product varieties viewed as close substitutes by consumers and produced using similar factor proportions. The latter is needed to conform to the definition of an industry stressed in the Heckscher–Ohlin theory of comparative advantage. Although we cannot prove that each of these over 1,300 product categories meets this definition, it seems unlikely that the categories generally are too broad.

and import other specific products that are produced using unskilled labor intensively. As another example, for some agricultural products, IIT measured over a year may reflect seasonal comparative advantages. The United States exports cherries in July but imports cherries in January.

Much intra-industry trade is driven by something other than comparative advantage, and the leading explanation focuses on the role of **product differentiation**— consumers view the varieties of a product offered by different firms in an industry as close but not perfect substitutes for each other. We can see the role of differentiation for the products shown in Figure 6.2. Product differentiation is rampant in perfumes and cosmetics, with strong brand names, exotic packaging, and wide-ranging claims for effectiveness and high quality. For clothes washing machines, brands from outside the United States, including Miele, Bosch, LG, Samsung, and Haier, compete with Whirlpool, Maytag, GE, and other U.S. brands. In integrated circuits there is differentiation by specific circuit design as well as by functional specification, with U.S. firms like Intel, Texas Instruments, and Micron battling with foreign firms like Toshiba, Samsung, and Infineon. The range of automobile models on offer is obviously very large. For cameras, consumers can choose from a range of brand names (including Canon, Sony, Samsung, Leica, Polaroid, and GE) and models that differ by features and quality. Books are inherently differentiated by title and author.

Product differentiation easily can be a basis for trade. Some buyers in a country prefer varieties of the product produced in a foreign country, so they want to import the product. The foreign varieties are not necessarily cheaper than the varieties produced by local firms. Rather, each foreign variety has different characteristics, and these buyers find the foreign varieties' characteristics to be desirable. At the same time, some foreign buyers prefer varieties produced by firms in this country, and these firms are able to export to the foreign country. Even if there are no relative cost differences of the type emphasized by theories of comparative advantage, there is international trade. And much of it can be intra-industry trade, with a country exporting and importing different variants of the same basic product.

Yet, it is not only product differentiation at work in this explanation. Taken to the extreme, each of us would want to buy the unique product variant that exactly matches our personal preference. This would be different from anyone else's exact variant, so the product variant would be completely customized to our own individual taste. But we know that this is not the case for the products shown in Figure 6.2. Each has a limited number of variants. The customization is limited. What limits the number of variants, and the amount of customization? The answer is some form of internal scale economy, so that there is a cost advantage to producing larger amounts of a specific variant.

MONOPOLISTIC COMPETITION AND TRADE

To understand why we see so much intra-industry trade, we need a model of trade driven by product differentiation and scale economies. Product differentiation is a deviation from the assumption of a homogeneous product, one of the standard assumptions used in the analysis of perfect competition, so we are entering the realm of imperfect competition. Our analysis is based on a mild form of imperfect competition called monopolistic competition. Edward Chamberlain pioneered this analysis in the 1930s, and Paul Krugman received a Nobel Prize in 2008 that cited his work in applying the model to international trade.

Monopolistic competition describes an industry with three main characteristics. First, for a general type of product, each of a number of firms produces a variant that consumers view as unique, so the product offering of each firm is *differentiated* from the product offerings of other firms. Consumers' perceptions of differences may be based on branding, physical characteristics, quality, effectiveness, or anything else that matters to the consumers. Each firm has some monopoly power based on its established production of its unique variety. At the same time, the variants of different firms are close substitutes for each other, so we analyze them together as part of a market for the general product. Second, there are some *internal scale economies* in producing a product variant. Third, there is *easy entry and exit* of firms in the long run (and the long run arrives rather quickly).

The third characteristic, easy entry and exit, is the same assumption used in perfect competition. This characteristic is powerful. Consider a firm that has a highly successful product variant and earns large economic profits. If entry is easy, other firms can readily introduce similar imitation or "me-too" variants to try to gain some of the profits. In the process, the sales and profits of the first firm decrease. In the long run, the typical firm in a monopolistically competitive industry earns zero economic profit (a normal rate of return on invested capital) for the same reason (easy entry and exit) that the typical firm in a perfectly competitive market earns zero economic profit in long-run equilibrium.

For our discussion here we will use automobiles as our running example of an industry that has many of the characteristics of monopolistic competition. It is like monopoly in that each firm produces unique models of cars, known by their brand names, so that the firm has some control over the price that it charges for each model. A Toyota Camry is somewhat different from a Honda Accord or a Volkswagen Passat. It is like competition because there are a fairly large number of producers, and there is entry of new producers into any segment of the market that looks attractive in terms of sales and profits. Chrysler pioneered the minivan segment with the Plymouth Voyager and Dodge Caravan. Once other firms saw how successful these models were, they developed and introduced their own minivans, including the Ford Windstar and the Toyota Sienna. In addition, new companies enter the market, for example, Kia and Hyundai from South Korea and, more recently, the emerging auto firms like Chery from China.

Let's look specifically at the product compact cars, with such models as the Ford Focus and the Honda Civic, and use our standard approach of comparing no trade with free trade. What would production and consumption of compact cars look like in a country if there were no international trade? What will change in the country (and in the world) if the country opens to trade with the rest of the world? Here in the text we will focus the analysis at the market or general product level. The box "The Individual Firm in Monopolistic Competition" provides a look at a firm producing a specific variant of the product (e.g., Ford and its Focus).

We would like to picture the entire market for compact cars, but this is challenging. There are a number of firms each producing its own unique model of a compact car. We will need to use a somewhat different approach from standard supply–demand analysis. In fact, it turns out to be useful to picture not the total quantity of compact cars produced and consumed but rather the total *number of variants (or models)* produced and consumed.

The Market with No Trade

Figure 6.4 shows what is happening in a monopolistically competitive national (say, U.S.) market for compact cars with no trade. The picture is built in three pieces, corresponding to the three key characteristics of monopolistic competition.

First, consider the price curve P. For buyers the models are *differentiated*. Still, as more compact car models are available in the market, consumers have access to more and closer substitutes for any one model. The demand for any one model becomes more price-elastic. As there are more models, each firm loses some pricing power as the market becomes more rivalrous. The price that the typical firm (e.g., Ford) can charge for its model (e.g., Focus) decreases as the number of models available in the market increases. The price curve P is downward sloping.

Second, consider the unit cost curve UC_{NUS}. Each firm could achieve *internal scale economies* and lower average cost if it could produce more units of its model. Yet, given the overall size of U.S. market demand for compact cars, an increase in the number of models produced means that the typical individual model will be produced at a smaller level of output. This crowding of models in the market reduces the ability of each firm to achieve scale economies. In fact, an increase in the number of models would drive scale economies "in reverse"—average cost would increase as the scale of production for the typical model decreased. The unit cost curve UC_{NUS} slopes upward. Note that a unit cost curve like UC_{NUS} is not the same as the individual firm's average

FIGURE 6.4

The U.S. Market for Compact Cars, No Trade

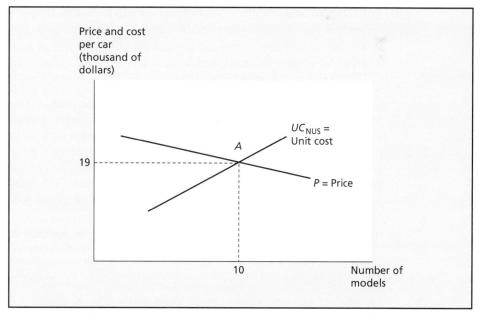

We can picture a monopolistically competitive market by showing how price and unit (or average) cost vary with the number of varieties (models) that firms are selling in the market. With more models on offer, price falls because buyers have more alternative models from which to choose. With more models on offer, average cost increases because each firm will produce at a smaller scale. With no trade the unit cost curve is UC_{NUS}. In long-run equilibrium, the typical firm earns zero economic profit, so the market equilibrium is determined by the intersection of the price curve and the unit cost curve. In the no-trade equilibrium the number of different models is 10, and the typical price is $19,000 per car.

cost curve (an average cost curve like the one shown in Figure 6.1). Rather, the unit cost curve is based on how the number of models affects where each firm can position itself on its individual average cost curve.

Third, *easy entry and exit* means that the typical firm earns zero economic profit on its model. Zero economic profit means that price equals unit (or average) cost, so the long-run equilibrium for the U.S. market for compact cars with no trade is at point A, the intersection of the price curve P and the unit cost curve UC_{NUS}.[3] In the no-trade equilibrium, 10 different models are produced and sold in the U.S. market, each at a price of $19,000 per car.

Opening to Free Trade

The top panel of Figure 6.5 pictures the world with no trade as two separate national markets for compact cars. The U.S. market with no trade is the same as that shown in Figure 6.4. The market in the rest of the world is assumed to be somewhat larger, so the no-trade unit cost curve UC_{Nf} for the rest of the world is somewhat farther to the right than is the no-trade unit cost curve for the United States UC_{NUS}. In the no-trade zero-profit equilibrium for the rest of the world, at point B the number of models is somewhat larger, 12 models, and the price is somewhat lower, $18,500. (One subtle note—the price curve is the same in both national markets because the overall size of the market does not directly influence consumers' buying decisions.)

If the world is now opened to trade, two things will happen:

• First, Ford (and other U.S. automakers) can export their models to foreign consumers because some buyers in the rest of the world find that they prefer the U.S. car models.

• Second, automakers in the rest of the world can export their models (for instance, Hyundai Elantra, Mazda3, and Mini Cooper) to the United States because some U.S. buyers prefer these foreign models.

Essentially, with free trade, the world becomes one market, as shown in the bottom panel of Figure 6.5. With the larger size of the overall global market for compact cars, rather than the two separated national markets with no trade, the unit cost curve for the world UC_W is farther to the right than either the no-trade U.S. curve UC_{NUS} or the no-trade curve for the rest of the world UC_{Nf}. (The world price curve is the same as that shown for the no-trade national markets.) The free-trade equilibrium for the world is at point E. The price of the typical car model is competed down to

---

[3]We can see why the intersection of the two curves is the long-run equilibrium by considering what would happen if the number of varieties is (temporarily) different from that shown by the intersection. Consider the price curve and the unit cost curve in Figure 6.4. If the number of models on offer is, say, 7, then the price of the typical model (shown by the height of the P curve for 7 models) is greater than the unit cost for the typical model (shown by the height of the UC_{NUS} curve). Firms are earning substantial economic profits on these 7 models, and the profits will attract the introduction of new, similar models by rival firms. As the total number of models on offer increases, the typical price falls and typical unit cost increases. The process continues until we have 10 models on offer. With 10 models, price equals unit cost, and there is no more incentive to introduce additional similar models. If, instead, the number of models begins at 14, the unit cost exceeds price. Each firm earns an economic loss, and some firms decide to exit by ceasing production of their models. The total number of models on offer decreases. The typical price increases, and the typical unit cost decreases, so the loss decreases. The market again is heading toward the zero profit (and zero loss) equilibrium at 10 models.

FIGURE 6.5

Markets for
Compact Cars,
No Trade and
Free Trade

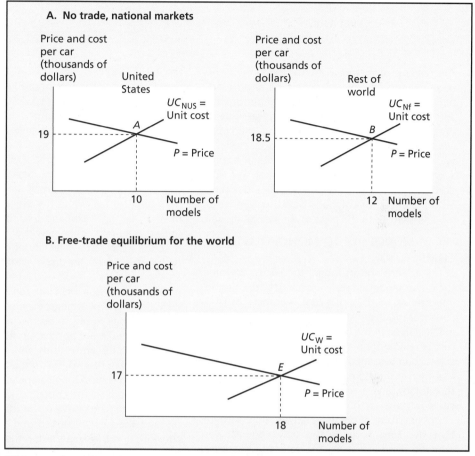

With no trade, each country must produce the models of compact cars that it consumes. With no trade, the size of each market is limited, so the unit cost curves are UC_{NUS} and UC_{Nf}. With no trade, the United States produces and consumes 10 different models, with a typical price of $19,000 per car, and the rest of the world produces and consumes 12 different models, with a typical price of $18,500 per car. With free trade, the world market is large (the combination of the two national markets), so the unit cost curve is UC_W. Consumers in both countries now have access to 18 models, and the typical price declines to $17,000 per car.

$17,000 and 18 different models will be offered for sale to consumers. For each country, some of these 18 models will be produced locally and some will be imported. Also, some of the country's production of its models will be exported.

Basis for Trade

What is the basis for Ford and each of the other firms in the United States to export their models of compact cars to the rest of the world? At first glance, it could be scale economies. But internal scale economies stem from engineering realities common to all auto producers. Auto firms in the rest of the world can achieve similar scale economies, so there may be no comparative advantage.

Extension   The Individual Firm in Monopolistic Competition

The analysis of monopolistic competition in the text focuses on the *market* for a type of differentiated product and examines the number of variants or models and the price of a typical variant. We can also picture what is happening to an *individual firm*—say, Ford—and its unique model—say, the Focus. By analyzing an individual firm in a monopolistically competitive market, we add depth to the analysis. We can better understand both the effects of entry and how the number of models is linked to the price of the typical model.

FROM MONOPOLY TO MONOPOLISTIC COMPETITION

Consider Ford and its model the Focus. We presume that moderate scale economies are of some importance, so the (long-run) average cost (AC) curve for producing the Focus is downward sloping, as shown in the graphs in this box. If average cost is falling, then we know that marginal cost is less than average cost. The exact shape of the marginal cost (MC) curve depends on production technology, and a reasonable shape for the MC curve is shown in the graphs.

To get started on the analysis, let's assume that the Ford Focus is the only compact car model offered in this market, so Ford has a pure *monopoly*. The demand for the Focus as the only compact car is strong, with the demand curve D_0 shown in the graph on the left at the top of the facing page. We assume that Ford sets one price to all buyers of the Focus during a period of time. Then, the marginal revenue for selling another car during this time period is less than the price the buyer pays for this car because Ford must lower the price to all other buyers to sell this one additional car. The marginal revenue curve (MR_0) is below the corresponding demand curve D_0.

How will Ford use its monopoly power to maximize its profit? Profit is the difference between revenue and cost, so Ford should produce and sell all units for which marginal revenue exceeds marginal cost. Maximum profit occurs when marginal revenue equals marginal cost, at point F in the graph, so Ford should produce and sell 1.2 million cars per year. Using the demand curve at point G, Ford should set a price of $31,000 per car to sell

the 1.2 million cars. The price of $31,000 per car exceeds the average cost of producing 1.2 million cars, shown in the graph as $15,000 per car. Ford earns total economic profit of $19.2 billion (equal to $16,000 per car times 1.2 million cars).

Will this high profit last? Other firms can see Ford's sales and its high profit. If *entry is easy,* then other firms will offer new, similar models. Here comes the competition part of *monopolistic competition*. As other firms offer similar models, some of what had been demand for the Focus is lost as some buyers shift to the new rival models. In addition, the increased availability of close substitutes probably increases the price elasticity of demand for the Focus. As a result of the entry of new competing models, the demand curve for the Focus shifts down and becomes somewhat flatter. If entry of new models is easy, then this process continues as long as there are positive profits that continue to attract entry. Entry stops only when economic profit is driven to zero, for Ford and its Focus (and for other firms producing competing models).

The graph on the top right side shows both the initial demand curve D_0 for the Focus monopoly and the new shrunken and flatter demand curve D_1 for the Focus after the entry of rival models. The Focus is still a unique model, and Ford still has some pricing power (the demand curve D_1 is still downward sloping). However, the best that Ford can do in the new long-run equilibrium of this monopolistically competitive market is to operate at point J. Ford sells 0.8 million cars at a price of $19,000 per car. Price equals average cost, and Ford earns zero economic profit.

FROM NO TRADE TO FREE TRADE

Assume that the monopolistic competition equilibrium for Ford shown in the top right-hand graph is part of the U.S. market equilibrium with no trade. What happens to Ford and its Focus when the U.S. market is opened to free trade with the rest of the world? Ford can now export Focuses to foreign buyers, and Ford faces new competition from imports of foreign models. Essentially, with free trade Ford is now part of a larger and more competitive world market for compact cars.

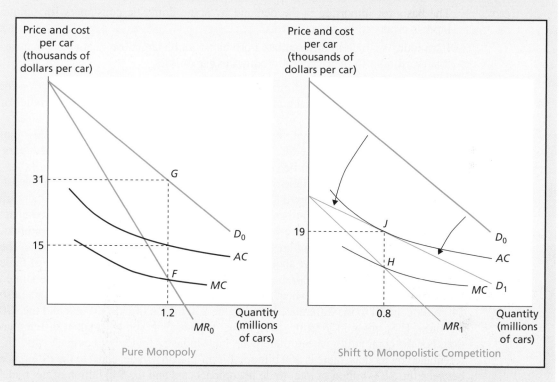

Pure Monopoly

Shift to Monopolistic Competition

With even more substitute models now available, demand for the Ford Focus becomes even more price elastic. And in the new long-run monopolistically competitive equilibrium with free trade, Ford still earns zero economic profit.

The graph at the right shows both the no-trade equilibrium for Ford and the new free-trade equilibrium. The new demand curve D_2 shows the combined U.S. and foreign demand for the Focus with free trade. In comparison with the no-trade demand curve D_1, the free-trade D_2 is somewhat flatter because of the larger number of competing models that are available (both U.S. and foreign models). In the new free-trade zero-profit equilibrium, the price of the Ford Focus is down to $17,000 per car, and Ford produces and sells 1 million cars per year, some to U.S. buyers and some to foreign buyers. With price equal to average cost at point L, Ford earns zero economic profit.

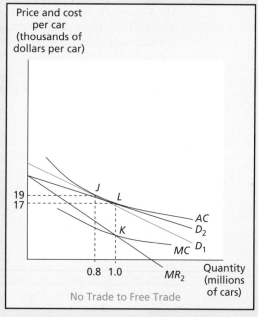

No Trade to Free Trade

Rather, in this setting *a country's trade is based on product differentiation.*

- The basis for exporting is the domestic production of unique models demanded by some consumers in foreign markets.
- The basis for importing is the demand by some domestic consumers for unique models produced by foreign firms.
- Intra-industry trade in differentiated products can be large, even between countries that are similar in their general production capabilities.

Scale economies play a supporting role, by encouraging production specialization for different models. Firms in each country produce only a limited number of varieties of the basic product.[4]

In addition to intra-industry trade, this product may also have some net trade—that is, the United States may be either a net exporter or a net importer of compact cars. The basis for the net trade can be comparative advantage.

Figure 6.6 provides an example of how net trade and intra-industry trade can coexist. We modify the world that we used in previous chapters slightly, so the two products are wheat and compact cars. Wheat is relatively land-intensive in production, and compact cars are relatively labor-intensive in production. Wheat is assumed to be a commodity, with no product differentiation, and compact cars are differentiated by model. The United States is relatively land-abundant and labor-scarce. Here is the pattern of trade that we predict. First, the Heckscher–Ohlin theory explains net trade, with the United States being a net exporter of wheat ($40 billion) and net importer of compact cars (also $40 billion, equal to the difference between the $30 billion of U.S. exports and the $70 billion of U.S. imports). Second, intra-industry trade is driven by product differentiation. For the commodity wheat, there is no intra-industry trade. For compact cars, differentiated by models, there is $60 billion of intra-industry trade, equal to the difference between the $100 billion of total trade in compact cars and the $40 billion of net trade. The share of intra-industry trade in total compact car trade is 60 percent ($60 billion of intra-industry trade as a percentage of the $100 billion of total trade).

Once we recognize product differentiation and the competitive marketing activities that go with it (for instance, styling, advertising, and service), net trade in an industry's products can also reflect other differences between countries and their firms. Net trade in a product can be the result of differences in international marketing capabilities. Or it can reflect shifting consumer tastes, given the history of choices of which specific varieties are produced by each country. For instance, Japanese firms focused on smaller car models, and they benefited from a consumer shift toward smaller cars in the United States following the oil price shocks of the 1970s. Japanese auto producers also marketed their cars skillfully and developed a reputation for high quality at reasonable prices. Japan developed large net exports in automobile trade with the United States during the 1970s and 1980s. Some of this was the result of comparative cost advantages, but another part was the result of focusing on smaller cars at the right time and skillful marketing.

---

[4]Product differentiation and the limited number of varieties produced in each country can also provide a base for examining the pattern of trade between different pairs of countries. See the box "The Gravity Model of Trade."

FIGURE 6.6

Net Trade and
Intra-Industry
Trade

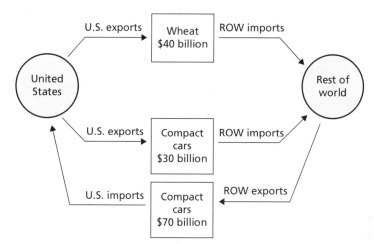

The United States has net exports of wheat of $40 billion and net imports of compact cars of $40 billion. There is also substantial intra-industry trade in compact cars, with the IIT share equal to 60 percent of total trade in compact cars.

Gains from Trade

Product differentiation, monopolistic competition, and intra-industry trade add major insights into the national gains from trade and the effects of trade on the well-being of different groups in the country. A major additional source of national gains from trade is the *increase in the number of varieties* of products that become available to consumers through imports, when the country opens to trade. For instance, the economic well-being of U.S. consumers increases when they can choose to purchase an automobile not only from the domestic models such as the Ford Focus but also from imported foreign models such as the Mini Cooper because some may prefer the Mini Cooper.

How large might the gains from greater variety be? Broda and Weinstein (2006) look at very detailed data on imports into the United States during 1972 to 2001 to develop an estimate. They conclude that the number of imported varieties more than tripled during this time period. They use estimates of how different the new varieties are to determine how much U.S. consumers gained from access to the new varieties. (The more different, the more the gain.) By 2001 the gain to the United States was about $260 billion per year, close to an average gain of $1,000 per person. Feenstra (2010) estimated that, as of 1996, the greater product variety obtained through international trade increased world well-being by an amount equal to about 12.5 percent of global GDP. If that 12.5 percent is still roughly correct, the increase in world well-being currently is about $10 trillion per year.

These national gains from greater variety accrue to consumers generally. They can be added to trade's other effects on the well-being of different groups within the country. Two additional insights result.

First, the opening (or expansion) of trade has little impact on the domestic distribution of factor income if the (additional) trade is intra-industry. Because extra exports occur as imports take part of the domestic market, the total output of the domestic industry is not changed much. There is little of the inter-industry shifts in production that put pressures on factor prices (recall the discussion in Chapter 5). Instead, with the expansion of intra-industry trade, all groups can gain from the additional trade because of gains from additional product variety. A good example is the large increase of trade in manufactured goods within the European Union during the past half-century. Much of the increase was expansion of intra-industry trade, so the rapid growth of trade actually led to few political complaints.

Second, gains from greater variety can offset any losses in factor income resulting from interindustry shifts in production that do occur. Groups that appear to lose real income as a result of Stolper–Samuelson effects will not lose as much; and they could actually believe that their well-being is enhanced overall if they value the access to greater product variety that trade brings. For instance, many people would be willing to give up a few dollars of annual income to continue to have numerous models of imported automobiles available for purchase.

Research pioneered by Melitz (2003) and Bernard et al. (2003) indicates yet another source of additional gains from trade, assuming (realistically) that firms in each country differ somewhat by cost levels (or quality levels) for their product models. With no trade, firms with different levels of cost can coexist, with lower-cost firms having lower prices and larger market shares. When the country opens to trade in this type of product, the increased global competition causes the demand curve facing a typical firm to become flatter and the typical price declines. In the more competitive global market, high-cost (or low-quality) national firms cannot compete and go out of business. Lower-cost firms can compete and export, so their production levels increase. Thus, opening to trade favors the survival and expansion of firms with lower cost levels (or higher levels of product quality).

We see a new way in which international trade drives national production toward firms with low opportunity costs. For comparative advantage trade (Ricardian or Heckscher–Ohlin), the restructuring is across different industries. For monopolistic competition trade, the restructuring is across firms of differing capabilities within the industry.

OLIGOPOLY AND TRADE

Monopolistic competition is a mild form of imperfect competition, but still one that has large implications for international trade. Oligopoly, the second type of imperfect competition examined in this chapter, is a stronger form. Some important industries in the world are dominated by a few large firms. Two firms, Boeing and Airbus, account for nearly all the world's production of large commercial aircraft. Three firms, Sony, Nintendo, and Microsoft, design and sell most of the world's video game consoles. Three firms, Companhia Vale do Rio Doce (CVRD), Rio Tinto, and BHP Billiton, mine more than half of the world's iron ore. Such concentration of production and sales in a few large firms is a major deviation from one of the assumptions of perfect competition, that there are a large number of small firms competing for sales in the market.

An industry in which a few firms account for most of the world's production is a global oligopoly. (In the extreme, one firm would dominate the global market—a global monopoly. Microsoft in operating systems for personal computers is an example.) How does global oligopoly (or monopoly) alter our understanding of international trade? We focus here on two aspects. First, there are implications of substantial scale economies for the pattern of trade. Second, there are implications of oligopoly (or monopoly) pricing for the division of the global gains from trade.[5]

Substantial Scale Economies

Exploiting *substantial* internal scale economies is an explanation for why a few large firms come to dominate some industries. If substantial scale economies exist over a large range of output, then production of a product tends to be concentrated in a few large facilities in a few countries, to take full advantage of the cost-reducing benefits of the scale economies. (In the extreme, production would be in one factory in a single country.) These countries will then tend to be net exporters of the product, while other countries are net importers. An example is the large civilian aircraft industry. Boeing concentrates most of its aircraft production in the United States, and Airbus concentrates most of its aircraft production in Western Europe.

Why do we see this pattern of producing-exporting countries and importing countries? History matters. Firms initially chose these production locations for a number of reasons. One prominent reason usually was comparative advantage—the companies could achieve low-cost production with access to required factor inputs at these locations.

However, even if a location initially was consistent with comparative advantage, cost conditions can change over time. Yet, the previously established pattern of production and trade can persist even if other countries could produce more cheaply. To see why, start with the fact that the established locations are already producing at large scale and have fairly low costs because they are achieving scale economies. Now consider the potential new location. The shifting comparative advantage can provide the new location with lower cost based on factor prices and factor availability, but that source of cost advantage may not be enough. To be competitive on costs with the established locations, the production level at this new location would also have to be large enough to gain the cost benefits of most of the scale economies. This may not be possible without an extended period of losses because (1) the increase in quantity supplied would lower prices by a large amount or (2) established firms in other locations may fight the entrant using (proactive) price cuts or other competitive weapons. With the risk of substantial losses, production in this potentially lower-cost location may fail to develop.

Oligopoly Pricing

Each large firm in an oligopoly knows that it is competing with a few other large firms. It knows that any action that it takes (such as lowering its price, increasing its

Extension   The Gravity Model of Trade

Another way of looking at international trade is to examine total exports and total imports between pairs of countries. That is, for a country like Australia, which countries does it export to and which countries does it import from? Australia exports mainly primary products, including coal and iron ore. The top 10 destination countries for its exports in 2012, in order from the largest down, were China, Japan, South Korea, India, the United States, Taiwan, New Zealand, Singapore, Britain, and Malaysia. Australia imports mainly manufactured products, including automobiles, machinery, and computers, as well as crude and refined petroleum. The top 10 source countries, again starting with the largest, were China, the United States, Japan, Singapore, Germany, Thailand, South Korea, Malaysia, New Zealand, and Britain.

In looking at these lists, we can note three things. The first is that they are mostly the same countries in the two lists. Eight of the top 10 are the same. The second is that many of these countries, including the United States, Japan, China, Britain, and Germany, have large economies. The third is that New Zealand is in both lists. Although New Zealand has a small economy, it is geographically close to Australia.

When we look at other countries, we see similar patterns for their major trading partners. Such observations have led to the development of the gravity model of trade, so called because it has similarity to Newton's law of gravity, which states that the force of gravity between two objects is larger as the sizes of the two objects are larger, and as the distance between them is smaller.

The *gravity model of international trade* posits that trade flows between two countries will be larger as

- The economic sizes of the two countries are larger.
- The geographic distance between them is smaller.
- Other impediments to trade are smaller.

In statistical analysis of data on trade between pairs of countries, the gravity model explains the patterns very well. Let's look at what we know and learn about each of these determinants.

ECONOMIC SIZE

Our theory of trade based on product differentiation and monopolistic competition can explain why the economic sizes of the countries matter. Consider first differences across the importing countries. Using basic demand analysis, we expect that an importing country that has a larger national income will buy (as imports) more of the product varieties produced in other countries. Now consider differences across the exporting countries. If the exporting country has a larger overall production capability, then it will have the resources to produce a larger number of varieties of the products. With more varieties offered to foreign buyers, it will sell more (as exports) to these foreigners.

Economic size is usually measured by a country's gross domestic product (GDP), which represents both its production capability and the income that is generated by its production. Consider Australia's trade with the United States and Canada. U.S. GDP is about nine times that of Canada, and Australia trades about nine times as much with the United States as it does with Canada. In statistical analysis, the elasticity of trade values with respect to country size (GDP) is usually found to be about 1 (so that, for instance, a country with twice the GDP tends to do twice the trade with a particular partner country, other things being equal).

DISTANCE

Most obviously, distance shows the importance of a cost that we have generally ignored in our theoretical analysis, the cost of transporting goods internationally. It costs more to transport goods longer distances. Consider Australia's trade with New Zealand and Ireland, the latter a country that is over seven times as far from Australia as is New Zealand. Even though Ireland's GDP is larger than that of New Zealand, Australia's trade with Ireland is only one-ninth that of its trade with New Zealand. (Not all of this huge trade difference is due to the large difference in distances because Australia and New Zealand also have a preferential trade agreement, but much of the difference is due to distance.)

In statistical analysis, a typical finding is that a doubling of distance between partner countries tends to reduce the trade between them by one-third to one-half. This is actually a surprisingly large effect, one that cannot be explained by the monetary costs of transport alone because these costs are not that high. This finding has led us to think about other reasons why distance matters.

One set of reasons is that countries that are closer tend to have more similar cultures and a greater amount of shared history, so the costs of obtaining information about closer trade partners are lower. Another set of reasons focuses on risk. Shipping things a longer distance, especially by ocean transport, takes a longer time. The longer time for shipment could lead to greater risks that the goods would be physically damaged or deteriorate. In addition, there is a greater risk that conditions could change in the importing country. For instance, the styles that are in fashion could change, or the importer could go bankrupt.

OTHER IMPEDIMENTS

Government policies like tariffs can place impediments to trade, as we will discuss in Chapter 8, and the gravity model can show how these reduce trade between countries. Perhaps the most remarkable finding from statistical analysis using the gravity model is that *national borders matter much more than can be explained by government policy barriers*. Even for trade between the United States and Canada, this *border effect* is very large.

A series of studies (starting with McCallum [1995] and including Anderson and van Wincoop [2003]) have used the gravity model to examine inter-provincial trade within Canada, interstate trade within the United States, and international trade between Canadian provinces and U.S. states. As usual, province and state GDPs are important, as are distances between them. The key finding is that there is also an astounding *44 percent less international trade* than there would be if the provinces and states were part of the same country. This extremely large border effect exists even though any government barriers are generally very low, and it is not easy to see what the other impediments could be. There's something about the national border. For Canada, the result is that provinces trade much more with each other and much less with U.S. states.

The gravity model has been used to examine the effects of many other kinds of impediments (or removal of impediments) to trade. Let's conclude with a sampling of some of the results:

- Countries that share a common language trade more with each other.

- Countries that have historical links (for example, colonial) trade more with each other.

- A country trades more with other countries that are the sources of large numbers of its immigrants.

- Countries that are members of a preferential trade area trade more with each other.

- Countries that have a common currency trade more with each other.

- A country with a higher degree of government corruption, or with weaker legal enforcement of business contracts, trades less with other countries.

advertising, or introducing a new product model) is likely to provoke reactions from its rivals. We can model this interdependence as a game. (Here we just give a flavor of this kind of analysis. We use game theory more formally in Chapter 11.)

Consider an example. Picture price competition between two dominant large firms as a choice for each firm between competing aggressively (setting a low price) or restraining its competition (setting a high price). The outcome of the game depends on which strategy each firm chooses. The best outcome for the two firms together is usually to restrain their price competition. They both can charge high, monopoly-like prices and earn substantial economic profits. However, if they cannot cooperate with each other, then the play of the game may result in both competing aggressively, and each earning rather low profits. To see why, imagine what could happen if one firm decides to restrain its competition and to set a high price. The other firm often has an incentive to compete by setting a lower price because it can increase its sales so much that it earns even more profit than it would earn by also setting a high price. The high-price firm loses sales and may earn very low profits. Both know the other is likely to act this way, so neither is willing to set a high price. Both compete aggressively with low prices, and both earn low profits. They are caught in what is called a *prisoners' dilemma.*

The firms can attempt to find a way out of the dilemma by cooperating to restrain their competition. The cooperation may be by formal agreement (though such a cartel arrangement is illegal in the United States and many other countries). The cooperation could be tacit or implicit, based on recognition of mutual interests and on patterns of behavior established over time. If they can cooperate, then they can both earn high profits. But the cooperation is often in danger of breaking down because each firm still has the incentive to cheat by lowering its price, to try to earn even higher profit.

Although game theory does not say for sure what is the outcome of this kind of game, it does highlight that cooperating with rivals is possible (though not assured) in an oligopoly. Firms in an oligopoly can earn economic profits, and these profits can be substantial if competition is restrained.

Pricing matters for the division of the global gains from trade. To see this, focus on export sales by the oligopoly firms. If the oligopoly firms compete aggressively on price, then more of the gains from trade go to the foreign buyers and less is captured by the oligopoly firms. If, instead, the oligopoly firms can restrain their price competition, then the oligopoly firms can earn large economic profits on their export sales. If a firm located in a country can charge high prices on its exports and earn high profits on its export sales, there are two related effects. First, the high export prices enhance the exporting country's terms of trade. Second, the high profits add to the exporting country's national income by capturing some of what would have been the consumer surplus of foreign buyers. More of the gains from trade go to the exporting country (or, perhaps more precisely, to the country or countries of the owners of the oligopoly firms), and less to the foreign buyers.

Putting all of this together, we see that the current pattern of national production locations for a global oligopoly may be somewhat arbitrary, and that the small number of countries that have the industry's production may obtain additional gains from trade if the firms in these countries can earn substantial economic profits on their exports. The national gain from having high-profit oligopoly firms in a country is a basis for national governments to try to establish local firms in the oligopoly industry or to expand the industry's local production and exporting. These issues are taken up further in the discussions of infant industry policy in Chapter 10 and of strategic trade policy in Chapter 11.

EXTERNAL SCALE ECONOMIES AND TRADE

Now let's turn to examine an industry that benefits from substantial *external* scale economies, as our third form of market structure that deviates from the standard case of perfect competition. External scale economies exist when the expansion of the entire industry's production within a geographic area lowers the long-run average cost for each firm in the industry in the area. External scale economies are also called agglomeration economies, indicating the cost advantages to firms that locate close to each other. As noted in the section on scale economies earlier in the chapter, examples of industries and locations that benefit from external scale economies include filmmaking in Hollywood, computer and related high-tech businesses in Silicon Valley, watch-making in Switzerland, and financial services in London.

To focus on the effects of *external* scale economies, we will conduct our formal analysis using the assumption that a large number of small firms exist in the industry in each location. That is, we assume that there are no (or only modest) *internal* scale economies, so that an *individual* firm does not need to be large to achieve low cost. We then have a case in which substantial external scale economies coexist with a highly competitive industry.

If expansion of an industry in a location lowers cost for all firms in that location, then new export opportunities (or any other source of demand growth) can have dramatic effect. Figure 6.7 pictures a national semiconductor industry that is competitive, but characterized by external scale economies. There is an initial equilibrium at point A, with many firms competing to sell 40 million units at \$19 a unit. Here the usual short-run supply and demand curves (S_1 and D_1) intersect in the usual way. The upward-sloping national supply curve is the sum of each small individual firm's view of its own costs. Each firm operates at given levels of industry production, which it cannot by itself affect very much. It reacts to a change in price according to its own upward-sloping supply curve, which is also its own upward-sloping marginal cost curve. The sum of these individual-firm supply curves is shown as national supply curve S_1.

What is new in the diagram is the coexistence of the upward-sloping short-run national supply curve S_1 with the downward-sloping long-run average cost curve, which includes the cost-reducing effects of the external scale economies. The national industry's downward-sloping average cost curve comes into play when demand shifts.

To bring out points about international trade, let us imagine that opening up a new export market shifts overall demand from D_1 to D_2. Each firm would respond to the stronger demand by raising output. If each national firm acted alone and affected only itself, the extra demand would push the market up the national supply curve S_1 to a point like B. The new export business raises the national industry's output, here

FIGURE 6.7

External
Economies
Magnify an
Expansion in
a Competitive
Industry

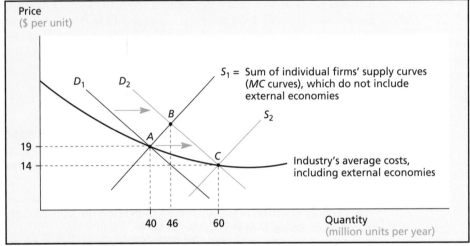

Results:

- In industries that can reap external economies (e.g., knowledge spillovers from firm to firm), a rise in demand triggers a great expansion of supply and lowers costs and price.
- Therefore, increasing trade brings gains to all consumers (home-country and foreign alike) as well as to the exporting producers.
- Corollary: Among nations having the same initial factor endowments, cost curves, and demand curves, whichever nation moved first to capture its export market would gain a cost advantage in this product.

initially from 40 at point A to 46 at point B. The increase in industry output brings additional external economies. For instance, there could be more development and exchange of useful information, which raises productivity and cuts costs throughout the national industry. This means, in effect, a sustained rightward movement of the national industry short-run supply curve, for instance, to S_2 in the new long-run equilibrium.

To portray the cost-cutting more conveniently than with multiple shifts of the supply curve, we can follow the national industry's long-run average cost curve, including external economies. The external economies lead to a decline in average cost as national industry output expands. As Figure 6.7 is drawn, we imagine that demand and supply expansion catch up with each other at point C, the new long-run equilibrium.

What are the welfare effects of the opening of trade for an industry with external economies? Producers of the product in an exporting country tend to gain producer surplus as a result of the expansion of industry output, although the decline in price will mitigate the gain. Producers in importing countries lose producer surplus. Consumers in the importing countries gain consumer surplus as price declines and their consumption increases. Consumers in the exporting country also gain consumer surplus as price declines and consumption quantity increases. Here is a definite contrast to the standard case (e.g., Figure 2.4), where local buyers suffer from price increases on goods that become exportable with the opening of trade.

What explains the pattern of trade that emerges in industries subject to external scale economies? Many of the issues are similar to those raised with respect to substantial internal scale economies. With no trade, each country must produce for its own consumption. If trade is opened, *production tends to be concentrated in a small number of locations*. Clusters of firms in some locations will expand production, as shown in Figure 6.7, and countries with these locations will export the product. In other countries, production will shrink or cease, and these countries will import the product.

It is not easy to predict which locations will expand and which will shrink or cease production. Sometimes it appears to be luck, with firms in one location deciding to expand at the right time to take the lead. Swiss watch-making seems roughly to fit. Or the size of the domestic market with no trade may be important if the larger domestic market permits domestic firms to be low-cost producers when trade is opened. Hollywood seemed to benefit from the early large size of the U.S. market for films. Or a push from government policy may be important. Early in its development Silicon Valley benefited from selling to the U.S. government for defense and aerospace applications. The outcome is analogous to the production of pearls. Which oysters produce pearls depends on luck or outside human intervention. An oyster gets its pearl from the accidental deposit of a grain of sand or from a human's introducing a grain of sand.

The external-economies case is one in which a lasting production advantage in an industry can be acquired by luck or policy even if there are no differences in countries' initial comparative advantages. The production locations and pattern of trade tend to persist even if other locations are potentially lower-cost. Other locations cannot easily overcome the scale advantages of established locations. As we also noted for the case for substantial internal scale economies, the government of an importing country may conclude that there is a basis for infant-industry policies that nurture the local development of the industry, an issue that we explore in Chapter 10.

**Summary:
How
Does
Trade
Really
Work?**

This chapter examined several theories that have broadened our answers to the four major questions about trade. The theories focus on

- **Product differentiation** and monopolistic competition.
- Substantial **internal scale economies** and global oligopoly.
- **External scale economies.**

According to the standard trade theory emphasizing comparative advantage, the similarity of industrialized countries in factor endowments and technological capabilities suggests little reason for trade among them. Yet we observe the opposite. Trade among industrialized countries represents a third of world trade. Furthermore, an increasing fraction of world trade consists of **intra-industry trade (IIT)**, in which a country both exports and imports items in the same product category. A challenge for trade theory is to explain why we have so much IIT and whether the standard model's conclusions about the gains from trade and the effects of trade still hold.

Much IIT involves trade in differentiated products—exports and imports of different varieties of the same basic product. **Monopolistic competition,** a mild form of imperfect competition, provides a good basis for understanding intra-industry trade. Firms producing their own varieties are able to export to some consumers in foreign markets even as they face competition from imports of varieties produced by foreign firms. **Net trade** in these differentiated products may still be based on comparative advantage.

Another fact is that some industries are dominated by a few large firms. Global **oligopoly** can arise when there are substantial scale economies internal to each firm. These large firms choose production locations to maximize their profits, and comparative advantages are likely to be prominent in such location decisions. Over time, the conditions may change, but, because of the scale advantages of the established places, the production locations and the trade pattern do not necessarily change.

Some other industries, while competitively populated by a large number of firms, also tend to concentrate in a few production locations because of scale economies that are external to the individual firm. External scale economies depend on the size of the entire industry in the location. It can be difficult to predict or explain which production locations prosper. Home market size, luck, and government policy may affect which country locations capitalize on the external economies.

Thinking about imperfect competition and scale economies also adds to our understanding of the gains from trade and the effects of trade on different groups. It does not contradict the main conclusions of the standard competitive-market analysis of Chapters 2 through 5. Rather, it broadens the set of conditions under which we see gains from trade, with some changes in how any gains or losses are distributed among the groups. Figure 6.8 summarizes gains and losses for three kinds of trade:

FIGURE 6.8
Summary of Gains and Losses from Opening Up Trade in Three Cases

	Kinds of Trade		
Group	**Standard Competition (Chapters 2–5)**	**Monopolistic Competition (IIT)* (This Chapter)**	**External Economies (This Chapter)**
Exporting country	Gain	Gain	Gain
Export producers	Gain	*	Gain
Export consumers	Lose	Gain	Gain
Importing country	Gain	Gain	Gain
Import-competing producers	Lose	*	Lose
Import consumers	Gain	Gain	Gain
Whole world	Gain	Gain	Gain

*In monopolistic competition that results in intra-industry trade (IIT), producers are both exporters and import-competing at the same time. If trade is mostly or completely IIT, then the effects on producers as a group tend to be small.
Note: The gains and losses to producers and consumers in all cases refer to changes in producer surplus and consumer surplus in the short run. In the long run, these gains and losses shift to the factors most closely tied to the export or import-competing industries (according to the Stolper–Samuelson theorem).

the standard competitive trade of Chapters 2 through 5 plus two of the three kinds of trade analyzed in this chapter. Oligopoly is not included because we do not have a single generally accepted model.

Relative to standard competitive trade, both trade based on monopolistic competition and trade based on external economies provide additional benefits to consumers, especially consumers of exportable products. In the case of monopolistic competition, the additional gains come from (1) access to greater product variety and (2) a tendency for additional competition to lower product prices. In the case of external economies, gains to consumers in the exporting country arise from the decline in the price for the good as the local industry expands and achieves greater external economies. Relative to standard competitive trade, trade based on monopolistic competition has less of an impact on producing firms and factor incomes because firms under pressure from import competition also have the opportunity to export into foreign markets.

Although not portrayed fully in Figure 6.8, global oligopoly (or monopoly) also has implications for well-being. Trade allows firms to concentrate production in a few locations, achieving scale economies that lower costs. Furthermore, a global oligopoly (or monopoly) firm can charge high prices and earn large economic profits on its export sales. In comparison with standard competitive trade, these high profits on exports alter the division of the global gains from trade, with more of the gains going to export producers and the exporting country.

Where does the theory of trade patterns stand?

The standard model of Chapters 2 through 5 has the virtue of breadth, allowing for both demand-side differences and production-side differences between countries to explain trade. The Heckscher–Ohlin variant of the standard model makes the stronger assertion that the explanation can focus on cross-country differences in the endowments of a few main factors used in production. This has the scientific virtue of giving more testable and falsifiable predictions than the broadest standard model (of which it is a special case). But, as we saw in Chapter 5, the tests of the Heckscher–Ohlin model give it only a middling grade. It is only part of the explanation of trade patterns.

Our ability to predict (explain) trade patterns is improved if we add technology differences and models based on scale economies and imperfect competition. Technology differences can be a basis for comparative advantage. We will explore in depth the relationship between technological progress and trade in the next chapter.

The monopolistic-competition model suggests that product differentiation can be a basis for both exporting and importing different variants, or models, of a type of product. Economic models based on substantial scale economies (internal or external) indicate that production tends to be concentrated at a small number of locations, but they do not precisely identify which specific countries will be the production locations. Historical luck and early government policy may have a major impact on the current production locations.

<table>
<tr><td>Key
Terms</td><td>Constant returns
  to scale
Scale economies
Internal scale economies</td><td>Monopolistic
  competition
Oligopoly
External scale economies</td><td>Inter-industry trade
Intra-industry trade (IIT)
Net trade
Product differentiation</td></tr>
</table>

Suggested Reading

Intra-industry trade is measured and interpreted by Grubel and Lloyd (1975), Greenaway and Milner (1986), and Brülhart (2009).

In his Nobel Prize acceptance speech, Krugman (2009) summarizes the role of scale economies in international trade analysis. Ottaviano and Puga (1998) survey analyses of external scale economies and the "new economic geography." Helpman (1999) surveys empirical testing of traditional and alternative trade theories. Antweiler and Trefler (2002) find that scale economies are important to understanding trade in at least one-third of the industries that they study. Helpman (2011, Chapters 4 and 5) provides an accessible survey of research on monopolistic competition in international trade. Melitz and Trefler (2012) summarize what we know about the gains from trade for monopolistically competitive industries with firms that differ by cost or quality. Bernard et al. (2007) survey research about firms that export.

Questions and Problems

◆ 1. "According to the Heckscher–Ohlin theory, countries should engage in a lot of intra-industry trade." Do you agree or disagree? Why?

2. Scale economies are important in markets that are not perfectly competitive. What is the key role of scale economies in the analysis of markets that are monopolistically competitive? What is the key role in oligopoly?

◆ 3. "Once we recognize that product differentiation is the basis for much international trade, there are likely to be more winners and fewer losers in a country when the country shifts from no trade to free trade." There may be several reasons why this statement is true. What are the reasons? Explain each briefly.

4. A country is the only production site in the world for hyperhoney infinite pasta, a wonderful product produced using a delicate, highly perishable extract obtainable from some trees that grow only in this country. Beyond a very small size, there are no internal or external scale economies—production is essentially constant returns to scale. Furthermore, there is no domestic demand for this product in the country, so all production will be exported. The country's government has the choice of forming the pasta-producing industry either as a monopoly or as a large number of small pasta producers that will act as perfect competitors. What is your advice to the country's government about which market structure to choose for the pasta industry?

◆ 5. "External scale economies are an influence on the pattern of international trade because they affect the number of varieties of a product that are produced in a country." Do you agree or disagree? Why?

6. The world market for large passenger jet airplanes is an oligopoly dominated by two firms: Boeing in the United States and Airbus in Europe.

   a. Explain why the market equilibrium might involve either a low price for airplanes or a high price for airplanes.

   b. From the perspective of the well-being of the United States (or Europe), why might a high-price equilibrium be desirable?

c. What price outcome is desirable for Japan or Brazil? Why?

d. If the outcome is the high-price equilibrium, does Japan or Brazil still gain from importing airplanes? Explain.

✦ 7. A monopolistically competitive industry exists in both Pugelovia and the rest of the world, but there has been no trade in this type of product. Trade in this type of product is now opened.

a. Explain how opening trade affects domestic consumers of this type of product in Pugelovia.

b. Explain how opening trade affects domestic producers of this type of product in Pugelovia.

8. You are a consumer of a product that your country imports. There is an increase in demand in the rest of the world for this type of product. You are wondering if this change will be good or bad for you (in your role as consumer of this product). Is it possible that your conclusion depends on whether (a) the product is undifferentiated and has a perfectly competitive market (so the standard model of Chapters 2–5 applies) or (b) the product is differentiated and has a monopolistically competitive market (so the model of this chapter applies)? Explain.

✦ 9. The global market for household dishwashers is monopolistically competitive. It is initially in a free-trade equilibrium, with 40 models offered, and a price of $600 for a typical dishwasher. In your answer use a graph like that shown in Figure 6.5. There is now a permanent increase in global demand for dishwashers generally, so the global market size increases by about 15 percent. Show graphically the effect on the number of dishwasher models offered, after the global market has adjusted to a new long-run equilibrium. Explain the process of adjustment to this new long-run equilibrium.

10. Return to the scenario described in Question 9, the initial free-trade equilibrium for dishwashers and the increase in global demand. In your answer use a graph like those shown in the box "The Individual Firm in Monopolistic Competition."

a. Show graphically and explain whether the typical individual firm earns an economic profit or a loss in the short run just after the general increase in global demand occurs.

b. Show graphically and explain the situation for the typical individual firm when the global market has adjusted to its new long-run equilibrium.

✦ 11. Here are data on Japanese exports and imports, for 2012, for the same seven products shown for U.S. trade in Figure 6.2:

Product	Japanese Exports ($ millions)	Japanese Imports ($ millions)
Perfumes (55310)	3	234
Cosmetics (55320)	1,291	1,183
Household clothes washing machines (77511)	3	967
Electronic microcircuits (77640)	27,997	17,456
Automobiles (78120)	97,276	10,882
Photographic cameras (88111)	11	26
Books and brochures (89219)	96	251

      a. For each product for Japan, calculate the IIT share.

      b. The weighted average of IIT shares for these seven products for 2012 for the United States (using the data from Figure 6.2) is 63.1 percent. For Japan for these seven products for 2012, what is the weighted average of the IIT shares? Which country has relatively more IIT in these seven products?

12. There are a small number of firms that make electric railroad locomotives. In 2012 world exports of electric railroad locomotives (SITC revision 3 number 79111) totaled about $1 billion. Germany exported $448 million (45 percent of the total), China exported $390 million (39 percent of the total), and Switzerland exported $78 million (8 percent of the total). Which economic model or theory from this chapter is most likely to explain these facts about the patterns of world trade and world production? Why?

✦ 13. Production of a good is characterized by external scale economies. Currently there is no trade in the product, and the product is produced in two countries. If trade is opened in this product, all production will be driven to occur in only one country.

      a. With free trade, why would production occur only in one country?

      b. Does opening trade bring gains to both countries? Explain.

14. You are an adviser to the Indian government. Until now, government policy in India has been to severely limit imports into India, resulting also in a low level of Indian exports. The government is considering a policy shift to much freer trade.

      a. What are the three strongest arguments that you can offer to the Indian government about why the policy shift to freer trade is desirable for India?

      b. Which groups in India will be the supporters of the policy shift toward freer trade? Which groups will be the opponents?

Chapter **Seven**

Growth and Trade

The world keeps changing, and trade responds. Real investments expand countries' stocks of physical capital. Population growth (including immigration) adds new members to the labor force. Education and training expand labor skills. Discoveries of resource deposits change our estimates of countries' endowments of natural resources. Land reclamation and other shifts in land use can alter the amount of land available for production. New technologies improve capabilities to produce goods and services. New products enter the market. Consumer tastes change, altering demands for various products. Each of these forces affects trade patterns.

The Heckscher–Ohlin theory is a snapshot of the international economy during a period of time. We can also use the H–O model to show the effects of changes over time. In a way we have already done this in previous chapters—the shift from no trade to free trade is an example of one kind of change that can occur over time.

This chapter focuses on changes in productive capabilities. These production-side changes are usually called **economic growth** (although we can also consider cases of decline). There are two fundamental sources of long-run economic growth:

- Increases in countries' endowments of production factors (e.g., physical capital, labor, and land).
- Improvements in production technologies (and other intangible influences on resource productivity).

In this chapter we will analyze the implications of economic growth, especially the implications for international trade flows and national economic well-being or welfare. Our analysis focuses on "before" and "after" pictures, with the after picture showing the economy after it fully adjusts (in the long run) to the growth that we are analyzing.

Some of the growth effects explored here will agree with common intuition, but some will not. In particular, we will discover two odd effects of growth. First, an increase in a country's endowment of only one of its production factors actually causes national production of some products to decline. This result is the basis for concerns that discovering and extracting new deposits of natural resources such as oil can retard a country's industrial development. Second, it is possible that expanding a country's ability to make the products that it exports can actually make the country worse off. This perverse outcome could be of concern to a country that is a large exporter of a primary commodity such as coffee beans or copper ore.

These surprising results are part of this chapter's tour of the variety of ways in which economic growth can affect trade and national well-being. The chapter also examines links between technology and trade, including technology differences as a basis for comparative advantage, the cycle of innovation of new technologies and diffusion of these technologies internationally, and the impact that openness to international trade can have on economic growth.

BALANCED VERSUS BIASED GROWTH

Growth in a country's production capabilities, whether from endowment increases or technology improvements, shifts the country's production-possibility curve outward. As the ppc shifts out, we are interested in knowing the effects on

- The general shape of the production-possibility curve.
- The specific production quantities for the different products, if product prices remain the same (as their pregrowth values).

The three panels in Figure 7.1 represent different possibilities for types of growth experienced by the United States. The first case, Figure 7.1A, is **balanced growth,** in which the ppc shifts out proportionately so that its relative shape is the same. In this case, growth would result in the same proportionate increase in production of all products if product prices remain the same. For instance, before the growth, production is at point S_1, 80 wheat and 20 cloth, and the relative price of cloth is 1 *W/C*. As a result of growth the ppc shifts out. At the same relative price (implying another price line parallel to the one through S_1), the country would produce at point S_2, 112 wheat and 28 cloth. Balanced growth could be the result of increases in the country's endowments of all factors by the same proportion. Or it could be the result of technology improvements of a similar magnitude in both industries.

With **biased growth** the expansion favors producing proportionately more of one of the products. In this case the shift in the production-possibility curve will be skewed toward the faster-growing product. Figure 7.1B shows growth that is biased toward producing more cloth. If the relative product price remains unchanged, production quantities do not change proportionately. For instance, with production initially at point S_1, growth biased toward cloth shifts production to a point like S_3 if the relative price remains at 1 *W/C*. Cloth production increases from 20 to 40 units. Wheat production in this case remains unchanged at 80. Other examples of this type of biased growth could have wheat production either growing somewhat (but by less than the percent increase in cloth production) or decreasing below 80.

Figure 7.1C shows growth that is biased toward wheat production. The ppc shift is skewed toward wheat. At the relative price of 1 *W/C*, the production point would shift from S_1 to a point like S_4. In this example, wheat production increases from 80 to 130 and cloth production remains unchanged. In other specific examples of growth biased toward wheat, cloth production might either increase by a lesser percentage than wheat production increases or decrease.

FIGURE 7.1 Balanced and Biased Growth

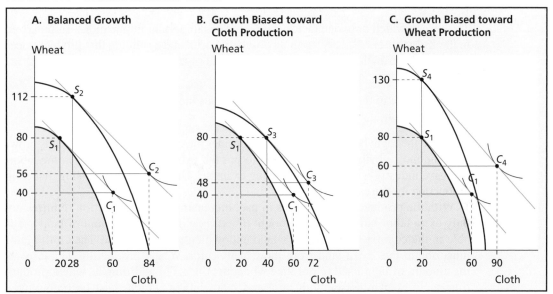

Before growth, the United States produces at point S_1 and consumes at point C_1. Balanced growth expands the ppc in a uniform or neutral way. Biased growth expands the ppc in a way skewed toward one good or the other. If the price ratio remains unchanged, then production growth (to points S_2, S_3, S_4) increases national income and increases consumption of both goods (points C_2, C_3, C_4). By altering production and consumption, growth may change the country's willingness to trade (the size of its trade triangle). For balanced growth and for growth biased toward wheat, the case of increased willingness to trade is shown. For growth biased toward cloth, the case of less willingness to trade is shown.

Biased growth arises when the country's endowments of different factors grow at different rates, or when improvements in production technologies are larger in one of the industries than in the other. A specific example of unbalanced growth in factor endowments is the situation in which one factor grows but the other factor is unchanged. A specific example of different rates of technology improvement is the situation in which technology in one industry is improving but technology in the other industry is not changing.[1]

[1]The case in which technology in one industry is improving but no other production-side growth is occurring actually looks a little different from the graphs in Figure 7.1B and C. For instance, growth biased toward cloth could occur if only cloth production technology is improving. In this case the ppc shifts out in a manner that is skewed toward cloth, *and the ppc intercept with the wheat axis does not change*. This wheat intercept shows no production of cloth, so the better cloth technology does not expand the production capability. The rest of the ppc shifts out, as any cloth production benefits from the improved cloth technology. A similar reasoning applies to an improvement only in wheat technology. In this case the ppc intercept with the cloth axis does not change, but the rest of the ppc shifts out.

GROWTH IN ONLY ONE FACTOR

The case in which only one factor is growing has important implications, summarized in the Rybczynski theorem: In a two-good world, and assuming that product prices are constant, growth in the country's endowment of one factor of production, with the other factor unchanged, has two results:

- An increase in the output of the good that uses the growing factor intensively.
- A decrease in the output of the other good.[2]

To see the logic behind this theorem, consider the case in which only labor is growing. The most obvious place in which to put the extra labor to work is in the labor-intensive industry—cloth in our ongoing example. Thus, it is not surprising that cloth production increases.

With the production techniques in use, increasing cloth production requires not only extra labor but also some amount of extra land. But the amount of land available in the country (the country's land endowment) did not grow. The cloth sector must obtain this extra land from the wheat sector. Wheat production decreases as the amount of land used to produce wheat declines. (In addition, as wheat production declines, it releases both land and labor, all of which must be reemployed into cloth production. Therefore, the proportionate expansion of cloth production will actually be larger than the proportion by which the overall labor endowment grows.)

Figure 7.2 shows the effects of this growth in the labor endowment. As a result of the growth, the ppc shifts out at all points. Even if the country produced wheat only, the extra labor presumably could be employed in wheat production to generate some extra wheat output. However, the outward shift in the ppc is biased toward more cloth production, the industry in which labor is the more important production factor. If the relative price is initially 1 *W/C* and remains unchanged, then growth shifts production from point S_1 to a point like S_5 on the new ppc. Cloth production increases from 20 to 35, and wheat production decreases from 80 to 74.

The Rybczynski theorem suggests that development of a new natural resource, such as oil or gas in Canada or Britain, may retard development of other lines of production, such as manufactures. (See the box "The Dutch Disease and Deindustrialization.") Conversely, rapid accumulation of new capital and worker skills can cause a decline in domestic production of natural resource products and make the country more reliant on imported materials. This happened to the United States in the 1800s. The United States shifted from being a net exporter to a net importer of minerals as it grew relative to the rest of the world. One of the causes of this shift was the rapid growth of production of manufactured goods as the United States accumulated skills and capital.

---

[2]The other important conditions and assumptions include (1) the country produces positive amounts of both goods before and after growth, with both factors used in producing each good; (2) factors are mobile between sectors and fully employed; and (3) the technology of production is unchanged. Rybczynski (1955) also explored the changes in the terms of trade that are likely to accompany factor growth, as we will do subsequently in this chapter. (You may abbreviate his name as "Ryb" when answering exam questions.)

FIGURE 7.2
Single-Factor
Growth: The
Rybczynski
Theorem

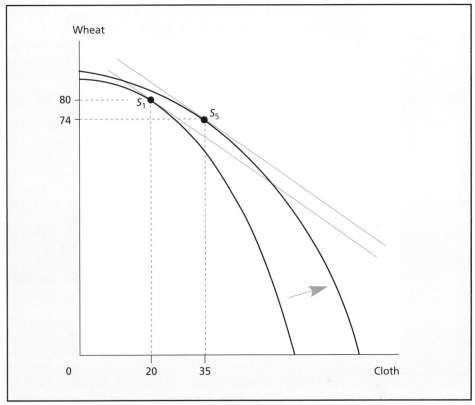

Growth in one production factor, with the other factor not growing, results in strongly biased growth. If only labor grows, the ppc shifts out in a way that is biased toward more cloth production. If the price ratio remains the same, the actual production point shifts from S_1 to S_5. The Rybczynski theorem indicates that cloth production increases and wheat production decreases.

CHANGES IN THE COUNTRY'S WILLINGNESS TO TRADE

Growth alters a country's capabilities in supplying products. Growth also alters the country's demand for products, for instance, by changing the income that people in the country have to spend. As production and consumption change with growth, a country's willingness to or interest in engaging in international trade can change. That is, even if the relative price between two products stays constant, the country could either

- increase its willingness to trade (it could want to export and import more) or
- decrease its willingness to trade (it could want to export and import less).

To analyze this further, we assume as usual that both goods are normal goods, so that an increase in income (with product prices unchanged) increases the quantities demanded of each of the goods.[3]

[3]An alternative assumption is that one of the two goods is inferior, so that quantity demanded of this inferior good would decrease as income increases. While this case is possible, it would complicate the discussion without adding major insights.

We can examine changes in the country's willingness to trade in each of the three cases of growth shown in Figure 7.1. In each graph the change in willingness can be shown by the change in the size of the trade triangle. The trade triangle is a handy way to summarize willingness to trade because it shows how much the country wants to export and import. Before the growth occurs we presume that the country was at a free-trade equilibrium with production at S_1 and consumption at C_1. The trade triangle connecting S_1 and C_1 shows exports of 40 wheat and imports of 40 cloth.

Consider first the case of balanced supply-side growth (Figure 7.1A). As we showed previously, production shifts to S_2 with growth. Proportionate expansion of production means that wheat production increases by 32 and cloth by 8. With the relative price constant, the price line shifts out. The country has more income and expands its consumption quantities for both products. However, this by itself is not enough to indicate the change in the country's willingness to trade. Here are the two major possibilities:

- If the consumption of wheat increases by less than 32, then the quantity of wheat available for export will increase. The size of the trade triangle and the country's willingness to trade will increase.

- If the consumption of wheat expands by more than 32, then the quantity of wheat available for export will decrease. The size of the trade triangle and the country's willingness to trade will decrease.[4]

The changes in the consumption quantities depend on the tastes of the consumers in the country. Tastes are summarized by the shapes of the community indifference curves and the specific community indifference curve that is tangent to the postgrowth price line. The case actually shown in Figure 7.1A has the new community indifference curve tangent to the new price line at point C_2, so that the quantities consumed expand proportionately to 56 wheat and 84 cloth. In this case, the increase in wheat consumption (16) is less than the increase in wheat production (32), so the trade triangle and the country's willingness to trade expand.

Suppose next that growth is biased toward cloth, the imported product, as shown in Figure 7.1B. Production shifts to S_3 with growth, raising cloth production with no change in wheat production. More wheat is consumed (as the consumption point shifts to a point like C_3),so there is less wheat available for export. In this case, the trade triangle and the country's willingness to trade shrink. A similar analysis applies to the growth shown in Figure 7.2, growth even more biased toward cloth production.

If the growth is sufficiently biased toward producing more of the good that is initially imported, the country's pattern of trade could reverse itself, making the country an exporter of cloth and an importer of wheat. For example, as noted at the end of the previous section, the United States shifted from exporting to importing minerals since the late 1800s. There is nothing immutable about the trade pattern—comparative advantage and disadvantage can reverse over time.

---

[4]We could also reach the same conclusions by focusing on changes in the quantities of cloth produced and consumed. In the order presented in the text, consumption of cloth would increase by more than production increases, so that desired imports increase, or consumption would rise by less, so that desired imports would decline. Of course, it is also possible that the quantities produced and consumed of cloth would increase by equal amounts (as would those for wheat), in which case the trade triangle and the country's willingness to trade would not change.

Case Study   The Dutch Disease and Deindustrialization

Developing a new exportable natural resource can cause problems. One, discussed later in this chapter, is the problem of "immiserizing growth": If you are already exporting and your export expansion lowers the world price of your exports, you could end up worse off. A second is the apparent problem called the Dutch disease, in which new production of a natural resource results in a decline in production of manufactured products (deindustrialization).

For the Netherlands, the origin of the disease was the development of new natural gas fields under the North Sea. It seemed that the more the Netherlands developed its natural gas production, the more depressed its manufacturers of traded goods became. Even the windfall price increases that the two oil shocks offered the Netherlands (all fuel prices skyrocketed, including that for natural gas) seemed to add to industry's slump. The Dutch disease has been thought to have spread to Britain, Norway, Australia, Mexico, and other countries that have newly developed natural resources.

The main premise of this fear is correct: Under many realistic conditions, the windfall of a new natural resource does indeed erode profits and production in the manufactured goods sector. Deindustrialization occurs for the same reason that underlies the Rybczynski theorem introduced in this chapter: The new sector draws production resources away from the manufacturing sector. Specifically, to develop output of the natural resource, the sector must hire labor away from the manufacturing sector, and it must obtain capital that otherwise would have been invested in the manufacturing sector. Thus, the manufacturing sector contracts.

Journalistic coverage of the link between natural resource development and deindustrialization tends to discover the basic Rybczynski effect in a different way. The press tends to notice that the development of the exportable natural resource causes the nation's currency to rise in value on foreign exchange markets because of the increased demand for the country's currency as foreign buyers pay for their purchases. A higher value of the nation's currency makes it harder for its industrial firms to compete against foreign products whose price is now relatively lower. To the manufacturing sector this feels like a drop in demand, and the sector contracts. The foreign exchange market, in gravitating back toward the original balance of trade, is producing the same result we would get from a barter trade model: If you export more of a good, you'll end up either exporting less of another good or importing more. Something has to give so that trade will return to the same balance as before.

Even though the Dutch disease does lead to some deindustrialization, it is not clear that this is really a national problem. Merely shifting resources away from the manufacturing sector into the production of natural resources is not necessarily bad, despite a rich folklore assuming that industrial expansion is somehow key to prosperity. The country usually gains from developing production of its natural resources, as long as this growth does not tip into the realm of the immiserizing.

DISCUSSION QUESTION
Why do many real-world examples of Dutch disease originate from developments in energy products?

Finally, consider growth that is biased toward wheat, as shown in Figure 7.1C. The country's demand for cloth increases as consumption shifts to a point like C_4, so it wants to import more. The strong growth of wheat production also increases the amount available for export. The trade triangle expands, showing the country's greater willingness to trade.

EFFECTS ON THE COUNTRY'S TERMS OF TRADE

Changes in a country's willingness to trade can alter the country's terms of trade if the country is large enough for its trade to have an impact on the international equilibrium. In turn, any change in the country's terms of trade affects the extent to which the country benefits from its growth.

In this section we first examine the case of a **small country,** one whose trade does not affect the international price ratio. We then examine the case of a **large country,** one whose trade can have an impact on the relative international price ratio (that is, an effect on the price the country receives for its exports, the price it pays for its imports, or both). Note that the definitions of *small country* and *large country* are based on the ability of the country to have a noticeable effect on one or more international prices. Even a country that we think of as having a small economy can be a large country. For instance, Ghana (which is a relatively small country, overall) is a major exporter of cocoa. A reasonable change in its export supply (say, an increase in its export supply by 10 percent due to an improvement in farming practices) would affect world cocoa prices. On the other hand, even a country that we think of as having a large economy (for instance, Japan) can be a small country for many products (examples would be milk and cheese), in the sense that reasonable changes in its own production or demand have no discernible effect on the world price of the product.

Small Country

If a country is small (that is, a price-taker in world markets), then its trade has no impact on the international price ratio (the country's terms of trade). The graphs shown in Figure 7.1 represent the full analysis of growth by the small country. In each of these cases the country gains from its growth in the sense that it reaches a higher community indifference curve (at point C_2, C_3, or C_4, depending on the type of growth).

Large Country

If a country is large, a change in its willingness to trade affects the equilibrium international price ratio. Consider first the case in which growth reduces the country's willingness to trade at any given price, as shown in Figure 7.3 (which reproduces the ppc shift of Figure 7.1B). The reduction in the country's demand for imports reduces the relative price of the import good (or the reduction in the country's supply of exports increases the relative price of the export good). This change in the equilibrium international price is an improvement in the country's terms of trade. In this case, the country gets two benefits from growth:

- The production benefit from growth as the ppc shifts out.
- The benefit from improved terms of trade as it receives a better price for its exports relative to the price that it has to pay for its imports.

In Figure 7.3 the improved terms of trade are shown in a flatter price line (a lower relative price of cloth, the import good). In response, the country shifts its production point to S_6 on the new ppc and decides to consume at a point C_6. If, instead, there were

FIGURE 7.3

Growth
Biased toward
Replacing
Imports in a
Large Country

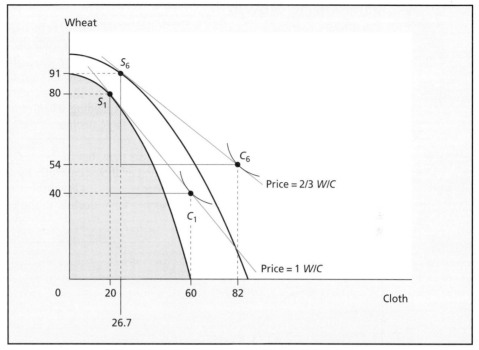

A large country can gain in two ways from an expanding ability to produce the import-competing
good—here, cloth. In addition to the gains from being able to produce more (already shown
in Figure 7.1B), it can improve its terms of trade. By demanding fewer imports (a decreased
willingness to trade), it makes cloth cheaper on world markets. After growth, the relative price of
cloth declines to 2/3 W/C in the example shown. The country's remaining imports cost less. Thus,
the country gains more from growth, as consumption shifts from C_1 to C_6 because the price line
becomes flatter.

no change in the terms of trade, with this ppc growth the country would reach the level
of well-being associated with the community indifference curve through C_3 (48 wheat
and 72 cloth) in Figure 7.1B. So, the actual improvement in the terms of trade permits
the country to reach the higher level of well-being associated with the community
indifference curve through C_6 (54 wheat and 82 cloth) in Figure 7.3.

Consider next the case in which growth increases the country's willingness to
trade. The increase in the country's demand for imports increases the relative price
of the import good (or the increase in the country's supply of exports reduces the
relative price of the export good). This change in the equilibrium international price
ratio is a deterioration in the country's terms of trade. In this case the overall effect
on the country's well-being is not clear. Growth brings a production benefit, but the
country is hurt by the subsequent decline in its terms of trade. (It receives a lower
price for its export products relative to the price that it pays for its import products.)

If the terms of trade do not decline by too much, then the country gains overall from
growth, but not by as much as it would if the terms of trade did not change. However,
if the adverse movement is large, a surprising outcome is possible.

Immiserizing Growth

What happens if the terms of trade decline a great deal in response to growth in the country's ability to produce its export good? If the terms of trade decline substantially, the country's well-being could fall. (Or, in the in-between case, the country's well-being could be unchanged.) The possibility of a decline in well-being is shown in Figure 7.4, in which a large improvement in wheat-production technology results in a shift in the ppc that is strongly skewed toward expanding wheat production.

For a relatively steep price line (showing a large decline in the country's terms of trade), the country's production is at point S_7 on the new ppc and its consumption at point C_7. The level of well-being for C_7 is less than that for point C_1 before growth.

This possibility is a remarkable result, first analyzed carefully by Jagdish Bhagwati. It is called the possibility of **immiserizing growth:** Growth that expands the country's willingness to trade can result in such a large decline in the country's terms of trade that the country is worse off.

FIGURE 7.4

Immiserizing
Growth in a
Large Country

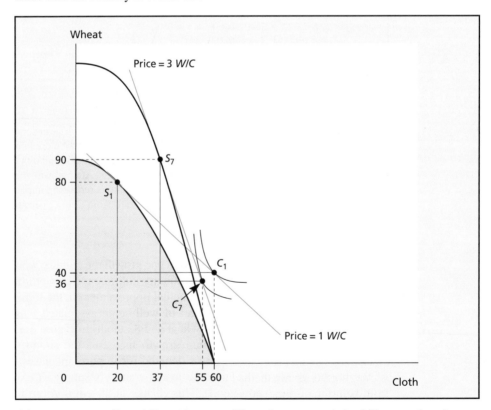

A large country actually could be made worse off by an improvement in its ability to produce the products it exports. Such a perverse case of immiserizing growth is shown here. By expanding its ability to produce wheat, its export good, the large country increases its supply of exports (expands its willingness to trade). This drives down the relative price of wheat in world markets. Looked at the other way, this causes an increase (here a tripling) of the relative price that it must pay for its imports of cloth. The decline in the country's terms of trade is so bad, in this case, that it outweighs the benefits of the extra ability to produce. Consumer enjoyment is lower at C_7 than at the initial consumption point C_1.

Three conditions seem crucial for immiserizing growth to occur:

1. The country's growth must be strongly biased toward expanding the country's supply of exports (increasing its willingness to trade), and the increase in export supply must be large enough to have a noticeable impact on world prices.
2. The foreign demand for the country's exports must be price inelastic, so that an expansion in the country's export supply leads to a large drop in the international price of the export product.
3. Before the growth, the country must be heavily engaged in trade, so that the welfare loss from the decline in the terms of trade is great enough to offset the gains from being able to produce more.

Countries that export a diversified selection of export products do not seem to be at much risk of experiencing immiserizing growth. A developing country that relies on one or a few primary products (agricultural or mineral products) is more at risk. For example, consider a country like Zambia that relies on a mineral ore (e.g., copper) for most of its export revenues. A discovery that leads to the opening of several new large mines would increase its ore exports and greatly reduce the international price of this ore. As a result of the decline in the price, the country could be worse off. For instance, the money value of Zambia's exports of copper ore could decline (if the price falls more than the export quantity increases), and Zambia then could not afford to import as much as before the growth.

It may seem foolish for a nation to undergo an expansion that makes itself worse off. But remember that the expansion would be undertaken, both in the model and in the real world, by individual competitive firms, each of which might profit individually from its own expansion. Individual rationality can sometimes add up to collective irrationality.

The possibility of immiserizing growth offers large countries a policy lesson that transcends the cases in which it actually occurs. By itself, the case of immiserizing growth is probably just a curious rarity. Even for large countries the necessary conditions listed above are not likely to be met very often. Yet a larger point emerges from Figures 7.3 and 7.4.

Any effect of growth in the national economy on the terms of trade affects the national gains from encouraging that growth. Suppose that the government is debating which industries to favor with tax breaks or subsidies and has to choose between encouraging import-replacing industries and encouraging export-expanding ones. In Figure 7.3 we found that the country reaped greater benefits if its expansion of import-competing capabilities causes a drop in the price of imports. By contrast, in Figure 7.4, expanding export industries is less beneficial because it lowers the relative price of exports. This is true whether or not the bad terms-of-trade effect is big enough to outweigh the gains from being more productive. So a large country has reason to favor import-replacing industries over export industries: *If* other things are truly equal, why not favor industries that turn world prices in your favor rather than against you?[5] We return to this point when discussing trade policy for developing countries in Chapter 14.

---

[5]Remember, however, that the whole reason for favoring import replacement here relates to turning international prices in this nation's favor. For the world as a whole, there can be no such gain and no immiserizing growth. One country's gains (losses) from changes in the terms of trade equal another country's losses (gains).

TECHNOLOGY AND TRADE

This chapter's discussion of biased growth can be linked to the general discussion of the basis for comparative advantage presented in Chapter 4. As we noted there, comparative advantage skews countries' capabilities for producing various products. In presenting the Heckscher–Ohlin theory, we spent much time discussing differences in factor endowments as the basis for comparative advantage.

Another basis for comparative advantage is differences in production technologies available in the various countries. Technology differences tend to skew production in each country toward producing the product(s) in which the country has the relatively better technology (that is, the technology of greatest advantage or least disadvantage).

Technology-based comparative advantage can arise over time as technological change occurs at different rates in different sectors and countries. For instance, improvements in the production technology used in the wheat industry in the United States over time would skew U.S. production capabilities toward producing larger amounts of wheat. The U.S. ppc would shift out in a way biased toward wheat production (as in Figure 7.1C). These technology improvements could include improved farming practices or better seed varieties. If the technology for wheat production is not improving in a comparable manner in the rest of the world, then the United States can develop a comparative advantage in wheat based on its relative technology advantage in wheat.

In some ways this technology-based explanation is an alternative that competes with the H–O theory. Technology differences can become an important cause (sometimes the dominant cause) of the pattern of trade in specific products. For instance, the fact that the United States became a net importer of steel products in the early 1960s can be explained in part by the adoption of newer production technologies for steel in Japan and other countries.

In other ways technology differences can be consistent with an H–O view of the world, at least one using an extended and dynamic H–O approach. To see this, we must consider the question of where the technological improvements come from.

Some technological improvement happens by chance or through the unusual efforts of individuals. However, most industrially useful new technology now comes from organized efforts that we call **research and development (R&D)**. This R&D is done largely by businesses and focuses on improvements in production technologies for existing products and on new production technologies for new or improved products. Products or industries in which R&D is relatively important—such as aircraft, semiconductors, and pharmaceuticals—are usually called *high technology*. Ongoing (and costly) R&D within these high-tech industries can create an ongoing stream of new and improved technology over time.

The most obvious link to the H–O theory is the national location of R&D itself. R&D is a production activity that is intensive in highly skilled labor—scientists and engineers in particular. Most of the world's R&D is done in the industrialized countries that have an abundance of this type of labor. Another factor of importance is capital willing to take the substantial risks involved in financing R&D investments. The relative abundance of *venture capital* (outsiders' purchase of ownership in new businesses) in the United States is the basis for a U.S. advantage, while other countries like Japan depend more on internal funding of R&D within their large corporations.

The national location of production using the new technology, which is what is shown explicitly in our ppc graph, is not so clear-cut. It seems reasonable that the first use in production could be in the same country in which the R&D was done. However, technology can spread internationally. This international spread or "trade" in technology is called **diffusion**. New technology is difficult to keep secret, and other countries have an incentive to obtain the technology improvements. Indeed, the creator of the new technology has the incentive to apply it in production in the national location(s) in which the new technology is most suitable (and therefore most profitable). H–O theory suggests that the suitable location matches the factor proportions of production using the new technology to the factor endowments of the national location.

Individual Products and the Product Cycle

One effort to find a pattern in these technology activities is the product cycle hypothesis, first advanced by Raymond Vernon. When a product is first invented (born), it still must be perfected. Additional R&D is needed, and production is often in small amounts by skilled workers. In addition, the major demand is mostly in the high-income countries because most new products are luxuries in the economist's sense. Close communication is needed between the R&D, production, and marketing people in the producing firm. All this suggests that both R&D and initial production are likely to be in an advanced developed country.

Over time, the product and its production technology become more standardized and familiar (mature). Factor intensity in production tends to shift away from skilled labor and toward less-skilled labor. The technology diffuses and production locations shift into other countries, eventually into developing countries that are abundant in less-skilled labor.

Trade patterns change in a manner consistent with shifting production locations. The innovating country is initially the exporter of the new product, but it eventually becomes an importer. Although it is dynamic and emphasizes additional considerations like demand and communication, many aspects of this product cycle hypothesis are consistent with H–O theory.

The product cycle hypothesis does fit the experience of products in many industries in the past century. Laptop computers are an example. Computer firms in the United States and Japan began R&D to design small, portable computers in the 1970s and early 1980s. The firms planned to meet expected demand by businesspeople and researchers in the United States and other high-income countries. Several early models were produced in the United States and Japan, and R&D continued. In the late 1980s and early 1990s, IBM, Toshiba, Texas Instruments, and other U.S. and Japanese firms introduced better models, with production in the United States and Japan, and some of this production was exported to buyers in other countries. As the components of the laptops became standardized, and as competition among sellers intensified through the 1990s, firms shifted much of the assembly production of laptops, first to Taiwan and later to China, to reduce production costs. In the process, the initial innovating countries became importers.

Nonetheless, the usefulness of the product cycle hypothesis is limited for several reasons. These have to do with the unpredictable lengths or progression of the phases of the cycle. In many industries—especially high-tech industries—product and production technologies are continually evolving because of ongoing R&D. Rejuvenation or replenished youthfulness is important. In addition, international diffusion often occurs within multinational (or "global") corporations. In this case, the cycle can essentially disappear. New technology developed by a multinational corporation in one of its research facilities in a leading developed country can be transferred within the corporation for its first production use in affiliates in other countries, including its affiliates in developing countries.

Openness to Trade Affects Growth

So far, most of the discussion in this chapter has looked at how growth in production capabilities can affect international trade. Clearly, growth can have a major impact on international trade. There is also likely to be an impact in the other direction, from trade to growth. Openness to international trade can have an impact on how fast a country's economy can grow—how fast its production capabilities are growing over time.

We can gain insights into this relationship by considering how openness to trade can affect the technologies that the country can use. As we noted previously, in the discussion of the product life cycle, there are two sources of new technology for a country: technology developed domestically and technology imported from foreign countries. If a country closes itself to international trade, it probably also cuts itself off from this second source of new technology. By failing to absorb and use new technologies developed in other countries, this closed country is likely to grow more slowly. Looked at in the other way, countries that are open to international trade (and international exchanges more generally) can grow faster. Let's consider more closely the reasons for this relationship. (We might also note that the relationship is actually complex, so none of these reasons is completely straightforward. We will focus on generally positive effects, without providing the caveats that may apply.)

Trade provides access to new and improved products. For our production-side analysis, capital goods are an important type of input into production that can be imported. Trade allows a country to import new and improved machinery, which "embodies" better technology that can be used in production to raise productivity. The foreign exporters can also enhance the process, for instance, by advising the importing firms on the best ways to use the new machines. Paul Romer, one of the pioneers of "new growth theory," has estimated that the gains from being able to import unique foreign capital goods that embody new technology can be much larger than the traditional gains from trade highlighted in Chapters 2–4.

More generally, openness to international activities leads the firms and people of the country to have more contact with technology developed in other countries. This greater awareness makes it more likely that the country will gain the use of the new foreign-developed technology, through purchase of capital goods or through licensing or imitation of the technology.

Openness to international trade can also have an impact on the incentive to innovate. Trade can provide additional competitive pressure on the country's firms. The pressure drives the firms to seek better technology to raise their productivity to build their international competitiveness. Trade also provides a larger market in which to earn returns to innovation. If sales into foreign markets provide additional returns, then the incentive to innovate increases, and firms devote more resources to R&D activities.

Focus on Labor   Trade, Technology, and U.S. Wages

Americans have reason to worry about trends in real wages since the early 1970s. One major trend has been a rising gap between the wages of relatively skilled workers and the wages of less-skilled workers. For instance, from the mid-1970s to the early 2010s, the ratio of the average wage of college graduates to that of high school graduates increased by about 30 percent. Many less-skilled workers have seen their wages decline in real (purchasing power) terms.

Meanwhile, the importance of international trade increased dramatically for the United States. The ratio of the sum of exports and imports to total national production (GDP) close to tripled from the early 1970s to the early 2010s. (Recall the data shown in the box "Trade Is Important" in Chapter 2, pages 18–19.) Do we see here the effects on U.S. wages of a "race to the bottom" driven by rising imports? More precisely, is this the Stolper–Samuelson theorem at work, as rising trade alters the returns to scarce and abundant factors in the United States?

Given the political implications of the trend toward greater wage inequality, economists have studied it carefully. While increasing trade presumably has had some effect on wage rates through the Stolper–Samuelson effect, economists have generally concluded that trade has not been the main culprit.

For the Stolper–Samuelson theorem to be the main culprit—the predominant effect—at least two other things should be true. First, the changes in factor prices should result from changes in product prices. Specifically, a decline in the relative price of less-skilled-labor-intensive goods should be behind the decline in the relative wages of less-skilled workers. Second, and more subtly, the change in the relative wage should induce industries to become more intensive in their use of the now cheaper less-skilled labor. (See the box "A Factor-Ratio Paradox" in Chapter 5, page 70.)

Neither of these two things appears to have occurred. Research on U.S. manufacturing industries indicates that there is no clear trend in the relative international price of manufactured goods that use less-skilled labor intensively. The data also show that most manufacturing industries became more intensive in their use of skilled labor and less intensive in less-skilled labor.

The lack of change in the relative prices of traded goods and the rising skill intensity of production are not consistent with the Stolper–Samuelson effect. The implication is that changes in international trade prices are not the predominant cause of the rising wage inequality. Other economists have concluded similarly that changes in the trade flows themselves (imports and exports) are not the predominant cause.

If not trade, then what? Most researchers have concluded that the major driving force changing demands for skilled and unskilled labor has been technological change. In fact, technological change may be pressuring relative wages in two ways.

First, technological progress has been faster in industries that are more intensive in skilled labor. As the cost and prices of some skill-intensive products decline, and the quality of these products is improved, demand for the products increases. As demand shifts toward skill-intensive products and their production increases, the demand for skilled labor expands, increasing the relative wage of skilled labor.

Second, the technological progress that has occurred within individual industries appears to be biased in favor of using more skilled labor. This bias increases demand for skilled labor even more, reinforcing the pressure for an increase in wage inequality. We see this bias in the shift toward greater use of computers generally and in the shift toward computer-controlled flexible manufacturing systems in manufacturing specifically.

The United Kingdom has also experienced rising wage inequality between skilled and unskilled workers, though the change is not as large as in the United States. In most other countries in Western Europe and in Canada, these pressures seem to have played themselves out somewhat differently. Labor market institutions like high minimum wages have prevented wage rates for less-skilled workers from declining so much. Instead, unemployment has increased since the early 1970s and has remained high. While inequality of earnings has not increased so much in Canada and Western Europe, unemployment, especially among the less skilled, has become a serious problem.

Openness to international trade thus can enhance the technology that a country can use, both by facilitating the diffusion of foreign-developed technology into the country and by accelerating the domestic development of technology. Furthermore, these increases in the current technology base can be used to develop additional innovations in the future. This is a key insight of the new growth theory mentioned above, which posits that economic policies and activities influence the growth rate. The current technology base provides a source of increasing returns over time to ongoing innovation activities. The growth rate for the country's economy (and for the whole world) increases in the long run.

Do we have clear evidence that openness to trade actually increases a country's economic growth? Jakob Madsen (2007) found that international trade in products has spurred international diffusion of technologies among industrialized countries, and that *foreign* technologies acquired through this diffusion have been the source of most productivity growth since 1870 in these industrialized countries. More broadly, many studies have used statistical analyses to examine the correlation between openness to international activities and national economic growth rates. For example, Estevadeordal and Taylor (2013) show that countries that reduced barriers to imports of capital goods and intermediate inputs grew by about 1 percent more per year since 1990 (than did countries that did not lower such barriers).

The preponderance of evidence favors a positive relationship. These studies do not absolutely prove that openness leads to increased growth, for two reasons. First, the positive correlation does not prove the direction of causation. Second, it is difficult to disentangle the effects of international openness from the effects of other government policies that can also increase economic growth, including policies that reform government taxation and spending, policies that strengthen the rule of law and protect private property generally, and less distorted exchange-rate policies.

Still, the evidence broadly is consistent with the proposition that international openness is good for long-run national economic growth, and there is no convincing evidence that openness to trade leads to slower long-run growth. We will take up the issue of trade and growth again in Chapter 14, when we discuss developing countries.

Summary

Economic growth (expansion of a country's production capabilities) results from increases in the country's endowments of factors of production or from technological improvements. Balanced growth shifts the country's production-possibility curve outward in a proportionate manner. If the product price ratio is unchanged, production of each product increases proportionately. Consumption of both products also increases. This alters the country's trade triangle and its willingness to trade unless the increases in quantities produced and consumed are equal. For instance, if the growth in production quantity of the exportable product exceeds the growth in its consumption quantity, then the trade triangle and the willingness to trade increase.

Biased growth shifts the ppc outward in a manner that is skewed toward one product. If the product price ratio is unchanged, production of this product expands, but production of the other product increases by a lesser proportion, stays the same, or declines. The Rybczynski theorem states that a kind of very biased growth, in which the endowment of only one factor is growing, results in a decrease in production by the sector that is not intensive in the growing factor. The Dutch disease is a real-world example. In the Dutch case the endowment growth was the discovery of natural gas deposits. Shifting labor and capital to the extraction of this gas led to a decline in the country's manufacturing sector.

If growth is biased toward producing more of the import-competing product, the country's trade triangle and its willingness to trade tend to shrink. If growth is biased toward producing more of the exportable product, the country's trade triangle and its willingness to trade tend to expand.

The trade of a small country has no impact on international prices. The analysis of growth in a small country is straightforward because its growth does not alter its terms of trade.

The trade of a large country does have an impact on international prices. If growth results in a large country becoming less willing to trade, then the relative price of the country's export product increases. In this case, growth benefits the country both by expanding its production capabilities and by improving its terms of trade.

If growth results in a large country becoming more willing to trade, then the relative price of its export product decreases. This deterioration in the terms of trade reduces the benefits to the country of growing productive capabilities. Indeed, it is possible that, if the terms of trade decline substantially, the country could be worse off after growing—a possibility called immiserizing growth.

The relationship of technology to the shape of the ppc indicates that differences in technology between countries can be a basis for trade. In some ways, this technology explanation competes with the Heckscher–Ohlin theory. The technology explanation of trade is that countries export products in which they have relative technology advantages. In other ways, technology differences can be linked to H–O. For instance, the research and development that leads to new technologies tends to be located in countries that are well endowed with the highly skilled labor (e.g., scientists and engineers) that is needed to conduct the R&D. The product cycle hypothesis is an attempt to offer a dynamic theory of technology and trade by emphasizing that the location of production of a product is likely to shift from the leading developed countries to developing countries as the product moves from its introduction to maturity and standardization.

Openness to international trade can also influence the rate of economic growth by affecting the rate at which the country's production technology is improving. With international openness, diffusion of new foreign technology into the country increases because of imports of capital goods that embody the foreign technology, or licensing or imitation of the foreign technology. Innovation by domestic firms increases because of competitive pressure and the greater returns available through foreign sales. Empirically, most studies find a positive relationship between the international openness of a country and the long-run economic growth rate of that country.

Key Terms			
	Economic growth	Dutch disease	Research and development
	Balanced growth	Small country	(R&D)
	Biased growth	Large country	Diffusion
	Rybczynski theorem	Immiserizing growth	Product cycle hypothesis

Suggested Reading

A classic theoretical study of the effects of technological progress on a country's economy and trade (using techniques similar to those presented in Appendix B) is Findlay and Grubert (1959). The product cycle hypothesis of trade is put forth in Vernon (1966), but doubts are voiced by Vernon himself (1979). Slaughter (2000), Lawrence (2008, chapter 3), and Haskel et al. (2012) survey the effects of trade and other influences on rising wage inequality. Anderson and Smith (2000) and Heitger and Stehn (2003) examine the effects of trade on wages in Canada and Germany, respectively.

Van den Berg and Lewer (2007) examine both theories and empirical evidence about how trade affects growth. Grossman and Helpman (1995) provide a technical survey of theories of the relationships between technology and trade. Romer (1994) and Rivera-Batiz and Romer (1991) present technical discussions of the effects of trade openness on growth. Keller (2004) offers a technical survey of economic research on international technology diffusion.

When you feel that you are nearing mastery of the theoretical material in Chapters 2 through 7, give yourself a test by looking at the first 10 paradoxes in Magee (1979). First look at Magee's listing of the paradoxes on his pages 92–93; then try to prove or explain them before looking at the answers.

Questions and Problems

◆ 1. Pugelovia's growth has been oriented toward expansion of its export industries. How do you think Pugelovia's terms of trade have been changing during this time period?

2. "An increase in the country's labor force will result in an increase in the quantity produced of the labor-intensive good, with no change in the quantity produced of the other good." Do you agree or disagree? Why? In your answer, use the logic of the Rybczynski theorem.

◆ 3. A number of Latin American countries export coffee and import other goods. A long-term drought now reduces coffee production in the countries of this region. Assume that they remain exporters of coffee. Explain why the long-term drought in the region might lead to an increase in the region's well-being or welfare. What would make this gain in well-being more likely?

4. "A country whose trade has almost no impact on world prices is at great risk of immiserizing growth." Do you agree or disagree? Why?

◆ 5. Why does the Heckscher–Ohlin theory predict that most research and development (R&D) activity is done in the industrialized countries?

6. If every new product goes through a product cycle, will the technological initiator (e.g., the United States or Japan) eventually develop chronic overall "trade deficits"?

◆ 7. Explain the effect of each of these on the shape and position of the country's production-possibility curve:

   a. A proportionate increase in the total supplies (endowments) of all factors of production.

   b. New management practices that can be used in all industries to improve productivity by about the same amount in all industries.

   c. New production technology that improves productivity in the wheat industry, with no effect on productivity in the cloth industry.

8. Which of the following can lead to a *reversal* of the country's trade pattern (that is, a shift in which a previously exported good becomes an imported good or a previously imported good becomes an exported good)? Consider each separately. Explain each.

   a. Growth in the country's total supply (endowment) of the factor that is initially scarce in the country.

   b. International diffusion of technology.

   c. Shifting tastes of the country's consumers.

✦ 9. A free-trade equilibrium exists in which the United States exports machinery and imports clothing from the rest of the world. The goods are produced with two factors: capital and labor. The trade pattern is the one predicted by the H–O theory. An increase now occurs in the U.S. endowment of capital, its abundant factor.

   a. What is the effect on the shape and position of the U.S. production-possibility curve?

   b. What is the effect on the actual production quantities in the United States if the product price ratio is unchanged? Explain.

   c. What is the effect on the U.S. willingness to trade?

   d. Assuming that the U.S. growth does affect the international equilibrium price ratio, what is the direction of the change in this price ratio?

   e. Is it possible that U.S. national well-being declines as a result of the endowment growth and the resulting change in the international price ratio? Explain.

10. A free-trade equilibrium exists in a two-region, two-product world. The United States exports food and imports clothing. A long-term drought now occurs in East Asia.

    a. What is the effect on East Asia's willingness to trade?

    b. Assuming that each region is large enough to influence international prices, how does East Asia's drought affect the equilibrium international price ratio?

    c. Show on a graph and explain the effect of all this on the following *in the United States:* (1) quantities produced of food and clothing, (2) quantities consumed of food and clothing, (3) U.S. well-being.

    d. Which group in the United States is likely to gain real income in the long run as a result of all this? Which group in the United States is likely to lose real income?

✦ 11. A free-trade equilibrium exists in which the United States exports food and imports clothing. U.S. engineers now invent a new process for producing clothing at a lower cost. This process cannot be used in the rest of the world.

    a. What is the effect on the U.S. production-possibility curve?

    b. What is the effect on the U.S. willingness to trade? (Assume that the United States remains an importer of clothing.)

    c. Assuming that the change in the United States is large enough to affect international prices, will the equilibrium international price of clothing rise or will it fall?

12. Continue with the scenario of question 11—the new process in the United States and the resulting change in the international equilibrium price ratio. Focus now on effects in the rest of the world.

    a. Show graphically and explain the effect on quantities produced, quantities consumed, and well-being in the rest of the world.

    b. Explain as precisely as possible why well-being changes in the rest of the world.

◆ 13. A country is initially in a free-trade equilibrium, in which it is producing 40 units of wheat and 64 units of cloth. The country exports cloth and imports wheat. Growth now occurs in the country's production capabilities. *If* product prices are unchanged, the country will shift to producing 50 units of wheat and 80 units of cloth.

   a. What kind of growth is this?

   b. The growth of the country actually causes a change in product prices. In the new free-trade equilibrium, the country actually produces 52 units of wheat and 77 units of cloth. Explain what has happened to result in the change from the initial equilibrium to this new equilibrium.

14. Country B is a small country that allows free trade with the rest of the world. There are two products, oats and newts. Country B initially can produce oats, but initially it cannot produce newts because it lacks the production technology for newts. Country B consumes some of both oats and newts. (In your graph for Country B, place oats on the horizontal axis and newts on the vertical axis.)

   a. Use a graph to show the initial free-trade equilibrium for Country B. (Choose a reasonable free-trade equilibrium international price ratio.) What is the quantity exported and the quantity imported?

   b. Now the technology for producing newts diffuses to Country B. Country B then can produce both products, with an increasing cost of trade-off in production. Show on your graph how this changes Country B's production possibilities.

   c. Let's examine the new free-trade equilibrium for Country B. Assume that in the new free-trade equilibrium, Country B produces positive amounts of both products. Which of the following is possible? Country B exports oats and/or Country B imports oats. For each case that you think is possible, show it on your graph and use your graph to explain why it is possible.

   d. In the initial situation (before the technology diffuses), what was the key driver of the trade pattern? In the new situation (after the technology diffuses), what is the key driver of the trade pattern?

◆ 15. During the 1950s both North Korea and South Korea were mostly closed to international trade. Both were very poor and had low rates of growth of production (or income) per person.

   Since the 1960s, North Korean government policy has continued to permit almost no international trade (and very limited contact with the outside world). In contrast, the South Korean government adopted a number of policy changes, including allowing more international trade with the rest of the world. Between 1970 and 2012, production per person in North Korea stagnated, while production per person in South Korea increased by more than eight times.

   You have been asked to make the case that trade policies and technologies probably were important contributors to the difference in growth rates between North Korea and South Korea since the 1960s. What will you say?

Chapter **Eight**

Analysis of a Tariff

Most economists favor letting nations trade freely, with few tariffs or other barriers to trade. Indeed, economists have tended to be even more critical of trade barriers than have other groups in society, even though economists have taken great care to list the exceptional cases in which they feel trade barriers can be justified. Such agreement among economists is rare. Why should they agree on this one issue?

The striking consensus in favor of free trade is based primarily on a body of economic analysis demonstrating that there are usually net gains from freer trade, both for nations and for the world. The main task of this chapter and Chapters 9–14 is to compare free-trade policies with a wide range of trade barriers, barriers that do not necessarily shut out all international trade. It is mainly on this more detailed analysis of trade policies that economists have based their view that free trade is generally better than partial restrictions on trade, with a list of exceptions. This analysis makes it easier to understand what divides the majority of economists from groups calling for restrictions on trade.

To see what is lost or gained by putting up barriers to international trade, let us take a close look at the effects of the classic kind of trade barrier, a tariff on an imported product. This chapter spells out who is likely to gain and who is likely to lose from a tariff and explains conditions under which a nation could end up better off from a tariff.

A tariff, as the term is used in international trade, is a tax on importing a good or service into a country, usually collected by customs officials at the place of entry. Tariffs come in two main types. A specific tariff is stipulated as a money amount per unit of import, such as dollars per ton of steel bars or dollars per eight-cylinder two-door sports car. An ad valorem (on the value) tariff is a percentage of the estimated market value of the goods when they reach the importing country. We will not pay much attention to this distinction because it makes almost no difference to our conclusions.

Tariff rates have been declining, but they are still important. Indeed, only one country in the world, Singapore, has almost no tariffs. (In addition, two autonomous customs areas, Hong Kong and Macau, have no tariffs.)

For the industrialized countries, average tariff rates in the 1930s were about 60 percent, in the aftermath of the infamous Smoot-Hawley tariffs that the United States enacted in 1930 and the increased rates adopted by other countries in response to the higher U.S. tariffs. Negotiated agreements since then have dropped most tariffs on nonagricultural products in these countries to very low levels. The key role of the General Agreement on Tariffs and Trade (GATT), which is now folded into the World

bal Governance   WTO and GATT: Tariff Success

During the past 65 years, governments of industrialized countries reached a series of global agreements that have reduced tariffs on their nonagricultural imports to very low levels. How did they accomplish this remarkable reduction? And what is the position of the developing countries in the process? To answer these questions, we take up the topic of *global governance*—practices and institutions that condition how national governments interact with each other—with a focus on international economic issues like trade.

GATT TO WTO
The story began during World War II, when the United States, Britain, and the other allies started to discuss how to ensure that the economic system worked better after the war than it had before the war. For trade, the goal was to find a way to avoid the virulent protectionism that had taken hold in many countries in the early 1930s. The United States, Britain, and their allies expected the key institution to be the International Trade Organization. However, it never came into existence because of opposition, led by members of the U.S. Congress, to what many viewed as the excessive breadth of the organization's proposed charter.

Instead, a "provisional" accord, the General Agreement on Tariffs and Trade (GATT), became the key institution. The GATT was signed in 1947 by 23 countries and focused squarely on international trade issues. The number of countries in the GATT rose to 38 in 1960, 77 in 1970, 84 in 1980, and 99 in 1990. A new global agreement in the early 1990s led to the creation of the World Trade Organization (WTO) in January 1995. The WTO, which subsumes and expands on the GATT, is now the organization that oversees the global rules of government policies toward international trade and provides the forum for negotiating global agreements to improve these rules.

The WTO (like the GATT before it) espouses three major principles:

- Reductions of barriers to trade.
- Nondiscrimination, often called the *most-favored nation (MFN)* principle.
- No unfair encouragement for exports.

As of early 2014 the WTO had 159 member countries, including Russia, which joined in 2012. In addition, 24 countries have been negotiating to become members. The WTO's headquarters are in Geneva, Switzerland.

NEGOTIATIONS LOWER TARIFFS
In the first decades of its existence the GATT focused on tariffs. In recent decades other ("nontariff") barriers have received more attention, and these are taken up in the next chapter.

Under the GATT, member countries pursued eight rounds of *multilateral trade negotiations* to lower barriers. The first five rounds focused on reductions in tariff rates, using item-by-item negotiations in which the largest trading countries agreed to mutual reductions and then extended these new lower tariffs to all members, following the MFN nondiscrimination principle. This meant that the negotiations were conducted among the largest industrial countries. In addition, it was quickly recognized that lowering barriers to trade in agricultural products would be fraught with controversy, so the negotiations focused on nonagricultural products.

The first round, Geneva 1947, achieved substantial tariff reductions (for instance, the average U.S. tariff rate was reduced by 21 percent). The next three rounds, Annecy 1949, Torquay 1950–1951, and Geneva 1956, achieved modest new reductions, as did the Dillon Round (1960–1961), which also took up the creation of a common external tariff schedule for the newly formed European Economic Community (now the European Union).

To accomplish more substantial tariff reductions, the Kennedy Round (1963–1967) shifted the process so that the industrialized countries began with an agreement to use a formula to lower all nonagricultural tariffs and then negotiated limited exceptions in which some products had lesser tariff cuts. This innovation worked—the average tariff reduction was 38 percent for nonagricultural imports into industrialized countries. The Tokyo Round (1973–1979) and the Uruguay Round (1986–1994) continued the process using formulas for cuts, with negotiated exceptions.

Industrialized countries' nonagricultural tariffs fell by an average of 33 and 38 percent, respectively.

DEVELOPING COUNTRIES

While the industrialized countries have negotiated tariff reductions, what has been the role of developing countries? Of the 23 founding members of GATT, 13 were developing countries, and now most WTO members are developing countries. However, until recently, developing countries played little role in the multilateral trade negotiations. Because they were seldom major exporters or importers of specific nonagricultural products, they were not active in the negotiations of the first five rounds. In the Kennedy Round there was formal recognition that developing countries did not need to offer tariff cuts even though they benefited from the tariff reductions by the industrialized countries. The Tokyo Round continued the approach, formalizing "special and differential" treatment for developing countries. In fact, most developing countries had not even agreed to maximum bound tariffs for most products, so they were free to raise their tariffs if they wanted to.

While the developing countries benefited from the tariff reductions by industrialized countries, they were not able to influence how the industrialized countries were lowering tariffs because they were not involved in the give-and-take of negotiating over mutual reductions. Industrialized countries shied from lowering tariffs on "sensitive" products, which were often the labor-intensive nonagricultural products that were the most promising products for expanding developing countries' manufactured exports.

In the 1980s many developing countries shifted toward a more outward-oriented strategy for development (see Chapter 14 for further discussion). Many unilaterally lowered their tariff rates. They also became more involved in the negotiations of the Uruguay Round, although ultimately the conclusion of the round still was dominated by negotiations among the industrialized countries, especially the United States and the European Union. As part of the Uruguay Round, many developing countries agreed to adopt bound rates for most of their tariffs, though these bound rates often remain above their actual rates. For example, Mexico has now bound most of its rates, but Mexico's average actual tariff rate of 8 percent is well below its average bound rate of 36 percent.

RECENT PROGRESS

Under the WTO, reduction of tariff barriers continues. First, a special negotiation led to the Information Technology Agreement of 1996. Each country adopting the agreement (initially 29 countries) commits to eliminate tariffs on imports of information technology goods (computers, telecommunications equipment, semiconductors, semiconductor manufacturing equipment, and related instruments and parts) and software. By 2014, 78 countries had adopted the agreement, so that 97 percent of global trade in these information technology products is (or soon will be) tariff-free.

Second, the developing countries that have joined the WTO since 1995 have generally lowered their actual tariff rates as a condition for joining and accepted bound rates equal to or very close to their actual rates. For instance, the average tariff rate of China, which joined the WTO in 2001, fell from 17 percent in 2000 to 11 percent in 2003. Third, reducing tariffs is an important part of the agenda for the current Doha Round of trade negotiations, a topic that will be examined further in the next chapter.

Overall, the liberalization procedures set up under the GATT and continued under the WTO have been remarkably successful in lowering industrialized countries' tariffs on nonagricultural products. In part the multilateral negotiations have succeeded because each country's government is able to defend its tariff-cutting "concessions" against the protests of domestic protectionists as the price the country must pay to give its exporters better access to other markets. This mercantilist logic is bad economics—we know instead that imports are something the country gains and exports are something the country gives up—but the logic seems to be useful politics.

Trade Organization (WTO), as a forum for these multilateral trade negotiations is described in the box "WTO and GATT: Tariff Success."

In 2012, tariff rates averaged 2.4 to 4.2 percent on nonagricultural products imported into the United States, Canada, the European Union, and Japan. But tariffs on some individual nonagricultural products are much higher, up to 55 percent in the United States, 25 percent in Canada, 26 percent in the European Union, and 463 percent in Japan. Tariff rates for agricultural products are higher for many industrialized countries, with average tariffs of 5 percent for the United States (highest rate 350 percent), average 16 percent for Canada (highest 551 percent), average 13 percent for the European Union (highest 605 percent), and average 17 percent for Japan (highest 692 percent).

Average tariff rates are higher in most developing countries. For example, for China, in 2012 the average tariff rate on nonagricultural imports was 9 percent, with a maximum rate of 50 percent, and the average tariff rate on agricultural imports was 16 percent, with a high rate of 65 percent. For Mexico, the average and maximum tariff rates were 6 and 50 percent for nonagricultural products and 21 and 254 percent for agricultural products.

A PREVIEW OF CONCLUSIONS

Our exploration of the pros and cons of a tariff will be detailed enough to warrant listing its main conclusions here at the outset. This chapter will discuss how

- A tariff almost always lowers world well-being.
- A tariff usually lowers the well-being of each nation, including the nation imposing the tariff.
- The "nationally optimal" tariff discussed near the end of this chapter is a possible exception to the case for free trade. When a nation can affect the prices at which it trades with foreigners, it can gain from its own tariff. (The world as a whole loses, however.)
- A tariff absolutely helps those groups tied closely to the production of import substitutes, even when the tariff is bad for the nation as a whole.

You may wish to review these conclusions after we have completed the analysis of import barriers in this chapter.

THE EFFECT OF A TARIFF ON DOMESTIC PRODUCERS

Intuition suggests that domestic producers that compete against imports will benefit from a tariff. If the government places a tax on imports of the product, the domestic price of the imported product will rise. Domestic producers can then expand their own production and sales, raise the price they charge, or both. The tariff, by taxing imports to make imports less competitive in the domestic market, should make domestic producers better off.

The demand and supply analysis of a tariff agrees with our intuition. It goes beyond intuition, though, by allowing us to calculate just how much a tariff benefits domestic producers.

We begin with a demand−supply view of the U.S. market for bicycles without any tariff. For most of this chapter, we deal with the simple case in which our nation is a competitive "price-taker" in the world markets for the products we trade. This is the same small country that we defined in the previous chapter. For a small country, the price that the country must pay the foreign sellers is not affected by how much the small country imports of the product.

In the free-trade situation shown in Figure 8.1, bicycles are imported freely at the given world price of $300. At this price consumers buy S_0 bikes a year from domestic suppliers and import M_0 bikes a year, buying a total of $D_0 = S_0 + M_0$ bikes. To use illustrative numbers, let's say that consumers buy $D_0 = 1.6$ (million bikes a year), domestic producers make $S_0 = 0.6$, and the remaining $M_0 = 1.0$ are imported.

Recall that **producer surplus** is the amount that producers gain from being able to sell bikes at the going market price. Graphically, producer surplus is the area above the supply curve and below the market price line. Let's review why this is producer surplus.

The supply curve tells us, for each possible quantity supplied, the lowest price that will draw out another bike produced and supplied. This is true because the supply curve indicates the marginal cost of each additional unit. A competitive producer will supply an additional unit as long as the price (the extra revenue) covers the marginal (or extra) cost. Thus, according to the supply curve S_d in Figure 8.1, some firm is willing to supply the very first bike for $210 (at point A). This firm receives the market price of $300, bringing a net gain (producer surplus) of $90 on this first unit.

FIGURE 8.1
The U.S. Market for Bicycles with Free Trade

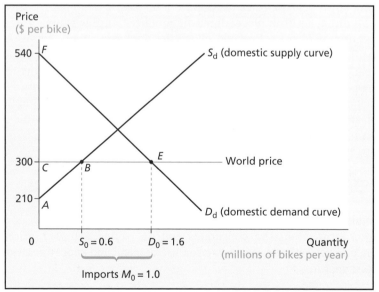

If the world price is $300 per bike, with free trade the country's consumers buy 1.6 million bikes, and its local firms produce 0.6 million bikes, so 1.0 million bikes are imported. With free trade domestic producer surplus is area *CBA* and domestic consumer surplus is area *FEC*.

Similarly, as we go up the supply curve from point *A* toward point *B*, we find that the vertical distance between the supply curve and the price of $300 shows the gains that producers are getting on each additional unit.

By summing the gain on each unit supplied, we see that producers receive the area of triangle *CBA* as producer surplus—the amount by which the price exceeds the incremental costs, unit by unit. We might immediately think that this is a measure of profit, and much or all of it could be profit. But it is possible that other resources used in production may also share in the producer surplus. For instance, the expansion of quantity produced could drive up wage rates for the type of labor used in the industry because the industry increases its demand for this labor.

Now imagine a tariff of 10 percent on imported bikes.[1] Because this is a small country, foreign exporters insist on continuing to receive $300 for each bike they export. So the 10 percent tariff is $30 per bike, *and* this amount is passed on to consumers. The domestic price of imported bikes rises to $330.

When the tariff is imposed, domestic producers can also raise the price that they charge for their bikes. If domestic and imported bikes are perfect (or very close) substitutes, then domestic producers raise their price to $330. When the tariff drives the domestic market price to $330, domestic firms respond by raising their output and sales, as long as the higher price exceeds the marginal cost of supplying the extra units.

Figure 8.2 shows the same bicycle market introduced in Figure 8.1. When the tariff is imposed, domestic producers expand output by 200,000 units, from S_0 to S_1. Each of these units from S_0 to S_1 is now profitable for some domestic firm to produce. The marginal cost of each of these units is between $300 and $330, which is less than the new, tariff-inclusive price of $330.

With the tariff in place, domestic producer surplus is area *g* + *a*, the area below the new $330 price line and above the domestic supply curve. As a result of the tariff, domestic producer surplus increases by area *a*, which equals $21 million per year. We can think of this as composed of two pieces. First, the rectangular part of area *a* covering the first 0.6 million bikes reflects the higher price received on units that are supplied even if there is no tariff. Second, the triangle at the right-hand end of area *a* reflects the additional producer surplus earned on the extra 0.2 million bikes supplied.

THE EFFECT OF A TARIFF ON DOMESTIC CONSUMERS

Intuition also suggests that buyers of a good imported from abroad will be hurt by a tariff. Domestic consumers end up paying a higher price, buying less of the product, or both. Again, we can use demand and supply analysis to calculate the consumer loss.

---

[1]The U.S. bicycle example is realistic in some ways. The Bicycle Manufacturers Association at times lobbied Congress for higher bicycle tariffs to stem import competition, but to no avail. Imports have now claimed over 90 percent of the U.S. market for bicycles.

FIGURE 8.2

The Effect
of a Tariff
on Domestic
Producers

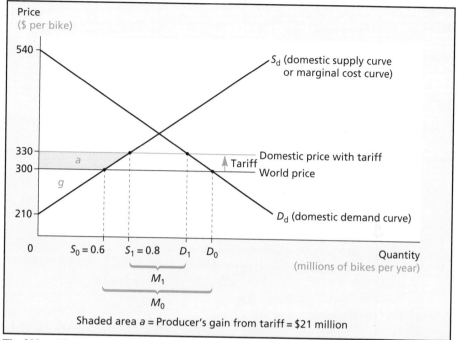

Shaded area a = Producer's gain from tariff = $21 million

The \$30 tariff on imports allows domestic producers to expand their production from S_0 to S_1. The \$30 bike tariff gives domestic producers extra surplus on all the bikes they would have produced even without the tariff (an extra \$30 × S_0) plus smaller net gains on additional sales [gain equaling ½ × \$30 × ($S_1 − S_0$)].

First, let's return to the free-trade situation (before the tariff is imposed) shown in Figure 8.1. With free trade domestic consumers buy D_0 bikes at the world price of \$300. Recall that **consumer surplus** is the amount that consumers gain from being able to buy bikes at the going market price. Graphically, consumer surplus is the area below the demand curve and above the market price line. To see this, recall that the demand curve tells us the highest price that some consumer is willing to pay for each additional bike. Thus, according to the demand curve in Figure 8.1, some consumer is willing to pay \$540 for the first bike (at point F). This consumer can buy the bike at the market price of \$300, so the consumer receives a net gain (consumer surplus) of \$240 on that first unit. As we go down the demand curve from point F to point E, we find that the vertical distances between the demand curve and the world price of \$300 show us the bargains that these consumers are getting. These consumers pay less for bikes than the maximum amount they would have been willing to pay. By summing the net gain on each unit purchased, we see that the entire area (FEC) between the demand curve and the \$300 price line tells us the total amount of consumer surplus.

Now the government imposes a tariff of 10 percent on imported bikes. Figure 8.3 shows the consumers' view of the bicycle market with the tariff. The tariff raises the price that consumers must pay for bikes (both imported and domestically produced) to \$330.

FIGURE 8.3

The Effect
of a Tariff
on Domestic
Consumers

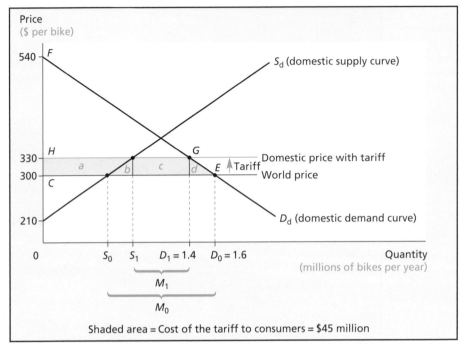

Shaded area = Cost of the tariff to consumers = $45 million

An import tariff of $30 raises the price that domestic consumers must pay for imported and domestic bikes. Quantity demanded falls from D_0 to D_1. The tariff costs consumers both the full $30 on every bike they continue to buy (a loss of $\$30 \times D_1$) and the net enjoyment on bikes they would have bought at the lower tariff-free price but do not buy at the higher price including the tariff [an additional loss of $\frac{1}{2} \times \$30 \times (D_0 - D_1)$].

By raising the price to $330, the tariff forces consumers who were buying the 1.6 million bikes to make a decision:

- Some will continue to buy bikes, paying $30 more per bike.
- Some will decide that a bike is not worth $330 to them, so they will not buy at the higher price.

In Figure 8.3, quantity demanded falls from D_0 to D_1, a decrease of 0.2 million bikes. The net loss to consumers is the shaded area $a + b + c + d$ because consumer surplus declines from triangle *FEC* to triangle *FGH*. Area $a + b + c$ is the loss of $30 per bike of consumer surplus for those who continue to buy bikes at the higher price. Area d is the loss of consumer surplus for those who stop buying bikes. In our example, the consumer surplus loss is $45 million per year.

What domestic consumers lose from the tariff (here $45 million) is larger than what domestic producers gain ($21 million). The reason is straightforward: Producers gain the price markup on only the domestic output, while consumers are forced to pay the same price markup on both domestic output and imports. Figures 8.2 and 8.3 show this clearly for the bicycle example. The tariff brings bicycle producers only area *a* in gains, but it costs consumers this same area *a* plus areas *b* + *c* + *d*. As far as the effects on bicycle consumers and bicycle producers alone are concerned, the tariff is definitely a net loss.

THE TARIFF AS GOVERNMENT REVENUE

The effects of a tariff on the well-being of consumers and producers do not exhaust its effects on the importing country. As long as the tariff is not so high as to prohibit all imports, it also brings revenue to the country's government. This revenue equals the unit amount of the tariff times the volume of imports with the tariff. In Figure 8.3 the total government revenue from collecting the tariff is area *c*, equal to $18 million per year (the tariff of $30 times the imports of M_1 = 0.6 million).

The country's government could do any of several things with the tariff revenue. The revenue could be used to pay for extra government spending on socially worthwhile projects. It could be matched by an equal cut in some other tax, such as the income tax. Or it could just become extra income for greedy government officials. Although what form the tariff takes can certainly matter, the central point is that this revenue accrues to somebody within the country. It counts as an element of national gain to be weighed in with the consumer losses and producer gains from the tariff.[2]

THE NET NATIONAL LOSS FROM A TARIFF

By combining the effects of the tariff on consumers, producers, and the government, we can determine the net effect of the tariff on the importing country as a whole.

The first key step is to impose a social value judgment. How much do you really care about each group's gains or losses? If one group gains and another loses, how big must the gain be to outweigh the other group's loss? To make any overall judgment, you must first decide how to weigh each dollar of effect on each group. That is unavoidable. Anybody who expresses an opinion on whether a tariff is good or bad necessarily does so on the basis of a personal value judgment about how important each group is.

The basic analysis uses the one-dollar, one-vote metric: *Every dollar of gain or loss is just as important as every other dollar of gain or loss, regardless of who the gainers or losers are.* Let's use this measure of well-being here just as we did in Chapter 2. Later we discuss what difference it would make if we chose to weigh one group's dollar stakes more heavily than those of other groups.

If the one-dollar, one-vote metric is applied, then a tariff like the one graphed in Figures 8.2 and 8.3 brings a clear net loss to the importing country and to the world as a whole. Figure 8.4 shows the same bicycle example. We have seen that the dollar value of the consumer losses exceeds the dollar value of the producer gains from

---

[2] We note a possible exception. Part of the tariff could be used up as real resource costs of administering and enforcing the tariff, so this amount would not represent a national gain.

FIGURE 8.4 The Net National Loss from a Tariff in Two Equivalent Diagrams

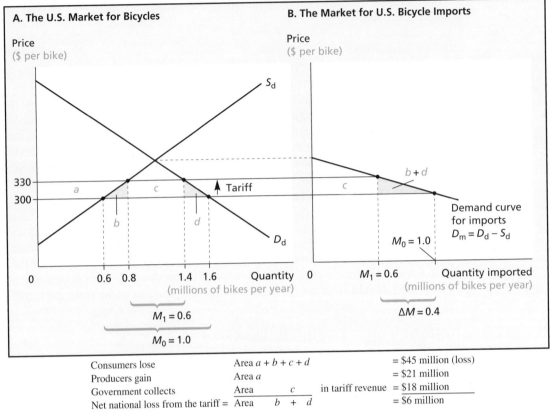

Consumers lose	Area $a + b + c + d$	= $45 million (loss)
Producers gain	Area a	= $21 million
Government collects	Area c in tariff revenue	= $18 million
Net national loss from the tariff =	Area $b + d$	= $6 million

For a small importing country, a tariff brings a net national loss. What it costs consumers is greater than what it brings producers plus the government's tariff revenue. The two reasons for the net loss are summarized in areas *b* and *d*. Area *b* (the production effect) represents the loss from making at higher marginal cost what could have been bought for less from foreign exporters. Area *d* (the consumption effect) represents the loss from discouraging import consumption that is worth more than what the nation would pay the foreign exporters.

the tariff. We have also seen that the country's government gains some tariff revenue. The left side of Figure 8.4 makes it clear that the dollar value of what the consumers lose (area $a + b + c + d$) exceeds even the sum of the producer gains (area *a*) and the government tariff revenues (area *c*). *The net national loss from the tariff is area* b *plus area* d.

The same net national loss can be shown in another way. The right side of Figure 8.4 shows the market for imports of bicycles. We can derive our demand curve for imports of bicycles by subtracting the domestic supply curve from the domestic demand curve for bicycles at each price (horizontally). That is, for each possible price, the quantity demanded of *imported* bicycles equals the domestic quantity demanded minus the domestic quantity supplied at that price.

We can use the right side of Figure 8.4 to show some of the same information that is shown on the left side. With free trade, the price of imports is $300. The country imports M_0 bikes. With the imposition of the tariff, the domestic price of imported bikes rises to $330. The country then imports only M_1 bikes. The government collects tariff revenue equal to area c.

The net national loss from the tariff is shown on the right side as the area of triangle $b + d$. To see that this triangle has the same area as the sum of the areas of the two triangles b and d on the left side, consider the heights and bases of the triangles. All of the triangles have the same height (the tariff per unit). The base of triangle b is the reduction in imports that are replaced by domestic production. The base of triangle d is the import reduction that results from the lower domestic consumption. The two bases add up to the total reduction in imports, the base of triangle $b + d$. With the same height and combined bases, the sum of the areas of triangles b and d equals the area of triangle $b + d$.

The net national loss from the tariff shown in Figure 8.4 is not hard to estimate empirically. The key information we need consists only of the amount of the tariff per unit and the estimated volume by which the tariff reduces imports, ΔM. The usual way of arriving at this information is to find out the percent price markup the tariff represents, the initial dollar value of imports, and the percent elasticity, or responsiveness, of import quantities to price changes. It is handy, and perhaps surprising, that the net national loss from the tariff can be estimated just using information on imports, as on the right side of Figure 8.4, without even knowing the domestic demand and supply curves. In our bicycle example, the net loss $b + d$ equals $6 million.

Why is there a net loss? What economic logic lies behind the geometric finding that the net national loss equals areas $b + d$? With a little reflection, we can see that these areas represent gains from international trade and specialization that are lost because of the tariff.

Area d, sometimes called the **consumption effect** of the tariff, shows the loss to consumers in the importing nation based on the reduction in their total consumption of bicycles. They would have been willing to pay prices above $300 and up to $330 to get the extra 200,000 bicycles. These extra 200,000 bicycles would have cost the nation only $300 a bike in payments to foreign sellers. Yet the tariff discourages them from buying these bicycles. Area d is a *deadweight loss* because what the consumers lose in area d, nobody else gains. Area d is the inefficiency for those consumers squeezed out of buying bicycles because the tariff artificially raises the domestic price.

Area b is a welfare loss based on the fact that some consumer demand is shifted from imports to more expensive domestic production. The tariff raises domestic production from 0.6 to 0.8 million bikes at the expense of imports. The domestic supply curve (which also shows the marginal cost of domestic production) is assumed to be upward sloping. Each extra bicycle costs more and more to produce, rising from a resource cost of $300 up to a cost of $330. The domestic resource cost of producing these bicycles is more than the $300 price at which the bicycles are available from foreign suppliers. This extra cost of shifting to more expensive home production, called the **production effect** of the tariff, is represented by area b. Like area d, it

Extension   The Effective Rate of Protection

To gain more understanding of how much protection is given to domestic producers by a country's tariffs, we need to take a closer look at how products are produced. We are interested in how tariffs affect domestic "value added" in an industry. Value added is the amount that is available to make payments to the primary production factors in the industry. That is, value added is the sum of wages paid to labor, the rents paid to landowners, and the profits and other returns to the owners and providers of capital.

In addition to these primary factors, firms also use various kinds of components and material inputs in production. This is more important than it sounds. It means that many tariffs matter to the industry, not just the tariff on the product it produces. Specifically, firms in a given industry are affected by tariffs on their purchased inputs as well as by the tariff on the product they sell. Firms producing bicycles, for example, would be hurt by tariffs on metal tubing or bicycle tires. This complicates the task of measuring the effect of the whole set of tariffs on an individual industry's firms.

To give these points their due requires a detailed portrayal of supply–demand interactions in many markets at once. To cut down on the elaborate details, economists have developed a simpler measure that does part of the job. The measure quantifies the effects of the whole tariff structure on one industry's value added per unit of output without trying to estimate how much its output, or other outputs and prices, would change. The effective rate of protection of an individual industry is defined as the percentage by which the entire set of a nation's trade barriers raises the industry's value added per unit of output.

The effective rate of protection for the industry can be quite different from the percent tariff paid by consumers on its output (the "nominal" rate of protection). This difference is brought out clearly by the example on the facing page.

What are the effects of a 10 percent tariff on bicycle imports and a 5 percent tariff on imports of tubing, tires, and all other material and component inputs into the bicycle industry? The 10 percent tariff on bicycles by itself raises their price and the value added by the bicycle industry by $30 per bike, as before. The 5 percent tariff on material and component inputs costs the bicycle industry $11 per bike by raising the prices of these inputs. The two sets of tariffs together would raise the industry's unit value added by only $19 per bike. But this extra $19 represents a protection of value added (incomes) in the bicycle industry of 23.8 percent of value added, not just 10 percent or less, as one might have thought from a casual look at the nominal tariff rates themselves.

This example illustrates two of the basic points brought out by the concept of effective rate of protection:

- A given industry's incomes, or value added, will be affected by trade barriers on its inputs as well as trade barriers on its output.

- The effective rate of protection will be greater than the nominal rate when the industry's output is protected by a higher rate than the tariff rates on its inputs.

We add three other insights. First, if the tariff rates on the inputs are the same as the tariff rate on the output, then this rate is also the effective rate of protection. (Try this by modifying our example by using a 5 percent tariff on bicycles.) Second, the effective rate of protection can be negative. The tariff structure can penalize value added in the industry. (Try this using a 2 percent tariff on bicycles.) Third, export producers are penalized with something like negative effective protection if their costs are increased by tariffs on the inputs they use in production. (Try this by changing our example to one in which the country's bicycle producers try to sell to foreign buyers at the world price of $300 per bike.)

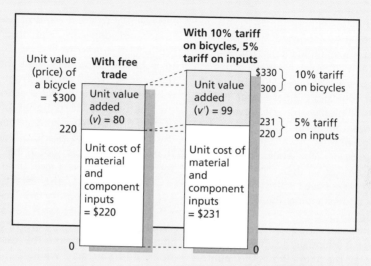

Illustrative calculation of an effective rate of protection

$$\text{Effective rate of protection for bicycle industry} = \frac{v' - v}{v} = \frac{\$99 - \$80}{\$80} = 23.8\%$$

To see who is getting protected by trade barriers, it helps (1) to distinguish an industry and its suppliers and (2) to look at the effects of the whole set of barriers, not just the one directly protecting the industry. In this case, the tariff on bicycles helps the domestic bike industry, but the tariffs on the material and component inputs the bicycle industry buys hurt it. The net result in this case is an "effective rate of protection" of 23.8 percent.

is a deadweight loss. It is part of what consumers pay, but neither the government nor bicycle producers gain it. It is the amount by which the cost of drawing domestic resources away from other uses exceeds the savings from not paying foreigners to sell us the 200,000 extra units.[3]

The basic analysis of a tariff identifies areas *b* and *d* as the net national loss from a tariff only if certain assumptions are granted. One key assumption is the one-dollar, one-vote metric. Use of this measure implies that consumers' losses of areas *a* and *c* were exactly offset, dollar for dollar, by producers' gain of area *a* and the government's collection of area *c*. That is what produced (*b* + *d*) as the net loss for the nation. Suppose that you personally reject this metric. Suppose, for example, that you think that each dollar of gain for the bicycle producers

---

[3]The text of this chapter focuses on tariffs, which are taxes or duties on imports. Some countries also impose duties on exports, and the box "They Tax Exports, Too" examines their effects.

Case Study   They Tax Exports, Too

Nearly all governments impose tariffs (taxes) on some imports into their countries. Most governments do not impose additional taxes (duties) on their exports. Still, WTO rules allow countries to impose export taxes. In the mid-2000s about half of WTO member countries did have some duties on their exports. Typically, this is a developing country (e.g., Argentina, Russia) imposing duties on its exports of one or more agricultural or other primary products. Why would some countries impose extra taxes on their exports? What effects do export taxes have? Let's start with the effects because understanding the effects provides clues to the reasons.

Consider a small exporting country, one whose supply of exports has essentially no effect on world prices of its exports. The figure shows the country and the world price P_0. If there is no export tax, the country produces the quantity S_0, consumes the quantity D_0, and exports the difference, $S_0 - D_0$. Now the country's government imposes an export tax equal to T dollars per unit exported (a rate that reduces but is not high enough to completely eliminate exports of this product). What changes (and what does not change)?

For a small country, the world price P_0 does *not* change. So, after the government collects the tax, domestic producers receive revenue net of tax on their exports of only $(P_0 - T)$. These producers will try to shift some sales to local consumers, who initially are willing to pay more. But as competitive domestic producers strive to make more domestic sales, the domestic price is also driven down to $(P_0 - T)$. At the new price of $(P_0 - T)$ received for both domestic sales and exports, the country's quantity produced falls to S_1, quantity consumed increases to D_1, and quantity exported decreases to $(S_1 - D_1)$.

Well-being changes, for groups within the country and for the country overall. Consumers gain surplus of area $g + h$, producers lose surplus of area $g + h + j + k + n$, the government gains export tax revenue equal to area k, and the country suffers deadweight losses equal to areas j and n. Area j is the inefficiency of domestic overconsumption of the product—the units from D_0 to D_1 are worth less to domestic consumers than the P_0 price that the country would receive from foreign buyers if instead these units were exported. Area n is the inefficiency of national underproduction of the product—the units from S_1 to S_0 cost the country less to produce than the price P_0 that foreign buyers would be willing to pay for them if they were produced and exported.

As you can see, the effects of an export tax for a small country are analogous to the effects of an import tariff for a small country. What about a large exporting country that imposes an export tax? This case is also analogous, and you may want to try to draw the graph yourself. The large exporting country has national monopoly power in the world market. It can use an export tax to limit its export supply and drive up the world price of the product. The country benefits from the higher world price for its export product, and there is a nationally optimal export tax that could maximize its net gains from enhancing its terms of trade in this way (assuming that the rest of the world is passive).

Why do we see some countries using export taxes (and other restrictions on exports)? The analysis provides insights. First, the country's government may use export taxes, as it would use any other tax, to raise revenue for the government. Second, the country's government may use export taxes to benefit local consumers of the product. The local consumers could be households. For example, in reaction to the increases in world food prices during 2007–2008, a number of countries (including Thailand, Vietnam, and India) increased export taxes or otherwise restricted exports of agricultural products like rice and sugar to keep local food prices low. Or the local consumers could be firms in other industries that use this product as an input into their production. The export tax artificially lowers their production costs and encourages the expansion of these user industries. Third, for a large country, the country's government may be using the export tax to gain national well-being at the expense of foreign buyers.

Are export taxes a good idea? For the first two reasons (more revenue or lower domestic prices), the government is achieving some other objective at the cost of the deadweight losses. For the third reason (exploiting national monopoly power), the country is risking retaliation by foreign countries, and the export tax is reducing global efficiency.

DISCUSSION QUESTION

In March 2012 the Indian government prohibited the export of cotton. What are the possible reasons for this export ban? Which one or two seem to be the most plausible reasons?

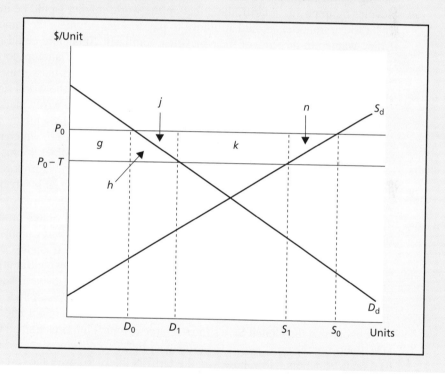

is somehow more important to you than each dollar of consumer loss, perhaps because you see the bicycle consumers as a group society has pampered too much. If that is your view, you will not accept areas *b* and *d* as the net national loss from the tariff. The same basic analysis of the tariff is still useful to you, however. You can stipulate how much more weight you put on each dollar of effect on bicycle producers than on each dollar for consumers. Then you can apply your own differential weights to each group's dollar stake to see whether the net effect of the tariff is still negative.

THE TERMS-OF-TRADE EFFECT AND A NATIONALLY OPTIMAL TARIFF

It is time to relax a key assumption we have been making. So far, this chapter has used the small-country assumption: We have assumed that the importing nation, here the United States, cannot affect the world price of the imported good. In particular, the tariff on bicycle imports did not affect the world price of bicycles, which stood fixed at $300, tariff or no tariff.

The small-country assumption is often valid. Many individual nations as importers have small shares of world markets for individual commodities. Any feasible change in a small country's demand for imports is so small that it has (almost) no effect on the big world market. For instance, if Costa Rica reduced its demand for imported bicycles by imposing a tariff, the effect on the world market would be imperceptible. Costa Rican importers would still have to pay foreign suppliers the same world price if they wanted to buy any of their bicycles. Similarly, Singapore could not expect to force foreign sellers of rice to supply it more cheaply. Any attempt to do so would simply prove that Singapore was a price-taker on the world market by causing rice exporters to avoid Singapore altogether, with little effect on the world rice price.

Yet in other cases a nation has a large enough share of the world market for one of its imports that the country's buying can affect the world price unilaterally. A nation collectively can have this **monopsony power** even in cases in which no individual buyer within the nation has it. For example, the United States looms large in the world auto market. If the U.S. government imposes a tariff on imported autos, the reduction in U.S. demand for foreign autos would have noticeable adverse effects on foreign exporters. In the face of lower U.S. demand, those exporters would fight to maintain sales by reducing their export prices. The United States probably has the same monopsony power to some extent in the world markets for many other goods.

A nation with such power over foreign selling prices could exploit this advantage with a tariff on imports. Let's look at a case in which a **large country** can affect the world price of a good it imports, just by imposing a tariff. In this case, the tariff has a **terms-of-trade effect.** Recall that in earlier chapters we defined the terms of trade as the ratio of the international prices of our exports to the international prices of our imports.

Suppose that the United States (now a large country) imposes a small tariff on bicycles. Imposing the tariff makes the price paid by U.S. consumers exceed the price paid to foreign suppliers. Now, however, the tariff is likely to lower the foreign price a bit as well as raise the domestic price a bit. To see why the foreign export price decreases, we need to watch what happens to the marginal costs of foreign exporters. Here is one way to think of the process:

- The United States imports fewer bicycles because the tariff increases the domestic price, so foreign firms export fewer and produce fewer.
- By removing demand pressure on foreign production, the marginal cost at the smaller level of foreign production is lower. (We will see that this is a movement down and to the left along the foreign export supply curve.)
- With lower marginal cost and weak demand, foreign firms will compete and lower their export price.

The lowering of the price paid to foreign suppliers of U.S. imports (an improvement in the U.S. terms of trade) is what makes it possible for the United States to gain as a nation from its own tariff. To be sure, there is still a loss in economic efficiency for the world. By discouraging some imports that would have been worth more to buyers than the price being paid to cover the foreign seller's costs—and by shifting some production to higher-cost domestic producers—the tariff still has its costs. And the United States bears part of these inefficiency costs. But as long as the tariff is small, for the United States its part of those costs is outweighed by the gains from continuing most of the previous imports at a lower price paid to foreign exporters. So, for tariff rates that are not too high, the United States as a nation is better off than with free trade.

Figure 8.5 shows the effects of a rather small tariff, in this case $6 per bicycle. As in Figure 8.4, the left side of Figure 8.5 shows the market for bicycles in the United States, and the right side shows the market for bicycle imports into the United States. Because the United States is a large country relative to foreign export capacity, the foreign supply-of-exports curve slopes upward (instead of being flat at a given world price, as it would be in Figure 8.4B).

With free trade, the market for bicycle imports clears at the price of $300, and the United States imports 1 million bikes. If the U.S. government then imposes a tariff of $6 per bike, the tariff drives a wedge of $6 between the price that foreign exporters receive and the price that U.S. buyers of imports pay. Even with this tariff wedge, the market still must clear. The quantity of exports (from the supply-of-exports curve) must equal the quantity of imports (from the demand-for-imports curve), given the $6 difference in price.

In Figure 8.5B, the $6 tariff drives up the domestic price of imports to $303 and lowers the price charged by foreign exporters to $297. The quantity traded declines by a small amount, to 0.96 million bikes. We can use these conclusions to show in Figure 8.5A what is happening in the U.S. market for bikes. If the domestic price rises to $303, the domestic quantity produced rises to 0.62 million bikes and the domestic quantity demanded declines to 1.58 million bikes.

What is the effect of the tariff on the national well-being of the United States? Consumer surplus decreases by area $a + b + c + d$, and producer surplus increases by area a. The government collects tariff revenue equal to area $c + e$ (the tariff of $6 per unit times 0.96 million units imported). Who *really* pays the tariff? For a large country, domestic consumers still pay part of the tariff, area c. The new wrinkle *for a large importing country* is that *foreign exporters also pay part of the tariff* (area e) because they lower their export price when the tariff is imposed. If foreigners pay part of our taxes, then this is a gain to the importing country (though not to the world as a whole).

What is the overall effect on the importing country if it imposes a small tariff? The importing country still loses areas b and d, the triangles of inefficiency that we also saw for the small-country case. This small loss is easily outweighed by the gain of area e, the part of the tariff that is absorbed by foreign exporters when they lower their export price. *For a suitably small tariff imposed by a large importing country, the importing country gains national well-being* because area e is larger than areas b and d. For tariff rates that are not too high, the United States is better off than with free trade. In the case of a $6 tariff, the net gain to the United States is $2.82 million, which is the gain of area e ($2.88 million) minus the loss of area $b + d$ ($0.06 million).

FIGURE 8.5   A Large Country Imposes a Small Tariff

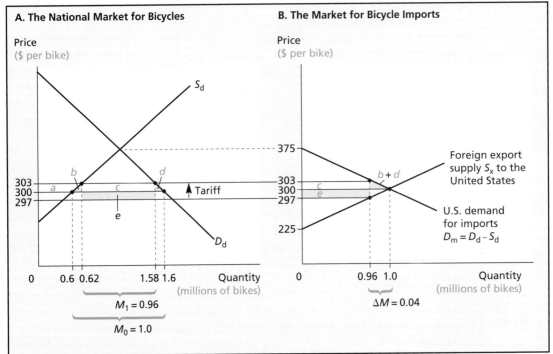

If the foreign export supply curve slopes up, an importing country collectively has some power over the price that it pays foreigners for its imports, even if individual importers have no such power. The importing country can exploit this monopsony power. Here, the United States imposes a relatively small tariff of $6 per bike imported. The United States has a net gain in well-being equal to area *e* minus areas *b* and *d*.

If a small tariff works for the nation with power over prices, higher tariffs work even better—but only up to a point. To see the limits to a nation's monopsony power, we can start by noting that *a prohibitive tariff cannot be optimal.* Suppose that the United States were to put a tariff on bicycle imports that was so high as to make all imports unprofitable. A tariff of over $150 a bike in Figure 8.5 would drive the price received by foreign suppliers below $225. Foreign suppliers would decide not to sell any bicycles to the United States at all. Lacking any revenues earned partly at the expense of foreign suppliers, the United States would find itself saddled with nothing but the loss of all gains from international trade in bicycles.

Is there a "best" tariff rate for the large importing country to impose, if it is purely driven by its own national well-being? The answer is yes, assuming that the rest of the world is passive. This best tariff is called the **nationally optimal tariff,** the tariff that creates the largest net gain for the country imposing it. For a large country, this optimal tariff lies between no tariff and a prohibitively high one.

The optimal tariff can be derived in the same way as the optimal price reduction for any monopsonist, any buyer with market power. Appendix D derives the formula for the optimal tariff rate. It turns out that the optimal tariff rate, measured as a fraction

FIGURE 8.6

The Nationally
Optimal Tariff

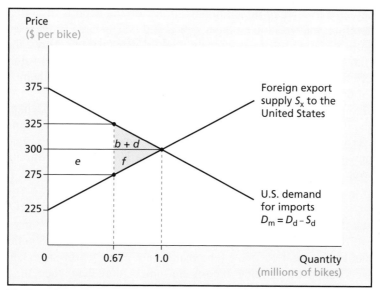

The large importing country in theory can gain the most by imposing an
optimal tariff. Here the nationally optimal tariff is $50 per bike, and the
importing country gains area e − area $b + d$. The foreign country is harmed,
losing areas e and f, and it may retaliate. Even without retaliation, the world
is worse off because of the nationally optimal tariff. The global inefficiency
equals area $b + d$ and area f.

of the price paid to foreigners, equals the reciprocal of the price elasticity of foreign
supply of our imports.

It makes sense that the lower the foreign supply elasticity, the higher our optimal
tariff rate. The more inelastically foreigners keep to supplying a nearly fixed amount
to us, the more we can get away with exploiting them. Conversely, if their supply is
infinitely elastic (the small-country case), facing us with a fixed world price, then we
cannot get them to accept lower prices. If their supply elasticity is infinite, our own
tariff hurts only us, and the optimal tariff is zero.

Figure 8.6 shows an optimal tariff for a large country. The nation gains the price
reduction on foreign bicycle imports, represented by area e. This considerably exceeds
what the nation loses by reducing its imports of bicycles (area $b + d$). The national
gain, $e − b − d$, is greater than the national gain at any other tariff rate.[4]

For the world as a whole, however, the nationally optimal tariff is still unambiguously bad. What the nation gains is less than what foreigners lose from our tariff.
Figure 8.6 shows this. The United States gains area e only at the expense of foreign
suppliers, dollar for dollar, leaving no net effect on the world from this redistribution of income through the price change. But foreign suppliers suffer more than that.

---

[4]As Figure 8.6 is drawn, the tariff rate does fit the optimal-tariff formula. The rate equals $50/$275,
or about 18.2 percent. The elasticity of foreign supply works out to be 5.5 at this point on the
foreign supply curve, so the tariff rate of about 18.2 percent is the reciprocal of 5.5.

They also lose area *f* in additional surplus on the exports discouraged by the tariff. Therefore, the world loses areas *b* + *d* and *f*. This large triangle (the shaded area in Figure 8.6) is a loss of part of the global gains from trade. Above the level of imports of 0.67 million a year (and up to 1.0 million), U.S. consumers value foreign bicycles more highly than it costs foreign suppliers to make and sell them. The tariff may be nationally optimal, but it still means a net loss to the world.

Even for large nations, it might be unwise to levy what looks like an optimal tariff. Even if individual foreign suppliers cannot fight back, their governments can. Foreign governments may retaliate by putting up new tariff barriers against our exports. Knowing this, even large countries like the United States restrain the use of their power in individual import markets.

Summary

A tariff is a tax on imports. It redistributes well-being from domestic consumers of the product to domestic producers and the government, which collects the tariff revenue. For a small country (one that cannot affect world prices), a tariff on imports lowers national well-being. It costs consumers more than it benefits producers and the government.

To reinforce your understanding of these basic effects of a tariff on well-being, imagine how you might describe each of them to legislators who are considering a tariff law. Remember what this performance in the policy arena requires. You have to speak in language that is clear to a wide audience. You can't use any diagram or equation—no legislator will be impressed by such abstractions. You can, however, use the following concise verbal descriptions to explain each of the key effects shown by lettered areas in Figures 8.2 through 8.4:

1. "By raising the price on strictly domestic sales, a tariff redistributes incomes from consumers to producers. The amount redistributed is the price increase times the average quantity of domestic sales." (This describes area *a*.)

2. "A tariff shifts some purchases from foreign products to home products. This costs more resources to make at home than to buy abroad." (This describes area *b*, the production effect.)

3. "A tariff makes consumers pay tax revenue directly to the government." (This describes area *c*.)

4. "A tariff discourages some purchases that were worth more than they cost the nation." (This describes area *d*, the consumption effect.)

5. "Both by shifting some purchases toward costly home products and by discouraging some purchases worth more than they cost the nation, the tariff costs the nation as a whole. The cost equals one-half the tariff amount times the drop in our imports." (This describes area *b* + *d*, the net national loss.)

The effects of tariffs on producer interests are further clarified by the concept of the effective rate of protection, which measures the percent effect of the entire tariff structure on the value added per unit of output in each industry. This concept incorporates the point that incomes in any one industry are affected by the tariffs on many products.

When a country as a whole can affect the price at which foreigners supply imports, the country has monopsony power. For such a large country, a positive tariff can increase national well-being because the tariff has a beneficial terms-of-trade effect. The nationally optimal tariff yields the largest possible gain. However, this tariff is optimal only if foreign governments do not retaliate with tariffs on our exports. With or without retaliation, the nationally optimal tariff is still bad for the world as a whole.

The World Trade Organization (WTO) was formed in 1995 as the successor to the General Agreement on Tariffs and Trade (GATT). The WTO oversees the global rules of government policies toward trade and provides a forum for negotiating global agreements to reduce barriers to trade. Beginning as the GATT, created in 1947, rounds of multilateral trade negotiations have been especially successful in reducing the tariffs that industrialized countries impose on their imports of nonagricultural goods.

Key Terms

Tariff	Small country	Effective rate of
Specific tariff	Producer surplus	protection
Ad valorem tariff	Consumer surplus	Monopsony power
General Agreement on	One-dollar, one-vote	Large country
Tariffs and Trade (GATT)	metric	Terms-of-trade effect
World Trade Organization	Consumption effect	Nationally optimal tariff
(WTO)	Production effect	

Suggested Reading

For summary information on countries' tariffs, see the annual *World Tariff Profiles* issued by the World Trade Organization. Greenaway and Milner (2003) discuss the concept of the effective rate of protection and its uses. Broda et al. (2008) provide a technical empirical analysis that finds support for optimal-tariff influences on tariff rates in countries that are not members of the WTO. Organization for Economic Cooperation and Development (2010) surveys export taxes and other restrictions.

Questions and Problems

◆ 1. What is the minimum quantitative information you would need to calculate the net national loss from a tariff in a small price-taking country?

2. "A tariff on imports of a product hurts domestic consumers of this product more than it benefits domestic producers of the product." Do you agree or disagree? Why?

◆ 3. What is the production effect of a tariff? How would you describe it in words, without reference to any diagram or numbers? How would you show it on a diagram, and how would you compute its value?

4. What is the consumption effect of a tariff? How would you describe it in words, without reference to any diagram or numbers? How would you show it on a diagram, and how would you compute its value?

✦ 5. You have been asked to quantify the effects of removing a country's tariff on sugar. The hard part of the work is already done: Somebody has estimated how many pounds of sugar would be produced, consumed, and imported by the country if there were no sugar duty. You are given the information shown in the table.

	Situation with Import Tariff	Estimated Situation without Tariff
World price	$0.10 per pound	$0.10 per pound
Tariff	$0.02 per pound	0
Domestic price	$0.12 per pound	$0.10 per pound
Domestic consumption (billions of pounds per year)	20	22
Domestic production (billions of pounds per year)	8	6
Imports (billions of pounds per year)	12	16

Calculate the following measures:
a. The domestic consumers' gain from removing the tariff.
b. The domestic producers' loss from removing the tariff.
c. The government tariff revenue loss.
d. The net effect on national well-being.

6. Suppose that Canada produces 1.0 million bicycles a year and imports another 0.4 million; there is no tariff or other import barrier. Bicycles sell for $400 each. Parliament is considering a $40 tariff on bicycles like the one portrayed in Figures 8.2 through 8.4. What is the maximum net national loss that this could cause Canada? What is the minimum national loss if Canada is a small country that cannot affect the world price? (*Hint:* Draw a diagram like Figure 8.4 and put the numbers given here on it. Next, imagine the possible positions and slopes of the relevant curves.)

✦ 7. As in Question 5, you have been asked to quantify the effects of removing an import duty; somebody has already estimated the effects on the country's production, consumption, and imports. This time the facts are different. The import duty in question is a 5 percent tariff on imported motorcycles. You are given the information shown in the table.

	Current Situation with 5 Percent Tariff	Estimated Situation without Tariff
World price of motorcycles	$2,000 per cycle	$2,050 per cycle
Tariff at 5 percent	$100 per cycle	0
Domestic price	$2,100 per cycle	$2,050 per cycle
Number of cycles purchased domestically per year	100,000	105,000
Number of cycles produced domestically per year	40,000	35,000
Number of cycles imported per year	60,000	70,000

Calculate the following:

a. The consumer gain from removing the duty.

b. The producer loss from removing the duty.

c. The government tariff revenue loss.

d. The net effect on the country's well-being.

Why does the net effect on the country as a whole differ from the result in Question 5?

8. For the international trade market for bicycles shown in Figure 8.5, demonstrate that a rather large tariff, for instance, a tariff that resulted in imports of 0.33 million bicycles, would not be an optimal tariff for the importing country.

✦ 9. This problem concerns the effective rate of protection. With free trade, each dollar of value added in the domestic cloth-making industry is divided as follows: 40 cents value added, 30 cents for cotton yarn, and 30 cents for other fibers. Suppose that a 25 percent ad valorem tariff is placed on cloth imports and a 1/6 tariff (16.7 percent) goes on cotton yarn imports. (There is no tariff on imports of other fibers.) Work out the division of the tariff-ridden unit value of $1.25 (the free-trade unit cloth value of $1 plus the cloth tariff) into value added, payments for cotton, and payments for other fibers. Then calculate the effective rate of protection.

10. What is the formula for the nationally optimal tariff? What is the optimal tariff if the foreign supply of our imports is infinitely elastic?

✦ 11. "A good way to understand why a large country can gain by imposing a tariff is that the country gets foreigners to pay some of its taxes." Do you agree or disagree? Why?

12. A small country has a straight-line, upward-sloping domestic supply curve and a straight-line, downward-sloping domestic demand curve for one of its key export products. The world price for this product is $150 per ton. The country currently has an export tax of $10 per unit, and it exports 10 million tons per year.

The country's government is considering reducing its export tax to $5 per ton, and it asks you to determine if this will reduce by half the inefficiency caused by the export tax. Use a graph to conduct your analysis and provide your response.

Chapter **Nine**

Nontariff Barriers to Imports

Protecting domestic producers against import competition

- Clearly helps those producers.
- Harms domestic consumers of the products.
- Probably hurts the importing nation as a whole.
- Almost surely hurts the world as a whole.

So it is with a typical tariff barrier, and so it is with other kinds of barriers against imports that we will analyze in this chapter. In fact, as tariff rates have declined in industrialized countries and many developing countries, the use of other barriers to provide protection to domestic producers has increased.

The major purpose of this chapter is to examine various kinds of nontariff barriers to imports and their effects. We also look at how large are deadweight losses from protection, in relation to the size of the whole national economy or to the extra producer benefits created by the protection. In addition, we continue our examination of the activities of the World Trade Organization, first in a box that looks at WTO rules about nontariff barriers and at the current Doha Round of multilateral trade negotiations, and then in a section at the end of the chapter that examines how trade disputes between countries can be resolved.

TYPES OF NONTARIFF BARRIERS TO IMPORTS

A nontariff barrier (NTB) to imports is any policy used by the government to reduce imports, other than a simple tariff on imports. Nontariff barriers can take many forms, including import quotas, discriminatory product standards, buy-at-home rules for government purchases, and administrative red tape to harass importers of foreign products.

An NTB reduces imports through one or more of the following direct effects:

- Limiting the quantity of imports.
- Increasing the cost of getting imports into the market.
- Creating uncertainty about the conditions under which imports will be permitted.

Figure 9.1 provides a listing of major types of NTBs and indicates the main way that each affects imports. Although antidumping duties and countervailing duties are not listed in the figure, they are also often considered NTBs. Because governments claim that they impose these kinds of measures in response to unfair practices by foreign exporters, we defer an in-depth discussion of antidumping and countervailing duties to Chapter 11. Here we will examine carefully several types of NTBs, listed in Figure 9.1.

How much protection do NTBs provide? Kee et al. (2009) estimate that NTBs are more important than tariffs in restricting world trade. One way to summarize the size of NTBs on a product is to estimate the equivalent tariff that would lead to the same reduction in import quantity as does the set of NTBs. (We will see explicitly what this means when we analyze the import quota in the next section.) Using this approach,

FIGURE 9.1   Major Types of NTBs

Type	Description	Direct Effect(s)
Import quota	Quantitative limit on imports	Quantity
Voluntary export restraint (VER)	Quantitative limit on foreign exports (based on threat of import restriction)	Quantity
Tariff quota	Allows imports to enter the country at a low or zero tariff up to a specified quantity; imposes a higher tariff on imports above this quantity	Quantity (if the tariff for potential imports above the specified quantity is so high that it is prohibitive, so that there are no imports above the specified quantity)
Government procurement	Laws and government rules that favor local products when the government is the buyer	Quantity (for instance, an outright prohibition) Cost of importing (for instance, special procedures for imports)
Local content and mixing requirements	Require specified use of local labor, materials, or other products	Quantity
Technical and product standards	Discriminate against imports by writing or enforcing standards in a way that adversely affects imports more than domestic products	Cost (to conform to standards or demonstrate compliance) Uncertainty (if approval procedures are unclear)
Advance deposit	Requires some of the value of intended imports to be deposited with the government and allows the government to pay low or zero interest on these deposits	Cost (forgone interest)
Import licensing	Requires importers to apply for and receive approval for intended imports	Cost (of application procedure) Uncertainty (if timing of, or basis for, approval is unclear)
Other customs procedures (classification of product, valuation of product, procedures for clearing)	Affect the amount of tariff duties owed or the quota limit applied; procedures can be slow or costly	Cost Uncertainty

and averaging across products, Kee et al. estimate that the country's NTBs create protection against imports that is the equivalent of an average tariff of 5.5 percent for the United States, 3.0 percent for Canada, 9.6 percent for the European Union, 8.5 percent for Japan, 6.4 percent for China, and 13.9 percent for Mexico.

The World Trade Organization has rules that try to limit the use of nontariff barriers, and it serves as a forum for negotiations to reduce NTBs. The first box of this chapter, "The WTO: Beyond Tariffs," describes the role of the WTO (and the GATT before it) in areas that extend outside its traditional focus on reducing tariffs on nonagricultural goods. Pressures for tariff and nontariff barriers to imports usually rise during recessions. The second box, "Dodging Protectionism," examines how the world managed to limit new import barriers that could have made the global financial and economic crisis worse.

THE IMPORT QUOTA

The best-known nontariff barrier is the **import quota** (or just **quota**), a limit on the total quantity of imports of a product allowed into the country during a period of time (for instance, a year). One way or another, the government gives out a limited number of licenses to import the quota quantity legally and prohibits importing without a license. As long as the quota quantity is less than the quantity that people would want to import without the quota, the quota has an impact on the market for this product.

There are several reasons why protectionists and government officials may favor using a quota instead of a tariff. For instance,

- A quota ensures that the quantity of imports is strictly limited; a tariff would allow the import quantity to increase if foreign producers cut their prices or if our domestic demand increases.
- A quota gives government officials greater power. As we will see below, these officials often have administrative authority over who gets the import licenses under a quota system, and they can use this power to their advantage (for instance, by taking bribes).

Note that these are not arguments showing that an import quota is in the national interest.

Let's compare the quota to a tariff as a way of impeding imports. A tariff increases the domestic price of the imported product and reduces the quantity imported. A quota reduces the quantity imported. Does a quota also increase the domestic price of the imported product? We will see that the answer is yes. In fact, we will see that, in most ways, the effects of a quota are the same as the effects of a tariff that leads to the same quantity of imports as the quota, if markets are perfectly competitive.

As we did with the analysis of the tariff, we begin our analysis of the quota with the small-country case and then proceed to the large-country case. Our analysis in the text assumes that all relevant markets are highly competitive. (The Extension box "A Domestic Monopoly Prefers a Quota" examines an alternative case.)

Quota versus Tariff for a Small Country

The effects of a quota on bicycles are portrayed in Figure 9.2 for a small importing country facing a given world price of $300 per bicycle. Recall that a country is "small"

FIGURE 9.2   The Effects of an Import Quota under Competitive Conditions, Small Importing Country

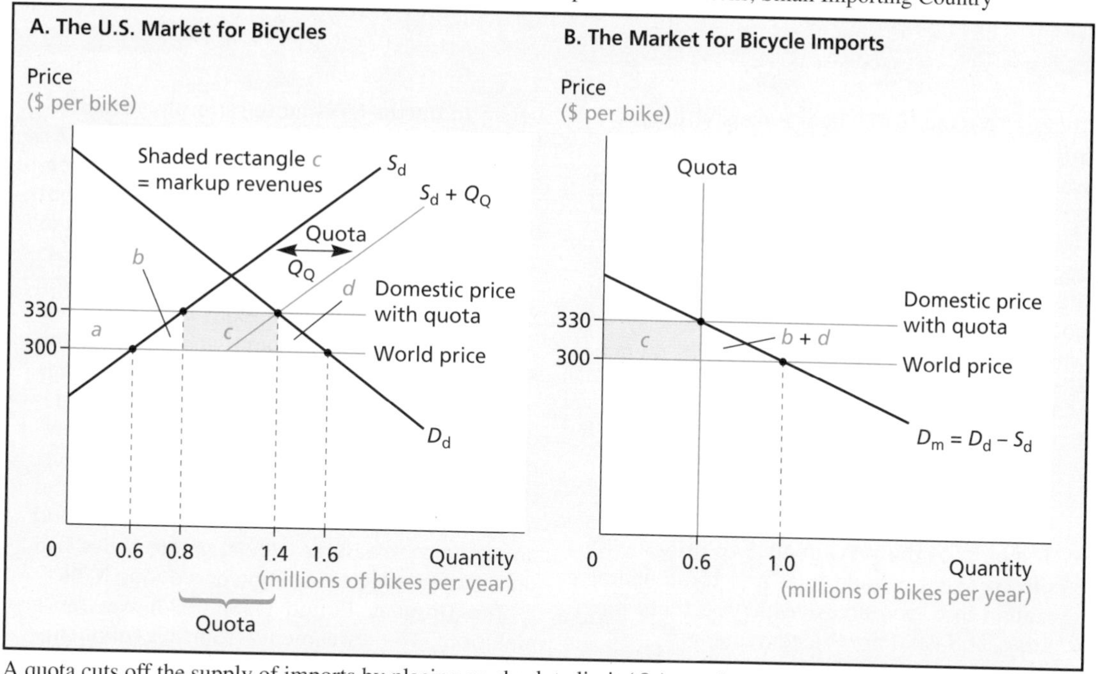

A quota cuts off the supply of imports by placing an absolute limit (Q_Q) on what can be bought from abroad. Under the competitive conditions shown here, the effects of an import quota are the same as those of a tariff that cuts imports just as much (with the possible exception of who gets shaded area *c*). To see this, compare the prices, quantities, and areas *a*, *b*, *c*, and *d* shown here with those shown in Figure 8.4.

if its decisions about how much to import of a product have no effect on the going world price of the product. That is, the foreign supply of exports to this small country is infinitely elastic at this price. In our example in Figure 9.2, the country would import 1.0 million bikes per year with free trade. The government then imposes a quota that limits imports to a smaller quantity, say, 0.6 million bikes per year.

   The quota alters the available supply of bicycles within the importing country. For all domestic prices at or above the world price, the total (domestic plus import) supply within the country equals the domestic supply curve plus the fixed quota quantity (Q_Q) of imports. At the domestic price of $300 there would be excess demand for bicycles in the importing country. The market in the importing country will clear only at the higher domestic price of $330, as shown by the intersection of the total available supply curve ($S_d + Q_Q$) and the domestic demand curve (D_d) on the left side of Figure 9.2. At the domestic price of $330, the domestic quantity supplied is 0.8 million, the quantity imported is the quota quantity of 0.6 million, and the domestic quantity demanded is 1.4 million. (We can see the same effect on domestic price by using the country's demand-for-imports curve shown in the right side of the figure. If the quota limits imports to 0.6 million, then the demand for imports indicates a price of $330.)

Global Governance   The WTO: Beyond Tariffs

The box "WTO and GATT: Tariff Success" in Chapter 8 introduced the World Trade Organization (WTO), which in 1995 subsumed the General Agreement on Tariffs and Trade (GATT). That box documented the success of the rounds of multilateral trade negotiations in reducing the tariffs imposed by industrialized countries on most nonagricultural goods. We now turn to examine three ways in which the WTO tries to go beyond tariffs on non-agricultural goods:

- As tariffs have declined, the use of nontariff import barriers has increased. How have the WTO and the GATT tried to limit and reduce nontariff barriers?
- The birth of the WTO in 1995 coincided with efforts to push trade rules and trade liberalization into new areas. What are these new areas, and what are the agreements?
- The current round of trade negotiations, the Doha Round, is an ambitious effort to push further, but as of late 2014 there had been modest progress. What are the key objectives of the Doha Round, and why the lack of progress?

NONTARIFF BARRIERS

The original GATT of 1947 included provisions that limited countries' use of some barriers to imports other than tariffs. Most important was a prohibition on the use of import quotas on non-agricultural goods. Countries complied by removing such quotas—another major success for the GATT. The agreement also stated that any governmental rules and regulations should not discriminate against imports; imports and domestic products should be treated equally, often called "national treatment." In addition, the agreement included provisions for national governments to take actions against foreign dumping using antidumping measures and against export subsidies using countervailing measures, topics that we will take up in Chapter 11.

As tariffs declined and NTBs (other than quotas) rose in importance, the GATT members began to discuss NTBs more seriously. Yet, negotiations have had less success in reducing NTBs. The protective effects of NTBs are harder to measure, so it is harder to get negotiated agreement on what constitutes an international exchange of "comparable" NTB reductions.

The Kennedy Round (1963–1967) included some NTB negotiations but the results were slim—one voluntary code on dumping and antidumping procedures. The Tokyo Round (1973–1979) made some progress and resulted in six voluntary codes on NTBs, covering customs valuation, import licensing procedures, government procurement, product standards and similar technical barriers, subsidies and countervailing measures, and dumping and antidumping measures. However, the codes had only modest effects in limiting or reducing NTBs.

The Uruguay Round (1986–1994) was more ambitious. The agreements from this round created the WTO, addressed a number of NTBs, and required that all countries joining the new WTO accept nearly all the NTB agreements. The Uruguay Round agreements also gave the new WTO a much stronger process for resolving disputes between countries about NTB and other trade issues. (Dispute settlement will be discussed in the final section of this chapter.)

The Uruguay Round agreements on NTBs are far-ranging and include new or revised codes on customs valuation, import licensing, import procedures, safeguards (temporary increased protection against import surges), subsidies, and dumping. Codes on technical standards established two rules to reduce the use of standards as subtle NTBs. Standards and regulations should not restrict imports more than the minimum necessary to achieve their legitimate objectives, and standards about food safety should be based on scientific evidence. Another major outcome was that governments agreed to phase out the global web of voluntary export restraints on textiles and clothing (a topic taken up in a case study later in this chapter). In addition, governments agreed to end the use of most other VERs, and they agreed to limit their use of domestic content requirements.

NEW AREAS

The Uruguay Round agreement established WTO rules to cover three areas that had received almost no attention in previous rounds. First, the treatment of agricultural goods was shifted to be similar to that of industrial goods. Tariffs (and tariff-rate quotas) have replaced many agricultural import quotas and other NTBs. In addition, governments agreed to limits on their domestic subsidies to agricultural production and to some reductions of their export subsidies for agricultural products. Overall, the effects of these changes have been modest. For instance, the new tariffs were usually set high enough that there has been little increase in total trade.

Second, the agreement on "trade-related intellectual property" created global rules requiring protections of patents, copyrights, and trademarks. The purpose is to get all governments behind efforts to prevent counterfeiting of branded products and pirating of technology, software, music, and films.

Third, the Uruguay Round established a new set of rules, the General Agreement on Trade in Services. Many countries limit international trade in services with legal red tape or with outright bans on foreign providers. This new agreement provides a framework for efforts to liberalize trade in services, although it contained little in the way of actual liberalizations. Subsequently, there was some progress. In 1997, 69 countries reached an agreement to open up national markets for basic telecommunications services, and 70 countries reached an agreement to remove restrictions in banking, financial services, and insurance.

THE DOHA ROUND

The effort to launch a new round of multilateral trade negotiations in the late 1990s was turbulent in two ways. First, the WTO, with its broader mandate, became a focal point for protests against globalization. Second, the governments

of the member countries had difficulty agreeing on what the new round should accomplish, a challenge because decision making in the WTO is generally by consensus.

Since the late 1990s protests have swirled around meetings of the WTO and other international organizations. Many groups have been involved, including human-rights activists, environmentalists, consumer-rights advocates, organized labor (unions), anti-immigration groups, animal-rights activists, and anarchists. It is not easy to summarize their positions toward the WTO, but prominent complaints and demands, some of them contradictory with others, have included:

- That the WTO is too powerful, undemocratic, and secretive and should be abolished or greatly reined in.
- That the WTO should expand the use of its powers to achieve goals other than free trade, especially such goals as environmental protection and better wages and working conditions in developing countries.
- That the WTO is the tool of big business and that freer trade benefits corporations and capitalists while hurting the environment, local cultures, and workers.

After failing to begin the new round at the WTO ministerial conference in Seattle in 1999, the next conference was in Doha, Qatar, in 2001. Developing countries believed that they had not received a fair deal in the Uruguay Round. They incurred substantial costs by accepting the mandatory NTB rules and the mandatory protections of intellectual property, but their benefits of greater access to export markets in the industrialized countries were limited by the slow end to the VERs on clothing and textiles and by the lack of actual liberalization of agricultural trade. Developing country governments pushed for a "development round" and vowed to be more active in the negotiations.

After much wrangling at the 2001 meeting, the ministers agreed on the agenda and

—Continued on next page

launched the Doha Round of trade negotiations. Each of the major players (the United States, the European Union, and the developing countries) compromised to reach the consensus. Key elements of the ambitious agenda include substantial liberalization of agricultural trade, reductions of tariffs on nonagricultural goods, liberalization of trade in services, provision of assured access by developing countries to low-cost medicines to protect public health, and refinement of rules governing various NTBs. (In a separate agreement reached in 2003, developing countries gained the right to import cheap generic versions of patented drugs in health emergencies.)

The Doha Round negotiations have been intermittent and mostly unproductive for more than a decade. A meeting in July 2008 seemed to make progress but collapsed when some developing countries, led by India and China, demanded a "safeguard" process that would allow them to easily increase tariffs on imports of agricultural products if and when such imports increased.

In December 2013 the WTO members reached a multilateral trade agreement about trade facilitation, a small part of the Doha agenda. Countries agreed to lower costs and to accept binding standards for customs and border procedures. Most of the benefits from the agreement will go to developing countries. However, in mid-2014 India blocked the process to adopt the agreement.

Discussions about other aspects of the Doha agenda have continued, but progress has remained elusive. The United States has resisted meaningful cuts in its agricultural subsidies. The European Union has sought to limit lowering its barriers to agricultural imports. India, Brazil, and other developing countries have been unwilling to reduce tariffs and to open up service sectors.

These effects on domestic price and quantities should sound familiar. They are the same as the effects of the 10 percent tariff shown in Figures 8.2 through 8.4. For a competitive market, the effects of a quota on price, quantities, and well-being are the same as those of an equivalent tariff, with one possible exception. Here are the effects that are the same. In comparison with free trade:

- The quota results in a higher price and larger production quantity, so domestic producers gain surplus equal to area *a*.
- With the higher price and smaller consumption quantity, domestic consumers lose surplus equal to area $a + b + c + d$.
- Area *b* is a loss to the country. The quota induces domestic producers to increase production from 0.6 to 0.8 million. The marginal costs of producing these additional bicycles at home rise up to $330 (along S_d), when these additional bicycles instead could be purchased from foreign exporters for only $300.
- Area *d* is also a loss to the country. The quota reduces quantity consumed from 1.6 million to 1.4 million. The consumer surplus lost on these bicycles is not a gain to anyone else.

Therefore, the quota creates the same two deadweight losses $(b + d)$, as does the tariff.

This leaves rectangular area *c*, the "possible exception" to the equivalence. With a tariff, area *c* is government tariff revenue. With a quota, what is it? Who gets it?

Global Crisis   Dodging Protectionism

If this bill is enacted into law, we will have a renewed era of prosperity . . .

Representative Willis Hawley, Republican of Oregon, June 1930

The global crisis that began in 2007 was the worst global economic crisis since the Great Depression of the 1930s. Protectionism played a key role in the Great Depression, but fortunately history did not repeat itself.

As the Great Depression began in 1929, the U.S. Congress was debating a bill to increase U.S. tariffs. The notorious Smoot-Hawley tariff bill was passed in June 1930. By itself, its tariff increases were not that large, adding several percentage points to average U.S. tariffs. But it did not lead to prosperity. Rather, other countries retaliated against the United States by enacting similar tariff increases. The average world tariff rose from 9 percent in 1929 to 20 percent in 1933. By 1933 world trade had fallen to only one-third its 1929 level. While much of this decline was the decrease in trade that accompanies macroeconomic reductions in national production and income levels, at least one-quarter of the decline was due to the rapid rise in protectionism around the world. Protectionism did not cause the Great Depression, but it did make it longer and worse than it otherwise would have been.

As the global crisis of the 2000s deepened, some countries again resorted to forms of protectionism. What happened, and how did we avoid a repeat of the 1930s? There were no widespread increases in tariffs (or in antidumping duties, which we will discuss in Chapter 11), although a few countries, Russia, Argentina, and Turkey, did increase tariffs by an average of about one percentage point. Overall, global tariff increases explain very little of the trade decline described in the box "The Trade Mini-Collapse of 2009" in Chapter 2. A number of countries increased nontariff barriers to trade:

- Some imposed tougher import licensing; for example, Argentina shifted to discretionary licensing for imports of car parts, televisions, shoes, and some other items.
- Some enacted more complicated customs procedures; for example, Indonesia limited imports of clothes, shoes, toys, and some other goods to only five ports of entry.
- Some adopted new product standards that blocked some imports; for example, China against certain European foods and beverages and India against Chinese toys.
- Some placed new "buy domestic" requirements on government spending as part of fiscal stimulus efforts; for example, new "Buy American" rules in the U.S. stimulus bill passed in 2009.

Still, overall the new protectionist measures were modest. The WTO estimated that less than 1 percent of world trade was affected.

Three forces were at work to limit increases in import barriers. First, world leaders did not want to repeat the experience of the 1930s. For example, in November 2008, at the meeting of the Group of 20 (G-20) major countries, leaders of these countries formally declared that they committed to "refrain from raising new barriers to investment or to trade in goods and services." Second, the WTO as a strong multilateral organization reinforced the resolve, through its agreed principles and rules and through its monitoring and reporting of trade policy developments. Third, in many countries the government policy response was focused more on bailouts (for example, financial institutions) and subsidies to domestic firms (for example, auto producers) than on directly limiting imports. Such subsidies can distort trade, but the subsidies did not lead to widespread policy retaliation or destruction of trade. Fortunately for the world, after the mini-trade collapse of late 2008 and 2009, world trade bounced back.

Ways to Allocate Import Licenses

The quota license to import is a license to buy the product from foreign suppliers at the world price of $300 and resell these units at the domestic price of $330. The quota results in a price markup (or economic rent) of $30 per unit imported. For all units imported with the quota, the markup totals to rectangular area c.

Who gets this rectangle of price markup? That depends on how the licenses to import the quota quantity are distributed. Here are the main ways to allocate import licenses:[1]

- The government allocates the licenses for free to importers using a rule or process that involves (almost) no resource costs.
- The government auctions off the licenses to the highest bidders.
- The government allocates the licenses to importers through application and selection procedures that require the use of substantial resources.

Let's look at each of these, examining who gets area c and whether this affects our view of the inefficiency of the quota.

Fixed Favoritism

Import licenses adding up to the total quota can be allocated for free on the basis of **fixed favoritism,** in which the government simply assigns the licenses to firms (and/or individuals) without competition, applications, or negotiation. In this case the importers lucky enough to receive the import licenses will get area c. Each of them should be able to buy from some foreign exporter(s) at the world price (playing different foreign exporters off against each other if any one of them tries to charge a higher price). The importers can resell the imports at the higher domestic price. The price difference is pure profit ($30 per bike in our example). Area c is then a redistribution of well-being from domestic consumers in the importing country to the favored importers with the quota licenses. Using the one-dollar, one-vote metric, this method of allocating the quota licenses does not create any additional inefficiency (as long as no resources are used up in allocating the quota rights).

One common way of fixing the license recipients and amounts is to give the licenses to firms that were doing the importing before the quota was imposed, in the same proportion to the amounts that they had previously been importing. This is how the U.S. government ran its oil import quotas between 1959 and 1973. Licenses to import were simply given to companies on the basis of the amount of oil they had imported before 1959. There is a political reason for allocating import licenses in this way. The importers generally will be hurt by the imposition of a quota, and they would then be a group opposing the quota. However, if they receive

---

[1]There is a fourth way that the quota licenses might be distributed. The importing country government could allocate the licenses to the exporting firms (or to others in the exporting country). In this case (but not in the three cases shown in the text), the exporters ought to be able to raise their export price, so this fourth case is essentially the same as that of the voluntary export restraint discussed in the next major section of this chapter.

the valuable quota licenses, they are much less likely to oppose the quota. Although they will have a lower volume of import business, the importing that they do will be very profitable.

Auction

The government can run an import license auction, selling import licenses on a competitive basis to the highest bidders. Would someone be willing to pay something to buy a quota license? Yes, because the right to acquire imports at the low world price and sell these imports at the higher domestic price is valuable. How much would some individuals be willing to pay in a competitive auction? An amount very close to the price difference—in our example, an amount very close to $30 per bike. If the winning bids in the auction are very close to this price difference, who gets area c? The government gets (almost all of) it, in the form of auction revenues. In this case, the auction revenues to the government will be (almost) equal to the revenues that the government would instead collect with the equivalent tariff.

Public auctions of import licenses are rare. They were used in Australia, New Zealand, and Colombia in the 1980s. In New Zealand, once or twice a year the government auctioned the rights to import over 400 different goods. For a sample of these auctions for which data are available, the bidders paid, on average, about 20 percent of the world price to acquire the quota licenses. The quotas for these products were equivalent to an average tariff of about 20 percent.

There is an informal variant of a quota auction that is probably more prevalent. Corrupt government officials can do a thriving business by selling import licenses "under the table" to whoever pays them the highest bribes. As with other forms of corruption, this variant of the auction entails some social costs that go beyond economic market inefficiency. Persistent corruption can cause talented persons to become bribe-harvesting officials instead of pursuing productive careers. Public awareness of corruption also raises social tensions over injustice in high places.

Resource-Using Procedures

Instead of holding an auction, the government can insist that firms (and/or individuals) that want to acquire licenses must compete for them in some way other than simple bidding or bribing. Resource-using application procedures include allocating quota licenses on a first-come, first-served basis; on the basis of demonstrating need or worthiness; or on the basis of negotiations. With first-come, first-served allocation, those seeking the licenses use resources to try to get to and stay at the front of the line. An example of allocation by worthiness is awarding quota licenses for materials or components based on how much production capacity firms have for producing the products that use these inputs. This approach encourages resource wastage because it causes firms to overinvest in production capacity in the hope of obtaining more quota licenses. An example of resource wastage from negotiation is the time and money spent on lobbying with government officials to press each firm's case for receiving quota licenses.

What amount of resources would be used by firms seeking quota licenses? It would be rational for the firms to use resources up to the value of the licenses themselves—that is, up to the value of area c. Using resources in this way is privately sensible for each

Extension   A Domestic Monopoly Prefers a Quota

The analysis of an import quota presented in the text presumes that the domestic industry in the importing country is highly competitive. With perfect competition we saw that the effect of the quota on domestic producer surplus is the same as the effect of a tariff that results in the same quantity of imports. In this case the domestic industry would not have a strong preference between the quota and the equivalent tariff.

Domestic industries are often highly competitive, but not always. Especially for a small country, in some industries no more than one or two domestic firms can achieve scale economies in production if they are selling only to local consumers. This would be true for industries like automobiles or steel.

If the domestic industry is a monopoly, would the monopoly have a preference between a tariff and a quota? The answer is yes. The monopoly prefers the quota (even if the monopoly does not get any of the price markup on the imports themselves). Let's look at this more closely. (We assume that the importing country is a small country, but the same idea holds for the large-country case.)

The domestic monopoly would like to use its market power to set the domestic price to maximize its profits. But with *free trade* the world price becomes the domestic price. Imports entering the country at the world price prevent the domestic monopoly from charging a higher price than the world price. If it did try to charge a higher price, most consumers would just buy imports. Free trade is a good substitute for national antitrust or antimonopoly policy.

If the country's government imposes a *tariff*, the domestic price rises to be the world price plus the tariff. The pricing power of the monopoly is still severely limited. If the monopoly tries to charge more than this tariff-inclusive price, again most consumers would just buy imports. Domestic consumers can buy as much of the imported product as they wish, as long as they are willing to pay the tariff-inclusive price. They will not pay more for the locally produced product.

If instead the country's government imposes a *quota*, the whole game changes. No matter how high the monopoly raises its domestic

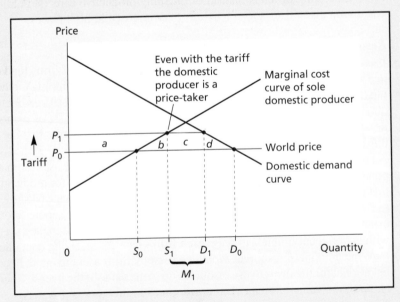

Tariff, domestic monopoly.

price, imports cannot exceed the quota quantity. Domestic consumers cannot just shift to imports because there is a strict limit on how much they can import. The marginal source of more of the product is now the domestic monopoly. After allowing for the quota quantity of imports, the domestic monopoly can set the domestic price to maximize its profits. In comparison to a tariff that results in the same quantity of imports, the domestic monopoly prefers an import quota because the monopoly can set a higher price and garner larger profits. However, these higher profits come at a cost to the importing country as a whole. If the domestic industry is a monopoly, the quota causes a larger net national loss.

A pair of graphs for the domestic monopoly can highlight the differences between the tariff and the quota. The figure on the previous page shows the case of the tariff. With free trade at the world price P_0, the monopolist cannot charge a price higher than P_0, so the monopoly produces all units for which its marginal costs are less than this free-trade price. The tariff raises the domestic price to P_1, but

the monopolist cannot charge a higher price than this tariff-inclusive price. The monopolist increases production from S_0 to S_1 and increases its profits by area a. Imports with the tariff are M_1. The net loss in national well-being because of the tariff equals area $b + d$.

The figure below shows what happens if this same M_1 quantity of imports is instead set as a quota. With the fixed quota quantity of imports, the monopoly views its market as domestic demand less this quota quantity (for all prices above the world price P_0). That is, the monopoly faces the downward-sloping net demand curve (the domestic demand curve minus the quota quantity). Using the net demand curve, the monopoly can determine the marginal revenue from lowering price to sell additional units. The monopoly maximizes profit when marginal revenue equals marginal cost, producing and selling quantity S_2 and charging price P_2.

In comparison with the tariff, the monopoly uses the quota to increase the product price ($P_2 > P_1$), to reduce the quantity that it produces and sells ($S_2 < S_1$), and to increase its profit. The monopoly prefers the quota, but the monopoly's

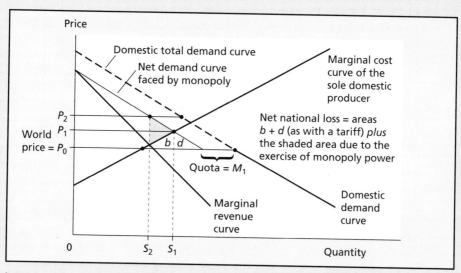

Import quota, domestic monopoly.

—Continued on next page

gain comes with some additional social cost. In comparison with the tariff, the economic inefficiency of the quota is larger. The nation as a whole loses not only area *b* + *d* but also the shaded area. The shaded area is the additional social loss from unleashing the monopoly's power to restrict production and raise prices. Additional consumers are squeezed out of the market, and they suffer an additional loss of consumer surplus that is not a gain for any other group.

We can combine this conclusion with the conclusions reached in the text. For the nation as a whole, at best the quota is no worse than an equivalent tariff as a way of impeding imports. The import quota is worse than the tariff in two cases:

- If quota licenses are allocated through resource-using application and selection procedures.
- If a dominant domestic firm can use the quota to assert its monopoly pricing power.

individual firm seeking to get the economic rents created by the licenses. But, from the point of view of the entire country, these *resources used up in the rent-seeking activities are being wasted* (compared to the other two ways of allocating quota licenses or compared to having no quota at all).

Resource-using procedures encourage rent-seeking activities, and some or all of area *c* is turned into a loss to society by wasting productive resources. The *inefficiency of the quota is greater than area b + d because it also includes some of area c.* In this case the quota is worse than the equivalent tariff in its effects on net national well-being.

Quota versus Tariff for a Large Country

Figure 9.3 shows the effects of a quota for a country whose import demand for this product is large enough to affect world prices. A large country faces an upward-sloping foreign supply-of-exports curve. With free trade, the country would import 1.0 million bicycles per year and the world price would be $300 per bicycle. The government then imposes an import quota that reduces the import quantity to 0.8 million bicycles. By looking at the right-hand side of Figure 9.3, we see the effects of the quota on prices. Domestic import buyers will pay $315 per bicycle if the import quantity is limited to 0.8 million. Foreign exporters will compete among themselves to make this limited amount of export sales, and they will bid the export price down to $285.

We can use these prices and the left-hand side of Figure 9.3 to see what is happening in the domestic market for the country that is importing bicycles. When the domestic price increases to $315, domestic quantity supplied increases to 0.7 million and domestic quantity consumed decreases to 1.5 million.

If we compare a quota to its equivalent tariff for the large-country case (by comparing Figure 9.3 to Figure 8.5), we reach the same general conclusion for the large-country case that we reached for the small-country case. With the same exception of who gets the price markup from the quota (area *c* + *e* in the large-country case), the effects of the quota are the same as those of the equivalent

FIGURE 9.3 The Effects of an Import Quota under Competitive Conditions, Large Importing Country

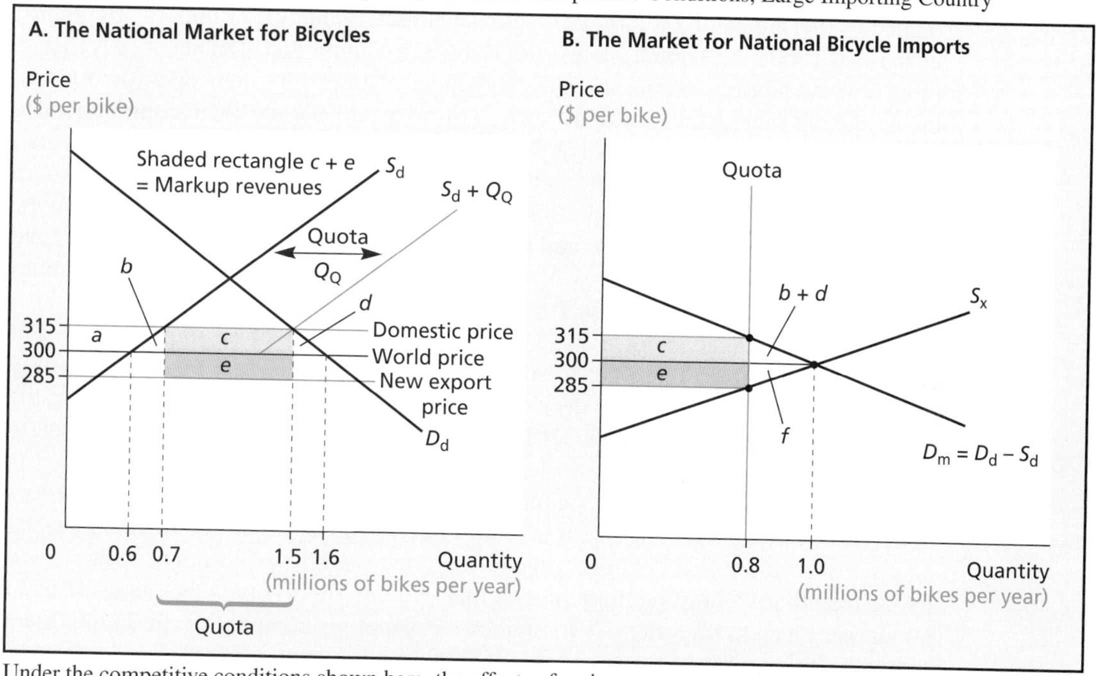

A. The National Market for Bicycles

Price
($ per bike)

Shaded rectangle $c + e$
= Markup revenues

S_d

$S_d + Q_Q$

Quota
Q_Q

b

a

c

d

e

315
300
285

Domestic price
World price
New export price

D_d

0   0.6 0.7   1.5 1.6   Quantity
(millions of bikes per year)

Quota

B. The Market for National Bicycle Imports

Price
($ per bike)

Quota

$b + d$

S_x

c

e

f

315
300
285

$D_m = D_d - S_d$

0   0.8   1.0   Quantity
(millions of bikes per year)

Under the competitive conditions shown here, the effects of an import quota are the same as those of a tariff that cuts imports just as much (with the possible exception of who gets shaded area $c + e$).

tariff. If the quota licenses can be distributed with minimal resource costs, then the effect on net national well-being of the import quota is the gain of area e less the loss of area $b + d$.

If the exporters are passive, then a large country can gain net national well-being by imposing an import quota, and there is an optimal quota that maximizes the gain in national well-being. The nationally optimal quota is 0.67 million bicycles per year, the same quantity of imports that results from the optimal tariff shown in Figure 8.6. The cautions for the use of an optimal quota are the same as those for the optimal tariff. The quota hurts the foreign country, and the foreign country may choose to retaliate. Even if the foreign country does not retaliate, the quota causes worldwide inefficiency. In comparison with free trade, the loss in world well-being is area $b + d$ plus area f in the right-hand side of Figure 9.3.

VOLUNTARY EXPORT RESTRAINTS (VERs)

A **voluntary export restraint (VER)** is an odd-looking trade barrier in which the importing country government compels the foreign exporting country to agree "voluntarily" to restrict its exports to this country. The export restraint usually requires that foreign exporting firms act as a cartel, restricting sales and raising prices. Yes, that's right—through the VER the importing country actually gives foreigners monopoly power, forces them to take it, and calls their compliance voluntary!

VERs have been used by large countries as a rear-guard action to protect their industries that are having trouble competing against a rising tide of imports. Beginning in the late 1960s the United States, the European Union, and Canada used VERs to limit imports while avoiding the embarrassment of imposing their own import quotas or raising their own tariffs, as such actions would violate their commitment to the international rules of the WTO. The countries most often forced to restrict their exports have been Japan, Korea, and the transition countries of Central and Eastern Europe. The box "VERs: Two Examples" describes both Japan's limit of car exports to the United States in the 1980s and the pervasive set of export quotas in textiles and clothing for almost half a century. Agricultural goods, steel, footwear, and electronics are other products that often have been restricted by VERs.

The graphical analysis of a VER is very similar to that of an import quota. For instance, we can use Figure 9.2 to show the effects of a VER for a small importing country. The amount Q_Q is now the export quota imposed by the VER. (Similarly, the graphs showing the effects of the VER for a large importing country would be nearly identical to Figure 9.3.)

Consider the small importing country shown in Figure 9.2. The two key differences between a VER (or any other form of export quota) and an import quota are the *effect on the export price* and *who gets area c,* the price markup or economic rent created by the quantitative limit on trade. Recall that with an import quota the quota rights to import are given to importers. If foreign export supply is competitive, these importers should be able to buy at the world price ($300 in our bicycle example) and sell these imports domestically at the higher price ($330). The price markup (area *c*) stays within the importing country.

With the VER, the exporting country's government usually distributes to its producers licenses to export specified quantities. The export producers should realize that there is much less incentive to compete among themselves for export sales. Instead, they should act as a cartel that has agreed to limit total sales and to divide up the market. Faced with limited export quantity (0.6 million bikes in Figure 9.2), the exporters should charge the highest price that the market will bear. *The export price rises to $330,* the highest price that import demanders will pay for this quantity. Therefore, *the foreign exporters now get area c* as additional revenue on the VER-limited quantity of exports.[2]

For the importing country, how does the cost of a VER compare to either an import quota or free trade? *In comparison to an import quota* (which uses minimal resources to administer), the VER causes a loss of area *c*. This is the amount paid to the foreign exporters rather than kept within the importing country. It is a national loss due to a deterioration in the importing country's terms of trade (the higher price paid to foreign exporters) because of the VER. *In comparison to free trade,* the net loss to the importing country because of the VER is area *b* + *c* + *d*. The VER may be a

---

[2]I learned of an interesting variation on this effect from one of my students a number of years ago. I noticed that each time I saw him outside of class he was driving a different expensive car. I complimented him on this, and he said that his family in India was doing very well. When I asked what they did, he said that they owned some of the VER rights to export clothing from India to countries like the United States. He said that his family actually did not bother to make clothing; instead they simply rented the export rights to local clothing manufacturers. Thus, his family did very well by getting some of area c created by the clothing VERs.

politically attractive way of offering protection to an import-competing industry, but it is also economically expensive for the importing country. (In addition, note that *for the world as a whole* the net loss in comparison to free trade is only area $b + d$. Area c is a transfer from consumers in the importing country to producers in the exporting country, so it is not a loss to the whole world.)

There is another important effect of the VER. For many products foreign producers can adjust the mix of varieties or models of the product that they export, while remaining within the overall quantitative limit. Usually, the profit margin on higher-quality varieties is larger, so the exporters shift toward exporting these varieties (a process called "quality upgrading"). As the Japanese firms implemented the VER on their auto exports to the United States, one part of their strategy was to shift the mix of models exported, away from basic subcompact cars (like the Honda Civic) and toward larger, fancier models (like the Honda Accord and eventually the Acura line). (In this auto case, there was one more notable effect. To avoid the sales limits created by the VER, Japanese automobile firms set up assembly operations in the United States. More generally, any import protection can serve as an incentive for direct investment into the importing country by the thwarted foreign exporters. We examine foreign direct investment in Chapter 15.)

OTHER NONTARIFF BARRIERS

In addition to quotas and VERs, there are many other kinds of nontariff import barriers. Indeed, we should be impressed with governments' creativity in coming up with new ways to discriminate against imports. Let's look more closely at three other NTBs from the vast toolkit used against imports. (The box "Carrots Are Fruit, Snails Are Fish, and X-Men Are Not Humans" provides more examples of creativity.)

Product Standards

If you are looking for rich variety and imagination in import barriers, try the panoply of laws and regulations pertaining to product quality, including those enforced in the names of health, sanitation, safety, and the environment. Such standards can be noble efforts to enhance society's well-being, by addressing market failures that lead to unsafe conditions and environmental degradation.

Standards that accomplish these goals need not discriminate against imports. But, if a government is determined to protect local producers, it can always write rules that can be met more easily by local products than by imported products. For instance, the standards can be tailored to fit local products but to require costly modifications to foreign products. Or the standards can be higher for imported products or enforced more strictly. Or the testing and certification procedures can be more costly, slower, or more uncertain for foreign products. Here are some examples to illustrate the ingenuity of the standard-setters.

In an obvious effort to protect domestic ranchers, the U.S. government in the past has found hidden health hazards in the way beef cattle are raised in Argentina. Similarly, the European Union (EU) has banned imports of beef from cattle that have received growth hormones, claiming that it is responding to public concerns about health dangers. The United States asserts that this is actually protection of European

Case Study   VERs: Two Examples

Voluntary export restraints provide for rich inter-play between economics and politics. Let's look at two examples. In the first, the United States forced one key exporter, Japan, to limit its exports of automobiles. In the second, a small VER, again between the United States and Japan, grew to become a wide-ranging set of export limits that covered many textile and clothing products, involved many countries, and lasted for decades.

AUTO VER: PROTECTION WITH INTEGRITY?

Before the mid-1970s import totals of automobiles into the United States were minuscule. Then, in the late 1970s sales of Japanese-made automo-biles accelerated in the United States. American buyers were looking for smaller cars in the wake of substantial increases in the price of oil. Japanese manufacturers offered good-quality smaller cars at attractive prices. Japanese cars were capturing a rapidly growing share of the U.S. auto market, U.S. production of cars was declining, American autoworkers were losing their jobs, and the U.S. auto companies were running low on profits.

In early 1981 the protectionist-pressure tacho-meter was in the red zone. Japanese auto exports were caught in the headlights, with Congress ready to impose strict import quotas if necessary. Ronald Reagan, the new U.S. president, had a problem. In March 1981, his cabinet was discuss-ing auto import quotas. Reagan's autobiography later explained his thinking at that moment:

> As I listened to the debate, I wondered if there might be a way in which we could maintain the integrity of our position in favor of free trade while at the same time doing something to help Detroit and ease the plight of thousands of laid-off assembly workers . . .
>
> I asked if anyone had any suggestions for striking a balance between the two positions. [Then–Vice President] George Bush spoke up: "We're *all* for free enterprise, but would any of us find fault if Japan announced without any request from us that they were going to *volun-tarily* reduce their exports of autos to America?"*

A few days later Reagan met with the Japanese foreign minister.

> Foreign Minister Ito . . . was brought into the Oval Office for a brief meeting . . . I told him that our Republican administration firmly opposed import quotas but that strong sentiment was building in Congress among Democrats to impose them.
>
> "I don't know whether I'll be able to stop them," I said. "But I think if you *voluntarily* set a limit on your automobile exports to the country, it would probably head off the bills pending in Congress and there wouldn't be any mandatory quotas."*

The Japanese government got the message and "voluntarily" agreed to make sure that Japanese firms put the brakes on their exports to the United States. Maximum Japanese exports to the United States for each of the years 1981 through 1983 were set at a quantity of 1.8 million vehicles per year, about 8 percent less than what they had exported in 1980. As total automobile sales in the United States increased substantially after the 1981–1982 recession, the export limit was raised in 1984 to 2 million and in 1985 to 2.3 million. The export restraint continued to exist until 1994, but from 1987 on actual Japanese exports to the United States were less than the quota quantity. By 1987 Japanese firms were producing large numbers of cars in factories that they had recently built in the United States.

As a result of the VER, the profits of U.S. auto companies increased, as did production and employment in U.S. auto factories. What did the VER cost the United States? One study estimated that the VER cost U.S. consumers $13 billion in lost consumer surplus and that it imposed a net loss to the United States of $3 billion. Other esti-mates of these costs are even higher. "Protection with integrity" does not come cheap.

TEXTILES AND CLOTHING: A MONSTER

In 1955, a monster was born. In the face of rising imports from Japan, the U.S. government convinced the Japanese government to "voluntarily" limit

Japan's exports of cotton fabric and clothing to the United States. In the late 1950s, Britain followed by compelling India and Pakistan to impose VERs on their clothing and textile exports to Britain. The VERs were initially justified as "temporary" restraints in response to protectionist pleas from import-competing firms that they needed time to adjust to rising foreign competition. But the monster kept growing.

The 1961 Short-Term Arrangement led to the 1962 Long-Term Arrangement. In 1974, the Multifibre Arrangement extended the scheme to include most types of textiles and clothing. The trade policy monster became huge. A large and rising number of VERs, negotiated country by country and product by product, limited exports by developing countries to industrialized countries (and to a number of other developing countries).

The monster even had its own growth dynamic. A VER is, in effect, a cartel among the exporting firms. As they raise their prices, the profit opportunity attracts other, initially unconstrained suppliers. Production of textiles and clothing for export spread to countries such as Bangladesh, Cambodia, Fiji, and Turkmenistan. As these countries became successful exporters, the importing countries pressured them to enact VERs to limit their disruption to the managed trade.

The developing countries that were constrained by these VERs pushed hard during the Uruguay Round of trade negotiations to bring this trade back within the normal WTO rules (no quantitative limits, and any tariffs to apply equally to all countries—most favored nation treatment, rather than bilateral restrictions). The Agreement on Textiles and Clothing came into force in 1995 and provided for a 10-year period during which all quotas in this sector would be ended. On January 1, 2005, after almost a half century of life, the monster mostly died.

We say "mostly" because for a few more years a small piece of the monster lived on. As part of its accession agreement to the World Trade Organization, China accepted that other countries could impose China-specific "safeguards" if its rising exports of textiles or cloth-ing harmed import-competing producers. As the United States phased out VERs, the U.S. government imposed such safeguards on some imports from China. By late 2005 a comprehensive agreement limited imports of 22 types of products from China. Similarly, the European Union imposed safeguard limits on imports from China on 10 types of products. Then, the monster finally took its last breaths. The EU limits expired at the end of 2007 and the U.S. limits expired at the end of 2008. (Still, we do not have free trade in textiles and clothing because many countries continue to have relatively high import tariffs in this sector. But the web of VERs has ended.)

Consumers are the big winners from the liberalization. Prices generally fell by 10 to 40 percent when the VERs ended. Another set of winners is countries, including China, India, and Bangladesh, that have strong comparative advantage in textiles and clothing but whose production and exports had been severely constrained by the VERs. On the other side, with rising imports, textile and clothing firms and workers in the United States and other industrialized countries have been harmed. Another set of losers is those developing countries, apparently including Korea and Taiwan, that do not have comparative advantage in textile and clothing production but that had become producers and exporters of textiles and clothing because the VERs had severely restricted the truly competitive countries. (This shows another type of global production inefficiency that resulted from the VERs.) These uncompetitive countries lost the VER rents that they had been receiving, and their industries shrank as those in countries such as China expanded.

DISCUSSION QUESTION

In late 1981, your father went to a Honda dealer in his home state and paid about $1,000 more for a Civic than he would have paid the year before. Why?

*Ronald Reagan (1990), pp. 253–254 and 255. Emphasis in the original.

Case Study　Carrots Are Fruit, Snails Are Fish, and X-Men Are Not Humans

Governments have shown perhaps their greatest trade-policy creativity when deciding in what categories different imported goods belong. Their decisions are by no means academic. The stakes are high because an import that falls into one category can be allowed into the country duty-free, whereas the same import defined as falling into a related category is subject to a high tariff or banned altogether.

You can bet that if definitions matter so much to trade policy, there will be intense lobbying over each product's official definition. Protectionists will insist that an imported product be defined as belonging to the category with the high import barrier, but importing firms will demand that it be put in the duty-free category. When such strong pressures are brought on government, don't always expect logic in the official definitions.

Some of the resulting rules are bizarre. For example, here are two included in regulations passed by the European Union (EU) in 1994:

- Carrots are a fruit. This definition allows Portugal to sell its carrot jam throughout Western Europe without high duties.
- The land snail, famously served in French restaurants, is a fish. Therefore, European snail farmers can collect fish farm subsidies.

The U.S. government has similarly bent the rules. In the early 1990s Carla Hills, then the U.S. trade representative, was compelled to call the same car both American and "not American." She told the Japanese government that car exports from U.S. factories owned by Japanese firms to Japan were Japanese, not American. They did not count when the U.S. government examined the size of American car exports to Japan. At the same time, she told European governments that the cars exported to Europe from these same Japanese-owned factories in the United States were American, so they were

not subject to European quotas on Japanese car imports.

With even greater ingenuity private firms have changed the look and the names of their products to try to get around each set of official definitions. For instance, a VER on down-filled ski *parkas* led to the innovation of two new products that were not subject to VERs. One product was a down-filled ski *vest* that had one side of a zipper on each armhole. The other product was a *matched pair of sleeves,* with one side of a zipper at the top of each sleeve. Once the two products were imported "separately," the distributor knew what to do.

As another example, Subaru once imported pickup trucks with two flimsy "rear seats" bolted to the truck bed to avoid the U.S. tariff of 25 percent on "regular" pickup trucks. To avoid the same 25 percent U.S. duty, Ford imports vans from Turkey as "passenger wagons" because the vans have both rear side windows and rear seats. Once past customs Ford removes and trashes the rear windows and seats, replaces the windows with metal panels, and sells them as small commercial delivery vans.

In some cases it is a U.S. judge that makes the call. In 2001, a judge ruled that cheap children's Halloween costumes (think *Scream*) were "fancy dress apparel," not the "flimsy festive articles" that the U.S. Customs Service had long considered them. The suit was a victory for the U.S. producer, Rubie's Costume Company, that brought it. Rather than entering duty-free, imported costumes (that competed with Rubie's) would be subject to a tariff up to 32 percent and be covered by the VERs on clothing. Trick or treat?

In 2003, another U.S. judge studied opposing legal briefs and more than 60 action figures, both heroes and villains. Among her conclusions were that the X-Men were not humans, nor were many of the others. She was not just playing around: Toys that depict humans are dolls, subject to 12 percent import tariffs, but toys that depict nonhumans are just toys, subject to a 7 percent tariff.

Such games have been played with great frequency over the definitions of products. As long as definitions mean money gained or lost, products will be defined in funny ways.

DISCUSSION QUESTION

During your foreign travel in South Asia, you acquired an expensive, elaborately woven textile, size 1 meter by 2 meters. At customs as you are returning home, the official asks if it is a rug or a decorative wall hanging. What do you reply?

beef producers because the scientific evidence indicates that beef from cattle that receive growth hormones is safe and poses no risk to human health.

The EU requires that foreign facilities producing dairy products and many other animal products be approved as meeting EU public health standards. But it has not devoted many resources to the approval process, leading to waits of months for simple approvals. Health regulations set by the Mexican government require inspection and approval of factories making herbal and nutritional products that are sold in Mexico. However, for a number of years the Mexican authorities were unable to inspect factories in other countries.

The U.S. government has complained that Japan's procedures for approving pharmaceuticals and medical devices is slow. For instance, the Japanese government often requires clinical trials on Japanese patients, even though such trials simply duplicate those completed successfully in other countries. Since the mid-1990s, South Korea has imposed many new standards for automobiles, including a unique antipinch requirement for electric windows and a unique emissions standard, that are costly for foreign automakers to meet. In addition, in May 2006 the Korean tax authority took actions implying that owners of foreign cars would be more likely to be subject to tax audits. Automobile imports into Korea are remarkably low.

Product standards usually do not raise tariff or tax revenues for the importing country's government. On the contrary, enforcing these rules uses up government resources (and businesses must use resources to meet the standards). The standards can bring a net gain in overall well-being to the extent that they truly protect health, safety, and the environment. Yet it is easy for governments to disguise costly protectionism in virtuous clothing.

Domestic Content Requirements

A **domestic content requirement** mandates that a product produced and sold in a country must have a specified minimum amount of domestic production value, in the form of wages paid to local workers or materials and components produced within the country. Domestic content requirements can create import protection at two levels. They can be a barrier to imports of the products that do not meet the content rules. And they can limit the import of materials and components that otherwise would have been used in domestic production of the products. For instance, local content requirements for automobiles, used by Malaysia and other countries, force local auto manufacturers to use more domestically produced automobile components and parts (for instance, sheet metal or seat covers). If the domestic content requirement is set high enough, it can force domestic production of such expensive parts as engines or transmissions.

A closely related NTB, sometimes called a **mixing requirement,** stipulates that an importer or import distributor must buy a certain percentage of the product locally. For instance, the Philippine government has required that certain retail stores in the country must source at least 30 percent of their inventory in the Philippines. Such mixing requirements have also been used to restrict imports of foreign entertainment. Canada has imposed "Canada time" requirements on radio and TV stations, forcing them to devote a certain share of their air time to songs and shows recorded in Canada. Similarly, the EU, led by France, has waged a sustained war against American entertainment, partly by stipulating that minimum percentages of various forms of entertainment must be from domestic studios.

Like product standards, domestic content and mixing requirements do not generate tariff or tax revenue for the government. The gains on the price markups are captured by the protected home-country sellers of the protected products. These requirements create the usual deadweight losses because the protected local products are less desired or more costly to produce.

Government Procurement

Governments are major purchasers of goods and services. One estimate is that government purchases of products that could be traded internationally amount to close to one-tenth of all product sales in the industrialized countries. Government procurement practices can be a nontariff barrier to imports if the purchasing processes are biased against foreign products, as they often are. In many countries the governments buy relatively few imported products and instead buy mostly locally produced products.

In the United States, the Buy America Act of 1933 is the basic law that mandates that government-funded purchases favor domestic products. For different types of purchases the bias takes different forms, including prohibitions on buying imports, local content requirements, and mandating that domestic products be purchased unless imported products are priced much lower (for instance, at least one-third lower). More than half of the states and many cities and towns also have "Buy American" or "buy local" rules for purchases by their governments.

Many other countries have similar rules and practices. For instance, in Japan the U.S. government has complained that the Japanese government has limited foreign sales of telecommunications products and services to the government and government-owned companies by using both standards that are biased toward local products and short time periods for bidding. In India the government requires that the computers it purchases have a minimum proportion of locally produced components. In Greece the specifications for the goods and services that the government plans to buy are often vague and tend to favor local suppliers. It also appears that the Greek government informally favors Greek and other EU firms when making purchasing decisions.

HOW BIG ARE THE COSTS OF PROTECTION?

We have examined the effects of tariffs and nontariff barriers to imports. How important are these effects? Are the costs large or small? Large or small relative to what? We'll look first at their importance for the whole national economy, and then at their size in relation to producer benefits from the protection.

As a Percentage of GDP

One popular way of weighing the importance of any economic cost or benefit is to see whether it is a big part of the national economy, which we usually measure by the value of domestic production (gross domestic product, or GDP). Surprisingly, our basic theory indicates that the costs of protection for a typical industrialized country may be small, even if we ignore any favorable changes in the country's terms of trade (the small-country assumption).

Consider a diagram like Figure 8.4B. For a small country that imposes a tariff, area $b + d$, the net national loss from the tariff, equals one-half the tariff per unit times the reduction in the import quantity. Using this equality and some mathematical manipulation, we can write the expression for the net national loss as a percentage of GDP:[3]

$$\frac{\text{Net national loss from the tariff}}{\text{GDP}} = \tfrac{1}{2} \times \text{Tariff rate} \times \frac{\text{Percent reduction in import quantity}}{} \times \frac{\text{Import value}}{\text{GDP}}$$

A similar expression applies to a product affected by an import quota or some other nontariff barrier. (The percentage increase in domestic price that results from the NTB replaces the tariff rate.) Furthermore, we can use this expression to examine the effect of all tariffs and nontariff barriers imposed by the country. (Roughly, we get this expression if we add up all the losses for all products protected against imports.)

---

[3]Here is how we get this formula. Our analysis of tariffs in Chapter 8 indicates that the net national loss (a money amount) is the area of the triangle $b + d$ (or the sum of the two triangles b and d). Recalling that the area of a triangle is equal to one-half of the product of the base (the change in imports as the result of the tariff) and height (the tariff money amount per unit, which is equal to the percentage tariff rate times the import price):

Net national loss from the tariff = $\tfrac{1}{2}$ · (Reduction of import quantity) · (Tariff rate · Import price)

Then, divide the first term in parentheses on the right side of the equation by the import quantity (so it becomes reduction in import quantity divided by import quantity, which is the percent reduction in import quantity, stated in decimal form) and multiply the second term by the import quantity (so we obtain import price times import quantity, which is import value, as part of the expression). We then have:

Net national loss from the tariff = $\tfrac{1}{2}$ · (Percent reduction of import quantity) · (Tariff rate · Import value)

Now divide both sides of the equation by the money value of GDP and rearrange terms to obtain the expression in the text.

How large is the loss? Suppose, for example, that a nation's import tariffs are all 10 percent and that they cause a 20 percent reduction in import quantities. Suppose that total imports affected by these tariffs are 20 percent of GDP. In this realistic case, the net national loss from all tariffs on imports equals $\frac{1}{2} \times 0.10 \times 0.20 \times 0.20$, or only 0.2 percent of GDP! The net national loss from import protection is not likely to be large for a country that has rather low tariff levels and that is not that dependent on imports. The cost of protection is now relatively small for industrialized countries because the governments of these countries have cooperated to lower their trade barriers so much during the past half-century. (We also note that that 0.2 percent of U.S. GDP is about $34 billion, an amount that most of us would not think to be absolutely small.)

However, we also know that estimates based on this simple calculation can underestimate the costs of protection as a share of GDP. Here are five ways in which the true cost is probably bigger than the calculation above shows:

- *Foreign retaliation.* If our country has introduced barriers, other governments may retaliate by putting new barriers against our exports. The true costs would be higher than any shown in the diagram or the calculation above. The costs would be much higher in the event of a trade war, in which each side counterretaliates with still higher import barriers.

- *Enforcement costs.* Any trade barrier has to be enforced by government officials. That is costly because the people enforcing the trade barrier could have been productively employed elsewhere. Part of the revenues collected by the government (area c in our diagram) is the waste of society's resources used to enforce the barrier. This is a loss to the country, not just a pure redistribution from consumers to the government.

- *Rent-seeking costs.* Local firms seeking protection may use techniques such as lobbying that also use resources. If this is the case, then part of the producer surplus created by protection (area a in our diagram) is also a loss due to wasted resources, rather than a pure redistribution from consumers to producers. In addition, firms and individuals may use resources to try to claim the tariff revenues or the price markup on the quota quantity of imports, another reason that some of area c could be a national loss due to wasted resources.

- *Rents to foreign producers.* VERs encourage foreign exporters to raise their export prices. This is a third reason that some or all of area c could be a loss to the importing country.

- *Innovation.* Protection can mute the incentive to innovate new technology because there is less competitive pressure. In addition, protection can cause a loss to national well-being because it reduces the number of varieties of products available in the domestic market.

For any or all of these reasons, the cost of protection could be noticeably larger than the estimates from the simple calculations above, but it is not easy to say how much larger.

As the Extra Cost of Helping Domestic Producers

The political reason for import barriers is often to enhance the incomes of a threatened domestic industry. How much does it cost society for each dollar of additional producer surplus for the protected industries?

To see how much it might cost society to create a dollar of protected income, let's return to the calculation that led to our conclusion that import barriers cost only 0.2 percent of GDP. In this case, the tariffs gave domestic producers a 10 percent hike in the price of their products. If the threatened industries were 25 percent of GDP, then their gains in producer surplus, as a percentage of GDP, would be close to 10 percent times 25 percent, or 2.5 percent of GDP. Every dollar transferred to provide income for the protected industries also costs society an additional 8 cents (equal to 0.2 divided by 2.5) in deadweight losses. Thus, every dollar of protected income costs the rest of society $1.08 (the $1.00 transferred plus the extra loss of $0.08), even in this example in which the level of protection is moderate.

INTERNATIONAL TRADE DISPUTES

Each country's government sets its own trade policies, but these policies also have effects on other countries. With regularity policies enacted by one country incite complaints from other countries that the policies are harmful or unfair. We mentioned this issue at the end of the previous chapter. If one country enacts an optimal tariff, the benefits to this country come at the expense of other countries, who are worse off because their terms of trade decline and their firms lose export opportunities. These other countries should complain and may take actions in response. Disputes about nontariff barriers are at least as likely. NTBs raised by one country hurt other countries, just as tariffs would. In addition, actions that one country takes for some other reason (for instance, the adoption of rigorous product standards to protect public health) can be viewed as unfair trade barriers by other countries.

How an international trade dispute is resolved is important to the countries involved and to the world. If other countries respond by raising their own barriers in retaliation, then the world is worse off, and it is likely that most or all of the countries involved are worse off because they are mutually losing some of the gains from trade. If, instead, negotiations and diplomacy lead the countries to find a resolution that removes offending trade restrictions, then the world benefits, as countries move closer to free trade. The trick is how to avoid the first outcome and make the second more likely.

Countries' governments can informally discuss and negotiate with each other, but institutions and rules also matter. From its inception in 1947, the General Agreement on Tariffs and Trade had a mechanism for hearing disputes in which a member believed that another member had taken actions that violated a GATT rule or obligation. However, the resolution process had a major shortcoming—any GATT member, including the country that had the dispute ruling go against it, could block adoption of a ruling. As rulings were blocked, frustration with the system grew. This led to movement in two directions. First, the United States adopted a law that promoted its right to seek its own resolution if other countries were using unfair trade practices. Then, as part of the Uruguay Round agreements, the newly created World Trade Organization was given a stronger dispute resolution process.

America's "Section 301": Unilateral Pressure

As the U.S. government became frustrated with the shortcomings of the GATT dispute resolution process, it enacted Section 301 of the Trade Act of 1974, which gives the

Focus on China   China in the WTO

After 15 years of complex and sometimes difficult negotiations, China became a member of the WTO in late 2001. To become a member, a country must gain acceptance from all WTO members (an example of WTO decision making by consensus). In this process, China agreed to make major changes in many of its trade policies and other economic policies—in some ways the commitments go well beyond those of members who joined many years ago.

Has China gained what it hoped from its membership in the WTO? Broadly, China has obtained substantial benefits from freer trade. China's trade continues to grow rapidly, as does its economy. China has gained the general benefits of WTO membership. China now has MFN treatment by other members. It has gained a seat at WTO-sponsored multilateral trade negotiations, although its role in the Doha Round negotiations was low-keyed until 2008.

As a WTO member, China qualified for the end of the VERs that limited its exports of clothing and textiles. As discussed in the box earlier in the chapter, when the VERs were removed, China's exports were limited for a few more years by safeguards imposed by the United States and the European Union. Still, its export of these products has grown rapidly during the past decade.

China's entry into the WTO has continued its integration into the global economy, and it became more attractive as a destination for direct investments by foreign firms (a topic taken up in more depth in Chapter 15). In turn, the operations of foreign firms in China have spurred its trade and economic growth. In addition, the WTO commitments have been useful in domestic politics, by strengthening the positions of reformers within the Chinese government leadership.

In pursuit of these economic benefits, what commitments did China make to join the WTO, and how has it been doing in meeting these commitments? Here are some major areas covered by the accession agreement.

- Tariff reductions: China had been reducing its tariff rates prior to joining the WTO, and it continued to do so. For industrial products, the average tariff rate has declined to 9 percent from 14 percent in 2001. Some reductions are dramatic. The tariff on autos declined from 80 percent to 25 percent, and tariffs on computers, telecommunications equipment, and other information technology products were eliminated. For agricultural products, China has dropped its average tariff to 16 percent from 23 percent in 2001. All tariff rates are bound (so that China cannot arbitrarily increase them in the future).

- Services: China agreed to a range of commitments under the General Agreement on Trade in Services to provide better market access for foreign services firms. For instance, China has removed or liberalized limits on the local activities of foreign firms engaged in banking, financial services, and insurance. Still, foreign firms have expressed some concerns that other rules and regulations have been used to limit their ability to benefit from the changes. High capital requirements have been imposed on foreign-owned banks and the process of gaining approvals for new office locations and for additional products has been costly and slow. Another concern is that China has failed to implement a process for approving the entry of foreign firms providing computer travel reservation services.

- Intellectual property: China agreed to bring its laws protecting intellectual property rights (patents, brand names and trademarks, and copyright) into conformity with WTO and other international standards and to enforce these laws. China's laws are generally in conformity. However, there remain major concerns that piracy and product counterfeiting are rampant and that the laws are not enforced.

Overall, China has made major changes, including amending several thousand laws and regulations. China generally has met the commitments that it made to join the WTO, though in some areas it has been slow or has taken other actions that offset some of its liberalizations.

By joining the WTO, China also became part of the WTO's dispute settlement system. After a slow start, China is now fully enmeshed in the system. Before 2007, China filed only one complaint and was the respondent to only four complaints from other countries (and three of these were about the same matter). Since 2007, China has lodged the third-largest number of complaints (behind the United States and the EU), and it has been the alleged violator more than any other WTO member.

From 2002 to early 2014, China filed 12 complaints in total, with the United States or the EU the respondent in all of them. In all but one of these cases, China alleged that the respondent had misused or misapplied antidumping duties, countervailing duties, or safeguards, types of contingent protection that we will examine in Chapter 11. Most of these cases led to decisions by panels after the countries could not reach agreements by consultation. Most panel decisions found that the United States or the EU had violated WTO rules, and they then implemented changes. For example, in the one case that did not involve contingent protection, in 2009 China complained that the United States had not followed WTO rules when it banned imports of Chinese poultry. After the panel ruled in favor of China's complaint, the United States removed the ban.

From the first case in 2004 to early 2014, China was the respondent in 31 cases that involved 19 distinct matters. In all the matters except one, the complainants included the United States or the EU (sometimes both). For three matters, consultations led to mutually agreed solutions in which China changed its policies. Five matters had not (yet) progressed past consultations, and the other 11 matters went to panels. Six panel decisions found that China had violated WTO rules,

and China then made changes to bring itself into conformity. As of early 2014, there were only two matters in which China had lost panel decisions but had not implemented changes within a reasonable time, and in one of these China seemed to be moving slowly to make changes.

Here are a few of the cases with China as the respondent. In 2004, the United States filed the first WTO case against China, alleging that China was using discriminatory domestic tax rates to favor integrated circuits that were designed or made in China. Negotiations led to a resolution in which China ended the tax differential.

The first complaints against China to go to a panel were filed in 2006 by the EU, the United States, and Canada, alleging that China was imposing tariffs on automobile parts that exceeded China's bound rate, through a form of domestic content requirement. In early 2008 the panel hearing the case ruled that the Chinese policy violated WTO rules, and China then changed its policies.

In 2010, the United States, the EU, and Mexico complained that China's limits on exports of certain raw materials provided unfair advantages to Chinese producers that used these raw materials as inputs. After the panel ruled against China, China removed its restrictions. In 2012 the United States, the EU, and Japan filed similar complaints that China was restricting exports of rare earths. In 2014, the WTO panel again ruled that China had violated WTO rules and commitments with its export restrictions.

China's role as a major player in the WTO dispute settlement system shows the value of the WTO processes. China has a legitimate way to address and attempt to resolve trade conflicts with two of its largest trade partners, the United States and the EU. In most dispute cases in which one of these countries is using procedures or enacting policies that do not conform to WTO rules and commitments, the country has eventually amended its procedures and policies to bring them in line with WTO rules.

U.S. president the power to negotiate to eliminate "unfair trade practices" of foreign governments. As part of the process, the U.S. government can threaten to enact new barriers to imports into the United States from the allegedly offending country if that country does not change its policies. (U.S. law also has "Special 301," which mandates an annual report on foreign countries that do not provide adequate protection to intellectual property.)

What are the effects of unilateral actions by the U.S. government to open foreign markets using a threat of retaliation? That depends on whether the threatened country gives in and removes the practices that the United States deems unfair. If it does, then the U.S. government achieves some of its objectives, and it probably is a move toward at least somewhat freer trade. About half of the 100 or so Section 301 cases since 1974 ended in this way, though the increases in U.S. exports usually were small.

However, if the other country does not accede to the U.S. demands to change its policies, and the U.S. government imposes trade sanctions (usually in the form of high tariffs on an arbitrary set of products imported from the other country), then carrying out the retaliation is likely to reduce the well-being of both sides. Unfortunately, nearly a quarter of Section 301 cases have led to such mutually harmful U.S. sanctions.

Not surprisingly, other countries resent U.S. government use of this law. They are irked by the self-righteous tone with which the United States has written and used 301. They rightly point out that 301 has allowed the United States to conduct its own unilateral "trade crimes" trials, deciding by itself what is unfair.

There has been a drop-off in Section 301 cases since the early 1990s. U.S. complaints are now much more likely to be sent to and resolved using the WTO dispute settlement process.

Dispute Settlement in the WTO

During the Uruguay Round of multilateral trade negotiations, governments recognized both the shortcomings of the then-existing GATT dispute process and the concerns about the unilateral approach embodied in U.S. Section 301. The World Trade Organization that came into existence in 1995 has a much stronger dispute settlement procedure than the GATT had.

If the government of a member country believes that another member country government is violating a commitment or WTO rule, it can file a complaint. The goal of the WTO is then to find a resolution to the dispute, including removing any violation that exists. The first step is consultations between the governments. If discussions cannot resolve the dispute, a panel of experts examines the case and reaches a decision. A country can appeal the decision by this panel, but it cannot block it just by objecting. If the complaint is upheld, the offending country is instructed to correct its policy. In most cases, the countries find a mutually acceptable solution to the dispute. But, if the offending country does not correct its policy or provide other compensation, then as a last resort the WTO can authorize retaliation by the complaining country against the offending country.

In its first 10 years (1995–2004), the WTO received an average about 32 complaints per year. Then, during 2005–2013, the average decreased to about 17 per year. For the entire period, in about 40 percent of these cases, the United States or the European Union has been the complaining country; in about 40 percent, the United States or the European Union has been the alleged violator (the respondent); and often it is one complaining about the other.

The dispute settlement procedure has also been widely used by other countries, though not so intensively. In about 45 percent of the cases, a developing country has brought the complaint, and in about 45 percent, a developing country is the alleged violator. Since joining the WTO in 2001, China has brought 12 complaints (as of early 2014), and it has been the alleged violator in 31 cases. (The box "China in the WTO" discusses disputes and other aspects of China's membership.) It is also worth noting that about half of the dispute cases are complaints about the types of nontariff barriers that we have discussed in this chapter.

WTO authorization of retaliation is rare, and actual imposition of trade sanctions against a recalcitrant violating country even rarer (about 2 percent of cases filed). The sanctions are usually in the form of high tariffs against a set of products exported by the violating country. The *threat* of retaliation appears to be useful in getting violating countries to correct their policies, but *actual* retaliation is problematic. It runs counter to the WTO's goal of trade liberalization, and it is likely to reduce the well-being of both countries involved and of the world as a whole. It is fortunate that such retaliation has been rare.

Summary

Nontariff barriers (NTBs) reduce imports by limiting quantities, increasing costs, or creating uncertainties. An import quota sets a maximum quantity of imports. If markets are competitive, a quota has the same effects as a tariff that results in the same import quantity, with one possible exception. Just as for imposing a tariff, imposing a quota raises the domestic price, reduces domestic quantity demanded, increases domestic quantity supplied, reduces domestic consumer surplus, increases domestic producer surplus, and, if the importing country is large, reduces the world price by reducing demand for the foreign product. The exception is what happens to what would be government revenue with a tariff. With a quota this amount is a markup of the domestic price over the world price for each unit imported. If the government *freely* gives away licenses to import under the quota, the lucky importers get this amount as extra profit. If the government *auctions* or sells the import licenses, the government can get the amount as revenue. If the government has a complicated process for obtaining import licenses, then some of this amount is lost to resource-using application procedures. For a small country, a quota is just as bad as a tariff, and it can be worse if resources are used up in pursuit of licenses to import or if the quota creates domestic monopoly power.

A form of protection that became important in the 1980s, especially in the United States and the EU, is the voluntary export restraint (VER) arrangement. Here the importing country threatens foreign exporters with stiff barriers if they do not agree to restrict exports by themselves. Under a negotiated VER arrangement, the main foreign exporters form a cartel among themselves, agreeing to cut export quantities. At the same time, they are allowed to charge the full markup on their limited sales to the importing country, where the product has become more expensive. A curious result is that the importing country, which insisted on the VER in the first place, loses even more than if it had collected a tariff or quota markup itself.

Other important nontariff barriers include domestic content requirements, mixing requirements, government procurement favoring domestic products, and a host of quality and safety standards that have protectionist effects.

The net costs of import barriers, both tariff and nontariff, often look small as a share of GDP when calculated in terms of the ordinary deadweight loss triangles. Yet this analysis overlooks foreign retaliation, enforcement costs, rent-seeking, and other considerations that can make import barriers more expensive. In relation to the boost provided to producer surplus in protected sectors, the net costs of import barriers are larger.

Global efforts to liberalize nontariff barriers have generally met with less success than the global efforts to reduce tariff rates. Under the GATT and the WTO, most import quotas have been eliminated, but the use of other NTBs has increased in recent decades. Multilateral trade negotiations in the Kennedy Round and the Tokyo Round resulted in voluntary codes for some types of NTBs, but these codes had modest effects. The Uruguay Round agreements have a wider set of NTB codes and rules that apply to all WTO members, including the phasing out of VERs on textiles and clothing.

The Uruguay Round agreements also began the process of liberalizing trade in agricultural products and trade in services, as well as requiring members to provide minimum levels of ownership protection for intellectual property. The current Doha Round of trade negotiations has an ambitious agenda, but progress has been stymied by the inability of the United States, the European Union, and developing countries (led by Brazil and India) to agree on how and how much to liberalize government policies toward agriculture and agricultural trade.

Beginning in the late 1970s, the United States, frustrated by the weakness of the dispute settlement procedures of the GATT, shifted toward using its Section 301 to try to resolve its complaints about foreign countries' trade practices and policies. Other countries resented the unilateral U.S. approach. With the advent of the much-improved dispute settlement process in the WTO, the United States has reduced its use of Section 301.

The WTO's dispute settlement procedures are generally viewed as successful. Many complaints are resolved by negotiated agreements between the countries to the disputes, and others are resolved after panels issue their formal rulings. If the WTO panel hearing a case finds that a country's policies are in violation of WTO rules, and the country does not change its policies, the WTO can approve retaliatory measures, usually that the complainant country can impose high tariffs on imports from the country in violation. The threat of retaliation can induce compliance by the violator country, but it also has a downside. If the country in violation does not change, and the retaliation is enacted, the countries involved in the dispute and the world are then worse off.

Key Terms	Nontariff barrier (NTB)	Resource-using application procedures	Domestic content requirement
	Import quota (quota)		
	Fixed favoritism	Voluntary export restraint (VER)	Mixing requirement
	Import license auction		Section 301

Suggested
Reading

World Trade Organization (2012) provides a broad survey of nontariff barriers to imports. Trionfetti (2000) examines government procurement as an NTB. Berry, Levinsohn, and Pakes (1999) provide a technical analysis of the VER on Japanese auto exports to the United States. Findlay and Warren (2000) present evidence on barriers to trade in services, and Hoekman (2000) looks at gains from liberalizing services trade. Footer and Graber (2000) examine barriers to trade in cultural goods and services (films, music recordings, and so forth).

Feenstra (1995) provides a technical survey of work estimating the effects of protection. Anderson and Wincoop (2004) provide a survey of the magnitudes of a broad range of policies and other influences that seem to impede international trade. Kee et al. (2010) and Evenett (2009) examine protectionism during the global crisis. Irwin (2011) explores the rise of protectionism during the Great Depression.

Destler (2005) and Pearson (2004) survey the development of U.S. trade policy. Hoekman and Kostecki (2001) examine the WTO's rules and activities. Jones (2004) explores the controversies surrounding the WTO and its activities. Bagwell and Staiger (2002) provide a conceptual analysis of why the WTO and its rules make economic sense. Bhattasali et al. (2004) analyze China's accession to WTO membership. Elliott (2006) and McCalla and Nash (2007) examine the issues of agricultural liberalization in the Doha Round negotiations. Bown (2009) critiques the role of developing countries in the WTO dispute settlement process. Using the gravity model described in the box in Chapter 6, Rose (2004) concludes that the WTO has not increased international trade, but a series of researchers, including Dutt et al. (2013), Liu (2009), and Subramanian and Wei (2007) counter with evidence that it has.

Questions
and
Problems

◆ 1. What are import quotas? Why do some governments use them instead of just using tariffs to restrict imports by the same amounts? Is it because quotas bring a bigger national gain than tariffs?

2. What are voluntary export restraint (VER) agreements? Why do some governments force foreign exporters into them instead of just using quotas or tariffs to restrict imports by the same amounts? Is it because VERs bring the importing country a bigger national gain than quotas or tariffs?

◆ 3. Under what conditions could an import quota and a tariff have exactly the same effect on price and bring the same gains and losses (given a tariff level that restricts imports just as much as the quota would)?

4. Define each of the following import policies and describe its likely effects on the well-being of the importing country as a whole: (a) product standards and (b) domestic content requirements.

◆ 5. To protect American jobs, the U.S. government may decide to cut U.S. imports of bulldozers by 60 percent. It could do so by either (a) imposing a tariff high enough to cut bulldozer imports by 60 percent or (b) persuading Komatsu and other foreign bulldozer makers to set up a VER arrangement to cut their exports of bulldozers to the United States by 60 percent. Which of these two policies would be less damaging to the United States? Which would be less damaging to the world as a whole? Explain.

6. The United States is considering adopting a regulation that foreign apples can be imported only if they are grown and harvested using the same techniques that are used in the United States. These techniques are used in the United States to meet various government standards about worker safety and product quality.

   a. As a representative of the U.S. government, you are asked to defend the new import regulation before the WTO. What will you say?

   b. As a representative of foreign apple growers, you are asked to present the case that this regulation is an unfair restriction on trade. What will you say?

✦ 7. A small country imports sugar. With free trade at the world price of $0.10 per pound, the country's national market is:

Domestic production	120 million pounds per year
Domestic consumption	420 million pounds per year
Imports	300 million pounds per year

The country's government now decides to impose a quota that limits sugar imports to 240 million pounds per year. With the import quota in effect, the domestic price rises to $0.12 per pound, and domestic production increases to 160 million pounds per year. The government auctions the rights to import the 240 million pounds.

   a. Calculate how much domestic producers gain or lose from the quota.

   b. Calculate how much domestic consumers gain or lose from the quota.

   c. Calculate how much the government receives in payment when it auctions the quota rights to import.

   d. Calculate the net national gain or loss from the quota. Explain the economic reason(s) for this net gain or loss.

8. A small country's protectionism can be summarized: The typical tariff rate is 50 percent, the (absolute value of the) price elasticity of demand for imports is 1, imports would be 20 percent of the country's GDP with free trade, and the protected industries represent 15 percent of GDP. Using our triangle analysis, what is the approximate magnitude of the economic costs of the tariff protection, as a percentage of the country's GDP? As a percentage of the gain of producer surplus in the protected sectors?

✦ 9. For a small country, consider a quota and an equivalent tariff that permit the same initial level of imports. The market is competitive, and the government uses fixed favoritism to allocate the quota permits, with no resources expended in the process. There is now an increase in domestic demand (the domestic demand curve D_d shifts to the right). If the tariff rate is unchanged, and if the quota quantity is unchanged, are the two still equivalent? Show this using a graph. Be sure to discuss the effects on domestic price, production quantity, and consumption quantity, on import quantity, and on producer surplus, consumer surplus, deadweight losses, and government revenue or its equivalent for the quota.

10. A Japanese friend asks you to explain and defend American use of Section 301. What will you say?

✦11. Suppose that the U.S. government is under heavy pressure from the Rollerblade and K2 companies to put the brakes on imports of Bauer in-line skates from Canada. The protectionists demand that the price of a $200 pair of in-line skates must be raised to

$250 if their incomes are to be safe. The U.S. government has three choices: (1) free trade with no protection, (2) a special tariff on in-line skates backed by vague claims that Canada is using unfair trade practices (citing Section 301 of the Trade Act of 1974), and (3) forcing Bauer to agree to a voluntary export restraint. The three choices would lead to these prices and annual quantities:

	With Free Trade	With an $80 Tariff	With a VER
Domestic U.S. price per pair	$200	$250	$250
World price per pair	$200	$170	$170
Imports of in-line skates (millions of pairs)	10	6	6

Note that the $80 tariff reduces imports by 4 million pairs a year, the same reduction that the VER arrangement would enforce.

a. Calculate the U.S. net national gains or losses from the tariff, and the U.S. gains or losses from the VER, relative to free trade. Which of the three choices looks best for the United States as a whole? Which looks worst?

b. Calculate the net national gains or losses for Canada, the exporting country, from the tariff and the VER. Which of the three U.S. choices harms Canada most? Which harms Canada least?

c. Which of the three choices is best for the world as a whole?

12. A small country initially has free trade in motorcycles, it has one local motorcycle producer, and imports account for over half of local motorcycle sales. The government has decided to impose a tariff of 20 percent, aimed to reduce motorcycle imports by about a third. The local producer proposes that a quota equal to two-thirds of the free-trade level of imports be imposed instead of the tariff because the quota will benefit the country by providing certainty about the import quantity. You are employed in the Ministry of the Economy and have been asked to provide a briefing on whether the government should use a tariff or a quota. What will you say in your presentation?

♦ 13. "In comparison to the GATT, two advantages of the WTO are that (a) the WTO has been more successful in completing rounds of multilateral trade negotiations and (b) the WTO has a better dispute settlement procedure." Do you agree or disagree? Why?

Chapter **Ten**

Arguments for and against Protection

Why do most countries have policies that limit imports? The previous two chapters found only bad barriers, ones that brought net harm to the world economy. Because free trade led to a fully efficient outcome for the world in our analysis, any trade barriers could only be bad. We did find one barrier, the nationally optimal tariff, that could be good for the country that imposed it. But it, too, was bad for the world as a whole, and it could end up being bad for the country that tried to impose it if other countries retaliate by raising their own tariffs on products that the first country exports.

A key objective of this chapter is to examine a variety of arguments proposing that import protection is good for the country (and perhaps for the world) because it allows the country to address some market shortcoming or to achieve some objective other than economic efficiency. We know that a tariff or nontariff barrier (NTB) to imports of a product can

- Increase domestic production of the product.
- Increase employment of labor and other resources in this domestic production.
- Decrease domestic consumption of the product.
- Increase government revenue.
- Alter the distribution of income or well-being in the country.

Corresponding to each of these effects, here are five generic arguments in favor of tariffs (or NTBs) that we will examine:

- If there is something extra good about local production of a product, then a tariff can be good for the country because the tariff leads to more domestic production of the product.
- If there is something extra good about employing people or other resources in producing a product, then a tariff can be good for the country because the tariff leads to more employment in the sector as local production of the product increases.
- If there is something extra bad about local consumption of a product, then a tariff can be good for the country because the tariff leads to less domestic consumption of the product.

- If there is something extra good about the government collecting more revenue, then a tariff can be good for the country.
- If it is desirable to enhance the incomes of factors used intensively in the import-competing industry, then a tariff can be good for the country.

In each of these cases, the tariff could also be good for the world as well. (We defer examination of one other generic argument for import protection, that foreign exporters are engaging in unfair trade, until the next chapter.)

Our analysis here will establish two main conclusions:

- There are valid "second-best" arguments for protection—situations in which protection could be better than free trade.
- Some other government policies are usually better than import barriers in these situations.

If there are few situations in which import protection is the best policy for a country, why do we see so many import barriers? The second part of the chapter focuses on the politics of protection. We examine how political actions by different self-interested groups in the country can influence political decisions about import barriers. Our political excursion indicates that institutions are important. Import protection is more likely in a representative democracy for products in which import-competing domestic producers organize into effective lobbies but domestic consumers do not.

THE IDEAL WORLD OF FIRST BEST

In the previous two chapters we assumed an ideal, or "first-best," world in which all *private* incentives aligned perfectly with benefits and costs to *society* as a whole. In a first-best world, any demand or supply curve can do double duty, representing both private and social benefits or costs. The domestic demand curve represented not only marginal benefits of an extra bicycle to its private buyer but also the extra benefits of another bicycle to society as a whole. The domestic supply curve represented not only the marginal cost to private producers of producing another bicycle at home but also the marginal cost to society as a whole.

The first row of Figure 10.1 summarizes what an economist means by a first-best world. The market price (*P*) acts as a signal to consumers and producers. Consumers buy the product up to the point where the price they are willing to pay, which equals the extra private benefits (*MB*) they receive from another unit, just equals the price that they must pay. The extra benefit to society (*SMB*) is just the extra benefit that the consumer gets. Producers supply the product up to the point where the price they receive just covers the extra costs (*MC*) of producing the product. The extra costs to society (*SMC*) of producing another unit of this product are just the extra costs that the individual firm incurs. That is, all five values are equal:

Price (*P*) = Buyers' private marginal benefit (*MB*) = Social marginal benefit (*SMB*)

= Sellers' private marginal cost (*MC*) = Social marginal cost (*SMC*)

FIGURE 10.1   Distortions and Their Effects

Situation	Incentives at the Margin	Effects
First-best world	$P = MB = MC = SMB = SMC$	Exactly the right amount is supplied and demanded.
Distortions		
External costs	$SMC > P (= MB = MC = SMB)$	Too much is supplied because suppliers make and sell extra units for which the social costs exceed the price (which equals MC and MB and SMB). Example: production that pollutes air or water.
External benefits	$SMB > P (= MB = MC = SMC)$	Not enough is demanded because demanders receive only private benefits equal to the price, not the full social benefits. Example: training or education that brings extra gains in attitudes or team skills.
Monopoly power	$P > SMC$	Not enough is demanded because the monopoly sets the price too high.
Monopsony power (a case not developed in this textbook)	$P < SMB$	Not enough is supplied because the monopsony sets its buying price too low. Example: a single firm that dominates a labor market and uses its power to set a low wage.
Distorting tax	P with tax $> SMC$	Not enough is demanded because the tax makes the price to buyers exceed the revenue per unit received by suppliers.
Distorting subsidy	P with subsidy $< SMC$	Too much is demanded because the subsidy makes the price to buyers lower than the revenue per unit received by suppliers.

P = Market price
MB = Private marginal benefit of an activity (to those who demand it)
MC = Private marginal cost of an activity (to those who supply it)
SMB = Social marginal benefit of an activity (to everybody affected)
SMC = Social marginal cost of an activity (to everybody affected)

In a first-best world free trade is economically efficient. Free trade allows the "invisible hand" of market competition to reach globally. Private producers, reacting to the signal of the market price, expand production in each country to levels that are as good as possible for the world as a whole. Private consumers, also reacting to price signals, expand their purchases of products to levels that make the whole world as well off as possible.

THE REALISTIC WORLD OF SECOND BEST

Our world is not ideal. Distortions exist, and they do not automatically cancel each other out. The distortions result from ongoing gaps between the private and social benefits or costs of an activity. We live in a **second-best world,** one that includes distortions. As long as these gaps exist between what private individuals use to make their decisions and the full effects of these decisions on society, *private actions will not lead to the best possible outcomes* for society.

There are two major sources of distortions in an economy. First, *market failures* are ways in which private markets fail to achieve full economic efficiency. Second, *government policies can distort an otherwise economically efficient private market.* Figure 10.1 provides information on six specific types of distortions, with the first four being types of private market failures and the last two being government policies that can create distortions.

The first two types of distortions in the figure are **externalities** or **spillover effects** (net effects on parties other than those agreeing to buy or sell in a market-place). The first example of an externality is the classic case of pollution. Consider the case of river pollution, an example we will explore at length in Chapter 13. If the sellers of paper products are not forced to do so, they do not reckon the damage done by the paper mills' river pollution as part of the cost of their production. So the pollution costs are not incorporated into the price of paper. Similarly, buyers of petroleum fuels do not reckon that the social cost of air pollution from using those fuels is part of the fuel price that they have to pay. If some costs of producing or consuming a product are ignored by the private decision-makers, then too much of the product is produced or consumed.

Our second example of an externality supposes that jobs in a certain import-competing sector generate greater returns for society than are perceived by the people who decide whether or not to take the jobs. These external benefits can happen, for instance, if working in the sector brings gains in knowledge, skills, and attitudes that benefit firms or people other than the workers and employers in the sector. In this example the social marginal benefits (SMB) of working in the sector are higher than the wage rate (or the price, P) that workers receive. If some benefits of the activity are ignored by private decision-makers, then too little of the activity occurs (in the example, too few people are hired into jobs in the sector).

In this chapter we focus on distortions caused by externalities. In fact, we focus on various kinds of external benefits that are the "extra good" that can accompany local production of a product or employment in producing the product. We only briefly mention here the other four types of distortions shown in Figure 10.1.

Monopoly power can create a distortion because a powerful seller restricts output to raise price and increase profits. For a domestic monopoly firm, free trade can eliminate this distortion by forcing the domestic firm to compete with foreign firms. Monopsony power can create a distortion because a powerful buyer sets a price that is too low.

In the absence of any other distortion, a tax creates a distortion by artificially raising the price to buyers. Our analysis of a tariff in Chapter 8 is an example of a tax distortion and the inefficiency caused by this distortion.

In the absence of any other distortion, a government subsidy creates a distortion by artificially lowering the price to buyers. Essentially, a subsidy is like a negative tax. We will examine subsidies later in this chapter and in the next chapter.

Government Policies toward Externalities

External costs and external benefits pose some of the most intriguing policy problems in economics. How should a society try to fix distortions caused by externalities? There are two basic alternative approaches for government policy. One approach is the *tax-or-subsidy approach* developed by British economist A. C. Pigou. The other approach is the *property-rights approach*, which builds on the ideas of Nobel Prize winner Ronald Coase.[1]

In this chapter we use the tax-or-subsidy approach because the trade policy debate is usually over taxes and subsidies (e.g., a tariff is a tax). While we explore how government taxes and subsidies, at their best, *can* cure externality distortions, remember that there is reason to debate whether such government interventions *will* work well in practice.[2] The idea is to explore the best possible cases for government interference with trade. At the same time, we have to keep in mind the real *possibility of government failure* to correctly identify problems and enact solutions.

The tax-or-subsidy approach says that we should spot distortions in people's and firms' private incentives and have a wise government policy correct the incentives with taxes or subsidies. What if social marginal cost exceeds private cost and market price ($SMC > MC = P = MB = SMB$), as in the pollution case? The government should levy a tax of ($SMC - MC$) to bring everything into equality by raising the market price to match the full social marginal cost (including the external costs created by the pollution). If the social marginal benefit exceeds the private benefit and the market price ($SMB > MB = P = MC = SMC$), as in the training case, let the government pay a subsidy of ($SMB - MB$) so that decision-makers in the marketplace recognize the full social returns.

Could trade barriers help to cure distortions caused by externalities? Even before we get to the details, we can see that the tax-or-subsidy approach can relate to the debate over trade barriers. If there is a distortion in our economy, perhaps cutting imports will help. A quick example is the worker-training case already mentioned. If the social benefit of having workers get training in a certain industry is greater than their current market wage, we could reap net social gains by protecting their jobs against foreign competition. This is the kind of issue that we return to repeatedly in this chapter.

The Specificity Rule

Externalities and other incentive distortions complicate the task of judging whether a trade barrier is good or bad for the nation as a whole. Realizing this, some scholars

---

[1]For example, the property-rights approach says that, if there is a problem of a paper mill polluting a river, we can make private incentives include all social effects by making the river someone's private property. Either let the downstream river users own it and charge the paper mill for any pollution, or let the paper mill own the river and demand compensation for cleaning it up. Choose between these two property-right assignments by choosing the one that costs less to implement and enforce. The property-rights approach will resurface in Chapter 13's treatment of international environmental issues.

[2]We can see this more broadly and also clear up a possible confusion. In Figure 10.1 a tax and a subsidy are listed as possible sources of distortions. That is, if the market otherwise gets to the first-best solution (because there is no other distortion), then introducing a tax or subsidy causes a distortion. If, instead, a distortion already exists, then the market will not get to the first-best outcome by itself. If a distortion already exists, then an appropriate tax or subsidy can improve the market outcome. But the wrong tax or subsidy could make things even worse.

have stressed that there is no cure-all prescription for trade policy in a second-best world. Once you realize that distortions exist, things become complicated. It seems that each situation must be judged on its own merits.

Yet we are not cast totally adrift in this world of distortions. We do not have to shrug and just say, "Every case is different. It all depends." There is a useful rule that works well in most cases. The **specificity rule** states that it is usually *more efficient to use the government policy tool that acts as directly as possible on the source of the distortion* separating private and social benefits or costs. In short, identify the specific source of the problem and intervene directly at this source.

The specificity rule applies to all sorts of policy issues. Let's illustrate it first by using an example removed from international trade. Suppose that the problem is crime, which creates fear among third parties and direct harm to victims. Since crime is caused by people, we might consider combating crime by reducing the whole population through compulsory sterilization laws or taxes on children. But such actions are obviously inefficient ways of attacking crime because less social friction would be generated (per crime averted) if we fought crime more directly through greater law enforcement and programs to reduce unemployment, a major contributor to crime.

The next sections of the chapter examine various arguments that restrictions on imports are a good way for the government to deal with distortions caused by spillover effects. As we will see in these cases, the specificity rule tends to cut against import barriers. *Although a barrier against imports can be better than doing nothing in a second-best world, the specificity rule shows us that some other policy instrument is usually more efficient* than a trade barrier in dealing with a domestic distortion.

PROMOTING DOMESTIC PRODUCTION OR EMPLOYMENT

Protectionists often come up with reasons that it is good to maintain high levels of domestic production of a product that is imported or high levels of employment of workers (and perhaps other resources) in this domestic production. They offer reasons that this is good *for the nation as a whole* (and not just for the firms and workers that receive the protection). In fact, most popular second-best arguments for protection can be viewed as variations on the theme of favoring a particular import-competing industry because there are extra social benefits to domestic production or employment in this particular import-competing industry. Here are several versions that we will examine in this chapter:

- Local production of this product produces spillover benefits because other firms and industries benefit from production know-how or management techniques introduced by the firms in this industry.
- Employment in this industry imparts new worker skills and attitudes, and some workers carry these when they switch jobs to work for other firms and industries.
- By producing now at high cost, firms in the industry can find ways to lower their costs over time.
- There are extra costs to workers if they are forced to switch to jobs in other industries.

- The country and its citizens take pride from producing this product locally.
- The product is essential to national defense.
- Employment in the industry is a way to redistribute income to poor or disadvantaged members of society.

In examining these proposed reasons that protection is good for the country, we consider the case of a *small country* (one whose trade has no impact on world prices), so that our analysis is not complicated by any effects of the trade barrier on the country's international terms of trade.

Let us turn first to the pros and cons of a tariff to promote domestic production or employment because this production or employment creates positive externalities (the first two of the reasons shown in the above list). Analysis of these two reasons is important, and we will be able to use the insights from this analysis in examining the other reasons in the list.

Let's look at the case in which a nation might want to encourage domestic production of bicycles because this production creates positive spillovers elsewhere in the country. It could achieve the production objective by putting a $30 tariff on imported bicycles, as shown in the diagram of the national bicycle market in Figure 10.2A. The nation loses area *b* by producing at greater expense what could be bought for less from abroad, and it loses area *d* by discouraging purchases that would have brought more enjoyment to consumers than the world price of a bicycle. But now something is added: The lower part of the diagram portrays extra social benefits (or spillover benefits) from local production, benefits that are not captured by the domestic bicycle producers. That is, we suppose that the *marginal external benefits* of making our own bicycles can be represented by the *MEB* curve at the bottom. By raising the domestic price of bicycles, the tariff encourages more production of bicycles. This increase in domestic production, from 0.6 to 0.8 million bikes, brings area *g* in extra gains to the nation.

Compared with doing nothing, levying the tariff in Figure 10.2A could be good or bad for the nation, all things considered. The net outcome depends on whether area *g* is larger or smaller than the areas *b* and *d*. To find out, we would have to develop empirical estimates reflecting the realities of the bicycle industry. We would want to estimate the dollar value of the annual spillover benefits to society and the slopes of the domestic supply and demand curves. The net national gain $(g - b - d)$ might turn out to be positive or negative. Until we know the specific numbers involved, all we can say, so far, is that the tariff might prove to be better (or worse) than doing nothing.

We should use our institutional imagination, however, and look for other policy tools. The specificity rule prods us to do so. The locus of the problem is really domestic production, not imports. What society wants to encourage is more domestic production of this good, not less consumption or fewer imports of it. Instead of a tariff, why not encourage the domestic production directly by rewarding firms for producing?

Society could directly subsidize the domestic production of bicycles by having the government pay bicycle firms a fixed amount for each bicycle produced and sold. This would encourage them to produce more bicycles. Any increase in production that a given tariff could coax out of domestic firms could also be yielded by a production subsidy. Figure 10.2B shows such a subsidy, namely, a $30 subsidy per bicycle

FIGURE 10.2 Two Ways to Promote Import-Competing Production

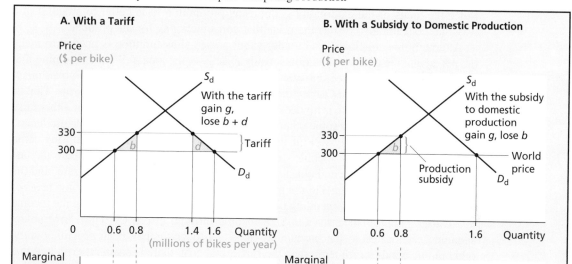

Compare the effects of two ways of getting the same increase in domestic output (0.2 million = 0.8 – 0.6 million) and in domestic jobs. Both the $30 tariff and the $30 subsidy to domestic production encourage the same change in domestic production. But the tariff also needlessly discourages some consumption of imports (the amount 0.2 million = 1.6 – 1.4 million) that was worth more to the buyers than the $300 each unit of imports would have cost the nation. The production subsidy is better than the tariff because it strikes more directly at the task of raising domestic production of this good.

produced domestically. The subsidy increases the revenue per unit sold to $330 ($300 paid by consumers and $30 paid by the government). This subsidy is just as good for domestic bicycle firms as the extra $30 in selling price that the tariff made possible. Either tool gets the firms to raise their annual production from 0.6 to 0.8 million, giving society the same external benefits.

The $30 production subsidy in Figure 10.2B is better than the $30 tariff in Figure 10.2A. Both generate the same external social benefits (area *g*), and both cause domestic firms to produce 0.2 million extra bicycles each year at a higher direct cost than the price at which the nation could buy foreign bicycles. (In both cases this extra cost is area *b*.) Yet the subsidy does not discourage the total consumption of bicycles by raising the price above $300. Consumers continue to pay $300 for each bicycle, equal to the world price of obtaining an imported bicycle. They continue to consume 1.6 million bicycles. Consumers do not lose the additional area *d*. This is a clear advantage of the $30 production subsidy over the $30 tariff.

What makes the production subsidy better is its conformity to the specificity rule: Since the locus of the externality is domestic production, it is better to attack it in a way that does not also distort the price that consumers pay for the product.

Although this conclusion is broadly valid, a special assumption is needed to make the net advantage of the production subsidy exactly equal area *d*. We are assuming that no other distortions between private and social incentives result when the government comes up with the revenues to pay the production subsidies to the bicycle firms. That is, we are assuming that there is no net social loss from having the government either raise additional taxes or reduce some other spending to pay this subsidy to bicycle producers. This assumption is strictly valid if the extra tax revenues going into the subsidy come from a head tax, a tax on people's existence, which should only redistribute income and not affect production and consumption incentives. Yet head taxes are rare, and the more realistic case of financing the production subsidy by, say, raising income taxes or cutting other government spending programs is somewhat murkier. Raising the income tax distorts people's incentives to earn income through effort. Or if the government spending reallocated to the production subsidy had previously been providing some other public goods worth more than their marginal cost, there is again an extra loss that can attend the production subsidy. Policymakers would have to consider these possible source-of-subsidy distortions. Yet it seems reasonable to presume that such distortions are less important than the distorting of consumption represented by area *d*.

If our concern is with *maintaining or expanding jobs,* rather than output, in the import-competing industry, the same results hold with a slight modification. A production subsidy would still be preferable to the tariff because it still achieves any given expansion in both bicycle production and bicycle jobs at lower social cost. We could come up with an even better alternative. If the locus of the problem is really the number of jobs in the bicycle industry, it would be even more efficient to use a policy tool that not only encourages production but also encourages firms to come up with ways of creating more jobs per dollar of bicycle output. A *subsidy tied to the number of workers employed* is better than a subsidy tied to output.[3] The box "How Much Does It Cost to Protect a Job?" examines the costs of using tariffs and NTBs to prop up jobs in import-competing industries.

So why do governments so often use import barriers instead of direct production or employment subsidies that are less costly to the economy? Once an industry's political lobby is strong enough to get government help, it uses its influence to get a kind of help that is sheltered from political counterattacks. The subsidy favored by our economic analysis provides less shelter. The subsidy is a highly visible target for fiscal budget cutters. Every year it has to be defended again when the government budget is under review. A tariff or other import barrier, however, gives much better shelter to the industry that seeks continuing government help. Once it is written into the law, it goes on propping up domestic prices without being reviewed. In fact, it generates government revenue (e.g., tariff revenue), giving it more political appeal. We examine the politics of protection in more depth later in this chapter.

---

[3]Alternatively, if the object is to create jobs and cure unemployment throughout the entire domestic economy, then it is logical to look first to economywide expansionary policies, such as fiscal policy or monetary policy, and not to policy fixes in any one industry.

THE INFANT INDUSTRY ARGUMENT

The analysis of using a tariff to promote domestic production helps us judge the merits of a number of popular arguments for protection. Of all the protectionist arguments, the one that has long enjoyed the most prestige among both economists and policymakers is the infant industry argument, which asserts that a temporary tariff is justified because it cuts down on imports while the infant domestic industry learns how to produce at low enough costs. Eventually the domestic industry will be able to compete without the help of a tariff. The infant industry argument differs from the optimal tariff argument by claiming that in the long run the tariff protection will be good for the world as well as for the nation. It differs from most other tariff arguments in being explicitly dynamic, arguing that the protection is needed only for a while.

The infant industry argument has been popular with aspiring countries at least since Alexander Hamilton used it in his *Report on Manufacturers* in 1791. The United States followed Hamilton's protectionist formula, especially after the Civil War, setting up high tariff walls to encourage production of textiles, ferrous metals, and other goods still struggling to become competitive against Britain. Similarly, Friedrich List reapplied Hamilton's infant industry ideas to the cause of shielding nascent German manufacturing industries against British competition in the early 19th century. The government of Japan has believed strongly in infant industry protection—sometimes, but not always, in the form of import protection. In the 1950s and 1960s in particular, Japan protected its steel, automobile, shipbuilding, and electronics industries before they became tough competitors and the import barriers were removed.

The infant industry argument will continue to deserve attention because there will always be infant industries. As some countries gain the lead in producing new products with new technologies, other countries will have to consider time and again what to do about the development of their own production of these new products.

How It Is Supposed to Work

Figure 10.3 provides a schematic for understanding the infant industry argument, using the example of small farm tractors. Now, as shown in the left side of the figure, no amount of production in this country is cost-competitive by world standards (the current domestic supply curve S_{dn} is everywhere above the world price of $3,000 per tractor). Apparently, no domestic production would occur now with free trade. If the country's government imposes a tariff of 33 percent, the domestic price rises to $4,000 per tractor and domestic firms produce 20,000 tractors. Now (and for as many years as this situation persists) we know that the country incurs inefficiencies of area b and area d because of the tariff.

The payoff to incurring these inefficiencies is that the infant industry grows up. As firms produce tractors, they find ways to lower their costs. Sometime in the future the domestic industry's supply curve will shift down to S_{df}. The government can then remove the tariff. As shown in the right side of the figure, the country will then have a tractor industry that can produce 50,000 tractors per year at costs that are competitive with world standards. This competitive domestic production creates producer surplus

FIGURE 10.3   The Infant Industry Argument

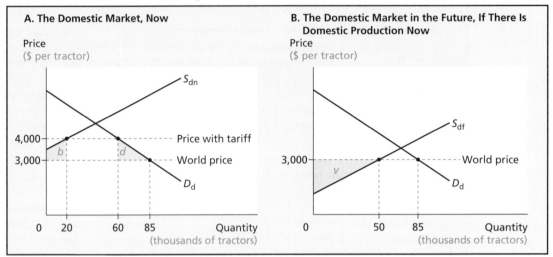

A. The Domestic Market, Now

Price
($ per tractor)

S_{dn}

4,000 ---- Price with tariff
b   *d*
3,000 ---- World price

D_d

0   20   60   85   Quantity
(thousands of tractors)

B. The Domestic Market in the Future, If There Is Domestic Production Now

Price
($ per tractor)

S_{df}

3,000 ---- World price
v

D_d

0   50   85   Quantity
(thousands of tractors)

With free trade now, there would be no domestic production. A tariff can induce domestic production now of 20,000 tractors per year. After a number of years of domestic production, the domestic firms will find ways to lower their costs, so the domestic supply curve in the future is lower. The government can remove the tariff in the future, and the future production of 50,000 tractors per year is cost-competitive by world standards.

of area v, surplus that would not exist if the country had not protected the industry in its early years. (For simplicity, the example assumes that the world price and the domestic demand curve do not change over time. This is not essential to the story. Also, the domestic industry is shown as still competing with imports in the future. This is not essential to the story, either. If the domestic cost curve falls low enough, the industry would become an exporter. The gain for the country in the future is still an area like v.)

How Valid Is It?

Whether the infant industry argument is a valid argument for a (temporary) tariff or other import barrier depends on whether the benefits to the country exceed the costs. The benefits are the stream of future producer surplus amounts (area v) that accrue to domestic producers once their production becomes cost-competitive by world standards. The costs are the deadweight losses (areas b and d) that the country incurs while the tariff is in place. It is not just that some domestic production in the future becomes cost-competitive. Rather, the cost-competitive future production must create enough surplus to exceed the deadweight losses of the tariff. Because this is an investment problem over time, we should carefully say that it is a valid argument if the present value of the stream of national benefits exceeds the present value of the stream of national costs.

The infant industry argument for protection looks great in theory. Still, there are important questions about how well it works in practice. Here are three questions to ask.

First, *is any government policy really needed?* The infant industry argument seems to be a story about firms that would make losses when they begin operations but eventually will become profitable. This is not an unusual business problem; in fact, it describes almost any new business. The standard solution is for the firm to obtain private financing, using personal wealth, borrowing from relatives and friends, obtaining bank loans, using venture capital, and so forth. If private financing is available, there is nothing left for the government to do.

Yet there are at least two reasons why there could be a beneficial role for government assistance. They both follow from distortions of the type that we have been examining in this chapter.

1. *There are imperfections in the financial markets.* Financial institutions like banks and stock markets may be underdeveloped or unwilling to take on certain kinds of risk. If the government cannot act directly to improve financial markets and institutions, then there could be a second-best argument for the government to provide assistance to the infant firms.

2. *The benefits from the early business investments do not accrue to the firms making these early investments.* Infant firms must spend a lot of money to learn about the product and the production process, to train workers, and to master the marketing of the product. They will not be able to earn profits on these early investments if follower firms can enter the industry later and imitate products and production technology, hire away experienced workers, and copy marketing practices. Competition from follower firms then means that the early firms do not earn much in the way of future profits. But if they probably will not earn future profits that can be used to pay back the loans, prudent lenders will not finance their early investments. Essentially, the early firms create positive externalities for the follower firms rather than future profits for themselves. In the face of this distortion, there could be a positive role for the government to provide assistance to the infant industry.

Second, *if the government is going to provide assistance, what government policy is best?* If the goal is to induce early production even when the early firms are not cost-competitive by world standards, we know that *a production subsidy is better than a tariff* or other import barrier. In Figure 10.3A, the national cost of a production subsidy in the early phase is only area *b*, not areas *b* and *d*. Other government policies could be even better if we can identify the exact reason why government intervention is needed. If the problem is imperfections in financial markets and institutions, the government should offer loans to the infant firms. If the problem is that the early firms train workers who then may leave and take their new skills to other firms, the government should offer a subsidy to defray some of the training costs. The specificity rule is very powerful in thinking about the best government policy to use to assist an infant industry. The rule cuts against the tariff.

Third, *will the infant industry really grow up?* It is cheap to claim to be a firm in an infant industry; it is much harder to become internationally competitive. If the tariff is truly temporary, then firms have a powerful incentive to grow up. But

Focus on Labor   How Much Does It Cost to Protect a Job?

Defenders of protection against imports claim that it is needed to protect domestic jobs. Although it sometimes sounds like any people who lose their jobs to increased imports are unemployed forever, we know that that is not true. Workers lose their jobs for many reasons, and nearly all of them then look for and find other jobs. It may take awhile and the new jobs may not pay as much (at first) as the previous jobs did, but they will be reemployed.

So the proponents of protection are really saying that restrictions on imports are needed to *maintain jobs in the import-competing industry that is receiving the protection.* We know that import barriers can maintain jobs in an import-competing industry by permitting domestic production at a level higher than it would be with free trade. But we also know from the discussion in the text that the specificity rule shows that an import barrier is not the best government policy to accomplish this objective.

Still, governments do use tariffs and non-tariff barriers to prop up domestic production and maintain jobs in import-competing industries. How large are the costs of doing so? We can examine the costs in two ways. First, how much does it cost domestic consumers of the product per job maintained? That is, what is the consumer surplus loss per job maintained? Second, what is the net cost to the country per job maintained?

We can turn to researchers at the Institute of International Economics to provide some estimates. Hufbauer and Elliott (1994) examined 21 highly protected industries in the United States, and Messerlin (2001) examined 22 highly protected industries in the European Union, both for 1990. Their estimates assume that the tariffs and import quotas do not affect world prices, the small-country assumption that is standard for this chapter.* Here is what they found:

| | Production Worker Jobs Maintained | Cost per Job Maintained ($ thousands) | |
		To Domestic Consumers	To the Nation
United States (21 industries)	191,764	169	54
European Union (22 industries)	243,650	191	99

*If, instead, the importing country is a large country, then including the effects of a change in the world prices would have almost no effect on the estimates of the cost to consumers per job maintained. For each industry both the numerator and the denominator of the calculation used to obtain the estimate would change by about the same proportion. Ignoring the world price change could result in estimates of the net cost to the country per job maintained that are larger than the costs actually are. If the importing country is large enough to drive down a product's world price when it imposes a tariff or quota, then the gains from the improved terms of trade would be set against the standard efficiency losses.

For the 21 industries in the United States, the jobs maintained by import protection represented about 10 percent of workers in these industries and less than 0.2 percent of the U.S. labor force. For the European Union, the maintained jobs were about 3 percent of workers in the 22 industries and less than 0.2 percent of the labor force.

These estimates show the high cost of maintaining industry jobs through high levels of

import protection. For the United States, consumers paid an average of about $169,000 per job maintained, and in Europe about $191,000 per job. Per year, this was over six times the average annual compensation for a manufacturing worker in each country. It would have been much cheaper for domestic consumers to simply pay these workers not to work than it was to maintain their jobs using import protection. For some specific industries the consumer cost per job maintained in the industry is breathtaking:

- For the United States, $600,000 for a sugar job and $498,000 for a dairy products job.
- For the European Union, $512,000 for an autoworker job and $474,000 for a chemical fiber job.

The net national cost per job was also high in both countries: $54,000 in the United States and $99,000 in the European Union. The net national cost per job was higher than the compensation earned by the typical manufacturing worker. It is worth noting that the average net national costs per job were this high because some of the protection was through VERs and similar policies that permit foreign exporters to raise their prices. Even if we remove these price markups lost to foreign exporters, the net national cost per job was still rather large—an average $18,000 in the United States and $42,000 in the European Union.

If our goal is to maintain jobs in these industries, the specificity rule says we can do better. Just paying the workers to have jobs in which they do nothing would be less costly. Indeed, the cost per person of a high-quality worker adjustment program that offers training and assistance to these workers to find well-paying jobs in other industries would be much less than the net national cost of maintaining these jobs through high import barriers.

the pressure is much less if the firms expect that they can ask for more time with the tariff because childhood is longer than they planned for. There is a danger that the industry remains high-cost behind the protection of the tariff for a long time. This is probably another reason to favor a subsidy. The subsidy is more likely to be temporary because there is likely to be ongoing political pressure to remove the subsidy.

There are cases of apparently successful infant industry protection, such as computers and semiconductors in Japan. The qualifier *apparently* is used because it is difficult to be sure that the eventual national benefits were more than the initial national costs, and because it is also difficult to show how much of a difference the government assistance actually made in the future success of the national industry. Another apparent success is Airbus in Europe, a case in which the governments provided subsidies and loans, not import protection. There are also many cases of failed infant industry protection. For instance, Brazil first offered "temporary" protection to its nascent automobile industry in 1952. More than 60 years later the tariff on imports is still 35 percent, and Brazil recently added an additional import tax that can be reduced if the car firm has sufficient local content or local research and development. It has been a long toddlerhood for auto production in Brazil.

In conclusion, how valid is the infant industry argument? Four conclusions emerge:

1. There can be a case for some sort of government encouragement.
2. A tariff may or may not be good.

3. Some form of government help other than a tariff is a better infant industry policy than a tariff.

4. It is hard for a government to know which industries to support because it is difficult to predict which industries can reduce their costs enough in the future to create net national benefits.

THE DYING INDUSTRY ARGUMENT AND ADJUSTMENT ASSISTANCE

The issues and results that arise in the infant industry debate also arise in the debate about saving dying industries from import competition. Once again, protection against imports might or might not be better than doing nothing. And, once again, doing something else is better than blocking imports.

Should the Government Intervene?

With regularity, rising imports of a product threaten the well-being and even the survival of import-competing domestic firms and industries. Time and again society faces a choice: Should the firms be allowed to shrink, perhaps to go out of business, or should they be protected?

If we are in a first-best world, the answer is clear. Since the social value of anything is already included in private incentives, ordinary demand and supply curves are already leading us to the right choice without any government intervention. If rising import competition is driving domestic producers out of business, so be it. Adjustment out of the industry is necessary so that the country can enjoy the net gains from increasing trade. It is true that there will be some losses to workers, managers, investors, and landowners. They must shift their resources into other uses that may not pay quite as well as the original uses did. These losses are already measured in the loss of producer surplus. Consumers gain more, and net national well-being increases.

There are, however, ways in which we could reject the rosy first-best view of the world. One important assumption is that the workers, managers, capital, and land quickly are reemployed in other uses, even if their pay is less. A protectionist would be right to insist that this adjustment does not always work so smoothly. For instance, firms in an import-competing industry are often concentrated in a small geographic area within the country. (For the United States examples include steel firms in the industrial Midwest from Pittsburgh to Chicago and clothing firms in North Carolina.) If large numbers of workers lose their jobs in one of these industries within a short time period, the labor market becomes "congested." Many people are looking for new jobs, and many do not have the skills that match the available jobs. Steelworkers do not easily start new careers as electronics workers next Monday in the same town. Many people will probably suffer through long spells of unemployment.

While these displaced workers and other resources are unemployed, they lose all income, not just the loss of producer surplus that would occur if they could easily shift into the next-best employment. In this case, the amount of their income that imports take away is a loss to society as well as to them. Wouldn't it be better for society to intervene? Wouldn't blocking the rising imports be better than standing by while the domestic industry withers?

The protectionist argument about a dying industry is just as valid as the arguments we examined in the past two sections. And the argument has the same flaws. In fact, it is the same argument, but in a different setting. The argument that workers and other resources will not quickly be reemployed outside the threatened industry can be recast in terms of Figure 10.2. The marginal external benefit (area *g* in Figure 10.2) of continuing production of 0.8 million bikes, instead of letting production shrink to 0.6 million bikes, is avoiding the costs of unemployment if resources are forced out of the bicycle industry. Area *g*'s extra benefits from maintaining the level of domestic production exist, in this case, because workers and other resources do not have to bear the lost income and other costs of shifting to employment in other industries. So it may be true that protecting a dying industry against imports is better than doing nothing. It depends, again, on whether area *g* is greater than areas *b* + *d* in panel A of Figure 10.2.

However, there is some other policy that works better than putting up import barriers. The specificity rule reminds us to look for the true source of the problem. The problem is really about employment or production, not imports. There is, again, no reason to make imports more expensive to consumers as long as we can help producers directly. If the problem is the cost of relocating to other geographic areas, then a subsidy for the costs of moving is better than import protection. If the problem is a mismatch of worker skills and available jobs, then a subsidy for the costs of retraining is better. Or, if the social losses can be avoided only by maintaining current production and employment in the threatened industry, then a subsidy to production (as we showed in Figure 10.2) or to employment in this industry is better.

In fact, governments do sometimes try to help import-threatened industries with something other than import protection. One example was the U.S. government's bailout loans to Chrysler at the end of the 1970s. Chrysler used the loans to make capital improvements that allowed it to survive and repay the loans on time. Of course, not all bailouts work so well. Many just end up being a continual drain on taxpayers, as rounds of new assistance are needed to keep the firms in business.

Trade Adjustment Assistance

Governments in a number of developed countries offer trade adjustment assistance to workers and firms in import-threatened industries. For instance, in the United States workers can petition the U.S. Department of Labor for this assistance. If the department accepts that this group of workers is being harmed by increased imports, workers who lose their jobs receive up to 30 months of unemployment compensation (much more than the 6 months that is usual in most states), and they are eligible for retraining programs and subsidies for job search and moving expenses.[4]

Trade adjustment assistance sounds like it is reasonably consistent with the specificity rule because it focuses on income losses, retraining, and job mobility. Nonetheless, it is controversial. In the United States it has been attacked from different sides. First, U.S. labor groups that originally backed it have felt betrayed

---

[4]In addition, an eligible worker who is over 50 years of age and whose annual earnings are less than $50,000 can receive a cash supplement equal to up to half of the wage difference if the earnings at a new job are less than the earnings at her previous job. Some other benefits had been available in earlier years but expired in 2011 or 2014.

because, in practice, it has provided so little support. The standards for eligibility are rather stringent. During 2009–2013 about two-thirds of the petitions for assistance were accepted. On average, about 150,000 workers per year qualify for assistance. Only about one-third of these workers use any of the assistance benefits. Labor groups believe that the assistance mainly provides temporary compensation (the extended unemployment benefits), and that the retraining has been rather ineffective. The retraining often does not result in new skills and good alternative employment.

From a different side, defenders of the free market question the whole concept of adjustment assistance for import-competing industries. They ask why society should single out this group for special aid. Jobs and incomes are affected by many different pressures for change in the economy, including shifts in consumer tastes, technological change, bad management decisions, government rerouting of highways, and bad weather. The government provides general unemployment compensation and some general support for retraining and relocation. Why should the government give more generous assistance to those whose jobs and incomes are affected by rising imports but not to those affected by the many other reasons that supply and demand shift in a market?

Free-market opponents of trade adjustment assistance also argue that this assistance creates perverse incentives. It encourages people to change their behavior for the worse. First, firms and workers are encouraged to gamble on entering or staying in import-vulnerable industries because they know that extra relief will be given if things work out badly. Second, workers are encouraged to remain unemployed for longer periods of time because they can receive unemployment compensation for a longer time. These perverse incentives (called *moral hazards* in discussions of insurance) do not automatically mean that the assistance program is bad. However, the net benefit of the program is reduced, and it may turn into a net cost because people change their behavior. (This set of problems affects many other government programs offering assistance. For instance, flood disaster relief helps victims of floods who have incurred large losses, but it also encourages people to settle in flood-prone areas.)

Thus, the economic case for a government to offer trade adjustment assistance is mixed. Still, there may be a good practical and political case for tying extra assistance to import injury. Where foreign trade is involved, free-trade advocacy is weakened because many of its beneficiaries, being foreign, have no votes in the national politics of the importing country. With no votes for foreign workers or firms, there is extra danger that injured workers and firms that lobby aggressively for sweeping protectionist legislation will prevail. More generous adjustment assistance for import-competing groups than for others may be an effective political step to forestall more protectionist policies.

THE DEVELOPING GOVERNMENT (PUBLIC REVENUE) ARGUMENT

Import tariffs can be justified by another second-best argument relating to conditions in developing countries. In a poor nation, the tariff as a source of revenue may be beneficial and even better than any feasible alternative policy, *both for the nation and for the world as a whole*.

For a developing nation with low living standards, the most serious "domestic distortions" may relate to the government's inability to provide an adequate supply of public goods. A low-income nation like Mali would receive large social benefits if it expanded such basic public services as the control of infectious diseases, water control for agriculture, and primary schooling. Yet the administrative resources of many poor nations are not great enough to capture these social gains.

The **developing government argument** states that in poor developing nations the import tariff becomes a crucial source, not of industrial protection but of government revenue. Revenue can be raised more cheaply by simply guarding key ports and border crossings with a few customs officials who tax imports than by levying more elaborate kinds of taxes. Production, consumption, income, and property cannot be effectively taxed when they cannot be measured and monitored.

The developing government argument is a valid reason why very low-income countries receive on average about 16 percent of their government revenue from customs duties, a higher dependence on customs than is found in equally trade-oriented high-income countries such as Canada. (On average for industrialized countries, taxes on international trade are about 1 percent of government revenues.) In principle, a developing-country government can use the tariff revenues to create net social gains, gains that may even benefit the world as a whole. This is not to say that every government that heavily taxes foreign trade is using the money to fund socially worthy investments. Foreign trade has also been heavily taxed by corrupt and wasteful governments. Based on available data for 2010, six of the seven countries that collected more than 20 percent of their total government revenues through import tariffs were also among the worse half of countries for perceived levels of government corruption.

OTHER ARGUMENTS FOR PROTECTION: NONECONOMIC OBJECTIVES

The other leading arguments for tariff protection relate to the national pursuit of noneconomic objectives, that is, goals other than achieving economic efficiency. The potential range of such arguments is limitless, but the view that people do not live by imported bread alone usually focuses on three other goals: national pride, national defense, and income distribution. Fortunately, a modified version of the specificity rule applies to a country pursuing a noneconomic objective: *To achieve the noneconomic objective with the least economic cost to the nation, use a policy that acts as directly as possible on the specific objective.*

National Pride

Nations desire symbols as much as individuals do, and knowing that some good is produced within our own country can be as legitimate an object of national pride as having cleaned up a previous urban blight or winning Olympic medals. As long as the pride can be generated only by something collective and nationwide, something not purchased by individuals in the marketplace, there is a case for policy intervention. If the pride is generated by domestic production itself, then the appropriate policy tool is a domestic production subsidy, not an import barrier. Only if the pride comes from increased self-sufficiency is restricting imports the best policy approach.

National Defense

The national defense argument says that import barriers would help the nation to have or to be ready to produce products that would be important in a future military emergency. It has a rich history and several interesting twists to its analysis. English mercantilists in the 17th century used the national defense argument to justify restrictions on the use of foreign ships and shipping services: If we force ourselves to buy English ships and shipping, we will foster the growth of a shipbuilding industry and a merchant marine that will be vital in time of war. Even Adam Smith departed from his otherwise scathing attacks on trade barriers to support the restrictive Navigation Acts where shipping and other defense industries were involved. The national defense argument remains a favorite with producers who need a social excuse for protection. In 1984, the president of the Footwear Industry of America, with a straight face, told the Armed Services Committee of Congress,

> In the event of war or other national emergency, it is highly unlikely that the domestic footwear industry could provide sufficient footwear for the military and civilian population . . . We won't be able to wait for ships to deliver shoes from Taiwan, or Korea or Brazil or Eastern Europe . . . [I]mproper footwear can lead to needless casualties and turn sure victory into possible defeat.[5]

The importance of having products ready for defense emergencies is clear. Yet a little reflection shows that none of the popular variants of the national defense argument succeeds in making a good case for an import barrier. That is, the popular national defense arguments fail to follow the specificity rule. For instance, if the objective is to maintain domestic production capacity for a product that is crucial to the national defense, then a production subsidy is the policy that has the lower cost to the nation.

The possibilities of storage and depletion also argue against the use of a tariff to create defense capability. If the crucial goods can be stored inexpensively, the cheapest way to prepare for the emergency is to buy them from foreigners at low world prices during peace. Thus, the United States could stockpile low-cost imported footwear instead of producing it domestically at greater cost. And if the crucial goods are depletable mineral resources, such as oil, the case for the tariff is even weaker. Restricting imports of oil when there is no foreign embargo or blockade causes us to use up our own resources faster, cutting the amount we can draw on when an embargo or blockade is imposed. It is better to stockpile imports at relatively low peacetime cost, as the United States has done with its Strategic Petroleum Reserve since the mid-1970s.

Income Redistribution

A third, less economic objective to which trade policy might be addressed is the distribution of income within the nation. Often one of the most sensitive questions in national politics is either "What does it do to the poor?" or "What effect does it have

---

[5]Quoted in *Far Eastern Economic Review,* October 25, 1984, p. 70.

on different regions or ethnic groups?" A tariff could sometimes be defended on the grounds that it restores equity by favoring some wrongly disadvantaged group, even though it may reduce the overall size of the pie to be distributed among groups. It is certainly important to know the effects of trade policy on the distribution of income within a country, a subject we have already examined in a number of previous chapters.

If the issue is inequity in how income is distributed within our country, why should trade policy be the means of redressing the inequity? Why not attack the problem directly? If, for example, greater income equality is the objective, it is less costly to equalize incomes directly, through tax-and-transfer programs, than to try to equalize incomes indirectly by manipulating the tariff structure. Only if political constraints are somehow so binding that the income distribution can be adjusted only through import policy would import barriers be justified on this ground.

THE POLITICS OF PROTECTION

We have now made much progress in our search for good import barriers. We have found a number of situations in which import protection could be better than free trade, but in nearly all of these some other form of government policy is even better.

If the economic case for import protection is so weak, why do most countries have many import barriers in place? Why are import barriers high for some products and low for others? In each country import barriers are adopted and maintained through a political process of decision-making. Understanding the answers to questions about why import barriers exist requires a mixture of political and economic insights. There is a growing literature on the "political economy of trade barriers." It focuses on activities by pressure groups and the self-interested behavior of political representatives who seek to maximize their chances of staying in office.

The Basic Elements of the Political–Economic Analysis

Let's take a look at the political process that leads to a decision about whether or not to impose a tariff on imports of a good, say, socks. As we have seen in previous chapters, imposing the tariff will have different effects on the well-being of different groups in the country, with both winners and losers. In addition, we presume that the tariff would cause some economic inefficiency—a decrease in national well-being because the losers lose more than the winners gain. When will such a tariff be enacted? Why?

There are a number of key elements in our political–economic analysis:

1. *The size of the gains for the winners from protection, and how many individuals are in the group of winners.* Let's call the total gains B_p, and presume that this is the producer surplus gained from securing government protection—the same thing as area *a* in diagrams like Figure 8.4. N_p is the number of individuals benefiting from the protection.

2. *The size of the losses for the losers from protection, and how many individuals are in the group of losers.* In the political fight, they gain by defeating the tariff. Their total gains are B_c, which we presume to be at least as large as areas *a* + *b* + *d* in

Figure 8.4. (Consumers may not view the tariff revenue area c as a loss to them if the government uses the revenue to reduce other consumer taxes or spends the revenue on projects valued by the consumers.) N_c is the number of individuals losing from protection (gaining from defeating protection).

3. *Individuals' reasons for taking positions for or against protection.* We presume that direct gains and losses of well-being (B_p and B_c) are reasons for taking positions. There may be other reasons. One is sympathy for groups who are suffering losses. Another is ideology or other closely held core beliefs about politics and economics.

4. *Types of political activities and their costs.* Individuals (and groups of individuals sharing a common interest) can engage in a range of different political activities. Assuming that the country has elections or referendums, individuals can vote. Individuals can themselves engage in lobbying of their government officials, in which the individuals provide information on their position, or they can hire others to lobby for them. Individuals can provide campaign contributions to politicians running for office. Or individuals can provide bribes or other side payments to attempt to gain the support of government officials. The costs of these different types of political activities include both money cost and the opportunity cost of any time or other efforts used in the activity.

5. *Political institutions and the political process.* We will closely examine two types of political processes: first, direct voting on the tariff by all individuals and, second, elected representatives voting on the tariff. These seem most relevant to a democratic system like that used in most industrialized and many developing countries. (Other possibilities include a single decision-maker or decision-making by an appointed committee of experts.)

When Are Tariffs Unlikely?

Under some circumstances, inefficient trade barriers would be rejected, and we would have a world closer to free trade than we observe. Let's consider two sets of circumstances.

Our first case is direct democracy. Consider what will happen if we have (1) a direct vote by individuals on each tariff (or import barrier), with (2) voting (almost) costless so that (almost) everyone votes, and (3) each person voting based on her direct interest as a winner or a loser from protection. Nearly always the number of losers, N_c (the number of consumers of the product), is larger than the number of winners, N_p (the number of people involved in production of the import-competing product). In the example of socks, nearly everyone buys socks, but only a small number of people work in (or provide substantial amounts of other resources like land or capital to) the sock industry. The sock tariff would be defeated by a large margin. Most trade barriers protect only a minority, and this is probably true even if many trade barriers are combined into a single vote.

The trade barriers that we see in most countries depart from what simple majority-rule democracy would give us. Indeed, countries usually do not use direct votes to set protection. Rather, a group of elected representatives or some other government officials decide. Winning the political fight is gaining the support of a majority of these representatives or officials.

Are forms of government like representative democracy inherently protectionist? Our second case shows that representative democracy can also lead to little or no protection. Consider what will happen if (1) each group is willing to devote all of its total gain (B_p and B_c) to political activity like lobbying or contributions and (2) politicians decide which side to support according to the amount of lobbying or contributions they receive. The fact that the tariff causes economic inefficiency means that B_c is larger than B_p. Those opposed to the tariff would be willing to spend up to B_c to prevent the tariff, while the protectionists would not rationally spend more than the smaller stake B_p. The inefficiency of the tariff (equal to $B_c - B_p$) dooms that tariff. Even if the political process does not work exactly like this, it still would tend to reject the more inefficient of protectionist proposals.

When Are Tariffs Likely?

Lobbying and contributions can lead to political decisions enacting protection if protectionist groups are more effective than other groups in organizing their political activities. In this case we reach a surprising conclusion: The group with the smaller number of individuals can be more effective. We can see two different reasons for this surprising conclusion. Both are based on the fact that each individual in the smaller group tends to have a larger individual gain.

First, consider what happens when there is some fixed cost per individual to being involved in any political activity. This cost could be a minimum amount of time that must be spent, or it could be the per person cost of organizing a group effort to engage in lobbying. If the benefit to an individual is less than the cost to participate, the individual will probably decide not to participate. The average gain per supporter of protection is B_p/N_p, and the average gain per opponent of protection is B_c/N_c. The individual gain tends to be larger as the number of individuals in the group is smaller. In our sock example, the number of sock producers is small, but the gain to each from protection is large (perhaps hundreds or thousands of dollars per year). The number of sock consumers is large, but the loss to each from protection is small (probably a few tens of dollars or less per year). If consumers' benefits from defeating the protectionist measure are small per person, many (or all) of them may decide that it is not worth it to fight protectionism. (That is, they see that B_c/N_c is less than the minimum per person cost of participating.) The protectionist minority is the only active interest group, and it gains the majority of representatives' votes.

Second, consider what happens when some members of the group can decide to "free-ride" on the contributions of others in the group. The free-rider problem arises whenever the benefits of a group effort fall on everyone in the group regardless of how much each individual does (or does not) contribute (in time, effort, voting, or money). Each selfishly rational individual tries to get a free ride, letting others advance the common cause. The free-rider problem usually affects a large, dispersed group more seriously than it affects a small, well-defined group. Conquering the free-rider problem is what political action groups—special interests—are all about.

Import-competing producers are motivated to participate in the politics of protection. They often overcome the free-rider problem to become a well-organized group with substantial resources to use in political activity. The group lobbies vociferously in favor of protection. The group uses campaign contributions to enhance the chances of electing representatives friendly to their position, to gain access to the representatives for lobbying, to influence the representatives' positions on votes, and reward those who vote in favor of industry protection. In contrast, each individual in the large, diffuse consumer group has a small incentive to become active and a large incentive to free-ride. But if all or most try to free-ride, the large group of consumers is not organized or has few resources to use for political activity. In our sock example, a trade association may organize and represent the interests of the sock-producing firms, and if the industry is unionized, the labor unions represent the interest of workers. An organization of sock consumers is unlikely.

The outcome is often that the well-organized protectionist lobby sways a majority of representatives, even though this protection is economically inefficient and hurts a majority of voters. Generally, the politicians in favor of protection trade a small reduction in the individual well-being of many voters, with some loss of votes possible in the next election, for the votes and largess of those protected, including the ability to use their campaign contributions to gain votes in the next election.

The tariffs imposed by the U.S. government on steel imports in 2002 provide a stark example of the political economy of protection. The small number of American steel firms are well organized as a political lobbying force. The industry employs only about 200,000 workers, about 0.1 percent of the U.S. workforce, but the United Steelworkers union is also politically active. Users of steel are much more dispersed. They did achieve some organization and mount a campaign to oppose the tariffs, but their effort was not as effective. In addition, steel firms and steelworkers are concentrated in a few states, including West Virginia, Pennsylvania, and Ohio, that were considered crucial for the 2002 and 2004 elections. In March 2002 the protectionists won—President George W. Bush announced new tariffs of up to 30 percent on imports of many types of steel. The box "How Sweet It Is (or Isn't)" presents another example by examining the political–economic forces in play for sugar protection.

In addition to this recognition of the important general role of lobbying and contributions by special interest groups, other specific features of the country's political institutions affect the political economy of protection. Here are two that are documented for the United States. First, the U.S. Senate gives exactly two senators to each state, regardless of population. States that are mainly rural and agricultural are overrepresented, providing extra support for protection of agricultural industries. Second, for the U.S. House of Representatives, in which there is one representative for each district, it helps to have the production activities of an import-competing industry spread over a substantial number of states or districts, so that a large number of representatives are likely to become a core of supporters for protection for the industry.

Applications to Other Trade-Policy Patterns

The simple model of political activity in a representative democracy can also explain other patterns besides the overall favoring of producer interests over consumer interests. Some of these patterns are extensions of the same producer-bias pattern; some are not.

The **tariff escalation** pattern is a general symptom of the importance of group size and concentration to effective lobbying. Economists have found that nominal and effective tariff rates rise with the stage of production. That is, tariff rates are typically

Case Study   How Sweet It Is (or Isn't)

Do you like to eat things that are sweet? If you do, and if you live in the United States, the European Union, or Japan, then you are a victim of your country's protectionist policies toward sugar. The domestic price of your sugar is about double the world price. For the United States, on average during 2000–2013, the domestic price of raw sugar was $0.24 per pound, while the world price was $0.14 per pound. For the United States, sugar protection costs consumers about $3.5 billion per year.

If you live in any of these countries, have you ever sent a letter to your legislative representative asking him or her to oppose sugar protection, a policy that is clearly against your interests? Have you contributed money or time to a group that lobbies the government to end sugar protection? Do you know anyone who has ever done so? Presumably not. Why not? While $3.5 billion per year sounds like a lot of money, it is only about $11 per person per year. As discussed in the text, the average gain for any one person to oppose this protection is small. It's not worth your effort.

The situation is a little different for sugar producers. For the United States, the increase in domestic producer surplus is about $1.5 billion per year. These gains are concentrated in a small number of firms. It is worth it for them to actively seek policies that restrain sugar imports. Two companies, American Crystal in North Dakota and Minnesota, and Flo-Sun in Florida, have been particularly active, contributing millions of dollars in recent years to Democratic and Republican congressional candidates and political parties. For Flo-Sun, owned by two brothers, Alfonso and Jose Fanjul, one estimate is that protectionist sugar policies add $65 million per year to their profits. A few million bucks to defend this profit stream is definitely a good investment.

Another group active in lobbying is the American Sugar Alliance, representing major U.S. sugar growers. In addition, the high domestic price for sugar expands demand for corn sweeteners, a close substitute for sugar. Corn farmers in the American Midwest like the sugar protection, and they have a major influence on the positions taken by their states' representatives and senators.

The Coalition for Sugar Reform, which includes food manufacturers that use sugar, consumer groups, taxpayer advocates, and environmental groups, is active in opposing sugar protection. It has some good arguments on its side. As Jeff Nedelman, a spokesperson for the coalition, said, "This is a corporate welfare program for the very rich."* The coalition points out that jobs are being lost as sugar-using firms shift production to other countries where sugar prices are cheaper. Furthermore, by polluting and disrupting water flows, the protected sugar production in Florida is also a cause of serious environmental decline in the Everglades. These are good points, but they are no match for the money and organization of the proponents of protection.

Foreign sugar producers, many of them poor farmers in developing countries, are also hurt by protectionist policies in importing countries. Researchers estimate that the world sugar price would rise by 17 percent if the United States removed its sugar policies. But it is not easy for foreign interests to have an effect on the U.S. political process. Foreigners don't vote, and political opponents can charge that legislators who openly side with foreigners against U.S. workers and companies are "anti-American."

So the sugar protection policies continue. For the United States, the net cost to the country is close to $2 billion per year. It is not that sugar is so large or important a part of the economy that we have to protect it. In the United States, about 6,000 people work growing sugar, and about 12,000 people work in sugar refining. If we shifted to free trade, employment would probably decline by about 3,000. The small number of people who lose their jobs could be reemployed with little trouble in other sectors of the economy. Instead, we see the pure political economy of protection, with the producer interests in this case much better organized and effective than the consumers are.

DISCUSSION QUESTION

A U.S. company (like Jelly Belly) makes its gourmet jelly beans in the United States, and sugar is about half the cost of production. Can the company change U.S. sugar policy? If not, what are its other options?

*As quoted in "Sugar Rules Defy Free-Trade Logic," *New York Times,* May 6, 2001.

higher on final consumer goods than on intermediate goods and raw materials sold to producing firms.[6] The explanation would seem to be that household consumers are a particularly weak lobby, being many people who are not well organized into dues-collecting lobbying associations. Consumer groups fight only weakly against the producers of final products, whose cause is championed by influential large firms and trade associations. When it comes to fights over protecting producers of intermediate goods, the story can be quite different. The buyers of intermediate goods are themselves firms and can organize lobbying efforts as easily as their suppliers can. The outcome of a struggle over tariffs on intermediate goods is thus less likely to favor protection.

The bias in favor of producer interests over consumer interests also shows up in multilateral negotiations to liberalize trade. There are curious guidelines as to what constitutes a fair balance of concessions by the different nations at the bargaining table. A concession is any agreement to cut one's own import duties, thereby letting in more imports. Each country is pressured to allow as much import expansion as the export expansion it gets from other countries' import liberalizations. It is odd to see import liberalization treated as a concession by the importing nation. After all, cutting your own import tariffs usually should bring net national gains, not losses. The concession-balancing rule is further evidence of the power of producer groups over consumer groups. The negotiators view their own import tariff cuts as sacrifices because they have to answer politically to import-competing producer groups but not to masses of poorly organized consumers. In addition, another producer group in the country—producers of exportable products—is active in lobbying to influence the trade negotiations. The balancing "concessions" by other countries to lower foreign import barriers bring benefits to export producers so that they politically support the multilateral trade liberalization.

So far we have presumed that each individual takes a position in favor of or against protection according to his or her own direct self-interest. But, in some cases, it seems that sympathy (or other reasons) determines an individual's position.

Interest groups are often victorious because they gain the sympathy of others, that is, of people who will not directly gain if policy helps the interest group. Political sympathy often surges when a group suffers a big income loss all at once, especially in a general recession. Sympathy creates this **sudden-damage effect.** The sympathy can spring from either of two sources. One is compassion for those suffering large income losses. Political sentiments often yield to pleas for protection when a surge of import competition wipes out incomes, just as we provide generous relief for victims of natural disasters. The other source shows up more when a deep recession hits the whole economy. In a recession, an increased number of people are at risk of having their incomes cut. More of them identify with the less fortunate, thinking, "That could be me." One policy response is to help those damaged by import competition, whose pleas are heard above the mild complaints of many consumers who would suffer small individual losses from import barriers. Thus, both a surge in import competition and a general recession raise sympathy for protectionism.

---

[6]The tariff escalation pattern does not apply to agricultural products in most industrialized countries, however. Farmers get at least as much effective protection as the processors and wholesalers to whom they sell.

Our discussion began in this section with the general question of why the overall level of trade barriers is higher than the analysis of economic efficiency would justify. But now that we have examined the political economy of trade barriers, we might easily ask the opposite question. Given the power of well-organized import-competing producers favoring protection, as well as the appeal of sympathy for local producers struggling against imports produced by foreign firms, why are our import barriers not so very high? One reason is that there are organized producer groups that are opposed to protection. These include firms that use imported products in their own production, the wholesalers and retailers who distribute imports, and export producers who generally favor free trade. A second reason is that we have used mutual "concessions" during multilateral trade negotiations to lower trade barriers. There is probably also a third reason. Economic ideology probably does have some impact. Politicians who espouse the merits of free enterprise, markets, and competition probably do see that protection is inconsistent with these concepts. This does make them somewhat less likely to support protection.

Summary

There are valid arguments for import barriers, though most are quite different from those usually given. One way or another, valid defenses of import barriers lean on the existence of relevant distortions (resulting from gaps between private and social costs or benefits) or noneconomic objectives.

In a second-best world where there are *distortions* in the domestic economy, imposing a tariff may be better than doing nothing. Whether or not it is better will depend on the details of the specific case. Yet, even when imposing the tariff is better than doing nothing, something else is usually better than the tariff. The specificity rule is a guideline that says: Use the policy tool that is closest to the true source of the distorting gap between private and social incentives. This rule cuts against import barriers, which are usually only indirectly related to the source of the distortion. Thus, many of the main arguments for blocking imports—such as maintaining jobs in an industry, the infant industry argument, and the national defense argument—are really arguments for government policies other than import barriers. The case for tariffs is most secure in the developing government setting. If a country is poor and its government limited in its administrative ability, then tariffs can be a vital source of government revenue to finance basic public investments and services.

Where, then, are the borders that separate good trade barriers from bad ones? Figure 10.4 maps those borders by summarizing the policy results of the main cases surveyed in this chapter plus Chapter 8's nationally optimal tariff plus two relevant cases coming up in the next chapter. Note the clear contrast in the answers in the two columns. In the middle column, the answer repeatedly is yes, an import barrier *can* be better than doing nothing, depending on factors discussed in this chapter. In the right column, the answer is generally no, the import barrier is not the best policy tool except in cases where the exact locus of the distortion is in international trade itself.

If analysis of economic efficiency indicates that import protection is often a bad policy and seldom the best policy, why do so many countries have so many import barriers? The political economy of trade barriers explains them in terms of the gains

FIGURE 10.4   Can an Import Barrier Be Better Than Doing Nothing, and Is It the Best Policy?

A Summary of Verdicts*

Goal to Be Promoted	Can an Import Barrier Be Better Than Doing Nothing?	Is an Import Barrier the Best Policy Tool?
Domestic production	Yes, it can	No
Domestic jobs	Yes, it can	No
An infant industry	Yes, it can	No
A developing government	Yes, it can	No
National pride	Yes, it can	No, unless only self-sufficiency can make the nation proud
National defense	Yes, it can	No
A fairer income distribution	Yes, it can	No
National monopsony power (a large country)	Yes, it can	For the nation, yes (if no retaliation); for the world, no (Chapter 8's nationally optimal tariff)
Antidumping (Chapter 11)	Usually, no	Usually, no
Counter a foreign export subsidy (Chapter 11)	Usually, no	For the nation, no; for the world, yes

Note: Remember that "Yes, it can" does not mean "Yes, it is." To see what separates situations when the import barrier is better than nothing from situations when it is worse, review the text of this chapter.
*In all verdicts except that for national monopsony power, the conclusions refer to a small country, so that the conclusions are not confounded by the possibility of optimal-tariff effects on the terms of trade.

for the winners from protection; the losses to those hurt by protection; the costs of engaging in political activities like voting, lobbying, and making campaign contributions; and the way that the political process works.

We can imagine political systems in which protection would be unlikely. If everybody voted directly, the majority would probably vote against a tariff or nontariff barrier because more people would be hurt as consumers than would be helped as producers of the product. Or, if everyone was willing to devote the entire amount that they would gain or lose to political activities like lobbying or campaign contributions, then political representatives would probably oppose protection because the loss to consumers would be larger than the gain to producers.

In reality, some groups are more effective than others at taking political actions to influence the votes of representatives. Producer groups are often more effective than consumer groups because the benefits of protection are concentrated in a small group of producers. The benefits are large enough to spur actions by individual producers, and the free-rider problem is more easily solved in a small group. In addition, support for protection often increases when the losses to the group hurt by rising imports generate sympathy among the rest of the population.

This approach also helps to explain other patterns. The group-size effect can explain the tariff escalation pattern. A few large firms buying intermediate goods make a stronger lobby against protection of the products they are buying than do masses of final consumers, each of whom has too small an interest to go to battle over consumer-good import policy. The ability of producer interests to lobby effectively also explains why, in international trade negotiations, each nation treats its own tariff reductions as if they were sacrifices. They are sacrifices for politicians who must answer to well-organized import-competing producer groups. And the concessions offered by other countries to reduce their trade barriers mobilize well-organized groups of export producers to support the multilateral agreement.

Key Terms

Second-best world	Infant industry argument	National defense argument
Externalities	Trade adjustment assistance	Free-rider problem
Spillover effects	Developing government	Tariff escalation
Specificity rule	argument	Sudden-damage effect

Suggested Reading

The theory of trade policy in a second-best world was pioneered by Nobel laureate James Meade (1955). Johnson (1965) and Bhagwati (1969) made major contributions, and Dixit (1985) provides a survey of related research.

Irwin (2009) examines economic and political arguments for protection. Kletzer (2001) discusses the experiences of U.S. workers who lost their jobs due to import competition. Baicker and Rehavi (2004), Kletzer and Rosen (2005), and Reynolds and Palatucci (2012) describe and analyze trade adjustment assistance in the United States. The Organization for Economic Cooperation and Development (2007) estimates the effects of protectionist sugar policies in a number of countries.

Two pioneering theories of political behavior and lobbying biases are Downs (1957) and Olson (1965). Grossman and Helpman (1994) provide an influential technical analysis of the political economy of trade barriers. Magee (2011) explores why tariffs are actually low.

Questions and Problems

♦ 1. A single firm's innovations in production technology often benefit the production of other firms because these other firms learn about the new technology and can use some of the ideas in their own production.

    a. Is there an externality here?

    b. How would an economist rank the following two policies in this situation? Why?

        i. A tariff on imports, to make sure that domestic production using the new technology occurs.

        ii. A subsidy to domestic production, to make sure that domestic production using the new technology occurs.

    c. What third policy (a tax or a subsidy to something) would the economist recommend as even better than these two?

2. What is the specificity rule?

✦ 3. A small price-taking nation imports a good that it could not possibly produce itself at any finite price. Can you describe plausible conditions under which that nation would benefit from an import tariff on the good?

4. What is the infant industry argument for putting up barriers to imports? What are its merits and weaknesses?

✦ 5. Can you describe plausible conditions under which a nation would benefit from subsidizing imports of a good?

6. What is the national defense argument for putting up barriers to imports? Why is import protection probably not the best approach?

✦ 7. "The infant industry argument is not really an argument for a tariff on imports of a product." Do you agree or disagree? Why?

8. The minister for labor of the small nation of Pembangunan is eager to encourage domestic production of digital clocks. A small clock industry exists, but only a few producers can survive foreign competition without government help. The minister argues that helping the industry would create jobs and skills that will be carried over into other industries by workers trained in this one. He calls for a 10 percent tariff to take advantage of these benefits. At the same cabinet meeting, the minister for industry argues for a 10 percent subsidy to domestic clock production instead, stating that the same benefits to the nation can be achieved at less social cost.

   a. Show the following diagrammatically:
      i. The effects of the tariff on domestic clock output and consumption.
      ii. The beneficial side effects of the tariff described by the minister for labor.
      iii. The net gains or losses for the nation as a whole.
      iv. All the same effects for the case of the production subsidy.
      v. The differences in the effects of the two alternatives on the government's budget. Which policy would appeal more to a deficit-conscious minister for finance?

   b. Can you describe a policy that captures the benefits of worker training better than either the 10 percent tariff or the 10 percent production subsidy?

✦ 9. Australia has only one firm that makes aircraft. Without assistance from the government, that firm has lost most of its business to imports from the United States and Europe. Which of the following policies would be most costly for the Australian nation as a whole, and which would be least costly?

   Policy A: Paying the lone Australian firm a *production* subsidy per plane, without protecting it against imports.

   Policy B: Imposing a *tariff* equal to the production subsidy in policy A.

   Policy C: Imposing an import *quota* that cuts imports just as much as policy B would.

10. Assume that the sock-importing countries are determined to expand their domestic production of socks. From the point of view of the sock-exporting countries, how would you rate each of these three policies that could be used by the sock importers? Why?

   Policy A: Subsidies to domestic sock production in the importing countries.

   Policy B: Tariffs on sock imports.

   Policy C: VERs on sock exports.

✦ 11. Do you favor or oppose the government policy of offering extra adjustment assistance to workers displaced by increasing imports? Why?

12. What is the free-rider problem, and how does it affect trade policy?

✦ 13. Elected legislative representatives are considering enacting a quota on imports of baseball bats, with the rights to import the quota amount of bats to be given for free to the three companies that currently distribute imported baseball bats. Identify the groups that have a direct interest in whether or not the quota is enacted. How effective do you think each will be in lobbying?

14. What is the tariff escalation pattern? Why does it exist in many countries?

✦ 15. In Chapter 2 we introduced the one-dollar, one-vote metric. If political decisions in a small country about imposing tariffs were based on this metric, how many tariffs would this country have?

16. A country currently has free trade in men's t-shirts, and the country imports half of its total domestic consumption. The government of the country has fully committed to the goal of reducing the quantity imported of t-shirts by one-third. The government is considering either a subsidy to domestic production or a tariff on imports to achieve its goal.

A friend who works in the foreign ministry knows that you are studying international economics, and she asks you to write a report comparing and contrasting the two policy alternatives (production subsidy or tariff). To make the report more authoritative, you are going to use at least one graph and one or more key concepts that you just learned in this chapter. What will you write and show in your report?

Chapter **Eleven**

Pushing Exports

Controversy over export behavior and export policy rivals the perennial fights over import barriers. On the export side, however, the fight takes on a somewhat different form. Here the fight usually centers on the artificial *promotion* of trade rather than on trade barriers. This chapter explores how both businesses and governments may push for more exports than their country would sell under ordinary competition. The underlying policy questions are: Can a country export too much for its own good or for the good of the world? Is that happening today? If so, what should an importing country do about another country's apparently excessive exports?

These questions do not arise in a vacuum. Governments, pressured by business and labor lobbies, have long fought over what producers in importing countries consider artificial and excessive exports from other countries. The heat of debate on this issue intensified during the past three decades. U.S. and European producers charged that Japan, China, India, Taiwan, South Korea, and other rapidly growing countries were engaging in "unfair trade" because exports from these countries were priced too low or subsidized by their governments. These countries were repeatedly accused of violating both the rules of ordinary competition and the rules of the World Trade Organization (WTO). In response, India, China, and several other countries enacted their own procedures and now bring many of their own cases charging unfair exporting by other countries.

To address the debate over unfair trade, we turn first to dumping, a way in which private firms may export more than competitive supply and demand would lead us to expect. Then we explore how governments push exports with outright or subtle subsidies.

DUMPING

Dumping is selling exports at a price that is too low—less than normal value (or "fair market value," as it is often called in the United States). There are two legal definitions of *normal value:*

- The long-standing definition of *normal value* is the price charged to comparable domestic buyers in the home market (or to comparable buyers in other markets). Under this traditional definition, dumping is international price discrimination favoring buyers of exports.
- The second definition of *normal value* arose in the 1970s. It is cost-based—the average cost of producing the product, including overhead costs and profit. Under

this second standard, dumping is selling exports at a price that is less than the full average cost of the product.

Why would an exporting firm engage in dumping? Why would it sell exports at a price lower than the price it charges for its product in its home market, or lower than its average cost? There are several reasons. To judge whether dumping is good or bad, it is important to understand the full range of reasons why dumping occurs.

Predatory dumping occurs when a firm temporarily charges a low price in the foreign export market, with the purpose of driving its foreign competitors out of business. Once the rivals are gone, the firm will use its monopoly power to raise prices and earn high profits.

Cyclical dumping occurs during periods of recession. During the part of the cycle when demand is low, a firm tends to lower its price to limit the decline in quantity sold. For instance, in a competitive market initially in long-run equilibrium, price equals full average cost (long-run average cost) for the representative firm. If an industry recession or an economywide recession then causes demand to decline, market price will fall below this full average cost in the short run. A firm continues to produce and sell as long as price exceeds average variable cost. If any of these sales are exports, the firm is dumping.

Seasonal dumping is intended to sell off excess inventories of a product. For instance, toward the end of a fashion season, U.S. clothing manufacturers may decide to sell off any remaining stock of swimsuits at prices that are below full average cost. That is, they have a sale. With production costs sunk, any price above the marginal cost of making the sale is sensible. If some of these low-priced sales are to Canada, the U.S. firm is dumping. Perishable agricultural products are also good candidates for seasonal dumping. A big harvest tends to lower the market price and to provide a larger quantity available for export. Similarly, dumping can be a technique for promoting new products in new markets. This is the equivalent of an introductory sale that an exporting firm could use to establish its product in a new foreign market.

Persistent dumping occurs because a firm with market power uses price discrimination between markets to increase its total profit. A firm maximizes profits by charging a lower price to foreign buyers if

- It has less monopoly power (more competition) in the foreign market than it has in its home market and
- Buyers in the home country cannot avoid the high home prices by buying the good abroad and importing it cheaply.

When these conditions hold, the firm can make home-country buyers pay a higher price and thus earn a higher total profit. This is not predatory; it is not intended to drive any other firms out of business. And it can persist for a long time—as long as these market differences continue.

Figure 11.1 shows such a case of profitable price discrimination under the simplifying assumption that the firm faces a constant marginal cost (and average cost) of production. (In addition, the marginal production cost is the same regardless of whether the product is sold in the home market or exported because essentially the same product is sold in both places.) The illustration is based on a real case that surfaced in 1989. The

FIGURE 11.1
Persistent
Dumping

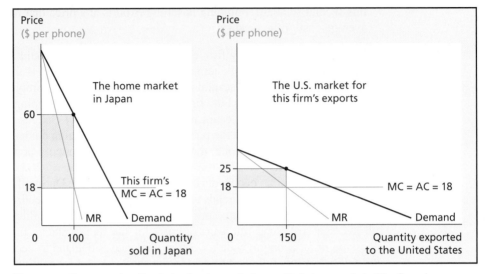

The monopolist uses price discrimination to maximize profits in two markets. The firm charges a higher price in the market where the demand curve is steeper. In this case, that is the home market in Japan, perhaps because in its home market the firm is protected from foreign competition. In the more competitive U.S. market, the firm charges a lower price for its exported product. Total profits are the sum of the two shaded rectangles. The price discrimination is viable only if there is no way for consumers in the high-price market to buy the product from the low-price market, and if policymakers in the importing country do not impose antidumping duties.

U.S. government determined that firms in Japan, Korea, and Taiwan were all guilty of dumping telephones in the U.S. market, causing injury to AT&T (the plaintiff) and other U.S. firms.[1] We illustrate with the case of a single Japanese firm (e.g., Matsushita).

What makes persistent dumping profitable is that, at any common price, the firm faces a less elastic (steeper) demand curve in its home market than in the more competitive foreign market. That is, home-country buyers would not change the quantity they buy very much in response to an increase in price, whereas foreign buyers would quickly abandon this firm's product if the firm raised its price much. Sensing this, the firm maximizes profits by equating marginal cost and marginal revenue in each market. In the U.S. market the profit-maximizing price is $25. With the $25 price U.S. consumers buy 150 telephones a year, at which level marginal revenue just equals the marginal cost of $18. In Japan's home market, where consumers see fewer substitutes for the major Japanese brands, the profit-maximizing price is $60. With the $60 price Japanese consumers buy 100 phones a year, and marginal cost equals marginal revenue at this quantity.

Price discrimination is more profitable for the firm than charging the same price in both markets. Charging the same price would yield lower marginal revenues in Japan

[1]The actual dumping case involved phone equipment for small businesses, although here we illustrate with the case of personal phones from Japan. The U.S. Department of Commerce estimated dumping margins (home-market price above price on sales to the United States) of 120 to 180 percent for major firms in Japan and Taiwan, but only a trivial difference for Korean firms. The Asian exporters had raised their share of the U.S. phone market for small businesses to 60 percent by 1989.

than in the United States. As long as transport costs and import barriers in Japan make it uneconomical for Japanese consumers to import low-priced telephones back from the United States, the firm continues to make greater profits by charging a higher price in the Japanese market. Often tariffs or nontariff barriers to import (back into the exporting country) are what keep the two markets separate. These barriers also protect the dumper against foreign competition in the higher-priced home market (Japan, in this example).

REACTING TO DUMPING: WHAT SHOULD A DUMPEE THINK?

Domestic firms competing against exports dumped into their market are likely to complain loudly to their government, charging that this is unfair. How should the importing country view dumping? What should be its government policy toward dumping?

In one sense the importing country's view is easy. It should welcome dumping and thank the exporting country. After all, we do not usually argue when someone tries to sell us something at a low price. This instinct seems clearly correct for persistent dumping. Compared to the high price in the exporting country, the importing country gets the gains from additional trade at the low export price. The importing country's terms of trade are better. The benefits to consumers are larger than the losses to the import-competing producers. To see this, consider what will happen to the importing country if it imposes a tariff on the dumped imports, to force the tariff-inclusive price up to about the level in the exporting country. In Figure 11.1, the duty would be 140 percent ($= [60 - 25]/25$). In this example the tariff of 140 percent is prohibitive. The Japanese firm would cease all exports to the United States. The United States thus would lose all net gains from trade in this product. Although there would be an increase in the surplus of domestic producers when the prohibitive duty was imposed, the loss of domestic consumer surplus would be larger. Through similar logic, the importing country generally should welcome seasonal and introductory-price dumping.

However, the other two types of dumping may not be so simple. There is a sound economic reason for the importing country to view predatory dumping negatively. Although the importing country gains from low-priced imports in the short run, it will lose because of high-priced imports once the exporting firm succeeds in establishing its monopoly power.

A key question is how frequently foreign firms use predatory dumping. Predatory dumping of manufactured goods was widely alleged during the international chaos of the 1920s and 1930s. In truth, there is no clear evidence that widespread predatory dumping has been practiced, despite a rich folklore about it. *Predatory dumping is likely to be rare* in modern markets. An exporting firm considering predatory dumping must weigh the sure losses from low prices in the short run against the possible but uncertain profits in the more distant future. Even if the firm could drive out its current competitors in the importing country, it may expect that, once it raises prices, new firms, including new exporters from other countries, will enter as competitors. The predatory exporter would not be able to raise prices or to keep them high for very long. Recent research suggests that no more than 5 percent of all cases of alleged dumping in the United States, the European Union, Canada, Mexico, and India show even a moderate possibility for predation (and it is possible that none of these cases involves predation).

Cyclical dumping is the most complicated kind of dumping for the importing country. Most cyclical dumping is probably the normal working of well-functioning, competitive global product markets. When demand declines, the market price falls in the short run. A firm will continue to produce, sell, and even export some amount of the product, as long as the revenue earned at least covers variable cost. This is exactly what we want to happen when there is a decline in demand. Production declines somewhat in many countries as the world price falls. There is an efficient global "sharing" of the decline in demand. Once the recession ends, demand, price, and global production will recover. (If instead too much production capacity continues to exist, then eventually there will need to be an efficient global sharing of capacity reduction before price can recover.)

The importing country may not be completely convinced that cyclical dumping is fair just because it is usually globally efficient. When demand declines by, say, 10 percent, which countries absorb how much of global reduction in output? Is it fair that the import-country firms have to reduce their output and suffer losses? In particular, if the decline in demand is a result of a national recession in the exporting country, why is it fair that the exporting country can "export some of its unemployment"?

As usual, it is not easy to answer the question of what is fair. The international sharing of recessions is one of the effects that comes with the general benefits of international trade. We can also recall the key lesson from the previous chapter—use the specificity rule. The real problem here is the concern about producer losses. For instance, if the key concern is about unemployed workers, the country should provide suitable unemployment insurance or adjustment assistance.

ACTUAL ANTIDUMPING POLICIES: WHAT IS UNFAIR?

Our discussion suggests that dumping is often good for the country importing the dumped exports but that two types of dumping could be bad for the importing country. Predatory dumping can be bad if it is successful, but success is probably rare. Cyclical dumping can sometimes unfairly harm the importing country, but much of the time it is probably the normal working of the competitive market. The implication is that the importing-country's government policy toward dumping (its antidumping policy) should examine each case and consider benefits and costs before imposing antidumping duties or other restrictions on dumped imports. In fact, actual government policies are not at all like this.

The WTO rules permit countries to retaliate against dumping if the dumping injures domestic import-competing producers. If the government in the importing country finds both dumping and injury, then the government is permitted to impose an **antidumping duty**—an extra tariff equal to the discrepancy (the dumping margin) between the actual export price and the normal value.

Antidumping cases throughout the world actually were infrequent until the late 1970s, and as of 1980 only about 34 countries had antidumping laws. Then more countries adopted antidumping laws, especially since 1990, and by 2010 more than 100 countries had them.

FIGURE 11.2   Top 9 Initiators of Antidumping Cases

	Number of Cases Initiated		Number of New Antidumping Measures	Antidumping Measures in Effect	Average Antidumping Duty Imposed*
	1986–1990	2008–2012	2008–2012	June 2013	
India	0	167	149	215	77%
Brazil	6	133	59	91	53
Argentina	0	81	52	89	85
European Union	182	79	43	111	43
United States	184	65	66	243	89
China	0	53	42	118	54
Australia	156	52	22	35	59
Pakistan	0	52	24	45	35
Turkey	12	47	33	120	11
World	736	982	634	1,374	NA

Notes: NA: Not available.

*For India, average 1992–2002, source Ganguli (2008); for the European Union, the United States, and China, average 2002–2004, source Bown (2010a); for other countries, average 1995–1999, source Congressional Budget Office (2001).

Other sources: Zanardi (2004); World Trade Organization, "Report (2013) of the Committee on Anti-Dumping Practices," G/L/1035, October 29, 2013; World Trade Organization, "Antidumping: Statistics on Antidumping," www.wto.org/english/tratop_e/adp_e/adp_e.htm.

Up to the late 1980s, the four "traditional users" of antidumping (the United States, the European Union, Canada, and Australia) accounted for over 90 percent of the cases, but then the use spread. Figure 11.2 shows the countries that are the major users of antidumping actions during 2008–2012. From 1986–1990 to 2008–2012 the number of cases worldwide increased by 33 percent, and the share of the four traditional users (including Canada, with 24 cases during 2008–2012) dropped to 22 percent of total cases. India had no antidumping cases until 1992, but by 2008–2012 it was the top initiator in the world. China enacted its antidumping policies in 1997 and quickly rose to be a major initiator. Argentina and Pakistan also went from zero to top 10.

Worldwide, the products most often involved in dumping cases are chemicals, steel and other metals, plastics and rubber products, machinery, textiles, and apparel. The countries whose exporters are most frequently charged with dumping are China, South Korea, Taiwan, the United States, Thailand, and Indonesia. For China, in 2009, about 2 percent of its exports were subject to antidumping measures in the importing countries.

Let's look more closely at U.S. antidumping policy. A case usually begins with a complaint from U.S. producers. The U.S. Department of Commerce examines whether dumping has actually occurred, and the U.S. International Trade Commission examines whether U.S. firms have been injured. In addition, negotiations may occur with foreign exporters. If they agree to raise prices or to limit their exports, then the case can be terminated or suspended. (This type of outcome has been common in cases involving steel and chemicals.)

In about 94 percent of it determinations, the Department of Commerce finds some amount of dumping—the law and the procedures are biased to make showing dumping easy. In cases in which the comparison is between the export price and the home market price, there are arcane rules about cost tests and ignoring export prices that are above the home market price. The upshot is that only low-priced exports tend to be compared to only high-priced home market sales. In cases in which export prices instead are compared to average cost, obtaining and interpreting data on the costs incurred by foreign exporters are often difficult, so the Commerce Department has leeway in determining what normal value is. Lindsey and Ikenson (2002), using actual data for 18 antidumping cases, examined them for specific biases in the methods used by the Department of Commerce. They concluded that in 10 of the 18 cases there actually was no dumping, and in 4 of the other 8 cases the actual dumping was less than half the amount found by the Department.

The injury standard is not strict, but injury is usually the key to the outcome of a case. In about two-thirds of the cases, the International Trade Commission finds material injury to U.S. import-competing industries.

If both dumping and injury are found, customs officials are instructed to levy an antidumping duty. More than half of the cases brought in the United States result in antidumping duties or an exporter agreement to restrain its export prices or volumes. (By comparing the two columns in Figure 11.2 for new cases initiated and new antidumping measures for 2008–2012, we can see that more than half of the cases in most of the other countries shown and in the world overall result in antidumping duties or exporter agreements.)

Recent research shows some clear patterns of effects from all this. Shortly after the complaint is filed, the prices of the exporters charged with dumping increase, probably to try to reduce the final dumping margin. Export quantities decrease because of the higher price and because of the uncertainty about the outcome of the case. If antidumping duties are imposed, the export quantities decrease further, by an average of 70 percent, and often to zero (as we noted for the case shown in Figure 11.1). The exporter also has an incentive to raise its export price. The antidumping duties are reduced or eliminated if a subsequent review by the Department of Commerce finds less or no dumping.

A study of the overall effects of imposing antidumping duties concluded that the United States suffers a loss of well-being of nearly $4 billion per year. About half of that amount is deadweight loss (like areas $b + d$ in Figure 8.5 or Figure 9.3). The other half is the transfer to foreign exporters that raises their prices (like area c in Figure 9.3). The net loss to the United States could be lower than this because the study does not attempt to quantify the value of avoiding any harmful effects from predatory dumping (probably minimal) and cyclical dumping (hard to measure).

Under current antidumping policies in the United States and a growing number of other countries, we get the following results:

1. The procedure is biased toward finding dumping.
2. The injury test considers only harm to import-competing producers. There is no consideration of whether predation or some other source of harm to the country is involved. There is little or no consideration of the benefits to consumers of the low-priced imports.

3. Overall, the process is biased toward imposing antidumping duties, even though this usually lowers the well-being of the importing country. Antidumping duties also generally lower world welfare.

See the box "Antidumping in Action" for specific examples that illustrate these conclusions.

If an exporting country's government believes that an importing country's government violated the WTO's rules in deciding to impose an antidumping duty, it can complain to the WTO. By early 2014 there had been 101 such complaints, including 47 about the laws and procedures of the U.S. government. As of early 2014, panels had been convened and reached decisions in close to half of these 101 cases. Usually, the panels found errors by the importing countries, including using inappropriate procedures, determining dumping margins (or subsidy rates) in a manner inconsistent with WTO rules, and determining injury using incomplete information or biased analysis. In some of the cases the importing country implemented changes (like revoking the duties) to bring their practices in line with WTO rules, but in others they have not (yet). While the WTO dispute settlement procedure can provide some guard against misuse of antidumping duties, the process is too slow to minimize the effects of such misuse.

Antidumping policy starts out sounding like it is about unfair exports. But a closer examination indicates that something else is going on. *Antidumping policy has become a major way for import-competing producers in a growing number of countries to gain new protection against imports, with the usual deadweight costs to the world and to the importing country.* As shown in Figure 11.2, the average antidumping duties imposed against foreign exporters are generally very high, much higher than most regular tariffs, so the deadweight losses can be large. There is also the cost of arguing the cases and gathering the data to prove or disprove dumping and injury. In addition, import-competing firms use the threat of a dumping complaint to prod exporters to raise their prices and restrain their competition—the *harassment effect*—even if no complaint is actually filed.

PROPOSALS FOR REFORM

Although there are exceptions, the current practice of retaliation against dumping is usually bad for the world and for the importing country.[2] Yet this practice is fully consistent with current WTO rules. Reform of the WTO rules is an important item on

---

[2]Here is an example in which retaliation against persistent dumping could bring gains to the whole world. If the "convicted" dumper ceases all price discrimination, continues to serve both markets with a single price that is not too high, and is rewarded by getting the duty removed, the world could end up better off from the temporary punitive use of the duty. The world is better off in the sense that output is redirected to the home-country buyers who value the good more highly at the margin. One example of this kind of gain is the outcome of a U.S. dumping case against Korean consumer electronics producers, which led to a lowering of the high prices Korean consumers had been paying for these products.

This is only one of a number of possible outcomes, and the others are usually bad for the world. For instance, the dumpers may move their export-market production to the importing country at some extra expense of world resources. Or they might abandon the controversial foreign market as not worth the bother if it is spoiled by an antidumping duty. The issue of dumping is complex. The text gives the welfare results that seem most likely.

Case Study   Antidumping in Action

Dumping laws and antidumping procedures sound technical and boring. The firms that use antidumping complaints to get protection from imports like it that way. Nobody else is much interested in what's going on. Yet the stakes are large. Maybe we should follow the money—now that's more interesting.

Here are three examples of antidumping in real life. One sad moral of these tales is that any exporter that succeeds in building market share is at risk of being accused of dumping, and defense against this charge will be very difficult.

A GAME OF CHICKEN
When it comes to chicken, Americans prefer white meat. South Africans prefer dark meat. Sounds like the basis for mutually beneficial trade. And it would be, if it weren't for those pesky dumping laws.

U.S. chicken producers noticed the differences in demand. They began exporting dark-meat chicken to South Africa. This created extra competition for South African chicken producers, but South African consumers gained more than local producers lost. That's the way trade works. In addition, U.S. chicken producers were happy. The price they received for their dark-meat exports was somewhat higher than the price they could get in the United States. This added to their profitability.

South African chicken producers scratched back. They charged U.S. producers with dumping by exporting dark-meat chicken at a price less than production cost. This is an ideal situation for a biased antidumping authority because there is no one way to determine this production cost. (What comes first, the dark meat or the white?) In 2000, the South African government determined that the U.S. firm Tyson was dumping by a margin of 200 percent (its export price was only one-third of its estimated production cost) and Gold Kiss was dumping by an incredible 357 percent margin. Something is fowl in South Africa. Good-bye gains from trade.

WHAT'S SO SUPER ABOUT SUPERCOMPUTERS?
In 1996 the Japanese company NEC won the contract to supply a supercomputer to a university consortium funded by the U.S. National Science Foundation, to be used for weather forecasting. This was the first-ever sale of a Japanese supercomputer to an agency of the U.S. government. It seemed to be a major setback for Cray Research, then the major U.S. supercomputer maker. But Cray thought it saw unfair trade.

With encouragement from the U.S. Department of Commerce, Cray filed a dumping complaint. NEC guessed that it was not likely to win with the Department of Commerce also acting as the judge, and it refused to participate in the case. Based on information provided by Cray, the U.S. government imposed antidumping duties on NEC supercomputers at the super rate of 454 percent (and at the almost super rate of 173 percent for supercomputers from Fujitsu, the other major Japanese producer). With these antidumping duties in place, no one in the United States would be buying NEC or Fujitsu supercomputers.

Not so super for U.S. users of supercomputers. Or for anyone in the United States who wanted accurate weather forecasts. NEC supercomputers were simply the best in the world for this purpose.

There's one more twist in this wired tale. Hey, maybe it isn't dumping after all. In 2001, Cray was in financial trouble, and its technology was lagging. In exchange for a $25 million investment by NEC and a 10-year contract to be the exclusive distributor of NEC supercomputers in North America, Cray asked the Department of Commerce to end the antidumping duty.

AMERICAN STEEL: THE KING OF ANTIDUMPING
If antidumping were like the Super Bowl, the American steel industry would be the winner. In early 2014 nearly half of all antidumping duties in effect in the United States were on steel products. As a comparison, steel accounts for about 2 percent of U.S. imports. How did one

industry that employs about 200,000 workers become the king of antidumping?

In the first half of the 20th century, the American steel industry was the world leader in output and productivity. In 1950 the United States produced about half of the world's total steel output. Since then the situation has changed dramatically. Steel producers in other countries increasingly have sourced high-quality raw materials globally (for instance, iron ore from Australia and Brazil). These foreign firms focused on raising productivity and lowering costs. They often had support from their national governments. At the same time, the managers of the large integrated American steel producers made poor decisions, including lagging innovation of technological improvements and payment of uncompetitive high wages and benefits to unionized workers. By 2013 American steel firms accounted for only about 5.5 percent of world production. Half of U.S. production was by minimills, another source of competitive pressure on the large integrated American firms (often called Big Steel).

American steel firms fought back. A large part of their strategy was the use of political lobbying and U.S. trade laws to attack imports. In the 1980s, to head off a large number of steel dumping complaints, the U.S. government forced the European Union and other countries to impose voluntary export restraints (VERs). As these VERs ended, on one day in 1992 American steel firms filed 80 dumping complaints against 20 countries. (Note that American steel producers buy about one-quarter of all steel imported into the United States, in the form of raw steel slabs that they use to make finished steel products. Amazingly, raw steel slab is apparently never dumped into the United States, but all kinds of finished steel products are.)

American steel firms are well organized. Statisticians at steel-producer organizations and at individual steel firms closely examine each month's trade data. When they see an increase of imports in a specific steel product, the American firms are likely to file a dumping complaint. The American firms actually "lose" or withdraw at least half of these complaints. But they don't really lose. For instance, in 1993, American firms filed dumping complaints against exporters of carbon steel rod. In the early months of the investigation, the price of this product in the United States increased by about 25 percent. Eventually, the American firms lost the cases or withdrew the complaints. An executive of a foreign-owned steel firm commented, "But who says they lost? I would say they won. Whatever they spent in legal fees, they probably recouped 50 times in extra revenue. That is the great thing about filing: Even if you lose, you win."*

Since the early 1990s there have been several other bursts of dumping cases filed by American steel firms. In the aftermath of the Asian crisis of 1997, demand collapsed in the crisis countries (especially Korea, Thailand, Indonesia, Malaysia, and the Philippines). Steel firms that had been selling to the crisis countries shifted sales to other countries. In 1998 imports of finished steel into the United States rose rapidly and prices for steel products typically fell by 20 to 25 percent. A strong case can be made that 1998 was a fairly typical down phase in the global cycle of a competitive industry. Still, American firms swung into action. They filed four major dumping cases in 1998 and four in 1999. The International Trade Commission found injury to U.S. steel firms in six of these cases, and the Department of Commerce found dumping margins of up to 185 percent. In the large case involving cold-rolled steel, imports declined by 20 percent in the months after the case was filed, even though the U.S. firms eventually "lost" the case when no injury was found.

As prices remained relatively low around the world, the U.S. steel firms continued to find new dumping. They brought five major cases in 2000 and six major cases in 2001.

*Mr. Nicholas Tolerico, executive vice president of Thyssen, Inc., a U.S. subsidiary of Thyssen AG, a German steel company. Quoted in *The Wall Street Journal*, March 7, 1998.

—Continued on next page

In early 2002 President Bush imposed new general tariffs of up to 30 percent on imports of steel, and the number of new dumping cases decreased. Under pressure from U.S. steel users and an adverse WTO ruling, he removed these tariffs in late 2003. But then global steel prices rose by more than 50 percent during 2004, driven by rapidly rising demand in China and other developing countries. With strong world prices continuing into 2008, there were few new antidumping suits in the United States.

As the global crisis hit in 2008, the steel industry went into recession and the share of the U.S. market served by imports increased. The U.S. industry filed seven new dumping cases in 2009. After a few years' lull, steel imports into the United States began to grow rapidly at the beginning of 2013, driven both by slowing demand for steel and excess capacity in the rest of the world and by strong demand in the United States (especially domestic demand for steel used in oil, natural gas, and automobile production). The great American steel machine that rolls out complaints about foreign dumping restarted, and the industry filed seven new dumping cases charging firms from 16 countries with dumping various steel products, the largest being tubular goods for oil production.

Steel remains the U.S. antidumping king, and the oil industry and many other users of steel in the United States pay the (higher) price.

DISCUSSION QUESTION

For the U.S. cases alleging dumping filed in 2013, why might the number of these cases that actually result in the imposition of antidumping duties turn out to be relatively low?

the agenda for the current Doha Round of multilateral trade negotiations. Three possibilities for reform are discussed in the following paragraphs.

First, *antidumping actions could be limited to situations in which predatory dumping is plausible.* This reform would focus on the type of dumping that is most likely to be bad for the world and for the importing country. It would also align antidumping policy with antitrust policy (as it is called in the United States; it is called competition policy, antimonopoly policy, or similar names in other countries). Pro-competition policies usually forbid any predatory action to gain monopoly power. This reform would try to limit the scope of antidumping policy. However, the procedures in a country could still be biased toward finding both dumping and something potentially predatory about it.

Second, *the injury standard could be expanded to require that weight be given to consumers and users of the product.* This change would shift the discussion toward injury to net national well-being, not just injury to domestic import-competing producers. Some countries, including the European Union, Canada, and Thailand, already have a "public interest test" in their antidumping regulations. This reform would try to limit the scope for antidumping actions in a general way rather than by focusing on one type of dumping.

This reform would also change an odd feature of current antidumping policy, that consumers will be substantially affected by dumping decisions but have no legal standing in the process. In fact, most antidumping actions involve intermediate goods like steel and chemicals. The buyers (like automobile firms) of these products are often well organized politically. They can be effective in opposing import protection on the intermediate products that they buy and use. Current dumping policies give import-competing producers of intermediate products an end run around this political battle. Reforming antidumping policy to include consumer interests would reopen the battle and probably reduce some of the bad use of antidumping policy.

Third, *antidumping policy could be replaced by more active use of safeguard policy,* another kind of increased import protection allowed by WTO rules. Safeguard policy is the use of temporary import protection when a sudden increase in imports causes injury to domestic producers. The intent is to give some time for import-competing firms and their workers to adjust to the increased import competition (recall the discussion of adjustment assistance in the previous chapter).

Defenders of antidumping policy often state that antidumping policy facilitates trade liberalization because it allows protection for industries that are hurt more than expected by increasing imports. This is really an argument for safeguard policy. Safeguard policy is better because:

- There is no need to show that foreign exporters have done anything unfair.
- The interests of consumers can be considered in the process that leads to the decision of whether or not to impose a safeguard, and what form it will take if imposed.
- The focus is on adjustment by the import-competing producers.
- There is pressure to adjust because the import protection is temporary.

Safeguard actions have not been much used in the United States. One famous case is Harley-Davidson in the 1980s. After a safeguard was imposed, Harley-Davidson came back so strongly and quickly in its battle with Japanese competitors (Suzuki and Honda) that it asked that the safeguard protection be removed earlier than scheduled. More recently, the tariffs on steel imposed by the U.S. government in 2002 were the outcome of the government's investigation of a request by American steel firms for safeguard relief. The tariffs that the U.S. government imposed in 2009 on imports of tires from China are another example. Clearly, safeguard actions such as these steel and tire tariffs can still be controversial, but at least all parties affected have a right to be heard in the debate.

EXPORT SUBSIDIES

Governments promote or subsidize exports more often than they restrict or tax exports.[3] Some government efforts to promote exports are not controversial according to international precepts (although there are questions about how effective they are). Government agencies like Export.gov of the U.S. Department of Commerce provide foreign-market research, information on export procedures and foreign government regulations, and help with contacting buyers. Government agencies sponsor export promotion events like trade fairs and organized trips. Governments establish export processing zones that permit imports of materials and components with easier customs procedures and low or no tariffs.

---

[3]In the United States this is not surprising because the U.S. Constitution prohibits the taxing of exports.

Governments also provide various forms of financial assistance that benefit their exporters. An export subsidy is controversial because it violates international norms about fair trade. Our analysis of export subsidies will conclude that export subsidies are usually bad from a world point of view. However, the international division of gains and losses turns out to be very different from what you would expect just by listening to who favors export subsidies and who complains about them. Export subsidies are bad for the countries that use them but are good for the countries that complain about them!

Governments subsidize exports in many ways, some of them deliberately subtle to escape detection. They use taxpayers' money to give low-interest loans to export-ers or their foreign customers. An example is the U.S. Export-Import Bank, or Eximbank. Founded in the 1930s, it has compromised its name by giving easy credit to U.S. exporters and their foreign customers but not to U.S. importers or their foreign sup-pliers. Governments also charge low prices on inputs (such as raw materials or domestic transport services) that go into production that will be exported. Income tax rules are also twisted to give tax relief based on the value of goods or services each firm exports.

Export subsidies are small on average, but they loom large in certain products and for certain companies. For instance, most Eximbank loans have been channeled toward a few large U.S. firms and their customers. Boeing, in particular, has been helped to extra foreign aircraft orders by cheap Eximbank credit. More broadly, the biggest export subsidies apply to agricultural products.

What are the effects on the country whose government offers the export subsidy? Let's examine the effects for a *competitive industry*, using our standard supply-and-demand framework. We will reach the following conclusions:

1. An export subsidy expands exports and production of the subsidized product. In fact, the export subsidy can switch the product from being imported to being exported.
2. An export subsidy lowers the price paid by foreign buyers, relative to the price that local consumers pay for the product. In addition, for the export subsidy to work as intended (the government subsidizes only exports, not domestic purchases), something must prevent local buyers from importing the product at the lower foreign price.
3. The export subsidy reduces the net national well-being of the exporting country.

Let's examine three cases to see the validity of these conclusions.

Exportable Product, Small Exporting Country

Figure 11.3 shows a small country, in this case a country whose exports of steel pipes do not affect the world price of $100 per pipe (standard length). With free trade the firms in the country's competitive steel-pipe industry produce 160 million pipes per year and export 90 million (= 160 − 70). The government of this country then decides to offer to its firms an export subsidy of $20 per pipe. The revenue per pipe exported then is $120, equal to the $100 price paid by foreign buyers plus the $20 sub-sidy. If a pipe firm can get $120 for each pipe exported, it will not sell to any domestic buyer at a price lower than $120. Of course, this is only possible if domestic buyers cannot just buy imported pipes from the world market at $100. Something must keep the export market separate from the domestic market. (This should sound familiar—it

FIGURE 11.3

Export Subsidy, Small Country, Exportable Product

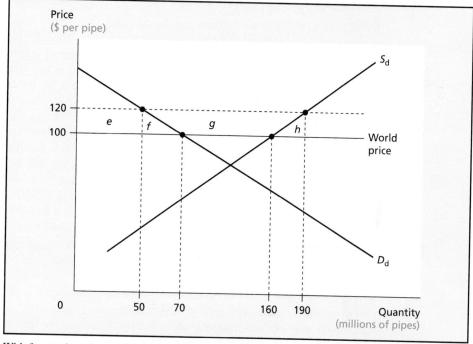

With free trade at the world price of $100, this small country exports 90 million steel pipes. If the country instead offers an export subsidy of $20 per unit exported, revenue per unit exported rises to $120, and the exporting firms must receive this amount as the selling price from domestic buyers as well. Domestic production rises from 160 to 190 million, domestic consumption falls from 70 to 50 million, and the country exports 140 million pipes. Domestic producers gain surplus equal to area $e + f + g$, domestic consumers lose surplus equal to area $e + f$, and the cost to the government of paying the export subsidy is area $f + g + h$. The net loss in national well-being because of the export subsidy is area f plus area h.

sounds like persistent dumping. In fact, receiving an export subsidy is another reason why an exporting firm would engage in dumping.)

What are the other effects of the export subsidy in this case? If revenue per unit rises to $120 (for both export and local sales), the quantity produced increases to 190 million. If the domestic price increases to $120, local quantity demanded decreases to 50 million. Quantity exported increases to 140 million (= 190 − 50).

Who are the winners and losers in the exporting country? Producers gain surplus equal to area $e + f + g$. Consumers lose surplus equal to area $e + f$. The cost to the government of paying the export subsidy is area $f + g + h$, equal to the export subsidy of $20 per pipe times the 140 million pipes exported with the subsidy.

The export subsidy has increased exports and production of this product, but is it good for the exporting country? Using our one-dollar, one-vote metric, the answer is no. After we cancel out the matching gains and losses, the net loss in national well-being is areas f and h. Area f is the **consumption effect** of the export subsidy, the lost consumer surplus for those consumers squeezed out of the market when the domestic price rises above the world price. Area h is the **production**

effect of the export subsidy, the loss due to encouraging domestic production that has a resource cost greater than the world price (the world standard for efficient production). Although these two triangles are on the opposite sides of the graph, because this is an exportable product rather than an importable product, they are the same kinds of effects shown for the import tariff in Figure 8.4. The loss of national well-being for this small exporting country is also a loss for the world.

Exportable Product, Large Exporting Country

We've just seen that a small exporting country harms itself by offering an export subsidy to its competitive exporting industry. Perhaps the result is different if the exporting country is large enough to affect the world price. Not so—in fact, it may be worse.

Figure 11.4 shows this case. With free trade the world price is $100 per pipe. When the exporting-country government offers the export subsidy of $20 per pipe, exporting firms want to export more to get more of the subsidy. To get foreign consumers to buy more of the exported product, the exporting firms must lower the export price. And, just as in the small-country case, domestic buyers in the exporting country must end up paying $20 more than the export price (assuming that they cannot import from the rest of the world at the new world price).

We can see the resulting equilibrium more easily in panel B of Figure 11.4. The export subsidy creates a wedge of $20 between the price that foreign importers pay and the revenue per unit that exporters receive. This $20 wedge "fits" (vertically) at the quantity traded of 110 million pipes. The new world price is $88, the price paid by the importers. The revenue per unit to the exporting firms, and the new price in the exporting country, is $108.

Panel A of Figure 11.4 shows what is happening in the exporting country. At $108 per pipe, production in the exporting country increases from 160 million to 172 million, and domestic consumption decreases from 70 to 62 million. Quantity exported increases from 90 million to 110 million.

As in the small-country case, the export subsidy has increased domestic production and exports of pipes. What are the effects on well-being in the exporting country? Producer surplus increases by area $e + f + g$. Consumer surplus falls by area $e + f$. The export subsidy costs the government $20 times the 110 million units exported. This government cost of $2.2 billion is area $f + g + h + i + j + k + l + m$ in panel A (or area $f + g + h + n + r + t + u$ in panel B).

The net loss to the exporting country is the shaded area in panel A or B. This net loss has three parts:

- The consumption effect (area f).
- The production effect (area h).
- The loss due to the decline in the exporting country's international terms of trade (area $i + j + k + l + m =$ area $n + r + t + u$).

The export subsidy gives a good bargain to foreign buyers. However, their gain is a loss to the exporting country from selling at a lower world price.

We can also use panel B to see the effect on world well-being. Area $n + r + t$ is increased surplus for the importing country. The net loss to the world is the triangular area $f + h + u$. This is the loss from too much trading of steel pipes.

FIGURE 11.4   Export Subsidy, Large Country, Exportable Product

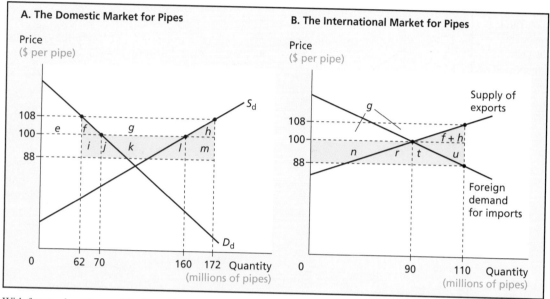

With free trade at the world price of $100, this large country exports 90 million steel pipes. If instead the country offers an export subsidy of $20, its extra exports drive the world price down to $88. The revenue per unit received by the exporting firms is $108, and domestic buyers pay a price of $108. The net loss of well-being for the exporting country is area $f + h + i + j + k + l + m$. The export subsidy both distorts domestic production and consumption and worsens the exporting country's international terms of trade. The inefficiency created for the world is area $f + h + u$.

Switching an Importable Product into an Exportable Product

"If you throw enough money at something, it will happen." This adage applies to export subsidies. They can turn an importable product into one that is exported. Let's see how.

To keep things from getting too complicated, we will examine the small-country case shown in Figure 11.5. With free trade at the world price of $2 per kilogram, the country would import 80 million kilos of butter (= 120 − 40). The government now offers an export subsidy of $2 per kilo and prevents domestic consumers from importing cheap foreign butter. The revenue per kilo exported now rises to $4, and domestic production increases to 90 million kilos. At the higher domestic price of $4 per kilo, domestic consumers reduce their butter purchases to 60 million kilos. With the export subsidy, the country is now an *exporter* of 30 million kilos.

The export subsidy switches an importable product into an exportable product. Domestic producers gain surplus of area *ACFE*. Domestic consumers lose surplus of area *ABJE*. The cost of the export subsidy to the government is area *BCHG*. The net loss of national well-being looks a bit peculiar because the triangles of the consumption effect and the production effect overlap each other. The net national loss (and the net loss to the world) is area *BJG* plus area *CHF*.

FIGURE 11.5

An Export
Subsidy Turns
an Importable
Product into
an Export

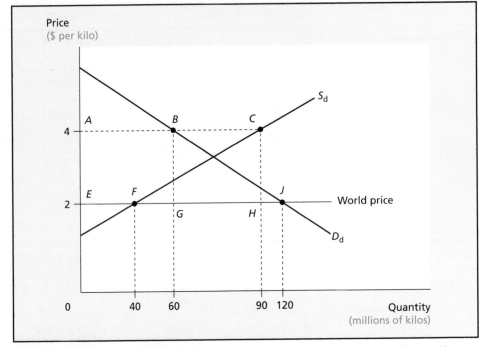

With free trade and no export subsidy, this small country imports 80 million kilos of butter. If instead the country's government offers an export subsidy of $2 per kilo, the revenue per unit received by producers doubles to $4. The country becomes an exporter of 30 million kilos of butter. The net loss of national well-being is the sum of a production deadweight loss of area *FCH* and a consumption deadweight loss of area *BJG*.

This example of using export subsidies to create exportables is not far-fetched! See the box "Agriculture Is Amazing."

At this point you might want to return to the conclusions stated at the beginning of this section. You should see that these conclusions apply to all three of our cases. If the market is competitive, an export subsidy is bad for the exporting country.

WTO RULES ON SUBSIDIES

As a result of the agreements reached in the Tokyo Round and Uruguay Round of trade negotiations, the WTO now has a clear set of rules for subsidies that may benefit exports. The WTO rules divide subsidies into two types:

- Subsidies linked directly to exporting are *prohibited,* except export subsidies used by the lowest-income developing countries. Example: A firm receives a tax break based on the amount that it exports.
- Subsidies that are not linked directly to exporting but still have an impact on exports are *actionable.* Example: Low-priced electricity is provided to assist production by local firms in an industry, and some of this production is exported.

If an importing country's government believes that a foreign country is using a prohibited subsidy or an actionable subsidy that is harming its industry, the importing country can follow one of two procedures:

- File a complaint with the WTO and use its dispute settlement procedure.
- Use a national procedure similar to that used for dumping (used more often).

If the importing country can show the existence of a prohibited or actionable subsidy and harm to its industry, it is permitted to impose a **countervailing duty,** a tariff used to offset the price or cost advantage created by the subsidy to foreign exports.

SHOULD THE IMPORTING COUNTRY IMPOSE COUNTERVAILING DUTIES?

How should the *importing country* respond to subsidized exports? Should the country simply enjoy the bargain? Or should the importing-country government heed the complaints from import-competing producers about unfair competition and impose a countervailing duty on the subsidized exports?

If the exporting country is large enough to affect world prices, then the export subsidy lowers the price that the importing country pays for these exports. As we saw in Figure 11.4B, the importing country overall is better off, but the import-competing industry is harmed. By WTO rules, the importing-country government is permitted to impose a countervailing duty. What happens if it does so?

To keep things from getting too complicated, let's use an extreme version of the large-country case examined in Figure 11.4. In this version, all of the export subsidy is passed forward to the buyers of imports in the foreign country. That is, the price charged to importers falls by the full amount of the export subsidy. Still, be warned: Even this simplified case can be confusing. We will focus on two different measures of well-being, one for the importing country and one for the world. We will make comparisons among three different situations: (1) free trade, (2) export subsidy with no countervailing duty, and (3) export subsidy plus countervailing duty.

Figure 11.6 shows the Canadian and international market for cold-rolled steel. With free trade, Canada imports 50 million tons per year from Brazil at the free-trade price of $300 per ton. Then, the Brazilian government offers a subsidy of $50 per ton exported. If all of this is passed on to buyers, the export price declines to $250 per ton. Canadian imports increase to 80 million tons, Canadian production declines to 130 million tons, and Canadian producer surplus declines by area *v*. Canadian consumption increases to 210 million tons, and Canadian consumer surplus increases by area *v* + *w* + *y* + *z*. The net Canadian gain from the Brazilian export subsidy is area *w* + *y* + *z*. Still, Canadian producers are harmed, and they complain about the unfair competition.

For the world, this is too much steel trade. Steel tons that each cost $300 of Brazilian resources to produce are valued at less than $300 per ton by Canadian buyers (as shown ton-by-ton on the Canadian demand-for-import curve).

FIGURE 11.6   A Foreign Export Subsidy and a Countervailing Duty

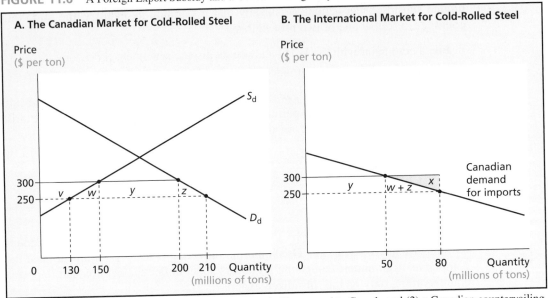

The diagram shows the effect of (1) a Brazilian export subsidy on steel to Canada and (2) a Canadian countervailing duty on imports of subsidized steel exports from Brazil. An odd pattern results: Each policy in turn brings a net loss to the country adopting it, yet for the world as a whole the Canadian countervailing duty undoes the harm done by the Brazilian export subsidy.

What happens if the Canadian government imposes a countervailing duty of $50 per ton of imported steel? The duty-inclusive price of imports rises back to $300. In this subsidy-plus-countervailing-duty situation, the world returns to the same price $300 and volume of trade (50 million tons) as with free trade. This makes good sense for *world efficiency* because the deadweight loss of excessive trade (area *x* in Figure 11.6B) is eliminated. For the world, the countervailing duty is a successful use of Chapter 10's specificity rule. In this case the world's problem is excessive exports of steel, and the countervailing duty directly affects exactly the problem activity.

Conclusions about the effects of the countervailing duty on *Canada's well-being* depend on what we compare to. *In comparison to the situation with the export subsidy and no countervailing duty,* Canada is worse off for imposing the countervailing duty. That's right—a countervailing duty in this case is bad for the country imposing it but good for the whole world. We can use Figure 11.6A to see the effect on the importing country of imposing the countervailing duty, given that an export subsidy exists. The duty-inclusive price rises to $300. Canadian producers gain area *v*, Canadian consumers lose area *v* + *w* + *y* + *z*, and the Canadian government collects area *y* as revenue from the countervailing duty. The net national loss to Canada of imposing the countervailing duty is area *w* + *z* (the standard result for imposing a tariff).

Let's look at a second valid comparison, the *comparison between free trade and the combination of the export subsidy and countervailing duty*. In both of these situations, the price in Canada is the same ($300), as are all quantities. The only difference is that the Canadian government is collecting revenue (area *y*) in the subsidy-and-duty situation. Who is effectively paying the countervailing duty? The Brazilian government! It pays the export subsidy to the Brazilian firms, who pass it on to import buyers in Canada through the lower export price. The Canadian import buyers then send it to the Canadian government when they pay the countervailing duty. The well-being of Canada is higher than it would be with free trade because the Brazilian government is now effectively paying Canadian taxes.

Because export subsidies are bad for the world as a whole, and retaliating against them is good for the world as a whole, WTO rules are wise to allow importing countries to impose countervailing duties. However, it turns out that subsidy complaints and countervailing duties are much less frequent than dumping complaints and antidumping duties. During 2008–2012 only 101 subsidy cases were initiated in the world, and in mid-2013 there were only 93 countervailing actions in effect.

The United States has been the largest user of countervailing duties, with 37 of these new cases and 52 of the countervailing duties in force. The European Union and Canada also make some use of countervailing duties. China, the United States, and India are the countries most frequently charged with subsidizing exports. Steel products are the most frequently involved. Countervailing duties also tend to be lower than antidumping duties. For instance, for the United States the average countervailing duty is about 10 percent.

While countervailing duties are often good for the world, they can also be misused in the same way that antidumping duties are misused. Import-competing producers have an incentive to complain about possible foreign subsidies to exports, in an effort to gain protection against these exports. Many activities of a government could have some element of subsidy in them. In antisubsidy cases, it is often possible for the complaining firms to establish that some kind of foreign subsidy exists that might benefit exports, perhaps with some help from a government process biased toward helping the import-competing domestic firms. Then, these firms can gain the protection of countervailing duties if they can show that they have been injured by the "subsidized" exports.

The softwood lumber dispute between the United States and Canada is an example of a controversial antisubsidy case. In early 2001 a VER limiting Canadian exports expired. U.S. lumber firms immediately renewed their complaint that Canadian lumber firms benefit from a subsidy because the Canadian government does not charge high enough fees for logging on government lands. The Canadian government contended that its fees were appropriate, so there was no subsidy. The U.S. government found otherwise. The U.S. Commerce Department concluded that the low fee was a subsidy of 19 percent and that Canadian lumber exporters also were dumping by an additional 8 percent on average. The U.S. International Trade Commission found injury to U.S. firms from the lumber imports that grew rapidly after the VER expired. U.S. lumber producers clearly gained surplus from the combined average duty of 27 percent against Canadian lumber. U.S. consumers lost. Most obviously, the cost of building a typical new home rose by over $1,000. Most new-home buyers could pay this, so they suffered a straight loss of money. The deadweight loss consumption effect occurred for the estimated 300,000 American families that could not afford the higher house prices. Most of them had modest incomes, and they reluctantly remained in less desirable housing.

Case Study   Agriculture Is Amazing

I don't want to hear about agriculture from any-body but you . . . Come to think of it,
I don't want to hear about it from you either.

President Kennedy to his top agricultural policy adviser

Agriculture is another world. Sometimes it seems as if the laws of nature have been repealed. From the late 1980s to the late 1990s, the desert kingdom of Saudi Arabia grew more wheat than it consumed, so it was a net exporter of wheat. Wheat is exported by other countries with unfavorable soils and climates, including Great Britain and France. And crowded, mountainous Japan has often been a net exporter of rice.

All this happens because governments are more involved in agriculture than in any other sector of the private economy. In 2012 government policies in industrialized countries provided about $259 billion of support to farmers, equal to about 19 percent of farmers' revenues. Government policies in the European Union (EU) provided $107 billion (19 percent of farm revenues), in the United States $30 billion (7 percent), and in Japan $65 billion (an amazing 56 percent of the revenues of Japanese farmers). The farmers' political lobbies in these countries are remarkably powerful, especially relative to the small role of agriculture in the economy (only about 2 percent of gross domestic product). Farmers producing rice, milk, sugar, and beef are the biggest recipients of these subsidies.

Close to half of the increased farm income is provided through price supports. For the typical *price support,* the government sets a minimum domestic price for the agricultural product, and the government buys any amounts that farmers cannot sell into the market at the minimum (support) price. Domestic farmers receive at least the minimum price when they sell, and domestic consumers pay at least the minimum price when they buy. All of this sounds domestic—domestic

minimum price, domestic farmers, domestic consumers. Yet something that starts "domestic" transforms itself on the way to the global markets.

The support price is almost always higher than the world price for the agricultural product. If the country would import the product with free trade, the price support requires that *imports be restricted.* Otherwise, cheap imports would flood into the country and undermine the price support. If the support price is not too high (less than or equal to the no-trade price for the country), then the price support is actually a form of import protection. The analysis of this type of price support mirrors that of import barriers presented in Chapters 8 and 9. Interesting, but not amazing yet.

If the country would export the product with free trade, but the support price is above the world price, then the country's farmers produce more than is purchased by domestic consumers. The government must buy the excess production at the high support price. The government could just destroy what it buys or let it rot, but that would be remarkably wasteful. The government could give it away to needy domestic families, but there are limits to how much can be given away before this free stuff starts to undermine regular domestic demand. The government could turn to the export market, which sounds like an excellent way to dispose of the excess national production. Perhaps it is, but the government will take a loss on each unit exported. This loss, the difference between the support price that the government pays and the lower world price that it receives, is an *export subsidy* from the government. Foreign buyers will not pay the high domestic support price; they buy only if the government offers a subsidized export price.

In this case, in which an exporting country sets a support price that is above the world price for the product, the price support policy is actually a combination of import protection and export subsidy. The analysis mirrors that accompanying Figures 11.3 and 11.4. We are getting closer to amazing.

Price supports can also s*witch agricultural products from being importable to being exported*. Wheat is an example for Britain, France, and other EU members. Butter and other dairy products in the EU are other examples of products that have become exports because of generous price supports. With free trade, wheat, butter, and other dairy products would be imported into the EU because the world prices of these products are lower than the EU's no-trade prices. (More simply, the EU has a comparative disadvantage in these products.) The EU's support prices are so high that EU farmers produce much more than is sold in the EU. The EU uses export subsidies to export some of its excess production. The analysis of this case mirrors that for Figure 11.5. Now that's pretty amazing. Domestic price supports morph into a combination of import protection and export subsidies that transform the country from an importer to an exporter of the products.

It takes a lot of government money to create amazement. The EU's Common Agricultural Policy (CAP) covers a broad range of agricultural products (including wheat, butter, and other dairy products). CAP spending represents over 40 percent of all EU fiscal expenditures. And the amazement brings a large national cost. The inefficiency of the CAP is equal to a loss of about 1 percent of the EU's gross domestic product.

Agriculture has also been another world for WTO rules. In contrast to the rules for industrial products, governments had been permitted to use import quotas and export subsidies. But things are changing. The agricultural provisions of the Uruguay Round trade agreement made agriculture less different, especially for developed countries. Governments converted quotas

and other nontariff barriers into tariff rates, a process called *tariffication*. Each developed country reduced its budget outlays for export subsidies by 36 percent and its volume of subsidized exports by 21 percent. Each developed country reduced its domestic subsidies to agriculture by 20 percent, with exceptions. The requirements for developing countries were less stringent.

The effects of these changes are not as large as one might expect. Most developed countries have maintained import protection through artful implementation of the agreement. Generally, highly protected products remain highly protected. The reduction of export subsidies has had some impact, especially in reducing subsidization of exports by the EU. The effects of the general reduction in domestic subsidies are moderate because major subsidy programs in the United States and the EU were exempt from the cuts.

After the Uruguay Round agreement, agriculture is becoming less different. One way is that tariffication has placed import barriers into a form in which they can be compared across countries. A second way is that there is now pressure to reduce the use of subsidies in agriculture. Countries can use the WTO dispute settlement process to examine excessive agricultural subsidies. Decisions in 2005 in two major cases—EU export subsidies for sugar and U.S. subsidies to cotton—found subsidies that violated WTO rules and agreements.

The Uruguay Round agreement also laid the groundwork for negotiations during the current Doha Round that are aimed to achieve more substantial liberalizations. In this sector that would be amazing.

DISCUSSION QUESTION

For the European Union, can a tariff or import quota turn butter into an EU export product? If not, why can a price support turn butter into an EU export product?

If the Canadian logging fee was a subsidy because it was too low, then world well-being was enhanced by the U.S. countervailing duty. However, if the Canadian fee was appropriate and not a subsidy, then the countervailing duty (and perhaps the antidumping duty) was simple import protection, with a net loss for the world. It is not an easy call for the referee of world efficiency.[4]

STRATEGIC EXPORT SUBSIDIES COULD BE GOOD

In the previous section we assumed competitive supply and demand, and we reached the conclusion that an export subsidy harmed the exporting country. For some industries this competitive assumption is wrong. Suppose instead that the real-world market in question features the clash of two giant firms, each of which could supply the whole market. The economics of an export subsidy looks very different if international competition in the industry consists of an oligopolistic duel between two firms for the global market. In this battle of giants, an export subsidy can be either good or bad, both for the exporting country and for the world.

To see the possibility of a good subsidy, let us imagine a simplified case inspired by the continuing real-world competition between Boeing of the United States and Europe's Airbus. Suppose that it becomes technologically possible for them to build a new kind of passenger plane, perhaps a superjumbo jet. To keep a clear focus on the key points, let us say that there is no inherent difference between Airbus and Boeing in the cost of making the new plane. Still, aircraft manufacture can benefit from scale economies—as a firm expands its planned output, the cost of making another unit drops as output rises. Either firm is capable of supplying the whole world market at a low cost. If only one firm captures the whole world market, it will reap some monopoly profits. If both firms produce, they will vie for sales and drive the price down to their marginal costs. In this rivalry case, they make no operating profits.

Figure 11.7 sets the stage by considering what might happen if Airbus and Boeing simultaneously face a decision about whether to make the new plane. For either of them, it is a tough decision. Let's look at it from Airbus's viewpoint. Should it choose to invest 8 in development costs and then produce the new planes (left column), or should it not invest and not produce (right column)? Well, that all depends on what Boeing does. If Airbus could be sure Boeing would stay out, it should definitely invest the 8 and produce, making the profit of 100 shown in the lower left box. But what if Boeing does produce? Then the two of them will have a price war and get no operating profits to offset their initial development investment of 8 each.

So choosing to enter the market looks risky for Airbus. It looks similarly risky for Boeing. As you can see by studying the payoffs for the two rows, Boeing would want to produce only if it could be sure that Airbus won't produce (upper-right box). But in a noncooperative game like this, neither firm can choose the outcome—each can

[4]This case led to several complaints to both the WTO and the North American Free Trade Agreement for dispute resolution. The duty rates declined and then were replaced in 2007 by a system in which the Canadian government will impose export taxes if the Canadian share of the U.S. market exceeds a specified percentage or if U.S. prices fall below a specified level.

FIGURE 11.7
A Two-Firm
Rivalry Game
with No
Government
Subsidies:
Airbus versus
Boeing

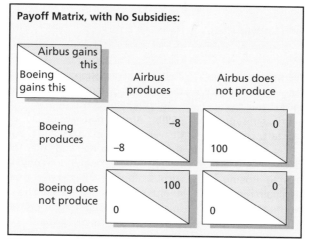

When two competing firms face each other with identical choices and no government help, there is no clear result to the game if both must decide simultaneously. Each would like to be the only producer, but if both decide to produce, both lose. Knowing this, both may decide not to produce.

only choose a strategy (column or row). The two firms might react to the threat of competition by producing nothing, leaving the world in the lower right-box—with no new planes.

Either government could break through the uncertainty by offering a subsidy to its producer, for instance, a subsidy that more than covers the producer's initial development costs. Again, let's take the European viewpoint. The governments of Britain, France, Germany, and Spain could agree to give subsidies to Airbus. If they give Airbus a start-up subsidy of 10, we could have the situation shown in panel A in Figure 11.8. Looking down the left column of possibilities, Airbus can see that it should definitely produce. Either it gains only 2 (invest 8, get 10 back in subsidies) in the face of competition from Boeing, or it gains a full 110 if Boeing is frightened off. And Boeing will be frightened off. Because Boeing is sure that Airbus will produce, Boeing's best choice is not to produce (no loss or gain is better than losing 8).

So, Airbus gains, and the world's consumers gain (an amount not shown here). Even Europe as a whole gains if Airbus makes the 110 in profits because after subtracting the subsidy of 10, the net gain to Europe is still 100. So here is a case of a subsidy that is good for the world as a whole and good for the exporting country (the European Union) as well. This subsidy is a form of **strategic trade policy,** in which government policy helps its own firm's strategy to win the game and claim the prize (here, 100 of economic profit).[5]

---

[5]Another form of strategic trade policy is protection of the home market if the home market is large and scale economies are important. The domestic firm can then use production to meet demand in its protected home market as the basis for low-cost production that allows it to compete aggressively in the foreign market. Aggressive exporting in this situation is sometimes called *strategic dumping*.

Global Governance   Dogfight at the WTO

In October 2004, the U.S. government filed a complaint with the World Trade Organization that the European Union had given and continued to give massive subsidies to Airbus in support of Airbus's production of civil aircraft. Later the same day the European Union filed a complaint that the U.S. government had given and continued to give massive subsidies to Boeing in support of its production of civil aircraft. The dogfight over airplane subsidies had moved to the WTO, with combat in the form of the two largest WTO dispute cases ever.

The story began in the late 1960s, when several national governments in Europe decided to offer infant industry support to a new airplane producer. The development of Airbus was slow, but in the 1980s it achieved a share of global deliveries of new civil aircraft (seating more than 100 passengers, distinct from smaller "regional" aircraft) of 10–20 percent. As the leading U.S. firm, Boeing complained to the U.S. government about the subsidies that Airbus was receiving. The U.S. government began discussions with the European Union. These talks culminated in a 1992 bilateral agreement to restrain subsidies offered by both sides:

- Direct government support for new airplane development (usually called launch aid) limited to no more than one-third of the total development cost, and only in the form of loans with minimum required interest rate and maximum repayment period.

- Indirect government support (for instance, research support offered through defense contracts) limited to no more than 4 percent of a firm's civil aircraft sales.

- No production or marketing subsidies, and limits on government financing assistance to airplane buyers.

The limit on launch aid restricted the major way that European governments have helped Airbus, and the limit on indirect support restricted the major way that the U.S. government has helped Boeing.

Airbus sales continued to grow. By the mid-1990s, Airbus had about 30 percent of new deliveries and in 2003–2004, Airbus had more than half. Boeing and the U.S. government became increasingly unhappy with continued Airbus subsidies. They stated that assistance that might have been suitable when Airbus was an infant was no longer appropriate when Airbus is grown up and clearly successful. In 2004 the U.S. government and the EU held discussions to consider revisions to the 1992 agreement but made no progress. In September the U.S. government announced that it was terminating the 1992 agreement as it filed the complaint under the general WTO subsidy rules.

The U.S. government complaint focused on the billions of dollars of launch aid from European governments to Airbus since its birth. The U.S. government argued that launch-aid loans provide subsidies because they have artificially low interest rates and pay-back terms that are conditional on future Airbus sales of the plane being developed. The U.S. government also complained that Airbus received billions of dollars of other government subsidies, including other low-cost loans, public investments to assist Airbus in its production, and R&D contracts that benefit its civil aircraft production. The United States specifically alleged that Airbus received $6.5 billion in subsidies in support of the development and production of the new superjumbo A380.

For its complaint the EU alleged that Boeing received billions of dollars in R&D contracts from the U.S. National Aeronautics and Space Administration and the U.S. Department of Defense, with the results of this research benefiting its civil aircraft production. The EU also stated that Boeing received other subsidies, including billions of dollars of tax breaks from federal, state, and local governments.

The WTO cases moved slowly. After filing the two complaints in October 2004, the U.S. government and the EU negotiated to attempt to resolve the issues, but they made little progress. In May 2005, the U.S. government asked the WTO to create a panel to hear and judge the case about its complaint, and the next day the EU responded by asking the WTO to create a panel for its complaint. For the U.S. complaint, the panel issued its report five years later, in June 2010. The U.S. government and the EU both appealed certain issues of law and legal interpretations in the panel decision, and the appeal report was adopted in June 2011. For the EU complaint, the panel issued its report almost six years later, in March 2011. Again, both sides appealed, and the appeal report was adopted in March 2012.

In the final ruling for the U.S. complaint, the WTO determined that the EU had provided actionable subsidies to Airbus that had harmed Boeing. The $15 billion of launch aid included substantial subsidies, and Airbus had received about $5 billion of other subsidies. The WTO recommended that the EU withdraw the subsidies or revise them to end the harm to Boeing. In the final ruling for the EU complaint, the WTO determined that the United States had provided subsidies to Boeing totaling at least $5 billion, mostly actionable R&D subsidies (about $3 billion) that had harmed Airbus and prohibited export tax subsidies ($2 billion). The WTO recommended that the U.S. government withdraw the subsidies or revise them to end the harm to Airbus.

In December 2011, the EU informed the WTO that it had brought its policies into compliance. The U.S. government disagreed, claimed up to $10 billion of continuing injury, and requested approval to retaliate. The WTO established an arbitration panel to consider retaliation, but the U.S. government and the EU requested suspension of the arbitration in January 2012. Much the same sequence played out for the other case. The U.S. government reported compliance in September 2012. The EU disagreed, claimed up to $12 billion in continuing injury, and requested approval to retaliate. The arbitration panel was established and then suspended in November 2012.

Thus, 10 years after the cases were filed, there is no resolution. It is not clear what this protracted and expensive battle has accomplished. The dogfight seems to have ended in an uneasy draw.

It's not so easy, though. Suppose that the U.S. government decides to subsidize Boeing's market entry in the same way that the EU subsidizes Airbus. Then we have the problem shown in panel B of Figure 11.8. Each firm sees a green light and decides to produce because each firm makes a positive profit regardless of whether or not the other produces. This is fine for the firms, but each government is spending 10. So *as nations*, the EU and the United States are each losing 8 (for each, this equals the 2 of profits that the firm shows minus the 10 of subsidy cost to the government). The only good news in panel B is hidden from view: The world's consumers gain. But if most of those consumers are outside the EU and the United States, these two nations are still net losers. (In the real world both the U.S. government and European governments provide subsidies to their aircraft manufacturers, and this has led to trade conflict, as discussed in the box "Dogfight at the WTO.")

FIGURE 11.8   A Two-Firm Rivalry Game with Government Subsidies: Airbus versus Boeing

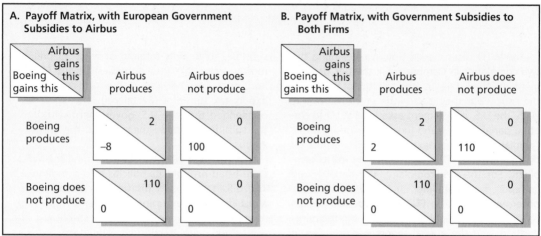

A. If the European government gives Airbus a subsidy of 10, to ensure Airbus a profit of 2 even with full competition, Airbus will choose to produce. Knowing that Airbus will produce, Boeing will choose not to produce. Airbus wins profits of 110. Because the airplane is built, consumers gain some surplus from the new product, and the world as a whole gains well-being. **B.** In this case, with each government offering a subsidy to its firm of 10, both firms will produce the airplane. For each country the cost of the subsidy (10) is greater than the gain to the firm (2). Each country loses by offering its subsidy, unless gains in national consumer surplus (not pictured here) are larger than this net loss of 8.

These simple examples bring out the two key points about an export subsidy or similar type of subsidy in a global duel between two exporting giants:

1. The subsidy *might* be a good thing for the exporting country, as shown in panel A in Figure 11.8, but
2. The case for giving the subsidy is fragile, depending on too many conditions to be a reliable policy.

In our example, we saw one condition that matters. If another national government also offers its firm strategic policy assistance, it is quite possible that both countries lose well-being. Another condition that matters is the possibility that there is no prize for the game. For instance, there may not be enough consumer demand for the new product, so economic profits will be negative instead of positive, even if there is only one producer. How would the government separate the false pleas of some of its firms for strategic help from the valid ones? While there is a theoretical case for the national benefit of strategic trade policy, we may be skeptical that a national government could actually use it effectively.

Summary

Dumping is selling exports at less than normal value—a price lower than the price in the home market or lower than the full average cost of production. Exporters may engage in dumping to drive foreign competitors out of business (predatory dumping), during recessions in industry demand (cyclical dumping), to unload excess inventory (seasonal dumping), or to increase profits through price discrimination (persistent dumping). The importing country benefits from the dumped exports because it pays a lower price for its imports. But the importing country could be hurt by predatory dumping (higher prices in the future) or by cyclical dumping (importing unemployment).

The WTO permits the importing country to retaliate with an antidumping duty if dumping is occurring and it is causing injury to the import-competing industry. It appears that the process of imposing antidumping duties has become a major source of new protection for import-competing producers because the process is biased to find dumping and impose duties. The American steel industry is an example of a set of firms that continually complain about dumping to gain relief from import competition. Proposals for reform of antidumping policy include limiting its use to cases where predatory dumping is plausible, incorporating consumer interests in the analysis of injury from dumping, and replacing antidumping policy with more use of safeguard policy, in which a government offers temporary protection to assist an industry in adjusting to increasing import competition.

Export subsidies are condemned by the WTO, with the exception of export subsidies to agricultural products. If the market is *competitive*, an export subsidy brings a loss to the country offering the subsidy and to the world as a whole by causing excessive trade. A countervailing duty against subsidized exports brings a loss to the importing country levying it but brings a gain to the world as a whole by offsetting the export subsidy. The combination of an export subsidy and an equal countervailing duty would leave world welfare unchanged, with taxpayers of the export-subsidizing country implicitly making payments to the government of the importing country.

In some situations it is at least possible that export subsidies will be good for the exporting nation and for the world as a whole. If export competition takes the form of an *oligopoly* game between two giant producers, each of which could dominate the market alone (e.g., Boeing versus Airbus), then a government can offer a subsidy to its exporter as a strategic trade policy. This firm then may capture more of the global market and bring gains both to the exporting nation and to the world as a whole. We do not know that such a case has occurred, but it is possible.

Key Terms			
	Dumping	Persistent dumping	Consumption effect
	Normal value	Price discrimination	Production effect
	Predatory dumping	Antidumping duty	Countervailing duty
	Cyclical dumping	Safeguard policy	Strategic trade policy
	Seasonal dumping	Export subsidy	

Suggested Reading

Bown (2011) surveys patterns of use of antidumping measures and countervailing duties. Niels (2000), Nelson (2006), and Niels and ten Kate (2006) provide surveys of a broad range of research on antidumping policy. Ethier (1982) presents the basic theory of dumping. Lindsey and Ikenson (2002) and Blonigen (2006) explore biases in the ways that the U.S. Department of Commerce determines dumping margins. Galloway, Blonigen, and Flynn (1999) present estimates of the effects of U.S. antidumping and countervailing duties. Finger and Nogues (2006) offer studies of the use of antidumping policies by Latin American countries. Aggarwal (2011) examines the effects of antidumping actions by India.

Read (2005) examines the U.S. safeguards imposed on steel imports in 2002. Tokarick (2005) provides estimates of the global effects of government subsidies and other support to agriculture in industrialized countries.

Brander (1995) provides a technical survey of strategic trade policy.

Questions and Problems

◆ 1. What are the two official definitions of *dumping*?

2. "U.S. antidumping policy uses its injury test to ensure that antidumping duties imposed by the U.S. government enhance U.S. national well-being." Do you agree or disagree? Why?

◆ 3. Which of the following three beverage exporters is dumping in the U.S. market? Which is not? How do you know?

	Banzai Brewery (Japan)	Tipper Laurie, Ltd. (UK)	Bigg Redd, Inc. (Canada)
Average cost	$10	$10	$10
Price charged at the brewery for domestic sales	10	12	9
Price charged at the brewery for export sales	11	11	9
Price when delivered to the U.S. port	12	13	10

4. What is persistent dumping? Does an exporter lose profit because of the low export price? Does persistent dumping harm the importing country?

◆ 5. You have been asked to propose a specific revision of U.S. antidumping policy to make the policy more likely to contribute to U.S. well-being. What will you propose?

6. What is a countervailing duty?

◆ 7. What would happen to world welfare if the United States paid exporters a subsidy of $5 for every pair of blue jeans they sold to Canada, but Canada charged a $5 countervailing duty on every pair imported into Canada? Would the United States gain from the combination of the export subsidy and import tariff? Would Canada? Explain. (In your answer, assume that the blue jeans market is perfectly competitive.)

8. Consider the case of an export subsidy for an importing country that has some monopsony power—that is, the case in which the foreign supply-of-exports curve is upward-sloping. Use a graph like that in Figure 11.4.

   a. In comparison with free trade, what is the effect of the export subsidy on the international price and the quantity traded?

   b. The importing country now imposes a countervailing duty that returns the market to the initial free-trade quantity traded. In comparison with the market with just the export subsidy, explain why the countervailing duty is good for the world. Explain why the countervailing duty can also increase the well-being of the importing country.

◆ 9. In the Airbus-versus-Boeing example in Figure 11.7, what strategy should the EU governments follow if the upper-left box (*a*) gives Airbus and Boeing each a sure gain of 5 or (*b*) gives Boeing a gain of 5 and Airbus a gain of 0? In each case, should the EU offer a subsidy to Airbus? Explain.

10. Consider the export subsidy shown in Figure 11.3. Assuming that the export subsidy remains $20, what are the effects of a decline in the world price from $100 to $90? Show the effects using a graph, and explain them.

◆ 11. You have been hired to write a defense of the idea of having a government plan to subsidize the expansion of an export-oriented industry, taking resources away from the rest of the economy. Describe how you would defend such an industrial targeting strategy as good for the nation as a whole.

12. You have been hired to discredit the argument you just presented in answering Question 11. Present a strong case against getting the government into the export-pushing business.

Chapter **Twelve**

Trade Blocs and Trade Blocks

Standard analysis of trade policy looks at equal-opportunity import barriers, ones that tax or restrict all imports regardless of country of origin. But some import barriers are meant to discriminate. They tax goods, services, or assets from some countries more than those from other countries. The analysis of Chapters 8 through 10 can now be modified to explain the effects of today's trade discrimination.

We look at two kinds of trade barriers that are designed to discriminate:

1. Trade blocs. Each member country can import from other member countries freely, or at least cheaply, while imposing barriers against imports from outside countries. The European Union (EU) has done that, allowing free trade between members while restricting imports from other countries.

2. Trade embargoes, or what the chapter title calls "trade blocks." Some countries discriminate against certain other countries, usually because of a policy dispute. They deny the outflow of goods, services, or assets to a particular country while allowing export to other countries, discriminate against imports from the targeted country, or block both exports to and imports from the target.

TYPES OF ECONOMIC BLOCS

Some international groupings discriminate in trade alone, while others discriminate between insiders and outsiders on all fronts, becoming almost like unified nations. To grasp what is happening in Europe, North America, and elsewhere, we should first distinguish among the main types of economic blocs. Figure 12.1 and the following definitions show the progression of economic blocs toward increasing integration:

1. A free-trade area, in which members remove trade barriers among themselves but keep their separate national barriers against trade with the outside world. Most trade blocs operating today are free-trade areas. One example is the North American Free Trade Area (NAFTA), which formally began at the start of 1994.

2. A customs union, in which members remove barriers to trade among themselves and adopt a common set of external barriers. The European Economic Community (EEC) from 1957 to 1992 included a customs union along with some other

FIGURE 12.1
Types of
Economic Blocs

Type of Bloc	Features of Bloc			
	Free Trade among the Members	Common External Tariffs	Free Movement of Factors of Production	Harmonization* of All Economic Policies (Fiscal, Monetary, etc.)
Free-trade area	✓			
Customs union	✓	✓		
Common market	✓	✓	✓	
Economic union	✓	✓	✓	✓

*If the policies are not just harmonized by separate governments but actually decided by a unified government with binding commitments on all members, then the bloc amounts to full economic nationhood. Some authors call this *full economic integration.*

agreements. The Southern Common Market (MERCOSUR), formed by Argentina, Brazil, Paraguay, and Uruguay in 1991, is actually a customs union.

3. A common market, in which members allow full freedom of factor flows (migration of labor and capital) among themselves in addition to having a customs union. Despite its name, the European Common Market (EEC, which became the European Community, EC, and is now the European Union, EU) was not a common market up through the 1980s because it still had substantial barriers to the international movement of labor and capital. The EU became a true common market, and more, at the end of 1992.

4. Full economic union, in which member countries unify all their economic policies, including monetary and fiscal policies as well as policies toward trade and factor migration. Most nations are economic unions. Belgium and Luxembourg have had such a union since 1921. The EU is on a path toward economic unity.

The first two types of economic blocs are simply trade blocs (i.e., they have removed trade barriers within the bloc but have kept their national barriers to the flow of labor and capital and their national fiscal and monetary autonomy). Trade blocs have proved easier to form than common markets or full unions among sovereign nations, and they are the subject of this chapter. Freedom of factor flows within a bloc is touched on only briefly here—we return to it in Chapter 15. The monetary side of union enters in Chapter 17 and beyond.

IS TRADE DISCRIMINATION GOOD OR BAD?

In 2014 about half of world trade occurred *within* functioning trade blocs, including:

- The 28 countries of the EU.
- The 4 remaining countries of the European Free Trade Area (EFTA).
- The preferential trade agreements that the EU has with 58 other countries (including the 4 EFTA countries).

- The 3 countries of NAFTA.
- The trade agreements that Mexico has with the EU, EFTA, Chile, Costa Rica, Colombia, El Salvador, Guatemala, Honduras, Israel, Japan, Nicaragua, Peru, and Uruguay, in addition to its membership in NAFTA.
- The 7 countries of the Central American Free Trade Area (CAFTA-DR).
- The free-trade areas that the United States has with Australia, Bahrain, Chile, Colombia, Israel, Jordan, Korea, Morocco, Oman, Panama, Peru, and Singapore, in addition to its memberships in NAFTA and CAFTA-DR.
- The 5 countries of MERCOSUR (with a sixth country, Bolivia, in the process of acceding to full membership) and its trade association agreements with Chile, Colombia, Ecuador, Guyana, Peru, and Suriname.
- The trade agreements that Turkey has with the EU, EFTA, and 16 other countries.

As of early 2014, there were almost 250 preferential trade agreements in force in the world, and over half of them had begun operating since 2000. Only four WTO members (Congo, Djibouti, Mauritania, and Mongolia) were not members of some trade bloc.

How good or how bad is all this trade discrimination? It depends, first, on what you compare it to. Compared to a free-trade policy, putting up new barriers discriminating against imports from some countries is generally bad, like the simple tariff of Chapters 8 through 10. But the issue of trade discrimination usually comes to us from a different angle: *Beginning with tariffs and nontariff barriers that apply equally regardless of the source country of the imports,* what are the gains and losses from removing barriers only between certain countries? That is, what happens when a trade bloc like the EU or NAFTA gets formed?

Two opposing ideas come to mind. One instinct is that forming a customs union or free-trade area must be good because it is a move toward free trade. If you start from an equally applied set of trade barriers in each nation, having a group of them remove trade barriers among themselves clearly means lower trade barriers in some average sense. Since that idea is closer to free trade, and Chapters 8 through 11 found free trade better with only carefully limited exceptions, it seems reasonable that forming a trade bloc allows more trade and raises world welfare. After all, forming a nation out of smaller regions brings economic gains, doesn't it?

On the other hand, we can think of reasons why forming a free-trading bloc can be bad, even starting from equally applied barriers to all international trade. First, forming the trade bloc may encourage people to buy from higher-cost partner suppliers. The bloc would encourage costly production within the bloc if it kept a high tariff on goods from the cheapest source outside the bloc and no tariff on goods from a more costly source within the bloc. By contrast, a uniform tariff on all imports has the virtue that customers would still do their importing from the low-cost source. Second, the whole idea of trade discrimination smacks of the bilateralism of the 1930s, when separate deals with individual nations destroyed much of the gains from global trade. The list at the beginning of this section indicates that we again have quite a tangled web of discriminatory agreements. Third, forming blocs may cause international friction simply because letting someone into the bloc will shut others out.

For all these reasons, World Trade Organization (WTO) rules are opposed to trade discrimination in principle. A basic WTO principle is that trade barriers should be lowered equally and without discrimination for all foreign trading partners. That is, the WTO espouses the most favored nation (MFN) principle. This principle, dating back to the mid-19th-century wave of free trade led by Britain, stipulates that any concession given to any foreign nation must be given to all nations having MFN status. WTO rules say that all contracting parties are entitled to that status.

However, other parts of WTO rules permit deviations from MFN under specific conditions. One deviation is special treatment for developing countries. Developing countries have the right to exchange preferences among themselves and receive preferential access to markets in the industrialized countries.

Another deviation permits trade blocs involving industrialized countries if the trade bloc removes tariffs and other trade restrictions on most of the trade among its members, and if its trade barriers against nonmembers do not increase on average. In fact, the WTO, and the GATT before it, has applied the rules loosely. No trade bloc has ever been ruled in violation.

THE BASIC THEORY OF TRADE BLOCS: TRADE CREATION AND TRADE DIVERSION

Trade discrimination can indeed be either good or bad. We can give an example of this and, in the process, discover what conditions separate the good from the bad cases. It may seem paradoxical that the formation of a trade bloc can either raise or lower well-being because removing barriers among member nations looks like a step toward free trade. Yet the analysis of a trade bloc is another example of the not-so-simple theory of the second best.

The welfare effects of eliminating trade barriers between partners are illustrated in Figure 12.2, which is patterned after Britain's entry into the EC (now the EU). To simplify the diagram greatly, all export supply curves are assumed to be perfectly flat. We consider two cases. In one, forming the trade bloc is costly because too much trade is diverted from lower-cost to higher-cost suppliers. In the other, forming the trade bloc is beneficial because it creates more low-cost trade.

In Figure 12.2A, the British could buy Japanese cars at £5,000 if there were no tariff. The next cheapest alternative is to buy German cars delivered at £5,500. If there were free trade, at point C, Britain would import only Japanese cars and none from Germany.

Before its entry into the trade bloc, however, Britain did not have free trade in automobiles. It had a uniform tariff, imagined here to be £1,000 per car, which marks up the cost of imported Japanese cars from £5,000 to £6,000 in Figure 12.2. No Britons buy the identical German cars because they would cost £6,500 (equal to the £5,500 price charged by the German producers plus the £1,000 tariff). The starting point for our discussion is thus the tariff-ridden point *A*, with the British government collecting (£1,000 times 10,000 = £10 million) in tariff revenues.

Now let Britain join the EU, as it did in 1973, removing all tariffs on goods from the EU while leaving the same tariffs on goods from outside the EU. Under the simplifying

FIGURE 12.2   Trade Diversion versus Trade Creation in Joining a Trade Bloc: UK Market for Imported Compact Cars

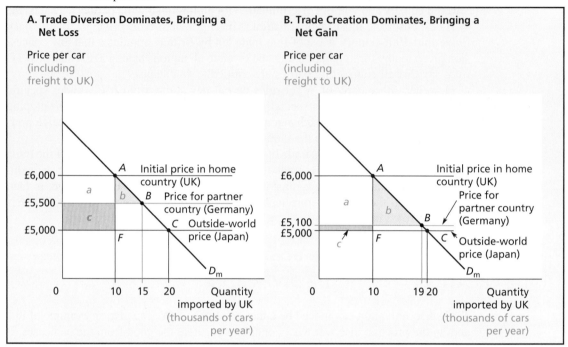

Starting from a uniform tariff on all compact cars (at point *A*), Britain joins the EU trade bloc, removing tariffs on imports from EU partners like Germany but not on imports from the cheapest outside source, Japan. With the flat supply curves assumed here, all the original imports of 10,000 cars from the cheapest outside source are replaced with imports from new partner countries (e.g., Germany). In panel A the shift from *A* to *B* creates 5,000 extra imports, bringing national gains for the UK (area *b*). But it also diverts those 10,000 cars from the cheapest foreign supplier to the partner country, imposing extra costs (area *c*). In this case, the loss exceeds the gain, bringing a net loss:

$$\text{Gain area } b = (1/2)(6{,}000 - 5{,}500)(15{,}000 - 10{,}000) = \text{Gain of £1.25 million}$$
$$\text{Loss area } c = (5{,}500 - 5{,}000)(10{,}000) = \text{Loss of £5 million}$$
$$\text{Net loss} = \text{£3.75 million}$$

In panel B, Germany's price is not much greater than that quoted by Japanese suppliers. Removing the tariff on German (and other EU) cars creates 9,000 new imports of cars, yielding the trade-creation gain shown as area *b*. The 10,000 cars are again diverted from the cheapest supplier (Japan), but this trade diversion costs less than that in panel A. So

$$\text{Gain area } b = (1/2)(6{,}000 - 5{,}100)(19{,}000 - 10{,}000) = \text{Gain of £4.05 million}$$
$$\text{Loss area } c = (5{,}100 - 5{,}000)(10{,}000) = \text{Loss of £1.00 million}$$
$$\text{Net gain} = \text{£3.05 million}$$

assumptions made here, German cars now cost only £5,500 in Britain (instead of that plus the £1,000 tariff), while the price of Japanese cars in Britain remains £6,000 because they still incur the tariff. British purchasers of imported cars switch to buying only German cars. In addition, seeing the price of imported cars fall to £5,500 in Britain, they buy more (at point *B*). Clearly, British car buyers have something to cheer about. They gain the areas *a* and *b* in consumer surplus, thanks to the bargain. But the British government loses all its previous tariff revenue, the area $a + c$ (£10 million). So, after we cancel out the gain and loss of *a*, Britain ends up with two effects on its well-being:

1. A gain from trade creation (in this case, from the extra 5,000 cars). Trade creation is the net volume of new trade resulting from forming or joining a trade bloc. It causes the national gain shown as area *b* in Figure 12.2. Area *b* represents two kinds of gain in the British economy: gains on extra consumption of the product and gains on replacement of higher-cost British production by lower-cost partner production.
2. A loss from trade diversion (in this case, from the 10,000 cars). Trade diversion is the volume of trade shifted from low-cost outside exporters to higher-cost bloc-partner exporters. It causes the national loss shown as area *c*.

This is the general result: The gains from a trade bloc are tied to trade creation, and the losses are tied to trade diversion.[1]

The net effect on well-being, the trade-creation gain minus the trade-diversion loss, could be positive or negative. In the first case (Figure 12.2A), the loss on trade diversion happens to dominate.

Our second case, Figure 12.2B, shows the opposite result. If the new bloc partners, such as Germany, were almost the lowest-cost suppliers in the world, then the gain from trade creation would dominate. If they can supply cars almost as cheaply as the Japanese, then there won't be much cost from diverting Britain's customers away from Japanese compact cars. The trade-diversion cost is only £100 on each of the diverted 10,000 cars. At the same time, there is a lot of trade creation. Removing the £1,000 tariff on German cars cuts the domestic price of imports from the old £6,000 on Japanese cars with tariff to £5,100 on German cars without tariff, resulting in a substantial gain. In the specific case shown in Figure 12.2B, there is a net national (and world) gain from the effects of the bloc on trade in this kind of automobile.[2]

---

[1]There is an alternative analysis assuming upward-sloping supply curves for all three countries, with similar but more widely applicable results (e.g., Harry G. Johnson, 1962). One point revealed by the upward-sloping supply analysis is that trade diversion may bring terms-of-trade gains to the bloc partners at the expense of the rest of the world. Diverting demand away from outside suppliers may force them to cut their export prices (i.e., the bloc's import prices). On the export side, diverting bloc sales toward bloc customers and away from outside customers may raise the bloc's export-price index. Thus, the bloc may gain from a higher terms-of-trade ratio (= export price/import price), a possibility assumed away by the flat outside-world supply curve in Figure 12.2.

Another point revealed is that trade diversion brings gains to the partner country that is exporting the product because its producers charge a higher price on exports to the importing partner and export a larger quantity to this partner. However, the exporting-partner gains are less than the importing-partner losses, so trade diversion still creates a net loss for the trade bloc and for the world. The flat-supply-curve case is used here because its diagram (or its algebra) makes the basic points more clearly.

[2]To imagine a case of pure trade creation, with no trade diversion at all, just switch the words *Germany* and *Japan* in either half of Figure 12.2. With Germany now the cheapest supplier, nobody in Britain would buy Japanese cars with or without the EU customs union. Forming the union expands trade from point *A* to point *C*, bringing the net gain *ACF*.

Reflecting on the one-good cases in Figure 12.2, you can figure out what conditions dictate whether the gains outweigh the losses. Here are two tendencies that make for greater gains from a trade bloc:

A. The lower the partner costs relative to the outside-world costs, the greater the gains. Any trade diversion will be less costly.
B. The more elastic the import demand, the greater the gains. The trade creation in response to any domestic price decline will be larger.

So the best case is one with costs that are almost as low somewhere within the bloc as in the outside world and highly elastic demands for imports. Conversely, the worst case is one with inelastic import demands and high costs throughout the trade bloc.

OTHER POSSIBLE GAINS FROM A TRADE BLOC

Researchers have identified several other possible sources of gains from forming a trade bloc. Several gains arise because *the trade bloc creates a larger market* (bloc-wide rather than only national) in which firms can sell their products with few or no trade barriers. It is easiest to see the possibility for these gains if we think of an extreme case in which the countries that form the bloc all had such high trade barriers before the bloc was formed that they traded little with each other or with the rest of the world. Furthermore, scale economies and product differentiation are important for some products. In this setting, here are four possible sources of additional gains from forming the trade bloc:

- *An increase in competition can reduce prices.* Before the bloc, firms in each country may have monopoly power in their separate national market, so prices are high in each national market. When the national markets are joined in the trade bloc, firms from the partner countries must compete with each other. The extra competition reduces monopoly power and reduces prices. The inefficiency of monopoly pricing is reduced.
- *An increase in competition can lower costs of production.* If a firm has monopoly power and substantial protection from foreign competition, there is little pressure on it to minimize costs or implement new technologies. When the national markets are joined in the trade bloc, the extra competition forces firms to pay more attention to reducing costs and improving technology. Studies by the consulting firm McKinsey have repeatedly shown that a key determinant of the differences in the productivity of firms in different countries is the intensity of competition the firms must face.
- *Firms can lower costs by expanding their scale of production.* Before the bloc is formed, the size of a firm is largely limited by the size of its own national market. If scale economies are substantial, the firm may not be large enough to exploit all of the scale economies. When the markets are joined in the trade bloc, each firm now has a larger market to serve. Some firms expand their size to take advantage of additional scale economies. (Other firms that cannot gain the scale economies fast enough may be driven out of business by these larger lower-cost firms. This is good for the trade bloc as whole, but some member countries may feel harmed if it is their firms that disappear.)

• *Consumers gain access to a larger number of varieties or models of a product.* Before the bloc is formed, consumers in the country are mostly limited to the versions of the product produced by domestic firms. When the markets are joined in the trade bloc, consumers can buy additional imported versions of the product produced by firms in the partner countries.

A final possible source of gains is the possibility that *forming the trade bloc increases opportunities for business investments.* Multinational firms (discussed further in Chapter 15) often seek foreign production locations based on the size of the market that can be served by their affiliates. By expanding the market that can be served inside the external trade barriers, a trade bloc can attract more foreign direct investment into the member countries. Global firms often bring better technologies, management practices, and marketing capabilities. If these "intangibles" diffuse to local firms (positive externalities), then the country gains an extra benefit from the direct investment by foreign firms. More broadly, by increasing the rate of return to business investments as the trade bloc opens new profit opportunities, the formation of the bloc can increase real investment and can therefore expand the overall production capacity of the partner countries.

Not all of these effects occur for every product or member country when a trade bloc is formed, but they do occur for some products and some members. They provide gains from being a member of a trade bloc that are in addition to the basic gains from trade creation.

THE EU EXPERIENCE

Europe has been the locus of the longest and deepest regional integration. The box "Postwar Trade Integration in Europe" provides the highlights of the chronology. In particular, the formation of the EU's customs union was the first major modern trade bloc. Numerous studies have examined its economic effects. Studies in the 1960s and 1970s tended to conclude that the net gains from forming the EU (then the EEC) were small but positive. For example, net gains on trade in manufactured goods calculated by Balassa (1975, p. 115) were a little over one-tenth of 1 percent of members' total GDP. That tiny positive estimate overlooks some losses from the EU and some likely gains. By concentrating on trade in manufactured goods, the literature generally overlooked the significant social losses from the EU's common agricultural policy. This policy protects and subsidizes agriculture so heavily as to bring serious social losses of the sort described in Chapter 11.[3] On the other hand, the studies of the 1960s and 1970s generally confined their measurements to static welfare effects like those in Figure 12.2, omitting possible gains from increased competition, scale economies, improved productivity incentives, and greater product variety.

---

[3]Trade diversion on agricultural products is one reason why empirical studies find that joining the EC in 1973 may have cost Britain dearly. The common agricultural policy meant that British consumers had to lose cheap access to their traditional Commonwealth food suppliers (Australia, Canada, and New Zealand). They had to buy the more expensive EU food products and had to pay taxes on their remaining imports from the Commonwealth, taxes that were turned over to French, Danish, and Irish farmers as subsidies. This cost Britain an estimated 1.8 percent of GDP in the 1970s, versus a static-analysis gain of less than 0.2 percent of GDP on manufactured goods. The Thatcher government later bargained for a fairer sharing of the burdens of farm subsidies.

Case Study   Postwar Trade Integration in Europe

1950–1952: Following the Schuman Plan, "the six" (Belgium, France, West Germany, Italy, the Netherlands, and Luxembourg) set up the European Coal and Steel Community. Meanwhile, Benelux is formed by Belgium, the Netherlands, and Luxembourg. Both formations provide instructive early examples of integration.

1957–1958: The six sign the Treaty of Rome setting up the European Economic Community (EEC, or "Common Market"). Import duties among them are dismantled and their external barriers are unified in stages between the end of 1958 and mid-1968. Trade preferences are given to a host of developing countries, most of them former colonies of EEC members.

1960: The Stockholm Convention creates the European Free Trade Area (EFTA) among seven nations: Austria, Denmark, Norway, Portugal, Sweden, Switzerland, and the United Kingdom. Barriers among these nations are removed in stages, 1960–1966. Finland joins EFTA as an associate member in 1961. Iceland becomes a member in 1970, Finland becomes a full member in 1986, and Lichtenstein becomes a member in 1991.

1967: The European Community (EC) is formed by the merger of the EEC, the European Atomic Energy Commission, and the European Coal and Steel Community.

1972–1973: Denmark, Ireland, and the United Kingdom join the EC, converting the six into nine. Denmark and the United Kingdom leave EFTA. The United Kingdom agrees to abandon many of its Commonwealth trade preferences. Also, *Ode to Joy* from Beethoven's Ninth Symphony is chosen as the EC's anthem.

1973–1977: Trade barriers are removed in stages, both among the nine EC members and between them and the remaining EFTA nations. Meanwhile, the EC reaches trade preference agreements with most nonmember

Mediterranean countries along the lines of earlier agreements with Greece (1961), Turkey (1964), Spain (1970), and Malta (1970).

1979: European Monetary System begins to operate based on the European Currency Unit. The European Parliament is first elected by direct popular vote.

1981: Greece joins the EC as its 10th member.

1986: The admission of Portugal and Spain brings the number of members in the EC to 12.

1986–1987: Member governments approve and enact the Single European Act, calling for a fully unified market by 1992.

1989–1990: The collapse of the East German government brings a sudden expansion of Germany and therefore of the EC. East Germans are given generous entitlements to the social programs of Germany and the EC.

1991–1995: Ten countries from Central and Eastern Europe establish free-trade agreements with the EC. All become EU members in 2004 and 2007.

End of 1992: The Single European Act takes effect, integrating labor and capital markets throughout the EC.

1993: The Maastricht Treaty is approved, making the EC into the European Union (EU), which calls for unification of foreign policy, for cooperation in fighting crime, and for monetary union.

1994: The European Economic Area is formed, bringing the EFTA countries (except Switzerland) into the EU's Single European Market.

1995: Following votes with majority approval in each country, Austria, Sweden, and Finland join the EU, bringing the number to 15. As it had done in 1972, Norway rejects membership in its 1994 vote.

1996: The EU forms a customs union with Turkey.

1999: Eleven EU countries establish the euro as a common currency, initially existing along with each country's own currency. Greece becomes the 12th member of the euro area in 2001.

2002: The euro replaces the national currencies of the 12 countries.

2004: Ten countries (Estonia, Lithuania, Latvia, Poland, Czech Republic, Slovakia, Hungary, Slovenia, Malta, and Cyprus) join the EU, bringing the total number to 25.

2007: Romania and Bulgaria join the EU, bringing the total number to 27. Slovenia joins the euro area.

2008: Cyprus and Malta join the euro area.

2009: Slovakia joins the euro area.

2011: Estonia joins the euro area.

2013: Croatia joins the EU, bringing the total number to 28.

2014: Latvia joins the euro area, bringing the total number of EU countries using the euro as their currency to 18.

DISCUSSION QUESTION
Which country do you think will be the next country to join the EU?

Here, unfortunately, is a research frontier still unsettled: We know that there are probably gains in addition to those from basic trade creation, but we lack full estimates of these other gains. For now, the empirical judgment is threefold: (1) On manufactured goods, the EU has brought enough trade creation to suggest small positive net gains. (2) The static gains on manufactures were probably smaller than the losses on the common agricultural policy. (3) But the net judgment still depends on what we believe about the unmeasured gains from competition, scale economies, productivity, and product variety.

In the 1980s the EU moved beyond being a customs union and toward being a single common market. The Single European Act, which took full effect at the end of 1992, forced many changes. First, it neutralized separate national product standards that had often been thinly disguised devices for protecting higher-cost domestic producers against competition from firms in other member countries. Examples included German beer purity regulations, Italian pasta protection laws, Belgian chocolate content restrictions, and Greek ice cream specifications. Second, capital controls on the flows of financial investments were removed. Third, restrictions on people working in other member countries were generally removed, although there are still some limits on licensed professionals such as lawyers.

How much benefit might such a miscellany of measures bring to the EU? It is hard to say, given the difficulty of measuring such key determinants as increased scale economies and increasing competition. Recent studies conclude that gains are probably 2 percent or less of GDP.

As indicated in the box "Postwar Trade Integration in Europe," in 2004 ten additional countries, including eight formerly communist countries in Central and Eastern Europe, joined the EU, in 2007 two more formerly communist countries joined, and in 2013 one more joined. These new members added about 27 percent to the EU's total population. But they are relatively poor, so they added less than 6 percent to its total GDP.

The basic requirements to join the EU are that the country have a functioning democracy, a commitment to respecting human rights, a market economy, and the capacity and willingness to adopt and to implement EU rules and standards. These 13 countries had to work intensely to meet the latter requirements. EU standards cover 31 major areas, and the documents listing them are 80,000 pages long.

Integration of the members that joined in 2004 and 2007 has been generally smooth. Still, some features of EU policies were phased in slowly for them. First, to control the costs to the EU budget, the subsidies that their farmers receive started at only one-fourth of the standard levels for the common agricultural policy. Second, the new members were not full members of the common market for labor. Citizens of the new members were not generally free to work in most other EU countries until seven years after the country joined the EU.

The new member countries experienced a mix of trade creation and trade diversion. One example of the basis for trade creation is the shift away from idiosyncratic national food safety laws and to the EU standards. Packaged food companies like Coca-Cola gain the benefits of easier product and packaging design and more flexibility in locating production facilities. One example of trade diversion is the new members' adoption of the EU's sugar policy, which leads to higher prices and purchases from other EU producers rather than from low-cost outside suppliers. The new members also gained from access to greater product variety. Overall, we think the gains are larger than the losses. Estimates of the economic effects of this enlargement indicate that the new members have seen a net gain in well-being of 2 to 8 percent of their GDP, with a small gain for the other EU countries.

The EU successfully grew over time from 6 members to 28 in 2013. The outlook for further expansion is less clear. The other countries of the Balkans (Serbia, Montenegro, Bosnia, Macedonia, and Albania) want to join, but it probably will be years before they qualify. Possible entry of such countries as Ukraine, Moldova, and Georgia, Eastern European countries that were part of the Soviet Union, is more distant. Turkey is eager to join, but the EU continues to be skeptical of Turkey's willingness to make the necessary political and economic policy changes, and it is concerned about its own ability to gainfully integrate such a large and poor country.

NORTH AMERICA BECOMES A BLOC

The North American Free Trade Area went from impossibility to reality in a few years during the late 1980s and early 1990s. The first step was the Canada–U.S. Free Trade Area (CUSFTA), an idea that had been debated since the 19th century. As late as 1986, when the two countries had a minor trade war over lumber and corn plus another tiff over Arctic navigational rights, there seemed to be little chance of forming a trade bloc. Yet the mood swung quickly, and negotiations that began in 1986 led to a free-trade area that came into force on January 1, 1989.

The second step was bringing Mexico into the picture. Starting in 1985, the Mexican government became increasingly determined to break down its own barriers to a freer, more privatized, more efficient Mexican economy. A series of reforms deregulated business and reduced barriers to imports of goods. Mexico's tariffs had been high and were raised even higher after the 1982 debt crisis forced Mexico to tighten its belt. By 1992, Mexico had slashed its tariffs to an average of only 10 percent. In 1990 the U.S. government and the Mexican government began negotiations on a trade agreement, and Canada joined the talks in 1991. The agreement was completed in 1992, and NAFTA, which replaced CUSFTA, came into existence on January 1, 1994.

NAFTA: Provisions and Controversies

NAFTA has eliminated nearly all tariffs and some nontariff barriers to trade within the area (some liberalizations occurred slowly and were not completed until 2008). It removed barriers to cross-border business investments within the area, and Mexico phased out performance requirements, including domestic content requirements and export requirements, that the Mexican government had previously imposed on foreign businesses operating in Mexico. NAFTA specifies open trade and investment in many service industries, including banking and financial services. NAFTA has its own set of dispute settlement procedures. Supplemental agreements call for better enforcement of labor and environmental standards, but these have had little effect. NAFTA does not, however, call for free human migration between these countries, nor does it denationalize Pemex, Mexico's huge government oil monopoly.

NAFTA was controversial, especially in Mexico and the United States, from the moment it became a strong political possibility in 1990. Critics in Mexico sounded the alarm that Mexican jobs would be wiped out, widening the already enormous gaps between rich and poor in Mexico. They also warned that the United States would use NAFTA to force Mexico to make many changes in its policies, weakening Mexican sovereignty. On the other side of the border, American labor groups were convinced that they would lose their jobs to Mexicans, whose wage rates were only a tiny fraction of those paid in the United States. This concern was dramatized by H. Ross Perot's famous claim in 1992 that NAFTA would cause a "great sucking sound" as many American jobs were instantly shifted to Mexico. Critics in the United States also decried that NAFTA rewarded and strengthened a corrupt political system in Mexico. In addition, environmentalists in both countries feared that NAFTA would lead to an expansion of the already serious pollution in Mexico, especially in the *maquiladora* industrial towns along the U.S.–Mexican border.

Proponents in Mexico hoped to use NAFTA to have some influence on U.S. trade policies like antidumping, a goal that the Canadians also had for the Canada–U.S. Free Trade Area. They also expected NAFTA to attract more investments into Mexico from foreign businesses using Mexico as a base for North American production. Proponents in the United States hoped to solidify the market-oriented reforms in Mexico, making Mexico a more dependable economic and political ally. But proponents of NAFTA were also extravagant in some of their claims, particularly when asserting that defeating NAFTA would send the Mexican economy into a giant depression, forcing an unemployed army to march over the U.S. border in search of jobs.

Concerns over jobs and the environment were so severe within the United States and Canada that they nearly defeated NAFTA. Yet in the end, the proponents prevailed and NAFTA became official at the beginning of 1994.

NAFTA: Effects

What have been the effects of NAFTA? There is broad agreement that NAFTA led to a substantial increase in total trade among the three countries, especially in the years up to the early 2000s. The standard view is that trade creation was larger than trade diversion. In this standard view, all three NAFTA countries have gained from NAFTA's trade expansion, with a gain in well-being to Mexico estimated at close to 2 percent of its GDP, a gain to Canada of close to 1 percent of its GDP, and a gain to the United States of perhaps 0.1 percent of its (very large) GDP.

There is a challenge to this standard view. Romalis (2007) presents a careful and detailed study of the effects of NAFTA in its first seven years (and of CUSFTA before it). He confirms the substantial effects on total trade, with the combination of CUSFTA and NAFTA increasing U.S.–Canadian trade by about 4 percent, and NAFTA increasing U.S.–Mexican trade by about 23 percent and Canadian–Mexican trade by about 28 percent. However, he finds that the large increases in total trade reflect both substantial trade creation and substantial trade diversion. Trade diversion is especially large for products that have relatively high tariffs against imports from outside countries because North American firms are often not low-cost producers of these products. For instance, imports of textiles and clothing were diverted away from low-cost suppliers in Asia. Romalis concludes that the gains from trade creation were about equal to the losses from trade diversion, so the net effect of expanding NAFTA trade on the well-being of each member country was very small.

NAFTA may also bring gains from increased competition in the larger area-wide market and from the increased ability for firms to achieve scale economies in this larger market. Studies of the effects on Canadian manufacturing industries during the first 10 years of free trade with the United States do show some large positive effects.

- Increased competition led to the demise of high-cost Canadian factories and the opening of low-cost ones.
- Average factory sizes did not become much bigger, which seems to question the role of increased scale economies. But there is evidence that fewer different products are being produced in these plants, so the scale economies are probably occurring through longer production runs of the smaller number of products.
- Increased competitive pressures and expanded export opportunities drove Canadian firms to innovate better products and improved production methods.

As a result of all of this, productivity in Canadian manufacturing increased about 14 percent more than it would have without the free-trade area.

NAFTA has created benefits for Mexico because it has made Mexico a more attractive place for business investments by foreign firms. With NAFTA firms look more favorably on locating production in Mexico to serve the entire NAFTA market (especially to serve the large U.S. market). The total amount invested by foreign businesses in their Mexican operations grew from $41 billion in 1993 to $403 billion in 2012. It is estimated that the investments would have been 40 percent lower without NAFTA.

As trade within NAFTA has grown, there has not been the massive shift of jobs toward Mexico that opponents in the United States predicted would result from

NAFTA. While U.S. imports from Mexico grew faster than U.S. exports to Mexico during 1993–2013, U.S. exports to Mexico still grew faster than U.S. exports to other countries. Any effects on the number of jobs in the United States are very small compared to the typical rates of overall job loss and job creation in the U.S. economy.

The large increases in NAFTA trade do have effects on workers in the United States, but they are the more subtle effects caused by shifting demands for different types of workers (the kind of effects that we highlighted in Chapter 5). Freer trade (in this case, NAFTA's discriminatory freeing of trade) absolutely hurts import-competing groups. NAFTA allows Mexico to better exploit its comparative advantage based on less-skilled labor in such products as apparel, field crops (e.g., tomatoes), and furniture and in such activities as product assembly. On the other hand, Mexico buys more U.S. financial services, chemicals, plastics, and high-tech equipment. The expansion of U.S. trade with Mexico spurred by NAFTA is pushing in the same direction as U.S. trade expansion with other developing countries, putting some downward pressure on the wages of less-skilled workers in the United States and increasing the incomes of more-skilled U.S. workers. In Mexico, too, there have been income losses, for instance, to small farmers growing corn (maize) who cannot readily shift to more lucrative crops. And there are income gains to others. For instance, in agriculture, NAFTA has facilitated large increases in Mexican exports of fruits and vegetables to the United States.

Rules of Origin

One other seemingly technical feature of NAFTA has received a surprising amount of attention. Because each member of a free-trade area maintains its own barriers against imports from outside the area, a member country must still police its borders, to tax or prohibit imports that might otherwise avoid its higher external barriers by entering through a lower-barrier partner country. Its customs officials must enforce **rules of origin** that determine which products have been produced within the free-trade area, so that they are traded freely within the area, and which products have not been produced within the area. These rules guard against a firm's ruse of doing minimal processing within the area and then claiming that the outside product is locally produced.

The NAFTA rules of origin are incredibly complex, covering over 200 pages with thousands of different rules for different products. Analysis of these rules has concluded that many of them are so strict that they are protectionist in two ways. First, the rules can limit the ability of firms in one member country to export freely to buyers in other member countries. They can create a nontariff barrier that hinders cross-member trade within the free-trade area. (The cost of documenting adherence to the rules can also be substantial, adding to the height of the NTB between the members.)

Second, the rules can create local content requirements that provide protection for the area producers of materials and components against rival suppliers of these materials and components from outside the area. Here is another, more subtle reason for producers from the rest of the world to lose. For instance, the rules of origin for clothing indicate that the clothing must be made with fabric produced within the area to qualify for duty-free shipping between NAFTA member countries. This rule benefits U.S. fabric producers and hurts the NAFTA sales of lower-cost fabric producers in Asia. It also reduces world well-being and North American well-being.

TRADE BLOCS AMONG DEVELOPING COUNTRIES

In several less-developed settings in the 1960s and 1970s, a different idea of gains from a trade bloc took shape. The infant industry argument held sway. It was easy to imagine that forming a customs union or free-trade area among developing countries would give the bloc a market large enough to support a large-scale producer in each modern manufacturing sector without letting in manufacturers from the industrialized countries. The new firms could eventually cut their costs through scale economies and learning by doing until they could compete internationally, perhaps even without protection.

For all the appeal of the idea, its practice "has been littered with failures," as Pomfret (1997) put it, and the life expectancy of this type of trade bloc was short. The Latin American Free Trade Area (Mexico and all the South American republics) lacked binding commitment to free internal trade even at its creation in 1960, and by 1969 it had effectively split into small groups with minimal bilateral agreements. Other short-lived unions with only minimal concessions by their members included a chain of Caribbean unions; the East African Community (Kenya, Tanzania, and Uganda), which disbanded in 1977; and several other African attempts. One centrifugal force was the inherent inequality of benefits from the new import-substituting industries. If scale economies were to be reaped, the new industrial gains would inevitably be concentrated into one or a few industrial centers. Every member wanted to be the group's new industrial leader, and none wanted to remain more agricultural. No formula for gains-sharing could be worked out. Even the Association of Southeast Asian Nations (ASEAN), with its broader industrial base, was unable to reach stable agreements about freer trade when this was tried in the late 1970s and early 1980s. Mindful of this experience, most experts became skeptical about the chances for great gains from developing-country trade blocs.

Yet the same institution can succeed later, even after earlier setbacks, especially if economic and political conditions have changed. As we have seen, the idea of a free-trade area between Canada and the United States failed to get launched for about a century before its time arrived.

The key change in many developing countries' trade policies since the 1970s, as we will examine in more depth in Chapter 14, has been a shift in philosophy, toward an outward, pro-trade (or at least pro-export) orientation. As in the case of Mexico, many developing countries have pursued economic reforms to liberalize government policies toward trade and business activity more generally. Forming a trade bloc can be a part of this thrust to liberalize (although, as we have seen, it is actually liberalizing internal trade while discriminating against external trade).

MERCOSUR (the Southern Common Market) is the most prominent of the current developing-country trade blocs. In 1991, Argentina, Brazil, Paraguay, and Uruguay formed MERCOSUR, which by 1995 had established internal free trade and common external tariffs (averaging 12 percent) for most products (although progress then stalled, so the customs union was not completed as of early 2014). One highly protected sector is automobiles, with an external tariff of about 34 percent (and an effective rate of protection of over 100 percent). In 1996, Chile and Bolivia became associate members and established free-trade areas with the MERCOSUR countries. Peru became an associate member in 2003, and Colombia, Ecuador, and Venezuela became associate members in 2004. In 2012 Venezuela became a full member.

Trade among MERCOSUR countries increased rapidly, rising from 9 percent of the countries' total international trade in 1990 to 23 percent in 1998. However, the Brazilian monetary crisis of 1999 and the Argentinean crisis in the early 2000s reversed this trend, partly because demand for imports declined generally as the economies of the countries weakened, and partly because Argentina and Brazil imposed some new barriers to trade between the bloc members. Intrabloc trade fell to 14 percent of the countries' total international trade in 2012.

One study of the effects of MERCOSUR concluded that it can increase real national incomes by 1 to 2 percent, with much of the gain coming from scale economies and the benefits of increasing competition among firms from different MERCOSUR countries. However, other observers are more cautious because trade within MERCOSUR increased most rapidly in protected capital-intensive products like automobiles, machinery, and electronic goods—products that are not consistent with the member countries' global comparative advantage. It is likely that substantial trade diversion is occurring in these products, and the losses from trade diversion must be set against other gains. MERCOSUR is a success in terms of survival, but its net effects on the well-being of its member countries are not clear.

TRADE EMBARGOES

Trade discrimination can be more belligerent—a trade block instead of a trade bloc. A nation or group of nations can keep ordinary barriers on its trade with most countries but insist on making trade with a particular country or countries difficult or impossible. To wage economic warfare, nations have often imposed *economic sanctions* or *embargoes,* which are discriminatory restrictions or bans on economic exchange. What is being restricted or banned can be ordinary trade, or it can be trade in services or financial assets, as in the case of a ban on loans to a particular country.

Waging economic warfare with trade embargoes and other economic sanctions dates back at least to the fifth century BC. In the 1760s the American colonists boycotted English goods as a protest against the infamous Stamp Act and Townshend Acts. In this case, the boycott succeeded—Parliament responded by repealing those acts.

The practice of economic sanctions was more frequent in the latter half of the 20th century than in any earlier peacetime era, and the use of sanctions increased during the 1990s. The United States practices economic warfare more readily than any other country. One estimate indicated that up to $20 billion of U.S. exports per year were blocked by sanctions in the mid-1990s, at a net cost to the country of about $1 billion per year. As of early 2014, the U.S. government had in place broad sanctions against Cuba, Iran, North Korea, Sudan, and Syria.

The effects of banning economic exchanges are easy to imagine. A country's refusal to trade with a "target" country hurts both of them economically, and it creates opportunities for third countries. But who gets hurt the most? The least? Magnitudes matter because they determine whether the damage to the target rewards the initiating country enough to compensate for its own losses on the prohibited trade.

FIGURE 12.3   Effects of an Embargo on Exports to Iran

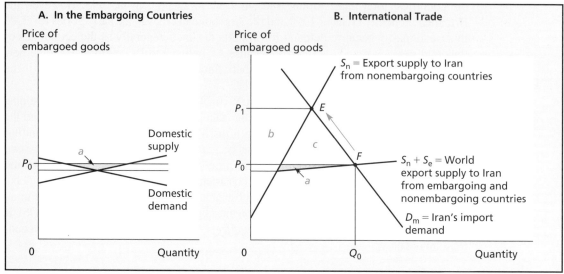

Moving from free trade (F) to an embargo (E) means

Embargoing countries lose	a
Iran loses	$b + c$
Other countries gain	b
World as a whole loses	$\overline{a + c}$

To discover basic determinants of the success or failure of economic sanctions, let us consider a particular kind: a total embargo (prohibition) on exports to the target country.[4] Figure 12.3 imagines a total embargo on exports to Iran. The example portrays one side of the restrictions that the United States, the European Union, Canada, and other countries have imposed on Iran for its nuclear program and pursuit of nuclear weapons capabilities. In addition to these restrictions on exports to Iran, the countries applying sanctions have also imposed severe restrictions on Iran's ability to make and receive payments through the global banking and financial system, so Iran's exports of oil and other products have also decreased. Still, Iran has been able to continue some trade with countries that have not joined the embargo.

In picturing international trade we will be careful to show export supply to Iran from both embargoing and nonembargoing countries, even before the embargo. The export supply to Iran from the nonembargoing countries is shown in Figure 12.3B as S_n, a limited and rather inelastic supply. The export supply from the embargoing countries (before they impose the embargo) is the difference between their domestic supply and domestic demand, which are shown in Figure 12.3A. If we add the two sources of export supply together, we get the total export supply, $S_n + S_e$, available to Iran before the embargo.

Before the embargo, Iran's import demand (D_m) equals the total export supply at point F on the right side of Figure 12.3. The price is P_0, and Iran imports Q_0.

[4]The case of an embargo on imports from the target country is symmetrical to the export case studied here. As an exercise at the end of this chapter, you are invited to diagram the import embargo case and to identify the gains and losses and what makes them large or small.

When countries decide to put an embargo on exports to Iran, part of the world export supply to Iran vanishes. In Figure 12.3B the export supply S_e is removed by the embargo. The remaining export supply to Iran is only S_n. With their imports thus restricted, Iranians find importable goods scarcer. The price in Iran rises from P_0 to P_1, as the free-trade equilibrium, F, shifts to the embargo equilibrium, E. The new scarcity costs Iran as a nation the area $b + c$ for reasons already described in Chapter 2 and Chapters 8 through 10.

The embargo also has a cost for the countries enforcing it because they lose exports to Iran and the world price (outside of Iran) declines somewhat. They lose area a, which is shown in Figure 12.3 in two equivalent ways:

• On the left as the difference between producer losses and consumer gains in the exporting countries.

• On the right as the loss of surplus on the exports that they no longer make to Iran.

Meanwhile, countries not participating in the embargo gain area b on extra sales to Iran at a higher price. What the world as a whole loses is therefore area $a + c$, the loss from restricting world trade.

Within countries on the two sides of the embargo, different groups will be affected differently. In the embargoing countries (e.g., Canada, the United Kingdom, the United States), the embargo lowers the price below P_0, slightly helping some consumers while hurting producers. Within Iran, there might be a similar division (not graphed in Figure 12.3), with some import-competing producers benefiting from the removal of foreign competition, while other groups are damaged to a greater extent.

If the embargo brings economic costs to both sides, why do it? Clearly, the countries imposing the embargo have decided to sacrifice area a, the net gains on trade with Iran, to try to achieve some other goal, such as forcing Iran to abandon or greatly limit its nuclear program. By their actions the embargoing governments imply that putting pressure on Iran is worth more than area a. The lost area a is presumably not a measure of economic irrationality, but rather a willing sacrifice for a noneconomic goal. As Figure 12.3 is drawn, the hypothetical export embargo is imagined to cause Iran more economic damage, measured by area $b + c$, than the embargoers' loss represented by area a.[5]

Embargoes can fail, of course. In a study of sanctions imposed between 1945 and 2000, Gary Hufbauer et al. (2007) conclude that sanctions failed to have a substantial impact on the policies of the target country in about two-thirds of the cases. There are two ways in which trade embargoes fail: political failure and economic failure.

Political failure of an embargo occurs when the target country's national decision-makers have so much stake in the policy that provoked the embargo that they

---

[5]In the real-world debate over sanctions, critics argue that the sanctions would harm large numbers of innocent civilians, whose right to a better government is a political outcome that sanctions are supposed to bring about. Thus, in the case of worldwide sanctions against South Africa (1986–1993), critics argued that the sanctions would lower incomes of "nonwhite" South Africans, the very groups the sanctions were supposed to help liberate. This may be correct in the short run, as all sides of the debate have long known.

To judge whether the sanctions are in the best interests of the oppressed within the target country, the best guide would be their own majority opinion. That opinion is not easily weighed in a context of disenfranchisement, press censorship, and tight police controls. The foreign governments imposing sanctions imply that the policy gains are worth more than their own loss of area a plus the short-run losses that they believe that oppressed groups in the target country are willing to sustain for the cause.

FIGURE 12.4 Two Kinds of Economically Unsuccessful Embargoes

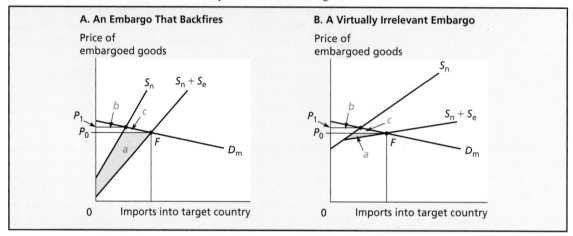

In panel A the cost to the embargoers, *a*, is much larger than the damage, *b* + *c*, to the target country. In panel B the costs to both sides are negligible because elasticities are so high.

will stick with that policy even if the economic cost to their nation becomes extreme. Such political stubbornness is very likely if the target country is a dictatorship and the dictatorship would be jeopardized by retreating from the policy that provoked the embargo. In such a case, the dictatorship will refuse to budge even as the economic costs mount.

An example of political failure of economically "successful" sanctions was Saddam Hussein's refusal to retreat from Kuwait or, after Iraq was driven from Kuwait, to step down from power. Defenders of the idea of pressuring Saddam Hussein with sanctions were right in asserting that sanctions would bring greater damage to the economy of Iraq than to the embargoing countries. One estimate is that the sanctions imposed a net cost to Iraq of $15 billion per year, equal to about half of Iraq's national income. Yet Saddam Hussein's grip on power was so firm that he was neither forced by internal pressure to step down nor forced to make a major change in certain policies, even if a majority of Iraqi citizens suffered great hardship. A counterexample is the UN-based sanctions imposed on South Africa, which succeeded in hastening the end of apartheid and the minority-rule police state.

The second kind of failure is **economic failure of an embargo,** in which the embargo inflicts little damage on the target country but possibly even great damage on the imposing country. Figure 12.4 shows two kinds of (export) embargoes that fail economically. In both cases, elasticities of supply and demand are the key.

In Figure 12.4A, the countries imposing the embargo have a very inelastic export supply curve, implying that their producers really depend on their export business in the target country. Banning such exports and erasing the supply curve S_e from the marketplace costs the embargoing nation(s) a large area *a*. The target country, by contrast, has a very elastic import demand curve D_m. It cuts its demand greatly when the price goes up even slightly, from P_0 to P_1. Apparently, it can do fairly well with supplies from nonembargoing countries (the S_n curve alone). Accordingly, it loses only the small areas $b + c$. Any nation considering an embargo in such a case must contemplate sustaining the large loss a, in pursuit of only a small damage $(b + c)$ to the target country. What works against the embargo in Figure 12.4A is the low elasticity of the embargoing country itself and the high elasticity of either the target country's import demand or its access to competing nonembargo supplies.

Figure 12.4B shows a case in which the embargo "fails" in the milder sense of having little economic effect on either side. Here the embargoing country is fortunate to have an elastic curve of its own (S_e) so that doing without the extra trade costs it only a slight area a. On the other hand, the target country also has the elastic demand curve D_m and access to the elastic competing supplies S_n. Therefore it sustains only the slight damage $b + c$ and presumably can defy the embargo for a long time.

So embargoes and other economic sanctions apply stronger pressure when the embargoing country or countries have high elasticities and the target countries have low ones. When is this likely to be true? Our analysis offers suggestions that seem to show up in the real world:

1. Big countries pick on small ones. A country (or group of countries) with a large share of world trade can impose sanctions on a small one without feeling much effect. In economic terms, the big country is likely to have highly elastic trade curves (like S_e in the examples here) because it can deal with much larger markets outside the target country. A small target country, on the other hand, may depend heavily on its trade with the large country or countries. Its economic vulnerability is summarized by low elasticities for trade curves like D_m and S_n. Little wonder that the typical embargo is one imposed by the United States on a small country like Nicaragua.

2. Sanctions have more chance of success if they are sudden and comprehensive when first imposed. Recall that the damage $b + c$ is larger, the lower are the target country's trade elasticities. Elasticities are lower in the short run than in the long run, and they are lower when a massive share of national product is involved. The more time the target country has to adjust, the more it can learn to conserve on the embargoed products and develop alternative supplies. Of course, quick and sudden action also raises the damage to the initiating country itself (area a), so success may be premised on the embargoing country's having alternatives set up in advance, alternatives that raise its elasticities and shrink area a.

3. As suggested by the definition and example of political failure, embargoes have more chance of changing a target government's policies when the citizens hurt by the embargo can apply political pressure on the stubborn head(s) of state, as in a democracy. In a strict dictatorship, the dictator can survive the economic damage to citizens and can hold out longer.

The first of these three points provides insight into why the effectiveness of unilateral sanctions imposed only by the United States has changed over time. In the 1950s, when the United States was predominant, its own sanctions could have some effect on countries like Iran and even Britain and France (in the Suez Canal dispute). With the growth of other countries and their economies, unilateral U.S. sanctions have become much less effective because S_n (from the rest of the world) has expanded and become more elastic.

In the 1990s, the United States shifted away from the use of unilateral sanctions (though it still uses some, as indicated by the list presented at the beginning of this section) and toward the use of sanctions imposed collectively by a coalition of countries. For instance, the United States pushed for UN mandates for sanctions that direct all countries to participate. Before 1990, the only UN-mandated sanctions were against South Africa and Rhodesia (now Zimbabwe). During the 1990s the UN established sanctions against Iraq, Serbia, Somalia, Libya, Liberia, Haiti, Angola, Rwanda, and Sierra Leone. However, these UN sanctions had limited success, while imposing often substantial costs on some of the embargoing countries. In the 2000s the UN has backed away from mandated sanctions. As of early 2014, the UN had only a small number of limited mandates in place, mostly arms embargoes of African countries that were involved in civil wars or other armed conflicts, as well as somewhat broader sanctions against Iran and North Korea.

Summary

The **trade bloc** revolution amassing since the 1990s has raised the importance of trade discrimination. The basic three-country model of a trade bloc shows that

- Its economic benefits for the partner countries and the world depend on its **trade creation,** the amount by which it raises the total volume of world trade.
- Its economic costs depend on its **trade diversion,** the volume of trade it diverts from lower-cost outside suppliers to higher-cost partner-country suppliers.

Other possible sources of gains to members of a trade bloc include increased competition that lowers prices or costs, enhanced ability to achieve scale economies, greater product variety, and the ability to attract more direct investment by foreign companies. Whether a trade bloc is good or bad overall depends on the difference between its gains from trade creation (and any other positive effects) and its losses from trade diversion.

The most common kind of trade bloc is the **free-trade area,** in which member countries remove tariffs and other barriers to trade among themselves but keep their separate barriers on trade with nonmember countries. In this case, member countries must use **rules of origin** and maintain customs administration on the borders between themselves to keep outside products from entering the high-barrier countries cheaply by way of their low-barrier partners. Examples of free-trade areas are the European Free Trade Area created in 1960 and the North American Free Trade Agreement (NAFTA), which came into existence in 1994.

The European Union from 1957 to 1992 was a **customs union,** in which member countries remove tariffs and other barriers to trade among themselves and adopt a common set of external tariffs. In 1992 the Single European Act promoted free movement of workers and capital, so the EU became a **common market**. (The act also required removal of many remaining nontariff barriers to trade among the member countries.) As the EU further integrates, including the adoption of the euro as a common currency by 18 of its members, the EU is moving toward **economic union,** in which all economic policies would be unified.

Efforts by developing countries to form trade blocs failed in the 1960s and 1970s, but they have become more successful since 1990. Trade among the MERCOSUR countries in South America expanded since the bloc was formed in 1991, but some of this expanded intrabloc trade is trade diversion.

Another form of trade discrimination is economic sanctions, or **trade embargoes**. Our basic analysis of an export embargo (which has effects symmetrical with those of an import embargo) reveals how the success or failure of such economic warfare depends on trade elasticities. Success is more likely when the target country has low trade elasticities, meaning that it cannot easily do without trading with the embargoing countries. Success is also more likely when the embargoing countries have high trade elasticities, meaning that they easily do without the extra trade. As the theory implies, embargoes are typically imposed by large trading countries on smaller ones, and success is more likely the quicker and more comprehensive the sanctions.

Key Terms

Trade bloc	Economic union	Political failure of an
Trade embargo	Trade creation	embargo
Free-trade area	Trade diversion	Economic failure of an
Customs union	Rules of origin	embargo
Common market		

Suggested Reading

The trade bloc literature is usefully surveyed by Freund and Ornelas (2010) and Pomfret (1997). Baldwin and Venables (1995) present a technical survey. Schiff and Winters (2003, Chapter 8) examine the effects of trade blocs on nonmember countries and on multilateral trade negotiations. Bhagwati (2008) examines the negative economic and political effects of preferential trade agreements. Magee (2008) uses the gravity model of trade to develop estimates of trade creation and trade diversion for a number of trade blocs.

On the economics of the European Union, see Neal and Barbezat (1998) and the Organization for Economic Cooperation and Development (2000). Baldwin and Wyplosz (2012, Chapter 9) provide overview and analysis of the EU's common agricultural policy. Mohler and Seitz (2012) develop estimates of gains from greater product variety for the EU's new members.

The effects of the North American Free Trade Area are plumbed by Hufbauer and Schott (2005). Jaramillo et al. (2006) explore the expected effects of the Central American Free Trade Agreement.

The economics and the foreign policy effects of trade embargoes are well analyzed by Hufbauer et al. (2007). Morgan et al. (2009) introduce a new dataset on sanctions imposed or threatened since 1970.

Questions and Problems

✦ 1. What is the difference between a free-trade area and a customs union?

2. Are trade blocs consistent with the most favored nation principle?

✦ 3. How are trade creation and trade diversion defined, and what roles do they play in the world gains and losses from a trade bloc?

4. Why are rules of origin needed for a free-trade area? How might they be protectionist?

♦ 5. Homeland is about to join Furrinerland in a free-trade area. Before the union, Homeland imports 10 million DVD recorders from the outside-world market at $100 and adds a tariff of $30 on each recorder. It takes $110 to produce each DVD recorder in Furrinerland.

   a. Once the free-trade area is formed, what will be the cost to Homeland of the DVD recorder trade diverted to Furrinerland?

   b. How much extra imports would have to be demanded by Homeland to offset this trade-diversion cost?

6. Which countries are likely to gain, and which are likely to lose, from the North American Free Trade Area? How are the gains and losses likely to be distributed across occupations and sectors of the Mexican economy? The U.S. economy?

♦ 7. Suppose that the United States currently imports 1.0 million pairs of shoes from China at $20 each. With a 50 percent tariff, the consumer price in the United States is $30. The price of shoes in Mexico is $25. Suppose that, as a result of NAFTA, the United States imports 1.2 million pairs of shoes from Mexico and none from China. What are the gains and losses to U.S. consumers, U.S. producers, the U.S. government, and the world as a whole?

8. In a presentation about Serbia's future entry into the European Union, the speaker indicates that the effects of trade creation will be equal to about 2 percent of Serbia's GDP, the effects of trade diversion will be equal to about 1 percent of Serbia's GDP, and the overall effects on Serbia will be a gain in national well-being equal to about 3 percent of its GDP. What do you think is the best explanation of how these numbers fit together? Is anything missing that you can fill in to make better sense of the numbers?

♦ 9. What kinds of countries tend to use economic embargoes? Do embargoes have a greater chance of succeeding if they are applied gradually rather than suddenly?

10. Draw a graph like Figure 12.3B. Initially the embargo is the one shown in this graph. Then, half of the nonembargoing countries switch and become part of the embargo. Use your graph to show how this changes the effects of the embargo. Specifically, what are the effects on the initial embargoing countries and on the target country? Does this shift make the embargo more or less likely to succeed? Why?

♦ 11. Which of the following trade policy moves is most certain to bring gains to the world as a whole: (*a*) imposing a countervailing duty against an existing foreign export subsidy, (*b*) forming a customs union in place of a set of tariffs equally applied to imports from all countries, or (*c*) levying an antidumping import tariff? (This question draws on material from Chapter 11 as well as from this chapter.)

12. Draw the diagram corresponding to Figure 12.3 for an embargo on imports from the target country. Identify the losses and gains to the embargoing countries, the target country, and other countries. Describe what values of elasticities are more likely to give power to the embargo effort and what values of elasticities are more likely to weaken it.

Chapter **Thirteen**

Trade and the Environment

Protection. For free traders, this word represents the consummate evil. For environmentalists, it is the ultimate good. Of course, for the trade community, "protection" conjures up images of Smoot and Hawley, while the environmental camp sees clear mountain streams, lush green forests, and piercing blue skies.

Daniel C. Esty, 2001

As nations interact more and more with each other, they have more and more effect on each other's natural environments. Often the international environmental effects are negative, as when activity in one nation pollutes other nations' air and water, or when it uses up natural resources on which other nations depend. These environmental concerns have become irreversibly global and are a growing source of international friction.

Inevitably, international trade has been drawn into the environmental spotlight, both as an alleged culprit in environmental damage and as a hostage to be taken in international environmental disputes. This chapter addresses the rising debate over the proper role of government policies in attacking environmental problems when the problems and policies have international effects.

IS FREE TRADE ANTI-ENVIRONMENT?

One attack on international trade is that it makes environmental problems worse. For instance, perhaps free trade simply promotes production or consumption of products that tend to cause large amounts of pollution. It is difficult to evaluate such a broad claim as this. But it is easy to find cases of the opposite, where government policies that limit or distort trade result in environmental damage. In the early 1980s, the United States forced Japan to limit its exports of autos to the United States. As a result, U.S. consumers tended to buy U.S. cars that were less fuel-efficient than the Japanese cars they could no longer buy, probably resulting in more pollution. Another well-researched case is the environmental effects of government policies that protect domestic agriculture. The web of import limits and export and production subsidies leads to excessive use of pesticides and fertilizers as protected farmers strive to expand production. Free trade would lead to farming that is more friendly to the environment.

Some kinds of trade can help efforts to protect the environment. Freer trade in capital equipment that incorporates environmentally friendly technologies and freer trade in environmental services can be conduits for improved environmental practices, especially in developing countries.

One fear of environmentalists is that free trade permits production to be shifted to countries that have lax environmental standards. Exports from these "pollution havens" then would serve demand in countries with tighter standards, with the result that total world pollution would be higher. However, research on relocation of production in response to differences in environmental standards finds that the effects are small. The costs to firms of meeting environmental protection regulations are usually small (less than 1 or 2 percent of sales revenues), even in the most stringent countries, so the incentive to relocate is usually small. Other determinants of production location, like standard comparative cost advantage, transport costs, and external scale economies, are usually more important. In addition, many multinational companies refrain from setting up high-pollution operations in lax countries because of fears of unexpected liabilities in cases of accidents, general risks to corporate reputations from appearing to cause excessive harm to the environment, and the costs of meeting more stringent regulations that are likely to be adopted in the future in these countries.

Let's turn to look at a concrete example of a recent global shift to freer international trade: the agreements reached during the Uruguay Round of trade negotiations. Does the expansion of trade resulting from these agreements harm or help the environment?

- Freer trade will alter the *composition* of what is produced and consumed in each country. As the composition of what is produced and consumed changes, the total amounts of pollution will change.
- There will be additional gains from trade. These gains could set up two different effects.
  - *a.* The *size* of the economy is larger. The increase in production and consumption probably leads to more pollution, other things being equal.
  - *b.* The higher *income* can lead to more pressure on governments to enact tougher environmental protection policies. For instance, stricter government policies may lead firms to clean up wastes before they are released into the environment or to switch to production methods that create less pollution per unit produced. Demand for a clean environment is a normal good.

Before examining the effects of the Uruguay Round, it's useful to look at how the size and income effects play against each other. How do rising production, consumption, and income in a country actually affect environmental quality? When income per person (our overall indicator of size and income) rises, does the environment deteriorate or improve? That is, which tends to be larger, the harm from the size effect or the environmental protection from the income effect?

There are likely to be different general patterns for this combined size–income effect, depending on what kind of environmental problem we are examining. Here are the three basic patterns:

1. *Environmental harm declines with rising income per person.* For some issues, the benefits of better environmental quality are so large that the income effect is dominant over (almost) the entire range of income per person. That is, the demand for better environmental quality as income rises is simply larger than any adverse effects from rising production scale.

2. *Environmental harm rises with rising income per person.* For some other issues, the benefits of preventing environmental harm are not considered to be large. The adverse effects from rising size dominate any modest increases in demand for better environmental quality.

3. *The relationship is an inverted U.* For yet other issues, the demand for better environmental quality is weak at first, perhaps because the focus when people are poor is on developing production to reduce the grip of material poverty. When income is low, people are willing to accept some environmental harm to increase production and income. This damage rises as economic activity rises. But, at some point at which the dire effects of poverty have been reduced enough, the demand for better environmental quality becomes more forceful. As incomes rise further, more stringent government regulation takes over. The environmental harm declines even though production and consumption are increasing.

Figure 13.1 provides some examples of these patterns for different environmental issues. Some very basic environmental dangers, including airborne heavy particles and lead in water, tend to fall as income rises, as shown in panel A. Some environmental problems rise with greater income, as shown in panel B. These include emissions of carbon dioxide, which we will discuss later in this chapter. The demand to reduce this pollutant is not particularly strong even when incomes are high. The harm from global warming is rather abstract, the costs of reducing these emissions are substantial, and the problem is global, so actions by any one country would have little effect on the problem.

Panel C of Figure 13.1 shows the inverted-U relationship.[1] The pollutants that fit this pattern tend to be those that cause harm within the region or country, so regional or national efforts to abate the pollution provide benefits to the people in that locale. This pattern has been found for such air pollutants as sulfur dioxide (which causes acid rain), airborne particulates, and lead and such water pollutants as fecal coliform (resulting from inadequate containment or treatment of human and animal wastes) and

---

[1]The inverted-U shape is sometimes called the environmental Kuznets curve, named after Nobel Prize winner Simon Kuznets. His research on the effects of economic development found an inverted-U relationship between per capita income and income inequality.

We should be careful interpreting and using this inverted-U shape. It is a statistical relationship and does not guarantee that any single country is on the curve or follows it as the country develops. There are also other influences, including the type of government (democracy generally is more responsive to popular demand for pollution control than is dictatorship) and the source of growth in national production and income (growth could be biased toward or against pollution-intensive sectors of the national economy).

FIGURE 13.1   Environmental Problems by Income Level

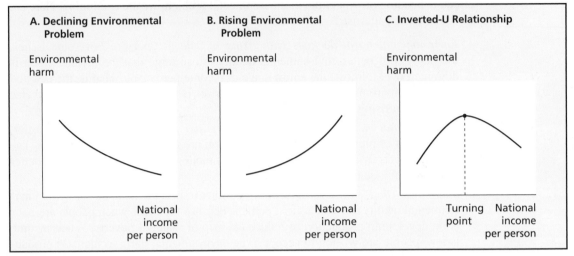

A. Declining Environmental Problem

B. Rising Environmental Problem

C. Inverted-U Relationship

Examples:
Concentration of heavy particles in urban air
Concentration of lead in water
Lack of dissolved oxygen in rivers
Percentage of population without safe water
Percentage of urban population without sanitation

Examples:
Carbon dioxide emissions per person
Urban waste per person

Examples (estimates of turning points):
Air pollution:
    Sulfur dioxide ($3,000–$10,700)
    Suspended particulate matter ($3,300–$9,600)
    Nitrogen oxides ($5,500–$21,800)
    Carbon monoxide ($9,900–$19,100)
    Lead from gasoline ($7,000)
Water pollution:
    Fecal coliform ($8,000)
    Arsenic ($4,900)
    Biological oxygen demand ($7,600)
    Chemical oxygen demand ($7,900)

Source of examples: Edward B. Barbier, "Introduction to the Environmental Kuznets Curve Special Issue," *Environment and Development Economics* 2, no. 4 (December 1997), pp. 369−81.

arsenic. Estimates of *turning points* (beyond which the pollution declines) often are at levels of income per person that are higher than those of most developing countries but lower than those of industrialized countries.

Now we have the tools that we need to examine the environmental effect of the Uruguay Round. Figure 13.2 shows the environmental effects that the trade changes resulting from the Uruguay Round have had on four air pollutants.

The *composition effects* tend to increase levels of all pollutants in the United States, the European Union, and Japan. With the exception of Latin America, the composition effects tend to reduce pollution in the developing countries. The reason for this pattern is Heckscher–Ohlin with a twist. As the world moves toward freer trade, production of capital- and skill-intensive products expands in the industrialized countries and shrinks in the developing countries. These products include most of the products that are environmentally "dirty," including iron and steel, the refining of other

FIGURE 13.2   Environmental Effects of the Uruguay Round (Percent Changes in Emissions for Each Type of Pollutant, in Each Place)

	Sulfur Dioxide			Suspended Particulates			Nitrogen Dioxide			Carbon Monoxide		
	Comp[1]	S & I[2]	Total[3]	Comp	S & I	Total	Comp	S & I	Total	Comp	S & I	Total
United States	0.4	−0.7	−0.3	0.2	−0.8	−0.6	0.1	0.0	0.1	0.1	−0.6	−0.5
European Union	0.3	−0.4	−0.1	0.2	−0.3	−0.1	0.1	0.2	0.3	0.2	−0.3	−0.1
Japan	2.0	−0.6	1.4	0.3	−0.5	−0.2	0.3	0.1	0.4	0.3	−1.0	−0.7
Latin America	0.5	0.7	1.2	0.4	0.6	1.0	0.6	0.9	1.5	0.2	0.8	1.0
China	−1.8	2.1	0.3	−0.9	2.0	1.1	−0.3	1.6	1.3	−0.1	1.8	1.7
East Asia	−3.1	1.8	−2.2	−3.0	1.7	−1.3	−0.1	2.0	1.9	−1.9	1.9	0.0
South Asia	−0.6	1.3	0.7	−0.4	1.4	1.0	−0.5	1.0	0.5	−0.5	1.3	0.8
Africa	−0.1	2.8	2.7	0.0	2.7	2.7	0.2	2.0	2.2	0.0	2.4	2.4
World	−0.3	0.2	−0.1	−0.1	0.1	0.0	0.1	0.5	0.6	0.0	0.1	0.1

[1]Composition effect.
[2]Combined size effect and income effect.
[3]Total change = Composition effect + Combined size effect and income effect.

Source: M. A. Cole, A. J. Rayner, and J. M. Bates, "Trade Liberalization and the Environment: The Case of the Uruguay Round," *World Economy* 21, no. 3 (May 1997), pp. 337–47.

metals, chemicals, petroleum refining, and pulp and paper. Production of unskilled-labor-intensive products, like textiles and apparel, shrinks in the industrialized countries and expands in the developing countries. Most less-skilled-labor-intensive products are environmentally "clean." Thus, as the composition of what is produced changes, pollution-intensive production tends to expand in the high-income industrialized countries and pollution-intensive production tends to decline in the low-income developing countries.

The gains from the Uruguay Round increase size and income. As shown in Figure 13.2, the combined *size and income effects* tend to lower pollution in the industrialized countries for sulfur dioxide, suspended particulates, and carbon monoxide because these countries are beyond the turning points in the inverted-U curves for these three pollutants. The combined size–income effects tend to increase nitrogen dioxide pollution in the European Union and Japan because the turning point for this pollutant is estimated to be at about the U.S. level of income per person. The combined size–income effects tend to increase pollution in the developing countries because their incomes are lower than the four turning points.

What actually happens to the environment in each place as a result of the Uruguay Round is the sum of the effects. The actual effects (the sums of the composition effects and the combined size and income effects) vary by country and by pollutant. The overall effects for the world are generally small, as are the effects for most countries and pollutants. Even for countries whose pollution increases, the monetary value of the usual gains from freer trade is a large multiple of the monetary cost of any extra pollution. For instance, for the world, the costs of the extra nitrogen dioxide pollution are less than 0.3 percent of the global gains from the freer trade. If we take a slightly different perspective, the world and the individual countries could prevent the extra pollution using only a small part of the gains that they get from the Uruguay Round agreements. In a more limited analysis, the same study that is the source of estimates shown in Figure 13.2 concludes that the Uruguay Round is likely to increase global emissions of carbon dioxide by 3.3 percent. This increase is somewhat larger than that for the other pollutants, but it is still only a small part of the global increase in carbon dioxide that has been occurring.

In summary, free trade is not inherently anti-environment. Relocation of production to avoid stringent environmental standards is small. Shifts toward freer trade cause a variety of changes, but the net effects on overall pollution usually seem to be small.

IS THE WTO ANTI-ENVIRONMENT?

Even if free trade is not itself anti-environment, environmentalists often complain that the global rules of the trading system, the rules of the World Trade Organization (WTO), prevent governments from pursuing strong environmental protection policies. There are some things that are not in doubt. Most important, a government that takes actions to control environmental damage caused by its own firms' production is *not* violating WTO rules. Beyond this, there are questions.

The main preoccupation of the WTO (and the GATT before it) is with liberalizing trade, but the rules also make special mention of environmental concerns. Article XX lists general exceptions to its free-trade approach. While Article XX begins by repeating the signing governments' fear that any exceptions are subject to abuse by protectionists, it does admit exceptional arguments for trade barriers. Two of those arguments are environmental exceptions to the case for free trade:

> Subject to the requirement that such measures are not applied in a manner which would constitute a means of arbitrary or unjustifiable discrimination between countries where the same conditions prevail, or a disguised restriction on international trade, nothing in this Agreement shall be construed to prevent the adoption or enforcement by any contracting party of measures:
> . . . (b) necessary to protect human, animal, or plant life or health;
> . . . (g) relating to the conservation of exhaustible natural resources if such measures
>   are made effective in conjunction with restrictions on domestic production
>   or consumption.

There is an obvious tension here. The signing parties conceded that environmental concerns might conceivably justify trade barriers, but they were suspicious that such concerns would be a mere facade, an excuse for protectionists to shut out foreign goods.

There are three important types of policies that may qualify for environmental exceptions. First, *consumption* of products can cause damage. WTO rulings make it clear that a country generally can impose product standards or other limits on consumption to protect the country's health, its safety, or the environment, even though such a policy will limit imports. A key is that the policy applies to all consumption, not just to imports. For instance, the WTO ruled that France can prohibit consumption and production of asbestos or asbestos-containing products within its borders, including prohibiting imports of these products. Similarly, the WTO ruled that the United States can impose a gas-guzzler tax on autos that get few miles per gallon, as long as the tax applies to all cars, both domestically produced and foreign.

At the same time, the WTO is vigilant against using environmental standards as disguised protectionism. The WTO ruled that U.S. regulations on average fuel economy of cars sold by each manufacturer violated WTO rules because they treated imports produced by foreign automakers differently from domestic autos. The WTO also ruled that U.S. policies on fuel additives violated the rules because they treated foreign-produced gasoline differently from domestically produced gasoline. The WTO ruled that a ban by Thailand on cigarette imports to promote health violated WTO rules because domestically produced cigarettes continued to be sold. In these three cases the issue was not the environmental health objective itself. Rather, it was the fact that imports were treated differently from domestically produced products without any overarching need to do so.

The WTO does also examine the basis for standards. As a result of the Uruguay Round, product standards to protect health or safety must have a scientific basis. This requirement tries to prevent a government from inventing standards that are written to limit imports. More controversially, it also may prevent a government from responding to public perceptions of risks, such as concern about genetically altered foods, if there is little scientific evidence supporting the public fears.

Second, *production in foreign countries* can cause environmental damage. Can a government limit imports of a foreign product produced using methods that violate the country's own environmental standards? As discussed in the box "Dolphins, Turtles, and the WTO," the position of the WTO has evolved to one that permits an environmental exception for national rules that limit imports of products produced using processes that harm the environment, but with strict standards:

- The rules must demonstrably assist in pursuing a legitimate environmental goal, and they must limit trade as little as possible.
- The rules must be applied equally to domestic producers and to all foreign exporting firms.
- The country imposing the rules should be engaged in negotiations with other involved countries to establish a multilateral agreement to address the environmental issue (if such agreement does not yet exist).

Again, the objective of the WTO is to allow countries to pursue environmental protection using policies that may affect international trade but to prevent countries from using environmental claims to create disguised protectionism.

Third, there are some environmental problems that are global in scope and that may require global solutions negotiated among many governments. Can a *multilateral environmental agreement* use controls on international trade to implement the agreement or sanctions on a country's trade to enforce the agreement? Two important multilateral agreements discussed later in this chapter—the Convention on International Trade in Endangered Species and the Montreal Protocol—use trade bans, even for trade with countries that have not signed the agreements. The WTO has not been asked to rule on these agreements. The WTO seems to be comfortable with this multilateral approach to well-defined environmental problems, but it has not actually issued any rulings endorsing them.

Global Governance   Dolphins, Turtles, and the WTO

Dolphins have long had a special appeal to humans because of their intelligence and seeming playfulness. The sympathy for dolphins, like the sympathy for all large animals, grows with income. It was inevitable that any threat to dolphins, even though they are not an endangered species, would mobilize a strong defense in the industrialized countries.

Most tuna are caught by methods that do not harm dolphins. But, for unknown reasons, large schools of tuna choose to swim beneath herds of dolphins in the Eastern Tropical Pacific Ocean. Before 1960, this posed no threat to dolphins. Fishing crews used hooks to catch tuna, and dolphins' sonar allowed them to avoid the hooks. However, the 1960s brought a new method for catching tuna, purse-seine fishing, in which speedboats and helicopters effectively herd the dolphins and tuna into limited areas, where vast nets encircle large schools of tuna. As the nets draw tight underwater, the dolphins, being mammals, drown. Six million dolphins have died this way since 1960.

The United States tried to stop this purse-seine netting with the Marine Mammals Protection Act of 1972, but with limited effect. The law can prohibit use of this method in U.S. waters, out to the 200-mile limit, and use of this method by U.S. ships anywhere in the world. Fishing fleets responded to the 1972 law by reflagging as ships registered outside the United States. Between 1978 and 1990, the share of U.S. boats in the Eastern Pacific tuna fleet dropped from 62 percent to less than 10 percent.

The United States still had some economic weapons at its disposal. The government pressured the three main tuna-packing and tuna-retailing firms (StarKist, Bumble Bee, and Chicken of the Sea) to refuse to buy tuna taken with dolphin-unsafe methods. While there were charges that at least one of the firms packed dolphin-unsafe tuna under its dolphin-safe label, the dolphin-safe scheme had some success. Through this and other forms of pressure, the estimated dolphin mortality in tuna fishing dropped from 130,000 in 1986 to 25,000 in 1991.

The United States did not let the matter rest there. In 1991, the U.S. government banned tuna imports from Mexico and four other countries. Mexico immediately protested to the GATT, where a dispute resolution panel handed down a preliminary ruling that the U.S. import ban was an unfair trade practice, a protectionist act against Mexico. The GATT panel ruled that the United States cannot restrict imports based on production methods used by firms in other countries. The EU also challenged the U.S. legislation as a violation of the GATT because it included a "secondary boycott" against tuna imports from any country importing dolphin-unsafe tuna from countries like Mexico that use this fishing method. In 1994, a GATT panel again ruled against the United States.

These rulings suggested that international trade rules would not endorse efforts by one country to use trade policy to impose its environmental policies outside of its borders, or to force other countries to change their environmental policies. Environmentalists were furious because they believed that principles of trade policy were placed ahead of environmental safeguards.

Within these constraints, what can the United States do if it wishes to save more dolphins? One possibility is to negotiate with other countries to get them to alter the methods they use to catch tuna, perhaps by offering other benefits in exchange. In 1995, six countries (including Mexico) agreed to adopt dolphin-friendly fishing. However, some fishing fleets could just reflag to yet other countries, so the best solution probably would be a global multilateral agreement on tuna fishing.

Sea turtles, a species threatened with extinction, present a similar case. Some shrimp are caught with nets that also trap and kill sea turtles. A U.S. law passed in 1989 requires shrimpers in U.S. waters to alter their nets with turtle-excluder devices, and it prohibits shrimp imports from countries whose rules do not require such devices to protect sea turtles.

The U.S. government initially applied the U.S. law to 14 Caribbean and Latin American countries, negotiated with them, and allowed them three years to implement changes in their fishing methods. Following a U.S. court ruling, the U.S. government extended the application of the law to other countries unilaterally and with only a four-month phase-in.

Four Asian countries filed a complaint with the WTO in 1997. In the ruling on the case, the WTO decided that

- Protection of sea turtles was a legitimate environmental purpose.
- The actual U.S. policies violated WTO rules because they did not apply equally to all foreign exporting countries.
- The actual U.S. policies were unacceptable because they required specific actions by the foreign countries (enacting laws and using turtle-excluder devices) and did not recognize alternative ways to protect sea turtles.
- The actual U.S. approach was also unacceptable because the U.S. did not undertake negotiations with the exporting countries affected by the extension of application of the law.

In response to the ruling, the U.S. government removed the discriminatory terms, recognized other turtle-protection methods, and began negotiations with the countries affected by the extension of the law. In 2001 the WTO ruled that, with these changes in place, the United States was in compliance with WTO rules, so it

could restrict imports of shrimp caught in ways that harm sea turtles. The WTO also ruled that good-faith negotiations toward a multilateral agreement were adequate—reaching an actual agreement was not a prerequisite for the United States to apply its law. At about the same time as the WTO rulings, the United States did reach agreements with a number of foreign countries to adopt rules to protect sea turtles.

Many environmentalists seem to believe incorrectly that WTO rules always favor free trade and so prevent a country from using trade-related measures as part of its efforts to protect the environment. The truth is more nuanced. The WTO is certainly vigilant against environmental policies and rules that unnecessarily limit trade or discriminate between foreign suppliers. Still, the WTO cannot force a member country to change its policies if the country does not want to. More important, the WTO generally accepts the legitimacy of protecting the environment and setting minimum environmental standards through negotiations between countries. The appellate body in the sea turtle case said in its report:

> We have not decided that protection and preservation of the environment is of no significance to the members of the WTO. Clearly it is. We have not decided that the sovereign states that are members of the WTO cannot adopt effective measures to protect endangered species, such as sea turtles. Clearly, they can and they should. And we have not decided that sovereign states should not act together bilaterally, plurilaterally, or multilaterally, either within the WTO or in other international fora, to protect endangered species or to otherwise protect the environment. Clearly, they should and do.

THE SPECIFICITY RULE AGAIN

To get a better grip on the links between trade and the environment, we must first revisit some key points of microeconomics. Environmental effects such as pollution call for special policies or institutional changes if, and only if, they are what economists call externalities. An **externality** exists when somebody's activity brings direct costs or benefits to anybody who is not part of the marketplace decisions to undertake the activity.[2] If your activity imposes a direct cost on somebody who has no impact on your buying or selling, he bears an external cost. If your activity brings him a direct benefit without his participation, he receives an external benefit.

Also recall that whenever an externality exists, there is a distortion, caused by a gap between private and social costs or benefits. Where there are distortions, a competitive market, in the absence of government policy, results in either too much or too little of the activity because the decision-makers consider only the private costs and benefits of their actions, not the full social costs and benefits.

Pollution is an externality that imposes an external cost on people who do not have any say over the pollution. That is, the social costs of production or consumption of the product are larger than the private costs that are recognized by the people in the market who make the decisions about producing and consuming. Social marginal cost (SMC, which includes the marginal external cost of the pollution) exceeds private marginal cost (MC, which does not include the marginal external cost). In the competitive market, price (P) equals private marginal cost and private marginal benefit (MB). If there are no external benefits, then private marginal benefit is the same as social marginal benefit (SMB). The distortion is that $SMC > MC = P = MB = SMB$. Because some social costs are ignored by market decision-makers, too much of the activity (production and/or consumption) occurs. For the last unit, the social cost of this unit exceeds the social benefit ($SMC > SMB$). This last unit is inefficient, and any other units for which SMC exceeds SMB are also inefficient. By adding more to social cost than they add to social benefit, these last units lower well-being for the society.

Because an externality leads to sub-par performance of a market, there is a role for government policies to enhance the efficiency of the market. The specificity rule is a useful policy guide. The **specificity rule** says to intervene at the source of the problem. It is usually more efficient to use the policy tool that is specific to the distortion that makes private costs and benefits differ from social costs and benefits.

If, for example, an industry is causing acid rain by discharging sulfurous compounds into the air, the best approach is a policy that restrains the discharge of the sulfur compounds themselves. That is usually better than, say, taxing electrical power because this latter approach would not send the electric companies the signal that

---

[2]The definition refers only to "direct" effects on others so as to exclude effects transmitted through prices. If people decide to smoke fewer cigarettes, their not polluting the public air reduces an *externality*—the external cost to those whose pleasure and health might be hurt by the smoke. But if the switch to nonsmoking drops the price of cigarettes, we will not call the implications of that price drop *externalities*. So externalities do not include the income losses to tobacco companies, the possibly lower wages for tobacco workers, the lower land values in tobacco-raising areas, and so on. Those are just market-price effects, not (direct) externalities. (We stick to this definition even though Alfred Marshall tried to confuse us by calling such market-price effects *pecuniary externalities*.)

the problem is their emissions of sulfurous compounds. Even worse would be more indirect measures like cutting down on all economic growth or all population growth to reduce the emissions.

There are several ways for a government to attack the externality directly. Two leading strategies represent different beliefs about the proper role of government in our lives:

- Use of *government taxes and subsidies*. The government could tax private parties to make them recognize the external costs that their actions (e.g., pollution) impose on others. (Correspondingly, it could pay them subsidies to get them to recognize the external benefits their actions give to others.)
- Changing *property rights* so that all relevant resources are somebody's private property. If somebody owns a resource, including even the right to pollute it, then what she decides to do with it depends on what others offer to pay for that resource. If she chooses to pollute (or to deplete the resource), it is because she was not offered enough by others to avoid pollution (or depletion). There is a new market for the private property, a market whose absence caused the externality in the first place.

Different as these two approaches are, they are both valid ways to attack an externality. Sometimes one is more practical, sometimes the other. In our discussions, we will often use the tax-and-subsidy approach, but we should keep in mind that the same efficiency-enhancing outcome could sometimes be achieved using the property-rights approach.

A PREVIEW OF POLICY PRESCRIPTIONS

Following the specificity rule, we can develop general guidelines for solutions to international externalities. If we could choose any kind of policy measure whatsoever, the specificity rule would take us on the most direct route: If the externality is pollution in some place, make the pollution itself more expensive; if resource depletion is excessive, make the depletor pay more. Often, though, we cannot hit the exact target, the externality itself. Often the only workable choices are policies toward some economic flow near the target, such as production, consumption, or trade in products related to the externality. What then?

When we have to choose between doing nothing and intervening in product markets *related to* externalities, as a substitute for controlling the externalities directly, we should follow guidelines like those summarized in Figure 13.3.

Figure 13.3 contains two sets of best-feasible prescriptions: one for the whole world acting as one government and one for a single nation unable to get cooperation from other governments. These represent the two extremes in international negotiations over issues like pollution or natural-resource depletion: The greater the scope for international cooperation, the more relevant is the column of prescriptions for a world with a single government. The more hopeless it is to gain cooperation, the more we must settle on the single-nation prescriptions in the right column.

If nations cooperate, as if they formed a single world government, there would be essentially no role for international trade policy. In the best of worlds, government would

FIGURE 13.3   Types of Externalities and Product-Market Prescriptions

Source of External Costs (e.g., Pollution) Harming Our Nation	Examples	If the Whole World Had Only One Government, Its Best Product-Market Policy Would Be	Best Product-Market Policy for Our Nation Acting Alone
Just our own production	Chemicals	Tax our production	Tax our production (as in Figure 13.4)
Just foreign production	Acid rain across borders; tuna and dolphins; ivory	Tax foreign production	Tax our imports
World production	CO_2 buildup from fossil fuels	Tax world production (or consumption)	Tax our production and imports
Just our own consumption	Tobacco, narcotics	Tax our consumption	Tax our consumption
Just foreign consumption	Mercury (used in small-scale gold mining)	Tax foreign consumption	Tax our exports
World consumption	CFCs	Tax world consumption (or production)	Tax our consumption and exports

Note: *Tax* here means "impose government restrictions." These could be taxes, quantitative limits, or outright prohibitions. Remember that only "best product-market policy" interventions are considered here. In many cases, a more direct approach would tax an input or specific technology (e.g., use of high-sulfur coal or fuel-inefficient automobiles) rather than the final product (e.g., electricity from power plants or road transportation). And in other cases, an optimal policy might manipulate more than one product market at once.

devise a way to tax the activity of pollution itself, to translate its concern about pollution into direct incentives. In the one-world-government column of Figure 13.3, the recommended policies are one step away from taxing pollution itself, taking the form of taxes on production or consumption. They are not taxes on exports or imports. This is because pollution and other externalities seldom arise from trade as such. The specificity rule accordingly calls for taxes near the source of the pollution, and taxes on production or consumption are closer to that target than taxes on international trade are.[3]

If one nation must act alone, trade barriers can be an appropriate second-best solution. That would happen if our nation suffered from transborder pollution, either from foreign production (e.g., foreign producers of our imported steel causing acid rain in our country) or from foreign consumption (e.g., foreign cars burning our exported gasoline upwind from our nation). In this situation, the only way that our nation can discourage the foreign pollution is by taxing imports of the products made by a polluting process (e.g., foreign steel) or by taxing exports of products that generate pollution when consumed (e.g., gasoline).

The rest of the chapter takes up discussion of each of three types of sources of external costs noted in Figure 13.3. First we look at issues when the external costs are ones we impose on ourselves—domestic pollution and similar national externalities.

[3]It may seem suspicious that Figure 13.3 mentions raising taxes but not lowering them or giving out subsidies. The reason is simply that the cases listed here are all cases of negative externalities, the kind that do harm and must be reduced by taxing the polluting activities. If Figure 13.3 had dealt with the mirror-image cases, in which there were external benefits rather than costs, it would have recommended lower taxes or subsidies.

Then we analyze cases in which the activity of another country imposes an external cost on our country—transborder pollution and similar cross-country externalities. Finally, we examine the challenges of global external costs—global pollution and similar worldwide externalities.

TRADE AND DOMESTIC POLLUTION

Economic activities sometimes produce significant amounts of *domestic pollution* (or similar environmental degradation). That is, the costs of the pollution fall only (or almost completely) on people within the country. *If there are no policies that force market decision-makers to internalize* these external costs, then we reach two surprising conclusions about trade with domestic pollution. First, *free trade can reduce the well-being of the country.* Second, *the country can end up exporting the wrong products;* it exports products that it should import, for instance.

To see this, consider the case of an industry whose production activity creates substantial pollution in the local rivers, lakes, and groundwater. For instance, consider the paper-making industry in a country like Canada. It is very convenient for paper companies to dump their chemical wastes into the local lakes, and the firms view this as a free activity (if the Canadian government has no policy limiting this kind of pollution). The Canadian companies are happy that the lakes are there, and the firms' operations thrive, producing profits, good incomes for their workers, and good products for their customers at reasonable prices.

Other Canadians have a different view, of course. Having the lakes turn brown with chemical waste spoils the scenery, the swimming, the fishing, and other services that they get from their lakes. The dumping of wastes into the lakes imposes an external cost on other users of the lakes.

The top half of Figure 13.4 shows the Canadian market for paper, with the domestic supply curve reflecting the private marginal cost of production and the domestic demand curve reflecting the private marginal benefits of paper consumption (which are also the social marginal benefits if there are no external benefits). The bottom half of Figure 13.4 shows the additional costs imposed on the country by the pollution that results from production of paper in the country. We keep track of this negative externality using the marginal external costs (MEC) of the pollution. (This figure is the analog of Figure 10.2, which showed the case of external benefits.) To keep the analysis simple, we assume that the external cost of the pollution is constant at $0.30 per ream of paper.

With no international trade (and no government policies limiting pollution), the paper market clears at a price of $1 per ream, with 2 billion reams produced and consumed per year. Because there is no recognition in the market of the cost of the pollution, this is overproduction of paper.

Consider the shift to free trade, with an international price of $1.10 per ream (and still no government policies limiting pollution). Domestic production expands to 2.3 billion reams, domestic consumption declines to 1.8 billion, and 0.5 billion reams are exported. For the case shown in Figure 13.4, free trade unfortunately makes the country worse off. The usual gain from trade is shown by the shaded triangle *a* in the

FIGURE 13.4   When Domestic Production Causes Domestic Pollution

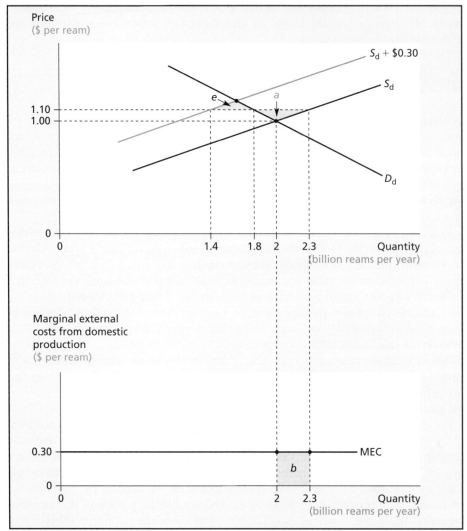

When domestic production causes pollution that imposes an external cost on the country, we find several surprising results about trade. If the government has no policy limiting this pollution, then domestic firms ignore the marginal external costs (MEC) of their pollution and operate along the supply curve S_d. If the world price is $1.10, then the country exports 0.5 billion reams of paper. In comparison with no trade, the country may be worse off, as it is here (gain of the shaded triangle *a* in the top of the figure, but loss of the shaded rectangle *b* in the bottom).

The country may also export the wrong products. Here it would be best if the country actually imported 0.4 billion reams. That would happen if a $0.30 tax, equal to the MEC, made domestic producers operate along the supply curve S_d + $0.30, which reflects all social costs.

upper graph, a gain of $25 million. But the extra production brings pollution that has an extra cost of the shaded area *b* in the lower graph, an external cost of $90 million ($0.30 per ream on the additional 300 million reams produced). Free trade reduces the well-being of the country by $65 million.

The country's government could avoid this loss by prohibiting exports of paper. But we know from the specificity rule that this is not the best government policy. The best policy attacks pollution directly, for instance, by placing a tax on pollution from paper production. If there is no way to reduce pollution per ream produced, then the tax should add $0.30 per ream to the firms' cost of production. The tax forces the firms to recognize the cost of pollution, and it alters their behavior. The domestic supply shifts up by the amount of the tax, to S_d + $0.30. This new supply curve now reflects all social costs, both the private production costs and the external pollution costs.

If this government policy is in place, what happens with free trade? Domestic consumers still buy 1.8 billion reams of paper, but now domestic producers supply only 1.4 billion reams. As shown, it is actually best for the country to import paper, not export it. Because the new supply curve (with the $0.30 tax) includes the external cost of pollution, we can read the effects of trade on the country from the top half of Figure 13.4, without referring to the bottom half. We find the usual triangle of gains from importing, the shaded triangle *e*.

From this example we see that pollution that imposes costs only on the local economy can still have a major impact on how we think about international trade. *With no government policy limiting pollution,* the country can end up worse off with free trade, and the trade pattern can be wrong. In the case of pollution caused by production that we examined, the country exported a product that it should instead import. (If, instead, the pollution cost is not so high, then the problem is that the country exports too much.)[4]

The country can correct this type of distortion by using a policy that forces polluters to recognize the external cost of their pollution. In our paper example, the government used a pollution tax, but instead it could establish property rights. For instance, people could be given the right to the water. Polluting firms then must pay the owners for the right to pollute. Or a limited number of rights to pollute could be created by the government, so that firms need to buy these rights if they want to pollute.

If domestic firms must pay the pollution tax (or pay for the right to pollute), they probably will not be happy. The pollution tax raises their production costs, and they produce and sell less. In addition, they face competition from imports at the world price of $1.10. Even if they accept the reason for the pollution tax, they may still complain about the imports. If other countries do not impose a similar pollution tax on their producers, then the domestic firms often complain that the imports are unfair. They claim that the lack of foreign pollution controls is a form of implicit subsidy, or that the foreign firms are engaged in "eco-dumping" based on lax foreign government policies.

What are we to make of these complaints? Should the country impose countervailing duties on imports from a country with different pollution policies? From the national

---

[4]What can happen if pollution is caused by consumption, not production? In this case the country tends to consume too much of the product, so the country could import a product that it should instead export (or, at least, it imports too much of the product).

perspective of the importing country, the answer is generally no. Foreign production may create pollution in the foreign country, but this has no impact on the importing country if the costs of this foreign pollution affect only foreigners. As with many other complaints about unfair exports, the best policy for the importing country is simply to enjoy the low-price imports. Indeed, under the rules of the World Trade Organization, lax foreign pollution policies are not a legitimate reason for imposing countervailing duties.

From the perspective of the whole world, it depends on why the foreign pollution policies are different from those of the importing country. It may be efficient for the foreign country to have different, and perhaps more lax, pollution policies. The pollution caused by foreign production may not be so costly because the foreign production itself creates less pollution, the foreign environment is not so badly affected, or foreigners place less value on the environment. In our paper example, the production process or the raw materials used in foreign production may create less pollution. Or the foreign country may have larger water resources or rainfall, in which case the pollution is not so damaging because the foreign environment has a larger "assimilative capacity." Or the foreign country may assign a high value to producing income to purchase basic goods because its people are poor and are therefore willing to accept some extra pollution more readily.

On the other hand, the foreign country may simply have policies that are too lax. From the point of view of the foreign country and the world, it would be better if it had tougher pollution policies. As a type of second-best approach, import limits by other countries can improve things. But these limits will not make the importing country better off, even though the limits might raise world well-being.

TRANSBORDER POLLUTION

In the previous section we considered pollution that had costs only to the country doing the pollution. While we reached some surprising conclusions about free trade in the absence of government policies limiting pollution, we also had a ready solution. The government should implement some form of policy addressing pollution that is occurring in its country. If each country's government addresses its own local pollution problems, then each can enhance its own national well-being. In the process, world well-being is also raised.

However, many types of pollution have transborder effects—effects not just on the country doing the pollution but also on neighboring countries. Examples include air pollution like particulates and sulfur dioxide that drifts across national borders and water pollution when the body of water (river or lake) is in two or more countries. Transborder pollution raises major issues for government policies toward pollution.

Suppose that a German paper company builds a large new paper mill on the Danube River, just to the west of where the river flows into Austria. It is very convenient for the paper company to dump its chemical wastes into the river, and it views this as a free activity (if the German government has no policy limiting this kind of pollution). Austrians have a different view. The dumping of wastes into the German Danube imposes an external cost on the Austrians and others (Slovaks, Hungarians, Serbs, Romanians, and Bulgarians) downstream.

FIGURE 13.5

A Classic Case of International Pollution with an Ideal Policy Solution

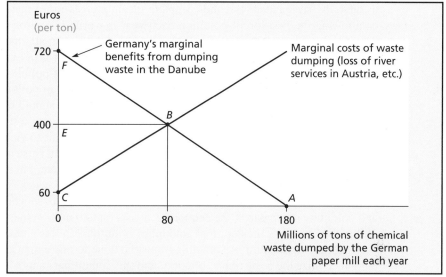

If there are no limits on pollution, then the German firm dumps 180 million tons. If the countries could negotiate the best solution, the pollution would be limited to 80 million tons.

The Right Solution

Figure 13.5 shows how we can determine the "right" amount of pollution, the amount that brings the greatest net gain to the world as a whole.[5] The figure focuses directly on pollution, without also showing the supply and demand for paper. It portrays Germany's benefits and Austria's costs from different rates of dumping waste into the Danube by the German paper mill. If left to itself, the German mill dumps as much as it wants into the Danube, ignoring the costs to Austria (and other nations). It will pollute until there is no more that it wants to dump at zero cost. That will be at point *A*, with the paper company dumping 180 million tons of waste per year. Point *A* is a disaster in Austria, where the river damage rises along the marginal cost curve in Figure 13.5.

Point *A* is also inefficient from a world perspective. Any pollution beyond 80 million tons is inefficient—it does more damage than it benefits the paper company. In the figure any waste dumping above 80 million tons has marginal costs that are above the marginal benefits. For instance, while the last few tons dumped bring the German firm almost no extra benefits (perhaps because these would be easy to avoid or clean up), these last few tons cost the Austrians about 700 euros per ton.

But, looking at it from the other side, we see that a total ban on dumping into the Danube would also be a mistake in this situation. The total ban, if effectively enforced, would force the paper mill to point *F*. Downstream users would be delighted, of course,

[5]Here, as in other chapters, the interest of the "world as a whole" is the sum of net gains to all parties, with each dollar (or euro) of gain or loss worth the same regardless of whose gain or loss it is. That is, we continue to follow the one-dollar, one-vote metric introduced in Chapter 2. To reject it, we would have to have another set of welfare weights, considering a dollar or euro of gain to the German firm to have a different value from the same value of gain or loss to Austrians.

to have the river clean. But the complete cleanup costs more than it is worth. That is, allowing the first ton of pollution each year is worth 720 euros to the paper company (perhaps because it is very costly to capture the last small amounts of waste for alternative disposal). Yet downstream users lose only 60 euros of extra enjoyment and income (at point C). The downstream cost of the first ton of pollution is not that high, probably because the river can assimilate this small amount of pollution without much damage. From a world viewpoint, the first ton of pollution should be allowed.

If Figure 13.5 correctly portrays the marginal benefits and costs, pollution up to 80 million tons adds to world well-being because the benefit to Germany from using the Danube for its waste is greater than the costs imposed on Austria. The paper company should be allowed to dump waste up to 80 tons per year, but no more than that. At point B, the benefits of using the river as a drain for wastes stop exceeding the costs of doing that. However offensive the idea may be to those who love clean water and don't buy much paper, the economist insists that 80 million tons, not zero tons (or 180 million tons), is the "optimal amount of pollution" in this situation.[6]

To get the right solution, something must be done to make the German paper company recognize the costs of its pollution, and this something cannot be too drastic. The specificity rule indicates that the best government policy is one that acts directly on the problem. A government can use the tax/subsidy approach to guide the use of the Danube to the optimal point B, if the government has good estimates of the marginal costs and benefits of the pollution. For instance, the government can tax the paper company 400 euros for every ton it dumps into the river. The company will respond by dumping 80 million tons a year (at point B) because up to that 80 millionth ton the company's gain from putting each extra ton of waste in the river exceeds the 400-euro tax. An efficient balance would be struck between the competing uses of the river.

A pollution tax like the one just described could well happen if "the government" were the Austrian government. But here the problem becomes international. Austria has no direct tax power over a paper mill in Germany, except to the extent that the mill happens to do business in Austria. More likely, the tax/subsidy option is in the hands of the German government because the paper mill is on the German side of the border. Germany might not tax the paper mill at all. Dumping 180 tons a year (at point A again) brings greater national gains to Germany than the world-efficient pollution tax at point B.

The likelihood that one country would decide to go on imposing an excessive external cost on other countries is a setback for the economist seeking global efficiency. To the efficiency-minded economist, it would not matter how we got to point B as long as we got there. But the German government has no incentive to tax the German company for its pollution.

We can imagine another way, assigning property rights, to try to get the efficient solution. A World Court could rule that the Danube is the property of the German paper company (or the German government) and that Austria must pay the German company to reduce its pollution. Or the World Court could rule that the Danube belongs to Austria and that the German company must buy the right to pollute for

---

[6]At point B, allowing 80 million tons of pollution (instead of none) brings the world a net gain of area BCF, or $(1/2) \times (720 - 60) \times 80 = 26.4$ billion euros per year.

each ton it dumps. The Nobel Prize–winning economist Ronald Coase pointed out that *either* court ruling could result in the same amount of pollution, as long as the property rights could be enforced. If the German company owned the river, the Austrian users would be willing to pay 400 euros per ton to reduce pollution to 80 million tons, and the German firm would agree to reduce its pollution to this level. If Austria owned the river, the German firm would be willing to pay 400 euros per ton for the right to dump 80 million tons, and the Austrians would accept this offer. Who gets the money depends on who owns the river, but in either case the same amount of pollution results.

This private-property approach has a major problem, however, when it comes to international disputes. There is no supreme world court that can enforce a property claim of one country's residents in another country. Austrians have no real legal recourse if the German paper mill insists on discharging all its wastes into the Danube. The Austrian government could threaten to take retaliatory actions against Germany. But it is unlikely that Austria would hold the right kind of power to force Germany to cooperate on the specific issue of the paper mill and the Danube if the Germans did not want to cooperate. The result is likely to be inefficient.[7]

We therefore get the same striking results for either the tax/subsidy approach or the property-rights approach. The good news is that any of several arrangements *could* give us the efficient compromise solution to the transborder pollution problem (at point *B*). The bad news is that the two countries often would not reach that efficient solution. Instead, negotiations would break down and each country would do as it pleased in its own territory. The result could be costly rampant pollution, as at point *A*, if the polluting firms can do as they please.

A Next-Best Solution

If international negotiations fail, the Austrian government must still consider what it can do on its own. If an international agreement is not possible, what can the government of the country that is being harmed by the other country's pollution do? It cannot tax or restrict the pollution-creating activity in the other country directly. But it may be able to have some influence by adopting policies toward international trade.

In our example, let's say that Austria imports paper from Germany and that Austrian paper production does not create much pollution (or this pollution is controlled by appropriate Austrian government policies). The Austrian government could attempt to reduce the dumping of waste into the Danube by limiting its imports from Germany (or, if possible, from the specific firm whose factory is responsible for the pollution).

[7]As it happens, the German–Austrian case is relatively benign in real life because Germany does care greatly about good relations with Austria, and both are members of the European Union. Yet the question "Whose river is it, anyway?" is destined to arise more and more often. Here are some examples: (1) Turkey has upstream control of the Euphrates, a vital resource for Syria and Iraq. (2) The potential for rising conflicts among China, Pakistan, and India over the waters of the Indus River system. (3) If the eight upstream nations use the Nile more intensively, there will be consequences for Egypt. (4) The Zambezi River will be the focus of disputes as Zambia, Angola, Botswana, Zimbabwe, and Mozambique construct dams to support irrigation projects. (5) Several drought-prone nations, most notably Mali and Niger, compete for the waters of the Niger River upstream from Nigeria. (6) The dams that have been built and the dams that are proposed could dramatically alter the flow of the Mekong River, affecting China, Myanmar, Thailand, Laos, Cambodia, and Vietnam.

If the decline in German paper exports reduces German paper production, then this also reduces the amount of waste that is dumped into the Danube. Austria gives up some of the gains from importing paper—that is, Austria suffers the usual deadweight losses from restricting imports. But Austria can still be better off if the gain from reducing the costs of the river pollution exceeds these usual deadweight costs. If instead Austria exports paper to Germany, then the Austrian government should consider subsidizing paper exports to Germany. The increase in Austrian exports can reduce German import-competing paper production, again leading to less dumping of waste.

There is a major problem with this indirect approach to addressing transborder pollution. The rules of the WTO generally prohibit the Austrian government from increasing its import tariffs or subsidizing its exports. Although, as we have seen, the rules also offer exceptions for measures intended to protect the environment, the WTO interprets this exception narrowly. So the WTO probably would not permit Austrian use of trade policy in response to lax German environmental policies.

NAFTA and the Environment

Environmental problems along the Mexico–U.S. border provide a real case of the challenges of transborder pollution. This issue was prominent in the fight over approving the North American Free Trade Agreement (NAFTA), adding to the concerns already discussed in the previous chapter, and it remains contentious in evaluations of the effects of NAFTA.

Mexico has a strong set of environmental protection laws and regulations on the books, comparable to those of the United States. But Mexican enforcement of these is weak. Weak enforcement is not surprising, and it is not only the result of limited administrative resources. Popular demand for clean air and water is a normal good. Nations feel they can afford to control many pollutants only when GDP per capita has reached high enough levels. Mexico has sacrificed air and water quality for economic development. Mexico City's smog is as bad as any in the world.

For the United States, a major concern is the pollution emanating from the Mexican side of the Mexico–U.S. border. The environmental problems in the border region arose well before NAFTA. In the 1960s, the governments of Mexico and the United States encouraged growth of industry just south of the border, where businesses could assemble goods for reentry into the United States without the usual tariffs and quotas. The arid border is not a forgiving place for a large industrial population. The absence of infrastructure for the several thousand *maquiladora* firms producing on the Mexican side, and the millions of people attracted by the jobs available, became (and remains) all too obvious. U.S. critics can point to unmanaged hazardous wastes, soil erosion, air pollution, raw sewage and other water pollution, lack of organized rubbish disposal, and lack of clean drinking water. While the pollution is most severe on the Mexican side of the border, major damage also affects the American side. Coal-fired power plants in northern Mexico cause serious air pollution in Texas, and Mexican water pollution is fouling the Rio Grande, a prime source of water for many U.S. towns.

Critics of NAFTA argued that freer trade would yield more environmental damage in the trade-oriented *maquiladora* zone, and they recommended rejecting NAFTA. In response to these criticisms, a side agreement on environmental issues was attached to NAFTA. It established a commission to investigate complaints about failure to enforce national environmental laws. It set up the North American Development Bank, owned by the U.S. and Mexican governments, to fund cleanup projects. Mexico also promised to enforce its environmental standards more effectively. With these additional provisions, environmental lobbying groups were actually divided about approving the final version of NAFTA.

What have been the effects since NAFTA began in 1994? NAFTA has not led to a decline in environmental standards in the United States, and it has not made Mexico a "pollution haven" for dirty industries, as some opponents had feared. But the institutions set up by the side agreement have had limited effects. The commission can investigate, but it has no power to mandate enforcement. It appears to have had little impact on Mexican enforcement of its environmental laws, which remains weak. The bank got off to a slow start, with few projects during its first five years. Since 1999 it has become more active, so that by December 2013 it had approved total funding (both loans and grants) of about $2.25 billion, although only half is to projects in Mexico, where the major problems exist. The projects supported have prevented conditions from deteriorating further, especially as population and business activities in the border area continue to grow. But, as Hufbauer and Schott (2005, p. 62) observe, the bank's project funding "still remains far below levels that would perceptibly improve border environmental conditions."

NAFTA has engendered a spirit of cooperation between the U.S. and Mexican governments, but the two countries still do not share the same views about the importance of ameliorating environmental damage. The environmental problems along the Mexico–U.S. border show how difficult it can be to address transborder pollution.

GLOBAL ENVIRONMENTAL CHALLENGES

Our discussion of transborder pollution focused on cases in which one country's activities impose external costs on neighboring countries. Things become even more controversial when the whole world's economic activities impose external costs on the whole world. Two important global environmental challenges are depletion of the ozone layer and global warming resulting from the buildup of greenhouse gases. Other challenges also have a global dimension, especially those that involve extinction of species or depletion of common resources such as fish stocks. We begin with an overview of important concepts and then examine specific applications.

Global Problems Need Global Solutions

Consider a global environmental problem like the depletion of the ozone layer caused by human release of chemicals. As we will see when we look at this in more detail, many types of activities release these chemicals, and the total of the global release causes the depletion. The harm of ozone depletion has global effects, with some countries more affected than others.

What would each country do if it sets its own policy toward this problem? From the purely national viewpoint, each country would recognize that chemical releases have some negative effect on its people, and it might use a policy to limit releases if it thought the national harm was large enough. But, for the whole world, total releases would be much too large. Each country would ignore the harm that its own releases did to other countries, so it would not be sufficiently stringent with its own environmental policy.

To get closer to the best global policy, the countries would need to find some way to cooperate. Each would need to tighten its standards compared to what it would do on its own. If each country does this, the whole world is better off. Many, but perhaps not all, of the countries will also each be better off. Each country incurs some costs in tightening its standards, but each also derives benefits from the reduction of the environmental damage.

Still, it may be very difficult to reach this global agreement. One problem is that there may be disagreement about the costs of the environmental damage or the costs of tightening standards. Science is unlikely to provide a definitive accounting, and countries differ in their willingness to take environmental risks. Even if this problem is not so large, others are likely to arise. Countries that suffer net losses from tightening may be unwilling to take part, unless they receive some other kind of compensation. Even countries that gain from the global agreement have a perverse incentive. A country can gain even more by free-riding. That is, it can gain most of the benefits if other countries abide by the agreement to tighten standards, even if this country does not, and it avoids the costs of tightening its own standards.

Because of the free-rider problem, a global agreement needs some method of enforcement, to get "reluctant" countries to agree in the first place and to assure that they abide by the agreement after it is established. There is no global organization that can provide these enforcement services. Countries can establish an enforcement mechanism as part of the global agreement, but it is not clear what it should be. It is generally not possible to impose fines directly. One possible penalty is some kind of trade sanctions to reduce the offending country's gains from trade. Such sanctions also have costs for the countries imposing the sanctions, and in any case they often do not work.

This is a sobering analysis. When an environmental problem causes only domestic costs, it is up to the government of the country to address it. When the problem is transborder but regional among a small number of countries, it is more difficult but still may be solvable by negotiations. When the problem is global, a global (or nearly global) multilateral agreement is needed, but negotiating and enforcing this agreement may prove to be very difficult or impossible. To gain more insight, let's turn to four global problems. We begin with a fairly effective global agreement to use trade policy to prevent the extinction of endangered species. Next we depict depletion of ocean fishing stocks and the lack of effective solutions to this global inefficiency. Then we portray a successful, nearly global agreement to reverse ozone depletion. We conclude with the most daunting of global environmental issues: greenhouse gases and global warming.

Extinction of Species

Extinction of species can be a natural process outside of human influence. Still, within the past half century the specific role of human activity in causing extinction has become recognized and controversial. There is a general belief that there is a loss when a species becomes extinct, perhaps because there may be future uses for the species (for instance, as a source of medicinal products). Thus, a global effort to prevent extinction of species can be economically sensible.

Human activities contributing to extinction include destruction of habitat, introduction of predators, and pollution. In addition, excessive hunting and harvesting can also cause extinction. The specificity rule indicates that the best global policy to preserve species would be a policy that promotes the species through such direct means as protected parks and wild areas; ranching, cultivation, and similar management intended to earn profits from the ongoing existence of the species; and zoos and gardens to maintain species in captivity. While there is no global agreement specifically to promote these best solutions, there is a global agreement that attempts to control the pressure of international demand as a source of incentives for excessive hunting and harvesting.

In 1973, over 100 nations signed the Convention on International Trade in Endangered Species of Wild Fauna and Flora **(CITES)**. With 180 member countries by 2014, CITES establishes international cooperation to prevent international trade from endangering the survival of species. An international scientific authority recommends which species are endangered. Commercial trade is usually banned for species threatened with extinction—about 900 species, including elephants, gray whales, and sea turtles. To export these products for noncommercial purposes, a nation must obtain an export permit from the central authority, and it must have a copy of an import permit from a suitable buyer in a country that signed CITES. Commercial trade is limited for an additional 34,000 species because free trade could lead to the threat of extinction.

No CITES-listed species has become extinct as a result of international trade. Some, including the rhino and the tiger, continue to decline, but CITES has probably slowed the declines. Generally, CITES seems to be fairly effective. This is impressive in that most member countries have incomplete national legislation, poor enforcement, and weak penalties for violating the trade bans or controls.

Much of the conflict over endangered species centers on Africa, with its unique biodiversity and its fragile ecosystems. The biggest fight so far has been over the fate of the African elephant, which is hunted for its ivory tusks.

The human slaughter of elephants accelerated at an alarming rate in the 1970s and 1980s. The African elephant population was cut in half within a span of only eight years in the 1980s. The problem was most severe in eastern Africa, north of the Zambezi River. The governments of Kenya, Tanzania, the Sudan, Zaire (now the Congo), and Zambia, while ostensibly committed to protecting elephants, were not preventing killing by poachers. The threat to elephants was weaker in southern Africa, south of the Zambezi, for three reasons: The governments of Zimbabwe, Botswana, South Africa, and Namibia enforced conservation more aggressively; agriculture was less of a threat to the wild animal population; and some elephants of Botswana and Zimbabwe had tusks of poor commercial quality.

In 1977, the African elephant was placed on the list of species with controlled trade. Public pressure from affluent countries to save the elephants became intense by the late 1980s. Although the African elephant did not fully meet the official definition, in 1989 it was moved to the list of endangered species. Also in 1989, most of the CITES countries signed a complete ban on exporting or importing ivory. Education and information on the plight of the elephant reduced demand for ivory, especially demand in affluent countries, and ivory prices plummeted from $100 per kilogram to $3 or $4 per kilogram in the 1990s. Poaching decreased (mostly a movement down the poachers' supply curve) and the elephant populations stabilized or increased. However, demand for ivory rose in the 2000s, especially increased Asian buying as incomes expanded there, and ivory prices rose to over $2,000 per kilogram by 2012. Poaching has increased in some parts of Africa, and illegal trade has increased.

Elephant numbers rose in the 1990s in the countries of southern Africa to such an extent that these countries argued that they had too many elephants. In 1997 these countries asked CITES to end bans for their elephants. They argued that they needed some economic use of elephants to justify the costs of managing the herds. In 1992 CITES had adopted the principle of "sustainable use," but CITES has moved very cautiously. For the countries of southern Africa, CITES has permitted limited hunting and a few sales of ivory.

CITES has generally been reasonably effective, but the situation of the elephant since 2000 shows the challenges facing CITES. First, a ban on exporting by itself restricts legal supply, so it raises the world price and encourages poaching and illegal trade. The ban works well only if it is coupled with a demand shift away from the animal. For a while demand for elephants' ivory did decrease, but demand has returned. Second, a ban adversely affects the people and the governments where the animal lives. To preserve the animal, it helps to make the animal valuable to the people who have other uses for the land. Africa's human population growth will bring more crop cultivation, and cultivation is simply incompatible with a roaming elephant population. Economic incentives to keep the animals in the wild can arise from tourism and from hunting and harvesting. If tourism is not enough, then the long-run solution probably is based on commercial hunting and trade that are consistent with sustainable use. For many species the ultimate success of CITES depends less on its precautionary bans and, paradoxically, more on its ability to encourage economic management for commercial uses.

Overfishing

The oceans, along with fish and other marine life, are one of the great global resources. However, major problems can develop because no one actually owns these resources. The world's fish catch has been roughly flat since 1990. About a quarter of the earth's 200 main fish stocks are overfished; sustainable catches could be larger if the stocks were better managed. For most fish species, overfishing does not pose a threat of extinction, but it does mean that populations are becoming smaller than they should be. Why are we squandering this resource? What can we do?

We have here an example of the "tragedy of the commons." With open access to fishing and no ownership, the incentive of each fishing firm is to catch as many fish as possible. There is no incentive to conserve. Even if one fishing firm did restrain its catch to maintain the fish stock, others would simply increase their catch. So all fish too much, and the fish stock declines. Rather than limiting their fishing industries, governments often make matters worse by subsidizing them. The result is severe overcapacity of fishing boats, perhaps twice as much ship tonnage as would be needed for a sustainable fish catch.

With good management of fishing stocks, the world catch of fish could be 10 to 20 percent larger than it is now. But even single nations have trouble managing their fishing activities. The fishing industry, with its overcapacity, pushes for lesser limits, even if this is helpful only in the short run. Global or multilateral agreements could enhance global fishing. But given the difficulty of negotiating and enforcing such agreements, effective ones are rare. The World Bank and the Food and Agriculture Organization (2009) estimate that the inefficiencies result in an annual global loss of $50 billion.

CFCs and Ozone

The 1940s brought new technologies for using chlorofluorocarbon compounds (CFCs) in several industries. About 30 percent of CFCs came to be used in refrigeration, air-conditioning, and heat pumps; about 28 percent in foam blowing; about 27 percent in aerosol propellants; and about 15 percent in dry cleaning and other industrial cleaning and degreasing. By the early 1970s, evidence had accumulated showing that CFCs and the halons used in fire extinguishers, while not directly toxic, were depleting ozone in the upper atmosphere. The chemical process is slow and complex. It takes 7 to 10 years for released CFCs to drift to the stratosphere, where their chlorine compounds interact with different climatic conditions to remove ozone. By 1985, the now-famous ozone holes were clearly detected in the stratosphere near the North and South Poles. Stratospheric ozone is an important absorber of ultraviolet rays from the sun, and its removal raises dangers of skin cancer, reduced farm yields, and climatic change.

In 1987, over 50 nations signed the **Montreal Protocol** on Substances that Deplete the Ozone Layer, and by 2014 the number of signatories had risen to 197 countries. The signing parties agreed to ban exports and imports of CFCs and halons. After more scientific evidence accumulated, most signatory nations agreed in 1990 to phase out their own production of these chemicals by 2000, with later deadlines and interim production limits for developing countries.

Note that the protocol called for outright bans and other quantitative limits, not a pollution tax or polluting-product tax like those discussed in Figures 13.3 through 13.5. The reason is that the scientific evidence suggested a steeply rising social-cost curve for CFC emissions into the atmosphere. With the cost curve so vertical, it did not make sense to use tax rates on a trial-and-error basis in the hope of achieving the large cut in pollution. It was better to legislate the bans and limits from the start, without waiting several years to see if some tax schedule had the right effects.

The Montreal Protocol is achieving much of the intended economic and environmental effects. Concentrations of chlorine-containing compounds in the stratosphere peaked and began to decline in 2000. Yet, because of the slow chemical process of recovery, the ozone holes will remain for a long time; ozone concentrations in the stratosphere will not return to normal levels until about 2070.

Why the success in this case? Why didn't nations try to free-ride by refusing to comply while demanding that others do so, as so often happens? Experts point to several factors that eased the signing and enforcement of the Montreal Protocol:

- The scientific evidence was clearer about CFCs and ozone than it is about other possible human threats to the atmospheric balance.
- A small group of products was involved, for which substitutes appeared to be technologically feasible with limited cost increases.

- Production of CFCs was concentrated in the United States and the EU, and in a few large publicity-conscious firms (mainly DuPont), so that agreement could be easily reached and enforced.

- The same higher-income countries that dominated production and use of these chemicals are also closer to the North and South Poles, so they expected to suffer most of the environmental damage themselves.

Greenhouse Gases and Global Warming

Finally, we turn to the most challenging environmental problem of all. Human activity is raising the concentration of carbon dioxide (CO_2) and other greenhouse gases in the earth's atmosphere. Most climate scientists believe that the rise of these gases is causing a pronounced warming of the earth's climate through a "greenhouse effect." The warming could bring desertification of vast areas and could flood major coastal cities and farm areas as it melts glacier ice and warms ocean water. It is hard to imagine a solution as clean and workable as the Montreal Protocol's phase-out of chlorofluorocarbons. The activities that release carbon dioxide, methane, and other greenhouse gases into the atmosphere are harder to do without than were CFC refrigerants and sprays. In addition, the damage from adverse climatic change would be spread around the globe unpredictably and unevenly.

To see the available options, we should first clear the air, so to speak, by noting some limits on the choices available. Three main points must be made at the outset: (1) The scientific facts are not fully established, (2) three palatable solutions will fall short of arresting the CO_2 buildup, and (3) international trade is not the cause or the cure.

First, the scientific facts about the greenhouse effect are less certain than the facts about CFCs and stratospheric ozone. We do know that atmospheric concentrations of CO_2 have risen by about 40 percent since 1750. The atmospheric concentrations continue to rise, and a reasonable estimate is that they will double during the 21st century if we do nothing to limit emissions. Human activity, especially the burning of fossil fuels, is the main source of the buildup.

The effects of the CO_2 buildup cannot be predicted precisely. We do know that there is a greenhouse effect—in fact, it is crucial to keeping the earth's surface and lower atmosphere warm. From 1900 the earth's average surface temperature has increased about 0.9°C (1.6°F), mostly since 1980. Most forecasts are that temperatures will rise by anywhere from 0.3°C to 4.8°C during the 21st century.

Even if the earth is getting warmer and CO_2 buildup is the main reason, the climatic changes and economic effects cannot be predicted with certainty. Nonetheless, the best available climate forecasts indicate that countries closer to the equator are likely to experience more adverse climate change, with potentially large economic losses for developing countries in Africa, South and Southeast Asia, and Latin America. Smaller relative economic losses, or even possible gains, are expected for most industrialized countries, China, Central and Eastern Europe, and Russia. Two areas that face a risk of catastrophic losses are India (if there is major change in monsoon patterns) and Europe (if the warming Atlantic current changes direction).

Scientific uncertainties do not justify doing nothing. The risks are real and indicate that a path of taking out "insurance" makes sense. We do not need radical actions that risk wrecking the world economy. We should move in the direction of cutting greenhouse-gas emissions, with adjustments in the future as scientific knowledge improves.

Second, it must be understood that three relatively palatable policy changes will fall far short of stopping the CO_2 buildup:

1. One desirable option is known as the "no-regrets" option. Let's just remove all those unwarranted *subsidies* to fossil fuel use, about $500 billion per year worldwide, subsidies that should have been removed anyway. Removing bad energy subsidies would reduce, at most, no more than 10 percent of the emissions, and the net global buildup of CO_2 would continue.

2. A second option would be to take CO_2 out of the atmosphere with afforestation, that is, by stopping deforestation and reforesting previously cleared land. Unfortunately, a mature forest does not absorb CO_2 from the atmosphere. It has achieved an equilibrium in which the absorption of atmospheric CO_2 by plant growth is approximately canceled by the release of CO_2 from decaying plant matter. Only growth of new forests absorbs CO_2 in significant degree. It would take perpetual growth of new forests equal in area to all current U.S. forests to cut the CO_2 buildup by 20 to 25 percent. Forests play much less role in the greenhouse-gas balance than does the burning of fossil fuels.

3. A third option that doesn't work is to wait for depletion of the earth's fossil fuels to push up the price of energy to a point where we stop raising the global CO_2 levels. Finite as planet Earth may be, there is no prospect of exhaustion, or even severe scarcity, of fossil fuels in the next few decades. Earth contains so much oil, coal, and other fossil fuels that our current fuel habits may exhaust our good air long before they exhaust our cheap fuel supplies. To clean up the air, we must artificially raise the price of fuel long before geology will do the job for us.

A third initial point is that international trade policy cannot be the best tool. If we are to attack greenhouse-gas emissions near their source, we must attack either total consumption or total production of fossil fuels, the main human source of greenhouse-gas emissions. International trade in fuels is large, but well below half the total fuel consumption. If we were to tax international trade as such, there would still be too much substitution of one source for another to achieve a large global reduction in emissions. If we relied on taxing international trade in fuels, fuel-importing countries like the United States would substitute home supplies for imports, and fuel-exporting countries like Mexico would divert their fuel from exports to home use.

Thus far, we have limited the search for solutions in three ways. First, scientific uncertainty urges an "insurance" approach, somewhere in between doing nothing and taking radical steps. Second, some hopes—the "no-regrets" reforms, afforestation, and naturally rising fuel scarcity—fall short as cures for the CO_2 buildup. Finally, trying to cut emissions by cutting international trade leaves too many options for substituting home fuel use for traded fuel.

Kyoto Protocol

What progress have we made in finding a more comprehensive way to address global warming? Actual world agreements so far have not been effective. Industrial countries committed in Rio de Janeiro in 1992 to keep their CO_2 emissions at 1990 levels, but they failed to do so.

With the **Kyoto Protocol,** reached in late 1997, industrialized countries, which at that time accounted for about 42 percent of global greenhouse-gas emissions, agreed to cut their emissions. In the first phase, industrialized countries agreed to reduce annual emissions to an average of about 5 percent below their 1990 levels by the years 2008–2012. Developing countries refused to make any commitments, however. They argued that they are poor and should not have to slow their economic growth. The Protocol came into effect in 2005, but the United States and Australia decided against ratifying it. (Australia subsequently signed on in late 2007, after an election changed the party in power.)

Each country with a required 2008–2012 emission level had to decide how to meet its target. The European Union has taken the lead in using tradable rights to emit carbon dioxide. This approach is a variation on the idea mentioned earlier in the chapter that property rights can be used to address pollution problems, in this case using property rights to pollute (rather than property rights to clean air). Each country allocates a limited number of rights to its individual firms that are the major sources of emissions. Then the firms can trade among themselves, as some firms lower emissions and have rights to sell, while other firms find that their emissions exceed their initial allocations and they must buy additional rights. The market for the rights sets the price of emitting the pollutant, in this case CO_2. Trading in carbon emission permits, mostly through the EU's Emission Trading Scheme, reached $106 billion in 2010 before falling off as it became clear that the EU would more than meet its target for an 8 percent emission reduction.

Even with the EU and some other industrialized countries meeting their targets for reducing emissions during the first phase, the Kyoto Protocol did not accomplish much. Worldwide, annual greenhouse-gas emissions increased by 39 percent during 1990–2010. Here are three major reasons that the Kyoto Protocol has had so little effect.

First, some other industrialized countries missed their targets. Canada committed to reducing its emissions by 6 percent, but its emissions actually increased by about 20 percent. To avoid possible penalties, Canada withdrew from the protocol in 2011. Australia committed to limiting its emissions increase to 8 percent, but its emissions actually increased by about 30 percent. Japan committed to reducing its emissions by 6 percent, but its own emissions were approximately unchanged. (Japan may still meet its commitment by buying credits for, and thus effectively funding, projects that reduced emissions in developing countries.)

Second, the United States, which accounted for about 20 percent of global greenhouse-gas emissions in 1997, decided not to take part. In March 2001 President George W. Bush indicated that the science was too uncertain for taking on such a costly process to reduce U.S. emissions. He also stated that it was unacceptable that developing countries, especially China, had made no commitments. He indicated that the U.S. government instead was urging voluntary actions by U.S. firms. Voluntary actions were not enough. Instead of its Kyoto target reduction of 7 percent, U.S. emissions actually increased by about 10 percent.

Third, and most important, annual greenhouse-gas emissions by developing countries increased dramatically, by 64 percent during 1990–2010. China's annual greenhouse-gas emissions tripled from 1990 to 2010, and China is now the largest emitter of greenhouse gases, accounting for 23 percent of worldwide emissions in 2010.

A Global Approach

At the 2012 United Nations climate conference, there were two developments. First, the countries agreed to the second and final phase of the Kyoto Protocol, but the participating industrialized countries (without the United States and Canada) committed to modest targets for their emissions in 2020, and Japan and Russia made no commitments. Second, the countries set a goal to negotiate a new, broader treaty to replace the Kyoto Protocol.

Can we imagine a policy approach that would be much more effective? What would it do, and how expensive would it be? Global problems require global solutions, and long-term problems usually require long-term solutions. The solution to excessive global warming should include the following elements:

• Economic incentives are used to encourage emission reductions.
• All countries are involved.
• The policy extends over decades.

Economic incentives are created by establishing a price for greenhouse-gas emissions, to reflect their external costs. Pricing emissions encourages reductions in two ways. First, with a cost now attached to emissions, the price of emission-intensive products increases, and consumers react by buying less. Second, producers have the incentive to look for technologies that generate fewer emissions per unit of product. Through both of these effects, the policy spurs emission reductions at low cost. Pricing of emissions can be achieved by a tax on emissions or by tradable rights to pollute such as those used by the European Union to meet its obligations in the Kyoto Protocol.

All countries should be involved, for both effectiveness and efficiency. With no policies restricting emissions (often called "business as usual"), emissions would continue to grow quickly in developing countries. There is no way to stabilize greenhouse gases in the atmosphere at reasonable levels without the participation of developing countries. Furthermore, the marginal costs of reducing emissions are generally lower in developing countries because they often do not make use of the most energy-efficient technologies and because they often rely heavily on coal to generate electricity. To achieve reductions in global emissions at low cost, much of the reduction should occur in developing countries.

The policies should be in place for a long time span because they should affect decisions about investments in long-lived capital equipment and decisions about research and development of new technologies that can lower future emissions. The price of emissions in the future is a key input into these investment and research decisions.

A number of researchers have examined global, long-term policies toward greenhouse-gas emissions. Let's consider the results of one study, reported by the International Monetary Fund in its April 2008 *World Economic Outlook*. The study examines several alternative policies, and we will look at the imposition of a tax on carbon dioxide emissions at the same rate in all countries.[8]

The global CO_2 tax would begin in 2013, at a rate of $3 per ton of CO_2 emissions, and rises by about $3 per year, to a level of $86 per ton in 2040, and then rises somewhat more slowly to a level of $168 per ton in 2100. (To get a feel for what this means for consumer prices, a tax of $86 per ton would result in an increase of about $0.80 in the price of a gallon of gasoline.) The rising CO_2 tax is chosen for two reasons. First,

---

[8]The study also examines different types of global schemes that use tradable rights to emit. For the same path of reduction of global emissions, the global costs in terms of income loss are similar under a carbon tax and the different emission-rights schemes. The choice of scheme does matter for the effects on different countries' national incomes.

FIGURE 13.6   Carbon Tax to Stabilize Atmospheric Carbon Dioxide

Country or Region	Annual CO_2 Emissions* (gigatons)			Real Annual National Income (U.S. $ trillions)		
		2040			2040	
	2010	Baseline	With CO_2 Tax	2010	Baseline	With CO_2 Tax
United States	6.2	11.0	3.5	12.0	25.7	25.1
Western Europe	3.7	5.4	4.4	10.5	20.9	20.4
Other industrialized countries	2.3	3.8	2.6	6.1	11.2	10.9
Russia and Eastern Europe	3.0	4.8	3.8	3.9	8.6	8.3
OPEC countries	1.4	3.6	0.8	1.0	2.9	2.3
Other developing countries	8.7	35.4	8.7	8.0	32.4	31.3
World	25.3	64.0	23.9	41.5	101.6	98.2

*From burning of fossil fuels.

Source: International Monetary Fund, *World Economic Outlook*, April 2008, Chapter 4. The author is grateful for data provided by Natalia Tamirisa.

it avoids large, unnecessary disruptions in the early years. Second, it is calibrated to achieve eventual stabilization of greenhouse-gas concentrations in the atmosphere at about 550 parts per million, a level that is expected to result in a manageable rise in average global temperatures. The policy results in annual emissions in 2100 that are only 40 percent of current levels.

How expensive is this policy approach? That is, how much does it reduce conventional measures of national income? The IMF study focuses on the effects in 2040, a year that is within our lifetimes. Figure 13.6 summarizes what the IMF study sees for both emissions and national incomes, contrasting starting values in the year 2010 (just before the CO_2 tax is enacted), the baseline values for the year 2040 (if no emissions policies are adopted—"business as usual"), and the values for 2040 with the global CO_2 tax policy.

Here are some key points that we can take from the information in Figure 13.6. First, in the absence of an emissions policy (the baseline), CO_2 emissions in 2040 are about 2.5 times the 2010 emissions, and much of the increase occurs in developing countries. Second, the CO_2 tax succeeds in restraining emissions, so that global emissions levels would be somewhat lower in 2040 than they are in 2010. Much of the effect of the tax is achieved by eliminating the growth of emissions in developing countries (other than Russia and Eastern Europe), with reductions in China being especially large. There is also a substantial reduction of emissions by the United States. Third, the emissions reduction is achieved at what seems to be a reasonable cost. With no policies (the baseline), world income would be 2.45 times as large in 2040 as it was in 2010. With the emission tax, world income is 2.37 times as large. Each country or region suffers some loss in national income, but, with the exception of the larger loss in the OPEC countries, it is equivalent to a reduction of only about 0.1 percentage point per year in the average annual economic growth rate.

The IMF study and others like it show that we can address the problem of global warming without imposing heavy damages on the global economy or on most if not all individual countries, if we can harness long-term economic incentives to achieve emissions reductions at low cost and if we can achieve participation by all countries (or, at least, all of the large emitter countries). The economics are promising. Still, it will be challenging to gain agreement from enough countries to negotiate and implement such a global approach to global warming.

Summary

International trade is not inherently anti-environment, and the best solution to environmental problems is seldom one that involves trade policy. The rules of the WTO are generally consistent with this application of the specificity rule. They permit countries to impose environmental standards on domestic production activities and on domestic consumption activities (including environment-based product standards). The WTO also offers limited environmental exceptions to its free-trade thrust. The WTO places strict requirements on a single country that attempts to use trade policy to punish what the country views as environmentally damaging production activities in other countries. The WTO seems willing to accept trade limits that are part of multilateral environmental agreements.

Because environmental problems like pollution involve an externality, government policies are usually needed to get markets to be efficient. In fact, if a country's government fails to implement a policy to limit pollution, free trade may make a country worse off and the country may end up exporting the wrong products.

Transborder pollution is an example of an international externality, in which production (or consumption) activities in one country impose external costs on neighboring countries. As with all external costs, the best solution is one that addresses the pollution directly, by imposing a tax on the pollution or by establishing property rights (to water or whatever is being polluted, or as limited rights to pollute). However, it is often challenging for the government of the country hurt by the pollution to gain the cooperation of the government of the country doing the pollution. For instance, little progress has been made in reducing environmental problems along the Mexico–U.S. border, even though a side agreement to NAFTA established a commission and a bank for this purpose.

In some cases the environmental problem is global: Global production or consumption is imposing a worldwide external cost. The best approach to a global environmental problem is a global cooperative agreement, but achieving one is usually difficult. Often, there are differences of opinion about the size of the external costs or the appropriate policies to adopt. Countries that suffer little or no harm have little incentive to cooperate and impose costs on themselves. More generally, countries have an incentive to free-ride on the efforts of others. Often an agreement has no real enforcement mechanism. Trade sanctions provide a possible threat against countries that do not abide by an agreement, but sanctions often do not work.

The chapter concluded with four examples of global environmental problems. Two have been addressed by successful global agreements. An agreement (CITES) on using trade limits and trade bans to prevent the extinction of species has been fairly effective. But the ultimate solution may well involve creating economic incentives for "sustainable use" (the propagation and economic management of the previously endangered species), as the discussion of elephants and ivory suggested. The global agreement on CFCs (the Montreal Protocol) has also been effective and should reverse the ozone damage over time. Success here seems to be based on clear scientific evidence, the rather small number of CFC producers, the availability of substitutes at reasonable cost, and the fact that the major producing countries were also those likely to suffer the most damage.

Two problems have not been addressed successfully. Because no one owns the oceans and their resources, *overfishing* has led to declines in fish stocks. The large number of fishing firms and their political activity to resist limits have prevented effective global agreements. *Global warming* as a result of the atmospheric buildup of CO_2 and other greenhouse gases is the most daunting global environmental problem. Science does not provide full guidance on the magnitude of the problem and its likely effects on different countries. All countries contribute to global emissions of greenhouse gases. The **Kyoto Protocol** is an attempt to address the problem, but it has had little effect. A better economic approach to managing global warming would include the pricing of emissions to provide economic incentives for achieving emission reductions at low cost, the involvement of all countries in the effort to reduce emissions, and the extension of the policy over decades to encourage and guide long-term investments and research.

Key Terms			
Externality		Transborder pollution	Montreal Protocol
Specificity rule		CITES	Kyoto Protocol

Suggested Reading

Copeland and Taylor (2004) provide an excellent survey of trade and environment issues. Esty (2001), Neumayer (2000), and Irwin (2009) present critical analyses of the controversies. Brunnermeier and Levinson (2004) survey research on the pollution-haven hypothesis. Kelly (2003) examines WTO dispute settlement rulings on environmental and health issues. For appraisals of global environmental problems, see the series of studies, *World Resources Report,* from the World Resources Institute.

On NAFTA and the environment, see Hufbauer and Schott (2005, Chapter 3). On greenhouse gases, see Chapter 4 of the International Monetary Fund's April 2008 *World Economic Report,* Tamiotti et al. (2009), Organization for Economic Cooperation and Development (2009), Aldy et al. (2010), and Nordhaus (2013).

Questions and Problems

◆1. Does a rise in national production and income per capita tend to worsen or improve air pollution, water pollution, and sanitation? Explain.

2. "One of the benefits of free trade is that it corrects the distortion caused by pollution." Do you agree or disagree? Why?

◆3. Which of the following probably violate the rules of the WTO?

   a. A country's government places a tax on domestic production to reduce pollution caused by this production.

   b. A country's government prohibits imports of foreign goods produced using production methods that would violate this importing country's environmental protection laws.

   c. A country's government places a tax on domestic consumption of goods (both imported and domestically produced) to reduce pollution caused by this consumption.

   d. A country's government restricts imports of a good to reduce pollution caused by consumption of this good.

4. Mining of metallic ores often causes harm to the environment in the area around the mines. Some countries impose strict policies to limit the environmental damage caused by this mining, but others do not. The mining companies in the strict countries complain that this is unfair and ask for limits on imports of ores and metals from the lax countries. As a government official interested in advancing the national interest in a strict country, how would you evaluate the request of your mining companies?

◆ 5. Oil spills from oceangoing tankers are rare but bring huge damages to coastlines when they occur within 200 miles of shore. Unfortunately, most tanker spills do occur on or near coasts. Rank the following alternatives according to how efficient they are in responding to the threat of oil spills. Explain your ranking.

   a. Each nation with an endangered coastline should impose a tax on all imported oil, a tax that raises enough revenue to compensate for any oil-spill damages.

   b. Each coastal nation should impose a tax on all domestically purchased oil, a tax that raises enough revenue to compensate for any oil-spill damages.

   c. Oil-carrying companies should be legally liable for all damages, in the courts of the countries whose national waters are polluted by the spills.

   d. Each coastal nation should intercept all oil tankers in national waters and charge them a fee that will cover the estimated costs of future oil spills.

   e. We might as well save ourselves the expense of trying to prevent spills. They are just accidents beyond the control of the shipping companies; they are part of the cost of having coasts.

6. Consider the example of domestic pollution shown in Figure 13.4. Suppose that the marginal external cost of the pollution is $0.05 per ream produced (instead of $0.30).

   a. With this different MEC, does free trade make the country better off or worse off?

   b. To gain the most from trade, should the country export or import paper? How much?

◆ 7. Which of the following would do most to cut the global buildup of carbon dioxide over the next 30 years?

   a. Elimination of all subsidies to energy use.

   b. Restoration of the original tropical rain forest.

   c. A tax that rises to $86 per ton of emitted carbon dioxide, as described in this chapter.

   d. The trend toward rising fuel scarcity, caused by exhausting the world's reserves of fossil fuels.

8. Assume that the production of cement also produces a substantial amount of air pollution and that a technology is available that can lower the pollution but with somewhat higher production costs for the cement. Because of the availability of raw materials in Lindertania, it produces large amounts of cement, and its exports supply most demand in Pugelovia. But the air pollution from Lindertania's production blows into Pugelovia, causing a noticeable deterioration in Pugelovia's air quality. Although Lindertania suffers some harm itself from this air pollution, it does not now have any policy to reduce the pollution. The Pugelovian government wants to address this air pollution problem.

   a. If the two countries' governments cooperate, what is the best solution to address the problem? Explain.

   b. If Pugelovia must come up with a solution on its own, what should the Pugelovian government do? Explain.

◆ 9. Use your no. 2 pencil to write down your views on this trade-and-environment debate:

According to the Rainforest Action Network (RAN), a rain-forest wood called jelutong is being logged at a dangerous rate in Indonesia. The reason is that pencil makers recently shifted about 15 percent of their production from the more expensive cedar wood to jelutong, saving $1 on every dozen pencils. The Incense Cedar Institute, which represents three major companies growing cedar in the United States, echoes the concerns of RAN about the threat to tropical rain forests. Speaking for the pencil makers, executives of Dixon Ticonderoga explain that the jelutong wood in Indonesia is not gathered from rain forests, but is planted and harvested on plantations.

What should be done about the use of jelutong wood in making pencils? Should the government of Indonesia block the export of jelutong wood? Should the government of the United States tax or prohibit jelutong imports? Defend your view. If you feel you need more information than is given here, what extra information would be decisive?

10. Draw a graph like the one in Figure 13.5, which shows the effects of transborder pollution. There is no governmental agreement on how to control the pollution, so the German firm is dumping 180 tons of waste into the river. There is free trade in paper, and Austria imports paper.

Now Austria imposes a 30 percent tariff on paper imports, which reduces Austrian imports of paper from Germany by 20 percent. As a result of imposing the tariff, Austria suffers standard deadweight losses from the tariff equal to €5 billion. Also as a result of the tariff, Germany produces less paper, and the German firm shown in the graph reduces its dumping of waste by 10 percent.

a. Using your graph, show the effect on Austria of this change in the waste dumping. Calculate the euro value of the effect of the change in waste dumping on Austria's well-being.

b. Overall, including both the standard effect of the tariff (not shown in the graph) and the effect of the change in waste dumping, is Austria better off or worse off (than it was before it imposed the tariff)?

◆ 11. Rhinoceroses are an endangered species. Worldwide, the number of rhinos has decreased 90 percent in the past 50 years, to about 28,000. Since 1977, CITES has had a ban on international trade in rhino parts. The most valuable part of a rhino is its horn, which can be sold for prices that have risen to close to $14,000 per kilogram. Given the very high price, illegal poaching, in which rhinos are killed for their horns, has increased rapidly. Interestingly, if done properly, the horn of a rhino can be harvested without killing the rhino, and the horn will grow back.

What challenges does CITES face in attempting to prevent international trade from contributing to the extinction of the rhino?

12. Why did the Montreal Protocol succeed in limiting global emissions of chlorofluorocarbons (CFCs), whereas the world has found it difficult to limit the emissions of CO_2? What differences between the two cases explain the difference in outcome?

Chapter **Fourteen**

Trade Policies for Developing Countries

Much of the world's attention focuses on the industrialized economies—especially the United States, Japan, and the countries of Western Europe. The attention is not surprising, given that these areas produce over half of world output and an even greater share of the supply of media services. Yet about 6 billion people (six-sevenths of the world's population) live in countries that are considered developing countries. One surprise is how widely the fortunes of these developing countries vary. Some have succeeded in developing and have experienced high growth rates. Others have experienced serious economic declines.

Figure 14.1 summarizes the best available measures of growth rates in real gross domestic product (GDP) per person for broad regions and for selected individual countries. The first point shown by Figure 14.1 is that the average product per person has grown faster in the developing countries than it has grown in the industrialized countries since 1990.[1] Yet, even with such a growth advantage, it would still take more

[1]Following the global convention, we use the term *developing countries* to refer to countries with low to moderate levels of income per capita.

The choice of terms to describe countries with low income levels has changed constantly over the past century. The general pattern of evolution has been toward increasingly optimistic, or even euphemistic, terminology in official international discourse. In the mid-20th century commentators could still speak of rich and poor countries. Soon, however, neither the high-income nor the low-income countries would abide such a stark contrast. From the mid-1950s to the mid-1960s, it was generally acceptable to speak of *underdeveloped countries* or *less developed countries*. With time, however, even terms like these were viewed as condescending.

From the 1960s through the 1980s, another attractive alternative presented itself. The *Third World* was a handy and relatively judgment-free way to contrast the low- and middle-income countries of the noncommunist world with the high-income market economies (First World) and the communist bloc (Second World). But in 1989–1991 the Second World vanished with the breakup of the communist bloc and the Soviet Union. Without a Second World, what does *Third World* mean? These formerly communist countries became the *transition economies,* and they are now part of the set of developing countries.

Diplomatic practice has retreated to the relatively benign term *developing country*. Few are bothered by two curious implications of this term: (1) that the high-income "developed" countries are no longer developing and (2) that countries whose incomes are dropping are "developing" if and only if their incomes are already low. Another name for developing countries is *emerging economies,* used especially for their emerging financial markets.

FIGURE 14.1   Real Growth Rates, 1990–2012, and Levels of Income per Capita, 2012

Region or Nation	Annual Growth Rate in per Capita GDP, 1990–2012	Per Capita GDP, 2012 (at international U.S. dollar prices)
Industrialized Countries	**1.4**	**40,571**
United States	1.5	51,749
Australia	1.8	43,818
Germany	1.4	42,700
Canada	1.3	41,298
United Kingdom	1.7	35,722
Japan	0.8	35,618
Developing Countries	**3.0**	**7,303**
European and Central Asian countries	1.8	12,282
Latin American and Caribbean countries	1.7	12,673
Arab countries	2.1	10,005
East Asian and Pacific countries	7.5	7,836
South Asian countries	4.3	3,506
Sub-Saharan African countries	0.9	2,356
Saudi Arabia	1.7	31,214
Russia	0.8	23,589
Poland	3.7	22,783
Chile	3.8	21,468
Turkey	2.4	18,551
Romania	1.9	18,063
Mexico	1.2	16,426
Mauritius	3.5	14,902
Venezuela	0.9	13,267
Brazil	1.6	11,716
South Africa	0.9	11,021
Thailand	3.5	9,660
China	9.4	9,083
Ukraine	−1.0	7,298
Indonesia	3.3	4,876
Philippines	1.9	4,339
India	4.8	3,870
Vietnam	5.5	3,787
Pakistan	1.8	2,741
Nigeria	2.1	2,620
Tajikistan	−2.0	2,192
Ghana	3.0	2,014
Bangladesh	3.7	1,851
Uganda	3.3	1,330
Congo, Democratic Republic of	−2.7	415

Note: Measures of gross domestic product per capita adjusted for purchasing power parity (at international dollar prices) are better than the often-cited estimates of average dollar incomes based on exchange-rate conversions. The purchasing power parity estimates reflect the ability to buy a broad range of goods and services at the prices prevailing in each country, whereas using exchange rates to convert other-currency values into U.S. dollars misleads by reflecting only the international prices of goods that are heavily traded between countries. As a rule, comparisons based on exchange-rate conversions overstate the relative poverty of low-income countries by failing to reflect the cheapness of their nontraded services. For more on purchasing power parity, see Chapter 19.

Sources: World Bank, *World Development Indicators.*

than a century for the developing countries to catch up with the average per capita income in the industrialized countries.

The most striking pattern shown in Figure 14.1, however, is the wide disparity in growth rates among the developing countries. Some are achieving supergrowth, while some have suffered declining income levels since 1990. Incomes have tended to grow fastest in East Asia. The "Four Tigers" (South Korea, Taiwan, Singapore, and Hong Kong) have grown so quickly over the past two decades that they now have relatively high incomes. South Korea's per capita GDP is about $30,000 and those of the other three Tigers are even higher. Several other countries in East Asia also achieved high growth rates, including China and Vietnam. At the rate achieved in 1990–2012, China's per capita income doubles in less than eight years.

However, in one-seventh of the developing countries for which we have data, income per person declined between 1990 and 2012. Most are countries in Africa and countries in Central and Eastern Europe and Central Asia that are making a transition from central planning to a market-based economy. The gaps in growth rates are much wider among developing countries than among high-income countries.

Why are the fortunes of developing countries so different, with some growing rapidly while others stay poor? Do differences in their trade policies play a role? Are there lessons about trade policy to be learned by studying what the supergrowing *newly industrializing countries (NICs)* did that countries with stagnating or declining incomes did not? This chapter reveals some clear answers and some still-unresolved questions about the trade-policy options for developing countries.

WHICH TRADE POLICY FOR DEVELOPING COUNTRIES?

Trade is important for developing countries. Exports of goods and services on average are about 37 percent of GDP in developing countries. (For developed countries exports are about 28 percent of GDP on average.) Developing countries are the source of about 46 percent of all world exports. About 42 percent of exports by developing countries go to industrialized countries, and these are about 38 percent of industrial-country imports.

What role can trade and trade policy play in development? How can trade and trade policy be used to boost incomes and economic growth in poor countries? Many developing countries have comparative advantages based on land (usually with a tropical climate) and in various natural resources "in the ground." Exploiting these comparative advantages would lead to exports of foods, fuels, and other primary products. Developing countries also generally have a comparative advantage based on less-skilled labor. This abundant labor could be used in combination with the land and natural resources in producing primary commodities, or it could be used in the production of less-skilled-labor-intensive manufactures. Developing countries could also seek to develop more advanced manufacturing industries using infant industry policies.

What should the government of, say, Ghana do about imports and exports if it is determined to reverse the economic stagnation that has held down the living standards of its people? To supplement the greater task of reforming its whole economy, Ghana has these basic trade-policy choices:

1. A trade policy that accepts and exploits the country's comparative advantages in *land and natural resources.* For Ghana this means encouraging greater exports of cocoa, coffee, gold, and other *primary products,* but offering no encouragement to industrial development by restricting imports or encouraging exports of manufactured products.

2. A trade policy that attempts to enhance the gains from exporting *primary products* by *raising the world prices* of these products. If the country's exports of a product are large enough, the country could use an *export tax* in a way that is similar to the nationally optimal import tariff of Chapter 8. If the country cannot accomplish much by itself, it could organize or join an *international cartel.* For Ghana, this means taxing exports of cocoa or organizing a cartel of cocoa producers or coffee producers.

3. A policy that taxes and restricts imports to protect and subsidize *new industries* serving the *domestic market.* For Ghana, this might mean forcing Ghanaians to buy more expensive domestic steel, televisions, and airline services. If the strategy nurtures infant industries successfully, firms in these industries eventually can compete at world prices.

4. A trade policy that encourages the development of *new industries* whose products can be readily *exported.* Most of these new industries would make manufactured products that exploit the country's comparative advantage in *less-skilled labor.* For Ghana, the new export production would probably be textiles, clothing, or the assembly of electrical products.

A developing country today does indeed face this choice alone, for the most part, without much international help other than negotiated trade liberalizations like the Uruguay Round.

In choosing a trade policy, should a developing country just follow the trade-policy guidelines laid out in Chapters 8 through 11? Or are developing countries so different that they need a separate trade-policy analysis? The basic answer is that the trade policy conclusions of Chapters 8 through 11 do apply to all countries, whether industrialized or developing. The pros and cons of restricting or subsidizing trade are the same, and the specificity rule still compels us to consider alternatives to trade policy when trade is not the source of the development problem. All that is different in this chapter is the degree of emphasis put on certain points.

Developing countries are different in that they face certain challenges that are less formidable, though still present, in a developed economy. These challenges fall into two categories:

1. *Capital markets work less efficiently in developing countries.* A defining characteristic of a lower-income country is that there are more barriers to the lending of money to the most productive uses. As a result, good projects must overcome a higher cost of capital (interest rate) than the rate at which capital is available to less promising sectors. One underlying reason is that property rights are less clearly defined, holding back the willingness to invest in new assets.

2. Similarly, *labor markets work less efficiently in developing countries.* The wage gaps between expanding and declining sectors are greater than those in higher-income countries. The wider wage gaps are an indirect clue that some labor is being kept from moving to its most productive use.

These differences imply some special tasks for the government of a developing country. There is a case for considering which sectors to protect or subsidize or give cheap loans to, if the government cannot quickly eliminate the barriers to efficient capital and labor markets. The government must also decide whether it is realistic to try to change the nation's comparative advantage, for instance, by increasing its investment in education and health care to expand the country's endowment of human skills. The shift from central planning to a market economy has required yet other policy decisions, as discussed in the box "Special Challenges of Transition."

We now explore the alternatives for trade policy for a developing country in the order that we presented them for Ghana: focus on exporting primary products, use export taxes or international cartels to influence the world prices of these primary products, use import protection to develop new manufacturing industries, or encourage the development of export-oriented new manufacturing industries.

ARE THE LONG-RUN PRICE TRENDS AGAINST PRIMARY PRODUCERS?

It seems natural that developing countries export primary products (agriculture, forestry, fuels, and minerals), and these are often called *traditional exports.* The majority of developing countries get half or more of their export revenues from primary products. Many developing countries have exports concentrated in one or a few products like petroleum, coffee, cotton, gold, sugar, timber, diamonds, and bauxite/aluminum.

A recurring idea is that developing countries' growth is held back by relying on exports of primary products. In the 1950s, Raul Prebisch and others argued that developing countries are hurt by a downward trend (and instability) in primary-product prices. International markets, ran the argument, distribute income unfairly. Since developing countries are net exporters of primary products, they are trapped into declining incomes relative to incomes in the industrialized world.[2]

Does the fear of falling prices sound reasonable? Economic analysis shows that there are at least two major forces depressing, and at least two forces raising, the trend in the prices of primaries relative to manufactures.

The relative price of primary products is depressed by Engel's law and synthetic substitutes.

---

[2]Be careful not to assume, as many discussions imply, that there is a tight link between being a developing country and being an exporter of primary products. Overall, the developing countries are only moderate net exporters of primary products and import significant amounts of them from North America, Australia, and New Zealand. And their comparative advantage in primary products varies greatly. Some developing countries (e.g., Nigeria) export mostly primary products, while others (e.g., South Korea) export almost no primary products and are heavily dependent on importing them.

Case Study   Special Challenges of Transition

In 1989, a massive transition from central planning to market economies began in the formerly socialist countries of Central and Southeastern Europe. With the breakup of the Soviet Union in 1991, the former Soviet Union countries joined this transition. This is the most dramatic episode of economic liberalization in history. What role have changing policies toward international trade played in the transition?

Prior to 1989–1991, central planning by each government directed the economies in these countries. National self-sufficiency was a policy goal. Imports were used to close gaps in the plan, and a state bureaucracy controlled exports and imports. When trade was necessary, the countries favored trade among themselves and strongly discouraged trade with outside countries. They tended to use bilateral barter trade, with lists of exports and imports for each pair of countries. The trade pattern had the Soviet Union specializing in exporting oil and natural gas (at prices well below world prices) and other countries exporting industrial and farm products.

As the transition began, these countries had a legacy of poor decision-making under central planning, including overdevelopment of heavy industries (like steel and defense), outdated technology, environmental problems, and little established trade with market economies. They needed to remove state control of transactions and undertake a major reorganization of production.

Transition involves accomplishing three challenging tasks: (1) shifting to competitive markets and market-determined prices, with a new process of resource allocation; (2) establishing private ownership, with privatization of state businesses; and (3) establishing a legal system, with contract laws and property rights. For success, the transition process must

- *Impose discipline on firms inherited* from the era of central planning.

- *Provide encouragement for new firms* that are not dependent on the government.

Opening the economy to international trade and direct investments by foreign firms can be part of both the discipline (through the competition provided by imports) and the encouragement (through access to new export markets and to foreign technology and know-how).

Domestic and international reforms usually advanced together in a transition country, and success requires a consistent combination of reforms. We can identify several different groups of countries that pursued reforms in different ways and at different speeds.

The Central European countries (Czech Republic, Hungary, Poland, Slovakia, and Slovenia), the Baltic countries (Estonia, Latvia, and Lithuania), and the Southeastern European countries (Albania, Bosnia, Bulgaria, Croatia, Macedonia, Montenegro, Romania, and Serbia) pursued strong, rapid liberalizations (except for Bosnia, Serbia, and Montenegro, which were involved in fighting). As we discussed in Chapter 12, the Central European and Baltic countries joined the European Union in 2004, Bulgaria Romania joined in 2007, and Croatia joined in 2013.

The members of the Commonwealth of Independent States (CIS, the countries that were formerly part of the Soviet Union, excluding the Baltic countries) have instead followed paths of less liberalization. Three countries, Belarus, Turkmenistan, and Uzbekistan, continue to resist enacting reforms. The other CIS countries (Armenia, Azerbaijan, Georgia, Kazakhstan, Kyrgyz Republic, Moldova, Russia, Tajikistan, and Ukraine) enacted partial reforms that were adopted slowly over time and that sometimes were reversed.

How do trade patterns evolve during transition? One pressure is clear, toward rapid growth of imports, especially consumer goods, based on pent-up demand. Transition countries must export to pay for their rising imports, and Western Europe and other industrialized countries are crucial as major markets for expanding their exports. However, exporting to demanding customers in the competitive markets of the industrialized countries was not going to be easy. Under central planning these countries had major deficiencies in their products and businesses, including poor product quality, lack of marketing capabilities, and lack of trade financing.

How successful have the transition countries been in reorienting their trade patterns? By 1998 the Central European, Baltic, and Southeastern European countries on average were selling over 60 percent of their exports to buyers in industrialized countries. Rapid and deep liberalizations, along with favorable geographic location close to the markets of Western Europe, have facilitated the shift by these countries to a desirable export pattern. They increased their exports of light manufactured goods like textiles, clothing, and footwear. They also used their low-cost skilled labor to expand export of such products as vehicles and machinery.

In contrast, most CIS countries did not reorient their exports much, and on average only about a quarter of their exports went to industrialized countries in the late 1990s. Many CIS countries resisted trade liberalizations and continued to produce low-quality manufactured products that could not be exported outside the region. As of early 2014, only 7 of the 12 CIS countries had become members of the World Trade Organization.

How does all of this combine to determine the success of economic transition? One broad indicator is the growth or decline of domestic production (real GDP). In the beginning transition is likely to cause a recession, as business practices and economic relationships are disrupted. Only after reforms begin to take hold can the economy begin to grow. This process is like that of the shift from no trade to free international trade. As we saw beginning in Chapter 2, the gains from opening to trade are based largely on disrupting previous patterns of production and consumption activities.

The evidence indicates that the depth and speed of reforms matter for the success of transition. In addition, as with developing countries generally, we see greater success for those countries adopting more open and outward-oriented trade policies.

The fast and deep reformers in Central and Southeastern Europe suffered through early-transition recessions that were not that deep and not that long. The recessions in the Baltic countries were somewhat longer and somewhat deeper. Then, starting between 1992 and 1996, each of these countries has generally had substantial and sustained growth.

The nine partial-reform and less open CIS countries have broadly performed the worst, even compared with the three nonreform CIS countries. Most partial-reform CIS countries experienced deep early-transition recessions, and three (including Russia) did not return to sustained growth until 1998 or later. They seemed to be caught in a trap in which special interests, oligarchs, and insiders who benefit from the partial reforms gain the political power to block or slow further reform. One advantage of speed in reform is that the reforms are enacted and the increased international trade and greater market competition impose discipline and offer encouragement, before such special interest groups have time to coalesce and exert their power.

DISCUSSION QUESTION
Based on the international economics of the situation, should a country like Ukraine strengthen its orientation toward the customs union that includes Russia and several other CIS countries or reorient itself more toward the European Union?

1. *Engel's law.* In the long run, per capita incomes rise. As they rise, demand shifts toward luxuries—goods for which the income elasticity of demand (percent rise in quantity demanded/percent rise in income causing the change in demand) is greater than 1. At the same time, the world's demand shifts away from staples—goods for which the income elasticity of demand is less than 1. The 19th-century German economist Ernst Engel (not Friedrich Engels) discovered what has become known as Engel's law: The income elasticity of demand for food is less than 1 (i.e., food is a staple). Engel's law is the most durable law in economics that does not follow from definitions or axioms. It means trouble for food producers in a prospering world. If the world's supply expanded at the exact same rate for all products, the relative price of foods would go on dropping because Engel's law says that demand would keep shifting (relatively) away from food toward luxuries.

2. *Synthetic substitutes.* Another force depressing the relative prices of primary products is the development of new human-made substitutes for these natural materials. The more technology advances, the more we are likely to discover ways to replace minerals and other raw materials. The most dramatic case is the development of synthetic rubber around the time of World War I, which ruined the incomes of rubber producers in Brazil, Malaysia, and other countries. Another case is the development of synthetic fibers, which has lowered demand for cotton and wool.

On the other hand, two other basic forces tend to raise the relative prices of primary products:

1. *Nature's limits.* Primary products use land, water, mineral deposits, and other limited natural resources. As population and incomes expand, the natural inputs become increasingly scarce, other things being equal. Nature's scarcity eventually raises the relative price of primary products, which use natural resources more intensively than do manufactures.

2. *Relatively slow productivity growth in the primary sector.* For several centuries productivity has advanced more slowly in agriculture, mining, and other primary sectors than in manufacturing. A reason is the tendency for cost-cutting breakthroughs in knowledge to be more important in manufacturing than in primaries. Slow productivity advance translates into a slower relative advance of supply curves in primary-product markets than in manufacturing markets, and therefore a rising relative price of primaries (or a falling relative price of manufactures), other things being equal.

So we have two tendencies that depress the relative price of primary products, and we have two that raise it. How does the tug-of-war work out in the long run? Figure 14.2 summarizes the experience since 1900.

It depends on when you look at the data and how far back into history you look. Studying Figure 14.2A, we can understand why the fear of falling relative primary prices was greatest in the 1950s (when Prebisch's argument achieved popularity) and the 1980s. Those were periods of falling primary prices. On the other hand, little was written about falling primary prices just before World War I, the historical heyday of high prices for farm products and other raw materials. Nor was there much discussion

FIGURE 14.2

The Relative Price of Primary Products, 1900–2013

Sources: Grilli and Yang (1988), updated using information on prices of primary products from International Monetary Fund, *International Financial Statistics,* and information on the unit values of manufactured-good exports from Pfaffenzeller et al. (2007), and United Nations Commodity Trade Statistics, *International Trade Statistics Yearbook, 2012.*

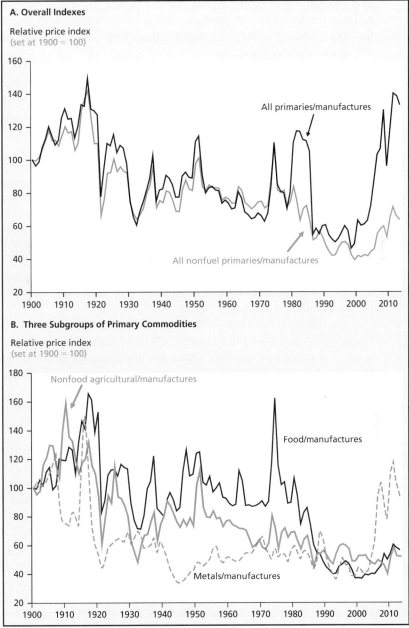

A. Overall Indexes

Relative price index (set at 1900 = 100)

All primaries/manufactures

All nonfuel primaries/manufactures

B. Three Subgroups of Primary Commodities

Relative price index (set at 1900 = 100)

Nonfood agricultural/manufactures

Food/manufactures

Metals/manufactures

For each commodity group, the relative price index is the ratio of the dollar-price index for the indicated primary products to the dollar-price index for exports of manufactures by industrialized countries.

of depressed prices during World War II, the Korean War of 1950–1953, the boom in primary-product prices in the early 1970s, or the run-up in commodity prices during the 2000s. During such times, many writers revived the Malthusian arguments about the limits to planet Earth.

To stand back from the volatile swings in commodity prices, let's look over as long a period as possible. For Figure 14.2, we can scan the period 1900–2013, though following some price series back to 1870 would tell a similar story. For the top panel, we also have to allow for the very large increase in energy prices since 1999, which causes a divergence between the relative price of all primary products and the relative price of nonfuel primary products at the end of the time period.

Figure 14.2 shows a fairly clear long-term trend. For the top panel, we can see that the general trend for relative nonfuel primary-product prices is downward. Statistically, if we fit the best trend line to the data over this entire time period, we find that these prices are declining at about 0.8 percent per year. (For all primary products, including energy fuels, the general trend is also downward, but the spike since the late 1990s pulls the trend line up somewhat. Statistically, the best trend line shows a price decline of about 0.4 percent per year.) Somehow, Engel's law and the technological biases toward replacing primary products have outrun nature's limits and the relative slowness of productivity growth in primary sectors. (Or, in shorthand, Prebisch outran Malthus.)

Some commodities have declined in price more seriously than others. The price of rubber snapped downward between 1910 and 1920 and has never really bounced back since. The relative prices of wool, cocoa, aluminum, rice, cotton, and sugar declined by more than half during the 20th century. In contrast, the relative prices of lamb, timber, and beef more than doubled.

While the net downward trend in primary prices stands as a tentative conclusion, there are two biases in the available measures, like those presented in Figure 14.2.

1. *The fall in transport costs.* The available data tend to be gathered at markets in the industrial countries. Yet technological improvements in transportation have been great enough to reduce the share of transport costs in those final prices in London, New York, or Tokyo. That has left more and more of the final price back in the hands of the primary-product exporters. Quantifying this known change would tilt the trend in the prices received by producers toward a flatter, less downward trend.

2. *Faster unmeasured quality change in manufactures.* We are using long runs of price data on products that have been getting better over time. Quality improvements (including those in the form of new products) are thought to have been more impressive in manufactures (and services) than in primary products. So what might look like a rise in the relative price of manufactures might be just a rise in their relative quality, with no trend in the relative price for given quality. This data problem is potentially serious, given that many 20th-century data have, for example, followed the prices of machinery exports per ton of exports, as if a ton of today's computers were the same thing as a ton of old electric motors.

When all is said and done, the relative price of primary products may have declined as much as 0.8 percent a year since 1900 (as in Figure 14.2), or there could have been almost no trend. There is a weak case for worrying about being an exporter of agricultural or extractive products on price-trend grounds.

INTERNATIONAL CARTELS TO RAISE PRIMARY-PRODUCT PRICES

Perhaps the developing-country producers of primary products can take actions to turn the price trends in their favor. Perhaps the primary-product exporters can become more powerful if they cooperate with each other, using international cartels or other types of concerted action.

The OPEC Victories

History records many attempts at international cartels (international agreements to restrict competition among sellers). The greatest seizure of monopoly power in world history was the price-raising triumph of the Organization of Petroleum Exporting Countries (OPEC)[3] in 1973–1974 and again in 1979–1980.

A chain of events in late 1973 revolutionized the world oil economy. In a few months' time, the 12 members of OPEC effectively quadrupled the dollar price of crude oil, from $2.59 to $11.65 a barrel. Oil-exporting countries became rich almost overnight. The industrial oil-consuming countries sank into their deepest recession since the 1930s. The relative price of oil (what the price of a barrel of oil could buy in terms of manufactured exports from industrial nations) tripled.

The sequel was a plateau of OPEC prosperity, a further jump, and then growing signs of weakness. From 1974 to 1978, the relative price of oil dipped by about a sixth, but stayed much higher than it had been at any time before 1973. Next came the second wave of OPEC price hikes, the second "oil shock," in 1979–1980. Led by the Iranian Revolution and growing panic among oil buyers, the relative oil price more than doubled. In the mid-1980s, however, OPEC weakened. The relative price of oil dropped suddenly in late 1985, from four to five times the old (pre-1973) real price in 1980–1984 to less than two times the old price for 1986–1989.

The tale of oil and OPEC in the 1970s and 1980s is one of two dramatic cartel victories and a subsequent retreat. The victories and the retreat both need explanation.

First the victories. The oil shocks of 1973–1974 and 1979–1980 were not the result of a failure of supply or exhaustion of earth's available resources. The world's "proved reserves" of known and usable oil were growing faster than world oil consumption. Nor were the costs of oil extraction rising much.

The 1973–1974 and 1979–1980 oil price jumps were human-made. The key was that world demand was growing far faster than *non-OPEC* supplies. Oil discoveries had been very unevenly distributed among countries. The share of OPEC countries in world crude oil production rose to over 50 percent by 1972. Furthermore,

---

[3]OPEC was created by a treaty among five countries—Iran, Iraq, Kuwait, Saudi Arabia, and Venezuela—in 1960. Since that time, the following countries have joined: Qatar (1961), Libya (1962), United Arab Emirates (1967), Algeria (1969), Nigeria (1971), and Angola (2007). Ecuador joined in 1973, withdrew in 1992, and rejoined in 2007. Indonesia joined in 1962 and withdrew in 2009. Gabon joined in 1975 and withdrew in 1995.

OPEC's share of proved reserves—roughly, its share of future production—was over two-thirds.

By the early 1970s, the United States was for the first time becoming vulnerable to pressure from oil-exporting countries. Largely immune to oil threats in earlier Middle East crises, the United States found itself importing a third of its oil consumption, part of it from Arab countries, by 1973. With their growing importance in world production, and with growing U.S. reliance on oil imports, OPEC countries were able to create a scramble among buyers to pay higher prices for oil in 1973 and again in 1979.

Classic Monopoly as an Extreme Model for Cartels

How big could the cartel opportunity be? That is, if a group of nations or firms were to form a cartel, as OPEC did, what is the greatest amount of gain they could reap at the expense of their buyers and world efficiency? If all of the cartel members could agree on simply maximizing their collective gain, they would behave as though they were a perfectly unified profit-maximizing monopolist. Because a commodity like oil is fungible, they would probably not be able to discriminate by setting different prices to different foreign buyers (except for standard distinctions by quality that we can safely ignore here). The cartel members acting as a monopoly would try to find the price level that would maximize the gap between their total export sales revenues and their total costs of producing exports. When cutting output back to the level of demand yielded by their optimal price, they would take care to shut down their most costly production units (e.g., oil wells) and keep in operation only those with the lowest operating costs.

Figure 14.3 portrays a monopoly or cartel that has managed to extract maximum profits from its buyers. To understand what price and output yield that highest level of profits, and what limits those profits, we must first understand that the optimal price lies above the price that perfect competition would yield, yet below the price that would discourage all sales.

If perfect competition reigned in the world oil market, the marginal-cost curve in Figure 14.3 would also be the supply curve for oil exports. Competitive equilibrium would be at point *C*, where the marginal cost of extra oil exports has risen to meet $40, the amount that the extra oil is worth to buyers (as shown by the demand curve).

The cartel members want to set a price higher than the competitive price, but their pricing power is limited by the negative slope of the demand curve for the cartel's product. This point is clear if we just consider the extreme case of a prohibitive price markup. If the cartel were foolish enough to push the price to $195 a barrel in Figure 14.3, it would lose all of its export business, as shown at point *A*. The handsome markup to $195 would be worthless because nobody would be paying it to the cartel. Thus, the cartel's best price must be well below the prohibitive price.

The cartel members could find their most profitable price by using the model of monopoly: The highest possible profits are those corresponding to the level of sales at which the marginal-revenue curve intersects the marginal-cost curve, at point *F* in Figure 14.3. These maximum profits would be reaped by selling 30 million barrels of export sales a day, at a price of $100 per barrel. The monopoly profits will be ($100 − $5) × 30 million barrels = $2.85 billion a day. If the cartel had not

FIGURE 14.3

A Cartel
as a Profit-
Maximizing
Monopoly

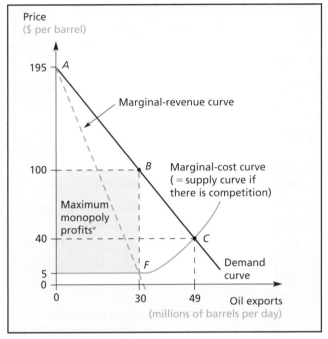

*Before subtracting any fixed costs.

If a cartel were so tightly disciplined as to be a pure monopoly, it would maximize profits according to the familiar monopoly model. It would not keep prices so low and output so high as to behave like a competitive industry, at point *C*. Why not? Because the slightest price increase, starting at point *C*, would give it net gains. Instead, the cartel would set price as high, with quantity demanded and output as low, as shown at point *B*. At this level of output (30 million barrels a day), profit is maximized because the marginal revenue gained from a bit more output raising and price cutting just balances the marginal cost of the extra output.

been formed, competition would have limited the profits of its members to the area below the $40 price line and above the marginal-cost curve. Given the demand curve and the marginal-cost curve, the profit gained by pushing price and quantity to point *B* is the best the cartel can do.

The cartel price that is optimal for its members is not optimal for the world, of course. For the 30 million barrels per day, the extra cartel profits above the $40 price line are just a redistribution of income from buying countries to the cartel, with no net gain or loss for the world. However, the cartel causes net world losses by curtailing oil exports that would be worth more to buyers around the world than those exports cost the cartel members themselves to produce. The world net loss from the cartel is represented in Figure 14.3 by the area *BCF* (which equals a little more than $900 million a day, as drawn in Figure 14.3). This area shows that what the cartel is costing the world as a whole is the gap between what buyers would have willingly paid for the extra 19 million barrels a day, as shown by the height of the demand curve, and the height of the marginal-cost curve between 30 million barrels and 49 million barrels.

The Limits to and Erosion of Cartel Power

How high is the cartel's profit-maximizing price if the cartel is functioning at full effectiveness? The theory of cartels provides some rules.[4] The first two rules follow from the monopoly model:

- The higher the marginal cost of production, the higher the price. In Figure 14.3, consider the effect on the monopoly price if the entire marginal-cost curve is higher than that shown.
- The higher the elasticity of demand, the lower the price. If demand is elastic, buyers easily find other ways of spending their money if the product price rises much. In Figure 14.3, consider the effect on the monopoly price of a different demand curve, one through point C and flatter (more elastic) than the curve shown.

However, even a well-functioning cartel usually does not control all of the world's production. If it doesn't, then we have two more rules:

- The larger the share of world production controlled by the cartel, the higher the price. Controlling more of the world production effectively increases the demand for the cartel's production (rather than having this demand lost to outside producers).
- The larger the elasticity of supply of noncartel producers, the lower the price. The elasticity of noncartel supply acts in the same way that the elasticity of demand does. The cartel refrains from raising the price too much because doing so results in too large a loss of its own sales.

These rules also suggest forces that work increasingly against cartels *over time*. When the cartel is first set up, it may well enjoy low elasticities and a high market share. Yet its very success in raising price is likely to set four anticartel trends in motion: sagging demand, new competing supply, declining market share, and cheating.

Sagging Demand

First, the higher price will make buying countries look for new ways to avoid importing the cartel's product. If the search for substitutes has any success at all, imports of the buying countries will drop over time for any given cartel price. These countries' long-run demand curve for imports of the product is more elastic than their short-run demand curve. This happened to OPEC. As theory predicts, and as some OPEC oil ministers had feared, the oil-importing countries slowly came up with ways to conserve on oil use, such as more fuel-efficient cars.

New Competing Supply

Second, the initial cartel success will accelerate the search for additional supplies in noncartel countries. If the cartel product is an agricultural crop, such as sugar or coffee, the cartel's price hike will cause farmers in other countries to shift increasing amounts of land, labor, and funds from other crops into sugar or coffee. If the cartel product is a depletable mineral resource, such as oil or copper, noncartel countries will

---

[4]Appendix D presents the mathematical formula for the optimal cartel price.

respond to the higher price by redoubling their explorations in search of new reserves. If the noncartel countries have any luck at all, their competing supply will become increasingly elastic with time. Again, that happened to OPEC—other countries discovered new oil at a faster rate.

Declining Market Share

Third, the cartel's world market share will fall over time. To raise the product's price without piling up ever-rising unsold inventories, the cartel must cut its output and sales. Since nonmembers will be straining to raise their output and sales, the cartel's share of the market will drop even if all of its members cooperate solidly. OPEC's share of world oil production fell from over half in the early 1970s to less than a third in 1985.

Cheating

Theory and experience add a fourth reason for a decline in cartel power—the incentive for members to cheat on the cartel agreement.

To see why, suppose that you are a member of the successful oil export cartel shown back in Figure 14.3. As a typical cartel member, you have enough oil reserves to pump and sell more than your agreed output (OPEC calls this your production quota) for as long in the future as you need to plan. Raising your output above your production quota might cost you only, say, $6 a barrel at the margin. Buyers are willing to pay close to $100 for each barrel you sell if the other cartel members are faithfully holding down their output. Why not attract some extra buyers to you by shaving your price just a little bit below $100, say, to $98? You can do so in the hope that your individual actions will not cause the cartel price to drop much, if at all. Theory says that this incentive to cheat tends to undermine the whole cartel. Perhaps some large members can keep the cartel effective for a while by drastically cutting their own outputs to offset the extra sales from the cheaters. Their aggregate size determines how long they can hold out.

OPEC members cheated on the cartel, even openly, just as theory would predict. Up to the mid-1980s, the largest producer, Saudi Arabia, had to hold the cartel together by cutting its production while others cheated. Then the Saudis themselves shifted to a more competitive stance, and the relative price of oil fell dramatically in late 1985.

The usual theory of cartels thus correctly explains why cartel profit margins and profits will erode with time.[5] Yet the theory does not say that cartels are unprofitable or harmless. On the contrary, it underscores the profitability of cartel formation to cartel members. Even a cartel that eventually erodes can bring fortunes to its members.

The Oil Price Increase since 1999

Following the price collapse of 1986, crude oil prices remained rather low (with the exception of a few months in 1990 during the time of Operation Desert Storm action against Iraq). By late 1998 the relative price of oil had fallen back to about its level in 1973. But then oil prices began to rise, from $11 per barrel in late 1998 to $34 per barrel

---

[5]These same reasons also imply that a cartel probably would be wise to charge a lower markup, even at the start, than the markup implied by short-run elasticities of demand and noncartel supply. The higher the initial markup, the faster the erosion of the cartel's market share and the lower the optimal markup that the cartel can charge later on.

in late 2000, and then remained rather flat to the beginning of 2004. Oil prices then climbed, with a price spike in 2007–2008 that had a peak price of over $140 per barrel in June 2008. With the recession that accompanied the global financial and economic crisis, oil prices collapsed to less than $40 per barrel in 2009. As global demand began to increase again, oil prices rose rapidly, moving above $100 per barrel in early 2011.

So, is this the reemergence of OPEC's monopoly power? Only partly. In the late 1990s and early 2000s OPEC did attempt with some success to reduce its production to raise the price. However, much of the price rise seems to reflect the broader dynamics of the industry, dynamics that are based on the competitive aspects of the market. Demand from China and India grew rapidly. Furthermore, the years of rather low oil prices discouraged investment in new crude oil production capabilities, leading to tight supply and a lack of spare production capacity. As a result of the demand increases and capacity limits, oil prices rose well above OPEC price targets in 2008. The big price rise in the mid- and late 2000s looks more like a boom period in a highly cyclical industry than it looks like the planned exercise of market power by the cartel.

Other Primary Products

Do theory and OPEC experience hold out hope for developing countries wanting to make large national gains by joining cartels in other primary products besides oil? Not much. There are good reasons for believing that international cartels would collapse faster, with less interim profit, for the non-oil primary products. For agricultural crops in particular, there is the problem of competing supply. Other countries usually can easily expand the acreage they devote to a given crop.

History agrees with this verdict. Of the 72 commodity cartels set up between the two world wars, only 2 survived past 1945. Of the few dozen set up in the 1970s, only 5 lived as late as 1985: cocoa, coffee, rubber, sugar, and tin. These 5 cartels have been so weak that they have had little effect on commodity markets since 1985.

Given the limits of international cartel power, a developing nation could still tax its own primary-product exports for the sake of economic development. In principle, the strategy could work well. A tax on exports of Nigerian oil, Ghanaian cocoa, or Philippine coconuts could generate revenues for building schools, hospitals, and roads.

Unfortunately, the political economy of some developing countries seems to divert the export-tax revenues away from the most productive uses (as we noted in Chapter 10 when discussing the developing government argument for import tariffs). So it has been with the three examples just imagined. Nigeria's oil revenues are lost in a swollen government bureaucracy and ravenous corruption. For two decades Ghana's cocoa marketing board used its heavy taxation of cocoa farmers to support luxury imports by officials. The Marcos government distributed the Philippine coconut-tax revenues among a handful of Marcos's friends and relatives.

IMPORT-SUBSTITUTING INDUSTRIALIZATION (ISI)

Exporting primary products is a way for many developing countries to use their comparative advantages based on land and natural resources. But reliance on such traditional exports brings risks, including what appear to be slowly declining relative prices of these products and exposure to the wide swings in world prices. Perhaps shifting the emphasis toward developing new industries, especially in manufacturing, is better for countries that want to grow more rapidly. After all, most high-income countries have industrialized.

To develop, officials from many countries have argued, they must cut their reliance on exporting primary products and must adopt government policies allowing industry to grow at the expense of the agricultural and mining sectors. Can this emphasis on industrialization be justified? If so, should it be carried out by restricting imports of manufactures?

The Great Depression caused many countries to turn toward **import-substituting industrialization (ISI).** In the early 1920s and again in the early 1930s, world prices of most primary products plummeted. Although these price declines did not prove that primary exporters were suffering more than industrial countries, it was common to suspect that this was so. Several primary-product-exporting countries, among them Brazil and Australia, launched industrialization at the expense of industrial imports in the 1930s.

The ISI strategy gained additional prestige among newly independent nations in the 1950s and 1960s. This approach soon prevailed in most developing countries whose barriers against manufactured imports came to match those of the most protectionist prewar industrializers. Though many countries have switched toward more pro-trade and export-oriented policies since the mid-1960s, ISI remains an important policy for developing countries.

ISI at Its Best

To see the merits and drawbacks of ISI, let us begin by noting the four main arguments in its favor. If ISI could be fine-tuned to make the most of these arguments, it would be a fine policy indeed.

1. *The infant industry argument* from Chapter 10 returns, with its legitimate emphasis on the economic and social side benefits from industrialization. These side benefits may include gains in technological knowledge and worker skills transcending the individual firm, new attitudes more conducive to growth, and national pride. As we saw in Chapter 10, the economist can imagine other tools more suitable to each of these tasks than import barriers. But in an imperfect world these better options may not be at hand, and protection for an infant modern-manufacturing sector could bring gains.

2. *The developing government argument* from Chapter 10 lends further support to ISI. Suppose that the only way that a government can raise revenues for any kind of economic development is to tax imports and exports. Such taxation can bring gains to a nation whose government cannot mobilize resources for health, education, and so on without taxing trade. ISI is a by-product of such taxation of foreign trade.

3. For a large country, replacing imports can bring better *terms-of-trade effects* than expansion of export industries. Here we return to a theme sounded first in the discussion of "immiserizing growth" in Chapter 7 and again during Chapter 8's discussion of the nationally optimal tariff. Replacing imports with domestic production will, if it has any effect at all on the foreign price of the continuing imports, tend to lower

these prices (excluding the tariff or other import charge) and offer the nation a better bargain. If you can affect the prices at which you trade, wouldn't it be better to expand your supply of import-competing industries, forcing foreigners to sell you the remaining imports at a lower price?

4. Replacing imports of manufactures is a way of using *cheap and convenient market information.* A developing country may lack the expertise to judge just which of the thousands of heterogeneous industrial goods it could best market abroad. But government officials (and private industrialists) have an easy way to find which modern manufactures would sell in their own markets. They need only look at the import figures. Here is a handy menu of goods with proven markets.

Experience with ISI

History and recent economic studies offer four kinds of evidence on the merits of ISI. Casual historical evidence suggests a slightly charitable view, while three kinds of detailed tests support a negative verdict.

In support of ISI, it can be said that today's leading industrial countries protected their industry against import competition earlier, when their growth was first accelerating. The United States, for example, practiced ISI from the Civil War until the end of World War II, when most American firms no longer needed protection against imports. Japan, in the 1950s, launched its drive for leadership in steel, automobiles, and electronics with heavy government protection against imports. When these industries were able to compete securely in world markets, Japan removed its redundant protection against imports into Japan.

Such a casual reading of history is at least correct in its premise: The industrialized countries did at times give import protection to industries that became their export strengths. But it is wrong to infer that most cases of industrial protection nurtured sectors that responded with strong productivity gains. On the contrary, even Japan, like the United States and most other industrialized countries, gave its strongest protection to sectors whose decline was long-lasting. ISI in the earlier history of these countries may well have slowed down their economic growth. Most of the infant industries, in other words, never grew up.

In contrast to the weaknesses of the evidence for ISI, the evidence against it takes three forms that in combination add up to a strong case. The first kind of test casting serious doubt on the merits of ISI is the estimation of its *static effects on national well-being,* using the methods introduced in Chapter 8. A series of detailed country studies quantified the welfare effects of a host of developing-country trade barriers in the 1960s and early 1970s, many of which were designed to promote industrialization. The barriers imposed significant costs on Argentina, Chile, Colombia, Egypt, Ghana, India, Israel, Mexico, Pakistan, the Philippines, South Korea, Taiwan, and Turkey. Only in Malaysia did the import barriers bring a slight gain, here because of a favorable terms-of-trade effect.[6]

By themselves, these standard calculations of welfare costs of trade barriers are vulnerable to the charge of assuming, not proving, that ISI is bad. Such calculations assume that all the relevant effects are captured by measures of consumer and

---

[6]See Balassa (1971), Bhagwati and Krueger (1973–1976), and Choksi et al. (1991).

producer surplus, without allowing protection any chance to lower cost curves as it is imagined to do in the infant industry case. It would be fair to demand firmer proof.

A second kind of test looks at what happens when a country *changes its trade-policy orientation* toward manufactures, away from restricting imports (ISI), and toward championing exports. Here there were two dramatic early cases. Until the late 1950s, Taiwan used ISI but then switched to a policy that encouraged exports. It subsequently achieved growth rates of about 10 percent per year. South Korea used ISI until policy reforms in the early 1960s increased its incentives for exports and lowered its import barriers. Its growth rate increased to about 10 percent per year. Hong Kong and Singapore also used policies that encouraged exports and achieved high growth rates. Other countries have achieved substantial effects. In the case of Ghana, the ISI strategy was part of a larger heavy hand of government that turned early growth into a 42 percent decline of Ghana's living standards over the decade 1974–1984. The country was saddled with costly industrial white elephants that never became efficient. Only after partial reforms that included a partial liberalization of trade policy did Ghana regain positive economic growth.

A third kind of test *compares growth rates of countries practicing ISI with growth rates of countries using policies that emphasize exporting.* The 1987 *World Development Report* presented the results of the World Bank's study of growth rates in 41 countries, which were placed into four categories according to their trade policy: strongly outward-oriented, moderately outward-oriented, moderately inward-oriented, and strongly inward-oriented. Hong Kong, South Korea, and Singapore followed strongly outward-oriented policies, with low trade barriers and some use of export subsidies. The strongly inward-oriented countries used high trade barriers. These included Argentina, Bangladesh, Chile (up to 1973), India, and Turkey (to 1973).

In the two time periods that the World Bank examined, 1963–1973 and 1973–1985, the average growth rate of real GDP per person was highest for the three countries with strongly outward-oriented trade policies (6.9 percent and 5.9 percent per year, respectively). The average growth rate in the countries with strongly inward-oriented trade policies was lowest in both periods (1.6 percent and −0.1 percent per year, respectively). An update in the 1994 *World Development Report* found that this pattern also held for the time period 1980–1992 (a 6.2 percent annual growth rate for strongly outward-oriented countries and a −0.4 percent annual growth rate for strongly inward-oriented countries).

In a 2002 study, the World Bank contrasted the experience of developing countries that have increased their integration into world markets since 1980 with the experience of other countries. The *newly globalizing developing countries,* as the World Bank calls them, are countries that

- had relatively low involvement in international trade and high tariffs in 1980 but then
- greatly increased their international trade (measured by the increase in the ratio of exports and imports to national GDP) and
- substantially lowered their tariff rates.

The 24 newly globalizing developing countries had a total population of 3 billion and included Argentina, Bangladesh, Brazil, China, Colombia, India, Nicaragua,

Thailand, and Uruguay. The other developing countries had a total population of about 2 billion and included many African countries and countries of the former Soviet Union. Most of these other developing countries concentrate on exporting primary products.

The World Bank found that the newly globalizing developing countries achieved average growth rates of GDP per person of 3.5 percent during the 1980s and 5.0 percent during the 1990s. These average growth rates were above their average annual growth rates in the 1960s (1.4 percent) and 1970s (2.9 percent). Their average growth rates in the 1980s and 1990s were also higher than the average growth rates of other developing countries (0.8 percent and 1.4 percent, respectively) and of the industrialized countries (2.3 percent and 2.2 percent, respectively). The differences between the newly globalizing and other developing countries do not seem to reflect favorable initial economic conditions for the new globalizers. In 1980 the people in the two groups had comparable average levels of education, and the newly globalizing countries on average had somewhat lower incomes per capita.

Such direct comparisons (as in these several World Bank studies) between *countries practicing* or *adopting freer-trade regimes* and *countries practicing a variant of ISI or resisting further liberalization of their trade policies* have the virtue of simplicity: They look directly at the two variables of interest (trade policies and economic growth). Yet here, as always, correlation cannot prove causation. By itself, this kind of evidence against ISI and restricting trade is subject to the suspicion that maybe some other force caused economic growth to be correlated with freer-trade policies. Or perhaps the causation ran the opposite way—perhaps successful growth itself brings freer-trade policies, even though policies departing from free trade helped promote growth. While it is not possible to answer these concerns fully, economists have conducted more complicated tests of the statistical significance of trade policy. After allowing for the effects of other variables such as investment, initial income, and education, the research tends to confirm that ISI-type trade barriers are a negative influence on economic growth.

If theory suggests that ISI can work well, why does experience make it look like a bad idea? There is no direct contradiction because theory only asserted that ISI *can* be better than free trade under certain conditions. It just so happens that those conditions have not held since the early 1960s. The theory failed, above all, in the assumption that an informed government tries to maximize national income. Real-world governments are ill-informed, and they lack the power to stop protecting industries that turn out to be inefficient. Worse, many governments have their own self-interest, which conflicts with the goal of maximizing national well-being. Embarking on a policy of ISI has so far not turned any economy into a supergrower like South Korea. More often, the ISI route is the road that turns a South Korea into a North Korea. ISI often results in industries in which domestic firms have high costs and domestic monopoly power and produce products of low quality.

Outward-oriented policies encourage domestic firms to make use of the country's abundant resources, and the firms can use sales into international markets to achieve scale economies. The efforts to succeed in foreign markets also mean that domestic firms face international competitive pressure, so that they are driven to raise product quality and resource productivity. The country can use its rising exports to pay for its rising imports. At the same time, an outward-oriented policy is not enough by itself to produce high growth rates. It must be part of a set of policies that minimize distortions in the economy, that nurture high rates of investment by establishing clear property rights and an impartial system of business law, and that provide such infrastructure as ports, airports, electricity, and communications.

EXPORTS OF MANUFACTURES TO INDUSTRIAL COUNTRIES

Since 1980, developing countries have turned increasingly toward our fourth trade-policy choice, emphasizing new exports of less-skilled-labor-intensive manufactured goods to the industrialized countries. As Figure 14.4 shows, the switch from primary-product exports to manufactured exports gained momentum in the 1980s and continued thereafter. Disillusionment with both primary-product cartels and ISI was probably a factor in the new push.

Is it wise for a developing nation to plan on being able to raise its exports of manufactures to the already industrialized countries? Should Mexico, Ghana, and India follow the example of South Korea, making strategic plans to become major exporters of manufactures? Would the same thing happen without planning, as in the market-directed development of Hong Kong and Taiwan?

For their part, the industrialized countries have not made the task easy. They have, in fact, discriminated against exports of manufactures from developing countries. Nontariff import barriers apply to a greater percentage of goods from developing countries than to goods from other industrial countries. As for tariffs, the rates are in principle nondiscriminatory. Tariff rates differ, however, by type of product. In general, the highest tariff rates among manufactures are those on textiles, apparel, and footwear—the kind of manufactures in which developing countries have their broadest comparative advantage.

Developing countries are thus justified in charging the industrial nations with hypocrisy. The industrial nations have not practiced the policies of free trade and comparative advantage that they have urged on developing countries. Furthermore, the departures of practice from preaching have been greatest on manufactures exported from developing countries. The Doha Round of multilateral trade negotiations is billed by the World Trade Organization as a "development round" in which a major focus will be improving access for the exports of developing countries into markets in both the industrialized countries and other developing countries. As of late 2014, the Doha

FIGURE 14.4 The Changing Mix of Exports from Developing Countries, 1970–2012

	1970	1980	1990	2000	2012
Nonfuel primary products	49.9%	18.7%	18.7%	11.5%	14.6%
Fuels	32.4	61.3	27.5	21.4	28.0
Manufactures	17.4	18.5	52.9	65.5	56.1

Note: Columns do not add to 100% because of a small amount of unclassified exports in each year.

Source: United Nations Conference on Trade and Development, *Handbook of International Trade and Development Statistics,* 1987 and 1995, and United Nations Conference on Trade and Development, UNCTADStat.

Round negotiations were at a standstill. You can watch to see if the round will achieve its vision of expanding trade for development.

Despite some discrimination against their exports, developing countries have been able to break into world markets for their exports of manufactures. One reason is that developing countries have been able to become exporters in standardized manufacturing lines where technological progress has cooled down, such as textiles, tires, and simple electrical appliances. A second reason is that developing countries have become locations for low-cost assembly of more technologically advanced products like computers, with multinational firms from the industrialized countries providing the advanced technology, the components, and the marketing and distribution of the finished products.

A third reason is that barriers against imports of manufactures from developing countries are not all that solid. Consider barriers based on voluntary export restraints, antidumping duties, or countervailing duties. These barriers can limit increases in exports from countries that have already succeeded in establishing their exports to the industrialized countries. But newcomers can gain market access for new manufactured-product exports because they are not hindered by such country-specific barriers. In this way a developing country can gain valuable new export markets, despite the protectionism of the industrialized countries, although there may eventually be limits on how large these export sales can grow.

All in all, betting on exports of manufactures is part of the most promising strategy for most developing countries. And as Figure 14.4 has made clear, the developing countries are relying more and more on this strategy.

Summary

The gaps in living standards are widening among developing countries. Developing countries in East Asia have grown quickly. For a number of poor countries in Africa, average incomes have been declining for several decades. And countries in transition from central planning to market economies experienced large declines in output and income during the early years of transition, with most countries of the former Soviet Union experiencing especially large declines.

Developing countries must decide what trade policies to adopt toward primary-product exports, industrial imports, and industrial exports.

A traditional fear about relying on exports of primary products is that the world market price trends are unfavorable to producers, especially those in developing countries. The evidence shows a downward trend in the relative prices of most primary products, as commonly feared. Two factors lowering the relative price of primary products are Engel's law and the development of modern synthetic substitutes for primary materials. Two opposing forces, which would tend to raise primary-product prices, are natural resource limits and the fact that productivity growth is often slower in the primary sectors than in the rest of the economy.

Joining an international cartel could bring gains to a developing country that exports the cartelized product. The greatest cartel success by far is OPEC's pair of price victories in 1973–1974 and 1979–1980. With all international cartels, even OPEC, success breeds decline. Four forces dictate the speed at which a cartel erodes: the rise in product demand elasticity, the rise in the elasticity of competing supplies, the decline in the share of the cartel in the world market, and the rise in cheating by members of the cartel. Because of supply conditions, it is unlikely that cartels in other primary products could achieve anything close to OPEC's success.

One strategy open to developing countries is that of **import-substituting industrialization (ISI).** It could raise national skill levels, bring terms-of-trade gains, and allow planners to economize on market information (because they can just take industrial imports themselves as a measure of demand that could be captured with the help of protection). Studies of ISI and related policies, however, show that income growth is negatively correlated with antitrade policies like ISI and positively correlated with outward-oriented policies that are closer to free trade.

Another strategy is to concentrate on developing exports of manufactured goods, especially those that are intensive in less-skilled labor. This has been a slowly prevailing trend since the 1960s, though ISI also remains practiced in developing countries. Relying on exports of manufactures has its risks, however. Developing nations have rightly complained about import barriers against their new manufactures erected by the industrialized countries. Such barriers have indeed been higher than the barriers on manufactures traded between industrialized countries. Still, evidence shows that an outward-oriented trade policy encouraging exports of manufactures is part of the most promising strategy for most developing countries.

Key Terms	International cartel	Organization of Petroleum Exporting Countries (OPEC)	Import-substituting industrialization (ISI)

Suggested Reading   Studies of the ISI and outward-oriented strategies are Choksi et al. (1991), Sachs and Warner (1995), Bruton (1998), World Bank (2002a), Panagariya (2004), and Estevadeordal and Taylor (2013). Waugh (2010) explores how extra trade costs for exports from developing countries limit their trade and lower their national incomes.

Grilli and Yang (1988) and Harvey et al. (2010) provide careful examinations of long-run trends in the relative prices of primary products. Gilbert (1996) discusses the failures of international commodity cartels.

The European Bank for Reconstruction and Development issues an annual *Transition Report.* Broadman (2005) examines trade policies in transition countries. World Bank (2002b) summarizes what we learned from the first decade of transition.

Questions and Problems   ✦ 1. List the main pros and cons of taking the import-replacing road to industrialization versus concentrating government aid and private energies on developing new manufacturing exports.

2. Under what conditions would ISI have the greatest chance of being better than any alternative development strategy? What other policies should accompany it?

✦ 3. "The terms of trade move against primary producers in the long run." What is the evidence in support of this proposition? How solid is the evidence?

4. You are an adviser to the government of a country whose exports are mainly a few primary products and whose imports are mainly manufactured products. You are asked to prepare a short report on the forces that are likely to drive the country's terms of trade during the next two decades. What will the main points of your report be?

✦ 5. The United States, China, India, Brazil, and Turkey are forming an international association known as Tobacco's Altruistic Raisers (TAR) to increase the world price of tobacco. TAR's members control 60 percent of world tobacco production. The price elasticity of world demand for tobacco is rather low in the short run but somewhat higher in the long run. The ability of other countries who are not TAR members to increase their production of tobacco is very small for a period of several years; but, with a few years to prepare, other countries could easily expand their tobacco production. You are asked to write a report on the outlook for TAR's success. What will you say in the report?

6. Drawing on material from this chapter and earlier chapters, weigh the pros and cons of restricting and taxing a country's exports of primary products. How could it raise the country's national income? What are the drawbacks of such a policy for a developing country?

✦ 7. Consider Figure 14.3, which shows what a cartel can do if it can act as a monopolist. In Figure 14.3, the cartel supplies the entire world market.

   a. What is the effect on the cartel's profit-maximizing price if a new outside source of supply now develops that can provide 10 million barrels of oil per day at any price above $5 per barrel? Show the effect using the graph. (Hint: With this new outside supply, what is the demand that remains for the cartel's oil?)

   b. Instead of the new outside source described in question *a*, consider instead a new outside source of supply that will provide amounts of oil that vary with the world price, according to the following schedule:

   Outside supply (millions of barrels per day) = (World price − 5)/2

   (For instance, if the world price is $15, the outside supply is 5 million barrels per day.) Show graphically and explain the effect on the cartel's profit-maximizing price of this new outside supply source.

8. In the 1987 World Bank study, India was categorized as having a strongly inward trade policy. During 1970–1990, India's average annual growth rate of real income per capita was about 2 percent. Around 1990, India shifted to an outward-oriented policy. What is your prediction for India's growth rate of income per capita since 1990? Do the data reported in Figure 14.1 support your prediction?

✦ 9. "As long as increasing exports of less-skilled-labor-intensive manufactured products are leading to rising employment and rising real wages for its workers, a developing country has no interest in improving its educational system." Do you agree or disagree? Why?

10. Ukraine has to decide on a trade-policy strategy to go with other reforms for promoting development. Comment on the merits and drawbacks of the following available choices:

   a. Unilaterally taxing its wheat exports.

   b. Forming a wheat-exporting cartel with Argentina, Australia, and Canada, which are also major wheat exporters.

   c. Choosing manufactures it could export (e.g., batteries), giving them a profitable home-market base protected by tariffs, and encouraging exports to other countries at competitive world prices.

◆11. Some developing countries (including Ghana) are encouraging development of local production of basic business services like call centers and data entry, to become an important destination for offshore outsourcing. Which of the four trade policies is most closely related to a national policy to grow this kind of services production? Why?

12. In 2008 India and Vietnam restricted their rice exports to prevent increases in their domestic rice prices, and world rice prices temporarily tripled. In 2011 the government of Thailand, at that time the leading rice-exporting country, implemented a policy to buy locally grown rice and withhold it from the market. The Thai government planned to export the rice at a profit after world rice prices had increased substantially. The actual outcome, as of early 2014, was that world rice prices were essentially unchanged and that Thailand had fallen to being the third-largest rice exporter. What factors probably contributed to the failure of the Thai government's plan?

Chapter Fifteen

Multinationals and Migration: International Factor Movements

In previous chapters we looked at the economic and political battles over international trade in goods and services. International movements of factors of production are often even more controversial, with the debates even more emotional as well. In this chapter we examine two major forms of international factor movements: those that occur through the foreign activities of multinational enterprises and those that occur through the international movement of people. In shifting our attention to international factor flows, we are relaxing the assumption that factors do not move internationally, an assumption that we have used through much of the discussion up to this point. That is, we now recognize that factors of production can and do move between countries in amounts that are often large enough to have economic effects and to grab political attention.

The global activities of multinational enterprises raise sensitive issues of whether their objectives conflict with the well-being of individual countries and whether they have the power to circumvent or overwhelm national-government sovereignty. Developing countries worry both that foreign firms will invest in them and that they won't. They fear exploitation on the one hand and inadequate access to foreign capital, technology, marketing, and management skills on the other. Industrialized countries worry about being both the sources and the recipients of direct investments. As direct investments flow out, don't these reduce product exports and employment opportunities at home? As direct investments flow in, won't foreigners establish undue influence and control over the local economy?

The first part of this chapter provides a broad survey of what we know about multinationals and foreign direct investment. We explore why direct investments occur. We also examine whether a home country or a host country has good reasons to try to restrict (or encourage) multinational direct investment.

These national issues are important because the policies of national governments remain powerful. All governments prohibit or restrict direct investments into certain lines of activity. Which lines are prohibited vary from one country to another, but the prohibitions are directed toward those activities that are regarded as particularly vulnerable to foreign influence—including natural resources, banking, newspapers, broadcasting, telecommunications, airlines, and defense industries. Governments also can regulate the local operations of foreign firms in a number of ways. They can require local participation in the ownership or management of the local operations, or they can require training, locally purchased components and parts, local research, or exports. Governments can also use tax policy to influence both the flows of direct investments and the division of the investment returns between the firms and the governments. On the other hand, many governments actively court multinational enterprises by offering various forms of subsidies to attract them to locate in their countries.

Of all the flows that take place between nations, none is more sensitive than the flow of humans. For those who migrate, the dangers are great but the average gain is high. A migrant risks disease or victimization by others and may fail to find a better income in the country of destination. Many migrants return home unsuccessful and disillusioned. Still, they experience great gains on average, as we might expect from so risky an activity. In some cases political and physical freedom itself is a large gain, as in the case of refugees from repressive regimes. In other cases, the economic gains stand out. Doctors, engineers, and other highly trained personnel from low-income countries such as India and Jamaica have multiplied their incomes several times over by migrating to North America, Australia, Britain, and the Persian Gulf. Mexican craftspeople and campesinos earn enough in Texas or California to retire early (if they wish) in comfortable Mexican homes. Turkish "guest workers" in Germany have also gained a comfortable living and a jump up the income ranks.

In the countries that receive migrants, ethnic prejudice, general xenophobia, and the direct economic stake of groups that fear competition from immigrants keep the issue especially sensitive. Anti-immigration groups have become more vocal since the early 1990s. In response to rising legal and illegal immigration from Mexico and Central America, the U.S. government enacted a federal law to deny even legal immigrants access to many social programs, though subsequent laws restored some of the benefits. Rising immigration into the European Union, including illegal immigration that may be larger than that into the United States, has alarmed some Europeans. In Austria, Denmark, France, Italy, and Switzerland, political parties opposed to immigration have sometimes used virulent rhetoric to try to gain votes. In Germany the government has put up new immigration barriers in response to the growing numbers of refugees from Eastern Europe.

The second part of this chapter examines the economics of international migration. We focus on people who migrate for economic reasons, to understand the effects on labor markets in the sending and receiving countries. As we did for the multinational enterprise, we then examine whether the sending or receiving country has reasons to restrict migration to prevent adverse effects on national well-being.

FOREIGN DIRECT INVESTMENT

The U.S. company Apple pays cash to acquire all of the equity shares of a German company that makes computer software. A U.S. investor named Pugel pays cash to buy 10,000 shares (0.1 percent of all outstanding equity shares) of a similar German company that also makes software. Both of these share purchases are international flows of financial capital from the United States to Germany. But only one is foreign *direct* investment. The key difference between the two investments is the degree to which each investor can control or influence the management of the company. In foreign *direct* investment the investor has, or could have, an effective voice in the management of the foreign company. **Foreign direct investment (FDI)** is the flow of funding provided by an investor or a lender (usually a firm) to establish or acquire a foreign company or to expand or finance an existing foreign company that the investor owns and controls. Apple's acquisition of the first German company is FDI.

In contrast, Pugel does not expect to have any influence on the day-to-day management of the second German company. Rather, Pugel is seeking financial returns by adding the 10,000 shares to his investment portfolio. Generally, the term *international portfolio investment* is used for all foreign securities investments that do not involve management control (that is, all that are not direct investments).

Both foreign direct investment and international portfolio investment are important ways in which financial capital moves between countries. During 2010–2012, the global flows of foreign direct investment and the global flows of international portfolio investment each averaged close to $1.7 trillion per year. In this chapter we examine the economics of foreign direct investment. We defer our analysis of international portfolio investment to Chapters 18 and 19 of the book because we need the discussion of foreign exchange rates contained there to analyze the financial returns and risks of international investing.

In many cases, including the acquisition of the German company by Apple, we can easily tell whether an investment is (or is not) FDI. In other cases, the investor acquires or owns part of the equity of the foreign company but not all of it. How much ownership is enough to the give the investor the ability to affect the management of the foreign firm? There is no clear-cut answer to this, but it is certainly at most half, and probably less than this. Someone who owns even, say, 20 percent of a firm can have some ability to influence the management of the firm.

The agreed international standard is 10 percent ownership.[1] That is, *foreign direct investment is any flow of lending to, or purchases of ownership in, a foreign firm in which the investor (usually a firm) has (or gains) ownership of 10 percent or more of the foreign firm.* Here are some examples of investments that do and do not fit the official definition of foreign direct investment:

U.S. Foreign Direct Investments	U.S. Portfolio Investments Abroad
Alcoa's purchase of 50 percent of the stock in a new Jamaican bauxite firm	Alcoa's purchase of 5 percent of the stock in a new Jamaican bauxite firm (this 5 percent is the full amount of ownership that Alcoa then has)
A loan from Ford U.S.A. to a Canadian parts-making subsidiary in which Ford holds 55 percent of the equity	A loan from Ford U.S.A. to a Canadian parts-making firm in which Ford U.S.A. holds 8 percent of the equity

[1]This 10 percent standard is used by the United States and many other countries, but not by all countries that report FDI data. In addition, another form of FDI recognized by the international standards involves a group of investors in a home country that establish control of a foreign affiliate, even if each investor individually owns less than 10 percent of the foreign firm.

Note that direct investment consists of any investment, whether new ownership or simple lending, as long as the investing firm owns (or acquires) over 10 percent of the foreign firm.

MULTINATIONAL ENTERPRISES

A firm that owns and controls operations in more than one country is a multinational enterprise (MNE). The parent firm in the MNE is the headquarters or base firm, located in the home country of the MNE. The parent firm has one or more foreign affiliates (subsidiaries or branches) located in one or more host countries.

The multinational enterprise uses flows of foreign direct investment to establish or finance its foreign affiliates. However, in two different ways a multinational firm is *more* than just the flow of foreign direct investment. First, foreign affiliates usually receive only part, and often a rather small part, of their total financing from the direct investment flows. Second, the multinational enterprise transfers many other things to its foreign affiliates in addition to the direct investment financing. The multinational enterprise typically provides its affiliates with a variety of intangible assets for the affiliates to use. These intangible assets can include proprietary technology, brand names, marketing capabilities, trade secrets, and managerial practices. In this section we focus on the first issue, the financing of the affiliates.

A foreign affiliate can obtain financing either from its parent (or other parts of the MNE) or from outside lenders and investors (for instance, banks or the buyers of bonds that the affiliate issues). Only the former is foreign direct investment, and it is often a small part of the total financing of the affiliate. For all MNEs in the world in 2012, foreign affiliates had about $87 trillion of financing in place, but only $23 trillion of that financing was provided by foreign direct investment by the multinational enterprises. Evidence for U.S.-based multinationals indicates that borrowing in the host countries provides more than half of the outside financing.

Why does FDI provide so little of the affiliates' total funding? An important reason is that a parent firm wants to reduce the risks to which its foreign activities are exposed. One risk is unexpected changes in exchange rates, which can alter the value of its direct investments. A good risk-reducing strategy for a parent company that has foreign-currency assets in its affiliates is to take on foreign-currency liabilities as well, by borrowing in foreign currencies that are used to finance the affiliate.

Another risk is political risk, the possibility that the government of a host country will alter its policies in ways that harm the multinational enterprise. For instance, the possibility of expropriation or nationalization of an affiliate by the host-country government is a political risk. Since World War I and the Russian revolution, host countries have shown willingness to seize the assets of multinationals, sometimes without compensating the investors. For example, in recent years the Venezuelan government has seized the local investments of Exxon Mobil (oil), Owens-Illinois (glass), Helmerich & Payne (drilling rigs), and many other companies in the electricity, cement, coffee, and oil industries. The Bolivian government took control of foreign-owned oil and natural gas operations in 2006, a foreign-owned electricity generation firm in 2010, and a foreign-owned electricity distribution firm in 2012. Realizing the danger of expropriation, many multinationals reduce their exposure to this kind of risk by matching much of the value of their physical assets in a host country with borrowings in that country. If political change brings expropriation, the parents also can tell the host-country lenders to try to collect their repayments from their own (expropriating) government. The shedding of liabilities offsets part or all of their asset losses in the country.

FDI: HISTORY AND CURRENT PATTERNS

Although data on foreign direct investment tell us only about one aspect of the global operations of MNEs, these data have the advantage that they are available for most countries and for long periods of time. We use data on FDI as general indicators of the importance of MNEs across countries and over time. Data on FDI are available for two related but different measures:

- *Flows* of FDI measure new equity investments and loans within MNEs during a period of time. This is the measure of FDI we used in the section in which we defined FDI.
- *Stocks* of FDI measure the total amount of direct investments that exist at a point in time. These stocks are the sums of past flows of FDI.

Let's look first at information on flows of FDI.

Foreign direct investment has been rising and falling, mainly rising, throughout the 20th century and into the 21st. It had its fastest growth, and took its largest share of all international investment, in the period dating roughly from the end of the Korean War (1953) to the first oil shock (1973–1974). During that period, direct investments were dominated by investment outflows from the United States. U.S. firms have historically shown a greater preference for FDI and direct control than have firms from other investing countries. Britain, France, and the oil-rich nations have channeled a greater proportion of their foreign investments into portfolio lending. Thus, the early postwar rise of U.S. FDI propelled U.S.-based multinationals into international prominence. In the 1970s and early 1980s, global FDI grew more slowly, being eclipsed by two waves of portfolio lending: the ill-fated surge of lending to developing countries in 1974–1982 and the surge of lending to the United States in the 1980s.

Global FDI was driven by increasing FDI by Japanese firms in the second half of the 1980s and by increasing FDI by U.S. firms, European firms, and firms based in South and East Asia since 1990. The global flows of foreign direct investment rose rapidly in the second half of the 1990s, as the value of cross-border mergers and acquisitions, mostly between firms in the industrialized countries, exploded. After reaching $1.4 trillion in 2000, FDI flows fell with the recession of the early 2000s. Then FDI flows grew rapidly again, to $2.2 trillion in 2007, again driven by a large increase in international mergers and acquisitions. With the sharp contraction in economic activity during the global financial and economic crisis, FDI flows fell to $1.2 trillion in 2009 and then recovered somewhat in the next years.

Foreign direct investment has also changed direction. First, in the 1970s and 1980s, it moved away from the developing countries, where it had met with resistance and expropriations climaxing in the 1970s. This trend reversed itself beginning in

FIGURE 15.1 Major Home Countries' Direct Investments, End of 2011 (Billions of U.S. Dollars)

Home Country	Total Outward FDI	Host Region					
		NAFTA[a]	European Union[b]	Other Industrialized	Latin America	Developing Asia	Other Developing[c]
United States	4,085	422	2,037	418	681	373	153
Britain	1,700	377	823	104	76	182	138
France	1,505	261	923	108	50	81	82
Germany	1,208	241	720	67	26	99	54
Switzerland	1,113	263	490	42	160	88	70
Netherlands	982	144	555	122	51	75	36
Japan	963	289	215	56	119	263	21
Canada	661	273	164	37	126	20	40
Spain	657	102	336	33	139	12	34

FDI shows noticeable regional patterns, with substantial direct investments between the United States and Canada, from Japan into the developing countries of Asia, and between European countries.

[a]North American Free Trade Area: Canada, Mexico, and the United States.

[b]For the 27 member countries as of 2010.

[c]Includes FDI not allocated to specific host countries.

Source: Organization for Economic Cooperation and Development, *OECD International Direct Investment Statistics: Foreign Direct Investment, Positions by Partner Country,* 2014; and United Nations Conference on Trade and Development, *Bilateral FDI Statistics 2014.*

about 1990, as FDI flows into developing countries increased dramatically. Growing domestic markets, low production costs, and reforms of economic policies attracted direct investment, especially into a small number of developing countries in South and East Asia and Latin America. Included in these is China, following its opening to foreign trade and investment that began in the late 1970s. Second, the United States attracted more FDI inflows than any other nation in the 1980s. The share of the United States then declined somewhat, but it continued to receive about one-seventh of new FDI flows during 2010–2012. Third, the deepening of integration in the European Union has encouraged FDI into and within the EU, and the formation of the North American Free Trade Area (along with Mexico's own policy reforms) has encouraged FDI into Mexico.

Let's turn now to information on the stocks of FDI. Recall that FDI stocks are the cumulation of the FDI flows that we have just been talking about. FDI stocks measure total amounts in existence as of the stated time. Figure 15.1 shows the geographic pattern of direct investment stocks by nine large home (or source) countries at the end of 2011. These nine countries are the source of about 62 percent of all existing direct investments. In fact, industrialized countries as a group are overwhelmingly the home countries of direct investments, accounting for about 79 percent of the world total.

The six columns toward the right in Figure 15.1 indicate different regions that host the direct investments. Reading across a row shows where the nine source countries invest. Half of U.S. direct investment is in Europe. The United States is also a major investor in Canada. (Most of the $422 billion of U.S. direct investment in the two other countries of NAFTA is in Canada.) Canada has placed about 40 percent of its direct investment in the United States. Japan has substantial direct investments in the developing countries of Asia, and it built a large position in the United States in the 1980s. Britain, France, Germany, the Netherlands, and Switzerland have close to half of their direct investments in other European countries, as well as substantial direct investments in the United States. Spain has about half of its direct investments in other European countries, and about a fifth in Latin American countries.

About 63 percent of the stock of direct investment is in industrialized countries. To a large extent, FDI involves firms from industrialized countries investing in other industrialized countries. With one exception, the major home countries are also major host countries. The exception is Japan. One way in which Japan is truly different from other major industrialized countries is that it is host to relatively little direct investment. In 2012, the stock of direct investment in Japan was only $205 billion, less than one-third of the FDI that Spain, a much smaller country, had received.

In which industries does FDI occur? That has changed over time. In 1970, about one-quarter of the world's direct investment was in the primary sector, mainly mining and extraction activities. About half was in the manufacturing sector, and about a quarter was in the services sector. The share of mining and extraction has since declined, especially in the 1970s as developing countries nationalized many firms and exerted greater control over the extraction of their natural resources. The share of manufacturing has declined to less than 30 percent, and the share of services has risen to over 60 percent. In manufacturing, firms that produce pharmaceuticals and other chemicals, electrical and electronic equipment, automobiles, machinery, and food tend to be active in direct investment, while firms in industries like textiles, clothing, and paper products tend to do rather little direct investment. Within the services sector substantial direct investment occurs in banking and other financial services; in business services such as consulting, accounting, and advertising; and in wholesaling and retailing.

WHY DO MULTINATIONAL ENTERPRISES EXIST?

This seems to be a silly question! The answer seems simple—because they are profitable. But the issue is more complicated than it sounds.

We should first dispose of one possible explanation, that multinationals are simply a way of shifting financial capital between countries based on national differences in returns and risks. Although return and risk must play a role in the decisions by firms about whether to make direct investments, this financial theory of direct investment is not adequate. It does not explain why these international investments would be large enough to establish managerial control over the foreign companies. If the challenge is to transfer capital from one country to another, international portfolio investment can accomplish this task better than direct investment by firms whose major preoccupation lies in production and marketing.

There is some agreement that five different pieces together provide a good explanation of why multinational firms exist (and why they are as large as they are). The five pieces are

1. Inherent disadvantages of being foreign.
2. Firm-specific advantages (to overcome the inherent disadvantages).

3. Location factors (that favor foreign production over exporting).

4. Internalization advantages (that favor direct investment over contracting with independent firms).

5. Oligopolistic rivalry (among multinational enterprises).

The combination of these pieces into a framework for understanding the multinational enterprise is often called the eclectic approach, with credit for the synthesis going to John Dunning.

Inherent Disadvantages

Our first step is to recognize that there are good reasons why multinational enterprises should not exist. An MNE has inherent disadvantages in trying to compete against foreign rivals by operating on their own turf. The multinational is at a disadvantage in this foreign production environment because it does not initially have the native understanding of local laws, customs, procedures, practices, and relationships. In addition, the firm has the extra costs of maintaining management control. It is expensive to operate at a distance, expensive in travel and communications, and especially expensive in misunderstanding. Furthermore, the MNE may lack useful connections with political leaders in the foreign country, or it could face actual or potential hostility from the foreign country's government.

Firm-Specific Advantages

What makes it possible for a multinational to overcome the inherent disadvantages of being foreign? To be successful, the multinational must have one or more firm-specific advantages—that is, one or more assets of the multinational enterprise that are not assets held by its local competitors in the host country (or, perhaps, by any other firm in the world). A firm's secret technology or its patents are a firm-specific advantage (examples: Siemens in electrical and electronic products, Pfizer in pharmaceuticals). Or, as in the case of petroleum refining (Royal Dutch Shell) or metal processing (Alcoa), the firm may gain advantage by coordinating operations and capital investments at various stages in a vertical production process. Because of heavy inventory costs and its knowledge of the requirements at each stage, the firm may be able to economize through synchronizing operations. Or the firm may have marketing advantages based on skilled use of advertising and other promotional methods that establish product differentiation—for instance, through highly regarded brand names (examples: Nestlé, Procter & Gamble). Or an advantage may inhere in superior management techniques (example: General Electric). Or, as for many of these large MNEs, it has access to very large amounts of financial capital, amounts far larger than the ordinary national firm can command. Some special advantage is necessary for the firm to overcome the disadvantages of operating at a distance in a foreign environment. It is costly for the firm to develop these assets (for instance, the cost of research and development to develop new technology, the marketing expenses to establish and maintain a strong brand name). The challenge to the firm is to maximize its returns on these assets.

We now have an enterprise that has firm-specific advantages such that it could operate profitably as a multinational. But should it? Even for the firm that has firm-specific advantages, it must also consider alternatives to foreign direct investment for earning profits from activities in a foreign market. It must be more profitable for a multinational enterprise to own and manage a foreign operation, rather than adopting some other way of earning profits. Let's focus on the situation in which a firm wants to earn profits by selling to local buyers in the foreign country. Here are two questions for the firm's managers:

1. Should the firm sell to foreign buyers by exporting from its home country, or should the firm set up local production in the foreign country to produce the products that are sold to the foreign buyers?
2. Should the firm license local firms in the foreign country to use its advantages in their own operations that serve the foreign buyers, or should the firm set up foreign operations that it owns and controls?

The answers to these questions bring location factors and internalization advantages into the explanation.

Location Factors

Location factors are all of the advantages and disadvantages of producing in one country (the home country) or in another country (the foreign country). We have already developed, in the previous chapters of the book, many of the location factors that we need to answer the question "Export or FDI?" Here are four key location factors from our previous explorations:

- *Comparative advantage:* the effects of resource availability (labor, land, and so forth) on the costs of producing in different countries.
- *Scale economies:* size advantages that favor concentrating production in a few locations and serving other national markets by exporting.
- *Governmental barriers to importing into the foreign country:* tariffs and nontariff barriers that make it difficult to export from the home country.
- *Trade bloc:* setup that favors FDI if the foreign country is a member of a free-trade area (or similar arrangement) but the home country is not a member because production in the foreign country can also be used to serve buyers in the other member countries.

There are other location factors that are important in some industries. High costs of transporting a product favor FDI to locate production units close to foreign buyers, rather than serving faraway buyers by exporting. Government taxes, subsidies, and regulations affect the profitability of producing in different countries. The need to adapt products to the specific tastes of foreign buyers can favor FDI because it is more effective to have close links among the local marketing group, the product redesign group, and the operations group that must produce the redesigned products at acceptable costs.

Location factors are key to answering the question "Export or FDI?" Note that the answer could go either way for a specific firm and product. In some cases it is more profitable to export from the home country, for instance, because the home country has a comparative advantage in the availability and low cost of the most important resource needed in producing the product. In other cases foreign production in an affiliate established by direct investment is more profitable, for instance, because the foreign country has high tariffs on imports of the product.

Internalization Advantages

Even if the firm rules out exporting as a way of serving the foreign market, it still has alternatives for earning profits from that foreign market. Instead of using foreign direct investment to set up an affiliate, the firm could sell or rent its firm-specific advantages to foreign firms for them to use in their own production. For instance, if the advantages are based on superior technology, a strong brand name, or better management practices, the firm could license one or more foreign firms to use these assets. A license is an agreement for one firm to use another firm's asset, with restrictions on how the asset can be used, and with payments for the right to use the asset.

In making the decision between FDI and licensing of foreign firms, the firm with the asset must weigh the advantages and disadvantages of each alternative. An important advantage of licensing foreign firms is that the firm avoids (most of) the inherent disadvantages of establishing and managing its own foreign operations. On the other side there are advantages to keeping the use of the firm-specific advantages within (internal to) the enterprise. Internalization advantages are the advantages of using an asset within the firm rather than finding other firms that will buy, rent, or license the asset. Internalization advantages exist because there are drawbacks to using the market for many firm-specific advantages, particularly intangible assets like technology, brand names, marketing techniques, and management practices.

Internalization advantages arise from *avoiding the transaction costs and risks of licensing* an independent firm. Negotiating the license is often costly and difficult. The licensor wants a high payment, and the licensee wants a low payment. The licensee is likely to be skeptical of claims by the licensor that the intangible asset is valuable and should command a high price. The licensor also wants to put various restrictions on how the licensee can use the asset, but the licensee wants to have as few restrictions as possible. Then, even if the license agreement can be negotiated, the licensor still faces some important risks. The licensee may not be as careful with the asset as the licensor would be. For instance, the licensee may let secret technology leak out to other competitors, or the licensee may itself apply the technology to other activities not covered by the license. Or the licensee may fail to maintain product quality, leading to news reports ("brand-name cola causes widespread illness in Austria") that harm the global reputation and value of the brand.

Foreign direct investment keeps the use of the assets under the control of the enterprise itself. It avoids many of the drawbacks of using the market for these kinds of assets. The advantages of internalization are based on the ability of the MNE's management to set the terms for the use of the assets in its foreign affiliates. The returns to the use of the assets are part of the profits earned by the affiliate, and the enterprise

---

[2]Buckley and Casson (1976) stressed the importance of internalization advantages for our understanding of MNEs. Magee (1977) developed a similar approach that stresses the importance of approbriability— the ability of an MNE to earn the best returns on its investment in intangible assets. The analysis by Nobel Prize winner Ronald Coase is also relevant. The economics of whether to engage in FDI is an international extension of the decision about the boundaries of the firm (whether to make or buy, whether to own or rent, and so forth).

can enforce policies to safeguard the ongoing value of its intangible assets. The multinational enterprise uses FDI to better appropriate the returns to its intangible assets.[2]

The importance of internalized use of firm-specific intangible assets explains why foreign direct investment occurs to a greater extent in high-technology industries (electronic products or pharmaceuticals, for example) and marketing-intensive industries (food products or automobiles, for example) than it does in standard-technology industries (clothing, for example) or less-marketing-intensive industries (paper products, for example).

Oligopolistic Rivalry

Many multinational enterprises are not the tiny firms that populate perfectly competitive markets. Instead, they are large firms that often compete among themselves for market shares and profits. They have used their intangible assets (like new technologies and strong brand names) to obtain large market shares. The same intangible assets drive their FDI. These multinationals are involved in global oligopolistic rivalry of the sort that we discussed in Chapters 6 and 11.

Multinationals can use their decisions about foreign direct investment as part of their strategies for competing. For instance, multinationals compete for location. A multinational sometimes seems to set up an affiliate that looks only marginally profitable, yet it does so with the stated purpose of beating its main competitors to the same national market. General Motors may set up a foreign affiliate in a developing country mainly because it fears that if it doesn't, Toyota will. With some regularity other multinational rivals then quickly respond by setting up their own affiliates in this country, to prevent the first mover from gaining any lasting advantage. Such follow-the-leader behavior results in a bunching of the timing of entries by rival multinationals into a host country. Most of the affiliates may have a tough time earning profits.

Multinationals can also use FDI to try to mute competition and enhance their market power. First, a multinational may acquire foreign firms that are beginning to challenge their international market position. Second, a multinational may set up an affiliate in the home country of one of its rivals, to establish a competitive threat to this rival. The message is "Don't compete too vigorously against me in other countries, or I will make life tough for you in your own home market."

TAXATION OF MULTINATIONAL ENTERPRISES' PROFITS

The profits of multinational enterprises come from the operations of the parent firms and their foreign affiliates. National governments impose taxes on business profits, and the taxation of the profits of multinational enterprises can become complicated and contentious. Let's look first at how the profits of these global firms are taxed and then at two important issues that arise from this taxation.

Part of how a multinational enterprise's profits are taxed is conceptually straightforward (although the details can be vexing). The host-country governments tax the profits of the local affiliates of the multinational, and the home-country government taxes the parent company's "local" profits earned on its own activities. A key question

Case Study CEMEX: A Model Multinational from an Unusual Place

Our discussion in the text stresses that multinationals succeed by using their firm-specific advantages throughout their global operations. We have also noted that most foreign direct investments are made by firms based in the industrialized countries. This is the story of CEMEX, a firm that rapidly has become multinational since 1990. The reasons for its multinational success fit very well with the advantages stressed in the eclectic approach. What makes the firm unusual is that it is based in Mexico. CEMEX is an example of a growing group of multinationals based in developing countries.

CEMEX began business in 1906. For most of its life this cement company focused on selling in the Mexican market. Cement is a product that is expensive to ship, especially overland, so cement plants ship mostly to customers within 300 miles of a plant. Shipment by water is moderately (but not prohibitively) expensive. Most cement producers in the 1980s were local producers with traditional business practices. New managers at CEMEX broke with tradition by introducing extensive use of automation, information technology, and a satellite-based communication network into CEMEX operations. They used the technology to improve quality control and to provide detailed information on production, sales, and distribution to top managers in real time. Delivery of ready-mix concrete is particularly challenging in cities. Traditionally, cement firms could ensure delivery only within a time period of about three hours. CEMEX pioneered the use of computers and a global positioning system to guarantee delivery to construction sites within a 20-minute window. These innovations became the company's firm-specific advantages.

Also in the 1980s CEMEX began to export more aggressively to the United States using sea transport, and it was increasingly successful. However, competing U.S. cement producers complained to the U.S. government, and in 1990 CEMEX exports to the United States were hit by a 58 percent antidumping duty. With exporting to the United States limited by the antidumping order, CEMEX looked for other foreign opportunities.

In 1991, it began exporting to Spain, and in 1992 it made its first foreign direct investment

by acquiring two Spanish cement producers. CEMEX minimized its inherent disadvantages by investing first in a foreign country with the same language as the firm's home country and a similar culture. In addition, CEMEX used its expansion into Europe as a competitive response to the previous move by the Swiss-based firm Holcim into the Mexican cement industry.

The management team sent by CEMEX to reorganize the acquired companies was amazed to find companies that kept handwritten records and used almost no personal computers. They upgraded the Spanish affiliates to CEMEX technology and management practices. The improvement in affiliate operations from this internal transfer of CEMEX's intangible assets was remarkable—profit margins improved from 7 percent to 24 percent in two years.

Since then, CEMEX has made a series of foreign direct investments by acquiring cement producers in Latin America (including Venezuela, Panama, the Dominican Republic, Colombia, and Costa Rica), the United States, Britain, the Philippines, Indonesia, and Egypt. CEMEX used the same type of process that it used in Spain to bring its technology and management practices into its new foreign affiliates, and generally achieved similarly impressive improvements in performance.

By 2000, CEMEX was the third largest cement producer in the world, behind Lafarge of France and Holcim. More than 60 percent of its physical assets were in its foreign affiliates. It was also the largest exporter of cement in the world (a fact consistent with the proposition discussed in the text that FDI and trade are often complementary). CEMEX is considered one of the best networked companies globally by computer industry experts, well ahead of its rivals. Its investments in developing and enhancing its firm-specific advantages have been paying off globally.

DISCUSSION QUESTION
In countries like Spain, Colombia, and the Philippines, why did CEMEX not just license independent local producers to use its operations technologies?

is, then, whether the home-country government also imposes any taxes on the profits earned by the foreign affiliates of the parent company.

Because the profits of these foreign affiliates have been taxed already by the host government, the home government usually tries to avoid double taxation of the foreign affiliate profits. While the exact rules vary by country, the outcome is that the home-country government collects few or no extra taxes on the profits of foreign affiliates.[3] Thus, the tax rate on the profits of a foreign affiliate is largely that imposed by the host government. Because tax rates vary across host countries, and because global multinational enterprises try to minimize the total taxes that they pay (as long as lower tax payments increase global after-tax profits), two important issues arise.

First, a multinational enterprise can shop around among countries and locate its affiliates in the jurisdictions of governments offering low tax rates. FDI allows a multinational enterprise to settle in countries with lower taxes. Whether this is good or bad from a world point of view depends on the uses to which tax revenues are put and whether the productivity of the investing firm is lower in the lower-tax country.

Second, multinational enterprises can use transfer pricing and other devices to report more of their profits in low-tax countries, even though the profits were actually earned in high-tax countries. Transfer pricing is the setting by the company of prices (or monetary values) for things that move between units of the company. Many things move between the parent and an affiliate or between affiliates of a multinational enterprise. These include materials and components, finished products, the rights to use technology and brand names, and financial capital. For accounting for each unit (the parent or an affiliate), each of these things must be assigned a price or value. Therefore, all multinationals must engage in setting these transfer prices.

The multinational can set transfer prices to achieve any of a number of enterprise objectives, and one of these is reducing the global taxes that the multinational pays. For instance, to lower its corporate income taxes, the MNE can have its unit in a high-tax country be overcharged (or underpaid) for goods and services that the unit buys from (sells to) an affiliate in a low-tax country. That way, the unit in the high-tax country doesn't show its tax officials much profit, while the unit in the low-tax country shows high profits. Profits are shifted from the unit in the high-tax country to the unit in the low-tax country. The result: net tax reduction for the multinational enterprise in question.

Here is a numerical example to show how this could work. An MNE produces a component in Germany where the tax rate on corporate income is, say, 50 percent. The component costs $8 per unit to produce in Germany, and the MNE sells all units that it produces there to its affiliate in Singapore, where the tax rate on corporate income is, say, 20 percent. The affiliate in Singapore uses this component and $7

---

[3]The United States imposes taxes on the portion of foreign affiliate profits sent home to the U.S. parents, but it also allows tax credits for taxes already paid to the host-country governments on these profits. Most other industrialized countries basically impose no taxes on the profits of the foreign affiliates of firms based in their countries.

of labor to produce a finished product that it sells to outside buyers for $20 per unit. Thus, for each unit sold to a final buyer the multinational has $5 of *before-tax* global profit ($20 – $8 – $7). But the multinational is most interested in the profit that it gets to keep after it pays its corporate income taxes. Its *after-tax* global profit depends on what transfer price it sets tor the sale of the component by its German affiliate to its Singapore affiliate. Here are three possibilities and the resulting after-tax global profit per unit:

Transfer Price of the Component	German Affiliate		Singapore Affiliate		Global MNE	
	Before-Tax Profit	After-Tax Profit	Before-Tax Profit	After-Tax Profit	Before-Tax Profit	After-Tax Profit
$13.00	$5.00	$2.50	$0.00	$0.00	$5.00	$2.50
10.00	2.00	1.00	3.00	2.40	5.00	3.40
8.00	0.00	0.00	5.00	4.00	5.00	4.00

Of the three possible transfer prices shown, the multinational achieves the highest global after-tax profit by using the lowest transfer price.

Governments know that multinational enterprises can use transfer prices to shift their profits and lower their taxes. Many governments attempt to police transfer pricing to ensure that the transfer prices used between units within a multinational enterprise are similar to the market prices that independent firms would pay to each other for similar transactions. However, determining whether transfer prices differ from market prices is complex and costly, so multinational enterprises usually have some scope to use transfer pricing to alter the taxes the multinationals pay (and to which countries they pay those taxes).

MNES AND INTERNATIONAL TRADE

It is natural to think of foreign direct investment in a host country as a substitute for exports by the parent firm (or other home-country firms) to the host country, just as we concluded in Chapter 5 that trade and international movements of production factors are substitutes. Yet it turns out that multinational enterprises are actually heavily involved in international trade. About one-third of the world's international trade in goods occurs as intrafirm trade between units of the multinational enterprises located in different countries. Another third of the world's international trade involves a multinational enterprise as the seller (exporter) or buyer (importer), trading with some other firm.

Why are multinational enterprises so involved in world trade? Especially, why is intrafirm trade so important? When are trade and FDI substitutes? Can FDI complement trade? We will answer these questions, first for the easier case in which a parent and its affiliates are engaged in different stages of overall production, then for the harder case in which the affiliate is largely doing the same types of production activities as the parent (or other affiliates).

As long as transport costs and trade barriers are low enough, FDI can be used to reduce total costs by locating different stages of overall production in different countries.

Compared with the situation in which the firm would perform most of these activities in a single country, FDI leads to more trade as the firm's overall production is spread across units in different countries.

For instance, for electronics products like televisions, communications equipment, and computer hard drives, each stage of production can be located according to the country's comparative costs advantage (or, in the case of marketing and distribution, according to the need to locate close to the customers for the final products). Design and development of new products are located in countries (often the home country) abundant in engineers and other skilled labor; production of components in countries with capabilities to make high-quality, complex products; and assembly in countries abundant in less-skilled labor. In this case, FDI is pro-trade, with large amounts of intrafirm trade as components produced by units in one set of countries are shipped to units in other countries for assembly, and the assembled final products are shipped to units around the world for sale to final customers.

Trade among parents and affiliates engaged in different stages of production shows that FDI and trade can sometimes be *complements*. Yet most FDI is not used primarily to locate different stages of production in different countries. Rather, most affiliates largely duplicate the production activities of the parent firm or affiliates located in other countries.

In the case in which foreign affiliates undertake the same kind of production as that of the parent firm or other affiliates, FDI and trade could be substitutes or complements. To some extent they are *substitutes*. In many industries a firm must find a reasonable trade-off between (1) centralizing production in one or a few locations and exporting to many other countries, to achieve scale economies (recall the discussion of scale economies from Chapter 6), and (2) spreading production to many host countries where the buyers are, to reduce transport costs, to avoid actual or threatened barriers to importing into these countries, or to gain local marketing advantages. When scale economies are less important, or when transport costs and trade barriers are higher, for example, the trade-off would tilt toward FDI. Foreign production through direct investment then substitutes for international trade.

However, the effects of this kind of FDI on trade are actually more complex. To some extent this FDI is also likely to *promote or complement trade,* for two reasons. First, the affiliates' production of the final product requires components and materials as inputs into production. Often it is most economic to acquire these components and materials from the parent firm, affiliates in other countries, or independent suppliers in other countries. Although trade in final products may decrease, trade in materials and components increases.

Second, this FDI can increase trade in final products because the affiliate improves the marketing of all of the firm's products in the host country. In many cases the affiliate produces only some of the firm's entire product line locally. Other items in the product line must be imported from the parent or other affiliates. The affiliate *displaces* some trade for the specific products that it produces, but it *expands* trade through better local marketing of other products produced by the multinational in other countries.

We have just seen that there are good reasons to think that FDI and trade could be substitutes, and good reasons to think that they could be complements. While each instance of FDI has its own outcome, can we say anything about the overall relationship?

Most studies conclude that FDI, on average, is somewhat complementary to international trade. For instance, studies of U.S., German, Japanese, French, and Swedish multinationals find that, controlling for other influences, FDI is associated with higher home exports of products in the same broad industry. The overall complementarity seems to reflect both higher home exports of components used in affiliate production and higher home exports of final goods (the latter applies to many but not all industries).

SHOULD THE HOME COUNTRY RESTRICT FDI OUTFLOWS?

To decide whether FDI should be restricted by the home (or source) country is a difficult task. Let's approach it using a framework similar to the approach we used to examine restrictions on international trade. We can then identify several key effects:

- The effect on workers and others who provide inputs into production in the home country.
- The effects on the owners of the multinational enterprises based in this home country.
- The effects on the government budget, especially the effects on government tax revenues.
- Any external benefits or costs associated with direct investments out of the country.

Notice that we are now dividing the producer side of the market into (1) workers and other providers of inputs and (2) the owners of the multinational enterprises. Our presumption is that the multinational enterprises are more mobile internationally than are the workers and some of the providers of other inputs.

A good starting point for policy judgments about FDI and multinationals is a static economic analysis of the effects of shifting some of the country's capital stock out of the country. If FDI shifts some of the home country's capital to other countries, then less is available to use in production at home. With less capital to use in production, workers may be harmed. Some workers will experience temporary unemployment as they adjust to the reduction in home production by the multinationals. If the demand for labor decreases in the home country, then the real wages of workers will decline broadly.

Representatives of organized (unionized) labor in the United States and Canada have fought hard for restrictions on the freedom of companies to set up affiliates producing overseas and in Mexico, arguing that their jobs are being exported. Basically, their protest is correct, even though there are indirect ways in which outbound FDI creates some jobs in the United States and Canada. Organized labor may be especially affected because firms faced with strong labor organizations in the home country often replace or threaten to replace home-country production and jobs with production and jobs in other countries.

Workers are not the only ones in the home country who lose from FDI. The home-country government in general loses. It receives few or no taxes from the part of the multinationals' profits that becomes the profits of their foreign affiliates, and spending on government services provided to the multinationals probably does not decline by as much as the tax revenues decline. Other home-country taxpayers then have the choice of paying more taxes or cutting back on government-funded public programs.

The owners of the multinationals are the key group that gains from the FDI. They receive increased returns to their equity investments as the returns to the multinational enterprises' assets increase. In fact, in the standard economic analysis, the gains to the owners can be greater than the losses to workers and the government. If the home country is made up of the workers, the owners, and the government, there can be a net gain for the country as a whole. But it also is possible that the gains to the owners are less than the losses to workers and to the home-country government. In addition, some of the owners of the multinationals can be foreign investors, so some of the owners' gains do not accrue to the home country.

There is one more effect of FDI outflows that can be important. FDI may carry external technological benefits out with it. For all the multinationals' attempts to appropriate all the fruits of their technology, many gains may accrue to others in the location of the firms' production, through training of workers and imitation by other local producers. If so, outward FDI takes those external benefits away from the home country.

When we put all the possible losses and gains from FDI outflows together, the economics of the situation do not provide clear guidance on whether the home country would gain or lose well-being by restricting FDI outflows. Both are possible.

What are the actual policies of home-country governments toward outward FDI? Industrialized countries, the source of most of the world's FDI, actually impose few restrictions on outbound FDI. If anything, their policies are somewhat supportive of outbound FDI because they impose little or no extra tax on affiliates' profits.

A key reason for the neutral-to-supportive home policies is that the multinationals have used their resources and common interests to enhance their political influence through lobbying. In particular, multinationals have been successful in emphasizing the competition among firms from different countries for global market shares and profits. In this competition, using foreign affiliates is often the best way for the multinationals to compete (for instance, through the affiliates' better marketing in the host countries, as we discussed in the previous section). Home-country governments generally refrain from restricting outbound FDI so that firms from the country can compete better globally. Indeed, multinationals sometimes gain enough political power to bend the foreign policy of a home-country government to their own ends. Historically, the governments of the United States, Britain, and other investing nations have been involved in costly foreign conflicts in defense of MNE interests that do not align with the interests of other voters in the home country.

SHOULD THE HOST COUNTRY RESTRICT FDI INFLOWS?

The effects of FDI on the host country, and the pros and cons of host-country restrictions on it, are symmetrical in form to those facing the home country.

First, the standard static analysis of foreign direct investment finds that workers in the host country gain from increased demand for their services, as do other suppliers of inputs to the affiliates of foreign multinationals. The host-country government gains from the taxes collected on affiliate profits, as long as these exceed the extra costs of any additional government services provided to the affiliates. Domestic firms that must compete with the affiliates lose. Overall there is a presumption that the host country gains well-being in this standard analysis. Workers and suppliers to the affiliates, along with the national taxing government, gain more than owners of competing domestic firms lose. One residual concern mirrors that of predatory dumping, that the foreign multinationals will exercise substantial market power to raise prices once they have thinned the ranks of the local competitors.

Second, as with the home country's perspective, the host country must weigh indirect economic effects when deciding what its policy toward incoming FDI should be. And again the main kind of effects to consider are positive externalities. Multinational enterprises bring technology, marketing capabilities, and managerial skills to the host country. While the multinational attempts to keep these intangible assets to itself, some of them do leak out to local firms. Workers in the affiliates receive training and insights into the practices of the multinational. Local firms can use the proximity to affiliates to learn about their technologies and practices.

The actual thrust of the policies of host-country governments toward MNEs has shifted dramatically in the past 40 years. From the 1950s to the 1970s, host-country policies, especially those of developing countries, were based more on ideology and politics than on economics. The ideology ascendant in many developing countries at that time stressed government intervention in the economy. National goals emphasized political and economic independence, national identity and autonomy, and self-reliance. There was skepticism about the workings of markets and the benefits of international trade. One result of this way of thinking was the focus of development policies on industrialization by import protection and import substitution, which we discussed in the previous chapter.

Skepticism and suspicion led to the characterization of MNEs as the instruments of injustice. Although there was recognition of the economic benefits that MNEs could bring to host countries, much of the discussion focused on complaints about MNEs. Here are some of the allegations: Economic gains were tilted toward MNEs because of their economic size and monopolistic power, leaving little for the host countries. MNEs used capital-intensive production methods that were not suitable to developing countries, and they "denationalized" the host country's industries by displacing local firms. MNEs acted as an extension of the power of their home-country governments, and they enlisted the support of home-country governments to pressure the host country in a confrontation. They also bought host-country politicians and bankrolled plots against the government, as International Telephone and Telegraph did against the Allende government in Chile in 1972–1973.

In short, at that time multinationals were seen by many as threats to the sovereignty (power) of host-country governments and to the well-being of the host countries. To reassert sovereignty and to minimize the alleged adverse effects of the local activities of foreign MNEs, many host-country governments adopted controls and restrictions on the entry and operations of MNEs. For instance, the governments of countries like India and Mexico adopted policies that required that a majority of ownership of any foreign affiliate be in local hands.

The economic effects of these inward-oriented government policies (antitrade and anti-FDI) came to be seen as quite negative. Instead, the countries that began to grow fastest were those that adopted outward-oriented policies. Heavy-handed government intervention sank in perceived value, and the strengths of using markets increasingly were accepted. Even developing countries that might have resisted this policy shift had to confront the problems of the high levels of international debt they had built up

Focus on China   China as a Host Country

In 1978 the Chinese government began a process of slowly opening China to direct investments by foreign multinationals. The cumulation of liberalizations paid off in the 1990s, when annual inflows of FDI increased 10-fold from 1991 to 1997. Inflows since then have remained strong, and during 2010–2012 China was the second-largest recipient of direct investment flows in the world (behind only the United States).* About half of FDI into China is in manufacturing, and foreign-affiliated firms account for about one-third of production value added in Chinese manufacturing.

Where is all of this FDI coming from? China has been unusual in that much of the FDI has come from developing countries located close to it, not from the industrialized countries whose firms are the source of most FDI worldwide. Firms from Hong Kong and Taiwan have been attracted to China because they were seeking low-cost labor and land (*location factors*) to produce products like clothing, toys, and shoes, and to assemble products like consumer electronics, for export to third countries. They faced rather low *inherent disadvantages*, based on their cultural and geographic proximity, and their moderate *firm-specific advantages*, based on their knowledge of their businesses, were sufficient to allow them to be generally successful in China. Firms from Hong Kong and Taiwan were also comfortable with forming joint ventures with Chinese firms—such joint ventures were previously mandated by the Chinese government and still are required for some industries.

*One should interpret economic data on China with some caution, though there is no doubt that China's inflows of FDI are large. In addition to the usual concerns about the accuracy of the data, there is one interesting feature of FDI into China that skews the data. Some substantial amount of the recorded FDI is actually not FDI at all, but what is called *round-tripping*. That is, firms and individuals in China find ways to shift funds out of China, usually to Hong Kong, and then use these funds to make "foreign" direct investments back into China. They do this to gain the incentives and favorable treatment given by the Chinese government to "foreign-owned" firms. A typical guess is that perhaps 20 to 25 percent of Chinese FDI inflows have actually been round-tripping.

The surge of FDI into China in the 1990s corresponded to the growth of FDI by the more typical MNEs based in industrialized countries. These firms, in such industries as autos, machinery, and chemicals, faced larger inherent disadvantages, but they also had more substantial firm-specific advantages. Increasingly they have used wholly owned Chinese subsidiaries rather than joint ventures, as they have gained experience in operating in China and as the Chinese government has become more tolerant of full foreign ownership. While some of their operations were geared to exporting, a key location factor for many of them has been using local production as the base for gaining sales in the rapidly growing Chinese market (incomes have grown rapidly, and a substantial urban middle class has developed). *Oligopolistic rivalry* among firms from industrialized countries reinforced the rush to China in some industries (for instance, autos). One constraint on firms from industrialized countries is that it has been very difficult to enter or expand by acquisition of local Chinese firms.

A key issue for a foreign firm in China is protection of its intellectual property (patents, trade secrets, brand names, trademarks, and copyrights). Like many other developing countries, China has good intellectual property laws but weak enforcement. A foreign firm contracting with an independent Chinese firm, say, for the production of its brand-name products, risks losing some control of its brand. This happened to the sneaker company New Balance when one of its contract manufacturers in China produced hundreds of thousands of pairs beyond what New Balance ordered and then sold the sneakers both locally and internationally. A foreign firm sees the *internalization advantages* of managing its intellectual property in China by owning and controlling its Chinese operations. For instance, the Japanese firm Matsushita Electric makes sure that each of its Chinese employees knows only a small part of the overall production process for its most advanced products, so no employee can leave with its advanced technologies.

Another use of location factors is to understand where within China the foreign-affiliated firms are located. Most FDI into China is located in the coastal areas of eastern China. These areas were opened to FDI earlier than the rest of the country; they have better transportation and communication infrastructure, including port facilities for exporting; and they have stronger consumer markets because they have higher per capita incomes. Guangdong Province alone is host to about one-sixth of all China's FDI. Its early advantages were that it borders on Hong Kong and that it had three of the first four Special Economic Zones, established by the central government in 1979 to offer foreign firms preferential treatment and fewer restrictions on their local operations.

Inflows of FDI are generally viewed as benefiting China's economic development. A study by the Organization for Economic Cooperation and Development concluded that FDI has assisted the development of new industries in China, offered new and better products to Chinese consumers, brought new technologies to China, offered employment to Chinese workers, provided them with training and experience that has allowed them to build their technological and managerial skills, and increased China's exports. For exports, China is a good example of how FDI and trade are complements—foreign-affiliated firms make over half of China's exports. In addition, other research suggests that the presence of foreign-affiliated firms has led to increases in the productivity of local firms. Part of this productivity effect may be spillovers of technologies and worker skills. Another part of the effect may be the pressure of increased competition, as local firms are forced to "dance with wolves."

Policies of China's government continue to influence FDI into China. China has a complex system of screening and approvals for the entry of foreign firms into China, including both public (published) rules and internal (unpublished) rules. Some screening and approval are done at the central (national) level, and some are done at the local level. There are four categories by industry or type of operation:

- Some types of FDI, including investments that bring in advanced and environmentally friendly technologies, are *encouraged*, so they receive incentives and privileges, like low taxes for extended time periods.
- Some types of FDI, including investments that use old technologies and investments in many mining and service industries, are *restricted*, so they get additional scrutiny before approval.
- Some types of FDI, including investments that would be highly polluting, investments in defense industries, and investments in traditional Chinese crafts, are *prohibited*.
- All other types of FDI not named in the first three categories are *permitted*.

The complexity and time needed to gain approvals act as a disincentive for foreign firms to invest in China. In addition, the Chinese government imposes some forms of operating requirements on foreign-owned affiliates. The ones related to exports and local content generally have declined as China has implemented the liberalizations that it committed to when it joined the WTO. The major remaining performance requirement is pressure from the Chinese government to transfer foreign technologies to Chinese firms (often, to the local partners in joint ventures), as General Electric is doing in its joint venture that produces and sells advanced electricity-generating turbines.

China's government also offers a variety of incentives to FDI, including tax breaks, low rents on land, and provision of infrastructure improvements. Overall, though, the Chinese government does not usually engage in "bidding wars" with other countries to attract FDI.

Beginning in 2006, the Chinese government began to shift its policy on inbound FDI, stating

—Continued on next page

that it would focus more on the quality of the investments and deemphasizing the quantity of investments. It tightened some restrictions on foreign acquisitions of Chinese publicly traded companies. In 2008 it implemented a change in its tax law, eliminating or starting the phase-out of many of the tax incentives that it had offered to foreign-owned firms. In 2011 it added to the list of encouraged investments: components for alternative-energy vehicles, next-generation Internet products, biotechnology, intellectual property consulting firms, venture capital firms, and waste-recycling firms. It moved from restricted to permitted medical facilities and services, financial leasing firms, distribution and import of newspapers and books, and carbonated soft drinks. It moved automobile design and manufacturing from encouraged to permitted. It moved domestic mail courier services and the construction of luxury villas to prohibited.

One way that China has looked different from much of the rest of the world is that most FDI into China has been in manufacturing. The changes in China's policy since 2006 are likely to shift manufacturing FDI away from unskilled-labor-intensive production (e.g., toys) and assembly (e.g., electronics products). It remains to be seen if there will also be a shift toward FDI in service industries. As part of the obligations that the Chinese government accepted to join the WTO, it agreed to liberalize entry and ownership limits in a range of services, including banking and finance, distribution, retail and wholesale, advertising, architecture, engineering, and law. In some of these industries the government has used regulations to slow the process. It now appears that with the recent policy shift the government will allow or encourage FDI in some service industries while becoming more restrictive in others.

by borrowing from banks. With the debt crisis of the early 1980s, lending by foreign banks and financing from other foreign portfolio investors dried up.

Although concerns about the MNEs' political and economic power did not disappear, policy discussions began to stress the static economic gains from direct investment into the country plus the possibility of technological and other beneficial spillovers. As an example of spillovers, a number of Irish workers in the local affiliates of foreign software firms have left their multinational employers to found their own software companies. MNEs were viewed more favorably as a source of inflows of foreign capital and as a set of investors that did not rush to the exits at the first whiff of trouble.

These advantages increasingly impressed developing-country governments that had previously restricted inward FDI. Since the mid-1970s, many governments have liberalized their previous restrictions on direct investments into their countries (including the shift by China, as discussed in the box "China as a Host Country"). Many governments instead now compete aggressively by offering special tax breaks and other subsidies as each government attempts to woo direct investors to locate affiliates in its country rather than some other country.

MIGRATION

We have now completed our look at the role of multinational enterprises as conduits for the international movement of such resources as technology, capabilities, and

FIGURE 15.2   Gross Immigration Rates into the United States, 1820–2012, and Canada, 1852–2012

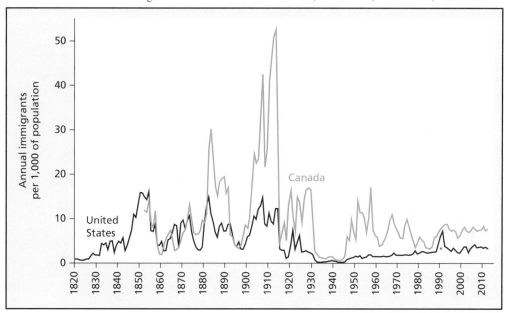

*The temporary jump in U.S. immigration, 1989–1991, reflected the amnesty granted to previously unrecorded immigrants and their families under the Immigration Reform and Control Act of 1986.

Source: U.S. annual rates, 1820–1970, from U.S. Bureau of the Census, *Historical Statistics of the United States, Colonial Times to 1970* (1976); 1971–1999, from U.S. Bureau of Census, *Statistical Abstract of the United States,* various years; and 2000–2012, from U.S. Department of Homeland Security, Office of Homeland Security, *2012 Yearbook of Immigration Statistics.* Canadian annual rates, 1852–1977, from Statistics Canada, *Historical Statistics of Canada,* second edition; and 1978–2012, from Citizenship and Immigration Canada, *Facts and Figures: Immigration Overview, Permanent and Temporary Residents, 2012.*

financial capital. For the rest of the chapter we will shift to examining the international movement of labor that accompanies emigration and immigration.

International migration is the movement of people from one country (the sending country) to another country (the receiving country) in which they plan to reside for some noticeable period of time. International migration has played an enormous role in the past expansion of receiving countries. Indeed, most of the populations of the Western Hemisphere and of Australia and New Zealand consist of descendants of those who immigrated in the past several centuries. In addition, since 1960 the fastest-growing migration has been from developing countries to industrialized countries.

The basic modern history of immigration flows into North America and Europe is sketched in Figures 15.2 and 15.3. Figure 15.2 shows that the rising tide of immigration into North America since World War II has still not reached its levels before World War I, when both Canada and the United States opened their doors to immigrants and even advertised in Europe to attract them. After World War I, the door swung toward shut. The United States severely restricted immigration in 1924, using a system of quotas by national origin, in response to unprecedented public fear of strange cultures, revolutionary radicalism, and job competition. Canada also switched from actively recruiting immigrants to limiting them, especially when hard times hit in the 1930s.

FIGURE 15.3   Net Immigration Rates into the European Union, 1960–2012

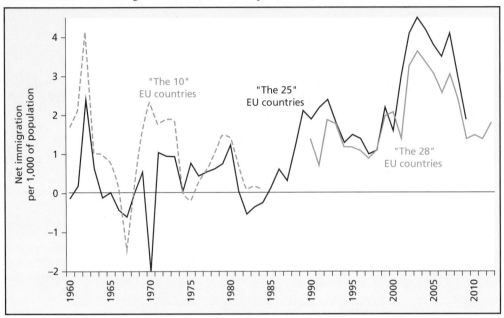

Net immigration = (Gross) immigration minus emigration.
"The 10" EU countries = the original six (Belgium, France, Germany, Italy, Luxembourg, and the Netherlands) plus the UK, Ireland, Denmark, and Greece.
"The 25" EU countries = the 25 member countries as of the end of 2004.
"The 28" EU countries = the 28 member countries as of the end of 2013.

Sources: European Communities, Statistical Offices (Eurostat), *Bevolkerungsstatistik* (Demographic Statistics), Brussels, 1986; Eurostat, *Population Statistics,* 2006 edition; and Eurostat, Statistics Database, Population.

After World War II, both countries relied on partial controls that favored immigrants arriving with training and experience. In 1965, the United States replaced the national-origin quotas with a system that gave preference to applicants with family relatives already in the United States, and subsequent changes opened the door to more refugees. In 1974, Canada also shifted to a liberal policy toward relatives. Family members and refugees began to arrive at a quickening rate in the 1980s. In the Immigration Reform and Control Act (IRCA) of 1986, the United States tried to solve two immigration policy problems at once: cutting the further inflow of "illegal" (undocumented) immigrants and giving amnesty (permanent residence rights) to those who came earlier. One result of IRCA was the temporary jump in legal immigration for 1989–1991, a jump that helped reawaken natives' concern about being burdened with a new wave of immigrants.

The doors in the European Union (EU) have also swung open, then shut, and then more open again, in this case within the shorter period since the EU was formed in 1957. In the 1950s and 1960s, the EU countries welcomed and even recruited workers from Turkey and other nonmember countries to help with the postwar reconstruction boom. In the early 1970s, however, the mood changed, as suggested by Figure 15.3. One EU country after another tightened up its immigration policy, partly out of rising cultural frictions and partly to protect jobs after the first oil crisis began to raise unemployment in 1974. Fewer immigrants were granted entry into the EU from 1974 to 1988. Then, the inflow began to rise again. The reason is not that EU immigration policy liberalized after 1988, but rather that a change in conditions outside the EU forced more immigrants through the same half-open doors. In particular, the rise of asylum seekers from the Balkan and other formerly communist countries made greater demands on those countries whose laws allowed for compassion toward refugees. The strain was particularly great on Germany because of its prosperity, the reunification of West and East Germany, Germany's proximity to the transition countries, and the German constitution's provision that refugees must be given safe haven. In 1993, Germany repealed the constitutional safe-haven guarantees and began clamping down on immigration.

HOW MIGRATION AFFECTS LABOR MARKETS

To see some important economic effects of migration, let's squeeze as much as we can out of a thrice-squeezed orange, the familiar demand–supply framework already used extensively in earlier chapters. To simplify the analysis, we aggregate the whole world into two stylized countries: a low-income "South" and a high-income "North." Let's start with a situation in which no migration is allowed, as at the points A in the two sides of Figure 15.4. In this initial situation northern workers earn $6.00 an hour and southern workers of comparable skill earn $2.00 an hour. (Realistically, we presume that factor-price equalization, as discussed in Chapter 5, does not hold, perhaps because of governmental barriers to free trade or differences in technologies.)

If all official barriers to migration are removed, southern workers can go north and compete for northern jobs. If moving were costless and painless, they would do so in large numbers until they had bid the northern wage rate down and the southern wage rate up enough to equate the two.

Yet moving also brings costs to the migrants. Monetary costs include the transportation and other expenses of migration, as well as lost wages while relocating. In addition, migrants usually feel uprooted from friends and relatives. They feel uncertain about many dimensions of life in a strange country. They may have to learn new customs and a new language. They may have to endure hostility in their new country. All these things matter, so much so that we should imagine that wide wage gaps would persist even with complete legal freedom to move. Thus only a lesser number of persons, 20 million of them in Figure 15.4, find the wage gains from moving high enough to compensate them for the migration costs (c), here valued at $1.80 per hour of work in the North. The inflow of migrant labor thus bids the northern wage rate down only to $5.00, and the outflow of the same workers only raises southern wages up to $3.20. The new equilibrium, at points B, finds the number who have chosen to migrate just equal to the demand for extra labor in the North at $5.00 an hour.

Those who decide to migrate earn $5.00 an hour in the North, but it is worth only as much as $3.20 in the South because of the costs and drawbacks of working in the

FIGURE 15.4 Labor-Market Effects of Migration

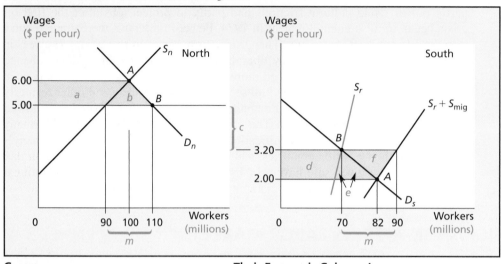

Group	Their Economic Gains or Losses	
Migrants	Gain area (e + f)	
Workers remaining in the South	Gain area d	
Southern employers	Lose area (d + e) }	Lose area e
Native northern workers	Lose area a	
Northern employers	Gain area (a + b) }	Gain area b
The world	Gains area (b + f)	

m = number of migrants = 20 million.

c = annuitized cost of migrating, both economic and psychic (being uprooted, etc.), which offsets $1.80 per hour of extra pay.

(By holding the labor demand curves fixed, we gloss over the small shifts in them that would result from the migrants' own spending.)

North. To measure their net gain, we take the area above the migrants' labor supply curve between the old and the new wage rates ($2.00 and $3.20), or areas e and f.[4]

It is not hard to identify the other groups of net gainers and losers in the two regions. Workers remaining in the South, whose labor supply curve is S_r, gain because the reduction in competition for jobs raises their wage rates from $2.00 to $3.20. We can quantify their gains as sellers of their labor with a standard surplus measure, area d, in the same way used to quantify the gains to producers as sellers of their products in previous chapters. Their employers lose profits by having to offer higher wage rates. The southern employers' loss of surplus is area $d + e$. (They lose surplus because they are buyers of now higher-priced labor, just as consumers as buyers of products lose

---

[4]The migrants' labor supply curve S_{mig} can be derived by subtracting the curve S_r from the combined curve $S_r + S_{mig}$. Note that their welfare gain does not equal the full product of ($3.20 – $2.00) times the 20 million unless their labor supply curve (S_{mig}) is perfectly vertical, in which case the amount of time they devote to work is independent of the wage rate. (Note that their supply curve can be interpreted as a curve showing the marginal opportunity cost of their time.)

surplus when the product price increases.) Employers in the North gain, of course, from the extra supply of labor. Having the northern wage rate bid down from $6.00 to $5.00 brings them area $a + b$ in extra surplus. Workers already in the North lose area a by having their wage rate bid down. So here, as in the analysis of product trade in earlier chapters, some groups absolutely gain and others absolutely lose from the new international freedom.

The analysis in Figure 15.4 shows some clear and perhaps unexpected effects on the well-being of entire nations (excluding those who migrate because it is debatable which country they belong to). Let's turn first to the effects on the North, here defined so as to exclude the migrants even after they have arrived. As a nation the North gains in standard economic terms—the gain to employers (and the general public buying their products) clearly outweighs the loss to "native" workers. Area b is the net gain. The case of restricting immigration cannot lie in any net national economic loss unless we can introduce substantial negative effects not shown in Figure 15.4.

The sending country, defined as those who remain in the South after the migrants' departure, clearly loses. Employers' losses of $d + e$ exceed workers' gain of d alone. So far it looks as though receiving countries and the migrants gain, while sending countries lose. The world as a whole gains, of course, because freedom to migrate sends people toward countries where they will make a greater net contribution to world production.

Does migration really work that way? Does it make wage rates more equal in different countries? Are competing workers harmed in receiving countries? Do immigrants eventually catch up with them in pay? Does the world as a whole gain? Several studies have shown that the predictions of Figure 15.4 are borne out by the history of migration, both in the great integration of the world economy before 1914 and again in experience since the mid-1970s. Here are some of the main findings of the empirical studies:[5]

- Freer migration makes wage rates in the migrant-related occupations more equal between countries.

- Directly competing workers in the receiving countries have their pay lowered, relative to less immigrant-threatened occupations and relative to such nonlabor incomes as land rents. For the United States, the proportion of immigrants who have not completed high school is relatively large, and the major group of workers hurt by rising immigration since 1980 consists of the least-skilled American workers (e.g., high school dropouts).

- Immigrants' earnings catch up partly, but not completely, within their own lifetimes. Numerous studies have traced their convergence toward the better pay enjoyed by native-born workers, but the deficit is not erased in the first generation after migration. The pay deficit has grown more pronounced in Canada and the United States since the 1970s.

- World output is raised by allowing more migration.

[5]For a sampling from this literature, see Borjas, Freeman, and Katz (1997, on the United States); Dustman, Frattini, and Preston (2013, on Britain); Pope and Withers (1993, on Australia); Bloom, Grenier, and Gunderson (1994, on Canada); and Friedberg and Hunt (1995).

SHOULD THE SENDING COUNTRY RESTRICT EMIGRATION?

Our analysis of the labor market shows that the sending country loses economic well-being because of emigration. Employers (and consumers of the products produced by these firms) lose more than the remaining workers gain. Before deciding that this means that the sending countries should try to restrict out-migration, it is important to look at several other important costs and benefits of emigration for the sending country.

First, let's look at the effects on the government budget. The sending-country government loses the future tax payments that the emigrants would have made (and perhaps also their military service). At the same time, those who emigrate no longer require government goods, services, and public assistance, so government spending also goes down. However, some public-expenditure items are true "public goods" in the economic sense that one person's enjoyment does not increase if there are fewer other users. That is, to provide the same level of benefits to the people who do not emigrate, the government has to continue spending the same amount of money. Examples of true public goods include national defense and flood-control levees.

Because some government spending is for true public goods, *the loss of future tax contributions is likely to be larger than the reduction in future government spending as people migrate from the sending country.* The likelihood of a net fiscal drain from emigration is raised by the life-cycle pattern of migration. People tend to migrate in early adulthood. This means that emigrants are concentrated in the age group that has just received some public schooling funded by the government, yet the migrants will not be around to pay taxes on their adult earnings. For this age group, the net loss to the sending country is likely to be largest for highly skilled emigrants—the *brain drain*. They have received substantial education at public expense, and they would pay substantial taxes on their above-average earnings if they stayed. For example, in some small developing countries, including Guyana, Haiti, Jamaica, Senegal, Mozambique, and Trinidad and Tobago, over half of the college-educated people have emigrated.

There is also a monetary benefit to the sending country that is not captured in the examination of the labor market effects of migration. Those who emigrate often send voluntary remittances back to relatives and friends in their home country. Globally, emigrants send home at least $400 billion in remittances per year. Remittances add over 20 percent to the national incomes of such countries as Haiti, Lesotho, Moldova, Nepal, and Tajikistan. *Sending countries that do not receive much in the way of remittances probably lose well-being, but those that receive substantial remittances probably gain well-being.*

What could the sending country do to try to restrict emigration or its negative effects? It could simply block departures. However, this would probably require severe restrictions on any foreign travel, with all of the losses that such travel restrictions would impose on the businesses and people of the country. A more defensible policy would be a tax on emigrants that is roughly equal to the net contributions the country has made to them through public schooling and the like. An alternative policy approach is to encourage return after the emigrant has been gone for a while, by appealing to national pride, offering good employment, and so forth. Taiwan and South Korea have encouraged the return of their scientists and engineers to work in their rapidly developing high-tech industries.

SHOULD THE RECEIVING COUNTRY RESTRICT IMMIGRATION?

Our analysis of the labor market shows that the receiving country gains economic well-being because of immigration, even if we ignore the gains to the migrants themselves. Employers (and consumers of the products produced by these firms) gain more than the native workers lose. Before deciding that this means that the receiving countries should not restrict in-migration, we should look at several other important costs and benefits of immigration for the receiving country.

Effects on the Government Budget

The effects here are symmetrical to those noted for the sending country. Immigrants pay taxes in their new country, and they use government goods and services. Some of the government goods and services are pure public goods, so we begin with a presumption that the tax payments are larger than the extra government spending required to serve the immigrants. However, there is a concern in many receiving countries that immigrants use government social services disproportionately. This suspicion was the basis for a 1996 U.S. law that made even legal immigrants ineligible for some forms of public assistance.

The true fiscal effects of immigrants are hard to measure, as discussed in the box "Are Immigrants a Fiscal Burden?" For immigration into the United States before 1980 or so, there is consensus that immigrants generally were major net taxpayers, not a fiscal drain. There is also consensus that the fiscal effects of an immigrant depend on the skill level of the immigrant. More-educated, more-skilled immigrants have higher earnings, pay larger taxes, and are less likely to use public assistance. For the United States since 1970, the fiscal balance is shifting toward immigrants being a fiscal burden because the average skill level of immigrants is declining relative to that of natives. Still, any net positive or net negative effect on the government budget from current immigration into the United States is probably small.

External Costs and Benefits

Other possible effects of migration elude both labor-market analysis and fiscal accounting. Migration may generate external costs and benefits outside private and public-fiscal marketplaces. Three kinds of possible externalities merit mention:

1. *Knowledge benefits.* People carry knowledge with them, and much of that knowledge has economic value, be it tricks of the trade, food recipes, artistic talent, farming practices, or advanced technology. American examples include migrants Andrew Carnegie, Albert Einstein, and many virtuosi of classical music. Often only part of the economic benefits of this knowledge accrues to the migrants and those to whom the migrants sell their services. Part often spills over to others, especially others in the same country. Migration may thus transfer external benefits of knowledge from the sending to the receiving country.

2. *Congestion costs.* Immigration, like any other source of population growth, may bring external costs associated with crowding: extra noise, conflict, and crime. If so, then this is a partial offset to the gains of the receiving country.

Case Study   Are Immigrants a Fiscal Burden?

It is widely suspected that immigrants are a fiscal burden, swelling the rolls of those receiving public assistance, using public schools, and raising police costs more than they pay back in taxes. This suspicion was the basis for a U.S. law that made immigrants (both legal and illegal) ineligible for some forms of public assistance. This suspicion, applied to illegal immigrants, was the basis for citizens first in California, and later in Arizona, to vote to deny public services to immigrants whose papers are not in order.

Are immigrants a burden to native taxpayers? The answer to this question is more complicated than it sounds, for two reasons:

- While some effects are easy to quantify using government data, other effects must be estimated without much guidance from available data.
- The full fiscal effects of a new immigrant occur over a long time—the immigrant's remaining lifetime and the lives of her descendants.

Let's look first at the effects of the set of immigrants that are in a country at a particular time. This kind of analysis provides a snapshot of the fiscal effects of immigrants during a year. We can see clearly what we can and cannot quantify well, but we do not see effects over lifetimes.

The Organization for Economic Cooperation and Development (2013, Chapter 3) examined the fiscal effects of immigrants in each of a number of countries during 2006–2008. Part of the analysis was relatively easy. The OECD researchers had good information on direct financial payments to and from the government. The immigrants' payments to the government include income taxes and social security contributions. Government payments to the immigrants include public pensions and transfers for public assistance, unemployment and disability benefits, family and child benefits, and housing support. If these were all the fiscal effects of immigrants, then, in most countries examined, immigrants made a positive net fiscal contribution. The first column of the

table shows the sizes of the net direct payments as a percent of GDP, for a few countries from the study. For Germany, the net effect of immigrants was negative because many immigrants in Germany are pensioners (Turks who arrived as guest workers in the 1960s and refugees from the former Soviet Union who arrived in the 1990s).

The remaining part is hard. Immigrants pay other kinds of taxes, including value added or sales taxes and, indirectly, corporate income taxes. And immigrants share in using all kinds of public services, including schools, medical care, training and labor market assistance, infrastructure, police, public administration, and defense. How much does immigrants' use of each of these items expand government spending on it? The answer varies by the type of service and immigrants' use. Immigrants probably have almost no effect on national defense expenditures. (Indeed, they might add effective soldiers.) Immigrants' use of education and health services probably does require additional government expenditures to maintain the same level of services to everyone else. Immigrants' use of transport infrastructure, police services, and similar items may require some expansion of government expenditure on these items. The hard part is that there is no good way to know how much immigrants expand government expenditures on most of these items. To go further, we must make assumptions.

The OECD researchers made assumptions to allocate these items (excluding defense spending and interest on government debt), generally by using per person estimates of the items. The second column of the table shows the estimates for the net fiscal effects of both the direct payments and the allocated items. Based on the assumptions used by the researchers, the allocated items are net negative for most countries, including the five shown here. For the United States, the estimated net fiscal effect of its immigrants shifts from a positive contribution to a negative "burden." However, perhaps the most defensible conclusions are that, for most countries including the United States, the current fiscal effects of immigrants are challenging to measure and probably are relatively small.

	Direct Payments, Net	Direct Payments and Allocated Items, Net
United States	0.03	−0.64
Britain	0.46	−0.01
Germany	−1.13	−1.93
Switzerland	1.95	1.42
Spain	0.54	0.07

Another way to look at the fiscal effects of immigrants is over their entire remaining lifetimes, and even to examine the fiscal effects of their descendants. For government programs that have costs for recipients of some ages but generate tax revenues from these same recipients at other ages, the lifetime approach is the more sensible way to calculate the fiscal effects of a small increase in immigration. One example is public schooling. Immigrants' children increase the cost of providing public schooling. But the schooling increases the children's future earnings, so the government eventually collects more taxes. Another example is social security. While working, immigrants pay social security taxes, but in the future they will collect social security payments.

Analysis of the fiscal effects of immigrants over lifetimes is complicated and requires many assumptions, including assumptions about how much immigrants add to costs as they consume various public services. Smith and Edmonston (1997, Chapter 7) examine the lifetime fiscal effects of typical immigrants in the United States as of 1996. Over the lifetime of the average immigrant (not including descendants), the net fiscal effect is slightly negative, about $3,000 net cost to native taxpayers. However, the effect depends strongly on how educated the immigrant is. (Education is used as an indicator of earnings potential based on labor skill or human capital.)

- The average immigrant who did not complete high school imposes a lifetime net cost of $89,000.
- The average immigrant who is a high school graduate imposes a net fiscal cost of $31,000.
- The average immigrant who has at least one year of college provides a lifetime net fiscal *benefit* of $105,000.

These findings indicate that the fiscal effects of immigrants depend very much on the levels of labor skills of the immigrants. More-educated, more-skilled immigrants have higher earnings, resulting in larger payments of taxes. Immigrants with greater skills and higher earnings are also less likely to use public assistance.

In addition, Smith and Edmonston conclude that the descendants of the typical immigrant provide a net fiscal benefit of $83,000. Thus, the typical immigrant and her descendants provide a net fiscal benefit of $80,000 (= −$3,000 + $83,000). Interestingly, this net fiscal benefit is not spread evenly over government units. State and local governments bear a net fiscal cost of $25,000, while the U.S. federal government receives a net benefit of $105,000.* We can see a clear basis for tension between states and the federal government over immigration policies. Especially, we can see the basis for California's efforts to limit its outlays for immigrants because California has by far the largest proportion of immigrants of any state.

DISCUSSION QUESTION

Immigrants, compared to natives in a country, tend to be young, to have lower wage rates, to be healthier, and to have more children. For fiscal effects for this country, how do these characteristics of immigrants matter?

*This differential is not unique to immigrants. The typical native-born child also imposes a net cost on state and local governments. They largely bear the costs of education, health care, and other transfers early in the child's life, while the federal government collects most of taxes paid after the child grows up.

3. *Social friction.* Immigrants are often greeted with bigotry and harassment—even from native groups that would benefit from the immigration. Long-lasting restrictions on the freedom to migrate, such as American discrimination against Asian immigrants beginning in the late 19th century, the sweeping restrictions during the "red scare" of the early 1920s in the United States, and Britain's revocation of many Commonwealth passport privileges since the 1960s, have been motivated largely by simple dislike for the immigrating nationalities. Although the most appropriate form of social response to this kind of prejudice is to work on changing the prevailing attitudes themselves, policymakers must also weigh the frictions in the balance when judging how much immigration and what kind of immigration to allow.

There is at least indirect support for the idea that admitting immigrants gradually would go far to removing social frictions and congestion costs. The United States experienced its worst surge of anti-immigrant feeling in the early 1920s, when the immigration rate was increasing toward the peak rate it had reached just before World War I. The immigration rate was higher then, just before and after World War I, than it is today, even if we add reasonable estimates of the number of unrecorded illegal immigrants. Even though some of the historic reasons for the anti-immigrant sentiment of that time (e.g., the Bolshevik Revolution) transcend economics, the high rate of immigration itself must have contributed to the fears and resentments of those Americans whose families had migrated earlier.

What Policies to Select Immigrants?

The major industrialized countries have policies to limit the rate of immigration. If a country is going to limit immigration, on what basis should it select the immigrants that it accepts? Our economic analysis offers some insights. Two features of the analysis are prominent. First, the types of immigrant workers admitted will affect which groups within the native population win and which groups lose as a result of the immigration. For instance, if relatively less-educated and less-skilled immigrants are admitted, these immigrant workers will compete for jobs against less-skilled native workers, further reducing their already low earnings. Second, the types of immigrants admitted will affect the net fiscal benefit or burden of immigration. To gain greater fiscal benefits, the country should admit young adults who have some college education. In addition, admitting highly educated and skilled immigrants is likely to enhance the external knowledge benefits we just mentioned.

Australian policies toward immigration seem to draw from these economic lessons. Australia has used a point system to screen applicants, focusing on those whose age and skills are likely to be beneficial to the Australian economy. New Zealand uses a similar point system, and Britain began one in 2008. Canada also uses a point system to screen some of its applicants, but about three-fourths of immigrants into Canada enter based on family links or refugee status.[6] Immigration into the United States is even more heavily skewed toward family and refugees, with about one-tenth entering based on their worker skills. For both the United States and

---

[6]To see how you score on the Canadian point system, go to www.cic.gc.ca/english/immigrate/skilled/

Canada, the results of these policies are that the average skill levels of their immigrants have been declining.

Economic analysis can make a strong case for a country like the United States or Canada to tilt its immigration policies toward encouraging and selecting more-skilled immigrants while reducing the number of less-skilled immigrants that it admits. Of course, economic objectives are not the only national goals. A shift toward pursuing national economic gain would come at a cost of achieving less toward other worthy goals, including promoting family reunification and providing humanitarian assistance to refugees. And the shift toward pursuing economic objectives would make the brain drain worse and leave more people in the rest of the world with lower income levels.

Summary

A **multinational enterprise (MNE)** is a firm that owns and controls operations in more than one country. Multinationals usually send a bundle of financial capital and intangible assets like technology, managerial capabilities, and marketing skills to their **foreign affiliates. Foreign direct investment (FDI)** is any flow of lending to, or purchase of ownership in, a foreign firm that is largely owned by residents of the investing, or home, country.

FDI grew rapidly for several decades after World War II, with the United States being the largest source country. FDI grew more slowly from the mid-1970s to the mid-1980s, but since the mid-1980s, FDI has grown rapidly. From the mid-1970s to the early 1990s, direct investment flows into developing countries slowed, but these flows then increased substantially. Nonetheless, most direct investment is from one industrialized country into another industrialized country. In the 1980s, the United States became an important host country, leaving Japan as the only major home country that is not also a major host to direct investment.

Explaining why multinational enterprises exist requires us to go beyond a simple competitive model. Multinationals can overcome the **inherent disadvantages** of being foreign by using their **firm-specific advantages**. Still, there are at least two alternatives to direct investment. The firm could export from its home country, but **location factors** often favor foreign production. The firms could rent or sell their advantages to foreign firms using licenses. Multinationals see **internalization advantages** to full control of the foreign use of their firm-specific advantages, especially their intangible assets like proprietary technology, marketing capabilities, brand names, and management practices. Negotiating **licenses** with independent foreign firms for them to use these assets would be costly and risky. Large multinationals are often involved in *oligopolistic competition* among themselves. For instance, one multinational attempts to gain an advantage by entering a foreign country first, and the others follow quickly to try to neutralize any advantage to the first firm.

The profits of foreign affiliates are taxed by the host-country government, but generally not taxed or taxed little by the home-country government. When multinationals shop around the globe for the lowest-cost sites, they favor low tax rates. Part of deciding which country to invest in involves the desire to keep taxes down. In addition, firms can use **transfer pricing** to shift some reported profits to low-tax countries.

FDI could lead to less international trade in products (substitute for trade) or to more (complement to trade). FDI used to locate different stages of production in different countries increases trade. FDI used to establish affiliate production of final goods for local sales substitutes for imports. But better marketing by the affiliate can also expand imports of other final goods produced by the multinational enterprise in other countries. And affiliate production of final goods often requires use of imported components and materials. Studies of FDI and trade conclude that they are somewhat complementary, on average.

The home (or investing) country gains from the basic market effects of FDI, as long as the government loss from collecting less corporate income tax revenue is not too large. The home country may have other reasons to restrict outward-bound FDI: the possibility that it loses external benefits that accompany FDI and the possibility of foreign-policy distortion from lobbying by multinationals. The actual policies of the industrialized countries (the major home countries) toward outbound FDI are approximately neutral.

The host country has less reason to restrict FDI than does the home country. It gains from the basic market effects of FDI, and it gains from positive external technological and training benefits. In the past three decades many developing countries have shifted from restricting FDI inflows to encouraging them. Political dangers remain, however, in the relationship between host-country governments and major multinational enterprises.

Free international migration of people, like free trade in products, is the policy most likely to maximize world income. Yet perfect freedom to migrate is politically unlikely. The main beneficiaries of such a liberal policy, the migrants themselves, have little political voice in any country. More vocal are groups that resent the departure of emigrants or, more often, the arrival of immigrants.

The labor-market analysis of migration flows shows who wins and who loses from extra migration, and by how much. The main winners and losers from migration are the ones intuition would suggest: the migrants, their new employers, and workers who stay in the sending country all gain; competing workers in the new country and employers in the old country lose. Yet the net effects on nations, defined as excluding the migrants themselves, may clash with intuition.

The sending country as a whole loses, both in the labor markets and in the negative effect on the government budget. However, if the emigrants make large enough remittances back to the country, the sending country can gain from emigration. A case can be made for a brain-drain tax that compensates the sending country for its public investments in the emigrants.

The receiving country is a net gainer according to the labor-market analysis. In addition, it has often been true that immigrants pay more to their new country in taxes than they receive in public services. However, the declining relative skill levels of immigrants to the United States suggests that the government-budget effect is not as positive as it once was, and may now be negative. Immigrants also cause externalities, both positive (new knowledge) and negative (congestion, social friction).

The reason for the U.S. drift toward immigrants being a net fiscal burden is that the relative education of immigrants has declined, as U.S. admission policy has given preference to family relatives and refugees since the mid-1960s. A country can improve the net economic effects of immigration by skewing its admissions toward selecting young, educated, and skilled adults and away from less-skilled persons. While this policy would improve the economic side of the immigration accounts, it may clash with other objectives such as reuniting families and providing humanitarian aid to refugees.

Key Terms

Foreign direct investment (FDI)	Inherent disadvantages	Transfer pricing
Multinational enterprise (MNE)	Firm-specific advantages	Intrafirm trade
Parent firm	Location factors	International migration
Home country	License	Sending country
Foreign affiliate	Internalization advantages	Receiving country
Host country		

Suggested Reading

Caves (2007) and Barba Navaretti and Venables (2004) provide good surveys of the economics of multinationals. Mutti (2003) and Organization for Economic Cooperation and Development (2008) examine the effects of tax differences on the location of MNE production activities. Brainard (1997) presents a careful analysis of the trade-off between FDI and trade. Moran (2011) examines FDI in developing countries. The annual *World Investment Report,* published by the United Nations Conference on Trade and Development, presents a broad discussion of trends and issues involving FDI and multinational enterprises.

Collier (2013) and Hanson (2009) provide surveys of migration and its economics. Jean et al. (2007) survey research on the experiences of immigrants in industrialized countries. Smith and Edmonston (1997); Borjas, Freeman, and Katz (1997); Borjas (1994 and 1995); and Card (2009) analyze U.S. immigration and immigration policy. Hanson (2006) surveys economic research on illegal immigration into the United States. Docquier and Rapoport (2012) and Gibson and McKenzie (2011) survey economic analysis of the brain drain.

Questions and Problems

✦1. "Most FDI is made to gain access to low-wage labor." Do you agree or disagree? Why?

2. "Industrialized countries are the source of most FDI because they have large amounts of financial capital that they must invest somewhere." Do you agree or disagree? Why?

✦3. "Multinational enterprises often establish affiliates using little of their own financial capital because they want to reduce their exposure to risks." Do you agree or disagree? Why?

4. What might be the reasons that Japan is host to little direct investment?

✦5. Why does much FDI occur in such industries as pharmaceuticals and electronic products, while little FDI occurs in such industries as clothing and paper products?

6. Which of the following is foreign direct investment?

   a. A U.S. investor buys 1,000 shares of stock of BMW AG, the German automobile company.

   b. Procter & Gamble lends $2 million to a firm in Japan that is half-owned by Procter & Gamble and half-owned by a Japanese chemical company.

    c. Mattel, a U.S.-based toy company, buys the 51 percent of its Mexican affiliate that it did not already own.

    d. Intel sets up an affiliate in Brazil using only two sources of financing for the affiliate: $100,000 of equity capital from Intel and a $1 million loan from a Brazilian bank to the new affiliate.

✦ 7. A firm has affiliates in both Japan, whose corporate income tax rate is 40 percent, and Ireland, whose corporate income tax rate is 15 percent. The major activity of the Irish affiliate is to produce a special component that it sells to the Japanese affiliate, initially at a price of $18 per unit. The cost of producing the component in Ireland has just risen from $12 per unit to $14 per unit. The controller of the MNE is considering three possible changes in the price of the component (for the sales between the Irish and the Japanese affiliate):

Ignore the cost increase, and leave the price at $18 (no price change).

Increase the price to $20, to reflect exactly the increase in cost.

Increase the price to $22, and, if necessary, explain the price increase by making general reference to unavoidable cost increases at the Irish affiliate.

    a. If the goal of the MNE is to maximize its global after-tax profit, which of these three should the controller choose? Why?

    b. What does each national government think of this use of transfer pricing?

  8. Labor groups in the United States seek restrictions on the flow of direct investment out of the country. Why? Is their opposition to FDI defending only their special interest, or might it also be in the national interest? Explain.

✦ 9. A country currently prohibits any FDI into the country. Its government is considering liberalizing this policy. You have been hired as a consultant to a group of foreign firms that want to see the policy loosened. They ask you to prepare a report on the major arguments for why the country should liberalize this policy. What will your report say?

10. "As Chinese companies expand their FDI into the United States by establishing new affiliates and expanding existing affiliates, U.S. imports from China will tend to decrease." Do you agree or disagree? Why?

✦11. What are two reasons that immigration into the United States was so low in the 1930s?

12. "The size of remittances can affect the conclusion about whether or not a sending country gains from international migration." Do you agree or disagree? Why?

✦13. For each of the following observed changes in wage rates and migration flows from the low-wage South to the high-wage North, describe one shift in conditions that, by itself, could have caused the set of changes:

    a. A rise in wage rates in both South and North, and additional migration from South to North.

    b. A drop in wage rates in both South and North, and additional migration from South to North.

    c. A drop in the northern wage rate, a rise in the southern wage rate, and additional migration from South to North.

14. Consider the labor-market effects of migration shown in Figure 15.4. What is the effect of a decrease in the annualized cost of migration (a decrease in *c*) on each group?

✦ 15. Review the areas of gain and loss to different groups in Figure 15.4. Why do the migrants gain only areas *e* and *f* ? Why don't they each gain the full southern wage markup ($3.20 − $2.00)? Why don't they each gain ($5.00 − $2.00)?

16. "Sending countries should cheer for emigration because the migrants improve their economic well-being." Do you think this statement is true or false? Why?

✦ 17. Japan currently has a very low rate of immigration because of very restrictive Japanese government policy. You are trying to convince your Japanese friend that Japan should change its laws to permit and encourage substantially more immigration. What are your three strongest arguments?

18. Your Japanese friend, from Question 17, is skeptical. What are her three strongest arguments that Japan should continue its policy of permitting little immigration?

✦ 19. Which of the following kinds of immigrants probably contributed the greatest net taxes, after deducting public-assistance and similar payments, to the U.S. government? Which probably contributed the least?

a. Political refugees arriving around 2000.

b. Electrical engineers arriving around 1990.

c. Earlier immigrants' grandparents, arriving around 2010.

Chapter **Sixteen**

Payments among Nations

In previous chapters we focused on international trade in products. This focus is justified by the need to understand the basis for international trade and the effects of various government policies toward trade. In that discussion countries seemed to exchange exports of goods and services for imports of goods and services. Little attention was given to the monetary and financial aspects of international transactions.

It is now time to add money and international finance to our discussion. We will recognize (1) that many international transactions are trades in financial assets like bonds, loans, deposits, stocks, and other ownership rights and (2) that nearly all international transactions involve the exchange of money (or some other financial asset) for something else—for a good, service, or a different financial asset.

This chapter examines the framework used to summarize a country's international transactions. The scorecard is the **balance of payments,** the set of accounts recording all flows of value between a nation's residents and the residents of the rest of the world during a period of time. The balance of payments shows us an abundance of information about a country's international activities. As we shall see in subsequent chapters, it is also key to understanding how people trade one country's money for that of another country. In addition, the exchanges documented in the balance of payments have major implications for macroeconomic concerns like growth, inflation, and unemployment.

ACCOUNTING PRINCIPLES

In balance of payments accounting, we need to keep track of flows of value both in and out of the country and (arbitrarily) assign a positive sign to one direction and a negative sign to the other direction:

- A **credit item** (measured with a positive sign) is an item for which the country must be paid. It sets up the basis for a payment by a foreigner into the country—that is, it creates a monetary claim on a foreigner.

- A **debit item** (measured with a negative sign) is an item for which the country must pay. It sets up the basis for a payment by the country to a foreigner—that is, it creates a monetary claim owed to a foreigner.

Examples of credit items include the country's exports of goods, purchases by foreign tourists traveling in this country, and foreigners' investing in a new issue of the country's government bonds. In each of these cases someone in the country is entitled to receive payment from a foreigner. Examples of debit items include the country's imports of goods, purchases by firms in this country of consulting services from providers located in foreign countries, and purchases by investors in this country of the equity shares of a foreign company from the foreigner that previously owned the shares. In each of these cases someone in the country is obligated to make a payment to a foreigner.

Each transaction between a country and the rest of world involves an exchange of value for value (if we ignore, for the moment, pure gifts). Each transaction has two items, one positive and one negative, of equal value. Balance of payments accounting is just an international application of the fundamental accounting principle of *double-entry bookkeeping*. (Appendix E provides examples of international transactions and how to identify and name the two items. Here in the text we simply take for granted that we are using double-entry bookkeeping.)

Double-entry bookkeeping has a key implication. If we add up all the positive items (credits) and all the negative items (debits) in a country's balance of payments, we know exactly what the total will be—*zero*! That is, with everything in, the country's balance of payments always "balances." So why is the balance of payments interesting? The interest comes in how we get to that all-in zero value. We look at smaller collections of positive and negative items by grouping them into categories. For each of these categories, we can examine the total of all of the credit and debit items in that category. While this total might best be called a "sub-balance," it is usually just referred to as a "balance." For any single category or any combination of categories that is not the entire balance of payments, the balance could be positive, zero, or negative, and this can be interesting. A balance that is positive is called a *surplus*, and negative balance is called a *deficit*.

A COUNTRY'S BALANCE OF PAYMENTS

There are three major broad categories of items that define the three major parts of a country's balance of payments: the current account, the financial account, and changes in official international reserves. Let's look at each of these categories and what goes into them using the example of the balance of payments of the United States for 2013, as shown in Figure 16.1.

Current Account

The current account includes all debit and credit items that are exports and imports of goods and services, income receipts and income payments, and gifts. Let's take a look at each of these.

Exports and imports of goods (also called merchandise) are easy to understand. But what are the major services that are exported and imported? Tourism or travel services include the expenditures of foreign visitors on such items as hotel rooms, meals, and transportation. In addition, nations trade transportation, insurance, education, financial, technical, telecommunications, and other business and professional services. Nations also pay each other royalties for use of technologies or brand names.

If we add up all the items for exports and imports of goods and services, we get the **goods and services balance,** an important balance within the current account.

FIGURE 16.1
U.S. Balance of
Payments, 2013
($ billions)

Source: Bureau of
Economic Analysis,
U.S. Department
of Commerce,
"U.S. International
Transactions: Fourth
Quarter and Year
2013," *Survey of
Current Business,*
April 2014.

Current Account	
Exports of goods and services	2,271
Imports of goods and services	−2,746
Income received from foreigners	789
Income paid to foreigners	−560
Unilateral transfers, net	−133
Current account balance	*−379*
Financial Account (excluding official international reserves)	
Changes in U.S. direct investments abroad	−360
Changes in foreign direct investments in the United States	193
Changes in U.S. holdings of foreign stocks and bonds	−389
Changes in foreign holdings of U.S. stocks and bonds	247
Changes in U.S. loans to foreigners and other investments	191
Changes in foreign loans to the U.S. and other investments	182
Financial account balance	*64*
Official International Reserves	
Changes in U.S. official holdings of foreign assets	3
Changes in foreign official holdings of U.S. assets	284
Changes in official international reserves, net	*287*
Statistical Discrepancy[a]	**28**
Other important balances:	
Goods and services balance	*−475*
Overall balance[b]	*−287*

[a]The statistical discrepancy is the net value of all errors and omissions in measuring the items. It equals the negative of the sum of the current account balance, the financial account balance, and the net changes in official international reserves. Here it equals −(−379 + 64 + 287).

[b]The overall balance is also called the official settlements balance. It equals the current account balance plus the financial account balance plus the statistical discrepancy because it is the total of all items except for the changes in official international reserves. (It is also equal to the negative of the net changes in official reserves.)

The balance on goods and services measures the country's net exports. It is often called the *trade balance,* although this somewhat imprecise term also sometimes refers to the goods (merchandise) trade balance.[1]

Income flows are mainly payments to holders of foreign financial assets. In addition to interest, these payments include dividends and other claims on profits by the owners of foreign businesses. Income flows also include payments to foreign workers who are only in the country for a short time, such as the honorarium paid to a U.S. professor for giving a talk at a Canadian university.

Unilateral (or unrequited) transfers are the items that keep track of gifts that the country makes and gifts that it receives. These credit and debit items are needed so that

---

[1]The United States reports the goods and services balance monthly. This provides monthly information that is meaningful for many economic analyses. Nonetheless, there is considerable noise or variation in these data, so be careful when interpreting month-to-month changes. The United States reports its complete balance-of-payments accounts quarterly.

there is a double entry for each gift. For instance, consider the situation in which the U.S. government gives Mali foreign aid in the form of wheat (that has been grown in the United States), perhaps in response to famine in Mali because of a severe drought there. The U.S. export of wheat would be measured as a credit and recorded. But there is no item of value moving in the other direction because Mali does not pay for the wheat. The accountants create a debit item that matches the value of the wheat export and call the debit item a unilateral transfer.

There are several types of unilateral transfers. In addition to government grants in aid to foreigners, private individuals also make unilateral transfers. One large kind of private transfer is international migrants' remittances of money and goods back to their families in the home country. Another kind of private aid is charitable giving, such as international disaster relief.

The net value of flows of goods, services, income, and unilateral transfers is the current account balance. As shown in Figure 16.1, the current account balance for the United States for 2013 is a deficit of $379 billion. Most of this current account deficit was the deficit in the goods and services balance.

Financial Account

The net value of flows of financial assets and similar claims (excluding official international reserve asset flows) is the private financial account balance.[2] The values reported in the financial account are for the *principal amounts* only of assets traded—any flows of *earnings* on foreign assets are reported in the current account. What counts as a credit and what counts as a debit in the financial account (and also for official reserves) can be a bit confusing. Here are four possible items:

1. A U.S. resident increasing his holding of a foreign financial asset (a stock, a bond, or an IOU from a loan) is a debit. The U.S. individual is making a payment now (or extending a loan now) to the foreigner, so funds are flowing out of the United States now (negative item).

2. A foreign resident increasing her holding of a U.S. financial asset (a stock, a bond, or an IOU from a loan) is a credit. The U.S. seller (or borrower) is receiving payment now (or getting a loan now) from the foreigner, so funds are flowing into the United States now (a positive item).

3. A U.S. resident decreasing her holding of a foreign financial asset (a stock, a bond, or an IOU from a loan) is a credit. The U.S. individual is receiving a payment now (or receiving repayment of a previous loan) from the foreigner, so funds are flowing into the United States now (positive item).

4. A foreign resident decreasing his holding of a U.S. financial asset (a stock, a bond, or an IOU from a loan) is a debit. The U.S. buyer (or borrower) is making a payment now (or repaying a previous loan) to the foreigner, so funds are flowing out of the United States now (a negative item).

[2]*Financial account* is the term that the International Monetary Fund (IMF) and most countries now use for what traditionally was called the *capital account*. Confusingly, the IMF also now has a separate, very small category that it calls the "capital account," made up mostly of capital transfers that traditionally were included in unilateral transfers. Our presentation of the financial account actually includes the combination of the IMF's financial account and capital account.

If we focus on the direction of movement of the financial asset itself, then the debits and credits are just like exports and imports of goods and services. In examples 2 and 3 above, the United States is *exporting financial assets,* and each is measured as a positive value. In examples 1 and 4 above, the United States is *importing financial assets,* and each is measured as a negative value. However, we often focus on which way the funds are flowing, so examples 2 and 3 are often called *capital imports* and examples 1 and 4 are often called *capital exports.*

Some varieties of private financial flows call for special comment here. *Direct investments,* discussed in depth in the previous chapter, are defined as any flow of lending to, or purchases of ownership in, a foreign enterprise that is largely owned and controlled by the entity (usually a multinational enterprise) doing this lending or investing. Foreign investments that are not direct include international flows of securities, loans, and bank deposits. The securities are bonds and stocks. A foreign investment in a bond or a stock that is not a foreign direct investment is sometimes called an *international portfolio investment,* indicating that the investor does not own a large share of the enterprise being invested in, but is just investing as part of a diversified portfolio.

As shown in Figure 16.1, the United States had a reported financial account surplus of $64 billion in 2013. Given the way that the debits and credits work, this means that foreign residents on net were increasing their holdings of U.S. financial assets relative to the increase in U.S. holdings of foreign financial assets.

Official International Reserves

The third major part of the balance of payments keeps track of changes in official holdings of international reserves. Official international reserve assets are money-like assets that are held by governments and that are recognized by governments as fully acceptable for payments between them. The distinction between private (or nonofficial) international financial assets and official international reserve assets is not quite the same as the distinction between private and government. The term *official* refers to assets held by *monetary*-type officials, not all government. Other ("nonofficial") government assets are included in the private category. The purpose of this distinction is to focus on the monetary task of regulating currency values, to which we return in discussing the overall surplus or deficit.

In the late 19th and early 20th centuries *gold* was the major official reserve asset. While gold is still held as a reserve asset, it is now little used in official reserve transactions. The majority of countries' official reserve assets are now *foreign exchange assets,* financial assets denominated in a foreign currency that is readily acceptable in international transactions. For the United States, these foreign exchange assets are euro (formerly German mark) and Japanese yen assets. For other countries these foreign exchange assets are often U.S. dollar assets. Two other small categories of official reserve assets are claims that a country has on the International Monetary Fund (IMF)—the country's reserve position in the fund and the country's holdings of special drawing rights (SDRs), a reserve asset created by the IMF.

As shown in Figure 16.1, the United States received substantial financing from changes in the holdings of official international reserves. (The signs of the values here are interpreted in the same way as those for the financial account.) The U.S. government had almost no change in its holdings of international reserves. The big change was that foreign monetary authorities increased their holdings of U.S. dollar-denominated official reserve assets (mostly U.S. Treasury bonds) by a huge amount—$284 billion. The surplus in net changes in official reserve assets ($287 billion) provided the majority of the funds that the United States needed to finance its current account deficit.

Statistical Discrepancy

At the bottom of the accounts comes the suspicious item *statistical discrepancy.* If the flows on the two sides of every transaction were correctly recorded, there would not be any statistical discrepancy. In fact, as shown in Figure 16.1, the statistical discrepancy for the U.S. balance of payments for 2013 was a credit of $28 billion, meaning that the credit items for the United States were less fully measured than its debit items. The accountants add the statistical discrepancy to make the accounts balance and to warn us that something was missed. In fact, the statistical discrepancy understates what was missed. It is the *net result of errors and omissions* on both the credit and debit sides. In truth, more than $28 billion of credits were missed, but some were offset by failure to measure all the debits.

How do the measurement errors arise? Which items appear to be most seriously undermeasured? For the United States, we suspect that much of the discrepancy is undermeasurement of private capital flows, so the true financial account balance for 2013 is probably a larger surplus. For some developing countries, capital flight, in which people send wealth to foreign countries, away from the rules and supervision of one's home government, is another source of mismeasurement. We can imagine that people and firms also sometimes have an incentive to hide or underreport imports of products and income from their offshore investments.

THE MACRO MEANING OF THE CURRENT ACCOUNT BALANCE

The current account balance (CA) has several meanings. The first meaning comes from the fact that all of the items in a country's balance of payments must add to zero (because it is double-entry bookkeeping). All of the items other than the current account items are flows of international financial investments, both private or nonofficial (in the financial account) and official (changes in official international reserve assets). Therefore, *the country's current account balance must equal* net foreign investment (I_f), the increase in the country's foreign financial assets minus the increase in the country's foreign financial liabilities.

- If the country has a *current account surplus,* then its foreign assets are growing faster than its foreign liabilities. Its *net foreign investment is positive*—it is acting as a *net lender* to the rest of the world.

- If the country has a *current account deficit,* then its foreign liabilities are growing faster than its foreign assets. Its *net foreign investment is negative*—it is acting as a *net borrower* from the rest of the world.

As we saw in Figure 16.1, the United States was financing its current account deficit in 2013 partly by building its liabilities to foreign private or nonofficial investors and lenders (the private financial account was in surplus) and partly by building its liabilities to foreign monetary authorities (which were increasing their holdings of official reserve assets denominated in dollars).

A country's current account balance is also linked to its national saving and domestic real investment. A country can do two things with its national saving (S):

- Invest at home in domestic capital formation, which is domestic real investment (I_d).
- Invest abroad in net foreign investment (I_f).

That is, national saving $S = I_d + I_f$. Looked at another way, the country's net foreign investment equals the difference between national saving and domestic investment ($I_f = S - I_d$) or, equivalently, *the country's current account balance equals national saving that is not invested at home* (CA $= S - I_d$).

For the United States in 2013, another way to look at its current account deficit is that U.S. national saving was low, relative to domestic real investment. To finance part of the U.S. real domestic investment, it had to rely on foreign funding. (We take up this interpretation again in Chapter 24, when we examine how the U.S. current account deficit is related to the U.S. government budget deficit, the latter being a form of national dissaving.)

A country's current account balance also is linked to domestic production, income, and expenditure. *A country's current account balance is the difference between its domestic production of goods and services and its total expenditures on goods and services.* Recall from basic macroeconomics that domestic production of goods and services (Y) equals the demand for the country's production,

$$Y = C + I_d + G + X - M$$

where

C = domestic household consumption of goods and services

I_d = domestic real investment in buildings, equipment, software, and inventories

G = government spending on goods and services

X = foreign purchases of the country's exports of goods and services

M = the country's purchases of imports of goods and services from other countries

C, I_d, and G all include purchases of both domestically produced and imported goods and services. Imports must be subtracted separately because imports are not demand for this country's products.

The country's total expenditures on goods and services (E, sometimes called absorption) simply equals consumption, domestic investment, and government spending:

$$E = C + I_d + G$$

Therefore, domestic product equals the country's total expenditures plus net exports, or $Y = E + (X - M)$. The country's current account balance is (approximately) equal to its net exports, so a country's current account balance is (approximately) equal to the difference between domestic product and national spending on goods and services:[3]

$$CA = X - M = Y - E$$

Yet another way to interpret the U.S. current account deficit in 2013 is that U.S. households, businesses, and government were buying more goods and services than they were producing.

To summarize, the current account balance turns out to be equal to three other things:

Current Account Balance	CA
= Net foreign investment	$= I_f$
= The difference between national saving and domestic investment	$= S - I_d$
= The difference between domestic product and national expenditure	$= Y - E$

We have illustrated these meanings using the U.S. current account deficit. What would they mean for a country with a current account *surplus*?

- The country has positive net foreign investment (that is, the country is acting as a net lender to or investor in the rest of the world).
- The country is saving more than it is investing domestically.
- The country is producing more (and has more income from this production) than it is spending on goods and services.

Note that we are not saying that any of these is good or bad (at least not yet). Right now we just want to know that they are all ways of looking at the same situation.

These identities help us see what must be changed if the current account balance is to be changed. Consider a country that seeks to reduce its current account deficit (that is, increase the value of its current account balance, making it less negative). One implication of our analysis is that an improvement in the country's current account balance *must* be accompanied by an increase in the value of domestic product (Y) relative to the value of national expenditure (E). If domestic production cannot expand much, then national spending on goods and services must fall in order to decrease imports or to permit more local production to be exported.

The identities also help us to understand what forces might be causing changes in the current account balance. To see some uses for the current account, let's look at how it has behaved since the early 1960s for the four countries in Figure 16.2. Figure 16.2 shows both the country's current account balance and its net exports of goods and services—its goods and services balance—each as a share of the country's gross domestic product. The two measures differ by the country's net income flows and transfers. (It is good to look at these latter two items here, especially income flows, although we usually ignore them in broad macroeconomic analysis.)

---

[3]In equating $X - M$, exports minus imports of goods and services, with the current account balance, we are ignoring income flows and unilateral transfers. This is one of several simplifications generally used in macroeconomic analysis. (Another is equating domestic product with national income.)

FIGURE 16.2

Current Account
Balances
and Goods
and Services
Balances for the
United States,
Canada, Japan,
and Mexico,
1963–2013

Source: International
Monetary Fund,
*International
Financial Statistics.*

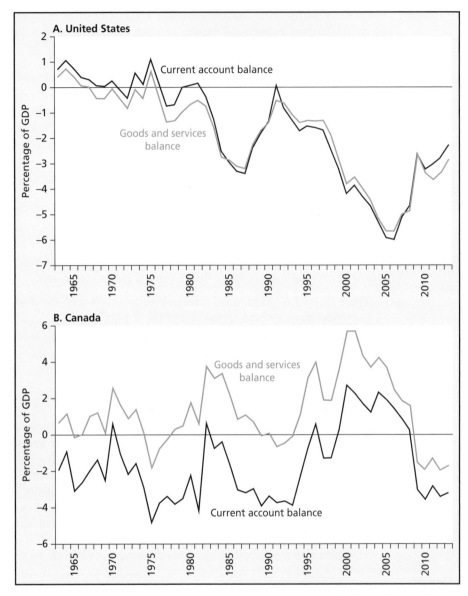

—*Continued on next page*

Panel a in Figure 16.2 shows that the United States has evolved from a net exporter and lender after World War II to a net importer and borrower. Up through the 1960s, the United States had a positive current account balance and a positive trade balance. The United States was a net exporter and lender largely because Europe and Japan, still recovering from World War II, badly needed American goods and loans. During the 1970s and up through 1981, a new pattern began to emerge. The United States became a net importer of goods and services but still kept its current account approximately in balance, thanks largely to interest and profit earnings on previous foreign investments. During the 1980s, the United States shifted into dramatic trade and current account

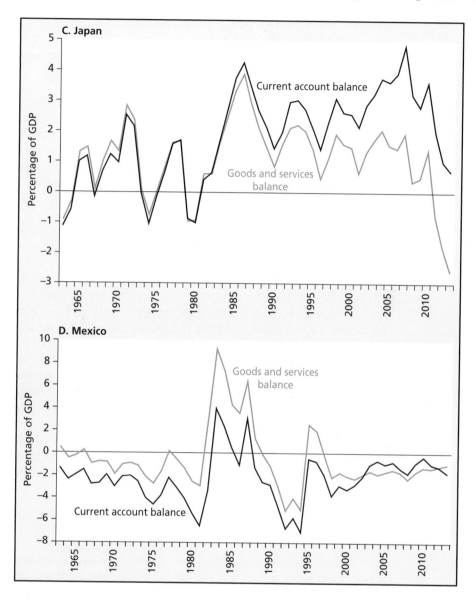

deficits, becoming the world's largest borrower. The underlying reason: Led by new federal government deficits, the United States cut its rate of national saving (S) much faster than its domestic investment (I_d) and therefore borrowed heavily from Japan and other countries (negative I_f = negative CA). The deficits declined in the late 1980s, but then began to increase again after 1991. By 2005–2006, the value of the U.S. current account deficit had grown to be about 6 percent of U.S. GDP, though it then decreased to about 3 percent of GDP in 2009.

Canadian experience up to the late 1990s fits a classic pattern of a borrowing country with good growth potential. Most of that time Canada borrowed from other countries (especially from the United States), as indicated by Canada's current account deficits. Canada used its typical goods and services surplus to pay foreign investors some of the earnings on their earlier investments. The payment of interest and profits on past borrowings is much of the gap between the goods and services balance and the current account balance in Figure 16.2 panel b.

Japan's goods and services balance and current account balance were nearly the same until the mid-1980s. These typically have been in surplus since the early 1960s. The surpluses became large and controversial in the 1980s, as Japanese goods gained major shares of foreign markets. Of course, the other way to look at this is that Japan's net foreign investment ($I_f = CA > 0$) became large in the mid-1980s. In those years Japanese foreign investment, including heavy lending to the United States, became the dominant force in international finance (although its role then diminished in the 1990s). Behind this shift to net foreign lending in the early and mid-1980s lay a widening gap between Japan's high national savings and its domestic capital formation ($CA = S - I_d > 0$). In addition, the rising net income from Japan's holdings of foreign assets has created a growing positive gap between the current account balance and the goods and services balance since the mid-1980s.

Until the debt crisis of 1982, Mexico was a consistent borrower. Its current account was in deficit (negative I_f), and net payments of interest and dividends to foreign creditors showed up as a widening gap between the goods and services balance and the current account balance. Figure 16.2 shows part of the tremendous shock Mexico felt when its debt crisis hit in 1982. Its trade balance jumped to a surplus of more than 9 percent of GDP in 1983, not because exports grew (they did not) but because Mexico had to cut out two-thirds of its imports in the belt tightening necessary to pay most of its swollen interest and repay principal to foreign creditors. Between 1983 and 1987, Mexico was actually a net "investor," in that it reduced its net foreign liabilities by running current account surpluses. From 1988 to 1994, Mexico returned to being a net foreign borrower ($CA < 0$). The peso crisis of late 1994 again forced Mexico into a radical readjustment of its current account, with a shift to a goods and services surplus in 1995 and 1996 and little net foreign borrowing (CA almost equal to zero) during those years. Moderate deficits reappeared in 1998.

THE MACRO MEANING OF THE OVERALL BALANCE

The **overall balance** should indicate whether a country's balance of payments has achieved an overall pattern that is sustainable over time. Unfortunately, there is no one indicator that represents overall balance perfectly. The indicator often used is based on the division of net foreign investment (or borrowing), I_f, into its two components: the net private (or nonofficial) capital flows, as shown by the financial account balance (FA), and the net flows of official reserve assets (OR). The **official settlements balance** (B) measures the sum of the current account balance plus the (nonofficial) financial account balance,[4]

$$B = CA + FA$$

---

[4]The official settlements balance also includes the statistical discrepancy because we assume that the discrepancy results from mismeasurement of private transactions.

Because all items in the balance of payments must sum to zero, any imbalance in the official settlements balance must be financed (or paid for) through official reserves flows:

$$B + \text{OR} = 0$$

If the overall balance B is in surplus, it equals an accumulation of official reserve assets by the country or a decrease in foreign official reserve holdings of the country's assets (that is, a debit in the official reserves account). If the overall balance is in deficit, it equals a decrease in the country's holdings of official reserve assets or an accumulation of foreign official reserve holdings of the country's assets (that is, a credit in the official reserves account). In some situations such changes in official reserve holdings can be specifically desired by the monetary authorities (for instance, gradually to increase the country's holdings of official reserve assets). In other situations these changes are not specifically desired and indicate an overall imbalance.

The official settlements balance measures the net flows of all private transactions in goods, services, income, transfers, and (nonofficial) financial assets. However, it is the counterbalancing items—the changes in official reserve holdings—that show the macroeconomic meaning of the official settlements balance. Most of the transactions by countries' monetary authorities that result in changes in official reserve holdings are official intervention by these authorities in the foreign exchange markets. The monetary authorities enter the foreign exchange markets to buy and sell currencies, usually exchanging domestic currency and some foreign currency. For instance, the monetary authority of a country can buy domestic currency and sell foreign currency. The selling reduces the authority's holdings of foreign exchange assets that count as official international reserves. Or the authority can sell domestic currency and buy foreign currency. The buying adds to its official international reserves.

As reported in Figure 16.1, the United States had an official settlements deficit of $287 billion in 2013. Foreign central banks added about this amount to their official reserve holdings of dollars, mostly by intervening in foreign exchange markets to buy dollars.

As we will see in the chapters that follow, foreign exchange intervention changes not only official international reserve holdings, it can also have impacts on many other economic variables. The intervention can affect exchange rates, money supplies, interest rates, private international flows of financial capital, domestic capital formation, domestic product, and exports and imports of goods and services.

THE INTERNATIONAL INVESTMENT POSITION

Complementing the balance of payments accounts (which record flows of transactions) is a balance sheet called the international investment position, a statement of the stocks of a nation's international assets and foreign liabilities at a point in time, usually the end of a year. Flows change stocks, and so it is with the balance of payments and the international investment position. For instance, if the country

FIGURE 16.3   U.S. International Investment Position at the End of Selected Years, 1897–2013 ($ billions)

	1897	1914	1930	1946	1960	1983	2013
U.S. investments abroad	$1.3	$5.0	$21.5	$39.4	$85.6	1,129.7	22,947.2
Private	0.7	3.5	17.2	13.5	49.3	924.9	22,407.3
Direct investments*	0.6	2.6	8.0	7.2	31.9	274.3	6,349.5
Other	0.1	0.9	9.2	6.3	17.4	650.6	16,057.8
U.S. government (nonofficial)	0.0	—	—	5.2	16.9	81.7	91.6
U.S. official reserve assets[†]	0.6	1.5	4.3	20.7	19.4	123.1	448.3
Foreign investments in the United States	3.4	7.2	8.4	15.9	40.9	868.2	28,297.7
Direct investments*	—	1.3	1.4	2.5	6.9	153.3	4,935.2
Other	3.4	5.9	7.0	13.4	34.0	714.9	23,362.5
U.S. net international investment position	**−2.1**	**−2.2**	**13.1**	**23.5**	**44.7**	**261.5**	**−5,350.5**

Direct investment refers to any international investment in a foreign enterprise owned in large part by the investor. For 1982 and subsequent years, direct investments are reported at estimated market values. For previous years, they are reported at historic cost.
[†]U.S. official reserve assets consist of gold and foreign exchange assets plus the reserve position at the IMF and Special Drawing Rights. For 1982 and subsequent years, reserve gold is reported at market values.

Sources: U.S. Bureau of the Census, *Historical Statistics of the United States: Colonial Times to 1970* (Washington, DC: U.S. Government Printing Office, 1976); and U.S. Bureau of Economic Analysis, *Survey of Current Business,* July 2013 and April 2014.

has a current account surplus for the year, its net foreign investment (as a flow) is positive. The country is adding to its holding of foreign financial assets (or decreasing its foreign liabilities). The value of its international investment position at the end of that year will be more positive (or less negative) than it was at the beginning of the year.[5]

The link between the two kinds of accounts relates to a subtle but common semantic distinction. We say that a nation is a *lender* or a *borrower* depending on whether its current account is in surplus or deficit during a time period. We say that a nation is a *creditor* or *debtor* depending on whether its net stock of foreign assets is positive or negative. The first set of terms refers to flows during a period of time, and the second set to stocks (or holdings) at a point in time. The box "International Indicators Lead the Crisis" discusses how the current account balances and international investment positions of Greece, Ireland, Portugal, and Spain foreshadowed the euro crisis.

Within the 20th century and into the 21st, the United States has come full circle in its international investment position. As shown in Figure 16.3, the nation was a net debtor before World War I. World War I abruptly transformed the United States into the world's leading creditor, and it reached a peak nominal creditor position by the end of 1983. However, the large current account deficits that the United States experienced during the 1980s required financing through increased international borrowing. The creditor position built up over 60 years was erased and reversed in the next 6 years. By early 1989, the United States again had become a net debtor, and the indebtedness keeps rising. Figure 16.3 dramatizes the change with the stark contrast in the net positions at the end of 1983 and the end of 2013.

[5]Changes in the market values of assets previously acquired can also change the international investment position.

Euro Crisis International Indicators Lead the Crisis

The beginning of the euro crisis is usually considered to be the announcement in October 2009 by the new Greek government that the country's fiscal deficit for the year would be much larger than the previous government had stated. If you had been watching two international indicators presented in this chapter, you would have been expecting that something was likely to go wrong in some of the countries in the euro area, with Greece as a leading candidate for trouble.

Consider the current account balances of several of the euro-area countries. The figure below shows the current account balances of four countries that all required bailout assistance during the crisis. The current account balances were close to zero up to about 1995. Beginning in 1995, the CA balances for both Portugal and Greece began to deteriorate. In 2008, as a percent of national GDP,

Greece's CA deficit reached about 15 percent and Portugal's CA deficit reached almost 13 percent. Spain's CA deficit began to deteriorate in 1997 and reached 10 percent of GDP in 2007. Ireland's CA deficit was not as problematic, but it did reach over 5 percent of the country's GDP in 2008.

Consider next the net international investment position for each country, again as a percent of the country's GDP, as shown in the figure on the next page. In 1999, when the euro was created, Greece, Spain, and Portugal were moderate net debtors, with negative net international investment positions equal to about 30 percent of GDP. (Ireland's data do not start until 2001, but its net debtor position was presumably less than 30 percent of GDP in 1999.) For Greece, Spain, and Portugal, the position steadily deteriorated. For Ireland, its net foreign debt

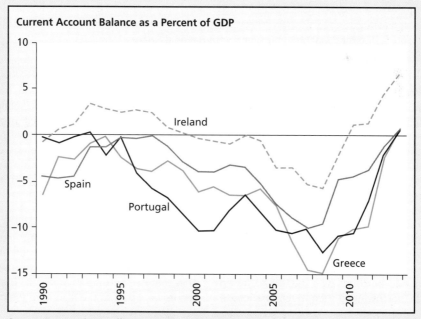

Source: Economist Intelligence Unit, *CountryData*.

—*Continued on next page*

Net International Investment Position as a Percent of GDP

Source: International Monetary Fund, *International Financial Statistics.*

exploded starting in 2007, as it entered into a massive banking crisis. By 2009, all had negative net international investment positions of between 90 and 110 percent. (In comparison, the net foreign debt shown in Figure 16.3 for the United States in 2013 was only 31.9 percent of U.S. GDP.)

For these countries, entry into the euro area (in 1999 for Ireland, Portugal, and Spain and in 2001 for Greece) lowered interest rates and encouraged borrowing, including foreign borrowing. Each country had its own borrowing pattern, as we discussed briefly in Chapter 1 and will discuss further in a "Euro Crisis" box in Chapter 21. The macroeconomic outcome was the same. Rising net foreign borrowing (I_f negative) financed a

growing current account deficit by financing national spending on goods and services (E) that exceeded national income from production of goods and services (Y). The flows of foreign borrowing led to the buildup of foreign debt.

Someone watching these indicators would have seen that, by 2008–2009, these countries' negative net international investment positions had become very large relative to the sizes of their national economies. With heightened sensitivity to risk from the global crisis that began in 2007 and intensified in 2008, foreign financial investors and lenders were unlikely to go on lending so freely to countries that had become so indebted. These developments were part of the lead-in to the euro crisis.

Summary   Basic definitions abound in this chapter. Terms introduced here appear constantly in the news media, and they will reappear throughout this book. Definitely review any of them that are not familiar at first sight.

A country's **balance of payments** is a systematic account of all the exchanges of value between residents of that country and the rest of the world during a given time period. Two flows occur in any exchange, or transaction, according to double-entry bookkeeping:

- A **credit item** $(+)$ is a flow for which the country is paid.
- A **debit item** $(-)$ is a flow for which the country must pay.

We can group the items into three major categories: those items that go into the current account, those items that go into the (private or nonofficial) financial account, and those items that are changes in **official international reserve assets** (countries' official holdings of gold, foreign exchange assets, and certain assets related to the IMF). Using these categories, we can create four important (net) balances:

1. The **goods and services balance** equals the net exports of both goods and services. It is often called the *trade balance.*
2. The **current account balance** equals the net credits minus debits on the flows of goods, services, income, and unilateral transfers.
3. The net private **financial account balance** equals net credits minus debits involving changes in nonofficial foreign financial assets and liabilities.
4. The **overall balance** (or **official settlements balance**) equals the sum of the current account balance and the private financial account balance (plus the statistical discrepancy from mismeasuring items in the current account and financial account). If the overall balance is in surplus, it is counterbalanced by an increase in the country's official reserve holdings or a decrease in its official liabilities to other countries' monetary authorities (debit items at the bottom of the accounts). If it is in deficit, it is counterbalanced by a decrease in the country's official reserve assets or an increase in its official liabilities (credit items at the bottom of the accounts).

The current account balance (CA) has special macroeconomic meaning. Because the current account balance equals **net foreign investment** (I_f), it also equals the difference between national saving (S) and domestic capital formation (I_d). A nation that is running a current account deficit, like the United States since 1982, is a nation that is saving less than its domestic capital formation. The current account deficit represents net foreign borrowing used to finance part of its relatively high level of domestic investment. The current account balance also equals the difference between domestic production of goods and services (Y) and national expenditures $(E$, expenditure on consumption, domestic capital formation, and government goods and services). Thus, yet another way of looking at the U.S. current account deficit is that the United States is buying more goods and services than it is producing (or spending more than its national income).

The overall balance is intended to indicate whether the overall pattern of the country's balance of payments has achieved a sustainable equilibrium. The official settlements balance does not quite match this concept, but it is still useful in macroeconomic analysis. It indicates the extent of official intervention in the foreign exchange markets—the buying and selling of currencies by the monetary authorities. As we will see in subsequent chapters, such intervention can have effects on exchange rates, money supplies, and many other macroeconomic variables.

A nation's **international investment position** shows its stocks of international assets and liabilities at a moment in time. These stocks are changed each year by the flows of private and official assets measured in the balance of payments. As a result of large current account deficits since the early 1980s, the United States switched from being the world's largest net creditor to being its largest net debtor.

Key Terms

Balance of payments	Current account balance	Overall balance
Credit item	Financial account balance	Official settlements
Debit item	Official international	balance
Goods and services	reserve assets	International investment
balance	Net foreign investment	position

Suggested Reading

Lane and Milesi-Ferretti (2007) develop and analyze estimates of the international investment positions of a large number of industrialized and developing countries. Higgins and Klitgaard (2014) discuss balance of payments aspects of the euro crisis. The balance-of-payments accounts of most nations are summarized in the IMF's *International Financial Statistics* and in its *Balance of Payments Statistics.* More detailed accounts for the United States appear regularly in the *Survey of Current Business,* and those for Canada are in the *Canada Yearbook.*

Questions and Problems

◆ 1. What is the current account balance of a nation with a government budget deficit of $128 billion, private saving of $806 billion, and domestic capital formation of $777 billion?

2. "A country is better off running a current account surplus rather than a current account deficit." Do you agree or disagree? Explain.

◆ 3. "National saving can be used domestically or internationally." Explain the basis for this statement, including the benefits to the nation of each use of its saving.

4. "Consider a country whose assets are not held by other countries as official international reserves. If this country has a surplus in its official settlements balance, then the monetary authority of the country is decreasing its holdings of official reserve assets." Do you agree or disagree? Explain.

◆ 5. Which of the following transactions would contribute to a U.S. current account surplus?

a. Boeing barters a $100 million plane to Mexico in exchange for $100 million worth of hotel services on the Mexican coast.

b. The United States borrows $100 million long-term from Saudi Arabia to buy $100 million of Saudi oil this year.

    c. The United States sells a $100 million jet to Turkey, and Turkey pays by transferring the $100 million from its bank account to the U.S. seller.

    d. A British investor buys $100 million of IBM bonds from the previous U.S. owner of these bonds, and the British buyer pays by transferring the $100 million from his bank account to the previous U.S. owner.

6. For each of the following changes (other things equal), has the value of the country's current account balance increased (become more positive or less negative), decreased (become less positive or more negative), or stayed the same?

    a. Net foreign investment out of the country increases.

    b. Exports of goods and services increase by $10 billion, and imports of goods and services increase by $10 billion.

    c. National expenditures on goods and services (E) increase by $150 billion, and production of goods and services (Y) increases by $100 billion.

    d. To assist recovery from a foreign disaster, the country gives a foreign transport authority a collection of transport equipment that has been produced in this (donor) country and that is valued at $500 million.

✦ 7. "For a country that has a surplus in its current account and wants to reduce this surplus, one way to do so would be to encourage its people to save more and spend less." Do you agree or disagree that such a shift would reduce the surplus? Explain.

8. You are given the following information about a country's international transactions during a year:

Merchandise exports	$330
Merchandise imports	198
Service exports	196
Service imports	204
Income flows, net	3
Unilateral transfers, net	−8
Increase in the country's holding of foreign assets, net (excluding official reserve assets)	202
Increase in foreign holdings of the country's assets, net (excluding official reserve assets)	102
Statistical discrepancy, net	4

    a. Calculate the values of the country's goods and services balance, current account balance, and official settlements balance.

    b. What is the value of the change in official reserve assets (net)? Is the country increasing or decreasing its net holdings of official reserve assets?

✦ 9. Which of the following can effectively provide financing for a country's current account deficit?

    a. Residents of the country sell foreign government bonds (that they had previously purchased) to residents of the foreign country.

    b. Residents of the country receive dividends and interest on their portfolio investments in foreign stocks and bonds.

    c. Foreign residents purchase newly issued equity in a number of the country's start-up companies.

10. For the past year, a country has $200 million of exports of goods and services, $160 million of imports of goods and services, $60 million of income received from foreigners, and −$40 million of net unilateral transfers. What is the range of values for income paid to foreigners, so that each of the following would be true?

   a. The country has a current account surplus.

   b. The country has a deficit for its goods and services balance.

   c. The country is a net borrower from the rest of the world.

♦ 11. What are the effects of each of the following on the U.S. international investment position?

   a. Foreign central banks increase their official holdings of U.S. government securities.

   b. U.S. residents increase their holdings of stocks issued by Japanese companies.

   c. A British pension fund sells some of its holdings of the stocks of U.S. companies in order to buy U.S. corporate bonds.

12. On December 31, a country has the following stocks of international assets and liabilities to foreigners.

   • The country's residents own $30 billion of bonds issued by foreign governments.

   • The country's central bank holds $20 billion of gold and $15 billion of foreign-currency assets as official reserve assets.

   • Foreign firms have invested in production facilities in the country, with the value of their investments currently $40 billion.

   • Residents of foreign countries own $25 billion of bonds issued by the country's companies.

   a. What is the value of the country's international investment position? Is the country an international creditor or debtor?

   b. If the country during the next year runs a surplus in its current account, what will the impact be on the value of the country's international investment position?

Chapter **Seventeen**

The Foreign Exchange Market

In foreign commerce, as in international dialogue, somebody has to translate. People in different countries use different currencies as well as different languages. The translator between different currencies is the exchange rate, the price of one country's money in units of another country's money. You can go only so far using just one currency. If an American wants to buy something from a foreign resident, the foreign resident will typically want to have the payment translated into her home currency.

This chapter introduces the real-world institutions of currency trading. It also begins to build a theory of exchange rates, starting with the role of forces that show up in the balance-of-payments entries of Chapter 16.

Much of the study of exchange rates is like a trip to another planet. It is a strange land, far removed from the economics of an ordinary household. It is populated by strange creatures—hedgers, arbitrageurs, the Gnomes of Zurich, the Snake in the Tunnel, the crawling peg, and the dirty float. Yet the student of exchange rates is helped by the presence of two familiar forces: profit maximization and competition. The familiar assumption that individuals act as though they are out to maximize the real value of their net incomes (profits) appears to be at least as valid in international financial behavior as in other realms of economics. To be sure, people act as though they are maximizing a subtle concept of profit, one that takes account of a wide variety of economic and political risks. Yet the parties engaged in international finance do seem to react to changing conditions in the way that a profit-maximizer would.

It also happens that competition prevails in most international financial markets despite a folklore full of tales about how wealthy speculators manage to corner those markets. There is competition in the markets for foreign exchange and in the international lending markets. Thus, for these markets, we can use the familiar demand–supply analysis of competitive markets. It is important also to make one disclaimer: It is definitely not the case that all markets in the international arena are competitive. Monopoly and oligopoly are evident in much of the direct investment activity discussed in Chapter 15 as well as in the cartels discussed in Chapter 14. Ordinary demand and supply curves would not do justice to the facts in those areas. Yet in the financial markets that play a large role in this chapter and the ones that follow, competitive conditions do hold, even more so than in most markets usually thought of as competitive.

THE BASICS OF CURRENCY TRADING

Foreign exchange is the act of trading different nations' moneys.[1] The moneys take the same forms as money within a country. The greater part of the money assets traded in foreign exchange markets are demand deposits in banks. A very small part consists of coins and currency of the ordinary pocket variety.

An exchange rate is the price of one nation's money in terms of another nation's money.[2] There are two basic types of exchange rates, depending on the timing of the actual exchange of moneys. The spot exchange rate is the price for "immediate" exchange. (For standard large trades in the market, immediate exchange for most currencies means exchange or delivery in two working days after the exchange is agreed, while it means one working day after the exchange is agreed for exchanges between U.S. dollars, Canadian dollars, and Mexican pesos.) The forward exchange rate is the price set now for an exchange that will take place sometime in the future. Forward exchange rates are prices that are agreed today for exchanges of moneys that will occur at a specified time in the future, such as 30, 90, or 180 days from now. This chapter focuses on foreign exchange in general and spot exchange rates specifically. Chapter 18 examines forward foreign exchange and its uses.

In today's increasingly international world, many online websites and newspapers keep track of exchange rates with quotations like those shown in Figure 17.1. Notice that each price is stated in two ways: first as a U.S. dollar price of the other currency and next as the price of the U.S. dollar in units of the other currency. The pairs of prices are just reciprocals of each other. Saying that the British pound sterling equals 1.6756 U.S. dollars is the same as saying that the U.S. dollar is worth 0.5968 British pound (0.5968 = 1/1.6756), and so forth. Each exchange rate can be stated in two ways. Each of the two ways sounds reasonable because both sides of the price are moneys. In contrast, for regular prices of goods and services, only one of the things being traded is money. So there is one natural way to quote the price (for instance, $9.00 per movie ticket). It is good practice to be careful to specify how an exchange-rate value is quoted, by stating the units in both the numerator and the denominator. As with other prices, the item that is being priced or valued is in the denominator. For instance, $1.6756/£ is the price or value of the pound.[3]

---

[1] The term *foreign exchange* also refers to holdings of foreign currencies.

[2] Exchange rates are one kind of price that a national money has. Another is its ability to buy goods and services immediately. This second kind of a price is the purchasing power of a unit of money—the reciprocal of the money cost of buying a bundle of goods and services. A third kind of price of money is the cost of renting it, and having access to it, for a given period of time. This is (roughly) the rate of interest that borrowers pay for the use of money, and it is analogous to other rental prices such as the price of renting an apartment or a car.

[3] Traders in the market also have conventions for stating exchange rates. In the market, most rates referring to the U.S. dollar are quoted as units of other currency per U.S. dollar, but some (the euro, British pound, Australian dollar, and New Zealand dollar) are quoted as U.S. dollars per unit of this currency. In addition, traders who are willing to buy or sell foreign exchange quote two exchange rates: one for buying and the other for selling. The resulting *bid-ask* spread is a source of profits to the traders. Furthermore, the difference between buying and selling rates (or the *bid-ask* spread) varies by size (or type) of trade. It is larger for smaller trades and largest for small transactions in actual currency and coins. The difference between buying and selling rates typically is very small for large trades in major currencies. We will ignore differences in buy and sell rates in most subsequent discussions, talking instead about the exchange rate as a single number.

FIGURE 17.1   Exchange Rate Quotations, May 30, 2014

The foreign exchange rates below apply to trading among banks in amounts of $1 million and more in late afternoon New York trading.

Country/currency	in US$	per US$	Country/currency	in US$	per US$
Americas			**Europe**		
Argentina peso	.1238	8.0784	**Czech Rep.** koruna	.04960	20.163
Brazil real	.4462	2.2410	**Denmark** krone	.1826	5.4750
Canada dollar	.9220	1.0846	**Euro area** euro	1.3632	.7336
Chile peso	.001821	549.10	**Hungary** forint	.004505	222.00
Colombia peso	.0005271	1897.00	**Norway** krone	.1674	5.9748
Ecuador US dollar	1	1	**Poland** zloty	.3290	3.0398
Mexico peso	.0778	12.8576	**Russia** ruble	.02866	34.895
Peru new sol	.3617	2.764	**Sweden** krona	.1495	6.6886
Uruguay peso	.04338	23.0525	**Switzerland** franc	1.1167	.8955
Venezuela b. fuerte	.157480	6.3500	1-mo forward	1.1171	.8952
Asia-Pacific			3-mos forward	1.1178	.8946
			6-mos forward	1.1192	.8935
Australian dollar	.9311	1.0740	**Turkey** lira	.4768	2.0972
1-mo forward	.9292	1.0762	**UK pound**	1.6756	.5968
3-mos forward	.9252	1.0808	1-mo forward	1.6753	.5969
6-mos forward	.9194	1.0876	3-mos forward	1.6745	.5972
China yuan	.1600	6.2486	6-mos forward	1.6731	.5977
Hong Kong dollar	.1290	7.7529	**Middle East/Africa**		
India rupee	.01686	59.309			
Indonesia rupiah	.0000857	11675	**Bahrain** dinar	2.6528	.3770
Japan yen	.009825	101.78	**Egypt** pound	.1398	7.1511
1-mo forward	.009827	101.77	**Israel** shekel	.2878	3.4742
3-mos forward	.009830	101.72	**Jordan** dinar	1.4115	.7085
6-mos forward	.009837	101.66	**Kuwait** dinar	3.5474	.2819
Malaysia ringgit	.3112	3.2135	**Lebanon** pound	.0006616	1511.45
New Zealand dollar	.8498	1.1768	**Saudi Arabia** riyal	.2666	3.7506
Pakistan rupee	.01013	98.695	**South Africa** rand	.0946	10.5729
Philippines peso	.0228	43.845	**UAE** dirham	.2723	3.6730
Singapore dollar	.7973	1.2542			
South Korea won	.0009794	1021.00			
Taiwan dollar	.03328	30.047			
Thailand baht	.03044	32.848			
Vietnam dong	.00004731	21135			

Source: *The Wall Street Journal*, May 31–June 1, 2014.

The foreign exchange market is not a single gathering place where traders shout buy and sell orders at each other. Rather, banks that act as dealers and the traders who work at these banks are at the center of the foreign exchange market. These banks and their traders use computers and telephones to conduct foreign exchange trades with their customers and with each other. The trading done with customers is called the *retail part of the market.* Some of this is trading with individuals in small amounts.

Case Study   Brussels Sprouts a New Currency: €

One of the currencies shown in Figure 17.1 was not there in the mid-1990s. On January 1, 1999, a major new currency, the euro (€), was born. The European Union (EU) created the euro, and 11 of the 15 EU countries began using it immediately, with Greece joining the club on January 1, 2001. For several years after the euro's birth in 1999, both the euro and the national currencies of these countries coexisted. Then, during the first two months of 2002, the national currencies of these 12 countries were completely replaced by the euro. The conversion rates were that 1 euro replaced each of

13.7603	Austrian schillings
40.3399	Belgium francs
5.94573	Finnish markka
6.55957	French francs
1.95583	German marks
0.787564	Irish punt
1,936.27	Italian lira
40.3399	Luxembourg francs
2.20371	Netherlands guilder
200.482	Portuguese escudos
166.386	Spanish pesetas
340.750	Greek drachma

Subsequently, Slovenia joined the euro area in 2007, Cyprus and Malta in 2008, Slovakia in 2009, Estonia in 2011, and Latvia in 2014, so that 1 euro has also replaced each of

239.640	Slovenian tolar
0.585274	Cyprus pound
0.429300	Maltese lira
30.1260	Slovakian koruna
15.6466	Estonian kroon
0.702804	Latvian lats

As recently as the late 1980s, the idea of merging the EU national currencies seemed like science fiction. But, in 1991, the EU countries drafted the Maastricht Treaty, and it became effective in 1993 after all EU countries approved it, some by close national votes. The Maastricht Treaty set a process for establishing a monetary union and a single unionwide currency, including a timetable and criteria for a country to join. But the system that preceded the euro, the Exchange Rate Mechanism of the European Monetary System, came under severe pressure in 1992–1993 and nearly collapsed. Monetary union still looked far away.

The national governments persisted, and people began to believe. In early 1998, 11 EU countries were deemed to meet the five criteria, covering each country's inflation rate, long-term interest rate, exchange-rate value of its currency, government budget deficit, and government debt. Three countries—the United Kingdom, Denmark, and Sweden—could have met the criteria but chose not to join the euro. Each had serious political concerns about the loss of national power and the loss of the national money as a symbol. The other EU country at that time, Greece, did not meet the criteria at first but joined two years later.

The euro is now one of the three major world currencies, along with the U.S. dollar and the Japanese yen. It is part of the growing integration within the EU, a process that also includes the "Europe 1992" drive for a single European market. The euro came under stress in 2010 and 2011 when rescue loans had to be granted to the governments of, first, Greece and then several other euro countries. In later chapters we will examine the implications of the euro for the macroeconomic performance of the EU countries.

DISCUSSION QUESTION

You are a Japanese citizen about to travel to France, Italy, and Slovenia for a vacation. Are you happy or unhappy that the euro exists?

We see this part of the market, for instance, when we travel to a foreign country, but individuals' exchanges are a very small part of overall foreign exchange trading. Most of the retail part of the market involves nonfinancial companies, financial institutions, and other organizations that undertake large trades as the customers of the banks that actively deal in the market. The trading done between the banks active in the market is called the *interbank part of the market.*

The banks active in foreign exchange trading are located in countries around the world, so this is a 24-hour market. On working days, foreign exchange trading is always occurring somewhere in the world. Although banks throughout the world participate, over half of foreign exchange trading involves banks in two locations: London and New York.

The total volumes traded in the foreign exchange market are enormous. Foreign exchange trading in 2013 has been estimated at about $5 trillion *per day,* which can be compared to a daily turnover of only about $500 billion for U.S. government securities and only about $300 billion for all stock trading around the world. Yet the number of people employed as foreign exchange traders in banks in this industry is several thousand for the world as a whole. (See the box "Foreign Exchange Trading.")

Most foreign exchange trading involves the exchange of U.S. dollars for another currency. Indeed, although some trades are made directly between currencies other than the U.S. dollar, many such trades are actually done in two steps. One foreign currency is exchanged for dollars, and these dollars are then exchanged for the other foreign currency. Because the dollar is often used in this way to accomplish trading between two other currencies, the dollar is called a *vehicle currency*.

Using the Foreign Exchange Market

In the customer or retail part of the spot foreign exchange market, individuals, businesses, and other organizations can acquire foreign moneys to make payments, or they can sell foreign moneys that they have received in payments. The spot foreign exchange market thus provides clearing services that permit payments to flow between individuals, businesses, and other organizations that prefer to use different moneys. These payments are for all of the types of items included in the balance-of-payments accounts, including payments for exports and imports of goods and services and payments for purchases and sales of foreign financial assets.

An example can show how this works. The example also demonstrates the role of demand deposits as the major form of money traded in the foreign exchange market. Consider a British firm that has purchased a small airplane (a corporate jet) from the U.S. producer of the plane and now is making the payment for it. If the British firm pays by writing a check in pounds sterling, the U.S. firm receiving the sterling check must be content to hold on to sterling bank deposits or sell the sterling for dollars. Alternatively, if the U.S. firm will accept payment only in dollars, then it is the British buyer who must sell sterling to get the dollars to pay the U.S. exporter.

Let's assume that the latter is the case. The British firm contacts its bank and requests a quotation of the exchange rate for selling pounds and acquiring dollars. If the rate is acceptable, the British firm instructs its bank to take the pounds from its demand deposit (checking) account, to convert these pounds into dollars, and to transfer the dollars to the U.S. producer. The British bank holds dollar demand deposits in the United States, at its correspondent bank in New York. The British bank instructs its correspondent bank in New York to take dollars from its demand

Case Study   Foreign Exchange Trading

In 2013, foreign exchange trading was an astounding $5 trillion per day. It is difficult to comprehend how large this number is. One comparison offers some guidance. In less than *four days* the amount of money traded in the foreign exchange market is a little larger than the value of U.S. production of goods and services for an *entire year*. In just the nine years from 2004 to 2013, global foreign exchange trading more than tripled. This rapid growth seems to be driven by large increases in trading by hedge funds, pension funds, and other financial institutions. These institutions have expanded their foreign exchange trading as they pursue international diversification of their financial investment portfolios. They also are increasingly using algorithms for computer-driven foreign exchange trading, including automated highfrequency trading.

What exactly is being traded in the huge global foreign exchange market? Where is the trading done? And who are the traders?

First, the what. In addition to spot and forward foreign exchange, there is one other traditional foreign exchange contract, the foreign exchange swap. A foreign exchange swap is a *package* trade that includes both a *spot exchange* of two currencies and an agreement to the reverse *forward exchange* of the two currencies (the future exchange back again). This type of package contract is useful when the parties to the trade have only a temporary need for the currency each is buying spot. In the 2013 global market, spot exchange was 41 percent of trading, forward exchange 14 percent, and foreign exchange swaps 45 percent. For all of this foreign exchange trading in 2013, the U.S. dollar was involved in 87 percent of all trades, the euro in 33 percent, the Japanese yen in 23 percent, the British pound in 12 percent, the Australian dollar in 9 percent, and the Swiss franc in 5 percent.

Second, the where. The global business was distributed in 2013 as follows:

United Kingdom	41%
United States	19
Japan	6
Singapore	6
Hong Kong	4
Switzerland	3
Other countries	21

About 60 percent of global trading is done in the United Kingdom (mostly London) and the United States (mostly New York). Even though the British pound itself is not that important in foreign exchange contracts, London is clearly the center of global foreign exchange trading.

Now, the who. Most foreign exchange trading is done by and through a network of dealer banks worldwide, banks that actively "make a market" in foreign exchange by quoting rates and being willing to buy or sell currencies for their own account. According to *Euromoney* magazine, in 2014 four banks conducted over half of the global trading in foreign exchange: Citigroup and Deutsche Bank, each about 16 percent, and Barclays Capital and UBS, each about 11 percent.

Most trading is done by several thousand traders who are employed at these several hundred banks. This is a surprisingly small number of traders, relative to the huge volume of trading conducted. There are good reasons why there are so few foreign exchange traders. One is the capital intensity of this business. It takes a lot of money and substantial investments in computer and telecommunications hardware and software, but only a few decision-makers. Another is the nature of the work itself.

Trading millions of dollars of foreign exchange per minute is a harrowing job; it's almost in the same category with being an air traffic controller or a bomb defuser. A trader should be somebody who loves pressures, makes quick decisions, and can take losses. Many who try it soon develop a taste for other work. Once an economics student visiting a foreign exchange trading room in a major bank asked a trader, "How long do people last in this job?" The enthusiastic answer: "Yes, it is an excellent job for young people."

DISCUSSION QUESTION

For foreign exchange trading, what is different about Asia, compared to Europe and the America? Do you think that this difference is surprising?

deposit account and transfer the dollars to the U.S. producer, by transferring them to the U.S. producer's bank for deposit into the producer's demand deposit account.[4]

As with most payments that are purely domestic, demand deposits are used in this foreign exchange trade and in completing the international payment for the airplane. The British firm uses the pounds in its demand deposit account to acquire the dollars needed. The U.S. producer uses its demand deposit account to receive the dollar payment. The British bank uses its dollar demand deposits in its correspondent bank in New York for two purposes: (1) as the dollars that it sells to its customer in the foreign transaction and (2) as the (same) dollars that are then transferred to the U.S. producer as payment.

Interbank Foreign Exchange Trading

A little less than 40 percent of foreign exchange trading is trading among the dealer banks themselves in the interbank (or interdealer) part of the foreign exchange market. What's being traded is still the same—demand deposits denominated in different currencies. But each deal is between one foreign exchange trader and another trader, not an "outside" customer.

The interbank part of the market serves several functions. Participation in the interbank (or interdealer) part of the market provides a bank with a continuous stream of information on conditions in the foreign exchange market through communications with traders at other banks and through observing the prices (exchange rates) being quoted. Interbank trading allows a bank to readjust its own position quickly and at low cost when it separately conducts a large trade with a customer. For instance, if Citigroup buys a large amount of yen from Toyota (and sells dollars to Toyota), Citigroup may be unwilling to continue holding the yen. Citigroup then can sell the yen to another bank (and buy dollars) quickly and at low cost. Interbank trading also permits a bank to take on a position in a foreign currency quickly if the bank and its traders want to speculate on exchange-rate movements in the near future. Such speculative positions are usually held only for a short time, typically being closed out by the end of the day.

About half of interbank trading occurs through brokers, and most brokered trading uses electronic brokering systems. The use of brokers provides anonymity to the traders until an exchange rate is agreed on for a trade. The other half of interbank trading involves traders at different banks in direct contact, mostly through electronic trading platforms. In addition, in the past decade the line between the customer part of the market and the interbank part of the market has blurred. A number of other financial institutions now have access to and trade on electronic platforms that previously had been a dealer-only part of the foreign exchange market.

Foreign exchange trading in this interbank part of the market is not for the little guy. Notice that the quoted interbank rates in Figure 17.1 are for amounts of $1 million or more. In fact, traders often save time by referring to each million dollars as a "dollar." With millions being exchanged each minute, extremely fine margins of profit or loss can loom large. For example, a trader who spends a minute shopping

---

[4]The British bank can also use dollars available at its own U.S. branch to carry out this payment in the United States if it has a branch there.

and secures 10 million pounds at $1.6756 per pound, instead of accepting a ready offer at $1.6757, has brought her bank an extra $1,000 within that minute. That's equivalent to a wage rate of $60,000 an hour. Correspondingly, anyone who reacts a bit too slowly or too excitedly to a given news release (e.g., announcement of rapid growth in the Canadian money supply, rumors of a coup in Libya, or a wildcat steel strike in Italy) can lose money at an even faster rate. On the average, these professionals make more than they lose, enough to justify their rates of pay. But foreign exchange trading is a lively and tense job. That department of a large bank is usually run as a tight ship with no room for "passengers" who do not make a good rate of return from quick dealings at fine margins.

DEMAND AND SUPPLY FOR FOREIGN EXCHANGE

To understand what makes the exchange-rate value of a country's currency rise and fall, you should proceed through the same steps used to analyze any competitive market. First, portray the interaction of demand and supply as determinants of the equilibrium price and quantity, and then explore what forces lie behind the demand and supply curves.

Within the foreign exchange market, people want to trade moneys for various reasons. Some are engaged in trading goods and services and are making or receiving payments for these products. Some are engaged in international flows of financial assets. They are investing or borrowing internationally and need to convert one nation's money to another money in the process of buying and selling financial assets, incurring and paying back debts, and so forth.

A nation's export of goods and services typically causes foreign moneys to be sold in order to buy that nation's money. For instance, the importer in a foreign country desires to pay using her currency, while the U.S. exporter desires to be paid in dollars. Somewhere in the payments process, foreign money is exchanged for dollars. We saw a specific example of this in the previous section on using the foreign exchange market. Thus, U.S. *exports of goods and services create a supply of foreign currency* and a demand for U.S. dollars to the extent that foreign buyers have their own currencies to offer and U.S. exporters prefer to end up holding U.S. dollars and not some other currency. Only if U.S. exporters are happy to hold on to pounds (or the UK importers somehow have large holdings of dollars to spend) can U.S. exports to Britain keep from generating a supply of pounds and a demand for dollars.

Importing goods and services correspondingly tends to cause the home currency to be sold in order to buy foreign currency. For instance, if a U.S. importer desires to pay in dollars, and the British exporter desires to be paid in pounds because she wants to end up holding her home currency, then somewhere in the payments process dollars must be exchanged for pounds. Thus, U.S. *imports of goods and services create a demand for foreign currency* and a supply of U.S. dollars to the extent that U.S. importers have dollars to offer and foreign exporters prefer to end up holding their own currencies. Only if foreign exporters are happy to hold on to dollars (or the U.S. importers somehow have large holdings of foreign currencies to spend) can U.S. imports keep from generating a supply of dollars and a demand for foreign currency.[5]

Similar reasoning applies to transactions in financial assets. Consider a U.S. insurance company that wants to replace some of its current holdings of U.S.-dollar-denominated bonds with British-pound-denominated bonds, perhaps because it expects a higher rate of return on the sterling investment. The company will need to sell dollars and buy pounds in the foreign exchange market, then use these pounds to make payment in the process of buying the pound-denominated bonds. U.S. *capital outflows create a demand for foreign currency* and a supply of U.S. dollars to the extent that the investors begin with dollars and a desire to invest in foreign financial assets that must be paid for in foreign currencies.

In another case, a British resident currently holding sterling demand deposits wishes to buy shares in Facebook. The person will need to sell pounds and buy dollars in the foreign exchange market, then use these dollars to make payment in the process of buying the stock. U.S. *capital inflows create a supply of foreign currency* and a demand for dollars to the extent that investors begin with foreign currency and desire to invest in U.S. financial assets that must be paid for in dollars.

All of these transactions create supply and demand for foreign exchange. The supply and demand determine the exchange rate, within certain constraints imposed by the nature of the foreign exchange system or regime under which the country operates.

Floating Exchange Rates

The simplest system is the floating exchange-rate system without intervention by governments or central bankers. The spot price of foreign currency is market-driven, determined by the interaction of private demand and supply for that currency. The market clears itself through the price mechanism. The two parts of Figure 17.2 show how such a system could yield equilibrium exchange rates for the pound sterling ($1.60/£) and the Swiss franc ($1.20/SFr) at the *E* points.

Let's digress for a little while, to examine the logic behind the slopes of the curves in Figure 17.2. We'll focus on the demand curve for foreign currency. What makes the demand curve slope downward? That is, why should a lower (higher) price of a currency generally mean that more (less) of it is demanded?

To see the likelihood of the downward slope, imagine that the exchange rate in Figure 17.2A has just shifted from $1.98 to $1.60. As the pound declines below $1.98, Americans will discover more uses for it. One use would be to buy wool sweaters in Britain. Before the pound sinks, a sweater selling for £50 in London would cost American tourists $99 (= 50 × $1.98). If the pound suddenly sank to $1.60, the same £50 wool sweater would cost American tourists only $80. They would start buying more. To pay for the extra sweaters, they would want more pounds sterling, to be paid to British merchants. As long as the level of business remains higher, there is more demand for pounds to conduct that business.

---

[5]International payments of income and unilateral transfers can also result in demand or supply of foreign currency. For instance, if a foreign company pays a dividend in its own currency, U.S. holders of its stock supply foreign currency if they want to take payment in dollars. As another example, some people in the United States and Canada demand foreign currency to send remittances and cash gifts to relatives in Italy, Mexico, or some other country from which they emigrated.

FIGURE 17.2   The Spot Exchange Market: Floating and Fixed Exchange Rates

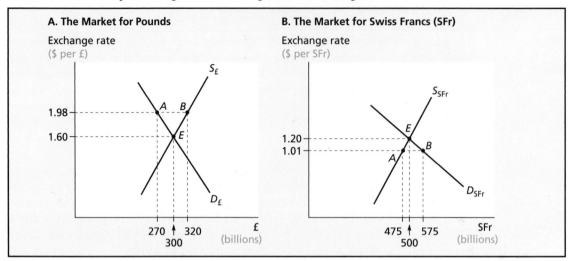

The demand and supply curves represent all demand and supply for that currency in the foreign exchange market, except for any official intervention by the official government monetary authorities (like central banks). With a *floating exchange rate,* the market reaches an equilibrium at points *E* in panels A and B. If the government wishes to *fix the exchange rate* at a different level, then it must intervene to buy or sell the currency to meet any difference between private (or nonofficial) quantity demanded and quantity supplied. In panel A, if the British government is committed not to let the pound fall below $1.98/£, the government must buy 50 billion pounds, equal to the gap *AB.* In panel B, if the Swiss government is committed not to let the franc rise above $1.01/SFr, the government must sell 100 billion Swiss francs, equal to the gap *AB.*

The case of British wool sweaters is just one illustration of the forces that would make the demand curve for a currency slope downward. There are usually many such responses of trade to a change in the exchange rate. A sinking pound means that Americans buy more cheese from British producers and buy less from cheesemakers in Wisconsin. There is more reason for Americans to buy British products and therefore more demand for pounds as a currency to facilitate such transactions. As long as a lower exchange rate raises the quantity demanded, the demand curve will slope downward.[6]

Now let's return to our market-driven floating exchange rate. What makes the floating exchange rate rise or fall over time? To answer we need to know the forces that shift the supply and demand curves. Again, let's focus on the demand curve. The demand curve is shifted by a variety of changes in the economy. Many of the demand-side forces relate to the balance-of-payments categories of the previous chapter. Shifts in demand away from U.S. products and toward UK products (caused

---

[6]Similar logic can be applied to examine the slope of the supply curve for foreign exchange, but the actual slope of the supply curve is not so clear-cut. We presume for now that the supply curve has the usual upward slope.

FIGURE 17.3

A Shift in
Demand for
Pounds in the
Spot Exchange
Market

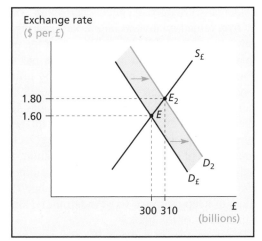

The demand curve for foreign exchange can be shifted to the right (or raised) by either of
the following changes related to the balance of payments:

A shift of U.S. demand toward the goods and services of other countries.
A rise in U.S. willingness to lend money to or invest in other countries.

If the demand curve shifts to the right, then the market equilibrium exchange-rate value
of the pound rises. (Chapter 19 discusses in more depth the forces that shift the demand
and supply curves and change the exchange rate.)

by forces other than changes in the exchange rate) would result in extra attempts
to sell dollars and buy pounds. This can be graphed as a shift to the right (or up) in
the demand curve for pounds. Similarly, a rise in U.S. residents' willingness to lend
money to UK borrowers or to invest in pound-denominated financial assets usually
requires that extra dollars be converted into pounds, thus shifting the demand curve
for pounds to the right.

In a floating-rate system, if for any reason the demand curve for foreign currency
shifts to the right (representing increased demand for foreign money), and the supply
curve remains unchanged, then the exchange-rate value of the foreign currency rises.
Such a shift is shown in Figure 17.3. The rightward shift in demand for pounds to D_2
increases the price of pounds from \$1.60 to \$1.80 per pound, as the market equilibrium shifts from E to E_2.

Fixed Exchange Rates

The other main foreign exchange regime is the fixed exchange-rate system. Here,
officials strive to keep the exchange rate virtually fixed (or pegged) even if the rate
they choose differs from the current equilibrium rate. Their usual procedure under
such a system is to declare a narrow "band" of exchange rates within which the rate
is allowed to vary. If the exchange rate hits the top or bottom of the band, the officials
must intervene. Let's return to Figure 17.2 to see how this could work.

In Figure 17.2A, consider an officially declared "par value" of $2.00, at which the pound is substantially overvalued relative to its market-clearing rate of $1.60 per pound. British officials have announced that they will support the pound at 1 percent below par (about $1.98) and the dollar at 1 percent above par (about $2.02). In Figure 17.2A, they are forced to make good on this pledge by officially intervening in the foreign exchange market, buying £50 billion (and selling $99 billion, equal to £50 billion times $1.98 per pound). This intervention fills the gap *AB* between nonofficial supply and demand at the $1.98 exchange rate.[7] Only in this way can they bring the total demand for pounds, private plus official, up to the 320 billion of sterling money supplied. If their purchases of pounds with dollars fall short, total demand cannot meet the supply and the price will fall below the official support price of $1.98. However, British officials wanting to defend the fixed exchange rate may not have sufficient reserves of dollars to keep the price fixed indefinitely, a point to which we will return several times in the rest of the book.

Another case of official intervention in defense of a fixed exchange rate is shown in Figure 17.2B. Swiss government officials have declared that the par value of the Swiss franc (SFr) shall be U.S. $1.00 and that the support points are $1.01 and $0.99. As the demand and supply curves are drawn, the franc is substantially undervalued at this fixed rate, relative to the market-clearing rate of $1.20 per franc. To defend the fixed rate, government officials must intervene in the foreign exchange market and sell 100 billion francs to meet the strong demand at $1.01. If the Swiss government officials cannot tolerate buying enough dollars to plug the gap *AB* and keep the exchange rate down at $1.01, they may give up and let the price rise.

Changes in exchange rates are given various names depending on the kind of exchange-rate regime prevailing. Under the floating-rate system a fall in the market price (the exchange-rate value) of a currency is called a **depreciation** of that currency; a rise is an **appreciation.** We refer to a discrete official reduction in the otherwise fixed par value of a currency as a **devaluation; revaluation** is the antonym describing a discrete raising of the official par. Devaluations and revaluations are the main ways of changing exchange rates in a nearly fixed-rate system, a system where the rate is usually, but not always, fixed.

Current Arrangements

Which countries have floating exchange rates for their currencies and which have fixed exchange rates? Here is an overview, without getting into everything now. First, most major currencies, including the U.S. dollar, the euro, the Japanese yen, the British pound, the Canadian dollar, the Australian dollar, and the Swedish krona, have floating exchange rates relative to each other. Second, the governments of a large number of other countries say they have floating exchange rates, though many use some amount of official exchange market intervention to "manage" the float. Third, some countries have fixed exchange rates between their currencies and the U.S. dollar. These countries include Hong Kong and Saudi Arabia. Fourth, some countries,

---

[7]Such official intervention could also be pictured as shifting the demand or supply curves. However, it seems more descriptive, when examining the defense of a fixed rate, to consider official exchange market intervention as filling the gap between quantity demanded and quantity supplied in the absence of the intervention.

including Denmark, Bulgaria, and former French colonies in Africa, fix the exchange-rate value of their currencies to the euro. We will examine these and other exchange-rate policies in more depth in Chapter 20.

ARBITRAGE WITHIN THE SPOT EXCHANGE MARKET

We have pictured foreign exchange as a single market for trading between two curren-cies. Yet we have also noted that trading occurs in different locations around the world. For instance, for a period of time each day, trading is occurring in both New York and London as well as in other money centers in Europe. Will the rates in the different locations be essentially the same at a point in time, or can they diverge as local supply and demand conditions differ? Furthermore, exchange rates exist for many different currencies, both rates representing the dollar price of various foreign currencies and the *cross-rates* between foreign currencies. Are these exchange rates and cross-rates related in some way, or can they have independent levels?

Arbitrage, the process of buying and selling to make a (nearly) riskless pure profit, ensures that rates in different locations are essentially the same, and that rates and cross-rates are related and consistent among themselves. What would happen if pounds were being exchanged at $1.70 per pound in London and $1.60 per pound at the same time in New York? If foreign exchange trading and money transfers can be done freely, then there is an opportunity to make a riskless profit by arbitraging between the two locations. Buy pounds where they are cheap (in New York) and simultaneously sell them where they are expensive (in London). For each pound bought and sold at the initial exchange rates, the arbitrage profit is 10 cents. Such arbitrage would occur on a large scale, increasing the demand for pounds in New York and increasing the supply of pounds in London. The dollar–pound exchange rate then would increase in New York and/or decrease in London. The two rates would be driven to be essentially the same (that is, within the small range reflecting transactions costs that prevent any further profitable arbitrage).

What happens if the exchange rate for the pound in terms of dollars is $1.60, the exchange rate for the Swiss franc in terms of dollars is $0.50, and the cross-rate between the franc and the pound is 3 francs per pound? Although it is more subtle, there is also an opportunity to make a riskless profit by arbitraging through the three rates—a process called **triangular arbitrage.** To see this, start with some number of dollars, say $150. Your $150 buys 300 francs (150/0.50). Use these francs to buy pounds at the cross-rate, and you have 100 pounds (300/3). Convert these pounds back into dollars and you end up with $160 (100 × 1.60). Your triangular arbitrage has made $10 profit for each $150 you started with. This profit occurs almost instantly and with essentially no risk if you establish all three spot trades at the same time.

As a large amount of this triangular arbitrage occurs, pressures are placed on the exchange rates to bring them into line with each other. The extra demand for francs tends to increase the dollar–franc exchange rate. The extra demand for pounds (paid for by francs) tends to increase the franc–pound cross-rate. The extra supply of pounds (to acquire dollars) tends to reduce the dollar–pound exchange rate. One or more of the exchange rates will change (due to demand and supply pressures) so that the cross-rate of francs per pound essentially equals the ratio of the dollar–pound exchange rate to the dollar–franc exchange rate. For instance, if only the cross-rate changes, then its value must shift to 3.2 francs per pound (1.60/0.50). At this cross-rate there is no further opportunity for profits from triangular arbitrage.

Just the threat of arbitrage of these types usually keeps the exchange rate between two currencies essentially the same in different locations and keeps cross-rates in correct alignment with other exchange rates. Opportunities for actual arbitrage of these types are rare.

Summary

A foreign exchange transaction is a trade of one national money for another. The exchange rate is the price at which the moneys are traded. The spot exchange rate is the price for immediate exchange of the two currencies. The forward exchange rate is the price agreed now for a currency exchange that will occur sometime in the future. Dealer banks and their traders are at the center of the foreign exchange market. They use computers and telephones to conduct foreign exchange trades with customers (the retail part of the market) and with each other (the interbank part of the market).

Spot foreign exchange serves a clearing function, permitting payments to be made between entities who want to hold or use different currencies. The exchange rate is determined by supply and demand, within any constraints imposed by the governmental choice of an exchange-rate system or regime. Under a freely flexible or floating exchange-rate system, market supply and demand set the equilibrium price (exchange rate) that clears the market. A floating exchange rate changes over time as supply and demand shift over time. Under a fixed exchange-rate system (also called a pegged exchange-rate system), monetary officials buy and sell a currency so as to keep its exchange rate within an officially stipulated band. When the currency's value threatens to fall below the bottom of its official band, officials must buy it by selling other currencies. When the currency's value presses against the top of its official price range, officials must sell it in exchange for other currencies.

Key Terms

Foreign exchange	Floating exchange-rate	Devaluation
Exchange rate	system	Revaluation
Spot exchange rate	Fixed exchange-rate system	Arbitrage
Forward exchange rate	Depreciation	Triangular arbitrage
Foreign exchange swap	Appreciation	

Suggested Reading

King et al. (2012) and Sager and Taylor (2006) describe the structure of and practices in the foreign exchange market. Two good textbook views are Eun and Resnick (2012, Chapter 5) and Eiteman, Stonehill, and Moffet (2013, Chapter 6). Cheung and Wong (2000) and Cheung and Chinn (2001) report information obtained from their surveys of foreign exchange traders. Fenn et al. (2009) examine opportunities for triangular arbitrage using detailed real-time data.

Questions and Problems

✦ 1. What are the major types of transactions or activities that result in demand for foreign currency in the spot foreign exchange market?

2. What are the major types of transactions or activities that result in supply of foreign currency in the spot foreign exchange market?

✦ 3. What has happened to the exchange-rate value of the dollar in each case?

   a. The spot rate goes from $1.25/SFr to $1.30/SFr.
   b. The spot rate goes from SFr 0.80/$ to SFr 0.77/$.
   c. The spot rate goes from $0.010/yen to $0.009/yen.
   d. The spot rate goes from 100 yen/$ to 111 yen/$.

4. A U.S. firm must make a payment of 1 million yen to a Japanese firm that has sold the U.S. firm sets of Japanese baseball-player trading cards. The U.S. firm begins with a dollar checking account. Explain in detail how this payment would be made, including the use of the spot foreign exchange market and banks in both countries.

✦ 5. A British bank has acquired a large number of dollars in its dealings with its clients. How could this bank use the interbank foreign exchange market if it was unwilling to continue holding these dollars?

6. A trader at a U.S. bank believes that the euro will strengthen substantially in exchange-rate value during the next hour. How would the trader use the interbank market to attempt to profit from her belief?

✦ 7. For each of the following, is it part of demand for yen or supply of yen in the foreign exchange market?

   a. A Japanese firm sells its U.S. government securities to obtain funds to buy real estate in Japan.
   b. A U.S. import company pays for glassware purchased from a small Japanese producer.
   c. A U.S. farm cooperative receives payment from a Japanese importer of U.S. oranges.
   d. A U.S. pension fund uses some incoming contributions to buy equity shares of several Japanese companies through the Tokyo stock exchange.

8. You have access to the following three spot exchange rates:

   $0.01/yen

   $0.20/krone

   25 yen/krone

   You start with dollars and want to end up with dollars.

   a. How would you engage in arbitrage to profit from these three rates? What is the profit for each dollar used initially?
   b. As a result of this arbitrage, what is the pressure on the cross-rate between yen and krone? What must the value of the cross-rate be to eliminate the opportunity for triangular arbitrage?

✦ 9. The spot exchange rate between the dollar and the Swiss franc is a floating, or flexible, rate. What are the effects of each of the following on this exchange rate?

   a. There is a large increase in Swiss demand for U.S. exports as U.S. culture becomes more popular in Switzerland.

   b. There is a large increase in Swiss demand for investments in U.S. dollar-denominated financial assets because of a Swiss belief that the U.S. economy and political situation are improving markedly.

   c. Political uncertainties in Europe lead U.S. investors to shift their financial investments out of Switzerland, back to the United States.

   d. U.S. demand for products imported from Switzerland falls significantly as bad press reports lead Americans to question the quality of Swiss products.

10. Assume instead that the spot exchange rate between the dollar and Swiss franc is a fixed or pegged rate within a narrow band around a central rate. For each change shown in Problem 9, assume that just before the change private (or nonofficial) supply and demand intersected at an equilibrium exchange rate within this narrow band. For each change shown in Problem 9, what intervention is necessary by the monetary authorities to defend the fixed rate if the change shifts the intersection of private supply and demand outside the band?

✦ 11. You are a foreign exchange trader and you receive the following two quotes for spot trading:
   • Bank A is willing to trade at $1.50 per Swiss franc.
   • Bank B is willing to trade at 0.50 Swiss franc per dollar.

  Is there an opportunity to make an arbitrage profit? If there is, explain what you will do. If there is not, why not?

12. You are an analyst following a medium-sized country that has a fixed exchange rate of 5 dinars per U.S. dollar (with a band of 2 percent above and below this par value). During March of last year you know that the country's monetary authority intervened in the foreign exchange market by buying U.S. $2 billion. During the next month (April) you know that the country's monetary authority intervened to sell U.S. $3 billion.

  What are *two different changes in the foreign exchange market* that could explain the different interventions during these two months? For each of the two changes, use a graph of the foreign exchange market to illustrate why the change resulted in the different interventions.

Chapter **Eighteen**

Forward Exchange and International Financial Investment

Many international activities lead to money exchanges in the future. This is true of many international trade activities, whose payments are not due until sometime in the (usually near) future. It is also true of international financial activities, which are specifically designed to create future flows of moneys as returns are received, debts are repaid, or financial assets are sold to others. A major challenge in conducting all of these activities is that we do not know for sure the exchange rates that will be available in the future to translate one country's money into another country's money.

This chapter examines future exchanges of moneys and the exposure to the risks of uncertain future exchange rates. It discusses how forward foreign exchange contracts can be used to reduce the risk exposure or to speculate on future exchange rates. Much of the chapter focuses on the returns to and risks of investments in foreign financial assets.

EXCHANGE-RATE RISK

Exchange rates change over time. In a floating-rate system, spot exchange rates change from minute to minute because supply and demand are constantly in flux. Indeed, as we have seen since the early 1970s, floating rates sometimes change quickly by large amounts as a result of large shifts in supply and demand. In a fixed-rate system, spot exchange rates also can change from minute to minute, but the range of the rate is typically limited to a small band around the par value as long as the fixed rate is defended successfully by the government authorities. Nonetheless, even in a fixed-rate system large changes can and do sometimes occur when the currency is devalued or revalued by the authorities. While some portion of the change in spot exchange rates in either system can be predicted by participants in the foreign exchange market, another part—often a large part—of exchange-rate change cannot be predicted.

A person (or an organization like a firm) is exposed to **exchange-rate risk** if the value of the person's income, wealth, or net worth changes when exchange rates change unpredictably in the future. This is a broad concept, but it has specific meanings in particular situations. If you are an American, take a vacation in Japan, and take

U.S. dollars along with you to convert into yen as needed to pay for your expenses and purchases, you are exposed to exchange-rate risk. The dollar value of the things that you buy and the number of things that you can afford to do will be affected by the dollar–yen exchange rates during your vacation. While you have some expectation of what those exchange rates will be, the actual rates will probably be different. From your point of view, the risk is that the yen could appreciate substantially so that it would take more dollars to obtain the same number of yen. The dollar prices of the things that you want to do and to buy will be higher; you will enjoy your vacation less. Of course, the yen might instead depreciate. In this case you will be pleasantly surprised by the increased buying power of your dollars. Still, as you begin your vacation you are exposed to exchange-rate risk because you do not know what will happen to the yen during your vacation.

Another example of exposure to exchange-rate risk is your first purchase of a financial asset denominated in a foreign currency—for instance, an investment in Mexican stocks. You may have heard that an investment in emerging markets is "where the action is." This may turn out to be too true. The dollar value of your investment depends not only on changes in the market prices of your Mexican stocks (valued in pesos) but also on changes in the dollar value of the peso. If the peso depreciates, the dollar value of your stock investment falls. Even if you expect some amount of peso depreciation, and incorporate that into the overall dollar return that you expect on your investment, the risk to you is that the peso could depreciate more than you are expecting.

The fact that exchange rates can change over time leads people to two types of responses. These appear contradictory, but actually just represent the responses of different people to different situations.

Some people do not want to gamble on what exchange rates will be in the future. They have acquired exposures to exchange-rate risk in the course of their regular activities, but they seek to reduce or eliminate their risk exposure by hedging. **Hedging** a position exposed to rate risk, here exchange-rate risk, is the act of reducing or eliminating a net asset or net liability position in the foreign currency.

Other people, thinking they have a good idea of what will happen to exchange rates, are quite willing to gamble on what exchange rates will be in the future. They are willing to take on or to hold positions that are exposed to exchange-rate risk. They are willing to bet that the rates are going to move in their favor so that they make a profit. **Speculating** is the act of taking a net asset position ("long") or a net liability position ("short") in some asset class, here a foreign currency.

These two attitudes have been personified into the concepts of hedgers and speculators, as though individuals were always either one or the other. Actually, the same person can choose to behave as a hedger in some situations and as a speculator in others.

THE MARKET BASICS OF FORWARD FOREIGN EXCHANGE

There are a number of ways to hedge an exposure to exchange-rate risk, or to take on additional exposure in order to speculate. For your vacation in Japan, you could hedge by buying yen (or yen-denominated traveler's checks) before you depart, thus having yen money to pay for your yen expenses and purchases.

For larger transactions involving international trade in goods and services, international financial investment, or pure speculation on future exchange-rate movements, forward foreign exchange and forward exchange rates are often useful. As we mentioned in the previous chapter, a **forward foreign exchange contract** is an agreement to exchange one currency for another on some date in the future at a price set now (the **forward exchange rate**).

Banks acting as foreign exchange dealers generally are willing to meet the needs of their customers for the specific size of the forward exchange contract (the amount of foreign exchange) and the specific date in the future for the exchange. Common dates for future exchange are 30, 90, and 180 days forward (one, three, and six months).[1] For instance, to buy £100,000 of 90-day forward sterling at $1.6745/£, you sign an agreement today with your bank that 90 days from now you will deliver $167,450 in dollar bank deposits and receive £100,000 in pound bank deposits. The exchange of these amounts will take place to carry out the forward contract, regardless of what the actual spot exchange rate turns out to be in 90 days. In the opposite trade, somebody agreeing now to sell 90-day forward sterling must deliver pounds at the agreed price of $1.6745/£ in 90 days. That person need not own any sterling at all until then, but the rate at which he gives it up in 90 days is already set now. *Do not confuse the forward rate with the future spot rate,* the spot rate that ends up prevailing 90 days from now. The actual spot price of sterling that exists in 90 days could be above, below, or equal to the forward rate. In this respect, a forward exchange rate is like a commodity futures price or a binding advance hotel reservation.

The forward exchange market is particularly convenient for large customers, typically corporations, that are viewed by their banks as acceptable credit risks. These customers typically do not need to commit anything other than the written agreement until the exchange actually occurs in the future. Some customers must pledge a margin that the bank can seize if the customer fails to fulfill the contract in the future, but this margin is only a fraction of the total size of the contract (because the bank only needs to recover any net loss on the other party's position).

Hedging Using Forward Foreign Exchange

Hedging involves acquiring an asset in a foreign currency to offset a net liability position already held in the foreign currency, or acquiring a liability in a foreign currency to offset a net asset position already held. Hedgers in international dealings are persons who have a home currency and seek a balance between their liabilities and assets in foreign currencies. In financial jargon, hedging means reducing both kinds of "open" positions in a foreign currency—both *long positions* (holding net assets in the foreign currency) and *short positions* (owing more of the foreign currency than one holds). An American who has completely hedged a position in euros has ensured that the future of the exchange rate between dollars and euros will not affect his net worth. Hedging is a perfectly normal kind of behavior, especially for people whose main business is not international finance. Simply avoiding any net commitments in

[1] In the usual forward exchange contract, the actual exchange of currencies will occur two (or one) days after the stated time period, to match the two-day (or one-day) delay in settling standard spot contracts. The discussion in this chapter ignores the two- or one-day delay in actually exchanging the currencies.

a foreign currency saves on the time and trouble of keeping abreast of fast-changing international currency conditions.

There are usually a number of ways to hedge a position that is exposed to exchange-rate risk. For many types of exposure, a forward exchange contract is a direct way to hedge. Consider a U.S. company that has bought some merchandise and will have to pay £100,000 three months from now. Assuming that this represents an overall net liability position in pounds (perhaps because the company has no other assets or liabilities in pounds), the company is exposed to exchange-rate risk. It does not know the dollar value of its liability because it does not know the spot exchange rate that will exist 90 days from now. One way to hedge its risk exposure is to enter into a forward contract to acquire (or buy) £100,000 in 90 days. If the current forward rate is $1.6745/£, then the company must deliver (or sell) $167,450 in 90 days. The company has an asset position in pounds through the forward contract (the company is owed pounds in the contract). This exactly matches its pound liability to pay for the merchandise, creating a "perfect hedge." The company now is assured that the merchandise will cost $167,450 regardless of what happens to the spot exchange rate in the next 90 days.[2]

Forward exchange contracts can be used to hedge exposures to exchange-rate risk in many other situations. A U.S. company that will receive a payment of £1 million in 60 days is unsure of the dollar value of this receivable because the spot exchange rate in 60 days is uncertain. It can hedge by selling pounds (and buying dollars) in a 60-day forward exchange contract, using the forward exchange rate to lock in the number of dollars it will receive. A British firm needing to pay $200,000 in 30 days on its dollar-denominated debt can hedge its exchange-rate risk exposure by buying dollars (and selling pounds) in a 30-day forward contract. A British individual inheriting $2 million that will be disbursed (in dollars) in 180 days can hedge by selling the dollars (and buying pounds) in a 180-day forward contract.

Speculating Using Forward Foreign Exchange

Speculating means committing oneself to an uncertain future value of one's net worth in terms of home currency. A rich imagery surrounds the term *speculator*. Speculators are usually portrayed as a class apart from the rest of humanity. These speculators are viewed as being excessively greedy—unlike us, of course. They are also viewed as exceptionally jittery and as adding an element of subversive chaos to the economic system. They come out in the middle of storms—we hear about them when the markets are veering

---

[2]There are several other ways in which the U.S. company can acquire an asset in pounds that hedges its pound liability. It could sell merchandise to someone else and bill the buyer in pounds payable in 90 days. Or it could use dollars that it has now to buy pounds now at the current spot rate and invest those pounds to earn interest for 90 days. The pound proceeds from the investment can then be used to pay the pound debt. Or it could enter into a long position (buying pounds) in a pound futures contract traded on an organized exchange. Or it could buy a currency option call contract that gives the company the right to buy pounds at a price set in the option contract (the exercise or strike price). Each of these establishes an asset in pounds that hedges its pound liability. The company's decision to hedge using a forward contract or one of the other methods depends on the cost of each method and how closely each method offsets its exposed position. In many cases the forward contract is a low-cost way of establishing the exact hedge desired by the company. Futures and options contracts are discussed further in the box "Futures, Options, and Swaps."

out of control, and then it is their fault. Although speculation sometimes has played such a sinister role, it is an open empirical question whether it does so frequently.

More to the present point, we must recognize that the only concrete way of defining speculation is the broad way just offered. A speculator is anybody who is willing to take a net position in a foreign currency, whatever his motives or expectations about the future of the exchange rate. There is nothing necessarily sinister about this. Still, banks and other international financial players often claim that they invest while others speculate, implying that the latter action is more risky and foolhardy. Yet there is no clear difference here. Any investment that is exposed to exchange-rate risk has a speculative element to it.

There are a number of ways deliberately to establish speculative foreign-currency positions. One direct way to speculate on the value of the future spot exchange rate is a forward foreign exchange contract. Forward foreign exchange provides the same bridge to future currency exchanges for speculators as for hedgers, and there are no credentials checks that can sort out the two groups in the marketplace. If a speculator thinks he has a fairly good idea of what will happen to the spot exchange rate in the future, it is easy to bet on the basis of that idea using the forward market. It is so easy, in fact, that the speculator can even bet with money he does not have in hand.

To illustrate this point, suppose that in May you are convinced that the pound sterling will take a dive from its current spot exchange-rate value of about $1.68 and be worth only $1.50 in August. Perhaps you see a coming political and economic crisis in Britain that others do not see. You can make an enormous gain by using the forward market. Contact a foreign exchange trader at your bank and agree to sell £10 million at the current 90-day forward rate of $1.6745. If the bank believes in your ability to honor your forward commitment in August, you do not even need to put up any money now in May. Just sign the forward contract. How will you be able to come up with £10 million in August? Given your knowledge of a coming crisis, there is nothing to worry about. Relax. Take a three-month vacation in Hawaii. From time to time, stroll off the beach long enough to glance at the newspaper and note that the pound is sinking, just as you knew it would. On the contract date in August, instruct your bank to settle the forward contract against the actual spot rate, which has sunk as you expected to $1.50. Effectively, in August you are buying £10 million in the spot market at $1.50 (total cost of $15 million) and selling the pounds at $1.6745 into the forward contract (total receipt of $16.745). You net a profit of $1.745 million for a few minutes' effort, a lot of foresight, and an understanding of "buy low, sell high." If you are smarter than the others in the marketplace, you can get rich using the convenient forward exchange market.

Your speculation may turn out differently, however. Suppose you are wrong. Suppose that Britain's prospects brighten greatly between May and August. Suppose that, when August comes around, the spot value of the pound has risen to $1.90. Now in August you must come up with $19 million to get the £10 million you committed to sell in the forward contract for only $16.745 million. It does not take much arithmetic to see what this means for your personal wealth. It is time to reevaluate your lifestyle.

What happens if in May *many* people expect the spot exchange-rate value of the pound to depreciate to $1.50 by August, and they are willing to speculate using the

Extension   Futures, Options, and Swaps

A forward foreign exchange contract is one type of agreement that can be reached now about an exchange of currencies that will occur in the future. This traditional form of future-oriented currency agreement has some relatives that have been introduced since the early 1970s. Someone wishing to hedge or speculate can now choose from among currency futures, currency options, and currency swaps in addition to traditional forward exchange.

Currency futures are contracts that are traded on organized exchanges, such as the Chicago Mercantile Exchange. By entering into a currency futures contract, you can effectively lock in the price at which you buy or sell a foreign currency at a set date in the future. This sounds very much like a forward foreign exchange contract, and it is. There are some differences, though. First, a futures contract is a *standard* contract (making it tradable on the organized exchange)—for instance, 12.5 million yen to be exchanged for dollars in March of next year. A forward contract can be *customized* by the bank to meet the needs of the customer. Second, if you enter into a futures contract, the exchange requires that you provide money as a *margin* to ensure that you will honor the contract. A margin might be required in a forward contract, but usually it is not. Third, the profits and losses on your futures contract accrue to you daily, as the contract is *"marked to market"* daily. Too many losses and you will receive a call to add to your margin account. The profit or loss on a forward contract usually is not taken until the *maturity* date. Fourth, and perhaps most important from your perspective, *almost anyone* able to put up a margin can enter into a futures contract, whereas banks usually are willing to enter into forward contracts only for large amounts (millions of dollars) with *highly creditworthy customers.* Futures contracts give ordinary people and small businesses access to a low-cost direct method for currency hedging or speculation.

For some purposes a major drawback to forward and futures contracts is that losses on your open positions can become very large. You

must honor your agreements. If the spot rate has moved in a way that is against your position, you will have to buy high and sell low, resulting in what can be a large loss. Some hedgers and speculators may dislike this feature. There is another alternative—an option contract.

A currency option gives the buyer (or holder) of the option the right, but not the obligation, to buy foreign currency (a call option) or to sell foreign currency (a put option) at some time in the future at a price set today. The price set into the contract now for the foreign exchange transaction that the holder may make in the future is called the *exercise price* or *strike price.* The option is a valuable right, and the buyer pays a *premium* (a fee) to the seller (or writer) of the option to acquire the option.

Let's say that you believe that the Swiss franc is going to appreciate substantially during the next month. The current spot price is $1.20 per franc and the current 30-day forward rate (or, for that matter, the current futures price for franc contracts maturing next month) is $1.21 per franc. You expect the spot value of the franc to be $1.26 in 30 days. If you speculate using a forward (or futures) contract, going long in francs, you will make a profit if the actual spot rate in 30 days is above $1.21 per franc. But if the actual spot rate in 30 days is below $1.21 per franc, you will make a loss, and the loss is larger the lower the spot rate is in 30 days. If the actual spot rate in 30 days is $1.14, you must buy francs at the forward price of $1.21 when the francs are worth only $1.14. You have a large actual loss.

You can instead speculate on the franc exchange rate using a currency option contract. The disadvantage of the option is that you must pay a premium to obtain it. (There is no comparable charge to obtain a forward contract.) The advantage of the option is that the size of any loss on the contract is limited to this premium— you cannot lose more. For instance, you can buy a 30-day currency call option that gives you the right to buy Swiss francs at an exercise price of $1.21 per franc. If the actual spot rate in 30 days is above $1.21 per franc, you exercise the option.

Your overall profit here is somewhat lower than the comparable forward contract because you had to pay the premium to buy the option. Still, your profit can be large if the actual spot rate in 30 days has moved well above the $1.21 exercise price. (You buy francs low by exercising the option and sell the francs high at the higher spot rate.) If the actual spot rate in 30 days is below $1.21, you let the option expire unexercised. You have lost the premium, but you are not required to lose any more, even if the actual spot rate is substantially below the exercise price.

Another important future-oriented currency agreement is the currency swap. In a currency swap two parties agree to exchange flows of different currencies during a specified period of time. For instance, Microsoft might enter into a swap with its bank in which Microsoft agrees (1) to deliver a large number of euros in exchange for a comparable number of dollars now, (2) every three months to make dollar interest payments and to receive euro interest payments, and (3) at the end of the swap to return the large number of dollars and receive back the comparable number of euros. Because Microsoft has committed to exchanging dollars for euros, at various times now and in the future, you might think that this sounds something like spot and forward foreign exchange contracts, and you would be right. A swap is basically a set of spot and forward foreign exchanges packaged into one contract. The advantages of the swap over a package of separate foreign exchange contracts are two: lower transactions costs by using one contract and a subtle but important decrease in risk exposure. In a swap any failure by the other side to honor the contract cancels all future obligations, while in the package of separates the other side might try to default on some contracts but force you to honor others.

Why would Microsoft want to enter into such a swap? One reason could be that Microsoft discovers that it has an unusual opportunity to issue euro-denominated bonds at a low interest rate, perhaps because EU investors strongly desire to add some Microsoft bonds to their portfolios.

But Microsoft actually needs dollars to finance the expansion of its business and wants to pay dollar interest on its debt. Microsoft can take advantage of the EU opportunity by issuing euro-denominated debt and then swapping the euros into dollars. Microsoft must pay euro interest to its EU investors, but it is receiving euro interest in the swap. These euro flows approximately equal each other, so Microsoft mostly is left with the obligation to pay dollar interest into the swap. Microsoft accomplishes two things with the structured combination of euro bonds and swap. First, Microsoft can lower its overall cost of financing by taking advantage of the unusually low interest cost in the EU, even though it really does not want euro-denominated debt. Second, Microsoft effectively does not have euro-denominated debt—the cash flows (on net) are converted through the swap into the dollar cash flows that Microsoft prefers to have.

Currency futures, options, and swaps are relatively recent additions to the set of foreign exchange products. The first foreign-currency futures contract was offered in 1972. The first exchange-traded foreign-currency option was offered in 1982. Foreign-currency options are also offered directly by banks and other financial institutions in customized contracts with their customers. The first major currency swap was contracted in 1981 between the World Bank and IBM (dollars for German marks and Swiss francs).

Exchange-traded currency futures and options are of some importance, with the equivalent of $244 billion and $143 billion in existence in December 2013. Still, most foreign exchange is transacted directly among banks, other financial institutions, and their customers. The size of the "over-the-counter" products (spot exchange, forward exchange, directly written currency options, and currency swaps) is much larger than the size of the exchange-traded foreign-currency futures and options. Currency swaps have become a big product, with $25.4 trillion of swap contracts in force in December 2013. And $11.9 trillion of directly written currency options existed in December 2013.

forward exchange market? They will sell pounds forward in large amounts. The increased supply of pounds forward will put downward pressure on the forward exchange-rate value of the pound, driving it toward $1.50. Generally, all speculators will not have the exact same view as to the expected future spot exchange rate. Nonetheless, *we hypothesize that speculators' pressures on supply and demand should drive the forward exchange rate to equal the average expected value of the future spot exchange rate.* For instance, the 90-day forward rate may indicate what informed opinion thinks the pound should be worth spot in 90 days' time. It would be an average expectation of the future spot value, much as the point spread in football betting is the number of points by which the average bettor expects the stronger team to win.

INTERNATIONAL FINANCIAL INVESTMENT

International financial investment has grown rapidly in recent decades. Decisions about international investments are based on the returns and risks of the available investment alternatives. How do we calculate the overall returns on financial assets denominated in foreign currencies? What are the sources of risk that apply specifically or especially to foreign financial investments? Can the investor hedge exposure to exchange-rate risk? The remainder of this chapter explores these questions about international financial investment. Although our discussion focuses on investing, most of the principles also apply to a borrower deciding whether to take out loans or issue securities denominated in foreign currencies.

Consider an investor who holds dollars now and plans to end up a year from now also holding dollars (or, at least, who calculates her wealth and returns in dollars). If she invests in a dollar-denominated financial asset like a U.S. government security or a dollar time deposit, then she will earn dollar returns and have dollar wealth a year from now. No currency translation is necessary. If she invests in a foreign-currency-denominated financial asset, like a British government security or a pound time deposit, her situation is not so simple. First, she must convert her dollars into pounds at the initial spot exchange rate. Then, she uses the pounds to buy the pound-denominated financial asset. She holds this asset, earning pound returns and having wealth in pounds a year from now. This can be converted back into dollars (either actually or simply to determine the dollar value of wealth) at some dollar–pound exchange rate that applies to foreign exchange transactions a year from now.

What exchange rate can be used to convert pounds back into dollars a year from now? There are two major alternatives, and these correspond to our concepts of hedging and speculation. First, she can contract now for the exchange of pounds back into dollars at the one-year *forward exchange rate* using a forward exchange contract. Her pound liability in the forward contract matches her pound asset position, so she has hedged her exposure to exchange-rate risk. She has a hedged or covered international investment. Second, she can wait and convert back into dollars at the *future spot exchange rate,* the one that will exist a year from now. She does not know for sure what this future spot exchange rate will be, so her investment is exposed to exchange-rate risk. This unhedged investment has a speculative element to it, and it is called an uncovered international investment.

FIGURE 18.1
Current and
Future Asset
Positions in
Two Currencies:
The "Lake"
Diagram

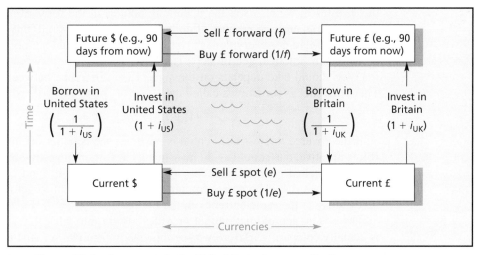

i_{US} = Current 90-day interest rate in the United States (not annualized)
i_{UK} = Current 90-day interest rate in Britain (not annualized)
e = Current spot price of the pound ($/£)
f = Current forward price of the pound, for exchange 90 days from now ($/£)
In moving from one currency to another at a point in time, or between the present and the future in
a single currency, the arrows show what action you are taking. The mathematical expressions show
what to multiply by, to convert from one to another. There are two ways to get from any one corner
to any other corner, and at least one of these two ways requires multiple conversions.

INTERNATIONAL INVESTMENT WITH COVER

We can compare domestic investment and covered international investment using
Figure 18.1, which shows ways of investing (or borrowing) as paths around a "lake."
People moving their assets from left to right are buying pounds and selling dollars,
whereas those transferring from right to left are buying dollars with pounds. People
moving upward in either country are investing or lending, whereas those moving
downward from future to current positions are either selling off interest-earning assets
or borrowing at interest. The corresponding expressions in terms of exchange rates
(the current spot rate, e, and the current forward rate, f) and current interest rates
(i_{US} and i_{UK}) show how the value of one's assets gets multiplied by each move. The
exchange rates are quoted as dollars per pound. The interest rates are measured for the
actual time period examined and are in decimal, not percent, form.[3]
  Studying how one gets from any corner to any other for any purpose, you will find
that the choice of the more profitable of the two possible routes always depends on
the comparison of two expressions. Suppose we want to convert present dollars into
future dollars. We could route our money through Britain, buying pounds in the spot
market, obtaining $1/e$ pound for each dollar. We would then invest these pounds at
interest and have $(1 + i_{UK})/e$ pound at maturity for each initial dollar. At the time of

[3]That is, the interest rates are not annual rates unless the time period is one year. If interest rates
are quoted as annualized rates, they must be converted. For instance, the 90-day interest
rate is approximately one-quarter the annualized interest rate.

the investment we also sell the upcoming pounds in the forward market (at the rate of f) to get an ensured number of dollars in the future. Overall, this yields $(1 + i_{UK}) \cdot f/e$ future dollars for every dollar invested now. Or we could simply invest our money at interest in America, getting $(1 + i_{US})$ future dollars for every present dollar. Which road we should take depends on the sign of the difference between the two returns. This difference is sometimes called the **covered interest differential** (CD):

$$CD = (1 + i_{UK}) \cdot f/e - (1 + i_{US})$$

If the covered interest differential is positive, one is better off investing in Britain. If it is negative, one should avoid investments in Britain, investing in America instead. Why is it called *covered*? Because the investor is fully hedged or covered against exchange-rate risk if he uses a foreign-currency investment to get from his own currency today to the same currency in the future.

There is an approximation that provides insight into what the covered differential is actually comparing. Before we see this handy formula, we first need to define the **forward premium** (F) as the proportionate difference between the *current* forward exchange-rate value of the pound and its *current* spot value:[4]

$$F = (f - e)/e$$

The forward premium (converted into a percentage) shows the rate at which the pound gains value between a current spot transaction to buy pounds and future selling of pounds at the forward rate that we can lock in today. (If F is negative, the pound is at a forward *discount* because it loses value between buying it at the current spot rate and selling it at the current forward rate.)

The handy approximation is that the covered interest differential is approximately equal to the forward premium on the pound plus the interest rate differential:[5]

$$CD = F + (i_{UK} - i_{US})$$

The formula shows that the net incentive to go in one particular direction around the lake depends on how the forward premium on the pound compares with the difference between interest rates.

There is another way to interpret the approximation. The overall covered return (in dollars) to a U.S. investor from investing in Britain is approximately equal to the sum of two components: the gain (or loss) from the spot and forward currency exchanges

---

[4]This is often stated on an annualized percent basis:

$$F = \frac{(f - e)}{e} \cdot \frac{360}{n} \cdot 100$$

where n is the number of days forward and a year is taken to be 360 days for convenience.

[5]To see the approximation involved, first complete the multiplication of terms in the first equation for CD:

$$CD = f/e + i_{UK} \cdot f/e - 1 - i_{US}$$

Next, add and subtract i_{UK}:

$$CD = f/e + i_{UK} \cdot f/e - i_{UK} - 1 + i_{UK} - i_{US}$$

Now group terms, using the fact that the forward premium $F = f/e - 1$:

$$CD = F + i_{UK} - i_{US} + i_{UK} \cdot F$$

If the British interest rate (i_{UK}) and forward premium on the pound (F) are small (in decimal form), then the last term (the product of two small numbers) is very small, and it is ignored in the approximation.

(the forward premium, F, on the pound) plus the interest return on the pound investment itself (i_{UK}). The covered interest differential is then approximately equal to the difference between the overall covered return to investing in pound-denominated assets ($F + i_{UK}$) and the return to investing in dollar-denominated assets (i_{US}).[6]

Covered Interest Arbitrage

The covered differential is such a handy guide to the profitable exchange between currencies that traders can use it to make arbitrage profits on any differential. Covered interest arbitrage is buying a country's currency spot and selling that country's currency forward, to make a net profit from the *combination* of the difference in interest rates between countries and the forward premium on that country's currency. Covered interest arbitrage is essentially riskless, although it does tie up some assets for a while. One way of engaging in this arbitrage is in fact the ultimate in hedging: We can start with dollars today and end up with a guaranteed greater amount of dollars today by going all the way around the lake.

To see how this arbitrage works, let's suppose that British and U.S. interest rates are i_{UK} = .04 (4 percent) and i_{US} = .03 (3 percent), respectively, for 90 days and that both the spot and forward exchange rates are \$2.00/£, so that there is neither a premium nor a discount on forward sterling ($F = 0$). Seeing that this means CD = .01 (1 percent), a New York arbitrageur uses his computer and sets up a counterclockwise journey around the lake. He contracts to sell, say, \$20 million in the spot market, buying £10 million. He informs his London correspondent bank or branch bank of the purchase and instructs that bank to place the proceeds in British Treasury bills that will mature in 90 days. This means that after 90 days he will have £10 million • 1.04 to dispose of. He covers himself against exchange-rate risk by contracting to sell the £10.4 million in the forward market, receiving \$20.8 million deliverable after 90 days. He could leave the matter there, knowing that his computer trip in and out of Britain will give \$20.8 million in 90 days' time, instead of the \$20.6 million he would have received by investing his original \$20 million within the United States. Or if he has excellent credit standing, he can celebrate his winnings by borrowing against the \$20.8 million in the United States at 3 percent, giving himself \$20,194,175 = \$20.8 million/ (1.03) right now, or about 1 percent more than he had before he used the computer. So that's \$194,175 in arbitrage gains minus any transactions fees, the use of part of a credit line in the United States, and a few minutes' time, not a bad wage. The operation is also riskless as long as nobody defaults on a contract. (The reader can confirm that if forward sterling instead were at a 2 percent discount [$F = -.02$ because $f =$ \$1.96] the New York arbitrageur would invest in the United States, buy forward sterling, borrow or sell bills in Britain, and sell pounds spot, making a net profit of about 1 percent.)

What happens if many people take advantage of an opportunity for interest arbitrage? Their activities will put pressures on the various rates. In the example in which, initially, the British interest rate is 4 percent, the U.S. interest rate is 3 percent, and both the spot and forward exchange rates are \$2.00/£, here are the pressures:

[6]The approximation is also useful because all rates can be stated on an annualized basis and in percent terms—the way we usually say them. In this case, F is the annualized percent forward premium (as defined in footnote 4) and the interest rates are annualized percent rates, regardless of the number of days forward being considered.

- As many arbitrageurs sell dollars and buy pounds for immediate delivery, the spot exchange rate tends to rise above \$2.00/£.
- As the arbitrageurs also buy dollars and sell pounds forward, the forward exchange rate tends to fall below \$2.00/£.
- As the arbitrageurs shift their funds from dollar-denominated investments to pound-denominated investments (or borrow dollars to fund the pound investments), U.S. interest rates tend to rise and British interest rates tend to fall.

If one or more of the rates change in these ways, the size of the covered interest differential shrinks. Where is all this heading?

Covered Interest Parity

John Maynard Keynes, himself an interest arbitrageur, argued that the opportunities to make arbitrage profits would be self-eliminating because rates would adjust so that the covered interest differential would be driven to zero. Since Keynes we have referred to the condition CD = 0 as **covered interest parity**. Here are two equivalent ways to think of covered interest parity:

- A currency is at a forward premium (discount) by as much as its interest rate is lower (higher) than the interest rate in the other country (that is, $F = i_{US} - i_{UK}$ in our example).
- The overall covered return on a foreign-currency investment equals the return on a comparable domestic-currency investment ($F + i_{UK} = i_{US}$).

In the numerical example on page 415, covered interest parity would exist if the forward rate were \$1.98/£ (rather than \$2.00/£). Then the forward discount on the pound of 1 percent (equal to the proportionate difference between the \$1.98 forward rate and the \$2.00 spot rate) would offset the amount by which the British interest rate (4 percent) was higher than the U.S. interest rate (3 percent). U.S. investors would earn only 3 percent on their covered investments in pound-denominated assets—the 4 percent interest minus the 1 percent lost in the currency exchanges. This 3 percent is equal to the rate that they receive on investments in dollar-denominated assets, so there would be no incentive for arbitrage.

Covered interest parity provides an explanation for differences between current spot and current forward exchange rates. A country with an interest rate that is lower than the corresponding rate in the United States will have a forward premium on its currency, with the percentage point difference in the interest rates equal to the percent forward premium. According to the exchange-rate quotations in Figure 17.1, the currencies of Japan and Switzerland have 90-day forward rates (in dollars per this currency) above their current spot rates. These currencies are at a forward premium, and we could confirm that Japanese and Swiss 90-day interest rates were less at that time than the interest rates on comparable assets denominated in U.S. dollars. The currencies of Australia and Britain have 90-day forward rates below their current spot rates, showing forward discounts that are connected to relatively high Australian and British interest rates.

Covered interest parity links together four rates: the current forward exchange rate, the current spot exchange rate, and the current interest rates in the two countries. If one of these rates changes, then at least one of the other rates also must change to maintain (reestablish) covered interest parity. For instance, if the spot exchange rate increases and the interest differential is unchanged, then the forward exchange rate also must rise to keep the forward premium steady. In this case, whatever moves the spot rate up (or down) will do the same to the forward rate. In fact, short-term interest differentials have not varied much over the past several decades for the major world currencies, so spot and forward rates between any two of these currencies have tended to go up or down together over time. That is, the current spot and current forward rates are highly positively correlated over time.[7]

INTERNATIONAL INVESTMENT WITHOUT COVER

Uncovered international financial investment involves investing in a financial asset denominated in a foreign currency without hedging or covering the future proceeds of the investment back into one's own currency. In the simplest case, the foreign currency proceeds will be translated back into domestic currency using whatever spot exchange rate exists at the future date (either actually or to calculate wealth and overall returns in one's own currency). The future spot rate is not known for sure at the time of the initial investment, so the investment is exposed to exchange-rate risk (assuming that the investor has no other offsetting liability in this currency).

At the time of the initial investment, the investor presumably has some idea of what the future spot rate is likely to be. The investor's *expected future spot rate* (e^{ex}) can be used to determine an expected overall return on the uncovered international investment. (This expected future spot rate is the same type of rate used in deciding whether to speculate using a forward contract.)

A kind of "lake" diagram similar to that used in Figure 18.1 applies here, but the top side of the lake refers to currency exchanges in the future at the future spot exchange rate. At the time of initiating the foreign investment ("ex ante"), we only have a notion or an expectation of what the future spot rate will be. Of course, once we get to the future date (the end or maturity of the foreign investment—"ex post"), we will know what the future spot rate actually is, and then we can determine the actual overall return on the uncovered foreign investment.

To see how this works, again consider that we want to convert present dollars into future dollars. We again could route our money through Britain, but in this case we decide not to cover against exchange-rate risk. We first buy pounds in the spot market, obtaining $1/e$ pound for each dollar. We then invest these pounds, and we will have $(1 + i_{UK})/e$ pound at maturity for each initial dollar. We have an expectation that we can convert these pounds back into dollars at the rate of e^{ex} to obtain $(1 + i_{UK}) \cdot e^{ex}/e$ future dollars expected for each dollar invested now. This can be compared to the future dollars $(1 + i_{US})$ that we could obtain simply by investing each present dollar in a dollar-denominated asset. The comparison is the **expected uncovered interest differential** (EUD):

$$\text{EUD} = (1 + i_{UK}) \cdot e^{ex}/e - (1 + i_{US})$$

[7]Covered interest parity also has implications for our earlier discussion of hedging a future pound liability. The goal is to get from current dollars to future pounds (needed to pay for the merchandise). If covered interest parity holds, then the cost of hedging using a forward contract (going up the lake and then across at the top toward the right) will essentially equal the cost of hedging by buying pounds spot now and investing these pounds for 90 days (going across the lake to the right at the bottom and then going up).

If this is positive, then the expected overall return favors uncovered investing in a pound-denominated asset. If it's negative, then the expected overall return favors staying at home.[8]

The expression for the expected uncovered interest differential is almost the same as the expression for the covered interest differential. The only difference is that the expected future spot rate, e^{ex}, replaces the forward rate, f. This is not surprising—the difference between the two is specifically the decision not to cover or hedge the exposure to exchange-rate risk by using a forward contract.

We can also show that the expected uncovered interest differential has a handy approximation. It approximately equals the expected rate of appreciation (depreciation if negative) of the foreign currency plus the regular interest rate differential:[9]

$$EUD = \text{Expected appreciation} + (i_{UK} - i_{US})$$

For a different view of this, note that the expected overall uncovered return (in dollars) to a U.S. investor from investing in Britain is approximately equal to the sum of the expected gain (or loss) from the currency exchanges (current spot and future spot) as the pound appreciates (or depreciates) during the time of the investment, plus the interest return on the pound investment itself. This expected overall return on the pound investment (expected appreciation $+ i_{UK}$) is compared to the return on investing in dollar-denominated assets (i_{US}) to approximate the expected uncovered interest differential.

Let's consider a numerical example similar to the one used in the section on covered investment. The current spot exchange rate (e) is \$2.00/£ and the current interest rates on 90-day investments are $i_{UK} = 0.04$ (4 percent) and $i_{US} = 0.03$ (3 percent). If a U.S.-based investor expects the spot rate (e^{ex}) to remain at \$2.00/£ in 90 days, what is the expected uncovered interest differential? Because he expects no change in the pound's exchange-rate value, the expected differential is 1 percent (equal to the interest rate differential, $4 - 3$) in favor of the pound investment. The investor expects a higher return to investing uncovered in pound assets, but he is not certain of the extra return. The actual spot exchange rate in 90 days could be quite different from what he is expecting.

If an uncovered foreign financial investment is exposed to exchange-rate risk, why would anyone want to invest uncovered? The answer has two components: one related to return and one to risk. First, the expected overall return on the uncovered investment may be higher than the return that can be obtained at home (EUD is positive), as in the numerical example just completed. Presumably, the investor would undertake such an uncovered investment if he expected to be adequately compensated for the risks that he is taking on, especially the exchange-rate risk that the actual future spot rate could be much lower than he is expecting.

However, the issue of risk exposure is really more subtle. It is not the risk of this individual investment that matters, but rather the contribution of this uncovered investment to the riskiness of the investor's full investment portfolio. While we will not develop this fully, analysis of portfolios indicates that the addition of an uncovered

---

[8]From the perspective of a UK investor considering an uncovered dollar investment, the expected uncovered interest differential is $(1 + i_{US}) \bullet e^{ex}/e - (1 + i_{UK})$, where the exchange rates are now measured as pounds per dollar.

[9]For the actual time period involved, the expected rate of appreciation equals $(e^{ex} - e)/e$. This is often stated on a percent annualized basis,

$$\frac{e^{ex} - e}{e} \bullet \frac{360}{n} \bullet 100$$

where n is the number of days in the future for the expected future spot rate.

foreign investment can sometimes increase overall riskiness, but in other cases it can instead lower it because of the benefits of diversification of investments. If it lowers overall riskiness, then the investor would look favorably on an uncovered foreign investment even if the expected uncovered interest differential is somewhat negative.

To see the importance of uncovered foreign investments and the expected uncovered interest differential, let's examine what is likely to be true if risk considerations are small. Risk considerations can be small if investors do not care much about risk exposures (they are *risk neutral*) or if the benefits of diversification indicate that additional uncovered investments add little or nothing to the overall riskiness of the investor's portfolio. In this case each investor is willing to undertake uncovered foreign investments if the uncovered interest differential is positive. As investors make shifts in their portfolios, they place supply and demand pressures on the current spot exchange rate, by buying or selling pounds for dollars to shift into or out of pound-denominated investments. (They may also place pressures on the interest rates as they buy and sell the financial assets themselves.)

Generally, the pressures on the rates will subside only when there is no further incentive for large shifts in investments. When the expected uncovered differential equals zero (EUD = 0), at least for the average investor, we have a condition called **uncovered interest parity.** (This parity is also called the "international Fisher effect," named for Irving Fisher, the economist who first proposed it.) Here are two ways to say it:

- A currency is expected to appreciate (depreciate) by as much as its interest rate is lower (higher) than the interest rate in the other country (for instance, expected appreciation of the pound = $i_{US} - i_{UK}$).
- The expected overall uncovered return on the foreign-currency investment equals the return on the domestic-currency investment (expected appreciation + $i_{UK} = i_{US}$).

Consider the rates used in our previous numerical example: British and U.S. interest rates of 4 and 3 percent and an expected future spot exchange rate of $2.00/£. For these rates uncovered interest parity holds if the current spot rate is $2.02/£. Then the expected depreciation of the pound of about 1 percent (from the current spot rate of $2.02 to a future spot rate of $2.00) matches the 1 percent by which British interest rates exceed U.S. interest rates (4 − 3).

If uncovered interest parity holds, then it links together four rates: the current spot exchange rate, the spot exchange rate that is currently expected to exist (on average) in the future, and the current interest rates in the two countries. As with covered interest parity, if one of these four rates changes, then at least one of the other rates must change to maintain or reestablish uncovered interest parity. Consider several possible changes that can lead to quick appreciation of the pound. If the interest rate in the United Kingdom increases, this can increase the current spot exchange-rate value of the pound, thus reducing the expected rate of further pound appreciation (or increasing the expected rate of pound depreciation) into the future (assuming that the value of the expected future spot rate is unchanged). If, instead, the value of the expected future spot rate increases and there is no change in interest rates, then the value of the current spot exchange rate must increase to maintain the same rate of further pound appreciation (or depreciation) expected into the future. We will look at these relationships more deeply in the next chapter, when we search for the determinants of spot exchange rates.

Case Study   The World's Greatest Investor

George Soros was born Dzjchdzhe Shorask (pronounced "Shorosh") in Budapest in 1930. The son of a lawyer, he became a global investment superstar, with a net worth in 2014 estimated at about $23 billion. In the years since its founding in 1969, his investment fund has earned an incredible average return of about 30 percent per year.

As a Jewish boy, he and his family struggled to evade the Nazis, and they managed to survive. In 1947 he went to England, expecting to continue his engineering studies. Instead, he enrolled in the London School of Economics and graduated in 1952. He began working at a small London brokerage, but he was frustrated by the lack of responsibilities.

In 1956, Soros moved to New York City, where he worked at two securities firms before joining the firm Arnold & Bleichroeder in 1963. In 1967, he became head of investment research, and he was successful at finding good investment opportunities in undervalued European stocks. In 1969, he founded an offshore hedge fund, using $250,000 of his own money and about $6 million from non-American investors whom he knew. (A hedge fund is an investment partnership that is not restricted by regulations of government agencies like the U.S. Securities and Exchange Commission. Each hedge fund can establish its own investment style and strategy, and these vary. While some hedge funds do use investment strategies that involve different kinds of hedging, others do not. The manager of a fund usually gets fees and a percentage of the profits, as well as having a substantial amount of his own money invested in the fund.)

Soon Soros left Arnold & Bleichroeder, taking his Soros Fund with him. While the 1970s were poor years for the U.S. stock market generally, the Soros Fund prospered. As the manager, Soros focused on finding undervalued sectors in the United States and other countries. He bought unpopular low-priced stocks and sold short popular high-priced stocks. He expected oil demand to outstrip oil supply, so he bought stocks of companies in oil-field services and oil drilling before the first oil shock in 1973. In the mid-1970s, he

invested heavily in Japanese stocks. In 1979, he changed the name of the fund to Quantum Fund, in honor of Heisenberg's uncertainty principle in quantum mechanics. In 1980, the fund return was 103 percent. It had grown to $380 million.

In 1981, *Institutional Investor* magazine named him "the world's greatest investor." But 1981 was a difficult year. The fund lost 23 percent, and one-third of his investors withdrew their investments. This was their mistake. Spectacular returns were still to come.

In August 1985, Soros became convinced that the U.S. dollar was overvalued relative to the Japanese yen and the German mark, and that a correction was coming soon. He decided to establish speculative investment positions to try to profit from the changes he expected. For instance, he borrowed dollars, used the dollars to buy yen and marks, and bought Japanese and German government bonds. In total, he established an $800 million position, a position larger than the entire capital of the fund. In late September the major governments announced the Plaza Agreement, in which they vowed to take coordinated actions (like intervention in the foreign exchange markets) to raise the values of other major currencies relative to the dollar. Within a month, as the dollar depreciated, Soros had profits of $150 million. The fund's total return for 1985 was 122 percent, as he had also invested in foreign stocks and long-term U.S. Treasury bonds. Of course, not all of his positions turned out so well. For instance, in 1987, the Quantum Fund lost up to $840 million when the U.S. and other stock markets crashed in October. But the fund still earned a return of 14 percent for the entire year.

In September 1992, Soros placed his most famous bet. Following German reunification in 1989, German interest rates increased, and the mark tended to appreciate. But most EU currencies were pegged to each other in the Exchange Rate Mechanism (ERM) of the European Monetary System. So the other countries had to raise their interest rates to maintain the pegged exchange rates. Soros predicted that the British government could not sustain this policy because the British economy was already weak and unemployment was high. He expected that Britain would either devalue the pound within the ERM or pull out of the ERM. In either case, the exchange-rate value of the pound would decline. He established his speculative investment positions short in pounds and long in marks, using pound borrowings and mark investments, as well as futures and options. And the positions were big—$10 billion. As Soros and other speculative investors established their positions, they sold pounds, putting downward pressure on the exchange-rate value of the pound. The central banks tried to defend the pegged rate, but soon the British government gave up and pulled out of the ERM. The pound depreciated against the mark. Within a month the Quantum Fund made a profit of about $1 billion on its pound positions, and a profit of up to $1 billion on other European currency positions. The *Economist* magazine called Soros "the man who broke the Bank of England."

After 1992, Soros turned over most trading decisions in the Quantum Fund to his chosen successor, Stanley Druckenmiller. The Quantum Fund continued to have some large successes and some large losses. In early 1997, Soros and Druckenmiller foresaw weakness in the Thai baht, and Quantum established short baht positions in January and February. The crisis hit in July, the Thai baht depreciated, and Quantum made money. But when the Thai baht and other Asian currencies continued to depreciate, they thought that the market had taken the rates too far. For instance, when the Indonesian rupiah fell from 2,400 per dollar to 4,000 per dollar, they established long positions in rupiah, and then lost money as the rupiah continued to fall beyond 10,000 per dollar.

In 1998, the Quantum Fund lost $2 billion on investments in Russia when Russian financial markets and the ruble collapsed. But the fund still earned more than 12 percent for the entire year. In 1999 the fund shifted to investing in tech stocks and was up 35 percent for the year. The tech investments and long positions in the euro took revenge in early 2000. For the first four months the fund was down 22 percent.

Weary of the battles, Druckenmiller resigned in April. Soros announced that the fund was shifting to investing with less risk and lower returns. Still, as the global financial and economic crisis began in summer 2007, Soros temporarily came out of retirement to trade with great success. During the crisis years 2007–2009, the Quantum Fund earned a phenomenal annual average return of 22 percent, and Soros himself earned over $7 billion. In 2011 Soros converted his fund to a family office, to manage only his investments and those of his family and foundations.

As he reduced his role in fund management, Soros turned to writing articles and books, philanthropy, and political activities. His writing is curious. He is deeply critical of excessive capitalism and individualism—what he calls "market fundamentalism." He believes that unregulated global financial markets are inherently unstable, and he calls for greater national regulation and the establishment of new global institutions like an international credit-insurance organization to guarantee loans to developing countries.

Soros is the quintessential international speculative investor. His name is synonymous with hedge funds, especially those that take large speculative positions. He has been denounced by government officials, like Prime Minister Mahathir Mohamad of Malaysia in 1997, as the source of immense and unjustified speculative pressures on their countries' currencies and financial markets. Soros continues to defend his own investment activities, stating that he merely perceived changes that were going to happen in any case. But, as his writings indicate, at a broader level he has mixed feelings about the current global financial system.

DISCUSSION QUESTION

In late 2012 Scott Bessent, chief investment officer of Soros' family office, concluded that coming political changes in Japan probably would lead to yen depreciation. His actions resulted in a gain of $1 billion during the next three months. What are some actions he probably took?

DOES INTEREST PARITY REALLY HOLD? EMPIRICAL EVIDENCE

The relationships among exchange rates and interest rates that we have discussed in this chapter are powerful concepts. Do these rate relationships hold for actual exchange rates and interest rates? Let's look at the evidence.

Evidence on Covered Interest Parity

Covered interest parity states that the forward premium should be (approximately) equal to the difference in interest rates. All of these rates can be seen in the foreign exchange markets and the short-term financial markets, so a test of covered interest parity is straightforward. The only further requirement is to identify comparable financial assets denominated in different currencies. Generally, we want to use financial assets with little or no risk of default so that any subtle differences in default risk do not muddy the empirical test.

Let's start by looking at broad evidence for major currencies for the time period that begins shortly after the world shifted to managed floating exchange rates in the early 1970s. Figure 18.2 shows the results from one careful study that examined the covered interest differentials between short-term financial assets in the United States and those in Germany, Japan, and France, starting in 1978. For Germany and Japan, the covered interest differential is consistently very close to zero (and thus within the small range created by modest transactions costs) beginning in about 1985. For France this is true beginning in about 1987. Since about the mid-1980s, covered interest parity has held for comparable short-term assets for these four currencies (and for a number of others not shown as well).

The divergences in the earlier period appear to reflect actual or threatened government capital controls, which are restrictions on the ability of financial investors to transfer moneys in or out of the country. Germany and Japan largely eliminated these capital controls in the early 1980s. With freer flows of moneys, covered interest arbitrage became possible, and covered interest parity has held between the United States and these two countries since the mid-1980s.

With the election of Mitterrand, a socialist, as president of France in 1981, foreign investors began to fear the imposition of more severe capital controls. This added a risk to covered investments into France, the *political risk* that investors would not be able to remove their moneys from France when they wanted to. Because of this additional risk, major deviations from covered interest parity arose in 1981, at times reaching an annualized covered interest differential of 10 percentage points. Foreign investors' fears were correct. France tightened its restrictions in 1981 and did not substantially liberalize these controls until 1986. Once the restrictions were removed and the risk that they might be reimposed subsided, covered interest parity began to hold in 1987.

Let's continue with a more granular look. How often do even small deviations from covered interest parity occur, and how quickly are they eliminated? Akram, Rime, and Sarno (2008) provide some answers using detailed second-by-second data for seven and a half months in 2004, for the euro, British pound, and Japanese yen, each relative to the U.S. dollar. For interest rates they use the rates on Eurocurrency deposits offered by large banks to their international customers. A bank active in the Eurocurrency market is willing to accept interest-paying deposits denominated in any of a number of currencies, not just the currency of the country in which the bank is located. (The box "Eurocurrencies: Not (Just) Euros and Not Regulated" says more about this market.)

FIGURE 18.2 Covered Interest Differentials: The United States against Germany, Japan, and France, 1978–1993

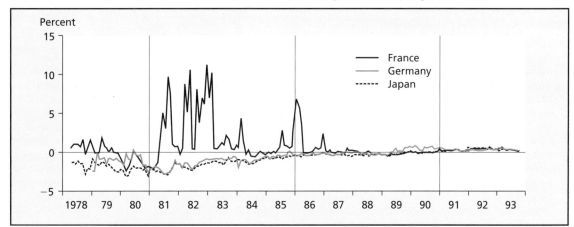

The (annualized) covered interest differential is measured in favor of the United States, $CD = F + i_{US} - i_F$, where F is the forward premium on the dollar and i_F is the interest rate for the other country (Germany, Japan, or France). The forward rate and the interest rates are 90-day rates. The interest rates are for commercial paper in the United States and for interbank borrowing in the other three countries.

Source: Pigott (1993–1994).

Previous studies found that, broadly, covered interest parity applies extremely well to Eurocurrency deposits. Akram, Rime, and Sarno use their detailed data to look very closely, and they find potentially profitable deviations from covered interest parity about 1 percent of the time for the euro, about 2 percent for the pound, and about 0.6 percent for the yen. These deviations, though profitable, are generally small and last briefly, usually less than a minute. While rapid-fire trading can find some opportunities for covered interest arbitrage, the opportunities also disappear quickly.

Overall, covered interest parity is an important and empirically useful concept. During normal times, it applies very well—forward and spot exchange rates are tightly linked to interest rates for major-currency countries and for a growing number of other countries that have liberalized or eliminated their restrictions on international movements of financial capital. However, even for major currencies, parity does not always apply during times of turmoil in financial markets, as discussed for the global financial and economic crisis and the euro crisis in the box "Covered Interest Parity Breaks Down."

Evidence on Uncovered Interest Parity

Uncovered interest parity states that the expected rate of appreciation of the spot exchange-rate value of a currency should (approximately) equal the difference in interest rates. Testing uncovered interest parity is much more difficult than testing covered interest parity. We have no direct information on people's actual expectations of exchange-rate changes.

One approach is to survey knowledgeable market participants about their exchange-rate expectations (and hope that they answer truthfully). The average expected future spot rate can then be used to calculate the expected appreciation and the expected

Case Study   Eurocurrencies: Not (Just) Euros and Not Regulated

The Eurocurrency market is a worldwide wholesale money market of enormous scope, one beyond the easy control of any government. The traditional definition of a Eurocurrency deposit is a bank deposit denominated in a currency different from the currency of the country where the bank is located. However, since 1981, the equivalent of Eurodollar deposits can be booked in the International Banking Facility of a U.S. bank. The better definition of a Eurocurrency deposit is a *bank deposit that is not subject to the usual government regulations* imposed by the country of the currency in which the deposit is denominated. Eurodollar deposits are dollar deposits that are not subject to the same regulations imposed by the U.S. banking authorities on regular dollar deposits. In fact, the prefix *Euro* has now come to be used in international finance to refer not to geographic location but rather to financial instruments or activities that are subject to little or no government regulation. Eurobonds are bonds that are issued outside of the usual regulations imposed by the country in whose currency the bond is denominated.

Eurocurrency deposits are large time deposits. In 2013, banks in various areas of the world, including Europe, North America, Asia, and the Caribbean, had Eurocurrency deposits totaling about $19 trillion. About three-fifths of these deposits are Eurodollar deposits. About one-fifth are euro Eurodeposits! (Yes, we have some confusing terminology—the *euro* as a currency is different from *Euro* as a prefix.) Eurosterling and Euroyen deposits are sizable too.

Eurocurrency deposits seem to have begun in Europe in the late 1950s. Several reasons explain the development and rapid growth of Eurocurrencies. European firms active in international trade began to hold dollars temporarily in their local banks that were willing to accept dollar deposits. The Soviet Union began to deposit U.S. dollars in European banks to keep the dollars out of the direct reach of the U.S. government during the Cold War. In the 1970s, Arab countries earning dollars on oil exports also feared possible restrictions if they placed their dollars on deposit in the United States, and turned to Eurodollar deposits. Most important to the long-run development of the market, banks involved in taking these deposits (and making loans with the funds) found that they could avoid various regulations.

One type of regulation that can be avoided is any restriction of international flows of moneys. Thus, in the late 1950s, the British government restricted the ability of British banks to lend pounds to foreigners but permitted them to lend dollars to foreigners. In the 1960s, the U.S. government attempted to restrict capital outflows. Borrowers turned to the Eurodollar market to obtain dollars that they could no longer borrow from the United States.

Other regulations that can be avoided in the Eurocurrency market are the standard regulations imposed on domestic banking activities. Countries that wish to attract Eurocurrency deposit activity generally do not impose reserve requirements on these deposits, or deposit insurance premiums, and they lighten or eliminate other regulations. Freedom from the burdens and extra costs of various regulations permits banks to offer somewhat higher interest rates on Eurocurrency deposits than are available on regular domestic bank deposits and perhaps also to charge somewhat lower interest rates on loans funded by these deposits. The lack of regulation implies that Eurocurrency deposit claims are somewhat riskier for depositors. They face somewhat more uncertainty about whether their claims will be honored if the bank should fail.

Eurocurrency deposits and loans are generally credited with enhancing the efficiency of international financial markets. Eurocurrencies offer large corporations, financial institutions, and governments another alternative as to where they can invest their funds to earn interest or where they can borrow to obtain low-cost financing. Some of the efficiencies here come from the lack of burdens and costs imposed by government regulations, while others come from additional and fierce competition among banks from many countries for the same business.

DISCUSSION QUESTION
If the Soviet Union and Arab oil-exporting countries had not been fearful of possible U.S government actions, would the Eurocurrency market still have developed into a large market?

FIGURE 18.3   Uncovered Interest Differentials: The United States against Germany
and Japan, 1991–2005

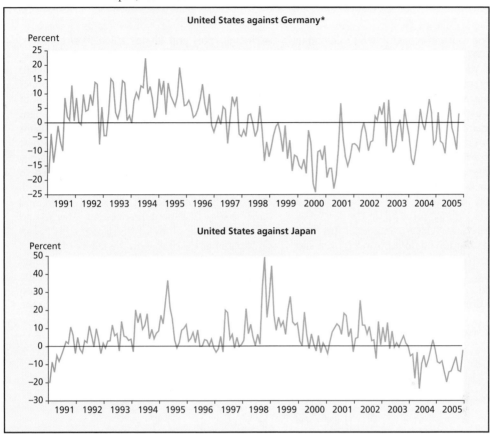

*The exchange rate is the German mark–U.S. dollar exchange rate through 1998 and the euro–U.S.
dollar exchange rate thereafter.

The (annualized) expected uncovered interest differential is measured in favor of the United States.
EUD = expected appreciation of the dollar $+ i_{US} - i_F$. The expected 90-day appreciation of the
dollar is based on forecasts of currency movements from *Consensus Forecasts*. Interest rates
are those on 90-day Eurocurrency deposits.

Source: Balakrishnan and Tulin (2006). The author is grateful for data provided by Ravi Balakrishnan and Volodymyr Tulin.

uncovered interest differential. Figure 18.3 shows the results of one study that reports
this differential. The two panels show the uncovered interest differential for the
United States relative to Germany and to Japan. In both panels it appears that market
participants often expected large uncovered interest differentials. This suggests that
uncovered interest parity does not hold nearly as closely as does covered interest parity.

A second approach is to examine actual returns on uncovered international investments to draw out inferences about expected returns and exchange-rate expectations.
Looking at the *actual* overall return (including both the foreign interest return and the
actual gain or loss on the currency exchanges) on any *one* uncovered foreign investment does not tell us much. The actual uncovered return may not equal the return on

Global Crisis and Euro Crisis Covered Interest Parity Breaks Down

The global financial and economic crisis that began in summer 2007 saw the disruption of many financial markets. While the foreign exchange market was less affected than many others, it still took its hits. One indication of the effect of the crisis on the foreign exchange market was the development of substantial deviations from covered interest parity for rates that would be at parity during normal times. With the euro crisis that began in 2010 and intensified in 2011, substantial deviations from covered interest parity reappeared.

The graph indicates how the crises affected covered interest parity, focusing on London interbank offered rates (LIBOR), interest rates that large banks in London use for borrowing from and lending to each other in various currencies. Similar to Figure 18.2, the graph here shows the annualized covered interest differential measured in favor of the United States, for the 90-day forward

exchange rates and 90-day LIBOR interest rates, relative to each of the euro and the British pound.

Up to August 2007, covered interest parity held well for these financial assets, a continuation of what we showed in Figure 18.2. The first part of the global crisis began in August when BNP Paribas announced that it could not value mortgage assets held by several of its mutual funds. By late August the covered interest differential had generally widened and fluctuated more. Rates returned to covered interest parity during January to mid-March 2008, when Bear Stearns nearly failed, and larger parity deviations reappeared. The second and much worse phase of the global crisis began on September 15, 2008, with the failure of Lehman Brothers. Deviations from covered interest parity widened, reaching over 2 percentage points for the euro relative to the dollar in late September and early October and over 3 percentage points for the

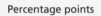

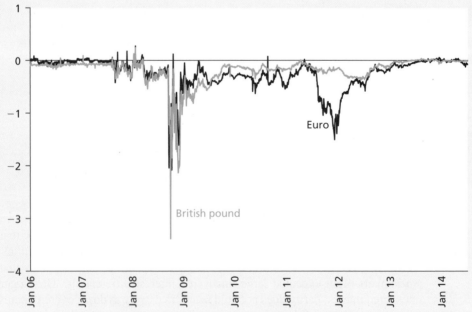

Covered Interest Differentials, the U.S. Dollar Relative to the Euro and the British Pound, 2006–2014

Source: Levich (2013). The author is grateful for data with updates provided by Richard Levich.

pound relative to the dollar in late September. After some large fluctuations, the differentials became smaller and less variable by early 2009. Still, covered interest differentials remained larger than they had been before August 2007. (Other major currencies, including the Swiss franc, Canadian dollar, Japanese yen, and Australian dollar, had similar parity deviations during the global crisis.)

At first, during 2010 and the first half of 2011, the euro crisis was focused on Greece, Ireland, and Portugal. There was no additional effect on deviations from covered interest parity. In mid-2011 new concerns arose that Spain and Italy, much larger countries, could require large bailout assistance; that Greece might be forced somehow to exit the euro area; and that the monetary union itself could enter a period of turmoil and possible collapse. With new concerns about bank obligations in euros, the deviations from covered interest parity for the euro relative to the dollar (but not for the pound relative to the dollar) widened to about 1.5 percentage points in late 2011. As the euro crisis abated, and as the financial system moved further away from the global financial crisis, the differentials became smaller.

Indeed, since early 2013, the rates have returned to a close fit for covered interest parity.

Why did we see such large deviations from covered interest parity? There were no government controls preventing international capital flows or preventing banks from lending to each other. Rather, the banks themselves were not exploiting the covered interest differentials that existed. While forward cover eliminates exchange-rate risk, it does not remove the risks of relying on the other parties to the arbitrage transactions to fulfill their sides of the contracts, both the future delivery of currency to settle forward foreign exchange contracts and the future repayment of loans. In normal times the risk of dealing with other large banks is considered minimal. But during the global crisis perceptions of such counterparty risks rose to high levels, based on the chance that other banks had large, unrevealed losses that could bring them down. Similar concerns arose during the euro crisis, though to a lesser extent and focused on the euro. Without a highly elastic supply of funds willing to undertake covered interest arbitrage, covered interest parity broke down.

a comparable domestic investment simply because the actual future spot exchange turned out to be somewhat different from the future spot exchange rate that was expected at the time of the investment. Nonetheless, if expected uncovered returns are typically at parity, then over a *large number* of investments the actual uncovered differentials should be random and on average approximately equal to zero. Various studies have shown that the actual uncovered differentials are not completely random and for some time periods are not on average equal to zero. Uncovered interest parity applies roughly, but there also appear to be deviations of some importance.

Why does uncovered interest parity not hold perfectly? One possible explanation is simple—exchange-rate risk matters. Investors will not enter into risky uncovered foreign investments unless they expect to be compensated adequately for the risk that this adds to their portfolios. Divergences from uncovered interest parity then reflect the risk premium necessary to compensate for exchange-rate risk. However, a number of studies conclude that the uncovered interest differential is often larger than the risk premium necessary to compensate for this risk.

To the extent that the differential is larger than that necessary to compensate for risk, it appears that the expectations of market participants about future spot exchange rates are biased. For some periods of time the market participants are consistently expecting an exchange-rate change that is different from what will actually occur. Research has attempted to determine the nature of the biases that may exist in market expectations of future spot exchange rates. One possible explanation is troubling. If the biases are simply consistent errors, the foreign exchange market is an inefficient market. Other possible explanations are more subtle and probably less troubling. One is that market participants learn slowly about exchange-rate behavior, but their forecasts are biased while they are learning. Another is that market participants (correctly) expect a large, rather sudden shift in an exchange rate at some point in the future. During the time before the large shift occurs, forecasts appear to be biased because they give some probability to the much different exchange rate that has not yet arrived. For instance, if the market expects a large devaluation of a now fixed-rate currency, the expected value of the spot exchange rate 90 days from now is an average of the current spot rate (if the devaluation does not occur within the next 90 days) and a much lower rate (if the devaluation does occur within the next 90 days). During the time before the devaluation actually occurs, the expected exchange rate appears to be biased—it is consistently lower than the actual (fixed) rate that continues to hold.

The conclusions that we reach are cautious. Uncovered interest parity is useful at least as a rough approximation empirically, but it appears to apply imperfectly to actual rates.

Evidence on Forward Exchange Rates and Expected Future Spot Exchange Rates

If there is substantial speculation using the forward exchange market, then the forward rate should equal the average market expectation of the future spot exchange rate. Although this seems quite different from the interest parity relationships, it is actually closely related to them. If covered interest parity applies to actual rates, then testing whether the forward rate is a predictor of the future spot exchange rate is the same as testing uncovered interest parity. The only difference between covered and uncovered interest parity is the replacement of the current forward exchange rate with the currently expected future spot exchange rate.

For currencies for which covered interest parity holds, conclusions about the forward rate are then the same as those about uncovered interest parity. The forward exchange rate is roughly useful as an indicator of the market's expected future spot rate or as a predictor of this future spot rate, but there are also indications of biases in the predictions. Some part of the biases probably reflects risk premiums, but another part appears to reflect biases in the forecasts themselves. In addition, the forward rate is not a particularly accurate predictor of the future spot exchange rate. The errors in forecasting are often large. Indeed, as we will see in the next chapter, no method of forecasting exchange rates into the near future is particularly accurate!

Summary

A person holding a net asset position (a *long* position) or a net liability position (a *short* position) in a foreign currency is exposed to **exchange-rate risk.** The value of the person's income or net worth will change if the exchange rate changes in a way that the person does not expect. **Hedging** is the act of balancing your assets and liabilities in a foreign currency to become immune to risk resulting from future changes in the value of foreign currency. Speculating means taking a long or a short position in a foreign currency, thereby gambling on its future exchange value. There are a number of ways to hedge or speculate in foreign currency.

A forward exchange contract is an agreement to buy or sell a foreign currency for future delivery at a price (the forward exchange rate) set now. Forward foreign exchange contracts are useful because they provide a straightforward way to hedge an exposure to exchange-rate risk or to speculate in an attempt to profit from future spot-exchange-rate values. An interesting hypothesis that emerges from the use of the forward market for speculation is that the forward exchange rate should equal the average expected value of the future spot rate.

International financial investment has grown rapidly in recent years. Investment in foreign-currency assets is more complicated than domestic investment because of the need for currency exchanges, both to acquire foreign currency now and to convert back the foreign currency in the future. If the rate at which the future sale of foreign currency will occur is locked in now through a forward exchange contract, we have a hedged or covered international investment. If the future sale of foreign currency will occur at the future spot rate, we have an uncovered international investment, one that is exposed to exchange-rate risk and therefore speculative.

As a result of covered interest arbitrage, to exploit any covered interest differential between the returns on domestic and covered foreign investments, we expect that covered interest parity will exist (as long as there are no actual or threatened government restrictions on international money flows). Covered interest parity states that the percentage by which the forward exchange value of a currency exceeds its spot value equals the percentage point amount by which its interest rate is lower than the other country's interest rate. For countries with no capital controls and for comparable short-term financial assets, covered interest parity normally holds almost perfectly when actual rates are examined empirically.

At the time of the investment, the expected overall return on an *uncovered* international investment can be calculated using the investor's expected future spot exchange rate. The overall expected return on the uncovered international investment can be compared to the return available at home. The expected uncovered interest differential is one factor in deciding whether to make the uncovered international investment. Exposure to exchange-rate risk must also be considered in the decision. If this risk is of little or no importance, then we hypothesize that uncovered interest parity will exist. The expected rate of appreciation of a currency should equal the percentage point amount by which its interest rate is lower than the other country's interest rate. Uncovered interest parity is not easy to test or examine empirically using actual rates because we do not directly know the expected future spot rate or the expected rate of appreciation. It appears that uncovered interest parity is useful as a rough approximation, but it does not apply almost perfectly. Rather, exchange-rate risk appears to be of some importance, and investors' expectations or forecasts of future spot exchange rates appear to be somewhat biased. (A similar conclusion is that, empirically, the forward exchange rate is a rough but somewhat biased predictor of the future spot exchange rate.)

Key Terms

Exchange-rate risk	Currency swap	Covered interest
Hedging	Covered international	arbitrage
Speculating	investment	Covered interest parity
Forward foreign exchange	Uncovered international	Expected uncovered
contract	investment	interest differential
Forward exchange rate	Covered interest	Uncovered interest parity
Currency futures	differential	Capital controls
Currency option	Forward premium	Eurocurrency deposit

Suggested Reading

Good presentations of theory and evidence on the parity relationships among forward exchange rates, spot exchange rates, and interest rates include Pigott (1993–94) and Marston (1995). Akram et al. (2008) examine the opportunities for covered interest arbitrage using detailed real-time data on exchange rates and interest rates. Levich (2013) and Baba and Packer (2009) analyze deviations from covered interest parity during the global crisis. Froot and Thaler (1990) and Levich (1989) discuss evidence about the efficiency or inefficiency of the foreign exchange market. A good textbook view of foreign exchange futures, options, and swaps is found in Eun and Resnick (2012, Chapters 7 and 14). Pojarliev and Levich (2012) explore the strategies of active currency investment managers. Bartram and Dufey (2001) provide an overview of portfolio aspects of international investment.

Questions and Problems

◆ 1. "For an investment in a foreign-currency-denominated financial asset, part of the return comes from the asset itself and part from the foreign currency." Do you agree or disagree? Explain.

2. You have been asked to determine whether covered interest parity holds for one-year government bonds issued by the U.S. and British governments. What data will you need? How will you test?

◆ 3. Explain the nature of the exchange-rate risk for each of the following, from the perspective of the U.S. firm or person. In your answer, include whether each is a long or short position in foreign currency.

   a. A small U.S. firm sold experimental computer components to a Japanese firm, and it will receive payment of 1 million yen in 60 days.

   b. An American college student receives a birthday gift of Japanese government bonds worth 10 million yen, and the bonds mature in 60 days.

   c. A U.S. firm must repay a yen loan, principal plus interest totaling 100 million yen, coming due in 60 days.

4. The current spot exchange rate is $0.010/yen. The current 60-day forward exchange rate is $0.009/yen. How would the U.S. firms and people described in question 3 each use a forward foreign exchange contract to hedge their risk exposure? What are the amounts in each forward contract?

◆ 5. The current spot exchange rate is $0.50/SFr. The current 180-day forward exchange rate is $0.52/SFr. You expect the spot rate to be $0.51/SFr in 180 days. How would you speculate using a forward contract?

6. The current spot exchange rate is $1.20/euro. The current 90-day forward exchange rate is $1.18/euro. You expect the spot rate to be $1.22/euro in 90 days. How would you speculate using a forward contract? If many people speculate in this way, what pressure is placed on the value of the current forward exchange rate?

◆ 7. You have access to the following rates:

Current spot exchange rate: $0.0100/yen
Current 180-day forward exchange rate: $0.0105/yen
180-day U.S. interest rate (on dollar-denominated assets): 6.05%
180-day Japanese interest rate (on yen-denominated assets): 1.00%
The interest rates are true 180-day rates (not annualized). You can borrow or invest at these rates. Calculate the actual amounts involved for the two ways around the lake (Figure 18.1) to get between each of the following.

  a. Start with $1 now and end with dollars in 180 days.
  b. Start with $1 now and end with yen in 180 days.
  c. Start with 100 yen now and end with yen in 180 days.

8. The following rates are available in the markets:

Current spot exchange rate: $1.000/SFr
Current 30-day forward exchange rate: $1.010/SFr
Annualized interest rate on 30-day dollar-denominated bonds: 12% (1.0% for 30 days)
Annualized interest rate on 30-day Swiss franc–denominated bonds: 6% (0.5% for 30 days)

  a. Is the Swiss franc at a forward premium or discount?
  b. Should a U.S.-based investor make a covered investment in Swiss franc–denominated 30-day bonds, rather than investing in 30-day dollar-denominated bonds? Explain.
  c. Because of covered interest arbitrage, what pressures are placed on the various rates? If the only rate that actually changes is the forward exchange rate, to what value will it be driven?

◆ 9. The following rates exist:

Current spot exchange rate: $1.80/£
Annualized interest rate on 90-day dollar-denominated bonds: 8% (2% for 90 days)
Annualized interest rate on 90-day pound-denominated bonds: 12% (3% for 90 days)
Financial investors expect the spot exchange rate to be $1.77/£ in 90 days.

  a. If he bases his decisions solely on the difference in the expected rate of return, should a U.S.-based investor make an uncovered investment in pound-denominated bonds rather than investing in dollar-denominated bonds?
  b. If she bases her decision solely on the difference in the expected rate of return, should a UK-based investor make an uncovered investment in dollar-denominated bonds rather than investing in pound-denominated bonds?
  c. If there is substantial uncovered investment seeking higher expected returns, what pressure is placed on the current spot exchange rate?

10. Here are today's rates:

    Spot exchange rate: 3.20 Polish zloty per U.S. dollar
    6-month forward exchange rate: 3.24 Polish zloty per U.S. dollar.
       You expect the spot exchange rate in 6 months to be 3.26 Polish zloty per U.S. dollar.

    Evaluate the validity of the following statement: "Given this information, you will profit from a forward exchange speculative position based on your expected future spot exchange rate, if the actual future spot exchange rate in 6 months is 3.25 zloty per U.S. dollar."

♦ 11. The following exchange rates exist on a particular day.

    Spot exchange rate: U.S. $1.400/euro
    Forward exchange rate (90 days): U.S. $1.427/euro
    The following (annualized) interest rates on 90-day government bonds also exist on this day:
    Euro-denominated bonds: 8%
    U.S. dollar–denominated bonds: 16%

    a. Financial investors in all countries have the expectation that the spot exchange rate in 90 days will be 0.7100 euro/U.S. dollar. Are investors expecting the euro will appreciate or depreciate during the next 90 days?
    b. Consider the comparison between investments in U.S. dollar–denominated bonds and euro-denominated bonds, with any foreign investment done as uncovered foreign investment. In which direction (between the United States and the euro area) will there be an incentive for uncovered investment to flow, based on a comparison of returns? Calculate the relevant returns and explain your answer.

12. Why is testing whether uncovered interest parity holds for actual rates more difficult than testing whether covered interest parity holds?

Chapter **Nineteen**

What Determines Exchange Rates?

Thinking in terms of supply and demand is a necessary first step toward understanding exchange rates. The next step is the one that has to be taken in any market analysis: finding out what underlying forces cause supply and demand to change.

We need to know what forces have caused the changes in exchange rates observed since the start of widespread "floating" back in the early 1970s. Figure 19.1 reminds us just how variable exchange rates have been. Between 1971 and the end of 1973, most currencies of other industrialized countries rose in value relative to the dollar, the average rise being about 20 percent. After 1973, when the modern era of floating exchange rates clearly took hold, we can see three types of variability for these exchange rates.

First, there are *long-term trends*. As shown in Figure 19.1A, over the entire period the Japanese yen, Swiss franc, and German mark (DM) tended to appreciate, with the Swiss franc almost quintupling in value, the yen more than tripling and the DM (fixed to the euro in 1999 and then retired in 2002) more than doubling. As shown in Figure 19.1B, over the period, and especially up to early 2000s, the Italian lira, British pound, Australian dollar, and Canadian dollar tended to depreciate. From 1970 to 2002, the lira (also fixed to and then replaced by the euro) lost about seven-tenths of its exchange-rate value against the dollar, the Australian dollar lost about a half, the pound lost about four-tenths, and the Canadian dollar lost about a third. Still other currencies, such as the Israeli shekel and Argentine peso, dropped so far in value that they would almost hit zero if we added them to Figure 19.1B.

Second, there are *medium-term trends* (over periods of several years), and these medium-term trends are sometimes counter to the longer trends. For instance, the Swiss franc, DM, and to a lesser extent the yen depreciated during the period 1980–1985. Another trend is the appreciation of the pound and the lira from 1985 to 1988. The decline in the dollar value of the euro from its introduction at the beginning of 1999 to late 2000, and then the euro's rise back up in value from late 2000 to early 2008, can be seen in either of two currencies shown (DM, lira) that it has replaced.

Third, there is substantial *short-term variability* in these exchange rates from month to month (and, indeed, from day to day, hour to hour, and even minute to minute).

We can look at the movements in the exchange-rate value of the dollar as the reverse of those for each foreign currency, or we can calculate the average movement against a set of other currencies. After the dollar's average value against the currencies of other industrialized countries fluctuated modestly from 1973 to 1980, nearly all observers were stunned as the

FIGURE 19.1   Selected Exchange Rates, 1970–2014 (Monthly)

*At the beginning of 1999, the German mark and Italian lira were fixed to the euro, and in 2002 the euro replaced these currencies. Each of these rates is tracking the U.S.$/euro exchange-rate movement from January 1999.

For each currency, the dollar price of that currency (e.g., $/£) is shown, with units adjusted so that its January 1970 value is 100. For any currency, an increase in the value shown from one time to another indicates that the currency increased in exchange-rate value (appreciated) relative to the U.S. dollar during that time period; a decrease in the value shown indicates that the currency depreciated relative to the U.S. dollar. For the currencies shown, the Japanese yen, Swiss franc, and German mark appreciated over the entire 44-year period, while the Italian lira, Australian dollar, and British pound sterling depreciated. The Canadian dollar tended to depreciate gradually to 2002 and then appreciated back to move above its 1970 value.

Source: International Monetary Fund, *International Financial Statistics.*

dollar rallied. By the time the dollar peaked in early 1985, it had gained over 50 percent in value since 1980 and was about 20 percent above its value in 1970. From early 1985 to early 1988, the dollar then fell (even more quickly) by a little more than it had risen in the previous five years. From early 1988 to 1995, the dollar fluctuated somewhat but did not show any pronounced overall trend. From 1995 to early 2002, the dollar's average value rose by about 40 percent. It then fell to about 12 percent below its 1995 value by early 2008, and in the following years to mid-2014 it fluctuated somewhat with no trend.

Why do we see large changes in the values of floating exchange rates? How does short-run variability turn into long-run trends? Why are medium-run trends sometimes opposite to these longer trends? This chapter presents what economists believe, what they think they know, and what they admit they do not know about this challenging puzzle.

A ROAD MAP

This chapter focuses on the determinants of exchange rates.[1] The first part of the chapter focuses on short-run movements in exchange rates. To understand exchange rates in the short run, we must focus on the perceptions and actions of international financial investors. We believe that rather little of the $5 trillion of foreign exchange trading that occurs each day is related to international trade in goods and services. Instead, most of it is related to the positioning or repositioning of the currency composition of the portfolios of international financial investors.

The **asset market approach to exchange rates** emphasizes the role of portfolio repositioning by international financial investors. As demand for and supply of financial assets denominated in different currencies shift around, these shifts place pressures on the exchange rates among the currencies. Fortunately, we have a head start on this analysis because we can use the concept of uncovered interest parity from Chapter 18 the previous chapter. Major conclusions of our analysis are that the exchange-rate value of a foreign currency (e) is raised *in the short run* by the following changes:

- A rise in the foreign interest rate relative to our interest rate ($i_f - i$).
- A rise in the expected future spot exchange rate (e^{ex}).

The second part of the chapter turns to long-term trends. Why do some currencies tend to appreciate over the long run, while others tend to depreciate? A key economic "fundamental" that appears to explain these long trends is the difference in national rates of inflation of the prices of goods and services. The concept of **purchasing power parity (PPP)** contains our core understanding of the relationship between product prices and exchange rates in the long run.

The third part of the chapter examines the role of money as a determinant of national product price levels and inflation rates. Through the link of money to price levels and inflation rates, the **monetary approach to exchange rates**

---

[1]The forces examined here are central not only to understanding what causes floating rates to change but also to understanding the pressures on a system of fixed rates. Whatever would make a floating currency sink or rise would also make a fixed exchange rate harder to defend. The material has more uses than simply the search for determinants of floating exchange rates. It also applies to the analysis of the balance of payments under a fixed-rate system or a managed floating rate.

emphasizes the importance of money supplies and demands as key to understanding the determinants of exchange rates. A major conclusion of the monetary approach is that the spot exchange rate *e,* the price of foreign currency in units of our currency, is raised *in the long run* by the following changes:

- A rise in our money supply relative to the foreign money supply (M^s/M_f^s).
- A rise in foreign real domestic product relative to our real domestic product (Y_f/Y).

The fourth part of the chapter shows one way in which the short term flows into the medium term and then into the long term. We examine the tendency for exchange rates to "overshoot," to change more than seems necessary in reaction to changes in government policies or to other important economic or political news. After the overshooting in the short run, the exchange rate moves in the medium run toward its long-run fundamental value.

The final part of the chapter examines two questions. First, how useful are these concepts and relationships—how well can we forecast future exchange rates? Second, how many different ways can we use to measure the exchange-rate value of a country's currency?

EXCHANGE RATES IN THE SHORT RUN

Economists believe that pressures on exchange rates in the short run can best be understood in terms of the demands and supplies of assets denominated in different currencies. In principle the asset market approach to exchange rates incorporates all financial assets. Fortunately, we can grasp its key elements by focusing on investments in debt securities, such as government bonds, denominated in different currencies. In the analysis here we build on the discussion of uncovered international financial investment and uncovered interest parity from the previous chapter. Recall that investors determine the expected overall return on an uncovered investment in a bond denominated in a foreign currency by using

- The basic return on the bond itself (the interest rate or yield).
- The expected gain or loss on currency exchanges (the expected appreciation or depreciation of the foreign currency).

While we may not believe that uncovered interest parity holds exactly, we still expect that there will be a noticeable relationship between the return on home-currency bonds and the expected overall return on foreign-currency bonds. These two returns will tend to be equal (or at least not too different). Emerging differences in these two returns will cause international financial investors to reposition their portfolios, and this repositioning creates the pressures that move the two returns toward equality.[2]

---

[2]This broad asset market approach built on uncovered interest parity is a kind of portfolio balance approach because it emphasizes the role of portfolio repositioning in the determination of exchange rates. However, the portfolio balance approach can go further than this. One further conclusion of the portfolio balance approach is that a change in the supplies of assets denominated in different currencies affects the deviation from uncovered interest parity (in the form of a risk premium) that is necessary to induce investors to hold (demand) all of these assets. This conclusion results because assets denominated in different currencies actually are not perfect substitutes for each other in investors' portfolios.

FIGURE 19.2   Determinants of the Exchange Rate in the Short Run

Change in Variable	Direction of International Financial Repositioning	Implications for the Current Spot Exchange Rate (e = Domestic currency/Foreign currency)
Domestic Interest Rate (*i*)		
Increases	Toward domestic-currency assets	e decreases (domestic currency appreciates)
Decreases	Toward foreign-currency assets	e increases (domestic currency depreciates)
Foreign Interest Rate (*i*$_f$)		
Increases	Toward foreign-currency assets	e increases (domestic currency depreciates)
Decreases	Toward domestic-currency assets	e decreases (domestic currency appreciates)
Expected Future Spot Exchange Rate (*e*^{ex})		
Increases	Toward foreign-currency assets	e increases (domestic currency depreciates)
Decreases	Toward domestic-currency assets	e decreases (domestic currency appreciates)

The analysis for each change in one of the variables assumes that the other two variables are unchanged.

Uncovered interest parity (whether exact or approximate) links together four variables: the domestic interest rate, the foreign interest rate, the current spot exchange rate, and the expected future spot exchange rate. (The two exchange rates together imply the expected appreciation or depreciation.) Change in any one of these four variables implies that adjustments will occur in one or more of the other three. We will focus on implications for the current spot exchange rate of changes in each of the other three variables. Figure 19.2 provides a summary of the effects.

The Role of Interest Rates

Foreign exchange markets do seem sensitive to movements in interest rates. Jumps of exchange rates often follow changes in interest rates. The response often looks prompt, so much so that press coverage of day-to-day rises or drops in an exchange rate often point first to interest rates as a cause.

If our interest rate (*i*) increases, while the foreign interest rate (*i*$_f$) and the spot exchange rate expected at some appropriate time in the future (*e*^{ex}) remain constant, the return comparison shifts in favor of investments in bonds denominated in our currency. If international financial investors want to shift toward domestic-currency assets, they first need to buy domestic currency before they can buy the domestic-currency bonds. This increase in demand for domestic currency increases the current spot-exchange-rate value of domestic currency (so *e* decreases). Given the speed with which financial investors can initiate shifts in their portfolios, the effect on the spot exchange rate can happen very quickly (instantaneously or within a few minutes).

Let's consider an example involving the United States, Switzerland, and 90-day bonds. Initially, the U.S. interest rate is 9 percent per year, and the Swiss interest rate is 5 percent per year. The current spot rate is $1.200 per Swiss franc (SFr), and the spot rate expected in 90 days is about $1.212 per SFr. The franc is expected to appreciate about 1 percent during the next 90 days, so the annual rate of expected appreciation is about 4 percent. (Uncovered interest parity holds at these rates, as the expected annualized overall return on the SFr-denominated bonds is about 9 percent, equal to 5 percent interest plus about 4 percent expected currency appreciation.) What happens if the U.S. interest rate increases to 11 percent? Given the other initial rates, the return differential shifts in favor of U.S.-dollar-denominated bonds. International financial investors have an incentive to shift toward dollar-denominated bonds, and this increases the demand for dollars in the foreign exchange market. The dollar tends to appreciate immediately. Furthermore, we can determine that the dollar should appreciate to about $1.194 per SFr, assuming that the interest rates and the expected future exchange rate do not change. Once this new current spot exchange rate is posted in the market, the SFr then is expected to appreciate during the next 90 days at a faster rate, equal to about 6 percent at an annual rate. This reestablishes uncovered interest parity (5 percent interest plus about 6 percent expected appreciation matches the 11 percent U.S. interest) and eliminates any further desire by international investors to reposition their portfolios.

If our interest rate instead decreases, with foreign interest rates and the expected future spot rate unchanged, the spot-exchange-rate value of our currency is predicted to decrease (e increases).

If the foreign interest rate (i_f) increases, the story is similar. Assuming that the domestic interest rate and the expected future spot exchange rate are constant, the return comparison shifts in favor of investments in bonds denominated in foreign currency. A shift by international financial investors toward foreign-currency bonds would require them first to buy foreign currency in the foreign exchange market. This increase in demand for the foreign currency increases the current spot exchange rate, e (the domestic currency depreciates).

Consider a variation on our previous example, still using 90 days and annualized rates. If the U.S. interest rate is 9 percent, the spot exchange rate is $1.200 per SFr, and the expected future spot rate is about $1.212 per SFr, what is the effect of an increase in the Swiss interest rate from 5 to 7 percent? The return differential shifts in favor of Swiss bonds. The increased demand for francs in the foreign exchange market results in a quick appreciation of the franc (and depreciation of the dollar). The current spot exchange rate must jump immediately to about $1.206 per SFr to reestablish uncovered interest parity.

If instead the foreign interest rate decreases, the spot rate, e, decreases. (The domestic currency appreciates.)

What happens if both interest rates change at the same time? The answer is straightforward. What matters is the interest rate differential $i - i_f$. If the interest rate differential increases, the return differential shifts in favor of domestic-currency bonds, and e tends to decrease. (The domestic currency appreciates.) If it decreases, e tends to increase.

The Role of the Expected Future Spot Exchange Rate

Expectations of future exchange rates can also have a powerful impact on international financial positioning, and through this on the value of the current exchange rate. Consider what happens when financial investors decide that they now expect the future spot exchange rate to be higher than they previously expected. Relative to the current spot rate, this means that they expect the foreign currency to appreciate more, or to depreciate less, or to appreciate rather than depreciate. Assuming that the interest rate differential is unchanged, the increase in the expected future spot rate alters the return differential in favor of foreign-currency-denominated bonds. The story from here is familiar. If international financial investors want to shift toward foreign-currency assets, they first need to buy foreign currency in the foreign exchange market before they can buy the foreign-currency bonds. This increase in demand for foreign currency increases the current spot exchange rate e. (The foreign currency appreciates; the domestic currency depreciates.) If instead the expected future spot exchange rate decreases, with the interest rate differential unchanged, the return differential changes in favor of domestic-currency investments, and the current spot-exchange-rate value of our currency increases (e decreases).

Consider another variation on our previous example. With the U.S. annualized interest rate at 9 percent, the Swiss annualized interest rate at 5 percent, and the current spot exchange rate at $1.200 per SFr, what happens if the spot exchange rate expected in 90 days increases from about $1.212 to about $1.236 per SFr (perhaps because international investors believe that the political situation in Switzerland will improve rapidly)? Relative to the initial current spot rate, investors now expect the franc to appreciate more in the next 90 days, at about a 12 percent annual rate (rather than the previously expected 4 percent). This shifts the return differential in favor of Swiss-currency bonds. Because investors desire to reposition their portfolios toward Swiss assets, demand for the franc increases in the foreign exchange market. The current spot exchange rate increases (the franc appreciates and the dollar depreciates). In fact, the spot exchange rate moves to about $1.224 per SFr. At this new spot rate, the franc then is expected to appreciate further by only about 4 percent (annual rate). Uncovered interest parity is reestablished, and there is no further incentive for international investors to reposition their portfolios.

As with a change in interest rates, the effect of a change in the expected future spot rate on the current spot exchange rate can happen very quickly (instantaneously or within a few minutes). This can be like a rapid-fire *self-confirming expectation*. In the Swiss franc example, the expectation that the franc would appreciate more than was previously expected resulted in a rapid and large appreciation of the franc. For another example, consider what happens if international financial investors shift from expecting no change in spot exchange rates (e^{ex} equals the initial e) to expecting a depreciation of the foreign currency (e^{ex} decreases so that it is then below the initial current spot rate e). The willingness of international investors to reposition their international portfolios away from foreign-currency bonds results in a depreciation of the foreign currency (e decreases)—exactly what they were expecting.

Given the powerful effects that exchange-rate expectations can have on actual exchange rates, we would like to know what determines these expectations. Many different things can influence the value of the expected future exchange rate.

Some investors, especially for expectations regarding the near-term future (the next minutes, hours, days, or weeks), may expect that the recent trend in the exchange rate will continue. They extrapolate the recent trend into the future. This is a **bandwagon.** For instance, currencies that have been appreciating are expected to continue to do so. The recent actual increase in the exchange-rate value of a country's currency leads some investors to expect further increases in the near future. If they act on this belief, the currency will tend to appreciate further. This bandwagon effect is the basis for fears that speculation can sometimes be *destabilizing* in that the actions of international investors can move the exchange rate away from a long-run equilibrium value consistent with fundamental economic influences. Expectations can be destabilizing if they are formed without regard to these economic fundamentals, which is quite possible if recent exchange-rate trends are simply extrapolated into the future. For example, the depreciation of the euro against the U.S. dollar after the euro was introduced in 1999 appears to have led to a bandwagon that drove continued depreciation of the euro into late 2000. (The euro fell in value from $1.18 in January 1999 to less than $0.83 in October 2000.)

Expectations can also be based on the belief that exchange rates eventually return to values consistent with basic economic conditions (for instance, purchasing power parity, which we will discuss in the next section). Expectations of this sort are considered *stabilizing* in the sense that they lead to stabilizing speculation, which tends to move the exchange rate toward a value consistent with some economic fundamentals such as relative national product price levels.

Changes in expectations can be based on various kinds of new information. The important part of the "news" is any *unexpected information* about government policies, about national and international economic data or performance, and about political leaders and situations (both domestic politics and international political issues and tensions). An example is that foreign exchange markets often react to news of official figures about a country's trade or current account balances, measures that largely reflect the balance or imbalance between a country's exports and imports of goods and services. There is logic to the market's reactions to such news. For instance, an unexpected increase in a country's trade deficit or (especially) its current account deficit indicates that the country requires an increasing amount of foreign financing of the deficit. If the increased foreign financing is not assured to be forthcoming, then the country's currency will tend to fall in the foreign exchange market. The increasing demand for foreign currency as part of the process of paying for the excess of imports over exports tends to appreciate the foreign currency and depreciate the domestic currency. If this logic is built into the changed expectations of international investors, then the exchange-rate change can occur quickly, rather than gradually as the trade imbalance would slowly add to market pressures.

THE LONG RUN: PURCHASING POWER PARITY (PPP)

In the short run, floating exchange rates are often highly variable, and there are times when it is not easy to understand why the rates are changing as they are. In the long run, economic fundamentals become dominant, providing an "anchor" for the long-term trends. Our understanding of exchange rates in the long run is based on the proposition that there is a predictable relationship between product price levels and exchange rates. The relationship relies on the fact that people choose to buy goods and services from one country or another according to the prices they must pay. We can present three versions of this relationship, depending on whether we are examining one product or a set of products, and whether we are looking at a snapshot of the product price–exchange rate relationship or how product prices and exchange rates are changing over time.

The Law of One Price

The law of one price posits that a product that is easily and freely traded in a perfectly competitive global market should have the same price everywhere, once the prices at different places are expressed in the same currency. In Chapters 2–4 we called this the equilibrium international, or world, price, although we did not specifically bring exchange rates into the picture. Now we can. The law of one price proposes that the price (P) of the product measured in domestic currency will be equated to the price (P_f) of the product measured in the foreign currency through the current spot exchange rate (e, Domestic currency/Foreign currency):

$$P = e \cdot P_f$$

The *law of one price works well for heavily traded commodities,* either at a point in time or for changes over time, as long as governments permit free trade in the commodity. Such heavily traded commodities include gold, other metals, crude oil, and various agricultural commodities.

Consider, for example, No. 2 soft red Chicago wheat, and suppose that it costs $4.80 a bushel in Chicago. Its dollar price in London should not be much greater, given the cheapness of transporting wheat from Chicago to London. To simplify the example, let us say that it costs nothing to transport the wheat. It seems reasonable, then, that the pound price of wheat will be £3.00 if the exchange rate is $1.60 per pound. The dollar price of the wheat in London then is $4.80 per bushel ($= 3.00 \cdot 1.60$). If it is not, it would pay someone to trade wheat between Chicago and London to profit from the price gap. For example, if an unexpected increase in British demand for wheat temporarily forces the price of wheat in London up to £3.75 per bushel, and the exchange rate is still $1.60 per pound, the dollar price in London is $6.00. As long as free trade is possible, we expect that the two prices would soon be bid back into equality, presumably somewhere between $4.80 and $6.00 per bushel for both countries. In the case of wheat (a standardized commodity with a well-established world market), we expect that arbitrage will bring the two prices into line within a week.

However, the law of one price does not hold closely for most products that are traded internationally, including nearly all manufactured products. It is not hard to find the culprits that explain the discrepancy. International transport costs are not negligible. Governments do not practice free trade. And many markets are imperfectly competitive. Firms with market power sometimes use price discrimination to increase profits by charging different prices in different national markets. One study concluded that the effect of the national border between the United States and Canada on product price differences is like adding thousands of miles of distance between Canadian and U.S. cities. *For many products the law of one price does not hold closely.*

Absolute Purchasing Power Parity

Absolute purchasing power parity posits that a basket or bundle of tradable products will have the same cost in different countries if the cost is stated in the same currency. Essentially, the average price of these products, often called the product-price level, or just price level, stated in different currencies is the same when converted to a common currency:

$$P = e \cdot P_f$$

Here P and P_f refer to the average product price or price level in the domestic and the foreign countries. The equation can be rearranged to provide an estimate of the spot exchange rate that is consistent with absolute PPP:

$$e = P/P_f$$

Absolute PPP is clearly closely related to the law of one price. The equations are the same, except that the price variables refer either to only one product (law of one price) or to a bundle of products (absolute PPP). If the law of one price holds for all the products, then absolute PPP will also hold (as long as the product bundle is the same in both countries). Even if the law of one price does not hold exactly, absolute PPP can still be a useful guide if the discrepancies tend to average out over the different products in the bundle.

Based on the evidence, however, absolute PPP does not fare much better than the law of one price in the real world. Divergences from absolute PPP can be large at any given time. (The divergences are even larger if nontraded products are included in the bundles. See the box "Price Gaps and International Income Comparisons.") In addition, we can get into technical difficulties of comparing index numbers if the information sources, like national governments, do not use the same bundles of products for the different countries. Nonetheless, there is evidence that large divergences from absolute PPP do tend to shrink over time for traded products.

Relative Purchasing Power Parity

Both the law of one price and absolute purchasing power parity are posited to hold at a point in time. Another version of PPP looks specifically at how things are changing over time. Relative purchasing power parity posits that the difference between changes over time in product-price levels in two countries will be offset by the change in the exchange rate over this time. The exact formula for relative PPP is

$$\left(\frac{e_t}{e_0}\right) = \frac{(P_t/P_0)}{(P_{f,t}/P_{f,0})}$$

where the subscripts indicate the values for the initial year, 0, and some later year, t, for each variable. Each ratio in parentheses shows the increase from the initial year to the later year for each variable. If you compare this equation to the second one for absolute PPP, you will see that relative PPP holds if absolute PPP holds for both the initial year and the later year. In addition, relative PPP may be useful as a guide to why exchange rates change over time, even if absolute PPP does not hold closely at specific times.

Relative PPP is often defined using an approximation:

$$\text{Rate of appreciation of the foreign currency} = \pi - \pi_f$$

Case Study PPP from Time to Time

Something like the purchasing power parity theory has existed throughout the modern history of international economics. The theory keeps resurfacing whenever exchange rates have become more variable as a result of wars or other events. Sometimes the hypothesis is used as a way of describing how a nation's general price level must change to reestablish some desired exchange rate, given the level and trend in foreign prices. At other times it is used to guess at what the equilibrium exchange rate will be, given recent trends in prices within and outside the country. Both of these interpretations crept into the British "bullionist–antibullionist" debate during and after the Napoleonic Wars, when the issue was why Britain had been driven by the wars to dislodge the pound sterling from its fixed exchange rates and gold backing, and what could be done about it.

The PPP hypothesis came into its own in the 1920s, when Gustav Cassel and others directed it at the issue of how much European countries would have to change their official exchange rates or their domestic price levels, given that World War I had driven the exchange rates off

their prewar par values and had brought varying percentages of price inflation to different countries. For instance, PPP was a rough guide to the mistake made by Britain in returning to the prewar gold parity for the pound sterling in 1925 despite greater price inflation in Britain than in Britain's trading partners.

With the restoration of fixed exchange rates following World War II, the PPP hypothesis again faded from prominence, ostensibly because its defects had been demonstrated, but mainly because the issue it raised seemed less compelling as long as exchange rates were expected to stay fixed.

After the resumption of widespread floating of exchange rates in the early 1970s, the hypothesis has been revived once again. It is now used as a standard for examining whether countries' currencies are undervalued or overvalued at their market exchange rates.

DISCUSSION QUESTION
Why was the PPP hypothesis less interesting when the major countries had fixed exchange rates and similar product-price inflation rates?

where π and π_f are the (product-price) inflation rates for the domestic and the foreign countries.[3] Relative PPP posits that the exchange rate changes over time at a rate equal to the difference in the two countries' inflation rates during that time period.

[3]To see the approximation, restate each variable at time t as being equal to its initial value at time 0 plus its change from time 0 to time t:

$$\left(\frac{e_0 + \Delta e}{e_0}\right) = \frac{[(P_0 + \Delta P)/P_0]}{[(P_{f,0} + \Delta P_f)/P_{f,0}]}$$

which equals

$$[1 + (\Delta e/e_0)] = \frac{[1 + (\Delta P/P_0)]}{[1 + (\Delta P_f/P_{f,0})]}$$

Multiplying the denominator to the left-hand side, multiplying out the expressions, and simplifying, we obtain,

$$(\Delta e/e_0) = (\Delta P/P_0) - (\Delta P_f/P_{f,0}) - [(\Delta e/e_0) \bullet (\Delta P_f/P_{f,0})]$$

If the rate of appreciation of the foreign currency $(\Delta e/e_0)$ and the foreign inflation rate $(\Delta P_f/P_{f,0})$ are small (in decimal form), then the last term (the product of two small numbers) is very small, and it is ignored in the approximation.

Case Study   Price Gaps and International Income Comparisons

There is tremendous social importance to international comparisons of income or production levels. To judge which countries are most in need of United Nations aid, World Bank loans, and other help, officials compare their incomes per capita. To judge whether South Korea has overtaken Japan in supply prowess, we compare Korean and Japanese gross domestic product per capita. All such comparisons are dangerous as well as unavoidable. The comparisons are likely to contain a host of errors.

One of the worst pitfalls comes in converting from one national currency to another. It turns out that the market exchange rate is a poor way to convert because the purchasing power parity hypothesis is not reliable when applied to all the goods and services that make up national expenditure or domestic production. Many of the products in such a broad bundle are not traded internationally. There is no direct reason (like arbitrage) to think that the prices of non-traded products should equalize internationally when stated in a common currency using market exchange rates, and they usually do not.

If the market exchange rate is unreliable, what should we use for comparing values of income per capita between countries? The principle is clear: We want to take the national income per capita measured using whatever prices exist in each country and convert these into values of national incomes per capita using a set of common international prices like those that would exist if PPP applied. That way, we are comparing how many units of a consistently priced bundle of goods and services the average resident of each nation could buy. But it is difficult to get data on the prices of a wide-ranging bundle of goods and services for every country.

That is where the United Nations International Comparisons Project (ICP) came in. Teams of researchers have done the hard work of measuring the prices of items in separate countries. What they have found, in effect, are the true levels of P and P_f for deflating the current-price national income figures. They confirm what was widely feared: On average for all goods and services, the

market exchange rate e is often far from the ratio P/P_f that absolute PPP says it would equal.

The accompanying table shows the typical pattern in departures from absolute PPP and the importance of replacing exchange-rate conversions of income per capita with the better comparisons based on common price levels.

If purchasing power parity really held, then every number in the right-hand column would be 100. The departures from that PPP norm are great enough to reshuffle some of the international rankings, making the better (PPP-based) measurements of the center column differ from the exchange-rate-based measures on the left. Two patterns are apparent in the figures. One is that the price-difference ratio in the right-hand column is above unity for most industrialized countries. Their PPP-measured real average income is not as high relative to that of the United States as the exchange-rate figures imply.

Another pattern is that the usual comparisons—the ones using exchange rates—overstate the real income gaps between rich and poor nations because the price-difference ratio is below unity for the lower-income countries in the bottom half of the list. For some of the poorest countries, the price disparity can be as large as 1:4, a substantial deviation from absolute PPP.

Why do lower-income countries have prices so much lower than U.S. prices? Most of the departures come from the wide international gaps in the prices of nontraded products like housing, haircuts, and other local services. The prices of nontraded products differ radically between lower-income and higher-income countries. The gaps in the prices of these products seem to be widened by two forces. One is the tendency for the price of land in towns and cities to be highly sensitive to the income of the country's residents. So a country with twice as high an income would have more than twice as high a cost for business and residential space, making space-intensive nontraded products cost much more. A second explanation is that, as a country develops, its productivity in making traded goods rises much faster than its productivity in making nontraded goods and services. The higher productivity in making traded goods tends to

Country	National Income per Capita, 2012, Relative to the United States = 100		Domestic Price Level (This Country/U.S.) as a Percentage of the Level Predicted by PPP
	Using the Exchange Rate	Using Common Prices	
Singapore	95	137	69
Norway	189	128	147
Switzerland	155	105	148
United States	100	100	100
Sweden	107	84	128
Germany	86	83	104
Australia	113	81	140
Canada	99	80	123
France	80	71	112
Japan	91	70	131
Britain	74	68	109
Italy	66	66	101
Israel	61	58	106
South Korea	43	57	76
Czech Republic	35	48	72
Russia	24	43	56
Poland	24	41	58
Chile	27	39	70
Turkey	21	35	59
Mexico	18	31	60
Brazil	22	27	82
Thailand	10	25	39
South Africa	14	23	63
China	11	21	53
Egypt	6	20	28
Indonesia	7	17	39
Nigeria	5	10	47
India	3	10	31
Pakistan	2	9	27
Ghana	3	7	44
Tanzania	1	3	34

Source: World Bank, *World Development Indicators.*

increase wage rates in more developed countries. Firms making nontraded goods and services must also pay these higher wage rates. With less productivity advantage, this results in costs and prices of nontraded products that are higher in more-developed countries.

DISCUSSION QUESTION

The table reports that Singapore's national income per capita was a little less than that of the United States, when compared using the market exchange rate for the Singapore dollar. Why is Singapore at the top of the list?

Relative PPP provides some strong predictions about exchange-rate trends, especially in the long term:

- Countries with relatively low inflation rates have currencies whose values tend to appreciate in the foreign exchange market.
- Countries with relatively high inflation rates have currencies whose values tend to depreciate in the foreign exchange market.

In fact, a strict application of relative PPP implies that each percentage point more of a country's inflation per year tends to be related to a 1 percent faster rate of depreciation of the country's currency (or slower rate of currency appreciation) per year, given the inflation rate in the other country. Relative PPP thus has an important message to offer countries, such as Switzerland, that seek to keep domestic prices stable when the rest of the world is inflating. If prices elsewhere are rising 10 percent a year, in the long run a country can keep its domestic prices stable only by accepting a rise of about 10 percent a year in the exchange value of its currency in terms of inflating-country currencies.

Relative PPP: Evidence

We just suggested that PPP holds reasonably well in the long run but poorly in the short run. We can examine specific evidence about PPP for recent decades. Figure 19.3 provides evidence on the long run during the current period of floating exchange rates. For each country included in samples of industrialized and developing countries, the average annual rate of change of its currency's exchange rate against the U.S. dollar is compared to the difference between the average U.S. inflation rate and the country's inflation rate.[4] Relative PPP predicts that, when the inflation differential is positive (the United States has a higher inflation rate, or the country has a lower one), the country's currency should appreciate. When the inflation differential is negative, the country's currency should depreciate. Looking across the countries in each sample, we can see that this relationship is clear. In fact, the relationships are very close to the one-to-one relationship implied by a strict version of relative PPP.[5]

We can also examine recent performance of PPP for both short and long periods using data on the exchange rates of individual countries over time. Figure 19.4 shows the actual exchange rates against the U.S. dollar and the exchange rates that would be consistent with PPP (relative to the base year 1975), month-by-month, for the German mark (DM) and Japanese yen. The exchange rate consistent with PPP is the rate that equals the ratio of the national price levels P/P_f (relative to the value of this ratio in

[4]The period is 1975–2012. The beginning year 1975 is somewhat arbitrary; it was chosen to be close to the beginning of the current floating-rate period and to allow several years of adjustment following the end of the previous fixed-rate period. Inflation rates are measured using the wholesale price index or a similar price index that includes only (or mostly) traded products.

[5]A standard statistical test of the relationship is to fit the best straight line to the data points using a simple regression. For the industrialized countries, the slope of the line (0.902) is not significantly different from 1 (and the intercept is not significantly different from zero). For the developing countries, the slope coefficient (0.965) also is not significantly different from 1 (and the intercept also is not significantly different from zero). The results show strong support for the one-to-one relationship. Furthermore, both straight lines fit the data very well. For industrialized countries about 92 percent of the variation in the rates of exchange-rate change across the countries is "explained" by the inflation rate differences and for developing countries about 99 percent is "explained."

FIGURE 19.3   Relative Purchasing Power Parity: Inflation Rate Differences and Exchange-Rate Changes, 1975–2012

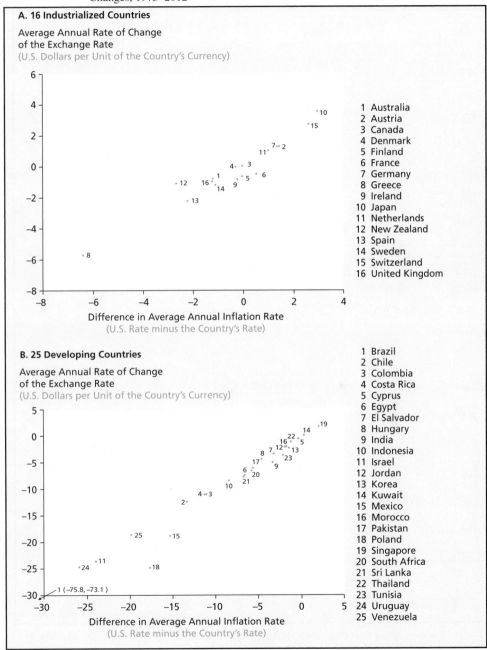

On average from 1975 to 2012, strong support is found for PPP. If the U.S. inflation rate is higher than the other country's inflation rate, the country's currency tends to appreciate; if the U.S. inflation rate is lower, the currency tends to depreciate.

Inflation rates are measured using wholesale (or similar producer-oriented) price indexes. Annual rates of change are calculated using the differences in natural logarithms.

FIGURE 19.4   Actual Exchange Rates and Exchange Rates Consistent with Relative PPP, Monthly, 1975–2014

*Beginning January 1999, the German mark is fixed to the euro, so its rate is tracking the U.S.$/euro exchange-rate movement from that date.

The exchange rate implied by PPP equals the ratio of national price levels P/P_f. The actual exchange rate can differ substantially from this PPP rate, and the divergences can persist for several years. Nonetheless, there is a tendency for the actual exchange rate to follow the PPP rate in the long run.

National price levels are measured by wholesale (or producer) price indexes.

Source: International Monetary Fund, *International Financial Statistics.*

the base year). If relative PPP always held, the actual exchange rate would equal the exchange rate implied by PPP. As we can see easily in the figure, the deviations of the actual exchange rate from its PPP value can be large and can persist for a number of years. The DM was substantially undervalued relative to the implied PPP value from 1981 through 1986, and then was somewhat overvalued for much of the first half of the 1990s. After the euro replaced the DM as Germany's currency beginning in 1999, the euro fell below its PPP value and then returned to and fluctuated around its PPP value. The yen tracked its PPP value reasonably well from 1976 through 1986 but then became overvalued. During 2005–2008 the yen returned to its PPP value, then again rose above its PPP value before again returning to its PPP value in 2013. In the long run there is a tendency for the actual exchange rates to move in a manner consistent with PPP.

If we examined evidence for other countries, we would generally reach similar conclusions: noticeable deviations from PPP in the short run but a tendency for PPP to hold in the long run. Based on a survey of rigorous studies, Froot and Rogoff (1995) conclude that it takes about four years on average for a deviation from PPP to be reduced by half for the exchange rates of major industrialized countries.

THE LONG RUN: THE MONETARY APPROACH

Purchasing power parity indicates that, at least in the long run, exchange rates are closely related to the levels of prices for products in different countries. But this also suggests the next question: What determines the average national price level or the rate at which it changes, the inflation rate? Economists believe that the money supply (or its growth rate) determines the price level (or the inflation rate) in the long run. This suggests that money supplies in different countries, through their links to national price levels and inflation rates, are closely linked to exchange rates in the long run. Indeed, this is not surprising. An exchange rate is the price of one money in terms of another. Trying to analyze exchange rates or international payments without looking at national money supplies and demands is like presenting *Hamlet* without the prince of Denmark.

Relative money supplies affect exchange rates. On the international front as on the domestic front, a currency is less valuable the more of it there is to circulate. Extreme cases of hyperinflation dramatize this fundamental point. The trillionfold increase in the German money supply in 1922–1923 was the key proximate cause of the trillion-fold increase in the price of foreign exchange and of everything else in Germany at that time. Hyperinflation of the money supplies is also the key to understanding why the currencies of Israel and several Latin American countries lost almost all their value during the 1970s and 1980s.

Money, Price Levels, and Inflation

The relationship between money and the national price level (or inflation rate) follows from the relationship between money supply and money demand. Why do we "demand," or hold, money? The key reason is that money is used as a medium of exchange. People and businesses want to hold a certain amount of money to be able to carry out transactions that require the exchange of money for other items. This transaction demand varies with the annual turnover of transactions requiring money, a turnover that is fairly well proxied by the money value of gross domestic product.

The link between domestic product and the demand for a nation's money is central to the quantity theory of demand for money. The **quantity theory equation** says that in a country the money supply is equated with the demand for money, which is directly proportional to the money value of gross domestic product. In separate equations for the home country and the rest of the world, the quantity theory equation becomes a pair:

$$M^s = k \bullet P \bullet Y$$

and

$$M_f^s = k_f \bullet P_f \bullet Y_f$$

where M^s and M_f^s are the home and foreign money supplies (measured in dollars and foreign currency, respectively), P and P_f are the home and foreign price levels, and Y and Y_f are the real (constant-price) domestic products. For each country, the nominal or money value of GDP equals the price level times the real GDP ($P \bullet Y$ and $P_f \bullet Y_f$). The k and k_f indicate the proportional relationships between money holdings and the nominal value of GDP. They represent people's behavior. If the value of GDP and thus the value of transactions increase, k indicates the amount of extra money that people want to hold to facilitate this higher level of economic activity. Sometimes quantity theorists assume that the ks are constant numbers, sometimes not. (The facts say that any k varies.) For the present long-run analysis, we follow the common presumption that each money supply (M^s and M_f^s) is controlled by each government's monetary policy alone and that each country's real production (Y and Y_f) is governed by such supply-side forces as factor supplies, technology, and productivity.

By taking the ratio of these two equations and rearranging the terms, we can use the quantity theory equations to determine the ratio of prices between countries:

$$(P/P_f) = (M^s/M_f^s) \bullet (k_f/k) \bullet (Y_f/Y)$$

Money and PPP Combined

Combining the absolute purchasing power parity equation with the quantity theory equations for the home country and the rest of the world yields a prediction of exchange rates based on money supplies and national products:

$$e = P/P_f = (M^s/M_f^s) \bullet (k_f/k) \bullet (Y_f/Y)$$

The exchange rate (e) between one foreign currency (say, the British pound) and other currencies (here represented by the dollar, the home currency in our example) can now be related to just the M^ss, the ks, and the Ys. The price ratio (P/P_f) can be set aside as an intermediate variable determined, in the long run, by the M^ss, ks, and Ys.

The equation predicts that a foreign nation will have an appreciating currency (e up) if it has some combination of slower money supply growth (M^s/M_f^s up), faster growth in real output (Y_f/Y up), or a rise in the ratio k_f/k. Conversely, a nation with fast money growth and a stagnant real economy is likely to have a depreciating currency.

Going one step further, we can use the same equation to quantify the percent effects of changes in money supplies or domestic products on the exchange rate. The equation implies that some key elasticities are equal to 1. That is, if the ratio (k_f/k) stays the same, then e rises by 1 percent for

- each 1 percent rise in the domestic money supply (M^s),
- each 1 percent drop in the foreign money supply (M_f^s),
- each 1 percent drop in domestic real GDP (Y), or
- each 1 percent rise in foreign GDP (Y_f).

The exchange rate elasticities imply something else that seems reasonable too: An exchange rate will be unaffected by balanced growth. If money supplies grow at the same rate in all countries, leaving M^s/M_f^s unchanged, and if domestic products grow at the same rate, leaving Y_f/Y unchanged, there should be no change in the exchange rate.

Changes in the ks would have comparable effects on the exchange rate in the long run, but we choose not to examine these here. Instead, let's look a little more closely at the effects of money supply and real income.

The Effect of Money Supplies on an Exchange Rate

Let's look at an example in which Britain is the foreign country and the United States is the domestic country. If, for instance, the supply of pounds were cut by 10 percent, each pound would become more scarce and more valuable. The cut would be achieved by a tighter British monetary policy. This contractionary policy would restrict the reserves of the British banking system, forcing British banks to tighten credit and the outstanding stock of sterling bank deposits, which represent most of the British money supply. The tighter credit would make it harder to borrow and spend, cutting back on aggregate demand, output, jobs, and product prices in Britain. With the passage of time, the fall in output and jobs should reverse, and the reduction in prices should reach 10 percent. Over time, relative PPP predicts that the pound should rise in value. The 10 percent cut in Britain's money supply should eventually lead to a 10 percent higher exchange-rate value of the pound.

The same shift should result from a 10 percent rise in the dollar money supply. If the U.S. central bank lets the dollar money supply rise 10 percent, the extra dollar money available should end up inflating dollar prices by 10 percent. For a time, the higher dollar prices might cause international demands for goods and services to shift in favor of buying the sterling-priced goods, which are temporarily cheaper. Eventually, relative purchasing power parity should be restored by a 10 percent rise in the exchange rate (e). One other result predicted above follows as a corollary: If the preceding equations are correct, a balanced 10 percent rise in all money supplies, both pounds and dollars, should have no effect on the exchange rate.

The Effect of Real Incomes on an Exchange Rate

The same kind of reasoning can be used to explore how long-run changes in real income and production should affect an exchange rate. Let us first follow this reasoning on its own terms and then add a word of caution.

Suppose that Britain's real income shifts up to a growth path 10 percent above the path Britain would otherwise have followed. This might happen, for instance, as a result of a spurt in British productivity. The extra transactions associated with the higher British production and income would call forth a new demand for holding pounds. If the extra productivity results in a 10 percent rise in real British national income, the quantity theory predicts a 10 percent higher transactions demand for the pound. But this extra demand cannot be met, assuming that Britain's money stock has not increased. Instead, the price level must decline in Britain by 10 percent so that the overall money value of British national income is unchanged. Essentially, in this case the increase in productivity is passed forward to buyers in the form of lower product prices. Then, according to relative PPP, the decline in British prices leads to a rise in the value of the pound. The rise again equals 10 percent. Again, we have two corollaries that can be seen from the equations: A 10 percent decline in U.S. real income should also raise *e* by 10 percent, and a balanced 10 percent rise in incomes in both Britain and the United States should leave the exchange rate the same.

A caution must be added to this tidy result, however. You can be misled by memorizing a single "effect of income" on the exchange rate. Income is not an independent force that can simply move by itself. What causes it to change has a great effect on an exchange rate. In the British productivity example, real income was being raised for a *supply-side* reason—Britain's ability to produce more with its limited resources. It is easy to believe that this would strengthen the pound by using the quantity theory equation (or by thinking about the extra British exports, made possible by its rising productivity, as something other countries would need pounds to pay for). But suppose that Britain's real income is raised by the Keynesian effects of extra government spending or some other aggregate-*demand* shift in Britain. This real-income increase might or might not strengthen the pound. If its main effect were to add inflation in Britain (or to make Britons buy more imports), then there would be reason to believe that the extra aggregate demand would actually lower the value of the pound.

Since the effects of aggregate demand shifts tend to dominate in the short run, while supply shifts dominate in the long run, the quantity theory yields the long-run result, the case in which higher production or income means a higher value of the country's currency.

To conclude this section, let's briefly return to the major-currency experience shown in Figure 19.1. Can we use the monetary approach to understand the long-term trends in some of the exchange rates shown in this figure? Over the long sweep of the flexible-exchange-rate era since the early 1970s, we know part of the reason why the Japanese yen rose: during the years to the early 1990s, Japan's stronger real economic growth (growth in Y), combined with the fact that its money supply did not grow much faster than the average, kept inflation down in Japan and raised the international value of the yen. The Swiss franc rose because Switzerland kept tight control over its money supply. The lira sank because Italy's money supply rose faster than average.

EXCHANGE-RATE OVERSHOOTING

Our view of exchange rates as being determined in the long run by purchasing power parity, with its emphasis on average rates of inflation over many years, seems quite removed from the view that exchange rates in the short run are buffeted by rapid shifts in investors' portfolio decisions, as we discussed earlier in the chapter. Yet the two must be related. The short run eventually flows into the long run. We have already

FIGURE 19.5
Overview of
Key Elements,
Exchange-Rate
Overshooting

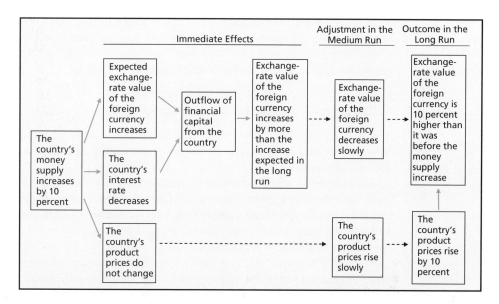

mentioned one basis for this flow. International investors form their expectations of future exchange rates partly on the belief that exchange rates will move toward their PPP values because eventually the economic fundamentals of money supply, GDP, and inflation rates become the key determinants of exchange rates.

It is useful to consider this relationship in more depth, to explore the phenomenon of **overshooting.** We will see that international investors can react *rationally* to news by driving the exchange rate *past* what they know to be its ultimate long-run equilibrium value. The actual exchange rate then moves slowly back to that long-run rate later on. That is, in the short run the actual exchange rate overshoots its long-run value and then reverts back toward it.

Figure 19.5 provides an overview of our story about how an exchange rate can overshoot its eventual long-run equilibrium value, even if all investors correctly judge the future equilibrium rate. Suppose that the domestic money supply unexpectedly jumps 10 percent at time t_0 and then resumes the rate of growth investors had already been expecting. Investors understand that this permanent increase of 10 percent more money stock should eventually raise the price of foreign exchange by 10 percent if they believe that purchasing power parity and the monetary approach hold eventually. In the long run, both the domestic price level (P) and the price of foreign exchange (the exchange rate e) should be 10 percent higher. So, the expected future spot exchange rate increases, with investors expecting that eventually the future spot exchange rate will be 10 percent higher.

Two realistic side effects of the increase in the domestic money supply intervene and make the exchange rate take a strange path to its ultimate 10 percent increase:

• Product prices are somewhat sticky in the short run, so considerable time must pass for domestic inflation to raise domestic prices (P) by 10 percent (relative to foreign prices, P_f).

• Because prices are sticky at first, the increase in the money supply drives down the domestic interest rate, both real and nominal.

With the domestic interest rate (i) lower, the return differential shifts to favor foreign-currency assets (assuming that the foreign interest rate (i_f) remains unchanged). Therefore, at the *initial* spot exchange rate, the overall return differential actually favors foreign-currency assets for two reasons:

- The foreign currency is expected to appreciate.
- The domestic interest rate has decreased.

The desire by investors to reposition their portfolios toward foreign-currency assets increases the demand for foreign currency and results in a quick appreciation of the foreign currency.

By how much will the foreign currency appreciate immediately? On the basis of only the expected appreciation of the foreign currency by 10 percent, the foreign currency would appreciate immediately by 10 percent. The decrease in the domestic interest rate creates additional supply–demand pressure, so the current spot exchange rate must rise immediately by *more than* 10 percent.

Figure 19.6 shows the time path of the exchange rate, including this immediate large change and then the adjustment in the medium run toward its new long-run equilibrium. After the initial jump in the exchange-rate value, the suddenly much higher spot rate will then slowly decline back toward its expected future value. That is, the new current spot rate e immediately rises above the new e^{ex} so that the foreign currency is then expected to depreciate slowly back toward the new expected rate. This is necessary to reestablish uncovered interest parity once the current spot rate adjusts. The domestic return is lower because of the lower domestic interest rate i. After the current spot rate overshoots, the overall return on foreign investments then also becomes lower. Even though the foreign interest rate (i_f) is unchanged, the overall expected foreign return is lower because the foreign currency is expected to depreciate from its now high value. Investors must have the prospect of seeing the foreign currency depreciate later in order to stem their outflow encouraged by relatively high foreign interest rates.

So, once the news of the extra 10 percent money supply is out, investors will quickly bid up the spot price of foreign exchange by more than 10 percent (Dornbusch, 1976). One test by Jeffrey Frankel (1979) suggested that perhaps the announcement of a surprise 10 percent increase in the domestic money supply would trigger a jump of the spot rate by 12.3 percent, before it begins retreating back to just a 10 percent increase.

Viewed another way, the overshooting is even larger. The exchange rate overshoots by even more in the short run if we compare the actual exchange rate to the path implied by PPP for each time period. Because the domestic price level rises only slowly toward its ultimate 10 percent increase, PPP alone implies that the exchange rate should rise only gradually toward its 10 percent increase. Thus, in the year or so after the money supply increase, little of the large increase in the actual spot exchange rate appears to be consistent with the limited amount of additional domestic inflation that occurs during that first year.

This case shows how exchange rates can be highly variable in the short run (driven by the reactions of international financial investors to policy surprises and other news), while at the same time exchange rates eventually change in the long run in ways consistent with PPP. The case also shows that it can be difficult to identify clearly cases of

FIGURE 19.6

Exchange-Rate Path, Exchange-Rate Overshooting

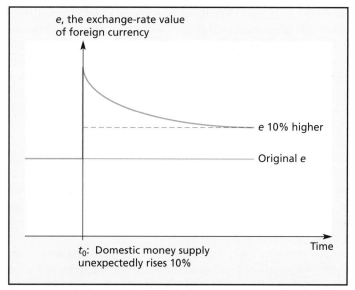

An unexpected 10 percent increase in the domestic money supply causes the spot-exchange-rate value of the country's currency to decline quickly by more than 10 percent, "overshooting" its eventual long-run value. Then the country's currency appreciates slowly until its exchange-rate value is 10 percent lower than what it was before the unexpected money-supply increase.

"destabilizing speculation." Exchange-rate movements that appear to be extreme and inconsistent with the economic fundamentals in the short run can be part of a process that is understandable, reasonable, and stabilizing in the long run.

HOW WELL CAN WE PREDICT EXCHANGE RATES?

We would like to be able to forecast exchange rates. One purpose of having theories is to predict tendencies in the real world. International experience since the switch to floating exchange rates in the early 1970s provides a rich data set against which to test the value of our theories.

How accurate would we want our theories to be in predicting changes in exchange rates? Clearly we should not expect perfect forecasts. But presumably we would expect a useful economic model at least to be able to outpredict a naive model that says the future spot exchange rate is predicted simply to be the same as the current spot exchange rate. This is a minimal standard. The naive model is equivalent to saying that the spot exchange rate follows a *random walk,* so we have no ability to predict whether it will go up or down. The predictions of any useful economic structural model presumably ought to be able to do better than this naive model.

Somewhat to our consternation, there is now general agreement that economic structural models are generally of no use in predicting exchange rates in the short run (for future periods up to about one year). Frankel and Rose (1995) and Rossi (2013) survey many studies that use various models based on many different economic fundamentals, including money supplies and real incomes, interest rates, expected inflation rates, and trade and current account balances. They conclude that structural economic models cannot reliably outpredict the naive alternative of a random walk for short forecast horizons.

The economic fundamentals stressed by purchasing power parity and the monetary approach are of some use in forecasting exchange rates farther into the future. There is value in predicting that some portion of any current deviation of an exchange rate from its estimated PPP value will be eliminated during the next years. Still, economists should be humble. Their forecast errors at these longer horizons are still large in an absolute sense, even though they are smaller than the (even larger) errors from simply predicting that the future exchange rate will be the same as the current exchange rate.

Why is it so difficult to predict exchange rates using economic models? There appear to be two parts to the answer.

First, and probably more important, the exchange rate reacts strongly and immediately to new information. Exactly because news is unexpected, it cannot be incorporated into any predictions. The reaction to such news often involves large movements in the exchange rate. Actual exchange-rate movements appear to overshoot movements in smoothly adjusting long-run equilibrium rates like those from PPP or the monetary approach. Studies have documented the immediate effects of a variety of different types of news on exchange rates, although some of these types seem to have power during some time periods but not others. For instance, the U.S. dollar tends to appreciate when there are unexpected contractions in the U.S. money supply, unexpected increases in U.S. interest rates (relative to foreign interest rates), unexpected growth in U.S. real GDP, unexpected increases in U.S. payroll employment, unexpected improvements in the U.S. trade or current account balance, and unexpected increases in the U.S. government budget deficit. In addition, casual observation indicates that the exchange rate reacts to new information concerning both actual events and changes in probabilities about what will happen, not only for economic variables such as those just mentioned but also for political variables such as elections, appointments, international tensions, and wars.

The second reason is that exchange-rate expectations can be formed without much reference to economic fundamentals. Surveys indicate that many foreign exchange market participants just extrapolate the latest trends up to one month ahead, the bandwagon effect that we discussed in an earlier section of this chapter. Because the actions taken by investors can make their expectations self-confirming, recent trends in exchange rates can be reinforced and persist for a while. If the resulting movement in the exchange rate appears to be simply inconsistent with any form of economic fundamentals, it is called a **bubble** (or *speculative bubble*). While it is difficult to identify such bubbles with complete certainty, the final stage of the appreciation of the dollar against many other currencies in 1984 and early 1985 appears to have been such a bubble. The strong possibility that bubbles occur in the foreign exchange market from time to time suggests that there is some economic inefficiency in foreign exchange markets. You may recall that we reached a similar conclusion at the end of Chapter 18, when we discussed why estimated deviations from uncovered interest parity appear to be too large to be explained completely by risk premiums.

FOUR WAYS TO MEASURE THE EXCHANGE RATE

In this chapter we have been examining the determinants of spot exchange rates. These "regular" exchange rates are the ones quoted in the foreign exchange markets and are technically termed **nominal bilateral exchange rates.** For a single focus currency like the U.S. dollar, there are actually more than a hundred different spot exchange rates with (more than a hundred) other currencies. For many purposes we are interested in only one or a few of these spot exchange rates with specific currencies, so we can ignore the other spot rates.

For other purposes, including those related to macroeconomic analysis, we are interested in knowing how the spot exchange-rate value of a country's currency is doing overall or on average. Furthermore, we probably do not want a simple average because some foreign countries are more important than others. Rather, we want a weighted average of the bilateral spot exchange rates. The weights show the importance of the other countries. For instance, an analysis of the effect of exchange rates on the country's exports and imports suggests using weights based on the country's amounts of international trade with the other countries. The weighted-average spot-exchange-rate value of a country's currency is called the **nominal effective exchange rate.** We have already used this idea in the introduction to this chapter, when we discussed the average value of the U.S. dollar against the currencies of other industrialized countries. In principle, the units used to measure the nominal effective exchange rate are "average foreign currency units per unit of this country's currency." Because we don't really have a measure of "average foreign currency units," the nominal effective exchange rate is usually measured as an index with some base time period equal to 100.

Another issue in exchange-rate analysis is the extent to which the actual exchange rate deviates from PPP. We showed this in Figure 19.4 by comparing the actual nominal bilateral exchange rates (for the DM and yen) to the values that the nominal exchange rates would be if they followed relative PPP (as P/P_f changed over time). The deviation from PPP can also be measured using the *real exchange rate (RER)*. By convention, we usually measure the real-exchange-rate value of the *domestic* currency:

$$\text{RER}_t = \frac{(P_t/P_0) \cdot (e'_t/e'_0)}{(P_{f,t}/P_{f,0})} \cdot 100$$

In this formula the use of e' to indicate the nominal exchange rate reminds us that we are now measuring the spot exchange rate as *foreign currency units per unit of domestic currency.* (More generally, the formula shows the real-exchange-rate value of the currency that is being priced in the nominal exchange rate (e'), and the product prices (P_t/P_0) in the numerator must be those of the country whose currency is being priced.) We can calculate a **real bilateral exchange rate** (relative to another specific country) and a **real effective exchange rate** (as a weighted average relative to a number of other countries).

The real exchange rate has no units, so we measure its value at a time t as an index number relative to a value of 100 in the base time period 0. If relative PPP holds continuously, then the value of the real exchange rate will always be 100. If relative PPP holds in the long run, then RER will tend to return to (or fluctuate around) the 100 value (assuming that the base year is chosen judiciously). If the actual nominal exchange-rate value of the currency being priced is above its implied PPP value, then the RER is above 100. In this case we say the currency is *overvalued relative to the PPP standard*. If the actual nominal exchange-rate value is below its implied PPP value, then the RER is below 100, and we say the currency is *undervalued relative to PPP*. In addition, increases in the RER values over time are called *real appreciations;* decreases are called *real depreciations*.

Figure 19.7 shows the nominal effective exchange-rate value of the U.S. dollar and its real effective exchange-rate value, during 1975–2014, for a broad sample including 37 other countries (18 industrialized and 19 developing countries). We can see that up to 2002 the dollar tended to appreciate on average on a nominal basis (especially because the dollar tended to appreciate nominally against the currencies of many developing countries like Mexico).

The real effective exchange-rate value of the U.S. dollar also fluctuates over time, but it stays closer to the 100 value. The tendency to return to the 100 value indicates that relative PPP tends to hold in the long run. Still, the divergences can be rather large at times, although the scale used in the graph does not show this so clearly.

FIGURE 19.7   Nominal and Real Effective Exchange-Rate Values of the U.S. Dollar, 1975–2014

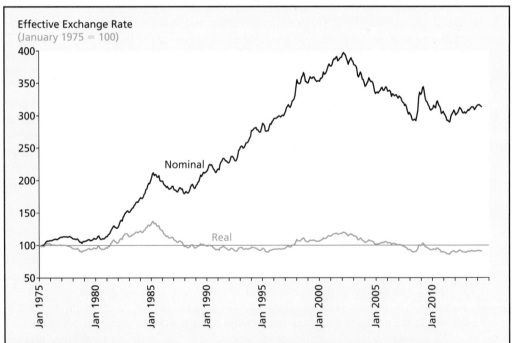

The nominal effective exchange rate shows the average spot exchange-rate of the U.S. dollar. The dollar tended to appreciate on average during 1975 to 2002. The real effective exchange-rate value is the average of real bilateral exchange rates. The real effective exchange rate of the U.S. dollar has fluctuated around a "neutral" value of about 100, consistent with relative purchasing power parity in the long run.

Source: Federal Reserve Board of Governors.

In particular, the dollar went through a large real appreciation (of nearly 50 percent) during 1980–1985. It then experienced a large real depreciation during the next three years that left the real exchange value of the dollar back close to its 100 value. During 1995–2002 the dollar again experienced a pronounced real appreciation, this time about 34 percent. It then fell back to about its 1995 level by early 2008.

Measuring the exchange-rate value of a country's currency is not as simple as it sounds. We have four ways to measure and to track the exchange-rate value: nominal bilateral, nominal effective, real bilateral, and real effective. Each has its uses. For instance, in a later chapter we will link the real effective exchange rate to the international price competitiveness of a country's products.

Summary

This chapter has surveyed what we know (and don't know) about the determinants of exchange rates. The asset market approach explains exchange rates as being part of the equilibrium for the markets for financial assets denominated in different currencies. We gain insights into short-run movements in exchange rates by using a variant of the asset market approach that focuses on portfolio repositioning by international investors, especially decisions regarding investments in bonds denominated in different currencies. If uncovered interest parity tends to hold (at least approximately), then any changes in domestic or foreign interest rates (i and i_f) or the expected future spot exchange rate (e^{ex}) create an uncovered interest differential and create pressures for a return toward uncovered interest parity. Focusing on the pressures on the current spot exchange rate e, the price of foreign currency, it tends to be raised by

- An increase in the interest rate differential ($i_f - i$).
- An increase in the expected future spot exchange rate (e^{ex}).

Changes in the expected future spot exchange rate tend to be self-confirming expectations in that the current spot rate tends to change quickly in the direction expected. Furthermore, there appear to be several types of influences on the expected future spot exchange rate, including recent trends in the actual spot rate, beliefs that the exchange rate eventually moves toward its PPP value, and unexpected new information ("news") about economic performance or about political situations. The rapid, large reaction of the current exchange rate to such news as a change in monetary policy is called overshooting. The current exchange rate changes by much more than would be consistent with long-run equilibrium.

Our understanding of the long-run trends in exchange rates begins with purchasing power parity (PPP). Absolute PPP posits that international competition tends to equalize the home and foreign prices of traded goods and services so that $P = e \cdot P_f$ overall, where the Ps are price levels in the countries and e is the exchange-rate price of foreign currency. Relative PPP focuses on the product-price inflation rates in two countries and the change in the exchange rate that offsets the inflation-rate difference. Relative PPP works tolerably well for longer periods of time, say, a decade or more. Over the long run, a country with a relatively high inflation rate tends to have a depreciating currency, and a country with a relatively low inflation rate tends to have an appreciating currency.

The **monetary approach** seeks to explain exchange rates by focusing on demands and supplies for national moneys because the foreign exchange market is where one money is traded for another. The transactions demand for a national money can be expressed as $k \bullet P \bullet Y$, a behavioral coefficient (k) times the price level (P) times the level of real domestic product (Y). The equilibrium $M^s = k \bullet P \bullet Y$ matches this demand against the national money supply (M^s), which is controlled by the central bank's monetary policy. A similar equilibrium holds in any foreign country: $M^s_f = k_f \bullet P_f \bullet Y_f$.

Combining the basic monetary equilibriums with PPP yields an equation for predicting the exchange-rate value of the currency of a foreign country; $e = (M^s/M^s_f) \bullet (Y_f/Y) \bullet (k_f/k)$. Ignoring any changes in the ks, we can use this equation to predict that the price of foreign currency (e) is raised by

- An increase in the relative size of the money supply (M^s/M^s_f).
- An increase in the relative size of foreign production (Y_f/Y).

Furthermore, the elasticities of the impact of (M^s/M^s_f) and (Y_f/Y) on e should approximately equal 1.

We would like to be able to use economic models to predict exchange rates in the future, but our ability to do so is limited. Economic models provide almost no ability to predict exchange rates for short periods into the future, say, about a year or less. This inability is based largely on the importance of unpredictable news as an influence on short-term exchange rate movements, but it may also reflect the role of expectations that extrapolate recent trends in the exchange rate, leading to **bandwagon** effects and (speculative) **bubbles.** We have some success in predicting exchange-rate movements in the long run. Over long periods, exchange rates tend to move toward values consistent with such economic fundamentals as relative money supplies and real incomes (the monetary approach) or, similarly, relative price levels (PPP).

We also presented four ways of measuring the exchange-rate value of a currency. The **nominal bilateral exchange rate** is the regular market rate between two currencies. The **nominal effective exchange rate** is a weighted average of the market rates across a number of foreign currencies. The **real bilateral exchange rate** incorporates both the market exchange rate and the product price levels for two countries. The **real effective exchange rate** is a weighted average of real bilateral exchange rates across a number of foreign countries. A *real exchange rate* can be used as an indicator of deviations from PPP or as an indicator of a country's international price competitiveness.

Key Terms		
Asset market approach to exchange rates	Absolute purchasing power parity	Nominal bilateral exchange rate
Purchasing power parity (PPP)	Relative purchasing power parity	Nominal effective exchange rate
Monetary approach to exchange rates	Quantity theory equation	Real bilateral exchange rate
Bandwagon	Overshooting	Real effective exchange rate
Law of one price	Bubble	

Suggested
Reading

Frankel and Rose (1995) and Rossi (2013) survey research on the determinants of exchange rates, including work based on the asset market approach and the monetary approach. Zettelmeyer (2004), using data on Australia, Canada, and New Zealand, shows that an unexpected tightening (loosening) of the country's monetary policy raises (lowers) domestic interest rates and appreciates (depreciates) the country's currency. Bjørnland (2009) offers a similar analysis, which also includes Sweden. Lyons (2001) provides an overview of a different approach to understanding exchange rates, one that focuses on actual trading activity. Menkhoff and Taylor (2007) examine the use of technical or chartist analysis by foreign exchange traders.

Froot and Rogoff (1995) survey a range of tests of purchasing power parity. The survey by Sarno and Taylor (2002) is more technical.

Questions
and
Problems

✦ 1. "Short-run pressures on market exchange rates result mainly from gradual changes in flows of international trade in goods and services." Do you agree or disagree? Why?

2. The following rates currently exist:

Spot exchange rate: $1.000/euro.

Annual interest rate on 180-day euro-denominated bonds: 3%.

Annual interest rate on 180-day U.S. dollar–denominated bonds: 4%.

Investors currently expect the spot exchange rate to be about $1.005/euro in 180 days.

  a. Show that uncovered interest parity holds (approximately) at these rates.

  b. What is likely to be the effect on the spot exchange rate if the interest rate on 180-day dollar-denominated bonds declines to 3 percent? If the euro interest rate and the expected future spot rate are unchanged, and if uncovered interest parity is reestablished, what will the new current spot exchange rate be? Has the dollar appreciated or depreciated?

✦ 3. The current rates are:

Spot exchange rate: $2.00/£.

Annual interest rate on 60-day U.S. dollar–denominated bonds: 5%.

Annual interest rate on 60-day pound-denominated bonds: 11%.

Investors currently expect the spot exchange rate to be $1.98/pound in 60 days.

  a. Show that uncovered interest parity holds (approximately) at these rates.

  b. What is likely to be the effect on the spot exchange rate if the interest rate on 60-day pound-denominated bonds declines to 8 percent? If the dollar interest rate and the expected future spot rate are unchanged, and if uncovered interest parity is reestablished, what will the new current spot exchange rate be? Has the pound appreciated or depreciated?

4. You observe the following current rates:

Spot exchange rate: $0.01/yen.

Annual interest rate on 90-day U.S. dollar–denominated bonds: 4%.

Annual interest rate on 90-day yen-denominated bonds: 4%.

  a. If uncovered interest parity holds, what spot exchange rate do investors expect to exist in 90 days?

b. A close U.S. presidential election has just been decided. The candidate whom international investors view as the stronger and more probusiness person won. Because of this, investors expect the exchange rate to be $0.0095/yen in 90 days. What will happen in the foreign exchange market?

◆ 5. As a foreign exchange trader, how would you react to each of the following news items as it flashes on your computer screen?

a. Mexico's oil reserves prove to be much smaller than touted earlier.

b. The Social Credit Party wins the national elections in Canada and promises generous expansion of the supply of money and credit.

c. In a surprise vote the Swiss government passes a law that will result in a large increase in the taxation of interest payments from Switzerland to foreigners.

6. Will the law of one price apply better to gold or to Big Macs? Why?

◆ 7. For your next foreign vacation, would it be better to go to a country whose currency is overvalued relative to PPP or one whose currency is undervalued relative to PPP (other attractions being equal)?

8. According to PPP and the monetary approach, why did the nominal exchange-rate value of the DM (relative to the dollar) rise between the early 1970s and the late 1990s? Why did the nominal exchange-rate value of the pound decline?

◆ 9. Mexico currently has an annual domestic inflation rate of about 20 percent. Suppose that Mexico wants to stabilize the floating market exchange-rate value of its currency (dollars/peso) in a world in which dollar prices are generally rising at 3 percent per year. What must the rate of inflation of domestic peso prices come down to? If the quantity theory of money holds with a constant k, and if Mexican real output is growing 6 percent per year, what rate of money growth should the Mexican government try to achieve?

10. To aid in its efforts to get reelected, the current government of a country decides to increase the growth rate of the domestic money supply by two percentage points. The increased growth rate becomes "permanent" because once started it is difficult to reverse.

a. According to the monetary approach, how will this affect the long-run trend for the exchange-rate value of the country's currency?

b. Explain why the nominal exchange-rate trend is affected, referring to PPP.

◆ 11. In 1990, the price level for the United States was 100, the price level for Pugelovia was also 100, and in the foreign exchange market one Pugelovian pnut (pronounced "p'noot") was equal to $1. In 2013, the U.S. price level had risen to 260, and the Pugelovian price level had risen to 390.

a. According to PPP, what should the dollar–pnut exchange rate be in 2013?

b. If the *actual* dollar–pnut exchange rate is $1/pnut in 2013, is the pnut overvalued or undervalued relative to PPP?

12. Here is further information on the U.S. and Pugelovian economies.

	1990			2013		
	M^s	Y	P	M^s	Y	P
United States	20,000	800	100	65,000	1,000	260
Pugelovia	10,000	200	100	58,500	300	390

a. What is the value of k for the United States in 1990? For Pugelovia?

b. Show that the change in price level from 1990 to 2013 for each country is consistent with the quantity theory of money with a constant k.

◆ 13. Consider our example of overshooting shown in Figure 19.6, in which the domestic money supply increased by 10 percent. Assume that the path of slow adjustment of prices is that the price level rises by about 2 percent per year for five years. What would the path of the nominal exchange rate be if PPP held for each year? Given the actual path for the exchange rate shown in Figure 19.6, does PPP hold in the short run? Does it hold in the long run?

14. A country has had a steady value for its floating exchange rate (stated inversely as the domestic currency price of foreign currency) for a number of years. The country now tightens up on (reduces) its money supply dramatically. The country's product price level is not immediately affected, but the price level gradually becomes lower (relative to what it otherwise would have been) during the next several years.

a. Why might the market exchange rate change a lot as this monetary tightening is announced and implemented?

b. What is the path of the market exchange rate likely to be over the next several years? Why?

◆ 15. The price levels in Canada and Switzerland were each 110 in 1995, and the nominal spot rate was 1.5 Swiss francs per Canadian dollar in 1995. The Canadian price level rose to be 160 in 2005, the Swiss price level rose to be 130 in 2005, and the spot exchange rate was 1.3 Swiss francs per Canadian dollar in 2005.

Did the Canadian dollar experience a real appreciation or a real depreciation (relative to the Swiss franc) between 1995 and 2005? (As part of your answer, use a calculation of the real exchange rate.)

16. Consider an effective exchange rate value of the euro in which the Canadian dollar gets a weight of 60 percent and the Japanese yen gets a weight of 40 percent. The nominal bilateral rates change from 2.0 euros per Canadian dollar to 1.9 euros per Canadian dollar and from 48 yen per euro to 50 yen per euro. Has the nominal effective exchange-rate value of the euro decreased? (That is, has the euro had a nominal effective depreciation?)

Chapter **Twenty**

Government Policies toward the Foreign Exchange Market

Chapters 16 through 19 presented the basic analysis of how currencies are exchanged and what seems to determine the exchange rate if the determination is left mainly to market forces. For better or worse, many governments do not usually just let the private market set the exchange rate. Rather, governments have policies toward the foreign exchange market in the form of policies toward exchange rates themselves, policies toward who is allowed to use the market, or both.

Our previous discussion suggests one reason why governments adopt such policies. Exchange rates, if left to private market forces, sometimes fluctuate a lot. They are prone to overshoot and may occasionally be influenced by bandwagons among investors or speculators. Exchange rates are very important prices—they can affect the entire range of a country's international transactions. One objective for government policy, then, can be to reduce variability in exchange rates.

Governments often have other reasons for adopting policies toward the foreign exchange market. A government may want to keep the exchange-rate value of its currency low, preventing appreciation or promoting depreciation. This benefits certain activities or groups in the country, including the country's exporters and import-competing businesses. Or, in a different setting, a government may want to do the opposite: keep the exchange-rate value of its currency high, preventing depreciation or promoting appreciation. This can benefit other activities or groups—for instance, buyers of imports. It can also be used as part of an effort to reduce domestic inflation by using the competitive pressure of low import prices. In addition, the government policy may reflect other, relatively noneconomic goals. The government may believe that it is defending national honor or encouraging national pride by maintaining a steady exchange rate or a strong currency internationally. Devaluation or depreciation may be feared as a confirmation of the ineptitude of the government in selecting policies.

This chapter has three objectives. First, it provides a framework for understanding the range of possible government policies toward the foreign exchange market. Second, it begins the analysis of these policies, focusing on the economics of official buying and selling of currencies in the market and the economics of restrictions on who can use the market. Third, it explores some lessons of history by surveying exchange-rate systems that have existed during the past 140 years, concluding with a description of the current system.

TWO ASPECTS: RATE FLEXIBILITY AND RESTRICTIONS ON USE

Government policies toward the foreign exchange market are of two types:

- Those policies that are directly applied to the exchange rate itself.
- Those policies that directly state who may use the foreign exchange market and for what purposes.

The first type of policy acts directly on price (the exchange rate), while the second type acts directly on quantity (by limiting some people's ability to use the foreign exchange market). We saw this distinction before when we examined tariffs and quotas as two forms of government policies toward imports. As in the case of imports, we expect that any one policy has impacts on both price and quantity in the market, even though the policy directly acts on only one of these. A policy toward the exchange rate affects the quantity of foreign exchange traded in the market (the turnover) and a policy restricting use has an impact on the exchange rate.

Government policies toward the exchange rate itself are usually categorized according to the flexibility of the exchange rate—the amount of movement in the exchange rate that the policy permits. In the simplest terms, governments choose between floating and fixed exchange rates, although, as we will see, the reality is often richer than this.

Government policies can also restrict access to the foreign exchange market. One policy choice is no restriction—everyone is free to use the foreign exchange market. The country's currency is *fully convertible* into foreign currency for all uses, for both trade in goods and services (current account transactions) and international investment activities (financial account transactions). The other policy choice is some form of **exchange control**—the country's government places some restrictions on use of the foreign exchange market. In the most extreme form of exchange control, all foreign exchange proceeds (for instance, proceeds resulting from foreign payments for the country's exports) must be turned over to the country's monetary authority. Anyone wanting to obtain foreign exchange must request it from the authority, which then determines whether to approve the request. Less extreme forms of control limit access for some types of transactions, while permitting free access for other types of transactions. For instance, in a common form of partial exchange control, the government:

- permits use of the foreign exchange market for all payments for exports and imports of goods and services (that is, the currency is *convertible for current account transactions*) and
- imposes some form of **capital controls,** by placing limits or requiring approvals for payments related to some (or all) international financial activities.

Another example of a less extreme form of restriction is limits on the use of the foreign exchange market for transactions related to broad types of imports, such as consumer luxury goods.

FLOATING EXCHANGE RATE

If government policy lets the market determine the exchange rate, the rate is free to go wherever the market equilibrium is at that time. This policy choice results in a clean float. Market supply and demand are solely private (nonofficial) activities. As private market supply and demand shift around, the value of the floating exchange rate changes. A clean float is the polar case of complete flexibility.

Even when the country's exchange-rate policy is to permit flexibility by floating the rate, the government often is not willing to simply let the rate go wherever private supply and demand drive it. Rather, the government often tries to have a direct impact on the rate through official intervention. That is, the monetary authority enters the foreign exchange market to buy or sell foreign currency (in exchange for domestic currency). Through this intervention, the government hopes to alter the configuration of supply and demand, and thus influence the equilibrium value of the exchange rate—the rate that clears the market. This policy approach—an exchange rate that is generally floating (or flexible) but with the government willing to intervene to attempt to influence the market rate—is called a managed float (if you are an optimist about the capabilities of the government) or a dirty float (if you are a pessimist). Often the government is attempting to lean against the wind to moderate movements in the floating rate. For instance, if the exchange-rate value of the country's currency is rising (and that of foreign currency falling), then the authorities intervene to buy foreign currency (and sell domestic currency). They hope that the intervention and the extra supply of domestic currency can slow or stop their own currency's rise in value (or, correspondingly, that the extra demand for foreign currency can slow or stop its decline). The actual effectiveness of intervention is controversial, and we will examine this issue further in Chapter 24. Nonetheless, most governments that choose a floating exchange-rate policy also do manage, or "dirty," the float to some extent.

FIXED EXCHANGE RATE

If the government chooses the policy of a fixed exchange rate, then the government sets the exchange rate that it wants. Often, some flexibility is permitted within a range, called a *band,* around this chosen fixed rate, called the *par value* or *central value.* Nonetheless, the flexibility is generally more limited than would occur if the government instead permitted a floating rate.

In implementing its choice of a fixed exchange rate, the government actually faces three specific major questions: To what does the government fix the value of its currency? When or how often does the country change the value of its fixed rate? How does the government defend the fixed value against any market pressures pushing toward some other exchange-rate value?

What to Fix To?

A fixed rate means that the value of the country's currency is fixed to something else, but what is this something else? As we will see later in this chapter, the answer about a century ago was to fix to gold. If several countries all fix the values of their currencies to specific amounts of gold, then arbitrage ensures that the exchange rates among the currencies will also be fixed at the rates implied by their gold values. That is, currencies tied to the same thing (such as gold) are all tied to each other. In principle, any other commodity or group of commodities could serve the same purpose—the gold standard is one example of the broader idea of a commodity standard.

The country could choose to fix the value of its currency to some other currency, rather than to a commodity. Since the end of World War II many countries have often fixed the value of their currency to the U.S. dollar. Any other single currency can serve the same purpose.

Or the country could choose to fix the value of its currency not to one other currency but to the average value of a number of other currencies. Why would a country choose to fix to such a *basket* of other currencies? The logic is the same as that of diversifying a portfolio (or not putting all your eggs in one basket). If the country fixes to one single other currency, then it will ride along with this other currency if the other currency's value experiences extreme changes against any third-country currencies. Fixing to a basket of currencies moderates this effect, in that the average value is kept steady.

What basket of currencies might the country fix to? There is one ready-made basket—the special drawing right (SDR), a basket of the four major currencies in the world.[1] Or a country can create its own basket. For instance, the country might be interested in maintaining a steady exchange-rate value to facilitate its international trade activities. In this case the basket would include the currencies of its major trading partners, and the importance of these other countries in the basket would be based on their importance in the country's trade. In designing its basket in this way, the country is using the same logic as that used to calculate an effective exchange rate.

No country today fixes its currency to gold or any other commodity. Although we examine the gold standard later in this chapter, the rest of our fixed-rate discussion presumes that a country fixes the exchange-rate value of its currency to one or more other currencies.

When to Change the Fixed Rate?

Once the country has chosen what to fix to, it establishes a specific value for its currency in terms of the item chosen. As the government attempts to maintain this fixed value over time, it faces the question of when to change the fixed rate.

The government may insist that it will never change the fixed rate. A permanently fixed exchange rate is useful as a polar case—the opposite of a clean float. However, it is not clear that the government's commitment is credible. The commitment is not truly binding—the government has the capability to alter its policy. Most probably, nothing is fixed forever. On this basis, we often use the term pegged exchange rate

---

[1] As we mentioned in Chapter 16, the SDR is a reserve asset created by the International Monetary Fund (IMF). The IMF periodically adjusts the specific composition of the SDR. As of 2011, one SDR equals the collection of U.S.\$0.66 plus 0.423 euro plus 12.1 Japanese yen plus British £0.111. Market exchange rates can then be used to compute the SDR's value in terms of any specific single currency.

in place of *fixed exchange rate,* in recognition that the government has some ability to move the peg value.

Although the fixed rate may not be fixed forever, the government may try to keep the value fixed for long periods of time. Nonetheless, in the face of a substantial or "fundamental" disequilibrium in the country's international position, the government may change the pegged-rate value. This approach is called an adjustable peg.

In other situations, the government may recognize that a specific pegged-rate value cannot be maintained for long. For instance, if the country has a relatively high inflation rate, then an attempt to maintain a pegged rate against the currency of a low-inflation country will quickly lead to large violations of purchasing power parity and declining international price competitiveness. Nonetheless, the country may prefer to maintain some form of pegged exchange rate, perhaps because it believes that a floating exchange rate would be too volatile. The solution chosen by some countries in this position is a crawling peg. With a crawling peg the peg value is changed often (for instance, monthly) according to a set of indicators or according to the judgment of the government monetary authority. If indicators are used, the discussion of Chapter 19 suggests one reasonable choice—the difference between the country's inflation rate and the inflation rate of the country whose currency it pegs to. If the inflation difference is used, the nominal pegged rate will track purchasing power parity over time, and this bilateral real exchange rate will be stabilized. Other indicators that might be used include the country's holdings of official international reserve assets (indicating pressure from the country's balance of payments), the growth of the country's money supply (indicating underlying inflation pressure), or the current actual market exchange rate relative to the central par value of the pegged rate (indicating, within the allowable band, the foreign exchange market pressure away from the par value).

In fact, the choice of the *width of the allowable band* is closely related to the issue of when to change the pegged rate. If the band is larger, then the actual exchange rate has more room to move around the par value. Market pressures can result in wider variations in the actual exchange rate, without necessarily forcing the government to face the decision of whether to change the pegged-rate value.

At this point, it is useful to summarize the main points of our survey. For government policies toward the exchange rate itself, we often frame the government decision as choosing between a floating or a fixed exchange rate. A floating exchange rate seems to permit substantial flexibility or variability in the actual rate, while a fixed rate seems to impose strict limits on this variability or flexibility. Although this proposition is true to a large extent, the reality is also more nuanced.

In a clean float, the rate is purely market-driven, but in a managed float the government takes actions such as exchange market intervention to influence the floating rate. In a heavily managed float, the exchange rate may show little flexibility—it is almost pegged, even though this is not the way that the government describes its choice.

Even with a fixed rate, much variability or flexibility may still exist for several reasons. The band around the central pegged rate can be wide, permitting substantial variability within the band. The exchange-rate value of the country's currency can also vary substantially with respect to other currencies that are not involved in the same type of peg. Furthermore, the government can change the pegged rate, sometimes frequently, as in a crawling peg.

The *polar cases of a clean float and a permanently fixed exchange rate* are useful in order to contrast the implications of a country's choice of exchange-rate policy. At the same time we must remember that in reality there is more of a *continuum in which the country permits more or less flexibility in the movements of the exchange-rate value* of the country's currency. A full analysis of a specific country requires examination of the true nature of government policy toward the exchange rate.

Defending a Fixed Exchange Rate

The third major question confronting a country that has chosen a fixed exchange rate is how to defend its fixed rate. The pressures of private (or nonofficial) supply and demand in the foreign exchange market may sometimes drive the exchange rate toward values that are not within the permissible band around the par value. The government then must use some means to defend the pegged rate—to keep the actual exchange rate within the band.

How does the government defend the fixed rate that it has announced? There are four basic ways:

1. The government can intervene in the foreign exchange market, buying or selling foreign currency in exchange for domestic currency, to maintain or influence the actual exchange rate in the market.
2. The government can impose some form of exchange control to maintain or influence the exchange rate by constricting demand or supply in the market. (A closely related approach would use trade controls such as tariffs or quotas to attempt to accomplish this result.)
3. The government can alter domestic interest rates to influence short-term capital flows, thus maintaining or influencing the exchange rate by shifting the supply–demand position in the market.
4. The government can adjust the country's whole macroeconomic position to make it "fit" the chosen fixed exchange-rate value. Macroeconomic adjustments driven by changes in fiscal or monetary policy can alter the supply–demand position in the foreign exchange market, for instance, by adjusting export capabilities, the demand for imports, or international capital flows.

We should also remember that there is a fifth option for the country—to surrender rather than defend:

5. The country can alter its fixed rate (devaluing or revaluing its currency) or switch to a floating exchange rate (in which case the currency usually will immediately depreciate or appreciate).

The four ways of defending a fixed rate are not mutually exclusive—a country can use several methods at the same time. Indeed, they are often closely interrelated. For instance, changing interest rates to influence short-term capital flows relates to overall macroeconomic management. In the next two sections of this chapter, we turn to a closer examination of the first two options: intervention and exchange control. Chapters 22–25 explore the broader implications of the country's foreign exchange policies for the whole national economy.

DEFENSE THROUGH OFFICIAL INTERVENTION

In defending a fixed exchange rate, the country's first line of defense is usually official intervention in the foreign exchange market. This is the defense that we introduced in Chapter 17, and we can now examine it in more depth. For much of our discussion in the first parts of this section, we will examine a country that has chosen to peg its currency to the U.S. dollar. We state the spot exchange rate value (*e*) as units of this country's currency per dollar. (The exchange rate stated this way is directly pricing the U.S. dollar, which is now considered the "foreign" currency.)

Defending against Depreciation

Consider first the case in which the pressure from private (or nonofficial) supply and demand in the foreign exchange market is attempting to drive the exchange rate above the top of its allowable band—the country's currency is tending toward depreciation. For instance, say that this is a Latin American country that is attempting to maintain a fixed rate of 25 pesos per dollar, with a band of plus or minus 4 percent (plus or minus 1 peso). As shown in Figure 20.1, nonofficial supply and demand are attempting to push the exchange rate to 28 pesos per dollar, the intersection where the market would clear on its own. If the country's monetary authority is committed to defending the fixed rate within its band using intervention, then the authority must enter into the foreign exchange market in its official role. It must sell dollars and buy domestic currency. To keep the currency in the allowable band, it must sell 3 billion dollars into the foreign exchange market at the rate of 26 pesos per dollar (the top of the band), so it is buying 78 billion pesos from the foreign exchange market.

We can also see how this intervention is reflected in the country's balance of payments. The relatively strong demand for dollars is generally related to strong demand by the country for purchases of foreign goods, services, and (nonofficial) financial

FIGURE 20.1

Intervention to Defend a Fixed Rate: Preventing Depreciation of the Country's Currency

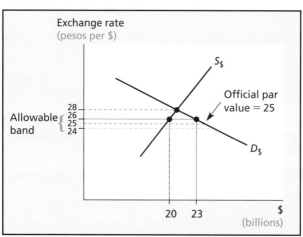

To prevent the market exchange rate from piercing through the top of the allowable band, the country's central bank must sell 3 billion dollars at the exchange rate of 26 pesos per dollar.

FIGURE 20.2
Official
Holdings of
Reserve Assets,
End of Year,
1970–2012
(Billions of U.S.
Dollars)

Source: International
Monetary Fund,
Annual Report,
various years.

	1970	1980	1990	2000	2012
Foreign exchange assets	45	381	806	1,935	10,950
Special drawing rights	3	15	28	24	294
Reserve position in the IMF	8	22	32	62	159
Gold	40	573	345	261	1,517
(millions of ounces)	(1,057)	(953)	(940)	(952)	(912)
Total reserve assets	96	991	1,211	2,282	12,920

Most official reserves are held as foreign exchange assets. The two reserve assets provided by the IMF are relatively minor. For official holdings of gold, the amount (ounces) decreased somewhat in the 1970s and again in the 2000s, but most of the variation in the value of official gold holdings is driven by changes in the dollar price of gold (here measured as the London market price).

assets (relative to the demand by foreigners for this country's goods, services, and nonofficial financial assets). This results in an official settlements balance deficit if the country's monetary authority intervenes to defend the fixed rate. The intervention provides the foreign exchange for the country to buy more (in total value) from foreigners than it is selling to them (for goods, services, and nonofficial financial assets). *Through intervention the monetary authority is financing the country's deficit in its official settlement balance.*

Where does the country's monetary authority get the dollars to sell into the foreign exchange market? This Latin American country cannot just create U.S. dollars. Rather, the authority either *uses its own official international reserve assets* (or some other similar government assets) to obtain dollars from some foreign source, most likely the U.S. monetary authority (the Federal Reserve), or it *borrows the dollars*. Let's examine each of these.

There are four major components to a country's official reserve assets: the country's holdings of foreign exchange assets denominated in the major currencies of the world, the country's reserve position with the International Monetary Fund, the country's holdings of special drawing rights, and the country's holdings of gold. To indicate the magnitudes, Figure 20.2 provides information on world holdings of official reserve assets.

As Figure 20.2 shows, total world holdings of official reserve assets have grown rapidly, and their composition has changed. In 1980 gold (measured at its market price) was over half of world official reserves, but then official holdings of foreign exchange assets grew rapidly. By 2012 foreign exchange assets were about 85 percent of world official reserves. These foreign exchange assets are mostly safe, highly liquid, interest-earning debt securities such as government bonds. Of these foreign exchange assets, close to two-thirds are U.S. dollar–denominated assets and almost one-fourth are euro-denominated assets. (There are also small amounts of assets denominated in British pounds, Japanese yen, and a few other currencies.)

If our Latin American country has official reserves in the form of dollar-denominated foreign-currency assets, it can sell these assets to obtain dollars that can then be used in its intervention. If the asset is denominated in some other major currency (such as euros or yen), the currency must be exchanged for dollars, and this can easily be accomplished because the other currency is readily traded.

If our country has a reserve position in the IMF, then it can obtain dollars from the IMF on request. If the country is holding SDRs, then it can use these SDRs to obtain dollars from the U.S. monetary authority or from the IMF. The SDRs actually act as a line of credit permitting the country to borrow dollars, and SDRs are counted as reserves because the country can automatically draw on this line. If the country has gold, then it can sell gold to obtain dollars, but officials today almost never use gold sales to obtain foreign currency.

In addition to using its reserve assets to obtain dollars, the country's monetary authority can borrow dollars. It may be able to borrow dollars (or other major currencies) from the monetary authorities of other countries. Some countries maintain arrangements called *swap lines* with each other to facilitate this type of official borrowing. The monetary authority also may be able to borrow dollars from private—that is, nonofficial—sources. Sometimes these borrowings are disguised to keep them secret from other participants in the foreign exchange market.

These borrowings usually are considered to be different from normal transactions in official international reserves because the country may not have "automatic" access to dollars through borrowings—the lender must be willing to make the loan. There is, however, a special case, the case of a country (like the United States) whose currency is readily held by the monetary authorities of other countries. If the country's currency is a reserve currency, then the country can effectively borrow through official channels by issuing assets that will be held as reserves by the central banks of other countries. Specifically, this has allowed the United States to run what French economist Jacques Rueff called *deficits without tears*. The United States, especially in the 1950s and 1960s, was given extraordinary leeway to finance its deficits. Needless to say, this option is probably not available to the Latin American country that was the focus of our previous example.

What is the implication of the other part of the intervention, that the country's monetary authority is buying domestic currency from the foreign exchange market? In buying domestic currency, the country's monetary authority is removing domestic currency from the economy. This will tend to reduce the domestic money supply unless the authority separately takes another action (called sterilization) to restore the domestic money back into the economy. If the authority does take action to prevent the domestic money supply from changing, then the authority is relying only on intervention to defend the fixed rate. This is called sterilized intervention.

If the monetary authority instead allows the intervention to reduce the money supply, then we have a clear interrelationship with two of the other defense methods. The change in the domestic money supply is likely to alter domestic interest rates, and these changes are likely to influence the entire macroeconomy of the country (including the country's price level).[2] We will examine these broader issues in depth in Chapters 23–25.

Defending against Appreciation

Consider now the case in which the pressure from private (or nonofficial) supply and demand in the foreign exchange market is attempting to drive the exchange rate, the

---

[2] The intervention may also change the foreign country's money supply as the monetary authority sells foreign currency, but we usually do not focus much on this effect.

FIGURE 20.3

Intervention to
Defend a Fixed
Rate: Preventing
Appreciation of
the Country's
Currency

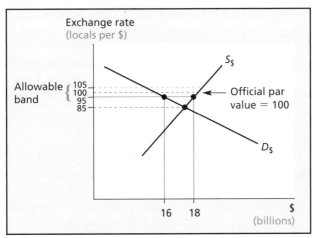

To prevent the market exchange rate from falling through the
bottom of the allowable band, the country's central bank must
buy 2 billion dollars at the exchange rate of 95 locals per dollar.

price of foreign currency, below the bottom of its allowable band—the country's currency is tending toward appreciation. For instance, say that this is an Asian country attempting to maintain a fixed rate of 100 "locals" per dollar, with a band of plus or minus 5 percent (plus or minus 5 locals). As shown in Figure 20.3, nonofficial supply and demand are attempting to push the exchange rate to 85 locals per dollar, the intersection where the market would clear on its own. If the country's monetary authority is committed to defending the fixed rate within its band using intervention, then the authority must enter into the foreign exchange market in its official role. It must buy dollars and sell domestic currency. To keep the currency in the band, it must buy 2 billion dollars from the foreign exchange market at the rate of 95 locals per dollar (the bottom of the band), so it is selling 190 billion locals into the foreign exchange market.

The relatively strong demand for locals is generally related to relatively strong demand by foreigners for the country's goods, services, and (nonofficial) financial assets. This results in an *official settlements balance surplus* if the country's monetary authority intervenes to defend the fixed rate. The intervention provides the local currency for the foreigners to buy more from the country than they are selling to the country (for goods, services, and nonofficial financial assets).

What does the country's monetary authority do with the dollars that it obtains from the foreign exchange market? It adds these dollars to its official international reserve holdings (or, if appropriate, repays prior official borrowings of dollars). Most likely, the authority will use the dollars to obtain U.S.-dollar-denominated foreign exchange assets, probably U.S. government bonds. The country's *holdings of official reserve assets increase*. Note that this case is closely related to the idea of a U.S. "deficit without tears." A U.S. deficit is a surplus for some other countries. If the other countries want to prevent an appreciation of their currencies, they may intervene to buy dollars. In the process, the United States finances its own official settlements deficit by issuing financial assets that other countries hold as their reserves.

What is the implication of the other part of the intervention, that the country's monetary authority is selling domestic currency into the foreign exchange market? This will expand the domestic money supply unless the authority separately *sterilizes* by taking another action to remove the additional domestic money from the economy. If the monetary authority does not (fully) sterilize, so that the domestic money supply does increase, then domestic interest rates and the entire macroeconomy of the country are likely to be affected.

Temporary Disequilibrium

A major issue for the use of intervention to defend a fixed exchange rate is the length of time for which the intervention must continue. How long will the gap between non-official supply and demand at the edge of the band persist? That is, how long will the imbalance in the official settlements balance persist at this exchange rate?

If imbalances are clearly temporary, then defending the fixed exchange rate purely through intervention can work and makes sense. In this case the monetary authorities can finance a succession of deficits and surpluses indefinitely. In fact, we can make a case that financing temporary deficits and surpluses is better than letting the exchange rate float around.

Consider, for example, a situation in which Canada maintains a fixed exchange rate with its major trading partner, Britain. The exchange rate (*e*) is in Canadian dollars per pound, the price of foreign currency if our home country is Canada. Figure 20.4 gives an example of a successful and socially desirable financing of temporary surpluses and deficits with a fixed exchange rate. We have imagined that the temporary

FIGURE 20.4

A Successful Financing of Temporary Deficits and Surpluses at a Fixed Exchange Rate

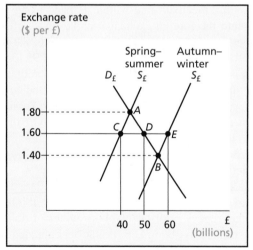

Autumn and winter: The monetary authority buys *DE* = £10 billion in foreign exchange. Spring and summer: The monetary authority sells *CD* = £10 billion in foreign exchange. Such official intervention increases well-being over the full cycle by area *ACD* plus area *BDE*.

fluctuations in the balance of payments and the foreign exchange market arise from something predictable, such as a seasonal pattern in foreign exchange receipts, with Canada exporting more and earning more foreign exchange (£) during the autumn–winter harvest season than during the nonharvest spring–summer season. To help the example along, let us assume that it is costly for producers of the export crop to refrain from selling it during the harvest season and that something also prevents private investors or speculators from stepping in and performing the equilibrating function being assigned to government officials here. If the officials did not finance the temporary imbalances, the exchange rate would drop to $1.40 at point *B* in the harvest season, when the nation had a lot of exports to sell, and it would rise to $1.80 in the off-season. In this instance there is some economic loss because it would be better if the people who wanted foreign exchange to keep up imports during the off-season did not have to pay $1.80 for foreign exchange that is readily available for only $1.40 during the harvest season. The officials can avoid this economic loss by stabilizing the price at $1.60. Their stabilization is made possible because they have somehow picked the correct price, $1.60, the one at which they can sell exactly as much foreign exchange during one season as they buy during the other, exactly breaking even while stabilizing the price.

The official financing of spring–summer deficits with autumn–winter foreign exchange reserves brings a net social gain to the world. This gain arises from the fact that the monetary authority gave a net supply of foreign exchange at $1.60 to people who would have been willing to pay up to $1.80 a pound during the spring–summer season, while also buying at $1.60 the same amount of foreign exchange from people who would have been willing to sell it for as little as $1.40. The net social gain is measured as the sum of areas *ACD* and *BDE* (or about $1 billion a year). In this case, official intervention was successful and superior to letting the exchange rate find its own equilibrium in each season.

For intervention to finance temporary disequilibriums to be the correct policy option, some stringent conditions must be met. First, it must be the case that private speculators do not see, or cannot take advantage of, the opportunity to buy foreign exchange in the fall and winter, invest it for a few months, and then sell it in the spring and summer. If private parties could do this, their own actions would bring the exchange rate close to $1.60 throughout the year, and there would be no need for official intervention.

It is also crucial that the officials correctly predict the future demand and supply for foreign exchange and that they predict what would be an equilibrium path for the exchange rate in the absence of their intervention. If they do not forecast correctly, their attempt to finance a deficit or a surplus at a fixed exchange rate can be costly because their accumulation of official reserves at some times will not balance against their loss of reserves at other times.

Disequilibrium That Is Not Temporary

What happens if the disequilibrium that results in an imbalance in the country's official settlements balance is not temporary? Rather, what if the disequilibrium is ongoing or *fundamental*? For a country that defends its fixed rate using intervention, the country's monetary authority is continually losing reserves (or borrowing foreign exchange) if the imbalance is a deficit, or it is continually accumulating reserves if the imbalance is a surplus.

If the domestic currency is facing *pressure toward depreciation* because of an *ongoing deficit,* the authority must *continually intervene to sell foreign currency.* Eventually its official reserves will run low, as will its ability to borrow foreign currencies. Furthermore, its problems can worsen if private investors and speculators observe its reserve losses and begin to bet heavily that the currency must be devalued. A *one-way speculative gamble* exists. As investors and speculators sell domestic currency and buy foreign currency, the gap that must be filled by official intervention widens, hastening the loss of reserves. As the country loses reserves, it also loses the ability to defend the fixed rate by intervention alone. It must shift to one of the other three defenses or surrender (devalue).

To see some of the economic costs of intervening to finance a "temporary" disequilibrium that turns out to be a fundamental disequilibrium, consider a stunning example of a failed defense of a currency—the depreciation of the Mexican peso in late 1994. The Mexican monetary authority was using a heavily managed "float" to effectively peg the Mexican currency at about 3.5 pesos per dollar. They were intervening to defend this value, and their holdings of official reserves declined from nearly $30 billion to about $6 billion during 1994. With their reserves so low, on December 20, 1994, they were forced to surrender, and the peso declined by about one-third, to about 5 pesos per dollar by year-end. They lost billions of dollars of taxpayers' money. Having bought pesos at about $0.29 per peso, they subsequently had to sell pesos at a much lower dollar value to buy dollars in order to rebuild their official reserves. Buying high and selling low is a formula for large losses.

If, in the opposite case, the domestic currency is facing *pressure toward appreciation* because of an *ongoing surplus,* the authority must *continually intervene to buy foreign currency.* The country eventually accumulates large international reserves. These eventually may be viewed as too large by the country itself for several reasons. First, the basic rate of return on this form of national wealth tends to be low, given the types of low-interest investments that are usually chosen for international reserve assets. Second, the value of foreign exchange assets will decline if the country eventually must "retreat" by revaluing its own currency (which devalues foreign currency). Furthermore, these reserves may be viewed as too large by other countries because some other countries are running deficits if this country is running a surplus and building its reserve holdings.

A recent example of a large buildup of official reserve assets is China, as we discussed in Chapter 1. With the yuan fixed to the U.S. dollar since the mid-1990s, China had official settlements surpluses, and these surpluses became large beginning in 2001. To defend the fixed exchange rate, China's monetary authorities intervened continually in the foreign exchange market to buy dollars and sell yuan. China's holdings of foreign exchange reserve assets more than quadrupled from the end of 2000 to mid-2005. The overall payments surpluses did not appear to be temporary and soon to be reversed. The Chinese government came under strong political pressure, especially from the United States and the European Union, to revalue its currency. In July 2005 the Chinese government instituted a small revaluation of the yuan, and then allowed the yuan to appreciate gradually for three years. After keeping the exchange value of the yuan steady from July 2008 to June 2010, the Chinese government then again gradually appreciated the yuan relative to the dollar. Throughout, the overall payments surpluses continued, and China's monetary authorities continued to intervene (buying dollars and selling yuan). By early 2014, the Chinese government had amassed $4 trillion of official reserves.

The intervention and the accumulation of official reserves expose the Chinese government to the risk of the same kind of currency losses as the Mexican government sustained in 1994. The difference is that the Chinese government officials will be stuck holding *foreign* currency that is worth less than they paid for it (the depreciating dollars), whereas the Mexican officials ended up holding less-valuable domestic currency. With the gradual appreciation of the yuan since 2005, the Chinese government has already experienced some losses on its official reserve holdings of U.S. dollar–denominated assets. The market and political pressures continue for more appreciation of the yuan. To the extent that the yuan's value eventually rises by a large amount against the dollar, the Chinese government will incur much larger losses.

These experiences do not prove that it is futile to try to keep exchange rates fixed. They do prove that, when the existing official exchange rate is becoming a disequilibrium exchange rate for the long run, trying to ride out the storm with intervention alone is costly. Something must be added. *Fundamental disequilibrium calls for adjustment, not merely financing.* However, it is not easy for officials to judge what constitutes fundamental disequilibrium. We are left with the knowledge that a fundamental disequilibrium is one that is too great and/or too enduring to be financed, but we have no clear way of identifying one until after it has happened.

EXCHANGE CONTROL

Among the options for defending a fixed exchange rate, one (exchange control) can be indicated as socially inferior to the others. Oddly enough, exchange controls are widely used. According to compilations of official policies done by the International Monetary Fund, in 2012, 56 countries, all developing countries, had fairly comprehensive exchange control policies in place, controls that included requirements to surrender export proceeds and restrictions on international portfolio investments. A large number of other countries had more limited forms of exchange control in place. For instance, about 35 other countries had substantial controls on financial transactions. A number of these countries are responding to persistent deficits in their external payments by defending a fixed exchange rate with elaborate government controls restricting the ability of their residents to buy foreign goods or services, to travel abroad, or to invest abroad.

Exchange controls are closely analogous to quantitative restrictions (quotas) on imports, already analyzed in Chapter 9. In fact, the analogy with import quotas fits very well, so well that the basic economics of exchange controls is simply the economics of import quotas expanded to cover imports of IOUs (investing abroad) and tourist services as well as imports of ordinary products. In Chapter 9, we demonstrated that an import quota is at least as bad as an import tariff using a one-dollar, one-vote analysis of changes in well-being. So it is with exchange controls as well: They are at least as damaging as a uniform tax on all foreign transactions, and probably they are worse.

FIGURE 20.5

The Best of the
Worst: Welfare
Losses from
Well-Managed
Exchange
Controls

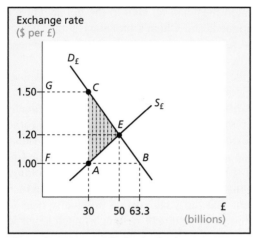

The exchange control limits the foreign currency
available to 30 billion pounds, the amount that is
earned by the country's exporters at the exchange
rate of $1.00 per pound. Even if only those who
value the foreign currency most highly (at $1.50 or
more per pound) get it, the country suffers a loss of
well-being of area *CEA*.

To show the economic case against exchange controls, it is useful to start with an
oversimplified view of exchange controls that is almost certain to underestimate the
social losses coming from real-world controls. Figure 20.5 sketches the effects of a
system of binding comprehensive exchange control that is about as well managed and
benign as we can imagine. Figure 20.5 imagines that the U.S. government has become
committed to maintaining a fixed exchange rate that officially values foreign currencies less, and the dollar more, than would a free-market equilibrium rate. This official
rate is $1.00 for the pound sterling, with similar subequilibrium rates for other foreign
currencies. The exchange control laws require exporters to turn over all their revenues
from foreign buyers to the U.S. government. The U.S. government, in turn, gives them
$1.00 in domestic bank deposits for each pound sterling they have earned by selling
abroad. At this exchange rate, exporters are earning, and releasing to authorities, only
£30 billion per month. This figure is well below the £63.3 billion per month that
residents of the United States want to buy at this exchange rate to purchase foreign
goods, services, and assets. If the U.S. government is committed to the $1.00 rate, yet
is not willing to intervene or to contract the whole U.S. economy enough to make the
demand and supply for foreign exchange match at $1.00, then it must ration the right
to buy foreign exchange.

Let us imagine that the U.S. officials ration foreign exchange in a sound but
seldom-tried way. Every month they announce that it is time for another public
auction-by-Internet. On January 21, they announce that anyone wanting sterling (or
any other foreign currency) for March must send in bids by February 15. A family
that plans to be in England in March could submit a form pledging its willingness to

pay up to $3 per pound for 700 pounds to spend in England and its willingness to pay $2.50 per pound for 1,000 pounds. An importer of automobiles would also submit a schedule of amounts of foreign currencies she wishes to buy at each exchange rate in order to buy cars abroad. Receiving all these bids, the government's computers would rank them by the prices willingly pledged, and the totals pledged would be added up at each price, thus revealing the demand curve $D_{£}$ in Figure 20.5. The government would announce on February 20 that the price of $1.50 per pound was the price that made demand match the available £30 billion. The family who wants to be in England for March would thus get £1,000 by paying $1,500 = £1,000 × $1.50 to the government. All who were willing to pay $1.50 or more for each pound would receive the pounds they applied for, at the price of only $1.50 a pound, even if they had agreed to pay more. Anyone who did not submit bids with prices as high as $1.50 would be denied the right to buy pounds during March.

This system would give the government a large amount of revenues earned from the exchange control auctions. Collecting $1.50/£ × £30 billion = $45 billion while paying exporters only $1.00/£ × £30 billion = $30 billion, the government would make a net profit of $15 billion, minus its administrative costs. This government profit could be returned to the general public either as a cut in other kinds of taxes or as extra government spending. Area *GCAF* in Figure 20.5 represents these auction profits taken from importers but returned to the rest of society, and it does not constitute a net gain or loss for society as a whole.

The exchange control just described does impose a *loss of well-being* on society as a whole, however. This loss is measured by the area *CEA*. To see why, remember the interpretation of demand and supply curves as marginal benefit and marginal cost curves. When the exchange controls are in effect and only £30 billion is available, some mutually profitable trades are being prohibited. At point *C*, the demand curve is telling us that some American is willing to pay $1.50 for an extra pound. At point *A*, the supply curve is telling us that somebody else, either a U.S. exporter or her customers, would be willing to provide an extra pound per year for $1.00. Yet the exchange controls prevent these two groups from getting together to split the $0.50 of net gain in a marketplace for pounds. Thus, the vertical distance *AC* = $0.50 shows the social loss from not being able to trade freely another pound. Similarly, each extra vertical gap between the demand curve and the supply curve out to point *E* also adds to the measure of something lost because the exchange controls hamper private transactions. All these net losses add up to area *CEA* (£5 billion).

Actual exchange control regimes are likely to have several other effects and costs. First, in practice, governments usually do not hold public foreign-currency auctions. Instead, they allocate the right to buy foreign currency at the low official rate according to more complicated rules. To get the right to buy foreign currency, we must go through involved application procedures to show that the purpose of the foreign purchase qualifies it for a favored-treatment category. Importing inputs for factories that would otherwise have to remain idle and underutilized is one purpose that often qualifies for priority access to foreign exchange, over less crucial inputs, imports of luxury consumer goods, or acquisition of private foreign bank deposits. One difference between actual exchange controls and our hypothetical one is that the actual controls often incur greater *administrative costs* to enforce the controls, as well as greater *private resource costs* in dealing with them. Another difference is that some *lower-valued uses may be approved in place of higher-valued uses.* The government is not necessarily serving the demanders toward the top of the demand curve. For both of these reasons the net loss is larger than area *CEA.*

Second, another effect of exchange controls—efforts to evade them—is predictable. People are frustrated when they are not allowed to buy foreign exchange, even though they are willing to pay more than the recipients of foreign exchange will get from the government when these holders sell their foreign currency. The frustrated demanders will then look for other ways to obtain foreign exchange. One way is to *bribe the government functionaries* in charge of determining the official approvals. Another is to offer more to the recipients of foreign exchange than the government is offering, thus making it worthwhile for the recipients to "sell direct," in violation of the exchange controls. In this way a second foreign exchange market—a **parallel market,** or black market—develops as a way for private demanders and sellers of foreign exchange to evade the exchange controls. Parallel markets exist in most countries that have exchange controls. The degree to which users of these illegal markets are punished varies widely. Some countries ignore violations of the exchange control, while others impose death penalties. If you visit a country that has exchange controls, be sure that you know the penalties before you use the parallel market. Your effort to take advantage of free-market economics might make you decidedly unfree.[3]

The costs of actual exchange controls are generally great enough to raise the question of what good purpose they are intended to serve. Because controls can be used to defend a fixed rate, we might imagine that they reduce economic uncertainty by holding fixed the external value of the national currency. Yet they are unlikely to help reduce uncertainty if they leave individual firms and households in doubt as to whether they will be allowed to obtain foreign exchange at the official price. Controls are likely to appeal mainly to government officials as a device for increasing their discretionary power over the allocation of resources. Controls undeniably have this effect. A charitable interpretation is that the extra power makes it easier for government officials to achieve social goals through comprehensive planning. A less charitable interpretation, consistent with the facts, is that officials see in exchange controls an opportunity for personal power and its lucrative exercise. In addition, the emergence of parallel markets or other methods to evade the controls calls into question their true effectiveness.

INTERNATIONAL CURRENCY EXPERIENCE

The first part of this chapter has laid out a framework for describing government policies toward the foreign exchange market and has examined some of the economics of official intervention and exchange control. The rest of the chapter surveys the

---

[3]In a number of countries the government itself creates two or more foreign exchange markets and rates—a dual- or multiple-exchange-rate system. Each rate applies to transactions of a specific type. For instance, a dual-rate system might have one rate for current transactions and another rate for financial transactions. In 2012, 24 developing countries had some form of dual- or multiple-exchange-rate system. As part of this type of policy, some form of exchange control is needed to direct each transaction to its appropriate rate. Again, the system creates incentives for evasion. For instance, transactions may be disguised to qualify for a more favorable rate.

historical experience of actual government policies since the establishment of a nearly worldwide gold standard over a century ago. It reports some lessons learned from that experience. The history leads into a description of the current system (or perhaps "nonsystem") in the final section of the chapter.

The Gold Standard Era, 1870–1914 (One Version of Fixed Rates)

Ever since 1914, the prewar gold standard has been the object of considerable nostalgia. In the decades after World War I, government officials in many countries believed that the experience of the gold standard proved the desirability of a fixed-exchange-rate system. Among scholars too, the "success" of the gold standard has been widely accepted and research has focused on *why,* not whether, it worked so well.

The international gold standard emerged by 1870 with the help of historical accidents centering on Britain. Britain tied the pound sterling ever more closely to gold than to silver from the late 17th century on, in part because Britain's official gold–silver value ratio was more favorable to gold than were the ratios of other countries, causing arbitrageurs to ship gold *to* Britain and silver *from* Britain. The link between the pound sterling and gold proved crucial. Britain's rise to primacy in industrialization and world trade in the 19th century enhanced the prestige of the metal tied to the currency of this leading country. Also, Britain had the advantage of not being invaded in wars, which further strengthened its image as the model of financial security and prudence. The prestige of gold was raised further by another lucky accident. The waves of gold discoveries both in the middle of the 19th century (California, Australia) and at the end of the century (South Africa, the Klondike) were small enough not to make gold suddenly too abundant to be a standard for international value. The silver-mining expansion of the 1870s and 1880s, by contrast, yielded too much silver, causing its value to plummet. Through such accidents, the gold standard, in which each national currency was fixed in gold content, remained intact from about 1870 until World War I.

Under the gold standard each country's government fixed its currency to a specified quantity of gold. The government also freely permitted individuals to exchange domestic currency for gold and to export and import gold. Through gold arbitrage the exchange rates between currencies then remained within a band (whose width reflected the transactions costs of gold movements between countries). Furthermore, changes in the government's gold holdings were linked to changes in the country's money supply—and thus to the country's average price level, its inflation rate, and other aspects of its macroeconomic performance.

The actual functioning of the gold standard was not this simple. Indeed, the process of actual payments adjustment under the prevailing fixed exchange rates puzzled Frank Taussig and his Harvard students after World War I. They found that international gold flows seemed to eliminate themselves very quickly, too quickly for their possible effects on national money supplies to change incomes, prices, and the balance of payments. The puzzle was heightened by the postwar finding of Arthur I. Bloomfield that central banks had done little to adjust their national economies to their exchange rates before 1914. Far from speeding up the economy's adjustment to payment surpluses or deficits, prewar central banks, similar to their successors in the interwar period, offset (sterilized) external reserve flows in the majority of cases, so that their national money supplies did not change much. What, then, actually kept the prewar balance of payments in line?

First, it must be noted that most countries were able to run payments surpluses before 1914, raising their holdings of gold and foreign exchange. This removed the cost of adjustment to fixed exchange rates because surplus countries were under little pressure to adjust. Widespread surpluses were made possible by, aside from the slow accumulation of newly mined gold in official vaults, the willingness and ability of Britain—and Germany to a lesser extent—to let the rest of the world hold growing amounts of its monetary liabilities. Between 1900 and 1913, for example, Britain ran payments deficits that were at least as large in relation to official (Bank of England) gold reserves as the deficits that caused so much hand-wringing in the United States in the 1960s. In fact, it would have been impossible for Britain to honor even one-third of its liquid liabilities to foreigners in 1913 by paying out official gold reserves. The gold standard was thus helped along considerably by the ability of the key-currency country to give the rest of the world liquid IOUs whose buildup nobody minded—or even measured.

There were times, of course, when Britain was called on to halt outflows of gold reserves that were more conspicuous than the unknown rise in its financial liabilities. The Bank of England showed an impressive ability to halt gold outflows within a few months, faster than it could have if it had needed to contract the whole British economy to improve the balance of payments. It appears that higher British interest rates, resulting from monetary tightening by the Bank of England, were capable of calling in large volumes of short-term capital from abroad, even when central banks in other countries raised their interest rates by the same percentage. This command over short-term capital seems to have been linked to London's being the financial center for the world's money markets. As the main short-term international lender (as well as borrower), London could contract the whole world's money supply in the short run if and when the Bank of England ordered private banks in London to do so. In this way, the prewar gold standard combined overall surplus for most countries with short-run defensive strength on the part of the main deficit country.

In retrospect, it is clear that the success of the gold standard is explained partly by the tranquility of the prewar era. The world economy was not subjected to shocks as severe as World Wars I and II, the Great Depression of the 1930s, and the OPEC oil price shocks of 1973–1974 and 1979–1980. *The gold standard looked successful, in part, because it was not put to a severe worldwide test.*

The prewar gold standard seemed to succeed for one other reason: *"Success"* was *leniently defined* in those days. Central banks were responsible only for fixing the gold exchange-rate value of the currency. Before World War I public opinion did not hold central bankers (or government officials) responsible for fighting unemployment or stabilizing prices. This easy assignment shielded officials from the policy dilemmas between defending a fixed exchange rate and stabilizing the domestic economy, which will be discussed in Chapter 23.

The pre-1914 tranquility also allowed some countries to have *favorable experiences with flexible exchange rates.* Several countries abandoned fixed exchange rates and gold convertibility in short-run crises. Britain itself did so during the Napoleonic

FIGURE 20.6
Selected
Exchange Rates,
1860–1913

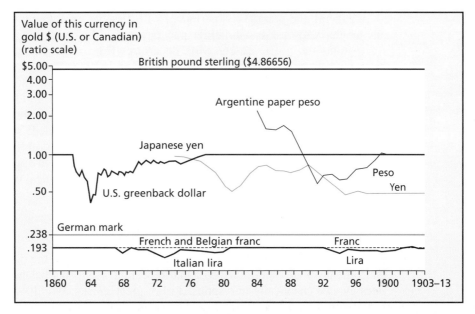

Sources: The data are annual averages of market exchange rates, except for the rates on the greenback dollar from 1862 through 1872, which are monthly averages for every third month. The Argentine paper peso rates are the John H. Williams gold premiums cited in Alec G. Ford, *The Gold Standard, 1880–1914: Great Britain and Argentina* (Oxford: Clarendon, 1962), p. 139. The Italian series is from Istituto Centrale di Statistica, *Sommario di Statistiche Storiche Italiane, 1861–1955* (Rome, 1958), p. 166. The gold value of the paper Japanese yen was calculated using the midrange New York dollar value of the metal-backed yen (Bank of Japan, Statistics Department, *Hundred Year Statistics of the Japanese Economy* [Tokyo, 1966], p. 318) and the average price of silver in paper yen for the period 1877–1886 (Henry Rosovsky, "Japan's Transition to Modern Economic Growth, 1868–1885," in *Industrialization in Two Systems*, ed. Henry Rosovsky [New York: Wiley, 1966], pp. 129 and 136). The U.S. greenback dollar series is the W. C. Mitchell series cited in Don C. Barrett, *The Greenback and Resumption of Specie Payments, 1862–1879* (Cambridge, Mass.: Harvard University Press, 1931, pp. 96–98). The virtually fixed rates are available in the *Economist* for prewar years.

Wars. Faced with heavy wartime financial needs, Britain suspended convertibility of the pound sterling into gold and let the pound drop by as much as 30 percent in value by 1813, restoring official gold convertibility after the wars. Other countries repeated the experience, as shown for selected countries in Figure 20.6. During the American Civil War, the North found itself unable to maintain the gold value of the paper dollar, given the tremendous need to print dollars to finance the war effort. The newly issued greenback dollars had dropped in value by more than 60 percent as of 1864, before beginning a long, slow climb back to gold parity in 1879 (accompanied by a substantial deflation of U.S. product prices). Heavy short-run financial needs also drove other countries off gold parity. War was the proximate culprit in the cases of Italy, Russia, and Austria-Hungary.

This experience with fixed and flexible exchange rates reveals some patterns. Most countries that abandoned fixed exchange rates did so in a context of growing payments deficits and reserve outflows. Note that in Figure 20.6 the end of fixed exchange rates was accompanied by a drop in the value of the national currency. This drop shows indirectly that *the fixed-rate gold standard imposed strain mostly on countries that were in payments deficit situations, not on countries in surplus.* Indeed, countries in surplus found it easy to continue accumulating reserves with a fixed exchange rate.

In general, the pre-1914 experiences with flexible exchange rates did not reveal any tendency toward destabilizing speculation. For the most part, the exchange-rate fluctuations did not represent wide departures from the exchange rate we would have predicted, given the movements in price indexes. Two possible exceptions relate to the U.S. greenback dollar and the Russian ruble. In 1864, the greenback dollar fell in value 49 percent between April and July, even though the wholesale price index rose less than 15 percent, suggesting that speculation greatly accelerated the drop in the greenback, which then promptly rebounded. Similarly, in 1888, political rumors caused a dive in the thinly marketed Russian ruble. With the exception of these two possible cases of destabilizing speculation, it appears that flexible rates were quite stable in the prewar setting, given the political events that forced governments to try them out.

Interwar Instability

If the gold standard era before 1914 has been viewed as the classic example of international monetary soundness, the interwar period has played the part of a nightmare that officials were determined to avoid repeating. Payments balances and exchange rates gyrated chaotically in response to two great shocks: World War I and the Great Depression. Figure 20.7 plots the exchange-rate history of the interwar period. The chaos was concentrated into two periods: the first few years after World War I (1919–1923) and the currency crisis in the depths of the Great Depression (1931–1934).

After World War I the European countries had to struggle with a legacy of inflation and political instability. Their currencies had become inconvertible during the war and their rates of inflation were much higher than that experienced in the United States, the new financial leader. In this setting, Britain made the fateful decision to return to its prewar gold parity, achieving this rate by April 1925. Although the decision has been defended as a moral obligation and as a sound attempt to restore international confidence as well as Britain's role at the center of a reviving world economy, the hindsight consensus is that bringing the pound back up to $4.86656 was a serious mistake. It appears to have caused considerable unemployment and stagnation in traded-goods industries, as theory would predict, because the high real exchange-rate value of the pound corresponded to a loss of international price competitiveness.

France, Italy, and some other European countries chose a more inflationary route for complicated political reasons. A succession of French revolving-door governments was unable to cut government spending or raise taxes to shut off large budgetary deficits that had to be financed largely by printing new money. Something similar happened in Italy, both before and immediately after the 1922 coup d'état that brought Mussolini to power. The ultimate in inflation, however, was experienced by Germany, where the money supply, prices, and cost of foreign exchange all rose more than a trillionfold in 1922–1923. Money became totally worthless, and by late 1923 not even a wheelbarrowful of paper money could buy a week's groceries. The mark had to be reissued in a new series equal to the prewar dollar value, with old marks forever unredeemable.

The early 1930s brought another breakdown of international currency relations. The financial community, already stunned by the early postwar chaos and the Wall Street collapse, became justifiably jittery about bank deposits and currencies as the Depression spread. The failure of the reputable Creditanstalt bank in Austria caused

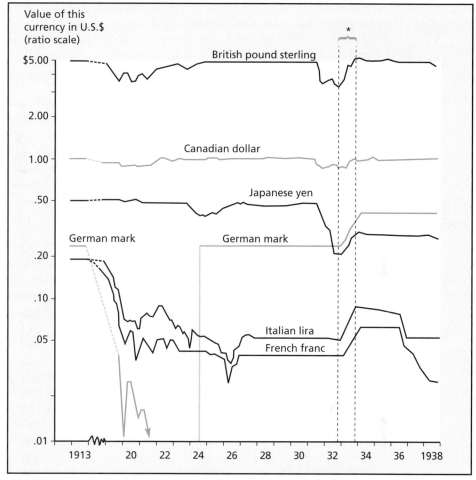

FIGURE 20.7
Selected Exchange Rates, 1913, 1919–1938 (Monthly)

Source: U.S. Federal Reserve Board, Board of Governors, *Banking and Monetary Statistics* (Washington, D.C., 1943).

*March 1933–February 1934: The United States raises the price of gold from $20.67 per ounce to $35 per ounce.

a run on German banks and on the mark because Germany had lent heavily to Austria. The panic soon led to an attack on the pound sterling, which had been perennially weak and was now compromised by Britain's making heavy loans to the collapsing Germans. On September 19, 1931, Britain abandoned the gold standard it had championed, letting the pound sink to its equilibrium market value. Between early 1933 and early 1934, the United States followed suit and let the dollar drop in gold value as President Franklin D. Roosevelt and his advisers manipulated the price of gold in an attempt to create jobs. Other countries also used devaluations, tariffs, and other trade restrictions to boost domestic employment. Such *beggar-thy-neighbor policies* (intended to benefit a country's economy at the expense of other countries) were widespread and probably added to worldwide depression (beggared almost everyone) as international trade shrank rapidly in the early 1930s.

What lessons does the interwar experience hold for policymakers? During World War II, expert opinion seemed to be that the interwar experience called for a compromise between fixed and flexible exchange rates, with emphasis on the former. Ragnar Nurkse, in his book *International Currency Experience,* written for the League of Nations in 1944, argued, with some qualifying disclaimers, that the interwar experience showed the instability of flexible exchange rates. Figure 20.7 adds some evidence to his premise: Exchange rates did indeed move more sharply during the interwar era than at any other time before the 1970s.

Yet subsequent studies have shown that a closer look at the interwar experience reveals the opposite lesson: *The interwar experience shows the futility of trying to keep exchange rates fixed in the face of severe shocks and the necessity of turning to flexible rates to cushion some of the international shocks.*

There is now general agreement that the working of the interwar gold standard contributed to the global spread of the Depression and made it more severe. In the late 1920s and early 1930s, the United States and France accumulated well over half the world's gold reserves, but they did not allow their domestic money supplies to increase. Instead, other countries, such as Britain, had to tighten their monetary policies to limit gold outflows. The pressure toward worldwide deflationary policies helped turn a recession into a nearly global depression. Then when Britain left the gold standard in 1931, the U.S. government responded by raising interest rates by 2 percentage points, to deter conversions of dollars into gold. With inappropriate contractionary monetary policy and widespread bank failures in the United States, the Depression deepened. As political pressure intensified to pursue other goals, like reducing domestic unemployment, central banks eventually gave up their defense of fixed rates. The gold standard ended, but not before much damage had been done.

Studies have also shown that, even during the unstable interwar era, speculation tended to be stabilizing—it was domestic monetary and fiscal policy that was destabilizing. This revisionist conclusion began to emerge from studies of Britain's fluctuating rates between 1919 and 1925. Both Leland Yeager and S. C. Tsiang found that the pound sterling fluctuated in ways that are easily explained by the effects of differential inflation on the trade balance. Relative to the exchange-rate movements that would be predicted by the purchasing power parity theory of the equilibrium exchange rate (see Chapter 19), the actual movements stayed close to the long-run trend. The cases in which Figure 20.7 shows rapid drops in currency values were cases in which the runaway expansion of the national money supply made this inevitable under any exchange-rate regime. This was true of France up until 1926; it was even more true, of course, of the German hyperinflation.

Closer looks at the currency instability of the early 1930s suggest a similar conclusion. The pound sterling, the yen, and other currencies dropped rapidly in 1931–1932 due to the gaping disequilibrium built into the fixed-exchange-rate system by the Depression (and, for Japan, by the invasion of Manchuria). Once fixed rates were abandoned, flexible rates merely reflected, rather than worsened, the varying health of national economies.

The Bretton Woods Era, 1944–1971 (Adjustable Pegged Rates)

Meeting at the Bretton Woods resort in New Hampshire in 1944, the monetary leaders of the Allied powers had an opportunity to design a better system. Everyone agreed that the system needed reform. The United States dominated the Bretton Woods

Global Governance   The International Monetary Fund

At the 1944 Bretton Woods conference, the governments of the 45 countries fashioned the Articles of Agreement for a new global monetary institution, the International Monetary Fund (IMF). The IMF began operating in 1946, and its membership has grown to 188 countries in 2014.

The IMF is owned by its member country governments. On joining the IMF, each member country contributes resources, called the country's *quota*. One-quarter of these contributed resources are assets generally recognized as official international reserves, and the other three-quarters are its own currency. The size of the quota is roughly related to the country's economic size, and the size of the quota determines the country's voting rights. The United States has about 17 percent of the voting rights, so the U.S. government has a veto power over certain decisions that require an 85 percent majority, especially amendments to the Articles of Agreement. Periodically the sizes of the quotas are increased to expand the IMF's financial resources. The IMF also can borrow from some of its members, and it receives voluntary contributions from some.

The IMF has several interlocking purposes. It promotes international monetary cooperation and the expansion of international trade among its members. It seeks to maintain orderly foreign exchange arrangements and to avoid competitive exchange-rate depreciations. It seeks to establish unrestricted convertibility of currencies for current account payments. And the IMF can make temporary loans to its members to provide time for them to correct international payments imbalances. Here we will look at the IMF's activities outside of its role as a lender to governments. A box in the next chapter examines IMF lending in depth.

ORDERLY FOREIGN EXCHANGE ARRANGEMENTS

The IMF's priorities and key activities have changed over time, as the international financial system has evolved. Initially, the IMF monitored the Bretton Woods system of fixed exchange rates, and it had

to approve if a country wanted to make a large devaluation or revaluation of the fixed rate for its currency. The IMF judged if the change was necessary and if it was of suitable magnitude to correct the fundamental disequilibrium.

With the demise of the Bretton Woods system of fixed exchange rates in the early 1970s, and the shift to the current "nonsystem" in which each country can set its own exchange-rate policies, the IMF had to search for a new way to pursue the objective of orderly exchange arrangements. The IMF has enunciated principles, including avoiding excessive exchange-rate volatility, refraining from manipulating exchange rates to prevent adjustment of the balance of payments or to gain unfair trade advantages, and avoiding ongoing exchange-rate misalignment that results from continual large official interventions in the foreign exchange market in one direction over a long period of time. To encourage compliance with these principles, the IMF conducts *surveillance* to monitor and to examine each member country's exchange-rate policies and its macroeconomic policies. However, the power of the IMF is limited. It can advise and recommend, but it cannot force a country to change its policies. There is no formal dispute system. Noncompliance could result in the IMF refusing to lend to a country, but many countries do not need to borrow and expect never to need to borrow from the IMF.

CURRENT ACCOUNT CONVERTIBILITY

In the aftermath of World War II, most countries had exchange controls on nearly all foreign transactions, so that international trade was inhibited. The IMF prodded countries to free up restrictions on foreign exchange transactions related to international trade and other current account transactions. By the early 1960s most industrialized countries had removed restrictions and achieved *current account convertibility*. A number of developing countries still have restrictions on current transactions, but the global trend is toward liberalization.

—Continued on next page

OTHER ACTIVITIES

Over time the IMF has taken on other activities. First, concerns about insufficient growth of the world's international reserve assets in the 1960s led the IMF to create Special Drawing Rights, described earlier in the chapter. The IMF made allocations that totaled 21 billion SDRs to its members in 1970–1972 and 1979–1981, and then allocations of another 183 billion SDRs in 2009. Even with the large 2009 allocations, the SDR is still only about 2 percent of the world's official international reserves (as shown in Figure 20.2).

Second, as a part of its role to promote international monetary cooperation, the IMF collects and publishes a broad range of national economic and financial data, presented in ways that make comparisons across countries easier. It also reports on and analyzes global economic trends and outlook, as well as global economic policy issues. Third, the IMF provides technical assistance and training in macroeconomic and financial sector policies, especially to government officials from low-income countries, as well as, in the 1990s, to officials from countries that were in transition from communism.

conference, just as it dominated the world economy and the world's gold reserves at the time. America wanted something like fixed exchange rates. Indeed, all leaders sought to get close to the virtuous fixed-exchange-rate case sketched in Figure 20.4. If only there were enough reserves to tide countries over temporary disequilibriums, and if only countries followed policies that made all disequilibriums temporary, we could capture those welfare gains from successful stabilization.

Two expert economists, John Maynard Keynes of Britain and Harry Dexter White of the United States, came up with workable plans to give the world a new central bank that would allow deficit countries enough reserves to ride out their temporary deficits. The grand design was fully fixed exchange rates defended by government intervention, with international reserves sufficient to permit defense by deficit countries. Keynes's plan also called for explicit automatic pressures on national governments running both surpluses and deficits to change their macroeconomic policies to serve the goal of balanced international payments.

In the end, however, the United States, Britain, and other governments could not accept the grand design. The Americans balked at putting billions of dollars at the disposal of other governments and at having to inflate the American economy just because it had a balance-of-payments surplus (as was then expected). Seeing the limits to what the Americans were prepared to give raised the fears of Britain and others about how they could adjust to their likely balance-of-payments deficits. In exchange, they insisted on the right to resort to devaluations and exchange controls when deficits threatened to persist.

The resulting compromise was what we have come to call the **Bretton Woods system.** Its central feature was the *adjustable peg,* which called for a fixed exchange rate and temporary financing out of international reserves unless a country's balance of payments was seen to be in "fundamental disequilibrium." A country in that condition might then change its "fixed" exchange rate to a new official par value that looked sustainable. The **International Monetary Fund (IMF)** was created as the global institution that promotes international monetary stability and lends reserves to member countries to finance temporary deficits. (The box "The International Monetary Fund" provides more information on the IMF and its activities.) The IMF is something like the global central bank that Keynes and White tried to design. Its resources and prerogatives, however, were more limited than Keynes and White envisioned. Also limited was the international community's ability to bend nations' macroeconomic policies to keep their international payments in line.

After the immediate postwar exchange-rate adjustments, which were completed by about 1950, the Bretton Woods system looked remarkably successful for almost two decades. Countries grew rapidly and unemployment stayed low. Most exchange rates stayed fixed for long time periods, as shown in Figure 20.8.

The strong economic growth probably contributed more to the look of success for monetary institutions than they contributed to the strong growth. The good growth climate was consistent with flexible exchange rates, too, to judge from the Canadian experience of managed floating during 1950–1962. As shown in Figure 20.8, the U.S. dollar–Canadian dollar exchange rate showed rather little movement. By itself this does not prove that the Canadian experience was one in which flexible rates worked well. However, detailed studies of Canada's floating rate have borne out this inference. Statistical analysis suggests that, if the exchange rate on the Canadian dollar had any effect on financial movements, this effect was in the stabilizing direction; that is, a lower value of the Canadian dollar tended to cause greater net capital inflows into Canada, as though investors expected the Canadian dollar to rise more when it was at

FIGURE 20.8

Selected Exchange Rates, 1950–1975 (Monthly)

Sources: For 1950–1956, Board of Governors of the Federal Reserve System, *Banking and Monetary Statistics, 1941–1970* (Washington, D.C., 1976); for 1957–1975, International Monetary Fund, *International Financial Statistics.*

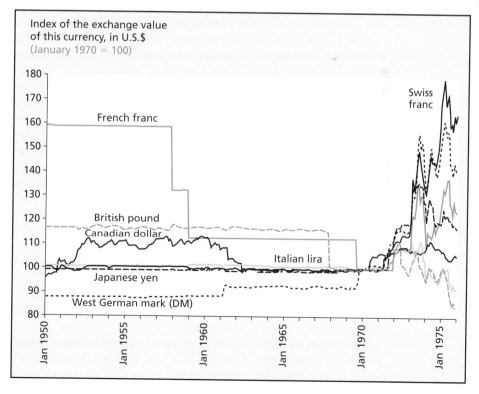

low levels. Other studies have confirmed that fluctuations in the exchange value of the Canadian dollar were no greater than we would have predicted by following movements in the relative U.S. and Canadian prices of traded goods. In this stable economic environment, the floating rate of the Canadian dollar was well behaved and almost as stable as the fixed rates of other currencies.

The One-Way Speculative Gamble

The postwar experience with adjustable pegged rates recorded only rare changes in exchange rates among major currencies up to 1971, as Figure 20.8 suggests. Yet the adjustable-peg system revealed a new pattern in private speculation, one that caused a great deal of official consternation. As the world economy grew, so did the volume of internationally mobile private funds. The new system of pegged but adjustable exchange rates spurred private speculators to attack currencies that were "in trouble." The adjustable-peg system then gave private speculators a one-way speculative gamble. It was always clear from the context whether a currency was in danger of being devalued or revalued. In the case of a devaluation-suspect currency, such as the pound sterling in the mid-1960s, the astute private speculator knew that the currency could not rise significantly in value. She thus had little to lose by selling the currency in the spot (or forward) market. If the currency did not drop in value, she had lost nothing but a slight gap between the domestic interest rate and the foreign interest rate (or between the forward rate and the spot rate), but if she was right and the currency was devalued, it might be devalued by a large percentage over a single weekend, bringing her a handsome return. In this situation, private speculators would gang up on a currency that was moving into a crisis phase.

This pattern of speculation under the adjustable-peg system meant serious difficulties for any government or central bank that was trying to cure a payments disequilibrium without adjusting the peg. A classic illustration of these difficulties was the attempt of Harold Wilson's Labor government to keep the pound worth $2.80 between 1964 and November 1967. When Wilson took office, he found that Britain's trade and payments balances were even worse than previous official figures had admitted. His government used numerous devices to make the pound worth $2.80: tighter exchange controls; higher interest rates; selective tax hikes; promises to cut government spending; and massive loans from the IMF, the United States, and other governments. Speculators who, in increasing number, doubted Britain's ability to shore up the pound were castigated by the chancellor of the Exchequer as "gnomes of Zurich." Yet, in the end, all of the belt-tightening and all of the support loans worked no better than had the attempt to make the pound worth $4.86656 from 1925 to 1931. On November 18, 1967, Britain devalued the pound by 14.3 percent, to $2.40. The gnomes had won handsomely. Those who had, for instance, been selling sterling forward at prices like $2.67 just before the devaluation were able to buy the same sterling at about $2.40, pocketing the 27 cents difference. The British government and its taxpayers lost a similar difference, by paying close to $2.80 to buy sterling that they had to concede was worth only $2.40 after November 18.

The existence of the one-way speculative gamble seems to make the adjustable peg of the Bretton Woods system look less sustainable than either purely fixed rates or purely flexible rates. If speculators believe that the government is willing to turn the entire economy inside out to defend the exchange rate, then they will not attack the exchange rate. Britain could have made speculators believe in $2.80 in the mid-1960s if it had shown its determination to slash the money supply and contract British incomes and jobs until $2.80 was truly an equilibrium rate. But as the speculators realized, few postwar governments are prepared to pay such national costs in the name of truly fixed exchange rates. Alternatively, the speculators might have been more cautious in betting against sterling if the exchange rate had been a floating equilibrium rate. With the float, speculators face a two-way gamble. Because the current spot exchange rate is an equilibrium rate and not an artificial official disequilibrium rate, the actual exchange rate in the future could turn out to be higher or lower than the current spot rate or the rate that speculators expect in the future.

Although the speculative attacks on an adjustable-pegged rate are certainly unsettling to officials, it is not clear that they should be called *destabilizing*. If the official defense of a currency is primarily just a way to postpone an inevitable devaluation and not a way to raise the equilibrium value of the currency, then it could be said that the speculative attack is stabilizing in the sense that it hastens the transition to a new equilibrium rate. Whether it performs this stabilizing function is uncertain, however. Officials may be induced to overreact to the speculative attack and to overdevalue the pegged rate.

The Dollar Crisis

The postwar growth of the international economy led to a crisis involving the key currency of the system, the U.S. dollar. Under the Bretton Woods system, other countries effectively pegged their currencies to the U.S. dollar. The dollar became the major reserve currency, and the U.S. government was committed to exchanging the dollars held as reserves by other countries' monetary authorities for gold at an official price of $35 per ounce. (The system is sometimes described as a *gold-exchange standard.*)

As the European and Japanese economies recovered from the war, and as their firms gained in competitive ability relative to that of U.S. firms, the U.S. payments position shifted into large official settlements balance deficits. In part, those deficits represented the fact that the monetary authorities of other countries wanted to run surpluses to increase their international reserves as international transactions generally grew rapidly. After a time, however, the deficits became a source of official concern in Europe and Japan. More and more dollars ended up in official hands. Something like this had happened in 1914, when other countries accumulated growing official reserves of sterling. In the postwar setting, however, few governments felt that they could be as relaxed about the gold backing of the U.S. dollar as the rest of the world had felt about the link between gold and Britain's pound before 1914. U.S. gold reserves dwindled as France led the march to Fort Knox (actually, the basement of the New York Federal Reserve Bank), demanding gold for dollar claims. It became questionable whether the U.S. dollar was worth as much gold as the official gold price implied.

In this situation, the United States had the option of shrinking the U.S. economy until foreign central banks were constrained to supply gold to the United States to pay for U.S. exports. Other alternatives were tight exchange controls and devaluing the dollar in terms of gold. Exchange controls were tried to a limited extent (in the form of the Interest Equalization Tax on lending abroad, the "Voluntary" Foreign Credit Restraint Program, and the like), but these controls ran counter to the official

U.S. stance of encouraging free mobility of capital between countries. Devaluation of the dollar in terms of gold would have marked up the dollar value of U.S. gold reserves but also would have brought politically distasteful windfall gains to the Soviet Union and South Africa (the two major gold producers).

Faced with these choices under the existing international rules, the United States opted for changing the rules. On March 17, 1968, a seven-country meeting hastily called by the United States announced the "two-tier" gold price system. The private price of gold in London, Zurich, and other markets was now free to fluctuate in response to supply and demand. The official price for transactions among the seven agreeing governments would still be $35 an ounce. Nonetheless, the U.S. overall payments deficits continued and had to be financed by increasing sales of U.S. foreign exchange reserves. Eventually, the United States would have to adjust, by restraining its economy, imposing exchange controls, or changing the international monetary rules. Again, the United States chose to change the rules.

In August 1971, President Nixon suspended convertibility of dollars into gold, effectively severing the official gold–dollar price link. He also imposed a 10 percent temporary additional tariff on all imports coming into the United States, to remain in place until other countries agreed to revalue their currencies against the dollar (so that the dollar was similarly devalued). Most major currencies then floated against the dollar until December 1971, when the Smithsonian Agreement attempted to patch the system back together. Under this agreement the DM was revalued by about 17 percent, the yen by about 13 percent, and other currencies by smaller percentages, overall creating an effective devaluation of the dollar of close to 10 percent, and the United States removed its import surcharge. The official dollar price of gold also was raised to $38 per ounce, but this was symbolic because the suspension continued. The agreement failed to save the system. By March 1973, most major currencies shifted to floating against the dollar. After effectively ending in 1971, the pegged-exchange-rate regime known as the Bretton Woods system was officially abandoned in 1973.

The Current System: Limited Anarchy

The current system is sometimes described as a *managed floating regime.* Since the early 1970s, a growing number of countries, including many major industrialized countries, have floating or relatively flexible exchange rates, but government authorities often attempt to have an impact through intervention or some other form of management of the floating or flexible exchange rates.

A noteworthy feature of the experience since 1973 is the extent of official resistance to floating. Some of this resistance is seen in the management of the float. For instance, at various times since 1973, the government of Japan has tried to hold down the dollar value of the yen, apparently to prevent a loss in the international price competitiveness of Japanese products. In the process, the Japanese central bank has bought huge numbers of dollars (which subsequently declined in yen value, anyway, as the yen did appreciate against the dollar). Another part of the resistance is seen in the substantial number of countries that continue to peg their currencies to the dollar or to other currencies.

The European Union has been a center of resistance to floating exchange rates, at least for the cross-rates among the EU currencies. The governments of the European

Economic Community (the forerunner of the European Union) strove to prevent movements in exchange rates among their currencies, first setting up the "snake" within the "tunnel" in December 1971. They agreed on maximum ranges of movement of the most appreciated versus the most depreciated member currency (the tunnel) and on maximum bands within which pairwise exchange rates could oscillate (the snake). This scheme was short-lived. Britain, Italy, and France soon allowed their currencies to drop well below the tunnel, leaving only a fixed set of exchange rates between the West German mark and the currencies of the Benelux countries. The governments of the European Community then developed a successor scheme, the Exchange Rate Mechanism (ERM) of the European Monetary System, in 1979. In the early 1990s, the governments of the European Union established a process for moving toward permanently fixed exchange rates and a single currency. At the beginning of 1999, the new common currency, the euro, came into existence, and in 2002 it replaced the national currencies of 12 of the then 15 EU countries.

The official desire for fixed or managed exchange rates has remained strong, but fixed or steady rates have been hard to maintain. Once the Bretton Woods system broke down, the U.S. government switched to advocacy of floating rates. It often (e.g., in the early 1970s, 1980–1984, and 1995–2014) has followed a policy of "benign neglect" toward the exchange-rate value of the dollar, with almost no official exchange-market intervention by U.S. monetary authorities during these long periods of time. At other times, especially in the late 1980s, the U.S. government has been active in managing the dollar float. After the dollar soared in value during 1981–1985, the U.S. government participated in two major international accords to manage exchange rates through coordinated intervention. The first accord, the Plaza Agreement of September 1985, was intended to promote a decline in the exchange-rate value of the dollar, and the dollar did fall. The second accord, the Louvre Agreement of February 1987, was intended to stabilize the exchange-rate value of the dollar against other major currencies. Formal coordination faded by the early 1990s, and as we have seen, exchange rates between the dollar and other major currencies still oscillate widely at times.

The series of exchange-rate crises in the 1990s and early 2000s shows how difficult it is to defend pegged rates or heavily managed floating rates in the face of large flows of private funds. When speculators believe they have spotted attempts by officials to maintain unrealistic exchange rates, they have a one-way speculative gamble that can overwhelm the defenses of the monetary authorities.

The first major crisis of the 1990s centered on the European Union. In the early 1990s, all EU countries but Greece had joined the ERM system of pegged rates among these currencies. (In addition, several European countries, including Sweden and Finland, also pegged to this system, although they were not formally part of it.) Following the shock of German reunification and the subsequent tight monetary policy followed by Germany, a major speculative attack hit the ERM in 1992 and 1993. Governments mounted defenses that included massive intervention, high short-term interest rates, and tightening of capital controls. Nonetheless, Britain and Italy surrendered and dropped out of the ERM in 1992, and Sweden and Finland ceased their peg to it. Several other currencies that remained in the system were devalued in 1992 and 1993. In addition, the bands for most currencies that remained in the system were widened in 1993 to 15 percent on each side of the central rate (from 2.25 percent) to deter speculation by permitting more room for the pegged rate to fluctuate.

During 1994–2002, a series of exchange crises hit developing countries, resulting in dramatic devaluations of pegged exchange rates or depreciations following abandonment of pegged or heavily managed rates. Here we provide a summary. We examine these crises in depth in the next chapter.

As discussed earlier in this chapter, after using a large part of its official reserve holdings to defend the peso exchange rate, the Mexican government had to abandon its heavily managed rate in late 1994. The CFA franc, a currency used by 13 African countries, was devalued by 50 percent in 1994, after it had been pegged at the same rate to the French franc for 45 years. In 1996, the Venezuelan government abandoned its pegged rate, and the bolivar declined by 42 percent in one day. In May 1997, the Czech government, after spending about 30 percent of its international reserves to defend the pegged rate it had maintained for 6 years, shifted to a floating exchange rate, and the koruna declined by about 10 percent during the first few days of the float.

In 1997, the Asian crisis hit. In July the Thai government gave up its pegged exchange rate for the Thai baht. By the end of the year the baht's value had fallen by 45 percent against the U.S. dollar. Then the Malaysian government floated its currency, and the ringgit fell by 35 percent. Soon Indonesia switched to a float, and the rupiah fell by 47 percent. In November the Korean government gave up its defense of the won, whose value then fell by 48 percent.

In 1998, the Russian government shifted to a floating rate and the ruble declined by 60 percent in value against the dollar in about a month and a half. From April 1998 to January 1999, the Brazilian government used about half of its official reserves defending the pegged value of the real. Capital outflows and other speculative pressures increased, and Brazil shifted to a floating rate in January 1999. In two and a half weeks the real declined by 39 percent. In early 2001 the Turkish government abandoned the pegged exchange rate for the lira, and its value fell by almost half during the year. In early 2002 the Argentinean government shifted to a floating exchange rate for its peso. The value of the peso plummeted, and Argentina's economy imploded.

After all of these schemes and crises, what is the current international monetary system? Perhaps it is best to describe it as a nonsystem—countries can choose almost any exchange-rate policies they want and change them whenever they want. The policies of various countries in mid-2013 are shown in Figure 20.9.

Column 1 in Figure 20.9 shows 17 countries that use some other country's currency as their own. (We examine this "dollarization" as an extreme form of a fixed exchange rate in Chapter 25.) Columns 2 and 3 show the 17 EU countries that use the euro as their currency, and the 24 countries whose currencies are pegged to the euro. Among these 24 countries are the EU members that participate in the continuation of the Exchange Rate Mechanism and the African countries that use the CFA franc. (At the beginning of 2014, Latvia joined the euro area, so it shifted from column 3 to column 2.)

Column 4 shows 43 countries that peg their currencies to the U.S. dollar. Column 5 shows 6 countries that peg to some other single currency, usually the currency of a larger neighboring country. Column 6 shows 12 countries that peg to a basket of currencies. The 17 countries shown in column 7 use a crawling pegged exchange rate in which the pegged value is changed frequently.

FIGURE 20.9 Exchange-Rate Arrangements, May 1, 2013[1]

		Currency Pegged To						
(1)	(2)	(3)	(4)	(5)	(6)	(7)	(8)	(9)
Use Foreign Currency (no separate local currency)[2]	Euro Area (use euro as currency)[3]	Euro[3]	U.S. Dollar	Other Currency	Currency Basket	Crawling Peg	Managed Float	Free Float
Andorra	Austria	**ERM II**	Angola	Bhutan (Indian rupee)	Algeria	Argentina	Afghanistan	Australia
Ecuador	Belgium	Denmark	Antigua & Barbuda	Brunei Darussalam (Singapore dollar)	Fiji	Botswana	Albania	Canada
El Salvador	Cyprus	Latvia	Aruba	Lesotho (S. African rand)	Iran	China	Armenia	Chile
Kiribati	Estonia	Lithuania	Azerbaijan	Namibia (S. African rand)	Kuwait	Croatia	Belarus	Czech Republic
Kosovo	Finland	**CFA Franc Zone**	Bahamas	Nepal (Indian rupee)	Libya	Dominican Republic	Brazil	Israel
Liechtenstein	France	Benin	Bahrain	Swaziland (S. African rand)	Morocco	Egypt	Burundi	Japan
Marshall Islands	Germany	Burkina Faso	Bangladesh		Myanmar	Ethiopia	Colombia	Mexico
Micronesia	Greece	Cameroon	Barbados		Samoa	Haiti	Gambia	Norway
Monaco	Ireland	Central African Rep.	Belize		Solomon Islands	Honduras	Ghana	Poland
Montenegro	Italy	Chad	Bolivia		Syria	Indonesia	Guinea	Somalia
Nauru	Luxembourg	Congo, Rep. of	Cambodia		Tonga	Jamaica	Hungary	Sweden
Palau	Malta	Cote d'Ivoire	Congo, Dem. Rep. of		Vanuatu	Kazakhstan	Iceland	United Kingdom
Panama	Netherlands	Equatorial Guinea	Costa Rica			Nicaragua	India	United States
San Marino	Portugal	Gabon	Curaçao and Sint Maarten			Rwanda	Kenya	
Timor-Leste	Slovak Republic	Guinea-Bissau	Djibouti			Singapore	Korea, South	
Tuvalu	Slovenia	Mali	Dominica			Tunisia	Kyrgyz Republic	
Zimbabwe	Spain	Niger	Eritrea			Uzbekistan	Liberia	
		Senegal	Georgia				Madagascar	
		Togo	Grenada				Malawi	
		Other	Guyana				Malaysia	
		Bosnia and Herzegovina	Hong Kong				Mauritania	
		Bulgaria	Iraq				Mauritius	
		Cape Verde	Jordan				Moldova	
		Comoros	Lao PDR				Mongolia	
		Macedonia	Lebanon				Mozambique	
		São Tomé & Principe	Maldives				New Zealand	
		Switzerland[4]	Oman				Nigeria	
			Qatar				Pakistan	
			St. Kitts & Nevis				Papua New Guinea	
			St. Lucia				Paraguay	
			St. Vincent & the Grenadines				Peru	
			Saudi Arabia				Philippines	
			South Sudan				Romania	
			Sudan				Russia	
			Suriname				Serbia	
			Tajikistan				Seychelles	
			Trinidad & Tobago				Sierra Leone	
			Turkmenistan				South Africa	
			Ukraine				Sri Lanka	
			United Arab Emirates				Tanzania	
			Venezuela				Thailand	
			Vietnam				Turkey	
			Yemen				Uganda	
							Uruguay	
							Zambia	

[1]Classification of each country is based on the country's actual (de facto) policy, as determined by the International Monetary Fund. For some countries the classification differs from the country's official (de jure) stated policy.

[2]These countries are often called "dollarized." All but Andorra, Kosovo, Monaco, Montenegro, and San Marino (euro); Kiribati, Nauru, and Tuvalu (Australian dollar); and Liechtenstein (Swiss franc) use the U.S. dollar as their currency.

[3]Latvia joined the euro area on January 1, 2014.

[4]One-sided arrangement, the Swiss National Bank does not allow the exchange rate value to fall below 1.2 Swiss francs per euro.

Source: International Monetary Fund, *Annual Report on Exchange Arrangements and Exchange Restrictions, 2013.*

Moving to the other end of the spectrum, column 9 shows 13 countries whose exchange rates are floating and mainly determined by market supply and demand. Included here are a number of industrialized countries. Column 8 shows that 46 countries have floating rates that are rather heavily managed. The monetary authorities of these countries influence the exchange rates through active intervention without committing to announced exchange-rate targets. The number of countries with floating exchange rates has grown during the past decades. In 1991, only 36 countries had floating exchange rates. By 2013 this number had risen to 59 countries (combining columns 8 and 9).

In summary, under the current system each country chooses its own exchange-rate policy. Two major blocs of currencies exist: currencies pegged to the U.S. dollar and currencies pegged to the euro. The exchange rates among the U.S. dollar, the euro, and such other major currencies as the Japanese yen, British pound, and Canadian dollar are floating rates, with some (usually small) amount of official management. Economists are still debating the merits and demerits of this "nonsystem," as well as the strengths and weaknesses of the policy choices made by individual countries. Critics of floating rates start at the obvious point: Floating exchange rates have fluctuated "a lot," "more than anyone expected." But pegged exchange rates have sometimes been difficult to maintain, so they are prone to currency crises.

Summary

The two major aspects of government policy toward the foreign exchange market are the degree of exchange-rate flexibility and restrictions (if any) on use of the market. Foreign exchange restrictions are called **exchange controls.**

Policies toward the exchange rate itself cover a spectrum. The polar case of complete flexibility is a **clean float,** with the exchange rate determined solely by nonofficial (or private) supply and demand. Governments often do not allow a clean float, but rather take actions (such as **official intervention**) to **manage** (or **dirty**) the float.

The other kind of exchange-rate policy is a **fixed,** or **pegged, exchange rate.** The government must decide what to fix to. The alternatives include a commodity like gold, a single other currency, and a basket of other currencies. The government also must decide the width of a band around the central fixed rate. The exchange rate has some flexibility around this par value, but the flexibility is limited by the size of the band. Although a permanently fixed rate is a polar case, it is nearly impossible for a government to commit never to change the fixed rate. If the exchange rate is not permanently fixed, then the government must also decide when to change the fixed rate. If the answer is seldom, the approach is called an **adjustable peg;** if often, it is called a **crawling peg.**

If the government chooses a fixed exchange rate, it must also decide how to defend the rate if private supply and demand pressures tend to push the actual rate outside the allowable band. One or more of four ways can be used to defend the fixed rate:

1. Use official intervention in the foreign exchange market, in which the monetary authority buys and sells currencies to alter the supply and demand situation.
2. Impose exchange controls to restrict or control some or all aspects of supply and demand.

3. Alter domestic interest rates to influence short-term capital flows.
4. Adjust the macroeconomy to alter nonofficial supply and demand.

The government may also exercise a fifth option—to surrender by changing the fixed rate (revaluation or devaluation) or by shifting to a floating exchange rate.

Government intervention in the foreign exchange market is closely related to official reserves transactions and the official settlements balance of the country's balance of payments. If the government attempts to prevent the exchange-rate value of its currency from declining, it must buy domestic currency and sell foreign currency in the foreign exchange market. The government can use its official reserve holdings as a source of foreign currency to sell in the intervention or it can borrow. This provides the financing for the country to run an official settlements balance deficit. If instead the government attempts to prevent the exchange-rate value of its currency from rising, it must sell domestic currency and buy foreign currency. The government can use the foreign currency that it buys to increase its official reserve holdings (or to repay past borrowings). The country's official settlements balance is in surplus.

Official intervention in the foreign exchange market also changes the country's money supply because the monetary authority is adding or removing domestic money as it carries out the intervention. The authority can use **sterilization** of the intervention to reverse the effect on the domestic money supply by taking some other action to remove or add the domestic money back to the economy.

Defense of the fixed rate using only intervention can work and make economic sense if the imbalances in the official settlements balance are temporary. This approach assumes that private speculators cannot perform the same stabilizing function and that officials correctly foresee the sustainable long-run value for the exchange rate. If these assumptions do not hold, the case for financing deficits and surpluses with a fixed exchange rate is weakened.

Defense using exchange control creates deadweight loss similar to that of an import quota, and it probably has high administrative costs. Efforts to evade exchange controls, including bribery of government officials and the development of an illegal **parallel market,** reduce the actual effectiveness of the controls.

The success or failure of different exchange-rate regimes has depended historically on the severity of the shocks with which those systems have had to cope. The fixed-rate **gold standard** seemed successful before 1914, largely because the world economy itself was more stable than in the period that followed. Many countries were able to keep their exchange rates fixed because they were lucky enough to be running surpluses at established exchange rates without having to generate those surpluses using contractionary macroeconomic policies. The main deficit-running country, Britain, could control international reserve flows in the short run by controlling credit in London, but it was never called upon to defend sterling against sustained attack. During the stable prewar era, even floating-exchange-rate regimes showed stability (with two brief possible exceptions).

The interwar economy was chaotic enough to put any currency regime to a severe test. Fixed rates broke down, and governments that believed in fixed rates were forced into flexible exchange rates. Studies of the interwar period show that the workings of the gold standard contributed to the depth of the Great Depression. Studies also show that speculation tended to be stabilizing. The large currency fluctuations were caused by the lingering economic effects of the first world war and by the instability of domestic monetary and fiscal policies in a number of countries.

Postwar experience showed some difficulties with the **Bretton Woods system** of adjustable pegged exchange rates set up in 1944. Under this system, private speculators were given a strong incentive to attack reserve-losing currencies and force large devaluations. The role of the dollar as a reserve currency also became increasingly strained in the Bretton Woods era. Under Bretton Woods, foreign central banks acquired large holdings of dollars through official intervention, when the United States shifted to running official settlements balance deficits. At first, these were welcomed as additions to official reserve holdings in these foreign countries, but the dollars became unwanted as the reserves grew too large. Foreign central banks' conversions of dollars into gold decreased U.S. official gold holdings, further reducing foreign officials' confidence in the dollar. The United States had to adjust its balance-of-payments position or change the rules. The United States opted for new rules, divorcing the private gold market from the official gold price in 1968, suspending gold convertibility and forcing a devaluation of the dollar in 1971, and shifting to general floating in 1973.

The current exchange-rate system permits each country to choose its own exchange-rate policy. Two major blocs exist, one of currencies pegged to the U.S. dollar and the other of the euro and currencies pegged to it. The euro is the successor to previous schemes, including the Exchange Rate Mechanism of the European Monetary System, as the countries that are members of the EU seek a zone of exchange-rate stability for transactions within the union.

The dollar bloc and the euro bloc float against each other, and the currencies of a number of industrialized countries—Australia, Canada, Japan, New Zealand, Sweden, and the United Kingdom—float independently. For countries with flexible exchange rates, most governments are skeptical of purely market-driven exchange rates, and they practice some degree of management of the floating rate.

Many developing countries have a pegged exchange rate of some sort, but the trend is toward greater flexibility and floating. A series of exchange-rate crises in the 1990s and early 2000s, including the Mexican peso in 1994, the Asian crisis (Thai baht, Malaysian ringgit, Indonesian rupiah, and South Korea won) in 1997, the Russian ruble in 1998, the Brazilian real in 1999, the Turkish lira in 2001, and the Argentinean peso in 2002, show the difficulty of defending a pegged rate against speculative flows of short-term capital when the speculators have a **one-way speculative gamble** against a currency that they believe is misvalued.

Key Terms			
	Exchange control	Pegged exchange rate	Bretton Woods system
	Capital controls	Adjustable peg	International Monetary
	Clean float	Crawling peg	Fund (IMF)
	Official intervention	Reserve currency	One-way speculative
	Managed float	Sterilization	gamble
	Dirty float	Sterilized intervention	
	Special drawing right	Parallel market	
	(SDR)	Gold standard	

<table>
<tr><td>

Suggested
Reading
</td><td>

Information on each country's policies toward the foreign exchange market can be found in the IMF's *Annual Report on Exchange Arrangements and Exchange Restrictions.* Edison et al. (2004) and Schindler (2009) examine capital controls.

For broad surveys of international currency experience during the past century, see McKinnon (1993 and 1996) and Giovannini (1989). The prewar gold standard is analyzed in more depth in Bloomfield (1959), Lindert (1969), and Bordo and Schwartz (1984). Meissner (2005) offers a statistical examination of the timing of countries' adoptions of the gold standard. Irwin (2012) links the gold standard to rising protectionism during the Great Depression.

A masterly survey of the interwar experience is Eichengreen (1992). Pioneering studies of the stability of fluctuating exchange rates in the interwar period are Yeager (1958), Tsiang (1959), and Aliber (1962).

For more detail on the Bretton Woods era, see Bordo and Eichengreen (1992). The dollar crisis under the Bretton Woods system was predicted and diagnosed in Robert Triffin's classic work (1960) and by Jacques Rueff (translation, 1972). Eichengreen (2007) considers how experiences under the Bretton Woods system illuminate current international monetary issues. Eichengreen (2011) discusses the history and the future of the U.S. dollar in the international monetary system.

Reinhart and Rogoff (2004) reassess exchange-rate policies since 1949. Calvo and Reinhart (2002) document the heavy management of floating exchange rates since 1973. Agénor (2004) examines the experiences of countries that exit from fixed-exchange-rate policies.
</td></tr>
</table>

Questions and Problems

◆ 1. What is the difference between a clean float and a managed float?

2. What is the difference between an adjustable peg and a crawling peg?

◆ 3. For a country that is attempting to maintain a fixed exchange rate, what is the difference between a temporary disequilibrium and a fundamental disequilibrium? Contrast the implications of each type of disequilibrium for official intervention in the foreign exchange market to defend the fixed exchange rate.

4. "The emergence of expectations that a country in the near future will impose exchange controls will probably result in upward pressure on the exchange-rate value of the country's currency." Do you agree or disagree? Why?

◆ 5. A government has just imposed a total set of exchange controls to prevent the exchange-rate value of its currency from declining. What effects and further developments do you predict?

6. The Pugelovian government is attempting to peg the exchange-rate value of its currency (the pnut) at a rate of three pnuts per U.S. dollar (plus or minus 2 percent). Unfortunately, private market supply and demand are putting downward pressure on the pnut's exchange-rate value. In fact, it appears that, under current market conditions, the exchange rate would be about 3.5 pnuts per dollar if the government did not defend the pegged rate.

   a. How could the Pugelovian government use official intervention in the foreign exchange market to defend the pegged exchange rate?

   b. How could the Pugelovian government use exchange controls to defend the pegged exchange rate?

   c. How could the Pugelovian government use domestic interest rates to defend the pegged exchange rate?

◆ 7. The Moroccan monetary authority is using a heavily managed float to keep the dirham at U.S.$0.12 per dirham. Under current foreign exchange market conditions, nonofficial supply and demand would clear at U.S.$0.15 per dirham.

   a. Using official intervention, what does the Moroccan monetary authority have to do to keep the exchange rate at U.S.$0.12 per dirham?

   b. If the monetary authority believes that this is a temporary disequilibrium, what does the authority expect to happen soon?

   c. If private investors and speculators believe that this is a fundamental disequilibrium, what actions are they likely to take?

8. The Danish central bank is committed to maintaining a fixed exchange rate of 7.46 Danish krone per euro, with a band of 2.25 percent on each side of this central rate. Under current conditions in the foreign exchange market, nonofficial supply and demand would intersect at a rate of about 7.1 krone per euro. The Danish central bank has sufficient international reserve assets and uses official intervention to defend the fixed rate.

   a. Draw a demand and supply graph of the foreign exchange market showing the central rate (7.46 krone per euro) and the positions of the nonofficial supply and demand curves.

   b. As a result of the official intervention, what will be the change in Denmark's holdings of international reserves? In your explanation, refer to your graph.

   c. If the Danish central bank does not sterilize its intervention, will the Danish money supply tend to increase, stay the same, or decrease? Why?

◆ 9. Under the gold standard the fixed price of gold was $20.67 per ounce in the United States. The fixed price of gold was £4.2474 per ounce in Britain.

   a. What is the "fixed" exchange rate (dollars per pound) implied by these fixed gold prices?

   b. How would you arbitrage if the exchange rate quoted in the foreign exchange market were $4.00 per pound? (Under the gold standard, you could buy or sell gold with each central bank at the fixed price of gold in each country.)

   c. What pressure is placed on the exchange rate by this arbitrage?

10. Consider the international currency experience for the period of the gold standard before 1914.

   a. What type of exchange-rate system was the gold standard and how did it operate?

   b. What country was central to the system? What was the role of this country in the success of the currency system?

   c. What was the nature of economic shocks during this period?

   d. What is the evidence on speculation and speculative pressures on exchange rates during this period?

◆ 11. What are the key features of the international currency experience in the period between the two world wars? What lessons did policymakers learn from this experience? Why are these lessons now questioned and debated?

12. Consider the international currency experience for the Bretton Woods era from 1944 to the early 1970s.

   a. What type of exchange-rate system was the Bretton Woods system? How did it operate?

    b. What country was central to the system? What was the role of this country in the success of the currency system?

    c. What is the evidence on speculation and speculative pressures on exchange rates during this period?

✦ 13. Why did the Bretton Woods system of fixed exchange rates collapse?

  14. The current exchange-rate regime is sometimes described as a system of managed floating exchange rates, but with some blocs of currencies that are tied together.

    a. What are the two major blocs of currencies that are tied together?

    b. What are the major currencies that float against each other?

    c. Given the discussion in this chapter and the previous Chapters 17–19, how would you characterize the movements of exchange rates between the U.S. dollar and the other major currencies since the shift to managed floating in the early 1970s?

Chapter Twenty-One

International Lending and Financial Crises

International financial capital flows have grown rapidly in the past several decades. The lenders (or investors) give the borrowers money to be used now in exchange for IOUs or ownership shares entitling them to interest and dividends later. International flows of financial claims are conventionally divided into different categories by type of lender or investor (private versus official), maturity (long-term versus short-term), existence of management control (direct versus portfolio), and type of borrower (private or government). For the first three distinctions, here are the key categories:

A. Private lending and investing
   1. Long-term
      a. Direct investment (lending to, or purchasing shares in, a foreign enterprise largely owned and controlled by the investor)
      b. Loans (to a foreign borrower, maturity more than one year, mostly by banks)
      c. Portfolio investment (purchasing stock or bonds with maturity of more than one year, issued by a foreign government or a foreign enterprise not controlled by the investor)
   2. Short-term (lending to a foreign borrower, or purchasing bonds issued by a foreign government or a foreign enterprise not controlled by the investor, maturing in a year or less)
B. Official lending and investing (by a government or a multilateral institution like the International Monetary Fund or the World Bank, mostly lending, both long-term and short-term)

In this chapter we take a close look at the causes and effects of bank lending and portfolio investment. (Foreign direct investment and the role of management control received their own separate analysis in Chapter 15.)

International lending and investing have been revolutionized. From before World War II to the early 1980s, the main lender was the United States, joined in the 1970s by the newly rich oil exporters. Since the early 1980s, the United States has been the world's largest net borrower, and the oil exporters also were net borrowers during 1983–1995. The dominant net lenders since 1980 have been Japan and Germany. With the rise of crude oil prices since the late 1990s, the oil exporting countries once again have become large lenders. The major type of lending has been private loans and portfolio investments, a shift from the official loans from governments and foreign direct investment that were dominant from the late 1940s to the early 1970s.

International lending can bring major benefits of two types. First, it represents intertemporal trade, in which the lender gives up resources today in order to get more in the future, and the borrower gets resources today but must be willing to pay back more in the future. Second, it allows lenders and investors to diversify their investments more broadly. The ability to add foreign financial assets to investment portfolios can lower the riskiness of the entire portfolio of investments through greater diversification. The chapter begins with an analysis of some of the benefits of international lending and borrowing. We focus on the benefits of intertemporal trade that takes advantage of different rates of return in different countries.

International lending is not always well behaved. International lending to developing countries swings between surges of lending and crises of confidence. During the financial crises, lending shrinks and lenders scramble to get repaid. The middle sections of the chapter examine the series of major crises that hit developing countries during 1982–2002. After describing the crises, we explore why these financial crises occur, how we try to resolve them, and what we might be able to do to make them less frequent.

Industrialized countries also experience financial crises. The final section of the chapter discusses the global financial and economic crisis that began in 2007 and intensified in 2008, noting similarities between crises in developing countries and what set off and spread the global crisis. A box toward the end of the chapter surveys the causes of the euro crisis that began in 2010.

GAINS AND LOSSES FROM WELL-BEHAVED INTERNATIONAL LENDING

If the world is stable and predictable, and if borrowers fully honor their commitments to repay, then international lending can be efficient from a world point of view, bringing gains to some that outweigh losses to others. In such a world, the welfare effects of international lending are parallel to the welfare effects of opening trade or those of allowing free labor migration.

Figure 21.1 shows the normal effects of allowing free international lending and borrowing. We divide the world into two large countries: "Japan," having abundant financial wealth and less attractive domestic investment opportunities, and an "America" in the image of Argentina, Brazil, Canada, and the United States, having less wealth relative to its abundant opportunities for profitable investment (for instance, in its new technologies or its open areas rich in natural resources). The length of the horizontal axis in Figure 21.1 shows total world wealth, equal to Japan's wealth (W_J) plus America's wealth (W_A). This wealth is used to finance capital investments. The vertical axes indicate rates of return earned on capital investments. (We often refer to an equilibrium rate of the return as the interest rate, although it may also incorporate the return to equity investment.) Capital investment opportunities in Japan are shown as the marginal-product-of-capital curve MPK_{Japan}, which begins at the left vertical

FIGURE 21.1

Gains and
Losses from
Well-Behaved
International
Lending

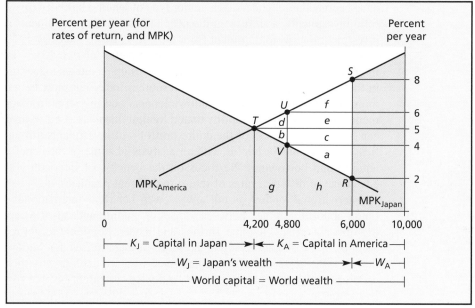

From no international lending (RS) to free lending (T):
   Japan   gains ($a + b + c$) = 27
   America gains ($d + e + f$) = 27
   World   gains (a through f) = 54
If Japan imposes a 2 percent per year tax on lending abroad (from T to UV):
   Japan   gains ($e - b$)   = 9
   America loses ($d + e$)   = 15
   World   loses ($b + d$)   = 6
If America imposes a 2 percent per year tax on borrowing abroad (from T to UV):
   Japan   loses ($b + c$)   = 15
   America gains ($c - d$)   = 9
   World   loses ($b + d$)   = 6

axis and ranks possible investments in Japan according to the returns the investments
produce. Investment opportunities in America are shown as the marginal-product-of-
capital curve $MPK_{America}$, which begins at the right vertical axis and ranks investments
in the opposite direction, from right to left.

We begin with a situation in which international financial transactions are prohibited. In this situation each country must use its financial wealth to finance its own
stock of real capital. If all Japanese wealth (W_J) is used domestically, Japan's lenders
must accept a low rate of return because the return on domestic capital investments
follows the declining MPK_{Japan} curve. Competition thus forces lenders in Japan to
accept the low rate of return of 2 percent per year at point R. Meanwhile, in America,
the scarcity of funds prevents any capital formation to the left of point S since W_A is
all the wealth that America has. Competition for borrowing the W_A of national
wealth bids the American rate of interest on lending up to 8 percent at point S. We
can also use this figure to show the value of total production in each country and

in the world, assuming that some capital is used in all production. If we add up the product of each unit of capital (the MPK), we get the total production by all capital, equal to the area under the MPK curve. With no international financial flows, the world's product equals the shaded area in Figure 21.1. Japan's product is the shaded area to the left of the vertical line through point R, and America's is the shaded area to the right.

Now imagine that there are no barriers to international finance. Wealthholders in Japan and borrowers in America have a strong incentive to get together. Why should one group lend at only 2 percent and the other borrow at 8 percent if, as we assume here, the riskiness or creditworthiness of the different borrowings is the same? Lenders in Japan should do part of their lending in America. Over time, their lending to America will allow more capital formation in America, with less capital formation in Japan. The international lending leads to a different equilibrium, one in which the worldwide rate of return is somewhere between 2 percent and 8 percent. Let's say that it ends up at 5 percent, at point T. In this situation the wealth of Japan exceeds its stock of domestic real assets by the same amount $(W_J - K_J)$ that America has to borrow to finance its extra real assets $(K_A - W_A)$.

With international financial freedom, world product is maximized. It equals everything under either the marginal product curve or all the shaded area plus area *RST*. This is a clear gain of area *RST* (or areas *a* through *f*) over the situation in which international lending was prohibited. The reason for this gain is that freedom allows individual wealthholders the chance to seek the highest return anywhere in the world.

The world's gains from international lending are split between the two countries. Japan's national income comes from two places:

• Its domestic production, which equals the area under its MPK_{Japan} curve down to point T (the product of the 4,200 of its wealth that it invests at home),

• *Plus* foreign source income on its investments in America, which equals area $a + b + c + g + h$ (the 5 percent return on the 1,800 that Japan has invested in America).

Japan gains area $a + b + c$ in national income through its foreign investment.

America's national income is the difference between two flows:

• Its domestic production, which equals the area under its $MPK_{America}$ curve down to point T (the product of the total 6,800 that is invested in America),

• *Minus* what it has to pay Japan for what it has borrowed from Japan, a payment equal to area $a + b + c + g + h$ (5 percent on the 1,800 that America has borrowed from Japan).

America also gains from its international borrowing, a gain of area $d + e + f$.

Within each country there are gainers and losers from the new freedom. Japanese lenders gain from lending at 5 percent instead of at 2 percent. That harms Japanese borrowers, though, because competition from foreign borrowers forces them to pay the same higher rate on their borrowings. In America borrowers have gained from being able to borrow at 5 percent instead of 8 percent. Yet American lenders will be nostalgic for the old days of financial isolation, when borrowers still had to pay them 8 percent. In addition, the smaller capital stock in Japan lowers the productivity and earnings of other resources (like labor and land) in Japan, whereas the larger capital stock in America raises the productivity and earnings of other resources in America.

TAXES ON INTERNATIONAL LENDING

We have compared free international lending with no international lending and have found the orthodox result: Freedom raises world product and national incomes. Another standard result also carries over from trade analysis: the **nationally optimal tax.** *If* a country looms large enough to have power over the world market rate of return, it can exploit this market power to its own advantage, at the expense of other countries and the world as a whole.

In Figure 21.1, Japan can be said to have market power. By restricting its foreign lending, it could force America's borrowers to pay higher interest rates (moving northeast from point *T* toward point *S*). Let us say that Japan exploits this power by imposing a tax of 2 percent per year on the value of assets held abroad by residents of Japan. This will bid up the rate that America's borrowers have to pay and bid down the rate that domestic lenders can get after taxes. Equilibrium will be restored when the gap between the foreign and the domestic rates is just the 2 percent tax. This is shown by the gap *UV* in Figure 21.1. Japan's government collects total tax revenues (area *e* + *c*) equal to the tax rate times the 1,200 of international assets that Japan continues to have after the adjustment to the tax. Japan has made a net gain on its taxation of foreign lending. It has forced America to pay 6 percent instead of 5 percent on all continuing debt. With a 2 percent tax, the markup, area *e*, is large enough to outweigh Japan's loss of some previously profitable lending abroad (triangle *b*). Setting such a tax at just the right level (which might or might not be the one shown here) gives Japan a nationally optimal tax on foreign lending.

Two can play at that game. Figure 21.1 shows that America also has market power: by restricting its borrowing, it could force Japan's lenders to accept lower rates of return (moving southeast from point *T* toward point *R*). What if it is America (instead of Japan) that imposes the 2 percent tax on the same international assets? Then all the results will work out the same as for the tax by Japan—except that the American government pockets the tax revenue (area *c* + *e*). America, in this case, gains income (area *c* minus area *d*) at the expense of Japan and the world as a whole. (If both countries impose taxes on the same international lending, the amount of international lending shrinks. At most, one country can gain compared to its position with free lending, and it is rather likely that both countries lose.)

INTERNATIONAL LENDING TO DEVELOPING COUNTRIES

International lending and borrowing are often well behaved and provide the sort of mutual benefits that we have discussed. Both lender and borrower usually benefit from the gains from intertemporal trade, as countries with net savings get higher returns and countries that are net borrowers pay lower costs. Additional gains arise as international financial investments are used to lower risk through portfolio diversification. Conflicts sometimes arise over tax policies, but these are manageable.

However, sometimes things go terribly wrong. There are periodic financial crises—international lending is sometimes not well behaved. For most of the rest of this chapter, we focus on the crises in developing countries since the early 1980s, in which lending from industrialized countries to these developing countries led to financial breakdowns rather than mutual benefits.

In a developing-country financial crisis, the borrowing country experiences difficulties in servicing its debts, and it often *defaults*—that is, fails to make payments as specified in the debt agreements. Lenders cut back or stop new lending, as the borrower is viewed as too risky. This section presents a brief history of capital flows to developing countries and the nature of developing-country financial crises. Subsequent sections look at why crises occur, how they are resolved, and suggestions for ways to reduce the frequency of crises.

The Surge in International Lending, 1974–1982

Before World War I there was a large amount of international lending, with Britain as the main creditor and the growing newly settled countries (the United States, Canada, Argentina, and Australia) as the main borrowers. To a large extent this international lending fit the well-behaved model of Figure 21.1, as lending sought out high returns (although defaults were also common).[1] During the 1920s, a large number of foreign governments issued foreign bonds, especially in New York, as the United States became a major creditor country. But in the 1930s, the Depression led to massive defaults by developing countries, which frightened away lenders through the 1960s. Lending to developing countries remained very low for four decades.

The oil shocks of the 1970s led to a surge in private international lending to developing countries. Between 1970 and 1980, developing-country debt outstanding increased more than seven-fold, with debt rising from 14.0 percent of the countries' national product in 1970 to 26.1 percent in 1980.

The oil shocks quadrupled and then tripled the world price of oil, and these shocks caused recessions and high inflation in the industrialized countries. How did the shocks also revive the lending? Four forces combined to create the surge. First, the rich oil-exporting nations had a high short-run propensity to save out of their extra income. While their savings were piling up, they tended to invest them in liquid form, especially in bonds and bank deposits in the United States and other established financial centers. The major international private banks thereby gained large amounts of new funds to be lent to other borrowers. The banks had the problem of "recycling" or reinvesting the "petrodollars." But where to lend?

Second, there was widespread pessimism about the profitability of capital formation in industrialized countries. Real interest rates in many countries were unusually low. One promising area was investment in energy-saving equipment, but the development of these projects took time. For a while the banks' expanded ability to lend

---

[1]The United States was the borrower in one of the default episodes. Britain lent substantial amounts to finance canals and cotton growing in the United States during 1826–1837. A depression began in 1837, and eight states had defaulted on their debts by 1843.

was not absorbed by borrowers in the industrial countries, which encouraged banks to look elsewhere. Attention began to shift to developing countries, which had long been forced to offer higher rates of interest and dividends to attract even small amounts of private capital.

Third, in developing countries, the 1970s was an era of peak resistance to foreign direct investment (FDI), in which the foreign investor, usually a multinational firm based in an industrialized country, keeps controlling ownership of foreign affiliated enterprises. Banks might have lent to multinational firms for additional FDI, but developing countries were generally hostile to FDI. Populist ideological currents and valid fears about political intrigues by multinational firms brought FDI down from 25 percent of net financial flows to developing countries in 1960 to 11 percent by 1980. To gain access to the higher returns offered in developing countries, banks had to lend outright to governments and companies in these countries.

Fourth, "herding" behavior meant that the lending to developing countries acquired a momentum of its own once it began to increase. Major banks aggressively sought lending opportunities, each showing eagerness to lend before competing banks did. Much of the lending went to poorly planned projects in mismanaged economies. But everyone was doing it.

The Debt Crisis of 1982

In August 1982, Mexico declared that it was unable to service its large foreign debt. Dozens of other developing countries followed with announcements that they also could not repay their previous loans. Several factors explain why the crunch came in 1982. Interest rates had increased sharply in the United States, as the U.S. Federal Reserve shifted to a much tighter monetary policy to reduce U.S. inflation. The United States and other industrialized countries sank into a severe recession. Developing countries' exports declined and commodity prices plummeted, while real interest rates remained high. The debtors' ability to repay fell dramatically.

At first the responses of the bank creditors depended on how much each bank had lent. Smaller banks (those holding small shares of all loans) headed for the exits and eliminated their exposure by selling off their loans or getting repaid. The larger banks could not extricate themselves without triggering a larger crisis, and they hoped that the problems were temporary. They rescheduled loan payments to establish repayment obligations in the future, and they loaned smaller amounts of new money to assist the debtors to grow so that repayment would be possible. Figure 21.2 provides information on financial flows to developing countries. Bank loans, which were most of the private long-term lending to developing countries in the early 1980s, declined from 1981 to 1985. As shown in Figure 21.3, the long-term foreign debt of developing countries nearly doubled between 1980 and 1985, the ratio of debt to national product rose from 26 percent in 1980 to 38 percent in 1985, and the share of export revenues that was committed to service the debt increased to 28 percent. As large banks reassessed the prospects for developing country debtors, they concluded that it was imprudent to lend more. The net flows of bank loans to developing countries remained low until 1995.

As the debt crisis wore on through the 1980s, it became clear that the debtor countries were suffering low economic growth and lack of access to international

FIGURE 21.2   Net Financial Flows to Developing Countries, 1981–2012 (Billions of U.S. Dollars)

Source and Type	1981	1982	1983	1984	1985	1986	1987	1988	1989	1990	1991	1992	1993	1994	1995	1996
Net long-term	78	75	56	47	43	42	44	52	50	57	71	99	158	160	180	210
Official loans	23	24	23	22	20	21	22	19	21	23	23	20	23	13	24	−1
Private debt	42	40	24	16	12	12	13	16	6	10	11	28	43	39	48	74
Bank and other loans	41	35	23	17	9	11	13	14	4	9	4	20	11	11	25	27
Bonds	1	5	1	−1	3	1	0	2	2	1	8	8	32	28	23	46
Portfolio equity (stocks)	0	0	0	0	0	0	0	0	2	3	6	9	30	26	14	23
Foreign direct investment	13	11	10	9	11	9	10	17	21	21	31	43	62	82	94	113
Net short-term	19	8	−15	−7	2	2	10	8	6	24	20	33	37	12	56	29
Total net financial flows	97	83	41	40	45	44	55	60	56	81	91	132	194	171	235	238

Source and Type	1997	1998	1999	2000	2001	2002	2003	2004	2005	2006	2007	2008	2009	2010	2011	2012
Net long-term	266	232	203	182	171	151	196	299	432	629	916	812	619	847	934	1,032
Official loans	7	19	15	5	12	−5	−12	−5	−5	−16	8	26	62	67	31	41
Private debt	83	60	25	21	−2	0	37	72	77	167	240	203	66	145	245	281
Bank and other loans	41	34	−10	−7	−18	−13	17	36	35	137	165	195	16	30	124	102
Bonds	43	26	35	28	16	13	20	36	42	30	76	8	50	116	121	179
Portfolio equity (stocks)	26	2	10	14	6	6	26	37	66	102	109	−41	111	123	3	98
Foreign direct investment	149	151	153	143	155	151	146	196	293	376	559	623	380	512	655	612
Net short-term	23	−48	−22	−10	17	4	40	67	85	78	138	3	47	256	175	103
Total net financial flows	289	184	181	172	188	155	236	366	517	707	1,055	815	666	1,103	1,109	1,135

Source: World Bank, *International Debt Statistics.*

finance, but that this cost was not leading to repayments that would end the crisis. In response, U.S. Treasury officials crafted the Brady Plan (named after U.S. Treasury Secretary Nicholas Brady). Beginning in 1989, each debtor country could reach a deal in which its bank debt would be partially reduced, with most of the remaining loans repackaged as "Brady bonds." By 1994, most of the bank debt had been reduced and converted into bonds. The debt crisis that began in 1982 was effectively over.

The Resurgence of Capital Flows in the 1990s

Beginning in about 1990, lending to and investing in developing countries began to increase again. Four forces converged to drive this new lending. First, the size and scope of the Brady Plan led investors to believe that the previous crisis was

FIGURE 21.3   Developing Countries' External Debt Outstanding, 1970–2012 (Billions of U.S. Dollars, Unless Otherwise Indicated)

Type of Debt	1970	1980	1985	1990	1995	2000	2005	2012
Long-term debt	61	386	679	987	1,375	1,635	1,794	3,406
Public and publicly guaranteed	45	323	599	932	1,174	1,184	1,229	1,766
Private nonguaranteed	15	63	80	55	199	450	565	1,641
Loans from the IMF	1	11	36	33	50	61	63	146
Short-term debt	9	112	118	174	319	269	481	1,278
Total debt	70	510	833	1,194	1,744	1,966	2,338	4,830
Debt/GNP ratio (percentage)	14.0	26.1	38.3	39.9	40.0	37.0	27.2	22.1
Debt service-exports of goods and services ratio (percentage)	16.2	20.6	27.8	21.9	19.3	21.1	13.8	9.8

Source: World Bank, *International Debt Statistics.*

being resolved. As each debtor country agreed to a Brady deal, it was usually able to receive new private lending almost immediately. Second, low U.S. interest rates again led lenders to seek out higher returns through foreign investments. Third, the developing countries were becoming more attractive places to lend as governments reformed their policies. Governments were opening up opportunities for financing profitable new investments as they deregulated industries, privatized state-owned firms, and encouraged production for export with outward-oriented trade policies. Fourth, individual investors, as well as the rapidly growing mutual funds and pension funds, were looking for new forms of portfolio investments that could raise returns and add risk diversification. Developing countries became the emerging markets for this portfolio investment.

Figure 21.2 shows the rapidly growing flows of investments into developing countries, as total net financial inflows increased from 1986 to 1997. The majority of this money went to a small number of developing countries viewed as the major emerging markets—Mexico, Brazil, and Argentina in Latin America and China, Indonesia, Malaysia, South Korea, and Thailand in Asia. The types of investments were different from those that drove the lending surge in the late 1970s. Foreign portfolio investors' net purchases of stocks and bonds rose from almost nothing in 1990 to about 30 percent of the total net financial flows in the mid-1990s. Bank lending was less important, but even bank lending increased substantially from 1994 to 1997.

The Mexican Crisis, 1994–1995

A series of crises punctured the generally strong flows of international lending to developing countries since 1990. The first of these struck Mexico in late 1994.

Mexico received large capital inflows in the early 1990s, as investors sought high returns and were impressed with Mexico's economic reforms and its entry into the North American Free Trade Area. But strains also arose. The real exchange-rate value of the peso increased because the government permitted only a slow nominal peso depreciation, while the Mexican inflation rate was higher than that of the United States, its main trading partner. The current account deficit increased to 6 percent of Mexico's GDP in 1993, although this was readily financed by the capital inflows. Mexico's banking system was rather weak, with inadequate bank supervision and regulation by the government. With the capital inflows adding funds to the Mexican banking system, bank lending grew rapidly, as did defaults on these loans. The year 1994 was an election year with some turmoil, including an uprising in the Chiapas region and two political assassinations. The peso came under some downward pressure. The government used sterilized intervention to defend its exchange-rate value, so its holdings of official international reserves fell.

Mexico's fiscal policy was reasonable, with a modest government budget deficit. Still, the fiscal authorities made the change that became the center of the crisis, by altering the form of the government debt. Beginning in early 1994, the government replaced peso-denominated government debt with short-term dollar-indexed government debt called *tesobonos*. By the end of 1994, there were about $28 billion of *tesobonos* outstanding, most maturing in the first half of 1995.

The crisis was touched off by a large flight of capital, mostly by Mexican residents who feared a currency devaluation and converted out of pesos. In December the currency was allowed to depreciate, but Mexican holdings of official reserves had declined to about $6 billion. The financial crisis arose as investors refused to purchase new *tesobonos* to pay off those coming due because it appeared that the government did not have the ability to make good on its dollar obligations. Each investor wanted to be paid off in dollars—a rush to the exit—but what was rational for each investor individually was not necessarily rational for all of them collectively. The Mexican government might not be able to repay all of them within a short time period. As investors reassessed their investments in emerging markets, they pulled back on investments not only in Mexico but also in many other developing countries (the "tequila effect").

The U.S. government became worried about the political and economic effects of financial crisis in Mexico, and it arranged a large rescue package that permitted the Mexican government to borrow up to $50 billion, mostly from the U.S. government and the International Monetary Fund (IMF).[2] The Mexican government did borrow about $27 billion, using the money to pay off the *tesobonos* as they matured and to replenish its official reserve holdings. The currency depreciation and the financial turmoil caused rapid and painful adjustments in Mexico. The Mexican economy went into a severe recession, and the current account deficit disappeared as imports decreased and exports increased.

As the rescue took hold, the pure contagion that led investors to retreat from nearly all lending to developing countries calmed after the first quarter of 1995. The adverse tequila effect lingered for a smaller number of countries, as investors continued to pull out of Argentina, Brazil, and, to lesser extents, Venezuela and the Philippines. Still, much of the Mexican financial crisis of 1994–1995 was resolved quickly. As shown in Figure 21.2, overall capital flows to developing countries continued to increase in 1995 and 1996.

---

[2]For information on IMF loans to countries with balance of payments problems, see the box "Short of Reserves? Call 1-800-IMF-LOAN."

The Asian Crisis, 1997

In the early and mid-1990s, foreign investors looked favorably on the rapidly growing developing countries of Southeast and East Asia. In these countries macroeconomic policies were solid. The governments had fiscal budgets with surpluses or small deficits; steady monetary policies kept inflation low, and trade policies were outward-oriented. Most of the foreign debt was owed by private firms, not by the governments.

A closer look showed a few problems. In Thailand and South Korea, much of the foreign borrowing was by banks and other financial institutions. Government regulation and supervision were weak. The banks took on significant exchange-rate risk by borrowing dollars and yen and lending in local currencies. And the lending boom led to loans to riskier local borrowers and rising defaults on loans. In Indonesia, much of the foreign borrowing was by private nonfinancial firms, which took on the exchange-rate risk directly.

The external balance of the countries also showed some problems. The real exchange-rate values of these countries' currencies seemed to be somewhat overvalued, and the growth of exports slowed beginning in 1996. With the exception of Thailand, the current account deficits were not large. Thailand's current account deficit rose to 8 percent of GDP in 1996. Still, the strong capital inflows provided financing for the deficits.

Crisis struck first in Thailand. Beginning in 1996, the expectation of declining exports led to large declines in Thai stock prices and real estate prices. The exchange-rate value of the Thai baht came under downward pressure. By mid-1997, the pressures had become intense. Banks and other local firms that had borrowed dollars and yen without hedging rushed to sell baht to acquire foreign currency assets. The Thai government could not maintain its defense, and the baht was allowed to depreciate beginning in July 1997.

Throughout the rest of 1997 the crisis spread to a number of other Asian countries, especially to Indonesia and South Korea, and also to Malaysia and the Philippines, as foreign investors lost confidence in local bank borrowers and the local stock markets, and as local borrowers scrambled to sell local currency to establish hedges against exchange-rate risk. Figure 21.4 shows the declines of 40 percent or more in the exchange-rate values of the currencies of Thailand, Indonesia, Korea, Malaysia, and the Philippines during the second half of 1997. (The figure also shows that the value of the Singapore dollar was affected much less, and the value of the Hong Kong dollar, fixed to the U.S. dollar through its currency board, not at all.)

In response, the IMF organized large rescue packages, with commitments to lend up to $17 billion to Thailand ($13 billion actually borrowed), up to $42 billion to Indonesia ($11 billion borrowed), and up to $58 billion to South Korea ($27 billion borrowed). As in Mexico, these large rescue packages and policy changes did contain the crises, though not without costs. The currency depreciations and the recessions did lead to improvements in the current account balance, largely through decreases in imports. However, these countries also went into severe recessions.

The Russian Crisis, 1998

Russia weathered the Asian crisis in 1997 reasonably well, but its underlying fundamental position was remarkably weak. It had a large fiscal budget deficit, and government borrowing led to rapid increases in government debt to both domestic and foreign

Global Governance   Short of Reserves? Call 1-800-IMF-LOAN

As we noted in the box "The International Monetary Fund" in the previous chapter, one of the IMF's major activities is lending to its members when appropriate to give them time to correct payments imbalances. These loans can be large and they can be controversial.

The IMF makes loans under a number of different programs, and maximum amounts of loans from the various programs are in proportion to a country's quota contribution to the IMF. Standard loans to assist a country to address its balance of payment problems are called *stand-by arrangements*, and the IMF also makes longer (extended fund) loans. These loans are made at market-based interest rates, with larger loans incurring a higher rate. Standard loans normally are to be repaid within five years.

With programs first offered in the mid-1970s, the IMF also makes loans at very low (concessional) interest rates to low-income countries. Facilities under the Poverty Reduction and Growth Trust make loans to assist countries with protracted or urgent balance of payments problems. The loans are to be repaid within 10 years. These low-rate loan programs seem to be a form of "mission creep," as they shift the IMF to a role as a development organization.

The accompanying figure shows IMF lending since 1970. Up to the early 1980s both industrialized countries and developing countries borrowed from the IMF. From 1980 to 2010 most IMF loans went to developing countries at market-based rates. The low-rate lending to poor developing countries is not large in total, with less than $10 billion outstanding. From 1987 to 2008 no industrialized country borrowed from the IMF. Then, Iceland borrowed in 2008, Greece borrowed in 2010, and Ireland and Portugal borrowed in 2011, as each of these countries experienced a crisis.

Let's focus on the major part of IMF lending, loans with market-based interest rates to countries with large payments deficits, countries whose official reserves are declining to low levels. The loans provide additional official reserve assets to the country. The country can use these additional reserves to buy time for the country to make orderly macroeconomic adjustments to reduce the deficit, without resorting to exchange controls or trade restrictions. Ideally, the adjustment can occur without excessive costs or disruptions to the country or to other countries.

The IMF only makes loans that it expects to be repaid. The IMF requires a borrowing country to agree to how it intends to correct its payments imbalance. That is, the IMF imposes conditionality—the IMF makes a loan only if the borrowing country commits to and enacts changes in its policies with quantified performance criteria. The policies should promise to achieve external balance within a reasonable time. The IMF disburses some loans in pieces over time. It withholds pieces if the performance criteria are not met. The policy changes that are usually included in an IMF adjustment program are not surprising. They include fiscal and monetary restraint, liberalization of restrictions on domestic markets and on international trade, and deregulation.

What is the record for these IMF loans? Do they work? One answer is repayment. Prior to the mid-1980s, nearly all loans had been repaid on time. However, from 1985 to 1992, rising amounts, reaching $4.8 billion, were not repaid on time. These overdue payments then declined and were about $2 billion during 2008–2013.

Do the loans assist payments adjustment? Evaluation of the effects of the loans and the conditions attached to them is difficult—what would have happened without them? Nonetheless, the programs accompanying IMF loans typically appear to result in increases in a country's exports, decreases in imports, and reduction in the payments deficits, but these changes are often temporary.

The conditions that a government is required to meet for a loan are often not popular domestically. The policy changes are usually contractionary, for instance, reductions in the rate of new lending by banks in the country. Indeed, the conditions are often resisted, and half or more of the lending programs break down because the conditions are not met by the country's government, as happened in Russia in 1998 and Argentina in 2001.

In the programs for the Asian crisis countries, the use of conditions seemed to get out of hand. The agreement with Indonesia had 140 conditions, and the agreement with the Philippines over 100. Some of these conditions required changes in basic economic structures and institutions, including changes in labor rules and business governance. Critics saw these structural conditions as unnecessary to address the external imbalances. In 2002 the IMF adopted guidelines to focus its conditionality on measures crucial to the needed macroeconomic adjustment, with fewer conditions that are easier to monitor for compliance. The fund hopes that this change will elicit more support for its requirements from the governments (and the people) of the borrowing countries.

Finally, you can see that the accompanying figure shows interesting recent developments. The amount of outstanding market-based IMF loans decreased dramatically from $107 billion at the end of 2003 to $16 billion in early 2008. Countries like Indonesia, Brazil, and Argentina were able to pay back their loans early, and there were no new major financial crises from 2002 through early 2008.

IMF lending expanded rapidly with the worsening of the global financial and economic crisis in 2008. During 2008–2010 the IMF reached agreements for market-rate lending arrangements for 28 countries. By mid-2014 IMF loans outstanding had reached a total of $125 billion. While the IMF seemed in danger of becoming irrelevant in early 2008 because it was lending so little, it has regained its importance in global governance with a host of new lending programs to countries in trouble, both small industrialized countries and developing countries.

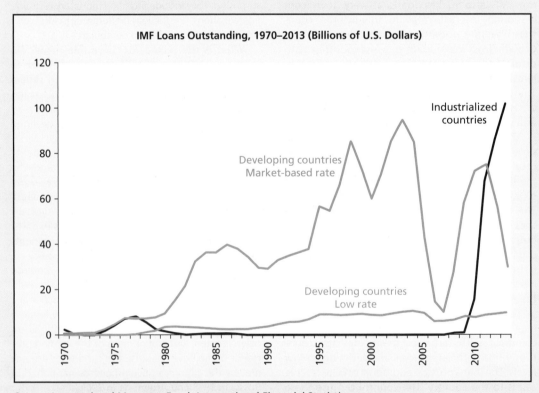

Source: International Monetary Fund, *International Financial Statistics.*

FIGURE 21.4 Exchange Rates, Asian Countries, 1994–2014

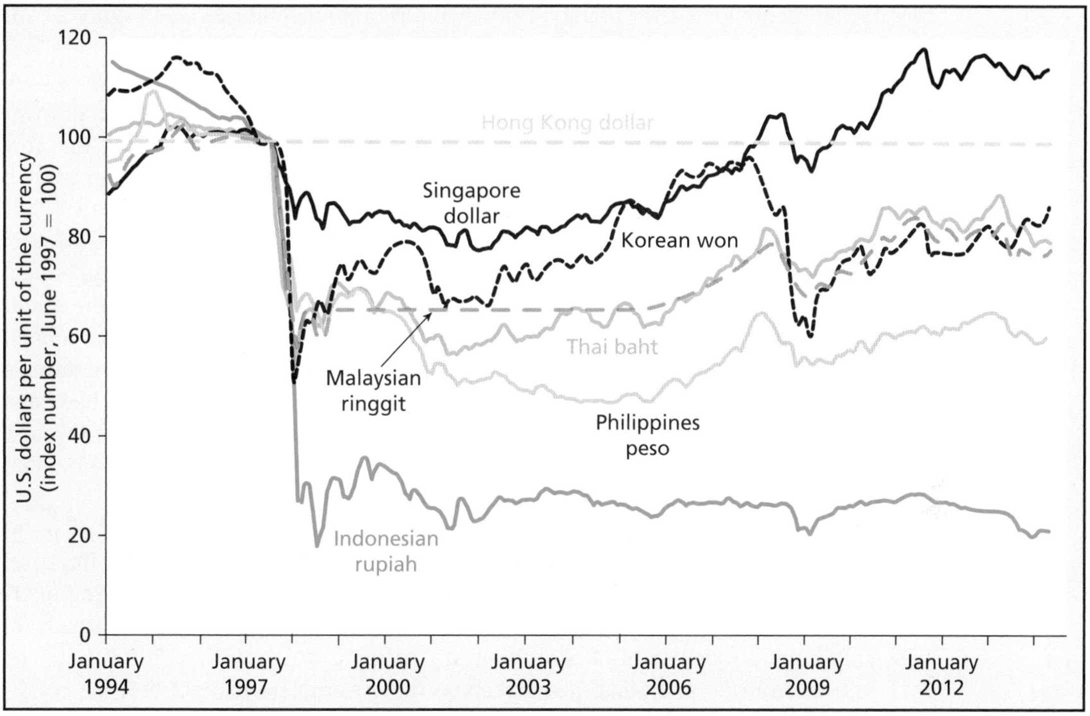

Source: International Monetary Fund, *International Financial Statistics.*

lenders. In mid-1998, lenders balked at buying still more Russian government debt. In July 1998, the IMF organized a lending package under which the Russian government could borrow up to $23 billion, and the IMF made the first loan of $5 billion. However, the Russian government failed to enact policy changes included as conditions for the loan. The exchange-rate value of the ruble came under severe pressure as capital flight by wealthy Russians led to large sales of rubles for foreign currencies. With substantial debt service due on government debt during the second half of 1998, investor confidence declined, with selling pressure driving down Russian stock and bond prices.

In August 1998, the Russian government announced drastic measures. The government unilaterally "restructured" its ruble-denominated debt, effectively wiping out most of the creditors' value. It placed a 90-day moratorium on payments of many foreign currency obligations of banks and other private firms, a move designed to protect Russian banks. And it allowed the ruble to depreciate by shifting to a floating exchange rate. Russia requested the next installment of its loan from the IMF, but the IMF refused because the government had not met the conditions for fiscal reforms.

Foreign lenders were in shock. They had expected that Russia was too important to fail and that the IMF rescue package would provide Russia with the funds to repay them. They reassessed the risk of investments in all emerging markets and rapidly sought to reduce their investments. The selloff caused stock and bond prices to plummet, with a general flight to high-quality investments like U.S. government bonds.

The reversal of international bank lending and stock and bond investing in 1998 led to a decline in net long-term financial flows to developing countries (see Figure 21.2).

Argentina's Crisis, 2001–2002

In the late 1980s, Argentina's economy was a mess, with hyperinflation of over 2,000 percent per year and a currency whose exchange value was in free fall. In a few years in the early 1990s everything changed, as it fixed its peso to the U.S. dollar using a currency board, reduced its inflation rate to almost zero, and grew rapidly up to 1998. It also strengthened its banking system and established sound regulation and supervision. Foreign investors saw all this and they liked it—foreign capital flowed into Argentina.

Beginning in 1997 the peso experienced a real appreciation, first because the dollar strengthened against other currencies and then because Brazil's currency depreciated by a large amount in 1999. The international price competitiveness of Argentina's products declined and its current account deficit increased. Its fiscal situation had been a weak point all along, and the fiscal deficit increased as the economy went through years of recession beginning in 1998. Much of the government debt was denominated in foreign currencies and owed to foreign lenders and bondholders.

In late 2000 Argentina reached agreement for a package of official loans of up to $40 billion, with $14 billion committed by the IMF. However, things did not improve, and the fiscal deficit remained a problem. Private capital inflows dried up. Rising interest rates in Argentina made the recession worse. In September 2001 the IMF made an unusually large disbursement of $6 billion to Argentina, but it was to be the last. The IMF refused to make additional loans because the government had not met the conditions set by the Fund for improvements in government policies.

The Argentinean people began to fear for the continuation of the fixed exchange rate and the soundness of the banking system. In response to depositor runs on banks, the government closed the banks in November. When the banks reopened in December, withdrawals were severely limited. Angry protest spawned looting and rioting, with 23 deaths. The country's president resigned, and Argentina then had four new presidents in two weeks.

In early 2002 the government surrendered the fixed exchange rate, and the peso lost about 75 percent of its value in the first six months of the year. The government defaulted on about $140 billion of its debt, much of it owed to foreigners. In addition, the peso depreciation caused huge losses in the banks because of some mismatch of dollar liabilities and dollar assets, and especially because of the terms under which the government mandated the conversion of dollar assets and liabilities into pesos. A number of banks closed, and the banking system was nearly nonfunctional. During 2002 real GDP declined by 11 percent, a huge recession after the economy had already endured several previous years of recession.

At first it appeared that Argentina's collapse would have few effects on other developing countries because it had been widely expected. But after a few months Argentina's problems did spread to its neighbors, especially Uruguay. Uruguay relied on Argentina for tourism and banking business. The tourism dried up, and Argentinean withdrawals from their Uruguayan accounts increased. After its holdings of official reserves plummeted defending Uruguay's crawling pegged exchange rate, the Uruguay government floated its currency in June; within two weeks, the currency had fallen by half. In August Uruguay received an IMF rescue package and used it to stabilize its financial situation. Still, it suffered a severe recession, with real GDP declining by over 10 percent during the year.

FINANCIAL CRISES: WHAT CAN AND DOES GO WRONG

International lending to developing countries brings benefits, but, as we just saw in the history of the past several decades, it also brings recurrent financial crises. How can we understand the frequency and scope of these crises? We gain major insights by focusing on five major forces that can, and do, lead to financial crises:

1. Waves of overlending and overborrowing.
2. Exogenous international shocks.
3. Exchange-rate risk.
4. Fickle international short-term lending.
5. Global contagion.

Waves of Overlending and Overborrowing

Our model of well-behaved lending, shown in Figure 21.1, assumes that lenders only lend (and that borrowers only borrow) for investment projects that generate the returns in the future that can be used to service the debt. This is not always true. In the late 1970s and again in the mid-1990s, lenders seemed to lend excessive amounts to some countries.

The classic explanation of overlending/overborrowing is that it results from excessively expansionary government policies in the borrowing country. These policies lead to government borrowing to finance growing budget deficits, and the government may also guarantee loans to private borrowers in order to finance the growing current account deficits. Lending to national governments, like the Mexican government in the late 1970s and early 1980s or the Argentinean government in the 1990s, seems to be low risk, but it's not. When the government realizes that it has borrowed too much, it has an incentive to default, and a financial crisis arises. (The box "The Special Case of Sovereign Debt" examines government defaults in more depth.)

The Asian crisis (and to a lesser extent the Mexican crisis of 1994–1995) presented a new form of overlending and overborrowing: too much lending to private borrowers rather than to national governments. In the 1990s, lending to banks in Asian countries seemed to be low risk because the countries' governments provided guarantees that creditors would be repaid. Large capital inflows lead to easy domestic credit. In a domestic lending boom, some of the lending is for current consumption, so that it is not invested to generate future returns.[3] Other lending goes to investments that are of low quality—projects that offer low returns or are too risky (too likely to fail to produce returns). More generally, the capital inflows and lending boom tend to inflate stock and real estate prices. For a while the capital inflows appear to be earning high returns, until the price bubble bursts.

---

[3]Borrowing for current consumption can be sensible if it is part of a strategy to smooth the country's consumption over time. It makes sense if the country's income will be higher in the future, so that part of the higher future income can be used to repay the loan. But borrowing for current consumption is also risky because it is not adding to future income potential.

Extension   The Special Case of Sovereign Debt

Most long-term debt of developing countries is *sovereign debt*—debt of the government of the country or debt of private borrowers that is guaranteed by the country's government. According to the information in Figure 20.3, sovereign debt was 94 percent of total long-term debt in 1990, and this was still 52 percent in 2012, notwithstanding the rising importance of investments in the securities of private companies.

Sovereign borrowers are different. They cannot be legally forced to repay if they do not wish to do so. Creditors cannot sue them in court or seize their assets. Granted, there have been times in the past when creditors could force repayments: Britain and France were able to take over Egyptian tax collections in the latter half of the 19th century after Egypt failed to repay English and French creditors, and creditors were backed by gunboats when they demanded repayment from Venezuela at the beginning of the 20th century. But the gunboat days are over. If Malaysia defaults on its debts, the United States and other lending countries cannot send gunboats to Malaysia. Nor can they send thugs to beat up the Malaysian finance minister.

If sovereign debtors cannot be forced to repay, why should they ever repay? The usual answer—that the debtor will repay on time to protect its own future creditworthiness—surprisingly turns out to be false, at least by itself. If fresh loans keep growing fast enough, the debtor country can afford to repay an ever-growing debt service. But this is no solution if the debtor never actually repays the full amount. When lenders tire of "repaying themselves" and cut their new lending, the debtor then defaults.

The answer to why sovereign debtors repay requires that they have something more to lose than just access to future loans. In domestic lending, collateral works well as the something more to lose. National laws allow the creditor to take over assets of the nonrepaying debtor, but only in amounts tied to the value defaulted.

Aside from creditworthiness, what might the sovereign debtor lose when it defaults? There are ways to create seizable international collateral, even though they are not perfect counterparts

to the collateral recognized by domestic law. If a debtor country has actual investments in the banks and enterprises of the creditor country, it should worry that these could be seized in retaliation, as when the United States froze Iranian assets in response to the Teheran hostage crisis in 1979–1981 and several countries froze Iraqi assets after Iraq invaded Kuwait in 1990. In practice, however, the international collateral mechanism is not finely tuned. The value of such assets is not necessarily close to the size of the possible default by the debtor country, and it may be legally difficult for the creditors to seize them.

There are two other sources of loss to the debtor country from default. First, the country can experience macroeconomic costs. We have seen that defaults linked to financial crises disrupt the domestic financial system and the domestic economy. The economy usually goes into a severe recession, exacting a large cost on the country. In addition, the debtor country may lose some ability to export and import if it loses access to trade financing or if new barriers are erected to its trade by the creditor countries. Second, the country can experience a general loss of reputation that results in a loss of other benefits. For instance, multinational firms may see the default as a sign of increased country risk. If multinationals fail to invest or they pull out of the country, it loses the spillover benefits from the technology, management practices, worker training, and marketing skills that the multinational firms bring to the country.

These extra losses create a true benefit–cost problem for the sovereign debtor considering default. And the answer to this benefit–cost problem indicates the limits to prudent lending to the sovereign borrower. The key forces are summarized in the accompanying graph. To simplify, let's examine the case in which the sovereign borrower owes full payment of all debt and interest at the end of the period, equal to the stock of debt (D) plus the interest due on this debt (iD). The debtor is considering full default, so that the straight line $(1 + i)D$ shows the benefits of not repaying. The debtor's cost (C) of not repaying also depends on the stock of debt, but

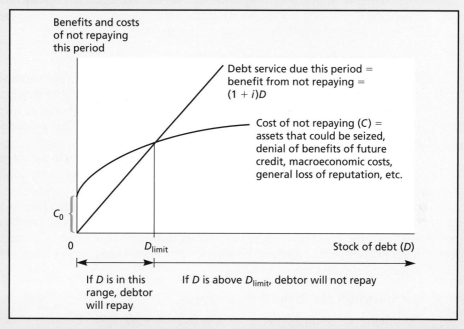

Benefits and costs of not repaying this period

Debt service due this period = benefit from not repaying = $(1 + i)D$

Cost of not repaying (C) = assets that could be seized, denial of benefits of future credit, macroeconomic costs, general loss of reputation, etc.

C_0

0   D_{limit} Stock of debt (D)

If D is in this range, debtor will repay

If D is above D_{limit}, debtor will not repay

only to some extent. There is a fixed cost (C_0) to any nonrepayment, regardless of the amount of debt. The fixed cost could be in the form of reduced creditworthiness, macroeconomic costs, or some loss of general reputation. Beyond C_0, the cost of not repaying probably rises with the amount of debt not honored, but not as fast as the stock of debt itself. Loss of access to future loans, asset seizures, macroeconomic costs, and more serious loss of general reputation are probably larger if the default is larger, but these losses are limited. A bigger default does not bring a much bigger penalty.

The fact that the cost of not repaying rises more slowly with extra debt than does the benefit of default means that the sovereign debtor repays debt faithfully as long as the debt is not too large. However, beyond some threshold amount of debt (D_{limit}), the willingness to repay disappears. Well-behaved lending occurs to the left of the limit because the cost of nonrepayment exceeds the amount of debt service that could be avoided.

Actual default can occur for any of several reasons. First, the borrower may amass debt larger

than D_{limit}. This is overlending and overborrowing, discussed in the text. We gain a subtle insight from the analysis here. Sovereign debtors may decide that it is not wise to repay even if they are able to repay. Second, a rise in the real rate of interest raises the benefit of not repaying. This is an upward rotation of the benefit line $(1 + i)D$ in the graph. If the sovereign debt just equaled D_{limit} before the increase in the interest rate, then it is now above the new D_{limit} for the higher interest rate. The country has the incentive to default. This is an example of how exogenous shocks (discussed in the text) apply to the special case of sovereign debt.

Should lenders make new loans if the sovereign debtor announces that it "cannot" repay without new loans to cover its current debt service? The graph suggests a negative answer. The debtor's announcement suggests that the stock of debt is already over the safe limit $(D > D_{\text{limit}})$. Extending more loans to cover current interest payments moves us farther to the right (D rises). The gap between the debtor's benefits and the costs of not repaying grows wider. Unless something else changes, default will occur.

Once foreign lenders realize that too much has been lent and borrowed, each has the incentive to stop lending and to try to get repaid as quickly as possible (before available money runs out). All cannot be repaid quickly, and a financial crisis erupts. The excessive lending/borrowing that can lead to a financial crisis is sometimes called a *debt overhang*—the amount by which the debt obligations exceed the present value of the payments that will be made to service the debt.

Exogenous International Shocks

When exogenous international shocks hit a country's economy, international lenders and the borrower must reassess the borrower's ability to meet its obligations to service its debt. For instance, a decline in export earnings, perhaps due to a decline in the world price of the country's key export commodity, makes it more difficult for the country to service its debt and thus more likely to default.

The experiences of the early 1980s and mid-1990s indicate that a change in U.S. real interest rates is a major exogenous shock. New funding flows to developing countries decrease, as fewer projects meet this higher required return. In addition, projects previously funded may not be profitable enough, leading to difficulties in servicing bank loans and to decreases in the market prices of stocks and bonds in the developing countries. Foreign investors can sour on their investments and try to sell them off before values decline further. The abrupt shift in flows can result in a crisis if the borrowers cannot adjust quickly enough.

Exchange-Rate Risk

Sometimes the form of the debts can help us understand financial crises. In the Mexican and Asian crises, private borrowers took on large liabilities denominated in foreign currency while acquiring assets valued in local currency. The borrowers took on these positions exposed to exchange-rate risk because they expected (hoped?) that the government would continue to defend the fixed or heavily managed exchange-rate value of the foreign currency. A major part of this uncovered foreign borrowing was the "carry trade," in which financial institutions borrow dollars or yen at a low interest rate, exchange the money to local currency, and lend in the borrowing country at a higher interest rate. This is very profitable as long as the exchange value of the local currency is steady (so that local currency can be exchanged back to dollars or yen at the same rate in the future, to repay the foreign borrowing).

When the likelihood of devaluation or depreciation becomes noticeable, the borrowers attempt to hedge their exposed positions by selling local currency, but this puts additional pressure on the government defense of the fixed exchange rate. If the government gives up the fixed rate, borrowers suffer losses to the extent that their positions are still unhedged. The losses make it more difficult for them to service their foreign debts. Foreign lenders then may reduce new lending and try to be repaid more quickly, leading to a financial crisis.

Fickle International Short-Term Lending

Another form of debt can help us understand financial crises. Short-term debt—debt that is due to be paid off soon—can cause a major problem because foreign lenders can refuse to refinance it. The inability of the Mexican government to refinance the large amount of short-term *tesobonos* that were coming due was a major contributor to the Mexican crisis of 1994–1995. In the Asian crisis, the large amount of short-term borrowing by banks that was coming due created a policy dilemma for the countries' governments. The governments could raise interest rates to attract continued foreign financing, but this would weaken local borrowers and hurt the banks' loan returns. Instead, the governments could guarantee or take over the banks' foreign borrowings, based on the need to prevent the local banks from failing. But the governments themselves did not have sufficient foreign exchange to pay off the debts, so they risked setting off a financial crisis on their own if foreign lenders demanded repayment.

Short-term debt is risky to the borrowing country because international lenders can readily shift from one equilibrium to another, based on their opinion of the country's prospects. In one equilibrium, the lenders refinance or roll over the short-term debt, and this can continue into the future. But a rapid shift to another equilibrium in which lenders demand repayment is also possible. If the borrowing country cannot come up with the payoff quickly, a financial crisis occurs.

Global Contagion

The four forces already discussed—overlending/overborrowing, exogenous shocks, exchange-rate risk, and short-term borrowing—provide major insights into why a financial crisis could hit a country. But the financial crises since 1980 were more than this. When a crisis hits one country, it often spreads and affects many other countries. It appears that international contagion is at work. Some contagion is the result of close trade links between the affected countries; thus, a crisis downturn in one country, like Argentina, has spillover effects in another country, like Uruguay.

Contagion can be an overreaction by foreign lenders as they engage in a scramble for the exits. Herding behavior can occur. Borrowers often do not provide full information to lenders. The high costs of obtaining accurate information on their own can lead some lenders to imitate other lenders who may have better information about the borrowers, or to fear that other borrowing countries are likely to have problems similar to those of the crisis country, even if there is no evidence that this is true.

Contagion can also be based on new recognition of real problems in other countries that are similar to those in the country with the initial crisis. The financial crisis in one country can serve as a "wake-up call" that other countries really do have similar problems. The crisis in Mexico led to a more severe tequila effect in countries that had problems similar to those of Mexico—currencies that had experienced real appreciations, weak banking systems and domestic lending booms, and relatively low holdings of official international reserves. In Asia the crisis in Thailand led to a recognition that Indonesia and South Korea had similar problems, including a weak banking sector, declining quality of domestic capital formation, a slowdown in export growth, and fixed exchange rates that may not be defensible for very long.

Analysis suggests that different forms of contagion are probably important and occur together in many crises. The initial reaction to a crisis in one country is often pure contagion, as international lenders pull back from nearly all investments in developing countries. Lenders then examine the other countries more closely. International lenders resume lending to those countries that do not seem to have problems. But the financial crisis spreads to those countries that seem to have similar problems.

Although the spread of the crisis has a basis in the recognition of actual problems, it is still a kind of contagion effect. Without the crisis in the first country, the other countries probably would have avoided their own crises.

RESOLVING FINANCIAL CRISES

A financial crisis in a developing country has serious negative consequences for the borrowing country and its economy. As new lending to the country dries up, the economy goes into recession. Also, a financial crisis in one country can threaten the economies of other countries and the broader global financial system, through contagion effects that reduce capital flows to other borrowers and can send some into their own crises. The two major types of international efforts to resolve financial crises have been rescue packages and debt restructuring. Let's look at each of these, how they work, and the questions that arise about these efforts.

Rescue Packages

When a financial crisis hits a country, that country's government usually seeks a rescue package of loan commitments to assist it in getting through the crisis. As indicated in the discussion of the history of lending to developing countries, the sizes of these rescue packages have been large since the mid-1990s, for example, $17 billion for Thailand and $58 billion for South Korea. The lenders generally included the IMF, the World Bank, and some national governments.

A rescue package can have several purposes. First, the loans in the rescue package compensate for the lack of private lending during the crisis. The money allows the country to meet its needs for foreign exchange, to provide some financing for new domestic investments, and to cushion the decline in aggregate demand and domestic production. Second, the package can restore investor confidence by replenishing official reserve holdings and by signaling official international support for the country and its government. This can stem the capital outflow, even if it does not immediately restart new private foreign lending to the country. Third, the IMF and the other official lenders in the rescue package hope that the package will limit contagion effects that could spread the crisis to other countries. As the leader in most of these efforts, the IMF is organizing an international safety net, in a way similar to national efforts (like deposit insurance and discount lending) to prevent problems at one bank from spreading to other banks in the national financial system. Fourth, the IMF imposes conditions as part of its lending, to require the government of the crisis country to make policy changes that should speed the end of the financial crisis. These policy reforms usually include tighter monetary policy and tighter fiscal policy, and they may include other structural reforms like liberalizing restrictions on international trade or improving regulation of the banking system (an issue that we will take up in the next section of the chapter).

One major question about these rescue packages is how effective they actually are. The rescue package for Mexico in 1995 seemed to be very successful in helping Mexico to resolve its financial crisis. The packages for the Asian countries in 1997 were at best moderately successful. The economies went into surprisingly deep recessions, and the exchange-rate values of the countries' currencies declined greatly before stabilizing. Russia was a nontest—Russia did not abide by the IMF conditions, so the package never took hold. The package for Argentina did not succeed in heading off a crisis, but it also was withdrawn before the crisis because the Argentinean government did not meet the IMF's conditions.

The other major question about the rescue packages is whether they actually increase the likelihood of financial crises because they encourage overlending and overborrowing. A large rescue package provides a bailout for lenders and borrowers when a crisis hits. But if lenders and borrowers expect to be bailed out, then they should worry less about the risk of a financial crisis. This leads them to lend and borrow more than is prudent—an example of moral hazard, in which insurance leads the insured to be less careful because the insurance offers compensation if bad things happen. Given the costs that the borrowers incur when a crisis hits, it seems that the moral hazard for them is probably not too large. Borrowers still lose a lot even with a rescue package.

The rescue package can create moral hazard for lenders. In the Mexican crisis of 1994–1995, the rescue package was used to pay off foreign investors, including full payment to the holders of the *tesobonos*. The lack of large losses to rescued creditors in the Mexican crisis probably encouraged too much international lending during 1996–1997 because the lenders worried too little about the risks of the lending.

In the Asian crisis, lenders to banks in the crisis countries were generally repaid in full, using money from the rescue packages. Still, the scope for moral hazard had its limits. Foreign investors in private bonds and stocks suffered large losses as the market prices of these securities declined, and foreign banks suffered large losses on loans to private nonfinancial borrowers.

The failure of the rescue package for Russia led to large losses for all foreign creditors. Many of these lenders were specifically relying on a rescue to limit their downside risk (moral hazard in action), so they received quite a surprise. Some of the caution in lending to developing countries in the years after the Russian crisis was probably the result of a reappraisal of the risks of this lending. This message was reinforced when Argentina defaulted in 2002 without any bailout appearing. Moral hazard in lending to developing countries has declined because lenders realize that rescue packages may not provide a bailout.

Debt Restructuring

Debt restructuring refers to two types of changes in the terms of debt:

- *Debt rescheduling* changes when payments are due, by pushing the repayments schedule further into the future. The amount of debt is effectively the same, but the borrower has a longer time to pay it off.
- *Debt reduction* lowers the *amount* of debt.

When a financial crisis hits a country because the country has more debt than it is willing or able to service, resolution of the crisis often requires debt restructuring. By stretching out payments or reducing debt, the borrowing country gains a better chance of meeting a more manageable stream of current and future payments for debt service. A key issue is the process of reaching a restructuring agreement among creditors and borrowers. There is a free-rider problem here. Each individual creditor has the incentive to hold out, hoping that others restructure their lending agreements, but not altering its own. Then the free rider can be repaid faster or fully, while other creditors that agreed to restructuring must wait longer or get less. But if free riding prevents a restructuring deal, then all creditors will probably lose, as the crisis is not resolved.

The debt crisis of 1982 dragged on through the 1980s partly because there was no framework for overcoming the coordination problem among the hundreds of banks that had lent to the crisis countries. In addition to the free-rider problem, legal clauses in many syndicated loan agreements limited debt restructuring. As we saw earlier, the Brady Plan of 1989 finally established a process for debt restructuring. It offered a menu of choices to the creditor banks, as well as coercion when necessary, to overcome the free-rider problem. In a typical Brady deal, each bank was offered a choice between partial debt reduction and continuance of its loan agreements along with required new lending to the crisis country. The debt reduction occurred when the bank exchanged its bank loans for a smaller amount of new bonds that were backed by collateral (usually U.S. government bonds). The borrowing country was able to establish the collateral by borrowing part of the value from the IMF and World Bank. (As usual, the IMF also imposed conditions for policy changes by the country along with its loan.) Brady deals succeeded in reducing the debt of 18 crisis countries by $65 billion, about one-third of their total debt. As the Brady deals resolved the lingering crisis, international lending to these countries resumed.

During the crises of the 1990s, restructuring of bank debt was smoother. The limited number of debtors and creditors eased the negotiations. The key issue that arose in the 1990s was the difficulty of restructuring bonds.

Most sovereign bonds issued internationally before 2003 could not in principle be restructured without the consent of all holders of the bond. There are often hundreds or thousands of bondholders, so negotiations can be complicated, and a few holdouts can try to prevent an agreement that the debtor country and most bondholders find acceptable. (In addition, any bondholder can sue to force immediate full repayment if the issuer defaults.) It is certainly possible to restructure such international bonds fairly smoothly, as the examples of Ecuador, Pakistan, and Uruguay show. But it can also be slow and acrimonious, as the examples of Russia and Argentina indicate.

Some international bonds include *collective action clauses,* which

- Provide that a qualified majority (often 75 percent) can bind all bondholders to the terms of a restructuring agreement.
- Require that all payments and recoveries from the issuer be shared evenly among the bondholders.
- Mandate that there can be no legal action against the issuer unless a minimum portion (often 25 percent) of bondholders agree to the suit.

Traditionally, bonds issued under New York State law did not include collective action clauses. In 2003, a path-breaking issue under New York law by Mexico did include a collective action clause, and it is now typical for bonds to include such clauses. As bonds with collective action clauses become the norm, the process of bond restructuring will be streamlined, to the benefit of both the issuers that run into problems and most bondholders, who are likely to receive better partial repayments.

REDUCING THE FREQUENCY OF FINANCIAL CRISES

Financial crises in developing countries impose large costs through sudden declines in access to lending and the macroeconomic costs of recessions and slow economic growth that usually accompany the crises. Financial crises also create large losses for international lenders though defaults, debt rescheduling, debt reduction, and declines in the market prices of bonds, stocks, and loans that are traded on secondary markets. While we have ways for trying to resolve crises once they occur, it would also be great to find ways to prevent financial crises from occurring, or at least to reduce their frequency.

There have been many proposals for improving the "international financial architecture." Four reforms enjoy widespread support and have been adopted by many countries. First, developing countries should pursue sound macroeconomic policies to avoid creating conditions in which overborrowing or a loss of confidence in the government's capability could lead to a crisis. Second, countries should improve the data that they report publicly to provide sufficient details on total debt and its components, as well as on holdings of international reserves, and they should report these data promptly. The belief is that with better data lenders will make more informed decisions on lending and investing, making overlending less likely and reducing the risk of pure contagion against emerging markets debt. While providing more information is not controversial, it has its limits. Developing-country governments have the incentive to provide misleading or incomplete data at exactly the times when lenders most need accurate information. Third, developing-country governments should avoid short-term borrowing denominated in foreign currencies to avoid crises that begin when foreign lenders abruptly demand repayment. In the next part of this section we look more closely at a fourth reform that enjoys widespread support—better regulation and supervision of banks in developing countries.

Other proposals for reform are more controversial, and in some cases serious competing proposals suggest moving in opposite directions. One proposal is that developing countries should end efforts to fix or heavily manage the exchange-rate values of their currencies. Among other possible benefits, the shift to more flexible exchange rates makes the existence of exchange-rate risk palpable, so private borrowers are less likely to build up large unhedged liabilities in foreign currencies. But a competing proposal is that developing countries should move to nearly permanently fixed exchange rates, with greater use of currency boards and dollarization. Such arrangements may discipline government macroeconomic policies to be more sound. In another set of competing proposals, one is that the IMF should expand its scope of activities, including being ready to offer large rescue packages if a number of large countries need assistance simultaneously. Backers of this proposal want the IMF to be able to quell panics and contagion more effectively by acting more like a global lender of last resort. The other is that the IMF should be abolished, or at least that its rescue activities be severely limited, because it creates substantial moral hazard with its lending. By encouraging overlending, it makes crises more likely. The IMF has recently greatly increased the total amount that it can lend, so the proponents of the expanding IMF are winning.

After we discuss proposals for better bank regulation, which is *not* controversial, we conclude the discussion of financial crises in developing countries with a look at a proposal that is controversial: expanding the use of capital controls to limit borrowing.

Bank Regulation and Supervision

Banks are considered to have a special role in an economy. They are at the center of the payments system that facilitates transactions in the economy. They acquire deposits from customers based on trust that the banks can pay back the deposits in the future, but if this trust is broken, depositors create a run on the bank as they all try to get their money out quickly.

In developing countries banks are often especially important because bank lending is also the major source of financing for local businesses. Stock and bond markets are often underdeveloped, but government regulation and supervision of banks in developing countries has often been weak. With weak regulation, banks engage in more risky activities. Banks make loans based on relationships—"crony capitalism" loans to bank directors, managers, friends of directors and managers, politically important people, and their businesses. Banks take on large exposures to exchange-rate risk by borrowing foreign currencies to fund local-currency loans. Banks operate with little equity capital, so they are more likely to take risks and require government rescues. In addition, the government often exerts direct influence on lending decisions, to favor some borrowers based on the government's strategy for economic development.

Thus, with weak supervision and an explicit or implicit guarantee that the government will rescue banks in trouble, banks have incentives to borrow too much internationally (and lenders are comfortable lending so much), and banks are more willing to take the risk of unhedged foreign-currency liabilities. A financial crisis becomes more likely.

There is a clear need for better government regulation and supervision of local banks in the borrowing countries. Regulators should require banks to use better accounting and disclose more information publicly, to use risk assessment and risk management to reduce risk exposures, to recognize bad loans and make provision for them, and to have more equity capital. The regulators should be willing to identify weak banks, to insist on changes in practices and management at these banks, and to close them if they are insolvent. In addition, the government probably should permit more foreign banks to operate locally because these foreign banks may bring better management and better techniques for controlling risks. Furthermore, a country's government should get the sequencing of its reforms right. To reduce the risk of a crisis, the country should solidify its regulation of banks and other financial institutions *before* it liberalizes its financial account and provides them with easy access to foreign-currency exposures.

In the abstract, the proposal for better bank regulation and supervision in developing countries is not controversial. The challenge is in the implementation. There is likely to be political resistance—from the banks, from the borrowers favored by crony capitalism, and from the government officials who lose some power to direct bank lending. Even if such political resistance can be overcome, there is also a shortage of people with the expertise to regulate banks effectively. Bank regulation and supervision meet world standards in some countries like Brazil, and supervision will continue to improve in developing countries more generally, but the improvement is likely to be a slow process.

Capital Controls

A controversial proposal for reducing the frequency of financial crises is to increase developing countries' use of controls or impediments to capital inflows.[4] Such controls could take any of several forms, including an outright limit or prohibition, a tax that must be paid to the government equal to some portion of the borrowing, or a requirement that some portion of the borrowing be placed in a deposit with the country's central bank. (If this deposit does not earn interest, then it is effectively a tax on the borrowing.) There are three ways in which such controls can reduce the risk of financial crisis. First, the controls can prevent large inflows that could result in overlending and overborrowing. Second, the controls can be used to discourage short-term borrowing. Third, the controls can reduce the country's exposure to contagion by limiting the amount that foreign lenders could pull out of the country.

Chile is usually offered as the example of a country that used controls on capital inflows successfully during the 1990s. The Chilean government required that a percentage of the value of new lending and investments into the country be placed in an interest-free deposit with the central bank for one year. And the government required that foreign investors keep their investments in Chile for at least one year. These requirements seem to have had their major effect by altering the mix of borrowing—less short-term debt. More recently, some developing countries have imposed or reimposed capital controls as financial inflows grew rapidly after the global crisis. For example, Brazil had ended its tax on capital inflows in late 2008 but reimposed a 2 percent tax on portfolio inflows in October 2009 and raised the rate a year later to 6 percent for foreign investments in Brazilian bonds.

What are the overall benefits and costs of controls on capital inflows? A major cost of the controls is the loss of the gains from international borrowing, to the extent that they discourage capital inflows. While they can provide benefits by reducing the risk of a financial crisis, they are a second-best policy. It would be better if the government of the borrowing country could identify the specific problems that might lead to a crisis and address these directly (recall the specificity rule from Chapter 10). For instance, if overborrowing or too much short-term foreign-currency borrowing occurs because of the excessive risks taken by local banks, the direct policy response is to improve bank regulation and supervision. If bank regulation cannot be improved immediately, then capital controls can be a second-best policy response. However, the capital controls are likely to lose their effectiveness over time, as investors and borrowers find ways to circumvent them. They probably only buy time for the government to adopt the direct policy improvement like better bank regulation. Furthermore, governments can also make mistakes with controls on capital inflows. For instance,

---

[4]Another possible use of capital controls is to limit capital outflows during a financial crisis. Malaysia adopted such controls as a temporary measure in 1998. The goal is to prevent continued capital flight and remove the pressures that it places on local financial institutions, local capital markets, and the exchange-rate value of the country's currency. Government fiscal and monetary policy can then be directed to addressing the internal imbalance of recession, with less fear that the shift to expansionary policies will worsen the financial crisis. Such controls are often only effective for a short time, as pressures build and investors find ways around the controls. The major cost of such controls is that they are likely to scare off new capital inflows in the future, even after the controls are removed, so that the country loses the gains from international borrowing.

South Korea removed controls on short-term bank borrowing while continuing to restrict longer-term capital inflows like foreign purchases of stocks and foreign direct investments. Korean banks then borrowed on a massive scale, and this became a key part of the Korean crisis of late 1997.

GLOBAL FINANCIAL AND ECONOMIC CRISIS

This time may seem different, but all too often a deeper look shows it is not.

Carmen M. Reinhart and Kenneth S. Rogoff, This Time
Is Different: Eight Centuries of Financial Folly (2009)

Following the Argentinean crisis of 2001–2002, no new financial crisis occurred in developing countries in the next years. Instead, world production and real incomes grew at a healthy annual rate of about 4 to 5 percent during 2004–2007. But conditions in financial markets were building toward the worst global financial and economic crisis since the Great Depression of the 1930s. This crisis arose not in the developing countries but rather in the industrialized countries. We conclude our examination of financial crises by describing how the global crisis happened and discerning the similarities with the developing-country crises we have already discussed in this chapter.

How the Crisis Happened

The story begins in the United States. With strong U.S. economic growth and low inflation, U.S. monetary policy was expansionary. Interest rates were moderate and there was little pricing of risk. Total U.S. debt outstanding, both bank loans and bonds, rose from 280 percent of U.S. GDP in 2002 to 340 percent of GDP in 2007. Banks increasingly pooled loans into asset-backed securities that could be sold to investors around the world, and these asset-backed securities were often structured into slices (called tranches), so that the top slices appeared to have very little risk. U.S. housing prices took off, rising by about 13 percent per year from 2002 to their peak in April 2006. The United States was in a credit boom, and one manifestation was a bubble in housing prices.

In 2007 the first signs of trouble appeared. More sub-prime mortgages, those made to high-risk borrowers, were going into default. Losses on securities backed by these mortgages began to mount. In August we got a clear sign that something was amiss, when the French bank BNP Paribas halted redemptions for three of its mutual funds because it was unable to value the sub-prime U.S. mortgage assets held by the funds. This shock was a wake-up call in the financial sector. Banks and other investors quickly wondered whether other financial institutions were impaired because they also held dodgy assets. Banks became reluctant to lend to each other—each wanted to build its own liquidity rather than risk that loans to other banks might not be repaid. Investors became wary about the issuers of asset-backed commercial paper, a kind of short-term debt security, and that market froze as new issues plummeted. More generally, banks tightened standards on new loans. U.S. stock prices reached a peak in October. In December a recession began in the United States, though at first it was mild. Losses on mortgage-backed financial securities totaled about $500 billion by early 2008.

In this first phase of the crisis, the key issue seemed to be limited access to funding for banks and other financial institutions. The credit boom had shifted to a credit crunch. The U.S. Federal Reserve and other central banks reacted as they usually do, using monetary policy to try to stabilize the financial sector and the economy. The Fed began to cut its interest rate target in increments beginning in August 2007, but banks and investors continued to be reluctant to lend and invest. So, in December, the Fed decided that it had to do more, and it introduced two unusual programs to provide additional liquidity. First, it began to auction funds to banks using the Term Auction Facility, to overcome banks' reluctance to borrow from the Fed using traditional discount loans. Second, the Fed began foreign central bank liquidity swaps with the European Central Bank and the Swiss central bank. The foreign central banks could use the swaps to obtain dollars, which they could then lend to their own banks, which were having trouble obtaining dollars through normal interbank borrowing. (The box "Central Bank Liquidity Swaps" in Chapter 24 discusses these swaps.)

While these central bank actions had some positive effects, conditions in financial markets remained unsettled. In March 2008 the investment bank Bear Stearns lost access to short-term funding and averted failure only when the New York Federal Reserve Bank arranged for J.P. Morgan Chase to purchase it.

Everything changed on September 15, when the investment bank Lehman Brothers failed. This shock pitched the world into the second, and much worse, phase of the global crisis. Things happened rapidly. Reserve Primary Fund, a money market fund, had invested in large amounts of debt issued by Lehman. On the next day, September 16, when many depositors tried to remove their funds, Reserve Primary had to "break the buck," paying depositors at less than the $1 promised par value. Scared depositors then pulled cash from other money market funds, and this had follow-on contractionary effects as these funds liquidated their investments. The commercial paper market, a big source of short-term funding, froze. Also on September 16, the insurance company AIG, which had issued very large amounts of credit default swaps without sufficient assets on hand to back them, was rescued from failure by an $85 billion loan from the Fed.

With the Lehman failure, financial institutions were much more unwilling to lend to each other. The freezing of financial markets and of lending deepened the U.S. recession, and the recession quickly became global. During the six months spanning late 2008 and early 2009, world real GDP declined at an annual rate of about 6 percent.

Central banks made valiant efforts to address the financial and economic implosion. From mid-September to November 2008 the Fed more than doubled the size of its assets. The Fed purchased massive amounts of financial assets to provide support for specific financial markets (including commercial paper and asset-backed securities) and for specific financial institutions (including not only AIG but also primary dealers and money market funds). The Fed also greatly expanded the liquidity swaps with foreign central banks. Then, starting in late 2008, as its holdings of other assets started to decline, the Fed purchased massive amounts of mortgage-related securities to provide support to the depressed housing sector in the United States. From April 2006 to April 2009, U.S. housing prices fell at an average annual rate of about 12 percent, and new construction plummeted.

Financial markets began to recover in early 2009, and by late 2009 most were operating reasonably. U.S. stock prices hit a low in March 2009 and then rose by over 50 percent in the next year. The U.S. recession ended in June 2009, but the recovery of the goods and services economy was much slower than the recovery of the financial markets. (Many developing countries, including China, recovered more quickly, and the growth of world real GDP was above 4 percent in 2010.)

Causes and Amplifiers

The global financial and economic crisis came out of the United States and Europe, and its effects were huge and worldwide. In previous sections of this chapter we examined key contributors to developing-country financial crises. Let's explore how our observations about developing-country crises help us to understand the global crisis that began in 2007.

The origin of the global crisis was centered in *overlending and overborrowing*. U.S. financial institutions, businesses, and households took on large amounts of new debt in the years leading up to 2007, and similar borrowing booms occurred during these years in quite a number of other countries, including Iceland, Ireland, Spain, Bulgaria, and New Zealand. (The box "National Crises, Contagion, and Resolution" examines the euro crisis that began in 2010.) Behind these big rises in debt were massive amounts of saving in other countries, especially Asian countries, including the dollars amassed by China in its foreign exchange market intervention to keep the yuan undervalued. The "global savings glut" was the source of funding for the overlending, channeled through large capital inflows that directly financed the large current account deficits of the United States and other countries. The savings glut put downward pressure on interest rates generally. The search for higher yields led to excessive investments in risky assets, so that the risk premiums built into interest rates on these assets fell to tiny levels. Cheap funding, especially for risky uses, was an important incentive for the overborrowing.

Another driver of overlending, especially in the United States, was the increasing ability of banks to package loans to households and businesses into asset-backed securities. These securities could be structured to perform the near-magic of turning risky loans, such as sub-prime mortgages, into apparently low-risk bonds that could readily be sold to investors around the world. For example, German savings banks bought large amounts of complex U.S. mortgage-backed securities.

In the United States, a number of European countries, South Africa, and New Zealand, lending booms led to bubbles in real estate prices and other asset prices. The overlending and overborrowing fed on itself, for instance, as higher house prices created the collateral for yet more loans, including home equity loans in the United States.

The overlending and overborrowing built a massive pile of combustibles, and *shocks* provided the fire sparks. The shock that began the first phase of the global crisis was the announcement by BNP Paribas in August 2007 that it could not value many of the sub-prime mortgage-backed assets held by several of its mutual funds. While we had seen rising losses on these types of securities, the announcement focused attention on how bad it had gotten. Then, in September 2008, the failure of Lehman Brothers provided the shock that started the second, much worse phase of the crisis.

After each shock, precarious *short-term lending* took over. In what came to be known as the "shadow banking system," financial institutions other than regular banks had grown in importance. The "shadow banks" included investment banks that became more active in lending and investing their own funds, mutual funds, hedge funds, and structured investment vehicles that regular banks increasingly used to move some of their financial activities "off the balance sheet." While regular banks can obtain funding from the deposits of households and businesses, shadow banks mostly rely on short-term funding from banks and other financial institutions and from debt markets.

After each shock, one form of *contagion* hit the financial system. Potential lenders and investors feared that other financial institutions had the same kinds of problems and losses that Paribas and Lehman had. Potential lenders and investors became much less willing to refinance or roll over short-term debt coming due. With such herding and scrambling for the exits, financial markets shifted rapidly from the previous high-confidence equilibrium of easy short-term lending to a low-confidence equilibrium of a near stop in short-term lending. For example, the market for commercial paper imploded. For the shadow banking system, this near stop is the equivalent of a run on the banks. The shadow banks that could not maintain funding for their assets had to sell the assets. Massive selling drove down asset prices, increasing the losses at these financial institutions and reinforcing the unwillingness to lend to them.

Because European financial institutions that had invested in U.S. mortgage-backed securities suffered losses, the seizing up of short-term lending easily crossed national boundaries. Other forms of contagion also contributed. Most important was international trade. When financial markets and lending froze in late 2008 following the Lehman failure, the United States and a number of other countries headed into deeper recessions. With production and incomes declining in these countries, they imported less. (We examined the collapse of international trade in the box "The Trade Mini-Collapse of 2009" in Chapter 2.) Declining imports meant declining exports for other countries, and their recessions deepened. Even countries, such as China, whose financial systems were resilient were still adversely affected by the loss of exports.[5]

Regulation and supervision of financial institutions are supposed to help us guard against such a cataclysm. In many ways regulation of regular banks in the United States (and in other industrialized countries) is competent and effective. However, financial innovations had opened and exploited holes in the regulatory system. Shadow banks performed many of the functions of regular banks but avoided much of the regulation. Regular banks were able to move some of their activities to lighter or no regulation by moving them off the balance sheet. Financial institutions had used their political power to lighten the regulation of financial derivatives, including the credit default swaps that almost brought down AIG. More generally, regulation became more difficult as the expansion of dealing among financial institutions created pervasive interconnections that greatly increase risks to the entire financial system.

Through overlending and overborrowing, shocks, the near stop to short-term borrowing, contagion, and gaps in financial regulation, we can see many parallels between developing-country financial crises and the global financial crisis that began in 2007. It would be good if we could learn from past crises. While we cannot hope to eliminate the possibility of future crises in industrialized countries, we can try to reduce the likelihood of another one being so destructive. Private players—financial institutions, investors, lenders, and borrowers—should use their historical memory to recognize the huge risks built by overlending and overborrowing. Government leaders should champion the design of better regulation and supervision of financial institutions.

[5]The case for using *capital controls* gets support from experience during the global crisis. Developing countries, including China and India, that had broad capital controls generally were less affected by the global crisis—they suffered less of a decline in real economic growth.

Euro Crisis   National Crises, Contagion, and Resolution

The global financial crisis that began in 2007 and intensified in 2008 affected the euro area and the rest of Europe. A recession began in the euro area during the first quarter of 2008. The recession was rather severe, but it ended by mid-2009, and the euro area began to grow again. The euro area appeared to be weathering the global crisis fairly well. There were indicators suggesting problems in some of the countries of the euro area, including the large current account deficits and large net foreign debts noted in the box "International Indicators Lead the Crisis" in Chapter 16. Still, most observers expected the euro area to recover at a good speed from the global crisis because the crisis was centered in the United States, not Europe.

Yet, in the next few years, crises would hit a series of euro countries and then threaten the euro itself. In October 2009, the newly elected government of Greece announced that the previous government had been misreporting government finances. The 2009 government budget deficit that was forecast to be less than 6 percent of Greek GDP would actually be more than 10 percent. Even before this, a housing price bubble had burst in Ireland, with house prices peaking in September 2007 and a rapid decline beginning in October 2008. In September 2008, to shore up confidence in a banking system that was experiencing rising bad loans, the Irish government guaranteed all deposits and debts of six major Irish banks.

How did large government budget deficits in one small euro-area country and a burst housing bubble in another lead the entire euro area into crisis? Shambaugh (2012) views the euro crisis as three interlocking crises that fed on each other. The figure below summarizes this view, with each arrow showing a major way in which intensification of one crisis tends to make the other crisis more likely or worse.

Because of the global crisis and recession, all euro countries in 2009 had weak macroeconomic performance. Greece was the first to enter a full crisis, through a sovereign debt crisis. For a number of years the Greek government had been underreporting its government budget deficits, but the truth came out in 2009, and the deficit for that year turned out to be almost 16 percent of GDP. Outstanding Greek government debt had increased from about 100 percent of GDP in 2005 to about 130 percent of GDP in 2009. With recognition of increased default risk, the prices of Greek government bonds decreased and the interest rates (yields) on the bonds increased. The Greek government by early 2010 was entering into a sovereign debt crisis, in which it could not pay such high interest rates on new borrowing. In May 2010 it received a bailout package of €110 billion from the European Union and the IMF. (Greece also received a second bailout program in 2012 that added €130 billion, bringing the total to more than the size of Greece's GDP.)

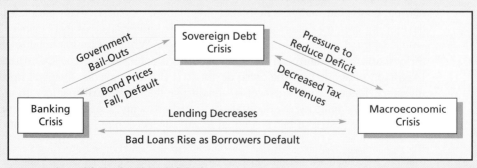

Source: Adapted from Shambaugh (2012).

Even with the bailout, the crisis worsened for Greece. Greek banks held Greek government bonds as assets, and losses as the prices of these bonds decreased threatened a banking crisis. When the banking crisis came with the Greek government's default on its privately held bonds in March 2012, the Greek government had to borrow to inject funds to bail out the banks. The sovereign debt crisis and the banking crisis interacted and reinforced each other.

The sovereign debt crisis, and the strict conditions that came with the bailout loans, forced the Greek government to change policies to reduce the fiscal deficit, by reducing government spending and raising taxes. But these fiscal changes ("austerity") reduced national demand and production, pushing Greece toward a macroeconomic crisis. Real GDP fell for six years (2007–2013), including annual declines of 7 percent in 2011 and 2012. Real GDP was 24 percent lower in 2013 that it had been in 2007 and unemployment was 27 percent. As production, spending, and income declined, government tax revenues decreased, making it harder to decrease the deficit to address the debt crisis. The sovereign debt crisis and the macroeconomic crisis reinforced each other.

The weakened Greek banks decreased their lending to private businesses and households, making the macroeconomic crisis worse. And, with declining sales and income because of the macroeconomic crisis, Greek businesses and households increasingly could not service their existing bank loans, further weakening the banks. By 2013 Greece was in depression, and its outstanding government debt was 175 percent of its GDP.

Ireland's crisis began differently, as a banking crisis. Irish banks had lent massively to private borrowers. When Ireland's housing price bubble burst, loans for housing and property went bad, and the Irish banks headed into crisis. The Irish government had to make good on its guarantee of bank liabilities. The Irish government went from a balanced budget in 2007 to a deficit of 30 percent of GDP in 2010, with outstanding government debt rising from a modest 25 percent of GDP to 91 percent. As investors perceived rising default risk, the prices of Irish government bonds fell and interest rate increased. The Irish government was forced to seek a bailout from the EU and the IMF, with the €85 billion program starting in November 2010. The Irish government reduced government spending and increased taxes. Fortunately, Ireland's macroeconomic crisis was not as severe as that of Greece, but its unemployment still averaged close to 15 percent during 2011 and 2012.

Portugal was the third European country to go into crisis, and it received a bailout program of €78 billion from the EU and IMF in 2011. The beginning of Portugal's crisis was a blend of the crises of Greece and Ireland, with excessive debt for both the government and private households, businesses, and excessive lending by Portuguese banks. Portugal's government budget deficit was 10 percent of GDP in 2009 and 2010, and its outstanding government debt increased from a reasonable 68 percent of GDP in 2007 to 129 percent in 2013. Its unemployment rate rose to 10 percent in 2013.

The crises in these three small countries then spread. Some of the spread was through international trade and international financial links, but contagion was more important. Investors and lenders focused next on Spain, where a housing price bubble had burst in late 2007. Spain had a large fiscal deficit starting in 2009, but at the end of 2010 its outstanding government debt was only 62 percent of its GDP. Still, the financial market became skittish. Between April and November 2011, Spanish government bond prices fell and interest rates jumped. Italy had had outstanding government debt of over 100 percent of its GDP since before the euro was born, but its government deficit was not especially large. With the contagion spreading, Italian government bond prices fell and interest rates jumped

—Continued on next page

during June–November 2011. Spain and Italy are not small countries, and it would have been impossible to provide them with bailouts of the same relative size as those to Greece, Ireland, and Portugal. Spain did receive a smaller assistance loan from the EU, eventually drawing a little over €40 billion to rescue its banks.

In July 2011 EU officials began to discuss that Greece would have to default on and restructure its privately held government debt. Fears that Greece would decide to (or be forced to) exit from the euro rose. The continued existence of the euro was in question.

In December 2011 and February 2012 the European Central Bank (ECB) provided huge longer term loans (called long-term refinancing operations) to a large number of European banks, and government bond markets calmed for a little while. Then market interest rates on Spanish and Italian government bonds spiked again during March to July 2012. Again, fears of Greek exit or even the collapse of the euro system intensified. Authorities reacted with two major changes that finally ended the worst of the crisis. In June 2012 euro-area leaders announced the first step toward an areawide banking union, with the ECB becoming the regulator of the area's large banks. More important, in July Mario Draghi, president of the ECB, announced forcefully that the ECB will do "whatever it takes to preserve the euro," adding, "And believe me, it will be enough." In September the ECB provided details of a program (Outright Monetary Transactions) under which the ECB would prevent distortions in financial markets by buying government bonds.

Draghi's statement and the new ECB program shifted bond markets from a low-confidence crisis equilibrium to a higher confidence, more stable equilibrium. The broad euro crisis of 2010–2012 effectively ended, and by 2014 market interest rates on government bonds for all countries except Greece had fallen back to reasonable levels (even Greece's rates were much lower than they had been at the peak of the crisis). Still, as of 2014 there was still some risk of renewed crisis. Outstanding government debt is still high—more than 100 percent of GDP in Greece, Ireland, and Portugal. And, macroeconomic performance remains weak (disastrous in Greece).

Summary

Well-behaved international lending (or international capital flows) yields the same kinds of welfare results as international trade in products. International lending increases total world product and brings net gains to both the lending and the borrowing countries, although there are some groups who lose well-being in each country. The lending-country government or the borrowing-country government can impose taxes on international lending. If either country has market power (that is, if it is able to affect the world interest rate), it can try to improve its well-being by imposing a **nationally optimal tax** on international lending. But if the other country retaliates with its own tax, both countries can end up worse off.

The history of international lending to developing countries shows surges of lending and recurrent financial crises. The dramatic increase of lending in the 1970s as banks recycled petrodollars led to the debt crisis beginning in 1982. This crisis stretched throughout the 1980s, with low capital flows to developing countries. The Brady Plan of 1989 led to the resolution of the crisis through debt reductions and the conversion of much bank debt to Brady bonds. Capital flows to developing countries increased dramatically during the 1990s, with more in the form of portfolio investments in bonds and stocks. However, we also saw a series of financial crises, including Mexico in 1994–1995, several Asian countries in 1997, Russia in 1998, and Argentina in 2001–2002.

We can identify five major forces that can lead to or deepen financial crises in developing countries. First, overlending and overborrowing can occur, as a result of government borrowing to finance expansionary government policies, excessive borrowing by banks, or the herding behavior of lenders seeking what seem to be high returns. For sovereign debt owed by borrowing governments, lending can turn out to be excessive even if the government has the ability to repay because the benefits of default exceed the costs. Second, exogenous shocks like increases in foreign (especially U.S.) interest rates can shift flows away from developing country borrowers and make repaying their debts more difficult. Third, borrowers, especially banks, can take on too many unhedged foreign currency liabilities, which then become very expensive to pay off if the local currency depreciates unexpectedly. Fourth, the borrowing country can borrow too much using short-term loans and bonds. The borrower can experience difficulties if foreign investors refuse to refinance or roll over the debt. And finally, **contagion** can spread the crisis from the initial crisis country to other countries. These other countries may be vulnerable because of problems with their policies or economic performance, but it is the contagion from the initial crisis country that leads foreign lenders to fear a crisis and pull back from lending to these other countries. Financial crises have elements of self-fulfilling panics, in which investors fear defaults, so they stop lending and demand quick repayment. If many lenders try to do this at once, the borrower cannot repay, and default and crisis occur.

The two major types of international efforts to resolve financial crises in developing countries are rescue packages and debt restructuring. A **rescue package** provides temporary financial assistance, can help to restore foreign investor confidence, and can try to limit contagion. In the crises since 1994, these packages have been large. A key question is whether the packages create substantial **moral hazard,** in which lenders believe that they can lend with little risk because a rescue will bail them out. **Debt restructuring** attempts to make debt service more manageable for the borrowing country. Debt rescheduling stretches out the repayments further into the future, and debt reduction lowers the amount of debt. Restructuring can be difficult because each individual creditor has the incentive to free ride, hoping others will restructure while the free-rider receives full repayment on time. The Brady Plan set up a process of successful restructuring of bank debt from the 1980s' crisis. International bonds can be more difficult to restructure, but it is becoming common for such bonds to include collective action clauses that streamline the restructuring process.

There are a range of proposals for reforms of the "international financial architecture" to reduce the frequency of financial crises in developing countries. Some are radical and unlikely, and others are controversial. Several are widely supported: Governments should have sound macroeconomic policies, they should provide better data for lenders and investors to use in their decision-making, they should minimize short-term debt, and they should improve their regulation and supervision of their banks. One controversial proposal is that developing-country governments should make greater use of controls on capital inflows. While this could limit overborrowing, short-term borrowing, and exposure to contagion, it could also reduce the benefits to be gained from international borrowing.

The global financial and economic crisis that began in 2007 and the euro crisis that began in 2010 show that major financial crises also originate in industrialized countries. For the global crisis, sub-prime mortgages that helped drive a housing price bubble in the United States were part of the tinder of overlending and overborrowing. The shock of the failure of Lehman Brothers in 2008 intensified the crisis. Contagion about similar problems at other financial institutions led investors and lenders to pull back from buying short-term assets. Financial institutions that relied on this short-term funding had to sell off their own assets and reduce their lending. As financial markets and lending froze, the world entered a severe recession. Actions by the U.S. Federal Reserve and other central banks may well have averted another depression like that of the 1930s.

Key Terms	Nationally optimal tax	Contagion	Moral hazard
	Conditionality	Rescue package	Debt restructuring

Suggested Reading

Obstfeld and Taylor (2004) provide a broad discussion of international capital movements. Agénor (2003) examines the benefits and costs of international financial openness. Henry (2007) surveys research on the effects of opening domestic stock markets to purchases by foreigners. Obstfeld (2012) views issues about international financial lending and investment flows through the lens of the current account balance. Rodrik and Subramanian (2009) offer skepticism about the effects of financial openness on developing countries.

Roubini and Setser (2004), Eichengreen (2002), Rogoff (1999), and Goldstein (1998) discuss developing-country financial crises and proposals for reform. Kindleberger and Aliber (2011) and Reinhart and Rogoff (2009) explore the history of centuries of crises. Panizza et al. (2009) survey the economics of sovereign default. Shambaugh (2012) and Pisani-Ferry (2014) provide overviews of the euro crisis.

Bird (2001) and Joyce (2004) survey evidence on the adoption and effects of IMF loan programs. Eichengreen and Mody (2004) analyze the inclusion of collective action clauses in international bonds. Ostry et al. (2011) examine the use of controls on capital inflows.

Questions and Problems

✦ 1. "It is best for a country never to borrow from foreign lenders." Do you agree or disagree? Why?

2. "Because a national government cannot go bankrupt, it is safe to lend to a foreign government." Do you agree or disagree? Why?

✦ 3. Why was there so much private lending to developing countries from 1974 to 1982, although there had been so little from 1930 to 1974?

4. What triggered the debt crisis in 1982?

✦ 5. Consider Figure 21.1. What is the size of each of the following? (Each answer should be a number.)

   a. World product without international lending.

   b. World product with free international lending.

   c. World product with Japan's tax of 2 percent on its foreign lending.

   What does the difference between your answers to parts *a* and *b* tell us? What does the difference between your answers to parts *b* and *c* tell us?

6. Consider Figure 21.1. In comparison with free international lending, what happens if each country imposes a 2 percent tax on the international lending (so that there is a total of 4 percent of tax)? What is the net gain, or loss, for each country?

✦ 7. How could each of the following cause or contribute to a financial crisis in a developing country?

   a. A large amount of short-term debt denominated in dollars.

   b. A financial crisis in another developing country in the region.

8. Consider the graph in the box "The Special Case of Sovereign Debt."

   a. Show graphically the effect of an increase in the interest rate (i). If the country's government would not default before this change, could this change lead to default?

   b. Show graphically the effect of an increase in the cost of defaulting. If the country's government would not default before this change, could this change lead to default?

✦ 9. How could each of the following reforms reduce the frequency of financial crises?

   a. Quick release of detailed, accurate information on the debt and official reserves of most developing countries.

   b. Use by more developing countries of controls to limit capital inflows.

10. "The global financial and economic crisis would have been resolved more quickly and with less cost if the IMF had provided rescue packages to the countries at the center of the crisis." Do you agree or disagree? Why?

✦ 11. An African country has a policy of fixing the exchange rate value of its currency to the U.S. dollar. Banks in the country have a business model in which the banks pay competitive interest rates to attract U.S. dollar deposits, and the banks then use these funds to make higher-interest loans denominated in the local currency. How likely would an unexpected devaluation of the local currency be to lead to banking crisis? Why?

12. The "Optimal Deadbeat" Problem: The World Bank is considering a stream of loans to the Puglian government to help it develop its nationalized oil fields and refineries. This is the only set of loans that the World Bank would ever give Puglia. If Puglia defaults, it receives no further funds from this set of loans from the World Bank. Whether the Puglian government repays the loan or defaults has no other impact on Puglia. The table on the next page shows the stream of loans to Puglia, the principal repayments and interest payments for the loans, and the increase in oil-export profits from the projects financed by the loans. Would it ever be in Puglia's interest to default on the loans? If not, why not? If so, why and when?

| | **Loan Effects ($ millions)** | | | |
Year	World Bank Loans and Repayments	Stock of Accumulated Borrowings at End of Year	Interest Payments on Borrowings (at 8 percent)	Profits on Extra Oil Export Sales
1	$200 (loan)	$200	0	0
2	100 (loan)	300	16	30
3	50 (loan)	350	24	45
4	0	350	28	60
5	50 (repayment)	300	28	60
6	50 (repayment)	250	24	60
7	50 (repayment)	200	20	60
8	50 (repayment)	150	16	60
9	50 (repayment)	100	12	60
10	50 (repayment)	50	8	60
11	50 (repayment)	0	4	60

Chapter **Twenty-Two**

How Does the Open Macroeconomy Work?

The analysis of Chapters 17–21 brought us part of the way toward a judgment of what kinds of policies toward foreign exchange would best serve a nation's needs. Chapters 19 and 20, in particular, spelled out some of the implications of different policies for the performance of the foreign exchange market, in terms of the efficiency—or inefficiency—of the market itself.

Our focus now shifts to the other kind of performance issue previewed when the basic policy choices were laid out at the start of Chapter 20. We address the challenge of *macroeconomic* performance—the behavior of a country's output, jobs, and prices in the face of changing world conditions. This chapter develops a general framework for analyzing the performance of a national economy that is open to international transactions. It provides a picture of how the open macroeconomy works. This framework will then be used in the next two chapters to examine macroeconomic performance in settings of fixed exchange rates and floating exchange rates.

There are many ways in which the national economy and the world economy interact. This chapter and the next two establish valuable conclusions about macroeconomic performance and policies. Based on these conclusions, Chapter 25 can provide a series of lessons about where the international macroeconomic system is headed and how well different exchange rate institutions work.

THE PERFORMANCE OF A NATIONAL ECONOMY

Each of us is comfortable judging our own performance in various activities. Did I perform in a sport up to the level at which I am capable? How did I perform on an examination relative to my own capabilities in the subject and relative to how others in the class performed? Judgments about performance also drive most macroeconomic analysis. How well is a country's economy performing? Is it performing up to its potential—for instance, its capabilities for producing goods and services? How close is it to achieving broad objectives that most people would agree are desirable, such as stability in average product prices (no inflation), low unemployment, and the maintenance of a reasonable balance of payments with the rest of the world?

We judge a country's macroeconomic performance against a number of broad objectives or goals. We can usefully divide these broad goals into two categories. The first category involves two objectives oriented to the domestic economy. One objective is keeping actual domestic production up to the economy's capabilities so that (1) the country achieves *full employment* of its labor and other resources and (2) the economy's production grows over time. Another domestic objective is achieving *price stability* (or, at least, a low or acceptable rate of product price inflation). These domestically oriented goals taken together define the goal of achieving internal balance.

The other category involves objectives related to the country's international economic activities. This is the problem of external balance, which is usually defined as the achievement of a reasonable and sustainable balance of payments with the rest of the world. Specifying a precise goal here is not so simple. Most broadly, the goal may be to achieve balance in the country's overall balance of payments. For instance, the goal may be to achieve a balance of approximately zero in the country's official settlements balance, at least over a number of years, so that the country is not losing official reserves or building up unwanted official reserves. This implies that the sum of the current account and the financial account (excluding official reserves transactions) should be approximately zero. If it is substantially different from zero for a long enough time, then we have the disequilibrium in the country's balance of payments (and exchange rate) that we discussed in Chapter 20. If the disequilibrium in the country's balance of payments becomes severe enough, it can lead to the kind of crises that we examined in Chapter 21.

For some purposes we focus on a somewhat narrower reading of external balance, one that focuses on the country's current account (or balance on goods and services trade). The goal here need not be a zero balance. Rather, it is a position that is sustainable in that the value for the current account balance can readily be financed by international capital flows (or official reserves transactions). Some rich industrialized countries probably achieve external balance by running a current account surplus because this allows the country to use some of its national saving to act as a net investor in the rest of the world (capital outflows or financial account deficit). Other countries that are in the process of developing their economies can achieve external balance while running a current account deficit. The deficit may include imports of machinery that directly are part of the development effort. The deficit can be financed by borrowing from the rest of the world (capital inflows or financial account surplus). As long as the surpluses and deficits on current account are not too large, the positions are sustainable over time. Each can become too large, however, and can become an external imbalance.

A FRAMEWORK FOR MACROECONOMIC ANALYSIS

To analyze the performance of an economy, we need a picture of how the economy functions. Such a picture is not without controversy—macroeconomists do not fully agree on the correct way to analyze the macroeconomy. One of the main difficulties has been to form a satisfactory framework for predicting both changes in domestic production and changes in the price level. We will use a synthesis that attempts to combine the strongest features from several different schools of thought. Our analysis of the behavior of the economy in the short run (say, a time period of one year or less) is relatively Keynesian in that the price level is not immediately responsive to aggregate demand and supply conditions in the economy. The price level is sticky or sluggish in the short run. Our view of the economy in the longer run is more classical. As we move beyond the short run, the price level does respond to demand and supply conditions. Furthermore, the amount of price inflation that the economy experiences eventually depends mainly on the growth rate of the country's money supply. In addition, the economy tends toward full employment in the long run. We have already developed some of the key features and implications of this long-run analysis in the discussion of the monetary approach in Chapter 19. Here and in the next two chapters we focus more on the economy in the shorter run. We want to develop a picture of how the economy works in the short run that is pragmatic and useful, even if it is not perfect.

The next three major sections of this chapter focus on the determinants of real GDP (representing both domestic product and national income) and the relationships between international trade and national income. Then the next major section adds the market for money and the country's overall balance of payments, resulting in a broad and flexible model of the open economy in the short run. To enhance the framework, the final two sections of the chapter take up issues related to product prices. These final sections explore the determinants of changes in the country's product price level (or its inflation rate) over time and the effects of international price competitiveness on a country's international trade.

DOMESTIC PRODUCTION DEPENDS ON AGGREGATE DEMAND

A major performance goal for an economy is to achieve production of goods and services that is close to the economy's potential. The economy's potential for producing is determined by the supply-side capabilities of the economy. Supply-side capabilities include both the factor resources (labor, capital, land, and natural resources) that the economy has available—the factor endowments from Chapters 4, 5, and 7—and intangible influences such as technology, resource quality, climate, and motivation. The intangibles determine the productivity of the resources.

The value of production of goods and services is the economy's real GDP (Y). Because production activity creates income (in the form of wages, profits and other returns to capital, and rents to landowners), real GDP is nearly the same thing as real national income.

In the short run (and within the economy's supply-side capabilities), domestic production is determined by aggregate demand (AD) for the country's products. Essentially, if someone demands a product, some business (or other organization) will try to produce it. Aggregate demand can be split into four components that represent different sources of demand: household consumption of goods and services (C); domestic investment (I_d) in new real assets like machinery, buildings, software, housing, and inventories; government spending on goods and services (G); and net exports of goods and services ($X - M$). Net exports capture two aspects of aggregate demand:

• Foreign demand for our exports (X) is an additional source of demand for our products.

- Our demand for imports (M) must be subtracted because these imports are already included in the other kinds of spending but actually represent demand for the products of other countries.

Equilibrium occurs when domestic production (Y, our GDP) equals desired demand for domestically produced goods and services:

$$Y = \text{AD} = C + I_d + G + (X - M) \qquad (22.1)$$

The level of actual domestic production (relative to the economy's potential for producing) tends to be closely related to the economy's labor unemployment rate. Increases of actual GDP (relative to potential) tend to decrease the unemployment rate, while decreases tend to increase the unemployment rate.

In order to focus on international trade issues, we can add up the national spending components into national expenditures (E) on goods and services:

$$E = C + I_d + G \qquad (22.2)$$

From basic macroeconomic analysis, we know something about the determinants of each of these components.

Household consumption expenditures are positively related to disposable income, and disposable income is (approximately) the difference between total income (Y) and taxes (T) paid to the government. Many taxes are based directly on income or are related indirectly to income because they are based on spending (for instance, sales or value-added taxes). Rather than carry around all of this detail, we will summarize the major determinant of consumption as income:

$$C = C(Y) \qquad (22.3)$$

remembering that the relationship incorporates taxes that have to be paid out of income before consumer spending is done. There are other influences on consumption, including interest rates that set the cost of borrowing to finance the purchase of items like automobiles, as well as household wealth and consumer sentiment about the future. To keep the analysis simple, we do not formally build these other influences into the framework. Instead, we can treat major changes in these other influences as shocks that occasionally disturb the economy.

Real domestic investment spending is negatively related to the level of interest rates (i) in the economy:

$$I_d = I_d(i) \qquad (22.4)$$

Higher interest rates increase the cost of financing the capital assets, thus reducing the amount of real investment undertaken. There are a number of other influences on real investment spending, including business sentiment about the future, current capacity utilization, and the emergence of new technologies that require capital investments in order to bring the technologies into use. Again, we can picture these other influences as a source of shocks to the economy.

We treat government spending on goods and services as a political decision. Decisions about government spending are a major part of a country's fiscal policy; the other part of fiscal policy is decisions about taxation.

TRADE DEPENDS ON INCOME

According to a host of empirical estimates for many countries, the volume of a nation's imports depends positively on the level of real national income or production:

$$M = M(Y) \qquad (22.5)$$

This positive relationship seems to have two explanations. One is that imports are often used as inputs into the production of the goods and services that constitute domestic product. The other explanation is that imports respond to the total real expenditure, or "absorption" (E), in our economy. The more we spend on all goods and services, the more we tend to spend on the part of them that we buy from abroad. Although a nation's expenditures on goods and services are not the same thing as its national income from producing goods and services, the close statistical correlation between income and expenditure allows us to gloss over this distinction. We can estimate the amount by which our imports increase when our income goes up by one dollar. This amount is called the marginal propensity to import (m).

It is also possible that the volume of our *exports* depends on *our* national income. If domestic national income is raised by a surge in domestic aggregate demand, there is a good chance that the increase in national income will be accompanied by a drop in export volumes, as domestic buyers bid away resources that otherwise would have been used to produce exports. Although such a negative dependence of export volumes on national-income-as-determined-by-domestic-demand is plausible, the evidence for it is somewhat sparse. We will assume that export volumes are independent of this country's national income.[1]

Exports nonetheless do depend on income—the *income of foreign countries.* If foreign income is higher, then foreigners tend to buy more of all kinds of things, including more of our exports. The amount by which their imports (our exports) increase if foreign income increases is the foreign marginal propensity to import.

EQUILIBRIUM GDP AND SPENDING MULTIPLIERS

With these pieces of the framework we can gain some major insights into macroeconomic performance in an open economy. To gain these insights we make a few assumptions that are useful now (but will be relaxed in later analysis). We assume that all price and pricelike variables are constant. In relation to our discussion so far, this means that the interest rate (in addition to the average product price level) is constant.

Equilibrium GDP

The condition for equilibrium real GDP is that it must equal desired aggregate demand, which in turn equals desired national expenditure plus net exports. Holding interest rates constant, our desired national expenditure depends on national income,

---

[1]Another way that export volumes can vary with our national income is through the supply side. A supply-side expansion of the economy permits production to increase, and some of this extra production may be available to increase exports.

as does our volume of imports. These relationships indicate that the value of aggregate demand itself depends on national income. The equilibrium condition is

$$Y = AD(Y) = E(Y) + X - M(Y) \tag{22.6}$$

Although our exports depend on foreign income, we initially ignore this (or assume that foreign income is constant).

Figure 22.1A illustrates the equilibrium level of domestic production and income, showing the matching between domestic product and aggregate demand at point *A*. At levels of domestic production below 100, the aggregate demand would exceed the level of production, as shown by the fact that the AD line is above the 45-degree line to the

FIGURE 22.1
Equilibrium
Domestic
Production in
an Open
Economy
Shown in Two
Equivalent
Ways

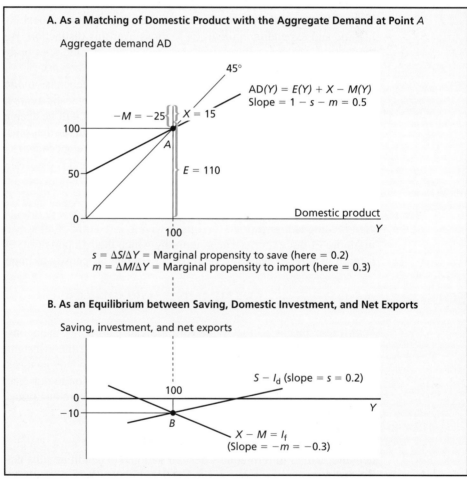

Panel A shows that we can use the fact that aggregate demand (AD) depends on domestic product and income (*Y*) to find the equilibrium in which domestic product equals desired aggregate demand. Panel B shows that we can find the same equilibrium domestic product by looking for the equality between net exports (*X − M*) and the difference between national saving and desired domestic real investment (*S − I_d*).

left of A. At any such lower levels of production, the combination of home and foreign demand for what this nation is producing would be so great as to deplete the inventories of goods held by firms, and the firms would respond by raising production and creating more jobs and incomes, moving the economy up toward A. Similarly, levels of production above 100 would yield insufficient demand, accumulating inventories, and cutbacks in production and jobs until the economy returned to equilibrium at point A.

Figure 22.1A does not demonstrate how the nation's foreign trade and investment relate to the process of achieving the equilibrium domestic production. To underline the role of the foreign sector, it is convenient to convert the equilibrium condition into a different form. National saving (S) equals the difference between national income (Y) and national expenditures on noninvestment items (C and G). Subtracting ($C + G$) from both sides of Equation 22.6 brings about an equilibrium between national saving, domestic investment, and net exports:

$$Y = E + X - M$$
$$(Y - C - G) = (E - C - G) + (X - M)$$

or

$$S = I_d + (X - M) \tag{22.7}$$

Recall from Chapter 16 that net exports are (approximately) equal to the country's current account balance, which in turn equals its net foreign investment (I_f). If we replace ($X - M$) with I_f, we see that this equilibrium condition is the same as saying that a country's desired national saving must match its desired domestic investment in new real assets plus its desired net foreign investment.

Figure 22.1B shows this saving–investment equilibrium in a way that highlights net exports (or the current account balance, approximately). As drawn here, Figure 22.1B shows a country having a current account deficit with more imports than exports of goods and services. For the equilibrium at point B, the country's domestic saving is less than its domestic investment, so the extra domestic investment must be financed by borrowing from foreigners (or selling off previously acquired foreign assets, including the country's official reserve assets). This could serve as a schematic view of the situation of the United States since 1982 because the United States has had a deficit in its current account balance financed by net capital inflows since then. In contrast, Japan has usually had its version of point B lying above the horizontal axis, representing a net export surplus and positive net foreign investment.

The Spending Multiplier in a Small Open Economy

When national spending rises in an economy in which actual production initially is below the economy's supply-side potential, this extra spending sets off a multiplier process of expansion of domestic production and income, whether or not the country is involved in international trade. Yet the way in which the country is involved in trade does affect the size of the spending multiplier. Suppose that the government raises its purchases of domestically produced goods and services by 10 units and holds them at this higher level. The extra 10 means an extra 10 income for whoever produces and sells the extra goods and services to the government. The extent to which this initial income gain gets transmitted into further domestic income gains depends on how the first gainers allocate their extra income. Let us assume, as we already have in Figure 22.1, that with each extra dollar of income, people within this nation

- save 20 cents (part of which is "saved" by the government as taxes on their extra income),
- spend 30 cents on imports of foreign goods and services, and
- spend 50 cents on domestically produced goods and services.

In other words, the marginal propensity to save (s, including the marginal tax rate) is 0.2; the marginal propensity to import (m) is 0.3; and the marginal propensity to consume domestic product ($1 - s - m$) is 0.5.

The first round of generating extra income produces an extra 2 units in saving, an extra 3 in imports, and an extra 5 in spending on domestic goods and services. Of these, only the 5 in domestic spending is returned to the national economy as a further demand stimulus. Both the 2 saved and the 3 spent on imports represent "leakages" from the domestic expenditure stream. Whatever their indirect effects, they do not directly create new demand or income in the national economy. (Here, we specifically rule out one indirect effect by assuming that this country is small and thus has no discernible impact on production or income in the rest of the world. If the country is small, then there is no indirect effect on foreign demand for our exports.) In the second round of income and expenditures, only 5 will be passed on and divided up into further domestic spending (2.5), saving (1), and imports (1.5). And for each succeeding round, as for these first two, the share of extra income that becomes further domestic expenditures is ($1 - s - m$) or ($1 - 0.2 - 0.3$) = 0.5.

The overall effects of this process are summarized in the spending multiplier. The **spending multiplier for a small open economy** is[2]

$$\frac{\Delta Y}{\Delta G} = \frac{1}{(s + m)} \tag{22.8}$$

In our example, the rise in government spending by 10 ultimately leads to twice as great an expansion of domestic production (an increase of 20) because the spending multiplier equals $1/(0.2 + 0.3) = 2$. The value of this multiplier is the same, of course, whether the initial extra spending is made by the government or results from a surge in consumption, a rise in private investment spending, or a rise in exports. Note also that the value of the multiplier is smaller in a small open economy than the multiplier in a closed economy. Had m been zero, the multiplier would have been $1/s = 5$.

We can also see the spending multiplier at work using either panel of Figure 22.1. In panel A, the increase in government spending of 10 shifts the AD line straight up by 10. Because of the slope of the AD line, the new intersection with the 45-degree line shows that domestic product increases to 120. In panel B, the increase in government spending of 10 is a *decrease of government saving* (the difference between tax revenue and government spending) by 10. The $S - I_d$ line shifts straight down by 10. Again,

---

[2]The multiplier formula can be derived from the fact that the change in production and income equals the initial rise in government spending plus the extra demand for the country's product stimulated by the rise in income itself:

$$\Delta Y = \Delta G + (1 - s - m) \bullet \Delta Y$$

so that

$$\Delta Y \bullet (1 - 1 + s + m) = \Delta G$$

because of the slopes of the lines, the intersection of the new $S - I_d$ line with the (unchanged) $X - M$ line indicates that domestic product increases to 120.

The spending multiplier of 2 works its effects not only on the rise in production but also on the rise in imports. Imports rose by 3 in the first round of expenditures, and they rise by twice as much, $6 (= 0.3 \times 20)$, over all rounds of new expenditures. With exports constant for this small country, the country's trade balance thus deteriorates by 6.

Foreign Spillovers and Foreign-Income Repercussions

We have described the propensity to import as a leakage, without considering what follow-on effects these imports can have. If the country is a small country, then any follow-on effects are very small, and we can ignore them. If, instead, the country is a large country, one whose domestic product and international trade are relatively large in the world economy, then these follow-on effects can be important, in two ways. First, changes in production and income of a large country have spillover effects on production and incomes in foreign countries. When a large country's extra spending leads to extra imports, the extra foreign exports noticeably raise foreign product and incomes. Second, the changes in foreign incomes alter foreign purchases of the first country's exports. If foreign incomes rise, foreign imports also rise, and the extra demand for its exports raises the country's product and income further.

Consider first foreign spillovers. The United States is a large country in the world economy, as is the euro area, the set of countries that use the euro as their currency. The United States accounts for about 19 percent of world production (measured using common international prices—measurement using purchasing power parity, as discussed in Chapter 19), and it accounts for about 13 percent of world imports. The euro area is also large, as it has about 13 percent of world production and 14 percent of world imports. Researchers at the International Monetary Fund examined what happens in other countries and areas of the world when national product in each of these two large countries increases by 1 percent, using data on actual national production during 1970–2005. Their results are summarized in Figure 22.2, with changes measured in percentages so that the values can be compared easily across countries and areas.

Here are some basic patterns. First, the United States and the euro area are each large enough to have noticeable effects on production and income in other countries. For instance, an increase of 1 percent in the domestic product of either the United States or the euro area would lead to an increase of 0.2 percent in the real GDP of other industrialized countries. Second, the importance of *close trading ties* is also evident. The United States has a relatively large effect on Canada, and the European Union has a relatively large effect on Africa.

Now consider that the effects kicked off by the rise in domestic product in a large country can feed back to affect it further. Figure 22.3 illustrates this process of foreign-income repercussions. An initial rise in our government purchases of goods and services, on the left, creates extra income in our national economy. Some fraction (s) of the extra income will be saved, some will be spent on domestic product, and some will be spent on imports. The fraction (m) spent on imports will create an equal amount of demand for foreign production, as well as income for foreign sellers (the foreign spillovers discussed above). The foreign countries, in turn, will save a fraction of this additional income (s_f), spend some in their own countries, and import a fraction (m_f) from us. We then divide that extra export income into saving, domestic

FIGURE 22.2   Foreign Spillovers of Changes in Domestic Product and Income

The Effect of a 1 Percent Increase of Real Domestic Product In	On Real Domestic Product In					
	Canada	Other Industrialized	Mexico	Other Latin America	Developing Asia	Africa
United States	0.5%	0.2%	0.4%	0.2%	0.1%	0.1%
Euro area	0.0	0.2	0.0	0.1	0.1	0.3

Each number gives the *percent* rise in the domestic product of the country or area whose column is named along the top that is caused by a 1 percent rise in the real domestic product of the country or area whose row is named on the left of the table.

Source: International Monetary Fund, *World Economic Outlook*, April 2007, Chapter 4.

purchases, and imports, and the cycle continues. Each round passes along a smaller stimulus until the multiplier process comes to rest with a finite overall expansion.

The process of foreign-income repercussions has implications for the size of the spending multiplier. For a large country, the foreign-income repercussions increase the size of the spending multiplier. *The more our country's imports affect foreign incomes, and the more the foreign countries have a propensity to import from our country, the more our true spending multiplier exceeds the simple formula 1/(s + m).*

The existence of foreign spillovers and foreign-income repercussions helps account for the parallelism in business cycles that has been observed among the major industrial economies. Since early in the 20th century, when America has sneezed, Canada, Europe, Japan, and many other countries have caught cold. Such a tendency was already evident in the business cycles in Europe and the United States in the mid-19th century, though the correlation between the European cycles and the U.S. cycles was far from perfect. The Great Depression of the 1930s also reverberated back and forth among countries, as each country's slump caused a cut in imports (helped by beggar-thy-neighbor import barriers that were partly a response to the slump itself) and thereby cut foreign exports and incomes. Correspondingly, the outbreak of the Korean War brought economic boom to West Germany, Italy, and

FIGURE 22.3

Foreign Trade and Income Repercussions Starting from a Rise in Our Spending

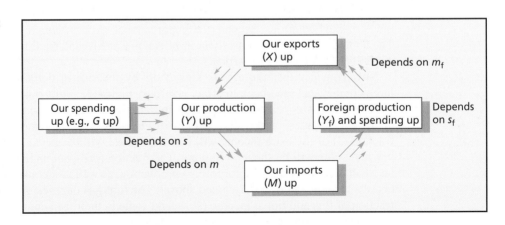

Japan, as surging U.S. war spending raised their exports and incomes, leading to a further partial increase in their purchases from the United States.

The same interdependence of incomes persists today. The *locomotive theory* posits that growth in one or more large economies can raise growth in other smaller countries that trade with these large countries. Growth in these large economies raises their imports, tending to pull the rest of the world along, with repercussions reinforcing the higher growth of all countries. The United States and the euro area are often considered to be key locomotives (a view supported by the estimates shown in Figure 22.2), and Japan also is large enough to contribute. Unfortunately, as we see with the global financial and economic crisis that began in 2007, the locomotives sometimes go in reverse, dragging the world into a global recession.

We also recognize one rising player. With its rapid growth of production and imports, China increasingly is playing the role of locomotive, especially to countries, such as Brazil, Malaysia, and even Japan, that export raw materials or components that China uses as inputs in its rapidly growing manufacturing industries.

A MORE COMPLETE FRAMEWORK: THREE MARKETS

The discussion of spending multipliers provides insights into macroeconomic performance, but it is too limited to be useful as a full framework for our analysis. We need to be able to picture three major components of the macroeconomy at the same time, adding the supply and demand for money and the country's overall balance of payments. In the process of developing this more complete framework, we can also drop the assumption that interest rates are constant. In fact, we will focus on the level of interest rates in the country as a second variable of major interest in addition to the country's real GDP.

Figure 22.4 sketches the basic approach, which is often called the Mundell-Fleming model, after its developers, Nobel Prize winner Robert Mundell and Marcus Fleming

FIGURE 22.4
An Overview of the Macromodel of an Open Economy

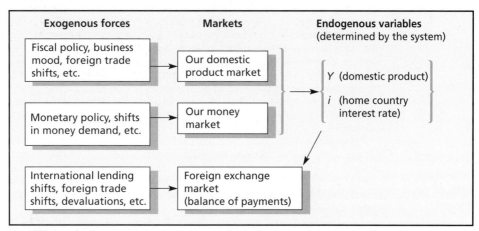

In addition to the linkages shown here, pressure in the foreign exchange market (or imbalance in the country's balance of payments) can feed back into and affect the country through the domestic product market or the money market. The ways in which this occurs depend on whether the country has a fixed or a floating exchange rate. These issues are taken up in the next two chapters.

of the International Monetary Fund. The three markets that give us a broader picture of the country's economy are shown in the center. The first two, the goods and services market and the market for money, directly determine two key variables of interest, the country's real GDP and its interest rate (Y and i). At the same time, these two variables have a major impact on the country's balance of payments and thus on the foreign exchange market. All three of the markets can be affected by different kinds of outside (exogenous) forces, shown on the left side of the figure. These outside forces represent shocks or disturbances that create pressures for macroeconomic changes.[3]

The Domestic Product Market

The aggregate demand for what our country produces depends not only on income (Y). It also depends on the interest rate (i) because a higher real interest rate discourages spending. We can picture these relationships in a graph as an IS curve. (IS stands for investment–saving.) The IS curve shows all combinations of domestic product levels and interest rates for which the domestic product market is in equilibrium. As in the previous section of this chapter, we can think of this equilibrium as following from the condition $Y = C + I_d + G + (X - M)$, or we can think of it as following from the condition that national saving equals the sum of domestic investment and net exports. If we use the latter, the domestic product market is in equilibrium when

$$\overset{+}{S(Y)} = \overset{-}{I_d(i)} + X - \overset{+}{M(Y)} \tag{22.9}$$

Here the signs above the equation indicate the direction of each influence in parentheses on the value of the variable it affects.[4]

To see why the IS curve slopes downward, let's start with one equilibrium point on it and then ask where other equilibriums would lie. Let us start at point A in Figure 22.5, where domestic product equals 100 and the interest rate is 0.07 (7 percent a year).

[3]This model of the open macroeconomy is not perfect, but it does allow us to examine the interrelationships among a large number of important macrovariables, and to examine the dynamics of national adjustments to achieve external balance. Here are some of the things that it does not do well. First, changes in the price level or the inflation rate are not modeled explicitly. Instead we infer that there are upward pressures on the price level or inflation rate when aggregate demand tries to push the economy beyond its supply-side potential. Second, the supply side of the economy is not modeled, so the approach cannot easily analyze supply-side shocks or long-run economic growth. Third, international capital flows are modeled as responsive to the difference in interest rates. However, a large effect cannot be sustained beyond the short run, once international investors have adjusted their portfolios. Fourth, expectations are not modeled explicitly, but instead they are brought in as exogenous forces.

Appendix G presents an approach that can address some of the issues raised in the first two points. This approach examines aggregate demand, aggregate supply, and price adjustment over time. We also briefly discuss, later in this chapter, how to add analysis of inflation to the Mundell-Fleming model. Furthermore, at several places in the analysis of this chapter and the next two, we will remind ourselves of how the third point about international capital flows should affect our interpretation of some of the results obtained using the Mundell-Fleming model.

[4]Additional influences of Y and i are possible. S may be a positive function of i, for instance, if higher interest rates reduce borrowing (that is, reduce negative saving) by households. I_d may be a positive function of Y, for instance, if high current production levels make the need for new investment to expand capacity more urgent. These additions would somewhat change the slope of the IS curve, but the picture would not be different in its essentials.

FIGURE 22.5

The IS Curve:
Equilibriums in
the Domestic
Product Market

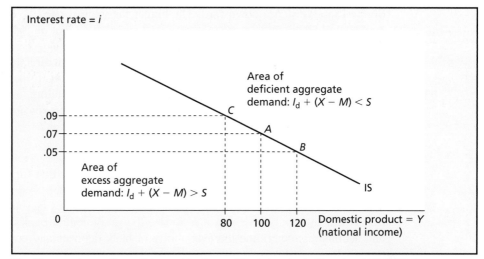

The IS curve shows all possible combinations of the interest rate (i) and real GDP (Y) that are
consistent with equilibrium in the goods and services sector of the national economy, given the state
of other fundamental influences. If any of these other fundamental influences changes,
then the entire IS curve shifts. Here are some changes in fundamental influences (usually
called exogenous shocks) that shift the IS curve to the right (or up):

- Expansionary fiscal policy (an increase in government spending or a tax cut).
- An exogenous increase in household consumption (for instance, due to improved consumer
  expectations about the future of the economy or an increase in wealth).
- An exogenous increase in domestic real investment (for instance, due to improved business
  expectations about the future of the economy).
- An exogenous increase in exports (for instance, due to rising foreign income, a shift in
  the tastes of foreign consumers toward the country's products, or an improvement in the
  international price competitiveness of the country's products).
- An exogenous decrease in imports (for instance, due to a shift in the tastes of local consumers
  away from imported products or an improvement in the international price competitiveness of
  the country's products).

To see what exogenous shocks can cause the IS curve to shift to the left (or down), reverse
all of these.

We somehow know that this combination brings an equilibrium in the domestic
product market. That is, given other basic economic conditions, having $Y = 100$ and
$i = 0.07$ makes domestic investment plus net exports, $I_d + (X - M)$, match national
saving, S. What would happen to the equilibrium in the product market if the interest rate is lower, say, only 0.05? The lower interest rate induces the nation to invest
in more domestic real capital. The higher level of aggregate demand (because I_d is
larger) results in a higher level of domestic product. (In fact, because of the spending
multiplier, the increase in domestic product is larger than the increase in real domestic
investment resulting directly from the lower interest rate.) According to the IS curve,
the higher level of domestic product matching aggregate demand for that low interest
rate is $Y = 120$, as represented at point B. Similarly, if point A is one equilibrium,
then others with higher interest rates must lie at lower production levels, as at point C.

So the IS curve slopes downward. The higher the interest rate, the lower the level of domestic product that is consistent with it. Points that are not on the IS curve find the domestic product market out of equilibrium.

Changes in any influence other than interest rates that can directly affect aggregate demand cause a shift in the IS curve. These are the exogenous forces or shocks noted in Figure 22.4. For instance, an increase in government spending, or an improvement in consumer sentiment that leads people to increase their consumption spending, increases aggregate demand and shifts the IS curve to the right.

The Money Market

The next market in which macroeconomic forces interact is that for the money of the nation. As usual, there is a balancing of supply and demand.

The supply side of the market for units of a nation's money is, roughly, the conventional "money supply." **Monetary policy,** the set of central-bank rules, regulations, and actions that determine the availability of bank deposits and currency in circulation, is the top influence on the money supply.

Our view of the demand for money is an extension of the money demand discussed in Chapter 19. There we posited that the (nominal) demand for money depends on the value of (nominal) GDP, which equals the price level P times Y (real GDP). Money is held to carry out transactions, and the value of transactions should be correlated with the value of income or production. The larger the domestic product during a time period such as a year, the greater the amount of money balances that firms and households will want to keep on hand to carry out their (larger) spending.

In addition to the benefits of money in facilitating transactions, there is an opportunity cost to holding money. The opportunity cost is the interest that the holder of money could earn if his wealth were instead invested in other financial assets such as bonds. Some forms of money (currency and coin, traveler's checks, zero-interest checking accounts) earn no interest. Others (interest-paying checking accounts) earn some interest, but the interest rate earned is generally relatively low. Interest forgone is an opportunity cost of holding money. This cost leads us to attempt to economize on our money holdings, and we attempt to economize more as the interest rate available on other financial assets rises. A higher interest rate tempts people to hold interest-earning bonds rather than money. That is, a higher interest rate reduces the amount of money demanded.

The demand for (nominal) money (L) is positively related to nominal GDP and negatively related to the level of interest rates available on other financial assets:

$$\overset{+ \quad -}{L = L(PY, i)} \qquad (22.10)$$

The equilibrium between money supply M^s and money demand is then

$$\overset{+ \quad -}{M^s = L(PY, i)} \qquad (22.11)$$

where the plus and minus signs again serve to remind us of the direction of influence of PY and i.

The money market equilibrium can be pictured as the "LM curve" of Figure 22.6. The **LM curve** shows all combinations of production levels and interest rates for

FIGURE 22.6

The LM Curve: Equilibriums in the Money Market

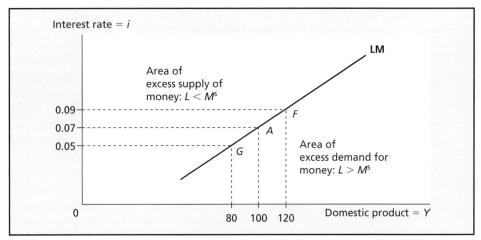

The LM curve shows all possible combinations of the interest rate (*i*) and real GDP (*Y*) that are consistent with equilibrium in the money sector of the national economy, given the state of other fundamental influences. If any of these other fundamental influences changes, then the entire LM curve shifts. Here are some changes in fundamental influences (exogenous shocks) that shift the LM curve down (or to the right):

- Expansionary monetary policy (increase in the money supply).
- Decrease in the country's average price level (for instance, due to a sudden decline in oil prices).
- Exogenous decrease in money demand (for instance, due to the introduction of credit cards that allow people to buy things without using money directly).

To see what exogenous shocks can cause the LM curve to shift up (or to the left), reverse all of these.

which the money market is in equilibrium, given the money supply (set by policy), the price level (*P*), and the money demand function (representing how people decide their money holdings). LM stands for liquidity–money, where money demand is viewed as demand for the most highly liquid financial assets in the economy.

To see why the LM curve slopes upward, begin with the equilibrium at point *A* and think of where the other equilibriums would lie. If the interest rate is higher, say, at 0.09, people would hold less money in order to earn the higher interest rate by holding bonds instead. To have the money market in equilibrium at that higher interest rate, people would have to have some other reason to hold the same amount of money supply as at point *A*. They would be willing to hold the same amount of money only if the level of domestic product and income is higher, raising their transactions demand for holding money. That happens to just the right extent at point *F*, another equilibrium. In contrast, going in the other direction, we can ask how people would be content to hold the same money supply as at point *A* if the interest they gave up by holding money were suddenly lower than at point *A*. By itself, the lower interest rate on bonds would mean a greater demand for money because money is convenient. People would be willing to refrain from holding extra money only if some other change reduced the demand. One such change is lower domestic product, meaning lower transactions demand for money. Point *G* is a point at which the lower interest rate and lower production leave the demand for money the same as at point *A*.

Changes in any of the influences on money supply and money demand other than the interest rate and domestic product represent exogenous forces that shift the entire LM curve. Consider an increase in the nominal money supply (M^s) by the central bank. If the price level (*P*) is sticky in the short run (so there is no immediate effect on the country's price level or inflation rate), then the increase in the money supply tends to reduce interest rates (or, equivalently, the increased money supply can support a higher level of domestic product and transactions). The LM curve shifts down (or to the right).

So far, we have two markets whose equilibriums depend on how domestic product (*Y*) and interest rates (*i*) interact in each market. For any given set of basic economic conditions (fiscal policy, the business mood, consumer sentiment, foreign demand for the country's exports, monetary policy, and so forth), these two markets simultaneously determine the level of domestic product and the level of the interest rate in the economy. The intersection of the IS and LM curves shows the levels of *Y* and *i* that represent equilibrium in both the market for goods and services and the market for money. For instance, if the IS curve from Figure 22.5 is added to Figure 22.6, the intersection is at point *A*. The short-run equilibrium level of real GDP (*Y*) is 100, and the equilibrium interest rate is 0.07 (7 percent).

The Foreign Exchange Market (or Balance of Payments)

The third market is the one where the availability of foreign currency is balanced against the demand for it. This market can be called either the *foreign exchange market,* if we want to keep the exchange rate in mind, or *the balance of payments,* if we are using the country's official settlements balance (*B*) to reflect the net private or nonofficial trading between our currency and foreign currency. To picture this third market, it is easier to think through the balance-of-payments approach.

The country's official settlements balance is the sum of the country's current account balance (CA) and its financial account balance (FA, which does not include official reserves transactions). The influences on *B* can be divided into trade flow effects and financial flow effects. How do our key variables—real product or income (*Y*) and the country's interest rate (*i*)—affect the country's balance of payments? Previous discussion has shown two major effects. First, the balance on goods and services trade (or the current account) depends negatively on our domestic product, through the demand for imports. Second, international capital flows depend on interest rates (both at home and abroad). A higher interest rate in our country will attract a capital inflow, provided that the higher domestic interest rate is not immediately offset by higher foreign interest rates.

The easy intuition that a higher interest rate in our economy will attract investment from abroad and give us a capital inflow is valid, but only in the short run (say, for a year or less after the interest rate rises). Over the longer run, this effect stops and is even reversed for at least two reasons:

1. A higher interest rate attracts a lot of capital inflow from abroad at first, as investors adjust the shares of their wealth held in assets from our country. Soon, though, the inflow will dwindle because portfolios have already been adjusted.

2. If a higher interest rate in our country succeeds in attracting funds from abroad and raising B in the short run, it may have the opposite effect later on for the simple reason that bonds mature and loans must be repaid. We cannot talk of using higher interest rates to attract capital (lending) to this country now without reflecting on the fact that those higher interest rates will have to be paid out in the future, along with repayments of the borrowed principal.[5]

For these reasons, the notion that a higher interest rate in our country can "improve" the balance of payments is valid only in the short run. We can use the short-run reasoning if the issue before us is the effect on B now. We will often use this short-run focus, but only with the warning that in the long run a higher interest rate has an ambiguous effect on the overall balance of payments.

We can express the dependence of the balance of payments (or the foreign exchange market) on production and interest rates with an equation. The official settlements balance, B, equals the current account balance, CA (which is approximately equal to net exports, $X - M$), plus the financial account balance, FA:

$$B = \overset{-}{\text{CA}(Y)} + \overset{+}{\text{FA}(i)} \tag{22.12}$$

Raising our domestic product lowers the current account surplus (or raises the deficit) because it gives us more demand for imports of foreign goods and services. Raising our interest rate, on the other hand, attracts an inflow of capital from abroad, raising our financial account surplus (or reducing the deficit).

To link the balance of payments with i and Y, we can also use the FE curve of Figure 22.7. For a given set of other basic economic conditions that can influence the country's balance of payments, the FE curve shows the set of all interest-and-production combinations in our country that result in a zero value for the country's official settlements balance.

The FE curve, like the LM curve, slopes upward. To see why, begin again with an equilibrium at point A. Let's say that this is the same point A as in the previous two figures, although it need not be. If point A finds our international payments in overall balance, how could they still be in balance if the interest rate is higher, say, at 11 percent? That higher interest rate attracts a greater inflow of capital, bringing

[5]The balance-of-payments cost of attracting the extra capital from abroad could be even greater than the interest rate alone might suggest. To see how, let us suppose that the home country (a) is a net debtor country and (b) is large enough to be able to raise its own interest rate even though it is part of a larger world capital market. Let us imagine Canada is in this position.

Suppose that a rise in Canada's interest rate from 9 percent to 12 percent succeeds in raising foreign investments into Canada from $500 billion to $600 billion. What interest will Canada pay out each year on the extra $100 billion of borrowing (a temporarily higher B)? The annual interest bill on the new $100 billion itself comes to $12 billion a year. But, in addition, to continue to hold the original investments of $500 billion within the country—that is, to "roll over" these bonds and loans as they come up for renewal or repayment—Canadian borrowers have to pay an extra $15 billion [= $500 billion $\times$ (.12 − .09)]. After the original bonds and loans have been rolled over, the total extra interest outflow each year will be the $12 billion plus the extra $15 billion, or payments of $27 billion just to hold on to an extra $100 billion in borrowings. That's an incremental interest cost of 27 percent, not just 12 percent. This is an expensive way to attract international "hot money."

FIGURE 22.7

The FE Curve:
Balance-of-
Payment
Equilibriums

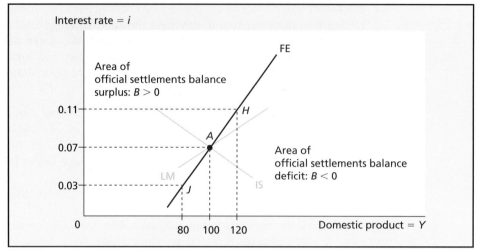

The FE curve shows all possible combinations of the interest rate (i) and real GDP (Y) that are consistent with an official settlements balance of zero for the country, given the state of other fundamental influences. If any of these other fundamental influences changes, then the entire FE curve shifts. Here are some changes in fundamental influences (exogenous shocks) that shift the FE curve to the right (or down):

- An exogenous increase in exports (for instance, due to rising foreign income, a shift in the tastes of foreign consumers toward the country's products, or an improvement in the international price competitiveness of the country's products).
- An exogenous decrease in imports (for instance, due to a shift in the tastes of local consumers away from imported products or an improvement in the international price competitiveness of the country's products).
- Exogenous changes that result in an increase in capital inflows or a decrease in capital outflows (for instance, a decrease in the foreign interest rate, an increase in the expected rate of appreciation of the country's currency, or a decrease in the perceived riskiness of investing in this country's financial assets).

To see what exogenous shocks can cause the FE curve to shift to the left (or up), reverse all of these.

an official-settlements-balance surplus unless something else also changes. With the higher interest rate, B could still be zero (no surplus, no deficit) if domestic product and income are higher. Higher product and income induce us to spend more on everything, including imports. The extra imports shift the balance of payments toward a deficit. In just the right amounts, extra production and a higher interest rate could cancel each other's effect on the balance of payments, leaving $B = 0$. That happens at point H. Correspondingly, some combinations of lower interest rates and lower production levels could also keep our payments in overall balance, as at point J.

How does the slope of the FE curve compare to the slope of the LM curve? As drawn in Figure 22.7, the FE curve is steeper. This is not the only possibility, though.

It depends on how responsive money demand and the balance of payments are to changes in the interest rate and domestic product. If, for instance, capital flows are very sensitive to interest rates, then the FE curve is relatively flat, flatter than the LM curve. The FE curve is relatively flat because only a small increase in the interest rate is needed to draw in enough capital to offset the decline in the current account if domestic product is higher. (Point *H* would be lower, with an interest rate that is not much above 0.07.) If capital flows are extremely sensitive to interest rates, then we have the case of **perfect capital mobility,** and the FE curve is essentially completely flat (a horizontal line).

What happens when some other condition or variable that affects the country's balance of payments changes? These are the exogenous forces of Figure 22.4. When one of these changes occurs, it shifts the FE curve (just as a change in an exogenous condition relevant to the IS curve or the LM curve causes a shift in that curve). For instance, an increase in foreign income increases demand for our exports, improving our balance of payments and shifting the FE curve to the right. Or an increase in foreign interest rates causes a capital outflow from our country, deteriorating our balance of payments and shifting the FE curve to the left.

Three Markets Together

Bringing the three markets together, we get a determination of the level of domestic product (*Y*), the interest rate (*i*), and the overall balance of payments (*B*). The economy will gravitate toward a simultaneous equilibrium in the domestic product market (on the IS curve) and the money market (on the LM curve). With *Y* and *i* thus determined, we also know the state of the balance of payments (*B*).

- The official settlements balance is in surplus if the IS–LM intersection is to the left of (or above) the FE curve.
- The official settlements balance is zero if the IS–LM intersection is on the FE curve (for example, point *A* in Figure 22.7).
- The official settlements balance is in deficit if the IS–LM intersection is to the right of (or below) the FE curve.

This section has given the same reasoning about three markets in three alternative forms: the causal-arrow sketch of Figure 22.4; the listing of Equations 22.9, 22.11, and 22.12; and the use of IS–LM–FE diagrams (Figures 22.5 through 22.7). The way that we use this framework—especially the way that we use the FE curve—depends on the type of exchange-rate policy that the country has adopted. As we will examine in the next chapter, if a country adopts a fixed exchange rate, then any divergence between the IS–LM intersection and the FE curve shows that official intervention is needed to defend the fixed rate. The official settlements balance is not zero—official intervention to defend the fixed rate results in official reserves transactions. As we will examine in Chapter 24, if the country adopts a clean float, then the official settlements balance must be zero, and somehow a triple intersection between the IS, LM, and FE curves must occur. In different ways, to be explored in each chapter, these situations create pressures for adjustments that affect the country's macroeconomic performance.

THE PRICE LEVEL DOES CHANGE

In developing the framework so far, we have generally ignored the product price level (*P*). We assumed that the price level is a constant for the short run, given by previous history. While this may be reasonable for most short-run analysis, it is clearly not appropriate generally. The price level does change over time for three basic reasons.[6]

First, most countries have some amount of ongoing inflation. This amount can be anticipated and built into inflation expectations. Generally, ongoing positive inflation requires sufficient ongoing growth of the country's nominal money supply. The role of ongoing inflation was prominent in Chapter 19, especially in discussing the monetary approach.

Second, strong or weak aggregate demand can put pressure on the country's price level. If the price level is somewhat sluggish, then this effect will not be felt in the immediate short run, but it will have an impact as the economy moves beyond the initial short run. The strength of aggregate demand must be evaluated against the economy's supply-side capabilities for producing goods and services. If aggregate demand is very strong, then actual production strains against the economy's supply capabilities. The economy will "overheat" and there will be upward pressure on the price level. (In a setting in which there is ongoing inflation, this really means that the price level will rise more than it otherwise would have, anyway. The inflation rate will increase.) If aggregate demand is weak, then product markets will be weak, creating downward pressure on the price level because of the "discipline" effect of weak demand. (Again, in a setting of ongoing inflation, this really means that the inflation rate will be lower than it otherwise would have been—the price level may still be rising, but it will rise more slowly.)

Third, shocks occasionally can cause large changes in the price level even in the short run. One example is an oil price shock. As oil prices rose dramatically during 2004–2008, inflation rates increased in the United States, the euro area, and most other oil-importing countries, although the effects were not as large as those during the two oil price shocks in the 1970s.

Another source of a price shock is a large, abrupt change in the exchange-rate value of a country's currency. As we will discuss in the next chapter, a large devaluation or depreciation is likely to cause a large increase in the domestic-currency price of imported products. The general price level tends to increase quickly because of both the direct effects of higher import prices and the indirect effects on costs and other prices in the country.

For subsequent analysis using our framework, the effect of strong or weak aggregate demand on the price level is of major interest. As we move beyond the initial short run, we do expect adjustment in the country's product price level. This can have an impact on the country's international price competitiveness, as discussed in the next section. If international price competitiveness is affected, then the country's current account balance changes. In addition, although we will not focus on this effect in subsequent analysis, a change in the price level changes money demand (through the *PY* term).

---

[6]Appendix G presents a formal framework for analyzing the adjustment of the price level over time.

If the nation's money supply is not changing in line with the change in money demand, then the LM curve will shift over time.[7]

TRADE ALSO DEPENDS ON PRICE COMPETITIVENESS

As previously discussed, a country's exports, imports, and net exports depend on production and incomes in this country and the rest of the world. Standard microeconomics indicates that demand for exports and imports each should also be affected by the prices of these products. Quantity demanded depends on both income and relative prices.

Our demand for imports depends not only on our income but also on the price of imports relative to the price (P) of domestic products that are substitutes for these imports. What is this relative price? Consider that an imported product (say, a bottle of French wine) is initially priced in foreign currency (say, 10 euros). Once imported into the United States, its foreign-currency price P_f is converted into dollars using the going (nominal) exchange rate (say, $1.40 per euro). The domestic-currency price of the import is then equal to $P_f \cdot e$ ($14.00 for the bottle), where the (nominal) exchange rate (e) is stated in units of domestic currency per unit of foreign currency. Our decision about whether to buy this import depends partly on its dollar price relative to the price of a comparable domestic product (say, a bottle of California wine). The price ratio is $(P_f \cdot e)/P$. This ratio may look familiar—it is essentially the real exchange rate introduced in Chapter 19 (but here the expression is measuring the real-exchange-rate value of the foreign currency).

Thus, by expanding our previous Equation 22.5, we see that the demand for imports has two major determinants:

$$M = M(Y, \overset{+}{P_f} \cdot \overset{-}{e}/P) \tag{22.13}$$

The volume of imports tends to be higher if our production and income are higher, but lower if imports are relatively expensive (meaning $P_f \cdot e/P$ is high).

Foreign demand for our exports depends not only on foreign income but also on the price of our products exported into the foreign market relative to the prices of their comparable local products (P_f). Our export product (say, a personal computer) is initially priced in our currency (say, $1,500). This can be converted into a foreign currency (say, yen) at the going (nominal) exchange rate (say, $e = $0.01 per yen). The foreign-currency price of our export is then equal to P/e. (Here $1,500/.01 = 150,000$ yen.) The foreign decision about whether to buy their domestic product (say, an NEC

---

[7]If the aggregate demand pressure continues for a sufficient period of time, it can also affect the ongoing rate of inflation. For instance, the United States went into the 1990–1991 recession with an ongoing inflation rate of about 4.5 percent. The weak aggregate demand that caused the recession (and slowed the subsequent recovery) reduced the actual inflation rate to less than 3 percent. In addition, the ongoing inflation rate expected to continue into the future (even when the economy had fully recovered from the recession) was reduced to about 3 percent, according to most estimates. (The expected ongoing inflation rate fell to 2.5 percent by the early 2000s, largely because technical changes lowered the measured inflation rate.)

computer) or our exported product is based partly on the relative price, which equals $P_f/(P/e)$, or $(P_f \cdot e)/P$. The higher this ratio, the less attractive is their domestic product, and the more attractive is our exported product.

Thus, the demand for our exports has two major determinants:

$$X = X(\overset{+}{Y_f}, \overset{+}{P_f \cdot e/P}) \tag{22.14}$$

The volume of our exports tends to be higher if foreign production and income are higher or if foreign substitute products are relatively expensive.

Thus, in addition to the income effects, net exports $(X - M)$ tend to be higher if the price competitiveness of our products is higher, both because the volume of exports tends to be larger and because the volume of imports tends to be smaller. Our general indicator of international price competitiveness is the ratio $(P_f \cdot e)/P$.[8] Our international price competitiveness improves if the foreign-currency price of foreign substitute products (P_f) is higher, the domestic-currency price of our products (P) is lower, or the nominal exchange-rate value of our currency is lower (e is higher). Over time, our price competitiveness improves if the foreign inflation rate is higher, our inflation rate is lower, or our currency appreciates less (or depreciates more).

A change in international price competitiveness can be incorporated into our IS–LM–FE framework. It is one of the other economic conditions (or exogenous forces) that can cause shifts in the curves. A change in international price competitiveness shifts two curves: the FE curve and the IS curve. To see this, consider an improvement in a country's international price competitiveness, perhaps because the country has had low product price inflation or because the country's currency has depreciated or devalued. The improved price competitiveness increases exports and decreases imports. The increase in net exports increases aggregate demand, so the IS curve shifts to the right. The current account improves, so the FE curve also shifts to the right.

Summary

The performance of a country's macroeconomy has both internal and external dimensions. We evaluate the country's internal balance against goals oriented toward the domestic economy. **Internal balance** focuses on achieving domestic production that matches the country's supply capabilities so that resources are fully employed, while also achieving price-level stability or an acceptably low rate of inflation. We evaluate

---

[8]While this ratio (essentially, the real exchange rate) is a useful broad indicator of a country's international price competitiveness, it is not perfect. For any particular product, the relative price is affected by several influences not usually captured in the ratio. First, transport costs and government barriers to imports can alter the price ratio by increasing the price of the imported product. Second, exporters may use strategic pricing so that the local-currency price of the imported product is not just the domestic-currency price in the home market converted at the going exchange rate. This reflects international price discrimination. It is particularly interesting here because exporters may resist passing through the full effect of any exchange-rate change into foreign-currency prices for their products. This is called *incomplete pass-through* or *pricing to market*. When the yen appreciated sharply from 1985 to 1987, Japanese firms did raise the dollar prices of the products that they exported to the United States, but by far less than the amount of the exchange-rate change. They did this, presumably, to minimize their loss of export sales. From the point of view of the U.S. economy, this means that the volume of imports did not fall as much as might have been expected following the large dollar depreciation.

external balance against goals related to the country's international transactions. **External balance** focuses on achieving an overall balance of payments that is sustainable over time.

A key aspect of how an open macroeconomy works is the relationship between domestic production and international trade in goods and services. International trade in goods and services is one component of total aggregate demand, which determines domestic product and income in the short run. In addition, domestic production and income have an impact on international trade, especially through the demand for imports.

These relationships influence how shifts in aggregate demand affect our domestic production. Holding interest rates (as well as the product price level and exchange rates) constant, we generally expect that an increase in some component of aggregate demand (like government spending) has a larger effect on domestic production—a phenomenon summarized in the spending multiplier. In a closed economy, the size of the multiplier is $1/s$, where s is the marginal propensity to save (including any government saving "forced" through the marginal tax rate). For the open macroeconomy, a rise in domestic product and income increases imports. The size of the **spending multiplier for a small open economy** is $1/(s + m)$, where m is the **marginal propensity to import.** The larger the country's propensity to import, the smaller is the spending multiplier. The leakage into imports, like the leakage into saving, dampens the effects of the initial extra spending on the ultimate change in domestic product and income.

If the country is not small, then changes in its demand for imports have noticeable effects on other countries, with several specific implications. First, any boom or slump in one country's aggregate demand can spill over to other countries. Second, the changes in production and income in the other countries can then feed back into the first country—**foreign-income repercussions.** These foreign-income repercussions make the true spending multiplier larger than the simple formula $1/(s + m)$. Swings in the business cycle (recession or expansion) are not only internationally contagious but also self-reinforcing, a conjecture easily supported by the experience of the 1930s and the global crisis that began in 2007. The locomotive theory posits that growth in the world's large economies (the United States, the euro area, Japan, and increasingly China) can spur growth in the entire world.

A more complete framework for analyzing a country's macroeconomy in the short run requires that we are able to picture not only domestic product, income, and aggregate demand but also supply and demand for money and the country's overall balance of payments. The IS–LM–FE approach, also called the Mundell-Fleming model, provides this framework.

The **IS curve** shows all combinations of interest rate and domestic product that are equilibriums in the national market for goods and services. Because lower interest rates encourage borrowing and spending, the IS curve slopes downward. The **LM curve** shows all combinations of interest rate and domestic product that are equilibriums between money supply and money demand. For money demand to remain equal to a given, unchanged money supply, the increase in money demand that accompanies a higher domestic product must be offset by a higher interest rate that reduces money demand, so that the LM curve slopes upward.

The FE curve shows all combinations of interest rate and domestic product that result in a zero balance in the country's overall international payments (its official settlements balance). The FE curve also generally slopes upward. An increase in domestic product and income increases demand for imports so that the country's current account and overall payments balance deteriorate. This can be offset (at least in the short run) by a higher interest rate that draws in foreign financial capital (or reduces capital outflows) so that the financial account (excluding official reserves transactions) improves.

The intersection of the IS and LM curves indicates the short-run equilibrium values for domestic product (Y) and the interest rate (i) for the country. The position of this IS–LM intersection relative to the FE curve indicates whether the official settlements balance is positive, zero, or negative.

Although we often assume that the country's product price level is constant in the short run, over time the price level changes. Most countries have some amount of ongoing inflation that is expected to continue. The monetary approach presented in Chapter 19 emphasizes that ongoing inflation is related to continuing growth of the money supply. In addition, the strength of aggregate demand relative to the economy's supply capabilities can affect the price level or inflation rate. If aggregate demand is too strong, the economy overheats and the price level or inflation rate rises. If aggregate demand is weak, the discipline effect of weak market demand tends to lower the price level or inflation rate. Furthermore, price shocks can cause large changes in the price level or inflation rate even in the short run.

International price competitiveness is another key determinant of a country's international trade in goods and services, in addition to the effects of national income on the country's imports and foreign income on the country's exports. If the price of foreign products relative to the price of our country's products is higher, our demand for imports tends to be lower and foreign demand for our exports tends to be higher. The real exchange rate is a useful general indicator of this relative price and thus of the country's international price competitiveness. A change in international price competitiveness shifts both the IS curve and the FE curve because the current account balance changes. For instance, if competitiveness improves, then exports increase and imports decline. The increase in aggregate demand shifts the IS curve to the right, and the improvement in the country's payments position shifts the FE curve to the right.

Key Terms	Internal balance	Spending multiplier for a	Monetary policy
	External balance	small open economy	LM curve
	Fiscal policy	Foreign-income	FE curve
	Marginal propensity	repercussions	Perfect capital
	to import	IS curve	mobility

Suggested
Reading

Bosworth (1993, Chapter 2) discusses the concepts of internal and external balance and develops the IS–LM–FE model. Hervé et al. (2011) and Dalsgaard et al. (2001) present empirical estimates of the domestic and foreign effects of policy changes using dynamic macroeconomic models that incorporate trade and other linkages among countries. Chapter 4 of the International Monetary Fund's April 2007 *World Economic Outlook* examines foreign spillovers of production and incomes and the correlation of business cycles across countries. Campa and Goldberg (2005) provide a statistical analysis of incomplete exchange-rate pass-through for industrialized countries.

Questions
and
Problems

✦ 1. According to Figure 22.2, on which country other than Canada does the United States have the largest impact? Why do you think that this is so?

2. "A recession in the United States is likely to raise the growth of real GDP in Europe." Do you agree or disagree? Why?

✦ 3. An economy has a marginal propensity to save of 0.2 and a marginal propensity to import of 0.1. An increase of $1 billion in government spending now occurs. (*Hint:* Assume that the economy is initially producing at a level that is below its supply-side capabilities.)

    a. According to the spending multiplier for a small open economy, by how much will domestic product and income increase?

    b. If instead this were a closed economy with a marginal propensity to save of 0.2, by how much would domestic product and income increase if government spending increased by $1 billion? Explain the economics of why this answer is different from the answer to part *a.*

4. A country has a marginal propensity to save of 0.15 and a marginal propensity to import of 0.4. Real domestic spending now decreases by $2 billion.

    a. According to the spending multiplier (for a small open economy), by how much will domestic product and income change?

    b. What is the change in the country's imports?

    c. If this country is large, what effect will this have on foreign product and income? Explain.

    d. Will the change in foreign product and income tend to counteract or reinforce the change in the first country's domestic product and income? Explain.

✦ 5. How does the intersection of the IS and LM curves relate to the concept of internal balance?

6. How does the FE curve relate to the concept of external balance?

✦ 7. Explain the effect of each of the following on the LM curve:

    a. The country's central bank decreases the money supply.

    b. The country's interest rate increases.

8. Explain the effect of each of the following on the IS curve:

    a. Government spending decreases.

    b. Foreign demand for the country's exports increases.

    c. The country's interest rate increases.

◆ 9. Explain the effect of each of the following on the FE curve:

   a. Foreign demand for the country's exports increases.

   b. The foreign interest rate increases.

   c. The country's interest rate increases.

10. Explain the impact of each of the following on our country's exports and imports:

   a. Our domestic product and income increase.

   b. Foreign domestic product and income decrease.

   c. Our price level increases by 5 percent, with no change in the (nominal) exchange-rate value of our currency and no change in the foreign price level.

   d. Our price level increases by 5 percent, the foreign price level increases by 10 percent, and there is no change in the (nominal) exchange-rate value of our currency.

◆ 11. According to the Board of Governors of the Federal Reserve System, the real effective exchange rate of the U.S. dollar (relative to the rest of the world) went from 110 in late 2002 to 100 in late 2003. Looked at the other way, the real exchange rate of the rest of the world relative to the dollar went from 91 in late 2002 to 100 in late 2003. Did the international price competitiveness of U.S. products improve or worsen from late 2002 to late 2003? Other fundamental things equal, what was the effect (if any) on the U.S. IS curve? On the U.S. FE curve?

12. Consider a small open-economy country, with $s = 0.25$ and $m = 0.15$. This country's economy is otherwise standard, but it has one unusual feature. When real GDP increases, the expanded sales to domestic buyers reduce the pursuit of export sales by domestic firms. That is, the export equation is $X = X(Y)$, and the "marginal propensity to export" (z) is -0.1, so that each \$1 increase in real GDP causes a \$0.10 decrease in exports.

   Is the size of the spending multiplier for this small open economy larger, the same, or smaller (than the spending multiplier for a country that is the same except that it does not have this unusual export behavior)? What is the mathematical expression for the spending multiplier for this country with the unusual export behavior?

Chapter **Twenty-Three**

Internal and External Balance with Fixed Exchange Rates

Fixed exchange rates can reduce the variability of currency values if governments are willing and able to defend the rates. This chapter examines the macroeconomics of a country whose government has chosen a fixed exchange rate.

Many major countries of the world have instead chosen floating rates (albeit with modest amounts of government management). Why study fixed rates? There are three important reasons. First, within the current system a substantial number of countries do fix their exchange rates. As shown in Chapter 20, there are two major blocs of currencies with fixed exchange rates. A large number of developing countries that fix their currencies to the U.S. dollar form the dollar bloc. The euro bloc includes the 18 European Union countries that use the euro, other EU countries that fix their currencies to the euro through the Exchange Rate Mechanism, and a number of countries outside the EU that fix their currencies to the euro. In addition, a number of other countries fix their moneys to currencies other than the dollar or the euro or to a basket of currencies. Second, in the current system a number of countries have floating rates in name, but the rates are so heavily managed by the governments that they are closer to being fixed rates in many respects. Third, there are continuing discussions about returning to a system of fixed rates among the world's major currencies. Proposals range from target zones, which would be a kind of crawling peg with wide bands, to a return to the gold standard. Before we can assess the desirability or feasibility of such proposals, we need to understand how a fixed exchange rate affects both the behavior of a country's economy and the use of government policies to influence the economy's performance.

The analysis of the chapter shows that defense of a fixed exchange rate through official intervention in the foreign exchange market dramatically affects the country's monetary policy. The intervention can change the country's money supply, setting off effects that tend to reduce the payments imbalance. But this process limits the country's ability to pursue an independent monetary policy. Defending the fixed rate also has an impact on fiscal policy, which actually becomes more powerful if international financial capital is highly mobile. In addition, intervention to defend the fixed rate affects how the country's economy responds to shocks, both shocks that come from within the country and shocks that are international in origin.

Fixed rates challenge government policymakers who are attempting to guide the country to both external balance (balance in the country's overall international payments) and internal balance (actual production equal to the economy's supply potential, or a high level of employment—"full employment"—without upward pressure on the country's inflation rate). Internal and external balance are often hard to reconcile in the short and medium runs. A government that pursues external balance alone, tidying up its balance of payments while letting inflation or unemployment get out of hand at home, may be thrown out of office. On the other hand, controlling domestic production alone, with fiscal or monetary policies, may widen a deficit or surplus in the balance of payments, jeopardizing the promise to keep the exchange rate fixed.

One possible solution is a subtle mixture of policies, with monetary policy assigned to reducing international payments imbalances and fiscal policy assigned to stabilizing domestic production (GDP). Another possible "solution" is surrender—to change the fixed rate by devaluing, revaluing, or shifting to a floating rate. The chapter looks at both ideas and concludes by considering the conditions that influence whether a change in the fixed rate will be successful in improving the country's internal and external macroeconomic performance.

FROM THE BALANCE OF PAYMENTS TO THE MONEY SUPPLY

Once a country's government has decided to have a fixed exchange rate, the government must defend that rate. As previously discussed, the first line of defense is official intervention—the monetary authority (central bank) buys or sells foreign currency in the foreign exchange market as necessary to steady the rate within the allowable band around the central value chosen for the fixed rate. Several implications follow from official intervention. First, the holdings of official reserves change as the central bank buys or sells foreign currency. Second, the country's money supply may change as the central bank sells or buys domestic currency as the other half of its official intervention.

Our goal in this and the next three sections of the chapter is to show how these effects occur and what implications they have for the country's macroeconomy. Let's begin with the assets and liabilities of the central bank that will be the core of our story. Here is a simplified balance sheet that shows these items:

Central Bank	
Selected Assets	**Selected Liabilities**
Domestic assets (D)	*Monetary base (MB)*
Debt securities	Currency
Loans to banks	Deposits from banks
International reserve assets (R)	
Foreign-currency assets	

FIGURE 23.1

Key Balance-
Sheet Items,
the Fed and the
ECB, December
31, 2013
(Billions of U.S.
Dollars)

Source: Federal
Reserve Board of
Governors, annual
report, 2013;
European Central
Bank, annual report,
2013.

	Federal Reserve (Consolidated System)	European Central Bank (Consolidated System)
Key Assets		
Securities (denominated in domestic currency)	3,952	852
Loans to banks (domestic currency)	0	1,037
Foreign-currency-denominated assets	24	361
Key Liabilities		
Currency (paper notes and coins)	1,198	1,318
Deposits from banks (domestic currency)	2,249	652

The differences in the holding of the key *domestic assets* reflects the difference in operating procedures. The Fed conducts its domestic monetary policy using *open market operations,* in which the Fed buys and sells U.S. government securities, so it holds a lot of these assets. The ECB conducts its domestic monetary policy mostly by *making loans (in euros) to banks and other financial institutions.* These are two alternative ways of regulating the two key liability items, which together form the monetary base. In addition, the sizes of securities holdings by the Fed and deposits from banks at the Fed are much larger than under normal conditions because of "quantitative easing" by the Fed. The ECB has conducted a milder form of quantitative easing, which has increased the sizes of its holdings of securities and its loans to banks.

The difference in holdings of *foreign-currency assets* mainly reflects history. The U.S. government seldom intervenes in the foreign exchange market, so the Fed has little need to hold international reserve assets. The ECB inherited its official reserve assets from the national central banks of the euro area. Historically, these national banks actively intervened, so they needed to hold substantial international reserves.

Figure 23.1 shows the magnitude of these items for the Federal Reserve, the U.S. central bank, and the European Central Bank (ECB), the central bank for the euro area.

The two key types of assets are **domestic assets** (*D*) and **international reserve assets** (*R*), especially the central bank's holdings of foreign currency and foreign-currency-denominated securities. The domestic assets are not international reserves because they are denominated in domestic currency. Two major types of domestic assets held by the central bank are (1) bonds and similar debt securities and (2) loans that the central bank has made to (regular) domestic banks or other domestic financial institutions.

On the other side of the balance sheet, the liabilities of interest to our story are (1) the domestic currency (paper money and coins) issued by the central bank and (2) the deposits that the country's (regular) domestic banks (or other domestic financial institutions) have placed with the central bank. The deposits from regular banks may be required by regulations of the central bank. In addition, the central bank often uses the deposits from banks in the process of settling payments between domestic banks (for instance, in the process of clearing checks drawn on one bank but payable to another). The total of these two central-bank liabilities, currency and deposits from banks, is called the **monetary base (MB).**

The country's **money supply** consists (mainly) of currency held by the public and various types of deposits (like checking accounts) that the public has at regular banks. The country's central bank has the ability to influence the total amount of these bank deposits from the public because banks are required to hold, or wish to hold, certain assets as bank reserves to "back up" these deposit liabilities. We presume that the types of assets that count as bank reserves are a bank's holdings of currency "in its vault" and the bank's holdings of deposits at the central bank. The amount of reserves that a bank is required to hold is typically some fraction of the deposits that the bank owes to its customers—a system called *fractional reserve banking.*[1]

In this setting the central bank controls the country's money supply by controlling its own balance sheet and by setting the reserve requirements that (regular) banks must meet. To see this, consider what happens if the central bank allows its liabilities (the monetary base) to increase. This will expand the money supply. If the increase is in the form of an increase in currency that is held by the public, then the money supply increases directly. If the increase is in the form of central bank liabilities that count as bank reserves (either currency in bank vaults or deposits from banks), then banks can increase the value of their deposit liabilities, and they can increase deposits by a multiple amount of the value of the increase in bank reserves. With fractional reserve banking, each dollar of extra bank reserves can back up several dollars of deposits (where *several* is the reciprocal of the reserve requirement fraction). The multiple expansion of the money supply with fractional reserve banking is called the *money multiplier process.*[2]

With this background on the country's central bank and its control of the country's money supply, let's return to the effects of official intervention used to defend the fixed exchange rate. If the country has an *official settlements balance surplus, so that the exchange-rate value of the country's currency is experiencing upward pressure,* the central bank must *intervene to buy foreign currency and sell domestic currency.* On its balance sheet this is

* an increase in official international reserve holdings ($R\uparrow$) and
* an increase in its liabilities (MB$\uparrow$ as the domestic currency is added to the economy).

[1]As you can see, the standard terminology seems intended to confuse us. *Bank* shows up in two ways. The country's *central bank* is the official monetary authority that controls monetary policy and (usually) is the authority that undertakes official intervention in the foreign exchange market. Regular banks, often just called *banks,* conduct regular banking business (making loans, taking deposits, transacting in foreign exchange) with regular customers (for instance, individuals, businesses, and government units) and among themselves (for instance, interbank loans and interbank foreign exchange trading). *Reserves* is an even more dangerous term. A central bank (or the country's relevant monetary authority if it is not exactly a central bank) holds *official international reserve* assets. Regular banks hold bank *reserves* as assets, usually in proportion to their deposit liabilities. Part of these bank reserves is usually in the form of deposits that these regular banks have at the central bank. (Just to add to the soup, there is another type of reserve in bank accounting—liability items such as reserves for bad loans—but these are not part of our main story.)

[2]This description of the central bank and the way in which it controls the country's money supply is appropriate for the United States (the Federal Reserve, or "Fed") and for many other countries. Still, some countries use different procedures (for instance, implementing monetary policy through limits on the expansion of loans by banks to their customers). Analysis of such countries would need to be modified somewhat to match their procedures, but the major conclusions to be reached in the sections below generally still apply.

The increase in liabilities can be in the form of an increase in actual currency outstanding (if the central bank delivers the domestic currency as currency itself). More likely, and more efficiently in terms of the process, the central bank delivers the domestic "currency" to a regular bank (the bank with whom it is transacting in the foreign exchange market) by increasing the deposits that the bank has at the central bank. In either case, the country's *money supply will increase*. If, as is likely, the reserves held by banks increase (because their deposits at the central bank increase or their holdings of vault cash increase), then the money supply can increase by a multiple of the size of the central bank intervention in the foreign exchange market.

If instead the *country's official settlements balance is in deficit and the exchange-rate value of the country's currency is under downward pressure,* the central bank must *intervene to sell foreign currency and buy domestic currency.* On its balance sheet this is

- a decrease in official international reserve holdings ($R\downarrow$) and
- a decrease in its liabilities (MB$\downarrow$ as the domestic currency is removed from the economy).

The central bank probably collects the domestic "currency" by decreasing the deposits that the regular bank involved in the foreign exchange transaction has at the central bank. Then the reserves held by banks decline (because their deposits at the central bank decrease), and the *money supply must decrease* by a multiple of the size of the central bank intervention in the foreign exchange market (the money multiplier in reverse).

The conclusion here is that official intervention alters the central bank's assets and liabilities in ways that change not only the country's holdings of official international reserve assets but also the country's money supply, unless the central bank does something else to attempt to resist the change in the money supply. Indeed, under fractional reserve banking, the change in the money supply will be a multiple of the size of the intervention.

FROM THE MONEY SUPPLY BACK TO THE BALANCE OF PAYMENTS

If official intervention changes the country's money supply, what are the implications for the country's balance of payments and for the country's macroeconomic performance in general? The change in the money supply sets off several effects that tend to reduce the payments imbalance.

Consider first the case in which the country begins with a surplus in its overall balance of payments. The surplus requires official intervention in which the central bank buys foreign currency and sells domestic currency. The domestic money supply increases "automatically" as the central bank increases its liabilities when it sells domestic currency. Figure 23.2 summarizes the effects of the increase in the money supply on the balance of payments.

As the central bank increases bank reserves, banks are more liquid and want to expand their business. They seek to make more loans. In the process, their competition to lend more is likely to bid down interest rates.

FIGURE 23.2 Expanding the Money Supply Worsens the Balance of Payments with Fixed Rates

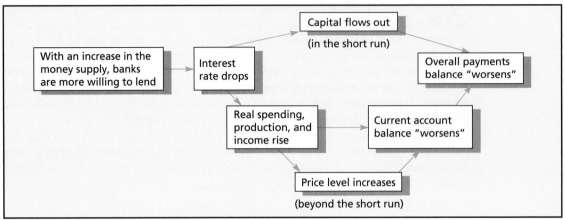

For a decrease in the money supply, reverse the direction of all changes.

The lowering of interest rates in the economy, at least in the short run, has several effects on the balance of payments. One is through the country's financial account. The decline in interest rates causes some holders of financial assets denominated in the domestic currency to seek higher returns abroad. The international capital outflow causes the financial account to "deteriorate" (become less positive or more negative).[3] This effect on the financial account can occur quickly, but it may not last long. Once portfolios are adjusted, any ongoing capital flows are likely to be smaller. In fact, the outflows could reverse when bonds mature or loans come due. (In addition, the extra foreign investment is likely to set up a stream of income payments that the country receives in the future.)

Another effect is on the current account because of changes in real income, in the price level, or in both. The decrease in domestic interest rates encourages interest-sensitive spending—for instance, through more borrowing to support additional new real investment projects. The expansion in spending results in an increase in real domestic product and income (assuming that there is some availability of resources to expand production in the economy). The rise in income increases imports of goods and services and "worsens" the current account balance. (A smaller surplus or a larger deficit results.) In addition, the extra spending can put upward pressure on the price level in the economy, especially if the expansion of aggregate demand pushes against the supply capabilities of the economy. If prices and costs in the economy rise, then the country's international price competitiveness deteriorates, and the country's current account worsens. Which of these two effects actually occurs depends on the starting point for the economy and the time frame involved. If the economy begins with unemployed resources, then the effect through real income is likely to be larger. If the

---

[3]We are assuming that the change in the domestic interest rate lowers the interest differential because foreign interest rates have not changed or have not changed as much. In addition, we are assuming that expectations of future spot exchange rates have not changed. For instance, international investors believe that the fixed rate will be maintained, so the expected future spot rate remains about equal to the current spot rate.

FIGURE 23.3

Payments
Adjustments
for a Surplus
Country with
Fixed Rates

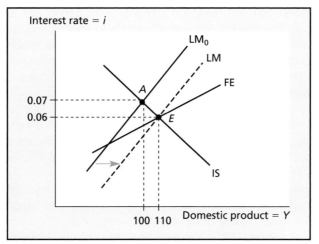

If the country begins at point *A* with a payment surplus,
intervention to defend the fixed exchange rate results in an
increase in the money supply. The LM curve shifts down or
to the right, and the surplus falls toward zero as the IS–LM
intersection shifts toward point *E*.

economy starts close to full employment, then the effect through the price level is likely
to be more important, at least beyond the short-run period when prices are sticky.

Thus, official intervention by a country that initially has a balance-of-payments
surplus can increase the money supply, and this increase in the money supply sets off
adjustments in the economy that tend to reduce the size of the surplus. Key features
of the adjustment can be pictured using an IS–LM–FE diagram. Suppose that the
economy is initially at point *A* in Figure 23.3, the intersection of the initial IS and
LM_0 curves. This point is to the left of the FE curve, showing that the country has a
surplus in its official settlements balance. Official intervention to defend the fixed rate
increases the money supply, shifting the LM curve down or to the right. As the LM
curve shifts down, the equilibrium interest rate decreases and domestic product and
income increase. The intersection of the IS curve and the new LM curve is moving
closer to the FE curve. If the price level does not change, then full adjustment has
occurred (probably over several years) when the LM curve has shifted down to the
triple intersection at point *E*. The equilibrium interest rate has fallen from 7 percent
to 6 percent, domestic product has risen from 100 to 110, and the official settlements
balance is zero (because the economy is on the FE curve).[4]

If the country instead begins with a deficit in its official settlements balance and
downward pressure on the exchange-rate value of its currency, then all of these effects
work in the reverse direction. The domestic money supply decreases and domestic
interest rates increase, at least in the short run. The rise in interest rates draws a
capital inflow, improving the financial account. The rise in interest rates also lowers

---

[4]If the price level also increases, then both the FE and IS curves will shift to the left as the country loses
international price competitiveness. The LM curve will shift by less, and the triple intersection will
occur with a somewhat lower real domestic product.

aggregate demand and real domestic product, reducing imports and improving the current account. The weak aggregate demand also puts downward pressure on the economy's price level, at least beyond the short-run period in which prices are sticky. This increases the country's international price competitiveness and improves its current account. The overall balance of payments improves—the deficit declines toward zero. The country's IS–LM intersection is initially to the right of the FE curve. The LM curve then shifts up or to the left, and eventually a triple intersection is achieved.

The thrust of the analysis is clear. If an external imbalance exists, intervention to defend the fixed rate changes the domestic money supply. The money supply change causes adjustments that move the country back toward external balance. So what is the problem? Possible problems are of two types.

First, the process is based on changes in the country's holdings of international reserve assets. For a country that begins with a payments surplus, the monetary authority will acquire official international reserve assets. For a deficit, the authority will lose official reserves. Officials may view either change as undesirable. However, this may not really be a problem if the authority *accepts that the money supply must change* (and the LM curve must shift). The central bank can simply use its *domestic* operations to speed up the adjustment. For instance, the country can use open market operations in which it buys or sells government securities.

In the surplus situation, the country could expand the money supply more quickly, and lower interest rates more quickly, by buying domestic government securities. This open market operation adds to both the domestic assets ($D\uparrow$) and the liabilities (MB$\uparrow$) of the central bank. By changing monetary conditions more quickly, external balance is achieved more quickly. Official reserve assets (R) increase by less because some of the increase in the domestic money supply is the result of the increase in domestic assets (D) held by the central bank.

In the deficit situation, the country could contract the money supply by selling domestic government bonds in an open market operation. Bank reserves decrease, the money supply contracts, and interest rates rise more quickly. The payments deficit shrinks more quickly, and external balance is achieved more quickly. Official international reserves do not decrease as much; instead, part of the money supply decrease is the result of a decrease in domestic assets held by the central bank.

A second possible problem with the adjustment toward external balance is that it may not be consistent with internal balance. In the surplus situation, the increase in the money supply can put upward pressure on the country's price level, and this pressure toward a positive (or higher) rate of inflation may be viewed as undesirable—a shift toward internal imbalance. In the deficit situation, the decrease in the money supply can result in a recession (declining real production), with rising unemployment.

STERILIZATION

Rather than allowing automatic adjustments to proceed (or speeding them up), the monetary authority instead may want to *resist* the change in the country's money supply. One reason for resistance is that the money supply change would tend to create an internal imbalance, as just described. Another is that the authority may believe that the international imbalance is temporary and will soon reverse. This is the case of temporary disequilibrium discussed in Chapter 20.

The central bank can keep the external surplus or deficit from having an impact on the domestic money supply by taking an *offsetting* domestic action. **Sterilization** is taking an action to reverse the effect of official intervention on the domestic money supply. If the central bank is intervening to defend the fixed rate in a situation of payments surplus by selling its national currency in exchange for foreign currency, the money supply tends to increase ($R\uparrow$ and $MB\uparrow$). This can be sterilized if the central bank, for instance, undertakes an open market operation in which the central bank sells domestic government bonds. While the intervention in currency markets tends to expand the money supply, the open market operation tends to reduce it by reducing both the domestic assets held by the central bank and the central bank liabilities that serve as the base for the domestic money supply ($D\downarrow$ and $MB\downarrow$). The effects on the monetary base and the money supply of the combination of intervention and sterilization tend to cancel out ($MB\uparrow = MB\downarrow$). The net effects of the sterilized intervention are to alter the composition of the central bank's assets (in this case, $R\uparrow$ and $D\downarrow$).

In the case of a deficit, the central bank can sterilize the official intervention (buying the nation's currency) by buying domestic government bonds with that same currency in an open market operation. In this case, the intervention reduces official reserve holdings ($R\downarrow$) and the central bank's liabilities ($MB\downarrow$). The sterilization increases the central bank's holding of domestic securities ($D\uparrow$) and increases its liabilities ($MB\uparrow$). The effects on the monetary base and the money supply tend to cancel out, and the net effects are on the central bank's assets ($R\downarrow$ and $D\uparrow$).

Because a sterilized intervention does not change the money supply, the LM curve does not change. In Figure 23.3 the economy's equilibrium remains at point *A*. There is no adjustment toward external balance. Often this is a wait-and-see or a wait-and-hope strategy. Perhaps something else will shift the FE curve toward point *A*, or some other source of change will shift the IS–LM intersection toward the FE curve. If nothing else moves the economy toward external balance, there are limits to the ability of the monetary authority to use sterilized intervention to continue to run a payments imbalance.

In the case of the payments surplus, the limit may be (1) the unwillingness of the central bank to continue to increase its holdings of official reserve assets or (2) the complaints by other countries about the country's ongoing surplus. China was in the middle of this scenario during 2005–2014. Previously, Taiwan saw this process play out in the 1980s, when its interventions resulted in official reserve holdings that grew rapidly to a value equal to about three-quarters of the value of its annual national income. Pressure by the U.S. government then induced Taiwan to allow its currency to appreciate quickly during 1986–1987.

In the case of a payments deficit, the limit is the inability of the central bank to obtain foreign currency to sell in the official intervention. The country's official reserve assets may dwindle toward zero (and it cannot borrow more foreign currencies because of its precarious international position). This limit can be dramatic—if international investors and speculators believe that the central bank is low in its holdings of official reserves, a currency crisis based on the one-way speculative gamble discussed in Chapters 20 and 21 can develop.

MONETARY POLICY WITH FIXED EXCHANGE RATES

The discussion of the preceding two sections has a major implication—*fixed exchange rates greatly constrain a country's ability to pursue an independent monetary policy.* To a large degree the country's monetary policy must be consistent with maintaining the value of the fixed rate. Payments imbalances place pressure for changes in the money supply driven by the intervention to defend the fixed rate. Sterilization can be used to resist these money supply changes, but there are limits to how long the country's central bank can use sterilization, especially if the central bank's holdings of official reserves are declining because of a payments deficit.

Even if the country begins with a payments balance, its ability to pursue an independent monetary policy is greatly constrained. To see this, consider a country that initially has an official settlements balance of zero. While the country has achieved external balance, the country may believe that it has not achieved internal balance. Specifically, it has a high unemployment rate and wants to expand its domestic product. To pursue this goal with monetary policy, it attempts to implement an expansionary monetary policy.

For a time this policy may increase real product. But the country's official settlements balance will go into deficit through the process shown in Figure 23.2. Both the current account and financial account will deteriorate. The country then must intervene to defend its fixed rate, selling foreign currency and buying domestic currency. This reduces the domestic money supply, effectively forcing the country to abandon its expansionary policy. Even if the central bank resists this for a while using sterilization, it cannot continue to sterilize indefinitely. Eventually, the country must allow its money supply to shrink (or pursue some other adjustment like an exchange-rate change).

This process can be seen in Figure 23.4, where the country is initially at point E, a triple intersection. The increase in the money supply shifts the LM curve down or to

FIGURE 23.4
Expansionary
Monetary Policy
with Fixed
Rates

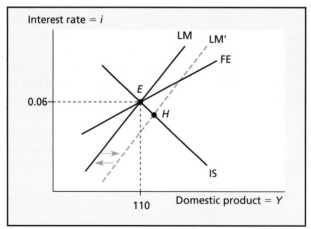

Starting from point E with an overall payments balance of zero, the country attempts to implement an expansionary policy. The LM curve shifts down or to the right, but at point H the payment balance is in deficit. Intervention to defend the fixed exchange rate decreases the money supply, and the LM curve shifts back up, eventually returning the country to point E.

the right. The IS–LM intersection at point *H* indicates that real domestic product has increased, but the new intersection is to the right of the FE curve, indicating a payments deficit. As the country intervenes to defend the fixed exchange rate, the money supply shrinks and the LM curve shifts back. If nothing else changes, the LM curve shifts back to the original triple intersection.

In this example, in contrast to the analysis in the earlier sections, we are starting from payments balance and conducting the analysis as "from the money supply to the balance of payments" and then "from the balance of payments back to the money supply." In the process we conclude that the ability to change the money supply is limited, and eventually stops, because of the feedback from the balance of payments and the need to defend the fixed rate.

FISCAL POLICY WITH FIXED EXCHANGE RATES

Fiscal policy is implemented by changing government spending and taxes. A change in fiscal policy affects the balance of payments through both the current account and the financial account. Let's examine the case of an expansionary fiscal policy, say, a rise in government purchases of goods and services. This case is summarized in Figure 23.5. (Contractionary fiscal policy is analyzed in the same way, with all of the changes occurring in the opposite direction.)

The extra government spending means a bigger government budget deficit (or a reduced budget surplus). We'll tell the story using a budget deficit. To finance the larger budget deficit, the government is borrowing more and driving up interest rates. The higher interest rates should attract a capital inflow, "improving" the country's financial account.

The extra government spending also increases aggregate demand and real domestic product (assuming that some resources are available to expand production).[5] The extra spending spills over into extra import demand, "worsening" our current account balance.

FIGURE 23.5
How Expansionary Fiscal Policy Affects the Balance of Payments with Fixed Rates

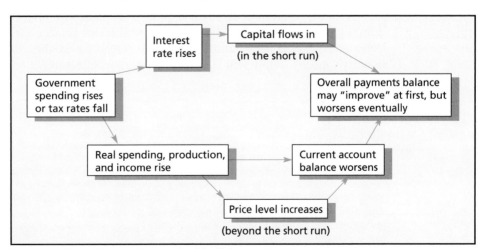

For contractionary fiscal policy, reverse the direction of all changes.

In addition, the extra aggregate demand may put upward pressure on the price level once we pass beyond the short-run period in which the price level is sticky. If the price level increases, then the country loses international price competitiveness, another reason that the current account deteriorates.

The effect on the country's overall balance of payments depends on the magnitudes of these changes. Given the worsening of the current account, we can examine the effect on overall balance as a question of how responsive international financial capital flows are to interest rate changes.

- If international capital flows are very responsive to interest rate changes (high capital mobility), then the capital inflows will be large, and the official settlements balance will go into surplus.
- If the capital flows are unresponsive (low capital mobility), then the financial account will improve only a little, and the overall balance will go into deficit.

The effect on the overall balance is probably also affected by timing—the capital inflows may be large at first, but they probably will dwindle as international portfolios are adjusted to the new economic conditions.

Figure 23.6 shows the effects of a fiscal expansion with fixed exchange rates in the short run assuming that the price level is steady. For both cases we begin with a triple intersection at point E. The shift to an expansionary fiscal policy shifts the IS curve to the right, to IS'. The new intersection with the LM curve is at point K, with a higher interest rate and a higher level of real domestic product.[6]

The two cases shown in Figure 23.6 differ in how responsive international capital flows are to changes in the interest rate. The left graph shows the case of high capital mobility so that the FE curve is relatively flat. The right graph shows the case of low capital mobility so that the FE curve is relatively steep. If capital flows are responsive, as in Figure 23.6A, then the new intersection point K lies to the left of the FE curve and the overall payments balance goes into surplus. If they are unresponsive (Figure 23.6B), then point K lies to the right of FE and the overall balance goes into deficit.[7]

The discussion so far has offered conclusions about the effects of a fiscal policy change on the domestic economy and on external balance. It might seem that we can stop here, but we should not. If the official settlements balance shifts into surplus or deficit, then official intervention is needed to defend the fixed exchange rate, and the country's money supply will change (although this effect might be postponed if the

---

[5]In the short run real GDP increases even if there is partial crowding out, as interest-sensitive domestic spending decreases somewhat when interest rates increase.

[6]Another way to see the pressure for a higher interest rate is to use the direct logic of the IS–LM analysis. The increase in real income and spending increases the transaction demand for money, but there is no increase in the money supply (assuming, at least initially, that the central bank does not permit any increase because of an unwillingness to shift its monetary policy). The extra money demand must be choked off by an increase in interest rates. (All of this represents a movement along the LM curve from E to K.)

[7]The slope of the FE curve does not matter much in analyzing monetary policy because there is no ambiguity in the direction of effects on the overall balance for an attempted shift in monetary policy such as that analyzed in Figure 23.4.

FIGURE 23.6 Expansionary Fiscal Policy with Fixed Exchange Rates

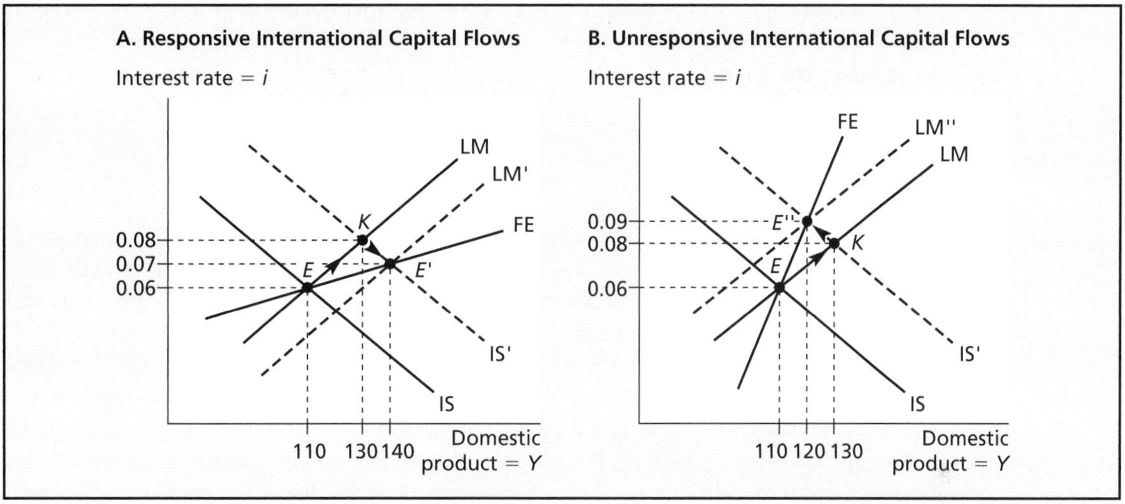

A. Responsive International Capital Flows

Interest rate = *i*

B. Unresponsive International Capital Flows

Interest rate = *i*

Expansionary fiscal policy shifts the IS curve to the right and the IS–LM intersection shifts from E to K. The effects of fiscal policy depend on how strongly international capital flows respond to the interest rate increase. In panel A, the overall payments balance goes into surplus. (K is to the left of FE.) In panel B, the overall payments balance goes into deficit. (K is to the right of FE.) In either case the payments imbalance leads to a change in the money supply (assuming that the central bank does not or cannot "sterilize" it). In panel A, intervention to defend the fixed rate increases the money supply, shifting the LM curve down, and the economy shifts toward a new full equilibrium at point E'. In panel B, intervention to defend the fixed rate decreases the money supply, shifting the LM curve up, and the economy shifts toward a new full equilibrium at point E".

intervention is sterilized). If the intervention is not sterilized, then interest rates and domestic product will be affected further as the money supply changes. The direction of this effect depends on whether the overall balance shifts into surplus or deficit.

If capital is highly mobile, then overall payments go into surplus, and the central bank must intervene by selling domestic currency and buying foreign currency. With no sterilization, the domestic money supply expands, reducing interest rates and supporting a further expansion in domestic product. In Figure 23.6A, the increase in the money supply shifts the LM curve down or to the right. It will eventually shift to the dashed LM', where a new triple intersection is achieved at point E'. In this case, fiscal policy becomes more powerful in increasing real GDP because the monetary authority expands the money supply as it intervenes to defend the fixed exchange rate.[8]

If capital mobility instead is low, then the overall payments deficit requires official intervention in which domestic currency is purchased and foreign currency is sold. If the intervention is not sterilized, then the domestic money supply decreases, raising

---

[8]If the price level also increases, the FE curve shifts to the left and the IS curve shifts back somewhat to the left. Real domestic product does not increase by as much in this case and in the one discussed in the next paragraph.

interest rates and reversing some of the increase in real domestic product. In Figure 23.6B the decrease in the money supply shifts the LM curve up or to the left, eventually to the dashed LM". In this case, expansionary fiscal policy loses some of its power to increase real GDP.

PERFECT CAPITAL MOBILITY

The case of perfect capital mobility is an extreme case of how international financial flows can alter the effectiveness of monetary and fiscal policies under fixed rates. Perfect capital mobility means that a practically unlimited amount of international capital flows in response to the slightest change in one country's interest rates.

Perfect capital mobility may be a good basis to analyze countries whose capital markets are open to international activity and whose political and economic situations are considered stable (so that no perceptions of political and economic risks limit capital inflows). Indeed, the success of a system of fixed exchange rates makes perfect capital mobility more likely. If investors are convinced that exchange rates will remain fixed, they will be more willing to move back and forth between currencies in response to small differences in interest rates.

For a small country (one that is too small to influence global financial markets by itself), perfect capital mobility implies that the country's interest rate must be equal to the interest rate in the larger global capital market. When exchange rates were fixed, this gave substance to the Canadian complaint that "Canadian interest rates are made in Washington."

If international capital flows are highly sensitive to slight, temporary interest rate changes, then they practically dictate the country's money supply, even in the short run. Why? Consider what happens if an incipient reduction of the money supply begins to increase the country's interest rates. The slightly higher interest rates draw a large capital inflow. Intervention to defend the fixed exchange rate requires selling domestic currency, thus expanding the money supply. Furthermore, sterilization is nearly impossible because of how large the capital inflows could be. Conversely, a nearly unlimited outflow of capital could occur if the country expanded its money supply and lowered interest rates slightly. The capital outflow forces the money supply back down to its original level to eliminate the slight drop in interest rates. The balance of payments rules the money supply. *Perfect capital mobility with fixed exchange rates robs monetary policy of its ability to influence interest rates or the domestic economy.*

For fiscal policy, perfect capital mobility actually means enhanced impacts on the domestic economy in the short run. Expansionary fiscal policies do not raise interest rates because the extra government borrowing is met by an influx of lending from abroad. Thus, the government borrowing does not crowd out private domestic borrowers with higher interest rates, allowing fiscal policy its full spending multiplier effects on the economy. In other words, with perfect capital mobility and interest rates set outside the country, fiscal expansion cannot be guilty of crowding out private real investment from lending markets. This extra potency of fiscal policy under fixed exchange rates and perfect capital mobility may be a poor substitute for the loss of monetary control because government handling of spending and taxes is often crude

FIGURE 23.7

With Perfect
Capital
Mobility,
Monetary
Policy Is
Impotent but
Fiscal Policy
Is Strong

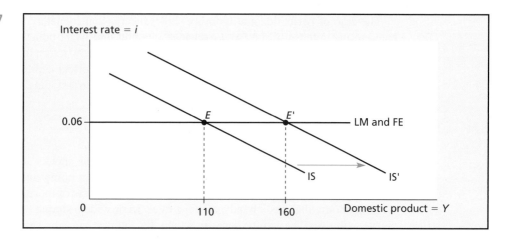

and subject to the vagaries of politics. Yet this is apparently a fact of life for small countries under truly fixed exchange rates and open capital markets (no capital controls).[9]

Figure 23.7 shows the effect of perfect capital mobility on the IS–LM–FE picture. The FE curve is flat because the tiniest change in interest rates would trigger a potentially infinite international flow of capital. If the global interest rate is 6 percent, then any point above the flat FE, corresponding to a domestic interest rate greater than 6 percent, results in a massive capital inflow and payments surplus. Any point below results in a massive capital outflow and payments deficit.

With perfect capital mobility the LM curve is also effectively flat and the same as FE. Any flood of international capital swamps any other influence on the nation's money supply. The money supply must be whatever is necessary to keep the domestic interest rate at 6 percent. Only the interest rate of 6 percent, dictated by financial conditions in the world as a whole, is consistent with equilibrium in the country's market for money. Under the conditions shown in Figure 23.7, the country has no independent monetary policy. The monetary authorities cannot change the domestic interest rate or control the money supply.

By contrast, fiscal policy takes on great power under these conditions. Raising government spending or cutting tax rates causes the usual rightward shift of the IS curve to IS'. As soon as the extra government deficit raises the home country's interest rate even slightly, there is a rush of capital inflow, as international investors seek the slightly higher interest rate in this country. The inflow raises the money supply until the interest rate is bid back down to 6 percent. So a rightward shift of the IS curve has a large effect on domestic product and no effect on the interest rate.[10]

---

[9]With perfect capital mobility, as with the other cases discussed in this chapter, we must remember that any attracted capital must be paid for later with reflows of interest and principal back to the foreign creditors.

[10]In fact, fiscal policy's impact on domestic product fits the spending multiplier formula of Chapter 22. For example, suppose that the country in Figure 23.7 had a marginal propensity to save of 0.2 and a marginal propensity to import of 0.3. This would make the multiplier equal to 2, according to Chapter 22. In this case, the rightward shift of $\Delta Y = 50$ from point E to point E' in Figure 23.7 could be achieved by $\Delta G = 25$.

The case of perfect capital mobility shows clearly that monetary policy is subordinated to the defense of the fixed exchange rate and that fiscal policy can be powerful with fixed exchange rates. For the rest of this chapter we now return to the case of moderate capital mobility and an upward-sloping FE curve. Perfect capital mobility can be considered the limiting case (flat) of the general case (upward-sloping) that we examine.

SHOCKS TO THE ECONOMY

From time to time a country's economy is hit by major shocks—both shocks that represent changes in basic conditions in the domestic economy and those that arise externally in the international economy. What are the effects of these exogenous forces on an economy that has a fixed exchange rate? To provide a simple base for our analysis, we will usually examine cases in which the country has achieved external balance (a triple intersection in the IS–LM–FE graph) just before the shock hits the economy.

Internal Shocks

One type of internal shock arises in the market for money. A domestic monetary shock alters the equilibrium relationship between money supply and money demand because (1) the money supply changes or (2) the way in which people decide on their money holdings changes. The latter can arise, for instance, from financial innovations like money market mutual funds, the spread of credit cards, or automated teller machines (ATMs). A domestic monetary shock causes a shift in the LM curve. Its effect on domestic interest rates and domestic product is quite limited with fixed rates. As we saw in our analysis of the attempt to run an independent monetary policy, a shift in the LM curve tends to reverse itself as the central bank must intervene to defend the fixed rate. A major effect of a monetary shock instead can be on the country's holdings of official reserve assets, if intervention is the basis for the money supply change that shifts the LM curve back toward its initial position.

Another type of domestic shock arises from exogenous changes in domestic spending on goods and services. A domestic spending shock alters domestic real expenditure (E) through an exogenous force that alters one of its components (consumption, real domestic investment, or government spending). A change in fiscal policy is one such shock. Another would be a change in the business mood or consumer sentiment, resulting in a change in real investment or consumption spending. The discussion of fiscal policy provides an example of the analysis of this type of shock. In addition, it is important to remember that effects on foreign countries will be transmitted through changes in our imports, and that this can have repercussions back to our economy if the induced changes in the foreign economies alter their imports from us.

International Capital-Flow Shocks

One type of external shock arises from unexpected changes in the country's financial account. An international capital-flow shock is the unpredictable shifting of internationally mobile funds in response to such events as a change in the foreign interest rate, rumors about political changes, or new restrictions (capital controls) on international asset holdings. Let's examine an international capital-flow shock in the form of a shift by international investors and speculators to a belief that the country's government is considering devaluing its currency in the near future. Although this is not necessary to the analysis, we begin with a country that has an external balance. (In this case the shift in belief is not related to a payments imbalance today—rather, it may be related to doubts about the political leadership of the country, or to a belief that the country may try to use devaluation to boost international price competitiveness in order to increase net exports and lower domestic unemployment.)

The shift in belief leads to a capital outflow as international investors attempt to reposition their portfolios away from assets denominated in this country's currency *before* the devaluation occurs. This type of capital outflow is a form of "capital flight," in which investors flee a country because of doubts about government policies. If the country begins with an external balance, then the overall balance shifts into deficit as the financial account deteriorates. There is downward pressure on the exchange-rate value of the country's currency, and the central bank must intervene to defend the fixed rate. The central bank buys domestic currency and sells foreign currency. If the intervention is not sterilized, then the domestic money supply shrinks. Interest rates increase and real domestic product decreases.

The increase in interest rates here becomes part of the defense of the fixed exchange rate. If the interest differential shifts in favor of this country, then international investors are more willing to keep investments in this country's financial assets (or are less interested in fleeing) even if there is some risk of devaluation. (Recall our discussions of uncovered financial investments in Chapters 18 and 19.) In fact, countries faced with a capital-outflow shock often immediately shift policy to raise short-term interest rates dramatically, for instance, from annual rates of less than 10 percent to annual rates of over 100 percent. This is an example of using monetary policy *actively* to reestablish external balance, rather than waiting for the slower effects of intervention on the domestic money supply to move the country toward external balance.

The effects of this shock are pictured in Figure 23.8. The economy begins at point E. The international capital-flow shock causes the FE curve to shift up or to the left. Once the FE curve has shifted, the official settlements balance is in deficit at point E. The central bank must intervene to defend the fixed rate. The central bank may attempt to keep the economy at point E by sterilizing the intervention. The central bank may hope that the disequilibrium in the overall balance is temporary, perhaps because the fears of the international investors will subside and the FE curve will shift back to the right in the near future.

However, if the monetary authority cannot or does not sterilize the intervention, then the LM curve will begin to shift up or to the left. If the new FE curve remains where it is, the LM curve must shift to LM', with a new triple intersection at point T. External balance has been reestablished at point T. Real domestic product has declined. The country now has an internal imbalance, in the form of low aggregate demand and higher unemployment, assuming that the country did not begin with the opposite imbalance of excessively strong aggregate demand. *Under fixed exchange rates, external capital-flow shocks can have powerful impacts on internal balance through the changes in the money supply driven by official intervention to defend the fixed rate.*

FIGURE 23.8

An Adverse
International
Capital-Flow
Shock

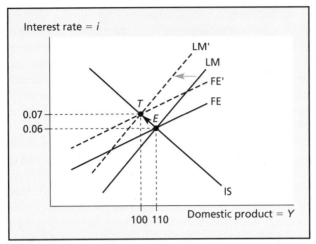

A shift of international capital flows away from the country
causes the FE curve to shift up or to the left, and the overall
payments balance goes into deficit. Intervention to defend the
fixed rate shifts the LM curve up or to the left. The economy
shifts toward a new full equilibrium at point *T*.

International Trade Shocks

A second type of external shock arises from exogenous changes in the country's
current account. An international trade shock is a shift in a country's exports or
imports that arises from causes other than changes in the real income of the country.
For instance, demand for a country's exports can change for many reasons. Export
shocks seem to be largest for countries specializing in exporting a narrow range
of products, especially primary commodities for which demand is sensitive to the
business cycle in importing countries. Instability has strongly affected exporters of
metals, such as Chile (copper), Malaysia (tin), and, to a lesser extent, Canada. Import
shocks can occur if our consumers unexpectedly alter their purchases between import
products and domestically produced substitutes, for instance, because of changing perceptions of the relative quality of the products. Trade shocks can also occur because
of shifts in the prices or availability of domestic and foreign products. An important
example of this type of shock is a shock to the price of a major import, such as oil for
most industrialized countries.[11]

[11]The analysis of an increase in the price of a major import is a bit complicated. Examples of such price
shocks for crucial imports are the oil shocks of 1973–1974 and 1979–1980, the smaller one of 1990,
and the more drawn-out oil price increase that peaked in 2008. The shock raises the price of imports of
this product and may lower the quantity of imports. The analysis is similar to that about to be discussed
in the text if the foreign price shock initially raises the total value of imports and lowers national
purchasing power (with the higher price acting as a "tax" on the economy imposed by the exporters).
These conditions hold if imports of the product take a large share of our national spending and our
demand for the product is price-inelastic (at least in the short run). An additional twist is that an oil price
shock can quickly increase the price level (*P*) so that the LM curve also shifts up or to the left as a result of
the shock.

An international trade shock alters the country's current account. Thus, it directly affects both the country's overall balance of payments and aggregate demand for the country's domestic production. For instance, a shift of foreign demand away from our exports, or a shift of our demand toward imports (and away from our own products), leads to a worsening of the current account and the overall balance (assuming that there is little effect on international capital flows). It also reduces aggregate demand, lowering real domestic product.[12] In addition, the country's central bank must intervene to defend the fixed rate by buying domestic currency and selling foreign currency. If the intervention is not sterilized, then the domestic money supply contracts, leading to a further decline in aggregate demand. External balance can be reestablished through these changes, but the internal imbalance of low aggregate demand and high unemployment will be increased.

Figure 23.9 shows the effects of this shock. Beginning at point E, the adverse international trade shock shifts the FE curve to the left and the IS curve to the left as well. At the new IS–LM intersection (point V), real domestic product declines (as does the domestic interest rate). With point V to the right of the new FE' curve, the country's overall payments are in deficit. Intervention to defend the fixed rate reduces the domestic money supply (assuming that it is not sterilized). The LM curve begins to

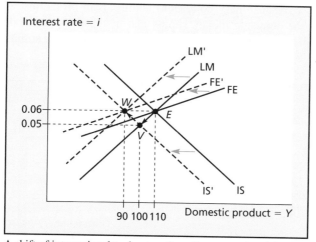

A shift of international trade away from the country's products causes the FE and IS curves to shift to the left, and the overall payments balance goes into deficit. Intervention to defend the fixed rate shifts the LM curve up or to the left. The economy shifts toward a new full equilibrium at point W.

[12]We are assuming that the current account actually does deteriorate even though the reduction in our real income will offset some of the initial decline by lowering the country's demand for imports through the domestic-income effect on imports. In Figure 23.9 this assumption ensures that point V is to the right of the new FE curve even if the FE curve is steeper than the LM curve.

shift up or to the left. External balance is reestablished at point *W* when the LM curve shifts to the dashed LM'. However, real domestic product has declined even more.[13]

Thus, as with international capital-flow shocks, *international trade shocks can have a powerful effect on the internal balance of a country with a fixed exchange rate.* The intervention needed to defend the fixed rate tends to magnify the effect of the shock on domestic production.

IMBALANCES AND POLICY RESPONSES

A country wants to achieve both internal balance and external balance. Yet its actual performance is often short of these goals. In many situations it has imbalances in both its internal and external situations as a result of shocks that hit the economy, or previous government policies that resulted in poor economic performance.

Internal and External Imbalances

Figure 23.10 catalogs the four possible cases in which the country has both internal and external imbalances. With fixed exchange rates, a country's policymakers could get lucky and face the straightforward problems represented by the upper-left and lower-right cells.

The government of a country experiencing high unemployment and a payments surplus can use expansionary policies to address both problems. Most obviously, an expansion of the domestic money supply can increase aggregate demand and lower unemployment, while also reducing the payments surplus (as summarized previously

FIGURE 23.10
Policies for Internal and External Balance

		State of the domestic economy	
		High unemployment	Rapid inflation
State of balance of payments	Surplus	Expansionary policy	??
	Deficit	??	Contractionary policy

In some situations a policy to change aggregate demand can serve both internal and external goals, but in some cases (marked "??" here) it cannot. To deal with high unemployment and a payments surplus, policymakers should expand aggregate demand (upper-left case). To deal with inflation and a payment deficit, they should cut aggregate demand (lower-right case). But with the other two combinations of imbalances, there is no clear prescription for aggregate-demand policy.

[13]As shown, the interest rate returns to 0.06. This is not the only possibility—the interest rate could be higher or lower, depending on the magnitudes of the curve shifts and the slopes of the curves.

in Figure 23.2). This shift occurs automatically if the country intervenes to defend the fixed exchange rate and does not sterilize, but the country can also speed it up by using active monetary policy to expand the money supply more quickly.

The government of a country experiencing an inflation rate that is viewed as being too high and a payments deficit can use contractionary policies to address both. Again, an obvious choice is a contraction of the money supply (or, perhaps more realistically, a reduction of the growth rate of the money supply).

Even in these cases the exact policy solution may be tricky because balance in one dimension may be achieved while part of the other imbalance remains. Nonetheless, the initial direction of the desirable policy change that reduces (if not eliminates) both imbalances is clear.

What about the other two cells in Figure 23.10? In broad terms the correct policy response is not clear. The dilemma of having to choose which goal to pursue has been felt most acutely by countries in the lower-left cell, where low aggregate demand has resulted in high unemployment, but the balance of payments is in deficit. This was the near tragedy of Britain after it rejoined the gold standard in 1925 at its prewar gold parity, with the high value for the pound making British products uncompetitive in international trade. This was the problem facing the United States in the early 1960s. France faced a similar problem in the early 1990s, as discussed in the box "A Tale of Three Countries."

In these cases, reducing unemployment called for raising aggregate demand with expansionary policies. However, this would worsen the trade balance and tend to worsen the overall balance. The dilemma was not well solved in any of the cases. Britain was driven off the gold standard in 1931. The United States reduced its unemployment rate with a series of fiscal policy changes (the tax cut of 1964, domestic "Great Society" spending programs, and Vietnam War spending), but the payments imbalance led toward the breakup of the Bretton Woods fixed-rate system. Through the mid-1990s, France continued to suffer from high unemployment.

The opposite dilemma faces governments worried about a rising or high inflation rate while the country is running a payments surplus (the upper-right cell of Figure 23.10). Saudi Arabia and several other Middle East oil-exporting countries that peg their currencies to the U.S. dollar found themselves in this situation in 2007–2008. Each had a surplus driven by tremendous growth of export revenues as oil prices rose dramatically. The rising revenues were fueling income growth that was overheating the domestic economy. Each country wanted to shift to contractionary monetary policy to fight the rising inflation. Instead, if each remained committed to defend the fixed exchange rate, it had to allow domestic monetary expansion as the government intervened to purchase dollars and sell its domestic currency.

The government of a country in one of the two dilemma cells has three basic choices:

1. It can abandon the goal of external balance, which eventually means that the country will abandon its fixed exchange rate.
2. It can abandon the goal of internal balance, at least in the short run, and set its policies (especially its monetary policy and money supply) to achieve external balance. This is sometimes called the "rules of the game" in a fixed-rate system such as the gold standard. Defending the fixed rate is the highest goal.

In 1992, unemployment in France was high and rising. Inflation was almost nothing. The French government seemed to respond by tightening up on money and raising interest rates.

Madness? Not really, but an example of the policy dilemma that can arise with fixed exchange rates. France was a member of the Exchange Rate Mechanism (ERM) of the European Monetary System. Membership committed the French government to keep the exchange rates between the French franc and the currencies of the other member countries within small bands around the central rates chosen for the fix.

To understand France we actually need to start with Germany, the largest member of the ERM. The Berlin Wall fell in 1989, and German unification proceeded rapidly over the next year, politically, financially, and economically. German government policy toward unification included support for the eastern part in the form of transfers, subsidies, and other government expenditures on such things as public infrastructure investments. This expansionary fiscal policy increased aggregate demand. Domestic production expanded rapidly in 1990 and 1991, and unemployment fell, but the economy began to overheat as demand exceeded production capabilities, so that the inflation rate increased. German policymakers, especially those at the Bundesbank (Germany's central bank), loathe inflation. History matters—the hyperinflation of the 1920s in Germany is considered to be the economic disaster of the past century for Germany.

In response to the rise in inflation, the German monetary authorities tightened up on monetary policy, after a spurt in money growth in 1990–1991 resulting from monetary unification. Interest rates rose. This monetary tightening slowed the economy during 1992–1993.

We can capture the main elements of the German story in an IS–LM picture. Germany began at point A. The fiscal expansion shifted IS_1 to IS_2, and the increased growth rate of the money supply shifted LM_1 to LM_2. At the new equilibrium point B, real domestic product was higher, but the economy was trying to push past its supply capabilities. In response to the internal imbalance of rising inflation, the Bundesbank reduced money growth, shifting LM_2 to LM_3.

Interest rates rose and domestic product declined as the economy moved toward point C.

In this way the German government adopted policies that focused almost completely on internal political and economic problems. (In fact, although we could add the FE curve to Germany's picture, we have instead omitted it to emphasize this internal focus of German policy.) Meanwhile, back in France . . .

In 1990, the French economy was already weak and weakening. The unemployment rate was 9 percent and rising. For internal reasons the French government probably wanted to shift to an expansionary policy. But it had an external problem. Rising interest rates in Germany could set off a capital outflow that would threaten the fixed exchange rate between the franc and the DM. France had to respond to this incipient external imbalance by tightening up on money and raising French interest rates. Unfortunately, for political reasons, fiscal policy could not turn expansionary. The assignment rule could not be used. Instead, the higher interest rates made the French economy worse. The growth rate of real French GDP declined from 1989 through 1993, and real GDP actually fell in 1993. The French unemployment rate rose from 1990 through 1994.

In France's picture, France began at point F, with aggregate demand already weak and unemployment high. The rise in Germany's interest rate shifted France's FE curve up or to the left (FE_1 to FE_2). To avoid capital outflows and a payments deficit, the French monetary authorities responded by tightening money, shifting LM_1 to LM_2. As the economy moved toward point H, demand and production weakened and the unemployment rate rose.

However, this was not always enough. International investors and speculators doubted the resolve of the French (and most other non-German members of the ERM) to stick to fixed exchange rates. Major speculative attacks occurred in September 1992, November 1992, and July 1993. In these the FE curve for France shifted sharply up or to the left. The French government responded with massive official intervention, buying francs and selling DM, and with high short-term interest rates to discourage the speculative outflows. Total intervention by all ERM members in September 1992 was over

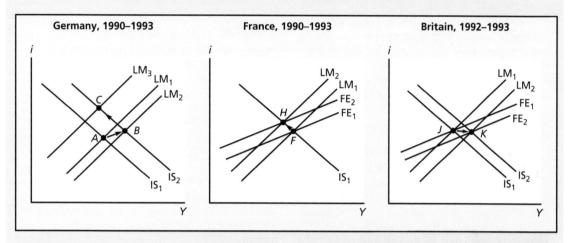

Germany, 1990–1993   France, 1990–1993   Britain, 1992–1993

$100 billion, with capital losses of about $5 billion to the central banks that bought currencies of the countries (Britain, Italy, Spain, and Portugal) that then devalued or depreciated anyway. Total intervention in July 1993 was also more than $100 billion, with the French central bank alone selling more than $50 billion of DM in defense of the franc. Official reserve holdings of the French central bank declined close to zero, but the French government was "successful." The franc was not devalued.

The third largest economy in the European Union is Britain. Britain's journey through these years was different. Britain was not a member of the ERM until joining in 1990, when it committed to a pound–DM rate of about 0.35. The next two years were not good for Britain. To defend the fixed rate, the growth rate of the British money supply had to be kept low (although at the same time British interest rates could decline, starting from a high level). A severe recession with two years of decline in real GDP hit, and the unemployment rate rose to about 10 percent. While Britain's and France's stories are broadly similar during these years, Britain's recession was worse.

In 1992, Britain's story diverged. As a result of the speculative attack on non-DM currencies in September 1992, Britain left the ERM. The British government spent close to half of its official reserves defending the pound before surrendering. Britain shifted to a floating exchange rate, and the pound depreciated by over 10 percent against the DM. This improved British price competitiveness.

In addition, the British government could allow its money supply to grow more quickly. Interest rates fell sharply in 1993 and real GDP began to grow. Britain's unemployment rate plateaued in 1993 and declined in 1994 (while the unemployment rate was still rising in both France and Germany). After declining in 1993, the inflation rate increased a little in Britain in 1994, but not even close to enough to reverse the gain in price competitiveness from the currency depreciation. Britain's depreciation of 1992 seems to have been successful.

Let's pick up Britain's picture as Britain left the ERM in 1992. (Its picture for 1990–1992 is similar to that of France.) The initial situation, just before the departure, is at point J. With the depreciation of the pound, the improvement in price competitiveness shifts FE_1 right to FE_2 and moves IS_1 right to IS_2. The money expansion shifts LM_1 right as well to LM_2. The British economy shifts toward point K, with higher real domestic production and a lower interest rate.

Tales have lessons. The lesson of this tale is that countries can be forced to choose between fixed exchange rates and control over their internal balance. When large countries choose internal balance, the choice gets tougher for smaller countries. Germany ran its policies mainly to satisfy internal objectives (like the United States in the 1960s). This created problems for other ERM members—conflicts for them between internal and external balance. Both France and Britain faced a dilemma: high unemployment and a tendency toward

—Continued on next page

payments deficits. For a while, both responded with tight money that tried to achieve external balance but made the internal imbalance (high unemployment) worse.

All of this did not completely convince international investors and speculators. With the speculative attack of September 1992, the paths diverged. France defended the fixed rate, at further cost to internal balance.

Britain surrendered, withdrawing from the ERM. This allowed Britain to address its internal imbalance. Expansionary policy and the competitiveness gained from the pound's depreciation rekindled economic growth. The unemployment rate declined.

The speculative attack in July 1993 led to a semi-surrender even by France and other ERM members. They widened the allowable bands around the central rates from plus or minus 2.25 percent to plus or minus 15 percent. This widening of the band forestalled any further speculative attacks. But, during the next years, the franc–DM rate seldom was more than 3 percent from its central value. France continued to direct its policies to keeping the franc exchange rate steady against the DM, and France's unemployment rate remained high.

DISCUSSION QUESTION

Explain whether or not the story could have turned out better if (a) Germany would have raised taxes in 1990 or (b) France would have reduced taxes in 1991.

	1988	1989	1990	1991	1992	1993	1994
Growth Rate of Real GDP (%)							
Germany	3.7	4.2	5.5	4.3	1.8	−1.2	2.7
France	4.2	3.9	2.4	0.6	1.2	−1.3	2.8
Britain	4.5	2.2	0.6	−2.1	−0.5	2.1	4.3
Unemployment Rate (%)							
Germany	8.7	8.9	7.2	5.5	5.8	7.3	8.2
France	10.0	9.4	9.0	9.4	10.3	11.7	12.3
Britain	8.4	6.3	5.8	8.0	9.8	10.3	9.4
Inflation Rate (%)							
Germany	1.3	2.8	2.7	3.5	4.0	4.2	3.0
France	2.7	3.5	3.4	3.2	2.4	2.1	1.7
Britain	4.9	7.8	9.5	5.9	3.7	1.6	2.4
Short-Term Interest Rate (%)							
Germany	4.0	6.6	7.9	8.8	9.4	7.5	5.3
France	7.5	9.1	9.9	9.5	10.4	8.8	5.7
Britain	9.7	13.6	14.6	11.8	9.4	5.5	4.8
Money Supply Growth Rate (%)							
Germany	7.5	4.6	8.4	9.4	6.7	8.1	7.8
France	4.1	8.1	3.8	−4.7	−0.2	1.4	2.8
Britain	7.6	5.7	2.6	3.0	2.5	5.6	7.3
Exchange Rate							
Franc/DM	3.4	3.4	3.4	3.4	3.4	3.4	3.4
Pound/DM	0.32	0.32	0.35	0.34	0.36	0.40	0.40

Source: Growth rate of real GDP, unemployment rate, (CPI) inflation rate, and money supply growth rate (M1 for France, M3 for Germany, and M0 for Britain) from Economic Intelligence Unit, *Country Report,* various issues for these three countries. Short-term (money market) interest rates and exchange rates from International Monetary Fund, *International Financial Statistics Yearbook,* 1998.

3. The government can try to find more policy tools or more creative ways to use the tools that it already has.

Giving up is unpopular, and the natural tendency is to search for more tools and creative solutions.

A candidate for addressing the dilemma of high unemployment and payments deficit is enhancement of the economy's supply capabilities. Why not come up with policies that create more national income by improving our productivity? Productivity improvements would enhance our ability to compete in international trade, thereby shifting demand to our products, expanding production and employment, and improving our current account balance. It sounds too good to be true. And it probably is. Policymakers usually have no fast, low-cost way of improving the economy's supply capabilities. That comes through sources of growth, such as the advance of human skills and technology, that respond sluggishly, if at all, to government manipulation.

A Short-Run Solution: Monetary–Fiscal Mix

There is a way to buy time and serve both internal and external goals using conventional demand-side policies while staying on fixed exchange rates. Looking more closely at the basic policy dilemma, Robert Mundell and J. Marcus Fleming noticed that monetary and fiscal policies have different relative impacts on internal and external balance. This difference can be the basis for a creative solution.

The key difference between the impacts of fiscal and monetary policies is that easier monetary policy tends to lower interest rates and easier fiscal policy tends to raise them, as noted in Figures 23.2 and 23.5. An expansion of aggregate demand and domestic product can be achieved with different mixes of fiscal policy and monetary policy, and the mix matters for the resulting level of the interest rate, at least in the short run. Expansion of domestic product can result in a low interest rate if it is driven mainly by expansionary monetary policy. Expansion can result in a high interest rate if it is driven mainly by expansionary fiscal policy. Because interest rates affect the country's payments balance, the interest rate is important. If the interest rate is lower, the payments balance deteriorates. If, instead, the interest rate is pushed high enough (for instance, by using very expansionary fiscal policy coupled with somewhat contractionary monetary policy), the payments balance improves (as long as capital flows are responsive to interest rate changes).

More generally, *monetary and fiscal policies can be mixed so as to achieve any combination of domestic product and overall payments balance in the short run.* Figure 23.11 illustrates the opportunities for solving one of the four policy challenges posed in Figure 23.10, namely, the case of excessive unemployment and payments deficits, starting at point Z. The goal is to raise the economy to full employment, which can be achieved at the level of domestic product Y_{full}. Shifting only one policy would not work, as we have seen, but shifting both can work. In this case, it is best to shift to tighter (contractionary) monetary policy to attract foreign capital with higher interest rates and to easier (expansionary) fiscal policy in pursuit of full employment. In the right amounts, the monetary tightening and fiscal easing can bring us exactly to full employment and payments balance. In Figure 23.11, this is achieved by shifting IS to IS' and LM to LM'.

FIGURE 23.11
How Monetary
and Fiscal
Policy Could
Combine to
Cure Both
Unemployment
and a Balance-
of-Payments
Deficit

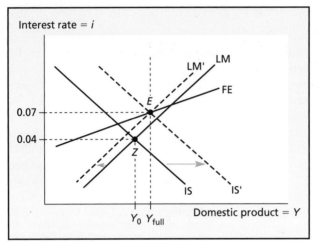

At the starting point Z, domestic product Y_0 is below the full
employment level Y_{full} and the balance of payments is in deficit.
To reach full employment and payments balance at point E,
combine the right amounts of tight monetary policy
and easy fiscal policy.

A similar recipe can be used to get from any starting point to internal balance and
payments balance. The principle is clear: As long as there are as many different policies as target variables, as in the present case of two policies and two targets, there is
a solution.

Furthermore, the pattern of policy prescriptions reveals a useful guideline for
assigning policy tasks to fiscal and monetary policy. This is Robert Mundell's
assignment rule: Assign to fiscal policy the task of stabilizing the domestic economy
only, and assign to monetary policy the task of stabilizing the balance of payments only.
We can see from Figure 23.12 that such marching orders would guide the two arms of
policy toward internal balance and payments balance. Studying the different cases in
Figure 23.12, you will find that the assignment rule generally steers each policy in the
right direction. There are exceptions, as Figure 23.12 notes, but even in these cases it is
likely that following the assignment rule does nothing worse than make the economy
follow a less direct route to the goal of internal and external balance.

The assignment rule is handy. It allows each arm of policy to concentrate on a
single task, relieving the need for perfect coordination between fiscal and monetary
officials. It also directs each arm to work on the target it tends to care about more
because the balance of payments (and exchange-rate stability) has traditionally been
of more concern to central bankers than to politicians who make fiscal decisions.

The rule might or might not work in practice. We have already mentioned problems
with the interest rate effect on capital flows that is supposed to guarantee the existence
of a solution. Furthermore, if either branch of policy lags in getting signals from the
economy and responding to them, the result could be unstable oscillations that are even
worse than having no policy at all. Or monetary policy may be run largely to accom-
modate the country's fiscal policy (and the need of the government to fund its deficit

FIGURE 23.12

Monetary–
Fiscal Recipes
for Internal
and External
Balance

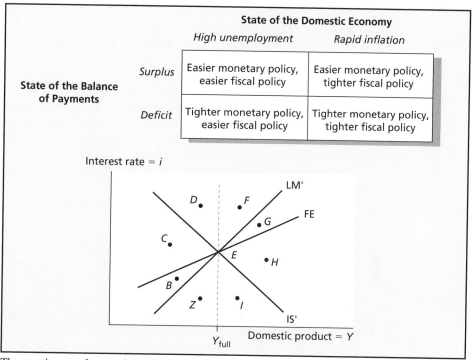

These recipes conform to the assignment rule: Assign monetary policy the task of balancing the country's international payments, and assign fiscal policy the task of bringing the domestic economy to full employment without excessive inflation. There are exceptional cases, however, when the assignment rule fails to follow the most direct route to the goal. In the diagram the assignment rule is wrong for monetary policy at points like *B* and *G*, and it is wrong for fiscal policy at points like *D* and *I*.

spending), in which case independent policies are not really possible. In addition, the mix influences both the composition of domestic spending and the level of foreign debt. A policy of high interest rates, such as that used in Figure 23.11, reduces domestic real investment. This can harm the growth of the economy's supply capabilities by reducing the growth of the capital stock. It also builds up foreign debt, which must be serviced in the future, reducing the amount of national income that the country keeps for itself.[14]

SURRENDER: CHANGING THE EXCHANGE RATE

If an imbalance in a country's overall balance of payments is large enough or lasts for long enough (a "fundamental disequilibrium"), the country's government may

---

[14]Another possible problem might seem to be the case of perfect capital mobility because the country has no control of its money supply. This is not a problem. In fact, the case of perfect capital mobility effectively forces the government to follow the assignment rule. Monetary policy must allow the money supply to be whatever is necessary to achieve external balance on the FE curve. Fiscal policy can then be directed toward achieving internal balance, addressing any problems of domestic unemployment or inflation pressures.

be unwilling to change domestic policies by enough to eliminate the imbalance. The country's government instead may conclude that surrendering the fixed rate is the best choice available. If the payments balance is in deficit, a devaluation may be used; if it's in surplus, revaluation may occur.

The government may hope that the exchange-rate change can adjust the external imbalance without excessive disruption to the domestic economy. Nonetheless, the exchange-rate change will affect aggregate demand, domestic production, unemployment, and inflation. In some situations these domestic changes represent a departure from internal balance. The internal effects of the exchange-rate change may then need to be offset by other policy changes, creating a rationale for a policy mix that includes the exchange-rate change and one or both of a fiscal policy change and a monetary policy change.

In other situations the internal effects of an exchange-rate change can themselves be desirable. Interestingly, these are precisely the dilemma cases of Figure 23.10. Consider a country that has a fixed exchange rate, a payments deficit, and a rather high unemployment rate (the lower-left cell in Figure 23.10). This country's government is not willing to allow an "automatic" adjustment to external balance through a decline in the money supply because this would raise interest rates, lower demand and production, and increase unemployment further. Instead, the government has been sterilizing its intervention. It is also not capable of following the assignment rule, perhaps because domestic politics precludes adopting the right policy mix.

What happens if this country devalues (or shifts to a floating exchange rate and allows its currency to depreciate)? What effects does this exchange-rate surrender have on external and internal balance?

The devaluation should improve international price competitiveness (as long as any changes in the domestic price level or the foreign price level do not offset the exchange-rate change).

- Exports tend to increase as firms from this country can lower the foreign-currency prices of their products (and as higher profits draw resources into producing for export).
- Imports tend to decrease as the domestic-currency prices of imported products rise (and as higher profits in producing domestic products that can now compete more successfully with imports draw resources into producing these import substitutes).

Thus, the current account tends to improve. The effects on the financial account are less clear-cut. The financial account may also improve. If some financial capital was fleeing the country in fear of the impending devaluation, then this flight could stop or even reverse once the devaluation was done. Overall, we expect an improvement in the payments balance (a decrease in the deficit).

If exports increase and imports decrease, then these changes increase aggregate demand and domestic production, reducing domestic unemployment. However, import prices in local currency increase, and this increase puts some upward pressure on the average price level or inflation rate in the country. The extra demand could also put upward pressure on the price level, but this effect may be small if the economy begins with high unemployment.

FIGURE 23.13

Devaluation of the Country's Currency

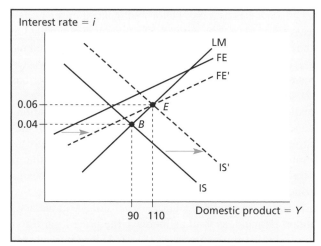

In response to the payments deficit at point *B*, the country's government devalues its currency. The devaluation improves its international price competitiveness, so it shifts the FE and IS curves to the right. If the devaluation is of the correct size, it can shift the economy toward a new full equilibrium at point *E*.

Figure 23.13 shows these effects in the IS–LM–FE diagram, assuming that the domestic price level is steady. The country begins at point *B* with a payments deficit. The (low) level of domestic production at *B* results in rather high unemployment. The devaluation improves the current account (and may improve the financial account), shifting the FE curve down or to the right. The increase in net exports as a result of the change in price competitiveness shifts the IS curve to the right. The figure shows that a devaluation (of the correct size) can shift the economy to a triple intersection (external balance) with a higher domestic product (and lower unemployment). The new equilibrium at point *E* may not exactly be internal balance (full employment), but it is a move in the correct direction.[15]

This sounds good—another possible answer to the dilemma of deficit and unemployment. In some cases it seems to work well. (See the discussion of Britain in the box "A Tale of Three Countries.") The comparable analysis, with all the signs reversed, indicates that a revaluation (or appreciation after the government allows the country's currency to float) can be an appropriate policy response to surplus and inflation (the upper-right cell in Figure 23.10) because it can lower a surplus while reducing inflation pressure in the economy by decreasing demand and lowering the local-currency price of imports.

This analysis posits clear, direct effects of a devaluation on aggregate demand and external balance. However, there are a number of ways in which things can turn out differently. Consider first aggregate demand. Recall our discussion in Chapter 21 of the

[15]If the price level also rises as a result of the devaluation, the FE and IS curves do not shift as much, and the LM curve shifts up or to the left. This reduces the effect on the payments balance and on domestic product. In fact, if the price level rises by enough, there is no gain in competitiveness and the benefits of devaluation on external and internal balance are lost.

role of currency mismatches as a risk factor for financial crises in developing countries. If many domestic firms have substantial net liabilities denominated in foreign currency (because they have borrowed or issued debt securities denominated in, for instance, U.S. dollars or euros), then the devaluation causes losses for these firms. The adverse balance-sheet effects force them to cut back on capital spending and other business activities. If this reduction is severe enough, the IS curve shifts to the left instead of to the right.

Consider next external balance. There are times that a devaluation fails to reduce the external imbalance. One possible reason for failure is taken up in the next section—the value of the current account may not actually increase because of low responsiveness of export and import volumes to the exchange-rate change. Another possible reason for failure is that the government pursues fiscal or monetary policies that themselves are driving to expand the payments deficit, and these are so strong that they overwhelm the benefits of the devaluation. For instance, expansionary monetary policy can expand income and import demand, as well as increase the price level through extra inflation so that the improved price competitiveness is lost. A third possible reason is that capital flows react in the "wrong" direction. For instance, a devaluation could lead to fears among international investors that the devaluation will not be successful in reducing the deficit (perhaps for one of the first two reasons). They then expect that another devaluation will be needed soon. Rising capital outflows (capital flight) could deteriorate the financial account and make the payments deficit bigger.

A key to external balance is how other government policies are used with the devaluation. If other government policies (especially monetary policy) can limit any increase in the country's price level or inflation rate, then the devaluation probably will improve the current account balance. International investors, seeing this, are less likely to fear that another devaluation will be needed. If the current account improves and the financial account does not deteriorate, then the devaluation will be successful in reducing the payments deficit.

HOW WELL DOES THE TRADE BALANCE RESPOND TO CHANGES IN THE EXCHANGE RATE?

According to the discussion in the preceding section, a change in the nominal exchange rate should alter net exports, at least as long as it alters international price competitiveness. The conclusion is straightforward for effects on the *volumes* (or quantities) of exports and imports, although we can still wonder about the speed or magnitude of the changes. However, the effect on the *value* of the trade balance is not so obvious because both prices and volumes are changing. Yet the effect on the *value* of net exports is what matters for the country's balance of payments and for its FE curve.

The value of the country's trade or current account balance, measured in foreign currency (here pounds) is

CA (our current account balance, measured in £/year) $= \quad P_x^£ \quad \bullet \quad X \quad - \quad P_m^£ \quad \bullet \quad M$

where $P^{£}_{x}$ and $P^{£}_{m}$ are the pound prices of the country's exports and imports and X and M are the quantities. Now consider the likely direction of changes in the trade prices and quantities when the country's currency (here the dollar) drops in value:

	£ Price of Exports	Quantity of Exports	£ Price of Imports	Quantity of Imports
Effects of a devaluation $=$ of the dollar	No change or *down*	• No change or *up*	$-$ No change or *down*	• No change or *down*

A dollar devaluation is likely to lower the pound price of exports (if it has any net effect on this price). This is because U.S. exporters are to some extent willing to lower pound prices while still receiving the same (or even higher) dollar prices because pounds are now worth more. If there is any effect of this price change on export quantities, the change is upward, as foreign buyers take advantage of any lower pound prices of U.S. exports to buy more from the United States. It is already clear that the net effect of devaluation on export value is of uncertain sign because pound prices probably drop and quantities exported probably rise. On the import side, any changes in either pound price or quantity are likely to be downward. The devaluation is likely to make *dollar* prices of imports look higher, causing a drop in import quantities as buyers shift toward U.S. substitutes for imports. If this drop in demand has any effect on the *pound* price of imports, that effect is likely to be negative. The sterling value of imports thus clearly drops, but if this value is to be subtracted from an export value that could rise or fall, it is still not clear whether the value of the net trade balance rises or falls. We need to know more about the underlying price elasticities of demand and supply in both the export and the import markets.

How the Response Could Be Unstable

A drop in the value of the dollar actually could worsen the trade balance. It would clearly do so in the case of *perfectly inelastic* demand curves for exports and imports. Suppose that buyers' habits are rigidly fixed so that they will not change the quantities they buy from any nation's suppliers despite changes in price. Examples might be the dependence of a non-tobacco-producing country on tobacco imports, or a similar addiction to tea or coffee, or to petroleum for fuels. In such cases of perfectly inelastic demand, devaluation of the country's currency backfires completely. Given the perfect inelasticity of import demand, no signals are sent to foreign suppliers by devaluing the dollar. Buyers go on buying the same amount of imports at the same pound price, paying a higher dollar price without cutting back their imports. No change in the foreign exchange value of imports results. On the export side, the devaluation leads suppliers to end up with the same competitive dollar price as before, but this price equals fewer pounds. U.S. exporters get fewer pounds for each bushel of wheat they export, yet foreigners do not respond to the lower price by buying any more wheat than they would otherwise.

In the case of perfectly inelastic demand curves for exports and imports, the changes in the current account are as follows:

$$CA^{£} \quad = \quad P^{£}_{x} \quad \bullet \quad X \quad - \quad P^{£}_{m} \quad \bullet \quad M$$
$$Down \ = \ (Down \ \bullet \ No\ change) \quad - \quad (No\ change \ \bullet \ No\ change)$$

FIGURE 23.14

Devaluation
Affects the
Trade Balance

A. How Devaluation Could Worsen the Trade Balance

Exchange Rate	$P^£_x$	•	X	–	$P^£_m$	•	M	=	$CA^£$
Before dollar devaluation: $1.60/£	1.00	•	80	–	1.00	•	120	=	–40
After dollar devaluation: $2.00/£	0.80	•	80	–	1.00	•	120	=	–56

The key to this case: Demand curves are inelastic, so the volumes of exports and imports do not change. Devaluing our currency just lowers the value of foreign exchange we earn on exports, worsening the trade deficit.

B. The Small-Country Case

Exchange Rate	$P^£_x$	•	X	–	$P^£_m$	•	M	=	$CA^£_m$
Before dollar devaluation: $1.60/£	1.00	•	80	–	1.00	•	120	=	–40
After dollar devaluation: $2.00/£	1.00	•	105	–	1.00	•	100	=	+5

The small-country case illustrates the ability of high demand elasticities to guarantee that devaluation improves the trade balance. The essence of the small-country case is that foreign curves are infinitely elastic, so the world (£) prices are not affected by our country's actions. On the export side, the infinite elasticity of foreign demand means that our own supply elasticity dictates what happens to the volume of exports (X). We probably export more, raising our earnings of foreign exchange. On the import side, the infinite elasticity of foreign supply means that our demand elasticity dictates what happens to volume (M). We probably import less, cutting our demand for foreign exchange.

Appendix H generalizes from such special cases, showing how larger demand elasticities raise the ability of devaluation to improve the trade balance.

A numerical illustration of this case is given in Figure 23.14A. There, devaluing the dollar merely lowers the value of foreign exchange the United States earns on exports, from 80 (= 1.00 × 80) to 64 (= 0.80 × 80), worsening the trade balance.

It might seem that this perverse, or unstable, result hinges on something special about the export market. This is not the case, however. It only looks as though the change is confined to the export side because we are looking at the equation expressed in sterling. If we had looked at the CA equation in dollar prices, the deterioration would still appear:

$$CA^\$ = P^\$_x \quad • \quad X \quad - \quad P^\$_m • \quad M$$
$$Down = (No\ change \quad • \quad No\ change) \quad - \quad (Up \quad • \quad No\ change)$$

Why the Response Is Probably Stable

In all likelihood, however, a drop in the value of the home currency improves the current account balance, especially in the long run. The reason, basically, is that export and import demand elasticities end up being sufficiently high, and, as Appendix H proves, this is enough to ensure the stable response.

One quick way to see why the case of perfectly inelastic demand does not prevail is to note its strange implications. It implies, first, that we make it harder for ourselves to buy foreign goods with each unit of exports (i.e., $P^£_x/P^£_m$ drops), yet this impoverishing effect fails to get us to cut our spending on imports. The result looks even stranger upside down. It implies that a country could succeed in cutting its trade deficit and at the same time buy imports more cheaply (in terms of the export good) by cleverly *revaluing* its currency (for example, raising the value of the dollar from $1.60/£ to $1.00/£). If that were a common occurrence, governments would have discovered it long ago, and they would have solved their trade deficits by happily raising the values of their currencies.

Over the long run, price elasticities tend to be higher, and each nation tends to face elastic curves from the outside world, both the foreign demand curve for its exports and the foreign supply curve for its imports. In the extreme *small-country case,* the home country faces infinitely elastic foreign curves. Foreign-currency (£) prices are fixed, and the current account balance is affected by a drop in our currency as follows:

$$CA^£ = (P^£_x \bullet X) - (P^£_m \bullet M)$$
$$Up = (No\ change \bullet Up) - (No\ change \bullet Down)$$

We know that, if the real volume of exports (X) changes, it will rise because the same pound price of exports means more dollars per unit for sellers. They will respond to the new incentive with extra production and export sales. Similarly, we know that any change in the real volume of imports (M) will be a drop because the same pound price for imports leaves the dollar-country consumers with a higher dollar price. In the small-country case, both sides of the current account move in the right direction: Export revenues rise and import payments decline. Figure 23.14B provides a numerical illustration that underlines the contrast with the pessimistic case of Figure 23.14A. The crucial role of elasticities, illustrated in the two halves of Figure 23.14, also emerges from the technical formulas of Appendix H.

Timing: The J Curve

The fact that the elasticities of response to a given change (here, the devaluation or depreciation of the dollar) usually rise over time brings a second key result: *Devaluation is more likely to improve the trade balance after a sufficient span of time has elapsed*. The current account balance may dip for several months after a devaluation or depreciation of the home currency. The changes in prices are likely to occur faster than any changes in trade quantities. The changes in trade quantities at first are small because it takes time for buyers to respond to the price changes by altering their behavior. Contracts previously concluded must expire or be renegotiated, and alternative sources of products must be identified and evaluated. Eventually the quantity responses become larger, as buyers do switch to lower-priced products. As quantity effects become larger, the current account balance improves.

Figure 23.15 gives a schematic diagram of what economists think is a typical response of the current account balance to a drop in the exchange-rate value of a country's currency. The typical pattern is called a J curve because of its shape over the first couple of years of response to devaluation. The value of the country's current account at first deteriorates, but then begins to improve. After a moderate time period, perhaps about 18 months, the value of the current account returns to where it started, and thereafter it moves above its initial value. This analysis indicates that it may take some time for a large devaluation or depreciation of the country's currency

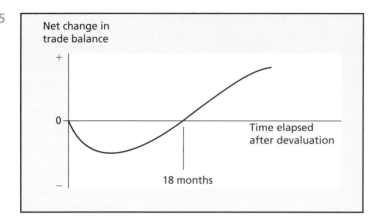

to have a positive impact on the country's current account. The shift in the FE curve is more complicated than in the previous section. In the short run the FE curve could (perversely) shift to the left unless a capital inflow (perhaps based on the anticipation of the eventual beneficial effects of the devaluation) stabilizes the curve. Eventually the FE curve should shift to the right, but perhaps not until a year or more after the devaluation.

Summary

If a country has a fixed exchange rate, it must defend the fixed rate chosen. The first part of this chapter examined four major implications of having a fixed exchange rate and defending it using official intervention.

The first implication is that intervention to defend the fixed rate alters monetary conditions in the country. Faced with an external imbalance in the country's overall international payments, the central bank defends the fixed rate by buying or selling domestic currency in the foreign exchange market. The intervention changes the central bank's liabilities that serve as the **monetary base** for the domestic **money supply.** The change in the domestic money supply then results in macroeconomic adjustments that tend to reduce the external imbalance. The domestic interest rate changes, altering international capital flows, at least in the short run. The change in real domestic product and income alters demand for imports. In addition, a change in the domestic price level can alter both exports and imports by changing the country's international price competitiveness.

The central bank can attempt to resist this monetary process through **sterilization,** which prevents the domestic money supply from changing. But there are limits to how long the central bank can use sterilized intervention to defend the fixed exchange rate. If the external imbalance continues, then the country's holdings of official reserves continue to change because the central bank is also selling or buying foreign currency as the other half of the intervention. Eventually the change in official reserve holdings forces the central bank to make some adjustment. For instance, if the central bank is selling foreign currency in its intervention, then eventually the central bank runs low on its holdings of official reserves.

The second implication is that a fixed exchange rate and its defense constrain a country's ability to pursue an independent monetary policy. If the country begins with an external deficit, the defense of the fixed rate eventually forces the country to contract its money supply. If the country begins with an external surplus, the defense of the fixed rate eventually forces the country to expand its money supply. If the country begins with an external balance, then any change in monetary policy and the money supply would create an external imbalance, and the intervention to defend the fixed rate would tend to reverse the monetary change.

The third implication is that the effects of fiscal policy are also altered by a fixed exchange rate. A change in fiscal policy causes the country's current and financial accounts to change in opposite directions in the short run, so the effect on the overall payments balance depends on how large the two changes are. If international financial capital flows are not that responsive to interest rate changes, then the resulting external imbalance following a fiscal policy change leads to intervention that changes monetary conditions in the other direction, reducing the effect of the fiscal policy change on domestic product. If international capital flows are sufficiently responsive, the resulting external imbalance leads to intervention that changes monetary conditions in the same direction, enhancing the effect of fiscal policy on real product. In the extreme case of perfect capital mobility, the fiscal change can have the full spending multiplier effect because the domestic interest rate remains unchanged and equal to the foreign interest rate. (However, with perfect capital mobility and a fixed exchange rate, the country has *no* independent monetary policy.)

The fourth implication is that defending a fixed exchange rate without sterilization alters how different exogenous shocks affect the country's macroeconomy in the short run. The effects of domestic monetary shocks are greatly reduced. The effects of domestic spending shocks on domestic product depend on how responsive international financial capital flows are to changes in the interest rate. If international capital is highly mobile, a domestic spending shock has more effect.

International capital-flow shocks can have major effects on the domestic economy because they require intervention to defend the fixed rate as the shock hits. For instance, a shift to capital outflow leads to intervention that results in a lower domestic money supply. Domestic interest rates tend to increase, and domestic product and income tend to decline.

International trade shocks affect the economy directly by changing aggregate demand. In addition, the resulting intervention to defend the fixed exchange rate causes a monetary change that generally reinforces the change in demand, resulting in a larger change in domestic product and income.

The second part of the chapter examined broad policy issues for countries that have fixed exchange rates. A country wants to achieve both internal and external balance. Yet stabilizing an open macroeconomy with a fixed exchange rate is not easy. If a country has only one policy for influencing aggregate demand (for instance, monetary policy that changes the money supply), it would have to be very lucky for the level of aggregate demand that is best for the domestic economy to turn out to be the one that keeps external payments in balance.

There is a way out of the dilemma if the country can use two policies (monetary and fiscal policies). Expansionary monetary and fiscal policies have opposite effects on domestic interest rates. The difference can be used to influence international capital flows in the short run. Monetary policy has a comparative advantage in affecting the external balance, whereas fiscal policy has a comparative advantage in affecting the domestic economy. We can thus devise a monetary–fiscal mix to deal with any pairing of imbalances in the external accounts and the domestic economy.

In fact, policymakers can follow a simple **assignment rule** with fair chances of at least approaching the desired combination of internal and external balance. When policies are adjusted smoothly and take quick effect, internal and external balance can be reached by assigning the internal task to fiscal policy and the external task to monetary policy.

Faced with a large or continuing external imbalance, a country's government may decide to react by surrendering—by changing the exchange rate: devaluing, revaluing, or shifting to a floating exchange rate that immediately depreciates or appreciates. A change in the exchange rate can reduce the external imbalance by altering the country's international price competitiveness. Changes in exports and imports alter the current account balance. The exchange-rate change also has an impact on internal balance. The export and import changes alter aggregate demand, and the change in the domestic prices of imported goods can alter the country's general price level or inflation rate.

However, it is not certain that the exchange-rate change actually does reduce the external imbalance. The effect on the *value* of the current account balance depends on changes in both the volumes (quantities) and the prices of exports and imports. Consider a devaluation. Measured in foreign currency, the price of exportable products tends to decrease, the quantity of exports tends to increase, and the price and quantity of imports tend to decrease. The value of exports can increase or decrease. If the value of exports decreases, the current account balance improves only if the decline in the value of imports is larger. A general condition that ensures that the current account balance improves is that the price elasticities of demand for exports and imports be sufficiently high so that the changes in the volumes of exports and imports are large enough. In practice, the price effects, especially the decrease in the foreign-currency price of exports, often occur quickly, while the volume effects occur more slowly but eventually become sufficiently large. The current account balance thus deteriorates at first, but after a period of months it tends to improve, tracing out a pattern called the **J curve.**

Key Terms

Domestic assets	Perfect capital	International capital-flow
International reserve	mobility	shock
assets	Domestic monetary	International trade
Monetary base	shock	shock
Money supply	Domestic spending	Assignment rule
Sterilization	shock	J curve

Suggested Reading

A technical treatment of the economics of fixed exchange rates is presented in Rivera-Batiz and Rivera-Batiz (1994, Chapter 14). Some of Robert Mundell's pioneering articles on internal and external balance and the implications of international capital mobility are reprinted in Mundell (1968, Chapters 16 and 18). The same path-breaking analysis was simultaneously developed by Fleming (1962). Chapter 3 of the International Monetary Fund's April 2007 *World Economic Outlook* examines the role of exchange-rate changes in reducing large current account deficits and surpluses.

Questions and Problems

◆ 1. "A country with a deficit in its overall international payments runs the risk of increasing inflation if it defends its fixed exchange rate by (unsterilized) official intervention in the foreign exchange market." Do you agree or disagree? Why?

2. A country with a fixed exchange rate has achieved external balance. Government spending then increases in an effort to reduce unemployment. What is the effect of this policy change on the country's official settlements balance? If the central bank uses unsterilized intervention to defend the fixed rate, will intervention tend to reduce the expansionary effect of the fiscal policy?

◆ 3. What does perfect capital mobility mean for the effectiveness of monetary and fiscal policies under fixed exchange rates?

4. What is the assignment rule? What are its possible advantages and drawbacks?

◆ 5. "According to the logic of the J-curve analysis, a country that revalues its currency should have an improvement in the value of its current account balance in the months immediately after the revaluation." Do you agree or disagree? Why?

6. The Pugelovian central bank intervenes in the foreign exchange market by selling U.S.$10 billion to prevent the Pugelovian currency (the pnut) from depreciating.

   a. What impact does this have on the Pugelovian holdings of official international reserves?

   b. What effect will this have on the Pugelovian money supply if the central bank does not sterilize? Explain.

   c. What effect will this have on the Pugelovian money supply if the central bank does sterilize (using an open market operation in Pugelovian government bonds)? Explain.

◆ 7. A country initially has achieved both external balance and internal balance. International financial capital is highly but not perfectly mobile, so the country's FE curve is upward sloping and flatter than the LM curve. The country has a fixed exchange rate and defends it using official intervention. The country does not sterilize. As a result of the election of a new government, foreign investors become bullish on the country. International financial capital inflows increase dramatically and remain higher for a number of years.

   a. What shift occurs in the FE curve because of the increased capital inflows?

   b. What intervention is necessary to defend the fixed exchange rate?

   c. As a result of the intervention, how does the country adjust back to external balance? Illustrate this using an IS–LM–FE graph. What is the effect of all of this on the country's internal balance?

8. A country initially has achieved both external balance and internal balance. The country prohibits international financial capital inflows and outflows, so its financial account (excluding official reserves transactions) is always zero because of these capital controls. The country has a fixed exchange rate and defends it using official intervention. The country does not sterilize. An exogenous shock now occurs—foreign demand for the country's exports increases.

   a. What is the slope of the country's FE curve?

   b. What shifts occur in the IS, LM, or FE curves because of the increase in foreign demand for the country's exports?

   c. What intervention is necessary to defend the fixed exchange rate?

   d. As a result of the intervention, how does the country adjust back to external balance? Illustrate this using an IS–LM–FE graph. What is the effect of all of this on the country's internal balance?

◆ 9. A country's government is committed to maintaining the fixed-exchange-rate value of its currency through central bank intervention in the foreign exchange market. The country's government also believes that its holdings of international reserve assets are barely adequate, and it would like to keep its holdings close to the current level. The country's international capital flows are relatively unresponsive to changes in interest rates. The country currently has an official settlements balance deficit. What, if anything, can the central bank do in this situation? For your answer, draw an IS–LM–FE graph and use it in your explanation.

10. A country has a fixed exchange rate. Initially, the country has a surplus in its overall international payments, as well as excessive aggregate demand that is putting upward pressure on the country's price level because the current level of real GDP (Y_0) is greater than the "full-employment" level of real GDP (Y_{full}). The country's international capital flows are noticeably responsive to changes in interest rates (the country's FE curve is upward sloping and flatter than its LM curve). Evaluate the ability of each of the following policies (separately, not in combination) to address the initial macroeconomic situation. In each answer, use an IS–LM–FE graph as part of the explanation.

   a. Sterilized intervention to defend the fixed exchange rate.

   b. A change in the fixed-rate value of the country's currency.

◆ 11. What is the mixture of monetary and fiscal policies that can cure each of the following imbalances?

   a. Rising inflation and overall payments deficit (e.g., point *H* in Figure 23.12).

   b. Rising inflation and overall payments surplus (e.g., point *F* in Figure 23.12).

   c. Insufficient aggregate demand and overall payments surplus (e.g., point *C* in Figure 23.12).

12. The Pugelovian government has just devalued the Pugelovian currency by 10 percent. For each of the following, will this devaluation improve the Pugelovian current account deficit? Explain each.

   a. People are very fixed in their habits. Both Pugelovian importers and foreign buyers of Pugelovian exports buy the same physical volumes no matter what.

   b. Pugelovian firms keep the Pugelovian pnut prices of Pugelovian exports constant, and foreign firms keep the foreign-currency prices of exports to Pugelovia constant.

Chapter Twenty-Four

Floating Exchange Rates and Internal Balance

One way to reconcile the goals of external balance and internal balance is to let the exchange rate take care of external balance and to direct macroeconomic policy toward the problem of internal balance. If the exchange rate is allowed to float cleanly, without government intervention, then the exchange rate changes to achieve external balance. If there are no transactions in official reserves, then the official settlements balance must be zero, and the exchange rate must change to whatever value is needed to achieve this external balance. Changes in the exchange rate are the "automatic" mechanism for adjusting to achieve external balance.

Even if a floating exchange rate is used to achieve external balance, this still leaves the problem of achieving internal balance. How does use of floating exchange rates affect the behavior of the economy and the effectiveness of monetary and fiscal policies that might be directed to achieving internal balance? The purpose of this chapter is to examine the macroeconomics of floating exchange rates. It first examines how monetary policy and fiscal policy work in an economy that has a floating exchange rate. Then it explores the impacts of various shocks on such an economy. The shocks are the same types that we examined in the previous chapter, so we can see how the choice of fixed or flexible exchange rates alters how the economy responds to different shocks.

In our analysis of floating exchange rates, we use the same basic model of the open macroeconomy that we developed in Chapter 22 and applied to fixed rates in Chapter 23. The key difference from the previous chapter is that the exchange rate is now a variable determined endogenously by the macroeconomic system rather than a rate set (and defended) by the government. With a floating rate, the exchange rate brings the foreign exchange market (or the overall balance of payments) into equilibrium by affecting people's choices about whether to buy goods and services abroad or at home and whether to invest in this country's financial assets or another country's financial assets. The impact on demand for goods and services then has a feedback effect on the country's domestic product.

The analysis of how a country with a floating exchange rate responds to a policy change or another type of economic shock can usefully proceed through three steps:

1. At the initial value of the exchange rate, what are the effects of the shock on the country's economy? In particular, does the shock push the official settlements balance away from a zero value?
2. If there is a tendency away from zero for the official settlements balance, what change in the exchange-rate value of the country's currency (appreciation or depreciation) is needed to move back to a zero balance?
3. What are the additional effects on the country's macroeconomy of this change in the exchange rate?

The additional effects indicate the "special" ways in which floating rates alter the behavior of the economy (just as the additional effects resulting from intervention to defend the fixed rate indicated the "special" ways in which fixed rates alter the behavior of the economy). The additional effects show how floating rates alter the effectiveness of government policies. They also suggest how floating rates alter the country's ability to keep internal balance in a changing world.

MONETARY POLICY WITH FLOATING EXCHANGE RATES

With floating or flexible exchange rates, monetary policy exerts a strong influence over domestic product and income. To see how, let us consider the case of a deliberate expansion of the domestic money supply. Such a change is implemented by using a domestic tool of monetary policy. For instance, the country's monetary authority might use open market operations to buy domestic securities. As the monetary authority pays for its securities purchase, it issues new liabilities that expand the country's monetary base and money supply.

An expansion of the money supply increases banks' willingness to lend, and interest rates decrease. Borrowing and spending rise. As we saw in Chapter 23, the drop in interest rates tends to worsen the overall balance of payments in the short run. The financial account tends to worsen as capital flows out of the country, and the current account worsens as imports rise. The demand for foreign currency is now greater than the supply. In the fixed-rate analysis of the previous chapter, the government had to intervene to defend the fixed rate against the pressure resulting from this payments deficit. With floating exchange rates, the pressure results in a depreciation of the exchange-rate value of the country's currency, as summarized in Figure 24.1.

Depreciation of our currency increases the international price competitiveness of the products produced by our country's firms (assuming that the nominal depreciation is larger than any increase in domestic prices and costs in the short run—a form of overshooting like that discussed in Chapter 19). The improvement in our firms' ability to compete with foreign firms is likely to improve our current account balance, as export volumes increase and import volumes decline. (Improvement in the current account balance occurs only after the initial stage of the J-curve has played itself out. This assumes that the stability conditions of Chapter 23 and Appendix H eventually hold. In this chapter we focus on situations in which the response is stable.)

FIGURE 24.1 Effects of Expanding the Money Supply with Floating Exchange Rates

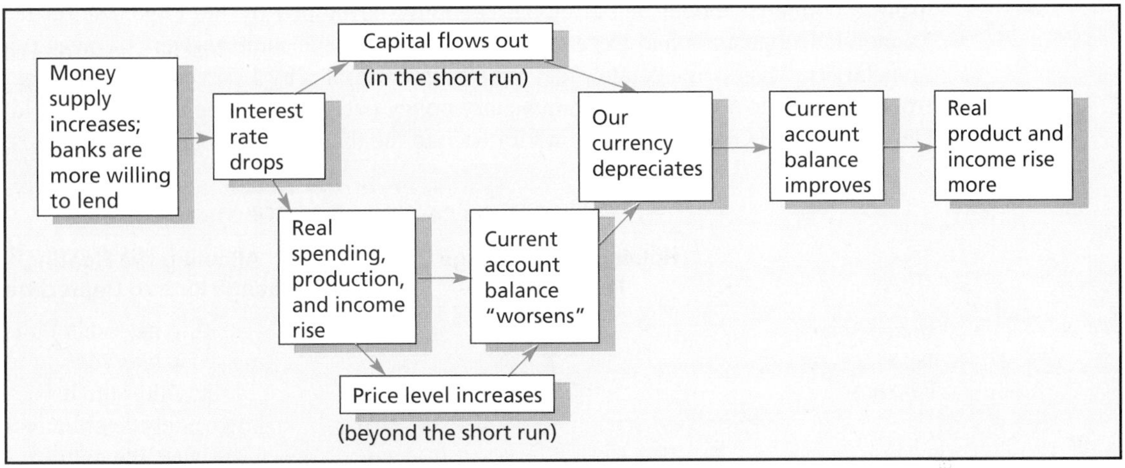

For a decrease in the money supply, reverse the direction of all changes.

The improvement in the current account balance lowers the overall payments deficit, reducing and eventually eliminating pressure for further depreciation of the exchange-rate value of our currency. External balance is restored through the exchange-rate change.

The new competitive edge for the country's firms raises aggregate demand for what the country produces. Such extra demand due to the depreciation augments the direct domestic effects of the increase in the money supply. Due to the extra demand, real domestic product and income may rise even more. However, the depreciation may also enhance the effects of monetary policy on the price level and inflation rate as well. The depreciation results in higher domestic prices for imported products, and the extra demand can create general upward pressure on prices.

Thus, under floating exchange rates, monetary policy is powerful in its effects on internal balance. The induced change in the exchange rate reinforces the standard domestic effects of monetary policy. Monetary policy gains power under floating exchange rates, whereas, as we saw in the previous chapter, it loses power under fixed exchange rates.

This general conclusion holds whatever the degree of capital mobility. Whatever the degree, expanding the money supply causes a depreciation, and this further expands aggregate demand. Consider, for instance, perfect capital mobility. Capital flows respond to both interest rates and the expected change in the exchange rate into the future. Perfect capital mobility implies that uncovered interest parity always holds because nearly unlimited flows of international financial capital occur if there is any deviation from this parity.[1] The overshooting discussed in Chapter 19 is a form of perfect capital mobility. There we saw that, if a monetary expansion reduced the domestic interest rate, the exchange-rate value of the country's currency would depreciate immediately by a large amount. The overshooting results in a large improvement in the country's international price competitiveness in the short and medium runs.

---

[1]For the fixed-rate analysis of Chapter 23, perfect capital mobility also implied uncovered interest parity, but the expected change in the exchange rate was assumed to be approximately zero if investors expected the fixed rate to hold into the future. With no change is expected in the fixed rate, uncovered interest parity means that the domestic interest rate is equal to the foreign interest rate.

How large are the follow-on effects from the currency depreciation? Simulations using a computer model of the global economy developed by the Organization for Economic Cooperation and Development (OECD) provide some answers.[2] Consider a monetary expansion in a country that reduces interest rates by 1 percentage point (e.g., from 6 percent to 5 percent), with monetary policy unchanged in the rest of the world. Here is what the OECD model shows for each of the three largest countries/currencies:

	Change in the Country's Real GDP after Two Years	
	Holding the Exchange Rate Steady	Allowing the Floating Exchange Rate to Depreciate
United States	0.5%	0.8%
Japan	0.7	0.9
Euro area	0.6	0.9

Thus, the induced depreciation of the country's currency increases the effect of the monetary expansion by about 50 percent on average.

We can see the effects of monetary policy in the IS–LM–FE picture used in the previous two chapters. Consider a country that begins with external balance—a triple intersection shown as point E_0 in Figure 24.2. The country's central bank now uses a domestic change (such as an open market purchase of domestic securities) to expand the domestic money supply, and the LM curve shifts down to LM'. Even if the exchange-rate value of the domestic currency is unchanged, the direct domestic effects of this policy change reduce the domestic interest rate from 6 percent to 5 percent and

FIGURE 24.2
Expansionary Monetary Policy with Floating Exchange Rates

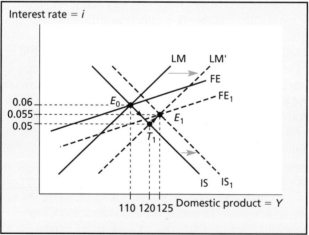

Starting from point E_0 with an overall payments balance of zero, the country implements an expansionary policy. The LM curve shifts down or to the right, but at point T_1 the payments balance tends toward deficit. The country's currency depreciates, and the FE and IS curves shift to the right, reestablishing external balance at E_1.

[2]Dalsgaard, André, and Richardson (2001).

increase real domestic product from 110 to 120. In addition, the country's balance of payments tends to go into deficit. (The intersection of LM' and the original IS curve at point T_1 is to the right of the initial FE curve.) The country's currency depreciates in the foreign exchange market. As the country's price competitiveness improves, exports increase and imports decrease. The current account balance improves, so the FE curve shifts to the right and the IS curve shifts to the right. If the floating exchange rate adjusts to maintain external balance (a zero balance in the country's official settlements balance), then the economy will be at a triple intersection of all three curves after the exchange rate has adjusted. The new triple intersection is point E_1. Because of the depreciation, real GDP increases even more, to 125. *Monetary policy is powerful in affecting real GDP in the short run under floating exchange rates.*[3]

FISCAL POLICY WITH FLOATING EXCHANGE RATES

How fiscal policy works with floating exchange rates is a little more complicated. Fiscal policy can affect exchange rates in either direction, as shown in Figure 24.3. The left side of the figure shows the same effects of expansionary policy as we saw in Chapter 23. The fiscal expansion bids up domestic interest rates as the government borrows more. Higher domestic interest rates tend to attract capital from abroad, at least temporarily. Meanwhile, aggregate spending, product, and income are raised by higher government spending and/or lower tax rates. This raises imports and worsens the current account balance. So there are two opposing tendencies for the country's

FIGURE 24.3   Effects of Expansionary Fiscal Policy with Floating Exchange Rates

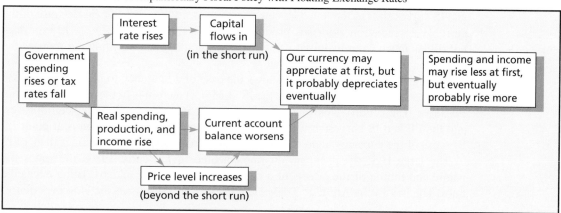

For contractionary fiscal policy, reverse the direction of all changes.

[3]The monetary expansion and the induced depreciation are also likely to increase the domestic price level through inflation, especially beyond the short run. If the domestic price level increases, then the LM curve shifts back up (or does not shift down by as much in the first place). The higher domestic price level reverses some of the gain in international price competitiveness, so the FE and IS curves also shift back (or do not shift by as much in the first place). The increase in real GDP is not as large. Indeed, in the long run, the currency depreciation will be exactly offset by the higher price level if money is neutral in the long run and purchasing power parity holds.

overall balance of payments and thus for the exchange-rate value of the country's currency. The interest rate rise tends to draw a capital inflow that strengthens the country's currency, but the rise in aggregate demand and imports weakens it. Which tendency will prevail? There is no firm answer. If capital is mobile internationally, then the capital inflow effect at first is probably large enough to appreciate the country's currency. Eventually the aggregate-demand effect is probably stronger and longer lasting, so eventually the currency depreciates.[4]

The "feedback" effects on the domestic economy depend on which way the exchange rate changes. If the country's currency at first appreciates, then the country loses price competitiveness. The country's exports decline and its imports increase. The decline in the country's current account reduces the expansionary effects of the fiscal change on the country's domestic product. That is, the expansionary effect is reduced by "international crowding out"—the appreciation of the country's currency and the resulting decline in the current account. If the country's currency instead (or eventually) depreciates, the enhanced price competitiveness and resulting increase in the current account give a further trade-based stimulus to domestic production.

The effects of fiscal expansion can be pictured using an IS–LM–FE graph. Figure 24.4 shows the two cases possible. In both cases the economy begins at the triple intersection E_0. The fiscal expansion directly shifts the IS curve to IS', increasing the domestic interest rate from 6 percent to 8 percent and boosting domestic product from 110 to 130.

The two cases differ by whether the country's overall payments balance tends to go into surplus or deficit. The left graph in Figure 24.4 shows the case of a tendency to surplus because the capital inflow effect is larger. In this graph the incipient payments surplus is shown by the IS'–LM intersection to the left of the initial FE curve. The country's currency appreciates, the current account balance worsens, and the FE and IS curves shift to the left. The new triple intersection is at point E_2. Because of the currency appreciation, domestic product declines somewhat from 130 to 125 (or does not rise as much from its initial value of 110). International crowding out reduces the expansionary thrust of the fiscal change.[5]

The right graph in Figure 24.4 shows the case of a tendency to deficit because the aggregate-demand effect is larger—the IS'–LM intersection is to the right of the initial FE curve. The country's currency depreciates, the current account balance improves, and the FE and IS curves shift to the right. The new triple intersection is at point E_3. Because of the currency depreciation, domestic product rises to 140 rather than 130.

The large U.S. fiscal expansion implemented in the early 1980s illustrates the nature and timing of the effects of a change in fiscal policy under floating exchange rates. The box "Why Are U.S. Trade Deficits So Big?" discusses the U.S. experience.

---

[4]The extreme case of perfect capital mobility is also consistent with this pattern. The initial interest rate increase leads to an immediate appreciation of the domestic currency. The exchange rate overshoots, so that the currency is expected subsequently to depreciate slowly. Uncovered interest rate parity is reestablished because the interest differential in favor of the country is offset by the expected depreciation.

[5]If the fiscal expansion causes the price level to increase, then the LM curve also shifts up, and both the FE and IS curves shift to the left somewhat (or do not shift as much to the right) as a result of some loss of international price competitiveness due to the higher domestic prices. For either of the two cases discussed here in the text, these additional shifts reduce the amount by which real domestic product increases from its initial value of 110.

FIGURE 24.4 Expansionary Fiscal Policy with Floating Exchange Rates

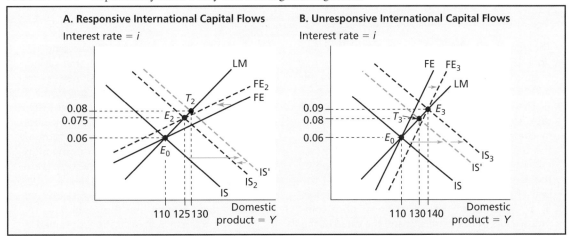

Expansionary fiscal policy shifts the IS curve to the right, and the IS–LM intersection shifts from E_0 to T_2 or T_3 initially. The effects of fiscal policy depend on how strongly international capital flows respond to the interest rate increase. In panel A, the overall payments balance tends toward surplus. (T_2 is to the left of FE.) In panel B, the overall payments balance tends toward deficit. (T_3 is to the right of FE.) In either case the payments imbalance leads to a change in the exchange rate. In panel A, the country's currency appreciates, and the FE and IS curves shift to the left, reestablishing external balance at E_2. In panel B, the country's currency depreciates, and the FE and IS curves shift to the right, reestablishing external balance at E_3. Here we assume that the LM curve does not move because the central bank can keep the money supply steady if it doesn't need to defend a fixed exchange rate.

SHOCKS TO THE ECONOMY

Major shocks occasionally strike a country's economy. What are the effects of these exogenous changes on a country that has a floating exchange rate? We will look at the same shocks that we examined in the previous chapter for a country with a fixed exchange rate so that we can contrast the results.

Internal Shocks

Domestic monetary shocks affect the equilibrium relationship between money supply and money demand, causing a shift in the LM curve. A change in the country's monetary policy is an example of such a shock. As we saw in the analysis of expansionary monetary policy, domestic monetary shocks have powerful effects on an economy with a floating exchange rate. If the monetary shock tends to expand the economy, then the exchange-rate value of the country's currency tends to depreciate, further increasing domestic product (or putting additional upward pressure on the country's price level or inflation rate). If the monetary shock tends to contract the economy, then the country's currency tends to appreciate, further decreasing domestic product.

Domestic spending shocks alter domestic expenditure, causing a shift in the IS curve. A change in fiscal policy is an example. As we saw for fiscal policy, the effect of this kind of shock on the exchange rate depends on which changes more: international capital flows or the country's current account.

Case Study   Why Are U.S. Trade Deficits So Big?

The United States has had a trade deficit every year since 1980. Why does the United States have this trade deficit? Why did it become very large in the mid-1980s and again starting in the late 1990s?

The United States has a floating exchange rate, so one place to look for an explanation is in changes in the real exchange-rate value of the U.S. dollar (recall our discussion of the real exchange rate in Chapter 19). The top graph in the accompanying figure shows the value of the real effective exchange-rate value of the dollar, as an indicator of the international price competitiveness of U.S. products, and the value of the U.S. trade balance (measured as a percentage of U.S. GDP, to make the size more comparable over time). It is clear that we may have a pretty good explanation here, if we allow for the lag of one to two years (recall the J curve from Chapter 23). That is, the dollar begins a large real appreciation in 1980 and the trade balance begins to deteriorate in 1982. The value of the dollar peaks in 1985 and begins a real depreciation that returns the real value in 1988 back to what it was in 1980. The trade balance begins to improve in 1987. The next big swing begins when the dollar starts another real appreciation in 1995. The trade balance deteriorates beginning in 1997. Then the dollar begins a real depreciation in 2002. This time the lag is somewhat longer—the trade balance begins to improve in 2006.

So an explanation of the large U.S. trade deficits is the change in international price competitiveness caused by exchange-rate swings. When the dollar experiences a real appreciation, the loss of price competitiveness hurts U.S. exports and encourages U.S. imports, so the trade balance deteriorates. The problem with this explanation is that it is not very deep. With a floating rate, the exchange-rate value of the U.S. dollar is an endogenous variable. We should probe further to find out what is behind the broad swings in the exchange rate and the trade balance.

One place to look is in the relationships between national saving and investment that we introduced in Chapter 16 and used again in Chapter 22. The bottom graph in the accompanying figure shows two aspects of national saving, private saving by households and businesses and government saving, which is the government budget surplus or deficit. If the government runs a surplus, then it is collecting more in tax revenues than it is spending, so the difference is a form of saving. If the government runs a deficit, then it is dissaving. The graph also shows domestic private investment and the trade balance again.

In the 1980s the closest relationship is between the government budget and the trade balance. In 1981 the Reagan administration obtained a major tax cut while government expenditures continued to grow. The government budget deficit increased to about 7.7 percent of GDP in late 1982 and remained at about 6 percent of GDP until 1987. In the graph the increase in the government budget deficit is shown as a decline in government saving in the early 1980s, with the line then remaining at about −6 percent for several years. Essentially, both the government budget deficit and the trade deficit increased in the first half of the 1980s and declined in the late 1980s. They came to be called the *twin deficits*.

Our model provides some insights into this relationship. Expansionary fiscal policy shifted the IS curve to the right, increasing both U.S. interest rates and U.S. national income. The rise in income alone tended to increase the trade deficit. The relatively high U.S. interest rates also drew large capital inflows and the real exchange-rate value of the dollar increased (as we saw in the top graph). In 1985 the capital inflows declined, so the large trade deficit became an important driver of the exchange-rate value of the dollar. The dollar began to depreciate in early 1985.

The explanation for the rise of the trade deficit in the second half of the 1990s is different. The government budget is not the explanation because the deficit began to decline in 1992. Instead, the explanation of the rising U.S. trade deficit in the late 1990s is the boom in real domestic investment. In the 1980s both private saving and private investment declined as shares of GDP.

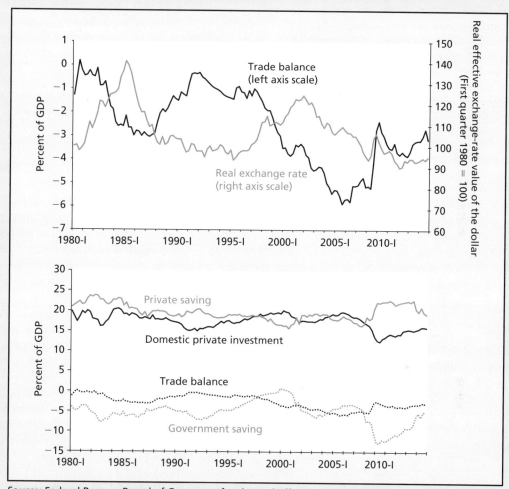

Source: Federal Reserve Board of Governors for the real effective exchange rate; U.S. government national income and product accounts for the other variables.

In the 1990s private saving continued to decline, but private domestic investment rose strongly, from 15 percent of GDP to about 20 percent. Businesses perceived major opportunities for profitable capital investments in the United States. So did financial investors, with a booming stock market drawing in large amounts of foreign capital. In terms of our macromodel, the story is much the same, though the driver is different (real domestic investment in the 1990s, fiscal policy in the 1980s). The increase in real domestic investment shifts the IS curve to the right. The trade balance deteriorates because of strong growth in U.S. GDP. The capital inflows appreciate the dollar, so the trade balance also deteriorates because of declining price competitiveness.

—Continued on next page

The stock market and real investment booms ended in 2000. As shown in the bottom graph, the decline in government saving (the rapid increase in the government budget deficit) again became the key driver of the growing trade deficit during 2000–2004. Then, with the onset of the global financial and economic crisis, the government budget deficit increased; private saving increased as households and businesses strove to reduce their debts; and domestic real investment, including new residential construction, collapsed. From late 2009 the overall effects of these changes on the trade balance was actually rather small.

DISCUSSION QUESTION

In mid-2014 you expected that, during the next several years, private saving would decrease and the government budget deficit would continue to decline. What was your forecast for the trade balance?

International Capital-Flow Shocks

International capital-flow shocks occur because of changes in investors' perceptions of economic and political conditions in various countries. For instance, an adverse shock to international capital flows, leading to a capital outflow from our country, can occur because foreign interest rates increase, investors shift to expecting more depreciation of our currency in the future, or investors fear negative changes in our country's politics or policies.

The capital outflow puts downward pressure on the exchange-rate value of the country's currency, and the currency depreciates. The depreciation improves the international price competitiveness of the country's products. Its exports increase and its imports decrease, improving the country's current account. The extra demand tends to increase its domestic product.

The effects of this shock are pictured in Figure 24.5. The economy begins at point E_0, a triple intersection. The adverse international capital-flow shock causes the FE curve to shift to the left to FE'. The country's overall payments balance tends to go into deficit, as the intersection of the (initially unchanged) IS–LM curves at E_0 is below FE'. The country's currency depreciates, shifting the FE and IS curves to the right. A new triple intersection occurs at point E_4, with domestic product and the interest rate higher.

Thus, under floating exchange rates, external capital-flow shocks can have effects on internal balance by altering the exchange rate and the country's international price competitiveness. Interestingly, an adverse shock tends to expand the domestic economy by depreciating the country's currency. We probably should add several cautions about this result. First, the reason for the capital-flow shift is important. If capital is flowing out because of political or economic problems in the country, then these problems may cause the economy to contract even though the exchange-rate depreciation is pushing in the other direction. Second, the capital outflow may disrupt domestic financial markets in ways that go beyond our basic analysis. Any disruptions in domestic financial markets may harm the broader domestic economy, also tending to contract it. We saw in Chapter 21 that a country often has domestic problems, large capital outflows, a depreciating currency, financial disruption, and a severe recession during a financial crisis. Thus, it is risky to conclude, on the basis of the simpler IS–LM–FE analysis, that an adverse capital-flow shock is simply good for the country's economy.

FIGURE 24.5

An Adverse
International
Capital-Flow
Shock

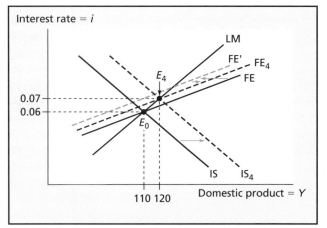

A shift of international capital flows away from the country
causes the FE curve to shift up or to the left, and the overall
payments balance tends toward deficit. The country's currency
depreciates, and the FE and IS curves shift to the right,
reestablishing external balance at E_4. Here again we assume
that the LM curve does not shift because the central bank
can keep the money supply steady.

International Trade Shocks

International trade shocks cause the value of the country's current account
balance to change. For instance, an adverse shock to international trade flows
might occur because of a decline in foreign demand for our exports, an increase in
our taste for imported products, or an increase in the price of an important import
such as oil.

An adverse international trade shock reduces both the current account and the
country's domestic product and income.[6] As the current account worsens, the overall
payments balance tends to go into deficit and the country's currency depreciates. The
improvement in price competitiveness leads to an increase in the country's exports and
a decline in imports. The current account improves and domestic product and income
rise. If all of this happens with no change in international capital flows, then the currency must depreciate enough to completely reverse the deterioration in the current
account, putting the overall payments balance back to zero.

Figure 24.6 shows the effects of this adverse international trade shock. The shock
causes the FE and IS curves to shift to the left. The intersection of IS' with LM at T_5
is below the new FE'. The country's currency depreciates, resulting in shifts back to
the right in the FE and IS curves. If nothing else changes (such as international capital

---

[6]We presume that the current account does actually decline. The shock itself worsens the current
account. The decline in national income lowers demand for imports, but we assume that this is not
enough to reverse the deterioration of the current account. In Figure 24.6, this assumption
ensures that the new IS'–LM intersection at T_5 is to the left of the new FE', even if the FE
curve is steeper than the LM curve.

FIGURE 24.6

An Adverse
International
Trade Shock

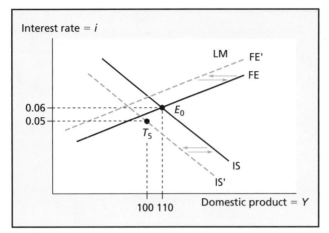

A shift of international trade away from the country's products
causes the FE and IS curves to shift to the left, and the overall
payments balance tends toward deficit. The country's currency
depreciates, and the FE and IS curves shift back to the right.
Here, to simplify the diagram, we imagine the case in
which external balance is reestablished at E_0.

flows or the domestic price level), then the curves shift back to their original positions,
and the new triple intersection is back to E_0.[7]

With floating exchange rates, the *effects of international trade shocks on internal
balance are mitigated by the effects of the resulting change in the exchange rate.* An
adverse trade shock tends to depreciate the country's currency, and this reverses some
of the effects of the shock. By reversing all of the directions of change, we would also
conclude that a positive trade shock appreciates the country's currency, reversing both
the improvement in the country's current account balance and the increase in demand
for the country's domestic product.

INTERNAL IMBALANCE AND POLICY RESPONSES

Shocks to the economy alter both the international performance of the country's
economy and its domestic performance. With floating exchange rates a change in
the exchange rate takes care of achieving external balance following a shock. If the
country's overall payments tend to go into deficit, then the country's currency depreciates, reversing the tendency toward deficit. If the country's overall payments tend to
surplus, then appreciation reverses the tendency to surplus.

A floating exchange rate does not ensure that the country achieves internal balance, but
changes in the floating rate do affect the country's internal balance. A depreciation tends
to expand the country's economy. If the country begins with excessive unemployment

---

[7]The depreciation of the currency may put some upward pressure on the country's price level
by increasing the domestic-currency price of imported products. If the overall domestic price
level increases, then the LM curve shifts up somewhat, and the new triple intersection will
still result in some decline in domestic product. Nonetheless, the decline is less than
what would occur without the currency depreciation.

before the exchange-rate change, then the expansionary thrust of the depreciation is welcome, as it reduces the internal imbalance. If the country instead begins with internal balance or with an inflation rate that is rising or too high, then the expansionary thrust of the depreciation will create or add to the internal inflationary imbalance.

An appreciation tends to contract the country's economy. If the economy begins with inflationary pressure, then this may be welcome. But if the economy is already in or tending toward a recession with excessive unemployment, then the exchange-rate change adds to the internal imbalance.

Government monetary or fiscal policy can be used to address any internal imbalances that do arise. If excessive unemployment is the internal imbalance, then expansionary monetary or fiscal policy can be used.[8] The size of the change in policy needed to address the imbalance depends on the change in the exchange rate that will occur. Monetary policy is powerful with floating exchange rates, so a relatively small change may be enough to reestablish internal balance. The power of fiscal policy is more variable and may be difficult to predict if it is difficult to predict the appreciation or depreciation of the exchange rate following the fiscal change.

INTERNATIONAL MACROECONOMIC POLICY COORDINATION

The dollar may be our currency but it's your problem.

U.S. Treasury Secretary John Connally, speaking to a group of Europeans (as quoted in Paul A. Volcker and Toyoo Gyohten, Changing Fortunes: The World's Money and the Threat to American Leadership, *New York: Times Books, 1992, p. 81)*

The policies adopted by one country have effects on other countries. With floating exchange rates these spillover effects happen in several ways, including foreign income repercussions as changes in incomes alter demands for imports, and changes in international price competitiveness as floating exchange rates change.

One danger is that a policy change that benefits the country making it can harm other countries. For instance, a shift to expansionary monetary policy causes the currencies of other countries to appreciate. This can appear to be a beggar-thy-neighbor policy in that the first country benefits from increased growth, but the exchange-rate appreciation can harm the price competitiveness and trade of other countries.

Another danger is that each country acting individually may fail to make a policy change whose benefits mostly go to other countries. If a number of countries could coordinate so that they all made this policy change, all would reap substantial benefits. For example, following the nearly global stock market crash of October 1987, the global financial system needed additional liquidity to counteract the decline in banking and financial activity. If any one central bank added liquidity, the rest of the global system would benefit, probably more than the individual country would. Each individual central bank might be slow to act, or reluctant to add liquidity aggressively, on its own. Fortunately, several central banks coordinated their actions to inject liquidity, and the financial markets stabilized.

---

[8]As the U.S. government attempted to address the recession resulting from the global financial and economic crisis, it confronted the vexing problem that monetary policy had already lowered domestic interest rates to about zero. The box "Liquidity Trap!" discusses how the U.S. Fed responded.

Global Crisis   Liquidity Trap!

Conventional monetary policy has a limit. It cannot reduce nominal interest rates below zero. Even interest rates that are as close to zero as they can go may not be enough to encourage borrowing and spending that will move the economy to its potential—that is, move real GDP to a level that results in "full employment" of the economy's resources. This problem, known as the *liquidity trap*, was experienced and analyzed during the Great Depression of the 1930s but then was almost forgotten for half a century. It seemed to be a curiosity because none of the world's major economies seemed to get anywhere close to it. It reappeared in discussions of Japan's lost decade in the 1990s, and it became disturbingly relevant for the United States and other countries with the global financial and economic crisis that began in 2007. Here's what happened in the United States.

In August 2007, with the onset of the first phase of the global crisis, financial institutions became less willing to lend to each other and to other borrowers. Households and businesses began to cut their spending. In our picture, the IS curve was shifting to the left. Beginning in August 2007, the U.S. Federal Reserve responded with conventional monetary policy, cutting its target for the Fed funds interest rate in steps from its starting value of 5.25 percent. The Fed was shifting the LM curve down to fight the shrinking IS curve. The Fed had some success for a while, as the recession was mild. By September 2008, the Fed funds target was down to 2 percent.

On September 15, Lehman Brothers failed and the crisis became intense. The Fed cut its Fed fund target in several more steps to 0–0.25 percent in mid-December. This is essentially as low as it can go. The economy was by then in a severe recession, but the United States was out of regular expansionary monetary policy. The graph shows the economy in this liquidity trap. Once interest rates in the economy, especially the short-term interest rates that are most directly influenced by conventional monetary policy, are close to zero, the LM curve becomes horizontal, as shown. If the IS curve shifts far enough to the left, to IS_L in the graph, the intersection is at point E_L in the liquidity trap. U.S. real GDP at Y_L was well below the economy's potential Y_{full}.

What can government policymakers do? Conventional monetary policy cannot shift the LM curve any lower in the area of its intersection with the IS_L curve. Fiscal policy is still available, and the U.S. government adopted a large fiscal stimulus in February 2009 to try to shift the IS curve to the right. However, this stimulus did not have that much effect, for several reasons. Other spending influences remained weak and were tending to push the IS curve to the left. Also, the actual fiscal stimulus occurred slowly, as various spending and tax-cut programs took time to implement. The fiscal stimulus probably prevented the economy from weakening further (preventing the IS curve from shifting further to the left), but it did not shift the IS curve much to the right.

The U.S. economy remained weak, with real GDP well below potential and a high unemployment rate. Because the government budget deficit had ballooned, more fiscal expansion was politically impossible. With the economy in the liquidity trap, the Fed turned to a form of unconventional monetary policy, *quantitative easing* (QE)—the central bank buying and holding massive amounts of securities—which the Bank of Japan had used with some success in the early 2000s. In the depth of the crisis, the Fed purchased large amounts of financial assets, expanding its assets from about $900 billion in September 2008 to almost $2.3 trillion in December. These purchases pushed large amounts of high-powered money into the banking system. The banks could not use this money to make new loans, so the banks deposited the funds at the Fed and held large amounts of excess bank reserves. As the crisis in the financial market eased in 2009, the Fed deliberately maintained its quantitative easing by keeping this high level of assets, and the Fed shifted the composition of its holdings toward mortgage-backed assets and longer-term U.S. Treasury bonds.

How can quantitative easing affect the economy? One can imagine several ways. First, the Fed may be able to lower long-term interest rates by buying large amounts of long-term bonds. With lower long-term interest rates, businesses and households are encouraged to take on long-term debt to finance purchases of buildings, machinery, and housing. Effectively, the IS curve shifts to the right. Estimates of the impact of the Fed's quantitative easing in 2008–2009 are that U.S. real GDP was about 1 to 2 percent higher by early 2011. Second, the large quantity of excess reserves that banks were holding could encourage some of them to make more loans, but this effect seems to be small. Third, some of the huge amount of dollar liquidity can flow into the foreign exchange market, depreciating the exchange-rate value of the dollar. During 2009,

the U.S. dollar had a real depreciation of about 6 percent. This effect of the unconventional monetary policy is conventional—the United States gains international price competitiveness. As shown in the graph, the IS and FE curves shift to the right to IS_{QE} and FE_{QE}, and U.S. real GDP increases to Y_{QE}. But other countries, including Brazil, Switzerland, and Japan, complained that the dollar depreciation resulting from U.S. quantitative easing was an appreciation of their currencies that undercut aggregate demand for their production.

U.S. recovery from the deep recession of 2007–2009 continued to be slow. In 2010 the Fed began a second round of quantitative easing (QE2), buying about $600 billion of Treasury bonds during November 2010 to June 2011. In late 2012 the Fed implemented a third round (QE3), buying about $1.5 trillion of bonds by late 2014. Each subsequent QE round seemed to have smaller effects on long-term interest rates and exchange rates, and the United States continued its slow growth. The United States had not yet escaped the liquidity trap.

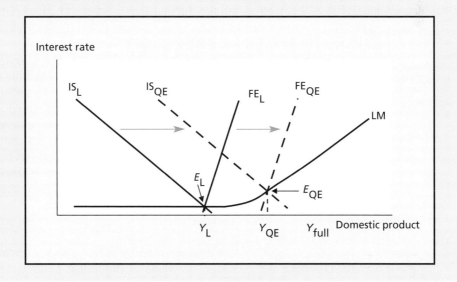

Given these spillover effects and interdependencies, it seems that it should be possible to improve global macroeconomic performance through international cooperation and international coordination. *International policy cooperation* refers to such activities as sharing of information about each country's performance, problems, and policies. Sharing of information occurs in many places, including high-level meetings of national finance ministers and heads of state as well as international organizations such as the International Monetary Fund and the Bank for International Settlements. International cooperation of this sort is not controversial.

International macroeconomic policy coordination is more than this. It is the joint determination of several countries' macroeconomic policies to improve joint performance. It implies the ability of one country to influence the policies of other countries and the willingness of a country to alter its policies to benefit other countries. In some situations coordination could be easy. For instance, in a deep global recession with no inflation, the advantages of mutual expansionary policies are clear. All countries can benefit if each country finds an alternative to beggar-thy-neighbor policies that harm other countries. In other situations coordination is more controversial.

We have several examples of major coordination efforts in the past 40 years. At the Bonn Summit of 1978, the United States agreed to implement policies to reduce U.S. inflation while also agreeing to reduce oil imports by decontrolling domestic oil prices. Germany agreed to increase its government spending to stimulate its economy. Japan also agreed to continue its expansionary policies, while taking steps to slow its growth of exports. In the Plaza Agreement of 1985, the major countries agreed to intervene in the foreign exchange markets to lower the exchange-rate value of the U.S. dollar (but there was no other substantial coordination of policies). In the Louvre Accord of 1987, the United States committed to reduce its fiscal deficit, while Germany and Japan committed to expansionary policies. All committed to stabilize the exchange-rate value of the dollar, if necessary through higher U.S. interest rates and lower interest rates in Germany and Japan, as well as through official intervention.[9] More recently, central banks undertook coordinated actions to try to address the global financial and economic crisis, as described in the box "Central Bank Liquidity Swaps."

We can see possible benefits of coordination by examining the Louvre Accord. Tightening of U.S. policies (both fiscal and monetary) would tend to slow down the U.S. economy, and slow down the economies of other countries by reducing U.S. demand for imports. Expansionary policies in Germany and Japan could offset the contractionary effects of the U.S. policy shift, not only in these two countries but also in other countries (including the United States) by expanding German and Japanese demands for imports. If this is done on a coordinated basis, the result can be a reduction of the U.S. current account deficit, reductions in the German and Japanese current account surpluses, and a stabilization of the exchange-rate value of the dollar, without a global recession caused by the tightening of U.S. policies.

If the benefits of international policy coordination seem clear, why do we actually see rather little of it? There seem to be several reasons. First, the goals of different countries may not be compatible. For instance, the United States may want to maintain growth while stabilizing the exchange-rate value of the dollar. Policymakers at the

---

[9]The box "Can Governments Manage the Float?" discusses the use of intervention to influence floating exchange rates.

Case Study   Can Governments Manage the Float?

Floating exchange rates allow a country to achieve external balance while maintaining control over its money supply and monetary policy. But floating exchange rates are also highly variable, more variable than we expected when many countries shifted to floating rates in 1973.

Governments that have chosen floating exchange rates worry about the large amount of variability, and nearly all manage the float to some extent. Some governments manage their floating rates closely. If the floating exchange rate is heavily managed, then it behaves more like a fixed exchange rate, and the analysis of the previous chapter is relevant. Other governments, including the governments of most major countries that have chosen floating rates, use management selectively. Occasionally the government intervenes in the foreign exchange market.

Is selective or occasional intervention effective in influencing exchange rates? Thirty years ago the conventional wisdom was clear. If the intervention is not sterilized, then it can be effective. However, it is effective not because it is intervention but rather because it changes the money supply. Unsterilized intervention is simply another way to implement a change in the domestic money supply and monetary policy. By changing the money supply, it can have a substantial effect on the exchange rate. If the intervention is sterilized, the conventional wisdom was that it would not be effective in changing the exchange rate, at least not much or for long. Yet interventions by the U.S., Japanese, and British monetary authorities, among others, are fully sterilized.

The conventional wisdom was based on studies that showed little effect of sterilized intervention. It was also based on the relatively small sizes of interventions. In a market where total daily trading was hundreds of billions of dollars, interventions that typically were less than $1 billion seemed too small to have much impact.

More recent studies have challenged this conventional wisdom. How might sterilized intervention be effective, even though it does not change the domestic money supply and is relatively small? The most likely way is by changing the exchange-rate expectations of international financial investors and speculators. Intervention can act as a signal from the monetary authorities that they are not happy with the current level or trend of the exchange rate. The authorities show that they are willing to do something (intervention) now and they signal that they may be willing to do something more in the future. For instance, the authorities may be willing to change monetary policy and interest rates in the future if the path for the exchange rate remains unacceptable. Sterilized interventions then can be a type of news that influences expectations. If international investors take the signal seriously, they adjust their exchange-rate expectations. Changed expectations alter international capital flows, changing the exchange rate in the direction desired by the authorities. For instance, in 1985 the major governments announced in the Plaza Agreement that they were committed to reducing the exchange-rate value of the dollar. They intervened to sell dollars. International investors shifted to expecting the dollar to depreciate by more than they had previously thought, and the exchange-rate value of the dollar declined rapidly.

Recent studies indicate that sterilized intervention can be effective. One indirect measure of effectiveness is whether the monetary authority makes a profit or a loss on its interventions over time. If the authority buys a currency and succeeds in driving its value up (and sells to drive the value down), the authority makes a profit (buy low, sell high). An early study found that central banks generally incurred losses on their intervention in the 1970s. However, a study of U.S. intervention during the 1980s found that the U.S. monetary authority made a profit of over $12 billion on its dollar–DM interventions and a profit of over $4 billion on its dollar–yen interventions during this period. Another study concluded that interventions during the mid- and late 1980s

—Continued on next page

significantly affected exchange-rate expectations in the direction intended.

Recently, a number of monetary authorities began releasing data on their daily intervention activities, information that had previously been kept secret. With these data the quality of statistical studies has improved dramatically. The typical findings are as follows:

- Intervention is usually effective in the short period of two weeks or less, in reversing the direction of the trend of the exchange rate, or at least in reducing the speed of the trend (when the authority is leaning against the wind).
- Larger interventions are more successful.
- Coordinated intervention, in which two or more monetary authorities intervene jointly to try to influence an exchange rate, is much more powerful than an intervention by one country of the same total size.
- The effectiveness of the intervention often diminishes after this two-week period, and often there is no discernible effect one month later.

Here is one example. After the introduction of the euro in 1999, the European Central Bank (ECB) intervened to influence the exchange-rate value of the euro on only four days, in the fall of 2000, after the euro's exchange-rate value had declined substantially during 1999–2000. On September 22 a coordinated intervention by the ECB and the monetary authorities of the United States, Japan, Canada, and Britain bought several billions of euros. The initial impact was to increase the euro's value by over 4 percent, though about half of the effect was lost during the remainder of the day. The intervention was successful in reversing the direction of the trend for about 5 days, and after 15 days the euro's decline was less than what it would have been if the previous trend had simply continued. Still, the euro's decline continued, and the ECB intervened again on November 3, 6, and 9. The same effects of reversing the trend for about 5 days and smoothing the decline for about 15 days occurred. These interventions may have had some lasting impact because at about this

time the value of the euro stopped its downward trend and began to vary around a trend that was essentially flat.

Here's another example. The Japanese government has been quite concerned about the variability of the yen's value. From early 1991 to 1995, the yen appreciated from 140 per dollar to 80. Then the yen depreciated to 146 in 1998, appreciated to about 100 in 2000, and then depreciated to about 125 by April 2001. Japan's monetary authority bought dollars (and sold yen) on 168 days during this time period, for total purchases of over $200 billion. It sold dollars (and bought yen) on 33 days, a total of $37 billion.

Ito (2003) reckons that these interventions were highly profitable for the Japanese government. It bought dollars at an average price of 104 and sold dollars at an average price of 130. It realized capital gains of $8 billion, earned an interest differential on its holdings of the dollars it bought of about $31 billion, and had an unrealized capital gain at the end of the period of $29 billion. In fact, the Japanese government seemed to have an unstated target exchange rate of about 125 per dollar. Sales of dollars were at rates above 125, and purchases below.

By combining days of intervention that are close together, Fatum and Hutchison (2006) identify 43 separate instances of intervention, 29 of buying dollars during 1993–1996 and 1999–2000 and 14 of selling dollars during 1991–1992 and 1997–1998. In 34 of these, Japan's monetary authority was clearly leaning against the wind—intervening against the trend during the previous two days. Of these, 24 reversed the trend for the two days after the intervention, and in another 5 the trend rate of exchange-rate change was lowered. The major failures occurred in the first half of 1995, when continual interventions could not prevent the yen from appreciating from 100 to the then-amazing level of 80 yen per dollar. However, even when the Japanese authorities succeeded during this short two-day window, there was generally little effect on the exchange rate a month after the intervention.

Coordinated interventions with the U.S. monetary authority (which occurred on 23 days during the decade) were *much* more powerful than interventions only by Japan. Ito estimates that, for 1996–2001, independent intervention of $2 billion by the Japanese authority moved the yen value by 0.2 percent on average. Coordinated intervention of $1 billion by each of the two authorities moved the yen value by about 5.0 percent.

After intervening rather little during 2001 and 2002, the Japanese government engaged in massive interventions during 2003 and the first quarter of 2004 to attempt to prevent appreciation of the yen. The government intervened on about 40 percent of these days and purchased a total of about $315 billion. Nonetheless, the yen did appreciate from 120 per dollar at the end of 2002 to 104 per dollar at the end of March 2004, although the appreciation might have been larger if there had been no intervention. The Japanese government then abruptly ended all intervention after March 2004, and the yen value was fairly steady for several years after the cessation.

Our beliefs about the effectiveness of sterilized intervention by the major countries is now cautious and nuanced. If the time frame is a few days, intervention seems often to be successful. If the time frame is one month or more, it usually seems to be unsuccessful. Still, there are times, such as late 2000 for the euro, when the monetary authorities believe that the market has pushed an exchange rate far from its fundamental value. As Michael Mussa, then chief economist for the International Monetary Fund, said a few days before the September 2000 euro intervention, "Circumstances for intervention are very rare, but they do arise. One has to ask, if not now, when?"

DISCUSSION QUESTION
On March 11, 2011, a devastating earthquake and tsunami hit Japan. Surprisingly, during the next week, the Japanese yen appreciated by 5 percent against the U.S. dollar. Should the Japanese central bank have intervened in the foreign exchange market? If so, how should it have intervened? If not, why not?

European Central Bank are mandated to focus solely on preventing inflation, so they may be unwilling to expand the money supply, lower interest rates, and expand the EU economy. It is simply difficult for a government to adopt policies that do not suit the economic and political conditions of its country, even if these policies would benefit other countries. Indeed, governments may disagree about how the domestic and global macroeconomy works. For instance, they may disagree about how much expansion is possible before inflation begins to increase noticeably.

Second, the benefits of international policy coordination may actually be small in many situations. Often the appropriate "coordinated" policies actually appear to be close to the appropriate policies that would be chosen by the countries individually (as long as blatant beggar-thy-neighbor policies such as new trade barriers are avoided). For instance, in 1987, the United States on its own probably should have shifted to somewhat contractionary policies and reduced its government budget deficit. In turn, both Germany and Japan, for their own benefit, probably should have shifted to more expansionary policies. Even in situations in which the coordinated policy actions are essentially what each government should do on its own, there can still be value to coordination, for two reasons. First, each government can use the commitment to international coordination to firm up domestic support for the policy changes. Second, the governments can use the high visibility of coordinated policy actions to try to enhance the effects on market psychology and expectations.

Global Crisis   Central Bank Liquidity Swaps

Central banks have often established swap lines among themselves, so that one central bank can quickly borrow from other central banks when the borrowing bank needs foreign currency for intervention in the foreign exchange market. The global financial and economic crisis brought a new kind of swap line, the *central bank liquidity swap*, innovated in December 2007 as part of a set of coordinated policies to address the crisis.

After the global crisis began in August 2007, many financial institutions that had become reliant on short-term funding from other financial institutions and from debt markets found it increasingly difficult to obtain this funding because heightened concerns about credit risk partially froze short-term lending and investing. To address the constricted short-term lending and credit markets, the U.S. Federal Reserve, the European Central Bank (ECB), the Bank of England, the Swiss National Bank, and the Bank of Canada announced on December 12 that they would inject $50 billion of funds into their banking systems, in the hope that the coordinated implementation of the unusual central bank loans would magnify their impact in encouraging regular banks to lend more fluidly.

Included among the lending programs were central bank liquidity swap lines provided by the U.S. Fed to the ECB and the Swiss central bank. These swaps addressed a specific problem. Banks outside the United States, especially banks in Europe, had dollar-denominated assets, but they did not have a base of deposits in dollars. In the crisis they lost ready access to dollar funding from other financial institutions (interbank) and from debt issues such as commercial paper purchased by money market funds. Interest rates on interbank lending (such as LIBOR, the London Interbank Offering Rate) rose well above normal levels, and there was still reluctance to lend.

The central bank liquidity swap is essentially a loan of dollars from the U.S. Fed. How does it work?

- The Fed exchanges dollars for the other country's currency with the foreign central bank.

- The foreign central bank lends the dollars to financial institutions in its country.

- The Fed holds the foreign currency passively, as collateral.

- At the maturity of the swap, the foreign central bank pays the Fed interest, and the two banks swap back the foreign currency and dollars.

The foreign central bank gets dollars that it can use, without dipping into its holdings of official international reserves. The Fed helps address the dollar shortage in the foreign banking system without direct credit risk exposure to foreign banks because its loan is to the foreign central bank.

The swap lines did allow the ECB and the Swiss central bank to lend to reduce the severity of the dollar shortage in the next months, and the limits on the total swap amounts outstanding were raised several times. With the intensification of the crisis after the failure of Lehman Brothers in September 2008, short-term funding again froze. Foreign financial institutions again lacked dollar funding, with short-term dollar interest rates like LIBOR soaring well above normal levels. Again the Fed worked with other central banks to address the problem. In September the Fed added liquidity swap lines with the central banks of Britain, Japan, Canada, Australia, Sweden, Norway, and Denmark, and in October with New Zealand, Brazil, Mexico, Korea, and Singapore. Also in October, the Fed removed limits on swap amounts with the ECB and the central banks of Switzerland, Britain, and Japan. There was a big increase in the value of swaps drawn and outstanding in October, and by December the swaps had peaked at nearly $600 billion outstanding, about half drawn by the ECB. Then the swaps decreased as dollar funding pressures decreased, and the program ended in February 2010.

Central bank liquidity swaps are an innovative form of international coordination that were effective in addressing dysfunction in dollar funding for foreign financial institutions during the crisis. The dollar loans made by the foreign central banks provided funding directly to their dollar-short banks. For their banks that already had plentiful dollars, the program assured these banks that they would have ready access to dollars in the future and encouraged the banks to lend their dollars rather than hoarding them. Studies show that the dollar loans from the swap lines contributed to the reduction of abnormally high interbank interest rates. Another indication of the success of the swap lines appeared a little later in 2010. With the euro crisis that began with Greece's government debt problems, dollar funding for foreign financial institutions again became constricted. In response, in May 2010 the Fed established new central bank liquidity swap lines with the ECB and four other central banks.

Major instances of international macroeconomic policy coordination are rare. Coordination is more likely when countries clearly see and agree to goals and the means to achieve these goals. In practice this means that the countries commit to doing what they largely should have done on their own. Even in these cases, governments often have difficulty delivering on their commitments. For instance, during the 1980s, international commitments by the U.S. government to reduce its government budget deficit seem to have had little impact.

Summary

With a cleanly floating exchange rate, the exchange rate changes to maintain external balance. If a country is tending toward a surplus in its overall international payments, the exchange-rate value of the country's currency will appreciate enough to reverse the tendency. If the country is tending toward a deficit, the currency will depreciate. The contrast with fixed exchange rates is clear. With a clean float external balance is not an issue, but the exchange-rate value can be quite variable or volatile.

Monetary policy is more powerful with floating exchange rates. After a shift in monetary policy, the exchange rate is likely to change in the direction that reinforces or magnifies the effect of the policy shift on aggregate demand, domestic product, national income, and price level. In contrast, as we saw in Chapter 23, with fixed exchange rates monetary policy loses power because the need to defend the fixed rate tends to reverse the policy thrust (assuming that the intervention is not or cannot be sterilized).

The effects of floating exchange rates on fiscal policy are not clear. Consider a fiscal expansion. If the resulting inflow of international financial capital is the dominant effect on external balance, then the country's currency appreciates. The loss of international price competitiveness leads to international crowding out, as the current account balance deteriorates. This reduces the effectiveness of fiscal policy in altering domestic product and income. If, instead, the initial deterioration in the current account balance is the dominant effect on external balance, then the country's currency depreciates. The gain in international price competitiveness improves the current account, and this enhances the effectiveness of fiscal policy. We also saw an ambiguity in how fixed exchange rates affect fiscal policy. But the conclusions are the opposite. With fixed exchange rates, fiscal policy is more effective in altering domestic product and income if capital is highly mobile internationally; it is less effective if capital is less mobile.

FIGURE 24.7
Ranking of
Exchange-Rate
Systems by
Unit Impacts
of Various
Exogenous
Shocks on
Domestic
Product and
Income

	More Disruptive–Less Stable	Less Disruptive–More Stable
Internal Shocks		
Domestic monetary shock	Floating	Fixed
Domestic spending shock	Floating*	Fixed*
External Shocks		
International trade shock	Fixed	Floating
International capital-flow shock	Fixed†	Floating†

Comparison is between (1) a fixed exchange rate defended by intervention with no sterilization, so adjustment is through money supply changes, and (2) a floating exchange rate with adjustment through exchange-rate changes. If sterilized intervention is used to defend the fixed exchange rate, this raises the disruptiveness of internal shocks, and it lowers the disruptiveness of external shocks, each relative to fixed rates with unsterilized intervention.

*This is the result if international capital flows are unresponsive to interest rate differences (low capital mobility), or if the current account change eventually is the dominant pressure on the exchange rate. The opposite result applies if the financial account change is the dominant pressure.
†The effect of the shock on national income is in the opposite direction for the two cases. The sense in which the shock is less disruptive under a floating exchange rate is that the induced exchange-rate change with floating exchange rates shifts the FE curve back toward its original position.

The ways in which different kinds of shocks affect the country's economy also differ according to whether the country has a fixed or floating exchange rate. Figure 24.7 summarizes the conclusions of the analysis of this chapter and Chapter 23. This figure indicates whether a particular shock would change domestic product and income more (be more disruptive or less stable) with fixed or with floating exchange rates. We can reach several general conclusions. First, internal shocks, especially domestic monetary shocks, are more disruptive to an economy with a floating exchange rate and are less disruptive with a fixed exchange rate. Second, external shocks, especially international trade shocks, are more disruptive to an economy with a fixed exchange rate and are less disruptive with a floating exchange rate. Floating exchange rates provide some insulation from foreign trade shocks.

While cleanly floating exchange rates can ensure that the country achieves external balance, they do not ensure internal balance. In several situations the exchange-rate change that reestablishes external balance can make an internal imbalance worse. If a country has rising inflation and a tendency toward external deficit, the depreciation of the currency can exacerbate the inflation pressures in the country. If the country has excessive unemployment and a tendency toward surplus, the appreciation of the currency can make the unemployment problem worse. To achieve internal balance, the country's government may need to implement domestic policy changes (contractionary to fight inflation, expansionary to fight unemployment).

In theory, international macroeconomic policy coordination can improve global macroeconomic performance. International policy coordination means that countries set their policies jointly. The benefits of coordination include the opportunity to consider spillover effects on other countries that arise from interdependence and the opportunity to avoid beggar-thy-neighbor policies that benefit one country at the expense of others. In practice, major instances of international policy coordination are infrequent.

Key Terms

Domestic monetary shock
Domestic spending
  shock

International capital-flow
  shock
International trade shock

International
  macroeconomic policy
  coordination

Suggested Reading

Genberg and Swoboda (1989) present a technical analysis of the effects of government policies on current account balances under floating exchange rates. International macroeconomic policy coordination is discussed in Bryant (1995) and Meyer et al. (2002). Cline (2005) and Iley and Lewis (2007) examine the U.S. current account deficit and the U.S. international investment position. Goldberg et al. (2011) provide an overview of central bank liquidity swaps.

Neeley (2011) and Sarno and Taylor (2001) survey the theory of and evidence on the use of sterilized intervention to manage floating exchange rates. Ito (2003) and Fatum and Hutchison (2006) examine Japan's intervention during the 1990s, and Fatum and Hutchison (2002) look at the ECB intervention in 2000.

Neely (2001) and Mihaljek (2005) present the results of surveys of central banks about their intervention practices. Menkhoff (2013) provides an overview of research on intervention by monetary authorities in developing countries. Aizenman and Glick (2009) find a high degree of sterilization of foreign exchange interventions for the Asian and Latin American countries they examine.

Questions and Problems

♦ 1. "Overshooting is the basis for the enhanced effectiveness of monetary policy under floating exchange rates." Do you agree or disagree? Why?

2. A country has a floating exchange rate. Government spending now increases in an effort to reduce unemployment. What is the effect of this policy change on the exchange-rate value of the country's currency? Under what circumstances does the exchange-rate change reduce the expansionary effect of the fiscal change?

♦ 3. "A drop in the foreign demand for our exports has a larger effect on our domestic product and income under floating exchange rates than it would under fixed exchange rates." Do you agree or disagree? Why?

4. Describe the effects of a sudden decrease in the domestic demand for holding money (a shift from wanting to hold domestic money to wanting to hold domestic bonds) on our domestic product and income under floating exchange rates. Is the change in domestic product and income greater or less than it would be under fixed exchange rates? (*Hint:* A decrease in the demand for money is like an increase in the supply of money.)

♦ 5. A country has a rising inflation rate and a tendency for its overall payments to go into deficit. Will the resulting exchange-rate change move the country closer to or further from internal balance?

6. Britain has instituted a contractionary monetary policy to fight inflation. The pound is floating.

   a. If the exchange-rate value of the pound remains steady, what are the effects of tighter money on British domestic product and income? What is the effect on the British inflation rate? Explain.

b. Following the shift to tighter money, what is the pressure on the exchange-rate value of the pound? Explain.

c. What are the implications of the change in the exchange-rate value of the pound for domestic product and inflation in Britain? Does the exchange-rate change tend to reinforce or counteract the contractionary thrust of British monetary policy? Explain.

◆ 7. In the late 1980s, the United States had a large government budget deficit and a large current account deficit. The dollar was floating. One approach suggested to reduce both of these deficits was a large increase in taxes.

　　a. If the exchange-rate value of the dollar remained steady, how would this change affect U.S. domestic product and income? How would it affect the U.S. current account balance and the U.S. financial account balance? Explain.

　　b. What are the possible pressures on the exchange-rate value of the dollar as a result of this change in fiscal policy? Explain.

　　c. If the dollar actually depreciates, what are the implications for further changes in U.S. domestic product and the U.S. current account balance? Explain.

8. What are the effects of a sudden surge in foreign money supplies on our domestic product and income under floating exchange rates? (*Hint:* The increase in the foreign money supplies will have an impact on demand for our exports and on international capital flows as well as on exchange rates.)

◆ 9. A country initially has achieved both external balance and internal balance. International financial capital is highly but not perfectly mobile, so the country's FE curve is upward sloping and flatter than the LM curve. The country has a floating exchange rate. As a result of the election of a new government, foreign investors become bullish on the country. International financial capital inflows increase dramatically and remain higher for a number of years.

　　a. What shift occurs in the FE curve because of the increased capital inflows?

　　b. What change in the exchange rate occurs to reestablish external balance?

　　c. As a result of the exchange-rate change, how does the country adjust back to external balance? Illustrate this using an IS–LM–FE graph. What is the effect of all of this on the country's internal balance?

10. A country initially has achieved both external balance and internal balance. The country prohibits international financial capital inflows and outflows, so its financial account (excluding official reserves transactions) is always zero because of these capital controls. The country has a floating exchange rate. An exogenous shock now occurs—foreign demand for the country's exports increases.

　　a. What shifts would occur in the IS, LM, and FE curves because of the increase in foreign demand for the country's exports if the exchange-rate value of the country's currency were to remain unchanged?

　　b. What change in the exchange-rate value of the country's currency actually occurs? Why?

　　c. As a result of the exchange-rate change, how does the country adjust back to external balance? Illustrate this using an IS–LM–FE graph. How does all of this affect the country's internal balance?

✦ 11. Each of the following indicates a series of foreign exchange interventions by the monetary authority of a country. For each, do you think that the authority effectively made a profit or not?

  a. The local currency is pesos. In January the authority intervenes to sell U.S. dollars at the rate $3.00/peso. In June it intervenes to buy dollars at $3.50/peso. In November it intervenes to sell dollars at $3.10/peso. In June of the next year it intervenes to buy dollars at $3.40/peso.

  b. The local currency is the yen. In February the authority intervenes to sell yen at $0.60/yen. In October it intervenes to sell yen at $0.55/yen. The next year it intervenes to sell yen in March at $0.51/yen. In April the exchange rate stabilizes at $0.50/yen, and the authority ceases its intervention.

  12. The exchange rates between the world's major currencies are floating. Each major country in the world is using its monetary policy to attempt to improve the country's international price competitiveness during the next few years. Is this a situation in which international macroeconomic policy coordination could be useful? Why or why not?

Chapter Twenty-Five

National and Global Choices: Floating Rates and the Alternatives

This chapter provides a capstone for our analysis of international economic and financial performance, by exploring the issues that surround countries' choices of policies toward the exchange rate.

What exchange-rate policy should a country use? Should it use a clean float in which private supply and demand determine the exchange rate? Should it commit to a fixed rate that it defends and attempts never to change? Should it generally use a floating, market-driven exchange rate but manage that rate to try to modify the market outcome some of the time? Should it use a fixed rate but be willing from time to time, or perhaps even quite frequently, to change the pegged-rate value?

Each country must choose its policy. The analysis of Chapters 16 through 24 provides a broad range of insights into the economics of this choice. This chapter pulls these insights together by exploring the key issues to consider. We will see that the issues suggest that each policy has both strengths and weaknesses, so different countries might wisely choose different policies.

The composite of all countries' choices results in the global exchange-rate system. At times in the past century, countries have created a coherent global regime around a single policy—fixing to gold during the gold standard, and the adjustable pegged system based on the U.S. dollar that we call the Bretton Woods system. At other times countries have made more varied choices, so characterizing the system during those times is not so easy. For instance, the period between the two world wars did not have a dominant policy, especially after the attempt to return to the gold standard broke down in the early 1930s.

In the current period different countries use different exchange-rate policies. Our analysis provides insights into their choices and into the general trend toward floating exchange rates. After discussing this trend, the chapter takes a look at three paths in the opposite direction, toward fixed exchange rates that are (nearly) permanent. The members of the European Union are on the most far-reaching of these paths, to a monetary union with a single European currency.

KEY ISSUES IN THE CHOICE OF EXCHANGE-RATE POLICY

A country must choose its exchange-rate policy from a menu of many alternatives. The aspect of the policy that we examine is the extent of flexibility that is permitted by the policy. On the one side is a policy that permits substantial flexibility, with a rate that is floating and largely (if not completely) market-driven. The polar case here is a cleanly floating exchange rate, but a lightly managed floating rate also fits the type. On the other side is a policy that fixes or pegs the exchange-rate value of the country's currency to a major foreign currency or a basket of foreign currencies.[1] A permanently fixed exchange rate is the polar case, but we should keep in mind that it is impossible for a country to commit never to change its policy.

Our previous analysis suggests that five major issues can influence the country's choice: the effects of macroeconomic shocks; the effectiveness of government policies; differences in macroeconomic goals, priorities, and policies; controlling inflation; and the real effects of exchange-rate variability. Let's look at each major issue and what it says about the advantages and disadvantages of floating or fixing. Figure 25.1 provides a road map that you can use as you read through this section of the chapter.

Effects of Macroeconomic Shocks

A country would look favorably on an exchange-rate policy that reduces the domestic effects of macroeconomic shocks. The performance of the country's economy is better if shocks are less disruptive because the economy is more stable. Our analysis of Chapters 23 and 24 indicates that the effects of various macroeconomic shocks depend not only on the exchange-rate policy but also on the type of shock.[2]

Internal shocks generally cause less trouble with a fixed rate than with a float.

A *domestic monetary shock* is less disruptive with a fixed exchange rate because the intervention to defend the fixed rate tends to reverse the shock and its effects. With a floating exchange rate the resulting change in the exchange rate would actually magnify the domestic effects of the monetary shock. For example, consider what happens if the demand for holding money increases unexpectedly, perhaps because people become wary of using credit cards and begin to pay more often with cash. The extra money demand increases domestic interest rates and reduces domestic product by discouraging interest-sensitive spending. The country's overall balance of payments tends toward surplus, as the financial account improves because of increased capital inflows and the current account improves because of lower domestic spending and demand for imports.

---

[1] A small number of often-vocal commentators believe that countries should return to fixing the values of their currencies to a commodity like gold. The box "What Role for Gold?" explores this possibility.

[2] Most of our discussion here continues to make the assumptions that product prices are rather sticky in the short run but that they do adjust to spending and monetary pressures in the long run. The discussion of the effects of shocks focuses on the short and medium runs, when shocks can cause cyclical movements in spending, production, and unemployment. In addition, our discussion of macroeconomic effects under fixed exchange rates focuses on the case in which the government does not or cannot sterilize, so the intervention does affect the domestic money supply.

FIGURE 25.1   Advantages of Floating Exchange Rates and Fixed Exchange Rates in Terms of Various Issues

Issue	Advantage of Floating Exchange Rates	Advantage of Fixed Exchange Rates
Effects of macroeconomic shocks	With floating rates external shocks, especially foreign trade shocks, are less disruptive.	With fixed rates internal shocks, especially domestic monetary shocks, are less disruptive.
Effectiveness of government policies	With floating rates monetary policy is more effective in influencing aggregate demand.	—
	With floating rates fiscal policy is more effective if capital flows are not very responsive to interest rates.	With fixed rates fiscal policy is more effective if capital flows are sufficiently responsive to interest rates.
Differences in macroeconomic goals and policies	Floating rates allow goals and policies to differ across countries.	Fixed rates require coordination or consistency of goals and policies across countries.
Controlling inflation	Floating rates allow each country to choose its own acceptable inflation rate.	With fixed rates countries should have about the same inflation rates. This creates a discipline effect on high-inflation countries (but low-inflation countries may "import" higher inflation).
Real effects of exchange-rate variability	Variability of floating rates is desirable. It shows that the market is working well as supply and demand shift. The rate variability reflects unstable economic and political environments. Real effects on international trade are not that large because much exchange-rate risk can be hedged.	Variability of floating rates, especially between the major currencies, is excessive. The rates may be driven at times by bandwagons and speculative bubbles. The variability causes undesirable real effects. Exchange-rate risk lowers trade volumes. Overshooting causes excessive resource shifts into and out of trade-oriented industries.
	A fixed rate is simply a form of price control. The fixed-rate value is often inefficiently low or high, causing inefficient resource allocations.	The relative stability of fixed rates may promote higher levels of international transactions, especially trade.

1. With a fixed exchange rate, the country's central bank must intervene to prevent the country's currency from appreciating. As the central bank sells domestic currency, the intervention increases the domestic money supply. The extra money demand is now met by an increased money supply, and interest rates can fall back toward their original level. The fall in interest rates spurs a recovery of interest-sensitive spending and domestic product.

Case Study   What Role for Gold?

Gold was at the center of the international monetary system during the gold standard. Individuals had the right to obtain or sell gold (in exchange for national currency) with the country's central bank at the fixed official gold price. Gold was also an important part of the Bretton Woods system of fixed exchange rates. The U.S. government was expected to buy or sell gold with foreign central banks (but not with individuals) at the official U.S. dollar price of gold.

What is the role for gold now? Gold remains an official reserve asset, but currently central banks make almost no official use of gold. Gold is also held by private individuals as part of their investments. Let's look at both the official role and private role for gold more closely.

OFFICIAL ROLE: THE ONCE AND FUTURE KING?

> You shall not crucify mankind upon a cross of gold.
> *William Jennings Bryan, U.S. presidential candidate, 1896*

Most observers of the current system are comfortable with the lack of a role for gold in official international activity. Indeed, some believe that central banks and the International Monetary Fund should sell off their current official holdings of gold. One reason to sell is that gold plays no active role and earns no interest. The part of national wealth (or IMF assets) held in gold could be invested more productively. Another reason is that the proceeds of gold sales could be used for assistance to the poorer countries of the world. Central banks and the IMF have made gold sales into the private market in recent decades (a process called *demonetization of gold*).

A small group of people are strong advocates of a return to a real gold standard in which countries tie their currencies to gold. These proponents believe that a return to a gold standard would greatly reduce national and average global rates of inflation by creating a strong discipline effect on countries' abilities to expand their money supplies. They also believe that a return to a gold standard would eliminate the variability of exchange rates by establishing full confidence in the system and by enforcing monetary adjustments to achieve external balance. By creating stability and confidence in national moneys and exchange rates, they believe, the return to a gold standard would stabilize and lower both nominal and real interest rates.

Most international economists oppose a return to the gold standard. To most, a gold standard is not nearly as stabilizing as its proponents claim, except perhaps in the very long run. The supply of new gold to the world is governed not by some master regulator, but rather by mining activities. A major discovery of new minable gold deposits leads to a rapid expansion of the world gold supply. As central banks bought gold to defend the fixed gold prices, national money supplies would expand rapidly and inflation rates would increase. On the other hand, if there were no new discoveries, and if current mines slowed output as mines were exhausted (or if major strikes or similar disruptions slowed output), national central banks would have to sell gold to defend their price (assuming that private demand continued to grow). National money supplies would shrink and countries would enter into painful deflations (with weak economic conditions forcing general price levels lower).

Looking at the other side of the market for gold, decreases in private demand for gold would require central banks to buy gold to defend their price, expanding money supplies. Increases in private demand would force central banks to sell gold, shrinking national money supplies.

Supply swings were evident even during the classical gold standard. Between 1873 and 1896, the British price level fell by about one-third, and it then inflated back up from 1896 to 1913. These

—Continued on next page

shifts were closely related to changes in the growth rates of world stocks of monetary gold, and these were closely related to cycles in mining driven by gold discoveries.

Between 1850 and 1873, the world gold stock grew by 2.9 percent per year, with discoveries leading to mining booms in California and Australia. This permitted money supplies to keep up with the growing real demand for money, so that price levels remained about steady. Between 1873 and 1896, the world gold stock grew by only 1.7 percent per year. This was not enough to keep up with continued growth in real money demand, and the general price level was forced down. Then from 1896 to 1913, new discoveries of gold led to mining booms in the Klondike (Canada) and the Transvaal (South Africa). The world gold stock rose 3.2 percent per year, faster than real money demand was growing, so the general price level increased. With such fluctuations in the growth of monetary gold, it is difficult to claim that the gold standard ensured steady expansion of the world money base (although the gold standard did limit money growth and inflation in the long run).

Because a gold standard probably would not be nearly as stable as its proponents claim, most international economists oppose a return to a gold standard. Bolstering their belief are the more typical arguments about the advantages of flexible or floating exchange rates, including independence in choosing priorities and using policies. In addition, the resource costs of expanding official gold reserves are themselves high. New gold must be mined. This seems to be an inefficient use of resources, to produce something that will largely sit in the vaults of central banks.

PRIVATE ROLE: A SOUND INVESTMENT?

The official link between gold and currencies effectively ended in 1968, and it seems unlikely to be revived. Even though its official role has largely ended, should gold play a role in the investments of private individuals? Holding gold

pays no interest, so the return to gold comes from increases in its price. (The return earned is actually lower than the price increase suggests because of the costs of buying and selling as well as the costs of storing and safekeeping.)

The accompanying graph shows the monthly dollar price of gold since 1970. There are three lessons from this graph. First, anyone who bought gold in the early 1970s earned a high rate of return through 1980, as the dollar price increased from under $100 per ounce to over $600 per ounce. Similarly, anyone who bought in the early 2000s earned a high return, as the gold price rose from less than $300 to about $1,800 in September 2011. For each of these time periods, the gold-price increase far exceeded general price inflation or the rates of return available on most financial assets.

Second, anyone who bought and sold gold from the early 1980s to the early 2000s generally was disappointed. The gold price stayed in the range of $250 to $500 per ounce. The gold price did not keep up with general price inflation, and it underperformed compared to the returns available on many financial assets like stocks and bonds.

Third, far from being stable, or tracking general price inflation as an "inflation hedge," the gold price has fluctuated a lot. It soared during 1979–1980, falling back during 1980–1982, rose strongly during 1982, and so forth.

Why has the price of gold jumped around so much during the past several decades? Shifts in supply have some impact, but major pressure often comes from shifts in demand. To a large extent gold is what frightened people invest in. This part of demand increases and decreases as fears and tensions rise and subside.

Suppose you are wealthy and live in an unstable region of the world. Clandestine gold ownership can protect you from having your assets seized or heavily taxed. Or suppose you fear an explosion of inflation. Holding real assets like gold provides at least some protection against the loss of purchasing power that will afflict most

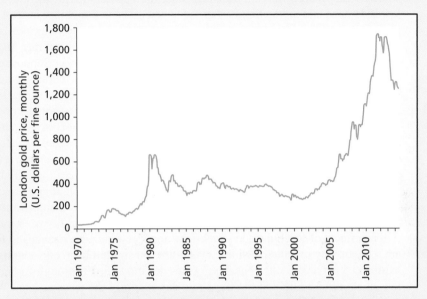

London gold price, monthly (U.S. dollars per fine ounce)

Source: International Monetary Fund, *International Financial Statistics.*

paper assets. Or suppose you are worried about financial and economic instability resulting from the global crisis that began in 2007, large fiscal deficits in the United States and Europe, the effects of quantitative easing by the Fed. You (and others) buy gold to move out of paper assets, and the price of gold rises rapidly.

Thus, private investments in gold are bets about the future course of gold prices. Over the long term the price of gold has roughly kept up with the rise of general prices (though past performance is no indicator of future performance). But for any short- or medium-term period of time, gold's value is anybody's guess. For a commodity that symbolizes stability, unpredictable shifts in demand and supply can and do cause large swings in gold's real price.

DISCUSSION QUESTION
Would adoption of a new gold standard by the industrialized countries result in better achievement of internal balance for these countries?

2. With a floating exchange rate, the tendency toward surplus causes the domestic currency to appreciate, reducing the country's international price competitiveness. As exports decline and imports rise in response to the shift in price competitiveness, the effect of the shock on the domestic economy is magnified. Domestic product tends to decline more.

The effects of a *domestic spending shock*, such as an unexpected change in real domestic investment spending or in consumption spending, or a sudden shift in fiscal policy, depend on how responsive international flows of financial capital are to interest rate changes. If capital mobility is low, then domestic spending shocks are also less disruptive with fixed rates than with floating rates. For instance, a decline in domestic spending tends to improve the country's current account balance as the demand for imports declines. If this is the dominant effect, the country's overall international payments also tend toward surplus. As in the monetary example, the payments surplus results in intervention that expands the domestic money supply if the country has a fixed exchange rate, and this tends to expand domestic spending, stabilizing the economy to some extent. With a floating exchange rate, the appreciation of the currency tends to lower demand and production further. Of course, if capital mobility instead is high, then the reverse is true—domestic spending shocks are more disruptive with fixed rates.

For *external shocks*, we reach opposite conclusions about stability and disruption. We can see this most clearly for *international trade shocks*. Suppose that foreign demand for our exports declines (or, for that matter, that our country's demand shifts toward imported foreign products and away from the comparable domestic products). The decrease in demand for our products tends to put the economy into a recession. In addition, the country's current account balance tends to deteriorate, and this tends to worsen the country's overall payments balance. With a fixed exchange rate, the central bank must intervene to defend the fixed rate by buying domestic currency. The resulting contraction of the domestic money supply reinforces the initial contraction of demand for our products, adding to the recession. With a floating exchange rate, the tendency to deficit depreciates the value of our currency. The improvement in price competitiveness boosts demand for our products, countering the recession tendency.

The effects of foreign trade shocks are important because changes in foreign trade are a major way in which business cycles are transmitted from one country to another. With fixed exchange rates business cycles are transmitted through foreign trade, and the intervention to defend the fixed rate can magnify the transmission. With floating exchange rates the transmission is muted because exchange-rate changes tend to insulate the economy from foreign trade shocks.

International trade shocks are particularly important for small developing countries, which are frequently affected by changes in the world prices (stated in foreign currency) of their exportable products. Christian Broda (2004) examined the effects of a 10 percent decrease in the price of a developing country's exports. He confirms that a floating exchange rate buffers the effects on the country. For a typical developing country that has a fixed exchange rate, the decline in the country's terms of trade causes a sharp decline of real GDP of about 2 percent in two years. For a typical developing country with a floating exchange rate, the two-year decrease in real GDP is only 0.2 percent. With a floating exchange rate, a quick nominal depreciation of the country's currency results in a 5 percent decrease in the real exchange-rate value of the country's currency. The country's enhanced price competitiveness increases exports and decreases imports, so the tendency toward declining GDP is offset.

International capital-flow shocks have domestic effects under both fixed and floating exchange rates, but there is a sense in which they are less disruptive under floating exchange rates. With a fixed exchange rate, an adverse capital-flow shift, which results in a capital outflow, requires intervention to defend the fixed rate by buying domestic currency. The reduction in the domestic money supply (if the intervention is not sterilized) has an adverse effect on the economy by raising interest rates and reducing spending. Under floating exchange rates, the currency depreciates. Any adverse effect that the capital outflow itself might have on the country's production is countered by the improvement in trade that results from better international price competitiveness.

The differences in the effects of shocks on the economy can have an impact on a country's choice of exchange-rate policy. If the country believes that it is buffeted mainly by internal shocks, the country favors a fixed exchange rate. If it believes that most shocks are external, then it favors a floating exchange rate.

However, we also must add a caution to this conclusion. While its conceptual basis is clear, its practical importance is actually debatable for several reasons. The most important reason is that the effects of shocks under fixed exchange rates depend on whether interventions are sterilized. The previous discussion has assumed that intervention is not sterilized. If, instead, the intervention is sterilized, the domestic money supply does not change. This reduces the stabilizing properties of fixed rates when internal shocks hit the economy, and it reduces the disruptive effects when external shocks hit. (Of course, continued sterilization may not be feasible if the payments imbalance persists, but the short-run behavior is still altered.)

The Effectiveness of Government Policies

Government policies' influence on aggregate demand and domestic product is altered by the type of exchange-rate policy chosen by the country. Monetary policy loses its control over the money supply if the country has a fixed exchange rate because monetary policy is constrained by the need to defend the fixed exchange rate. If the country tries to implement an expansionary monetary policy, the payments balance tends to go into deficit, and intervention to defend the fixed rate reduces the domestic money supply and reverses the monetary expansion. Indeed, if the country has a payments deficit for any reason, the intervention reduces the domestic money supply. If instead the country tries to implement a contractionary monetary policy, the payments balance tends to go into surplus, and the intervention to defend the fixed rate increases the domestic money supply and reverses the monetary contraction. In fact, a payments surplus for any reason expands the domestic money supply.

The country's monetary authority can attempt to regain some control over domestic monetary policy by sterilizing to reverse the effect of the intervention on the money supply, but there is a limit to how long it can continue to sterilize. Indeed, if international capital is highly or perfectly mobile, sterilized intervention cannot work. With perfect capital mobility, a country that is committed to defending a fixed exchange rate loses it power to have an independent monetary policy (because its monetary policy, such as it is, must be directed to defending the fixed exchange rate). The impossibility for a country to maintain a fixed exchange rate, to permit free capital flows, and to have a monetary policy directed toward domestic objectives is often called the *inconsistent trinity* or *trilemma*.

Monetary policy gains effectiveness under floating exchange rates. The resulting change in the exchange rate reinforces the thrust of the policy change. A shift to expansionary monetary policy results in a depreciation of the country's currency. The improvement in price competitiveness further expands demand for the country's products. A shift to contractionary policy appreciates the country's currency, resulting in a further reduction in demand for the country's products.

The effectiveness of fiscal policy depends on how responsive international capital flows are to interest rates. If capital is highly mobile, then fiscal policy gains effectiveness under fixed rates. The intervention to defend the fixed rate reduces the change in domestic interest rates, so that there is less domestic crowding out. With floating exchange rates and highly mobile capital, fiscal policy loses effectiveness. The resulting exchange-rate change leads to international crowding out. If capital is not that mobile, or if capital flows decline beyond a short-run period, the reverse is true. Fiscal policy then loses effectiveness with a fixed exchange rate and gains effectiveness with a floating rate.

The country's choice of exchange-rate policy can be influenced by its impact on the effectiveness of fiscal policy. A country whose capital markets are closely linked to the rest of the world, so that capital is highly mobile, will view a fixed exchange rate more favorably if it wants fiscal policy to be highly effective in the short run. A country whose capital flows are less responsive, or one that is worried about the effectiveness of fiscal policy beyond the short-run period when capital flows are responding, will look more favorably on floating rates.

While the impact of fiscal policy effectiveness on the choice of exchange-rate policy is conditional, the impact of monetary policy effectiveness is straightforward. *If a country desires to use monetary policy to address domestic objectives, then the country will favor a floating exchange rate.* A floating rate frees monetary policy from the need to defend the exchange rate.

Differences in Macroeconomic Goals, Priorities, and Policies

Government policymakers in each country must decide on the goals and objectives of macroeconomic policy. Even if countries generally pursue the same set of macroeconomic performance goals—including real economic growth, low unemployment, low inflation, and external balance—the priorities that governments place on the goals can differ, as can the specific policies adopted to achieve the goals.

For fixed exchange rates between the currencies of two or more countries to be successful, a kind of consistency or coordination between the countries involved is necessary. A country choosing a fixed exchange rate must follow policies that permit successful defense of the rate, given the policies and performance of the other countries linked by the fixed rates. If the policies diverge noticeably, large payments imbalances are likely to develop, making the defense of the fixed rates difficult or impossible.

One example is that countries should be willing to refrain from policy changes that lead to large international capital flows, or coordinate such changes in policies across countries. For instance, a big reduction in the taxes that one country imposes on financial investments can lead to large international capital flows into the country. If the other countries must intervene to defend the fixed rates as capital flows out of their countries, their international reserve holdings decline, threatening their ability to continue to defend the fixed rates. To maintain fixed rates, the first country may need to temper policy changes such as this. Or the other countries may need to adopt their own policy changes to mute the incentives for capital flows. For instance, the other countries could also lower their taxes on financial investments, or they could raise their interest rates. These changes would create a kind of consistency or coordination that reduces the threat to the viability of the fixed-rate system.

Another example is the priority that each country places on controlling inflation, or the trade-off that each country is willing to make between inflation and unemployment. For instance, during the years of the Bretton Woods system, Germany and Switzerland placed the highest priority on maintaining a very low inflation rate. The United States was less concerned with inflation and more concerned with growth and employment.

Even if there is no long-run trade-off between inflation and unemployment, such differences in priorities can still influence policy in the short run. The United States was willing to risk somewhat higher inflation to reduce unemployment in the short run, while Germany and Switzerland were not. The United States ended up with a higher inflation rate than Germany or Switzerland, and neither side was willing to compromise to achieve consistency. The fixed rates could not be maintained. We examine the relationship of inflation rates and exchange-rate policy in more depth in the next section.

Floating exchange rates are tolerant of diversity in countries' goals, priorities, and policies. As long as the country is willing to let the exchange rate change according to market pressures, external balance in the country's overall payments is maintained, whatever the country's policies. International policy coordination is still possible across countries, as we discussed in the previous chapter, but it is not necessary. There is no doubt that floating exchange rates permit a country to be more independent in its choices of policies, but we should also be a little cautious with this proposition. Policymakers in a country often are concerned about movements in the exchange-rate value of the country's currency, so their policy choices are somewhat constrained, even with floating rates. For instance, in the early 1980s unemployment rates were high in a number of the major European countries. However, they did not shift to expansionary policies because their currencies were already weak against the dollar. In fact, they tightened up and raised their interest rates to prevent their currencies from weakening further.

Controlling Inflation

The relationship between the choice of exchange-rate policy and a country's inflation rate is an important issue for the country. In addition, this issue has broad meaning for global macroeconomic performance, especially for the average rate of global inflation.

Countries that choose to fix the exchange rates among their currencies are committing to have similar inflation rates over the long run. This is the prediction of purchasing power parity—a nominal exchange rate can be steady only if the difference in inflation rates between the countries is about zero. The logic is based on the need to maintain reasonable price competitiveness for the products of each country. If inflation rates are consistently different over a substantial period of time, and exchange rates are fixed, a low-inflation country steadily gains international price competitiveness, leading to current account surpluses. A high-inflation country steadily loses price competitiveness, leading to deficits. These continuing and growing surpluses and deficits are not sustainable, and something needs to adjust. The inflation rate in the low-inflation country can increase, the inflation rate in the high-inflation country can decrease, or the exchange rate can change. If inflation rates change, then the fixed rate can be maintained, but the inflation difference instead can result in surrender of the fixed rate.

A number of implications follow from the conclusion that countries that fix their exchange rates should have similar inflation rates. First, proponents of fixed rates argue that fixed rates create a discipline effect on national tendencies to run high inflation rates. *For the fixed rate to be sustained, a country cannot have an inflation rate that is much above the inflation rate(s) of its partner(s).* In fact, a country embarking on a serious effort to reduce its high inflation rate may deliberately choose to fix its currency to the currency of another country that has a lower inflation rate. The high-inflation country is using the discipline effect as part of its anti-inflation program.

The high-inflation country hopes that the peg to the other country's currency can establish the credibility of its anti-inflation program. If it can gain credibility, it has a greater chance of success because people will lower their estimate of how much inflation will occur in the future. If inflation expectations are lowered, then it is easier to lower actual inflation and keep it low. Argentina used this strategy successfully in the early 1990s. In 1989, prices in Argentina rose by about 3,000 percent; in 1990, they climbed by about 2,300 percent. Argentina began an anti-inflation program and, in 1991, fixed the value of the peso to the U.S. dollar. The discipline of this peg helped reduce the growth rate of the money supply and the inflation rate in Argentina. By 1994, Argentinean inflation had dropped to about 4 percent, nearly the same as that in the United States, and it remained close to zero through the rest of the 1990s.

Second, a fixed-rate system in which most countries participate may also impose price discipline to lower the average global rate of price inflation. The fixed-rate system puts more pressure on governments whose countries have international deficits than on governments that have surpluses:

- Deficit countries face an obvious limit on their ability to sustain deficits; they soon run out of reserves and creditworthiness. Even if they attempt to sterilize their interventions, they must tighten up on their money supplies fairly quickly if they are to maintain the fixed rate. This forces them to contract, which lowers their money growth and inflation rate.

- Surplus countries, in contrast, face only more distant and manageable inconveniences from perennial surpluses. As long as they are willing to accumulate additional official reserves, they should be able to use sterilized intervention for an extended period.

Thus, the deficit countries tend to lower their money growth, while the surplus countries tend not to raise theirs. Overall *there is less money growth in the world and a lower average inflation rate.*

With the price discipline of fixed exchange rates, there is a greater chance that countries have similar inflation and that the average inflation rate may be somewhat lower than the average that each country would choose on its own. If the system has a leading country, such as the United States in Bretton Woods, then countries tend to have to match the inflation rate of this lead country. For countries that would have had a higher inflation rate, the system is imposing a discipline effect. But other countries might prefer an even lower inflation rate.

This observation leads to the third implication. With fixed exchange rates, a country that prefers to have a lower inflation rate than that of other countries, especially the lead country in the system, will have difficulty maintaining this low inflation rate. It will tend to "import inflation" from the other countries. Germany complained of this pressure in the 1960s as the inflation rate in the United States rose.

In contrast to all of this, *floating exchange rates simply permit countries to have different inflation rates.* According to purchasing power parity, high-inflation countries tend to have depreciating currencies and low-inflation countries tend to have appreciating currencies. The nominal exchange-rate changes maintain reasonable price competitiveness for both types of countries in the long run. Proponents of floating rates generally view this as a virtue. Different countries' policymakers may have different beliefs as to what an acceptable inflation rate is. These beliefs may be the result of historic events, such as the hyperinflation of the 1920s in Germany, which has resulted in a strong German preference for very low inflation. Or they may be the result of a series of decisions about acceptable trade-offs of a little more inflation in order to reduce unemployment. This was the situation of the United States in the 1970s, and it resulted in rather high inflation. Or the government may choose to "finance" its large budget deficit by printing money (rather than by borrowing through the issue of government bonds). The rapid money growth leads to high rates of inflation. This has been the case in some developing countries.

Opponents of floating exchange rates suggest that the ability of each country to choose its own policies toward inflation results in more inflation worldwide. The exchange rate does not impose any discipline on money growth and inflation. Instead, with floating exchange rates a country can be caught in a vicious circle in which (1) high inflation leads to currency depreciation and (2) the depreciation increases the domestic currency prices of imports, so the high inflation rate is reinforced. Continuing high inflation requires further depreciation and so forth. Domestic money growth simply accommodates this dynamic.

The world experience in the first decade after the shift to general floating in 1973 seemed to be consistent with the concerns of these opponents of floating rates. Average world inflation in the 1970s was substantially higher than it had been in the 1950s or 1960s. The seeds for some of this higher inflation had been sown, especially in the United States, beginning in the fixed-rate 1960s. In addition, the two oil shocks of the 1970s presumably would have resulted in higher average inflation even if exchange rates had remained fixed. Nonetheless, some of the higher inflation was probably the result of the removal of the discipline of fixed rates.

The world experience since the early 1980s indicates that the tendency toward higher inflation with floating rates actually may not be a serious problem. The inflation rates in many of the major countries whose currencies have generally been floating—including Japan, the United States, and Britain—fell noticeably and remain low. Since the early 1990s, inflation rates in most developing countries have also been low. The experience since the early 1980s indicates that *what really matters in controlling national inflation rates is the discipline and resolve of the national monetary authorities.*

Real Effects of Exchange-Rate Variability

A major concern about floating exchange rates is that they are highly variable. Some variability presumably is not controversial, including exchange-rate movements that offset inflation rate differentials and exchange-rate movements that promote an orderly adjustment to shocks. However, the substantial variability of exchange rates within fairly short time periods like months or a few years is more controversial. What are the possible effects of exchange-rate variability that might concern us?

If the variability simply creates unexpected gains and losses for short-term financial investors who deliberately take positions exposed to exchange-rate risk, we probably would not be much concerned. However, we would be concerned if heightened exchange-rate risk discourages such international activities as trade in goods and services or foreign direct investment. Exchange-rate variability then would have *real effects*, by altering activities in the part of the economy that produces goods and services.

Consider international trade in goods and services. Does exchange-rate variability create risk that leads to lower volumes of trade? First, simple short-run variability may have little direct impact on trade activities. Anyone engaged in international trade has a range of foreign exchange contracts, including forward foreign exchange, currency futures, and currency options, that can be used to hedge exposures to exchange-rate risk in the short run, for many (but not all) currencies in the world. These contracts usually can be obtained with low transaction costs. Second, exchange-rate variability beyond the short run can affect the real investments that must be made to support export-oriented production. If exchange-rate variability raises the riskiness of these real investments, they tend to be lower if firms are risk-averse. This form of exchange-rate risk is more difficult to hedge because (1) longer maturities of many contracts do not exist or are rather expensive to buy and (2) the specific amounts of payments that might need to be hedged several years in the future are themselves often highly uncertain.

Economists have studied the overall effect of increased exchange-rate risk on the volumes of international trade activities. Early studies typically found almost no effect of exchange-rate variability on trade volumes. More recently, Klein and Shambaugh (2010, Chapter 9) use the gravity model of trade to show that countries with a fixed exchange rate between their currencies trade more with each other and that greater exchange-rate variability has a small negative effect on trade.

Overshooting raises another concern about the real effects of the variability of floating exchange rates. When exchange rates overshoot, they send signals about changes in international price competitiveness that seem, to some observers, to be far too strong. Big swings in price competitiveness create incentives for large shifts in real resources. If overshooting leads to a large appreciation of the country's currency (for instance, the U.S. dollar in the early 1980s), this creates the incentive for production resources to move out of export-oriented and import-competing industries, as the country loses a large amount of price competitiveness. New capital investment in these industries is strongly discouraged and some existing facilities are shut down. However, as the overshooting then reverses itself, these resource movements appear to have been excessive. Resources then must move back into these industries.

Relative price adjustments are an important and necessary part of the market system. They signal the need for resource reallocations. The concern here is not with relative price changes in general. The concern is with the possibility that the dynamics of floating exchange rates sometimes send false price signals or signals that are too strong, resulting in excessive resource reallocations.

This discussion of exchange-rate variability and the real effects of this variability leads into a broader debate. Proponents and defenders of floating exchange rates agree that variability has been high and that some real effects occur. But they believe that this is what markets should do. Exchange rates as prices send signals about the relative values of currencies. These signals represent the summary of information about the currencies that is available at that time. As economic and political conditions change, the prices and signals should change. The variability of exchange rates represents the ongoing market-based quest for economic efficiency.

The proponents of floating rates believe that the supporters of fixed rates delude themselves by claiming that the lack of variability of fixed rates is a virtue. A fixed exchange rate is simply a form of *price control*. Price controls are generally inefficient because the price is often too high or too low. That is, with a fixed rate the country's currency is often overvalued or undervalued by government fiat.

Furthermore, a fixed rate is sometimes changed, often suddenly and by a large amount, when the peg is adjusted through a devaluation or a revaluation. This *sudden change* can be highly disruptive, and it often occurs in a crisis atmosphere brought on by large capital flows as speculators believe that they have a one-way speculative gamble on the direction of the exchange-rate change. In addition, with the comfort of a fixed exchange rate, financial institutions and others in the country that borrow foreign currencies can ignore or underestimate their exposure to exchange-rate risk. They do not hedge their currency risk exposure. When a devaluation occurs, their losses can contribute to a deep financial crisis for the country.

Detractors and opponents of floating exchange rates believe that floating exchange rates are *excessively variable* and that this variability has real effects that are inefficient. Some of these detractors view the variability of floating rates as excessive because the exchange rates themselves are sometimes inefficient, as they are affected by speculative bandwagons and bubbles that do not reflect the underlying economic fundamentals. Other detractors, while conceding that floating exchange rates are reasonably efficient prices from the point of view of their function within the international *financial* system, believe that floating exchange rates do not serve the *broader economy* well. Variability and over-shooting may have a logic in international finance, but they nonetheless cause undesirable real effects like discouragement of international trade and excessive resource shifts.

To these opponents, with floating exchange rates the market often undervalues or overvalues a country's currency, at least in relation to the signals that should be sent to the goods-and-services part of the economy. Exchange rates should make transactions between countries as smooth and easy as possible. To the opponents of floating rates, exchange rates, like money, serve their transactions functions best when their values are *stable*.

NATIONAL CHOICES

We have just examined five major issues that can affect a country's choice of its exchange-rate policy. Each country must make its own decision, and that decision depends on the balancing of a number of factors, including the economic issues explored here as well as political concerns. While each country will have its own important issues because of its own economic and political situation, we can none-theless discern in our set of five issues several factors that are likely to be of major importance for most countries.

There are several strong arguments in favor of a country adopting a floating exchange rate. First, a floating exchange rate provides more effective use of two important tools for adjusting toward internal and external balances. Exchange-rate changes can promote adjustment to external balance, and monetary policy can be directed toward achieving internal balance because it does not need to be directed toward defending the exchange rate. Second, a floating exchange rate permits a country to pursue goals, priorities, and policies that meet its own domestic preferences and needs, with less concern about how these will put pressure on the exchange rate. Third, the country does not need to defend a fixed rate against speculative attacks, a task that is increasingly difficult as large amounts of internationally mobile capital can be shifted quickly from country to country.

The strongest argument against a country adopting a floating exchange rate is that floating rates have been disturbingly variable since 1973. This variability increases exchange-rate risk, and this risk does seem to have some effect in discouraging international activities such as trade in goods and services. In addition, overshooting of floating exchange rates may have promoted too much adjustment into or out of trade-oriented production from time to time. A major advantage of fixed rates is the substantial reduction in variability and exchange-rate risk if the fixed rate can be defended and the peg is not adjusted too often.

In Chapter 20 we presented countries' current choices of exchange-rate policy. We saw that a growing number of countries use some form of floating-rate policy. The world has been shifting toward floating exchange rates. The advantages of independence in crafting and using policies to attain domestic objectives make the choice of a floating exchange rate increasingly attractive. Put the other way, an increasing number of governments are unwilling to subordinate money supply, interest rates, and other policies to defending a fixed exchange rate.

The governments of these countries generally do not adopt the polar case of a clean float. Rather, they use some form of management of the float. While they like the advantages of adopting a floating exchange rate, they are also worried about the variability of floating rates. Through management of the float, the government attempts to moderate wide swings without becoming chained to an officially announced fixed rate that would give speculators a clear one-way bet at times.

There are still questions about the management of the float. A government can make mistakes, or act out of political motives, so that the government is attempting to resist exchange-rate trends that are justified by the economic fundamentals. There are also questions about how effective the management can be, at least for the exchange-rate values of the major currencies. Intervention often seems to have little impact on the floating rate, and even with management the floating rates are often substantially variable. Still, overall, *for many countries, a managed floating exchange rate seems to be a reasonable compromise choice*. It gains much of the policy independence while offering governments some ability to reduce exchange-rate variability.

While the global trend is toward floating, a number of countries continue to maintain fixed exchange rates. For most of these countries, the compelling argument is that floating exchange rates are too variable. A number of these countries are smaller countries that fix to the currency of a major trading partner (or to a basket of currencies of major trading partners). For these countries reducing exchange-rate risk to promote smooth trade and avoiding overshooting that would disrupt their trade-oriented industries seem to be the major objectives in choosing an exchange-rate policy. These countries are willing to sacrifice some economic policy autonomy to obtain exchange-rate stability.

However, a fixed exchange rate that is adjustable—a *soft peg* that provides substantial leeway for the country's monetary authority to change or abandon the fixed value—sometimes invites attack through a one-way speculative gamble if the country is reasonably open to international capital flows. Such a speculative attack can all but force the monetary authority to surrender, as in Mexico in late 1994; Thailand, Indonesia, and South Korea in 1997; Brazil in early 1999; and Turkey in 2001. In response, some countries have adopted or are considering arrangements that create more permanent fixes (often called *hard pegs*).

EXTREME FIXES

The general trend in national exchange-rate policies is toward greater flexibility. But some countries have moved in the opposite direction—to exchange rates that are not only fixed but also rather difficult or nearly impossible to change. In this section we examine currency boards and "dollarization," two "extreme" forms of fixed rates that can be adopted by a single country. In the final section of the chapter we examine what may be the ultimate form of fixed rates—a monetary union among several countries that agree to a single, unionwide currency.

Currency Board

A currency board attempts to establish a fixed exchange rate that is long-lived by mandating that the board, acting as the country's monetary authority, should focus almost exclusively on maintaining the fixed rate. A currency board holds only foreign-currency assets (official reserve assets). The board issues domestic-currency liabilities only in exchange for foreign-currency assets that it acquires. Because the board owns no domestic-currency assets, it has no ability to sterilize. This arrangement increases the credibility of a country's commitment to maintaining the fixed exchange rate by automatically linking the domestic money supply to the defense of the fixed rate. For instance, if increased private selling is putting downward pressure on the exchange-rate value of the country's currency, the currency board defends the fixed rate by buying domestic currency and selling foreign currency. As the board buys domestic currency, the domestic money supply decreases. This money supply decrease sets in motion the adjustments discussed at length in Chapter 23, and the currency board has no power to resist. With no domestic assets, the currency board cannot sterilize the intervention—the domestic money supply must decrease.

Several very small countries have had currency boards since before 1970, and Hong Kong established one in 1983 to defend the value of its dollar. During the 1990s, four transition countries—Estonia, Lithuania, Bulgaria, and Bosnia/Herzegovina—established currency boards. Argentina set up a currency board in 1991, but it abandoned the board amid the turmoil of its 2002 financial crisis.

The experience of Argentina shows the advantages and disadvantages of a currency board. Argentina's government established a currency board to signal its commitment to stop the country's hyperinflation, by imposing strict discipline to limit the growth of Argentina's money supply. As we saw earlier in the chapter, this effort was successful in its early years. With inflation quickly reduced, interest rates decreased and economic growth increased. After almost no growth of its real GDP during the 1980s, Argentina's annual real growth averaged nearly 4 percent during 1992–1998.

However, the Argentinean economy was vulnerable to adverse external shocks. The fallout from the Mexican peso crisis caused a recession during 1995. In this period of foreign financial turmoil, international investors pulled back from investments in Argentina, its money supply shrank, and its interest rates increased. In addition, concerns about whether Argentina would maintain its fixed rate led to speculative outflows that further decreased Argentina's money supply. In the mid-1990s Argentina did stick with its currency board and the fixed dollar–peso exchange rate, but probably at the cost of a deeper recession.

Argentina experienced the same pressures in the late 1990s because of the series of crises in Asia, Russia, and Brazil. As we saw in Chapter 21, this time the outcome was bad. A recession began in 1998 and persisted. Other shortcomings of its government policies, including a lack of fiscal discipline, overregulation, and corruption, interacted with the recession. After rather desperate attempts to shore up the currency board arrangement by preventing people from using their bank accounts, the government gave up and shifted to a floating exchange rate. Argentina by then was in the middle of a severe financial and economic crisis.

The currency board arrangement worked well in Argentina for a number of years, and it has worked well for the other countries that have currency boards. But a currency board does not force a country to follow sensible fiscal and regulatory policies, and it leaves the country more exposed to adverse foreign shocks. In addition, Argentina's experience shows another potential drawback of a currency board, the difficulty of finding an *exit strategy* that does not add disruption to the country's economy.

"Dollarization"

So much of barbarism, however, still remains in the transactions of most civilized nations, that almost all independent countries choose to assert their nationality by having, to their own inconvenience and that of their neighbors, a peculiar currency of their own.

John Stuart Mill, 1870

A currency board establishes a strongly fixed exchange rate, but it is still at risk of a speculative attack. It is a hard peg, but perhaps still not hard enough because the country's government could decide to shift to some other exchange-rate policy for its currency.

A more extreme form of fixed exchange rate is for the country's government to abolish its own currency and use the currency of some other country. Because the other currency is often the U.S. dollar, this arrangement is called dollarization. This is a harder peg, but even this is not permanent. The government still cannot credibly commit never to change the exchange rate. That is, the government can still "de-dollarize" and reintroduce local currency, as Liberia did in the early 1980s. Panama, Micronesia, the Marshall Islands, Timor-Leste, and Palau use the U.S. dollar as their official local currency, and several other very small countries use the currency of a large neighboring country as their own currency. In September 2000 Ecuador dollarized in an effort to turn around its struggling economy. At the beginning of 2001 El Salvador dollarized in a smooth transition from the fixed rate between the colón and the dollar that it had maintained for many years. In 2009 Zimbabwe dollarized to escape from hyperinflation.

In comparison with a well-maintained fixed exchange rate with the dollar, what are the advantages and disadvantages of full dollarization? The major advantage for a country like El Salvador is *removing the exchange-rate risk* that its government might devalue or depreciate the local currency in the future. This eliminates the risk of a speculative attack on the currency.[3] It also eliminates the risk premium (to compensate lenders for this exchange-rate risk) that is built into local-currency

---

[3]An international crisis is still possible, as the experience of Panama shows. Foreign investors can run for the exits if they fear either default on government debt that is rising quickly because of large fiscal deficits or losses because of weaknesses in the local financial system.

interest rates. For El Salvador, interest rates fell by about 5 percentage points as the country dollarized. Another advantage is the *elimination of the transaction costs of currency exchanges* between the local currency and the dollar. The major disadvantage of full dollarization is the *loss of interest income on the country's holdings of international reserve assets* that are used in the process of full dollarization. The government must replace all local currency with dollars. To do this the government uses its official holdings of U.S. government bonds to obtain dollars. In El Salvador's case, the loss of interest income is equal to about 0.6 percent of its GDP. That is, with dollarization the *seigniorage profit* from issuing currency in El Salvador goes to the U.S. government (the issuer of dollar bills) rather than to El Salvador's government (the issuer of colones).[4]

With full dollarization, El Salvador completely cedes its monetary policy to the United States. The U.S. Fed will make its monetary policy decisions based on economic conditions in the United States, with almost no concern for economic conditions in El Salvador. This sounds like a major drawback, but El Salvador was already fully committed to defending the fixed exchange rate, so it had already almost completely given up its own monetary policy, anyway.

The dollarization of Ecuador is a more aggressive use of this policy because Ecuador shifted from a flexible exchange-rate value for the sucre. In the two years prior to dollarization, Ecuador had defaulted on its foreign debt and its currency had lost 73 percent of its dollar value. Dollarization was shock treatment for an economy that had serious problems. This treatment was fairly successful. Inflation fell from 96 percent in 2000 to 13 percent in 2004. Real GDP grew by an annual average of 4.5 percent during 2001–2004. Still, international trade was one problem in the transition. With an inflation rate higher than that of the United States during the first several years after dollarization, Ecuador lost international price competitiveness. Its non-oil exports were hurt, and its imports increased.

THE INTERNATIONAL FIX—MONETARY UNION

Since the breakup of the Bretton Woods fixed-rate system, the countries of the European Union have attempted to establish and maintain fixed exchange rates among their currencies. In 1979, they established the European Monetary System, and a subset of the countries established fixed exchange rates among their currencies through the Exchange Rate Mechanism (ERM). The Maastricht Treaty, approved in 1993, committed the countries to a monetary union and a single currency, the euro. In a monetary union, exchange rates are permanently fixed and a single monetary authority conducts a single, unionwide monetary policy.[5] Eleven EU countries established the monetary union in

---

[4]El Salvador's government could attempt to negotiate an agreement with the U.S. government to gain a share of the forgone interest, but the U.S. government has not appeared to be receptive to encouraging dollarization by sharing seigniorage profits with other countries.

[5]Other monetary unions are the CFA franc zone and the East Caribbean Currency Union among eight Caribbean island countries. The CFA franc zone has two groups, the eight members of the West African Economic and Monetary Union and the six members of the Central African Economic and Monetary Community.

1999, with seven more countries joining during 2001–2014. This final section of the chapter examines the economics of monetary union as the ultimate fixed exchange-rate arrangement, by looking at the experience of the EU during the past several decades.

Exchange Rate Mechanism

In 1979, Germany, France, Italy, the Netherlands, Belgium, Denmark, Ireland, and Luxembourg began to fix the exchange rates among their currencies as participants in the Exchange Rate Mechanism. Spain joined the ERM in 1989, Britain in 1990, Portugal in 1992, Austria in 1994, Finland in 1996, and Greece in 1998.

The ERM was an adjustable-peg system. There were 11 realignments during the first nine years, 1979–1987, with a tendency for the Belgian, Danish, French, and Italian currencies to devalue. Then from 1987 through 1992, there were no realignments. In fact, the discipline effect on national inflation rates seemed to work quite well. Germany was generally regarded as the lead country in the system due to its economic size and the prestige of its central bank. Germany maintained a low inflation rate, and the other ERM countries were disciplined by the fixed exchange rates to lower their inflation rates toward the German level.

By mid-1992, the ERM seemed to be working very well. As part of "Europe 1992," the general effort to dismantle barriers to permit free movements of goods, services, and capital within the EU, most countries had removed capital controls by 1990. The EU countries had completed the drafting of the Maastricht Treaty, which contained the plans for monetary union, and they were in the process of approving it.

The ERM exchange rates came under serious pressure beginning in September 1992. Several things contributed to the severity of the pressure. International investors became worried that the exchange-rate values of several currencies in the ERM were not appropriate. For instance, the Italian lira appeared to be overvalued, given that the Italian inflation rate had remained above that of the other ERM members. In addition, international investors became worried by policy tensions among the ERM members. German policymakers were placing full emphasis on reducing and controlling German inflation, while policymakers in several other countries, including France and Britain, probably preferred to shift the emphasis to reducing unemployment. Furthermore, in a general vote in 1992, Denmark rejected the Maastricht Treaty, and the upcoming French vote was expected to be close. These votes raised doubts about eventual monetary union, and they raised doubts about the countries' current commitments to fixed exchange rates. Finally, the removal of capital controls meant that international investors and speculators could move large amounts of financial capital quickly from one country and currency to another. Official defense of the fixed rates was difficult in the face of these large speculative flows.

As international investors and speculators shifted to expecting devaluations against the DM by a number of ERM countries, large amounts of capital flowed and the central banks mounted massive defenses. Italy and Britain surrendered and left the system. As speculative attacks continued in late 2002 and early 2003, the Spanish, Portuguese, and Irish currencies were devalued. Another large speculative attack occurred in July 1993. The ERM widened the allowable band for exchange-rate movements around the central fixed rates, but there was no realignment. With the exception of devaluations of the Spanish and Portuguese currencies in 1995, exchange rates among the ERM currencies were calm after 1993. Italy rejoined in 1996.

The ERM illustrates many of the points made in the first half of the chapter about the strengths and weaknesses of fixed exchange rates. The ERM exchange rates were generally steadier than floating rates were during this period, although occasional realignments disturbed the stability. The fixed rates applied pressure on other ERM countries to reduce their inflation rates toward the German level. Differences in goals between Germany and several other ERM countries in the early 1990s led to strains in the system, and these other countries could not use monetary policy to address their internal imbalances. The removal of capital controls made the defense of the fixed rates through official intervention more difficult in 1992 and 1993. In fact, several countries temporarily reimposed or tightened their capital controls as part of their defense efforts. These controls helped in the defense of the fixed exchange rates, but they ran counter to the broad efforts to create a single EU market.

European Monetary Union

In 1991, the EU countries completed the draft of the Maastricht Treaty (named for the Dutch town where it was negotiated) to set a process for establishing a monetary union and a single, unionwide currency. After several close national votes, including a defeat in Denmark that was later reversed, all EU countries approved the treaty, and it became effective in November 1993.

The Maastricht Treaty specified the procedure for the establishment of the European Monetary Union. To participate in the monetary union, a country had to meet five criteria:

- The country's inflation rate must be no higher than 1.5 percentage points above the average inflation rate of the three EU countries with the lowest inflation rates.
- Its exchange rates must be maintained within the ERM bands with no realignments during the preceding two years.
- Its long-term interest rate on government bonds must be no higher than 2 percentage points above the average of the comparable interest rates in the three lowest-inflation countries.
- The country's government budget deficit must be no larger than 3 percent of the value of its GDP.
- The gross government debt must be no larger than 60 percent of its GDP (or the country must show satisfactory progress to achieving these two fiscal requirements in the near future).

The criteria were intended to measure whether the country's performance had converged toward that of the best-performing EU countries so that the country was ready to enter the monetary union.

In May 1998, a summit of EU leaders decided which countries met the five criteria and would be members of the new euro area. With some liberal use of the "satisfactory progress" exception for the government debt criterion, 11 countries were deemed to meet the criteria and chose to join the monetary union. Britain, Denmark, and Sweden could have qualified but chose not to join the union. Greece did not then qualify but was able to join two years later. The 12 countries that joined the EU in 2004 and 2007 are eligible to join the monetary union and adopt the euro if they meet the five criteria. Slovenia joined in 2007, Cyprus and Malta in 2008, Slovakia in 2009, Estonia in 2011, and Latvia in 2014.

The European Central Bank (ECB) was established in 1998 as the center of the European System of Central Banks, a federal structure that also includes the national central banks as operating arms. On January 1, 1999, the monetary union began and the ECB assumed responsibility for monetary policy in the euro area.

Modeled after the Bundesbank (the German central bank), the ECB is designed to be independent from direct political influence and is mandated to conduct unionwide monetary policy to achieve price stability. It has defined price stability as a consumer price inflation rate of less than but close to 2 percent per year. Its decisions about changes in monetary policy are made by its governing council, composed of the heads of the member national central banks and the six members of the executive committee. While the council is not overtly political, there is room for national economic interests to sway unionwide policy decisions.

As the ECB began its operations, there were concerns about how effectively it would function. As shown in Figure 25.2, the exchange-rate value of the euro declined from its introduction in 1999 to late 2000. Among the factors that probably contributed to the euro's weakness were confusing and poorly worded statements by ECB officials. The early operating issues were then largely resolved.

What can the EU countries achieve with monetary union and what did they give up or risk? The European Monetary Union provides examples of many of the issues that we discussed in the first half of the chapter.[6]

The gains from monetary union are based on the elimination of all exchange-rate concerns. The shift to a common currency is a permanent fix and more. It ends exchange-rate variability and risk. It ends one-way speculation about changes in pegged exchange rates. It eliminates all foreign exchange transaction costs. Monetary union is

FIGURE 25.2
Nominal Exchange-Rate Value of the Euro, 1999–2014

Source: International Monetary Fund, *International Financial Statistics.*

[6]This discussion is also largely an application of the analysis of an *optimum currency area*—the size of the geographic area that shows the best economic performance with fixed exchange rates (or one currency) within the area and floating exchange rates with currencies outside the area.

part of the broad drive to European integration and single European markets. Estimates of the increase in international trade of products within the euro area range from 10 to 15 percent. In addition, the elimination of transaction costs and exchange-rate risks has led to greater integration of European financial markets, especially markets for government and corporate bonds, with the potential for greater gains from intertemporal trade (international lending and borrowing).

The risks and possible losses from the European Monetary Union are the result of economic shocks that affect different member countries in different ways. Economic conditions sometimes vary across the countries. Especially, weak demand causes recessions or slow growth in some countries. For example, Germany's domestic product grew by less than 1 percent per year during 2000–2005. Demand in other countries grows too quickly, causing inflation pressures. For example, Ireland's domestic product grew by over 6 percent per year during the early 2000s, and it experienced rapidly rising wages and a housing price bubble. With monetary union, each country has given up both the ability to run an independent monetary policy that could respond to domestic imbalances and the ability to use exchange-rate changes as an adjustment tool.

In the absence of national monetary policy and national exchange rates, there are three mechanisms that can reduce national imbalances within the monetary union— cross-national resource movements, national price-level adjustments, and fiscal policies. We have seen a major test of these mechanisms during the euro crisis that began in 2010 and its aftermath. Chapter 1 and the box "National Crises, Contagion, and Resolution" in Chapter 21 provide overviews of the euro crisis.

One way to adjust national imbalances is for workers to move from areas of weak demand to areas of strong demand. If labor mobility is high, adjustments to internal imbalances can be speeded by people moving from places where unemployment is high to places where demand for labor is strong. Regional migration is an important way that different regions in the United States adjust to local shocks. Most studies conclude that labor mobility across EU countries (and even within these countries) is relatively low and is likely to remain low. Less than 3 percent of EU citizens live in an EU country other than the one in which they were born. Even mobility between regions within countries is small. Adjustment also could occur with capital moving to seek out and employ underutilized resources like unemployed labor. But, given rigidities in labor markets and labor practices, capital may not move in this way—in fact, capital may instead flee from problem areas to those that are booming.

A second way to adjust is through changes in cross-national price competitiveness (changes in national real exchange rates). Countries with high unemployment can boost aggregate demand by using improved price competitiveness to increase national exports and to decrease national imports. However, for the euro crisis, we saw the limits to this kind of adjustment. As shown in the box "International Indicators Lead the Crisis" in Chapter 16, by 2008 Greece, Portugal, and Spain had developed large current account deficits. Here we see a drawback of monetary union, the inability to devalue in the face of fundamental disequilibrium. Instead of being able to adjust the country's nominal exchange rate to build international price competitiveness, Greece, Portugal, and Spain each had to pursue an "internal devaluation." Each tried to reduce wages and other costs relative to other EU countries, such as Germany, a process that proved to be difficult and painful.

With cross-national resource movements unlikely to be helpful, and with "internal devaluation" to build international price competitiveness being slow, the remaining adjustment mechanism is fiscal policy, at the union level or at the national level. For the euro area (and for the broader European Union), there is almost no unionwide fiscal policy. The EU fiscal budget in total is only about 1 percent of EU GDP. There are almost no "automatic stabilizers" across countries. That is, higher tax revenues from the growing countries are not "automatically" shifted to the recession countries through lower taxes and larger expenditures in the recession countries. And there is no active unionwide fiscal policy to help the recession countries.

That leaves each country's national fiscal policy as a government tool to improve the country's domestic performance, but in a monetary union national fiscal policy is a two-edged sword. National fiscal policy can be used to move the country toward internal balance, and it will be powerful if capital flows are very elastic, as they are likely to be in a well-functioning monetary union. However, national fiscal policy can also become a source of instability, a source of negative shocks for the country and possibly for the monetary union. A country's government will feel less pressure to keep its fiscal deficit under control if it believes that the union's central bank or the governments of other countries in the union will come to its rescue if the deficit becomes unmanageable.

As part of the process of moving toward monetary union, the German government insisted on the *Stability and Growth Pact*, which mandates that national government budget deficits should be no more than 3 percent of GDP, with temporary exceptions for unusual external shocks or severe national recessions. Countries that violate the rule were to be subject to monetary sanctions. Such a rule can reduce the risk that excessive fiscal deficits become a source of instability. The rule also limits the use of national fiscal policy to address internal balance, and it can at times turn national fiscal policy into a destabilizer. For instance, if the government budget deficit begins close to 3 percent and a mild national recession hits, the government may be compelled to raise taxes or cut government expenditures to prevent the deficit from rising above 3 percent. These fiscal changes would make the recession worse.

With slow growth in several euro-area countries, including Germany and France, in the early 2000s, the fiscal situations in these countries deteriorated. The budget deficits of Germany and France moved above 3 percent of their GDP and stayed there for several years. It made no sense for them to aggressively raise taxes or cut spending, which would have made their economies even weaker. The EU decided not to impose fines (although strictly the pact called for fines), and it became clear that the pact was largely unenforceable. In early 2005 the EU countries revised the pact to recognize a much broader set of exceptions.

The dual roles of national fiscal policy were at the center of the euro crisis, beginning with Greece in 2010. After joining the euro area in 2001, Greece looked fairly successful, with annual real GDP growth that averaged about 4 percent to 2007, but its growth was based too much on fiscal deficit spending and foreign borrowing. Although the data were misreported for years by the Greek government, we now know that Greece had never met the 3 percent deficit limit. With the recession caused by the global financial and economic crisis, Greece's fiscal deficit and debt rose to high levels. By April 2010 the Greek government effectively lost access to regular borrowing—the interest rate at which the Greek government could issue new government bonds rose to prohibitively high levels. Either the Greek government had to instantly slash government spending and enact a massive tax increase or it needed an official rescue. In May 2010 the Greek government received a large official rescue loan program to provide funds to cover the ongoing Greek government deficit.

The crisis spread to other countries. Several other countries had precarious fiscal deficits. Ireland's government took on huge debts when it rescued the country's banks. Ireland received a large bailout program in November 2010. In May 2011 Portugal had to be rescued with another large bailout program. By mid-2011, investors were also increasingly concerned about the government deficits and debts of Spain and Italy, and interest rates on their bonds jumped. In March 2012, with Greek government debt equal to more than 150 percent of its GDP, Greece required a second bailout program, and Greece's government defaulted on most of its privately held debt.

Greece, Portugal, and Ireland went into severe national recessions. In addition to structural reforms (liberalizing regulation of labor markets and product markets) that may eventually improve national economic performance, the terms of the bailout programs included reductions in government expenditures and increases in taxes to reduce the fiscal deficit. Such austerity forced national fiscal policies to make the recessions worse.

The bailouts were actually a form of unionwide fiscal policy compelled by the national crises. Although some of the funding for the rescue loans came from the International Monetary Fund, most of the funding came from other euro-area countries. In 2010, the countries created the temporary European Financial Stability Facility, and in 2012 they replaced it with the European Stability Mechanism, with a permanent lending capacity of €500 billion. (This may sound like a lot, but it probably would not have been large enough to rescue a country like Spain or Italy.)

Again led by Germany, the euro area has also attempted to establish a fiscal compact that tightens up the limits on national fiscal deficits and debt. New rules and a new treaty require, with some exceptions, that each country achieve a near-zero structural fiscal balance in the medium term and have in place a program steadily to reduce a structural fiscal deficit that is initially too large.[7] If a country is not in compliance, the European Commission, the EU's executive body, can recommend financial sanctions, which are imposed automatically unless the European Council, an EU body of national ministers, specifically rejects the recommendation. In addition, each country must incorporate the structural balance rules into its core national laws.

The member countries of the euro area have a strong political commitment to EMU and the single currency. The euro crisis calmed in 2012, and the euro survived. Still the tension remains between national fiscal policy as a tool for stabilizing the macroeconomy of a euro-area country and national fiscal policy as a source of instability for the country and for the monetary union.

More broadly, the problems in the euro area make it even less likely that countries in another part of the world will establish their own monetary union. As we have noted in this chapter, the major trend in the world outside of the European Union is toward floating exchange rates with their promise of some degree of national independence in economic policies.

---

[7]The structural fiscal deficit (also called the cyclically adjusted fiscal deficit) is the estimated size of the fiscal deficit if the country's economy were operating at its potential (what we called "full employment" real GDP in Chapter 23). It ignores the part of the fiscal deficit that is driven by automatic stabilizers. For example, total tax revenues collected automatically decline as GDP and income decline in a recession, and expenditures on assistance to unemployed workers automatically increase.

Summary

A major decision for a country's government is its choice of exchange-rate policy. This chapter has examined the extent of rate flexibility that a country's policy allows. We discussed what five major issues say about the advantages and disadvantages of choosing a floating rate or a fixed rate. You may want to review Figure 25.1 for a summary of this discussion.

For each issue there are usually ways in which the issue favors a floating rate and other ways in which the issue favors a fixed rate. Because countries differ in their economic situations, policymaking institutions, economic histories, and political interests, different countries can view the balance of advantages and disadvantages differently, leading to different policy choices. Indeed, as economic and political conditions change over time, the policy chosen by a country can change.

In a country's choice between a more flexible rate and a more fixed-rate policy, several points are typically prominent. Strong arguments in favor of a floating exchange rate include the country's ability to use independent monetary policy and exchange-rate changes to adjust internal and external imbalances; the country's ability, more generally, to pursue goals and policies that meet its own domestic needs; and the difficulty of defending fixed rates against speculative attacks, given the large and growing amounts of financial capital that can move quickly between countries. The strongest argument in favor of a fixed exchange rate is that floating rates have been too variable, and this excessive variability disrupts and discourages international trade and other international transactions.

In recent decades, countries have shifted toward choosing more flexible exchange rates. Countries generally attempt to manage the float in order to moderate the variability of the floating rate, although the effectiveness of this management, at least for the major currencies, is questionable.

Still, a number of countries continue to have fixed exchange rates. However, soft pegs (fixed rates that are easily adjustable) can be difficult to sustain because they seem at times to encourage speculative attacks. Some countries use forms of hard pegs (fixed rates that are more nearly permanent). A currency board is a monetary authority that holds only international reserve assets, so sterilization is not possible. With a currency board, the country's money supply is automatically linked to the intervention to defend the fixed exchange rate. Dollarization involves completely replacing the local currency with a foreign currency (for instance, the U.S. dollar). Monetary conditions in the country are almost completely controlled by the foreign central bank (for instance, the U.S. Federal Reserve).

The most ambitious fixed-rate effort is occurring in the European Union, where 18 EU countries are members of the European Monetary Union, established in 1999 and based on the Maastricht Treaty of 1993. In a monetary union, exchange rates are permanently fixed and a single monetary authority conducts a unionwide monetary policy. For the European Monetary Union, the countries use a single currency, the euro, and the European Central Bank (ECB) conducts unionwide monetary policy.

The European Monetary Union is the successor to the fixed exchange rates of the Exchange Rate Mechanism (ERM) of the European Monetary System, established in 1979. Under the ERM, the fixed exchange rates were generally less variable than comparable floating exchange rates, although the fixed ERM rates were occasionally adjusted in realignments. Inflation rates in other ERM countries declined toward the low German inflation rate. However, following the removal of capital controls by some ERM countries, differences in macroeconomic goals between Germany and some other ERM countries led to speculative attacks in 1992 and 1993. After 1993, the ERM exchange rates were generally steady.

The European Monetary Union can be used to indicate the major advantages and disadvantages of a monetary union. The gains flow largely from reduced transactions costs and reduced exchange-rate risk. For the European Monetary Union, with its shift to a single currency, these gains are substantial.

The major source of disadvantages is that economic shocks can affect member countries differently, with some countries in recession and others growing quickly. When this occurs, the countries will need ways to adjust their internal imbalances, but each country no longer has national monetary policy or national exchange-rate policy. Fiscal policy at the union level could be useful, by providing automatic stabilizers as well as active fiscal policy changes. If unionwide fiscal policy is not sufficient, each nation may need to use national fiscal policy actively. In addition, labor mobility can assist in adjusting imbalances, as people move from areas of high unemployment to areas of low unemployment. The European Monetary Union faces its major challenges in this broad area of shocks, national imbalances, and policy and adjustment responses. The member countries are different and experience different internal imbalances, there is almost no fiscal policy at the union level, national fiscal policies are limited, and labor mobility is low. The euro crisis that began with Greece in 2010 shows some of the challenges that face the euro-area countries as a monetary union.

Key Terms	Price discipline	Exchange Rate	European Monetary Union
	Currency board	Mechanism (ERM)	European Central Bank
	Dollarization	Monetary union	(ECB)

Suggested Reading

The classic article favoring floating exchange rates is Friedman (1953). Fischer (2001) explores the unsustainability of soft pegs. Shambaugh (2004) provides a technical analysis of the relevance of the inconsistent trinity to recent national experiences with fixed and floating exchange rates. Klein and Shambaugh (2010) and Ghosh et al. (2010) analyze the differences between countries that have fixed exchange rates and those that have floating exchange rates. Goldstein (2002) surveys other options and presents the case in favor of managed floating.

Wolf et al. (2008) look at currency boards. Mundell (1961), McKinnon (1963), and Tower and Willett (1976) examine fixed rates within optimum currency areas. De Grauwe (2009), Lane (2006), and Wyplosz (2006) provide an overview and analysis of the European Monetary Union. De Haan et al. (2005) examine the ECB's monetary policy. Jagelka (2013) uses the gravity model (described in Chapter 6) to estimate the trade effects of euro adoption by Slovenia, Slovakia, Malta, and Cyprus. Pisani-Ferry (2014) provides an overview of the euro crisis.

1. "Countries whose currencies are linked to each other through fixed exchange rates usually should pursue very different monetary and fiscal policies." Do you agree or disagree? Why?

2. "If most countries adhered to a system of fixed exchange rates, global inflation would be lower." Do you agree or disagree? Why?

3. A country is worried that business cycles in other countries tend to disrupt its own economy. It would like some "insulation" from foreign business cycles. Why would this country favor having a floating exchange rate?

4. "If a country's government decides to have a flexible exchange rate, then it should have a clean float." Do you agree or disagree? Why?

5. A country now has a floating exchange rate. Its government would like to fix the exchange-rate value of its currency to another currency. You have been hired as an advisor to the country's government. Suggest three major criteria for deciding what other country's currency to fix to. Why is each important?

6. The variability of floating exchange rates since 1973 has been higher than most economists expected.
   a. Why are some economists not concerned about this?
   b. Why are other economists quite worried about this?

7. A new government has been elected in a country that now has a high inflation rate and a floating exchange rate. The new government is committed to reducing the country's inflation rate.
   a. If the government continues to use a floating exchange rate, what will the government need to do to reduce the high inflation rate?
   b. As part of its effort to reduce the country's inflation rate, why might the country's government consider a change to using a currency board and a fixed exchange rate with one of the major currencies of the world?

8. What is a currency board? Is having a fixed exchange rate with a currency board that defends the fixed rate better for a country than having a fixed exchange rate and a standard central bank that defends the fixed rate?

9. What is dollarization? Is dollarization better for a country than having a fixed exchange rate and a standard central bank that defends the fixed rate?

10. According to the Maastricht Treaty, what are the five convergence criteria for an EU country to be allowed to join the European Monetary Union? What logic do you see for having each as a requirement? Which of the five criteria seem to be more or less important as a basis for excluding a country from the monetary union?

11. The time is 2015. After the end of the worst of the euro crisis in 2012, the European Monetary Union and the euro have worked reasonably well. Britain has remained outside. You are attempting to convince a British friend that Britain should join the monetary union as soon as possible. What are your two strongest arguments?

12. Consider the same scenario in the previous question. Your British friend is trying to convince you that Britain should stay out of the monetary union. What are her two strongest arguments?

Appendix **A**

The Web and the Library: International Numbers and Other Information

The Internet and the World Wide Web have fundamentally changed how we do international research. If you want to explore international trade competition, a recent financial crisis, a trade dispute between the United States and the European Union, the policy of the Korean government toward exchange rates, or almost any other topic in international economics, useful information is available. You can find a lot of it by putting the topic name into a good search engine. You usually will get links to several useful Web sites. (You will probably also get links to a number of less useful sites, and sometimes even links to sites whose information is not reliable. One aspect of good Web research is identifying the best sites and validating the information you obtain.) Of course, some sources of information are available only in hard copy, so access to a good library is also important for many research projects.

This appendix presents some of the best sources of international data and information. Figure A.1 shows a number of useful Web sites, ranging from those maintained by official international organizations to those maintained by individual experts.

The rest of the appendix presents information sources that can be found in hard copies in libraries. Many of the sources that are shown below are now available on the Web—check the Web site of the issuing organization or use a good search engine. To assist you if you are trying to locate these in hard copy, the first parts of their typical Library of Congress call numbers are in parentheses.

For many research projects, you want to take a close look at the international economic dealings of a single country. One useful source is usually that country's statistical yearbook. Here are some examples:

- U.S. Bureau of the Census, *Statistical Abstract of the United States* (HA37.U4).
- Statistics Canada, *Canada Year Book* (HA744.581).
- Great Britain, Central Statistical Office, *Annual Abstract of Statistics* (HA1122.A33).
- Japan, Statistical Bureau, *Japan Statistical Yearbook* (HA1832.J36).
- Australian Bureau of Statistics, *Year Book Australia* (HA3001.B5).

FIGURE A.1
Useful Web
Sites

Creator/Description	Address
Official International Organizations	
World Trade Organization	www.wto.org
International Monetary Fund	www.imf.org
World Bank	www.worldbank.org
Organization for Economic Cooperation and Development	www.oecd.org
Bank for International Settlements: Information on foreign exchange markets, international banking, and national central banks, including links to many central bank sites	www.bis.org
United Nations: National statistics	http://unstats.un.org/unsd
United Nations Conference on Trade and Development: National statistics, including extensive data on foreign direct investment	www.unctad.org (click on Statistics)
International Trade	
International Trade Centre: Data on trade by product and country	www.intracen.org/itc/market-info-tools/trade-statistics
U.S. Trade Representative: Information on foreign barriers to U.S. exports and other trade policy issues	www.ustr.gov
International Trade Administration, U.S. Department of Commerce: Information on U.S. dumping and subsidy cases	http://trade.gov/enforcement
U.S. International Trade Commission: Information on dumping and subsidy cases and on other trade policy issues	www.usitc.gov
U.S. Export.gov: Information on foreign markets for U.S. exports	http://export.gov
Canadian International Trade Tribunal: Information on dumping and subsidy actions by the Canadian government	www.citt.gc.ca/
Canadian Trade Commissioner Service: Information on foreign markets for Canadian exports	www.tradecommissioner.gc.ca
European Commission, Trade: Information on EU trade policy and foreign barriers to EU exports	http://ec.europa.eu/trade
Global Trade Watch: Alternative views on trade policy and globalization issues, presented by Ralph Nader's group Public Citizen	www.citizen.org/trade

FIGURE A.1
continued

Creator/Description	Address
Exchange Rates and International Finance	
OANDA, the Internet arm of Olsen & Associates, LLC: Exchange-rate data and news	www.oanda.com
Pacific Exchange Rate Service (University of British Columbia): Exchange-rate data and information	http://fx.sauder.ubc.ca
Ministry of Finance, Japan: Information on foreign exchange intervention by the Japanese government	www.mof.go.jp/english/international_policy/reference/feio/index.htm
National, Regional, and International Data	
U.S. federal government: Access to a wide range of data and information	www.fedstats.gov
St. Louis Federal Reserve Bank: Data on United States and other countries	http://research.stlouisfed.org/fred2
U.S. Bureau of Economic Analysis: U.S. balance of payments data	www.bea.gov/International
European Union	http://europa.eu/index_en.htm
Statistics Canada	www.statcan.gc.ca/start-debut-eng.html
Central Banks	
U.S. Federal Reserve System	www.federalreserve.gov
European Central Bank	www.ecb.europa.eu/home/html/index.en.html
Bank of Japan	www.boj.or.jp/en
Other Useful Sites	
Resources for Economists on the Internet: Links to a broad range of sites with economics information	www.rfe.org
WebEc International Economics: Many useful links	www.helsinki.fi/WebEc/framef.html
Michigan State University: Links to many useful sites and a glossary	http://globaledge.msu.edu/reference-desk
University of Auckland, Offstats: Data and links to sites with data	www.offstats.auckland.ac.nz
Nationmaster: Comparative national data and tools for displaying the data	www.nationmaster.com
Peterson Institute for International Economics: Information on its publications, including some available online	www.iie.com
World Economic Forum: Reports and discussions of global issues	www.weforum.org
Abyz News Links: Links to the Web sites of newspapers from around the world	www.abyznewslinks.com

You may find statistical yearbooks for other countries in the Library of Congress's HA_ range.

If you want to compare countries in the same region, you can get numbers for all the countries in the region from such compilations as the following:

- United Nations, Economic Commission for Latin America and the Caribbean, *Statistical Yearbook for Latin America and the Caribbean* (HA751.A58).
- United Nations, *African Statistical Yearbook* (HA1955.U5).
- European Bank for Reconstruction and Development, *Transition Report* (HC331.E2).

For analysis of global issues for developing countries, see the World Bank's annual *World Development Report* (HC59.7.W659). At http://data.worldbank.org, the World Bank provides access to World Development Indicators and other sets of data. For most of the main economic aggregates, you can also see the International Monetary Fund's *International Financial Statistics* (HG3881.I626), which covers more than just international finance. The United Nations Development Project produces its annual *Human Development Report* (HD72.H85), which focuses on measures of living conditions, education, and male–female differences in achievements.

Some global volumes cover specific aspects of international economics that are evident from their titles:

- United Nations, *International Trade Statistics Yearbook* (HF91.U47).
- United Nations, *National Accounts Statistics* (HC79.I5.N388).
- International Monetary Fund, *Balance of Payments Statistics* (HG3882.B34).
- United Nations Conference on Trade and Development, *World Investment Report* (HG4538.W67).
- Organisation for Economic Cooperation and Development, *International Direct Investment Statistics Yearbook* (HG4583.I58).
- International Monetary Fund, *Direction of Trade Statistics* (HF1016.I652).
- International Monetary Fund, *Annual Report on Exchange Arrangements and Exchange Restrictions* (HG3834.I61A3).
- World Bank, *International Debt Statistics*, formerly *Global Development Finance* (HJ8899.W672).

- United Nations Environment Programme, *Year Book* (HC79.E5 U55).

- International Organization for Migration, *World Migration Report* (JV6006.W67).

Multilateral organizations produce other useful periodic reports, including the World Trade Organization, *Annual Report* (HF1371.A56); the International Monetary Fund, *World Economic Outlook* (HG230.3.O4); and the Bank for International Settlements, *Annual Report* (HG1997.I6A3).

Here is one more useful resource: Alan V. Dearforff, *Terms of Trade: A Glossary of International Economics* (HF1373.D43), provides definitions, graphs, and explanations.

Appendix **B**

Deriving Production-Possibility Curves

The shape of the production-possibility curve used so much in the theory of international trade depends on the factor supplies of the country and on the technology for combining these factors to produce outputs. The usual device for portraying the state of technology is the **production function,** which expresses the output of any one commodity as a function of its inputs.

Geometrically, the production function for each commodity can be shown in two dimensions by plotting the various combinations of two factors needed to produce given amounts of the commodity in question. Figure B.1 shows several **production isoquants,** each showing the different combinations of land and labor that could yield a given level of output. The smooth isoquants of Figure B.1A portray a case in which land and labor are partial substitutes for one another in cloth. Starting from a point like W, it would be possible to keep the same cloth output per year (i.e., stay on the isoquant T–T) with less labor if we used enough more land, as at V. By contrast, in Figure B.1B, the production function has a special form (sometimes called the Leontief production function) in which land and labor are not substitutes at all. Thus, starting from point W, we cannot give up any labor inputs without falling to a lower output isoquant, regardless of how much extra land is added. Thus the isoquant moves vertically up from point W to points like Z demanding the same labor inputs. Some industries are thought to resemble this special case, though the factors of production are usually partial substitutes for one another, as in Figure B.1A.

What combination of resources should be used to produce a specific amount of output of a product? If the factors are partial substitutes, then the lowest-cost combination of resources to use depends on the factors' prices. The relative prices of the two factors are summarized in factor-price slopes like that of **isocost lines** S–S and S'–S' in Figure B.1A, which are parallel. This slope shows the ratio of the wage rate for labor to the rental rate for land—the number of acres of land use that can be traded for each hour of labor in the marketplace. For given factor prices, isocost lines farther from the origin indicate higher total costs.

To minimize the cost of producing a specific level of output, a firm would seek the lowest isocost line, the one that is just tangent to the isoquant for that output level. For instance, if factor prices are shown by the slope of line S–S, then the least-cost way of

FIGURE B.1   Production: Isoquants and Expansion Paths

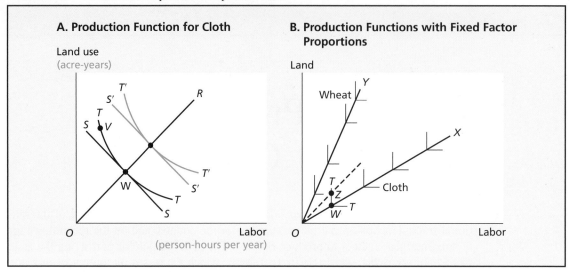

producing the output level for isoquant *T–T* is to use the combination of labor hours and land acres shown by point *W*. If land then becomes cheaper relative to labor, the factor-price slope would be steeper than *S–S*. Firms should substitute the lower-priced land for labor, and production would shift to a point like *V*.

How would the use of labor and land increase if the industry wanted to expand output, assuming that factor prices are constant? In Figure B.1A, we have shown the often-imagined case in which any expansion of output would be achieved along the *expansion path R*, a straight line from the origin as long as the factor-price ratio is still the slope *S–S*. In Figure B.1B the factor proportions would always be fixed, on the more labor-intensive expansion path (*X*) for cloth and the more land-intensive expansion path (*Y*) for wheat, regardless of the relative prices of land and labor.

To know the most efficient combinations a nation can produce, we must now combine the technological possibilities represented by the production-function isoquants with the nation's total supplies of land and labor. A handy device for doing this is the *Edgeworth–Bowley box diagram,* in which the dimensions of the box represent the amounts of land and labor in a country, which we call Britain. These factor supplies are assumed to be homogeneous in character and fixed in amount.

Figure B.2 shows an Edgeworth–Bowley box for production functions with fixed factor proportions and constant returns to scale (so that a proportionate increase in all inputs used to produce a product results in an increase in the product's output by the same proportion). The production function for cloth is drawn with its origin in the lower-left corner of the box at *O*, and with its isoquants, *T–T*, *T'–T'*, and so on, moving out and up to the right. Its expansion path is *OX*. If all the labor in Britain (*OR*) were used to make cloth, only *RX* of land would be required, and *O'X* of land would be left unemployed. At *X*, the marginal physical product of land would be zero.

The production function for wheat is drawn reversed and upside down, with its origin at *O'* and extending downward and to the left. Its expansion path is *O'Y*. At *Y*, all the

FIGURE B.2
Edgeworth–
Bowley Box
Diagram with
Fixed Factor
Proportions

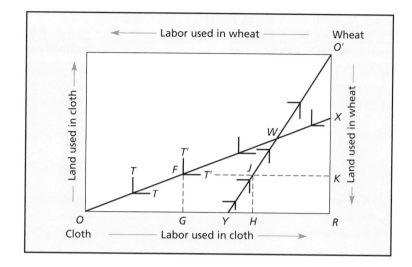

land and *YR* of labor would be employed, but *OY* of labor would be unemployed. *OX* and *O'Y* intersect at *W*, which is the only production point in the box diagram where there can be full employment and positive prices for both factors. At any other point on either expansion path, say, *F* on *OX*, land and labor will be able to produce at *J* on the expansion path for wheat; *OG* of labor will be engaged in cloth, and *HR* in wheat. *RK* of land will be employed in cloth, and *O'K* in wheat. But *GH* of labor will be unemployed.

The curve *OWO'*, as in Figure B.2, is in effect a production-possibility curve, showing the various combinations of wheat and cloth that can be produced in Britain, given the factor endowments of the country. The only point providing full employment of the two factors and positive factor prices is *W. OWO'* does not look like a production-possibility curve because it is given in terms of physical units of land and labor, rather than physical units of production. If we remap the *OWO'* curve in Figure B.2 from factor space into commodity space in terms of units of wheat and cloth and turn it right side up, it is a production-possibility curve, kinked at *W*, as in Figure B.3.

FIGURE B.3
Production-
Possibility
Curve
Derived from
Edgeworth–
Bowley Box
Diagram with
Fixed Factor
Proportions

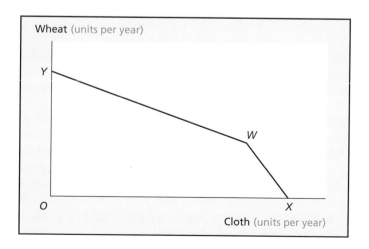

FIGURE B.4   Production-Possibility Curve with Identical Factor Proportions

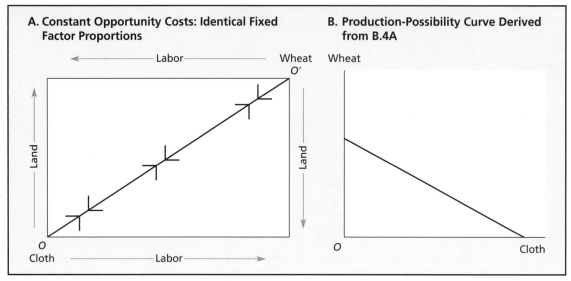

A. Constant Opportunity Costs: Identical Fixed Factor Proportions

B. Production-Possibility Curve Derived from B.4A

If cloth and wheat were produced with fixed factor coefficients, and these were identical, the two expansion paths would coincide, as in Figure B.4A. In this case, if production also involves constant returns to scale for both products, then the production-possibility curve becomes a straight line, as in Figure B.4B. Because land and labor are always used in the same combination, they might well be regarded as a single factor. This is equivalent to Ricardo's labor theory of value and its resultant straight-line production-possibility curve. A similar straight-line production-possibility curve would be produced for any economy in which the production functions are constant returns to scale and identical factor-intensity for the two commodities.

When there is the possibility of substitution between factors in the production of a commodity, there is no unique expansion path. Instead, a separate expansion path can be drawn for any given set of factor prices. To determine the production-possibility curve, we can draw in the isoquants for both commodities and trace out a locus of points of tangency between them. This locus represents the efficiency path, or the maximum combinations of production of the two goods that can be produced with the existing factor supplies. It is shown in Figure B.5A. To see why it is an efficient path, suppose that production were to take place at *W*, away from the efficiency locus. *W* is on cloth isoquant 7 and on wheat isoquant 5. But there is a point *T*, also on cloth isoquant 7, that is on a higher isoquant (6) of wheat. It would therefore be possible to produce more wheat without giving up any cloth. There is also point *T'* on wheat isoquant 5 that is on cloth isoquant 8. It would be equally possible to produce more cloth and the same amount of wheat. Any point off the locus of tangencies of isoquants of the two production functions is therefore inefficient, insofar as it would be possible to get more output of one commodity without losing any of the other, by moving to the locus.

When the Edgeworth–Bowley box is used for picturing production, it shows not only the efficient combinations of outputs but also factor combinations and factor

FIGURE B.5 Production-Possibility Curve with Variable Factor Proportions

A. Maximum Efficiency Locus under Variable Factor Proportions

B. Production-Possibility Curve Derived from B.5A

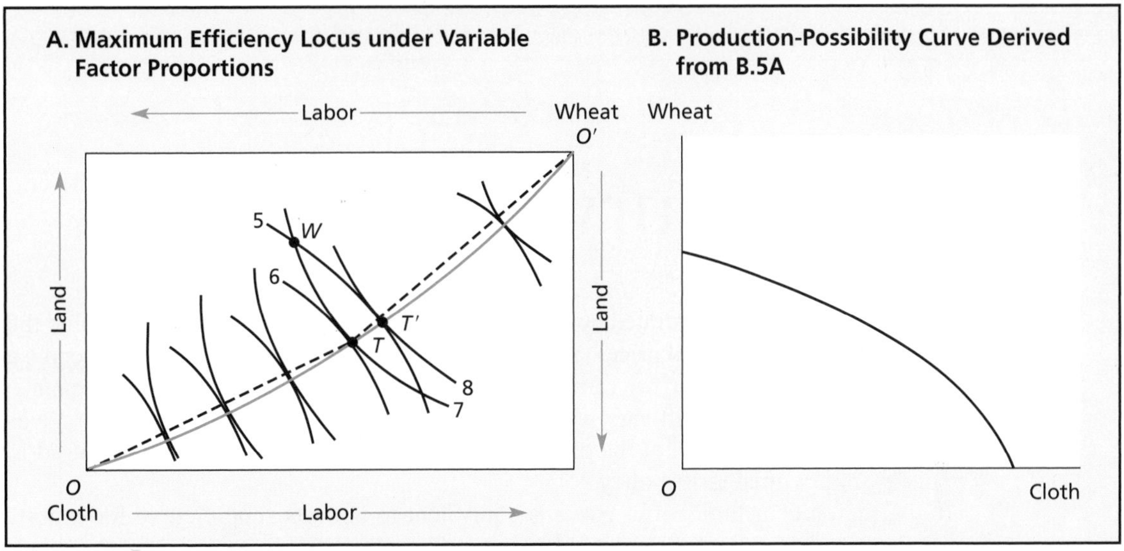

prices. If production is at T, the factor proportions in cloth are represented by the slope of the dashed line OT, and the factor proportions in wheat by the dashed line $O'T$. The relative price of land and labor with these outputs is represented by the slope of the line tangent to the isoquants at T.

If the production function for each product shown in Figure B.5A is constant returns to scale, then the bowed shape of the efficiency locus translates into the bowed-out production-possibility curve in Figure B.5B. One way to see the basis for this is first to recognize that production along the diagonal of this Edgeworth–Bowley box would result in a straight-line "production-capability" curve. (The logic is essentially the same as that sketched for the case of identical constant-returns-to-scale production functions.) Because moving off the diagonal to produce instead on the efficiency locus increases output for all points except the corners of the box, the actual production-possibility curve lies outside of this straight line connecting the end points (where the country is completely specialized in producing only one product, corresponding to the corners of the Edgeworth–Bowley box). The resulting production-possibility curve is bowed out.

Appendix C

Offer Curves

In Chapter 2 we demonstrated how to use supply and demand curves to determine the equilibrium international price with free trade. Another geometric device that serves a similar function is the **offer curve,** which shows how the export and import quantities a nation chooses will vary with the international price ratio. This appendix gives the geometric derivation of the offer curve. Appendix D shows how it can be used in discussing optimal tariff policy.

A region or nation's offer curve is equivalent to both its supply curve for exports and its demand curve for imports. (For examples of the latter two curves, see the center panel of Figure 2.3.) It graphs trade offers as a function of the international price ratio. And it can be derived from the same production-possibility curves and community indifference curves used extensively in Chapter 4.

Figure C.1 shows the derivation, starting from the usual production and consumption trade-offs. For each international price ratio, the behavior of the United States produces a quantity of exports willingly offered in exchange for imports at that price ratio. At 2 W/C, the United States does not want to trade at all, as shown at S_0. At 1 W/C, the United States would find cloth cheaper, and wheat more valuable, than without trade. It would be willing to export 40 billion wheat units and import 40 billion cloth units, by efficiently producing at S_1 and consuming at C_1. A price of 1/2 W/C would again induce the United States to offer 40 billion of wheat exports, but this time in exchange for 80 billion of cloth imports. Each offer of exports for imports is pictured as a trade triangle with corners at the production and consumption points for the price ratio.

Each of these offers is plotted on the lower half of Figure C.1 (as points O, O_1, and O_2), where the axes are the exports and imports to be exchanged, and the slope of any ray from the origin is a price ratio. The resulting curve O_{US} is the U.S. offer curve. A similar derivation produces the rest of the world's offer curve, O_{RW}. Only at the equilibrium price of 1 W/C, at point O_1, will the United States and the rest of the world be able to agree on how much to trade.

There is another way to derive the same offer curve for a country. We can use *trade indifference curves*, which show the levels of well-being attained by a country for different amounts of imports received and exports paid. Imports add to national well-being by expanding consumption while exports detract from well-being because they are not available for local consumption. A trade indifference curve pictures the trade-off that the country would be willing to make while remaining at the same level

FIGURE C.1

Deriving the
Offer Curve

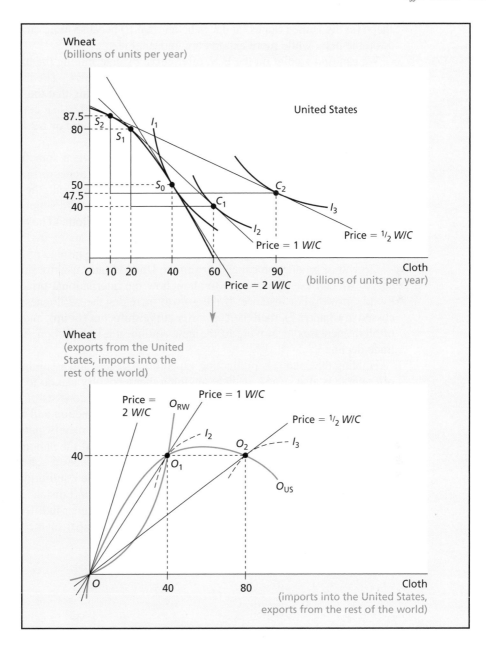

of overall well-being. The bottom half of Figure C.1 shows two U.S. trade indifference curves: I_2 and I_3.[1] These two trade indifference curves correspond to the levels of U.S. well-being shown by community indifference curves I_2 and I_3 in the top half of the figure. The trade indifference curves have the upward slope and rather peculiar

---

[1] The trade indifference curves for the country can be derived from its production-possibility curve and community indifference curves.

shape for the United States (and I_3 is better than I_2) because more cloth imports are the desirable item, while more exports are undesirable.

We can find a point on the U.S. offer curve by determining the highest trade indifference curve that can be reached if the price ratio is 1 W/C. The highest trade indifference curve, and therefore the highest level of well-being that the United States can reach at this price ratio, is the tangency with trade indifference curve I_2 at point O_1. Thus, O_1 is a point on the U.S. offer curve. For the price ratio of 1/2 W/C, the tangency is with I_3, so O_2 is another point on the U.S. offer curve.

Offer curves can be used to analyze what happens when something fundamental changes. For instance, the implications for the United States of a shift in the offer curve of the rest of the world are straightforward. If it shifts out, the two offer curves' intersection shifts from point O_1 to a point like O_2. The extra supply of cloth exports from the rest of the world decreases the relative price of cloth. (The price line becomes flatter.) This represents an improvement in the U.S. terms of trade, and the United States is better off, reaching an indifference curve like I_3 instead of I_2.

Growth of production capabilities in the United States usually shifts the U.S. offer curve. We can use offer curves to show how the international price ratio is affected by this growth. For instance, if the growth increases the willingness to trade (as discussed in Chapter 7), then the U.S. offer curve shifts out (or up), and the relative price of cloth increases in moving to the new equilibrium intersection. The U.S. terms of trade decline.[2]

Holding the country's production capabilities steady, and assuming that the foreign offer curve is also steady, is there anything that a country can do to improve its well-being by moving its own offer curve? Not if the nation consists of large numbers of private individuals competing against each other in production and consumption with no government intervention. Such private competition merely puts us on the offer curve in the first place and does not shift the curve. Yet if the nation acted as a single decision-making unit, there is the glimmering of a chance to squeeze more advantage out of trade in Figure C.1. Starting at the free-trade equilibrium O_1, the United States might be able to come up with a way to move a short distance to the southwest along the foreign offer curve O_{RW}, reaching somewhat higher indifference curves than at O_1. How could this be done? Through an optimal tariff of the sort discussed in Appendix D, where the offer curves reappear.

---

[2]We cannot use the original trade indifference curves to analyze the effects of this growth on U.S. well-being because the growth in the U.S. production capabilities means that the United States has a new set of trade indifference curves. Chapter 7 shows how changes in well-being can be examined using production-possibilities curves and community indifference curves once the change in the equilibrium price ratio is determined.

Appendix **D**

The Nationally Optimal Tariff

DERIVING THE OPTIMAL TARIFF

In the latter part of Chapter 8 we presented the nationally optimal tariff for a country that can affect the foreign-supply price of its imports without incurring retaliation by the foreign country. This appendix derives the formula for the nationally optimal tariff using both the demand–supply framework of Chapter 8 and the offer-curve framework of Appendix C. An analogous formula is derived for the optimal export duty, both for a nation and for an international cartel.

As we saw in the demand–supply framework, a small increase in an import tariff brings an area of gain and an area of loss to the nation. Figure D.1 compares these two areas for a tiny increase in the tariff above its initial amount per unit, which is the fraction t times the initial price P paid to foreign exporters. The extra gains come from being able to lower the foreign price on continuing imports, gaining the level of imports M times the foreign price drop dP/dt. The extra losses come from losing the extra imports (dM/dt) that were worth tP more per unit to consumers than the price (P) at which foreigners were willing to sell them to us.

The optimal tariff rate is that which just makes the extra losses and extra gains from changing the tariff equal each other. That is, the optimal tariff rate t^* as a share of world price is the one for which

$$\text{Extra gains} - \text{Extra losses} = M\frac{dP}{dt} - t^*P\frac{dM}{dt} = 0$$

so that

$$t^* = \frac{dP/dt}{dM/dt}\frac{M}{P}$$

Since the foreign supply elasticity is defined as

$$s_m = \frac{dM/dt}{dP/dt} \cdot \frac{P}{M}$$

along the foreign supply curve, the formula for the optimal tariff is simply $t^* = 1/s_m$, as stated in Chapter 8. If the world price is fixed beyond our control, so that $s_m = \infty$,

FIGURE D.1
The Gains and
Losses from a
Slight Increase
in the Tariff, in a
Demand–Supply
Framework

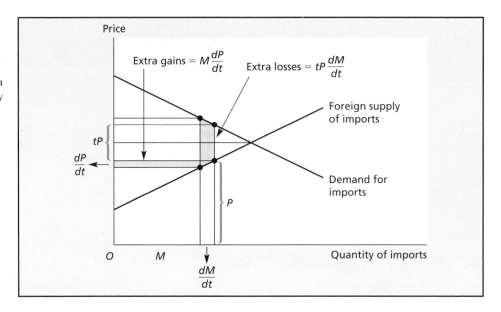

then the optimal tariff rate is zero. The more inelastic the foreign supply, the higher the optimal tariff rate.[1]

OPTIMAL EXPORT TAXES

We can derive the optimal rate of *export* duty in the same way. Just replace all terms referring to imports with terms referring to exports and redraw Figure D.1 so that the extra gain at the expense of foreign buyers of our exports comes at the top of the tariff gap instead of at the bottom. It turns out, symmetrically, that the optimal export duty equals the absolute value of $1/d_x$, or the reciprocal of the foreign demand elasticity for our exports.

The formula for the optimal export duty can also be used as the optimal rate of markup of an international cartel. Since both the international cartel maximizing joint profits from exports and the single nation optimally taxing its exports are monopolistic profit maximizers, it stands to reason that the formula linking optimal markup to foreign demand elasticity should hold in both cases. So the optimal markup for an

[1]Figure D.1 makes it easy to show that the nationally optimal tariff is lower than the tariff rate that would maximize the government's tariff revenue, even when the foreign supply curve slopes upward. The optimal tariff in Figure D.1 is one that equates the "extra gains" area with the "extra losses" area. But at this tariff rate a slight increase in the tariff still brings a net increase in government tariff revenue. By raising the tariff rate slightly, the government collects more duty on the remaining imports, M, while losing the "extra losses" area on the discouraged imports. However, its gain in revenue on M is not just the "extra gains" area already introduced, but this plus the thin unlabeled rectangle above the tP gap, which takes the form of a higher price to consumers importing M. A slight increase in the tariff would still raise revenue even when it brings no further net welfare gains to the nation. It follows that the revenue-maximizing tariff rate is higher than the optimal tariff rate. Thus a country would be charging too high a rate if it tried to find its nationally optimal tariff rate by finding out what rate seemed to maximize tariff revenues.

international exporting cartel is $t^* = |1/d_c|$, or the absolute value of the reciprocal of the world demand elasticity for the cartel's exports.

We can extend the formula to show how the optimal export markup for cartel members depends on the other elasticities and the market share discussed in Chapter 14's treatment of cartels like OPEC. We can link the elasticity of demand for the cartel's exports to world demand for the product, the supply of perfect substitutes from other countries, and the cartel's share of the world market by beginning with a simple identity:

$$\text{Cartel exports} = \text{World exports} - \text{Other countries' exports}$$

or

$$X_c = X - X_0$$

Differentiating with respect to the cartel price yields

$$\frac{dX_c}{dP} = \frac{dX}{dP} - \frac{dX_0}{dP}$$

This can be reexpressed in ways that arrive at an identity involving elasticities:

$$\frac{dX_c/dP}{X} = \frac{dX/dP}{X} - \frac{dX_0/dP}{X}$$

$$\frac{dX_c}{dP}\frac{P}{X_c}\frac{X_c}{X} = \frac{dX}{dP}\frac{P}{X} - \frac{dX_0}{dP}\frac{P}{X_0}\frac{X_0}{X}$$

The cartel's share of the world market is defined as $c = X_c/X = 1 - (X_0/X)$. The elasticity of demand for the cartel's exports is defined as $d_c = (dX_c/dP)(P/X_c)$; the elasticity of world export demand for the product is $d = (dX/dP)(P/X)$; and the elasticity of noncartel countries' competing export supply of the product is $s_0 = (dX_0/dP)(P/X_0)$. Substituting these definitions into the equation above yields

$$d_c \cdot c = d - s_0(1 - c)$$

so that

$$d_c = \frac{d - s_0(1 - c)}{c}$$

Now since the optimal markup rate is $t^* = |1/d_c|$, this optimal cartel markup rate is

$$t^* = \frac{c}{|d - s_0(1 - c)|}$$

The optimal markup as a share of the (markup-including) price paid by buying countries is greater, the greater the cartel's market share (c), the lower the absolute value of the world demand elasticity for exports of the product (d), or the lower the elasticity of noncartel countries' export supply (s_0).

THE OPTIMAL TARIFF AGAIN WITH OFFER CURVES

The nationally optimal tariff on imports (or exports) can also be portrayed using the offer-curve framework of Appendix C, though this framework is less convenient for showing the *formula* for the optimal tariff. A trade-taxing country can use the tariff to move its own offer curve until it reaches the point on the foreign offer curve that maximizes the country's well-being. Figure D.2 shows this optimal tariff for a wheat-exporting country. Our country, the wheat exporter, has pushed its offer curve to the right by making the price of imported cloth in units of wheat higher within the country than the price received by our foreign cloth suppliers. At point T domestic consumers must pay for cloth at the domestic price ratio SR/RT, giving up SR in wheat for RT in cloth. The foreign suppliers receive only OR in wheat for their RT of cloth. The government has intervened to collect tariff revenue at the tariff rate SO/OR.

Figure D.2 shows that this particular tariff rate happens to be optimal because at point T the foreign offer curve is tangent to I_0, the best indifference curve we can reach through trade. The optimal tariff is positive because the foreign offer curve is not infinitely elastic. If it were infinitely elastic, in the form of a fixed world price line coming out of the origin, our optimal tariff would be zero because no other tariff can

FIGURE D.2

An Optimal Tariff, Portrayed with Offer Curves

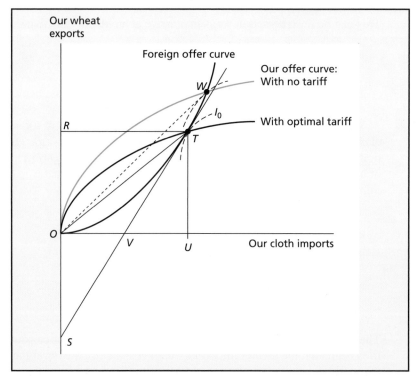

At point T, foreign sellers are paid only OR of our wheat for OU of their cloth. But domestic buyers have to pay the OR plus the tariff revenue of OS in extra wheat to get that OU of cloth. While that is bad for our cloth consumers in their role as cloth consumers, our nation gets to the better trade indifference curve I_0, helped by the fact that foreign suppliers pay some of the tariff, in effect, when they are forced to accept a lower world price (the slope OT) than the price reflected by the slope OW, which they would receive for cloth with no tariffs.

put us on as high an indifference curve as we can reach on our free-trade, no-tariff offer curve. The same principle emerges here as in the demand–supply framework: The more elastic the foreign trading curve, the lower is our optimal tariff.

Deriving the formula for the optimal tariff rate is more complicated with offer curves than with demand and supply curves. The elasticity of the foreign offer curve is conventionally defined differently from a foreign supply curve, and defined in a way that is hard to identify in the offer-curve diagram itself. Any country's offer-curve elasticity is conventionally defined as the ratio of the percent response of its import demand to a percent change in the relative price of its imports:

$$\text{Offer-curve elasticity } (E_{OC}) = \frac{-(\%\ \text{change in } M)}{[\%\ \text{change in } (X/M)]}$$

Since the change in the price ratio X/M is not easy to spot on an offer-curve diagram like Figure D.2, let's convert this definition into a more usable equivalent:

$$E_{OC} = \frac{-(\%\ \text{change in } M)}{(\%\ \text{change in } X) - (\%\ \text{change in } M)}$$

$$= \frac{-1}{\dfrac{(\%\ \text{change in } X)}{(\%\ \text{change in M})} - 1} = \frac{1}{1 - \left(\text{slope } \dfrac{\partial X}{\partial M}\right)(M/X)}$$

This last expression can be translated into a relationship among line segments in Figure D.2. We now take the foreigners' point of view since it is their offer curve we are trying to interpret. The foreigners export cloth and import wheat. Thus the slope showing how a change in cloth exports relates to a change in their wheat imports at point T is the ratio RT/SR, and the ratio (M/X) is OR/RT. Therefore the elasticity of their offer curve becomes

$$E_{OC} = \frac{1}{1 - \dfrac{RT}{SR}\dfrac{OR}{RT}} = \frac{1}{1 - \dfrac{OR}{SR}} = \frac{SR}{SR - OR} = \frac{SR}{SO}$$

(Some authors derive an equivalent ratio on the cloth axis: $E_{OC} = UO/VO$.)

We can now see the close link between the optimal tariff rate at point T and the elasticity of the foreign offer curve:

$$t^* = \frac{SO}{OR} = \frac{SO}{SR - SO} = \frac{1}{\dfrac{SR}{SO} - 1}$$

or

$$t^* = \frac{1}{E_{OC} - 1}$$

This expression seems to differ slightly from the formula relating to the foreign supply elasticity for our imports, derived above. But the difference is only definitional. The elasticity of the foreign offer curve is defined as the elasticity of the foreigners' wheat imports with respect to the world price of wheat, not the elasticity of their cloth exports (supply of our cloth imports) with respect to the world price of cloth. Since the ratio of the foreigners' cloth exports to their wheat imports is just the world price of wheat, the foreign offer-curve elasticity [(Percent change in wheat)/(Percent change in cloth/wheat)] is equal to one plus their elasticity of supply of our import, cloth. So the above expression is equivalent to the reciprocal of the foreigners' supply elasticity of our import good, as in the demand–supply framework.[2]

[2]One word of caution in interpreting the optimal tariff formula relating to the foreign offer curve: The tariff rate can equal the formula $1/(E_{oc} - 1)$ for *any* tariff rate, not just the optimal one. To know that the rate is optimal, as at point *T*, you must also know that the foreign offer curve is tangent to our trade indifference curve.

Appendix **E**

Accounting for International Payments

In Chapter 16 we examined the uses and meanings of a country's balance of payments, which records all flows of economic value between a country's residents and the residents of the rest of the world. We noted that the balance of payments is based on *double-entry bookkeeping*. Each transaction between a resident of our country and a resident of the rest of the world includes two items:

- A *credit item* (measured with a positive sign) is what we give up in the transaction, so that it creates a reason for a payment by the foreigner into the country—a monetary claim on the foreigner.

- A *debit item* (measured with a negative sign) is what we receive in the transaction, so that it creates a reason for a payment by our country to a foreigner—a monetary claim owed to a foreigner.

The assumption of double-entry bookkeeping is that each transaction is an exchange of value for equal value. (For something that is given away, this equality is not true, but in this case we create an artificial item to maintain the system.)

This appendix shows how accounting for the balance of payments works, by examining five illustrative transactions between the United States and the rest of the world during a short period of time. For each transaction, we will post the items to relevant parts of the balance of payments, and then we will create a simplified balance of payments for the United States for this time period using these five transactions.

FIVE TRANSACTIONS

First, suppose that Northern Illinois Gas, a U.S. utility company, buys $34 million in natural gas from a Canadian firm. It does not pay in cash immediately, but instead issues a promissory note saying that it will pay the bill (plus interest that will accrue over time) one year later. For the U.S. balance of payments, two accounting entries are made for the transaction that occurs now:

	Credit (+)	Debit (−)
	($ million)	($ million)
Import of goods (natural gas)		$34
Change in foreign loans to the U.S. (promissory note)	$34	

The debit entry probably seems easier and more natural than the credit entry in this case. It is clear that importing natural gas is an inflow of something valuable for which the United States must pay. But why should the promissory note be recorded as a credit item? Because the Canadian seller of the gas has received something valuable in exchange, the right to be paid in the future. Effectively, the Canadian seller is providing the funds to Northern Illinois now (in exchange for the promissory note), so that Northern Illinois can use those funds now to "pay for" the natural gas that it is importing.

Consider a second international transaction, in which Brazilian soccer fans spend $6 million as tourists in the United States during a soccer tournament, and they pay for their hotels, meals, and transportation by using the deposits that they have at a New York bank. The two flows are entered in the U.S. accounts as

	Credit (+)	Debit (−)
	($ million)	($ million)
Exports of services (travel)	$6	
Change in foreign investments in the U.S. (reduction in U.S. bank obligations to foreign residents)		$6

Again, one entry fits intuition more easily than the other. It is easy to see that sales of tourist services to Brazilians are a U.S. export, for which the United States must be paid. If this is a credit item, then the other item must be a debit item. Reducing a liability to foreigners is something of value that the United States must pay for now. Effectively, the New York bank is providing the funds to the Brazilian tourists so that they can use these funds to pay for their expenditures.

For our third transaction, suppose that the U.S. Treasury pays $25 million in interest on its past borrowing from Swiss investors, paying with checks on a New York bank. The two accounting entries are

	Credit (+)	Debit (−)
	($ million)	($ million)
Income paid to foreigners (interest payment)		$25
Change in foreign investments in the U.S. (increase in U.S. bank obligations to foreign residents)	$25	

The payment of interest is payment of income to foreign residents, so this is a debit. The means of payment is a credit. The private New York bank on which the U.S. government wrote the checks now has a new liability to residents of Switzerland. The bank uses the borrowing from foreigners to cancel an equal checking-account obligation to the U.S. government, which has less claim on the private bank now that it has written the checks.

In our fourth transaction the U.S. monetary authority in its official role becomes concerned that the exchange rate value of the dollar may appreciate against the Japanese yen. It decides to purchase yen-denominated bank deposits from a major Tokyo bank and pay by transferring $15 million of its New York bank deposits to this Tokyo bank. For this transaction, here are the entries for the U.S. balance of payments:

	Credit (+)	Debit (−)
	($ million)	($ million)
Change in U.S. official holdings of foreign assets (increase in yen financial assets)		$15
Change in foreign investments in the U.S. (increase in U.S. bank obligations to a foreign resident)	$15	

Here we have a purely financial exchange. Effectively, the U.S. monetary authority is transferring part of its dollar bank deposits to a foreigner (the Tokyo bank) to get the funds that it uses to pay for the yen deposits. (There are two things to note about the accounting. First, the increase in U.S. holdings of foreign assets is measured as a negative item. This is simply based on the choice of how the credit, or positive, and debit, or negative, items are defined. Second, the yen value of the Tokyo bank deposits is converted into its dollar equivalent because all values must be measured in the same currency.)

So far we can see that every transaction has two equal sides. If we add up all the credits as pluses and all the debits as minuses, the net result is zero. Let's turn to a case that might look like a violation of this accounting balance.

The fifth transaction involves giving something away. Suppose that the U.S. government simply gives $8 million in foreign aid to the government of Egypt in the form of wheat from U.S. government stockpiles. The correct way to record the credit and debit items is:

	Credit (+)	Debit (−)
	($ million)	($ million)
Exports of goods (wheat)	$8	
Unilateral transfer (aid to Egypt)		$8

The $8 million credit is easy because this is just the export of a good, for which the United States ordinarily would be paid. The accountants get around the fact the United States is not paid by inventing a debit item for the unilateral transfer (gift) to Egypt. We can imagine that the United States receives $8 million of goodwill—or gratitude—from Egypt. That goodwill is something received, a debit, for which the United States pays in wheat. In this way, even a one-way flow is transformed by accounting fiction into a two-way flow, preserving the all-in zero balance of double-entry bookkeeping.

Current Account	
Exports of goods and services	+6 + 8 = +14
Imports of goods and services	−34
Income paid to foreigners	−25
Unilateral transfers, net	−8
Current account balance	−53
Financial Account (excluding official international reserves)	
Changes in foreign loans to the U.S. and other investments	+34 − 6 + 25 +15 = +68
Financial account balance	+68
Official International Reserves	
Changes in U.S. official holdings of foreign assets	−15
Changes in official international reserves, net	−15
Other important balances	
Goods and services balance	−20
Overall balance	+15

PUTTING THE ACCOUNTS TOGETHER

To arrange the credit and debit items from the separate transactions into a useful summary set of accounts, group them according to the major types of flows. Figure E.1 does this for our set of five transactions. For the five transactions, the United States has a current account deficit of $53 million, but this is more than offset by a (private or nonofficial) financial account surplus of $68 million. Thus, the United States has an overall payments (or official settlements balance) surplus of $15 million, and the United States has increased its holdings of official reserve assets by this amount.

Appendix **F**

Many Parities at Once

In Chapter 18 we introduced two parity conditions relating interest rates in different countries and exchange rates. In Chapter 19 we introduced another parity condition, purchasing power parity, that linked the prices of goods in different countries through exchange rates. These parity conditions are all based on people's ability to arbitrage between countries. As long as there are different ways of starting with one asset or product and ending up with another asset or product, the prices at which the assets or products can be exchanged will be closely related.

These parity conditions reveal relationships between foreign exchange markets and such macroeconomic phenomena as inflation and real interest rates. To see the relationships, let's think about the fact that investors can move between currencies and products. To simplify here, let us think about uniform products that can be bought or sold in either country. In addition to holding currencies today or in the future, you can hold products today or in the future. Investors must worry about price trends for products as well as price trends for currencies. Suppose, for example, you fear more inflation in the prices of products in Britain than in America over the next 90 days. How should your decision about where to hold your wealth relate to this fear and to the interest rates and trends in exchange rates? If others share your fear, what will happen to currency and commodity markets?

There are a number of links here, portrayed by Figure F.1. The central rectangle is just the lake diagram of Figure 18.1 revisited. Now, however, there also are ways to buy and sell products with currencies. You can trade either currency for products today at the dollar price $P_\$$ or the sterling price $P_£$. If you start with today's dollars, your way of buying products depends on the relative prices shown at the bottom of Figure F.1. You might just take, say, \$10,000 and buy $10,000/P_\$$ in current products with it. Or you could take a more roundabout route, using the \$10,000 to buy £10,000/e worth of sterling and then using it to buy $10,000/(eP_£)$ in products today. Do whichever is cheaper. That is, you have an incentive to travel the cheaper of the two routes between today's dollars and today's products. The availability of this choice means that the two prices will tend to be bid into line: $P_\$ = eP_£$. This is the (absolute) purchasing power parity (PPP) condition discussed in Chapter 19. As argued in that chapter, it is a general tendency that works reasonably well over decades, but only more roughly over shorter periods because of trade barriers, the costs of transactions and transportation, and the underlying differences in the goods whose prices are being compared.

FIGURE F.1
Spot and
Forward
Positions in
Currencies and
Products

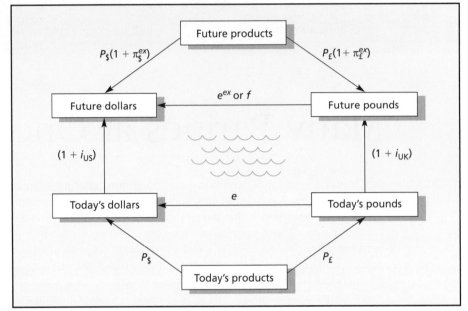

Moving with the arrow, multiply the value of your goods or money by the expression.
Moving against the arrow, divide by it.

Symbols: $P_\$$, $P_£$ = today's price level for goods (wheat, DVD movies, etc.) in terms of \$, £; $\pi_\$^{ex}$, $\pi_£^{ex}$ = the expected rate of inflation in the dollar and sterling goods' price levels; e, f = the spot and forward prices of the £ (in \$/£); e^{ex} = the expected future level of the spot price of the £ (not to be confused with the present forward price of it); i_{US}, i_{UK} = the interest rates on widely marketed assets (e.g., treasury bills) in America and Britain. (Ignore transactions fees and ignore futures markets in goods such as grain futures.)

A version of purchasing power parity should also hold for the future. If it doesn't, there may be unexploited chances for profitable arbitrage. Buying goods with dollars in the future should look equally cheap whether we expect to buy directly at the future dollar price or at the future pound price of goods times the dollar price of getting each pound. These different prices will depend on how much price inflation people expect between now and the future (say, 90 days from now). If people expect dollar prices to go up by the fraction $\pi_\$^{ex}$ and pound prices to go up by the fraction $\pi_£^{ex}$, then these average expectations should be tied to what future exchange rate people expect (e^{ex}). Their expectations should equate the direct and indirect dollar prices of goods shown at the top of Figure F.1, or $P_\$(1 + \pi_\$^{ex}) = e^{ex}P_£(1 + \pi_£^{ex})$. This condition can be called *expected future PPP*. It is only a rough tendency, like today's PPP, when actual changes in prices are used as measures of the expected changes $\pi_\$^{ex}$ and $\pi_£^{ex}$.

The tendencies toward purchasing power parity today and in our expectations about the future provide links among expected price inflation, interest rates, and exchange rates. Recall from Chapter 18 that the forward price of the pound, f, should equal e^{ex}, the average expectation about the future value of the spot rate. Combining the equality $e^{ex} = f$ with the interest parity conditions of Chapter 18 gives further results shown in Figure F.2's summary of key parity conditions.

FIGURE F.2

International Parities

1. **Purchasing power parity (PPP) today:** $eP_{£} = P_{\$}$, roughly (see Chapter 19).
2. **Expected future PPP:** $e^{ex}P_{£}(1 + \pi_{£}^{ex}) = P_{\$}(1 + \pi_{\$}^{ex})$, roughly, so that $e^{ex}/e = (1 + \pi_{\$}^{ex})/(1 + \pi_{£}^{ex})$, or, approximately, Expected appreciation of £ = Expected \$ inflation − Expected £ inflation.
3. **Covered interest parity:** $(f/e) = (1 + i_{US})/(1 + i_{UK})$ definitely.
4. **Speculators' forward equilibrium:** Forward rate measures average expected future spot rate, or $e^{ex} = f$, we think.
5. **Uncovered interest parity:** $(e^{ex}/e) = (1 + i_{US})/(1 + i_{UK})$, we think.
   Combining parities 2, 3, and 5, we see that

   $$e^{ex}/e = f/e = (1 + i_{US})/(1 + i_{UK}) = (1 + \pi_{\$}^{ex})/(1 + \pi_{£}^{ex}),$$

   or, approximately,

   Expected appreciation of £ = Premium on forward £
   = Difference between \$ and £ interest rates
   = Expected difference between \$ and £ inflation rates

   So we expect real interest rates to be roughly equal internationally:
6. **Real interest rate equilibrium:** $(1 + i_{US})/(1 + \pi_{\$}^{ex}) = (1 + i_{UK})/(1 + \pi_{£}^{ex})$ or, approximately, $(i_{US} - \pi_{\$}^{ex}) = (i_{UK} - \pi_{£}^{ex})$.

One result that emerges from all these arbitrage equilibriums is that real interest rates should tend to be the same across countries. This is only a rough long-run tendency. In fact, expected real interest rates, as best (such) expectations can be measured, can differ noticeably between countries for years at a stretch. There is nonetheless a tendency toward equality.

Figure F.2 shows some of the intricacy we must expect from increasingly globalized financial and product markets. To illustrate, let us return to a question posed above: What would happen if more inflation in Britain were expected in the near future? If you alone have this new perception of higher British inflation, you can act on it by moving away from sterling into dollars or products over any of the routes shown in Figure F.1. As long as your fear is confirmed, you will gain from the eventual general exodus from sterling. If everyone eventually agrees with your quick interpretation of the latest news, then prices and rates must change. The nominal interest rate must rise in Britain and the forward premium on the pound must decline, as the parity conditions in Figure F.2 show.

The moral of Figures F.1 and F.2 is that interest rates, exchange rates, and expected inflation rates are tied together. Whatever affects international differences in one is likely to affect international differences in the other two. It should be stressed, though, that one parity is much more reliable than the others. That one is the covered interest parity condition.

Appendix **G**

Aggregate Demand and Aggregate Supply in the Open Economy

In Chapter 22 we noted that a difference between the actual level of real GDP and its full-employment level will put pressure on the country's product price level or inflation rate. The formal IS–LM–FE model that we used in Chapters 22, 23, and 24 does not have an explicit role for the adjustment of the country's level of prices. This appendix develops a model of a country's macroeconomy that focuses on price adjustment over time. The standard way to analyze price adjustment is to picture the economy as a combination of aggregate demand and aggregate supply.

THE AGGREGATE DEMAND CURVE

A country's **aggregate demand curve** shows the level of real GDP that represents a short-run equilibrium for each possible price level, given fundamental conditions in the economy. We presume that this short-run equilibrium incorporates all adjustments to a triple intersection in the IS–LM–FE picture for the country. That is, for a country with a fixed exchange rate, the aggregate demand curve includes induced intervention to defend the fixed exchange rate (as discussed in Chapter 23). If the country instead has a floating exchange rate, the aggregate demand curve includes the induced adjustment of the exchange rate value (as discussed in Chapter 24).

Figure G.1A shows an aggregate demand curve. To see how it is derived, consider that we start at point A, where we know that aggregate demand level Y_1 corresponds to price level P_1. What is the effect on the level of aggregate demand if the price level changes to P_2? At this higher price level, the level of aggregate demand changes for two reasons:

- First, the nominal demand for money increases (see equation 22.10 in Chapter 22). The LM curve shifts to the left, and the level of aggregate demand tends to decrease.
- Second, the increase in the country's price level decreases the country's international price competitiveness. The IS curve shifts to the left, and the level of aggregate demand tends to decrease.

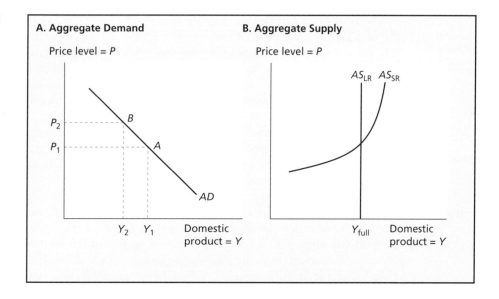

For both of these reasons, the level of aggregate demand falls to Y_2 at point B if the price level increases to P_2.[1] The aggregate demand curve AD is downward-sloping.

The AD curve shifts if there is a change in anything fundamental (other than the price level) that affects the level of aggregate demand in the economy. Examples include exogenous changes in consumption and domestic real investment, changes in fiscal policy, and a devaluation by a country using a fixed exchange rate.

AGGREGATE SUPPLY

Figure G.1B shows two types of aggregate supply curves. The **long-run aggregate supply curve** (AS_{LR}) is vertical and corresponds to the full-employment level of real GDP. This level of real GDP, also called potential real GDP, is the output the country can produce using the factor resources available in the country and the technologies in use in the country. (It corresponds to production being on the country's production possibility curve we used in Chapters 3–5 and 7.) We presume that markets in the country work well enough that the economy tends toward full employment in the long run. That is, in the long run, prices fully adjust so the economy achieves full employment of its resources. The AS_{LR} curve shifts if there are changes in factor resource availability or changes in technologies used in production.

[1]The decrease in international price competitiveness also shifts the FE curve to the left. In addition, the new IS–LM intersection is not necessarily on the new FE curve. If not, then with a fixed exchange rate there will be intervention to defend the fixed rate. Or, with a floating exchange rate, the exchange rate will change. The adjustments to external balance will alter the specific slope of the AD curve, but it will still be downward-sloping. There is no general rule that says that the aggregate demand curve is necessarily steeper or flatter with a fixed or floating exchange rate, and we will ignore any differences in the slope in the remainder of this appendix.

The **short-run aggregate supply curve** (AS_{SR}) is upward sloping because some prices in the economy do not adjust quickly. That is, some prices are sticky in the short run. For instance, a dry cleaner does not continuously adjust its prices as it sees what business arrives. Instead, the dry cleaner has a price list that it sticks to, and it typically changes the price list infrequently. Similarly, tuition at most universities is adjusted at most once per year. Essentially, the short-run supply curve is anchored by a set of prices that are given for the short-run time period.

To see the slope of the short-run aggregate supply curve, consider first an extreme case. If no prices can change in the short run, then the short-run aggregate supply curve would be a horizontal line (up to some high level of real GDP). If instead some prices change in the short run but others do not, then the aggregate supply curve is upward sloping. That is, it is "in-between" the horizontal aggregate supply curve where no prices change and the long-run aggregate supply curve where all prices are completely flexible. We also presume that the economy in the short run can operate beyond its long-run full-employment level of production, so part of the short-run aggregate supply curve is to the right of the long-run aggregate supply curve. Essentially, it is possible for people to work more hours than they normally want to, and for firms to run their machines more than they normally do, but this high level of factor use cannot be sustained for long periods of time.

The short-run aggregate supply curve shifts because the level of the sticky prices that anchors the curve changes over time. In fact, this is the essence of the slow price adjustment that characterizes the macroeconomics of many countries. The short-run aggregate supply curve also shifts if there is a shock to the country's price level, or if there is a shift in the long-run aggregate supply curve.

THE PRICE ADJUSTMENT PROCESS: AN EXAMPLE

Before we analyze various kinds of shocks that can hit an open macroeconomy, let's first look at the nature of price adjustment as the economy moves beyond a short-run period of time. Consider Figure G.2, in which the country's economy is at a short-run equilibrium at point A_1. Because A_1 is to the left of the AS_{LR}, the actual level of production, Y_1, is below the full-employment level, Y_{full}. The level of aggregate demand is low, relative to the economy's potential for producing goods and services.

With weak product markets and high levels of unemployment of labor and other resources, there is downward pressure on product and factor prices. As the economy moves beyond the short run, the price level falls as the short-run aggregate supply curve falls from AS_{SR1} to AS_{SR2}. The decline in the price level from P_1 to P_2 moves the economy down its aggregate demand curve from A_1 to A_2. This occurs because interest rates fall as the nominal demand for money decreases, and the country gains international price competitiveness as its price level declines. Interest-sensitive spending increases and net exports increase, so real GDP increases, from Y_1 to Y_2.

The process continues until the short-run aggregate supply curve has shifted down to AS_{SR3}, and the price level has declined to P_3. At this triple intersection the economy is now in a long-run equilibrium operating at potential real GDP Y_{full}. However, the process of getting to this long-run equilibrium may be slow and painful if there is

FIGURE G.2

The Price
Adjustment
Process

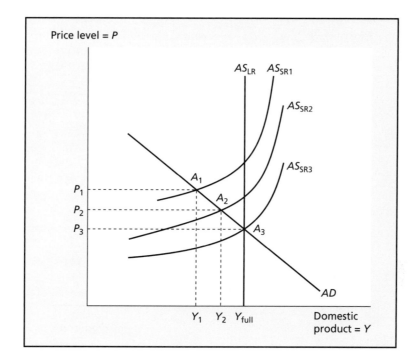

resistance to reductions in product prices, wages, and other resource prices. There may be a case for speeding up the process of achieving full employment by using expansionary government policy to shift the *AD* curve to the right, rather than waiting for the price adjustment.

SHOCKS AND PRICE ADJUSTMENT

The aggregate demand–aggregate supply model can be used to gain additional insights into the effects of shocks in the open macroeconomy. We are building on what we have already learned in Chapters 23 and 24 using the IS–LM–FE analysis. We will first examine the same four types of shocks that we examined in those chapters, for both a fixed exchange rate and a floating exchange rate. We will then turn to look at two types of shocks to aggregate supply.

Internal Shocks

As we saw in Chapter 23, a *domestic monetary shock* has no effect with a fixed exchange rate, assuming that the country's monetary authority cannot or does not sterilize. The monetary shock is neutralized by the induced adjustments in the domestic money supply as the country's monetary authority intervenes to defend the fixed rate. So there is nothing for the *AD–AS* analysis to show.

A domestic monetary shock does have an effect with a floating exchange rate. Figure G.3 shows the effect of a shift to an expansionary monetary policy, which shifts the *AD* curve to the right, from AD_1 to AD_2. If the economy starts from a

FIGURE G.3

Domestic
Monetary
Shock, Floating
Exchange Rate

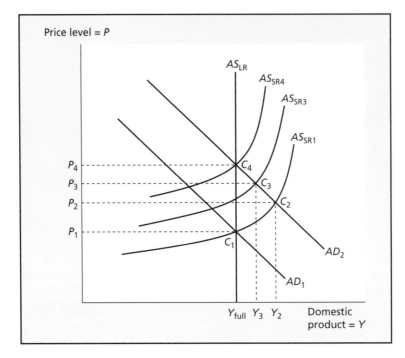

position of long-run equilibrium at point C_1 (P_1 and Y_{full}), the economy shifts to point C_2, with a higher price level P_2 and a higher real GDP Y_2. Excessively strong aggregate demand is driving the price level up, and inflation is rising. As the economy moves beyond the initial short run, even the sticky prices begin to increase, and the short-run aggregate supply curve shifts up from AS_{SR1} to AS_{SR3}. The price level rises to P_3. The higher price level takes some of the strength out of the level of aggregate demand because the interest rate is increasing back up as the nominal demand for money increases and because the country is losing international price competitiveness as the price level rises. This process continues until the aggregate supply curve has shifted up to AS_{SR4}, and the economy is back to production Y_{full} with a higher price level, P_4. In the long run, expansionary monetary policy causes inflation and a higher price level, the relationship that we focused on in Chapter 19 when we discussed the monetary approach to exchange rate determination. In the short and medium runs, the slow price adjustment is a key part of exchange rate overshooting that was also discussed in Chapter 19.

A *domestic spending shock* causes a shift in the aggregate demand curve. The magnitude of the shift may differ depending on whether the country has a fixed or floating exchange rate, but the general direction is the same. For instance, a shift to an expansionary fiscal policy causes a shift to the left in the *AD* curve. If the economy begins at full employment, then the price-adjustment story is similar to the one that we just looked at for monetary policy with a floating exchange rate. Actual real GDP is temporarily above its long-run potential, the inflation rate and the price level increase, and production falls back to Y_{full}.

FIGURE G.4

An International
Capital Flow
Shock: Fixed
Exchange Rate
or Floating
Exchange Rate

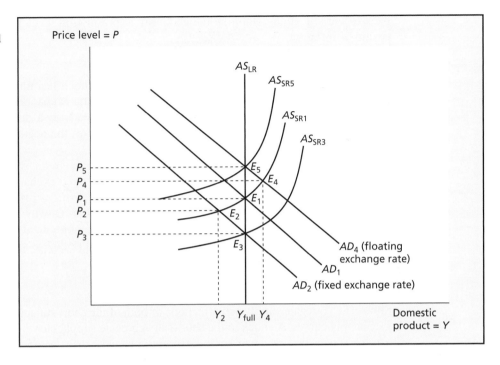

International Capital Flow Shock

An international capital-flow shock shifts the aggregate demand curve because of the induced effect on the money supply (fixed exchange rate) or on the exchange rate (if it is floating). Consider an adverse shock in which investors are pulling their financial capital out of the country. In Figure G.4 the country begins at point E_1, and then the shock hits. If the country has a *fixed exchange rate*, the intervention to defend the fixed rate requires that the country's monetary authority sell foreign currency and buy domestic currency. The country's money supply shrinks and the *aggregate demand curve shifts to the left*, from AD_1 to AD_2. The country goes into a recession and production falls from Y_{full} to Y_2. Downward price adjustment could eventually return the economy to full employment as the economy will move down the AD_2 curve to point E_3. But this could be a slow process. Expansionary fiscal policy could be used to speed the process, by shifting the aggregate demand curve back to the right.

Consider now that the country instead has a *floating exchange rate*, again starting from point E_1 in Figure G.4. The capital outflow results in a depreciation of the country's currency. The depreciation improves the country's international price competitiveness and the *aggregate demand curve shifts to the right*, from AD_1 to AD_4. The strong aggregate demand causes the price level to increase, and the price adjustment process is moving the economy toward point E_5. If the economy is overheating, there is a case for a shift to contractionary monetary policy or contractionary fiscal policy. If contractionary policy is used to shift the aggregate demand curve back to the left, it can stabilize the economy at production level Y_{full} and avoid the period of inflation.

International Trade Shock

With a floating exchange rate, an international trade shock has no lasting effect on the economy, once we include the induced change in the exchange rate. As we saw in Chapter 24, an adverse international trade shock leads to a depreciation of the country's currency, and the currency depreciation reverses the negative effect on real GDP. There is nothing for the *AD–AS* analysis to show.

With a fixed exchange rate, an adverse international trade shock reduces the country's net exports and the intervention to defend the fixed exchange rate leads to a reduction in the domestic money supply. Both of these changes result in a reduction in aggregate demand. The economy goes into a recession. Downward adjustment in the country's price level will return the economy to full employment over time, but the country instead could use a shift to expansionary fiscal policy to shift the *AD* curve back to the right and speed the adjustment.

Shocks to Aggregate Supply

Shocks to aggregate supply can affect one or both of the short-run and long-run aggregate supply curves. A shock to the short-run aggregate supply curve, sometimes called a price shock, occurs when some economic change causes a quick and substantial change in the price level. A shock to the long-run aggregate supply curve occurs when some economic change alters the full-employment level of real production, perhaps because of a change in the amount of resources available or a change in the technology used in production. Let's examine two types of aggregate supply shocks, an oil price shock in an oil-importing country and a large improvement in technology.

Oil price shock. In the 1970s two major oil-price shocks hit the world economy, a smaller shock occurred in 1990, and a more spread-out oil price increase occurred in the 2000s. When an oil-price shock hits, it has several effects on the economy of an oil-importing country. First, it causes a sudden jump upward in the country's price level because oil and the products produced from oil are important to and used throughout the economy and because the short-run demand for oil is price inelastic. Second, the higher oil prices can have long-lasting adverse effects on the country's supply capabilities. For instance, some capital equipment that can be used profitably when oil prices (or energy prices more generally) are low is uneconomic to use when oil (energy) costs are higher. Third, the jump in oil prices tends to increase the value of imports, so the country's trade balance deteriorates. That is, the oil price shock also causes an international trade shock. Here we focus more on the first two effects.

Figure G.5 shows an oil-importing country, initially in long-run equilibrium at point F_1. An oil-price shock now hits—a sudden large increase in world oil prices. The price shock causes an upward shift in the short-run aggregate supply curve from AS_{SR1} to AS_{SR2}. The decline in the useful capital stock causes a shift to the left in the long-run aggregate supply curve from AS_{LR} to AS'_{LR}. (We presume, as seems realistic, that the shift in the short-run curve is large relative to the shift in the long-run curve.) The economy shifts in the short run to point F_2, the intersection of the new short-run

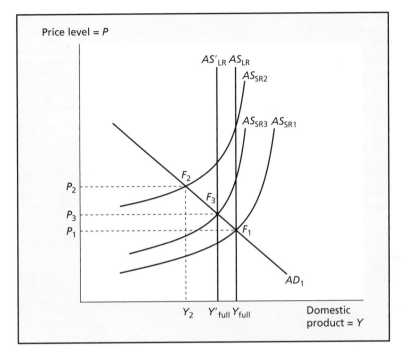

aggregate supply curve with the aggregate demand curve.[2] The country is experiencing two macroeconomic problems at the same time:

- The unemployment rate is increasing because the economy goes into recession as real GDP declines.
- The inflation rate is rising because of the oil price shock.

This combination of rising unemployment and rising inflation is sometimes called stagflation.

If there is no response by government policies, then the economy will adjust back toward long-run equilibrium as the economy moves beyond the short run. At the high price level, the weak level of aggregate demand puts downward pressure on prices and wages. Once again, a process of downward price adjustment can shift the short-run aggregate supply curve down and move the economy back toward full employment at point F_3. Because of the adverse effect of the oil price shock on the economy's production capabilities, the new level of potential real GDP is lower, only Y'_{full}.[3]

How should government policies respond to the oil price shock? The policy decision-makers face a dilemma. If they respond by loosening policy to fight the recession, the aggregate demand curve shifts to the right. The recovery from recession is faster, but the country experiences additional price inflation. If the policymakers

[2]If the country has a fixed exchange rate, the adverse international trade shock also causes the aggregate demand curve to shift to the left.

[3]If, instead, there is no change in the long-run aggregate supply curve, then the downward price adjustment must return the economy all the way back to point F_1.

FIGURE G.6
Technology
Improvement
Increases
Potential GDP

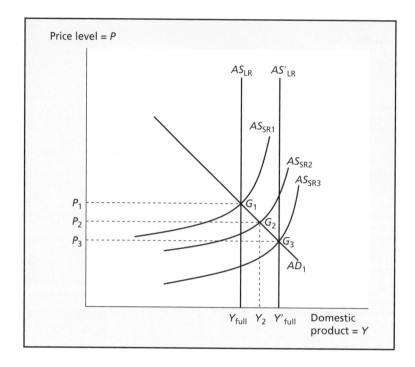

instead tighten policy to fight the rising inflation, the aggregate demand curve shifts to the left and the recession is deeper and longer. There are no easy decisions for policymakers in responding to an oil price shock.

Technology improvement. Another kind of shock to aggregate supply is a period of rapid improvements in production technology in the economy. We can use Figure G.6 to illustrate this case. Again the economy begins in a long-run equilibrium at point G_1. The improvement in technology then shifts both the long-run and the short-run aggregate supply curves to the right, as the economy's production capabilities expand. In the short run, the economy moves to an equilibrium at point G_2, with an increase in real GDP and a somewhat lower price level as some of the technology improvement is passed forward to consumers in the form of lower prices. However, the economy is still short of its new potential GDP Y'_{full}. If there is no change in government policy, the price level will continue to fall as the economy moves beyond the short run. The full adjustment to the new technology is the triple intersection at point G_3 as the short-run aggregate supply falls to AS_{SR3}. Government policymakers could speed the adjustment to the new potential real GDP by using expansionary policy to shift the aggregate demand curve to the right.

DEVALUATION OF A FIXED EXCHANGE RATE

Our final example of using *AD–AS* analysis is the devaluation of a fixed exchange rate, from its initial fixed value to a new lower fixed value for the country's currency. Figure G.7 shows the effects of a currency devaluation.

FIGURE G.7
Devaluation
of a Fixed
Exchange Rate

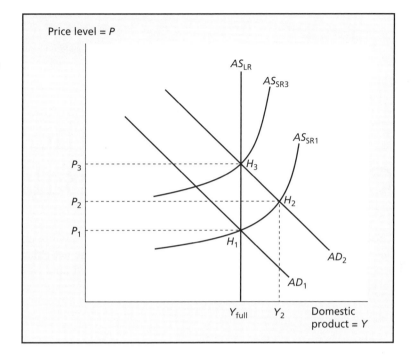

If the country begins at point H_1, the currency devaluation results in an increase in aggregate demand as the country gains international price competitiveness, so the aggregate demand curve shifts from AD_1 to AD_2. Assuming that the short-run aggregate supply curve is unaffected, real GDP increases from Y_{full} to Y_2. There is some upward pressure on the price level, which rises from P_1 to P_2. As the economy moves beyond the short run, the strong aggregate demand causes further upward pressure on the price level and the short-run aggregate supply shifts up. The economy is headed for a new long-run equilibrium at point H_3, with a higher price level of P_3 and production returned to Y_{full}.

The *AD–AS* analysis of devaluation brings out two important points. First, the devaluation has little effect in the long run. The gain in price competitiveness from the decline in the nominal exchange-rate value of the country's currency is offset by the rise in domestic prices. This is the reversion to purchasing power parity in the long run that we examined in Chapter 19. Second, there is a risk that the devaluation could have little effect even in the short run. The devaluation results in an increase in the domestic currency price of imports. If people in the country also quickly raise domestic prices and wages when they see or anticipate that import prices are rising, the short-run aggregate supply curve shifts up quickly. The country quickly moves to point H_3. There is little effect of the devaluation because the higher domestic inflation has quickly offset the devaluation.

Devaluation and the Current Account Balance

This appendix extends Chapter 23's explorations of the possible effects of a drop in the value of the home currency on the trade balance or the net balance on the current account.[1] It derives a general formula for such effects and applies it to some special cases that establish the range of possible results.

CURRENT ACCOUNT ELASTICITIES

The current account (or trade) balance defined in foreign currency (here, pounds, the foreign currency) is[2]

$$CA_£ = V_x - V_m = P_x^£ X - P_m^£ M \tag{H.l}$$

where V_x is the value of exports and V_m is the value of imports. To derive the elasticity of the current account balance with respect to the exchange rate, begin by differentiating the balance:

$$dCA_£ = dV_x - dV_m \tag{H.2}$$

or

$$dCA_£/V_m = dV_x/V_m - dV_m/V_m \tag{H.3}$$

Let us define

$E_{ca} = \dfrac{dCA_£/V_m}{de/e} =$ The elasticity of the current account balance with respect to e, the exchange rate (measured as the price of the foreign currency, \$/£)

$E_x = \dfrac{dV_x/V_x}{de/e} =$ The elasticity of the value of exports with respect to the exchange rate, e

$E_m = \dfrac{dV_m/V_m}{de/e} =$ The elasticity of the value of imports with respect to the exchange rate, e

[1]There are other determinants of the current account balance besides the exchange rate, of course. We focus on the role of exchange-rate changes.

[2]The derivation follows that given in Jaroslav Vanek (1962).

Then if we divide both sides of (H.3) by the proportion of change in the exchange rate (de/e), we get

$$E_{ca} = \frac{V_x}{V_m} E_x - E_m \tag{H.4}$$

Deriving the formula for the effect of the exchange rate on the current account balance amounts to deriving a formula relating E_{ca} to the underlying elasticities of demand and supply for exports and imports.

EXPORT AND IMPORT ELASTICITIES

The export (or import) value is defined as the product of a trade price and a traded quantity. We therefore need to derive expressions giving the elasticities of these trade prices and quantities with respect to the exchange rate. Let's do so on the export side. There the supply, which depends on a dollar price ($P_x^\$ = P_x^\pounds \cdot e$), must be equated with demand, which depends on a pound price. We start with the equilibrium condition in the export market, differentiate it, and keep rearranging terms until the equation takes a form relating elasticities to the change in export prices:

$$X = S_x(P_x^\pounds e) = D_x(P_x^\pounds) \tag{H.5}$$

$$dX = \frac{\partial S_x}{\partial P_x^\$}(edP_x^\pounds + P_x^\pounds de) = \frac{\partial D_x}{\partial P_x^\pounds} dP_x^\pounds \tag{H.6}$$

$$dX/X = \frac{\partial S_x}{\partial P_x^\$}\frac{1}{S_x}(edP_x^\pounds + P_x^\pounds de) = \frac{\partial D_x}{\partial P_x^\pounds}\frac{1}{D_x} dP_x^\pounds \tag{H.7}$$

Multiplying within each of the latter two expressions by ratios based on $P_x^\$/e = P_x^\pounds$ and dividing all three expressions by de/e yields

$$\frac{dX/X}{de/e} = \left[\frac{\partial S_x}{\partial P_x^\$}\frac{P_x^\$}{S_x}\right]\left(\frac{dP_x^\pounds/P_x^\pounds}{de/e} + 1\right) = \left[\frac{\partial D_x}{\partial P_x^\pounds}\frac{P_x^\pounds}{D_x}\right]\frac{dP_x^\pounds/P_x^\pounds}{de/e} \tag{H.8}$$

The expressions in brackets on the left and right are the elasticities of export supply (s_x) and demand (d_x), respectively, so that

$$\frac{dX/X}{de/e} = s_x\left(\frac{dP_x^\pounds/P_x^\pounds}{de/e} + 1\right) = d_x\frac{dP_x^\pounds/P_x^\pounds}{de/e} \tag{H.9}$$

and the percent response of the pound price of exports to the exchange rate is

$$\frac{dP_x^\pounds/P_x^\pounds}{de/e} = \frac{s_x}{d_x - s_x} \tag{H.10}$$

This has to be negative or zero because d_x is negative or zero and s_x is positive or zero. (The response of the dollar price of exports to the exchange rate equals this same expression plus one.)

Recalling that the value of exports equals the price times the quantity of exports, we can use the fact that any percent change in this export value equals the percent price change plus the percent quantity change:

$$E_x = \frac{dX/X}{de/e} + \frac{dP_x^{£}/P_x^{£}}{de/e}$$ (H.11)

From (H.9) and (H.10), we get the relationship between the elasticity of the value of exports and the elasticities of demand and supply of exports:

$$E_x = \frac{d_x s_x}{d_x - s_x} + \frac{s_x}{d_x - s_x} = \frac{d_x + 1}{(d_x/s_x) - 1}$$ (H.12)

which can be of any sign.

Going through all the same steps on the imports side yields expressions for the responses of the pound price of imports, the quantity of imports, and the value of imports with respect to the exchange rate:

$$\frac{dP_m^{£}/P_m^{£}}{de/e} = \frac{d_m}{s_m - d_m} \ (\leq 0)$$ (H.13)

$$\frac{dM/M}{de/e} = \frac{s_m d_m}{s_m - d_m} \ (\leq 0)$$ (H.14)

and

$$E_m = \frac{s_m + 1}{(s_m/d_m) - 1} \ (\leq 0)$$ (H.15)

THE GENERAL TRADE BALANCE FORMULA AND THE MARSHALL–LERNER CONDITION

We have now gathered all the materials we need to give the general formula for the elasticity of response of the current account (or trade) balance to the exchange rate. From (H.4), (H.12), and (H.15), the formula is

The elasticity of the trade balance with respect to the exchange rate =

$$E_{ca} = \frac{V_x}{V_m} \left(\frac{d_x + 1}{(d_x/s_x) - 1} \right) - \frac{s_m + 1}{(s_m/d_m) - 1}$$ (H.16)

By studying this general formula and some of its special cases, we can determine what elasticities are crucial in making the trade balance response stable (i.e., in making E_{ca} positive). It turns out that

the more elastic are import demand and export demand, the more "stable" (positive) will be the response of the current account balance.

Demand elasticities are crucial, but supply elasticities have no clear general effect on the trade balance response.

FIGURE H.1

Devaluation and the Trade Balance: Applying the General Formula to Special Cases

	Assumed Elasticities	Effect of Devaluation on the Trade Balance
Case 1: Inelastic demands	$d_m = d_x = 0$	Trade balance worsens: $$E_{ca} = -\frac{V_x}{V_m} < 0$$
Case 2: Small country	$s_m = -d_x = \infty$	Trade balance improves: $$E_{ca} = \frac{V_x}{V_m} s_x - d_m > 0$$
Case 3: Prices fixed in buyers' currencies	$d_m = d_x = -\infty$	Trade balance improves: $$E_{ca} = \frac{V_x}{V_m} s_x + s_m + 1 > 0$$
Case 4: Prices fixed in sellers' currencies	$s_x = s_m = \infty$	It depends: $$E_{ca} = \frac{V_x}{V_m}(-d_x - 1) - d_m \gtreqless 0$$

In Case 4, if trade was not initially in surplus, then the Marshall–Lerner condition is sufficient for improvement: $|d_x + d_m| > 1$.

These results can be appreciated more easily after we have considered four important special cases listed in Figure H.1. The perverse result of a trade balance that worsens after the domestic currency has been devalued is the *inelastic-demand case*, discussed in Chapter 23. As shown in Figure H.1, this Case 1, in which $d_m = d_x = 0$, yields clear perversity regardless of the initial state of the trade balance. The "J curve" of Chapter 23 is based on the suspicion that this case may sometimes obtain in the short run, before demand elasticities have had a chance to rise.

A second special case, also discussed in Chapter 23, is the *small-country case*, in which both export prices and import prices are fixed in terms of foreign currencies in large outside-world markets. This Case 2 is represented in Figure H.1 by infinite foreign elasticities: $s_m = -d_x = \infty$. In the small-country case, devaluation or depreciation of the home currency definitely improves the current account balance.

Consistent with the emphasis on the importance of demand elasticities is the extreme result for Case 3. With *prices fixed in buyers' currencies*, for example, by infinitely elastic demands for imports both at home and abroad ($d_m = d_x = -\infty$), the general formula yields the most improvement.

The fourth special case considered here is one in which *prices are kept fixed in sellers' currencies*. This fits the Keynesian family of macromodels, in which supplies are infinitely elastic and prices are fixed within countries. In Case 4, the net effect of devaluation on the current account balance depends on a famous condition, the **Marshall–Lerner condition,** which says that the absolute value of the sum of the two demand elasticities must exceed unity: $|d_x + d_m| > 1$. This is sufficient for a stable result if the current account balance is not initially in surplus (i.e., if $V_x \leq V_m$, as is typical of devaluations). While the Marshall–Lerner condition strictly is definitive only in a narrow range of models, it is a rougher guide to the likelihood of the stable result because it reminds us of the overall pattern that higher demand elasticities give more stable results.

Suggested Answers to Odd-Numbered Questions and Problems

Chapter 2

1. Consumer surplus is the net gain to consumers from being able to buy a product through a market. It is the difference between the highest price someone is willing to pay for each unit of the product and the actual market price that is paid, summed over all units that are demanded and consumed. The highest price that someone is willing to pay for the unit indicates the value that the buyer attaches to that unit. To measure consumer surplus for a product using real-world data, three major pieces of information are needed: (1) the market price, (2) the quantity demanded, and (3) the slope (or shape) of the demand curve in terms of how quantity demanded would change if the market price increased. Consumer surplus could then be measured as the area below the demand curve and above the market-price line.

3. The country's supply of exports is the amount by which the country's domestic quantity supplied exceeds the country's domestic quantity demanded. The supply-of-exports curve is derived by finding the difference between domestic quantity supplied and domestic quantity demanded for each possible market price for which quantity supplied exceeds quantity demanded. The supply-of-exports curve shows the quantity that the country would want to export for each possible international market price.

5. There is no domestic market for winter coats in this tropical country, but there is a domestic supply curve. If the world price for coats is above the minimum price at which the country would supply any coats (the price at which the supply curve hits the price axis), then in free trade the country would produce and export

coats. The country gains from this trade because it creates producer surplus—the area above the supply curve and below the international price line, up to the intersection (which indicates the quantity that the country will produce and export).

7. It is true that opening trade bids prices into equality between countries. With a competitive market this also means that marginal costs are equal between countries. But ongoing trade is necessary to maintain this equilibrium. If trade were to stop, the world would return to the no-trade equilibrium. Then prices would differ, and there would be an incentive for arbitrage. The ongoing trade in the free-trade equilibrium is why prices are equalized—trade is not self-eliminating.

9. The demand curve D_{US} shifts to the right. The U.S. demand-for-imports curve D_m shifts to the right. The equilibrium international price rises above 1,000. It is shown by the intersection of the new U.S. D_m curve and the original S_x curve.

11. For the first country, for any world free-trade equilibrium price above $2.00 per kilogram, the country will want to export raisins. For the other country, for any world free-trade equilibrium price above $3.20 per kilogram, this other country will also want to export raisins. With only sellers (exporters) internationally and no buyers (importers) internationally, the international market cannot be in equilibrium. Instead, at this high price, there is an excess supply of raisins. As the graphs on the next page show, at the price of $3.50 per kilogram, both countries want to export—at that price, domestic quantity supplied exceeds domestic quantity demanded for each country.

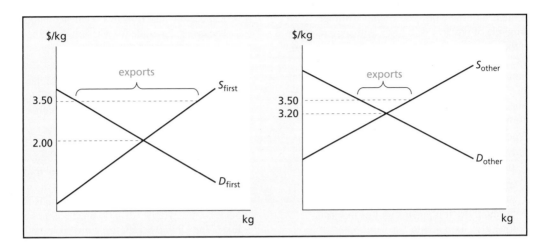

13. a. With no international trade, equilibrium requires that domestic quantity demanded (Q_D) equals domestic quantity supplied (Q_S). Setting the two equations equal to each other, we can find the equilibrium price with no trade:

$$350 - (P/2) = -200 + 5P$$

The equilibrium no-trade price is $P = 100$. Using one of the equations, we find that the no-trade quantity is 300.

   b. At a price of 120, Belgium's quantity demanded is 290 and its quantity supplied is 400. With free trade Belgium exports 110 units.

   c. Belgian consumer surplus declines. With no trade it is a larger triangle below the demand curve and above the 100 price line. With free trade it is a smaller triangle below the demand curve and above the 120 price line.

   Belgian producer surplus increases. With no trade it is a smaller triangle above the supply curve and below the 100 price line. With free trade it is a larger triangle above the supply curve and below the 120 price line. The net national gain from trade is the difference between the gain of producer surplus and the loss of consumer surplus. This net national gain is a triangle whose base is the quantity traded (110) and whose height is the change in price ($120 - 100 = 20$), so the total gain is 1,100.

Chapter 3

1. Disagree. This statement describes absolute advantage. It would imply that a country that has a higher labor productivity in all goods would export all goods and import nothing. Ricardo instead showed that mutually beneficial trade is based on comparative advantage— trading according to maximum relative advantage. The country will export those goods whose *relative* labor productivity (relative to the other country *and* relative to other goods) is high, and import those other goods whose relative labor productivity is low.

3. Disagree. Mercantilism recommends that a country should export as much as it can because of the purported benefits of large exports. In its original form mercantilism argued that exports were good because the country could receive gold and silver in payment for its exports. In its modern form exports are good because they create jobs in the country. Mercantilism does not hold local consumption to be as important an objective as gold and silver (original version) or employment (modern version).

5. Using the information on the number of labor hours to make a unit of each product in each country, you can determine the relative price of cloth in each country with no trade. With no trade, the relative price of cloth is 2 W/C ($= 4/2$) in the United States, and it is 0.4 W/C ($= 1/2.5$)

in the rest of the world. Using the arbitrage principle of buy low–sell high, you acquire cloth in the rest of the world, giving up 0.4 wheat unit for each cloth unit that you buy. You export the cloth to the United States and sell each cloth unit for 2 wheat units. Your *profit* is 1.6 (= 2.0 – 0.4) wheat units for each unit of cloth that you export from the rest of the world.

(You could also explain the arbitrage as buying and exporting wheat from the United States.)

7. a. Pugelovia has an absolute disadvantage in both goods. Its labor input per unit of output is higher for both goods, so its labor productivity (output per unit of input) is lower for both goods.

   b. Pugelovia has a comparative advantage in producing rice. Its relative disadvantage is lower (75/50 < 100/50).

   c. With no trade, the relative price of rice would be 75/100 = 0.75 unit of cloth per unit of rice.

   d. With free trade the equilibrium international price ratio will be greater than or equal to 0.75 cloth unit per rice unit and less than or equal to 1.0 cloth unit per rice unit (the no-trade price ratio in the rest of the world). Pugelovia will export rice and import cloth.

9. a. With no trade, the real wages in the United States are 1/2 = 0.5 wheat unit per hour and 1/4 = 0.25 cloth unit per hour. The real wages in the rest of the world are 1/1.5 = 0.67 wheat unit per hour and 1/1 = 1.0 cloth unit per hour. The absolute advantages (higher labor productivities) in the rest of the world translate into higher real wages in the rest of the world.

   b. With free trade the United States completely specializes in producing wheat. The U.S. real wage with respect to wheat remains 0.5 wheat unit per hour. Cloth is obtained by trade at a price ratio of one, so the U.S. real wage with respect to cloth is 0.5 cloth unit per hour. The gains from trade for the United States are shown by the higher real wage with respect to cloth (0.5 > 0.25). As long as U.S. labor wants to buy some cloth, the United States gains from trade by gaining greater purchasing power over cloth. With free trade the rest of the world completely specializes in producing cloth. Its real wage with respect to cloth is unchanged at 1.0 cloth unit per hour. Its real wage with

respect to wheat rises to 1.0 wheat unit per hour because it can trade for wheat at the price ratio of one. The rest of the world gains from greater purchasing power over wheat.

   c. The rest of the world still has the higher real wage. Absolute advantage matters—higher labor productivity translates into higher real wages.

11. For the United States (left side of Figure 3.1), the new trade line still begins at the production point S_1, and it is steeper than the initial trade line shown in the figure. The intercept of the new trade line with the horizontal axis is 50/1.2 = 41.7 (rather than 50 for the initial trade line). The United States still gains from trade—it can consume more than it can consume with no trade (at point S_0). But the United States gains less when the world price is 1.2 W/C because the new trade line is inside of the initial trade line. The United States is not able to consume at the initial trade-enabled consumption point C.

   For the rest of the world (right side of Figure 3.1), the new trade line begins at the production point S_1 and is steeper than the trade line shown in the figure. The intercept of the new trade line with the vertical axis is 100 × 1.2 = 120 (rather than 100 for the initial trade line). The rest of the world gains from trade—it can consume more than it can consume with no trade (at point S_0). And the rest of the world gains more when the world price is 1.2 W/C, because the new trade line is outside of the initial trade line. The rest of the world is able to consume at points on the new trade line that allow more consumption of both goods than at the initial trade-enabled consumption point C.

Chapter 4

1. Disagree. The Hecksher–Ohlin theory indicates that two countries will trade with each other because of differences in their relative endowments of the various factors that are needed to produce the products. Each country will export products that use its relatively abundant factors intensively and import products that use its relatively scarce factors intensively. Even if there are no technology differences that otherwise could drive international trade, the Heckscher–Ohlin theory indicates that the countries may still trade a lot

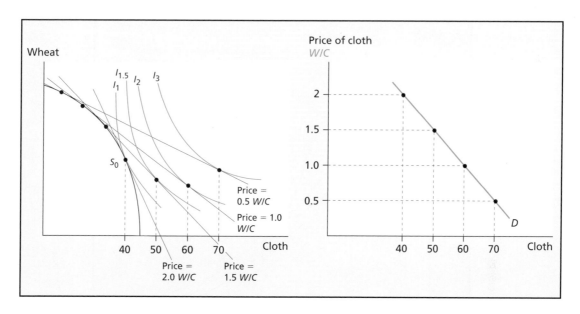

with each other as long as there are differences in the relative availability of factor inputs between the countries.

3. Pugelovia has 20 percent of the world's labor [20/(20 + 80)], whereas it has 30 percent [3/(3 + 7)] of the world's land. Pugelovia is land-abundant and labor-scarce relative to the rest of the world. H–O theory predicts that Pugelovia will export the land-intensive good (wheat) and import the labor-intensive good (cloth).

5. To derive the country's cloth demand curve, we need to find the price line for each price ratio, and then find the tangency with a community indifference curve. The tangency indicates the quantity demanded at that price ratio. The price line has the slope indicated by the price ratio, and it is tangent to the country's production-possibility curve. (This tangency indicates the country's production at this price ratio.) As each price ratio is lower, the tangency with the production-possibility curve shifts to the northwest, as shown in the graph above. As the price line shifts and becomes flatter, the tangency with a community indifference curve shifts to the right. Representative numbers are shown, with each decrease of price by 0.5 increasing quantity demanded by 10.

7. a. With increasing marginal opportunity cost, Puglia's production-possibility curve has a

bowed-out shape, as shown in the graph on the next page. With no international trade, the country produces and consumes at the point at which one of Puglia's community indifference curves (I_1) is tangent to the production-possibility curve at point N. The slope of the price line at this tangency indicates that the no-trade relative price of pasta is 4.

b. The world relative price of pasta (3) is lower than Puglia's no-trade relative price (4), so Puglia will import pasta. Looked at the other way, the world relative price of togas (1/3) is higher than Puglia's no-trade price (1/4), so Puglia will export togas. In the graph on the next page the price line whose slope indicates a relative price of 3 T/P is tangent to the production-possibility curve at point R. With free trade, production of pasta declines in Puglia and resources shift to producing togas. With the price line based on the relative price of 3 T/P and production at point R, Puglia chooses its consumption to reach the highest possible community indifference curve (I_2), the one that is tangent to this price line at point V.

c. Puglia gains from trade. One way to see this is that trade allows Puglia to consume amounts of the two products that are beyond its own abilities to produce these products (point V is

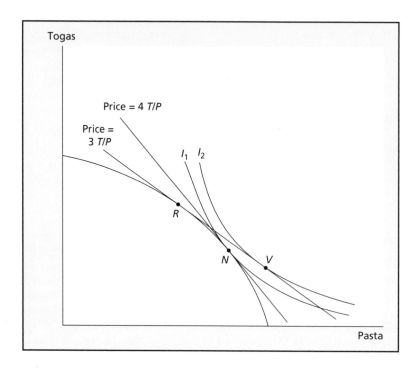

outside of the ppc). Another way to see this is that Puglia reaches a higher community indifference curve (I_2 is better that I_1).

9. In Figure 4.4A, the shape of the U.S. production-possibility curve skews toward producing wheat, and the rest of the world production-possibility curve skews toward producing cloth. The Heckscher–Ohlin theory has a specific explanation for the skew. The United States has relatively a lot of the factor inputs (e.g., land) that are most important for producing wheat, so the United States is relatively strong at producing wheat. The rest of the world has relatively a lot of the factor inputs (e.g., labor) that are most important for producing cloth, so the rest of the world is relatively strong at producing cloth.

11. a. They could make 7 wheat, with no cloth production.

   b. They could make 6 cloth, with no wheat production.

   c. The ppc is not a straight line between (6 cloth, 0 wheat) and (0 cloth, 7 wheat). Rather, it has four parts with different slopes.

Here is a tour of the ppc, starting down on the cloth axis (x axis). They could produce anything from (6 cloth, 0 wheat) up to (5, 2) by having A shift between cloth and wheat while the others make only cloth. Then they could make anything from (5, 2) up to (3, 5) by keeping A busy growing wheat and B and C busy at cloth, while D switches between the two tasks. Then they could make anything from (3, 5) up to (2, 6) by choosing how to divide C's time, keeping B in wheat making and A and D in cloth. Finally, they could make anything between (2, 6) and (0, 7) by varying B's tasks while the others make cloth.

   Study this result to see how the right assignments relate to people's comparative advantages. Note that, with four different kinds of comparative advantage, there is a bowed-out curve with four slopes. In general, the greater the number of different kinds of individuals, the smoother and more bowed out the curve. Therefore, we get an increasing-cost ppc for the nation, even if every individual is a Ricardian constant-cost type.

Chapter 5

1. Mexico is abundant in unskilled labor and scarce in skilled labor relative to the United States or Canada. With freer trade Mexico exports a greater volume of unskilled-labor-intensive products and imports a greater volume of skilled-labor-intensive products. According to the Stolper–Samuelson theorem, a shift toward freer trade then increases the real wage of unskilled labor in Mexico, reduces the real wage of unskilled labor in the United States or Canada, decreases the real wage of skilled labor in Mexico, and increases the real wage of skilled labor in the United States or Canada.

3. Disagree. Opening up free trade does hurt people in import-competing industries in the short run—essentially due to the loss of producer surplus. The long-run effects are different because people and resources can move between industries, but everyone will not gain in the long run. If trade develops according to the Heckscher–Ohlin theory, then the owners of the factors of production that are relatively scarce in the country lose real income. Because the country imports products that are intensive in these factors, trade effectively makes these factors "less scarce" and reduces their returns.

5. Leontief conducted his research shortly after World War II, when it seemed clear that the United States was abundant in capital and scarce in labor, relative to the rest of the world. According to the Heckscher–Ohlin theory, the United States then should export capital-intensive products and import labor-intensive products. But in his empirical work using data on production in the United States and U.S. trade flows, Leontief found that the United States exported relatively labor-intensive products and imported relatively capital-intensive products.

7. Yes. The Heckscher–Ohlin theory states that a country will export products that require (in their production) relatively large amounts of the country's relatively abundant factor inputs. First, consider the relatively abundant factor inputs in China and South Korea. As shown in Figure 5.3 (reading across the row for China), China is relatively abundant in medium-skilled labor, with 27.8 percent of the world total. (China is also abundant in physical capital and unskilled labor.) South Korea is relatively abundant in highly skilled labor and physical capital, with 2.6 and 2.3 percent of the world's total, respectively. Second, apply this information to the product examples. China, abundant in medium-skilled and unskilled labor, exports basic bulk-carrying ships, which require relatively intensive general use of labor in production. South Korea, relatively abundant in highly skilled labor, exports complex ships, which depend more on the relatively intensive use of highly skilled labor for technical work and design.

9. a. With prices of 100, the two equations are
$$100 = 60w + 40r$$
$$100 = 75w + 25r$$
Solving these simultaneously, the equilibrium wage rate is 1 and the equilibrium rental rate is 1. The labor cost per unit of wheat output is 60 (60 units of labor at a cost of 1 per unit of labor). The labor cost per unit of cloth is 75. The rental cost per unit of wheat is 40. The rental cost per unit of cloth is 25.

b. With the new price of cloth, the two equations are
$$100 = 60w + 40r$$
$$120 = 75w + 25r$$
Solving these simultaneously, we see that the new equilibrium wage rate is about 1.53 and the new equilibrium rental rate is 0.2.

c. The real wage with respect to wheat increases from 0.01 (or 1/100) to about 0.0153 (or 1.53/100). The real wage with respect to cloth increases from 0.01 (or 1/100) to about 0.01275 (or 1.53/120). On average the real wage is higher—labor benefits from the increase in the price of cloth. The real rental rate with respect to wheat decreases from 0.01 (or 1/100) to 0.002 (or 0.2/100). With respect to cloth it decreases from 0.01 (or 1/100) to about 0.0017 (or 0.2/120). On average the real rental rate is lower—landowners lose real income as a result of this increase in the price of cloth.

d. These results are an example of the Stolper–Samuelson theorem. Wheat is relatively intensive in land, and cloth is relatively intensive in labor. The increase in the price of cloth raises the real income of labor (its intensive factor) and lowers the real income of the other factor (land).

11. The total input share of labor in each dollar of cloth output is the sum of the direct use of labor plus the labor that is used to produce the material inputs into cloth production:

$$0.5 + 0.1 \times 0.3 + 0.2 \times 0.6 = 0.65$$

The total input share of capital is calculated in the same way:

$$0.2 + 0.1 \times 0.7 + 0.2 \times 0.4 = 0.35$$

Cloth is labor-intensive relative to the country's import substitutes ($0.65 > 0.55$). Thus the country's trade pattern is consistent with the Heckscher–Ohlin theory. This labor-abundant country exports the labor-intensive product.

Chapter 6

1. Disagree. The Heckscher–Ohlin theory indicates that countries should export some products (products that are intensive in the country's abundant factors) and import other products (products that are intensive in the country's scarce factors). Heckscher–Ohlin theory predicts the pattern of interindustry trade. It does not predict that countries would engage in a lot of intra-industry trade, which involves both exporting and importing products that are the same (or very similar).

3. There are two major reasons. First, product differentiation can result in intra-industry trade. Imports do not lead to lower domestic output of the product because exports provide demand for much of the output that previously was sold at home. Output levels do not change much between industries, so there are (1) little shift between industries in factor demand and (2) little pressure on factor prices. There are likely to be fewer losers from Stolper–Samuelson effects. Second, there is a gain from trade that is shared by everyone—the gain from having access to greater product variety through trade. Some groups that otherwise might believe that they are losers because of trade can instead believe that they are winners if they place enough value on this access to greater product variety.

5. Disagree. External scale economies are cost or quality advantages to firms in an industry that locate close to each other, that is, in the same small geographic area. The key influence of external scale economies on the pattern of international trade is that they lead to a small number of locations producing much of the world output of the industry's product because firms in these locations benefit from the external scale economies. Countries that have such centers of large production become the exporting countries, and countries without them, the importing countries. The activities of firms in these centers could include the creation of product varieties, but they need not. Variety is not necessary to the explanation of why external scale economies affect the pattern of trade.

7. a. Consumers in Pugelovia are likely to experience two types of effects from the opening of trade. First, consumers gain access to the varieties of products produced by foreign firms, as these varieties can now be imported. Consumers gain from greater product variety. Second, the additional competition from imports can lower the prices of the domestically produced varieties, creating an additional gain for domestic consumers.

   b. Producers in Pugelovia also are likely to experience two types of effects from the opening of trade. First, imports add extra competition for domestic sales. As we noted in the answer to part a, this is likely to force domestic producers to lower their prices, and some sales will be lost to imports. Second, domestic producers gain access to a new market, the foreign market. They are likely to be able to make additional sales as exports to consumers in the foreign market who prefer these producers' varieties over the ones produced locally there.

9. We can use a graph like Figure 6.5, as shown on the next page, to examine the change in the number of models. In the initial situation, the global market was in equilibrium with 40 models and a typical price of $600 per washer. The increase in global demand shifts the unit cost curve from UC_0 to UC_1. Here is one way to see why the unit cost curve shifts this way. For any given number of models, each firm would

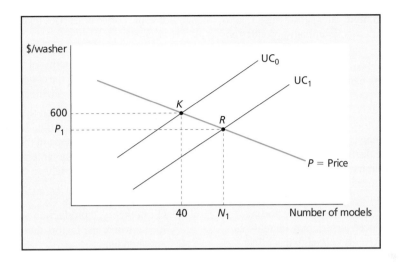

be able to produce more units of its own version with greater demand, so each firm would be able to achieve additional scale economies that would lower its unit cost. Therefore, the unit cost curve shifts down. With the new unit cost curve UC_1, the new long-run equilibrium is at point R, with a typical price P_1 less than $600 and the number of models N_1 larger than 40. How did we get from the initial equilibrium to the new long-run equilibrium? With the increase in global demand, the firms producing the initial 40 models began to earn economic profits. The positive profits attracted the entry of additional firms that offered new models. With the entry of new firms and new models, the demand for each of the established firms' models eroded. In addition, the arrival of new close substitute models increased the price elasticity of demand for each model. The decrease in demand for each model and the increase in the price elasticity forced each firm to lower the price of its model. The new long-run equilibrium occurs when the typical firm is back to earning zero economic profit on its model. This occurs with a larger total number of models offered, and with a lower price for the typical model.

11. a. Here is the calculation for perfumes: IIT share $= 1 - [|3 - 234|/(3 + 234)] = 0.025$ (or 2.5%). Using the same type of calculation for the other products, here are the IIT shares for each product:

Perfumes	2.5%
Cosmetics	95.6
Household clothes washing machines	0.6
Electronic microcircuits	76.8
Automobiles	20.1
Photographic cameras	59.5
Book and brochures	55.3

b. For Japan, total trade in these seven products is $157,676 million. The weighted average of the IIT shares is

$(6/157,676) \times 2.5 + (2,366/157,676) \times 95.6 + (6/157,676) \times 0.6 + (34,912/157,676) \times 76.8 + (21,764/157,676) \times 20.1 + (22/157,676) \times 59.5 + (192/157,676) \times 55.3 = 37.6\%$

The United States has relatively more IIT in these products.

13. a. External scale economies mean that the average costs of production decline as the size of an industry in a specific geographic area increases. With free trade and external economies, production will tend to concentrate in one geographic area to achieve these external economies. Whichever area is able to increase its production can lower its average costs. Lower costs permit firms in this area to lower their prices so

that they gain more sales, grow bigger, and achieve lower costs. Eventually production occurs in only one country (or geographic area) that produces with low costs.

b. Both countries gain from trade in products with external economies. The major effect is that the average cost of production declines as production is concentrated in one geographic area. If the industry is competitive, then the product price declines as costs decline. In the importing country, consumers' gains from lower prices more than offset the loss of producer surplus as the local industry ceases to produce the product. In the exporting country, producer surplus may increase as production expands, although this effect is countered by the decrease in the price that producers charge for their products. In the exporting country, consumer surplus increases as the product price declines. Thus the exporting country can gain for two reasons: an increase in producer surplus and an increase in consumer surplus.

Chapter 7

1. By expanding its export industries, Pugelovia wants to sell more exports to the rest of the world. This increase in export supply tends to lower the international prices of its export products, so the Pugelovian terms of trade (price of exports relative to the price of imports) tend to decline.

3. The drought itself reduces production in these Latin American countries and tends to lower their well-being. (Their production-possibility curves shrink inward.) But the lower export supply of coffee tends to raise the international price of coffee, so the terms of trade of these Latin American countries tend to improve. The improved terms of trade tend to raise well-being. (The purchasing power of their exports rises.) If their terms of trade improve enough, the countries' well-being improves. The greater purchasing power of the remaining exports is a larger effect than the loss of export (and production) volumes. The gain in well-being is more likely (1) if these Latin American countries represent a large part of world coffee supply, so that their supply reduction can have a noticeable impact on the world price; (2) if foreign demand for coffee is price-inelastic (as it probably is), so

that the coffee price rises by a lot when supply declines; and (3) if exports of coffee are a major part of the countries' economies, so that the improvement in the terms of trade can have a noticeable benefit to the countries. (This answer is an example of immiserizing growth "in reverse.")

5. R&D is a production activity that is intensive in the use of highly skilled labor (scientists and engineers) and perhaps in the use of capital that is willing to take large risks (e.g., venture capital). The industrialized countries are relatively abundant in highly skilled labor and in risk-taking capital. According to Heckscher–Ohlin theory, a production activity tends to locate where the factors that it uses intensively are abundant.

7. a. This is balanced growth through increases in factor endowments. The production-possibility curve shifts out proportionately, so that its relative shape is the same.

b. This is balanced growth through technology improvements of similar magnitude in both industries. The production-possibility curve shifts out proportionately, so that its relative shape is the same.

c. The intercept of the production-possibility curve with the cloth axis does not change. (If there is no wheat production, then the improved wheat technology does not add to the country's production.) The rest of the production-possibility curve shifts out. This is growth biased toward wheat production.

9. a. The entire U.S. production-possibility curve shifts out, with the outward shift relatively larger for the good that is intensive in capital. If the U.S. trade pattern follows the Heckscher–Ohlin theory, then this good is machinery. Growth is biased toward machinery production.

b. According to the Rybczynski theorem, the quantity produced of machinery increases and the quantity produced of clothing decreases if the product price ratio is unchanged. The extra capital is employed in producing more machinery, and the machinery industry must also employ some extra labor to use with the extra capital. The extra labor is drawn from the clothing industry, so clothing production declines.

c. The U.S. willingness to trade increases. With growth of production and income, the United States wants to consume more of both goods. Demand for imports of clothing increases because domestic consumption increases while domestic production decreases. (Supply of exports also increases because the increase in domestic production of machinery is larger than the increase in domestic consumption.)

d. The increase in demand for imports tends to increase the international equilibrium relative price of clothing. (The increase in supply of exports tends to lower the international equilibrium relative price of machinery.)

e. The change in the international equilibrium price ratio is a decline in the U.S. terms of trade. U.S. well-being could decline— immiserizing growth is possible. If the decline in the terms of trade is large enough, then this negative effect can be larger than the positive effect of growth in production capabilities.

11. a. The U.S. production-possibility curve shifts out for all points except its intercept with the food axis. This is growth biased toward clothing production.

b. The U.S. willingness to trade probably decreases because the United States is now capable of producing its import good at a lower cost. Although the extra production and income lead to an increase in U.S. demand for clothing, the expansion of the supply of clothing that results from the improved technology is likely to be larger, so U.S. demand for clothing imports probably decreases.

c. The decrease in U.S. demand for imports reduces the equilibrium international relative price of clothing. The U.S. terms of trade improve.

13. a. With unchanged product prices, wheat production increases by 25 percent [= (50 − 40)/40]. Cloth also increases by 25 percent [= (80 − 64)/64]. This is balanced growth.

b. Along the new production-possibility curve, the change in product prices has caused production of wheat to increase from 50 to 52 units, and production of cloth to decrease

from 80 to 77 units. The relative price of wheat increased (or, equivalently, the relative price of cloth decreased).

15. South Korea allowed more international trade with the rest of world, and this probably contributed in important ways to the country's rapid growth since the 1960s. First, the country benefited from the standard gains from trade. Factor inputs were reallocated across industries toward their most productive uses, raising the value of national production and income. South Korean households gained by buying cheaper and more varied foreign products. Second, and probably more important, the country's firms benefited from access to foreign technologies. Through imports Korean firms gained access to innovative machinery that brought new and better technology into the country. Korean firms more generally gained greater awareness of foreign technologies. Once aware, they could find ways to bring these technologies into use in Korea, through import purchases, licensing, and imitation. Third, international trade puts competitive pressure on South Korean firms (e.g., Samsung) to raise their productivity, through more cost-effective employment of factors and through improved products and production technology. South Korean firms increased their own research and development activities to try to gain their own technology advantages. In contrast, North Korea largely remained closed to the rest of the world. It did not achieve gains from trade, and its production does not quickly incorporate foreign technology. It remains a very poor country.

Chapter 8

1. You can calculate it if you know only the size of the tariff and the amount by which it would reduce imports. (See Figure 8.4.)

3. The production effect of a tariff is the deadweight loss to the nation that occurs because the tariff encourages some high-cost domestic production (production that is inefficient by the world standard of the international price). Producing the extra domestic output that occurs when the tariff is imposed has a domestic resource cost that is higher than the international price that the country would have to pay to the foreign

exporters to acquire these units as imports with free trade. The domestic resource cost of each unit produced is shown by the height of the domestic supply curve. Thus, the production effect is the triangle above the free-trade world price line and below the domestic supply curve, for the units between domestic production quantity with free trade and domestic production quantity with the tariff. It can be calculated as one-half of the product of the change in domestic price caused by the tariff and the change in production quantity caused by the tariff.

5. (a) Consumers gain $420 million per year.
(b) Producers lose $140 million per year.
(c) The government loses $240 million per year. (d) The country as a whole gains $40 million a year.

7. (a) Consumers gain $5,125,000. (b) Producers lose $1,875,000. (c) The government loses $6,000,000 in tariff revenue.
(d) The country as a whole loses $2,750,000 each year from removing the tariff. The national loss stems from the fact that the tariff removal raises the world price paid on imported motorcycles. In question 5, removing the duty had no effect on the world price (of sugar).

9. The $1.25 is made up of 60 cents of value added, 35 cents of cotton payments, and 30 cents of payments for other fibers. The effective rate is (60¢ – 40¢)/40¢ = 50%.

11. Agree. Consider the example shown in Figure 8.5. The free-trade world price is $300 per bike. The country then imposes a $6 tariff. Because the country is large, the price charged by exporters falls to $297 per bike. With the $6 tariff, the domestic price rises to $303 per bike. Area *e* is the gain to the country by paying less to foreign exporters ($297 rather than $300 for each bike imported). We can look at this in a different way, focusing on who pays the tariff. The total tariff revenue collected by the government is area *c* plus area *e* ($6 times the number of bikes imported). Who actually pays this tariff revenue? Compared to the no-tariff (free-trade) initial situation ($300 per bike), domestic consumers pay $3 per bike ($303 – $300) and foreign exporters effectively pay (or absorb) the other $3 per bike ($300 – $297). That is, the foreign exporters in

total effectively pay area *e*, a part of the total tariff revenue collected by the government. This is another way to look at why a large country can gain by imposing a tariff.

Chapter 9

1. Import quotas are government-decreed quantitative limits on the total quantity of a product that can be imported into the country during a given period of time. Here are three reasons why a government might want to use a quota rather than a tariff: (1) Quotas ensure that imports will not exceed the amount set by the quota. This can be useful if the government wants to assure domestic producers that imports are actually limited. (2) A quota gives government officials greater power and discretion over who gets the valuable right to import. (3) The government may accede to the desires of domestic producers who could have monopoly pricing power if import competition is removed at the margin. For instance, a quota would be preferred by a domestic monopoly because the monopoly could raise its price with no fear of growing imports as long as a quota limits the quantity imported.

A quota does not bring a greater national gain. From the point of view of the national interest, a quota is no better than an equivalent tariff, and it may be worse.

3. This would happen if the domestic product market were perfectly competitive and the import quota rights were auctioned off competitively.

5. The tariff would be less damaging to the United States because it gives the United States the tariff revenue that instead would be a price markup pocketed by foreign bulldozer makers with a VER. Both would bring the same overall loss in world welfare.

7. a. The change in producer surplus is a gain of $0.02 per pound for the 120 million pounds that are produced with free trade *plus* the producer surplus on the increased production of 40 million pounds. The latter is 1/2 × $0.02 per pound × 40 million pounds (assuming a straight-line domestic supply curve). The gain in producer surplus totals $2.8 million.

b. The change in consumer surplus is a loss of $0.02 per pound for the 400 million pounds that the consumers continue to purchase

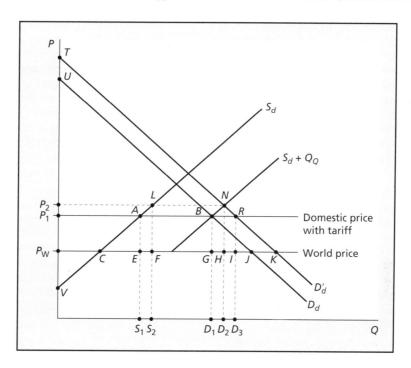

after the quota is imposed *plus* the loss of consumer surplus on the 20 million pounds that consumers no longer purchase because of the quota. The latter is $1/2 \times \$0.02 \times 20$ million (assuming a straight-line domestic demand curve). The loss in consumer surplus totals $8.2 million.

c. The right to import is a right to buy sugar at the world price of $0.10, import it, and sell it domestically at the price of $0.12. If the bidding for the rights is competitive, then the buyers of the rights bid $0.02 per pound. The government collects $4.8 million (= $0.02 per pound $\times$ 240 million pounds).

d. The net loss to the country is $0.6 million. By limiting imports, the quota causes two kinds of economic inefficiency. First, the increased domestic production is high-cost by world standards. The country uses some of its resources inefficiently producing this extra sugar rather than producing other products. Second, the consumers squeezed out of the market by the higher price lose the consumer surplus that they would have received if they were allowed to import freely.

9. Before the demand increase, as shown in the graph above, the tariff and the quota are essentially equivalent (domestic price P_1, domestic production quantity S_1, domestic consumption quantity D_1, import quantity $D_1 - S_1$, domestic producer surplus VAP_1, domestic consumer surplus UBP_1, deadweight losses AEC and BGJ, and government tariff revenue or quota import profits $ABGE$). With the increase in demand to D_d', the unchanged tariff and the unchanged quota are no longer equivalent:

	Tariff	Quota
Domestic price	P_1	P_2
Production quantity	S_1	S_2
Consumption quantity	D_3	D_2
Producer surplus	VAP_1	VLP_2
Consumer surplus	TRP_1	TNP_2
Deadweight losses		
Production	AEC	LFC
Consumption	RIK	NHK
Tariff revenue or quota import profits	$ARIE$	$LNHF$

After domestic demand has increased, the domestic price is higher with the quota than with the tariff, domestic quantity produced is higher with the quota than with the tariff, domestic quantity consumed is lower with the quota than with the tariff, domestic producer surplus is larger with the quota than with the tariff, domestic consumer surplus is smaller with the quota than with the tariff, and the deadweight losses are larger with the quota than with the tariff.

11. a. Relative to free trade, the tariff gives the United States a terms-of-trade gain of $180 million and an efficiency loss of $100 million for a net gain of $80 million. In terms of Figure 9.3, this is area e minus area $(b + d)$. The VER costs the United States $300 million (area c) plus $100 million $(b + d$ again) for a loss of $400 million. For the United States, then, the tariff is best and the VER is worst.

   b. If the United States imposes the $80 tariff, Canada loses $180 million (area e) and $60 million (area f) for a total loss of $240 million. By contrast, if the United States and Canada (Bauer) negotiate a VER arrangement, Canada gains $300 million on price markups (area c) and loses $60 million (area f) for a net *gain* of $240 million. For Canada, the U.S. tariff is the most harmful, whereas the VER actually brings a net gain.

   c. For the world as a whole (United States plus Canada here), either the tariff or the VER brings a net loss of $160 million (areas $b + d$ and f). Free trade is still best for the world as a whole.

13. Partly disagree, partly agree. (a) The WTO has been less successful than the GATT at completing rounds of multilateral trade negotiations. Under the GATT its member countries reached eight multilateral trade agreements, culminating in the Uruguay Round agreement that created the WTO. The WTO has started one round, the Doha Round, in 2001, and, as of 2014, it has not been completed. (b) The WTO does have a better dispute settlement procedure than did the GATT. Under the WTO process, a country's government that is found to be in violation of

its WTO commitments is instructed to change its policy, offer compensation in some way, or face possible consequences (a retaliatory action by the complaining country). The country's government that is found to be in violation cannot simply block the decision (as it could under the GATT procedure). For the WTO procedure, most cases in which violations are found result in the countries' governments changing their policies.

Chapter 10

1. a. Yes, there are external benefits—a positive spillover effect. The benefits to the entire country are larger than the benefits to the single firm innovating the new technology. Other firms that do not pay anything to this firm receive benefits by learning about and using the new production technology.

   b. The economist would say that the production subsidy is preferable to the tariff. Both can be used to increase domestic production, but the tariff distorts domestic consumption, leading to an unnecessary deadweight loss (the consumption effect).

   c. The economist would use the specificity rule. The actual problem is that innovating firms do not have enough incentives to pursue new production technologies (because other firms get benefits without paying). The economist would recommend some form of subsidy to new production technology as better than a production subsidy or tariff. The technology subsidy could be a subsidy to undertake research and development, or monetary awards or prizes for new technology once it is developed.

3. One such set of conditions described in this chapter is the developing government argument. If the government is so underdeveloped that the gains from starting or expanding public programs exceed the costs of taxing imports, then the import tariff brings net national gains by providing the revenue so badly needed for those programs. Another answer could be: Tax imports if our consumption of the product brings external costs. For example, a country that does not grow tobacco could tax tobacco imports for health reasons.

5. Yes, even though no such case was explicitly introduced in this chapter. Think about distortions and ask how a nation could have too little private incentive to buy imports. The most likely case is one in which buying and using foreign products could bring new knowledge benefits throughout the importing country, benefits that are not captured by the importers alone. To give them an incentive matching the spillover gains to residents other than the importers, the national government could use an import subsidy.

7. Agree. The infant-industry argument states that a domestic industry that is currently uncompetitive by world standards (uncompetitive against low-priced imports) will, if it can begin producing with assistance from the government, grow up to become internationally competitive in the future. Whether this is really an argument for a tariff depends on whether a tariff is the best policy that the government can use to assist the domestic industry to get its production started. The specificity rule indicates that the best government policy is one that attacks the problem directly. Using the specificity rule, the infant-industry argument is actually an argument for government assistance (a subsidy) to some aspect of domestic production, not for a tariff.

9. Policy A, the production subsidy, would be the lowest cost to the country. By comparison, the tariff (Policy B) would raise the domestic price of aircraft, which will distort buyer decisions and thwart the growth of the domestic airline industry. The tariff adds a deadweight loss (the consumption effect). Policy C, the import quota, would be the most costly to the country. The sole Australian producer would gain monopoly power, and it will raise the domestic price even higher. The deadweight loss will be larger.

11. In favor: Adjustment assistance is designed to gain the benefits of increased imports by encouraging workers to make a smooth transition out of domestic production of the import-competing good. A key problem is that workers pushed out of import-competing production suffer large declines in earnings when forced to switch to some other industry or occupation. Adjustment assistance can overcome this problem by offering workers retraining, help with relocation, and temporary income support during retraining and relocation. Adjustment assistance represents an application of the specificity rule. It is better than using a tariff or nontariff barrier to limit imports and resist shrinking the domestic industry. And politically, it can reduce the pressure to enact these import barriers.

Opposed: Workers are faced with the need to relocate and develop new skills for a variety of reasons—not only increased imports but also changing consumer demand and changing technologies. There is nothing special about increasing imports, and workers affected by increasing imports deserve no special treatment. In fact, offering adjustment assistance could encourage workers to take jobs in import-competing industries that are shrinking because they have the social insurance offered by adjustment assistance. In addition, adjustment assistance is not that effective. It does offer temporary income assistance to those who qualify, but it is much less successful at effective retraining and smooth relocation.

13. Imposing the quota will create one clear winner—domestic baseball bat producers. It will create one clear loser—domestic consumers of baseball bats. And it will create one group that may have mixed feelings—the three import distributors—because they will have a smaller volume of business, but the profit margin on the limited business that they conduct will be larger. Baseball bat producers probably will be an effective lobbying group because there are a small number of firms that need to organize to lobby (and they may already have a trade association). Baseball bat consumers are unlikely to be an effective lobbying group because each has a small stake and it would be difficult to organize them into a political group. The three import distributors should be an effective lobbying group if they can agree among themselves whether to favor or oppose the quota.

15. None. The loss in consumer surplus from imposing a tariff is larger than the gain in producer surplus. (The consumer loss is also larger than the combined gains of producer surplus and government tariff revenue, if the latter has "votes.")

Chapter 11

1. One definition of dumping is selling an export at a price lower than the price charged to domestic buyers of the product within the exporting country. This definition emphasizes international price discrimination. The second definition is selling an export at a price that is lower than the full average cost of the product (including overhead) plus a reasonable profit margin. This definition emphasizes pricing below cost (counting some profit as a cost of capital).

3. Tipper Laurie, because its at-brewery price is lower for exports to the United States than for domestic sales. Bigg Redd, because its at-brewery export price is below average cost.

5. The objective of the revision is to make antidumping policy contribute to U.S. national well-being. The policy should be targeted toward addressing predatory dumping and aggressive cyclical dumping. It should take into account domestic consumer interests as well as domestic producer interests. It generally should not impose antidumping duties on persistent dumping that involves international price discrimination in favor of U.S. buyers. The specific provisions could include one (or more) of the following. First, the definition of dumping should be changed. Dumping should be defined as pricing an export below the average variable cost (or marginal cost) of production. This change will permit the definition of dumping to be focused on overly aggressive pricing that is often characteristic of predatory dumping or aggressive cyclical dumping. Second, the test for injury should include consideration of benefits to domestic consumers from low-priced imports, in addition to harm to domestic producers. The injury test should be a test of effect on net national well-being. Alternatively, a radical change would be to abolish the antidumping law and substitute use of safeguard policy. Another radical alternative is to abolish the antidumping law and instead focus on prosecuting any predatory dumping using U.S. antitrust laws that prohibit monopolization.

7. The $5 export subsidy would lower the price charged to Canadian buyers, but the $5 countervailing duty would raise the price back up. If Canadian buyers are paying the same price (inclusive of the export subsidy and the countervailing duty) that they would pay with free trade (no export subsidy and no duty), then they are importing the same quantity that they would import with free trade. World well-being is the same in both cases because all of the quantities are the same.

   The United States would lose. The U.S. government pays a subsidy of $5 for each pair of blue jeans to Canada. The export price is lower, but the quantity exported is the same as with free trade. Canada would gain the $5 on each pair. The gain would be collected as government revenue from the countervailing duty. Otherwise, the domestic price in Canada and all quantities are the same as with free trade. Because Canada's gain equals the U.S.'s loss, this is another way to see that the well-being of the world as a whole is the same as it would be with free trade.

9. a. In this case, Airbus would gain by producing even without government intervention. Airbus would gain 5 if Boeing did produce and 100 if Boeing did not produce. There would be no reason for European governments to subsidize Airbus.

   b. In this case, Boeing is sure to produce because Boeing gains whether or not Airbus produces. The EU should recognize this. With Boeing producing, the net gain for Airbus without government help is zero. If none of Airbus's customers were in Europe, there would be no reason to encourage Airbus to produce. Notice, however, that consumers might be better off if Airbus did produce. You can see this either by noticing that production by Airbus would deprive Boeing of 100 in profits taken from consumers (presumably by charging higher prices) or by reasoning that more competition is a good thing for consumers. Either way, the EU would have reason to subsidize Airbus if its consumers could reap gains from the competition.

11. One way to build the case is to claim that the industry is a global oligopoly, with substantial scale economies and high profit rates (like the Boeing–Airbus example in this chapter).

The nation can gain if the country's firm(s) can establish export capabilities and earn high profits on the exports. Another way to build the case is to claim that this industry is an infant industry (discussed in Chapter 10). If the industry could get some assistance, it would grow up and generate new producer surplus when it is strong enough to export.

Chapter 12

1. Members of a customs union have the same tariff on each category of imported good or service, regardless of which member country receives the imports. In this case, there is no need to scrutinize goods that move between countries in the customs union, even if the product might have been imported from outside the union.

   In a free-trade area, by contrast, each member country can have a different tariff rate on the import of a product. Therefore, the free-trade area needs to scrutinize goods that move between countries in the free-trade area to make sure that they were not imported from outside the area into a low-tariff country and then shipped on to a high-tariff country in an effort to avoid the high tariff.

3. Trade creation is the increase in total imports resulting from the formation of a trade bloc. Trade creation occurs because importing from the partner country lowers the price in the importing country, so that some high-cost domestic production is replaced by lower-priced imports from the partner, and because the lower price increases the total quantity demanded in the importing country. Trade diversion is the replacement of imports from lower-cost suppliers outside the trade bloc with higher-cost imports from the partner. It occurs because the outside suppliers remain hindered by tariffs, while there is no tariff on imports from the partner. Trade creation creates a gain for the importing country and the world. Trade diversion creates a loss for the importing country and the world. The importing country and the world gain from the trade bloc if trade creation gains exceed trade diversion losses.

5. (a) 10 million DVD recorders times ($110 – $100) = $100 million. (b) To offset this

$100 million loss, with linear demand and supply curves, the change in imports, ΔM, would have to be such that the trade-creation gain (area b in Figure 12.2) has an area equal to $100 million. So $1/2 \times (\$130 - \$110) \times \Delta M = \$100$ million requires $\Delta M = 10$ million, or a doubling of Homeland's DVD recorder imports.

7. This case resembles that shown in Figure 12.2A, assuming the United States is a price-taking country.

   U.S. consumers gain, as the domestic price drops from $30 to $25. We cannot quantify the dollar value of their consumer-surplus gain without knowing the level of domestic consumption or production.

   U.S. producers would lose from the same price drop, though again we cannot say how much they would lose. (We do know, however, that the consumer gain would exceed this producer loss plus the government revenue loss by the triangular area $(1/2) \times \$5 \times 0.2$ million = $0.5 million.)

   The U.S. government would lose the $10 million it had collected in tariff revenue on the imports from China.

   The world as a whole would gain the triangular area $(1/2) \times \$5 \times 0.2$ million = $0.5 million, but lose the rectangular area $(\$25 - 20) \times 1$ million = $5 million because of the diversion of 1.0 million pairs from the lower-cost producer (China) to the higher-cost producer (Mexico). So overall, the world would lose $4.5 million.

9. Trade embargoes are usually imposed by large countries that are important in the trade of the target country. An embargo has a better chance to succeed if it is imposed suddenly rather than gradually because a sudden interruption of economic flows damages the target country by a large amount for some time before it can develop alternatives. (In economic terms, for a good that the target imports, its import demand tends to be more inelastic in the short run, and the supply of exports from alternative (non-embargo) countries tends to be more limited and more inelastic in the short run as well.)

11. The "most certain" is (a), a countervailing duty, which, for a competitive industry, brings net gains for the world as a whole if it just offsets the foreign export subsidy that provoked it.

Whether the world as a whole gains from a customs union depends on whether it brings more trade creation than trade diversion. Whether the world gains from an antidumping duty also depends on the specifics of the case, as explained in Chapter 11.

Chapter 13

1. There are two effects. First, rising production and consumption bring rising pollution if the techniques used to produce and consume are unchanged. Second, rising income brings increased demand for pollution control because a cleaner environment is a normal good. As Figure 13.1 shows, there are three basic patterns that arise for different types of pollution and related issues like sanitation. For some types of pollution, the first effect is larger, and pollution rises with rising income and production per person. For other types, the second effect is generally larger, so pollution declines with rising income and production per person. For yet other types, there is a turning point, so pollution at first rises and then falls as income and production per person increase.

3. Both (b) and (d). For item (b), the WTO places strict requirements on a country using trade limits to punish a foreign country for having environmental standards for production in the foreign country that are different from those of the importing country. If the country does not recognize that other methods for controlling this pollution may also be acceptable, or if the country is acting unilaterally rather than negotiating with the foreign countries, then the WTO is likely to view the policy as a violation of WTO rules. For (d), the WTO would consider the pollution issue to be a pretext for unacceptable protectionist import barriers because the imported products are not the only source of the pollution.

5. While there is some room for interpretation here, the specificity rule definitely prefers (c), followed by (d), then (a), and then (b).

    The defeatism of (e) is misplaced. Oil spills are the result of shippers' negligence to a large extent, and not just uncontrollable acts of God.

    One drawback to (a) and (b) is that they force each nation's importers or consumers to pay insurance against shippers' carelessness. The more direct approach is to target the shippers themselves. In addition, many oil spills ruin the coastlines of nations that are not purchasers of the oil being shipped, making it inappropriate to charge them.

    It might seem that the most direct approach, (c), is unrealistic because it is hard to get full damages from the oil-shipping companies in court. Yet it is not difficult to make them pay for most or all of the damages. A key point is that the most damaging spills occur within the 200-mile limit, meaning that they occur in the national waters of the country suffering the damage. Full legal jurisdiction applies. The victimized country can legally seize oil shippers' assets, apply jail sentences, and even demand that a shipping company post bonds in advance of spills in exchange for the right to pass through national waters.

    As for (d), intercepting and taxing all tankers in national waters is a reasonable choice. Its workability depends, however, on the cost of such coast-guard vigilance. If all tankers entering national water must put into port, they could be taxed in port. That is unlikely, however, and it might be costly to pursue them all along the 200-mile coast. Furthermore, such a tax, like many insurance schemes, makes the more careful clients (shippers) pay to insure the more reckless.

7. Item (c). This tax would lead to substantial reductions in the use of fossil fuels, the major source of human-made greenhouse gases. The other items would have small effects over the next 30 years.

9. No trade barriers are called for by the information given here. If the wood is, in fact, grown on plantation land that would have been used for lower-value crops, there is no clear externality, no basis for government intervention. Only if the plantations would have been rain forest and only if there were serious environmental damage (e.g., extinction of species or soil erosion) from the clearing of that rain forest land for plantations would there be a case for Indonesia's restricting the cultivation of jelutong. As for the greenhouse-gas effects of cutting more tropical rain forest, they could easily be outweighed by the longer growing life of cedar trees in the temperate zone.

11. For the rhino, as an endangered species, CITES bans commercial international trade in horns (and other parts). One challenge for CITES is making this ban work. If the ban is combined with education of potential buyers to decrease demand, then the price of horns decreases and the incentive to poach (in which a rhino is killed to obtain its horn) decreases. However, poaching is difficult to police, and the ban on international trade is difficult to enforce. If demand is strong, the price of horns increases and the incentive to poach increases. A second challenge for CITES is deciding whether or not to shift away from a ban on commercial international trade and toward a policy of "sustainable use" for rhinos. Horns can be harvested without killing the rhino. If such harvesting is developed as a business, those who run the business have the incentive to keep rhinos alive, so their horns can be harvested more than once over time. The goal is to align economic incentives with protection and preservation of the species. But there may then be a third challenge for CITES. If it allows commercial trade in rhino horns that are harvested without killing the rhino, it may become easier for horns obtained by poaching to be traded internationally because it may be difficult to design a system that distinguishes between harvested and poached horns. So, a system of sustainable use and commercial trade for harvested horns could also create a conduit that enables increased poaching.

Chapter 14

1. The four arguments in favor of ISI are the infant-industry argument, the developing-government argument, the chance to improve the terms of trade for a large importing country, and economizing on market information by focusing on selling in the local market rather than in more uncertain foreign markets. The drawbacks to ISI are the deadweight losses from the inefficiencies of import protection, the danger that government officials directing the policy will try to enrich themselves rather than the country, and the lack of competitive pressure on local firms to "grow up" by reducing costs, improving technology, and raising product quality. The arguments in favor of a policy of promoting manufactured exports are that it encourages use of the country's abundant resources (comparative advantage), export sales can help to achieve scale economies, and the drive to succeed in foreign markets creates competitive pressure. A major drawback is the importing countries may erect trade barriers that limit the exporter's ability to expand its exports of manufactures.

3. The available data do indicate that the relative prices of primary products have declined since 1900, perhaps by as much as 0.8 percent per year. But there are biases in the data. Some of the decline could reflect declining transport costs, and some could be offset by the rising quality of manufactured products that is not reflected in the price comparison. The true trend decline is probably less than 0.8 percent per year, and it may even be no decline.

5. For its first few years, TAR has the ability to be successful as an international cartel if its member countries can agree on and abide by its policies. TAR will have several advantages during its first few years. It has a fairly large share of world production, so its actions can have a substantial impact on the world price. The price elasticity of demand is rather low, so it can raise the world price without too much of a falloff in world sales. It will not face much pressure from outside suppliers because they cannot enter or increase their production quickly. The biggest challenges facing TAR in its first few years are establishing its policies and having its members comply with them. The five countries may have different views on how much to increase the price in the first few years, they may disagree on how much each of them should reduce their own production to limit global supply, and so forth. Even if they can reach agreement on the cartel's policies, each of them has an incentive to cheat on the agreement. Given how different the five countries are, agreeing to and abiding by the cartel policies are major challenges.

   In the longer run, the cartel is unlikely to remain successful, even if it achieves success in its first few years. If it succeeds in raising the world price in its first years, two forces come into play that erode its effectiveness over time.

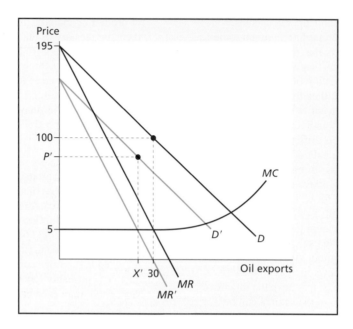

First, the price elasticity of demand becomes larger, so world sales of tobacco decline if the price is kept high. Second, new outside suppliers can enter into production, and existing outside suppliers can expand their production. The cartel members are squeezed from both sides. The price that maximizes the cartel's total profit declines. Furthermore, it becomes more difficult, and eventually impossible, to reach agreement on which cartel members should continue to reduce their own production to keep the world price above its competitive level by limiting total global supply.

7. a. The demand that remains for the cartel's oil falls by 10 million barrels per day, for any price above $5 per barrel. In the graph above, this is a shift of the demand curve for cartel oil to the left, from D to D'. The new demand curve for the cartel's oil is parallel to the original demand curve and lower by 10 million barrels. Its intercept with the price axis is below $195. (Using the equation for the market demand curve, $P = 195 - (95/30) \times Q_D$, the intercept for the new demand curve is $163.33.) The marginal revenue curve for the cartel also shifts down and to the left, from MR to MR'. The intersection of the new marginal revenue curve and the

(unchanged) marginal cost curve for cartel production occurs when oil exports are X', less than 30 million barrels, and the new profit-maximizing price for the cartel is P', less than $100 per barrel.

b. The quantity demanded for the cartel's oil is unchanged if the market price is $5 per barrel, but each $1 increase in the market price takes away another 0.5 million barrels from the demand remaining for the cartel's oil. The new demand curve for the cartel's oil is shown as the colored line D'' in the graph on the next page. With the new outside supply the quantity demanded of the cartel's oil falls to zero at a price less than $100. (The price intercept of the new demand curve for the cartel's oil is $78.55.) Because both the old and the new straight-line demand curves show the same quantity demanded at a price of $5, the new marginal revenue curve MR'' intersects the original marginal revenue curve MR at $5 per barrel. This point is also the intersection with the cartel's marginal cost curve, so the cartel continues to produce 30 million barrels. Because of the new and elastic outside supply of oil, the cartel's new profit-maximizing price P'' is much less than $100.

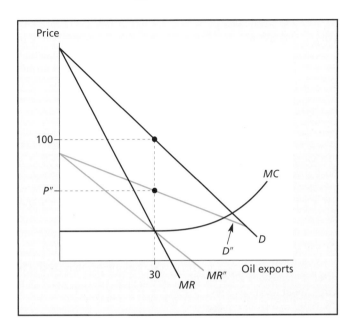

9. Disagree. The country is doing well using exports of manufactured products as an important part of its development strategy. However, there is a limit to how far this policy can carry the country. Competitiveness in less-skilled-labor-intensive products depends on low wages. Real wages cannot rise too high, or the country will begin to lose its ability to compete for foreign sales. In addition, other developing countries with lower wages may shift to a similar strategy based on exports of these products, adding to the international competition that the country's exporters face. If the country is to continue to develop, it probably needs another dimension for its strategy. As we noted back in Chapter 3, payment of high wages depends largely on workers' being able to achieve high levels of productivity. Workers with more skills are more productive and can be paid more. A better educational system is part of a national effort to equip the country's people with skills and with the ability to learn new skills.

11. The four types of trade policies that a developing country can use in its effort to promote growth of its economy are expanding primary product exports, raising the prices of its primary product exports, restricting imports to encourage the growth of import-replacing domestic production, and promoting exports of new products (other than primary products) that make use of the country's comparative advantage. The policy of encouraging development of local production of basic business services is an example of the fourth policy. Business services are not primary products, so it is not an example of the first two. Basic business services are not major import item, and the demand to be served is mostly not within the country, so it is not an example of the third. Rather, basic business services are products that can be produced using the country's abundant low-skilled and medium-skilled labor and that can be exported to buyers in other countries. The most successful country that has pursued this strategy is India, and other developing countries have been adopting policies to add this set of products to their development strategies.

Chapter 15

1. Disagree. Most FDI is in industrialized countries, especially the United States and Europe. Wages are not low in these countries. This FDI instead is used to gain access to large markets and to

gain the insights and marketing advantages of producing locally in these markets.

3. Agree. One exposure is to exchange-rate risk. The home-currency value of the assets of foreign affiliates will vary as exchange rates vary. If foreign-currency borrowings and other liabilities are used to finance the affiliates' assets, they provide a hedge against exchange-rate risk by more closely balancing foreign-currency assets and liabilities. Another exposure is to the risk of expropriation. The host government sometimes exercises its power to seize the affiliates of multinational firms. If most of the affiliates' assets are financed by local borrowings and other local liabilities, then the parent firms lose less because they can refuse to honor the liabilities once the assets are seized.

5. There are inherent disadvantages of FDI arising from lack of knowledge about local customs, practices, laws, and policies and from the costs of managing across borders. Therefore, firms that undertake FDI successfully generally have some firm-specific advantages that allow them to compete successfully with local firms in the host country. Major types of firm-specific advantages include better technology, managerial and organizational skills, and marketing capabilities. These types of firm-specific advantages are important in industries such as pharmaceuticals and electronic products. The firms that have the advantages can undertake FDI successfully. These types of firm-specific advantages are less important in industries such as clothing and paper products. Fewer firms possess these types of advantages, and there is less FDI in these industries.

7. a. To maximize global after-tax profit, the controller should try to show as much profit as possible in Ireland and as little profit as possible in Japan, because Ireland's tax rate of 15 percent is lower than Japan's tax rate of 40 percent. If possible, the controller should choose the third alternative, to raise the price of the component to $22. For each unit of the component exported from Ireland to Japan, this shifts $2 of profit from Japan to Ireland in comparison with the second alternative (price of $20) and it shifts $4 of profit compared to the first alternative (keep the price at $18). For each unit of the component exported, tax paid

in Japan is reduced by $0.80 (or $1.60) and the extra tax paid in Ireland is only $0.30 (or $0.60). For each unit exported, the increase in global after-tax profit is $0.50 compared to the second alternative and $1.00 compared to the first alternative.

b. Ireland's government may be pleased with this change in transfer price. More profits are shown in the country, so its tax revenues are higher than they would be if the transfer price were lower. Japan's government is likely to be displeased. Its tax revenues are lower. It can try to police transfer pricing to ensure that the "correct" prices are used to show the "correct" amount of profit in the affiliates in Japan.

9. Key points that should be included in the report:
   (1) FDI brings new technologies into the country.
   (2) FDI brings new managerial practices into the country.
   (3) FDI brings marketing capabilities into the country. These can be used to better meet the needs of the local market. They may be particularly important in expanding the country's exports by improving the international marketing of products produced by the multinational firms that begin production in the country.
   (4) FDI brings financial capital into the country and expands the country's ability to invest in domestic production capabilities.
   (5) The local affiliates of the multinationals raise labor skills by training local workers.
   (6) Technological (and similar) spillover benefits accrue to the country as it hosts FDI because some of the multinationals' technology, managerial practices, and marketing capabilities spread to local firms as they learn about and imitate the multinational's intangible assets. Taken together, these first six items increase the country's supply-side capabilities for producing (and selling) goods and services.
   (7) In addition, the country's government can gain tax revenues by taxing (in a reasonable way!) the profits of the local affiliates established by the foreign multinationals.

11. First, in 1924, the United States passed a law that severely restricted immigration, using a system of quotas by national origin. Second, the Great Depression, with its very high rates of labor unemployment, probably reduced the economic incentive to immigrate because potential immigrants would expect that it would be very difficult to find employment.

13. a. A rise in labor demand in the North.

   b. A "push" factor in the South, such as labor force growth or decreased demand for labor.

   c. A drop in the cost or difficulty of migration.

15. The migrants don't gain the full Southern wage markup from $2.00 to $3.20 because some of their extra labor was supplied only at a marginal cost of their own time that rose from $2.00 to $3.20. That's shown in Figure 15.4 by the fact that the curve $S_r + S_{mig}$ leans further out to the right than does the curve S_r.

   As for the full international wage gain from $2.00 up to $5.00, it is true that the migrants do get paid that full extra $3. However, $1.80 of it is not a real gain in their well-being. It's just compensation for the economic and psychic costs of migrating.

17. Here are several arguments. First, standard economic analysis shows that there are net economic gains to the Japanese economy, even if the gains to the immigrants are not counted. Japanese employers gain from access to a larger pool of workers, and these gains are larger than any losses to Japanese workers who must compete with the new immigrants (see Figure 15.4). Second, some of the immigrants will take on work that most Japanese shun, such as janitorial work. These immigrants view this work as an opportunity and better than what they had back in their home countries. Third, if immigrants are selectively admitted, the Japanese government can assure that they are net contributors to public finance—that they will pay more in taxes than they add to the costs of running government programs. The Japanese government should favor young adult immigrants, including many with skills that will be valued in the workplace. This effect on public finance is especially important for Japan because it has a rapidly aging native population, so the costs of providing social security payments

to retirees is going to rise quickly in the next decades. Fourth, immigrants bring with them a range of knowledge that can create spillover benefits for Japan. The immigrants bring food recipes, artistic talent, know-how about science and technology, and different ways of doing things. Japan wants to increase the creativity of its people and firms to be more successful in high-tech and information-intensive industries. Immigrants can be a source of creative sparks.

19. The greatest net contributors were probably (b) electrical engineers arriving around 1990, whose high average salaries made them pay a lot of U.S. taxes and draw few government benefits. As for who contributed least, one could make a case for either (a) the political refugees or (c) the grandparents. The political refugees, as people who had not been preparing themselves for life in a new economy until displaced by political events, are generally less well equipped to earn and pay taxes in the economy when they arrive. The grandparents are also likely to pay little taxes and may make some claims on government aid networks, though their qualification for Social Security is limited.

Chapter 16

1. National saving (S) equals private saving plus government saving (or dissaving if the government budget is in deficit). For this country, national saving equals $678 billion (or $806 – $128). The current account balance equals the difference between national saving and domestic real investment (I_d). For this country, the current account balance is a deficit of $99 billion (or $678 – $777).

3. Saving can be used to make investments. The country can use its national saving to make domestic real investments in new production capital (buildings, machinery, and software), new housing, and additions to inventories or it can use its national saving to invest in foreign financial assets. If it uses its national saving to make domestic real investments, benefits to the nation include the increases in production capacity and capabilities that result from new production capital and the housing services that flow from a larger stock of housing. If it uses its national saving to make foreign investments, benefits to the nation include the dividends,

interest payments, and capital gains that it earns on its foreign investments, which add to the national income of the country in the future.

5. Transaction *c* contributes to a surplus in the current account because it is an export of merchandise that is paid for through an item in the financial account. (Transaction *a* leaves the current account unchanged because it is both an export and an import. Transaction *b* contributes to a deficit in the current account because it is an import. Transaction *d* affects no items in the current account.)

7. Disagree. A shift to saving more would tend to increase the surplus, not reduce it. The current account balance equals net foreign investment, and net foreign investment is the difference between national saving and domestic real investment. If national saving increases, then net foreign investment tends to increase, and the current account balance tends to increase (the surplus tends to increase).

9. a. A capital inflow (a credit or positive item in the country's financial account or in its transactions in official international reserve assets) can provide financing for a current account deficit. Yes, this item can provide financing. When residents of the country sell previously acquired foreign bonds, they have a monetary claim on the foreign buyers—a positive item in the financial account of the country's balance of payments.

b. No, this item is not a financing item. Residents receiving income from foreign sources is part of the current account. It is already included in the calculation of the overall current account deficit.

c. Yes, this item can provide financing. The start-up companies have a monetary claim on the foreign buyers of the equity—a positive item in the financial account of the country's balance of payments.

11. a. The U.S. international investment position declines—an increase in foreign investments in the United States (an increase in what the United States owes to foreigners).

b. The U.S. international investment position rises—an increase in private U.S. investment abroad (an increase in U.S. claims on foreigners).

c. The U.S. international investment position is unchanged. The composition of foreign investments in the United States changes, but the total amount does not change.

Chapter 17

1. *Imports of goods and services* result in demand for foreign currency in the foreign exchange market. Domestic buyers often want to pay using domestic currency, while the foreign sellers want to receive payment in their currency. In the process of paying for these imports, domestic currency is exchanged for foreign currency, creating demand for foreign currency. *International capital outflows* result in a demand for foreign currency in the foreign exchange market. In making investments in foreign financial assets, domestic investors often start with domestic currency and must exchange it for foreign currency before they can buy the foreign assets. The exchange creates demand for foreign currency. Foreign sales of this country's financial assets that the foreigners had previously acquired and foreign borrowing from this country are other forms of capital outflow that can create demand for foreign currency.

3. a. The value of the dollar decreases. (The SFr increases.)

b. The value of the dollar decreases. (This is the same change as in part *a*.)

c. The value of the dollar increases. (The yen decreases.)

d. The value of the dollar increases. (This is the same change as in part *c*.)

5. The British bank could use the interbank market to find another bank that was willing to buy dollars and sell pounds. The British bank could search directly with other banks for a good exchange rate for the transaction or it could use a foreign exchange broker to identify a good rate from another bank. The British bank should be able to sell its dollars to another bank quickly and with very low transactions costs.

7. a. Demand for yen. The Japanese firm will sell its dollars to obtain yen.

b. Demand for yen. The U.S. import company probably begins with dollars, and the Japanese producer probably wants to receive payments in yen. Dollars must be sold to obtain yen.

c. Supply of yen. The Japanese importer probably begins with yen, and the U.S. cooperative probably wants to receive payment in dollars. Yen must be sold to obtain dollars.

d. Demand for yen. The U.S. pension fund must sell its dollars to obtain yen, using these yen to buy the Japanese shares.

9. a. Increase in supply of Swiss francs reduces the exchange-rate value ($/SFr) of the franc. The dollar appreciates.

b. Increase in supply of francs reduces the exchange-rate value ($/SFr) of the franc. The dollar appreciates.

c. Increase in supply of francs reduces the exchange-rate value ($/SFr) of the franc. The dollar appreciates.

d. Decrease in demand for francs reduces the exchange-rate value ($/SFr) of the franc. The dollar appreciates.

11. Yes. State both exchange rates in the same way and then buy low, sell high. Bank A is quoting a rate of 0.67 Swiss franc per dollar (= 1/1.50), and this can be compared to Bank B's quote of 0.50 Swiss franc per dollar. Arbitrage: Buy dollars from Bank B, and sell dollars to Bank A. Pocket 0.17 Swiss franc for each dollar. (Equivalently, buy Swiss francs from Bank A at $1.50 per franc and simultaneously sell them to Bank B at $2.00 per franc.)

Chapter 18

1. Agree. As an investor, I think of my wealth and returns from investments in terms of my own currency. When I invest in a foreign-currency-denominated financial asset, I am (actually or effectively) buying both the foreign currency and the asset. Part of my overall return comes from the return on the asset itself—for instance, the yield or rate of interest that it pays. The other part of my return comes from changes in the exchange-rate value of the foreign currency. If the foreign currency increases in value (relative to my own currency) while I am holding the foreign asset, the value of my investment (in terms of my own currency) increases, and I have made an additional return on my investment. (Of course, if the exchange-rate value of the foreign currency goes down, I make a loss on the currency value, which reduces my overall return.)

3. a. The U.S. firm has an asset position in yen—it has a long position in yen. The risk is that the dollar exchange-rate value of the yen in 60 days is uncertain. If the yen depreciates, then the firm will receive fewer dollars.

b. The student has an asset position in yen—a long position in yen. The risk is that the dollar exchange-rate value of the yen in 60 days is uncertain. If the yen depreciates, then the student will receive fewer dollars.

c. The U.S. firm has a liability position in yen—a short position in yen. The risk is that the dollar exchange-rate value of the yen in 60 days is uncertain. If the yen appreciates, then the firm must deliver more dollars to buy the yen to pay off its loan.

5. For forward speculation the relevant comparison is between the current forward exchange rate and the expected future spot exchange rate. Comparing these two rates, we hope to make a profit by buying low and selling high. You expect the Swiss franc to be relatively cheap at the future spot rate ($0.51) compared with the current forward rate ($0.52). To speculate you should therefore enter into a forward contract today that requires that you sell (or deliver) SFr and buy (or receive) dollars. If the spot rate in 180 days is actually $0.51/SFr, then you can buy SFr at this low spot rate, deliver them into your previously agreed forward contract at the higher forward rate, and pocket the price difference, $0.01, for each franc that you agreed to sell in the forward contract.

7. a. Invest in dollar-denominated asset: $1 \times (1 + 0.0605) = \$1.0605$. Invest in yen-denominated asset: $\$1 \times (1/0.0100) \times (1 + 0.01) \times (0.0105) = \$1.0605$.

b. Invest in dollar-denominated asset: $\$1 \times (1 + 0.0605) \times (1/0.0105) = 101$ yen. Invest in yen-denominated asset: $\$1 \times (1/0.0100) \times (1 + 0.01) = 101$ yen.

c. Invest in dollar-denominated asset: 100 yen $\times (0.01) \times (1 + 0.0605) \times (1/0.0105) = 101$ yen. Invest in yen-denominated asset: 100 yen $\times (1 + 0.01) = 101$ yen.

9. a. From the point of view of the U.S.-based investor, the expected uncovered interest differential is $[(1 + 0.03) \times 1.77/1.80] - (1 + 0.02) = -0.0072$. Because the differential is negative, the U.S.-based investor should stay at home, investing in dollar-denominated bonds, if he bases his decision on the difference in expected returns. (The approximate formula could also be used to reach this conclusion.)

   b. From the point of view of the UK-based investor, the expected uncovered differential is $[(1 + 0.02) \times (1/1.77) \times 1.8] - (1 + 0.03) = 0.0073$. (Note that the position of the interest rates is reversed and that the exchange rates are inverted so that they are pricing the dollar, which is now the foreign currency. Note also that this differential is approximately equal to the negative of the differential in the other direction, calculated in part a.) Because the differential is positive, the UK-based investor should undertake an uncovered investment in dollar-denominated bonds if she bases her decision on the difference in expected returns. (Again, the approximate formula could be used to reach this conclusion.)

   c. If there is substantial uncovered investment flowing from Britain to the United States, this increases the supply of pounds in the spot exchange market. There is downward pressure on the spot exchange rate to drop below $1.80/pound. The pound tends to depreciate. (The dollar tends to appreciate.)

11. a. For the expected future value of the euro, the future spot exchange rate expected in 90 days is U.S.$1.408/euro ($= 1/0.71$). This value is larger than the current spot rate, $1.400/euro, so investors are expecting the euro to appreciate.

   b. *With the United States as the home country of the investor, for each dollar invested:* Invest in the euro-denominated bond, expected in 90 days: $[(1/1.400) \times (1 + 0.08/4) \times 1.408] = \$1.026$ Invest in the dollar-denominated bond, in 90 days: $(1 + 0.16/4) = \$1.04$ There is no incentive for flows from the United States to the euro area, based on the

comparison of returns ($1.026 < 1.04$). *With the euro area as the home country of the investor, for each euro invested:* Invest in the dollar-denominated bond, expected in 90 days: $[(1/(1/1.400)) \times (1 + 0.16/4) \times (1/1.408)] = \text{€}1.034$ Invest in the euro-denominated bond, in 90 days: $(1 + 0.08/4) = \text{€}1.02$ The uncovered interest differential favors investing in the United States ($1.034 > 1.02$), so uncovered investment will tend to flow from the euro area to the United States to invest in dollar-denominated bonds. The 90-day expected return in the United States (3.4%) is 1.4 percentage points higher than the 90-day return in the euro area (2.0%). (Note that the approximation formula could be used for all calculations.)

Chapter 19

1. Disagree. First, exchange rates can be quite variable in the short run. This much variability does not seem to be consistent with the gradual changes in supply and demand for foreign currency that would occur as trade flows change gradually. Second, the volume of trading in the foreign exchange market is much larger than the volume of international trade in goods and services. Only a small part of total activity in foreign exchange markets is related to payments for exports and imports. Most is related to international financial flows. International financial positioning and repositioning are likely to be quite changeable over short periods of time, explaining the variability of exchange rates in the short run.

3. a. If we use the approximation formula, uncovered interest parity holds (approximately) when the foreign interest rate plus the expected rate of appreciation of the foreign currency equals the domestic interest rate. Using the pound as the foreign currency, we find that it is expected to change (depreciate) at an annual rate of -6%, or $(1.98 - 2.00)/2.00 \times 360/60 \times 100$. The uncovered annualized return on a pound-denominated bond is expected to be approximately $11\% - 6\% = 5\%$, which equals the annual return of 5% on

a dollar-denominated bond. Uncovered interest parity holds approximately. (We could also use the full formula from Chapter 18 to show that the uncovered expected interest differential is approximately zero.)

b. This shifts the uncovered differential in favor of investing in dollar-denominated bonds. The additional demand for dollars in the foreign exchange market results in an appreciation of the dollar. To reestablish uncovered interest parity with the other rates unchanged, the expected annual rate of change (depreciation) of the pound must be 3 percent, so the spot rate now must change to about $1.99/pound. The pound depreciates.

5. a. Sell pesos. Weaker Mexican exports of oil in the future are likely to lower the peso's exchange-rate value.

   b. Sell Canadian dollars. The expansion of money and credit is likely to lower the exchange-rate value of the Canadian dollar because Canadian interest rates will decline (in the short run) and Canadian inflation rates are likely to be higher (in the long run).

   c. Sell Swiss francs. Foreign investors are likely to pull some investments out of Swiss assets (and to invest less in the future), reducing the exchange-rate value of the franc.

7. As a tourist, you will be importing services from the country you visit. You would like the currency of this foreign country to be relatively cheap, so you would like it to be undervalued relative to PPP. If it is undervalued, then the current spot exchange rate allows you to buy a lot of this country's currency, relative to the local-currency prices that you must pay for products in the country.

9. According to purchasing power parity, attaining a stable exchange rate between the peso and the dollar requires that the Mexican inflation rate fall so that it is about equal to the 3 percent inflation in the United States. If k is constant, then the rate of growth of the Mexican money supply must fall to about 9 percent (or 6 percent real growth in Y + 3 percent inflation in Mexican prices, P).

11. a. If we use 1990 as the base year, the nominal exchange rate of $1/pnut corresponds to a ratio of U.S. prices to Pugelovian prices of 100/100. According to PPP, this relationship should be maintained over time. If the price level ratio changes to 260/390 in 2013, then the nominal exchange rate should change to $0.67/pnut. The pnut should depreciate during this time period because of the higher Pugelovian inflation rate (the reason why Pugelovia's price level increased by more than the U.S. price level increased).

    b. If the actual exchange rate is $1/pnut in 2013, then the pnut is overvalued. Its exchange-rate value is higher than the rate that would be consistent with PPP (using 1990 as the base year).

13. If PPP held, the exchange rate (e) should rise steadily by 2 percent per year for five years, ending up 10 percent higher after five years. This matches the path of changes in the domestic price level (relative to the foreign price level) during these five years. PPP does not hold in the short run because the actual exchange rate jumps immediately by more than 10 percent (rather than rising gradually by about 2 percent per year). In the medium run, the actual rate remains above its PPP value, but the two are moving closer together, as the actual rate declines and the PPP rate rises over time. In the long run, PPP holds. According to PPP, the exchange rate eventually should be 10 percent higher, and it actually is 10 percent higher.

15. Because the nominal spot exchange rate declined from 1.5 to 1.3 SFr per Canadian dollar, the Canadian dollar experienced a *nominal* depreciation. However, the Canadian inflation rate was greater than the Swiss inflation rate. The change in the real exchange rate incorporates all three changes. The real exchange-rate value of the Canadian dollar in 2005 (relative to a base value of 100 in 1995) is

$$\frac{\left(\frac{160}{110}\right) \times \left(\frac{1.3}{1.5}\right)}{\left(\frac{130}{110}\right)} \times 100 = 106.7$$

Between 1995 and 2005 the Canadian dollar experienced a *real* appreciation (106.7 > 100). The nominal depreciation was not enough to offset the higher rate of Canadian price inflation.

Chapter 20

1. In a clean float, the government allows the exchange-rate value of its currency to be determined solely by private (or nonofficial) supply and demand in the foreign exchange market. The government takes no direct actions to influence exchange rates. In a managed float, the government is willing to and sometimes does take direct actions to attempt to influence the exchange-rate value of its currency. For instance, the monetary authorities of the country may sometimes intervene in the market, buying or selling foreign currency (in exchange for domestic currency) in an effort to influence the level or trend of the floating exchange rate.

3. The disequilibrium is the difference between private demand for foreign currency and private supply of foreign currency at the fixed level of the exchange rate. Official intervention by the central bank can be used to defend the fixed exchange rate, selling foreign currency if there is an excess private demand or buying foreign currency if there is an excess private supply. Another way to see the disequilibrium is that the country's overall payments balance (its official settlements balance) is not zero.

   A temporary disequilibrium is one that will disappear within a short period of time, without any need for the country to make any macroeconomic adjustments. If the disequilibrium is temporary, official intervention can usually be used successfully to defend the fixed exchange rate. The country usually will have sufficient official reserve holdings to defend the fixed rate if there is a temporary private excess demand for foreign currency (or a temporary overall payments deficit); the country usually is willing and able to accumulate some additional official reserves if there is a temporary private excess supply of foreign currency (or temporary overall payments surplus). Indeed, for temporary disequilibriums the well-being of the country can be higher if the government stabilizes the currency by defending the fixed exchange rate through official intervention, as Figure 20.4 shows.

   If the disequilibrium is fundamental, then it tends to continue into the future. The country cannot simply use official intervention to defend the fixed exchange rate. The country will run out of official reserves (if its defense involves selling foreign currency), or it will accumulate unacceptably large official reserves (if the defense involves buying foreign currency). Thus, a major adjustment is necessary if the disequilibrium is fundamental. The government may surrender the fixed rate, changing its value or shifting to a floating exchange rate. Or the government may adjust its macroeconomy to alter private demand and supply for foreign currency.

5. The exchange controls are intended to restrain the excess private demand for foreign currency (the source of the downward pressure on the exchange-rate value of the country's currency). Thus, some people who want to obtain foreign currency, and who would be willing to pay more than the current exchange rate, do not get to buy the foreign currency. This creates a loss of well-being for the country as a whole because some net marginal benefits are being lost. Furthermore, these frustrated demanders are likely to turn to other means to obtain foreign currency. They may bribe government officials to obtain the scarce foreign currency. Or they may evade the exchange controls by using an illegal parallel market to obtain foreign currency (typically at a much higher price than the official rate).

7. a. Nonofficial supply and demand are pressuring the dirham to appreciate above the central bank's informal target value. The Moroccan monetary authority has to intervene in the foreign exchange market to sell dirhams and buy dollars.

   b. For this situation in the foreign exchange market to be a temporary disequilibrium, the Moroccan monetary authority expects that nonofficial supply and demand will shift in the near future, so that the market will be close to clearing at $0.12 per dirham without official intervention. That is, the central bank expects that nonofficial demand for the dirham will decrease (shift to the left) and/or that nonofficial supply of dirhams will increase (shift to the right).

   c. If private investors and speculators believe that this is fundamental disequilibrium, then they expect that the monetary authority will need to continue to intervene, selling dirhams and buying dollars. The private investors and speculators may believe that the Moroccan monetary authority will not or cannot continue to intervene in this way for a long period of time. Instead, the Moroccan central bank will decide to allow the dirham to appreciate. To profit from the coming large dirham appreciation, investors and speculators should increase their long positions in dirhams, for example, by shifting into dirham-denominated financial investments. To make these investments, investors and speculators increase the demand for dirhams on the foreign exchange markets. (The actions by the investors and speculators also make dirham appreciation more likely. The size of intervention by the Moroccan authority needed to defend the informal target rate increases, and the Moroccan monetary authority is more likely instead to allow the dirham to appreciate.)

9. a. The implied fixed exchange rate is about $4.87/pound (or 20.67/4.2474).

    b. You would engage in triangular arbitrage. If you start with dollars, you buy pounds using the foreign exchange market (because as quoted the pound is cheap). You then use gold to convert these pounds back into dollars. If you start with $4, you can buy one pound. You turn in this pound at the British central bank, receiving about 0.2354 (or 1/4.2474) ounces of gold. Ship this gold to the United States and exchange it at the U.S. central bank for about $4.87 (or 0.2354 × 20.67). Your arbitrage gets you (before expenses) about 87 cents for each $4 that you commit.

    c. Buying pounds in the foreign exchange market tends to increase the pound's exchange-rate value, so the exchange rate tends to rise above $4.00/pound (and toward $4.87/pound).

11. Key features of the interwar currency experience were that exchange rates were highly variable, especially during the first years after World War I and during the early 1930s. Speculation seemed to add to the instability, and governments sometimes appeared to manipulate the exchange-rate values of their currencies to gain competitive advantage. One lesson that policymakers learned from this experience was that fixed exchange rates were desirable to constrain speculation and variability in exchange rates, as well as to constrain governments from manipulating exchange rates. These lessons are now debated because subsequent studies have shown that the experience can be explained or understood in other ways. Exchange-rate changes in the years after World War I tended to move in ways consistent with purchasing power parity, which suggests that the fundamental problems were government policies that led to high inflation rates in some countries. The currency instability of the early 1930s seems to be reflecting the large shocks caused by the global depression. Indeed, the research suggests that it may not be possible to keep exchange rates fixed when large shocks hit the system.

13. The Bretton Woods system of fixed exchange rates collapsed largely because of problems with the key currency of the system, the U.S. dollar. The dollar's problems arose partly as a result of the design of the system and partly as a result of U.S. government policies. As the system evolved, it became a gold-exchange standard in which other countries fixed their currencies to the U.S. dollar, largely held U.S. dollars as their official reserve assets, and intervened to defend the fixed exchange rates using dollars. The United States was obligated to exchange dollars for gold with other central banks at the official gold price. This caused two problems for the system. First, other central banks accumulated dollar official reserves when the United States ran a deficit in its official settlements balance. In the early years of Bretton Woods this was desirable, as other central banks wanted to increase their holdings of official reserves. But in the 1960s, this became undesirable as the U.S. deficits became too large. Expansionary U.S. fiscal and monetary policies led to the large U.S. deficits and to rising inflation in the United States. Second, other central banks saw their rising dollar holdings and a declining U.S. gold stock, and they began to question whether the United States could continue to honor the official gold price.

The U.S. government probably could have maintained the system, at least for longer than it actually lasted, if it had been willing to change its domestic policies, tightening up on government spending to contract the economy and cool off its inflation. The United States instead reacted by changing the rules of Bretton Woods, severing the link between the private gold market and the official gold price in 1968 and suspending gold convertibility and forcing other countries to revalue their currencies in 1971. An agreement in late 1971 reestablished fixed exchange rates after a short period in which some currencies floated, but most major currencies shifted to floating in 1973.

Another contributor to the collapse of the system was the ability of investors to take one-way speculative gambles against currencies that were perceived to be candidates for devaluation. The adjustable-peg system gave speculators a bet in which they could gain a lot if the currency was devalued but would lose little if it was not. Most governments did not have large enough holdings of official reserves to defend the fixed exchange rate against a determined speculative attack.

Chapter 21

1. Disagree. Borrowing from foreign lenders provides a net gain to the borrowing country, as long as the money is used wisely. For instance, as long as the money is used to finance new capital investments whose returns are at least as large as the cost of servicing the foreign debt, then the borrowing country gains well-being. This is the gain of area $(d + e + f)$ in Figure 21.1.

3. The surge in bank lending to developing countries during 1974–1982 had these main causes: (1) a rise in bank funds from the "petrodollar" deposits by newly wealthy oil-exporting governments; (2) bank and investor concerns that investments in industrialized countries would not be profitable because the oil shocks had created uncertainty about the strength of these economies; (3) developing countries' resistance to foreign direct investment, which led these countries to prefer loans as the way to borrow internationally; and (4) some amount of herding behavior by

bank lenders, which built on the momentum of factors (1) through (3) and led to overlending.

5. a. World product without international lending is the shaded area. We first need to calculate the intercepts for the two MPK lines. The negative of the slope of MPK_{Japan} is 1 percent per 600, so the intercept for Japan is 12 percent. The "negative" of the slope of $MPK_{America}$ is also 1 percent per 600, so the intercept for America is about 14.7 percent. Japan's product is the rectangle of income from lending its wealth at 2 percent (120) plus the triangle above it (300), which is income for everyone else in Japan. America's product is the rectangle of income from lending its wealth at 8 percent (320) plus the triangle above it (about 134), which is income to everyone else in America. Adding up these four components yields a total world product of 874.

    b. Free international lending adds area *RST* (54), so total world product rises to 928.

    c. The 2 percent tax results in a loss of area *TUV* (6), so total world product falls to 922.

7. a. A large amount of short-term debt can cause a financial crisis because lenders can refuse to roll over the debt or refinance it and instead demand immediate repayment. If the borrowing country cannot meet its obligations to repay, default becomes more likely.

    b. Lenders can become concerned that other countries in the region are also likely to be hit with financial crises. This contagion can then become a self-fulfilling panic. If lenders refuse to make new loans and sell off investments, the country may not be able to meet its obligations to repay, so default becomes more likely. And the prices of the country's stocks and bonds can plummet as investors flee.

9. a. If lenders had detailed, accurate, and timely information on the debt and official reserves of a developing country, they should be able to make better lending and investing decisions, to avoid overlending or too much short-term lending. Better information should also reduce pure contagion, which is often based on vague concerns that other developing countries might be like the initial crisis country. In addition, developing countries that must report such detailed information are more likely to have prudent

macroeconomic policies, so that they do not have to report poor performance.

b. Controls on capital inflows can (1) limit total borrowing by the country to reduce the risk of overlending and overborrowing, (2) reduce short-term borrowing if the controls are skewed against this kind of borrowing, and (3) reduce exposure to contagion by reducing the amount of loans and investments that panicked foreign lenders can pull out when a crisis hits some other country.

11. The likelihood of a banking crisis following an unexpected depreciation of the local currency is fairly high. Banks in this country appear to have substantial exposure to exchange rate risk. The banks are short dollars because their liabilities (the deposits) denominated in dollars appear to be unhedged against exchange rate risk—the dollar liabilities exceed any assets that they may have denominated in dollars. (Looked at the other way, the banks are long the local-currency—the loans.) An unexpected devaluation of the country's currency would lead to large losses for the banks because the local-currency value of their liabilities would increase. If the losses are large enough, a banking crisis is likely. Because of the large losses, the banks would become insolvent (negative net worth) and may have to cease functioning. Even if the banks are not immediately bankrupt, depositors may create a run on the banks, as the depositors fear losing their deposits and try to withdraw their deposits quickly. The banks would not be able to find sufficient funds to pay the depositors quickly and would have to suspend payments.

Chapter 22

1. Mexico. The United States and Mexico have close trading ties, with most of Mexico's exports destined for the United States. If national production and income increase in the United States, the relatively large increase in Mexican exports to the United States increases Mexico's domestic product by a substantial amount. For countries other than Mexico and Canada, the shares of their exports that go to the United States generally are lower.

3. a. The spending multiplier is $1/(0.2 + 0.1) = 3.3$, so domestic product will increase by $3.3 billion.

b. For a closed economy, the spending multiplier is $1/0.2 = 5$, so domestic product will increase by $5 billion. The spending multiplier is larger for a closed economy than for a small open economy because there is no import "leakage" for the closed economy. For both economies, as production and income rise following the initial increase in spending, some of the extra income goes into saving (and to pay taxes), so that the next rounds of increases in production and income are smaller. For the open economy, as production and income rise, there is an additional leakage out of the domestic demand stream as some of the country's spending goes to additional imports. Spending on imports does not create extra demand for this country's production. The next rounds of increases in the country's production and income become smaller more quickly, resulting in a smaller multiplier.

5. The intersection of the IS and LM curves indicates a short-run equilibrium in the country's market for goods and services (the IS curve) and a short-run equilibrium in the country's market for money (the LM curve). The intersection indicates the equilibrium level of the country's real domestic product and income (its real GDP) and the equilibrium level of its interest rate. We evaluate internal balance by comparing the actual level of domestic product to the level that we estimate the economy is able to produce when it is fully using its supply-side production capabilities. If the short-run equilibrium level of domestic product is too low—less than this "full-employment" level—the country has an internal imbalance that results in high unemployment. If the short-run equilibrium level of domestic product is pushing to be too high—more than its "full-employment" level—the country has an internal imbalance that results in rising inflation (driven by excessive demand).

7. a. A decrease in the money supply tends to raise interest rates (and lower domestic product). Thus, the LM curve shifts up (or to the left).

b. An increase in the interest rate does not shift the LM curve. Rather, it results in a movement along the LM curve.

9. a. An increase in foreign demand for the country's exports tends to drive the country's overall international payments into surplus. To reestablish payments balance, the country's domestic product and income could be higher (so imports increase) or the country's interest rates could be lower (to create a capital outflow and reduce the country's financial account balance). Thus, the FE curve shifts to the right or down.

   b. An increase in the foreign interest rate tends to drive the country's overall international payments into deficit because of capital outflows seeking the higher foreign returns. To reestablish payments balance, the country's domestic product could be lower (to reduce imports) or its interest rates could be higher (to reverse the capital outflow). Thus, the FE curve shifts to the left or up.

   c. An increase in the country's interest rate does not shift the FE curve. Rather, it results in a movement along the FE curve.

11. The real exchange rate value of the dollar decreased from 110 to 100, so the U.S. dollar had a real depreciation. The United States gained international price competitiveness. (For the import and export functions shown in equations 22.13 and 22.14, the ratio ($P_f \times e/P$) is an indicator of the U.S. international price competitiveness. Stated this way, the real exchange rate is measuring the real exchange-rate value of the foreign (rest of the world) currency—the nominal exchange rate e is valuing foreign currency and the foreign currency product price index P_f is in the numerator. The rest of the world experienced a real appreciation (from 91 to 100), so the rest of the world lost international price competitiveness.) A change in international price competitiveness drives a change in the country's net exports and current account, so the IS and FE curves shift. An improvement in international price competitiveness tends to increase exports and to decrease imports. Aggregate demand for U.S. products increases, so the IS curve shifts to the right. The current account balance tends to improve, so the FE curve shifts to the right.

Chapter 23

1. Disagree. The risk is rising unemployment, not rising inflation. The deficit in its overall international payments puts downward pressure on the exchange-rate value of the country's currency. The central bank must intervene to defend the fixed exchange rate by buying domestic currency and selling foreign currency in the foreign exchange market. As the central bank buys domestic currency, it reduces the monetary base and the country's money supply falls. The tightening of the domestic money supply puts upward pressure on the country's interest rates. Rising interest rates reduce interest-sensitive spending, lowering aggregate demand, domestic product, and national income. The risk is falling real GDP and rising unemployment.

3. Perfect capital mobility essentially eliminates the country's ability to run an independent monetary policy. The country must direct its monetary policy to keeping its interest rate in line with foreign interest rates. If it tried to tighten monetary policy, its interest rates would start to increase, but this would draw a massive inflow of capital. To defend the fixed exchange rate, the central bank would need to sell domestic currency into the foreign exchange market. This would increase the domestic money supply, forcing the central bank to reverse its tightening. If it tried to loosen monetary policy, interest rates would begin to decline, but the massive capital outflow would require the central bank to defend the fixed rate by buying domestic currency. The decrease in the domestic money supply forces the central bank to reverse its loosening.

   Perfect capital mobility makes fiscal policy powerful in affecting domestic product and income in the short run. For instance, expansionary fiscal policy tends to increase domestic product, but the increase in domestic product could be constrained by the crowding out of interest-sensitive spending as interest rates increase. With perfect capital mobility the domestic interest rate cannot rise if foreign interest rates are steady, so there is no crowding out. Domestic product and income increase by the full value of the spending multiplier.

5. Agree. Consider the value of the country's current account measured in foreign currency (superscript F):

$$CA^F = (P^F_x \times X) - (P^F_m \times M)$$

According to the logic of the J-curve analysis, the price changes resulting from the exchange-rate change occur first, and the effects on export and import volumes occur more slowly. The revaluation quickly increases the foreign-currency price of the country's exports (because it now takes more foreign currency to yield the same home-currency price). Therefore, the current account improves in the months immediately after the revaluation. (Eventually the revaluation leads to a decrease in export volume, an increase in import volume, and perhaps an increase in the foreign-currency price of imports, so eventually the current account value is likely to decrease.)

7. a. The FE curve shifts to the right or down.

   b. The capital inflows drive the country's overall international payments into surplus. They put upward pressure on the exchange-rate value of the country's currency. The central bank must intervene to defend the fixed exchange rate by selling domestic currency in the foreign exchange market.

   c. As the central bank intervenes by selling domestic currency in the foreign exchange market, the country's monetary base and its money supply increase. The increase in the money supply lowers domestic interest rates. The lower interest rates encourage interest-sensitive spending, raising aggregate demand, domestic product, and income. External balance is reestablished through two adjustments. First, domestic product and income are higher, so imports increase. Second, the country's interest rates are lower, so the capital inflows are discouraged and capital outflows are encouraged.

   The increase in the country's domestic product and income alters its internal balance. If the country began with high unemployment, then this would be welcome as a move toward internal balance. If, instead, the country does not have the resources to produce the extra output, the country would develop the internal imbalance of rising inflation as the economy tries to expand and overheats.

   In the IS–LM–FE graph below the increased capital inflows shift the FE curve to the right to FE′. The country's international payments are then in surplus as the intersection of the original IS and LM curves at E_0 is to the left of FE′. The intervention to defend the fixed rate shifts the LM curve down (or to the right). External balance is reestablished at the new triple intersection E_1.

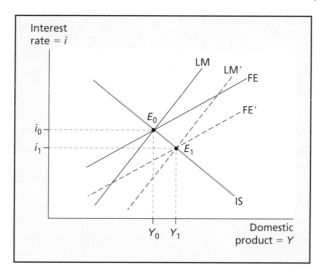

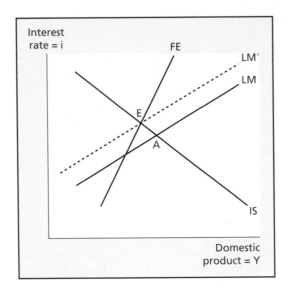

9. The country initially has an overall payment deficit. In the IS-LM-FE graph above, the IS-LM intersection at point A is to right of the FE curve. (The FE curve is steeper than the LM curve because international capital flows are relatively unresponsive to changes in interest rates.) If the country's central bank does nothing else, it would have to intervene in the foreign exchange market to defend the fixed exchange rate value because the country's currency is under pressure to depreciate. The central bank would need to buy domestic currency and sell foreign currency (e.g., U.S. dollars). If the country does not sterilize, then the country's LM curve will slowly shift to the left, and eventually the payments deficit will be eliminated when the LM curve reaches LM', with the new triple intersection at point E. But, if the country uses its international reserve holdings as the source of the foreign currency it sells in the intervention, then the country's holdings of official international reserves will decrease.

Is there anything that the central bank can do to avoid (or to minimize) the loss of international reserves? The central bank could take a domestic action to shift the LM curve more quickly to the left. For example, the central bank could use domestic open market operations to sell national government bonds, and the domestic money supply will shrink more quickly. The LM curve

will shift to the left. The overall payments deficit will decrease more quickly, with less intervention to defend the fixed-rate value and less loss of international reserves. In the graph, the domestic monetary action shifts the LM curve quickly to LM'. (Another possibility is that the country's central bank could borrow the foreign currency, for example, from other central banks. Its gross holdings of official reserve assets would remain steady, but its holdings net of what it owes would decrease, and it will eventually need to repay the loans.)

11. a. Tighten fiscal policy to address the internal imbalance of rising inflation and tighten monetary policy to address the external imbalance of the deficit.

b. Tighten fiscal policy to address the internal imbalance of rising inflation and loosen monetary policy to address the external imbalance of the surplus.

c. Loosen fiscal policy to address the internal imbalance of low demand and loosen monetary policy to address the external imbalance of the surplus.

Chapter 24

1. Agree. The change in the exchange rate that occurs when there is a change in monetary policy is the basis for the enhanced

effectiveness of monetary policy under floating exchange rates. For instance, when monetary policy shifts to be more expansionary, the decrease in the country's interest rate results in a depreciation of the country's currency. This is essentially overshooting (although overshooting also emphasizes that this depreciation is very large). It is overshooting relative to the path of the exchange rate implied by PPP, so that the depreciation improves the country's international price competitiveness. The improvement in price competitiveness enhances the effectiveness of the policy. The country exports more and shifts some of its spending from imports to domestic products, further increasing aggregate demand, domestic product, and income.

3. Disagree. Under floating exchange rates the decrease in our exports reduces demand for our currency in the foreign exchange market, so our currency depreciates. The depreciation improves our international price competitiveness, so exports tend to rebound somewhat, and some spending is shifted from imports to domestic products. This increase in aggregate demand counters the initial drop in demand for our exports, so the adverse effect on our domestic product and income is lessened. This exchange-rate adjustment is not possible if the exchange rate is fixed. In addition, with a fixed exchange rate our overall international payments go into deficit when our exports decline. The central bank then intervenes to defend the fixed rate by buying domestic currency. The reduction in the domestic money supply raises our interest rate and makes the decline in our domestic product larger.

5. The tendency for the overall international payments to go into deficit puts downward pressure on the exchange-rate value of the country's currency, and it depreciates. This moves the country further from internal balance. The depreciation of the currency tends to increase aggregate demand by making the country's products more price-competitive internationally. The extra demand adds to the inflationary pressure. In addition, the depreciation raises the domestic-currency price of imports, adding to the inflation pressure.

7. a. The increase in taxes reduces disposable income and reduces aggregate demand. U.S. domestic product and income will fall (or be lower than they otherwise would be). If national income is lower, spending on imports will be lower, so the U.S. current account will improve. The increase in taxes reduces the government budget deficit. The government borrows less, and U.S. interest rates are lower. If international capital flows are responsive to changes in interest differentials, then the lower U.S. interest rates lead to capital outflows (or less capital inflows). The U.S. financial account declines.

b. The pressures on the exchange-rate value of the dollar depend on which change is larger: the improvement in the current account or the deterioration in the financial account. If the effect on capital flows is larger, then demand for dollars will decrease (relative to the supply of dollars) in the foreign exchange market, so the dollar will depreciate. If the current account change is larger, then the supply of dollars (relative to demand) will decrease, so the dollar will appreciate.

c. If the dollar depreciates, then the United States gains international price competitiveness. U.S. exports increase and imports decrease. The current account improves further. The increase in exports and shift of domestic spending from imports to domestic products add some aggregate demand, so domestic product and income rebound somewhat (or do not decline by as much).

9. a. The FE curve shifts to the right or down.

b. The country's international payments tend toward surplus. The extra demand for the country's currency leads to its appreciation.

c. The appreciation reduces the country's international price competitiveness, so the country's exports decrease and its imports increase. The current account worsens, reducing the overall surplus. In addition, the decrease in aggregate demand as the current account worsens reduces domestic product and income. Money demand declines and the

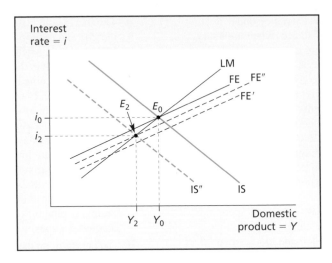

country's interest rate declines. The decline in the interest rate discourages some capital inflow or encourages some capital outflow. The financial account worsens, so the overall surplus also falls for this reason. The combined effects on the current and financial accounts reestablish external balance. The declines in aggregate demand and domestic product affect the county's internal balance. If rising inflation was initially a problem, then this change is desirable. However, the decrease in aggregate demand could instead create or add to an internal imbalance of high unemployment.

In the graph above the increased capital inflows shift the FE curve to the right or down to FE'. The country's currency appreciates, so the FE curve shifts back to the left somewhat to FE", and the IS curve shifts to the left to IS" as the country loses international price-competitiveness. The new triple intersection is at point E_2. External balance is reestablished, the interest rate is lower, and domestic product is lower, relative to the initial equilibrium at point E_0.

11. a. The central bank probably made a profit. The central bank bought pesos at $3.00/peso, sold pesos at $3.50/peso, bought pesos at $3.10/peso, and sold pesos at $3.40/peso. The central bank bought pesos low and sold them high. (You reach the same conclusion if you look at the dollar sales and purchases.

The central bank bought dollars at 0.286 peso/dollar and 0.294 peso/dollar, and it sold dollars at 0.333 peso/dollar and 0.323/dollar.) To determine the exact profit or loss, you need to bring in dollar and peso interest rates.

b. The central bank probably made a profit. The central bank sold yen at $0.60/yen, $0.55/yen, and $0.51/yen. Then, with the exchange rate value stabilized, the central bank could, if it wanted to, buy yen to replace those it had sold, at the price $0.50/yen. The central bank sold yen high and could rebuy them low. (You reach the same conclusion if you look at dollar purchases. The central bank bought dollars at 1.67 yen/dollar, 1.82 yen/dollar, and 1.96 yen/dollar. The central bank could then sell the dollars at 2.00 yen/dollar.) To determine the exact profit or loss, you need to bring in dollar and yen interest rates.

Chapter 25

1. Disagree. Countries must follow policies that are not too different if they are to be able to maintain the fixed exchange rates. The policies need not be exactly the same, but the policies must lead to private demand and supply in the foreign exchange market that permits the countries to defend the fixed rates successfully. The most obvious need for consistency is in policies toward inflation rates. For fixed rates to be sustained, inflation rates must be the same or very similar for the countries involved.

If inflation rates are the same, then fixed
rates are consistent with purchasing power
parity over time. If, instead, the inflation rates
are different, then with fixed exchange rates
the high-inflation countries will lose price-
competitiveness over time. Their international
payments will tend toward deficits, and the
fixed rates will not be sustainable in the face
of the "fundamental disequilibrium." Another
need for consistency is in policies that can
have a major influence on international capital
flows. If policies lead to large capital flows,
especially outflows, they may overwhelm
the government's ability to defend the fixed
exchange rate.

3. A floating exchange rate provides some
insulation from foreign business cycles
because the rate tends to change in a way
that counters the spread of the business cycle
through international trade. For instance,
when a foreign country goes into recession, its
demand for imports declines. This lowers the
focus country's exports, reducing its aggregate
demand, and it tends to go into recession. With
floating exchange rates, the focus country's
international payments tend to go into deficit
when the country's exports decline, and the
country's currency depreciates. The depreciation
improves the country's international price-
competitiveness. Its exports rebound somewhat,
and it shifts some spending away from imports
and toward domestic products. Therefore,
aggregate demand rises back up. The tendency
toward recession is not so strong, so floating
exchange rates provide some insulation from
foreign business cycles.

5. Possible criteria include the following. First, if
the country wants to shift to a fixed exchange
rate to promote international trade by reducing
exchange-rate risk, then it should consider
fixing its exchange rate to the currency of
one of its major trading partners. Second,
the country should look for a country whose
priorities and policies are compatible with
its own. For instance, if the country wants
to have and maintain a low inflation rate,
then it should consider fixing its rate to the
currency of a foreign country that has and is
likely to maintain policies that result in a low
inflation rate. Third, the country should look

for a foreign country that is seldom subject to
large domestic shocks. With a fixed exchange
rate, any economic shocks in the foreign
country will be transmitted to this country.
(From this country's point of view, these are
external shocks.) The country will lose the
ability of floating exchange rates to buffer the
disruptiveness of these external shocks, so it
should consider fixing its rate to the currency
of a foreign country that has a relatively stable
domestic economy.

7. a. In the short run the country must implement
policies to reduce aggregate demand. The
reduction in aggregate demand will create
the discipline of weak demand in putting
downward pressure on the inflation rate.
Tightening up on monetary policy is one way
to do this in the short run, and it is crucial to
reducing the inflation rate in the long run. In
the long run the growth of the money supply
is the major policy-controlled determinant
of the country's inflation rate. The floating
exchange rate can be affected by these policy
changes, but the key to reducing the inflation
rate is getting domestic policies pointed in
the right direction.

   b. The major countries of the world generally
have low inflation rates. Adopting a
currency board and a fixed exchange rate
with one of these currencies may help the
country reduce its inflation rate for several
reasons. First, the country is accepting
the discipline effect of fixed exchange
rates. If the country's demand expands
too rapidly or its inflation rate is too high,
its international payments tend to go into
deficit. By intervening to defend the fixed
exchange rate, the country's currency
board will buy domestic currency. This
tends to force a tighter monetary policy
on the country. Second, the shift to the
currency board and fixed exchange rate can
enhance the credibility of the government's
policy, signaling that the government is
truly serious about reducing the country's
inflation rate. Actually reducing the
inflation rate is easier if people expect that
it is going to decrease. Third, with a fixed
exchange rate the local-currency prices
of imported goods tend to be steady. The

steady prices of imports not only reduce the country's measured inflation rate directly but also put competitive pressure on the prices of domestic products, so these prices do not rise as much.

9. Dollarization is the process of a country (unilaterally) replacing its own currency with the currency of some other country, for general use in transactions within the country. Compared to using the national currency, having a national central bank, and maintaining a fixed exchange rate between the country's currency and the currency of the other country, dollarization has advantages and disadvantages, so dollarization may be better or worse for the country. Advantages: First, dollarization eliminates the exchange rate risk that the country's government could change the fixed rate value in the future (although there is some small risk that a dollarized country could reintroduce its own currency). Second, dollarization eliminates transactions costs between the local currency and the foreign currency. Disadvantages: First, the dollarized country loses the seigniorage profit from issuing its own currency. (Instead, the foreign central bank earns the seigniorage profit, which can be viewed as the profit from issuing zero-interest money as a financial asset.) Second, the dollarized country loses the ability to adjust its exchange rate as a tool of macroeconomic policy. The dollarized country also loses the ability to conduct its own monetary policy, although this ability would still be much diminished if instead the country was committed to the fixed exchange rate to the foreign currency.

11. There are several strong arguments. Here are four. First, joining the monetary union and adopting the euro will eliminate the transactions costs of exchanging pounds for euros. Resources used for this purpose can be shifted to other uses. The lower costs will encourage more British trade and investment with the member countries of the euro area. Second, joining the monetary union will eliminate exchange-rate risk between the pound and the euro. Again, trade and investment with the euro area are encouraged. Third, the risk of rising British inflation is reduced, to the extent that the European Central Bank, with its mandate to keep inflation in the euro area to 2 percent or below, is likely to be better at controlling inflation than the British central bank would be. And finally, the shift to the euro can enhance the role of London as a center of international finance. As long as Britain stays out of the monetary union, European financial activities may drift away from London to other centers (Frankfurt, Paris) where the euro is local currency.

References*

Agénor, Pierre-Richard. "Benefits and Costs of International Financial Integration: Theory and Facts." *World Economy* 26, no. 8 (August 2003), pp. 1089–1118.

———. "Orderly Exits from Adjustable Pegs and Exchange Rate Bands." *Journal of Policy Reform* 7, no. 2 (June 2004), pp. 83–108.

Aggarwal, Aradhna. "Trade Effects of Anti-Dumping in India: Who Benefits?" *International Trade Journal* 25, no. 1 (January–March 2011), pp. 112–158.

Aizenman, Joshua, and Reuven Glick. "Sterilization, Monetary Policy, and Global Financial Integration." *Review of International Economics* 17, no. 4 (September 2009), pp. 777–801.

Akram, Farooq, Dagfinn Rime, and Lucio Sarno. "Arbitrage in the Foreign Exchange Market: Turning on the Microscope." *JIE* 76, no. 2 (December 2008), pp. 237–253.

Aldy, Joseph E., Alan J. Krupnick, Richard G. Newell, Ian W. H. Parry, and William A. Pizer. "Designing Climate Mitigation Policy." *JEL* 48, no. 4 (December 2010), pp. 903–934.

Aliber, Robert Z. "Speculation in the Foreign Exchanges: The European Experience, 1919–1926." *Yale Economic Essays* 2 (1962), pp. 171–245.

Anderson, James E., and Eric van Wincoop. "Gravity with Gravitas: A Solution to the Border Puzzle." *AER* 93, no. 1 (March 2003), pp. 170–192.

———. "Trade Costs." *JEL* 42, no. 3 (September 2004), pp. 691–751.

Anderson, Michael A., and Stephen L. S. Smith. "Canadian Trade and Wages: Lessons from the Past, Prospects for the Future." *World Economy* 23, no. 8 (August 2000), pp. 1005–1029.

*Often-cited journals:
AER = American Economic Review
JEL = Journal of Economic Literature
JEP = Journal of Economic Perspectives
JIE = Journal of International Economics
JPE = Journal of Political Economy

Antweiler, Werner, and Daniel Trefler. "Increasing Returns and All That: A View from Trade." *AER* 92, no. 1 (March 2002), pp. 93–119.

Baba, Naohiko, and Frank Packer. "From Turmoil to Crisis: Dislocations in the FX Swap Market before and after the Failure of Lehman Brothers." *Journal of International Money and Finance* 28, no. 8 (December 2009), pp. 1350–1374.

Bagwell, Kyle, and Robert Staiger. *Economics of the World Trading System*. Cambridge, MA: MIT Press, 2002.

Baicker, Katherine, and M. Marit Rehavi. "Policy Watch: Trade Adjustment Assistance." *JEP* 18, no. 2 (Spring 2004), pp. 239–255.

Balakrishnan, Ravi, and Volodymyr Tulin. "U.S. Dollar Risk Premiums and Capital Flows." IMF Working Paper WP/06/160, June 2006.

Balassa, Bela. *European Economic Integration*. Amsterdam: North-Holland, 1975.

———. *The Structure of Protection in Developing Countries*. Baltimore: Johns Hopkins University Press, 1971.

Baldwin, Richard E., and Anthony J. Venables. "Regional Economic Integration." In Grossman and Rogoff (1995).

Baldwin, Richard E., and Charles Wyplosz. *Economics of European Integration,* 4th ed. New York: McGraw-Hill, 2012.

Barba Navaretti, Giorgio, and Anthony J. Venables. *Multinational Firms in the World Economy*. Princeton, NJ: Princeton University Press, 2004.

Barro, Robert J., and Jong Wha Lee. "A New Data Set of Educational Attainment in the World, 1950–2010." *Journal of Development Economics* 104 (September 2013), pp. 184–198.

Bartram, Söhnke M., and Gunter Dufey. "International Portfolio Investment: Theory, Evidence and Institutional Framework." *Financial Markets, Institutions & Instruments* 10, no. 3 (August 2001), pp. 85–155.

Bems, Rudolfs, Robert C. Johnson, and Kei-Mu Yi. "The Great Trade Collapse." *Annual Review of Economics* 5 (2013), pp. 375–400.

Bernard, Andrew B., Jonathan Eaton, J. Bradford Jensen, and Samuel Kortum. "Plants and Productivity in International Trade." *AER* 93, no. 4 (September 2003), pp. 1268–1290.

Bernard, Andrew B., J. Bradford Jensen, Stephen J. Redding, and Peter K. Schott. "Firms in International Trade." *JEP* 21, no. 3 (Summer 2007), pp. 105–130.

Bernhofen, Daniel M., and John C. Brown. "An Empirical Assessment of the Comparative Advantage Gains from Trade: Evidence from Japan." *AER* 95, no. 1 (March 2005), pp. 208–225.

Berry, Steven, James Levinsohn, and Ariel Pakes. "Voluntary Export Restraints on Automobiles: Evaluating a Trade Policy." *AER* 89, no. 3 (June 1999), pp. 400–430.

Bhagwati, Jagdish N. "Immiserizing Growth: A Geometrical Note." *Review of Economics Studies* 25, no. 3 (June 1958), pp. 201–205.

———. *In Defense of Globalization*. New York: Oxford University Press, 2004.

———. *Termites in the Trading System: How Preferential Agreements Undermine Free Trade*. New York: Oxford University Press, 2008.

———. *Trade, Tariffs and Growth*. Cambridge, MA: MIT Press, 1969.

——— and Anne Krueger. A series of volumes on *Foreign Trade Regimes and Economic Development*. New York: Columbia University Press for the National Bureau of Economic Research, 1973–1976.

Bhattasali, Deepak, Shantong Li, and Will Martin, eds. *China and the WTO: Accession, Policy Reform, and Poverty Reduction Strategies*. Washington, DC: World Bank and Oxford University Press, 2004.

Bird, Graham. "IMF Programs: Do They Work? Can They Be Made to Work Better?" *World Development* 29, no. 11 (November 2001), pp. 1849–1865.

Bjørnland, Hilde C. "Monetary Policy and Exchange Rate Overshooting: Dornbusch Was Right after All.'" *JIE* 79, no. 1 (September 2009), pp. 64–77.

Blonigen, Bruce. "Evolving Discretionary Practices of U.S. Antidumping Activity." *Canadian Journal of Economics* 39, no. 3 (August 2006), pp. 874–900.

Bloom, David E., Gilles Grenier, and Morley Gunderson. "The Changing Labor Market Position of Canadian Immigrants." Working Paper no. 4672. National Bureau of Economic Research, March 1994.

Bloomfield, Arthur I. *Monetary Policy under the International Gold Standard, 1880–1914*. New York: Federal Reserve Bank of New York, 1959.

Bordo, Michael D., and Barry Eichengreen, eds. *Retrospective on the Bretton Woods International Monetary System*. Chicago: University of Chicago Press, 1992.

——— and Anna J. Schwartz, eds. *A Retrospect on the Classical Gold Standard, 1821–1931*. Chicago: University of Chicago Press, 1984.

Borjas, George J. "The Economic Benefit from Immigration." *JEP* 9, no. 2 (Spring 1995), pp. 3–22.

———. "The Economics of Immigration." *JEL* 32, no. 4 (December 1994), pp. 1667–1717.

———, Richard B. Freeman, and Laurence F. Katz. "How Much Do Immigration and Trade Affect Labor Market Outcomes?" *Brookings Papers on Economic Activity*, no. 1 (1997), pp. 1–90.

Bosworth, Barry P. *Saving and Investment in a Global Economy*. Washington, DC: Brookings Institution, 1993.

Bowen, Harry P., Edward E. Leamer, and Leo Sveikauskas. "Multicountry, Multifactor Tests of the Factor Abundance Theory." *AER* 77, no. 5 (December 1987), pp. 791–809.

Bown, Chad P. "China's WTO Entry: Antidumping, Safeguards, and Dispute Settlement." In *China's Growing Role in World Trade*, ed. Robert C. Feenstra and Shang-Jin Wei. Chicago: University of Chicago Press, 2010.

———. *Self-Enforcing Trade: Developing Countries and WTO Dispute Settlement*. Washington, DC: Brookings Institution Press, 2009.

———. "Taking Stock of Antidumping, Safeguards, and Countervailing Duties, 1990–2009." *World Economy* 34, no. 12 (December 2011), pp. 1955–1998.

Brainard, S. Lael. "An Empirical Assessment of the Proximity-Concentration Trade-Off between Multinational Sales and Trade." *AER* 87, no. 4 (September 1997), pp. 520–544.

Brander, James A. "Strategic Trade Policy." In Grossman and Rogoff (1995).

Broadman, Harry G., ed. *From Disintegration to Reintegration: Eastern Europe and the Former Soviet Union in International Trade.* Washington, DC: World Bank, 2005.

Broda, Christian. "Terms of Trade and Exchange Rate Regimes in Developing Countries." *JIE* 63, no. 1 (May 2004), pp. 31–58.

———, Nuno Limão, and David E. Weinstein. "Optimal Tariffs and Market Power: The Evidence," *AER* 98, no. 5 (December 2008), 2032–2065.

Broda, Christian, and David Weinstein. "Globalization and the Gains from Variety." *Quarterly Journal of Economics* 121, no. 2 (May 2006), pp. 541–585.

Brülhart, Marius. "An Account of Global Intra-Industry Trade, 1962–2006." *World Economy* 32, no. 3 (March 2009), pp. 401–459.

Brunnermeier, Smita B., and Arik Levinson. "Examining the Evidence on Environmental Regulations and Industry Location." *Journal of Environment & Development* 13, no. 1 (March 2004), pp. 6–41.

Bruton, Henry J. "A Reconsideration of Import Substitution." *JEL* 36, no. 2 (June 1998), pp. 903–936.

Bryant, Ralph C. *International Coordination of National Stabilization Policies.* Washington, DC: Brookings Institution, 1995.

Buckley, Peter, and Mark Casson. *Future of Multinational Enterprise.* New York: Macmillan, 1976.

Calvo, Guillermo A., and Carmen M. Reinhart. "Fear of Floating." *Quarterly Journal of Economics* 117, no. 2 (May 2002), pp. 379–408.

Campa, José Manuel, and Linda S. Goldberg. "Exchange Rate Pass-Through into Import Prices." *Review of Economics and Statistics* 87, no. 4 (November 2005), pp. 664–678.

Card, David. "Immigration and Inequality." *AER* 99, no. 2 (May 2009), pp. 1–21.

Caves, Richard E. *Multinational Enterprise and Economic Analysis*, 3rd ed. New York: Cambridge University Press, 2007.

Cheung, Yin-Wong, and Menzie David Chinn. "Currency Traders and Exchange Rate Dynamics: A Survey of the US Market." *Journal of International Money and Finance* 20, no. 4 (August 2001), pp. 439–471.

Cheung, Yin-Wong, and Clement Yuk-Pang Wong. "A Survey of Market Practitioners' Views on Exchange Rate Dynamics." *JIE* 51, no. 2 (August 2000), pp. 401–419.

Choksi, Armeane M., Michael Michaely, and Demetris Papageorgiou. *Liberalizing Foreign Trade*. Oxford, England: Basil Blackwell, 1991.

Chor, Davin. "Unpacking Sources of Comparative Advantage: A Quantitative Approach." *JIE* 82, no. 2 (November 2010), pp. 152–167.

Cline, William R. *United States as a Debtor Nation.* Washington, DC: Institute for International Economics, 2005.

Cohen, Daniel, and Marcelo Soto. "Growth and Human Capital: Good Data, Good Results." *Journal of Economic Growth* 12, no. 1 (March 2007), pp. 51–76.

Collier, Paul. *Exodus: How Migration Is Changing Our World.* New York: Oxford University Press, 2013.

Congressional Budget Office. "Antidumping Action in the United States and around the World: An Update." CBO Paper, June 2001.

Copeland, Brian R., and M. Scott Taylor. "Trade, Growth, and the Environment." *JEL* 42, no. 1 (March 2004), pp. 7–71.

Dalsgaard, Thomas, Christophe André, and Pete Richardson. "Standard Shocks in the OECD Interlink Model." Organization for Economic Cooperation and Development, Economics Department Working Paper no. 306, September 6, 2001.

Davis, Donald R., and David E. Weinstein. "An Account of Global Factor Trade." *AER* 91, no. 5 (December 2001), pp. 1423–1453.

———. "The Factor Content of Trade." In *Handbook of International Trade, Volume 1*, ed. E. Kwan Choi and James Harrigan. Malden, MA: Blackwell, 2003.

Deardorff, Alan V. "Testing Trade Theories and Predicting Trade Flows." In Jones and Kenen, eds., *Handbook*, vol. I, 1984.

De Grauwe, Paul. *Economics of Monetary Union*, 8th ed. New York: Oxford University Press, 2009.

de Haan, Jakob, Sylvester C.W. Eijffinger, and Sandra Waller. *European Central Bank: Credibility, Transparency, and Centralization*. Cambridge, MA: MIT Press, 2005.

Destler, I. M. *American Trade Politics*, 4th ed. Washington, DC: Institute for International Economics, 2005.

Dixit, Avinash. "Tax Policy in Open Economies." In *Handbook of Public Economics*, ed. Alan Auerbach and Martin Feldstein. New York: North-Holland, 1985.

Docquier, Frédéric, and Hillel Rapoport. "Globalization, Brain Drain, and Development." *JEL* 50, no. 3 (September 2012), pp. 681–730.

Dornbusch, Rudiger. "Expectations and Exchange Rate Dynamics." *JPE* 84, no. 6 (December 1976), pp. 1161–1176.

Downs, Anthony. *An Economic Theory of Democracy*. New York: Harper & Row, 1957.

Dunning, John H. *Theories and Paradigms of International Business Activity: Selected Essays of John H. Dunning, Volume 1*. Cheltenham: Edward Elgar, 2002.

Dustmann, Christian, Tommaso Frattini, and Ian P. Preston. "The Effect of Immigration along the Distribution of Wages." *Review of Economic Studies* 80, no. 1 (January 2013), pp. 145–173.

Dutt, Pushan, Ilian Mihov, and Timothy Van Zandt. "The Effect of WTO on the Extensive and Intensive Margins of Trade." *JIE* 91, no. 2 (November 2013), pp. 204–219.

Edison, Hali J., Michael W. Klein, Luca Antonio Ricci, and Torsten Sløk. "Capital Account Liberalization and Economic Performance: Survey and Synthesis." *IMF Staff Papers* 51, no. 2 (2004), pp. 220–256.

Eichengreen, Barry. *Exorbitant Privilege: The Rise and Fall of the Dollar and the Future of the International Monetary System*. New York: Oxford University Press, 2011.

———. *Global Imbalances and the Lessons of Bretton Woods*. Cambridge, MA: MIT Press, 2007.

———. *Gold Fetters: The Gold Standard and the Great Depression, 1919–1939*. New York: Oxford University Press, 1992.

———. *Financial Crises and What to Do about Them*. New York: Oxford University Press, 2002.

——— and Ashoka Mody. "Do Collective Action Clauses Raise Borrowing Costs?" *Economic Journal* 114, no. 495 (April 2004), pp. 247–264.

Eiteman, David K., Arthur I. Stonehill, and Michael H. Moffet. *Multinational Business Finance*, 13th ed. Upper Saddle River, NJ: Prentice Hall, 2013.

Elliott, Kimberley Ann. *Delivering on Doha: Farm Trade and the Poor*. Washington, DC: Center for Global Development, Institute for International Economics, 2006.

Estevadeordal, Antoni, and Alan M. Taylor. "Is the Washington Consensus Dead? Growth, Openness, and the Great Liberalization, 1970s–2000s." *Review of Economics and Statistics* 95, no. 5 (December 2013), pp. 1669–1690.

Esty, Daniel C. "Bridging the Trade-Environment Divide." *JEP* 15, no. 3 (Summer 2001), pp. 113–130.

Ethier, Wilfred J. "Dumping." *JPE* 90, no. 3 (June 1982), pp. 487–506.

Eun, Cheol S., and Bruce G. Resnick. *International Financial Management*, 6th ed. New York: McGraw-Hill/ Irwin, 2012.

Evenett, Simon J. "Crisis-Era Protectionism One Year after the Washington G20 Meeting: A GTA Update, Some New Analysis, and a Few Words of Caution." In *Great Trade Collapse: Causes, Consequences and Prospects*, ed. Richard Baldwin. VoxEU, 2009, www.voxeu.org/reports/global_trade_collapse.pdf.

Fatum, Rasmus, and Michael M. Hutchison. "ECB Foreign Exchange Intervention and the Euro: Institutional Framework, News and Intervention." *Open Economies Review* 13, no. 4 (October 2002), pp. 413–425.

———. "Effectiveness of Official Daily Foreign Exchange Market Intervention Operations in Japan." *Journal of International Money and Finance* 25, no. 2 (March 2006), pp. 199–219.

Feenstra, Robert C. "Estimating the Effects of Trade Policy." In Grossman and Rogoff (1995).

———. *Product Variety and Gains from International Trade*. Cambridge, MA: MIT Press, 2010.

———. Robert Inklaar, and Marcel P. Timmer. "The Next Generation of the Penn World Table," 2013. Available for download at www.ggdc.net/pwt.

Fenn, Daniel J., Sam D. Howison, Mark McDonald, Stacy Williams, and Neil F. Johnson. "The Mirage of Triangular Arbitrage in the Spot Foreign Exchange Market." *International Journal of Theoretical and Applied Finance* 12, no. 8 (December 2009), pp. 1105–1123.

Findlay, Christopher, and Tony Warren, eds. *Impediments to Trade in Services: Measurement and Policy Implications*. New York: Routledge, 2000.

Findlay, Ronald, and Harry Grubert. "Factor Intensities, Technological Progress, and the Terms of Trade." *Oxford Economic Papers* 11, no. 1 (February 1959), pp. 111–121.

Finger, J. Michael, and Julio J. Nogues, eds. *Safeguards and Antidumping in Latin American Trade Liberalization: Fighting Fire with Fire*. Washington, DC: World Bank, 2006.

Fischer, Stanley. "Distinguished Lecture on Economics in Government—Exchange Rate Regimes: Is the Bipolar View Correct?" *JEP* 15, no. 2 (Spring 2001), pp. 3–24.

Fleming, J. Marcus. "Domestic Financial Policies under Fixed and Floating Exchange Rates." *IMF Staff Papers* 9 (March 1962), pp. 369–377.

Footer, Mary E., and Christoph Beat Graber. "Trade Liberalization and Cultural Policy." *Journal of International Economic Law* 3, no. 1 (March 2000), pp. 115–144.

Frankel, Jeffrey A. "On the Mark: A Theory of Floating Exchange Rates Based on Real Interest Differentials." *AER* 69, no. 4 (September 1979), pp. 610–622.

——— and Andrew K. Rose. "An Empirical Characterization of Nominal Exchange Rates." In Grossman and Rogoff (1995).

Freund, Caroline, and Emanuel Ornelas. "Regional Trade Agreements." *Annual Review of Economics* 2 (2010), pp. 139–166.

Friedberg, Rachel M., and Jennifer Hunt. "The Impact of Immigrants on Host Country Wages, Employment, and Growth." *JEP* 9, no. 2 (Spring 1995), pp. 23–44.

Friedman, Milton. "The Case for Flexible Exchange Rates." In his *Essays in Positive Economics*. Chicago: University of Chicago Press, 1953.

Froot, Kenneth A., and Kenneth Rogoff. "Perspectives on PPP and the Long-Run Real Exchange Rate." In Grossman and Rogoff (1995).

Froot, Kenneth A., and Richard H. Thaler. "Anomalies: Foreign Exchange." *JEP* 4, no. 3 (Summer 1990), pp. 179–192.

Galloway, Michael P., Bruce A. Blonigen, and Joseph E. Flynn. "Welfare Costs of the U.S. Antidumping and Countervailing Duty Laws." *JIE* 49, no. 2 (December 1999), pp. 211–244.

Ganguli, Bodhisattva. "The Trade Effects of Indian Antidumping Actions." *Review of International Economics* 16, no. 5 (November 2008), pp. 930–941.

Genberg, Hans, and Alexander K. Swoboda. "Policy and Current Account Determination under Floating Exchange Rates." *IMF Staff Papers* 36, no. 1 (March 1989), pp. 1–30.

Ghosh, Atish R., Jonathan D. Ostry, and Charalambos Tsangarides. "Exchange Rate Regimes and the Stability of the International Monetary System." International Monetary Fund Occasional Paper 270, 2010.

Gibson, John, and David McKenzie. "Eight Questions about Brain Drain." *JEP* 25, no. 3 (Summer 2011), pp. 107–128.

Gilbert, Christopher L. "International Commodity Agreements: An Obituary Notice." *World Development* 24, no. 1 (January 1996), pp. 1–19.

Giovannini, Alberto. "How Do Fixed Exchange-Rate Regimes Work: The Evidence from the Gold Standard, Bretton Woods and the EMS." In *Blueprints for Exchange Rate Management*, ed. Marvin Miller, Barry Eichengreen, and Richard Portes. London: Center for Economic Policy Research, 1989.

Goldberg, Linda S., Craig Kennedy, and Jason Miu. "Central Bank Dollar Swap Lines and Overseas Dollar Funding Costs." *FRBNY Economic Policy Review* 17, no. 1 (May 2011), pp. 3–20.

Goldberg, Pinelopi Koujianou, and Nina Pavcnik. "Distributional Effects of Globalization in Developing Countries." *JEL* 45, no. 1 (March 2007), pp. 39–82.

Goldstein, Morris. *Asian Financial Crisis: Causes, Cures, and Systemic Implications*. Washington, DC: Institute for International Economics, 1998.

———. *Managed Floating Plus*. Washington, DC: Institute for International Economics, 2002.

Golub, Stephen S. *Labor Costs and International Trade*. Washington, DC: AEI Press, 1999.

Gonzaga, Gustavo, Naércio Menezes Filho, and Cristina Terra. "Trade Liberalization and the Evolution of Skill Earnings Differentials in Brazil." *JIE* 68, no. 2 (March 2006), pp. 345–367.

Greenaway, David, and Chris Milner. *The Economics of Intra-Industry Trade*. Oxford, England: Basil Blackwell, 1986.

———. "Effective Protection, Policy Appraisal and Trade Policy Reform." *World Economy* 26, no. 4 (April 2003), pp. 441–456.

Grilli, Enzo R., and Maw Cheng Yang. "Primary Commodity Prices, Manufactured Goods Prices, and the Terms of Trade of Developing Countries: What the Long Run Shows." *World Bank Economic Review* 2, no. 1 (January 1988), pp. 1–47.

Grossman, Gene M., and Elhanan Helpman. "Protection for Sale." *AER* 84, no. 4 (September 1994), pp. 833–850.

———. "Technology and Trade." In Grossman and Rogoff (1995).

Grossman, Gene M., and Kenneth Rogoff, eds. *Handbook of International Economics*, vol. III. New York: North-Holland, 1995.

Grubel, Herbert G., and P. J. Lloyd. *Intra-Industry Trade: The Theory and Measurement of Trade in Differentiated Products*. New York: John Wiley & Sons, 1975.

Hanson, Gordon H. "Illegal Migration from Mexico to the United States." *JEL* 44, no. 4 (December 2006), pp. 869–924.

———. "The Economic Consequences of International Migration of Labor." *Annual Review of Economics* 1 (September 2009), pp. 179–207.

———. "The Rise of the Middle Kingdoms: Emerging Economies in Global Trade." *JEP* 26, no. 2 (Spring 2012), pp. 41–63.

Harvey, David I., Neil M. Kellard, Jakob B. Madsen, and Mark E. Wohar. "The Prebisch–Singer Hypothesis: Four Centuries of Evidence." *Review of Economics and Statistics* 92, no. 2 (May 2010), pp. 367–377.

Haskel, Jonathan, Robert Z. Lawrence, Edward E. Leamer, and Matthew J. Slaughter. "Globalization and U.S. Wages: Modifying Classic Theory to Explain Recent Facts." *JEP* 26, no. 2 (Spring 2012), pp. 119–139.

Heckscher, Eli. "The Effects of Foreign Trade on the Distribution of Income," originally published in 1919. In *Readings in the Theory of International Trade*, ed. Howard S. Ellis and Lloyd M. Metzler. Philadelphia: Blakiston, 1949.

Heitger, Bernhard, and Jürgen Stehn. "Trade, Technical Change, and Labour Market Adjustment." *World Economy* 26, no. 10 (September 2003), pp. 1481–1501.

Helpman, Elhanan. "The Structure of Foreign Trade." *JEP* 13, no. 2 (Spring 1999), pp. 121–144.

Helpman, Elhanan. *Understanding Global Trade*. Cambridge, MA: Belknap Press of Harvard University Press, 2011.

Henry, Peter Blair. "Capital Account Liberalization: Theory, Evidence, and Speculation." *JEL* 45, no. 4 (December 2007), pp. 887–935.

Hervé, Karine, Nigel Pain, Pete Richardson, Franck Sédillot, and Pierre-Olivier Beffy. "The OECD's New Global Model." *Economic Modelling* 28, nos. 1–2 (January–March 2011), pp. 589–601.

Higgins, Matthew, and Thomas Klitgaard. "The Balance of Payments Crisis in the Euro Area Periphery." *Federal Reserve Bank of New York Current Issues in Economics and Finance* 20, no. 2 (2014).

Hoekman, Bernard. "The Next Round of Services Negotiations: Identifying Priorities and Options." *Federal Reserve Bank of St. Louis Review* 82, no. 4 (July/August 2000), pp. 31–47.

——— and Michel Kostecki. *Political Economy of the World Trading System: The WTO and Beyond*, 2nd ed. New York: Oxford University Press, 2001.

Hufbauer, Gary Clyde, and Kimberly Ann Elliott. *Measuring the Costs of Protection in the United States*. Washington, DC: Institute for International Economics, 1994.

——— and Barbara Oegg. *Economic Sanctions Reconsidered*, 3rd ed. Washington DC: Peterson Institute for International Economics, 2007.

Hufbauer, Gary Clyde, and Jeffrey J. Schott. *NAFTA Revisited: Achievements and Challenges*. Washington, DC: Institute for International Economics, 2005.

Iley, Richard A., and Mervyn K. Lewis. *Untangling the US Deficit: Evaluating Causes, Cures, and Global Imbalances*. Northampton, MA: Edward Elgar, 2007.

Irwin, Douglas A. *Against the Tide: An Intellectual History of Free Trade*. Princeton, NJ: Princeton University Press, 1996.

———. *Free Trade under Fire,* 3rd ed. Princeton, NJ: Princeton University Press, 2009.

———. *Peddling Protectionism: Smoot-Hawley and the Great Depression*. Princeton, NJ: Princeton University Press, 2011.

———. *Trade Policy Disaster: Lessons from the 1930s*. Cambridge, MA: MIT Press, 2012.

Ito, Takatoshi. "Is Foreign Exchange Intervention Effective? The Japanese Experiences in the 1990s." In *Monetary History, Exchange Rates, and Financial Markets: Essays in Honour of Charles Goodheart, Vol. 2*, ed. Paul Mizen. Northampton, MA: Edward Elgar, 2003, pp. 126–153.

Jagelka, Tomáš. "Bilateral Trade and the Eurozone: Evidence from New Member Countries." *World Economy* 36, no. 1 (January 2013), pp. 48–63.

Jaramillo, Carlos Felipe, Daniel Lederman, Maurizio Bussolo, David Gould, and Andrew Mason. *Challenges of CAFTA: Maximizing the Benefits for Central America*. Washington, DC: World Bank, 2006.

Jean, Sebastian, Orsetta Causa, Miguel Jimenez, and Isabelle Wanner. "Migration in OECD Countries: Labour Market Impact and Integration Issues." Organization for Economic Cooperation and Development, Economics Department Working Paper no. 562, September 2007.

Johnson, Harry G. *Money, Trade and Economic Growth*. Cambridge, MA: Harvard University Press, 1962.

———. "Optimal Trade Policy in the Presence of Domestic Distortions." In *Trade, Growth and the Balance of Payments*, ed. Robert E. Baldwin. Chicago: Rand McNally, 1965.

Jones, Kent. *Who's Afraid of the WTO?* New York: Oxford University Press, 2004.

Jones, Ronald W., and Peter B. Kenen, eds. *Handbook of International Economics*. Two volumes. New York: North-Holland, 1984.

Joyce, Joseph P. "Adoption, Implementation and Impact of IMF Programmes: A Review of the Issues and Evidence." *Comparative Economic Systems* 46, no. 3 (September 2004), pp. 451–467.

Kee, Hiau Looi, Cristina Neagu, and Alessandro Nicita. "Is Protectionism on the Rise? Assessing National Trade Policies during the Crisis of 2008." World Bank Policy Research Paper 5274, April 2010.

Kee, Hiau Looi, Alessandro Nicita, and Marcelo Olarreaga. "Estimating Trade Restrictiveness Indices." *Economic Journal* 119, no. 534 (January 2009), pp. 172–199.

Keller, Wolfgang. "International Technology Diffusion." *JEL* 42, no. 3 (September 2004), pp. 752–782.

Kelly, Trish. "WTO, the Environment and Health and Safety Standards." *World Economy* 26, no. 2 (February 2003), pp. 131–151.

Kindleberger, Charles P., and Robert Aliber. *Manias, Panics, and Crashes*, 6th ed. New York: Palgrave Macmillan, 2011.

King, Michael R., Carol Osler, and Dagfinn Rime. "Foreign Exchange Market Structure, Players and Evolution." In *Handbook of Exchange Rates*, ed. Jessica James, Ian W. Marsh, and Lucio Sarno. Hoboken, NJ: John Wiley & Sons, 2012.

Klein, Michael W., and Jay C. Shambaugh. *Exchange Rate Regimes in the Modern Era*. Cambridge, MA: MIT Press, 2010.

Kletzer, Lori G. *Job Loss from Imports: Measuring the Costs*. Washington, DC: Institute for International Economics, 2001.

——— and Howard Rosen. "Easing the Adjustment Burden on U.S. Workers." In *United States and the World Economy: Foreign Economic Policy for the Next Decade*, ed. C. Fred Bergsten. Washington, DC: Institute for International Economics, 2005.

Krugman, Paul R. "Increasing Returns, Monopolistic Competition, and International Trade." *JIE* 9 (1979), pp. 469–479.

———. "The Increasing Returns Revolution in Trade and Geography." *AER* 99, no. 3 (June 2009), pp. 561–571.

Lane, Philip R. "The Real Effects of European Monetary Union." *JEP* 20, no. 4 (Fall 2006), pp. 47–66.

——— and Gian Maria Milesi-Ferretti. "The External Wealth of Nations Mark II: Revised and Extended Estimates of Foreign Assets and Liabilities, 1970–2004." *JIE* 73, no. 2 (November 2007), pp. 223–250.

Lawrence, Robert Z. *Blue-Collar Blues: Is Trade to Blame for Rising US Income Inequality?* Policy Analyses in International Economics, vol. 85. Washington, DC: Peterson Institute for International Economics, 2008.

Leamer, Edward E., and James Levinson. "International Trade Theory: The Evidence." In Grossman and Rogoff (1995).

Leontief, Wassily. "Domestic Production and Foreign Trade: The American Capital Position Reexamined." *Economia Internazionale* 7 (February 1954), pp. 3–32.

———. "Factor Proportions and the Structure of American Trade: Further Theoretical and Empirical Analysis." *Review of Economics and Statistics* 38, no. 4 (November 1956), pp. 386–407.

Levich, Richard M. "Interest Rate Parity." In *Evidence and Impact of Financial Globalization*, vol. 3, ed. Gerard Caprio. Amsterdam: Elsevier, 2013.

———. "Is the Foreign Exchange Market Efficient?" *Oxford Review of Economic Policy* 5, no. 3 (October 1989), pp. 40–60.

Lindert, Peter H. *Key Currencies and Gold, 1900–1913*. Princeton, NJ: Princeton University Press, 1969.

Lindsey, Brink, and Dan Ikenson. "Antidumping 101: The Devilish Details of 'Unfair Trade' Law." Cato Institute Trade Policy Analysis No. 20, November 21, 2002.

Liu, Xuepeng. "GATT/WTO Promotes Trade Strongly: Sample Selection and Model Specification." *Review of International Economics* 17, no. 3 (August 2009), pp. 428–446.

Lyons, Richard K. *Microstructure Approach to Exchange Rates*. Cambridge, MA: MIT Press, 2001.

Madsen, Jakob B. "Technology Spillover through Trade and TFP Convergence: 135 Years of Evidence for the OECD Countries." *JIE* 72, no. 2 (July 2007), pp. 464–480.

Magee, Christopher S. P. "New Measures of Trade Creation and Trade Diversion." *JIE* 75, no. 2 (July 2008), pp. 349–362.

———. "Why Are Trade Barriers So Low?" *Economic Affairs* 31, no. 3 (October 2011), pp. 12–17.

Magee, Stephen P. "Information and Multinational Corporations: An Appropriability Theory of Direct Foreign Investment." In *New International Economic Order*, ed. Jagdish N. Bhagwati. Cambridge, MA: MIT Press, 1977, pp. 317–340.

———. "Twenty Paradoxes in International Trade Theory." In *International Trade and Agriculture: Theory and Policy*, ed. Jimmye Hillman and Andrew Schmitz. Boulder, CO: Westview, 1979, pp. 91–116.

Marston, Richard C. *International Financial Integration: A Study of Interest Differentials between the Major Industrial Economies*. New York: Cambridge University Press, 1995.

McCalla, Alex F., and John Nash, eds. *Reforming Agricultural Trade for Developing Countries, Volume One: Key Issues for a Pro-development Outcome of the Doha Round*. Washington, DC: World Bank, 2007.

McCallum, John. "National Borders Matter: Canada-U.S. Regional Trade Patterns." *AER* 85, no. 3 (June 1995), pp. 615–623.

McKinnon, Ronald. "International Money in Historical Perspective." *JEL* 31, no. 1 (March 1993), pp. 1–44.

———. "Optimum Currency Areas." *AER* 53, no. 1 (March 1963), pp. 717–725.

———. *Rules of the Game*. Cambridge, MA: MIT Press, 1996.

Meade, James. *Trade and Welfare*. Oxford, England: Oxford University Press, 1955.

Meissner, Christopher. "A New World Order: Explaining the International Diffusion of the Gold Standard, 1870–1913." *JIE* 66, no. 2 (July 2005), pp. 385–406.

Melitz, Marc J. "The Impact of Trade on Intra-Industry Reallocations and Aggregate Industry Productivity." *Econometrica* 71, no. 6 (November 2003), pp. 1695–1725.

——— and Daniel Trefler. "Gains from Trade When Firms Matter." *JEP* 26, no. 2 (Spring 2012), pp. 91–118.

Menkhoff, Lukas. "Foreign Exchange Intervention in Emerging Markets: A Survey of Empirical Studies." *World Economy* 36, no. 9 (September 2013), pp. 1187–1208.

——— and Mark P. Taylor. "The Obstinate Passion of Foreign Exchange Professionals: Technical Analysis." *JEL* 45, no. 4 (December 2007), pp. 936–972.

Messerlin, Patrick A. *Measuring the Costs of Protection in Europe: European Commercial Policy in the 2000s*. Washington, DC: Institute for International Economics, 2001.

Meyer, Laurence H., Brian M. Doyle, Joseph E. Gagnon, and Dale W. Henderson. "International Coordination of Macroeconomic Policies: Still Alive in the New Millennium?" Board of Governors of the Federal Reserve System, International Finance Discussion Paper no. 723, April 2002.

Mihaljek, Dubravko. "Survey of Central Banks' Views on Effects of Intervention." In *Foreign Exchange Market Intervention in Emerging Markets: Motives, Techniques and Implications*. Bank for International Settlements Papers no. 24, May 2005.

Mohler, Lukas, and Michael Seitz. "The Gains from Variety in the European Union." *Review of World Economics* 148, no. 3 (September 2012), pp. 475–500.

Moran, Theodore H. *Foreign Direct Investment and Development: Launching a Second Generation of Policy Research*. Washington, DC: Peterson Institute for International Economics, 2011.

Morgan, T. Clifton, Navin Bapat, and Valentin Krustev. "The Threat and Imposition of Economic Sanctions, 1971–2000." *Conflict Management and Peace Science* 26, no. 1 (February 2009), pp. 92–110.

Mundell, Robert. *International Economics*. New York: Macmillan, 1968.

———. "A Theory of Optimum Currency Areas." *AER* 51, no. 4 (September 1961), pp. 657–665.

Mutti, John H. *Foreign Direct Investment and Tax Competition*. Washington, DC: Institute for International Economics, 2003.

Neal, Larry, and Daniel Barbezat. *Economics of the European Union and the Economies of Europe*. New York: Oxford University Press, 1998.

Neely, Christopher J. "A Foreign Exchange Intervention in an Era of Restraint." *Federal Reserve Bank of St. Louis Review* 93, no. 5 (September/October 2011), pp. 303–324.

———. "The Practice of Central Bank Intervention: Looking under the Hood." *Federal Reserve Bank of St. Louis Review* 83, no. 3 (May/June 2001), pp. 1–10.

Nelson, Douglas. "The Political Economy of Antidumping: A Survey." *European Journal of Political Economy* 22, no. 3 (September 2006), pp. 554–590.

Neumayer, Eric. "Trade and the Environment: A Critical Assessment and Some Suggestions for Reconciliation." *Journal of Environment and Development* 9, no. 2 (June 2000), pp. 138–159.

Niels, Gunnar. "What Is Antidumping Policy Really About?" *Journal of Economic Surveys* 14, no. 4 (September 2000), pp. 467–492.

——— and Adriaan ten Kate. "Antidumping Policy in Developing Countries: Safety Valve or Obstacle to Free Trade?" *European Journal of Political Economy* 22, no. 3 (September 2006), pp. 618–638.

Nordhaus, William. *Climate Casino: Risk, Uncertainty, and Economics for a Warming World*. New Haven: Yale University Press, 2013.

Nurkse, Ragnar. *International Currency Experience: Lessons of the Interwar Period*. Geneva, Switzerland: League of Nations, 1944.

Obstfeld, Maurice. "Does the Current Account Still Matter?" *AER* 102, no. 3 (May 2012), pp. 1–23.

——— and Alan M. Taylor. *Global Capital Markets: Integration, Crisis, and Growth*. New York: Cambridge University Press, 2004.

Ohlin, Bertil. *International and Interregional Trade*. Cambridge, MA: Harvard University Press, 1933.

Olson, Mancur. *The Logic of Collective Action*. Cambridge, MA: Harvard University Press, 1965.

Organization for Economic Cooperation and Development (OECD). *Economic Impact of Export Restrictions on Raw Materials*. Paris: OECD, 2010.

———. *Economics of Climate Change Mitigation: Policies and Options for Global Action beyond 2012*. Paris: OECD, 2009.

———. *European Union's Trade Policies and Their Economic Effects*. Paris: OECD, 2000.

———. *International Migration Outlook 2013*. Paris: OECD, 2013.

———. *Sugar Policy Reform in the European Union and in World Sugar Markets*. Paris: OECD, 2007.

———. *Tax Effects on Foreign Direct Investment: Recent Evidence and Policy Analysis*. Paris: OECD, 2008.

O'Rourke, Kevin H., Alan M. Taylor, and Jeffrey G. Williamson. "Factor Price Convergence in the Late Nineteenth Century." *International Economic Review* 37, no. 3 (August 1996), pp. 499–530.

O'Rourke, Kevin H., and Jeffrey G. Williamson. "Were Heckscher and Ohlin Right? Factor-Price Convergence in Economic History." *Journal of Economic History* 54, no. 4 (December 1994).

Ostry, Jonathan D., Atish R. Ghosh, Karl Habermeier, Luc Laeven, Marcos Chamon, Mahvash S. Qureshi, and Annamarie Kokenyne. "Managing Capital Inflows: What Tools to Use?" International Monetary Fund Staff Discussion Note SDN/11/06, April 2011.

Ottaviano, Gianmarco I. P., and Diego Puga. "Agglomeration in the Global Economy: A Survey of the 'New Economic Geography.'" *World Economy* 21, no. 6 (August 1998), pp. 707–731.

Panagariya, Arvind. "Miracles and Debacles: In Defence of Trade Openness." *World Economy* 27, no. 8 (August 2004), pp. 1149–1171.

Panizza, Ugo, Federico Sturzenegger, and Jeromin Zettelmeyer. "The Economics and Law of Sovereign Debt and Default." *JEL* 47, no. 3 (September 2009), pp. 651–698.

Pearson, Charles S. *United States Trade Policy: A Work in Progress.* New York: John Wiley & Sons, 2004.

Pfaffenzeller, Stephan, Paul Newbold, and Anthony Rayner. "A Short Note on Updating the Grilli and Yang Commodity Price Index." *World Bank Economic Review* 21, no. 1 (2007), pp. 151–163.

Pigott, Charles A. "International Interest Rate Convergence: A Survey of the Issues and Evidence." *Federal Reserve Bank of New York Quarterly Review* 18, no. 4 (Winter 1993–1994), pp. 24–37.

Pisani-Ferry, Jean. *Euro Crisis and Its Aftermath.* New York: Oxford University Press, 2014.

Pojarliev, Momtchil, and Richard M. Levich. *New Look at Currency Investing.* New York: Research Foundation of CFA Institute, 2012.

Pomfret, Richard. *Economics of Regional Trading Arrangements.* Oxford: Clarendon Press, 1997.

Pope, David, and Glenn Withers. "Do Migrants Rob Jobs? Lessons of Australian History, 1861–1991," *Journal of Economic History* 53, no. 4 (December 1993), pp. 719–742.

Read, Robert. "The Political Economy of Trade Protection: The Determinants and Welfare Impact of the 2002 US Emergency Steel Safeguard Measures." *World Economy* 28, no. 8 (August 2005), pp. 1119–1137.

Reagan, Ronald. *An American Life.* New York: Simon & Schuster, 1990.

Reinhart, Carmen M., and Kenneth S. Rogoff. "Modern History of Exchange Rate Arrangements: A Reinterpretation," *Quarterly Journal of Economics* 119, no. 1 (February 2004), pp. 1–48.

———. *This Time Is Different: Eight Centuries of Financial Folly.* Princeton, NJ: Princeton University Press, 2009.

Reynolds, Kara M., and John S. Palatucci. "Does Trade Adjustment Assistance Make a Difference?" *Contemporary Economic Policy* 30, no. 1 (January 2012), pp. 43–59.

Ricardo, David. *On the Principles of Political Economy and Taxation.* London: John Murray, 1817.

Rivera-Batiz, Francisco L., and Luis A. Rivera-Batiz. *International Finance and Open Economy Macroeconomics*, 2nd ed. New York: Macmillan, 1994.

Rivera-Batiz, Luis A., and Paul M. Romer. "Economic Integration and Endogenous Growth." *Quarterly Journal of Economics* 106, no. 2 (May 1991), pp. 531–556.

Robertson, Raymond. "Trade and Wages: Two Puzzles from Mexico." *World Economy* 30, no. 9 (September 2007), pp. 1378–1398.

Rodrik, Dani, and Arvind Subramanian. "Why Did Financial Globalization Disappoint?" *IMF Staff Papers* 56, no. 1 (March 2009), pp. 112–138.

Rogoff, Kenneth. "International Institutions for Reducing Global Financial Instability." *JEP* 13, no. 4 (Fall 1999), pp. 21–42.

Romalis, John. "NAFTA's and CUSFTA's Impact on International Trade." *Review of Economics and Statistics* 89, no. 3 (August 2007), pp. 416–435.

Romer, Paul. "New Goods, Old Theory, and the Welfare Cost of Trade Restrictions." *Journal of Development Economics* 43, no. 1 (February 1994), pp. 5–38.

Rose, Andrew K. "Do We Really Know That the WTO Increases Trade?" *AER* 94, no. 1 (March 2004), pp. 98–114.

Rossi, Barbara. "Exchange Rate Predictability." *JEL* 51, no. 4 (December 2013), pp. 1063–1119.

Roubini, Nouriel, and Brad Setser. *Bailouts or Bail-Ins? Responding to Financial Crises in Emerging Economies.* Washington, DC: Institute for International Economics, 2004.

Rueff, Jacques. *The Monetary Sin of the West*. Trans. Roger Glemet. New York: Macmillan, 1972.

Ruffin, Roy J. "The Missing Link: The Ricardian Approach to the Factor Endowments Theory of Trade." *AER* 78, no. 4 (September 1988), pp. 759–772.

Rybczynski, T. M. "Factor Endowments and Relative Commodity Prices." *Economica* 22, no. 84 (November 1955), pp. 336–341.

Sachs, Jeffrey D., and Andrew M. Warner. "Economic Reform and the Process of Global Integration." *Brookings Papers on Economic Activity*, no. 1 (1995), pp. 1–95.

Sager, Michael J., and Mark P. Taylor. "Under the Microscope: The Structure of the Foreign Exchange Market." *International Journal of Finance and Economics* 11, no. 1 (January 2006), pp. 81–95.

Samuelson, Paul A. "International Factor-Price Equalization Once Again." *Economic Journal* 59, no. 234 (June 1949), pp. 181–197.

Sarno, Lucio, and Mark P. Taylor. "Official Intervention in the Foreign Exchange Market: Is It Effective and, If So, How Does It Work?" *JEL* 39, no. 3 (September 2001), pp. 839–868.

———. "Purchasing Power Parity and the Real Exchange Rate." *IMF Staff Papers* 49, no. 1 (2002), pp. 65–105.

Schiff, Maurice, and L. Alan Winters. *Regional Integration and Development*. Washington, DC: World Bank, 2003.

Schindler, Martin. "Measuring Financial Integration: A New Data Set." *IMF Staff Papers* 56, no. 1 (March 2009), pp. 222–238.

Schott, Peter K. "One Size Fits All? Heckscher–Ohlin Specialization in Global Production." *AER* 93, no. 3 (June 2003), pp. 686–708.

Shambaugh, Jay C. "Effect of Fixed Exchange Rates on Monetary Policy." *Quarterly Journal of Economics* 119, no. 1 (February 2004), pp. 301–352.

———. "The Euro's Three Crises." *Brookings Papers on Economic Activity*, no. 1 (Spring 2012), pp. 157–211.

Slaughter, Matthew J. "What Are the Results of Product-Price Studies and What Can We Learn from Their Differences?" In *Impact of International Trade on Wages*, ed. Robert C. Feenstra. Chicago: University of Chicago Press, 2000, pp. 129–170.

Smith, Adam. *Wealth of Nations*. Originally published 1776. New York: Random House (Modern Library edition), 1937.

Smith, James P., and Barry Edmonston, eds. *New Americans: Economic, Demographic, and Fiscal Effects of Immigration*. Washington, DC: National Academy Press, 1997.

Stolper, Wolfgang F., and Paul A. Samuelson. "Protection and Real Wages." *Review of Economic Studies* 9 (November 1941), pp. 58–73.

Subramanian, Arvind, and Shang-Jin Wei. "The WTO Promotes Trade, Strongly but Unevenly." *JIE* 72, no. 1 (May 2007), pp. 151–175.

Suranovic, Steven M. "A Positive Analysis of Fairness with Applications to International Trade. " *World Economy* 23, no. 3 (March 2000), pp. 283–307.

Tamiotti, Ludivine, Anne Olhoff, Robert Teh, Benjamin Simmons, Vesile Kulaçoğlu, and Hussein Abaza. *Trade and Climate Change*. Geneva, Switzerland: World Trade Organization, 2009.

Tokarick, Stephen. "Who Bears the Cost of Agricultural Support in OECD Countries?" *World Economy* 28, no. 4 (April 2005), pp. 573–593.

Tower, Edward, and Thomas D. Willett. "The Theory of Optimum Currency Areas and Exchange Rate Flexibility." *Special Papers in International Economics*, no. 11. Princeton, NJ: Princeton University, May 1976.

Trefler, Daniel. "The Case of the Missing Trade and Other Mysteries." *AER* 85, no. 5 (December 1995), pp. 1029–1046.

———. "International Factor Price Differences: Leontief Was Right!" *JPE* 101, no. 6 (December 1993), pp. 961–987.

——— and Susan Chun Zhu. "Structure of Factor Content Predictions," *JIE* 82, no. 2 (November 2010), pp. 195–207.

Triffin, Robert. *Gold and the Dollar Crisis*. New Haven, CT: Yale University Press, 1960.

Trionfetti, Federico. "Discriminatory Public Procurement and International Trade." *World Economy* 23, no. 1 (January 2000), pp. 1–23.

Tsiang, S. C. "Fluctuating Exchange Rates in Countries with Relatively Stable Economies: Some European Experiences after World War I." *IMF Staff Papers* 7 (October 1959), pp. 244–273.

Van den Berg, Hendrik, and Joshua J. Lewer. *International Trade and Economic Growth*. Armonk, NY: M. E. Sharp, 2007.

Vanek, Jaroslav. *International Trade: Theory and Economic Policy*. Homewood, IL: Richard D. Irwin, 1962.

Vernon, Raymond G. "International Investment and International Trade in the Product Cycle." *Quarterly Journal of Economics* 80, no. 2 (May 1966), pp. 190–207.

———. "The Product Cycle Hypotheses in a New International Environment." *Oxford Bulletin of Economics and Statistics* 41 (November 1979), pp. 255–267.

Waugh, Michael E. "International Trade and Income Differences." *AER* 100, no. 5 (December 2010), pp. 2093–2124.

Wolf, Holger C., Atish R. Ghosh, Helge Berger, and Anne-Marie Gulde. *Currency Boards in Retrospect and Prospect*. Cambridge, MA: MIT Press, 2008.

Wolf, Martin. *Why Globalization Works*. New Haven, CT: Yale University Press, 2004.

World Bank. *Globalization, Growth, and Poverty: Building an Inclusive World Economy*. Washington, DC: World Bank, 2002a.

———. *Transition the First Ten Years: Analysis and Lessons for Eastern Europe and the Former Soviet Union*. Washington, DC: World Bank, 2002b.

——— and Food and Agriculture Organization of the United Nations. *Sunken Billions: The Economic Justification for Fisheries Reform*. Washington, DC: World Bank, 2009.

World Trade Organization. *World Trade Report 2012*. Geneva, Switzerland: World Trade Organization, 2012.

Wyplosz, Charles. "European Monetary Union: The Dark Sides of a Major Success." *Economic Policy* 21, no. 46 (April 2006), pp. 207–261.

Yeager, Leland B. "A Rehabilitation of Purchasing-Power-Parity." *JPE* 66, no. 6 (December 1958), pp. 516–530.

Zanardi, Maurizio. "Anti-Dumping: What Are the Numbers to Discuss at Doha?" *World Economy* 27, no. 3 (March 2004), pp. 403–433.

Zettelmeyer, Jeromin. "Impact of Monetary Policy on the Exchange Rate: Evidence from Three Small Open Economies." *Journal of Monetary Economics* 51, no. 3 (April 2004), pp. 635–652.

Index